Handbook of Distance Education

SECOND EDITION

Edited by

Michael Grahame Moore
The Pennsylvania State University

LEA LAWRENCE ERLBAUM ASSOCIATES, PUBLISHERS
2007 Mahwah, New Jersey   London

Director of Editorial: Lane Akers
Editorial Assistant: Anthony Messina
Cover Design: Tomai Maridou
Full-Service Compositor: MidAtlantic Books and Journals, Inc.

This book was typeset in 10/12 pt. Times, Italic, Bold, and Bold Italic with Helvetica.

Lawrence Erlbaum Associates, Inc., Publishers
10 Industrial Avenue
Mahwah, New Jersey 07430
www.erlbaum.com

Library of Congress Cataloging-in-Publication Data

ISBN 978-0-8058-5847-1 — 0-8058-5847-4 (case)
ISBN 978-1-4106-1764-4 — 1-4106-1764-5 (e book)

Books published by Lawrence Erlbaum Associates are printed on
acid-free paper, and their bindings are chosen for strength and durability.

Printed in the United States of America

10   9   8   7   6   5   4   3   2   1

Contents

Part VI
GLOBAL PERSPECTIVES

Preface

Michael Grahame Moore

When the first edition of this *Handbook* was published in 2003, it was in response to a perceived need for an authoritative compilation of the research in what is arguably the most significant development in education of the past quarter century. Across the educational spectrum, distance education continues to be a topic of great interest to policy makers, administrators, teachers, and students. Its value as a means of opportunity for learners while also improving the quality of teaching is now widely recognized—as much by professors in universities and community colleges as by trainers in corporations and the armed forces—in continuing professional education of teachers; physicians and nurses; public accountants; pharmacists; leaders of voluntary organizations; managers in the corporate boardroom; and workers seeking new skills on the factory floor. Thankfully, what I described in the first edition as the "recent frenzy" of precipitant innovation driven by excitement about Internet technology has subsided to a considerable extent, as those who got caught up in that early excitement discovered for themselves the limitations as well as the opportunities offered by the technology. Communication through computer technologies is now an everyday affair for teachers, most of whom have settled down to the more interesting work involved in learning the pedagogy of designing and delivering quality programs through technology. Administrators must also perform the particularly difficult task of channeling their faculty away from typical classroom roles and into those more appropriate for the information age. Meanwhile students are learning faster as they becoming familiar with the tough-but-rewarding effort that distance study demands. These students must share in the management of their own learning, particularly by juggling their schedules to make time to complete course readings and meet assignment deadlines.

In this environment of gradually maturing understanding about distance education as it increasingly becomes part of the educational mainstream, a growing number of students are looking for opportunities in academic study of this field, and a growing number of educational institutions are offering distance education programs of study, particularly at the graduate level. Evidence of this can be seen, for example, in the increasing number of doctoral dissertations that include the terms *distance education* or *distance learning* in their titles, averaging, at the most modest estimate, about 100 each year since the beginning of the decade. As editor, I am aware of the enormous increase in interest among faculty that has led to an almost overwhelming supply of research articles submitted to *The American Journal of Distance Education*, as well as noting the number of new online journals that happily absorb what the established journals cannot publish. The extent of this growth in scholarship of distance education becomes even more apparent when we take into account the many research studies and other published works that focus on one or other of the component parts of this field, or one of its many applications—reported in terms such as *distributed learning, telelearning,* and *e-learning*; as well as *open learning, blended learning* and *flexi-learning.* Each of these subsets of distance education has generated its own following of specialists, each with its own journals, conferences, and evolving theory—an excellent development and a further sign of the maturation of the field. This splitting of the field into component disciplines brings with it one problem: by focusing on what is published under the terminology of one part of the field, students might not always connect with relevant knowledge that is packaged under the label of one of the other of the field's component parts. The chapters in Part I of this book should help in the development of a perspective that enables the reader to recognize both the specific trees as well as the wood of which they are a part, and to help that, I will repeat the definition of the broad field: "Distance education is all planned learning that normally occurs in a different place from teaching, requiring special techniques of course design and instruction, communication through various technologies, and special organizational and administrative arrangements" (Moore & Kearsley, 2005, p. 2). This definition should help readers differentiate between educational environments in which technology is used to enhance what some authors call "contiguous"—and others, "face-to-face"—teaching, and distance education, in which the student is entirely or "normally" in a different location from the instructor, and the use of technology is not an option but is a defining characteristic of their relationship.

The definition also serves to remind us that the field of study is both broad and deep. It certainly includes the study of communications technology, but far more attention is given to the design of teaching and facilitation of learning, as well as administrative, organizational, and policy issues and historical and comparative studies. These are the themes around which this *Handbook* is organized. Following Part I, dealing with historical and conceptual foundations, subsequent parts cover: learning; design and teaching; policies, administration, and management; the main providers; and global perspectives. This last, Part VI, serves to demonstrate that because distance education is powered by the same information and communication technologies that have already transformed our economies and societies from national to global, it is quintessentially the educational model for the 21st-century global society, with all the promise and problems that this suggests. Consequently, although this *Handbook* has been prepared primarily for use in North American universities, most of the research it reports will be relevant where-ever in the world there is study and research about distance education. This applies particularly to chapters about learning, course design, and teaching, but the thoughtful reader in other countries will surely benefit from chapters in Part IV that deal with policy and administrative issues, albeit in an American context, such as faculty participation, copyright and other legal problems, program evaluation, and cost-effectiveness. Similarly, though Part V reports the main American distance education providers, its contents will be recognizable wherever distance education is being developed alongside conventional teaching, in so-called dual-mode agencies—by far the most common administrative structure for distance education worldwide, in spite of the well-deserved reputation and enormous influence of the single-mode, national, open universities.

RATIONALE FOR THIS *HANDBOOK*

In the preface to the first edition, I described the rationale for the *Handbook,* and I would like to repeat this explanation because understanding why the book was prepared will help potential readers judge its suitability for their needs and suggest how best to use it.

The motivation for producing this work has two roots. First, as editor of *The American Journal of Distance Education* for more than twenty years and as adviser of doctoral students during that same period, I have noted that one of the most common causes of difficulty and failure is a common view of research as nothing more than mere empiricism. This is a perspective that sees the beginning and end of the research process as gathering, analyzing, and reporting data. The "literature review" that typically is the second chapter in a dissertation or comprises the opening section of a research article is too often approached as a tedious chore imposed by convention that has to be got through as quickly as possible before getting to the "real thing"—which is to gather and report data. These data may be the results of a survey or a case study, or very occasionally, an experiment; however, the data gathered in too many studies submitted for publication, and even reported in some dissertation studies, have little or no value simply because the research question that the data is supposed to address has little or no connection to the previous state of knowledge as reported in the literature. It is so sad to see students (and others who should know better) investing time and energy to design a study and collect data that address questions that have already been answered, are beyond being answered given the present state of knowledge, or—not quite so seriously—connect with some part of the literature but lose effectiveness by not linking to a more general theoretical framework. As suggested above, if a question is asked in terms of a technology, whether it is the Internet, video conference, or even correspondence study, there is a danger that relevant knowledge is missed if the researcher fails to review the research on the same question that was conducted in programs using a different technology. To illustrate, consider the wisdom of setting out to research gender differences in interaction in a Web-based distance learning program without reference to research about gender differences in programs delivered by video teleconferencing. Consider the wisdom of studying how much reading is appropriate for learners of a given educational level in a course designed for Web delivery without considering findings about students' reading capacities that have been obtained by one of the correspondence schools.

There is an obverse to this concern, however, which is that specialists in distance education have to be open to adopting into their theory, research, and practice, knowledge generated in fields such as instructional systems, educational policy, and educational psychology that are foundational to distance education itself, as well as adjunct fields such as comparative education, history, and economics. Just as it is impossible to research distance education on the basis of adjacent research alone, it is also unwise not to integrate such research where it is relevant, as is often the case. So it is with the potential of such cross-fertilization in mind that this book has a number of chapters by authors whose academic reputations have been established in adjacent fields. However, whether considering the use of research from established distance education publications or applying that from related fields, the main point remains—and deserves to be repeated—that good research must be based on a good foundation in previous research. Thus, the principle rationale for this *Handbook* is to provide a structured guide to what is already known about distance education, as well as encourage better grounded research.

The second root motivation for this collection is closely related to the first. Experience as a consultant to a wide range of institutions, states, national governments and international agencies over several decades has led to the conclusion that a similar impatience for moving to action without adequate comprehension of previous experience characterizes not only the research, but virtually all American practice in this field as well. Just as it is hard to imagine that, in any other field of inquiry, researchers could set out to gather data without thorough knowledge of what research had been previously undertaken, so it is hard to imagine that other professions would set up departments, design courses, recruit teachers, invest millions of dollars, make appearances before Congressional committees, and so on without a substantial review of previous practice in their field, without a thorough knowledge of what had succeeded and what had failed, and the reasons for those successes and failures. Yet in distance education, it happens all the time. University professors, generally knowledgeable in an academic subject with experience of lecturing to groups in a classroom, are driven into designing courses for delivery on the Web with little or no knowledge about how to design programs suitable for learning in what is essentially an individual mode of study, requiring skill in teaching through textual communications. Often they see the desirability of building an online learning community, and go at it, *ab initio*, unaware of the research about learning communities in audio and video teleconferencing programs—not that it is suggested that the online procedures are identical, but that there is knowledge that is transferable.

Thus, this book is intended to be a source of information for students and researchers to help them "know what is known" before they begin a search for new knowledge and to help practitioners and policy makers know what is known before they plan, design, and deliver new programs. It should be emphasized, especially to the researcher, that this is a key only. No synthesis or summary of other people's research can be a substitute for the knowledge provided by that research itself; each of these chapters merely points the way to that literature. Our approach, and the way we expect the book to be used, can be explained by reference to the following instruction we gave our authors when their contributions were commissioned: "The method we are using is that of literature review. We are not primarily reporting our own research nor our own opinions. Our research and our opinions will rightly shape the way we view and manipulate the literature. But the goal is that we point the way to the end of each chapter where we have a rich, extensive, up-to-date list of references that should be the 'required reading' for any graduate student who wanted to begin research in your part of the field."

Our recommendation is that students skim the whole book early on in their studies, and after deciding on an area for research, take the relevant chapters as the starting point for identifying the literature in that area. The next step is to locate each of the items listed in the references of the chosen chapters and thus dig deeper and deeper into the literature until mastery is achieved. Lest that seems too easy, it has to be added that knowledge in this field, like most others, does not lend itself to watertight compartmentalization. It is *vital* to be aware that something of value for any research question can be found within a chapter having a principal focus quite different from the question on which one is focused. In this book, for example, we have two chapters about historical research in Part I, but references to history can be found dotted throughout the book. Similarly, it is impossible to separate important references to learning from those of teaching, while much that is addressed to administration is relevant to both. The process of literature research is not easy, but it can be guaranteed that time and effort spent in this foundation work will result in better research and better practice.

In this *Handbook*, as in the first edition, we have assembled some of the most respected authorities in the North American field of distance education, with some distinguished foreign contributors as well as some "rising stars." In extending our invitations, we aimed to deal with another problem commonly encountered in advising students and in reviewing research. This is the problem of *authority*. Along with my plea to give more attention to building a solid theoretical foundation for their research and practice (i.e., "knowing what is known"), I would like to ask students and other readers to try to develop a critical perspective on what is published, recognizing that not all that is published is of equal value. Before one can effectively use literature, it is necessary to learn who are the authors and which publications are most trustworthy—that is, that have greater authority. This is a bigger problem today, when anyone can publish anything on the Web and when search engines make it very easy to gather whatever was published there, but give no clue about its quality.

In this book, at least, the reader can be assured that the authors have considerable authority. At a minimum, every one has published research in *The American Journal of Distance Education*, itself the result of considerable competition and a rigorous review process. Most are veterans of many years of research, writing, practice, and study; the authors of many of the principal publications in the field. Such "authorities" are in great demand in a field that is insatiable in its need for real expertise. Consequently, I must express thanks to them for volunteering time and expertise to contribute to this book. I wish to express my thanks also to Jessica T. Moore, senior education producer at *US News and World Report*, for her editorial assistance and for sharing ideas about design of quality programs for Web delivery. I thank Joe Savrock, my assistant at *The American Journal of Distance Education*, for his editorial work and for preparing the indexes, and also graduate student Will Diehl for helping Joe. Finally, once again I thank publisher Lawrence Erlbaum and his staff, particularly editorial director Lane Akers, for their ongoing encouragement and support of our publication efforts.

REFERENCE

Moore, M. G., & Kearsley, G. (2005). *Distance education: A systems view* (2nd ed.). Belmont, CA: Wadsworth.

The Handbook in Brief:
An Overview

Michael G. Moore

This Handbook is about research and other scholarship in distance education and is organized in six parts, as follows:

Part I.   Historical and conceptual foundations
Part II.   Learners, learning, and learner support
Part III. Design and teaching
Part IV.   Policy, administration, and management
Part V.   Audiences and providers
Part VI.   Global perspectives

PART I: HISTORICAL AND CONCEPTUAL FOUNDATIONS

Part I consists of two chapters dedicated to the history of distance education and six that deal with theory. In the opening chapter, Linda Black introduces some of the pioneer researchers and early publications, and mentions a few landmark events in the history of scholarship. In this first encounter, readers will have an experience that will be repeated in every chapter of this book, which is the recognition of how much opportunity there is for research in this field. In this first case, the opportunity is to catch hold of one of the many threads that Black provides and pull on it—that is, to do historical research. In this area, virtually nothing has been studied in depth. For example, apart from William Rainey Harper, founder of American university distance education, and William Lighty, pioneer of teaching by radio, there are no scholarly biographies of the founders of the field. What an incredibly rich treasure trove of opportunities this offers to, for example, the student wanting to write a doctoral dissertation!

Following Black—who, incidentally, makes it clear that right from the beginning the scholarship of distance education has been an international enterprise, built on strong relationships between scholars in North America and overseas, particularly those in Europe—Charles Feasley and Ellen L. Bunker in chapter 2 elaborate on this theme when they describe the 70-year history of the International Council for Distance Education (ICDE), the organization that was mainly responsible for facilitating the international linkages referred to in the first chapter. The focus on ICDE in chapter 2 is preceded by an account of national and regional associations in the United States. One of these is the National Home Study Council, the mention of which serves to further raise our awareness of the historical depth of this field, whereas mention of the Public Broadcasting Service, the National Teleconference Network, and the Sloan Foundation alert us also to its extraordinarily breadth. To help us bring order to the variety of organizations, Feasley and Bunker provide a typology, classifying them into (a) pioneering organizations, (b) curriculum organizations, (c) technology organizations, (d) regional and virtual consortia, and (e) international associations. Students will become aware of a variety of other conceptual systems that authors in subsequent chapters have devised as a way of dealing with the common problem of making sense out of a mammoth volume of information. Such conceptual frameworks, especially those that are used and reused and acquire authority, can be useful tools for achieving control and mastery of the subject.

Chapter 3 is itself such a tool. This chapter consists of meta-analyses of research articles published in the four principal scholarly journals, published in Australia, Canada, the United Kingdom, and the United States. The analysis of trends in research as reported in these journals is placed in this location in the book as a kind of advance organizer, a way of helping the reader position some of the leading theorists and researchers they will encounter later in this *Handbook*. After reporting on the relative popularity of different research methods and topics, Youngmin Lee and his fellow authors in chapter 3 provide tables showing the names of the most frequently cited authors and the most referenced articles and books. These tables should be helpful to students learning to identify the recognized authorities; indeed, if one wanted to take a crash course in distance education, one could hardly do better than to read the 15 books listed in Table 6 of this chapter.

The remainder of Part I consists of five chapters about the theory of distance education. They begin with Farhad (Fred) Saba's discussion of the systems approach to theory building, and its special relevance for understanding emerging post-modern social systems, of which distance education is an example. Readers who remember Black's brief mention of Wedemeyer's pioneering projects will build on their understanding of that history with Saba's explanation of the Articulated Instructional Media (AIM) project, an early attempt to apply a systems approach to teaching. Saba also provides an introduction to my own theoretical work and explains how his own research was based on the theoretical foundation of what I called "transactional distance." I suggest that before moving forward, readers will benefit from spending a little time reflecting on the significance of Saba's Figure 3, showing the hierarchy of nested systems levels, including its use as a tool or map for use in navigating the contents of the remaining chapters of this book.

No book on the scholarship of distance education would be complete without representation of both Otto Peters and Börje Holmberg, both of whom were introduced in chapter 1 as among the field's first theorists, with work dating from the 1960s and 1970s. I asked them both to comment on the current relevance of their theory and to list some of the research that it has generated, and agreed to do the same with regard to transactional distance theory. In reply, Peters discusses the theory of industrialized education in its historical, organizational, sociological, cultural, anthropological, economic, and pedagogical dimensions. Holmberg explains his theory, focused on the personal relationship between distant learner and the instructing agency, with an emphasis on the characteristic of empathy in that relationship. Here the reader might consider how these two conceptual systems are congruent with the "nested systems" described by Saba; are these terms describing the same phenomena, with different labels? If not, are any of Saba's levels of system subordinate or superordinate to those of Peters and Holmberg?

In chapter 7, D. Randy Garrison and Walter Archer present a model of distance education that is defined by yet another set of variables, broader than Holmberg's but not as broad as Peters'. These variables are social presence, cognitive presence, and teaching presence. It is recommended that this chapter should be read in association with chapters that follow in Parts II and III, dealing with collaborative interaction (chapter 25) and modes of interaction (chapter 24). The reader might also compare Garrison and Archer's chapter with that of William Anderson (chapter 9) to compare two different views of distance education: (a) one that sees it as a group activity in a virtual classroom and (b) the other as an essentially private and individual process of independent study. It is not suggested that the two views are incompatible, or not equally legitimate, but only that it will be helpful to be able to recognize situations and publications that hold one or the other set of assumptions that underlie these two perspectives.

The last chapter in Part I introduces some of the research based on the theory of transactional distance. When first conceptualized and for many years after (until the arrival of Saba, in fact), transactional distance theory was the only American theory of distance education and is generally cited with Peters and Holmberg as one of the principal foundation theories. It has been referred to in several previous chapters in this part, and will be referred to further in subsequent chapters, particularly in chapter 18. Quite often the concepts contained in transactional distance theory are employed in other theories under different labels. For example, it is recommended that when the student reads chapters 21 and 22 on teaching in directed, negotiated, and informal learning environments, he or she should keep at hand the explanation of transactional distance given in chapter 18 and use this explanation to make comparisons. Similarly, the concept of dialogue is not the same as interaction, but research on interaction is often relevant to expanding understanding of dialogue, and vice versa. In general, it is worth taking time to look at the various theories side by side to see the relationships among them. Each succeeds in a different way in summarizing knowledge, in summarizing reality. In some cases the reality is global; for example, Peters' view. In others it is relatively molecular, as is Holmberg's view. Transactional distance, empathy, and community of inquiry are primarily pedagogical theories, each illuminating teaching and learning from a different angle. Students are advised to try to understand each of these different interpretations, and eventually to accommodate them into their own theoretical perspectives.

PART II: LEARNING AND LEARNERS

In Part II, we focus specifically on learning and learners. To start, W. Anderson picks up where Part I ended, with reference to autonomous learning leading to an explanation of the concept of independent learning, one of the key learner characteristics associated with distance education (which was at one time known as "independent study"). W. Anderson explains the relationship of distance education to the even broader theory of adult learning, and shows how recent scholars have revisited earlier ideas about adult self-directed learning represented by Malcolm Knowles and Alan Tough, looking particularly to develop understanding about the controlling roles played by teachers. W. Anderson's summary of research on learner autonomy and student outcomes points to a later chapter (chapter 12) that discusses student satisfaction, and his review of research on metacognition introduces themes that will be picked up in several later chapters, particularly by Michael Hannafin and his colleagues in chapter 10, and by Priya Sharma and her colleagues in chapter 21. References to Peters, Garrison, and Moore, authors of chapters in Part I, further remind readers that knowledge in this field, like others, is not developed or acquired linearly, nor can it be neatly compartmentalized. Consequently, chapters read earlier in the book will be better understood by frequent rereading, as one becomes increasingly familiar with concepts that will appear and reappear in varying depth and complexity.

The chapter by Michael Hannafin, Janette R. Hill, Liyan Song, and Richard West represents what was described in the Preface as work by scholars in adjacent fields to distance education. Here it is the research on cognitive psychology, and learning in what Hannafin and colleagues refer to as "technology enhanced distance learning environments," meaning those in which the communication is Web-based, or what many people nowadays call "e-learning." Beginning with a body of knowledge acquired in classrooms, a wealth of potential research and practical applications for distance educators is suggested by what this chapter reports about metacognition (see W. Anderson earlier), prior knowledge, and motivation (consider, for example, the impact of these finding on decisions to be made during the course design process).

Kayleigh Carabajal's, Deborah LaPointe's, and Charlotte N. Gunawardena's chapter 11, "Group development in online distance learning groups," builds on the "community of inquiry" perspectives in chapter 7, as well as the systems theory perspective of chapter 4. They introduce several different social psychology models that explain the behavior of individuals in groups, and follow this with a discussion of group dynamics in virtual groups, where interaction is mediated by online communications technology.

In chapter 12, Mike Allen and colleagues provide a very brief summary of their meta-analysis of some of the literature about students' attitudes to distance learning, consisting mainly of comparisons of satisfaction with learning in face-to-face environments. This is followed, in chapter 13, by Cathy Cavanaugh's meta-analyses of effectiveness of distance education in elementary and high-school education, referred to as K–12. Focusing on recent studies of online delivery and virtual schools, the chapter discusses student characteristics (notably, differences in the learning autonomy of children as compared to adults), considerations in course design and instruction, and administrative and policy studies.

The four chapters that complete this part are all on the general theme of learner support. In the first, Cheria Kramarae explains "why gender matters" and discusses some of the kinds of support needed by women students. These include support in dealing with problems arising from the content of courses; gender differences in learning and teaching styles (suggesting that women prefer the collaborative over independent study pedagogies introduced in earlier chapters); differences in ownership of technology and readiness for college-level study online; and pressures arising from the time needed for study and its financial cost. Similar problems are encountered by all students to some extent during an academic career, which is why successful distance education institutions are those that have good learner support systems, the subject of Robert F. Curry's chapter 15. In chapter 16, Shelley Kinash addresses the needs of disabled students and the support services available to them. To finish this part, Stephen H. Dew reviews the literature of library support, beginning with a list of published resources for librarians, prominently those of the Distance Learning Section of the Association of College Research Libraries.

PART III: DESIGN AND INSTRUCTION

Rick Shearer opens Part III with a discussion of some of the complex decisions that face instructional and course designers when choosing from among the various technologies available for delivery of distance education programs. As I have explained elsewhere (see Moore & Kearsley, 2005, pp. 6–7), the interface of learners with both content and instructors is through one or more media: either (a) text in a variety of forms, (b) audio, (c) video, or (d) artifacts. One of the designer's problems is to choose from among the large range of possible media combinations, as well as the technology best suited to deliver that combination of media. This chapter discusses the merits of various technologies in terms of their suitability for learners with different degrees of learner autonomy; effectiveness in delivering interaction; accessibility; and cost. In setting his discussion within the framework of transactional distance theory, Shearer's chapter can also be read in conjunction with chapter 8.

Chapter 19, by Curtis J. Bonk and Vanessa P. Dennen, builds on Shearer's introduction of design issues, presenting a more detailed look at factors to be considered when designing courses for delivery on the Web. The authors provide five frameworks that display some of the multitude of variables related to learner psychology; student-student and student-instructor interaction; levels of technology integration; instructor and student roles; and alternative pedagogical strategies. The authors suggest that each of these frameworks can contribute to the development of research agendas as well as the development of instructional tools, instructional design benchmarks, instructor training, and teaching resources.

Instructional design is also the focus of Som Naidu's chapter, which begins with a reiteration of some of the main responsibilities of the instructional designer—worth placing alongside Shearer's discussion of the same subject. The special focus of this chapter is the challenge of designing programs that support activity-based distance learning, a pedagogy grounded in principles of situated learning and constructivist learning theory (see chapter 7), that permits "learning by doing," focusing more on learning activities than on "declarative subject matter content." Here is an aspiration that proved extremely difficult (though not impossible) to achieve in the days of correspondence instruction and has become more viable through creative use of new technology, though it requires understanding and good decisions on the part of course designers.

Chapters 21 and 22 discuss teaching-learning relationships. These are classified into three types: (a) those in which learning is "directed" by teachers, (b) those that are "negotiated," and (c) those that are "informal." These two chapters, which follow a common structure, broaden our understanding of several core themes encountered in previous chapters, including: (a) the role of interaction in learning; (b) the use of resources, including learning objects; (c) the strategy of scaffolding; and (d) assessment, which has not yet been considered in detail. In chapter 21, "Learning in directed distance learning environments," Sharma and colleagues focus on teaching that is "rooted in objectivist models of knowledge acquisition, where external information is organized and strategies developed to ensure consistent acquisition of knowledge and skill. In this type of learning environment, "an expert establishes learning goals and means in accordance with the norms and practices of a specific discipline or community." By contrast, in chapter 22, Janette R. Hill and her colleagues discuss "negotiated" distance learning environments, in which "learning goals and means are jointly determined, balancing individual with externally established priorities." Finally, they describe "informal" environments in which "learners identify the learning goals, deploy individual learning approaches, and assume responsibility for assessing their learning."

The relation of this typology to earlier discussions about learner autonomy, independent learning, and teacher control should be apparent.

Diane Davis is a long-established authority on teaching through text. In chapter 23, she discusses designing teaching to be delivered by text on the Web, including use of textbooks, journal articles, and other forms of text in Web-based courses. Just as Shearer explained that different technologies are optimally suited to different aspects of the teaching and learning communication processes (the concept of "articulation" first identified by Wedemeyer and introduced in chapter 1), so Davis explains that there is a wide range of types of text media. Good instruction therefore depends on each being selected to take advantage of its special strengths before being integrated into the total instructional package (readers will recognize Curtis J. Bonk's and Vanessa P. Dennen's "technology integration" here). Readers should also obtain further insight into one of the principal dimensions of transactional distance as they follow Davis' elaboration of the concept of structure.

Terry Anderson and Alex Kuskis devote their chapter to a more in-depth treatment of interaction. Dialog in transactional distance originally referred to interaction between teacher and learner, but T. Anderson and Kuskis, building on what I can describe as a very simple (since I wrote it!), three-part typology of interaction that adds learner-learner and learner-content interaction, discuss these and several other kinds of interaction. They are interaction between (a) learners and institutions, (b) teachers and content, (c) teachers and teachers, and (d) content and content. This advances the ideas about interaction far beyond my early conceptualization, placing them in the context of online communications, but also connecting with such concepts as communities of inquiry, constructivist learning theory, and collaborative learning, all of which readers have already encountered in earlier chapters. In relation to the design issues raised earlier in this part, the challenge remains—as stated in different ways by Shearer; Bonk and Dennen; Davis; and T. Anderson and Kuskis—to "get the mixture right." In the terminology of transactional distance theory, getting the balance right between the extent of dialog and the extent of structure appropriate for learners of varying abilities to control their learning is the core and enduring design challenge.

Further developing a discussion that has been introduced in several previous chapters, Morris Sammons explores the meaning of collaboration and what can be done to encourage and facilitate it. The discussion touches on several important concepts that readers should recognize, including scaffolding (see Sharma; Naidu), social presence (Hannafin, et al.; W. Anderson; T. Anderson & Kuskis; Garrison & Archer), learning objects (T. Anderson & Kuskis) and one that I was pleased to see that has not appeared before, transactional presence.

The subject of learning objects now comes center stage, as Susan Moisey and Mohamed Ally describe this "promising means of achieving efficiencies and enhanced flexibility in course design and development." I urge every reader to give careful and thoughtful consideration to this subject. The learning object concept offers enormous value in terms of improved quality of teaching, not only because of the way that "mass customization" of content should give us better text, audio and video materials than can be produced by multiple competing teachers and institutions, but also because of the way it releases human and other resources from content creation to facilitating collaborative groups, communities of inquiry, constructivist learning, and other forms of interaction. Unfortunately, there seems to be much uninformed prejudice about learning objects that is impeding what Moisey and Ally describe as "potential to change the way instruction is produced and delivered on a worldwide scale."

The last chapter chosen for Part III is more self-consciously focused on technology than previous chapters, but it is also very much about learning and learners. Chris Dede and his collaborators discuss their hypothesis about the "neomillennial" learning styles they see emerging in the next generation of students as a result of the everyday use of video, audio, and text media in video games, multiuser virtual environments, cell phones, etc. Predicting that over the next decade, how people will learn will be shaped by ubiquitous access to information through workstations and laptop computers, interactions through multiuser virtual environments and the experience of "augmented realities," the authors posit "psychological immersion" as the distinguishing characteristic of future technologies. It is intriguing to consider the implications for course designers, instructors, and administrators of such student habits as "seeking, sieving, and synthesizing," "Napsterism," and "multitasking."

PART IV: POLICIES, ADMINISTRATION, AND MANAGEMENT

If it can be argued that, in formal education, good teaching helps achieve good learning, then it might also be argued that both are dependent on the quality of administrators and managers. It is the perspectives, problems and research-related questions of those who have to set up and manage distance education institutions or programs within institutions that we focus on in Part IV. Opening this set of chapters, Michael Simonson explains the importance of policy itself, "a natural step in the adoption of an innovation," and lists seven types of issues that require a policy at the institutional level (though each would be a policy issue at a state or national level as well). Several of these policy areas address subjects that appeared in previous chapters, including student support, academic advising and library services, while others will be dealt with in later chapters, such as faculty issues and legal issues. Not touched on in Simonson's chapter is the seminal policy question of whether to introduce or develop a distance education program in the first place, and this is the question addressed by Ryan Watkins and Roger Kaufman in their chapter on strategic planning (chapter 29). A model is presented that the authors believe should guide policy makers in acquiring the kind of understanding of needs and opportunities that should precede a decision to introduce or expand a distance education program. Without such study, they believe it is likely that "by the time the impact of a possibly ineffective intervention (e.g. distance education) is known, the institution has sustained damage and/or the ideal time for addressing the problem/opportunity has passed."

Faculty issues have become prominent among policy-maker debates and have demanded much attention from managers and administrators as well. Here Linda L. Wolcott and Kay Shattuck review research related to the faculty's motivation for participating in distance education, highlighting the importance of policy that encourages participation, and management action to provide appropriate rewards. While the issue is not settled, Wolcott and Shattuck's review strongly suggests that managers are not likely to encourage sustained participation (and presumably attention to quality performance) by offering external rewards such as increases in salary. More appreciated by faculty are steps that enhance the quality of the faculty's work, such as providing good support services, good training, and overt commitment to distance education by the institution's leadership.

This last factor, institutional leadership, is the subject of special attention by Michael F. Beaudoin in chapter 31. Beaudoin begins where Wolcott and Shattuck (and indeed others, such as Dede and his colleagues and Watkins and Kaufman) leave off, with a recognition of the demands made by the changing character of teaching and learning on the institution's leadership. A common thread in many such discussions about the future of education and the challenge to the administration is well summed up by Beaudoin: "Indecision and immobility during these tumultuous times could prove fatal to a number of institutions, and it is the presence of effective distance education leadership in such an uncertain milieu that could well make the difference between success or failure, or indeed survival."

The organizational structure of distance education in the United States cannot be understood without an understanding of accreditation, and this is the subject of chapter 32. As Amy Kirle Lezberg explains in her opening sentence, "Unlike most other countries in the world, the United States has never had a Ministry of Higher Education directly regulating the quality of its postsecondary institutions of learning. . . . Instead, in order to operate legally, academic institutions must, like other businesses, be licensed by one of the fifty states, each of which sets individual rules governing entities incorporated within its borders." What she calls "the primary mechanism for assuring employers, governments, and most importantly students and their families that degree granting institutions are offering acceptable levels of education" are private regional accrediting agencies. The chapter gives fascinating glimpses into the evolution of the acceptance of distance education in the United States, as represented by the very recent changes in attitude of the accrediting agencies. Their responsibilities—apart from the specialist Distance Education and Training Council—were, for over a hundred years, geographically defined and so they gave little or no attention to courses that were not located on a campus within their jurisdiction. It was during the 1980s that these traditional agencies began to recognize and implement procedures for examining and evaluating distance education programs. In my view rather optimistically, Lezberg writes that "by the beginning of the twenty-first century, none (of the agencies) had any problem in finding sufficient numbers of appropriately experienced people to review their standards, (and) staff their visiting teams." I say "optimistic" since it has been suggested that what these "appropriately experienced people" often bring to the task of evaluating distance education programs are their very traditional understanding about what is required of a teacher and teaching institution, and so the standards they apply are often guided by the question whether the distance learning is the same as "the real thing." The set of rules intended to guide evaluation of distance programs that was drawn up in 2000 is summarized in Lezberg's chapter, and can be seen as an illustration of the tension between attempts to accommodate the changes driven by new technology and protection of traditional privileges of faculty and the teaching institutions. Another particularly interesting story is that of "the move from strict regionalism to national cooperation," in which Lezberg explains some of the gradual steps made in the United States to the kind of standardization of quality controls that are usually built into the "industrialized system" of most national distance education systems in other countries.

Closely related to the subject of accreditation is that of program evaluation, which is the focus of Melody M. Thompson's and Modupe E. Irele's chapter 33. Some of the guidelines for good practice we met in Lezberg's chapter reappear here, preceded by a quotation that nicely illustrates the skepticism of traditional academia: "How can a teaching/learning process that deviates so markedly from what has been practiced for hundreds of years embody quality education?" The answer, of course, is that if we evaluate the quality of outputs and not inputs (i.e., what is learned and not what teachers do), there is ample evidence that this process provides quality education. Obtaining such data requires a good evaluation design and that depends on knowing specifically what it is intended be learned, which is related closely to good course design, discussed in Part II of this book. Chapter 33 begins with a summary of the rationale for both past ("Is it as good?) and contemporary ("How do we cope"?) evaluations, explains the purposes of evaluation, discusses the evaluation process itself, and reports on some notable evaluation studies. As stated before, regarding this and all chapters, the reader is strongly advised not to read the chapter in isolation from others, but to look at the many threads that connect it to those in the chapters that precede it in this part as well as in Part II and elsewhere. To take a less-than-obvious example, what Saba says about a systems approach to theory might not at first sight appear to be closely related to Thompson and Irele's discussion of evaluation, but assuredly, each chapter will be better understood by carefully considering how evaluation acts as a driver of course design or the reciprocal relationship of evaluation and policy on faculty issues. The relation to accreditation, institutional leadership, and the chapter that follows next in Part III, which discusses costs should be very obvious.

Turning to the question of costs, we find an explanation (Alistair Inglis, chapter 34) of the principal factors that impact cost and how these affect the viability of programs of different types. Beginning with a reference to the expectations of increased productivity that marked the general introduction of new technology into education nearly twenty years ago, Inglis reminds us of the fundamental difference between two different types of distance education: namely, the difference between programs that are extensions of the classroom and those that are based on learning packages—what Inglis calls "resource-based delivery." The terminology is different, but the distinction was noted earlier between the virtual class represented by, among others, Garrison in chapter 7 and the independent learner (who uses the learning package), represented by W. Anderson in chapter 9. As Inglis states, "The reason for drawing this distinction between classroom-based and resource-based models of delivery is that the differences between the two models are critical to the economics of distance education delivery." A central concept in understanding distance education is that of "economy of scale." Several times since we were introduced to Wedemeyer's and Peters' ideas about a systems—or industrial revolution in thinking about teaching, turning it from a craft to a collaborative team activity—we have seen how it is through use of specialist experts and integrated multimedia that distance education can advance the quality of teaching. Until now the cost implications have not been addressed in depth, though referred to among others by Shearer, Bonk, and Denham. The core issue is how to support the large investments needed to pay for the teams of specialist educators and media producers and the production facilities needed for high quality mediated programs; the answer is, as Inglis explains, to spread the total cost over large numbers of students. Maintaining large numbers and sustain quality instructor-to-learner interaction is a challenge not only to faculty but even more to the administration, since the answer lies in part in employing a larger proportion of faculty on a part-time basis, thus releasing the funds needed for program design and production. This is a step that few managers in dual mode institutions have been prepared to take, with the result that many of their programs are of less-than-high quality, while also offering scope for more businesslike for-profit competitors.

Another thorny issue involving the faculty is the subject of the last chapter in Part IV, this being "intellectual property". Tomas A. Lipinski explains that laws passed recently have been intended to encourage distance education, but there are "new obligations that the educator and institution must undertake before advantage of those provisions can be made." Uppermost among these obligations are those concerning ownership of educational materials. The chapter provides a detailed review of some of the copyright issues, noting that "controversy over the ownership and control of faculty created or enhanced educational materials in support the distance education curriculum continues to be unresolved." The controversy centers on questions regarding when faculty members own the rights to material they develop, and when ownership belongs to their employing institution. Put most simply, could any of the authors of this book be sued by their employing institutions if any part of what they included in their chapter had been written as part of a lecture given in the course of their regular teaching (i.e., as "work for hire")? According to one judgment cited by Lipinski, the answer is that the author would lose such a case. Intriguing issues arise that are philosophical, and perhaps methodological and legal, such as "a distinction between what is taught and how it is taught," meaning that "if a professor elects to reduce his lectures to writing, the professor and not the institution employing him owns the copyright." If a lecture, even when written, is not content but is a teaching process, then what of the written teaching that constitutes an online study guide? If these faculty ownership issues make up what we might call the "supplier's problem," there is a second type of copyright problem, which can be called the "consumer's problem." This consists of our obligations when we are teaching, not to infringe on the ownership rights of others. Has any reader (to quote a case from Lipinski) "posted copyright material without permission on their web-site"? See the chapter to find out what happened in court!

PART V: AUDIENCES AND PROVIDERS

In Part V, eight separate chapters report on some of the main consumers and suppliers of distance education programs, focusing in turn on elementary and high schools, community colleges, and universities; training in the corporate sector, continuing professional education; and the armed forces, ending with a discussion of the very important post-modern phenomenon: the virtual, or network, organization.

To begin, Tom Clark reviews distance education in the education of children in the elementary and secondary schools ("K–12"). The chapter reviews some of the historical trends from the 1920s through to the development of today's virtual schools, including the evolution of audio- and video-based courses as well as professional development for school teachers. Some of the factors affecting the current state of K–12 virtual and distance education include demographic factors, changing attitudes in society and schools to use of technology, the emergence of for-profit vendors, access and equity issues, and the impact of federal and state policies. Following this discussion of pre-college schooling, Christine Mullins provides a review of distance education in the community colleges. As she writes in opening her chapter, "community colleges have led the way in the adoption of distance education for good reason." More than 60% of community college students are part-time students and nearly half are in full-time employment. The community college sees distance education as a way "to fulfill their philosophical mission to provide affordable 'open access' to higher education to all students regardless of their educational financial or ethnic background." Community colleges have been especially important in American distance education as developers and distributors of high-quality, high-production value video programs, often referred to as "telecourses." By complementing these highly polished video presentations with the interactivity available by using the Internet, the community college is well placed to provide an example of superior-quality distance education to the rest of the higher education sector, where video-based instruction has never been taken up to the same extent as in the community college. In her chapter, Mullins reviews for us "a little history" and reports on the take-up of online delivery methods and adds further to our understanding of quality assurance, faculty training, student support services and the emergence of virtual networks.

Also building on a subject touched upon in several previous chapters, Donald E. Hanna's chapter makes more explicit some of the issues about organizational change in higher education. Distance education is "inevitably about changing existing organizational practices through the development of new structural, pedagogical, and technological models." However, as Hanna explains, universities are very conservative, and while able to cope with what he calls "procedural and technological changes," these institutions have difficulty contemplating structural and cultural changes. He reviews the history of organizational change in dual-mode (typically American) universities, single-mode universities such as the United Kingdom's Open University and Athabasca University, and—though not mutually exclusive—for-profit universities. Echoing a theme that has been touched on in Clark's as well as in Mullins' chapters, and anticipating Andrew Woudstra's and Marco Adria's chapter, he introduces the concept of "strategic alliances." After his historical recapitulation of the evolution of distance education in higher education explained as a change process, Hanna introduces the vitally important variable of organizational culture. To understand the extent to which higher educational institutions succeed in distance education, it is necessary to examine neither technology nor pedagogy alone, but to study the dynamics of the institutional culture, for it is the culture and the propensity for innovation within the culture that determines the extent to which change, and therefore success with technology and pedagogy, occurs.

The next four chapters share a common interest in the application of distance education in work settings, the emphasis being on training adults to sustain and enhance their business and professional knowledge and skills. First, Zane L. Berge offers a chapter about the part distance education plays in meeting the training needs of modern business corporations. Echoing Hanna's thesis, in this chapter, the theme of organizational change comes quickly into focus, and "many changes" says Berge, in agreement with Hanna, "have to do with philosophy and in turn, organizational culture." Introducing the significance of the changing global economy (a subject to be taken up further in the chapters that make up Part VI), Berge explains the importance of distance education as a contribution to corporate competitiveness at a time when the shift from "an industrial economy to a knowledge-based economy has companies competing to control intellectual assets, not physical assets." After expanding on the theme of "business needs for distance training and education," Berge reports what are considered to be the steps to be taken by a management that proposes to take advantage of distance education (with strong resonance to Watkins' and Kaufman's chapter on strategic planning).

Moving the focus from corporate training, Gary W. Kuhne and George E. Krauss continue the theme of distance education as a means of coping with the continuously changing state of knowledge, as they address its use in continuing professional education (CPE). Although defining "professional" in its most inclusive sense, the chapter focuses primarily on the continuing education of health professionals, specifically doctors and nurses, as well as accountants. The chapter also provides a more brief review of CPE for insurance agents and lawyers. The conclusion—which suggests there are many opportunities for research related to many other professions—is that "distance education could soon become the preferred way of enabling professionals to keep abreast of changing profession-specific knowledge and skills, maintain and enhance their professional competence, assist their progress from novice to expert practitioners, and advance their careers through promotion and other job changes."

Following the discussion of the corporate and continuing professional education sectors, we next have two contributions representing distance education in the armed forces. From the time in the 1960s when the United States Armed Forces Institute was the largest distance teaching organization in the world until now, when we read about such high profile initiatives as the "E-army university," the army, navy, marine corps and navy have been leaders in the application of communications technologies in continuing education and training. In chapter 41, Philip J.-L.Westfall reports on the evolution and current status of distance education in the US Air Force, and then Walter R. Schumm, David E. Turek, and colleagues provide a similar description in the case of the army. Statistics alone are impressive when one reads about the military sector. Westfall tells us that the US Air Force's Extension Course Institute provides over 450 courses to a quarter of a million students each year, while the Air Technology Network delivers over 3,500 hours of interactive video broadcasts, amounting to 260,000 student hours of training a year. The US Air Force, like the other services, is a partner in the Advanced Distributed Learning Initiative, which includes the development of "sharable content object reference model" and is thus the principal forum for the development of learning objects, a cutting-edge initiative we looked at in chapter 26 of this book. In discussing developments in the army, Walter R. Schumm and his colleagues compare what they consider to be the weaknesses of traditional "legacy" distance education and recent "electronic" distance education. In February of 2006, a statement of policy to promote distance education included as comprehensive a definition of distance education as one will find: "the delivery of standardized individual, collective, and self-development training to soldiers and units at the right place and right time, using multiple means and technologies, with synchronous and asynchronous student-instructor interaction." For reasons known to the army (possibly to outlive the apparently unsatisfactory memory of "legacy" programs"), the title was, unfortunately I feel, changed from Army Distance Learning Program to Army Distributed Learning Program. If we can forgive the confusion caused by relabeling, the policy that supports the program is exemplary; distance education "will become the primary method of training, except where resident training is justified." This perfectly reflects the more sophisticated view about the relationship of distance and resident training, which is that the latter, usually more costly, should not be discounted in any training strategy, but only used when the normally lower cost and more efficient method of distance education cannot result in the learning outcomes desired by the program. If resident training was *not* used when it was unnecessary, sufficient funds would be released for the development of the distance education program (the cost policy problem mentioned in connection with chapter 34). As is so often the case, the armed forces are more pragmatic and less constrained by "legacy" than most formal education institutions.

To end Part V, we focus explicitly on a topic that has emerged in several earlier chapters, including those by Clark, Mullins, and Hanna. The virtual organization, also conceived as an organization with the structure of a network, has become a core concept of the postmodern global society. "The network continues to constitute the single most important structural and organizing principle in the short history of distance education," state Woudstra and Adria. Theorists and practitioners outside of distance education "have used the principles of the network to develop approaches to e-commerce, community development, and e-government that have transformed entire industries," yet it remains "largely un-theorized in the distance education literature and unrecognized within the practices and processes of distance education." To the extent this is true—and I would argue that what is here referred to as "network" has been an integral element in the systems approach to the design and delivery of distance education— the student would be well advised to research in as much depth as possible what is represented by this chapter. One can safely study distance education that is grounded on the traditional model of education in which supplying institutions hold monoplistic control over cohorts ("classes") of learners, but if one believes that this is giving way to a demand-driven model— to what Dede and colleagues called a "postmillennial" model, in which largely autonomous learners will draw different components of their study programs from any one of a miscellany of providing institutions—then the network is the organizational model of the future, and research on this area will be groundbreaking. As Woudstra and Adria make clear, it is not only the learner but also the teacher and the administrator who would be well advised to anticipate the shift from institutional provision of programs to network design and delivery as the educational system of the future. The authors propose some "strategies as potentially helpful for distance educators who are considering organizing or reorganizing their operations with the intention of creating a network organization, virtual organization, or virtual community." Once again, as so often in our *Handbook,* a key theme is that "the task for managers and advocates of virtual distance education is to devise organizational and management processes that will encourage change and allow it to be measured."

PART VI. GLOBAL PERSPECTIVES

Although the *Handbook of Distance Education* is designed primarily for use by educators in North America, contributors include nationals of many countries. This alone can be taken as a reflection of the global nature of this field, a field that since its beginning has always been more international than conventional education, as can be seen in the opening chapters of the book. Today the flow of information and ideas about distance education is merely part of the phenomenon of globalism, the closer integration of national societies and economies that is itself to a large extent a consequence of the spread of powerful communications and information technologies. For this last part of the *Handbook*, we have commissioned a group of international scholars to help us understand some of these global dimensions of the field. Their perspectives give a glimpse of some of the directions that the field is likely to take in the years ahead, as our countries, cultures, and economies become more and more integrated.

In the opening chapter of this part, the idea of internationalization is introduced by Robin Mason as "cross-border activity, borderless education, globalized education, even trade in education." Mason writes, "The university is in some ways the most international, and the best positioned, institution to promote genuine globalization." She explains how the concept of globalization appeals differently to different players in the international arena, and points out some of the significant issues: accessibility; quality assurance; cultural differences in learning and teaching; and pressures arising from commercialization of education. The chapter reports some examples of important cross-national programs and suggests areas for future research.

One of the core problems mentioned by Mason is that of cultural diversity and the problems of teaching and learning across cultures, and this is the focus of the chapter by Charlotte N. Gunawardena and Deborah LaPointe. After defining culture ("not only do nationalities and ethnic groups have cultures, but so do communities, organizations and other systems"), the authors discuss intercultural communication, cultural perceptions of social presence, cultural differences in group dynamics, and the role of language. A very nice illustration is the example of how we refer to ourselves; in English, we have few words, usually "I" and "we"; in Japanese, "what you call yourself and others is totally dependent on the relationship between you and the other person, and often it is dependent on the status differential." Gunawardena and LaPointe follow their analysis with some suggestions for accommodating cultural issues during the design process. Again, I am reminded of Saba's chapter in Part I in which he encourages us to see how each relatively small decision or issue—for example, what particular text layout (Davis) to choose for a particular presentation—has to be seen in the context of the larger frames within which it is nested. The frame under consideration here is one that, until now, Americans have almost entirely failed to comprehend: how phenomena appear when seen through the eyes of persons of a non-American culture. There is much to learn before we can hope to succeed in the post-millennial networked global society.

In this global society, one of the most important challenges facing distance education is to meet expectations that it will be the means of opening opportunity to the educationally deprived in the same way that it has been motivated by the need to open opportunity domestically. This is the theme of chapter 46, in which John Daniel, Wayne Mackintosh, and William C. Diehl explain the advantages of "mega-universities" as the only viable strategy for meeting the need for tertiary (i.e., higher) education in developing countries. The problem is that "around the world today we need the equivalent of one large new university to open every week just to keep participation rates in higher education constant." It is impossible to meet the need for access at acceptable cost and quality (the "eternal triangle") except through distance education on a large scale. The chapter amplifies some earlier explanations about the benefits of economies of scale and division of labor of teaching, and proceeds to discuss some trends. These include the future role of information and communication technologies, the university response to the challenge of educational entrepreneurship, and the problem of the "digital divide" between developed and developing countries.

Representing one of the most important players in the global economy, namely, the international aid and development agencies, Michael Foley describes the World Bank's Global Development Learning Network (GDLN). He explains the Bank's policy regarding the development of knowledge as a means of combating poverty, and the gradual change in its distance education methodology from a focus on delivering training alone to a broader approach in which training works alongside practical problem solving in a process of knowledge development.

The last two chapters in the *Handbook,* though having many differences, both ask that as we prepare for our participation in the new, fast-changing global society, we take time to reflect on our past experience as well as current practice in a process of reevaluating the relevance of what we do and how we do it.

Looking from the vantage point of one who spent many years in leadership positions at UNESCO—the United Nations Educational, Scientific and Cultural Organization—Jan Visser believes there is a discrepancy between what we do in education and its overriding purpose, which is development. The question, he says, should not be simply how "distance education has improved access to and participation in education and at what cost, but rather: does distance education contribute to a better world?" Since many educational practices "violate the attainment of agreed purposes," the starting place for reform is to develop a "more comprehensive picture of what learning is." One of the implications for distance education in the global society, Visser concludes, is that "the overriding vision in learning must be on problems." Surely, the independently arrived at agreement between Foley from the World Bank and Visser from UNESCO on the importance of problem-centered learning as a key to development in the global society is worth a great deal of consideration.

Drawing on history and rethinking the ends and means of distance education in the global society are also core themes in the last chapter in the *Handbook*. This chapter, written by Australian scholars Terry Evans and Daryl Nation, could as well be placed in the beginning of the book as the end, since it deals primarily with theoretical issues. It goes beyond theory, however, as it attempts to position reflections on these issues in terms of a "critical debate," and it is for that reason—in the hope that we can end the book in a mood of debate—that the chapter has been located here. The debate has to take into account some of the pervasive, over-arching "big issues" that have been met throughout the book. These include "the tensions between the globalizing forces of contemporary life and the ways people live and learn"; the meaning of development, including the "access versus invasion" dilemma; "the global-local tension . . . which operates through to the level of the individual person"; the promise and the limitations of constructivism, that has "ridden a populist wave to become a fashionable theoretical position on which to build educational practices." To begin to engage with these issues, we are pointed back to the history of distance education and invited to revisit foundation theories of learning and social structure. In considering the future of distance education, we are asked to include the proposition that its future might depend on those who work in new forms of distance education developing better understanding of "the expertise and understanding that decades of the research, theory and practice in distance education could provide."

Surely there could be no better justification for the *Handbook* itself.

In concluding this overview, I hope readers will be as strongly impressed as I was when writing it that if this field of distance education is to be understood, it has to be understood in systems terms. Once again, Farhad Saba's chapter in Part I is particularly helpful in theorizing the core reality of this field—multidimensional, the component parts of which are comprehensible in themselves, but only in part. No part can be understood without some understanding of the subfields in which that part is, to use Saba's term, "nested." Thus as we read Part VI and reflect on the future of the field in the global society, understanding has to begin with study of the past; as we study Part V and try to understand the role of distance education in providing learning for each of the principal client populations, not only is it helpful to understand what delivery systems have worked historically and are in use currently internationally, but it is necessary to understand the instructional design and delivery practices of those systems, past and present. And of course, instructional design cannot be divorced from learning theory or from teaching theory. So in the use of this *Handbook*. I hope readers will find not only a key to each of their specializations, but also will be able to see where those specializations fits into the "bigger picture."

Technology is, of course, part of that big picture, but as must be apparent from this overview of chapters, anyone who thinks that distance education is merely adding technology to the existing tools and procedures of the classroom fails to understand the field. Distance education is, at the same time, a set of values about opening opportunity and leveling inequalities; a pedagogy based on readjustment of the control of learning that conventionally lies with teachers, and becomes redirected to give greater responsibility to the learner; it includes a set of instructional design principles and procedures as well as special methods of facilitating interaction; it leads to special leadership and managerial practices especially to the disintegration of traditional structures and the constitution of network systems; it demands a rethinking of educational policy as well as developing forms of institutional organization that changes the balance of capital (i.e., technology) and labor (teachers). Distance education holds enormous promise of better teaching, better quality of learning, and far more economical returns to public and private institutions for money invested in education and training. None of this can happen without careful and deliberate planning, without a vision and clear policy, which ultimately can only be possible where there is enlightened leadership. Leadership is needed to motivate and explain, and to defuse the anxieties of the mass of "late adopters," who while ready to adopt new technology, are far more cautious about changing the roles of teachers or the apportionment of human and financial resources, without which technology is bound to fall short of its promise.

The ultimate value of a book such as this *Handbook* is that it provides the information that will enable teachers, students, administrators, and policy makers to develop the knowledge needed to perform their roles better in better systems. Of course, providing information is not the same thing as developing knowledge. By reading each chapter of this book, the reader will acquire information. Then it is up to the reader to use that information as the source of knowledge by, for example, experimenting with new ways of designing a course, or teaching it, or administering it or studying in it, or undertaking systematic research about it. Becoming more knowledgeable in these ways, each of us then has the opportunity to contribute to the pool of information about the field, particularly by reporting our experiences and the results of our systematic research. The value of such reports lies directly in proportion to the extent to which the answers they provide are related to the preexisting state of knowledge—in other words, to the theory. Thus we come full circle to what was said in the preface to this *Handbook:* add to what is known through research, but first know what is known so that the research is well justified. The ultimate and fundamental reason for the study of the chapters that follow is to help each reader know what is known as the basis for exploring forward. Contributing authors, the publisher, and the editor extend the wish that every reader who turns the page with this mission in mind is blessed with success.

REFERENCE

Moore, M. G., & Kearsley, G. (2005). *Distance education: A systems view* (2nd ed.). Belmont, CA: Wadsworth.

I

HISTORICAL AND
CONCEPTUAL FOUNDATIONS

1

A History of Scholarship

Linda M. Black
Mountain State University and
The Pennsylvania State University

Although isolated studies of distance education in its original form of correspondence study were undertaken from the early decades of the last century, scholarship in the sense of a sustained, growing body of knowledge generating theory through systematic research, really began in the 1950s. The first advocates for research in this field were Gayle B. Childs of Kansas State University (see Almeda, 1988) and Charles A. Wedemeyer at the University of Wisconsin (see Moore, 1987b). After writing his doctoral dissertation on correspondence education in public schools, Childs (1949) initiated one of the first studies of educational television, funded with a substantial grant from the Ford Foundation (Wright, 1991, p. 43). As advocate for research into correspondence education at the National University Extension Association (NUEA), Childs participated in a milestone study of completion rates. Data was gathered on 42,068 college enrollments in 32 institutions and 17,520 high school enrollments in 24 institutions (Childs, 1966, p. 130). Research, although not yet a "notable emphasis in the field of correspondence study" (Childs, 1966, p. 126), began to develop momentum during the 1960s. The Correspondence Study Division (CSD) of the NUEA and the National Home Study Council (NHSC) collaborated in the Correspondence Education Research Project (CERP), a national survey of correspondence study in U.S. higher education, reporting for the first time data which showed that correspondence instruction could be as effective as classroom methods (see MacKenzie, Christensen, & Rigby, 1968, pp. 104–105).

The other pioneering advocate for research in distance education, Wedemeyer, was director of correspondence at the University of Wisconsin-Madison where he conceived and implemented his Articulated Instructional Media Project (AIM). In this, Wedemeyer demonstrated that by deconstructing the teaching process into specialties, employing specialists to work on each as members of a teaching team, and connecting (i.e., "articulating") a variety of communications media to deliver the program, the quality of programs would exceed what could be provided by individuals working alone, or that could be delivered by any one medium (Wedemeyer & Najem, 1969). Of monumental importance in the history of distance education, Wedemeyer's ideas were incorporated into the design of the revolutionary new Open University of the United Kingdom (UKOU), the first publicly funded, national, autonomous, degree-granting, distance teaching university.

In Europe, also during the 1960s, the beginning of scholarly writing is associated with two pioneers: Börje Holmberg in Sweden and Otto Peters in Germany. Holmberg's (1960) *On the*

Methods of Teaching by Correspondence has been described (for example, Larsson, 1992, p. x) as initiating the first European awareness of a pedagogy of correspondence study. Otto Peters began his research at the Education Center of Berlin and, beginning in 1969, at the German Institute for Distance Education Research (DIFF) at the University of Tübingen. He undertook an inventory of distance education in more than 30 countries, and developed his theory of "industrialized education" (Peters, 1967, 1973; Keegan, 1994). Chapters by Peters and by Holmberg (chap. 5 and chap. 6, respectively) appear later in this *Handbook*.

As the 1970s progressed, a number of phenomena about distance education—among them, favorable research findings; educational reforms and socioeconomic justifications for distance education; improved attitudes about it; increased funding for research; and the birth of large, single-mode distance institutions with specialized academic researchers—combined to raise interest in distance education research. One result was the growth of research centers, among the most important being the University of Wisconsin-Extension in Madison, Wisconsin; the Institute of Educational Technology (IET) at the UKOU; the Education Center of Berlin; the DIFF at Tübingen; the Central Institute for Distance Education Research (ZIFF) at the FernUniversität, Hagen, Germany; the Centre for Distance Education (CDE) at Athabasca University, Canada; and the American Center for the Study of Distance Education (ACSDE) at The Pennsylvania State University.

While research topics in the United States were typically limited to studies to compare conventional, face-to-face classroom with mediated distance delivery and studies comparing the effectiveness of technologies and media, popular topics, internationally, went beyond such comparison studies. For example, at the UKOU, studies investigated students' characteristics and attrition rates, underrepresentation of society's disadvantaged segments, traditional academic credentialing, and resistance to distance education as well as instructional effectiveness (e.g., McIntosh, Calder, & Swift, 1976; Glatter & Wedell, 1971).

In 1988, the ACSDE sponsored what was described as the First American Symposium on Research in Distance Education, bringing together some 50 American leaders in distance education with the aim of setting a national research agenda. The book *Contemporary Issues in American Distance Education* (Moore, 1990) carried edited papers from the symposium and provided the first compilation of American scholarly articles reflecting the state of the research at that time. In 1990, the ACSDE sponsored a similar event, this time to focus on international research. "Research in Distance Education: Setting a Global Agenda for the Nineties," was held in Venezuela in cooperation with the International Council of Correspondence Education (ICCE). Representatives from five continents proposed a global research agenda comprising (a) research on computer conferencing; (b) a meta-analyses of researchers' values and assumptions; (c) comparative institutional studies; (d) analyses of students' life experiences; (e) methods and technologies of small island countries; (f) representation of women in distance education materials; and (g) influences of planning and personal, institutional, instructional contexts on student performance (Paulsen & Pinder, 1990, pp. 83–84).

By the beginning of the 21st century, the "no significant difference" phenomenon had been firmly and repeatedly substantiated (Saba, 2003, pp. 6, 18). In the seminal work on this subject, Dubin and Taveggia (1968) had analyzed data from 7 million academic records to conclude that it was not difference in instructional method that determined student performance. Three decades later, Russell (1999, see http://www.nosignificantdifference.org/) summarized 355 research studies that show "no significant difference" in the effectiveness of face-to-face and distance education, citing as the earliest study a dissertation on this subject published in 1928. Contemporary scholars seem to agree that "within group" differences are more important than such "between group" differences (Bates, 2000; Saba, 1999, 2003; Smith & Dillon, 1999a, 1999b), and that future studies have to focus on multiple perspectives and confounding factors of media attributes, or to investigate the specific contributions each technology and media can make to learning, evaluating their merit in terms of access, flexibility, costs, and potential to support quality teaching and learning.

Beginning in 1995, a number of factors, including less generous funding, the retirement of some leading figures, the co-option of distance education research questions by a wider population of academic specialists such as computer scientists and information technologists, impacted the research centers. The DIFF reorganized to become a broad-based education research center and donated its distance education materials to the ZIFF. The IET is now associated with the U.K.'s Centre for Research in Education and Educational Technology (CREET), a center established in 2004 to employ multidisciplinary research teams. The overall productivity of the ACSDE has decreased significantly since Michael G. Moore gave up the directorship in 2002. These early centers performed well their purpose of establishing distance education as a field of study. Current changes, such as moving centers' journals and other publications from public higher education to commercial publishers, are intended to ensure longevity of the scholarship initiated by these centers. Meanwhile, new research centers have emerged (Moore & Kearsley, 2005, pp. 257–287). Prominent among these are the Center for Research in Distance Education (ASF) at the Carl von Ossietzky University of Oldenburg, Germany; the Distance Education Centre at the University of Southern Queensland, Australia; the Norwegian Center for Distance Education (SEFU); the Centre for Flexible and Distance Learning at the University of Auckland, New Zealand; and the South African Institute for Distance Education (SAIDE). Most open universities have their research centers; examples are the Center for Research in Distance and Adult Learning at the Open University of Hong Kong; the Staff Training and Research Institute of Distance Education (STRIDE) at the Indira Ghandi National Open University (IGNOU), India; the Institute of Distance Education at Korea National Open University; and the research center at the Sukhothai Thammathirat Open University (STOU) in Thailand.

SHORT HISTORY OF THEORY

Like research, to which it is intimately related, theory began to emerge during the 1960s and 1970s. The first theorizing attempted to show correspondence teaching as a form of "guided didactic conversation" (Holmberg, 1960), as "industrial production" (Peters, 1967); and as a systems method (Wedemeyer, 1971). Wedemeyer redefined correspondence instruction as "independent study," a philosophical theory connecting communications theory and andragogy to define the learner as independent not only in space and time but also potentially independent in controlling and directing learning (Wedemeyer, 1971). Taken up by M. G. Moore as "learner autonomy," this became part of a foundational theory that together with course structure and dialog became known as the theory of transactional distance (Moore & Kearsley, 2005, pp. 223–227). Other early theoretical writing of some significance include Bååth's (1979) "correspondence study in light of contemporary teaching models;" "the helping organization" (Delling, 1985); and "continuity of concern for students learning at a distance" (Sewart, Keegan, & Holmberg, 1983, pp. 48–49).

A year to remember is 1980! Desmond Keegan, cofounder and coeditor of the Australian journal *Distance Education*, published in the first issue a synthesis of leading theories of distance education. These were "four generally accepted definitions of distance education." The four definitions were those of Holmberg, Peters, Moore, and the July 1971 Law of France, which regulated distance education in that country (Keegan, 1980, pp. 13–36).

From his analysis of these theories, Keegan (1980) concluded that distance education can be defined by six elements: (a) separation of teacher and student; (b) influence of an educational organization; (c) use of technical media; (d) two-way communication; (e) possibility of occasional seminars; and (f) participation in the most industrial form of education. Keegan's became "the most widely cited definition of distance education" (Moore & Kearsley, 2005, p. 229). More recent additions to the corpus of theoretical work include Simonson, Schlosser, and Hanson's (1999) "equivalency theory," Saba's (2003) systems theory, and Garrison, Anderson, and Archer's (2003) theory of communities of inquiry.

PROFESSIONAL DEVELOPMENT OF DISTANCE EDUCATORS

Prior to the 1960s, the private U.S. Hadley School for the Blind was one of the few correspondence institutions to provide in-service professional development for its instructors (Black, 2004, p. 214). Hadley's tutors—full-time, face-to-face teachers at other institutions hired on a part-time basis to tutor Hadley's distance students—were trained to apply distance teaching-learning strategies and methods. Holmberg participated in creating training courses for the European Association of Distance Learning (EADL), while Peters created "Weekly Information Sheets," for DIFF professors and also for *Funkkolleg*, a radio college. Wedemeyer organized faculty lectures on correspondence teaching and during the 1970s developed the first graduate seminars. M. G. Moore, Wedemeyer's research assistant, continued the seminars at Wisconsin from the mid-1970s to the mid-1980s and then developed a three-course graduate program and special certificate in distance education at The Pennsylvania State University from 1986. Moore's training programs used computer- and audio-conferencing technology to deliver instruction to students in Mexico, Finland, and Estonia.

Beginning in the 1960s, professionalizing courses were delivered face-to-face for Third-World countries by the German Foundation for International Development, Bonn; the International Extension College (IEC), London; the Swedish Authority for Work in Developing Countries (SIDA); the University of Wisconsin-Extension; and the ICCE. Professionalizing courses were also delivered by correspondence and by other technologies and media by a number of institutions and organizations, including Australia's South Australia College of Advanced Education, Canada's Open Learning Institute of British Columbia, Germany's FernUniversität, Sweden's Hermods Correspondence School, the United Kingdom's Open University, and in the United States, the University of Wisconsin and Penn State University. A 1993 project, "The Bangkok Project," under the auspices of the International Council for Distance Education (ICDE), was the first successful attempt to show that online networking could provide cost-effective yet meaningful interactions among distance education professionals (Anderson & Mason, 1993, p. 15). Among current highly regarded programs of professional development are the Penn State World Campus' adult education master's program, which includes Moore's distance education courses; and master's degrees in distance education at Athabasca University, the UKOU, and the University of Maryland University College (UMUC) in partnership with the University of Oldenburg, Germany.

Two associations of importance today for sponsoring distance education professionalizing projects are the Commonwealth of Learning (COL) and the United Nations Educational, Scientific and Cultural Organization's (UNESCO) Institute for Information Technologies in Education (IITE). COL, a resource for training in the policies, methodology, and practice of open, distance, and technology-mediated learning, describes its professionalizing projects on its Web site (http://www.col.org). IITE has sponsored a course "Information and Communication Technologies in Distance Education" (http://unesdoc.unesco.org/images/0012/001293/129395e.pdf) to teach professionals in developing regions of the world such as Africa, Asia, and Eastern Europe.

LECTURES, SEMINARS, SYMPOSIA, WORKSHOPS, AND CONFERENCES

In 1891, the First National Extension Conference brought together educators interested in correspondence study (Watkins, 1991, p. 4). A marginalized group in higher education, the correspondence educators continued to network in an effort to enjoy mutual support. The CSD/NUEA activities of the 1950s and 1960s and the ICCE conferences of 1948 and 1953 impacted favorably on correspondence instruction's status within higher education, helped stimulate an international correspondence movement, and established some U.S. correspondence educators as international leaders (Bunker, 2003, pp. 52–55).

A 1962 conference, "Conference on New Media," funded by the U.S. Department of Education (Erdos, 1992, pp. 68–72) brought together specialists in audio-visual media, programmed instruction, field service bureaus, motion picture, radio, and television production, and correspondence study with Wedemeyer and Childs as keynote speakers. A 1988 workshop initiated by the Independent Study Division (ISD, successor to the Correspondence Study Division) also brought together representatives from a variety of fields, including instructional systems designers, correspondence educators, communications technologists, and others. When correspondence experts joined experts from other fields, new research agendas originated. Study questions moved from print-based correspondence learning to audioconferenced and teleconferenced learning; from one-on-one, individualized communication between instructors-tutors to group-based, two-way communication between instructors-students; and from increasing persistence to increasing learner motivation though new communications media (Black, 2004, pp. 171–172).

During the 1970s, these evolutionary trends accelerated. At distance education conferences, there was an influx of specialists not only from other fields but also from the Third World. In fact, Third-World countries submitted the majority of the papers considered for the Open University of the United Kingdom's (UKOU's) 1979 10th anniversary conference (Neil, 1981). Regional conferences during the 1980s in Europe were funded by a variety of groups; e.g., the European Council for Education by Correspondence (EHSC), the European Association of Distance Teaching Universities (EADTU), the European Union (EU), the United Kingdom's Council of Educational Technology (CET), and the European Council for Education by Correspondence (CEC). In the United States, the University of Wisconsin-Extension in Madison, WI sponsored its First Annual Conference on Distance Teaching and Learning in 1985 with Michael G. Moore as keynote speaker. With changing travel habits, conferences became increasingly international. The International Council for Open and Distance Education (ICDE) world conferences have grown in size as well as frequency, and are historically important to the origins and development of scholarship in the field. The conferences from 1938 to 2001 are described by Bunker (2003; also see Chapter 2 in this *Handbook*).

FILMS, STUDY/LEARNING GUIDES, DIRECTORIES, ESSAYS, NEWSLETTERS, BIBLIOGRAPHIES, OCCASIONAL PAPERS, MONOGRAPHS, AND JOURNALS

Among early publications that helped lay the foundation for the field of study and scholarship are the newsletters of the National University Extension Association (NUEA, 1952, as cited in Wright, 1991, p. 42) and the National Home Study Council's (NHSC) *Home Study Review*. Other sources include Wedemeyer's 1963 film "The Postage Stamp Classroom," a story about correspondence study (Wright, 1991, p. 49) and his *Brandenburg Memorial Essays on Correspondence*

Instruction (1963, 1966). Wedemeyer was also responsible for initiating ICCE's newsletters in 1971. Other newsletters of note are those of the Australian and South Pacific External Studies Association (ASPESA), initiated in 1974, and the Council of Educational Technology's (CET's) *Open Learning Guides* of the 1970s, created by the United Kingdom's National Extension College (NEC) (Lewis & Paine, 1985, p. vii).

Bibliographies represent valuable scholarship. Of historical significance are those of Childs (1960), Mathieson (1971), and Holmberg (1968, 1977). Among historically important reports are: Wedemeyer's (1968) Report on the University of South Africa and his report on the AIM Project (Wedemeyer & Najem, 1969). Historically important documents should include the ICCE conference proceedings and occasional papers by Australia's Deakin University, the Netherlands' Open Universiteit, the *Broadsheets on Distance Learning* by the United Kingdom's International Extension College; and publications of Spain's *Universidad Nacional de Education a Distancia* (UNED). Of most importance, historically in the United States, are monographs, research reports, and books of readings by the American Center for Study of Distance Education (ACSDE).

Early journals published articles aimed at improving practice rather than scholarship, examples being the NHSC's *Home Study Review*; *Epistolodidaktika*, first published in Germany in 1963 and subsequently by the European Home Study Council; the UK Open University's *Teaching at a Distance*, first published in 1975 and changing its title in 1986 to *Open Learning*.

During the 1980s, several journals were developed with the declared aim of reporting research and theory rather than practice. Most important among these are *Distance Education*, started in 1980 by the Australian and South Pacific External Studies Association (ASPESA); the *Journal of Distance Education*, started in 1986 by the Canadian Association of Distance Education (CADE); and the *American Journal of Distance Education (AJDE)*, founded in 1987 by Michael G. Moore at The Pennsylvania State University. The *AJDE* paved the way for greater external visibility and recognition of distance educators by the higher education community in the United States and abroad (Moore, 1987a). The journal also provided budding U.S. distance education scholars—often a marginalized group in higher education—a place to publish, "increasing the opportunity for the exchange of ideas and information," according to Childs (Almeda, 1988, p. 70).

Other important journals and publications that have appeared in recent years include the Athabasca University's *International Review of Research in Open and Distance Learning* and the Sloan Foundation's *Journal of Asynchronous Learning Networks (JALN)*.

BOOKS, DISSERTATIONS, AND DATABASES

Two of the first books in the field, both published in 1926, are *The University Afield* by Hall-Quest and *Correspondence Schools, Lyceums, Chautauquas* by Noffsinger (Pittman, 1990, pp. 68–70). Another book of great historical interest is *University Teaching by Mail: A Survey of Correspondence Instruction Conducted by American Universities* by Bittner and Mallory (1933), which illuminates correspondence study's origins and its integration into American universities. In the 1960s and 1970s, three books contributed richly to emerging scholarship in America (Pittman, 1990, pp. 69–71): (a) *Correspondence Instruction in the U.S.: A Study of What It Is, How It Functions, and What Its Potential May Be* (MacKenzie et al., 1968); (b) *New Perspectives in University Correspondence Study* (Wedemeyer & Childs, 1961); and (c) *The Changing World of Correspondence Study: International Readings* (MacKenzie & Christensen, 1971); Wedemeyer's (1963, 1966) edited monographs, *The Brandenburg Memorial Essays,* provided important evidence about the broadening use of correspondence education at an international level.

Catalyzed first by the emergence and proliferation of the open universities in the 1970s and 1980s, and then by the advent and increasing popularity of online delivery, the quantity of books, dissertations, and databases about distance education has exploded. Among the most valuable for the study of scholarship are, according to Australian commentators Evans and Nation (2003, p. 779): *Learning at the Back Door: Reflections on Nontraditional Learning in the Lifespan* (Wedemeyer, 1981) and *Distance Education: International Perspectives* (Sewart, Keegan, & Holmberg, 1983, 1988). Three other books of value in the study of history are (a) *The Distance Teaching Universities* (Rumble & Harry, 1983), (b) *The Ivory Towers Thrown Open* (Reddy, 1988), and (c) *Distance Education in Canada* (Mugridge & Kaufman, 1986).

In the United States, Moore's (1990) extremely important anthology *Contemporary Issues in American Distance Education* was the first compilation reporting the state of scholarship and practice in distance education. Another anthology, Garrison and Shale's (1990) *Education at a Distance: From Issues to Practice* included a historical chapter "Origins of Distance Education in the United States" by Moore's student, Sherow, and Wedemeyer (1990), including a brief explanation of Wedemeyer's AIM system and its relationship to the UKOU and the influence of both on distance education.

An outstanding book for historians is *The Foundations of American Distance Education: A Century of Collegiate Correspondence Study* by Watkins and Wright (1991). According to the distinguished historian Von Pittman (2003, p. 23), this "represents the single most important contribution to the history of collegiate correspondence study published" since Moore (1990). Watkins' and Wright's history begins in 1982 with the founding of the University of Chicago's correspondence study program and covers the next 100 years of achievements, ideas, issues, and research in collegiate distance education.

Renee Erdos, the first distance educator awarded a Fulbright Scholarship and President of ICCE in the late 1960s, studied the educational systems at 18 correspondence study institutions in Asia, Canada, Europe, and the United States and reported her impressions and findings in her *Teaching Beyond the Campus* (Erdos, 1992). Another highly valuable book is Sarah Guri-Rosenblits' (1999) *Distance and Campus Universities.*

Peters' ideas became known to English-speaking scholars through Keegan's (1994) *Otto Peters on Distance Education: The Industrialization of Teaching and Learning* and more recently through Peters' (2001) *Learning and Teaching in Distance Education: Analysis and Interpretations from an International Perspective* and his *Distance Education in Transition: New Trends and Challenges*, 4th edition (Peters, 2004).

Moore and Kearsley's (1996, rev. ed., 2005) *Distance Education: A Systems View* has become a standard textbook in the United States and has been translated into Chinese, Korean, and Japanese. Moore and Anderson's (2003, 2004 paperback) *Handbook of Distance Education* has become a definitive scholarly reference book.

Important doctoral dissertations of the 1960s to the 1970s include *William Henry Lighty: Adult Education Pioneer* by Axford (1961), which "stands alone as a comprehensive account of the career of a seminal figure in collegiate correspondence study" (Pittman, 1990, p. 72); *Die Didaktische Struktur des Fernunterrichts. Untersuchungen zu einer Industrialisierten Form des Lehrens und Lernens* by Peters (1973); *Investigation of the Interaction Between the Cognitive Style of Field Independence and Attitudes to Independent Study Among Adult Learners Who Use Correspondence Independent Study and Self-Directed Independent Study* by Moore (1976); and *College-Sponsored Correspondence Education in the United States: A Comparative History of Its Origins (1873–1915) and Its Recent Developments* by Gerrity (1976), a dissertation that is "arguably the best single historical work on collegiate correspondence education" (Pittman, 1990, p. 70).

One of the earliest, comprehensive, extensive databases (published in German) of international distance training and education systems was created by Peters in the 1960s as part of his comparative research and theoretical work (Keegan, 1993, pp. 2–3). Another of the earliest, large centralized databases—i.e., the International Center for Distance Learning (ICDL)—was established at the UKOU (Harry, 1986, 1992). One of the first online databases of information, ideas, and discussions, the DEOS-L listserv was developed under Moore's direction at the ACSDE at Penn State in 1991, had 4,000 participants in 60 countries by 1996, and is still running. A relatively new online database is the Global Distance Education Network (GDENet), initiated by Moore at the World Bank to provide access to information about distance education in developing countries. GDENet, was linked to the International Center for Distance Learning and also to the Commonwealth Of Learning. GDENet (www.gdenet.org) is now linked to a UNESCO's Higher Education Open and Distance Learning Knowledge Base (http://portal.unesco.org/education/en/ev.php-URL_ID=428438&URL_DO=DO_TOPIC&URL_SECTION=201.html).

Prominent editors such as Desmond Keegan, Fred Lockwood, and Michael G. Moore are important for creating whole series of publications on distance education that have promoted and advanced scholarship. In the United States, under Moore's leadership, the ACSDE published more than 20 monographs between 1987 and 1997 (e.g., Moore & Thompson, 1990, 1997; Munro, 1998; Wagner & Koble, 1998). The ACSDE also published several important edited books, for example, Moore and Shin's (2000) historical collection of interviews with distance education leaders of the 1980s and 1990s.

In recent years, there has been an explosion in the number of doctoral dissertations as well as master's papers. They now comprise a valuable body of unpublished secondary literature (Pittman, 2003). An April 5, 2006, a keyword search of the term "correspondence study" in the UMI Dissertation Abstracts Online database produced only 40 citations, 20 of which were dated from 1981 to 2001, and 20 from 1932 to 1976. On the same date, a keyword search of the term "distance education" produced 1178 citations with 947 of the citations dated from 1995 to 2006, and 231 dated from 1981 to 1994. The earliest data-based publication under "distance education" was dated 1981.

CONCLUSION

Pioneering scholars of distance education have provided a broad, rich foundation of scholarly activity. Scholarly activity developed in three waves. It stirred prior to 1960 and grew increasingly professionalized from 1960 until the mid-1990s through today, Beginning in 1995, scholarly activity exploded. There are many exciting opportunities for historical study, and the resources listed in this chapter would be good places to start.

REFERENCES

Almeda, M. B. (1988). Interview: Speaking personally with Gayle B. Childs. *The American Journal of Distance Education, 2*(2), 68–74.

Anderson, T., & Mason, R. (1993). International computer conferencing for professional development: The Bangkok Project. *The American Journal of Distance Education, 7*(2), 5–18.

Axford, R. (1961). William Henry Lighty: Adult education pioneer (Doctoral dissertation, University of Chicago, 1961). *Dissertation Abstracts International,* ADD X1961, AAT T-07764.

Bååth, J. A. (1979). *Correspondence in light of a number of contemporary teaching models.* Kristianstads Boktryckori AB Kristianstad. Malmö, Sweden: Liber-Hermods. (This is the revised, translated version of a research project: "2-Way Communication in Correspondence Education," 1978, originally written in Swedish, by Bååth.)

Bates, A. W. (2000). *Managing technological change: Strategies for college and university leaders.* San Francisco: Jossey-Bass.

Bittner, W. S., & Mallory, H. F. (1933). *University teaching by mail: A survey of correspondence instruction conducted by American universities.* New York: Macmillan.

Black, L. M. (2004). A living story of the origins and development of scholarship in the field of distance education. (Doctoral dissertation, The Pennsylvania State University, 2004). *Dissertation Abstracts International, DAI-A 65/12,* p. 4496. AAT 3157520.

Bunker, E. L. (2003). The history of distance education through the eyes of the International Council for Distance Education. In M. G. Moore, & W. G. Anderson (Eds.), *Handbook of distance education* (pp. 49–66). Mahwah, NJ: Lawrence Erlbaum Associates.

Childs, G. B. (1949). Comparison of supervised correspondence study pupils and classroom pupils in achievement in school subjects. (Doctoral dissertation, University Of Nebraska-Lincoln, 1949). *Dissertation Abstracts International,* ADD W1949.

Childs, G. B. (1960). *An annotated bibliography of correspondence study 1897–1960.* New York: National University Extension Association, Committee on Research, Correspondence Study Division.

Childs, G. B. (1966). Review of research in correspondence study. In C. A. Wedemeyer (Ed.), *The Brandenburg memorial essays on correspondence instruction—II* (pp. 126–141). Madison, WI: The University of Wisconsin-Extension.

Delling, R. M. (1985, August). *Towards a theory of distance education.* Paper presented at the ICDE Thirteenth World Conference, Melbourne, Australia.

Dubin, R., & Taveggia, T. C. (1968). The teaching-learning paradox: A comparative analysis of college teaching methods. Eugene, OR: Center for the Advanced Study of Educational Administration. ERIC Document ED 026 966.

Erdos, R. (1992). *Teaching beyond the campus.* Australia: Fast Books, a Division of Wild and Woolley Pty. Ltd., Glebe.

Evans, T., & Nation, D. (2003). Globalization and the reinvention of distance education. In M. G. Moore, & W. G. Anderson (Eds.), *Handbook of distance education* (pp. 777–792). Mahwah, NJ: Lawrence Erlbaum Associates.

Garrison, D. R., Anderson, T., & Archer, W. (2003). A theory of critical inquiry in online distance education. In M. G. Moore, & W. G. Anderson (Eds.), *Handbook of distance education* (pp. 113–128). Mahwah, NJ: Lawrence Erlbaum Associates.

Garrison, D. R., & Shale, D. (Eds.). (1990). *Education at a distance: From issues to practice.* Malabar, FL: Robert E. Krieger Publishing Co.

Gerrity, T. W. (1976). *College-sponsored correspondence education in the United States: A comparative history of its origins (1873–1915) and its recent developments (1960–1975).* (Doctoral dissertation, Columbia University Teachers, 1976). *Dissertation Abstracts International, DAI-A 37/02,* p. 4496. AAT 7617282.

Glatter, R., & Wedell, E. G. (1971). *Study by correspondence.* London: Longman Group.

Guri-Rosenblits, S. (1999). *Distance and campus universities.* Oxford: Pergamon.

Hall-Quest, A. L. (1926). *The university afield.* New York: Macmillan Company.

Harry, K. (1986). The International Center for Distance Learning of the United Nations University: Resources and services. *Journal of Distance Education, 1*(1), 77–79.

Harry, K. (1992). The development of information and documentation work in distance education. In G. E. Ortner, K. Graff, & H. Wilmersdoerfer (Eds.), *Distance education as two-way communication: Essays in Honour of Börje Holmberg* (pp. 210–224). Frankfurt am Main: Peter Lang.

Holmberg, B. (1960). *On the methods of teaching by correspondence.* Lund, Sweden: Lunds Universitets Arsskrift (The Lund University Yearbook), n.f. Avd. 1, Bd. 54, No. 2. (1962; reprinted in entirety in the U.S. N.H.S.C.'s *Home Study Review* journal and in German as *Über die Lehrmethoden im Fernunterrich*).

Holmberg, B. (1968). *Studies in education by correspondence: A bibliography.* Malmö: Sweden: European Council for Education by Correspondence (CEC).

Holmberg, B. (1977). *Distance education: A survey and bibliography.* London: Kogan Page; New York: Nichols Publishing Co.

Keegan, D. (1980). On defining distance education. *Distance Education, 1*(1), 13–36.

Keegan, D. (Ed.). (1993). *Theoretical principles of distance education.* London: Routledge.

Keegan, D. (Ed.) (1994). *Otto Peters on distance education: The industrialization of teaching and learning.* London: Routledge.

Larsson, H. (1992). Living eulogy—Börje Holmberg: Scholar, teacher, and gentleman. In G. E. Ortner, K. Graff, & H. Wilmersdoerfer (Eds.), *Distance education as two-way communication: Essays in honour of Börje Holmberg* (pp. viii–xi). Frankfurt am Main and New York: Peter Lang.

Lewis, R., & Paine, N. (1985). *Open learning guide 6: How to communicate with the learner.* London: Council for Educational Technology.

MacKenzie, O., & Christensen, E. L. (Eds.). (1971). *The changing world of correspondence study: International readings.* University Park: Pennsylvania State University Press.

MacKenzie, O., Christensen, E. L., & Rigby, P. H. (1968). *Correspondence instruction in the United States: A study of what it is, how it functions, and what its potential may be.* New York: McGraw-Hill Book Co. Sponsored by the American Council on Education and the National Commission on Accrediting: Supported by the Carnegie Corporation of New York.

Mathieson, D. E. (1971). *Correspondence study: A summary review of the research and development literature.* New York: National Home Study Council/ERIC Clearinghouse on Adult Education.

McIntosh, N., Calder, J., & Swift, B. (1976). *A degree of difference. A study of the first year's intake to the Open University of the U.K.* Gulidford: Society for Research in Higher Education.

Moore, M. G. (1976). Investigation of the interaction between the cognitive style of field independence and attitudes to independent study among adult learners who use correspondence independent study and self-directed independent study. (Doctoral dissertation, University of Wisconsin-Madison, 1976). *DAI-A 37/06*, p. 3344. AAT 7620127.

Moore, M. G. (1987a). Editorial: Words of welcome and intent. *The American Journal of Distance Education, 1*(1), 1–5.

Moore, M. G. (1987b). Interview: Speaking personally with Charles A. Wedemeyer. *The American Journal of Distance Education, 1*(1), 59–64.

Moore, M. G. (1990). (Ed.). *Contemporary issues in American distance education.* New York: Pergamon Press.

Moore, M. G., & Anderson, W. G. (Eds.). (2003). *Handbook of distance education.* Mahwah, NJ: Lawrence Erlbaum Associates.

Moore, M. G., & Kearsley, G. (1996). *Distance education: A systems view.* Belmont, CA: Wadsworth.

Moore, M. G., & Kearsley, G. (2005). *Distance education: A systems view* (2nd ed.). Belmont, CA: Wadsworth.

Moore, M. G., Mackintosh, W., Black, L., Mushi, H., Shimlopilami, R. K., Sa, C., Thompson, E., & Norrie, J. (2002). *Information and Communication Technologies in Distance Education: A Specialized Training Course.* UNESCO: Institute for Information Tecnologies in Education.

Moore, M. G., & Shin, N. (Eds.). (2000). Speaking personally about distance education: Foundations of contemporary practice. *Readings in Distance Education No. 6 of the American Center for the Study of Distance Education (ACSDE).* University Park, PA: The Pennsylvania State University, ACSDE.

Moore, M. G., & Thompson, M. M. (1990). The effects of distance learning: A summary of literature. *Monograph No. 2 of the American Center for the Study of Distance Education (ACSDE).* University Park, PA: The Pennsylvania State University, ACSDE.

Moore, M. G., & Thompson, M. M. (1997). The effects of distance learning. *Monograph No. 15 of the American Center for the Study of Distance Education (ACSDE).* University Park, PA: The Pennsylvania State University, ACSDE.

Mugridge, I., & Kaufman, D. (Eds.). (1986). *Distance education in Canada.* London: Croom Helm.

Munro, J. S. (1998). Presence at a distance: The educator-learner relationship in distance learning. *Monograph No. 16 of the American Center for the Study of Distance Education (ACSDE).* University Park, PA: The Pennsylvania State University, ACSDE.

Neil, M. W. (1981). *Education of adults at a distance: A report of the Open University's Tenth Anniversary Conference.* London: Kogan Page in association with the Open University Press.

Noffsinger, J. S. (1926). *Correspondence schools, lyceums, chautauquas.* New York: The Macmillan Company.

Paulsen, M. F., & Pinder, P. W. (1990). Workshop report: Research in distance education: Setting a global agenda for the nineties. *The American Journal of Distance Education, 4*(3), 83–84.

Peters, O. (1967). *Das Fernstudium an Universitaten und Hochschulen: didaktische Struktur und vergleichende Interpretation: Ein Beitrag zur Theorie der Fernlehre* [Distance education at universities and higher education institutions: Didactical structure and comparative analysis—A contribution to the theory of distance education]). Weinheim und Berlin: Beltz—Padagogisches Zentrum: Veroffentlichungen, Reihe B, vol. 8. Second half of the monograph: Available at http://www.umuc.edu/ide/seminar/peters.html; also published in D. Sewart, D. Keegan, & B. Holmberg (Eds). (1983). Distance education: International perspective (pp. 95–113). London: Croom Helm. Distance education and industrial production: A comparative interpretation in outline, 1967. Available at http://www.umuc.edu/ide/seminar/peters.html

Peters, O. (1973). (Doctoral dissertation). *Die didaktische struktur des Fernunterrichts. Untersuchungen zu einer industrialisierten form des lehrens und lernens.* Weinheim: Beltz. Tubinger Beitrage zum Fernstudium, vol. 7.

Peters, O. (2001). *Learning and teaching in distance education: Analysis and interpretations from an international perspective* (Rev. ed.). London: Kogan Page. (First published in German as *Didaktik des fernstudiums* by Luchterhand Verlag, 1997).

Peters, O. (2004). *Distance education in transition: New trends and challenges* (4th ed.). Oldenburg, Germany: Bibliotheks—und Informationssystem der Universitat Oldenburg.

Pittman, V. (1990). Correspondence study in the American university: A historiographic perspective. In Michael G. Moore (Ed.), *Contemporary issues in American education* (pp. 67–80). New York: Pergamon Press.

Pittman, V. (2003). Correspondence study in the American university: A second historiographic perspective. In M. G. Moore, & W. Anderson (Eds.), *Handbook of distance education* (pp. 21–35). Mahwah, NJ: Lawrence Erlbaum.

Reddy, G. R. (1988). *The ivory towers thrown open.* Stosius Inc., Advent Books Division.

Rumble, G., & Harry, K. (1983). *The distance teaching universities.* PalgraveMacmillan.

Russell, T. (1999). *The no significant difference phenomenon: A comparative research annotated bibliography on technology for distance education.* U.S. IDEC.

Saba, F. (1999). Review of lead article: Toward a systems theory of distance education. *The American Journal of Distance Education, 13*(2), 24–31.

Saba, F. (2003). Distance education theory, methodology, and epistemology: A pragmatic paradigm. In M. G. Moore, & W. G. Anderson (Eds.), *Handbook of distance education* (pp. 3–20). Mahwah, NJ: Lawrence Erlbaum Associates.

Sewart, D., Keegan, D., & Holmberg, B. (Eds). (1983). *Distance education: International perspectives.* London: Croom Helm.

Sewart, D., Keegan, D., & Holmberg, B. (Eds). (1988). *Distance education: International perspective* (Rev. ed.). New York: Routledge.

Sherow, S., & Wedemeyer, C. A. (1990). Origins of distance education in the United States. In D. R. Garrison, & D. Shale (Eds.), *Education at a distance: From issues to practice* (pp. 7–22), Malabar, FL: Robert E. Krieger.

Simonson, M., Schlosser, C., & Hanson, D. (1999). Theory and distance education: A new discussion. *The American Journal of Distance Education, 13*(1), 60–75.

Smith, P. L., & Dillon, C. L. (1999a). Comparing distance learning and classroom learning: Conceptual considerations. *The American Journal of Distance Education, 13*(2), 6–23.

Smith, P. L., & Dillon, C. L. (1999b). Toward a systems theory of distance education: A reaction. *The American Journal of Distance Education, 13*(2), 32–36.

Wagner, E. D., & Koble, M.A. (1998). Distance Education Symposium 3: Course design. *Monograph No. 14 of the American Center for the Study of Distance Education (ACSDE).* University Park, PA: The Pennsylvania State University, ACSDE.

Watkins, B. L. (1991). A quite radical idea: The invention and elaboration of collegiate correspondence study. In B. L. Watkins, & S. J. Wright (Eds.), *The foundations of American distance education: A century of collegiate correspondence study.* (pp. 1–35). Dubuque, Iowa: Kendall-Hunt.

Watkins, B. L., & Wright, S. J. (Eds.). (1991). *The foundations of American distance education: A century of collegiate correspondence study.* Dubuque, IA: Kendall-Hunt.

Wedemeyer, C. A. (1963). *The Brandenburg memorial essays on correspondence instruction—I.* Madison, WI: The University of Wisconsin—University Extension.

Wedemeyer, C. A. (1966). *The Brandenburg memorial essays on correspondence instruction—II.* Madison, WI: The University of Wisconsin—University Extension.

Wedemeyer, C. A. (1968), No. 302763, Assessment Report of February, 1968. *University of South Africa (UNISA): Report and recommendations.* Published by UNISA: Pretoria, South Africa.

Wedemeyer, C. A. (1971). Independent study. In L. C. Deighton (Ed.), *The encyclopedia of education, vol. 4* (pp. 548–557). New York: Free Press.

Wedemeyer, C. A. (1974). Characteristics of open learning systems. In *Open learning systems.* Washington: National Association of Educational Broadcasters.

Wedemeyer, C. A. (1981). *Learning at the back door: Reflections on nontraditional learning in the lifespan.* Madison, WI: The University of Wisconsin Press.

Wedemeyer, C. A., & Childs, G. B. (1961). *New perspectives in university correspondence study.* Chicago: The Center for the Study of Liberal Education for Adults.

Wedemeyer, C. A., & Najem, R. E. (August, 1969). *AIM—From concept to reality: The Articulated Instructional Media Program at Wisconsin.* Syracuse, NY: Syracuse University Publications in Continuing Education.

Wright, S. J. (1991). Opportunity lost, opportunity regained. In B. L. Watkins & S. J. Wright (Eds.), *The foundations of American distance education: A century of collegiate correspondence study* (pp. 37–66). Dubuque, IA: Kendall-Hunt.

2

A History of National and Regional Organizations and the ICDE

Charles Feasley
Oklahoma State University

Ellen L. Bunker
Distance Education Consultant

Although the United States continues to have a substantially decentralized system of higher education, emerging information and computer technologies (ICT) shift quality control processes toward increased voluntary centralization. In contrast to many countries, the United States has had no national curriculum in postsecondary education (or lower levels). This situation stems from the facts that (a) most postsecondary funding is not from the national government and (b) most funds from the national government are connected to a voluntary system of institutional and professional accrediting groups. However, the large front-end expenditures that are required to develop and deliver many distance education offerings have stimulated individual colleges and universities to form consortia within metropolitan areas, states, regions, nations, and groups of nations. In addition, partnerships have emerged among postsecondary institutions and business corporations, especially those that have development and/or instructional delivery capabilities.

In order to examine the evolution of distance education organizations of importance to U.S. distance educators, five types have been identified: national pioneering organizations; curriculum specializing organizations; technology networking organizations; regional and virtual consortia; and international linking organizations.

National pioneering organizations are so named in recognition of historically broad geographic representation of their membership as well as the diverse media coverage and complex scope of their distance education goals.

Curriculum specializing organizations focus on small segments of the total curriculum within postsecondary education. The first example of this type is the American Distance Education Consortium (ADEC), whose curricular focus is on the agricultural sciences. The two other examples, the Association for Media-Based Continuing Education for Engineers (AMCEE) and the National Technology University (NTU), give emphasis to engineering, industrial sciences, and management of technology. Curriculum specializing organizations usually have a national membership.

Examples of technology networking organizations are the National University Telecommunications Network (NUTN), the Instructional Telecommunications Council (ITC), the Public Broadcasting Service's Adult Learning Services (PBS), and the Sloan Consortium. They were each established for a national membership that shared a common interest in a particular type of delivery system (satellite conferencing, video courses, broadcast television, and Internet computing, respectively).

The fourth type of distance education organization, regional and virtual consortia, has differing geographic distributions of members and goals that are reflective of preexisting regional parent organizations.

International linking organizations, the fifth distance education type, are nongovernmental, multipurpose organizations with members from multiple regions of the world. The example that is discussed in this chapter is the International Council for Open and Distance Education (ICDE), which is the oldest (founded 1938) and most widely used distance education association, with institutional members in 140 countries. It has been of strong interest to U.S. distance educators from the start. Many international organizations have links to ICDE, but are really regional in nature (examples include the Southeast Asian Ministers of Education Organization, the Organization of American States, and the European Commission). Also, ICDE has a formal link to the broad international policy organization UNESCO, the United Nations Educational, Scientific, and Cultural Organization.

CASE STUDIES AND A CAUTION

Lewis (1983, pp. 14–15) provided a broadly representative, yet richly detailed early picture of the overlapping activities between postsecondary education and the telecommunications industry. Within his examples of evidence of technological impact on postsecondary education, Lewis mentioned three organizations that are examined in more detail in this chapter: PBS, AMCEE, and NUTN.

All 70 case studies within Lewis (1983, p. 17) are helpful because they include comparable descriptions with regard to 16 categories of information:

Organization

Telecommunications Program

Educational Mission

Telecommunications Technology

Curriculum

Faculty Roles

Delivery System

Enrollment

Administrative Structure

Finances

Noteworthy Features

Problems Encountered

Observations about Distance Learning

Future Plans

Resources Available

Contact Person

Lewis noted that one of the more striking trends associated with the use of telecommunications technologies by educators is the extent of formal and informal collaborations among educational institutions (1983, p. 22). A more current and more international review of cooperative approaches to distance education can be found in Feasley (1995).

Although there are more reference choices for program descriptions today, caution is necessary. Just as enthusiasm for different new delivery technologies prompted the formation of the technology networking organizations discussed in this chapter, current zealousness about online education can prompt neutral observers to conclude that distance learning consortia are associations or partnerships that cooperate to provide Internet education. It is hoped that both publishers and readers consider the word *online* as a generic umbrella term meaning "readily available," so that many off-line offerings using videotape, audiotape, computer disk, CD-ROM, and print delivery systems are not overlooked.

NATIONAL PIONEERING ORGANIZATIONS

Increasingly, writers have noted that the history of correspondence instruction within U.S. higher education offers many insights for distance learning policy today. For example, Berg (1999, p. 15) listed how correspondence courses (a) did not try to replace traditional higher education; (b) were aimed at nontraditional student populations who did not have access to higher education; and (c) grew out of the university extension movement, not through the university proper. As evidence, Berg provided a useful chronology of many historical events, especially the 1926 Carnegie Corporation study on private correspondence schools, which found that (a) there were more students enrolled in correspondence schools than in all the traditional higher education institutions combined, but that (b) there were no standards yet to protect the public from poor quality or fraud (1999). For a comprehensive historical and philosophical examination of nontraditional education, readers are directed to Wedemeyer (1981).

Soon after the Carnegie study in 1926, a trade association known as the National Home Study Council (NHSC) was founded to promote sound educational and business practices among the home study schools (Fowler, 1981, p. 234). The author of the 1926 Carnegie study, John Noffsinger, served as the first executive director of the NHSC and initiated reform efforts, including the promulgation of a list of minimum standards for proprietary schools (Pittman, 1990, p. 68).

As noted later in this chapter, in 1959 NHSC was approved by the U.S. Office of Education as a nationally recognized accrediting agency, which enabled students in NHSC member schools to be eligible for federal aid without the schools being accredited by the seven regional associations that accredit most schools, colleges, and universities in the United States. In 1994, with 56 institutions serving three million students, NHSC was renamed the Distance Education and Training Council (DETC), while continuing to be a national accrediting agency to both the U.S. Secretary of Education and to the Commission on Recognition of Postsecondary Accreditation ("NHSC Get New Name," 1994). More recently, DETC's national purview and long-standing Accreditation Commission activity have attracted new members from other continents.

A large oversight within Berg's history of correspondence instruction is his failure to mention in any way the National University Extension Association (NUEA) or its renamed successor, the National University Continuing Education Association (NUCEA), while stating that traditional higher education correspondence courses did not have a separate group of standards (1999, p. 15). In a compendium of historical documents commemorating the seventy-fifth anniversary of NUCEA, details are provided of the important role that U.S. non-profit correspondence study professionals played in the establishment of NUEA in 1915, the adoption in

1922 of Standards for Extension Credit Courses (applicable to both class and correspondence courses), and the recommendation in 1931 of a set of correspondence study standards to supplement the 1922 Standards (Rohfeld, 1990).

Also, Watkins (1991), Wright (1991), and Pittman (1991) were able individually to utilize a wide range of primary and secondary historical resources to document the same conclusion that U.S. university-based correspondence practitioners played a key role in the establishment of NUEA and its early creation of standards for correspondence courses. Regardless of variations in the materials used, the common hypothesis drawn by authors has been that the existence of both types of correspondence study programs (non-profit and proprietary) appeared to spur each type into more vigorous attention to issues of quality, especially as documented through research.

While Pittman has published evidence of how the notoriety of some proprietary home study schools has had a negative impact on collegiate correspondence programs, he noted Noffsinger's assertion that proprietary schools could never have succeeded if collegiate programs had not popularized the correspondence method (1990, p. 68).

In 1915, more surprising praise was offered by Charles R. Van Hise, president of the University of Wisconsin and presiding officer of the first annual NUEA conference. He said that proprietary schools, not universities, first found the opportunity to instruct by correspondence, exactly as education in medicine and law were not first developed by universities, but by proprietary schools (Van Hise, 1915, 1990, p. 27). Almost half a century later the two renowned practitioners/scholars of American correspondence study, Charles Wedemeyer and Gayle Childs (1961), conceded that progress in the field was still hampered by its association in the popular mind with the sleazy promotional and financial operations of some of the proprietaries (cited in Pittman, 1992, p. 40). Despite such disappointments, Wedemeyer and Childs provided leadership within NUEA both in researching the effectiveness of different methods of instruction and in establishing good standards of practice. Later, Duning (1987) and Pittman (1987) helped explain the roles played by research and flexible technology use within the resiliency of the American collegiate correspondence study.

In 1955, when NUEA adopted a division structure and correspondence study was included among the five charter units, division members gained a new sense of group coherence and common purpose. But, after the U.S. Office of Education designated the NHSC's Accrediting Commission as a nationally recognized accrediting agency in 1959, the new Correspondence Study Division feared a direct impact on its own member institutions. As a result, the Division offered a special workshop to over half of its members to create a Criteria and Standards document, which was approved by the Division in 1962 and by the NUEA board a year later (Pittman, 1991, p. 126). In 1980, the Correspondence Study Division was renamed the Independent Study Division (ISD) to reflect the fact that many types of technologies were being used in addition to correspondence study's print-only image. Since that time, in addition to revising the Criteria and Standards document, ISD members operated almost two dozen different committees which achieved goals that included conducting an annual research survey; establishing an archive at Penn State University; conducting an oral history project; and giving awards for excellence in catalogs, courses, publications, and professional service.

In 1980, the parent organization name changed from NUEA to the National University Continuing Education Association (NUCEA) (Rohfeld, 1990, p. 139). Then, in 1999, NUCEA dropped the word *National* from the organization's name to attract international member schools, thereby becoming UCEA.

At the same time as the renaming to UCEA, while retaining a Board of Directors and keeping regions, the organization re-engineered itself significantly by eliminating all twenty division specializations, which had been popular with the preponderance of individual members. Instead, three broader units were created: the Commission of Futures and Markets, the Commission on Leadership and Management, and the Commission on Learning and Instructional Technologies. Within each commission with adequate numbers of interested members there may be established communities of practice. In the Distance Learning Community of Practice, there has been some re-establishment of the activities of the former Divisions of Educational Telecommunications and Division of Independent Study (Duning, Van Kekerix, & Zaborowski, 1993, p. 220, 222).

However, even before the NUCEA re-engineering was under serious discussion, substantial reallocations of annual conference programming sessions away from the divisions and toward the national conference committee and staff, prompted the creation of a new separate organization (AACIS) for professionals who serve individual learners rather than students who learn in groups. AACIS is the acronym for the American Association for Collegiate Independent Study, which held its fourteenth annual national conference in fall 2006 (AACIS, 2006). About twice as many independent study professionals are members of AACIS as were members of Independent Study Division of UCEA because the AACIS annual conference costs half as much to attend as that of UCEA and the AACIS annual dues are half as much as those of UCEA.

Although the United States Distance Learning Association (USDLA) has not been in existence for the majority of the 20th century as is the case for both the University Continuing Education Association and the Distance Education and Training Council (USDLA was formed in 1987), USDLA has been classified as a National Pioneering Organization for two reasons. First, on the national level, it had successfully involved U.S. senators and representatives in its regular conferences and national policy forums in 1991, 1997, and 1999 to develop and publish national policy recommendations that have been the basis for legislative and administrative proposals. Second, with its several thousand members, USDLA has stimulated broad participation across the United States by beginning in 1993 to establish local chapters in many states and one for the employees of the federal government. Pescatore (2000) provided a good description of one of the larger chapters of USDLA, the Oklahoma Distance Learning Association, which consists of members in all the sectors that use distance learning, including schools, telemedicine, business, and the military. In contrast, McAuliffe (2000) and Flores (2000) describe how the Federal Government Distance Learning Association works on the integration of existing infrastructure with emerging technologies that can reach the populations of military and civilian users directly at their job sites. USDLA established a Distance Learning Accreditation Board in December 2004 that includes an on-site visit by a peer-review team after the U.S. or non-U.S. institution's completion of a detailed self-study document (USDLA, 2006). This process is similar to that used by other accrediting bodies.

CURRICULUM SPECIALIZING ORGANIZATIONS

The Association for Media-Based Continuing Education of Engineers (AMCEE) is a private non-profit association that was formed in 1976 by representatives of 12 engineering schools (Lewis, 1983). Currently there are 22 engineering universities involved, which offer hundreds of different courses covering 16 technical and engineering-related disciplines (AMCEE, 2006).

AMCEE is known to feature non-credit short courses that are videotaped in high quality studio environments and offered with specially designed study guides and regular textbooks as support material. AMCEE chose this blend to take advantage of the logistical and financial benefits of videotaped classes and the pedagogical and marketing advantages of studio-produced non-credit courses (Duning, Van Kekerix, & Zaborowski, 1993).

Past discussions by the AMCEE Board of Directors generated the development of the National Technological University.

The National Technological University (NTU) was established in 1984 as a private, non-profit, accreditation-seeking institution that broadcasted via satellite carefully chosen courses from 24 top engineering schools in the United States. It earned full accreditation status from the North Central Association of Schools and Colleges in 1986 and then achieved the maximum length 10-year review cycle (Bagley, 2000). Over time more than 50 universities have contributed over 1400 courses to fulfill all requirements of the 18 NTU Master of Science degrees that were offered for highly mobile engineers, scientists, and technical managers. Most students were full-time employees of the more than 250 corporations and universities that received the courses via satellite, videotape or the Internet.

In 1999, NTU created a for-profit learning service organization called National Technological University Corporation (NTUC) to perform certain functions it feels are essential in securing clients ("NTU Changes to Keep Up With Corporate Markets," 1999). Yet, subsequent to that event, NTU was purchased by Sylvan Learning Systems. And in January 2005, the renamed successor to Sylvan, Laureate Education, converted NTU into the NTU School of Engineering and Applied Science at Walden University, another Laureate business (NTU, 2006).

AG*SAT was formed by 23 land-grant institutions in 1989. During spring 1992, seven credited courses were offered nationwide via satellite and other distance learning technologies. The courses originated from seven different land-grant institutions and were used by 18 of 35 affiliated AG*SAT institutions (Levine, 1992). Not long afterward, AG*SAT was renamed the American Distance Education Consortium (ADEC).

In an interview, ADEC president Janet K. Poley provided a description of the 60-member consortium's extensive activities in grant management, professional development, public education, technology research, and international outreach (Anderson, 2000). Presently, ADEC's structure includes a board of directors, a program panel, principal contact officers, and ADEC staff, plus an expanded membership as a result of its Western Hemisphere Initiative (ADEC, 2006). In a recent, high profile partnership between ADEC, the Sloan Consortium, and the Southern Regional Electronic Campus, institutions that were impacted by Hurricanes Katrina and Rita were able to provide courses for their students during an intensive eight-week semester using ADEC's National Science Foundation developed internet satellite technology (J. K. Poley, personal communication, December 14, 2005).

TECHNOLOGY NETWORKING ORGANIZATIONS

E. M. Oberle (1990) provided a helpful case study of the early years of the National University Teleconference Network (NUTN) from its founding in 1982 with less than 70 universities into an organization whose membership at the time was four times larger and included a much more diverse mixture of postsecondary educational institutions than at its start. A bandwagon effect was notable from the very beginning when only 5% of the charter members had access to satellite-receive capability. But, subsequently, the heavy financial burden on the long-time host institution, Oklahoma State University, prompted the transfer of NUTN headquarters to Old Dominion University. Also, after the initial years, the third word of the organization name was changed from *Teleconference* to *Telecommunications*.

Oberle (1990) also explained how non-member institutions such as high schools, businesses and industries, associations, and government agencies could receive NUTN programs and services. Oberle also identified training and international contacts as additional benefits; the benefits have expanded since then through NUTN partnerships with many of the other organizations mentioned in this chapter. A key reason for the ongoing success of NUTN has been sustained broad participation of its leaders in its overall advisory board and in specialized resource/planning groups.

The Instructional Telecommunications Council (ITC) is an affiliated council of the American Association of Community Colleges. Prior to assuming its present ITC name in 1981, the group was much smaller in membership and was known as the Task Force on Uses of Mass Media in Learning. The name change was partly to reflect broader interests than producing and marketing (Zigerell, 1982). ITC's location in Washington, D.C., enables it to serve as a legislative liaison. The results of an early ITC policy meeting on adult learners were summarized by Brock (1991). ITC has also influenced local institutional policies and practices on telecommunications by publishing for presidents and trustees (RDR Associates, 1998) and for academic administrators and faculty (Tulloch & Sneed, 2000). ITC represents nearly 600 institutions in the United States and Canada, including single institutions, regional and statewide systems, for-profit organizations, and non-profit organizations. Two-year colleges comprise a majority of its membership. Current benefits of membership include a newsletter and listserv, grant information, awards, publications, and research (ITC, 2006). The respect that ITC has garnered in those areas can be noted in the Kellogg Foundation's selection of ITC as the coordinating home for the National Alliance of Virtual Colleges (Young, 2001).

The impressive beginning of PBS's Adult Learning Services (ALS) in 1981 has been described by Brock (1990) and Lewis (1983) as having enabled 555 colleges and universities to enroll 53,000 students in television-assisted courses (telecourses) during its initial year of operation.

In an interview with PBS's Director of Learning Innovations, Shirley M. Davis, which was published in *The American Journal of Distance Education* (Hardy, 2000), Davis described a picture in which ALS served 500,000 students per year in partnership with 1,000 colleges and universities and public television stations in every state. A major factor in the growth of ALS was noted to be an expansion of offerings to include 85 telecourses (enough to enable students to pursue an associate degree at the more than 200 institutions that are part of PBS's Going the Distance project) and 30 to 40 live satellite events each year for the professional development of faculty and administrators (Hardy, 2000, p. 72). However, in a surprise to many people, ALS was closed at the end of September 2005 (PBS, 2006). The closing probably resulted from budget cuts and a shift in predominant distance education usage from television courses to those that utilize the Internet.

The skyrocketing popularity of Internet/online courses was stimulated by the Sloan Foundation, which began its "Learning Outside the Classroom" program in 1993; within ten years, 244 grants totaling $48 million were awarded to 118 institutions. At the same time, the Sloan Consortium (a users' group) was established and has attracted over 1,000 member institutions which benefit from a journal, a magazine, training opportunities, book reviews, summaries of best practices, research reports, and results from annual surveys of over 1,000 chief academic officers (CAOs). Within the 2003 Sloan survey report, *Sizing the Opportunity*, one key finding was that a majority of the CAOs believed the learning outcomes for online education are equal to or greater than those for face-to-face instruction. In the 2004 Sloan survey report, *Entering the Mainstream*, a majority of institutions (53.4%) agreed that online education is a key part of their long-term strategy. In the 2005 survey results, *Growing by Degrees* (2005), 65% of the institutions report that core faculty members teach online courses more than they do face-to-face courses. All three survey reports and other resources are available for free downloading on the Sloan Consortium Web site (2005).

REGIONAL AND VIRTUAL CONSORTIA

Case studies have been written about the U.S. government's most ambitious attempt to create an open university on a traditional university base, the University of Mid-America (UMA). A prelude activity, the State University of Nebraska (SUN), was created in 1971 by President D. B. Varner of the University of Nebraska and the head of the Nebraska Educational Television Network, Jack McBride. Early in its existence the need to involve more universities in order to share the cost of developing and delivering high quality course materials became clear. This need prompted Varner to obtain participation from 10 public universities in six surrounding states in successful proposals to the U.S. Department of Education, which provided funding from 1974 through 1982. But, because of funding agency reorganizations, the end of the funding was announced three years in advance, prompting various related, but unsuccessful, efforts to find money to establish a separate American Open University that could award course credits and degrees (McNeil, 1993).

McNeil's full analysis merits careful review, yet two key problems were his lack of clarity about goals (within both the funding agency and UMA's participating universities) and lack of coherence in curricular planning (1993). Subsequent U.S. initiatives at the state and regional levels appear to place greater emphasis on degree and certificate goals, plus build upon ongoing planning committees.

In addition to state governments (such as those of California, Kentucky, and Minnesota) starting their own individual virtual universities, many states have formal interstate compacts, such as the 16 states in the Southern Regional Education Board (founded in 1948) and the 14 states in the Western Interstate Commission for Higher Education (founded in 1956), which have fostered two of the larger virtual universities in the USA: Southern Regional Electronic Campus (SREC) and Western Governors University (WGU), respectively. In each case there was an ongoing internal technology resource group, the SREB Educational Technology Cooperative and the Western Cooperative for Educational Telecommunications (Western Cooperative), to draft extensive virtual university/portal plans, then remain available for further assistance.

Because of its effective leadership and some national government funding, the Western Cooperative developed documents with standards for electronic offerings which have been used in whole or substantial part by all of the U.S. regional accrediting associations and many virtual providers since it was published by the Council of Regional Accrediting Commissions in 2001. More recently the Western Cooperative developed the first generally accepted basis for evaluating distance learning programs, Principles of Good Practice for Electronically Offered Degree & Certificate Programs (Western Cooperative, 2005).

Published literature offers some useful comparisons of three early U.S. virtual universities that had been given considerable publicity: WGU, SREC, and the California Virtual University (CVU). The establishment of WGU in 1996 prompted a serious review of the stand-alone virtual organization by traditional institutions and state policy makers (Twigg, 2003, p. 4; Epper & Garn, 2003, p. 51). During 2002–2003, the Western Cooperative and the State Higher Education Executive Officers (SHEEO) surveyed 61 virtual organizations in 45 states that were neither singular institutions nor multi-state arrangements. From the 51 responses representing 40 states, Epper and Garn (2003) recommended that the earlier virtual college or university taxonomy proposed by Wolf and Johnstone (1999) to show variations on consortial collaboration be expanded to include a second dimension for the degree of business practice implementation.

Because Western Governors University was initially using program provider institutions from multiple regional accrediting areas, it stimulated the formation of a new Inter-Regional Accreditation Committee. Since then, WGU has received full accreditation from four regional associations (WGU, 2006). Another national objective that has been achieved by WGU was to become identified as a designated federal aid demonstration program wherein certain calendar and tracking conditions may be waived.

Because most virtual providers do not seek to offer direct degrees or attain their own accreditation, they are primarily marketing Web sites (with searchable databases for offerings) and sources for services (student support, faculty training, etc.) Most virtual universities have used pilot and expanding phases of offerings, subsequently including private colleges and private sector programs (Winer, 1998).

Unlike other state virtual institutions, the California Virtual University (CVU) had emphasized the global export of education in direct challenge to other institutions. However, if diversity of funding, even including corporate support, is confined to just the one state's environment, local economic downturns can be more devastating than at Western Governors University, which has secured support from international corporations and distance learning providers in different regions of the country. In addition to the contrast between goals and funding, the derailment of CVU (Blumenstyk, 1999) was also likely to stem from being too dependent upon three systems of faculty-centered providing institutions (Berg, 1999). The influence of faculty in regard to CVU may have been strengthened because of the success faculty had experienced in derailing the establishment of a for-profit limited-liability corporation to be set up by the California State University system with four technology companies. However, the successor to CVU, the California Virtual Campus, with 137 institutional participants, appears to have a more stable environment as part of the Web site for the Professional Development Center of the California Community Colleges System (California Virtual Campus, 2006). Organizations of all types have been exploring how to succeed on a global level.

INTERNATIONAL LINKING ORGANIZATION

The International Council for Open and Distance Learning (ICDE), perhaps the largest and best-known of international distance education associations, had its beginnings in the second quarter of the 20th century. It was inspired by visionary educators using correspondence education, many of whom also participated in other early pioneering organizations mentioned previously.

The idea for holding an international conference came from J. W. Gibson, director of High School Correspondence Instruction for the province of British Columbia and a visitor attending The National Conference on Supervised Correspondence Study in New York in 1936. Gibson shared knowledge he had about correspondence education in several countries and suggested an international conference be held. Delegates at the New York conference were enthusiastic about the idea (Broady, 1938).

At the second conference, held in 1948, the delegates voted unanimously to establish a more permanent International Council (Broady, 1948). At the third conference, held in 1953 in Christchurch, New Zealand, a committee presented a proposed "Constitution and Rules" for the Council which was adopted by the delegates. As these rules helped the Council became more established, conferences began to follow a more regular schedule (see Table 2.1).

At the second conference delegates voted to form a permanent association and selected the name of The International Council on Correspondence Education (ICCE). The association retained this name until the conference in 1982 when the name changed to the International Council for Distance Education (ICDE). In a research study of the accumulated proceedings from the conferences of ICDE, Bunker (1998) searched for themes and patterns of interest to distance educators today. Several notable shared assumptions, practices, and aims appear in the data from

TABLE 2.1.
ICCE/ICDE Conferences—Year and Location

	Year	Location
1	1938	Victoria, British Columbia, Canada
2	1948	Lincoln, Nebraska, USA
3	1950	Christchurch, New Zealand
4	1953	State College, Pennsylvania, USA
5	1958	Banff, Alberta, Canada
6	1961	Gearhart, Oregon, USA
7	1965	Stockholm, Sweden
8	1969	Paris, France
9	1972	Warrenton, Virginia, USA
10	1975	Brighton, United Kingdom
11	1978	Delhi, India
12	1982	Vancouver, British Columbia, Canada
13	1985	Melbourne, Queensland, Australia
14	1988	Oslo, Norway
15	1990	Caracas, Venezuela
16	1992	Bangkok, Thailand
17	1995	Birmingham, United Kingdom
18	1997	State College, Pennsylvania, USA
19	1999	Vienna, Austria
20	2001	Düsseldorf, Germany
21	2004	Hong Kong, China
—	2005	Delhi, India
22	2006	Rio de Janeiro, Brazil

the proceedings which characterize the discourse community of ICCE/ICDE. In addition, several trends, important developments, and key ideas and events give valuable insight into alternatives facing the field of international distance education today.

First, the discourse from the ICCE/ICDE conferences reveals an unremitting allegiance to the belief in the value of providing access to education for all learners, no matter how dispersed or disadvantaged by economic, personal, or political situations. Over the years of the conferences, this general commitment to access did not change.

Second, the commitment to access was followed closely by a commitment to education of equal value to that which could be received by traditional education. In order to ensure this equality, distance educators, as evidenced by the data of the Bunker study, constantly sought academic credibility for their educational offerings. Because correspondence/distance education was an alternative to conventional education, distance educators were required to prove the efficacy of their efforts. The discourse in the proceedings contains constant references to quality, standards, accreditation, status, and credibility in both the teaching/learning and the administration/management domains of distance education. These issues of credibility led participants in the conferences to discuss means of improving instruction, interacting with learners, applying communications technologies, and supporting learners. Together, the two motivations of access and equity are present in many different forms in the data from the early years of the conference.

Third, concerns for academic credibility led ICDE practitioners to persistently call for more research into the methods and practices of distance education. References to the need for more research appear in the data from all conferences. At the first conference, the need for research was recognized and a research committee was established. This committee became an ongoing part of the early ICCE/ICDE organizational structure.

The discourse on research also shows throughout the proceedings a consistent acknowledgment that the amount of research and the dissemination of the results are inadequate. These statements are usually accompanied, however, by the concession that improvement has "recently" been made. For example, Buck states in 1948 that a small amount of "objective research in this field has been done, but not nearly enough" (Buck, 1948, p. 90). Wedemeyer notes in 1965 that there has "never been sufficient scholarship poured into this field" (Wedemeyer, 1965, p. 16). In reporting as chair of the research committee in the 1969 conference, Childs writes that there is a "substantial and growing worldwide body of literature relating to correspondence instruction. . . . It must be noted, however, that even though the volume of literature may be increasing this does not indicate any great upsurge in research activity. Evidences of carefully done research are still hard to come by" (Childs, 1969, p. 40). In the 1982 conference proceedings, the editors write that the "particular symptom of the general weakness of research on learning at a distance until very recently" has been characterized by a wide gap between reality and rhetoric, but they note the hope "that future writing will give increasing importance to rigorous studies with properly defined variables and boundaries" (Daniel, Stroud, & Thompson, 1982, p. 86). Again in 1992, research concerns merited a chapter in the proceedings. The editors note that an historical analysis shows that research is a fairly recent phenomenon, but, in contrast to the past, reports in this conference contain research from around the world (Scriven, et al., 1993, p. 322).

Fourth, international representation is a distinctive feature of ICCE/ICDE and emerges as a theme and pattern in the analysis. All discourse related to origin; policies and philosophies; conference planning and conference themes directly support the commitment for international representation. The sense expressed in the discourse of a "mutual esteem" for all distance educators from all countries providing all types of education is consistent and powerful within the Council. Sustained effort is shown in the choice of themes and topics to include representation from different countries. In fact, the support for wide international representation became even more pronounced in the 1960s and 1970s when the number of countries represented at the conference jumped from the earlier core of four countries (Australia, Canada, New Zealand, and the United States) to a much larger and more widely distributed group of countries. Topics directly related to international issues and concerns are part of nearly all conferences.

Fifth, the amount of discourse devoted to educational technology in the ICCE/ICDE conference proceedings is relatively small given the general excitement that usually accompanies the emergence of new communications technologies and given that distance education must rely on some form of media to provide interaction. Discourse about technology was present in every conference in some form, even when not given enough status to merit even a conference sub-theme. However, through all the conferences, educational technology remained a part, and only a part, of the total discourse about distance education. For most of the conferences it remained only one of five to twelve subsections forming the organization of the conference. The patterns show that this has changed little over the years of the conference, even though more and more papers began appearing in the sections devoted to educational technology. The emphasis remained on correspondence/distance education as a whole, with technology serving as a mediator for that education.

In conclusion, the five primary trends found in the ICCE/ICDE conference proceedings include (a) the importance of access as a key value for distance educators, (b) the commitment to quality, (c) the need for research to inform practices, (d) the high value placed on international participation and representation in the membership of the Council, and (e) the role of educational technology in distance education and its place in the discourse of the conferences.

These five general patterns are still reflected in the conference themes of the recent international conferences for ICDE. For example, the themes for the 2005 conference (ICDE, 2005) held in New Delhi, India, were given as

- Internationalization: collaboration and networking
- ICT-enabled education
- Quality and accreditation
- Globalization, culture and ODL
- Distance education for development.

FUTURE CHALLENGE AND PROMISE

The substantially decentralized system of higher education in the United States has helped produce the rich array of formal and informal collaboration among institutions discussed in this chapter. The national pioneering organizations, curriculum specializing organizations, technology networking organizations, regional and virtual consortia, and the international linking organization of ICDE, as each has developed throughout the last century, have all aimed at assisting institutions and learners involved in learning at a distance. Considered together, these organizations represent a wide assortment of institutions. The patterns of organization and development, sources and security of funding, governing principles, and successes and failures can all be used to provide guidance and experience to today's distance educators.

While each organization discussed represents different institutions and combinations of institutions and individuals, this combined experience can enhance decisions of policy and practice in future offerings of distance education. For example, since the five values identified in the literature from more than 60 years of ICDE conferences have remained constant throughout that time, these values—broad access, equal quality, research-guided practice, international participation, and appropriate technology use—are promising foci for future challenges. Likewise, other issues that are faced by distance education programs and institutions, such as the ever-present matters of financing or accreditation, can be addressed through studying the methods, patterns, or services of these national, regional, and international organizations. In that way, the concerns of faculty, administrators, accrediting teams, or potential students can be more easily resolved. The extensive numbers, types, and purposes of these organizations can be a constructive and beneficial guide to all users and providers of distance education today.

REFERENCES

American Association for Collegiate Independent Study, AACIS. (2006). *AACIS Membership.* Retrieved January 15, 2006, from http://www.AACIS.org/aboutUs.htm.

American Distance Education Consortium, ADEC. (2006). *About ADEC.* Retrieved January 20, 2006, from http://www.adec.edu.

Association for Media-based Continuing Education for Engineers, Inc., AMCEE. (2006). *About AMCEE.* Retrieved January 16, 2006, from http://www.amcee.org/about_who.asp

Anderson, B. (2000). Speaking personally with Janet K. Poley. *The American Journal of Distance Education, 14*(3), 75–81.

Bagley, J. (2000, July 18). Interview with Gearold Johnson, academic vice president, National Technological University. *Information Technology in Postsecondary Education, 3*(13), 4–5.

Berg, G. A. (1999). Contemporary implications of the history of correspondence instruction in American higher education. *Education At a Distance, 13*(3), 11–17.

Blumenstyk, G. (1999). California Virtual University will end most of its operations. *Chronicle of Higher Education, 45*(30), A30.

Broady, K. O. (1938). Minutes of first general meeting. In *Report of the First International Conference on Correspondence Education* (p. 10). Victoria, BC: The Department of Education.

Broady, K. O. (1948). Foreword. In *Proceedings of the Second International Conference on Correspondence Education* (pp. 1–2). Lincoln, NE: The University of Nebraska Extension Division.

Brock, D. (1990). Research needs for adult learners via television. In M. G. Moore (Ed.), *Contemporary Issues in American Distance Education* (pp. 172–181). Oxford, England: Pergamon Press.

Brock, D. (1991). *Symposium on Telecommunications and the Adult Learner.* Washington, DC: Instructional Telecommunications Council.

Buck, G. J. (1948). The plan of the second conference. In *Proceedings of the Second International Conference on Correspondence Education* (pp. 97–101). Lincoln, NE: The University of Nebraska Extension Division.

Bunker, E. L. (1998). *An historical analysis of a distance education forum: The International Council for Distance Education world conference proceedings, 1938 to 1995.* Unpublished doctoral dissertation, The Pennsylvania State University, State College.

California Virtual Campus, CVC. (2006). *About CVC.* Retrieved January 9, 2006, from http://www.cvc.edu/catalog.

Childs, G. (1969). Committee on research reports from chairmen of standing committees. In *Proceedings of the Eighth International Conference of the International Council on Correspondence Education* (pp. 40–49). Paris, France: International Council for Correspondence Education.

Daniel, J. S., Stroud, M. A., & Thompson, J. R. (1982). Preface. In *Learning at a distance: A world perspective* (p. 4). Edmonton: Athabasca University/International Council for Correspondence Education.

Duning, B. S. (1987). Independent study in higher education: a captive of legendary resilience. *The American Journal of Distance Education 1*(1), 37–46.

Duning, B. S., Van Kekerix, M. J., & Zaborowski, L. M. (1993). *Reaching Learners Through Telecommunications.* San Francisco: Jossey-Bass Publishers.

Epper, R. M., & Garn, M. (2003). *Virtual college and university consortia: a national study.* Retrieved November 10, 2005, from http://www.wcet.info/resources/publication/vcu.pdf.

Feasley, C. E. (1995). International perspectives on cooperative approaches to distance education. In Sewart, D. (Ed.), *One World, Many Voices: Quality in Open and Distance Learning* (pp. 77–80). Birmingham, England: International Council for Distance Education and the Open University.

Flores, J. (2000, August). Distance learning booms in government market. *Government Video, 11*(9), 86.

Fowler, W. A. (1981). The national home study council: Distance education leadership for five decades. *Distance Education, 2*(2), 234–239.

Hardy, D. W. (2000). Speaking personally with Shirley M. Davis. *The American Journal of Distance Education, 14*(2), 71–74.

International Council for Distance Education. (2005). *Open and distance education in a global environment: Opportunities for collaboration.* New Delhi, India: International Council for Distance Education. Retrieved December 12, 2005, from http://www.ignou.ac.in/icde2005/index.htm.

Instructional Telecommunications Council, ITC. (2006). *About ITC.* Retrieved January 19, 2006, from http://www.itcnetwork.org.

Levine, T. K. (1992). *Going the Distance: a Handbook for Developing Distance Degree Programs.* Washington, D.C.: Annenberg/Corporation for Public Broadcasting.

Lewis, R. (1983). *Meeting Learners' Needs Through Telecommunications: A Directory and Guide to Programs.* Washington, D.C.: American Association for Higher Education.

McAuliffe, T. (2000, August). Education connection. *Government Video, 11*(9), 6.

McNeil, Donald R. (1993). The rise and fall of a consortium: the University of Mid-America. In L. Moran & I. Mugridge (Eds.), *Collaboration in Distance Education*, (pp. 123–131). New York, NY: Routledge.

Moore, M. G., & Kearsley, G. (1996). *Distance Education: A Systems View.* Belmont, CA: Wadsworth Publishing.

National Home Study Council, NHSC. (1994, Spring). NHSC gets new name after 68 years: Distance Education and Training Council. *DETC News, 1,* 1.

National Technological University (NTU) changes to keep up with corporate market (1999, May 11). *Information Technology in Postsecondary Education, 2*(9), 7.

National Technological University, NTU (2006). *About NTU.* Retrieved January 16, 2006, from http://www.ntu.edu.

Oberle, E. M. (1990). The national university teleconference network: A living laboratory for distance learning research. In M. G. Moore (Ed.), *Contemporary Issues in American Distance Education* (pp. 81–95). Oxford, England: Pergamon Press.

Pescatore, M. J. (2000, August). Oklahoma professionals convey importance of distance learning. *Government Video, 11*(9), 68–69.

Pittman, V. V. (1987). The persistence of print: Correspondence study and the new media. *The American Journal of Distance Education, 1*(1), 31–36.

Pittman, V. V. (1990). Correspondence study in the American university: A historiographic perspective. In M. G. Moore (Ed.), *Contemporary Issues in American Distance Education* (pp. 67–80). Oxford, England: Pergamon Press.

Pittman, V. V. (1991). Academic credibility and the "image problem": The quality issue in collegiate independent study. In B. L. Watkins & S. J. Wright (Eds.), *The Foundations of American Distance Education: A Century of Collegiate Correspondence Study* (pp. 109–134). Dubuque, IA: Kendall/Hunt Publishing.

Pittman, V. V. (1992). Amateurs, tough guys and a dubious pursuit: Crime and correspondence study in popular culture. *The American Journal of Distance Education, 6*(1), 40–50.

Public Broadcasting Service, PBS. (2006). *PBS Adult Learning Service.* Retrieved January 23, 2006, from http://www.pbs.org/als-r/pbscampus.html.

RDR Associates, Inc. (1998). *New Connections: A Guide to Distance Education.* Washington, D.C.: Instructional Telecommunications Council.

Rohfeld, R. W. (Ed.). (1990). *Expanding Access to Knowledge: Continuing Higher Education.* Washington, D.C.: National University Continuing Education Association.

Scriven, B., Lundin, R., & Yoni Ryan, Y. (1993). Commentary: Chapter 5—distance education—theory and research. In *Distance education for the twenty-first century: Selected papers from the 16th World Conference of the International Council for Distance Education* (pp. 322–323). Bangkok, Thailand: International Council for Distance Education.

Sloan Consortium (2005). *Sizing the Opportunity; Entering the Mainstream; Growing by Degrees.* Retrieved December 6, 2005, from http://www.aln.org/publications/freedownloads.asp.

Tulloch, J., & Sneed, J. (Eds.). (2000). *Quality Enhancing Practices in Distance Education: Teaching and Learning.* Washington, D.C.: Instructional Telecommunications Council.

Twigg, C. A. (2003). *Expanding Access to Learning: The Role of Virtual Universities.* Retrieved December 26, 2006, from http://www.center.rpi.edu/Monographs/ExpAccess.html

United States Distance Learning Association. USDLA (2006). *Resources.* Retrieved December 27, 2006, from http://www.usdla.org/html/resources/accreditation.htm

Van Hise, C. (1915/1990). The university extension function in the modern university, (pp. 20–35). In R. W. Rohfeld (Ed.), *Expanding Access to Knowledge: Continuing Higher Education.* Washington, D.C.: National University Continuing Education Association (original work published in 1915).

Watkins, B. L. (1991). A quite radical idea: The invention and elaboration of collegiate correspondence study. In B. L. Watkins & S. J. Wright (Eds.), *The Foundations of American Distance Education: A Century of Collegiate Correspondence Study* (pp. 1–25). Dubuque, IA: Kendall/Hunt Publishing.

Wedemeyer, C. A. (1965). Correspondence education in the world of today. A general survey of the field, ideas, principles, trends, new developments. In *Proceedings Seventh International Conference of the International Council on Correspondence Education* (pp. 8–18). Stockholm, Sweden: International Council on Correspondence Education.

Wedemeyer, C. A. (1981). *Learning at the Back Door: Reflections on Nontraditional Learning in the Lifespan.* Madison, WI: University of Wisconsin Press.

Wedemeyer, C. A. (1985). Correspondence study. In T. Husen & T.N. Postlewaite (Eds.), *International Encyclopedia of Education* (pp. 1026–1030). London, England: Pergamon Ltd.

Wedemeyer, C. A., & Childs, G. B. (1961). *New Perspectives in University Correspondence Study*. Chicago: Center for the Study of Liberal Education for Adults.

Western Cooperative for Educational Telecommunications. (2005). *Principles of Good Practice for Electronically Offered Higher Education Degree and Certificate Programs.* Boulder, CO: Western Interstate Commission for Higher Education. Retrieved January 21, 2006, from http://www.wcet.info/resources/accreditation/.

Western Governors University. (2006). *About WGU: Accreditation.* Retrieved January 21, 2006, from http://wgu.edu/about_WGU/accreditation.asp.

Winer, R. M. (1998). Three virtual universities gear up for fall openings. *Education at a Distance, 12*(11), 12–14.

Wolf, D. B., & Johnstone, S. M. (1999, July/August). Cleaning up the language: Establishing a consistent vocabulary for electronically delivered academic programs. *Change, 31*(4), 34–39.

Wright, S. J. (1991). Opportunity lost, opportunity regained: university independent study in the modern era. In B. L. Watkins & S. J. Wright (Eds.), *The Foundations of American Distance Education: A Century of Collegiate Correspondence Study* (pp. 37–66). Dubuque, IA: Kendall/Hunt Publishing.

Young, J. R. (2000). Virtual universities pledge to ease transfer and encourage other kinds of collaboration. *The Chronicle of Higher Education, 46*(35), A45.

Zigerell, J. (1982). Video vitality: consortium has it. *Community and Junior College Journal, 45*(2), 16–18.

3

Trends in Research:
A Content Analysis of Major Journals

Youngmin Lee
Korean Educational Development Institute, Korea

Marcy P. Driscoll and David W. Nelson
Florida State University

Most researchers acknowledge that understanding trends and issues of both topics and methods is pivotal in the advancement of research. To that end, Anglin and Morrison (2000) analyzed distance education research as reflected in two distance education journals: *The American Journal of Distance Education* and *Distance Education*. Koble and Bunker (1997) identified trends in research and practice by exploring articles published in *The American Journal of Distance Education* during a nine-year period. Berge and Mrozowski (2001) reviewed four distance education journals and also dissertations, based on the categorization system that originally came from Sherry's (1995) study.

In the same tradition, this chapter seeks to answer the following questions by examining research topics, methods, and citation trends by using content analysis: (a) What general research topics have been the focus of articles that report distance education research? (b) What specific topics have been discussed in distance education research articles? (c) Which research methods have been applied and are prevalent in distance education research? (d) Whose inquiry conveys a major impact on distance education research? and (5) What implications might the findings of this study have on future distance education research? These questions are the primary issues. Once these research topics, methods, and influential researchers are identified, they can be used to review current research trends and explore potential research directions. In addition, this information can bolster the theoretical foundation of the field and present empirical guidance for the practitioners in the field.

METHOD

Selection of Articles for Analysis

Four journals were reviewed in this study: *The American Journal of Distance Education*, the *Journal of Distance Education*, *Distance Education*, and *Open Learning*. These journals were selected because of their recognition among researchers as the most prominent in the distance education field, and because they had been used as data sources in previous studies. The total number of articles selected in this study was 553.

- For *The American Journal of Distance Education*, all articles (excluding editorials, commentaries, and book reviews) published from 1997 to 2005 (volume 11 to volume 19) were selected and classified. The number of articles selected from this journal was 120.
- For the *Journal of Distance Education*, all articles (excluding editorials, "For Your Information," dialogues, and "In Review") published from 1997 to 2005 (volume 12 to volume 20, number 1) were selected and classified. The number of articles chosen was 92.
- For *Distance Education*, all articles (excluding editorials and introductions) published from 1997 to 2005 (volume 18 to volume 26) were selected and classified. The number of articles selected from this journal was 152.
- For *Open Learning*, all articles (editorials and book reviews) published from 1997 to 2005 (volume 12 to volume 20) were selected and classified. The number of articles chosen was 189.

Classification of Topics

Two categorization systems were considered and developed to classify these articles by their topics and methods. Initially, the topic classification system was constructed based on the works of Sherry (1995), Kleemann (2000), Phipps and Merisotis (1999), and Khan (1997). By referring to those studies, a new categorization system to account for distance education research topics was developed. This system consists of the following six topics:

- Design-related topics: needs assessment, course scheduling, course design, instructional strategy development, course material design, and visual design;
- Development-related topics: course support system and material development, Web-based learning management system building, online tools development, and online testing system development;
- Management-related topics: learning resource management, troubleshooting, attrition rates, faculty and staff support, learner support, and technical support;
- Evaluation-related topics: program quality control, assessment of learning outcomes, benefits and cost analysis, Return on Investment (ROI), evaluation of supporting systems;
- Institutional and operational-related topics: administration, academic affairs, accreditation, certification, policy, payment, and budgeting; and
- Theory and research-related topics: distance education theory building, review of literature, introduction to new research methods, culture and gender issues, learning style, history of distance education, and copyright law.

A thematic analysis method, which uses a volume of data in an attempt to identify core meanings from those data (Boyatzis, 1998), was also used to identify what specific research topics were addressed. From a thematic analysis, the most frequently used themes (i.e., detailed topics) by year can be identified as those given a greater consideration by researchers in the distance education field. These core meanings were found through selection of three major keywords from each article in each journal, which were classified and cumulated by year.

Classification of Research Method

In developing the research-method classification system, the categories posited by Berge and Mrozowski (2001), Koble and Bunker (1997), Anglin and Morrison (2000), and Klein (2002) were used. Based on the classification schemes of those authors, a new method classification system for sorting the types of research method was developed. The research methods are as follows:

- Theoretical inquiry: a theoretical review of literature and conceptual study for proposing new ideas in distance education;
- Experimental research: a study examining the effect of independent variable(s) on dependent variable(s);
- Case study: a study aimed at investigating a single individual, group, program, or organization, qualitatively;
- Evaluation research: a study aimed at determining the impact of a project, program, model, or software;
- Developmental research: a study aimed at designing, developing, and evaluating an existing or newly developed model, process, product, or technique;
- Survey research: a study addressing the distribution and return of responses in nonexperimental situations; and
- Combination of inquiries: a study synthesizing two or more research methods.

Research was further classified to identify the types of statistical methods authors employed. To increase the precision of classification, an interrater reliability test was conducted. This test defined the extent to which different coders, each coding the same content, came to the same coding decisions. The first author and two research assistants trained by him took part in the interrater reliability test (Krippendorff, 1980).

Finally, the reference lists from each journal were examined using the research topics and methods. The names of each author and coauthor in the reference lists were chosen and numbered, and only the first author was collected to identify his or her significant impact on a particular area of research or theory. Only the first author was cited because of the assumed primacy of his or her contribution to the research paper (Anglin & Towers, 1992) and to avoid an avalanche of superfluous data that could result from examining the publications of secondary authors. From the resulting analysis, we are better able to infer whose inquiry conveys a major impact on distance education (Anglin & Towers).

RESULTS AND DISCUSSION

Results are categorized separately by the general research topics, specific topics, research methods, statistical methods, and citation index.

General Research Topics Investigated

An analysis of research topics indicated that approximately 201 (36%) were classified as theory and research topics, 118 (21%) as design topics, 76 (14%) as evaluation topics, 54 (10%) as institution and operation topics, 53 (10%) as development topics, and 51 (9%) as management topics. The frequencies of topics by year are presented in Table 3.1.

The result of this analysis was different from that of other studies largely because of differences in the classification of articles but also because the current study included more recent publications. The study by Anglin and Morrison (2000) showed that over 70% of the articles were classified as primary research that accounts for conceptual as well as theoretical studies. The study by Berge and Mrozowski (2001) imparted that over 75% of the articles were associated with descriptive research. The study of Koble and Bunker (1997) also classified a large number of studies as theoretic. The foundation topic (i.e., theory, model, or history) ranked first in Rourke and Szabo's (2002) study. Compared to these results, the development and institution topics seemed to decrease gradually and make up a relatively small portion of the topics. The reliability coefficient of the three coders' classification of research topics was .86.

Specific Research Topics Identified with Keywords

Three prominent keywords were selected from each article. A total of 213 keywords were identical with others in 1997, 207 keywords in 1998, 195 keywords in 1999, 192 keywords in 2000, 183 keywords in 2001, 159 keywords in 2002, 165 keywords in 2003, 171 keywords in 2004, and 177 keywords in 2005. Table 3.2 presents the analysis of keywords by publication year.

Keywords that show increased frequency in recent years include "interaction," "learners' perception," "collaboration," "professional development," and "support." These keywords were closely related with the theory and research topic, and the design research topic. Cross-cultural issues ranked first in 2001 because it was the topic of a special issue of the journal *Distance Education* (volume 22, number 1). In most cases, however, cultural issues in distance education have not been prioritized by researchers in the field. Moreover, learning object issues ranked first in 2005 because it was the topic of a special issue of *Open Learning* journal (volume 20, number 1).

Research Methods Used

Coding for research method revealed that 185 (32%) of the 553 articles published in the four journals were case studies, 103 (19%) described theoretical inquiry, 76 (14%) were survey research,

TABLE 3.1.
Distance Education Research Topics

Topic	1997	1998	1999	2000	2001	2002	2003	2004	2005	Total	
Design	19	14	16	18	21	14	8	5	3	118	(21%)
Development	10	3	7	4	4	5	7	3	10	53	(10%)
Management	6	8	10	9	6	6	4	2	0	51	(9%)
Evaluation	10	12	8	7	6	4	9	8	12	76	(14%)
Institution & Operation	7	11	9	6	4	1	6	4	6	54	(10%)
Theory & Research	19	21	15	20	20	23	21	34	28	201	(36%)
Total	71	69	65	64	61	53	55	56	59	553	(100%)

Note: The percentages of research topics by publication year are presented in parentheses.

TABLE 3.2.
Distance Education Research Specific Topics by Keyword

Rank	1997	1998	1999	2000	2001	2002	2003	2004	2005
1	Interaction (12)	Program quality (8)	Learners' perception (5)	Collaboration (10)	Cross-cultural issues (11)	Problem-based learning (8)	Interaction (8)	Interaction (6)	Learning object (6)
2	Program evaluation (8)	Learners' perception (7)	Video-conferencing (4)	Learners' perception (8)	Faculty support (5)	Interaction (7)	Learner support (7)	Retention (4)	Interactivity (4)
3	Collaboration (8)	Program's effectiveness (5)	Learners' participation (4)	Video-conferencing (5)	Video-conferencing (4)	Learners' attitude (6)	Learners' perception (4)	Teaching (3)	Collaboration (3)
4	Video-conferencing (7)	Faculty support (5)	Learners' attrition (4)	Program's effectiveness (4)	Collaboration (4)	Learners' perception (4)	Synchronous Communication (3)	Collaboration (3)	Professional development (3)
5	Learning outcome (6)	Interaction (4)	Collaboration (3)	Learners' achievement (4)	Barrier to online learning (3)	Flexible learning (4)	Quality (3)	Learners' perception (3)	Asynchronous discussion (2)
6	Online learning model (5)	Instructor's leadership (4)	Program evaluation (3)	Need analysis (4)	Assessment of outcomes (3)	Learners' satisfaction (4)	Adult learner (2)	Support (3)	Dialogue (2)
7	Program quality (4)	Theory development (4)	Metacognition (3)	Program evaluation (4)	Interaction (3)	Tutor (4)	Critical thinking (2)	Characteristics (2)	Critical thinking (2)
8	Faculty support (4)	Institution issues (4)	Learners' achievement (3)	Faculty support (3)	Learners' performance (3)	Program evaluation (3)	Online instruction (2)	Professional development (2)	Satisfaction (2)
9	Learners' perception (3)	Learning strategy (3)	Faculty support (3)	Self-directed learning (3)	Program's quality (3)	Faculty support (3)	Time issue (2)	Persistence (2)	Support (2)
10	Learners' satisfaction (3)	Assessment of outcomes (3)	Tutor (3)	Cost issues (3)	Learners' persistence (3)	Scaffolding (3)	Discussion (2)	Dropout (2)	Competency (2)

Note: Frequency of key word is in parentheses.

71 (13%) were experimental research, 38 (7%) were developmental research, 38 (7%) were evaluation research, and 42 (8%) were implemented with combined inquiries. Table 3.3 presents the frequencies and percentages of research methods reported by authors in the four journals by year with totals across years. The reliability coefficient of the three coders' identification of research method was .86.

   This analysis indicates that case studies were used more than other methods in all years, but that the number of published experimental studies rose to nearly meet the number of case studies in 2002. These case studies investigated single individuals, groups, programs, or organizations qualitatively. Cumulatively, across years, the case-study method is followed in frequency by theoretical inquiry, survey research, and experimental research, respectively. Although the results of Berge and Mrozowski (2001) reported two-thirds of their studies as descriptive studies, followed by case studies, the results they obtained are not decidedly different from the results obtained in this study. If theoretical inquiry, evaluation research, development research, and survey were incorporated into Berge and Mrozowski's category of descriptive study, the proportion would approach two-thirds.

Statistical Methods Used

Studies were specified to report the scope of statistical methods that researchers in the field have applied during the years under investigation. However, the result of this analysis has limited generalization because the number of studies using statistical methods is small relative to the number of methods used. The researchers in the field frequently used analysis of variance, t-test, regression, chi-square, and factor analysis. Moreover, they used discriminant analysis, the Mann-Whitney U-test, structural equation modeling, and other methods. Table 3.4 presents the frequencies of statistical methods used in studies published in the four journals by year and the totals for each statistical method during the years under investigation.

Citations of Authors

The citations of primary authors in the four journals by subsequent authors were examined as a means by which to infer the relative impact the authors have made on the field of research in distance education. The total number of citations was 13,209. The cited authors were ranked by the order of the total number of citations in the four journals. We followed the reasoning of Anglin and Towers (1992) who indicated that an author could be cited because of his or her impact on a

TABLE 3.3.
Distance Education Research Methods

Method	1997	1998	1999	2000	2001	2002	2003	2004	2005	Total (%)
Theoretical inquiry	12	15	12	14	13	12	3	13	9	103 (19%)
Experimental research	5	5	9	6	10	12	8	7	9	71 (13%)
Case study	28	26	26	20	25	13	16	20	11	185 (32%)
Evaluation research	9	3	4	3	2	2	7	4	4	38 (7%)
Developmental research	10	2	2	6	3	3	2	1	9	38 (7%)
Survey research	7	11	8	12	4	6	13	8	7	76 (14%)
Combined inquiries	0	7	4	3	4	5	6	3	10	42 (8%)
Total	71	69	65	64	61	53	55	56	59	553 (100%)

TABLE 3.4.
Frequency of Statistical Methods

Statistical Method	1997	1998	1999	2000	2001	2002	2003	2004	2005	Total (%)
t-test	1	1	2				2	6	2	14 (16%)
ANOVA, ANCOVA	1	1	2		1	3	3	2	1	14 (16%)
Regression	2		1		3	2	1	0	4	13 (15%)
Chi-square	1	1		2	3	1	1	0	2	11 (14%)
Correlation			1	1	1	2	0	1	1	7 (9%)
MANOVA, MANCOVA						1	1	0	1	3 (3%)
Factor analysis		1	1	2	2	2	2	1	3	14 (16%)
Cluster analysis			1				0	0	0	1 (1%)
Path analysis		1	1				0	0	0	2 (2%)
Meta analysis				1		1	0	1	0	3 (3%)
Other							0	3	1	4 (5%)
Total	5	5	9	6	10	12	10	14	15	86 (100%)

particular area of inquiry, significant theory, research design, or theoretic perspective. Reviewed by those criteria, frequently cited authors were nominated primarily because of their impact on the field. The nominated authors published numerous articles and books or chapters and seemed to construct their own theories in distance education, whether narrowly or broadly.

Some of the authors examined were cited only in one or two journals. Although we took into account the number of articles published in each journal, selection biases might still have interfered in the analysis. For example, T. D. Evans was ranked tenth in authors' number of citations but was frequently cited in the *Journal of Distance Education* and *Open Learning*. The authors Rumble, Laurillard, Thorpe, Jegede, Peters, and Biggs were cited in the same way. Two reasons can be inferred from the skewedness in citations. This study considered only the first authors in citation, and secondary authors might have been instrumental in the development of theory or the investigation of effects. The number of citations might have been somewhat different had the coauthors also been counted. However, this study collected only the first authors to accentuate their significant contribution to the research designs and results. As another reason, an author's research topics might motivate a researcher in a certain country to call attention to a certain issue depending on the country in which the research was conducted. Many case studies focusing on individual country issues were found in the studies that were analyzed. The frequencies of citations of primary authors by journal are presented in Table 3.5.

Cited Books, Book Chapters, and Articles

All books, chapters, and articles cited in the articles appearing in the four journals were ranked (Tables 3.6 and 3.7). The first-ranked book was Moore and Kearsley's *Distance Education: A Systems View* ($n = 42$) and the first-ranked article or chapter was Moore's "Three Types of Interaction" ($n = 27$).

Future Research

The results of this study, combined with recommendations by other authors, suggest several areas in which future research in the field of distance education can develop.

TABLE 3.5.
Frequency of Cited Primary Author by Journal

Rank	Author	AJDE	DE	Open	JDE	Total
1	Moore, M. G.	72	43	39	31	185
2	Garrison, D. R.	30	33	22	42	127
3	Harasim, L. M.	7	31	18	38	94
4	Mason, R.	3	37	33	18	91
5	Kember, D.	4	40	33	12	89
6	Jonassen, D. H.	6	28	18	12	64
7	Holmberg, B.	12	5	36	6	59
8	Rumble, G.	3	14	39	2	58
9	Bates, A. W.	7	28	17	5	57
10	Evans, T. D.	1	21	29	2	53
11	Hiltz, S. R.	8	14	7	22	51
11	Berge, Z. L.	9	20	5	17	51
13	Biggs, J. B.	4	24	8	5	41
14	Laurillard, D.	2	18	18	2	40
15	Thorpe, M.	1	5	30	2	38
16	Gunnawardena, C. N.	10	13	8	6	37
16	Daniel, J. S.	5	6	23	3	37
16	Henri, F.	10	9	1	17	37
19	Peters, O.	0	6	24	6	36
19	Keegan, D. J.	2	5	25	4	36
19	Collis, B.	2	24	7	3	36
22	Burge, E. J.	1	7	8	19	35
23	Marton, F.	1	7	17	7	32
24	Kearsley, G.	2	13	6	11	32
25	Jegede, O. J.	2	24	3	2	31
25	Oliver, R.	5	19	5	2	31
27	Davie, L. E.	2	4	7	15	28
28	Lewis, R.	1	4	19	3	27
29	Kolb, D.	4	10	8	4	26
29	Keegan, D.	4	11	6	5	26

Note: AJDE = American Journal of Distance Education; DE = Distance Education; Open = Open Learning; JDE = Journal of Distance Education

First, practices that reflect educational and psychological theory are rarely found in distance education journals. Almost 30% of articles published have been classified as case studies that investigate an individual, a group, a program, or an organization qualitatively. However, many studies focus primarily on describing a case rather than the description of unique theory supporting distance education. One of the limitations of the case study is that it may be useful only to the researchers and practitioners involved in similar projects (Anglin & Morrison, 2000). Given the comparatively small number of theory-based studies in the field of distance education, why so few theory-based studies have been published remains an unanswered question. One answer may be a lack of theory-driven research methodology for distance education. Social and cognitive theories involving self-regulation and cognitive load are beginning to fill the theoretic void, but no general theory dedicated to distance learning has emerged.

Second, many research methods have been applied to analyze research topics. Particularly noteworthy is the multiple-inquiry method (combined inquiry, multimethod, mixed method),

TABLE 3.6.
Frequency of Cited Books

Rank	Title of Book	Total
1	Moore, M. G., & Kearsley, G. (1996). *Distance education: A systems view*. New York: Wadsworth.	42
2	Harasim, L., Hiltz, S. R., Teles, L., & Turoff, M. (1995). *Learning networks: A field guide to teaching and learning online*. Cambridge, MA: MIT Press.	29
3	Laurillard, D. (1993). *Rethinking university teaching: A framework for the effective use of educational technology*. London: Routledge.	27
4	Harasim, L. M. (1990). *Online education: Perspectives on a new environment*. New York: Praeger.	20
5	Bates, T. (1995). *Technology, open learning, and distance education*. New York: Routledge.	19
6	Rumble, G. (1999). *The costs and economics of open and distance learning*. London: Kogan Page.	14
6	Kember, D. (1995). *Open learning courses for adults*. Englewood Cliffs, NJ: Educational Psychology Publications.	14
8	Daniel, J. S. (1996). *Mega-universities and knowledge media: Technology strategies for higher education*. London: Kogan Page.	10
9	Mason, R. (1994). *Using communications media in open and flexible learning*. London: Kogan Page.	9
10	Evans, T. D. (1994). *Understanding learners in open and distance education*. London: Kogan Page.	8
10	Evans, T. D., & Nation, D. E. (1989). *Critical reflections on distance education*. London: Falmer Press.	8
12	Holmberg, B. (1995). *Theory and practice of distace education*. London and New York: Routledge.	7
13	Jonassen, D. H. (1996). *Handbook of research for educational communications and technology*. New York: Macmillan	5
14	Jonassen, D. H., Peck, K. L., & Wilson, B. G. (1999). *Learning with technology: A constructivist perspective*. Upper Saddle River, NJ: Merrill/Prentice Hall.	4
14	Keegan, D. (1993). *Theoretical principles of distance education*. New York: Routledge.	4

which combines two or more methods and is gradually increasing in frequency to answer the diverse questions raised in the distance education research (Anglin & Morrison, 2000; Goldman, Crosby, Swan, & Shea, 2005). For results, the researcher sometimes produces descriptive data as well as a model that explains the descriptive data more specifically. However, validity and reliability issues seem to be of minor concern among many researchers who apply these methods. Few studies report the result of power analysis, which is essential to generalize the result in other contexts.

There is a rising frequency of reported experimental studies, as compared with other research methods. However, most authors of experimental research did not explain how they obtained adequate sample size or the predictive power of their findings, nor did many report

TABLE 3.7.
Frequency of Cited Journal Articles and Book Chapters

Rank	Title of Article/Chapter	Total
1	Moore, M. G. (1989). Three types of interaction. *The American Journal of Distance Education, 3*(2), 1–6.	27
2	Moore, M. (1993). Theory of transactional distance. In D. Keegan (Ed.), *Theoretical principles of distance education* (pp. 22–38). London: Routledge.	17
3	Garrison, D. R. (1997). Computer conferencing: The post-industrial age of distance education. *Open Learning, 12*(2), 3–11.	14
4	Garrison, D. R. (1993). A cognitive constructive view of distance education. An analysis of teaching-learning assumptions. *Distance Education, 14,* 199–211.	13
4	Burge, E. (1994). Learning in computer conferenced contexts: The learners' perspective. *Journal of Distance Education, 9*(1), 19–43.	13
6	Jonassen, D., Davidson, M., Collins, M., Campbell, J., & Haag, B. B. (1995). Constructivism and computer-mediated communication in distance education. *The American Journal of Distance Education, 9*(2), 7–26.	12
7	Bates, A. W. (1990). Third generation distance education: The challenge of new technology. *Research in distance education, 3*(2), 10–15	11
7	Garrison, D. R., & Baynton M. (1987). Beyond independence in distance education: The concept of control. *The American Journal of Distance Education, 1*(3), 3–15.	11
9	Kember, D., Lai, T., Murphy, D., Siaw, I., & Yuen, K. S. (1994). Student progress in distance education courses: A replication study. *Adult Education Quarterly, 45*(1), 286–301.	10
9	Garrison, D. R. (1987). Researching drop-out. *Distance Education, 8,* 95–101.	10
11	Bates, A. W. (1997). The impact of technological change on open and distance learning. *Distance Education, 18*(1), 93–109.	8
11	Garrison, D. R. (1990). An analysis and evaluation of audio teleconferencing to facilitate education at a distance. *The American Journal of Distance Education, 4*(3), 13–24.	8
11	Mason, R., & Kaye, T. (1990). Toward a new paradigm for distance education. In L. Harasim (Ed.), *Online education: Perspectives on a new environment,* 15–38. New York: Praeger.	8
14	Peters, O. (1983). Distance teaching and industrial production: A comparative interpretation in outline. In D. Seward, D. Keegan, & B. Holmberg (Eds.), *Distance education: International perspectives,* 95–113. New York: Routledge.	6
15	Marton, F., & Säljö, R. (1976). On qualitative differences in learning. I. Outcome and process. *British Journal of Educational Psychology, 46,* 4–11.	5

effect size, confidence intervals, or even alpha level. Moreover, many experimental researchers did not indicate whether or not they assigned participants randomly in their studies, which makes their conclusions questionable. It is evident that publication of experimental research in the field of distance education is not yet held to the standards of experimental research in other fields of social science.

Third, action research is a paradigm championed by Nunes and McPherson (2003) for distance education, in which an instructor is actively involved with learners in conducting the research. In this paradigm, the research itself can be integrated with instructional practice and professional development. It might lead to more focused theory development than detached observation would.

REFERENCES

Anglin, G. J., & Morrison, G. R. (2000). An analysis of distance education research: Implications for the instructional technologist. *Quarterly Review of Distance Education, 1,* 189–194.

Anglin, G. J., & Towers, R. L. (1992). Reference citations in selected instructional design and technology journals, 1985–1990. *Educational Technology Research & Development, 40*(1), 40–43.

Berge, Z. L., & Mrozowski, S. (2001). Review of research in distance education, 1990 to 1999. *The American Journal of Distance Education, 15*(3), 5–19.

Boyatzis, R. E. (1998). *Transforming qualitative information: Thematic analysis and code development.* Thousand Oaks, CA: Sage.

Goldman, R., Crosby, M., Swan, K., & Shea, P. (2005). Qualitative and quisitive research methods for describing online learning. In S. R. Hiltz & R. Goldman (Eds.), *Learning together online: Research on asynchronous learning networks,* pp. 103–120. Mahwah, NJ: Erlbaum.

Khan, B. H. (1997). Web-based instruction: What is it and why is it? In B. H. Khan (Ed.), *Web-based instruction,* pp. 5–18. Englewood Cliffs, NJ: Educational Technology Publications.

Kleemann, G. (2000). *Distance learning and student affairs defining the issues.* Retrieved January 12, 2007, from http://www.ed.gov/about/bdscomm/list/acsfa/distnaspa.pdf

Klein, J. D. (2002). Empirical research on performance improvement. *Performance Improvement Quarterly, 15*(1), 99–110.

Koble, M. A., & Bunker E. L. (1997). Trends in research and practice: An examination of *The American Journal of Distance Education* 1987 to 1995. *The American Journal of Distance Education, 11*(2), 19–38.

Krippendorff, K. (1980). *Content analysis: An introduction to its methodology.* Beverly Hills, CA: Sage.

Nunes, M. B., & McPherson, M. (2003). Action research in continuing professional distance education. *Journal of Computer Assisted Learning, 19,* 429–427.

Phipps, R., & Merisotis, J. (1999). *What's the difference? A review of contemporary research on the effectiveness of distance learning in higher education.* Washington, DC: The Institute for Higher Education Policy. Retrieved January 12, 2007, from http://www.ihep.com/Pubs/PDF/Difference.pdf

Rourke, L., & Szabo, M. (2002). A content analysis of the *Journal of Distance Education* 1986–2001. *Journal of Distance Education, 17*(2), 63–74.

Sherry, L. (1995). Issues in distance learning. *International Journal of Educational Telecommunications, 1*(4), 337–365.

4

A Systems Approach in Theory Building

Farhad Saba
San Diego State University

While the field of distance education is rapidly growing, its theoretical base needs further articulation if distance education is going to offer a solid paradigm. Several questions should be addressed in this regard:

- What is the most appropriate approach for theory building in a field that is growing quickly in the number of institutions, practitioners, and students involved?
- How can we understand the relationships between ideas, research results, and practice in a discipline that has its roots in several related fields from which it borrows heavily for its conceptual development?
- As complex and colorful as distance education is, and may become in the future, how can we cast a wide net enough to capture distance education in its entirety while making it readily understandable?

The task is daunting. The literature in this field is immense. A recent Google search of "distance education" returned 112 million results in 16 seconds! Of course, one can guess that not all of this information is useful or even valid, but it shows how much our field has grown and challenges our ability to describe it fully in a parsimonious theoretical expression. The first edition of this *Handbook* (Moore & Anderson, 2003) highlighted the growth of the field much more precisely than a Google search.

In this impressive volume, Moore, the lead editor of the *Handbook*, brought together a remarkable group of thinkers to discuss recent advances in our field, as well as to present a comprehensive and coherent view of its intellectual history, scholarship, and practice. However, unless you are fortunate enough, as I am, to have been coached by Dr. Moore, you may not have readily recognized the relationship between his work on the theory of transactional distance and the earlier work of Charles A. Wedemeyer, one of the most distinguished pioneers in distance education. You may also have had to delve deep to see how the theoretical work of Holmberg, Moore, and Wedemeyer are interrelated. These are just two examples among numerous interconnected ideas that have formed the core intellectual foundation of distance education. These conceptual relationships have contributed to distance education's common history of research and practice and made it worthy of being called a discipline.

This current chapter, therefore, is about relationships. It is intended to cast a net wide enough to fully encompass the vast theoretical foundation of distance education while still articulating it in easily understood models. This chapter will demonstrate the necessity and centrality of the systems approach as a robust philosophy, methodology, and technology capable of organizing and describing conceptual relationships for building a contemporary theory of distance education and for developing principles that can guide its practice. It will show why the traditional scientific approach, while helpful in certain respects, is not sufficient to explain the postmodern paradigm of distance education. The traditional scientific approach must be augmented with methods from systems science if it is to represent a comprehensive and coherent theory of distance education. Finally, this chapter will present specific philosophical underpinnings, research methods, and technologies for theory building, research, and practice in distance education that are more appropriate for our postmodern era.

TRADITIONAL SCIENCE

In broad terms, the traditional scientific method based on the Cartesian dictum has been to "break down every problem into as many separate simple elements as might be possible" (Weinberg, 2001, p. 183). Understanding any particular field is difficult, if not impossible, if it is not broken down into manageable and understandable chunks. However, in fields concerned with human behavior—including education, political science, and management, as well as small group and interpersonal communication—it is not enough to merely observe and report about isolated parts, because they do not tell the entire story. For example, certain aspects of an organization might be revealed by observing the behavior of each individual within the organization. However, it is clear that the workings of the organization as a whole are far more complex than the sum of each individual's behavior. As Capra (1996) put it, the "great shock" of 20th-century science was that reality could not be understood merely by Cartesian analysis. Synthesis and understanding of the relationships between phenomena are at least as important, if not more so, particularly when living systems and human organizations are concerned.

SYSTEMS SCIENCE

The systems approach to research and development was conceptualized in the 1930s (Bertalanffy, 1968) in order to understand the complexity of a range of phenomena that did not lend itself to simple cause-and-effect relationships. Skyttner (2002) posited that classical science, due to partitioning and specialization, became incapable of solving complex problems ranging from the spread of communicative diseases to over-bureaucratization in social services. He explained, "The interaction of system-variables are so interlinked to each other that cause and effect can seldom be separated. One separate variable thus can be both cause and effect. An attempt to reduce complexities to their constituent and build an understanding of the wholeness through the knowledge of its parts is no longer valid" (p. 33).

In introducing the systems approach, Skyttner said, "General systems theory is a part of the systems paradigm which complements the traditional scientific paradigm . . . with a kind of thinking that is better suited to biological and behavioural realms" (p. 50). He further explained,

> This more comprehensive systems paradigm attempts to deal with processes such as life, death, birth, evolution, adaptation, learning, motivation and interaction. . . . It also attends to explanations, values, beliefs, and sentiments, that is, to consider the emotional, mental, and intuitive components of our being as realities. Consequently, the scientist becomes *involved* and is allowed to show *empathy.* (pp. 50–51)

In the recent past, scientists from a wide range of disciplines including physics (Capra, 1982, 1996), biology (Wilson, 1998), psychology (Damasio, 1994), and education (Banathy, 1992), to name a few, have questioned modern science's Cartesian reductionist thinking (Appleyard, 1993) and have foreseen the development of the postmodern systems science. Capra (1982) said,

> The new vision of reality we have been talking about is based on the awareness of the essential interrelatedness and interdependence of all phenomena—physical, biological, psychological, social and cultural. It transcends current disciplinary and conceptual boundaries and will be pursued within new institutions. At present there is no well established framework, either conceptual or institutional, that would accommodate the formulation of the new paradigm, but the outlines of such a framework are already being shaped by many individuals, communities, and networks that are developing new ways of thinking and organizing themselves according to new principles. (p. 265)

Today, there are a few institutions, such as the Santa Fe Institute (http://www.santafe.edu) that devote themselves solely to systems science by "emphasizing multidisciplinary collaboration in pursuit of understanding the common themes that arise in natural, artificial, and social systems" (Santa Fe Institute homepage, para. 1).

SYSTEMS THINKING IN DISTANCE EDUCATION

Systems thinking in distance education is not new. Moore (1999) and Moore and Kearsley (2005) trace its origin to Wedemeyer's founding of the Articulated Instructional Media (AIM) project in 1969 at the University of Wisconsin-Madison. The project not only broke "the ancient mold of extension, adult, and higher education," it created an integrated approach to the use of media for educating mature learners. Moore and Kearsley (2005) stated,

> Wedemeyer's idea regarding students was that using a variety of media meant that not only could content be better presented than through any one medium alone, but also meant that people with differing learning styles could choose the particular combination that was most suited to their needs. To bring together the expertise needed to produce such integrated multimedia programs, AIM invented the idea of the course design team, formed of instructional designers, technology specialists, and content experts. (p. 33)

Wedemeyer also assembled pioneering thinkers in the field to share their thoughts. This collaboration greatly contributed to the development of the British Open University through Harold Wiltshire and Walter James, who were close colleagues of Wedemeyer (Garrison, 2000; M. G. Moore, personal communication, December 2005).

In 1984, while resuming my research in the field after 10 years of managing distance education programs, I came across two articles by Moore (1973, 1983). Building on Wedemeyer's work in these articles, Moore had set forth structure, dialog, autonomy, and transactional distance as key constructs in independent adult learning. While reading these articles, I noticed the obvious dynamic relationships between these constructs proposed by Moore. He explained that variability in dialog and structure indicates four types of individual learning:

1. Programs with no dialogue and no structure ($-$D $-$S)
2. Programs with no dialogue, but with structure ($-$D $+$S)
3. Programs with dialogue and structure ($+$D $+$S)
4. Programs with dialog, but no structure ($+$D $-$S)

Looking at these classifications, I had one of those rare—aha!—insights that leads to creative work. Moore, by defining the relationship between dialog and structure in mathematical terms, had already started the preliminary development of a system dynamics model. It was all right there in front me! How could I possibly ignore the opportunity to test Moore's hypotheses by developing a system dynamics model?

This brainstorming led me to formalize Moore's hypotheses in system dynamics. I presented the results in an article submitted to the *American Journal of Distance Education* (Saba, 1989). It was with great surprise that I received a call a few months after the publication of the article. I was informed that I would receive the great honor of being the first recipient of the Charles A. Wedemeyer award for a research article. In a rare historic event, standing next to Dr. Moore, I received the award from Dr. Wedemeyer in Madison, Wisconsin. This system's particular causal loop had come full circle (see Figure 4.1).

More recently, Moore and Kearsley (2005) reiterated their systems view of distance education: "A distance education system consists of all the component processes that operate when teaching and learning at a distance occurs. It includes learning, teaching, communication, design, and management" (p. 9).

They also presented a conceptual model of distance education, which includes primary components such as teaching, learning, program/course design, technology, management, policy, and

FIGURE 4.1. Michael G. Moore, Charles Wedemeyer, and Farhad Saba (left to right).

organization, and defined the relationship between these components and the broader educational system, which includes economics, psychology, sociology, history, culture and philosophy (Moore & Kearsley, 2005).

They augmented this conceptual model with a systems model in which main components and processes were defined. These include

- a body of knowledge to be taught and learned
- a subsystem to organize this body of knowledge into materials and activities for students, such as courses
- a subsystem that delivers the courses to learners
- teachers who interact with learners as they engage with these materials and activities (courses) to construct their knowledge base
- learners in their individual environments
- a subsystem that monitors and evaluates outcomes so that interventions are possible when failures occur
- an organization with a policy and a management system to integrate these elements.

Embedded in this model are elements that instructional designers have been using since the 1970s to develop new programs, courses, and instructional materials. Instructional Systems Design (ISD), the instructional design model, follows a linear process that begins with identifying and analyzing the needs of the learner. Such analyses enable the instructional designer to design, develop, and implement instruction, and to evaluate the results in terms of learning outcomes. Ideally, the instructional designer leads a team of other specialists and is often guided by a subject matter expert.

Other scholars have also contributed to systems thinking in distance education. Concentrating on public policy, Pacey and Keough (2003) presented a model that offers feedback between policy goals and objectives (input) and intended/observed outcomes (output). Components influencing the behavior of the model are content, resources, and activities for programs offered. Granger and Bowman (2003) echoed Wedemeyer's systems approach to division of labor in distance education:

> A systems perspective on instructional design for distributed learning also gives emphasis to a need to restructure the role of faculty in the development of courses and programs. It is not realistic for a single teacher to design, develop, and teach effective distributed learning courses, and conventional structures in colleges and universities have not supported the advancement of collaborative distributed learning development. (p. 178)

Shaffer (2005) proposed a model of the socio-economic environment of distance education while criticizing the field. He claimed that "much research is published as disembodied pieces of information that lack coherence" (n.p.) and called for the development of a standard model.

A SYSTEMS APPROACH TO DISTANCE EDUCATION

This overview illustrates how a systems approach to distance education has been applied to various functions of the field, ranging from management practices to instructional design, policy analysis, and theory building. Systems thinking in these studies include several dimensions that must be explained if we are to develop a comprehensive view of how it can illuminate future theory building. A review of these dimensions will also be helpful to scholars who may not have had the opportunity to address systems theory fully, and may have shied away from incorporating it into their research. In addition, such a review might facilitate the development of a coherent concept of distance education that could potentially lead to establishing systemic organizational and pedagogical practices.

These dimensions are

1. Systems as philosophy and theory
2. Systems as a methodology for theory building in distance education
3. Systems as technology for research and practice

The remainder of this chapter will describe these dimensions and explain their applications to building a systems theory of distance education.

1. Systems as Philosophy

Premodern philosophy viewed the universe as one cohesive entity, comprised of interdependent parts. As modernism gained influence, this holistic view was replaced by an atomistic vision. Today, a new systemic view of the world is reemerging, defining the postmodern era. Table 4.1, based on Laszlo (2001), shows a comparison of the modern atomistic view of the world with a postmodern reemerging systemic view.

In addition to a robust philosophy, the systems approach offers a specific method for theory building, research, and development, which is explained in the next section.

TABLE 4.1.
Comparison of the Modern Atomistic View of the World with the Postmodern Systemic View

Modern Atomistic World View	Postmodern Systemic World View
Classical world view was anthropocentric. Man is perceived as mastering and controlling nature.	Man is an integral part of nature.
Nature is a giant machine with intricate but replaceable parts.	Nature is endowed with irreplaceable elements and an innate but non-deterministic purpose for choice, flow, and spontaneity.
People and objects are viewed as separate from their environments and from one another.	People and objects are perceived within the context of their environments and in relation to one another. Interconnectedness, communication, and community are emphasized.
All things are distinct and measurable material entities.	Matter is conceived as a configuration of energies that flow and interact. It allows for probabilistic processes, self-creativity, and unpredictability.
The purpose of life is the accumulation of material wealth through competition.	Acquiring knowledge is the purpose of life. Education, communication, human services, and cooperation are emphasized.
Science and technology are Eurocentric.	Valid contributions of people from other regions of the world are welcome.

2. Systems as a Methodology for Theory Building in Distance Education

If the ideal of the traditional scientific approach was to isolate one element in order to study its affect on another, then the purpose of systems science, in contrast, is to study a phenomenon in relation to its environment. As such, in defining a field, the theorist must identify the boundaries of a system by determining its key components. This is the most important task of a theorist who is building a model for a relatively young field of study, such as distance education. A precise description of key components and their relationships is necessary if we are to avoid conceptual confusion. Relative to one another, and collectively in relation to their environment, these components constitute a system that ideally represents a field of practice.

The current literature on distance education is replete with verbal descriptions of concepts, but lacks a formal and precise account of how these concepts relate to one another. Occasionally, an author might provide a diagram that clarifies the relationships between concepts. However, these mental models are rarely formalized as testable mathematical models. Identifying components of a system, articulating them, and depicting the relationships among them graphically are necessary, but not sufficient. Such relationships must also be defined in mathematical terms. This is where the systems model has the potential to be empirically validated.

For example, in the previous section titled, "Systems Thinking in Distance Education," I showed, how during reviewing the literature in adult, distance, and open education, I came across Moore's theoretical statements and decided to formalize them in system dynamics equations. Moore (1983) hypothesized that transactional distance in education is determined by the two variables of structure and dialog. Next, I articulated the relationships between these components in the following hypotheses: (a) when structure increases, transactional distance increases and dialog decreases; (b) when dialog increases, transactional distance decreases and structure decreases.

By now, Rick Shearer had joined me as a research colleague. We proceeded to illustrate these hypotheses in the causal loop diagram shown in Figure 4.2.

Notice that these statements imply a dynamic relationship between system components. That is, the mathematical values of system components increase or decrease as time progresses. Time is an inescapable reality affecting our lives. We cannot avoid its progression. Yet, research in education is often oblivious to the impact time has on phenomena. A robust theory of distance education must take the dynamic nature of teaching and learning into consideration.

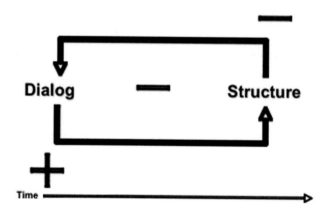

FIGURE 4.2. Causal loop of transactional distance.

In system dynamics, components are mainly of two kinds: *levels* and *rates*. (There are others, but for simplicity's sake, we will discuss only these two.)

Let's use an analogy to understand the concepts of levels and rates. A level is analogous to the amount of water in a pool at any given point in time. More water may pour in from a faucet while some may also drain out. However, the water level at any single point in time is determined by the interactions of: (a) the water level in the pool immediately prior to opening the faucet, or the drain; (b) the rates at which water pours into the pool and drains out once the faucet and drain are opened.

If we conceptualize transactional distance as a *level*, as we did in our 1994 study (Saba & Shearer, 1994), structure would increase the mathematical value of transactional distance, and dialog would decrease it.

But our work is not done yet. One more step must be taken. This relationship between structure and dialog must be defined in an algebraic equation.

$$\text{Transactional} \times \text{Distance }(t) = \text{Transactional} \times \text{Distance }(t - dt)$$
$$+ (\text{structure} - \text{dialog}) \times dt$$

In this equation, the level of transactional distance at any point in time [Transactional $\times$ Distance (t)] is equal to its prior level [Transactional $\times$ Distance $(t - dt)$], plus the rate of structure, minus the rate of dialog [structure $-$ dialog], multiplied by the time interval (dt).

This equation, along with a few other necessary equations, constitutes a system that can be computer-simulated and tested. Data can be collected to determine the rate of dialog and structure in an instructional session. The model can then be run based on actual empirical observations to test and verify it as we demonstrated in our 1994 study (Saba & Shearer, 1994).

In constructing models using system dynamics, it is paramount to distinguish between linear and non-linear systems. In linear systems, such as traditional instructional design models, the resulting behavior of the system (output) is the sum of responses to simpler inputs. The learner, for example, who receives instruction developed on a previous needs assessment, is expected to exhibit behavior that shows the desired learning outcomes have been achieved.

In non-linear dynamic systems, the output of the system is greater than the sum of the simpler inputs. Systems designed with the non-linear cognitive processes of the learners in mind take autonomy, and creativity into account. While distance educators continue to use the traditional ISD model for developing objectives-based instruction, a comprehensive systems model of distance education must also include learner autonomy, constructivist learning as well as self-organized non-linear dynamic processes of the brain. Ideally in such a system, learners would master all of the prescribed instructional objectives determined by the needs assessment. However, some unanticipated learning outcomes can occur due to the autonomous behavior of the learner. The biological capability of the brain to self-organize has been neglected in education for developing a learning theory for the future. (Abraham, 2003).

To summarize the process of model building, Roberts, Anderson, Deal, Goret and Shaffer (1983) presented the following guidelines:

1. Problem Definition—At this stage the "problem" (developing a theoretical model of distance education, in this case) is defined.
2. System Conceptualization—Components of the system are identified and their relationships are formalized in mathematical equations.
3. Model Behavior—The behavior of the theoretical model is observed in a test performed on the computer, running hypothetical data.

4. Model Evaluation—The theoretical model is evaluated and refined based on observation of the results of its behavior.
5. Model Analysis—Data is collected and the theoretical model is observed based on running actual data.

Model analysis can be a perpetual process when new data is collected and the model is retested. Sometimes anomalies are observed that lead to further refinement of the model and may ultimately result in a paradigm shift (Kuhn, 1970). However, few if any studies are replicated in the field of distance education. This should be a major concern for theorists and researchers in our field. A practice we must adopt from the traditional scientific method is replicating published research studies. This allows gaps in the existing knowledge base to surface and be articulated in more precise terms so that theorists and researchers will be able to work toward bridging them. It is to be hoped that in the process, conceptual confusion will be minimized. Unfortunately, little attention is being paid to the literature of our field by those involved in current research. Rather than building upon existing concepts, and frameworks many researchers are beginning anew, developing terminology, concepts, and models that are not based on valid, existing constructs that form the foundations of distance education.

HIERARCHY OF NESTED SYSTEM LEVELS

The equation previously discussed addressed one aspect of the teaching and learning process. The learner behaves based on his or her need for dialog while the instructor strives to maintain a certain level of structure to ensure that learning objectives are achieved; thus, the dynamic defines transactional distance at each point in time. Open systems, by definition, however, behave in response to their environment, as compared to closed systems, which do not interact with their surroundings. They affect and are affected by their environment. Transactional distance is an open system residing in a larger environment in the Instructional Systems Level, which is in turn part of a larger system in the hierarchical model proposed by Saba (2003; see Figure 4.3.)

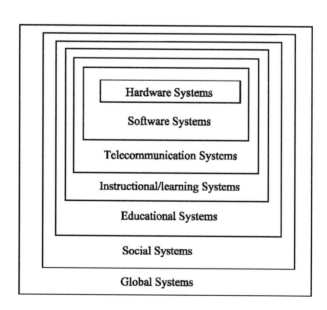

FIGURE 4.3. Hierarchy of distance education systems.

For example, Global Systems Level affects the availability, price, quality, and performance of Hardware Systems Level, which in turn determines what can and cannot be achieved at other levels of the hierarchy.

As such, the theoretical analysis/synthesis that we undertook to define one aspect of the Instructional Systems Level must be extended to define the other system levels as well. Each system level must be analyzed for defining its constituents. In doing so, we might mitigate Holmberg's (2005) reservation about developing a comprehensive theory of distance education, and instead move toward building an inclusive and coherent theory for the field. This carefully defined structure is capable of supporting and accommodating valid current theoretical constructs. In addition, it can incorporate future constructs as they emerge. Ideally, future theories would originate from within this model to minimize conceptual confusion.

THEORY BUILDING VS. PRESCRIPTIVE MODELS

Models developed by the systems dynamic method described in this chapter are intended for building a theory of distance education that is inspired by current knowledge, research, and practice. They may be adopted by practitioners to guide program development, implementation, and evaluation. However, as Dubin (1978) clarified, modeling for theory building should not be confused with offering prescriptive approaches for practice. Perhaps more than any other field, education often leaps directly from theory building to practice without the benefit of developing practitioner-oriented principles inspired by theoretical models. New theoretical models are often operationalized without the requisite testing and analysis needed to develop appropriate guidelines for practice. Progress in our field, and the development of sound prescriptive models, demand that there be a close and iterative relationship between theory building and practical application. Ultimately, they must inform and influence one another. Practitioner-oriented guidelines developed from sound theory must be put into practice and then tested. The resulting learning outcomes must be evaluated. This data influences theory and indicates where modifications to the theory or model should be made. In this cyclical process, new guidelines are developed and implemented based on adjustments to the original theory.

3. Systems as Technology

In traditional sciences the laboratory is the place where experiments are conducted. In systems science, however, the computer is the instrument as well as the "virtual" place for research and theory building. Skyttner (2002) posited, "When creating theories regarding the information world and complex living systems, different kinds of virtual worlds are necessary. There, the computer works as a laboratory and in its digital universe artificial intelligence and artificial life is created" (p. 38).

Computer models for theory building and research occupy substantial space within these virtual worlds. Describing the increasingly important role of computer modeling for advancing scientific discoveries, Feurzeig and Roberts (1999) explained,

> From the time of Galileo until fairly recently, there were two complementary ways of doing science: experiment and theory. Now there is a third way. Computer modeling, a child of our time, is a powerful new paradigm serving as a bridge between the traditional processes of experiment and theory and as a synergistic catalyst to both. The use of computer models as tool for furthering scientific knowledge is fast becoming a key component of current scientific research. We don't

know what scientific discoveries will be made in the twenty-first century. But we can be sure explorations and experiments with computer models will play a paramount role in making major advances possible. (p. xv)

These models are capable of simulating various contingencies based on hypothetical scenarios or actual data. A growing number of simulation software has entered the market, especially since the advent of the personal computer. The computer has brought the laboratory to the desktop.

In building a systems theory of distance education, I have used system dynamics in most of my work. Envisaged by J. W. Forrester in the 1960s, system dynamics was originally used to model industrial processes. For instance, in manufacturing, the relationships between suppliers of raw materials, rate of production, and customer orders were seen as being interrelated, rather than viewed as a series of unrelated functions. Since then, system dynamics has been used for modeling a variety of phenomena ranging from population patterns of wildlife to the future of planet Earth in general.

In recent years, algorithms enabling simulations of system dynamics models have been developed for the computer, unlike in the 1970s when running system dynamics models were only possible on mainframes involving cumbersome and time-consuming processes. What used to take hours to accomplish is now possible in minutes or seconds on a computer. Surprisingly, the most challenging part of producing and running a model is not actually building it on the computer and calculating and programming the required mathematical equations. It is conceptualizing the model itself, determining its components and their functions and relationships. Today, software such as STELLA and Vensim make it relatively easy to construct system-dynamics models. With built-in equations and a graphic interface, model builders can focus their efforts on the conceptual integrity of their models, spending less time on writing all of the necessary equations.

SUMMARY AND CONCLUSION

Growth in the amount of literature of the field and an expanding community of practice have introduced new challenges in building a theory of distance education. Piecemeal approaches to theory building have created more conceptual confusion, rather than clarifying the nature of a multifaceted field concerned with constructs of varying complexity. These constructs range from learner autonomy relative to the instructor's need for imposing structure, to the application of distance education in different countries and across borders.

The systems approach as a philosophy, methodology, and technology concerned with relationships among phenomena was proposed to encompass a wide variety of theoretical constructs in a hierarchical model. This model can accommodate developments at the global level as well as less complex levels as shown in Figure 4.3. Transactional distance was presented to illustrate how a dynamic model can be constructed relative to the concepts such as autonomy and structure. Transactional distance, however, is itself a component of the Instructional Systems Level. The same theory building process should be followed to identify and define theoretical components and their behaviors at all system levels.

Following these guidelines is likely to lead to a unified theory of distance education with flexibility. As new ideas and concepts are developed, they can be incorporated into the systems model, and their integrity and validity can be tested. A systems approach to distance education provides the breadth necessary to understand a field that includes theories and methods of praxis from various disciplines. Yet it also represents elements of everyday practice that range from the management of complex hardware at one system level to the intricacies and politics of different cultures working together at another system level. The task is enormous, but systems thinking is the path that offers the greatest potential.

REFERENCES

Abraham, J. L. (2003). Dynamical systems theory: Application to pedagogy. In W. Tschacher, & J. P. Dauwalder (Eds.), *The dynamical systems approach to cognition* (pp. 295–307). Singapore: World Scientific.

Appleyard, B. (1993). *Understanding the present: Science and the soul of modern man.* New York: Doubleday.

Banathy, B. H. (1992). *A systems view of education: Concepts and principles for effective practice.* Englewood Cliffs, NJ: Educational Technology Publications.

Bertalanffy, L. V. (1968). *General system theory: Foundations, development, applications* (Rev. ed.). New York: George Braziller.

Capra, F. (1982). *The turning point. Science, society and the rising culture.* New York: Simon and Schuster.

Capra, F. (1996). *The web of life: A new scientific understanding of living systems.* New York: Anchor Books.

Damasio, A. (1994). *Descartes' error: Emotion, reason and the human brain.* New York: G. P. Putnam's Sons.

Dubin, (1978). *Theory building* (Rev. Ed.). New York: The Free Press.

Feurzeig, W., & Roberts, N. (1999). *Modeling and simulation in science and mathematics education.* New York: Springer-Verlag.

Garrison, R. (2000, June). Theoretical challenges for distance education in the 21st century: A shift from structural to transactional issues. *International Review of Research in Open and Distance Learning.* Retrieved December 10, 2005, from http://www.irrodl.org/content/v1.1/randy.html

Granger, D., & Bowman, M. (2003). Constructing knowledge at a distance: The learner in context. In M. G. Moore & W. G. Anderson (Eds.), *Handbook of distance education* (pp. 169–180). Mahwah, NJ: Lawrence Erlbaum Associates.

Holmberg, B. (2003). A theory of distance education based on empathy. In M. G. Moore & W. G. Anderson (Eds.), *Handbook of distance education* (pp. 79–86). Mahwah, NJ: Lawrence Erlbaum Associates.

Kuhn, T. S. (1970). *The structure of scientific revolutions* (2nd ed.). Chicago: University of Chicago Press.

Laszlo, E. (2001). *The systems view of the world: A holistic vision for our time.* Cresskill, NJ: Hampton Press.

Moore, M. G. (1973). Toward a theory of independent learning and teaching. *Journal of Higher Education, 44*(9), 661–680.

Moore, M. G. (1983). The individual adult learner. In M. Tight (Ed.), *Adult learning and education* (pp.153–168). London: Croom Helm.

Moore, M. G. (1999). Charles Wedemeyer, In memoriam. *The American Journal of Distance Education, 13*(3), 1–6.

Moore, M. G. Personal communication, December 18, 2005.

Moore, M. G., & Anderson, W. G. (Eds.). (2003). *Handbook of distance education.* Mahwah, NJ: Lawrence Erlbaum Associates.

Moore, M. G., & Kearsley, G. (2005). *Distance education: A systems view.* Belmont, CA: Thomson Wadsworth.

Pacey, L., & Keough, E. (2003). Public policy, institutional structures, and strategic implementation. In M. G. Moore & W. G. Anderson (Eds.), *Handbook of distance education* (pp. 401–416). Mahwah, NJ: Lawrence Erlbaum Associates.

Roberts, N., Andersen, D., Deal, R., Garet, M., & Shaffer, W. (1983). *Introduction to computer simulation: A system dynamics modeling approach.* Reading, MA: Addison-Wesley.

Saba, F. (1989). Integrated telecommunications systems and instructional transaction. *The American Journal of Distance Education, 2*(3), 17–24.

Saba, F. (2003). Distance education theory, methodology, and epistemology: A pragmatic paradigm. In M. G. Moore & W. G. Anderson (Eds.), *Handbook of distance education* (pp. 3–20). Mahwah, NJ: Lawrence Erlbaum Associates.

Saba, F., & Shearer, R. L. (1994). Verifying key theoretical concepts in a dynamic model of distance education. *The American Journal of Distance Education, 8*(1), 36–59.

Santa Fe Institute (n.d,) Homepage. Retrieved from http://santafe.edu

Shaffer, S. C. (2005). System dynamics in distance education and a call to develop a standard model. *International Review of Research in Open and Distance Learning*. Retrieved December 10, 2005, from http://www.irrodl.org/content/v6.3/shaffer.html

Skyttner, L. (2002). *General systems theory: Ideas & applications*. Singapore: World Scientific.

Weinberg, G. M. (2001). *An introduction to general systems thinking*. (Silver anniversary ed.). New York: Dorset House Publishing.

Wilson, E. O. (1998). *Consilience: The unity of knowledge*. New York: Knopf.

5

The Most Industrialized Form of Education

Otto Peters
FernUniversität in Hagen

The reception and integration of the theory of distance education as *the most industrialized form of learning and teaching* is not easy because of its *unconventional* approach and even more so because of its *complexity.* Many educationists find it inadequate to apply industrial criteria to a pedagogical phenomenon and are not aware of the complexity of this theory. Usually they know and refer to a mere interpretation of distance education which compares it roughly to the industrialized production process. This limited comprehension gave rise to misinterpretations and misunderstandings, some of which I was able to clear up some years ago (Peters, 1989).

At present, as we pass through the information-and-knowledge society, the situation is changing. We are affected by the digitization of our world. The information explosion is bringing about an era of super-industrialism. Awareness of the present transformation of social and societal processes such as learning and teaching has grown. This may motivate experts to study as well the *broader* meaning of the theory of industrialized education, as this form of education caused similar structural changes in the 19th and 20th centuries and is now part of the present transformation process of teaching and learning.

If the theory is analyzed thoroughly, seven dimensions can be identified: historical, organizational, sociological, cultural, anthropological, economical, and pedagogical. These were described in detail in 1965, published in German in 1967, and published in English in 1994 (Keegan, 1994, 128–169).

THE FULL RANGE OF THE THEORY

Historical Dimension

Hypothesis: Principally, distance and online education are not stopgaps, chance solutions, strange side-effects, or mere surrogates for traditional education. They are in line with inherent trends in the history of learning. Structurally speaking, they represent the most advanced stages of the development of learning up to now. This was caused, accelerated, and reinforced by its industrialization.

57

When we consider distance education in a more general, far-reaching sense, a new dimension emerges for understanding this form of education. Undoubtedly, distance education is a part and a result of the historical development of teaching and learning. Since it is not possible to refer to all periods of this historical development, I will refer to extremes only. In archaic times (a) only a few people of the religious and political class were involved, (b) priestly functions were performed, (c) teachers exercised power over learners, (d) learners were often included in the teacher's family, (e) technical media were not used, and (f) individual teachers taught at fixed times at fixed places. Instruction was strongly under the influence of conventions. In other words, learning took place under extremely elitist, sacral, hierarchical, familial, personal, and traditional influences.

Analyzing the historical development of these six aspects we cannot but realize that, mainly under the influence of industrialization, each of them was transformed step-by-step into the opposite. Learning became egalitarian; secularized; and emancipated from hierarchical pressure, individual teachers, and fixed times and places. It became technically mediated and computerized. Personal and social bonds deteriorated; basically, it became depersonalized. A close analysis of these developments shows that, in contrast to classroom education and to other forms of face-to-face instruction, distance and online education have reached extreme categories in all the lines of structural development mentioned. With regard to this unique development it is also fair to argue again that distance education is clearly the most industrialized form of education, whereas face-to-face instruction has not reached this stage as it can still be more or less characterized by comparisons to elements of the artisan production process.

Organizational Dimension

Hypothesis: Distance education relies and depends on a great number of elements borrowed from the theory and practice of industrial production.

An in-depth analysis and interpretation of the process of distance education reveals structural elements that are practically and theoretically the same as their equivalents in the industrial production process—for example, professional planning and preparation, formalization, standardization, mechanization, automation, digitalization, rationalization, division of work, mass production, repeatability, and centralization. Teaching becomes an objectified process. With the help of implementation strategies and of specific technologies it is produced as a commodity, which can be mass-produced and distributed to students in a region, state, nation, or group of nations. Remarkable and even amazing parallels become clearly apparent. However, it must be emphasized again that so far we are talking about the first dimension of the theory only, which is usually referred to in the literature.

Economic Dimension

Hypothesis: Due to its industrialized structure, distance education has a close affinity with business and advances the commercialization of education.

The striking difference between the artisan and industrialized modes of producing goods is the possibility of mass production and mass distribution based on machines, processes, and materials that are used in industry, transport, and communication. Entrepreneurs recognized the economies of large scale and exploited the new chance to make profits that considerably exceeded traditional gains in the artisan economy. Many founders of early correspondence schools came up with the idea of applying methods from the industrial production process to the teaching-and-learning process in order to operate at lower costs and higher profits. It is significant that many founders were entrepreneurs themselves, usually publishers (in Germany: Langenscheidt, Hachfeld & Bonnes, Walter Schultz) or newspaper proprietors (in the United States). They had already acquired experience with self-learning material, textbooks, and the organization of publications and printing (Ehmann, 1978, p. 15). The economies of scale were also a convincing argument used by politicians who planned to establish cost-effective open universities during the last decades of the 20th century.

The commercialization of teaching and learning went hand-in-hand with their industrialization. This led as well to grave misuses of correspondence instruction (hard selling and "degree mills") and did lasting damage to its image. After the Second World War this misuse became a public nuisance which had to be curbed by legislation (Norway, the Netherlands, Germany, and the United States) and by the establishment of accreditation agencies for distance teaching courses. The possibility of establishing additional funds was also a motivation for U.S.-American universities to use distance education in their extension departments or for Australian universities to cater to distance students in Southeast Asian countries.

Two present trends accentuate the commercial potential inherent in industrialized teaching and learning: globalization and educational consumerism.

- The globalization of communication led to the emergence of a global educational market that is dominated by commercial competition. As distance education is not bound to places or times, it lends itself more easily to transnational systems than local schools or on-campus universities. Their peculiar industrialized structure enables distance learning institutions to export education on a large scale through international cooperation and the establishment of worldwide instructional systems (e.g., Penn State University's World Campus).

- This development is furthered and promoted by an increasing reinterpretation of teaching and learning by neo-liberal economists (Overbeek, 1993). They "promote a free-market orientation to the supply and trade of services. Education is considered such a service" (Moore & Kearsley, 2005, p. 300). Education is no longer a cultural and social good but instead becomes a private good to be sold according to requirements of the market. Distance teaching institutions become "providers of services," distant students "consumers." Educational and pedagogical goals lose their original significance as the "needs of the economy have precedence as market solutions are the rule" (Usher, Briant, & Johnston, 1997; Moore & Kearsley, 2005, p. 301). Productivity and consumption are the ultimate criteria for the development of consumerism, and also of distance education. They substitute or depreciate cultural, scholarly, and humanistic goals.

Cultural Dimension

Hypothesis: Distance education depends on a general societal atmosphere in which people have progressive attitudes, believe in innovation and development, strive for personal success, and are active and upwardly mobile.

Distance education sprang up and developed in the era of industrialization not only because of the new technical means of printing and transportation, but also because of new particular cultural conditions. These conditions shaped human behavior in a revolutionary way. This can be illustrated already by one example from many: people in pre-industrial societies were tradition-directed (Riesman, 1958), which means that their observation of the external rules of behavior was regulated and forced upon them by customs, habits, ceremonies, rites, and etiquette. Their attitude was modest and humble. People in industrialized societies, however, are inner-directed

(Riesman, 1958). This means that they have become able to disengage from strict traditional rules of behavior and to act at their own discretion. They learned how to take the initiative in order to realize new career prospects that were provided in great numbers in industrialized societies for the first time in history. They endeavored to be efficient, to control themselves permanently and to fight the "devil of indolence," to work hard for years in order to be rewarded later. They felt a desire to improve the conditions of their lives by professional and social advancement. Many new goals of life emerged.

The relevance of such developments for the emergence of distance education can easily be seen. Distance education as a mass phenomenon would have been unthinkable in a tradition-directed, pre-industrial society.

Sociological Dimension

Hypothesis: With the help of sociological criteria from the industrial production process it is possible to describe characteristic traits of the teaching-learning process in distance education more precisely.

The industrial production process is in the center of sociological research (Friedmann 1952; 1953; 1959; Galbraith, 1987; Beck, 1996) and focuses on rapid changes of our time caused by industrialization. It is advantageous to analyze distance education in its sociological aspects as well. Sociology—in contrast to theory of education—has fully understood and clearly explained the effects of technology and industrialization on social change. I will refer here to one aspect only.

Jürgen Habermas (1968, p. 61) observed that Talcott Parsons' catalogue of possible alternatives of value orientation can also be used to characterize the change of dominant attitudes as a consequence of the transition from traditional to modern society. Parsons presented the following four pairs of value orientations: affectivity/affective neutrality, particularism/universalism, ascription/achievement, and diffuseness/specificity. It is easy and revealing to describe classroom instruction by pointing to its affectivity, particularism, ascription of certain qualities, and diffuseness. On the other hand, distance education can be characterized by affective neutrality, universalism, achievement, and specificity.

Anthropological Dimension

Hypothesis: Industrialization has not only changed the relations of human beings to their physical and social environment, but also themselves. "Industrial human beings" and "information human beings" can be distinguished clearly from pre-industrial human beings.

The main factor that brought about this change is the extent to which human beings use technical media and technology in order to compensate for their biological deficiencies, their lack of specialized organs and instincts, and for their inability to adapt to a particular species-specific environment, for their "morphological helplessness" (Gehlen, 1958). Technology is used to substitute, intensify, and relieve their organs. In a general sense, technology belongs to them and mirrors their being.

The industrialization of education can be understood as the development of a complex technical system of teaching and learning, which human beings are forced to use as they no longer are able to cope with all the instructional and training tasks of the advanced industrial and knowledge society using their natural organs. A few examples: the voice of teachers is extended in order to reach students everywhere on this planet. Their eyes and ears, which inform them about the learning behavior of the students, are substituted and intensified by systematic collection of data with the help of computers. Their notorious forefingers, which draw and guide the attention of students, are extended and intensified by graphical representations and sensory stimuli techniques;

their memory is extended and intensified by powerful storing techniques. Even some of their intellectual abilities are extended by networking in a virtual reality.

Seen in a larger anthropological context the construction of complex technological systems of learning and teaching and their implementation can be interpreted as a real proof of the capacity of human beings to react to fundamental changes in society. It is a building block for the secondary environment that people must create in order to survive. At the same time, teachers and students are subject to processes of alienation as the traditional teacher/student relationship is disrupted.

Pedagogical Dimension

Hypothesis: Under the strong impact of industrialization, distance education became a unique form of teaching and learning that differs in decisive structural elements from face-to-face education and requires different approaches.

The impact of industrialization on the pedagogical structure of distance learning and on the behavior of students and faculty is profound. The original proximity between learner and teacher changes into distance. Consequently, an entirely new and singular learning and teaching method must be established, new learning and teaching behaviors have to be shaped, new learning styles must be developed, and students must become used to new learning environments and climates. A model of a teacher interacts with many students at a time and yet with each single student asynchronously. The students interact with a teaching system in a mediated way and learn by means of a two-way exchange of information. Communication media and pre-produced teaching materials assume an extraordinary importance, never experienced before in the history of learning. The roles of teachers change drastically. Their work is divided into separate functions that are performed by specialists who work together in teams. This requires new concepts and a reorganization of instructional design, as well as unusual pedagogical implementation strategies.

One important educational aspect of a learning system of this type must be singled out. Students are obliged to become active, to assume responsibility, and to organize their learning with regard to time and location. In this situation they have many opportunities to become autonomous and self-regulated with regards to goals, methods, and media as well. Quite often, presentational teaching and receptive learning are substituted by activated self-learning. Industrialized learning causes and reinforces a dramatic pedagogical paradigm shift.

EXPLANATIONS

Continuous Relevance

Quite often the argument is put forward that the theory of the most industrialized education is no longer valid as the era of industrialism is fading out in our growing information-and-knowledge society. However, if we look deeper we become aware that the original approaches and many processes of industrialization are still changing our world, even at an accelerated pace and with far-reaching critical consequences. We have experienced the periods of neo-industrialism and of post-industrialization. Now many of these industrialized processes are changing as a consequence of their digitization. In spite of these stages of transformation, these industrial production processes were not discontinued, but only modified structurally. These periods have not substituted each other, but remain side by side. They accelerate, reinforce, and improve industrial processes in order to make them more efficient and profitable. They intensify and radicalize industrialized production. We can observe enormous increases in the production, distribution, and networking of information and communication and diagnose the consequences.

On closer inspection we realize that the basic principles of industrialization remain: rationalization, planning and control mechanisms, the use of advanced technology and scientific knowledge, an (internationally) extended division of labor, the extension of distribution areas, the constant improvement of the product, the differentiation of sub-systems, and partly even mass production and a remarkable increase of commercialism. The German philosopher and sociologist Helmut F. Spinner (2000, p. 140), calls our present society a "super-industrialized information and communication society."

Another aspect is that most open universities, which quite often cater to several hundreds of thousands of students each, still have to rely on an industrialized structure, and in particular on the principle of mass production in spite of the theoretical advances referred to and the wealth of additional new digitized communication possibilities, which can take place only in smaller networked groups.

Purpose

Generally speaking, theories accomplish an understanding of reality—in this case, the reality of distance education. The function of the theory of the most industrialized education can be indicated by stating that it is basically descriptive, analytical, and explanatory, and to a certain degree predictive and prescriptive as well.

The theory *describes* all elements of the overall process of distance education and focuses on macro-pedagogical perspectives. It offers a frame of reference to planners, teachers, learners, and evaluators. In contrast to this, face-to-face pedagogical situations are mainly based on micro-pedagogical approaches. The theory describes the circumstances which caused the creation of distance education and its transformations in its three or four generations.

This theory helps to *analyze* and to interpret a complex system which consists of professional specialists, media, learners and teachers, support services, and quality management. It provides an overview and facilitates calculated interventions.

Why is it adequate to interpret distance education by applying this theory? It helps to understand the reality of learning and teaching at a distance. It raises our awareness of the specific character, the "essence" of this form of learning, and of the social processes on which it is based. It makes crystal-clear that this form differs from all pre-industrial forms of learning and teaching. It relates distance education to the history of learning, our cultural development, technological advances, the world of industrial production, commercialism, and a humanitarian mission. And it helps to imagine possible future developments of learning.

This theory is basically descriptive and analytical. It describes the circumstances which caused the creation of distance education and explains relevant changes in three generations of distance education as they can be related to relevant changes of industrial production. It raises the awareness of educationists that distance education in all its generations is basically and structurally a unique form of education (sui generis) and cannot be equated with face-to-face education. This is difficult, as we have all been educated in face-to-face learning arrangements and have internalized this kind of education, which induces us to judge distance education by satisfying criteria of classroom or on-campus education. Nevertheless, this general awareness is necessary because learning and teaching behavior must be adapted to an entirely different structural framework in order to prevent severe dysfunctions. This awareness certainly exists when a curriculum-planning director differentiates as follows: "This should be done in an artisan way and this in an industrialized way," or when a student, in order to characterize the present dilemma of many teachers, writes an essay entitled "Back to the Craftsman's Method?"

Distance teaching institutions have a humanitarian mission, because they are committed to the idea of helping the neglected and underserved on a grand scale. John Daniel (1998) used to call this the "legacy of distance education." The existence of neglected and underserved persons, who make up considerable sections of the population, is another typical feature of industrialized societies.

Reception

The theory was conceived in the middle of the 1960s and first published in 1967 (Peters, 1967; 1973). German scholars clearly did not appreciate it as they were not at all familiar with distance education and its specific problems at that time. But, more importantly, they were seized by the 1968 students' movement that focused on the emancipation of the *traditional* students from suppression by academic hierarchies. They felt that social processes cannot be planned and calculated. They rejected the use of technology in general, but especially in teaching and learning. There was practically no response from German-speaking educators.

The first description of the theory in English was published by Mackenzie and Christensen (1971, pp. 225–228). In 1983, David Sewart translated a relevant chapter of the author's 1973 book and edited it, together with Desmond Keegan and Börje Holmberg, in *Distance Education. International Perspectives* (Sewart, Keegan, & Holmberg, 1983). It was Desmond Keegan's (1986) book, *The Foundation of Distance Education*, that made a lasting impact on distance educators. He devoted a whole chapter to the industrialization of distance education and discussed it at international conferences. At that time, the theory was especially convincing to experts who were involved in establishing open universities in the 1970s and 1980s as they combined technical, organizational, and management innovations and appeared to be the empirical proof of the theory. Open universities are the most industrialized distance learning institutions. Keegan (1994) later reinforced this impact by editing a book containing selected translated writings of this author. It is subtitled *The Industrialization of Teaching and Learning*. In subsequent years Desmond Keegan's strong impulses in the literature provoked animated international discussions. Since then the theory has been dealt with in all scholarly books on distance education and is included in many online Master of Arts courses on Distance Education, the last and most striking example being the online Master of Arts course "Foundations of Distance Education" of the University of Maryland University College (UMUC).

Contrasting Views

There are problematic aspects to this theory. Industrialization is founded on ideas of the Age of Enlightenment, according to which we are able to plan and construct our social life and our conditions of life can be improved by goal awareness and by applying knowledge and rational approaches, advanced planning strategies, and technology. The industrialization of education means that we adhere to the optimistic belief of constant progress in the expansion of educational opportunities in order to improve society by improving education.

However, in our postmodern or trans-modern society, we cannot but sense that these ideas and assumptions have lost much of their original importance. Postmodern interpretations of our society cause us to accept that some of these concepts of enlightenment are now no longer valid. Critics diagnosed the end of history, the end of humanity, the disempowering of the subject, and even the end of education. The idea that it might be possible to plan the education of masses of students by using a digitalized system of distance education seems to be obsolete. Things become worse when we see that the consciousness and the attitudes of postmodern learners do indeed differ from those of industrial human beings. This creates clashes of opinions and difficulties in understanding.

On the other hand we see that industrialized education is still taking place and is even increasing with regard to volume and significance. Its importance is even growing as more and more universities and corporations establish systems of distance education, especially under global aspects. Educational experts continue to plan and implement distance education in a rationalized, strictly goal-oriented way. They profit from the division of labor, the use of technology, systematic approaches, and mass production. They see that distance education is becoming more and more commercialized and continue teaching at a distance in spite of learners' changes of attitudes. The possible transformation into neo- and post-industrial structures may alleviate this approach (Peters, 2000, p. 121).

The only way out of these contrasting views is to admit that, according to Jean-François Lyotard, our postmodern society can be characterized by the "awareness of radical plurality, even heterogeneity and incompatibility of individual kinds of discourses" (Pries & Welsch, 1991, p. 372). We must be ready to cope with this situation by exhibiting tolerance.

Empirical Legitimacy

The strongly industrialized nature of distance education is evident to anyone able to recognize and analyze the structure of pedagogical situations and processes and to compare them to the structure of industrialized production processes. The awareness of impressive analogies is desirable and necessary, as most educationists do not see or even deny them. Therefore, we might think it necessary to support this evidence scientifically. "Comparison" is the method to be applied here. This approach would be by no means unusual, as it has been successfully applied in cross-cultural surveys (Murdock, 1949) and cross-polity surveys (Banks & Textor, 1965). This required research project could be called "cross-social-technological processes survey." The comparison should include an analysis of several generations of industrialized production and several generations of distance education. The hypothesis for this kind of research is that all models of distance education, from the simplest 19th century correspondence school to the most complex 20th century open university and the 21st century virtual university, show strong structural affinities to industrialized production processes. This insight can be created and reaffirmed by logical deduction. A further hypothesis could be that, traditionally, there is no awareness of the industrialized character of distance education even among distance education educators and students. At present, however, this awareness is increasing and the readiness to adapt pedagogical decisions to this structure is growing. Proof of this process could be established by opinion polls.

RELATIONS TO TWO OTHER THEORIES

When trying to relate the theory of industrialized learning to Moore's theory of *Transactional Distance* and Holmberg's theory of the *Empathetic Learning and Teaching Conversation* it appears that significant differences and similarities can be diagnosed.

In Search of the Specific Character of Distance Education

Moore's theory of transactional distance (Moore, 1977; Moore & Kearsley, 2005) is a convincing contribution to the theory of distance education, as Moore has ingeniously succeeded in pointing to a characteristic feature of distance education that cannot be found in any other form of learning and teaching. He interprets "geographical distance" in distance education as unique in the sense that it is a relative, continuous phenomenon that can be made more or less distant by employing pedagogical approaches. Although the same can be said about "distance" in face-to-face instruction, it should be realized that the relative proximity in classrooms has never been of concern to pedagogical theorists. Moore's concept, however, attributes special significance to situations in which teacher and student are separated by geographical distance. For him, this distance can be influenced by three pedagogical categories: dialogue, structure, and autonomy. Structure in particular, which is mainly defined as the structure of printed or otherwise mediated courses especially designed for distance education, is typical of distance education. And his concept of autonomy also refers to the special requirements and possibilities of isolated students learning at a distance, and opens up new ways of self-learning for them. This interplay of the three pedagogical categories and their specific influence on distance constitutes the very core of the pedagogical structure of distance education.

Holmberg's theory of distance education as an "empathetic teaching learning conversation" (Holmberg, 2005, p. 121) does not characterize distance education in the same plausible way. Empathetic teaching learning conversations take place in classroom teaching at schools and colleges as well. It is therefore not the fundamental characteristic of distance education. The same can be said about the specific quality of this conversation. Holmberg emphasizes the necessity of creating personal relations between teachers and students in order to promote study pleasure and motivation (Holmberg, 1981, pp. 30–32). His empathy approach (Holmberg, 2005, p, 37), however, is again not typical for distance education, but a general pedagogical goal and requirement of most teaching. The humanistic psychology (Rogers, 1965) and humanistic pedagogy (Tausch & Tausch, 1977) movements promoted the idea of the teacher's "empathy" as a general pedagogical requirement from the 1950s—without referring to distance education. The only justification for this approach is that students engaged in distance education are normally isolated and may require more empathetic communication than traditional students. Holmberg also stresses the peculiarity of distance education, namely that mediated dialogues enable one-to-one communication in which empathetic dialogues are more likely to arise. He focuses on a single element of instruction, but believes that his theory "is also an attempt to explain what distance education really is" (Holmberg, 1985, p. 27). His real contribution is the highly competent description of the pedagogical forms that guided conversation can take in "good" distance education. But this means that his theory does not cover "bad" distance education.

The theory of the most industrialized education emphasizes a criterion that clearly separates distance education from face-to-face education, as it draws a clear dividing line between them and reveals the real nature, the "essence," of this form of education.

Description and Prescription

Moore's theory is principally descriptive, in the sense that it does not explicitly recommend a specific model of learning and teaching at a distance. It describes three teaching behaviors: the provision of dialogue, structure, and autonomy—together with the corresponding teaching and learning behaviors. As such they are not typical for distance education because they also make up important elements of face-to-face education. In distance education, however, these teaching behaviors assume prime importance because they influence the transactional distance. Furthermore, they relate to each other in different ways in specific learning situations. Moore has no preferences, nor does he recommend special configurations of these approaches. His theory is based on a distant, neutral, and explicit description.

However, the theory suggests implicitly that distance education should be made up of these three teaching-learning behaviors. This means that Moore wishes to innovate and improve distance education, because traditional distance teaching courses, and many newer forms of distance education and of online learning as well, have severe deficiencies, especially with regard to dialogue and autonomy. By describing that dialogue, structure, and autonomy as fundamental elements of distance education, Moore offers the means for improving distance education and for enhancing its pedagogical quality. Thus his descriptive theory appears also as a prescriptive one.

Holmberg is also concerned with a weakness of traditional distance education: its lack of two-way communication. Insofar, there is a point of contact with Moore's "dialogue." Holmberg intends to improve the practice of distance education. He conceives it as a form of learning in which there is a strong and continued rapport between teacher and students. This is to be achieved by talking to each other in written form or over the telephone, something which is certainly a sound and laudable pedagogical endeavor. Clearly his theory is a prescriptive one, and in fact he calls it "prescriptive" himself.

The theory of the most industrialized form of education is mainly a descriptive one. The approach is cold, analytical, exploring. Value judgments are avoided. The author tries to reveal structural peculiarities and their transformation of the whole process without any recommendations. He is by no means a supporter of industrialization or a promoter of industrialized education. On the contrary, he believes that industrialization will disrupt and finally destroy not only our traditional forms of education, but also our *Lebenswelt* on the whole. But again, this theory is implicitly prescriptive as well, because it heightens the awareness of societal and pedagogical change and of possible dysfunctional teaching and learning behavior, which necessarily occurs whenever a person thinks and acts in terms of face-to-face learning although working at a distance.

Scope

The three theories differ considerably in their broadness.

Holmberg's theory focuses on one aspect of learning and teaching in distance education that relates to a limited, restricted aspect only. It refers to one part of a micro-pedagogical process. This is not at all typical for his general concept of distance education because, as a distinguished author and practitioner, he is certainly familiar with all the other aspects as well. His impressive publications show this clearly. His theory implies that teacher/student rapport is of fundamental importance in distance education. Insofar, we can imagine hypothetical links to the whole of the teaching-learning process in distance education. But taking his theory alone as a basis for our comparison, we can see that it covers only a section of the learning process.

Holmberg's theory is based on the idea that in distance education "the presentation of learning matter cannot be confined to dissimilation of information. As an educational endeavor it must engage students in intellectual activity that makes them try out ideas, reflect, compare and apply critical judgments to what is studied" (Holmberg, 1989, p. 41). He considers and stresses the importance of the affective aspects of such an approach. He calls this an "overarching principle." By selecting this aspect he aims at the very core of the pedagogical process—in both face-to-face instruction and in distance education. But again it assumes specific significance in distance education, because students learn in an isolated situation by themselves and need support. Many traditional commercial correspondence schools (and many online teaching institutions as well) succumb to the temptation to limit their activity to the distribution of printed or e-mailed teaching texts. Obviously, Holmberg intends to curb this practice. His convincing recommendation of introducing empathetic mediated conversations is a genuine pedagogical approach as well, but covers only one aspect of a complex process. Insofar the scope of this theory is comparatively small.

Moore's theory deals with the main peculiar characteristic of distance education: the manipulation of "distance" by pedagogical approaches. This original approach aims at, and relates to, distance education in its entirety. It makes distance educators aware of a central peculiarity of this form of education. His micro-pedagogical concept is critical for all course developers, tutors, correctors, and moderators and can enhance their work. Insofar, this theory covers a broader area of distance education.

The theory of the most industrialized form of education is a broad one. It is true that at first sight it seems to cover the organizational side of the teaching-learning process in distance education only and seems to be rather narrow. However, at second sight we realize that it is a complex and multifaceted theory that indicates how the process of industrialization has also changed the pedagogical structure of teaching and learning in a decisive way. Furthermore, the seven dimensions of this theory offer further explanations of the complex meaning of distance education. This theory is based on a macro-pedagogical approach.

Final Comment

The *Encyclopaedia Britannica* defines the word *theory* as "any of the proposals put forth to explain changes in behavior produced by practice. . ." The theories explicated and referred to in this article comply with this definition. They contribute to a better understanding of an egregious breach of educational tradition. They help readers to become aware of and understand the severe pedagogical paradigm change that was caused by mechanization, automation, computerization, and digitization. These advances made it possible and necessary to develop distance education both in its early form of correspondence education and in its advanced forms in open and virtual universities. All transformations of distance education require fundamental "changes in behavior" as they are developed beyond fixed times, fixed places, and fixed habits. The three theories help us to understand these changes.

REFERENCES

Banks, A., & Textor, R. B. (1965). *A. C.–P. S.* Cambridge, MA: MIT Press.

Beck, U. (1996). Das Zeitalter der Nebenfolgen und die Politisierung der Moderne. In Ulrich Beck, Anthony Giddens, & Scott Lash, *Reflexive Modernisierung*. Frankfurt am Main, Germany: Suhrkamp.

Daniel, Sir John. (1998). Knowledge Media for Mega-Universities: Scaling up New Technology at the UK University. Keynote speech at the 1998 Shanghai International Open and Distance Education Symposion. Shanghai Television University: Symposion Abstracts, 3.

Ehmann, C. (1978). *Fernstudium in Deutschland.* Köln, Germany: Verlagsgesellschaft Schulfernsehen.

Friedmann, G. (1952). *Der Mensch in der mechanisierten Produktion.* Köln, Germany: Bund-Verlag.

Friedmann, G. (1953). *Zukunft der Arbeit: Perspektiven der industriellen Gesellschaft.* Köln, Germany: Bund-Verlag.

Friedmann, G. (1959). *Grenzen der Arbeitsteilung.* Frankfurt am Main, Germany: Europäische Verlagsanstalt.

Galbraith, J. K. (1987). *A history of economics.* London.

Gehlen, A. (1986, 13th ed. 1958). *Der Mensch. Seine Natur und seine Stellung in der Welt.* Bonn: Athenäum.

Habermas, J. (1968, 61). *Technik und Wissenschaft als Ideologie.* Frankfurt am Main, Germany: Suhrkamp.

Holmberg, B. (1981). *Status and Trends of Distance Education.* London: Kogan Page.

Holmberg, B. (1985). *Status and Trends of Distance Education. Revised edition.* Lund, Germany: Lector Publishing.

Holmberg, B. (1989). *Theory and Practice of Distance Education.* London: Routledge.

Holmberg, B. (2005) *The Evolution, Principles and Practices of Distance Education.* Oldenburg, Germany: Bibliotheks- und Informationssystem der Universität Oldenburg.

Keegan, D. (1986). *The Foundations of Distance Education*. London: Croom Helm.

Keegan, D. (Ed.) (1994). *Otto Peters on Distance Education. The Industrialization of Distance Education*. London: Routledge.

Mackenzie, O., & Christensen, E. L. (1971). *The Changing World of Correspondence Study*. University Park, PA: Penn State University Press.

Moore, M. G. (1977. *A model of independent study*. In Kurt Graff & Rudolf Manfred Delling (eds.) *Epistolodidaktika, Beiträge zu Problemen des Fernunterrichts, 1*, pp. 6–40. Hamburg: Walter Schultz Verlag.

Moore, M. G., & Kearsley, G. (2005, 2nd edition). *Distance education. A systems view*. Belmont, CA: Thomson Wadsworth.

Murdock, G. P. (1949). *Social Structure*. New York: Macmillan.

Overbeek, H. (Ed.) (1993). *Restructuring hegemony in the global political economy: the rise of transnational neo-liberalism in the 1980s*. London: Routledge.

Peters, O. (1967). *Das Fernstudium an Universitäten und Hochschulen*. Weinheim, Germany: Beltz.

Peters, O. (1973). *Die didaktische Struktur des Fernunterrichts*. Weinheim, Germany: Beltz.

Peters, O. (1989). The iceberg has not yet melted: Further reflections on the concept of industrialisation and distance teaching. *Open Learning 4*(3), 3–8.

Peters, O. (2000). *Learning and Teaching in Distance Education* (pp. 128–169). London: Kogan Page.

Pries, C., & Welsch, W. (1991). *Ästhetik im Widerstreit*. Weinheim, Germany: Wiley-VCH .

Riesman, D. (1958). *Die einsame Masse. Eine Untersuchung der Wandlungen des amerikanischen Charakters*. Reinbek, Germany: Rowohlt. In English: *The Lonely Crowd*. New Haven, CT: Yale University Press, 1950.

Rogers, C. A. (1965). *Client Centered Therapy*. Boston: Houghton Mifflin Company.

Sewart, D., Keegan, D., & Holmberg, B. (Eds.) (1983). *Distance Education. International Perspectives*. Beckenham, Germany: Croom Helms.

Spinner, H. F. (2000). Informations- und Kommunikationsgesellschaft. In Bernhard Schäfers, *Grundbegriffe der Soziologie*. Opladen, Germany: Leske + Budrich, pp. 140–148.

Tausch, R., & Tausch, A. M. (1977, 8th ed.) *Erziehungspsychologie*. Göttingen, Germany: Hogrefe.

Usher, R., Briant, I., & Johnston, R. (1997). *Adult Education in the Postmodern Challenge: Learning beyond the Limits*. London: Routledge.

6

A Theory of Teaching-Learning Conversations

Börje Holmberg
FernUniversität, Germany

My approach to distance education, describing its most effective application as a teaching-learning conversation—first tentatively mentioned in a monograph (Holmberg, 1960), and later (Holmberg, 1985; 1995) developed into a theory generating testable hypotheses—is based on the very general observation that feelings of empathy and personal relations between learner and teacher support motivation for learning and tend to improve the results of learning. This is something of a truism, something constantly experienced in teaching-learning situations irrespective of historical, political, and sociocultural contexts. As this general insight is not consistently applied to distance education, there seems to be good reason to look into its particular appropriateness in this kind of education. Its relation to Moore's and Peters' understandings of distance education is discussed in the last section of this contribution to the theory debate (cf. Moore, 1983; Moore & Kearsley, 2005; Peters, 1973, 1989, 1998).

The latest wording of my theory, given in my book (Holmberg, 2005), is this:

> Distance education is based on deep learning as an individual activity. Learning is guided and supported by non-contiguous means which activate students, that is, by mediated communication, usually based on pre-produced courses. The development of courses may apply large-scale methods and may also be carried out for small groups of students. Subject-matter presentation and mediated interaction are the two constituent components of distance education, for which a supporting organisation is responsible.[1]

As individual study requires a certain amount of maturity, self-discipline, and independence, distance education can be an application of independent learning at the same time as it is apt to further develop study autonomy. Central to the learning and teaching in distance education are personal relations, study pleasure, and empathy between students and those representing the supporting organisation.

---

[1] In some online learning, today a popular application of distance education, these two elements merge. Cf. Thorpe, 2002, p. 106.

Feelings of empathy and belonging promote students' motivation to learn and influence the learning favorably. Such feelings can be developed in the learning process independently of any face-to-face contact with tutors. They are conveyed by students' being engaged in decision making; by lucid, problem-oriented, conversation-like presentations of learning matter that may be anchored in existing knowledge; by friendly, un-delayed, non-contiguous interaction between students and tutors, counselors, and other staff in the supporting organization; and by liberal organizational-administrative structures and processes.

It should be stressed that what is meant by conversation-like presentations applies to mediated, usually printed texts or texts provided by computer. This theory includes both elements of understanding and explanation (*Verstehen* and *Erklären* in Dilthey's sense; cf. Bollnow, 1967).

I thus regard empathy and personal relations between the parties involved in the teaching-learning process as central to distance education. These feelings are brought about by real and simulated dialogue. Real dialogue occurs in distance education in interaction in writing, on the telephone, by computer, and so forth, based on students' assignments and in spontaneous questions and answers, comments, and suggestions, whereas simulated dialogue is created by a conversational way of course writing. This thinking is based on the following postulates:

1. Feelings of a personal relation between the learning and teaching parties promote study, pleasure, and motivation.
2. Such feelings can be fostered on the one hand by well-developed self-instructional material, and on the other hand by interaction.
3. Intellectual pleasure and study motivation are favorable to the attainment of study goals and the use of proper study processes and methods.
4. The atmosphere, language, and conventions of friendly conversation favor feelings of personal relations according to postulate 1.
5. Messages given and received in conversational form are easily understood and remembered.
6. The conversation concept can be successfully applied to distance education and the media available to it.

These six postulates attempt to describe a reality that gives rise to the idea of a kind of simulated conversation brought about by course texts being written not as neutral handbook pieces, but as personal communications to students including explicit advice and suggestions as to what to do and what to avoid; clear statements about what is particularly important; relevant references to what the student has already learned; reasons for stressing certain points; and so forth. The course text may say, simulating a conversation, "This is tricky. You may well draw the conclusion that . . . , but look out. In course unit *x* we discussed . . . and then found that. . . . Consider this and ask yourself. . . ."

Suggestions like this belong to study guides at an advanced level when the basic content of the study is found in scholarly literature or handbooks, but can well be part of self-contained courses at lower levels that cover the whole of the learning matter.

This personal, conversation-like way of writing attempts to involve the student emotionally, to make him or her develop a feeling of belonging, to encourage him or her to ask questions and comment. The empathy-encouraging presentation must then be followed up by real interaction, that is, in tutor comments on submitted assignments and other contacts between students and tutors.

This is what I call the empathy approach to distance education.

For a long time I referred to this thinking as a theory of didactic conversation, which I regret as to many (most?) speakers of English the adjective didactic indicates an authoritative approach laying down what applies in an authoritarian way, which is opposed in nature and tendency to the examination by argument that conversation represents. I owe this insight primarily to Helen Lentell (1997), whose contribution I commented on in Holmberg (1999).

HYPOTHESES SUGGESTED

As I believed (and believe) in the possibility of testing this thinking in the way Karl Popper (1980) and his school of critical rationalists test theories—that is, by trying to prove hypotheses derived from it wrong, falsifying them—I specified a number of such explicit, testable hypotheses. In Holmberg (1995), I worded seven hypotheses on distance learning, thirteen on distance teaching, and seven on the organization and administration of distance education.

Self-evident examples of testable hypotheses immediately derived from the theory by its characteristics being specified are

- Pre-produced courses characterized by a conversational style with invitations to an exchange of views and with attempts to involve the students emotionally are favorable to learning and goal attainment.
- Extensive, friendly, helpful, and cooperative tutor comments on submitted assignments contribute to emotional involvement and to study success.
- Feelings of rapport with tutors and the supporting organization—that is, emotional involvement—support study motivation and promote study pleasure.
- Intellectual pleasure favors deep learning, the use of problem-oriented study processes, the attainment of study goals, and the development of study independence.
- Participation in goal considerations and planning encourages personal commitment to learning and the attainment of study goals.
- Personal (not necessarily or primarily contiguous) contacts with tutors and other representatives of the supporting organization promote emotional involvement.
- Dialogue and emotional involvement facilitate learning and make for study success.

On the testability and testing of these and other general hypotheses derived from the theory (see Holmberg, 1995, pp. 176–180), all can be expressed as *if . . . then* or *the . . . the* propositions.

HYPOTHESES TESTED AS PART OF THE STUDY
OF THE EMPATHY APPROACH

The gist of the theory was for the purpose of testing summarized in four overarching hypotheses, viz.,

1. The stronger the characteristics of a teaching-learning conversation, the stronger the students' feelings of personal relationship between them and the supporting organization.
2. The stronger the students' feelings that the supporting organization is eager to make the learning matter personally relevant to them, the greater their personal involvement.
3. The stronger the students' feelings of personal relations with the supporting organization and of being personally involved with the learning matter, the stronger the motivation and the more effective the learning.
4. The more independent and scholarly experienced the students, the less relevant the characteristics of teaching-learning conversations.

By three empirical investigations (Holmberg, Schuemer, & Obermeier, 1982), these overarching hypotheses as one unified theory were subjected to rigorous falsification attempts in the spirit of Popper (1980). Thus the testing was carried out under circumstances as unfavorable as possible to the theory. Instead of testing the hypotheses on groups of students at elementary levels or students with little experience of study who could be expected to be more dependent on empathy than more advanced students, the target groups investigated were university students (of English and education) and postgraduate students.

In one of the studies, participants were divided into (a) an experimental group taking a course version written according to the principles of a teaching-learning conversation and (b) a control group taking an original more handbook-like course, with each version containing exactly the same subject content. In a second study, the first part of the course was written in the style of a teaching-learning conversation, while the second part was a traditional, original course version. The third study concentrated on students' attitudes toward the teaching-learning conversation.

With extremely few exceptions, the students who took part in the investigations stated that they felt personally involved by the conversational presentations, their attitudes were favorable to them, and they did marginally better in their assignment attainments than the students belonging to the control groups. A full report on the testing is provided in Holmberg, et al. (1982).

DISCUSSIONS OF THE THEORY OF TEACHING-LEARNING CONVERSATIONS IN JOURNALS AND OTHER PUBLICATIONS

Wholly or partly independently of my own theoretical approach, similar thinking was presented by others at an early stage. In this context I can refer to Lewis (1975), Rowntree (1975; identifying his concept called "tutorial in print"), Pask (1976), Thomas and Harri-Augstein (1977), Sparkes (1982), Forsythe (1986), Juler (1990), and Inglis (1995). Discussions directly referring to my theory occur in a great number of publications, among them, Keegan (1983), Rekkedal (1985), Mitchell (1992), Rumble (1992), Peters (1998), Moore and Kearsley (2005), and elsewhere.

On the whole, my thinking has been accepted. One writer (Mitchell, 1992) even thinks that I have underestimated the importance of teaching-learning conversations in that he (indirectly) rejects the fourth of my overarching hypotheses, which suggests a limitation of the relevance of the theory that Mitchell regards as uncalled for.

A very interesting critical analysis of my theory was carried out by Rumble (1992), who pays particular attention to the epistemological principles it is based on, which is a somewhat watered-down Popperian approach. Popper (1980) considers "the theorist's interest in explanation . . . as irreducible to the practical technological interest in the deduction of predictions," although he finds prediction important for the testing of theories "to find out whether they cannot be shown to be false" (p. 61). Evidently, my theory is not what Popper would call "nomological," as it cannot be said to apply everywhere and under all circumstances. It is impossible to postulate any automatic cause-effect principle in the learning and actions of human beings. Educational theories, one of which is mine, have to be limited to statements indicating that if such-and-such a measure is taken under specific circumstances, then this is likely to facilitate learning.

The requirements that my theory are meant to satisfy are that it should

- have internal consistency as a logical system.
- establish functional relationships between the teaching and the outcomes of learning.

- be capable of generating hypotheses and prescriptions.
- be expressed in such a way that research data capable of possibly refuting (falsifying) the theory can be collected.

Rumble (1992) scrutinizes these epistemological concerns in a rewarding way. He is no doubt right when he states that my theory (and, implicitly, predictive theories of distance education in general) are "unlikely" to "be conclusively falsifiable in the same way that, for example, the discovery of a black swan falsified the theory 'All swans are white'" (p. 112).

A more generally negative view of my approach was expressed by Peters (1998):

> Scientific thinking is targeted, logical, systematic, and conscious of its methods and cannot be brought about with the help of constant conversation. . . . How can academic contents be imparted in a "clear, somewhat colloquial language". . . . How can authors of academic texts be advised to write in a personal style, not to exceed a defined density of information and to address students emotionally as well. . . . Is it not the case that with most contents, a strict objectivity of the analysis and exposition is required? Is it not so that efforts made step-by-step to open up and understand a dense and initially inaccessible text provide more intellectual pleasure than the feeling of taking part in a simulated conversation? (p. 22)

This criticism is, as I showed in Holmberg (1999), based on a misunderstanding. Naturally, distance students at the university level have to read complicated academic texts, which cannot possibly be expected to be written in a personal, conversational style. It is in the guides to this literature, that is, the texts written specifically for the distance students, that the conversational style should be used. These are what we call study-guide or commentary courses. Nevertheless, as shown above, we have at lower levels self-contained distance courses which provide the students with all they need: (a) factual presentation, (b) questions for repetition, (c) exercises in application, and (d) assignments for submission. In these self-contained courses, the conversational style serves the support of motivation and goal attainment just as it does in the study-guide courses that help students to read learned texts.

What should be discussed here is, apart from the applicability of my empathy approach, the proper use of study-guide courses and self-contained courses (see Holmberg, 2005, pp. 38, 57–58). The question is, what sense does it make to develop distance education courses for university study as alternative course literature? Do not guides to the study of appropriate, available literature and internet sources serve distance students more effectively?

THE THEORY OF TEACHING-LEARNING CONVERSATION AS RELATED TO THE THEORY OF TRANSACTIONAL DISTANCE AND THE VIEW OF DISTANCE EDUCATION AS AN INDUSTRIAL FORM OF TEACHING AND LEARNING

There is no contradiction between my theoretical approach and those of Peters and Moore. It is compatible with them and I agree with both. However, both Peters and Moore disassociate themselves from or are at least guarded in their appreciation of mine.

Peters finds my theory weak as it is concerned with only one aspect of distance education (Black, 2004, p. 195). While I agree with the reason for his view, my theory is mainly concerned with explanation and methodology, teaching, and learning, and contributes nothing to our knowledge about the societal background (but undoubtedly something to the understanding of distance education). I find it difficult to follow him when he says it is weak. It represents, after all, a methodology which, if applied consistently, revolutionizes the style of presentation characterizing printed distance education courses. Peters also seems to think it used to be important, but is less so now (Black ibidem). This cannot be accurate unless my first identification of the empathy approach is seen as an early eye-opener to its reality and applicability. My approach is either to be seen as correct (because it has not been falsified) or misleading; if the former, is it weak? As far as I know, no one has falsified or tried to falsify it. What in my view makes it important to stress it is that a great many course writers do not at all apply the principles of the empathy approach.

In this context, it is interesting to see that application of the empathy approach mitigates the industrialization of distance education that Peters identifies (but hardly favors), as well as the extreme transactional distance with little dialogue that Moore describes.

Moore prefers Peters' theoretical approach to mine (Black, 2004, p. 195), a stand I cannot repudiate, as the two are incommensurable. Peters' as well as Moore's later approaches[2] are not only educational theories, but also something of social ones. Both Peters and Moore basically contribute to our understanding of distance education in the sense of what Dilthey (1973) means by *Verstehen*, whereas my presentation does this to a small degree only, its gist bearing on *Erkenntnis*, explanation of possible cause-effect relations, that is, methodology.

Moore also describes my theory as "a bitty or micro theory" (Black, 2004, p. 195), which is acceptable if the methods of learning and teaching are considered small concerns. He also compares it with Wedemeyer's approach, which is said to provide a macro picture. If—as I believe is correct—we take Wedemeyer's (1981) "new guidelines for instruction" (on p. 36 of his great work *Learning at the Back Door*) as a summary of his approach and compare it with my theory presentation above, it will be evident that the requirements insisted on by Wedemeyer belong to, and are, indeed, prerequisites of mine. I feel I belong to the same school of liberal educational thinking as Wedemeyer did.

While I express my respect for Moore's and Peters' theoretical approaches, I thus claim that my own theory is relevant, contributes to the understanding of distance learning, and has the potential to influence the learning, the teaching, and the administration of distance education.

REFERENCES

Black, L. (2004). A living story of the origins and development of scholarship in the field of distance education. Unpublished doctoral thesis, The Pennsylvania State University, University Park.

Bollnow, O. F. (1967). *Dilthey. Eine Einführung in seine Philosophie.* Stuttgart: Klett.

Dilthey, W. (1973). Der Aufbau der geschichtlichen Welt in den Geisteswissenschaften. *Gesammelte Schriften* VII. Stuttgart: Teubner.

Forsythe, K. (1986). *Understanding the effectiveness of media in the learning process.* Victoria: Learning Systems Knowledge Network.

Garrison, D. R., Anderson, T., & Archer, W. (2000). *Critical inquiry in a text-based environment: Computer conferencing in higher education.* The Internet and Higher Education, 2(2–3), 87–105.

Holmberg, B. (1960). On the methods of teaching by correspondence. *Lunds Universitets Årsskrift* N. F. Avd. 1 Bd 54: 2. Lund: Gleerup.

---

[2]However, in his doctoral thesis, Moore (1976) made an empirical study of the hypothesis that autonomous students are particularly attracted by distance methods of learning. This was confirmed at the same time as it was shown that distance students do not reject guidance.

Holmberg, B. (1985). The feasibility of a theory of teaching for distance education and a proposed theory. *ZIFF Papiere* 60. Hagen: FernUniversität.

Holmberg, B. (1995). *Theory and practice of distance education.* New York: Routledge.

Holmberg, B. (1999). The conversational approach to distance education. *Open Learning, 14*(3), 58–60.

Holmberg, B. (2005). *The evolution, principles and practices of distance education.* Oldenburg: Bibliotheks- und Informationssystem der Universität Oldenburg.

Holmberg, B., Schuemer, R., & Obermeier, A. (1982). *Zur Effizienz des gelenkten didaktischen Gespräches.* Hagen: FernUniversität, ZIFF.

Inglis, A. (1995). Towards a dialogic theory of tele-education. In D. Sewart (Ed.), *One world, many voices* 2, (pp. 364–367). Milton Keynes: The Open University (ICDE).

Juler, P. (1990). Promoting interaction: Maintaining independence: Swallowing the mixture. *Open Learning, 5*(2), 24–33.

Keegan, D. (1983). *Six distance education theorists.* Hageen: FernUniversität, ZIFF.

Lentell, H. (1997). Professional development. Distance education, correspondence tuition, and dialogue. *Open Praxis, 1,* 44–45.

Lewis, N. B. (1975). Conversational man. *Teaching at a Distance, 2,* 68–70.

Mitchell, I. (1992). Guided didactic conversation: The use of Holmberg's concept in higher education. In G. E. Ortner, K. Graff, & H. Wilmersdoerfer (Eds.), *Distance education as two-way communication. Essays in honour of Börje Holmberg* (pp. 123–132). Frankfurt am Main: Peter Lang.

Moore, M. G. (1976). Investigation of the interaction between the cognitive style of field independence and attitudes to independent study among adult learners who use correspondence independent study and self-directed independent study. Unpublished doctoral thesis, University of Wisconsin: Madison.

Moore, M. G. (1983). Self-directed learning and distance education. *ZIFF Papiere* 48. Hagen: Fern Universität.

Moore, M. G., & Kearsley, G. (2005). *Distance education. A systems view.* Belmont, CA: Wadsworth.

Pask, G. (1976). Conversational techniques in the study and practice of education. *British Journal of Educational Psychology, 46,* 12–25.

Peters, O. (1973). *Die didaktische Struktur des Fernunterrichts. Untersuchngen zu einer industrialisierten Form des Lehrens und Lernens.* Weinheim: Beltz.

Peters, O. (1989). The iceberg has not melted: Further reflections on the concept of industrialisation and distance teaching. *Open Learning, 4*(3), 3–8.

Peters, O. (1998). *Learning and teaching in distance education: Analyses and interpretations from an internatinoal perspective.* London: Kogan Page.

Popper, K. (1980). *The logic of scientific discovery.* London: Hutchinson.

Rekkedal, T. (1985). *Introducing the personal tutor/counsellor in the system of distance education.* Oslo: NKI.

Rowntree, D. (1975). *Student exercises in correspondence texts.* Milton Keynes: The Open University Institute of Educational Technology.

Rumble, D. (1992). Explanation, theory and practice in distance education. In G. E. Ortner, K. Graff, & H. Wilmersdoerfer (Eds.), *Distance education as two-way communication. Essays in honour of Börje Holmberg* (pp. 102–122). Frankfurt am Main: Peter Lang.

Sparkes, J. J. (1982). On choosing teaching methods to match educational aims. *ZIFF Papiere* 39. Hagen: FernUniversität.

Thomas, L. F., & Harri-Augstein, E. S. (1977). Learning to learn: The personal construction and exchange of meaning. In M. J. A. Howe (Ed.), *Adult learning: Psychological researcch and applications.* London: Wiley.

Thorpe, M. (2002). Rethinking learner support: The challenge of collaborative online learning. *Open Learning, 17*(2), 105–119.

Wedemeyer, C. A. (1981). *Learning at the back door.* Madison: The University of Wisconsin Press.

7

A Theory of Community of Inquiry

D. Randy Garrison
University of Calgary

Walter Archer
University of Saskatchewan

Theoretical interests and developments in the field of distance education have progressed from a preoccupation with organizational and structural barriers to transactional (teaching and learning) concerns (Garrison, 2000). This transformational shift is the result of recent advances in communications technology coupled with a focus on collaborative-constructivist learning theories (Garrison & Archer, 2000). The emergence of new asynchronous and synchronous communications technology has made possible collaborative distance education experiences. The transactional era of distance education has been made possible by the capability of computer-mediated communication (CMC) to create and sustain a community of learners at a distance. The theoretical challenge faced by distance education is to construct transactional frameworks and models that will explain, interpret, and shape the new form of educational practice that has been made possible by highly interactive communications technologies.

Online learning was once the exclusive domain of distance educators; however, it has now aroused widespread interest among educators in general as the Internet has developed and matured. In particular, the World Wide Web (WWW) has transformed online learning "from a single-media (text) to a multimedia environment" (Garrison, 1997, p. 4). Online learning now integrates CMC applications such as asynchronous computer conferencing, and recently, synchronous audio and videoconferencing. Despite the increasing adoption of online learning, our understanding of this educational technology has lagged well behind adoption rates.

Online learning has been utilized extensively to enhance classroom learning as well as to increase access to educational experiences at a distance. Articles on the educational uses of CMC in general and asynchronous computer conferencing in particular began appearing in the 1980s. One of the first articles to cause distance educators to take note was by Roxanne Hiltz (1986). She argued that CMC could be used to build a "virtual classroom." Paulsen and Rekkedal (1988) discussed the potential of CMC and stated that "the most exciting challenge in the long run will be to apply the new technology to create new and more efficient learning situations, rather than replicate the traditional classroom or distance learning environment" (p. 363). These insights were prescient.

This same message was carried forward by Kaye (1987, 1992; Mason & Kaye, 1989), another early researcher in online learning. Kaye (1987) rightly noted that CMC is "qualitatively different from other interpersonal and group communication media" (p. 157). Kaye (1992) also recognized that computer conferencing represented a new form of collaborative learning that goes beyond information exchange and necessitates moderated critical discourse to realize new and worthwhile understanding. Lauzon and Moore (1989) were the first to recognize that the potential of computer conferencing represented a new generation of distance education characterized by networked, asynchronous group communication. Like her contemporaries, Harasim (1987, 1989, 1990) argued strongly "that on-line education . . . represents a unique domain of educational interaction" (Harasim, 1989, p. 50). She argued for instructional designs to accommodate collaborative online learning, thus adopting constructivist learning approaches. Henri (1992) advocated and provided a framework to systematically study computer conferencing. She identified both cognitive and social dimensions of computer conferencing that enhance learning outcomes. This may have been the first coherent theoretical approach to studying this communications technology.

A THEORETICAL FRAMEWORK AND MODEL

Much of the research and practice associated with online learning during the 1990s focused on and took advantage of the social and democratic features of the technology (Gunawardena, 1991, 1995; Harasim, 1990). Some researchers attempted to broaden the focus to include cognitive elements and focused on the ability of this medium to support higher-order learning (Garrison, 1997; Newman, Johnson, Cochrane, & Webb, 1996). Another key area of research was the role of the moderator as facilitator of the learning process (Fabro & Garrison, 1998; Feenberg, 1989; Gunawardena, 1991; Kaye, 1992). It is these three essential elements—social, cognitive, and teaching—that form the core of the framework outlined next.

Garrison, Anderson, and Archer (2000) constructed a comprehensive conceptual framework designed to capture the educational dynamic and guide understanding of online learning effectiveness in higher education. The first assumption was that an educational experience intended to achieve higher-order learning outcomes is best embedded in a community of inquiry composed of students and teachers (Lipman, 1991). This assumption is also consistent with the educational philosophy of Dewey (1959), who described education as the collaborative reconstruction of experience. The context for this study is not independent learning, but rather a collaborative-constructivist learning experience within a community of inquiry. This is a sharp departure from theories of distance education that idealize student independence.

Before describing the core elements of the framework, however, it is necessary to digress to a very brief discussion of the importance of the communication mode within which this online community of inquiry is created. Currently, online learning is predominantly a text-based, asynchronous form of interaction in which communication occurs through written language, without the paralinguistic and nonverbal communication characteristic of classroom-based learning. While the absence of paralinguistic and nonverbal communication may create an initial barrier for at least some learners, there are compensating advantages. The use of the written word may encourage discipline and rigor, and the asynchronous nature of the communication may encourage reflection, resulting in more complex contributions to the discussion and demonstrating more advanced stages of critical thinking (Archer, Garrison, & Anderson, unpublished, 2001; Feenberg, 1989). However, more basic research in this area is required if we are to understand and apply this knowledge.

Community of Inquiry

FIGURE 7.1.   Community of inquiry framework.

   The community of inquiry described in this model is defined by three overlapping elements: (a) social presence, (b) cognitive presence, and (c) teaching presence (see Figure 7.1). As noted previously, a number of scholars have devoted considerable attention to and the creation of a favorable climate or social presence in an online learning environment. Within the community of inquiry model, social presence is defined as the ability of learners to project themselves (i.e., their personal characteristics) socially and emotionally, thereby representing themselves as "real" people, in a community of inquiry. From a review of the literature, three broad categories of social presence, along with indicators of these categories, were identified (Garrison et al., 2000). Through the analysis of the transcripts of online courses, adjustment, and reapplication, these categories and their associated indicators were refined (Rourke, Anderson, Garrison, & Archer, 2001). The resulting instrument was used to detect and quantify levels of social presence in different online courses.
   The second element in the framework is cognitive presence. We define cognitive presence as "the extent to which learners are able to construct and confirm meaning through sustained reflection and discourse in a critical community of inquiry" (Garrison, Anderson, & Archer, 2001). The concept of cognitive presence is grounded in the critical thinking literature and more specifically operationalized by the practical inquiry model derived to a large extent from the work of Dewey (1933). This model consists of four phases of critical inquiry which are idealized and, as such, are not sequential or immutable. The four phases are the (a) triggering event, (b) exploration, (c) integration, and (d) resolution. Categories corresponding to each of these phases were developed and tested, along with descriptors and indicators of each category (Garrison et al., 2001).
   The finding of interest was that most of the discussion analyzed was coded in the exploration category (42%). Only 13% of the responses were coded in the integration or meaning construction category, and fewer yet (4%) in the resolution or application category. This is consistent with other studies (Celentin, in press; Kanuka & Anderson, 1998; McKlin, Harmon, Evans, & Jones, 2001; Meyer, 2004; Newman et al., 1996). Several explanations are possible. One is that

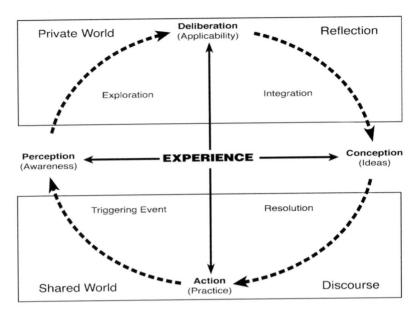

FIGURE 7.2.   Practical inquiry.

the course objectives addressed in the computer conference were not congruent with achieving the higher-order learning outcomes characteristic of the later phases of critical thinking. The most likely explanation, however, is inconsistent facilitation and poor direction. This is supported by other research (Celentin, in press; Garrison & Cleveland-Innes, 2005; Meyer, 2003; Pawan, Paulus, Yalcin, & Chang, 2003; Picciano, 2002; Shea, Li, Swan, & Pickett, in press; Swan & Shih, in press; Vaughan & Garrison, 2005).

We now turn to teaching presence, the third element of the framework. As previously alluded to, teaching presence is crucial for realizing intended learning outcomes. Teaching presence is defined as "the design, facilitation and direction of cognitive and social processes for the purpose of realizing personally meaningful and educationally worthwhile learning outcomes" (Anderson, Rourke, Garrison, & Archer, 2001). Resulting from this definition and the results of validation work, three categories of teaching presence emerged: (a) design and organization, (b) facilitating discourse, and (c) direct instruction. A set of indicators correspond to each of these categories. The preliminary analysis of teaching presence revealed important differences between the transcripts of the online courses studied. The frequency of the teacher responses in each category was largely attributable to both instructional approaches and subject differences. The conclusion is that teaching presence is a very complex process that must be studied in the context of a wide range of factors such as intended learning outcomes, instructional strategies, student characteristics, and practical factors such as class size and the familiarity of participants with the technology.

The previous description represents the theoretical framework and initial findings associated with a major research project to study higher-order learning in an online learning environment. Clearly much work remains to be done; however, this framework provides a foundation and perspective for systematically and comprehensively studying the complexities of online learning in an educational context. We now turn our attention to pedagogical implications associated with the adoption of online learning.

PEDAGOGICAL ISSUES

Practice to date in online learning has been largely technology driven. Ubiquitous and inexpensive Internet and communications technology has allowed many educators to adopt online learning. However, their motivations for adopting this technology are mixed and are often not based upon sound educational and pedagogical reasoning.

The focus and challenge here is to understand pedagogically the use of online learning to achieve higher-order learning objectives. This means going beyond enhancing course packages and using e-mail to contact tutors, or putting videos of lectures online. The premise is that educators must first understand that online learning has unique properties that make it possible to create a critical community of learners not constrained by time or place. Educators must also be able to develop pedagogical principles and guidelines that will directly facilitate deep and meaningful approaches to teaching and learning. In other words, we must ensure that we encourage critical thinking online and have as the outcome of the educational experience critical thinkers who have learned to learn.

While there are numerous guidelines and suggestions as to how to conduct online learning (e.g., Berge, 1995; Paulsen, 1995; Salmon, 2000), these are generally disparate methods for ensuring participation; however, the use of online learning in pedagogically sound ways that make optimal use of its unique properties means using it for more than merely participating in an optional discussion forum or accessing information more efficiently. As Fraser (1999) suggests, the extent to which we have not taken advantage of the "expanded horizons for communicating ideas . . . is the extent to which you have done nothing of pedagogical value by using the Web" (p. B8). In Fraser's (1999) words, doing anything with these new media that does not expand our horizons is "pedagogically pointless." This is particularly applicable to online learning in general, and to computer conferencing in particular.

The challenge facing researchers and teachers in distance education is the development of a more sophisticated understanding of the characteristics of new technology and how we might harness this potential to enhance critical thinking and higher-order learning. As important as critical thinking is as an educational process and goal, we educators often fall far short of achieving it (Garrison et al., 2001). Reasons include a lack of metacognitive understanding of the inquiry process and a lack of purposeful and sustained commitment to facilitating and directing critical discourse and reflective thinking. In this regard, there is an absence of systematic empirical research into how to facilitate critical thinking and inquiry (Kuhn, 1999). In terms of fostering critical thinking skills, Kuhn states that "teachers have been offered remarkably little in the way of concrete examples of what these skills are—what forms they take, how they will know when they see them, how they might be measured" (p. 17).

This is certainly the case in distance education, but in this context the problem is compounded by a technology and communication medium whose characteristics have not been well researched. McLoughlin and Luca (2000) stated that online learning has become mainstream, but "there is limited empirical evidence that online learning and asynchronous text based communications support the higher order forms of learning" (p. 1). Distance educators have much work to do to investigate the nature of online learning and demonstrate that it can support critical thinking and higher-order learning.

The literature certainly suggests that a stronger teaching presence is required in online learning (Garrison & Cleveland-Innes, 2005; Meyer, 2003; Shea et al., in press; Swan & Shih, in press). Teaching presence shapes cognitive and metacognitive processing. Teachers must be able to understand and design learning activities that facilitate higher-order learning outcomes. A model that has shown promise is the practical inquiry model discussed briefly here and described more extensively elsewhere (Garrison & Archer, 2000; Garrison et al., 2000; Garrison & Anderson, 2003). This provides a model for systematically identifying the phases of critical thinking and associated skills and activities. It also provides a metacognitive model of the inquiry process that students can use to help them monitor their own learning. For example, activities should be designed and moderated so as to focus on the appropriate phase of critical thinking and ensure that the learners progress to the next phase and gain a metacognitive understanding of the process in which they are engaged (Garrison, 2003). Kuhn (1999) reinforced this point when she argued "The development of metacognitive understanding is essential to critical thinking because critical thinking by definition involves reflecting on what is known and how that knowledge is justified." (p. 23)

Unfortunately, the simple adoption of technology does not resolve issues related to the teaching of critical thinking and metacognitive understanding. Moreover, it does not fundamentally change approaches to teaching and learning for the better. It has been argued elsewhere that technology can have both a strong and weak influence on the educational transaction (Garrison & Anderson, 2000). The weak approach is to enhance, and thereby reinforce, existing teaching practices. On the other hand, the

> stronger influence of technology on teaching would fundamentally change our outcome expectations, and thereby, how we approach the teaching and learning transaction. . . . Here the focus is on the quality of learning outcomes (i.e., developing critical thinkers) and adopting approaches to teaching and learning that are congruent with such outcomes. (Garrison & Anderson, 2000, p. 25)

Teaching presence is the unifying force in developing a community of inquiry and ensures that discussions progress to resolution. However, the first challenge in this regard is to develop a comprehensive understanding of the properties of online learning and the implications for supporting an educational community of inquiry using this medium. While we have begun the process of providing a coherent framework, much work remains in understanding the pedagogical implications of using online learning in a variety of contexts and for a variety of purposes. The power and potential of the technology may be enormous but realizing this potential will depend on conceptual models and principles, as well as well founded guidelines and techniques. To help identify these principles, Garrison (2006) used the community of inquiry framework to develop a list of principles with direct pedagogical implications:

1. Establish a climate that will create a community of inquiry.
2. Establish critical reflection and discourse that will support systematic inquiry.
3. Sustain community through expression of group cohesion.
4. Encourage and support the progression of inquiry through to resolution.
5. Evolve collaborative relationships where students are supported in assuming increasing responsibility for their learning.
6. Ensure that there is resolution and metacognitive development.

Much research is now being conducted to understand the potential of online learning to enhance and extend the educational experience. It is important that online learning be used in the service of intended and worthwhile educational goals. Online learning can be a catalyst to transform our educational practices for the better. However, transformation is never accomplished without resistance. Threatened disruption of existing organizational structures inevitably creates issues that must be addressed if the transformation is to succeed.

ORGANIZATIONAL ISSUES

The current structure and organization of most universities and colleges is largely historical and . . . largely unsuited to new forms of technological delivery (Bates, 2000, p. 36).

As Postman (1992) argued, not only do new technologies compete with old ones but surrounding "every technology are institutions whose organization—not to mention their reason for being—reflects the world-view promoted by the technology" (p. 18). This section concentrates on the great majority of educational institutions whose current organization reflects the world-view promoted by the technology of face-to-face classroom instruction, and who are having this world-view challenged by the rapidly expanding technology of online learning (Tait & Mills, 1999).

For educational institutions built around face-to-face classroom instruction, the advent of online learning presents both an opportunity and a threat, but invariably is a serious disruption to the current worldview. Educational institutions have before them the opportunity to use this new mode of instruction to improve the instruction offered to on-campus students, and to reach out to other learners who are not able or willing to enroll in face-to-face, on-campus programs. The threat is at least twofold: that other providers will serve these potential off-campus students and begin to attract students who currently attend on campus (Kirkpatrick & Jakupec, 1999; Marchese, 1998); that a move to embrace online learning will seriously compromise the academic values held by the institution (Katz & Associates, 1999; Noble, 1997, 1998).

We have argued elsewhere (Archer, Garrison, & Anderson, 1999) that distance education, for conventional institutions of higher education, is what Harvard business professor Clayton M. Christensen (1997) refers to as a "disruptive technology"—that is, it is a new technology that requires an organization to do things in a fundamentally different way. This contrasts with what Christensen (1997) refers to as a "sustaining technology," a new technology that represents simply an improvement on current practices. Archer et al. (1999) suggest that educational institutions can benefit by paying attention to the insights derived by Christensen and others (e.g., Day & Schoemaker, 2000) regarding ways in which established business firms (analogous to established educational institutions) can cope successfully with disruptive technologies. Although start-up firms, unhampered by large size (and need for large profits), inertia, and entrenched organizational culture, have an inherent advantage when dealing with disruptive technologies, Christensen (1997, p. 99) describes how established firms have successfully adopted such technologies. Applying Christensen's insights to higher education, we have argued (Archer et al., 1999), that one key strategy for educational institutions could be to incubate the disruptive technology of online learning in areas of the organization where they are needed and valued and where the early adopters can learn from mistakes. However, it has since become apparent to us that the educational form that has come to be known as blended learning is another very promising method through which educational institutions can adopt online learning with minimal disruption to their established structures and values.

BLENDED LEARNING

Moving online learning to a more central role and making it an integral element of conventional, campus-based institutions rather than a disruptive attack on their structures and values represents a significant challenge. Blended learning has the potential to do just this, and thereby transform educational institutions (Garrison & Kanuka, 2004). The attractiveness of blending face-to-face and online learning is the assumption that designers can organically integrate the best of each mode. In this regard, blended learning, as contrasted with purely online learning, may be seen less as a disruptive technology since it does not reject the traditional core values of higher education associated with communities of inquiry. It has the potential to address both effectiveness and efficiency challenges facing much of higher education today. Online learning is more openly considered when contextualized in a more conventional, campus-based context. It also encourages educators and researchers to rigorously examine the properties of online learning and how they can support communities of inquiry and high levels of learning. The challenge is to thoughtfully integrate online learning with the sustaining technology of higher education. This requires considerable reflection, discussion and rethinking.

We leave to other scholars the discussion of the impact of online learning on "autonomous distance teaching institutions" (Keegan, 1993) whose organization reflects the structural worldview and technologies that, in most cases, are much older than online learning. The best known set of institutions falling into this category is the "mega-universities" described by Daniel (1996). We also leave to other scholars (e.g., those cited in Keegan, 1993, p. 73) the discussion of what Keegan (1993) refers to as the "Australian integrated mode." However, we would suggest that this is less of an integrated mode than a two-track approach that serves two distinct student populations, an approach in which face-to-face and distance study exist in separate spheres. In essence, dual-mode institutions juxtapose sustaining and disruptive technologies. While this model is a possible option for the evolution of many campus-based institutions (Johnson, 1999), achieving this balanced approach to on- and off-campus delivery will meet resistance. The risk is in a clear separation of on-campus and online courses and a perceived difference in preference and quality. The online course will be viewed as a substitute for the real thing based upon contextual contingencies.

CONCLUSION

Online learning facilitated by computer-mediated communication, and more specifically, computer conferencing, is radically changing education. Discussions of the effects of these technologies on education are not mere speculations about what the future might bring; these changes are rapidly becoming part of modern educational practice at all levels. A number of commentators have suggested that the impact of these changes might be so great that our current educational institutions might not survive (e.g., Duderstadt, 1999; Perelman, 1992).

With the widespread adoption of online learning, there is a distinct convergence of distance and campus-based educational institutions (Garrison & Kanuka, in press). Convergence is occurring around the growing recognition and desire to enhance interaction and discourse. As Shale (2002) pointed out, the interactive potential of communications technology reveals a "growing convergence between conventional and distance learning modes . . ." (Introduction, para. 1). Online learning is certain to be at the heart of this convergence. With its interactive capabilities, online learning is at the source of the erosion of the distinction between distance and campus-based institutions. Forward looking institutions recognize the interactive potential of online learning and are taking a step back and rethinking how they wish to approach teaching and learning.

Whatever its impact on the educational system as a whole, the adoption of online learning, with its unique properties to support asynchronous collaborative learning, represents a new era in distance education. The challenge for the field of distance education is to continue to develop theoretical models for online learning that will imagine its potential and guide its practical application; however, of paramount importance is to understand how we can use online learning to support and facilitate critical thinking and higher-order learning outcomes. Much work remains to be done in studying and developing the dynamic patterns of pedagogical practice that will facilitate productive online educational transactions.

The strategic approach advocated here begins with a coherent model that focuses on collaborative and constructive discourse. The community of inquiry framework could be used to provide a model metacognitive awareness for critical discourse and reflection online. Without such awareness there is a serious question as to whether researchers will have the means to systematically study this complex process, and whether students will have the cognitive map within which to learn how to learn and become self-directed, cognitively autonomous learners.

REFERENCES

Anderson, T., Rourke, L., Garrison, D. R., & Archer, W. (2001). Assessing teaching presence in a computer conferencing context. *Journal of Asynchronous Learning Networks, 5*(2). Retrieved December 19, 2006, from http://www.sloan-c.org/publications/jaln/v5n2/index.asp

Archer, W., Garrison, D. R., & Anderson, T. (1999). Adopting disruptive technologies in traditional universities: Continuing education as an incubator for innovation. *Canadian Journal of University Continuing Education, 25*(1), 13–30.

Archer, W., Garrison, D. R., & Anderson, T. (unpublished, 2001). *The textuality of computer mediated communication: Consequences for the use of CMC in education.*

Bates, A. W. (2000). *Managing technological change: Strategies for college and university leaders.* San Francisco: Jossey-Bass.

Berge, Z. L. (1995). Facilitating computer conferencing: Recommendations from the field. *Educational Technology, 35*(1), 22–30.

Celentin, P. (in press). Online training: Analysis of interaction and knowledge building patterns among foreign language teachers. *Journal of Distance Education.*

Christensen, C. M. (1997). *The innovator's dilemma: When new technologies cause great firms to fail.* Boston: Harvard Business School Press.

Daniel, J. S. (1996). Mega-universities and knowledge media: Technology strategies for higher education. London: Kogan Page.

Day, G., & Schoemaker, P. (2000). Avoiding the pitfalls of emerging technologies. *California Management Review, 42*(2), 8–33.

Dewey, J. (1933). *How we think.* (Rev. ed.). Boston: D. C. Heath.

Dewey, J. (1959). My pedagogic creed. In J. Dewey, *Dewey on education* (pp. 19–32). New York: Teachers College, Columbia University. (Original work published 1897)

Duderstadt, J. J. (1999). Can colleges and universities survive in the Information Age? In R. N. Katz and Associates, *Dancing with the devil: Information technology and the new competition in higher education* (pp. 1–25). San Francisco: Jossey-Bass.

Fabro, K. R., & Garrison, D. R. (1998). Computer conferencing and higher-order learning. *Indian Journal of Open Learning, 7*(1), 41–54.

Feenberg, A. (1989). The written word: On the theory and practice of computer conferencing. In R. Mason & A. Kaye (Eds.), *Mindweave: Communication, computers and distance education* (pp. 22–39). Oxford: Pergamon Press.

Fraser, A. B. (1999). Colleges should tap the pedagogical potential of the World-Wide Web. *The Chronicle of Higher Education, 48*, p. B8.

Garrison, D. R. (1997). Computer conferencing: The post-industrial age of distance education. *Open Learning, 12*(2), 3–11.

Garrison, D. R. (2000). Theoretical challenges for distance education in the 21st Century: A shift from structural to transactional issues. *International Review of Research in Open and Distance Learning, 1*(1), 1–17.

Garrison, D. R. (2003). Cognitive presence for effective asynchronous online learning: The role of reflective inquiry, self-direction and metacognition. In J. Bourne & J. C. Moore (Eds.), *Elements of quality online education: Practice and direction*: Vol. 4. the Sloan C Series (pp. 29–38). Needham, MA: The Sloan Consortium.

Garrison, D. R. (2006). Online collaboration principles. *Journal of Asynchronous Learning Networks, 10*(1). Retrieved December 19, 2006, from http://www.sloan-c.org/publications/jaln/v10n1/v10n1_3garrison.asp

Garrison, D. R., & Anderson, T. (2000). Transforming and enhancing university teaching: Stronger and weaker technological influences. In T. Evans & D. Nation (Eds.), *Changing university teaching: Reflections on creating educational technologies*. London: Kogan Page.

Garrison, D. R., & Anderson, T. (2003). *E-Learning in the 21st century: A framework for research and practice*. London: Routledge/Falmer.

Garrison, D. R., Anderson, T., & Archer, W. (2000). Critical inquiry in a text-based environment: Computer conferencing in higher education. *The Internet and Higher Education, 2*(2–3), 87–105.

Garrison, D. R., Anderson, T., & Archer, W. (2001). Critical thinking, cognitive presence, and computer conferencing in distance education. *The American Journal of Distance Education, 15*(1), 7–23.

Garrison, D. R., & Archer, W. (2000). *A transactional perspective on teaching-learning: A framework for adult and higher education*. Oxford, UK: Pergamon.

Garrison, D. R., & Cleveland-Innes, M. (2005). Facilitating cognitive presence in online learning: Interaction is not enough. *The American Journal of Distance Education, 19*(3), 133–148.

Garrison, D. R., & Kanuka, H. (2004). Blended learning: Uncovering its transformative potential in higher education. *The Internet and Higher Education, 7*(2), 95–105.

Garrison, D. R., & Kanuka, H. (in press). Changing distance education and changing organizational issues. In W. J. Bramble & S. Panda (Eds.), *Economics of distance and online learning: Theory, practice and research*. New York: Lawrence Erlbaum Associates.

Gunawardena, C. N. (1991). Collaborative learning and group dynamics in computer-mediated communication networks. *Research Monograph of the American Center for the Study of Distance Education* (9) (pp. 14–24). University Park, PA: The Pennsylvania State University.

Gunawardena, C. N. (1995). Social presence theory and implications for interaction and collaborative learning in computer conferences. *International Journal of Educational Telecommunications, 1*(2/3), 147–166.

Harasim, L. M. (1987). Teaching and learning online: Issues in computer mediated graduate courses. *Canadian Journal of Educational Communication, 16*(2), 117–135.

Harasim, L. M. (1989). Online education: A new domain. In R. Mason & A. R. Kaye (Eds.), *Mindweave: Communication, computers, and distance education* (pp. 50–62). New York: Pergamon.

Harasim, L. M. (Ed.). (1990). Online education: Perspectives on a new environment. New York: Praeger.

Henri, F. (1992). Computer conferencing and content analysis. In A. R. Kaye (Ed.), *Collaborative learning through computer conferencing: The Najaden papers* (pp. 117–136). Berlin: Springer-Verlag.

Hiltz, S. R. (1986). The "virtual classroom": Using computer mediated communication for university teaching. *Journal of Communication, 36*(2), 95–104.

Johnson, S. (1999). Introducing and supporting change towards more flexible teaching models. In A. Tait and R. Mills (Eds.), *The convergence of distance and conventional education* (pp. 39–50). New York: Routledge.

Kanuka, H., and Anderson, T. (1998). Online social interchange, discord, and knowledge construction. *Journal of Distance Education, 13*(1), 57–75.

Katz, R. N., & Associates (1999). *Dancing with the devil: Information technology and the new competition in higher education*. San Francisco: Jossey-Bass.

Kaye, T. (1987). Introducing computer-mediated communication into a distance education system. *Canadian Journal of Educational Communication, 16*, 153–166.

Kaye, T. (1992). Learning together apart. In T. Kaye (Ed.), *Collaborative learning through computer conferencing* (pp. 1–24). New York: Springer-Verlag.

Keegan, D. (1993). A typology of distance teaching systems. In K. Harry, M. John, & D. Keegan (Eds.), *Distance education: New perspectives* (pp. 62–76). London: Routledge.

Kirkpatrick, D., & Japupec, V. (1999). Becoming flexible: What does it mean? In A. Tait & R. Mills (Eds.), *The convergence of distance and conventional education* (pp. 51–70). New York: Routledge.

Kuhn, D. (1999). A developmental model of critical thinking. *Educational Researcher, 28*(2), 16–25.

Lauzon, A., & Moore, G. (1989). A fourth generation distance education system: Integrating computer-assisted learning and computer conferencing. *The American Journal of Distance Education, 3*(1), 38–49.

Lipman, M. (1991). *Thinking in education.* Canbridge: Cambridge University Press.

Marchese, T. (1998, May). Not-so-distant competitors: How new providers are remaking the postsecondary marketplace. *AAHE Bulletin.*

Mason, R., & Kaye, A. R. (1989). *Mindweave: Communication, computers, and distance education.* New York: Pergamon.

McKlin, T., Harmon, S. W., Evans, W., & Jones, M. G. (2002). Cognitive presence in web-based learning: A content analysis of students' online discussions *ITForum Paper #60.* Retrieved October 11, 2005, from http://it.coe.uga.edu/itforum/paper60/paper60.htm

McLoughlin, C., & Luca, J. (2000). Cognitive engagement and higher order thinking through computer conferencing: We know why but do we know how? *Teaching and Learning Forum 2000.* Retrieved December 19, 2006, from http://cleo.murdoch.edu.au/confs/tlf/tlf2000/mcloughlin.html

Meyer, K. A. (2003). Face-to-face versus threaded discussions: The role of time and higher-order thinking. *Journal of Asynchronous Learning Networks, 7*(3), 55–65.

Meyer, K. A. (2004). Evaluating online discussions: Four different frames of analysis. *Journal of Asynchronous Learning Networks, 8*(2), 101–114.

Newman, D. R., Johnson, C., Cochrane, C., & Webb, B. (1996). An experiment in group learning technology: Evaluating critical thinking in face-to-face and computer-supported seminars. *Interpersonal Computing and Technology, 4*(1), 57–74.

Noble, D. F. (1997, October). Digital diploma mills: The automation of higher education. *Bulletin of the Canadian Association of University Teachers.*

Noble, D. F. (1998, March). Digital diploma mills: Part II. *Bulletin of the Canadian Association of University Teachers.*

Paulsen, M. (1995). Moderating Educational Computer Conferences. In Z. Berge & M. Collins (Eds.), *Computer mediated communication and the online classroom* (pp. 81–90). Cresskill, NJ: Hampton Press, Inc.

Paulsen, M. F., & Rekkedal, T. (1988). Computer conferencing: A breakthrough in distance learning, or just another technological gadget? In D. Sewart & J. S. Daniel (Eds.), *Developing distance education* (pp. 362–364). Paper submitted to the 14th World Conference, Oslo, August.

Pawan, F., Paulus, T. M., Yalcin, S., & Chang, C. (2003). Online learning: Patterns of engagement and interaction among in-service teachers. *Language Learning & Technology, 7*(3), 119–140.

Perelman, L. J. (1992). *School's out: Hyperlearning, the new technology, and the end of education.* New York: William Morrow & Co..

Picciano, A. G. (2002). Beyond student perceptions: Issues of interaction, presence, and performance in an online course. *Journal of Asynchronous Learning Networks, 5*(2), 18–35.

Postman, N. (1992). Technopoly: The surrender of culture to technology. New York: Alfred A. Knopf.

Rourke, L., Anderson, T., Garrison, D. R., & Archer, W. (2001). Methodological issues in the content analysis of computer conference transcripts. *International Journal of Artificial Intelligence in Education, 12*(1), 8–22.

Salmon, G. (2000). *E-moderating the key to teaching and learning online.* London: Kogan Page.

Shale, D. (2002). The hybridization of higher education in Canada. *International Review of Research in Open and Distance Learning, 2*(2). Retrieved December 19, 2006, from http://www.irrodl.org/index.php/irrodl/issue/view/12

Shea, P., Li, C.S., Swan, K., & Pickett, A. (in press). Teaching presence and the establishment of community in online environments: A preliminary study. *Journal of Asynchronous Learning Networks.*

Swan, K., & Shih, L. F. (in press). On the nature and development of social presence in online course discussions. *Journal of Asynchronous Learning Networks.*

Tait, A., & Mills, R. (Eds.). (1999). *The convergence of distance and conventional education.* New York: Routledge.

Vaughan, N., & Garrison, D. R. (2005). Creating cognitive presence in a blended faculty development community. *Internet and Higher Education, 8,* 1–12.

8

The Theory of Transactional Distance

Michael Grahame Moore
The Pennsylvania State University

TRANSACTIONAL DISTANCE THEORY:
HISTORICAL SIGNIFICANCE

When first published, (Moore, 1972, 1973) what became known as the "theory of transactional distance" (Moore, 1980) was an attempt to establish the identity of a previously unrecognized field of educational research. In an educational culture in which all research questions were grounded in the assumption that "instruction refers to the activity which takes place during schooling and within the classroom setting" (Association of Supervision and Curriculum Development, 1971), this theory would identify and describe teaching and learning that did *not* take place in classrooms, but took place in *different* locations. Named (for the first time in English) "distance education," what had hitherto been an activity on the margins of educational practice was defined in terms of variables sufficiently robust to enable subsequent research and further theorizing by an ever-growing number of students and academics. As a result, whatever specific issues might engage these scholars of a later generation, it is only by rather convoluted and even bizarre argument that any contemporary writer would argue that there is no such field of research and study as distance education. True, there are those who fail to recognize the broader dimensions of the field, as they focus on one or another of its component parts or one of its many applications—expressed in terms such as *distributed learning, tele-learning*, and *e-learning*—and others who by accident or design conflate distance education and "contiguous" (Moore, 1972, p. 76) education, using such terms as *open learning, blended learning*, and *flexi-learning*. However, even such muddling of concepts does not detract from the general recognition that there is a universe of educational programs and practices that are distinctly different from those in which teachers and learners work in the same space and time, a field worthy of study and research, and practices in that field which are also worth study and training. It is this recognition and acceptance of the identity of distance education that is the first claim of transactional distance as an educational theory.

To further appreciate the theory, it is the *character* of that identity that must be understood, for this was the first American theory to define the field in *pedagogical* terms. By 1970, though having no recognizable theory, distance education had existed in practice for almost 100 years, beginning as correspondence study through the mail and later being supplemented by radio and television programs, the use of the telephone, and the computer. As long as this practice was defined solely by the technology, the few research questions that were generated were also stated as studies of the technology—usually how education through that technology might best resemble "real" teaching, i.e., teaching in classrooms. This began to change with the theory of transactional distance, which showed that teaching and learning in separate locations is better understood not as an aberration from the classroom, but as a significantly different pedagogical domain. This domain was first identified by Charles Wedemeyer, who called it "independent study," a term that described the behavior of people who did not study in class but learned alone, either by directing their own study, or studying with the help of teaching in the form of correspondence courses (Wedemeyer, 1971).

ORIGINS OF TRANSACTIONAL DISTANCE THEORY

The rationale for a theory dealing with this kind of teaching and learning was argued in a 1972 presentation to the World Conference of the International Council for Correspondence Education (ICCE), as follows:

> "As we continue to develop various nontraditional methods of reaching the growing numbers of people who cannot or will not attend conventional institutions but who choose to learn apart from their teachers, we should divert some of our resources to the macro-factors, i.e. describing and defining the field . . . discriminating between the various components of this field; identifying the critical elements of the various forms of learning and teaching, in short building a theoretical framework which will embrace this whole area of education." (Moore, 1973, p. 661)

Distance education was defined in that presentation as "the family of instructional methods in which the teaching behaviors are executed apart from the learning behaviors . . . so that communication between the learner and the teacher must be facilitated by print, electronic, mechanical, or other device" (Moore, 1972, p. 76). The research method used to identify "the critical elements" in this form of learning and teaching was an analysis of a large selection of program descriptions and other literature, from which emerged a theory consisting of three sets of "macro-factors." The first of these, derived from analysis of curricula, is described as the teaching-learning program's "structure"; the second, derived from analysis of communication between teachers and learners, is the "dialogue" in the program. The third describes the roles of learners, in terms of the extent to which they exercise degrees of "autonomy" in deciding what to learn, how to learn, and how much to learn. The pervasive requirement in all distance education environments for learners to exercise degrees of self-management was reflected in Wedemeyer's definition of independent study as well as informed by the (then) radical writings of Carl Rogers (1969), Abraham Maslow (for example Maslow, 1968), and other "humanistic" psychologists.

The term *distance education* originated at the University of Tübingen in Germany, where researchers in the 1960s wrote about *fernstudium* ("distance study") to describe how certain industrial principles, such as division of labor and use of technology, could be applied in the craft of teaching. The terms *dialogue, structure*, and *transaction* originated with adult education professor Robert Boyd. The term dialogue was chosen deliberately in preference to "interaction" in recognition of Boyd's argument that the latter term includes relationships that are manipulative and negative and that an alternative term should define the kind of helping, constructive, and positive exchanges that are required in a teaching-learning relationship. Boyd's teaching theories were heavily influenced by Gestalt psychology, and it was from this that the importance of identifying programs according to their structure originated. The term *transactional distance* was first used in the 1980 *Handbook of Adult Education* (Boyd & Apps, 1980). Originating with John Dewey, the concept of transaction "connotes the interplay among the environment, the individuals and the patterns of behaviors in a situation" (Boyd & Apps, 1980, p. 5). Thus the transaction in distance education is the interplay of teachers and learners in environments that have the special characteristic of their being spatially separate from one another. What emerged as the theory of transactional distance was a typology of all educational programs having this distinguishing characteristic of separation of learner and teacher. It accommodates all extremes of such programs, from those that are relatively highly structured and quasi-industrial, owing a lot to behaviorist and cognitive theories of learning, to those reflecting the Humanists' perspective of a learner-centered pedagogy, in which learners with varying degrees of autonomy engage in a relatively high degree of dialogue with a more-or-less supportive tutor. (It should be noted that the terms *relatively*, *varying degrees,* and *more or less* are significant, since transactional distance theory describes the fullest range of *all possible* degrees of structure, dialogue, and autonomy.) Because this is a point that is often overlooked, it bears repeating that transactional distance is relative rather than absolute. Teaching-learning programs are *not* dichotomously either "distance" or "not distance," but they have "more distance" or "less distance." One has more dialogue than another and less structure than another, allowing greater learner autonomy than another. Commenting on the significance of this, the distinguished German scholar Otto Peters (one of the Tübingen group mentioned earlier) wrote:

> "[B]y showing the transactional distance not as a fixed quantity but as a variable, which results from the respective changing interplay between dialogue, the structured nature of the teaching program being presented, and the autonomy of the students, it (the transactional distance theory) provides a convincing explanation of the enormous flexibility of this form of academic teaching. It also provides an insight into the pedagogical complexity of distance education—." (Peters, 1998, p. 42)

It should be added, however, that distance education can also be defined in organizational or administrative terms, and then a dichotomy is possible and indeed helpful as it enables us to focus on the special administrative arrangements that are needed. When so defined we can say that a program in which the sole or principal form of communication is through technology is a distance education program, and those in which technology-mediated communication is ancillary to the classroom is not a distance education program. Either type of program can also be evaluated in terms of transactional distance, for each has a structure, dialogue, and learners with a degree of autonomy. To repeat, transactional distance is a theory of the pedagogy of distance education, not a theory of its organizations.

MORE ABOUT STRUCTURE, DIALOGUE AND AUTONOMY

More about Structure

An educational course consists of one or more lessons, each containing such elements as learning objectives; content themes; presentations of information, case studies, pictorial and other illustrations; activities and exercises, questions for discussion, projects, and tests. Each of these might be very strictly specified by the designer(s), leaving little room for a student's or instructor's deviation. You only have to imagine the content of courses designed for medical, nursing, military, or other technical training to see how such rigid standardization would be appropriate. To achieve the most efficient structure, a design team might test parts of the course on a pilot group of students to find out, for example, precisely how long it will take each student to accomplish each objective, and the suitability of the test questions aimed at evaluating performance; they might measure the reading speed of the sample of students and then tailor the number of pages of reading required for each part of the course. To ensure all students achieve precisely the same degree of competence, instructors may be provided detailed marking schemes. During the instruction, they may monitor the progress of each student very frequently and give regular feedback and remedial activities for those that need them, and so ensure that every student has accomplished each step of the course in a tightly controlled sequence. Each student might have to follow the exact same sequence of reading and activity; audio and video tapes may be synchronized very tightly and linked to specific pages in a study guide or Web site; synchronous discussions may be carefully organized minute by minute to ensure participation by each student, according to a carefully scripted plan. A recorded television program, for example, is highly structured, with virtually every activity of the instructor and every minute of time scripted and every piece of content predetermined. There is little or no opportunity for any student to deviate according to personal needs from what the instructors have planned for that period of time. This describes a course or program that has a high degree of structure. By comparison, other courses are designed with a loose structure in which students can follow any of several different paths, or many paths, through the content, or may negotiate significant variations in the program with the instructor(s). Such a course might allow students to browse a loosely determined set of Web pages or view a CD-ROM or a set of video tapes at their own speed, study a set of recommended readings, and only submit written assignments when they feel ready. They may be told to call an instructor if, and only if, they need advice. Such would be a course with much lower structure than the former. Since structure expresses the rigidity or flexibility of the course's educational objectives, teaching strategies, and evaluation methods, it describes the extent to which a course can accommodate or be responsive to each learner's individual needs and preferences. Since individualizing requires communication between the learner and instructor, this last observation indicates that dialogue plays a part in determining structure, while also being determined by structure, and further—(showing how complex are the interactions among these sets of variables)—it has to be added that more autonomous students may, perhaps with a minimum of dialogue, impose their own structure on their learning program.

More about Dialogue

Dialogue is a particular kind of interpersonal interaction, and it happens after a course is designed, within the environment determined by the course structure when teachers exchange words and other symbols with learners, aimed at the latter's creation of knowledge. Interaction is not always constructive, but dialogue by definition is. Dialogue has a synergistic character, as each party in the exchange builds upon comments of the other. In dialogue, "each party . . . is a respectful and active listener; each is a contributor and builds on the contributions of the other party or parties." (Moore, 1993, p. 26).

Courses of instruction may allow almost continuous dialogue between student and teacher, or none, and there is a range of variations between the extremes. The extent and nature of dialogue in any course is determined by numerous factors and overarching all is the structure of the course. For example, a teaching institution using synchronous videoconferencing on the Web (a potentially highly dialogic medium) but holding the view that the role of the student is to assimilate information by listening and taking notes, might design its courses with highly structured lessons and dialogue limited to asking factual questions of the teacher and receiving answers. Obviously another particularly important variable affecting dialogue is the medium of communication. In a traditional text-based correspondence course there is the potential for each learner to engage in a relatively highly dialogic relationship with the instructor, though the pace of such dialogue is slow when it is conducted by traditional mail. A greater degree of dialogue is likely if the same course is taught on the Web, wherein, even though the communication medium is mostly text, there can be rapid and frequent responses by teacher to student. A tutorial between an instructor and a single student conducted in real-time by telephone is likely to be a highly dialogic process, while a similar audio teleconference between groups would probably have a lower degree of dialogue (for each student). Some courses, such as those using CD-ROMs or "teach yourself" books, are highly structured and have virtually no dialogue with live instructors. Other determinants of the extent of dialogue in a course or lesson are (a) the subject matter of the course, (b) the personality of the teacher, (c) the propensity of a learner to competently participate in the dialogue, and (d) cultural and language differences between instructors and students. Dialogue is of course also powerfully affected by the abilities of students to manage their side of the process. Highly autonomous learners are able to cope with a lower or higher degree of dialogue, but less autonomous learners need a relatively high degree of dialogue.

TRANSACTIONAL DISTANCE IS A FUNCTION OF DIALOG AND STRUCTURE

In the typical recorded video telecourse program the teaching is highly structured and there is minimal teacher-learner dialogue (we have to say "minimal" because there is a kind of vicarious dialogue between the learner as he/she uses the tapes and the instructors who prepared them, as the learner experiences what Holmberg has called an "internal didactic conversation"). With such a high degree of structure and little or no dialogue, the transactional distance is high. By comparison, in the typical correspondence course there is more dialogue, though restricted by the technology, and there is a little less structure, so it has less transactional distance. In typical Web-based programs there is considerable dialogue and relatively low structure, so the extent of transactional distance is relatively low. It should be clear that the extent of dialogue and the degree of structure varies from course to course. It is not simply a matter of the technology, though that definitely imposes limitations; it also depends on the teaching philosophy of the instructor, the capacity of learners, and the nature of the subject.

How the variables of dialog and structure interact to determine transactional distance can be seen in a simple two-dimensional graph (Figure 8.1).

MORE ON LEARNER AUTONOMY

The Humanistic psychologists, particularly Carl Rogers (1969), were responsible for establishing the idea of "learner autonomy," supported by empirical research—notably that of Alan Tough (1971)—that demonstrated that students have, in different degrees, the ability to develop a personal learning plan, to find resources for study in their work or community environments, and to evaluate for themselves when progress was satisfactory. During the research that led to the development of the theory of transactional distance, it became apparent that some programs allow or demand the greater exercise of learning autonomy than others and that there are conditions under which greater learner autonomy may be exercised and others where a lower degree of autonomy is more appropriate.

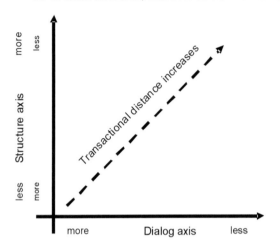

As dialog increases, transactional distance decreases
As structure increases, transactional distance also increases

FIGURE 8.1.   Relationship of dialog, structure and transactional distance.

Thus it was hypothesized, and demonstrated, that teaching-learning programs can be organized, not only according to the extent of structure and dialogue, but also according to the extent of self-management, or learner autonomy, permitted by each program.

Here is how the idea was first explained, in 1972:

> In our efforts to explore various aspects of learner autonomy in distance teaching and learning programs, we have tried to prepare a system that makes it possible to order programs according to the kind and extent of autonomy the learner is expected or—permitted to exercise. We are placing programs in appropriate positions on a continuum, with those permitting the exercise of most autonomy at one extreme and those permitting the least at the other. For every program, we seek to identify the relationship between learners and teachers, and where control of each instructional process lies, by asking:
>
>   Is learning self initiated and self-motivated?
>
>   Who identifies goals and objectives, and selects problems for study?
>
>   Who determines the pace, the sequence, and the methods of information gathering?
>
>   What provision is there for the development of learners' ideas and for creative solutions to problems?
>
>   Is emphasis on gathering information external to the learner?
>
>   How flexible is each instructional process to the requirements of the learner?
>
>   How is the usefulness and quality of learning judged?

By this subjective, inductive method we can put together a typology of distance teaching programs, "classified by the dimension of learner autonomy" (Moore, 1972, p. 83).

Applying these criteria, programs were classified on a range from AAA, meaning the learner had full autonomy in deciding what to learn (Goals), how to learn (Execution), and how much to learn (Evaluation) at one extreme; to NNN at the other extreme, describing a program in which the learner had absolutely no freedom to make any decisions about the learning program. These

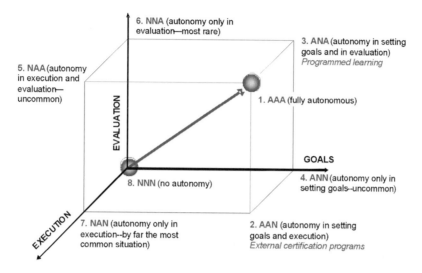

FIGURE 8–2.   Dimensions of autonomy in distance teaching-learning programs.

are only theoretical constructs, because no one is entirely without freedom or absolutely without constraint. Between these theoretical poles lie all teaching-learning programs. This can be illustrated in a model (Figure 8.2).

Since this has sometimes been misunderstood, it should be noted that it was not suggested that all learners are fully or even highly autonomous. It is recognized that learners vary in their ability to exercise autonomy, and might want to have greater autonomy in some courses than in others. It is very appropriate for educators to allow the exercise of more or less autonomy. Also, it has not been suggested that highly autonomous learners do not need teachers. It is the relationship of such learners to teachers that is different than that between teachers and less autonomous learners, with the latter needing more emotional support from the teacher and the former only needing instrumental support, i.e., information and the advice necessary to "get the job done."

RELATIONSHIP OF AUTONOMY
AND TRANSACTIONAL DISTANCE

In a course with little transactional distance, learners receive information, directions, and guidance through ongoing dialogue with their instructors and through instructional materials that allow modifications to suit their individual needs, learning style, and pace. Such a program with a lower degree of transactional distance is invariably more attractive to learners who are less secure in managing their own learning. More autonomous learners appear more comfortable with less dialogue, receiving some information, direction, and guidance in that way, and more through structured course materials. If there is minimal dialogue or structure, in a program of high transactional distance, students are forced to find their own information and make decisions for themselves about what to study, when, where, how, and to what extent. In other words, the greater the transactional distance the more the learners have to exercise autonomy.

This relationship is illustrated in Figure 8.3.

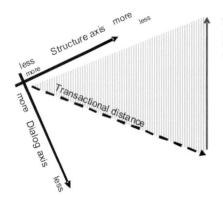

FIGURE 8.3. Relationship of autonomy and transactional distance.

SIGNIFICANCE OF TRANSACTIONAL DISTANCE THEORY:
AUTHORITATIVE OPINIONS

In the broadest sense, theory consists of the total accumulation of knowledge as it is recorded in the literature of a field. More narrowly, a theory is a synthesis or summary of this knowledge—often represented by symbols, diagrams, or models—which takes on authority as more and more scholars and researchers find it useful in place of a full review of the literature. Consequently the questions that are important about any theory are "how useful has it been as a summary of what is known?" and "how helpful has it been as a tool for analysis of practice and for generating questions for research?" In search of a response to these questions, we might begin by citing the opinions of eminent scholars and researchers and—more tellingly perhaps—we should look for cases in which it has been used as the theoretical foundation for empirical research.

Among early recognition of the theory of transactional distance was its inclusion by Desmond Keegan, co-founder of the Australian journal *Distance Education,* in the first issue of that journal, as one of the "generally accepted definitions" of distance education (Keegan, 1980). Keegan's definitions became the most widely cited in the field, especially after the publication of his *Foundations of Distance Education* (Keegan, 1986). In another early recognition, Greville Rumble, a leading authority on the administration of distance education institutions, expressed the view that "the most fruitful use of the term 'distance' is that proposed by Moore in the expression 'transactional distance,' which defines the nature and degree of separation of teacher and learner in the educational process" (Rumble, 1986, p. 7). More recently Alan Tait, Dean of Education at the United Kingdom Open University, asked in an editorial in the *International Review of Research on Open and Distance Learning* what "in essence (is) changed by the revolution in media we have undergone over the last decade?" and in reply says: "My own approach firstly would be to return to Moore's theory of transactional distance and use that to evaluate what is happening in terms of learning and teaching in any e-learning programme." When tested in that way, he concludes, "Moore's theory remains, in my view, the crucial framework of ideas against which such assertions as represented here can be tested," and "the core of distance in Moore's theory—that the space between the learner and the structure of teaching must be mediated by dialogue, offering the learner the opportunity to be an active participant—remains valid . . ." (Tait, 2003, p. 5).

For the most recent example, we turn to one of the best-known American researchers, Farhad Saba, whose research has done most to elaborate on the original concept of transactional distance and its constructs. In one of his more recent statements, Saba said that "if the theory of transactional distance is taken to its logical conclusion it subsumes concepts that are based on physical attributes, such as electronics in e-Learning, blendedness in blended learning, and wired or wireless telecommunication in online learning. Furthermore the theory of transactional distance extends well beyond these lower level system components and includes fundamentals of psychology, sociology and education and other related areas of educational science . . . a clear understanding of the concept of transactional distance and its centrality to the future of practice, research and policy formation is necessary if distance education is going to grow and develop in the foreseeable future." (Saba, 2005, p. 4)

Finally, a good idea of the extent to which this, or any, theory is recognized can be gleaned from how often it is cited in the principal scholarly journals and conference proceedings. In such a content analysis of the presentations at 17 conferences of the International Council for Distance Education between 1938 and 1995, Bunker rated Moore's writings—which means primarily transactional distance—as third out of 93 authorities cited (Bunker, 1998). More recently, Lee, Driscoll, and Nelson (2005) report that the chapter on transactional distance in Keegan's *Theoretical principles of distance education* (Keegan, 1993) is the second most widely cited item, after the same author's article on interaction.

SIGNIFICANCE OF TRANSACTIONAL DISTANCE THEORY: USE IN RESEARCH

Transactional distance has been used extensively, both formally and informally, as a theoretical framework for research. Its informal use cannot be described with any accuracy, not only because it has been so extensive but also because often in such cases the theoretical source is not cited. Occasionally such uncited use is deliberate, but usually the failure to acknowledge the theory is because the ideas it represents are now so much a part of the general knowledge of the field that their source is either not known, or not considered noteworthy. Leaving such cases aside, we can provide here a brief mention of some of the dissertations and other studies in which the theory has been formally acknowledged as the basis of the research.

Saba has already been mentioned. In his early studies, he used computer simulation (Saba, 1988; Saba & Twitchell, 1988) to develop a model based on principles of systems dynamics that operationalized dialogue, structure, and autonomy, and tested the hypothesized changes in each of these that resulted from changes in others. In a subsequent project, Saba and Shearer (1994) used discourse analysis to identify 10 categories of teacher-learner transactions and again demonstrated how changes in dialogue, structure, and teacher-learner control effected changes in each of the others. Saba and Shearer's instrument has been adapted for use by others, as for example by Shinkle (2001) in an analysis of dialogue by e-mail in a doctoral distance education program. Enhancements and modifications of dialogue and structure have been proposed as, for example, what Braxton (1999) called a "refined theory of transactional distance." Along with Saba and Shearer and others, Braxton also attempted to create an instrument to measure transactional distance. An instrument developed by Zhang (2003) measured transactional distance in Web-based courses, not only between student and teacher, but also student and student, student and content, and student and interface procedures. Based on an analysis of 58 research articles in five distance education journals, Jung (2001) suggested that in Web-based instruction, the dialogue variables include academic, collaborative, and interpersonal interaction; while the structure variables are content expandability, content adaptability, and visual layout; and learning variables are learner autonomy and collaboration. Gallo (2001) used transactional distance theory in an attempt to identify the competencies needed for success as distance learners, and proposed a training program to develop these competencies. Shin (2001) expanded the idea of transactional distance by postulating and testing a concept of transactional presence. Caspi, Gorsky, and Chajut (2003) developed what they called a "restructured model of transactional distance" consisting of four kinds of dialogue, and used it to examine the effect of group size on students' behavior in asynchronous discussion groups.

Bischoff (1993) and Bischoff, et al. (1996) reported the effect of electronic mail in lowering transactional distance in public health and nursing courses delivered by videoconferencing. In what were probably the first cross-cultural studies, Gayol (1996) and Bunker, Gayol, Nti, and Reidell (1996) examined transactional distance in courses delivered by audio-conferencing and electronic mail to students in four countries. The effects of differences in culture on transactional distance among foreign graduate students in the United States was studied by Walker Fernandez (1999), and effects of cultural differences on transactional distance in computer science courses delivered on the Web have been reported by Lemone (2005). M. H. Moore (1999) used transactional distance theory in a study of the effects of changing a sales training program from an individual, self-directed package to a group method using videoconferencing. Vrasidas and MacIsaac (1999) studied course structure and dialogue in computer mediated instruction, and found that quality of dialogue is significantly affected by prior experience. In a study of mathematics taught on the Internet, Anderson (1999) found that students and faculty reported that their dialogues were meaningful, though they were relatively highly structured, and that while these courses facilitated learner autonomy, for some students the level of autonomy was uncomfortable and the students wanted more dialogue with instructors. Atkinson (1999) described instructor strategies such as humanizing and the use of visual techniques as ways of increasing dialogue to reduce transactional distance in video-based courses. Hopper (2000) found that students who reported a perception of high transactional distance did not think it impeded their achievement or satisfaction with their learning experience. Transactional distance was among variables examined by Rovai (2000) to see what makes a sense of community in asynchronous learning networks, and later (Rovai, 2002) he described steps to increase a sense of community by facilitating dialogue. Chen, Y. (2001) found that in a Web-based course, previous experience with distance education and in-class learner support had no effect on students' perception of the transactional distance, but the learner's skill in using the Internet and the extent of the dialogue that occurred between instructor and learners and among learners themselves had significant effects. Clouse (2001) found that transactional distance in an online course was lower in a chat mode and higher in a threaded discussion. Dron (2002) reported an online course explicitly designed to have a high degree of dialogue, in which an unanticipated reversion by instructors to increased structure occurred, with negative effects on both quality and quantity of dialogue. Subsequently Dron, (2004) discussed how students' self-organization (i.e., the exercise of autonomy) in a highly structured learning environment can lead to increased dialogue, and thus a program in which both structure and dialogue are high. Williams (2003) includes implications for transactional distance theory in a discussion of research on retention and barriers to success in an online graduate program. Wikeley and Muschamp (2004) developed a model for the delivery of professional doctorate programs at a distance, arguing that dialogue might be increased through a structure that allowed greater adaptability of content by instructors. Edstrom (2002) discussed transactional distance in the classroom, and how it can be reduced through use of information and communication technologies. Wheeler (2002) concluded that transactional distance can explain why "remote students expect a great deal more from their instructors than their local peers in terms of social and practical support. . ." (p. 425). Lee and Gibson (2003) concluded from a study of adult learners taking a computer-mediated course that instructors should encourage dialogue, allow for structural flexibility, encourage critical reflection, and permit students to take on some degree of control. Witte and Wolf (2003), in a study of mentoring, recommended that instructors "should consider the perceived transactional distance as well as keeping the various types of mentoring interaction, facilitation, and structured student collaboration in mind when organizing materials and assignments" (pp. 98–99). Lowell (2004) found that significant predictors for perceived distance among students in online courses were dialogue, social presence, and fluency. Pruitt (2005), in a study of students in three delivery modalities (Internet, telecourse, compressed video), found dialogue, structure, and learner autonomy to be significant in predicting self-ratings of performance and grades. Stein, Wanstreet, et al. (2005) concluded that satisfaction with the course structure and with dialogue led to satisfaction with perceived knowledge gained. Dupin-Bryant (2004) identified teaching behaviors necessary to account for transactional distance in a survey of 225 instructors at nine land-grant universities. Avive, Erlich, Ravid, and Gava (2003) evaluated dialogue in two Open University of Israel courses, one more structured than the other, and found that high levels of critical thinking were more evident in the structured environment. Also at the Open University of Israel, Gorsky, Caspi, and Trumper (2004) investigated dialogue in a physics course and Gorsky, Caspi, and Tuvi-Arid (2004) in a chemistry course. Gorsky and Caspi, concluded that transactional distance could be explained primarily in terms of dialogue, though they also said that dialogue was supported by "structural resources" such as "instructional design, group size and accessibility of students and instructors" (2005, p. 140). Offir and colleagues describe how an analysis of verbal and nonverbal interactions revealed the strategies teachers use to reduce transactional distance. They report that "data, indicating significant cross-context changes in teacher-student interaction patterns validate Moore's (1972, 1993) transactional distance theory"; they believe their "empirical evidence of changes in specific categories of interaction also expands the conceptualization of the dialogue variable" (Ofir, et al. 2004, p. 101).

Among studies that focus primarily on learner autonomy, Munro's (1991) study reported a relationship between dropping out of distance learning programs and perceived deficiencies in dialogue. Emulating, though not replicating, Moore's (1976) study of learner autonomy and the cognitive style of field dependence-independence, Brenner (1996) investigated field dependence-independence of learners who studied by video and text, and found no relationship between field independence and achievement. Richardson (1998) also failed to find a relationship between students' field independence, their course evaluations, preference for independent learning, course completion, or level of autonomy. In her study of learner autonomy among nurses returning to college, Thompson (1998) used questionnaires based on Baynton's (1992) derivation of transactional distance theory, and concluded the distance learners did not show greater autonomy than traditional students, which she believed was probably due to the high degree of structure in both their programs. Chen (1997) and Chen and Willits (1998, 1999) who studied teaching strategies in videoconference courses concluded that "the more independent the students reported themselves to be, the more frequently they indicated in-class interaction." This finding of a positive relationship between dialogue and autonomy was later confirmed by Huang (2000) who gathered data about Web-based courses. Kanuka, Collett, and Caswell (2002) investigated the effects of integrating asynchronous Internet communication into distance courses and wrote:

> "Finally, in terms of Moore's theory of the relationship between structure and dialogue versus learner autonomy, the outcomes of this study not only support this idea, but also provide additional insights and clarification. While structure is a relatively straightforward concept that that tends not to be in need of further clarification, in agreement with Garrison and Baynton (1987), we find that autonomy is a complex and multi-faceted construct. However, while Garrison and Baynton describe autonomy in terms of power, control and support, the participants in this study referred to autonomy in terms of flexibility."

COMMENT ON TRANSACTIONAL DISTANCE THEORY
RELATIVE TO HOLMBERG AND PETERS

To indicate the relationships between transactional distance, Peters' theory of industrialized education, and Holmberg's conversation theory, we should refer to Saba's chapter in this book (Chapter 4), and specifically to his Figure 8.3 in which he shows some of the main systems nesting within a global system. Saba explains that "transactional distance is an open system residing in a larger environment in the instructional systems level which is in turn part of a larger system in the hierarchical model" (Saba 2007 p. 51). Looked at in this way, Peters' model of the educational process can be seen as a higher-level system within which the phenomena explained by transactional distance are nested. Transactional distance is better understood, and becomes of significant practical value, when we appreciate the more global concepts that Peters' theory provides, particularly division of labor—which explains the fundamental distinction between the roles of those who design a program's structure and those that facilitate the dialogue aimed at converting its information into personal knowledge. In the same way, Holmberg's model should be seen as a lower-level system nested within the transactional distance system. What transactional distance refers to as "dialogue" Holmberg prefers to call "conversation," and the value added by his theory is the more detailed explication of some, *though not all*, of the dynamics within dialogue as defined in transactional distance. As with all systems of thinking, the value of each of these theories is reciprocal, in that it is necessary to look from one to the other as one pursues further understanding of their relationships at the macro-level on the one hand and micro-level on the other, regardless of which level one begins.

I specifically wish to address Dr. Holmberg's complaint (p. 74) at my use of the expression "a bitty or micro-theory." In light of what I have just explained above, I feel no need to apologize for the word "micro" since it should be obvious that knowledge of micro-factors are, ultimately, at least as important as knowledge of larger systems. (If the point is not obvious, just think "DNA" or "the atom"!) However I should be more apologetic about the term "bitty," which was the word that came to mind in a tape-recorded interview that I had no chance to review, because it sounds more unappreciative than was intended. My true opinion was expressed elsewhere in that interview when I said about the Holmberg and Peters theories that it was "not fair really to compare. It's like comparing the management of the apples and oranges distribution point in a supermarket to the management of a supermarket. . . . One is more macro and one more micro level. That isn't to say there isn't a place for each. There is." (Black, 2004).

I know that Holmberg understands this perspective, as he demonstrates with his reference (ibid in this book) to Wedemeyer's "New guidelines for instruction." However, it is in his choice of words for that same reference that I find a reason for concern about the way Holmberg presents his theory, for here, as elsewhere, he seems to position his micro-theory at a higher level on the hierarchy of systems and sub-systems than is appropriate. Certainly his teaching-as-conversation can be placed *within* Wedemeyer's model, just as it can be placed within transactional distance and within the industrialized system, but that is not the same thing as locating it at a parallel level to either of these. To return to the previous metaphor, describing the (important) fruit department of the supermarket as the supermarket itself does not improve our understanding of either the larger system or the smaller. There is a second issue, and that is the extent to which Holmberg drifts from theoretician to proselyte. It is as if *teaching-as-conversation* is not as much a scientific description of how people behave as it is a behavior that he advocates. For example, in his chapter in this book Holmberg writes, "It is in . . . the texts written specifically for the distance students that the conversational style *should* be used" (p. 73) and "I thus regard empathy and personal relations between the parties involved in the teaching learning process as central to distance education." This surely is *not* an objective description of reality—because we know that the character of relationships between teachers and learners varies enormously and many teachers do *not* show empathy, veering as often towards the impersonal as the personal. Holmberg in fact exposes his vulnerability on this issue when he writes about his experiment: "With extremely few exceptions the students who took part in the investigations stated that they felt personally involved by the conversational presentations . . ." (ibid, p. 71)Given Holmberg's declared affection for a Popperian approach to research, surely the existence of even one "exception"—one student who prefers not to be personally involved by conversational presentations—is sufficient to "falsify" the theory? Rather than declare that all teaching *should be* conversational, it would be more helpful to describe what kinds of students benefit and do not benefit from such an approach, and what alternatives are available to each. I would suggest—following Robert Boyd who warned against teachers allowing their students to become emotionally dependent (Boyd, 1966; see also Anderson's explanation in this book, chapter 9)—that impersonality, absence of empathy, and high transactional distance are highly desirable for certain students, those with a high degree of learner autonomy. Just as it is desirable for some students to have a high degree of dialogue (conversation), so for others it is equally desirable that they have little. Our theories have to describe the full range of such relationships, without advocacy towards any.

CONCLUSION

Transactional distance theory provides the broad framework of the pedagogy of distance education. It allows the generation of an almost infinite number of hypotheses for research into the interactions between course structures, dialogue between teachers and learners, and the student's propensity to exercise control of the learning process. This chapter has summarized the genesis of the theory, and listed some of the research projects it has spawned, which now serve to point the way for future research. Before proceeding in that direction, potential researchers should look more closely at some of the studies reviewed above, and then, when results are in, they will be able to report them with reference to this literature, and in terms of the underlying theory. It is as a framework for such a scientific approach, as contrasted to the haphazard "wouldn't it be nice to know. . ." approach that is unfortunately too prevalent in education, that transactional distance theory, like other theories, is most valuable.

REFERENCES

Anderson, D. (1999). *Mathematics and distance education on the Internet: An investigation based on transactional distance education theory*. Unpublished doctoral dissertation, Columbia University, New York.

Anglin, G. J., & Morrison, G. R. (2000). An analysis of distance education research: Implications for the instructional technologist. *Quarterly Review of Distance Education, 1*, 189–194.

Association of Supervision and Curriculum Development. (1971). Criteria for assessing the formal properties of theories of instruction. In R Hyman (Ed), *Contemporary thought on Teaching.* (p. 123). Englewood Cliffs, NJ: Prentice-Hall.

Atkinson, T. R. (1999). *Toward an understanding of instructor-student interactions: A study of videoconferencing in the postsecondary distance learning classroom*. Unpublished doctoral dissertation, Louisiana State University, Baton Rouge.

Aviv, R., Erlich, Z., Ravid, G., & Geva, A. (2003). Network analysis of knowledge construction in asynchronous learning networks. *Journal of Asynchronous Learning Networks, 7* (3). Retrieved January 2, 2007, from http://www.sloan-c.org/publications/jaln/v7n3/index.asp.

Baynton, M. (1992). Dimensions of "control" in distance education: A factor analysis. *American Journal of Distance Education, 6*(2), 17–31.

Berge, Z. L., & Mrozowski, S. (2001). Review of research in distance education, 1990–1999. *The American Journal of Distance Education, 15*(3), 5–19.

Bischoff, W. R. (1993). *Transactional distance, interactive television, and electronic mail communication in graduate public health and nursing courses: implications for professional education.* Unpublished doctoral dissertation, University of Hawaii, Honolulu.

Bischoff, W. R., Bisconer, S. W., Kooker, B. M., & Woods, L. C. (1996). Transactional distance and interactive television in the distance education of health professionals. *American Journal of Distance Education, 10*(3), 4–19.

Black, L. M. (2004). *A living story of the origins and development of scholarship in the field of distance education (Borje Holmberg, Michael G. Moore, Otto Peters).* Unpublished doctoral dissertation, Pennsylvania State University, University Park.

Boyd, R. (1966). A psychological definition of adult education. *Adult Leadership, 13*, 160–162.

Braxton, S. N. (1999). *Empirical comparison of technical and non-technical distance education courses to derive a refined transactional distance theory as the framework for a utilization-focused evaluation tool.* Unpublished doctoral dissertation George Washington University, Washington DC.

Brenner, R. J. (1996). *An analysis of the transactional distance in asynchronous telecourses at a community college using the group embedded figures test.* Unpublished doctoral dissertation, East Tennessee State University, Johnson City.

Bunker, E., Gayol, Y., Nti, N., & Reidell, P. (1996). A study of transactional distance in an international audioconferencing course. *Technology and Teacher Education Annual*, 40–44. Phoenix, AZ: Association for the Advancement of Computing in Education.

Bunker, E. L. (1998). *An historical analysis of a distance education forum: The International Council for Distance Education world conference proceedings, 1938 to 1995.* Unpublished doctoral. dissertation Pennsylvania State University, University Park.

Caspi, A., Gorsky, P., & Chajut, E. (2003). The influence of group size on non-mandatory asynchronous instructional discussion groups. *The Internet and Higher Education, 6*(3), 227–240.

Chen, Y. (1997). *The implications of Moore's theory of transactional distance in a videoconferencing learning environment.* Unpublished doctoral. dissertation, Pennsylvania State University, University Park.

Chen, Y. & Willits, F. (1998). A path analysis of the concepts in Moore's theory of transactional distance in a videoconferencing learning environment. *Journal of Distance Education, 13*(2), 51–65.

Chen, Y. J., & Willits, F. K. (1999). Dimensions of educational transactions in a videoconferencing learning environment. *The American Journal of Distance Education, 13*(1), 45–59.

Chen, Y. J. (2001). Dimensions of transactional distance in world wide web learning environment: A factor analysis. *British Journal of Educational Technology, 32*(4), 459–470.

Clouse, S. F. (2001). *The assessment of student performance and satisfaction outcomes with synchronous and asynchronous interaction methods in a student-centered distributed learning environment.* Unpublished doctoral dissertation, University Of Montana, Missoula.

Dron, J. (2002). *Achieving self-organisation in network-based learning environments.* Unpublished doctoral dissertation, University of Brighton, Brighton, UK.

Dron, J., Seidel, C., & Litten, G. (2004). Transactional distance in a blended learning environment. *ALT Journal, 12*(2), 163–174

Dupin-Bryant, P. (2004). Teaching styles of interactive television instructors: A descriptive study. *The American Journal of Distance Education, 18*(1), 39–50.

Edstrom, R. (2002). *Flexible education in the upper secondary school: Extended classrooms and a decreased transactional distance.* Unpublished doctoral dissertation, Uppsala University, Uppsala, Sweden.

Gallo, J. A. (2001). *A distance learning and training model.* Unpublished doctoral dissertation, Pennsylvania State University, University Park.

Garrison, D. R., & Baynton, M. (1987). Beyond independence in distance education: The concept of control. *The American Journal of Distance Education, 1*(3), 3–15.

Gayol, Y. (1996). The use of computer networks in distance education: analysis of the patterns of electronic interaction in a multinational course. In C. C. Gibson (Ed.), *Distance education symposium 3: Learners and learning* (pp. 61–70). University Park, PA: The American Center for the Study of Distance Education.

Gorsky, P., Caspi, A., & Trumper, R. (2004). University students' use of dialogue in a distance education physics course. *Open Learning, 19*(3), 265–277.

Gorsky, P., Caspi, A., & Tuvi-Arid, I. (2004). Use of instructional dialogue by university students in a distance education chemistry course. *Journal of Distance Education, 19*(1), 1–19

Gorsky, P., & Caspi, A. (2005, March). Dialogue: a theoretical framework for distance education instructional systems. *British Journal of Educational Technology, 36*(2), pp. 137–44.

Hopper, D. A. (2000). *Learner characteristics, life circumstances, and transactional distance in a distance education setting.* Unpublished doctoral dissertation, Wayne State University, Detroit.

Huang, H. (2000). *Moore's theory of transactional distance in an online mediated environment: Student perceptions on the online courses.* Unpublished doctoral dissertation, Seattle Pacific University, Seattle, WA.

Jung, I. (2001). Building a theoretical framework of web-based instruction in the context of distance education. *British Journal of Educational Technology, 32*(5), 525–534).

Keegan D. (1980). On defining distance education. *Distance Education, 1*(1), 13–35.

Keegan D. (1986). *The foundations of distance education.* London: Croom Helm.

Keegan D. (1993). *Theoretical principles of distance education.* New York: Routledge.

Kanuka, H., Collett, D., & Caswell, C. (2002). University instructor perceptions of the use of asynchronous text-based discussion in distance courses. *American Journal of Distance Education, 16*(3), 2.

Koble, M., & Bunker, E. (1997). Trends in research and practice: An examination of The American Journal of Distance Education 1987 to 1995. *The American Journal of Distance Education, 11*(2), 19–38.

Lee, Y., & Driscoll, M. P., & Nelson, D. (2005). The past, present, and future of research in distance education: Results of a content analysis. *The American Journal of Distance Education, 18*(4), 225–241.

Lee, J., & Gibson, C. C. (2003). Developing self-direction in an online course through computer-mediated interaction. *The American Journal of Distance Education, 17*(3), 173–187.

Lemone, K. (2005). Analyzing cultural influences on ELearning transactional issues. In Richards, G. (Ed.), *Proceedings. World Conference on E-Learning in Corporate, Government, Healthcare, and Higher Education 2005* (pp. 2637–2644). Chesapeake, VA: AACE.

Lowell, N. (2004). *An investigation of factors contributing to perceived transactional distance in an online setting.* Unpublished doctoral dissertation, University of Northern Colorado, Greeley.

Maslow, A. H. (1968). Some educational implications of the humanistic psychologies, *Harvard Educational Review, 38*(4), 685–696.

Moore, M. G. (1972). Learner autonomy: The second dimension of independent learning. *Convergence, 5*(2), 76–88. Retrieved January 2, 2007, from http://www.ajde.com/Documents/learner_autonomy.pdf

Moore, M. G. (1973). Towards a theory of independent learning and teaching. *Journal of Higher Education,* (44), 661–679. Retrieved January 2, 2007, from http://www.ajde.com/Documents/theory.pdf

Moore, M. G. (1976). *Investigation of the interaction between the cognitive style of field independence and attitudes to independent study.* Unpublished doctoral dissertation, University of Wisconsin, Madison.

Moore, M. G. (1980). Independent study. In R. Boyd & J. Apps (Eds.), *Redefining the discipline of adult education* (pp. 16-31). San Francisco: Jossey-Bass. Retrieved January 2, 2007, from http://www.ajde.com/Documents/independent_study.pdf

Moore, M. G. (1993). Theory of transactional distance. In D. Keegan (Ed.), *Theoretical Principles of Distance Education* (pp. 22–29). New York: Routledge. Retrieved January 2, 2007, from http://www.uni-oldenberg.de/zef/cde/found/readings/moore93.pdf

Moore, M. H. (1999). *The effects of two instructional delivery processes of a distance training system on trainee satisfaction, job performance and retention.* Unpublished doctoral dissertation, Ohio State University, Columbus.

Munro, P. (1991). *Presence at a distance: The educator-learner relationship in distance education and dropout.* Unpublished doctoral dissertation, University of British Columbia, Vancouver.

Offir, B., Lev, Y., Y. Lev, Barth, I., & Shteinbok, A. (2004). An integrated analysis of verbal and nonverbal interaction in conventional and distance learning environments. *Journal of Educational Computing Research, 31*(2), 101–118.

Peters, O. (1998). *Learning and teaching in distance education Analysis and interpretation from an international perspective.* London: Kogan Page.

Pruitt, D. (2005). *Transactional distance and learner autonomy as predictors of student performance in distance learning courses delivered by three modalities.* Ph.D. dissertation, Tulane University, New Orleans.

Richardson, J. T. (1998). Field independence in higher education and the case of distance learning. *International Journal of Educational Research, 29*(3), 241–250.

Rogers, C. (1969). *Freedom to learn.* Columbus, OH: Charles E. Merril Publishing Company.

Rovai, A. P. (2000). Building and sustaining community in asynchronous learning networks. *The Internet and Higher Education, 3*(4), 285–297.

Rovai, A. P. (2002, April). Building sense of community at a distance. *International Review of Research in Open and Distance Learning.*

Rumble, G. (1986). *The planning and management of distance education.* New York: St. Martin's Press.

Saba, F., & Twitchell, D. (1988). Research in distance education. A system modeling approach. *The American Journal of Distance Education, 2*(1), 9–24.

Saba, F. (1988). Integrated telecommunications systems and instructional transaction. *The American Journal of Distance Education, 2*(3), 17–24.

Saba, F., & Shearer, R. (1994). Verifying key theoretical concepts in a dynamic model of distance education. *The American Journal of Distance Education, 8*(1), 36–57.

Saba, F. (2000, June). Research in distance education: A status report. *International Review of Research in Open and Distance Learning, 1*(1). Retrieved January 2, 2007, from http://www.icaap.org/iuicode.org/iuicode?149.1.1.3

Saba, F. (2005). *Is distance education losing its identity? Or what should we call our field these days: Presentation at 22nd Annual Conference on Distance Teaching and Learning, University of Wisconsin-Madison, August.* Retrieved January 2, 2007, from http://www.uwex.edu/disted/conference/Resource_library/proceedings/05_1662.pdf

Shin, N. (2001). *Beyond interaction: Transactional presence and distance learning.* Unpublished doctoral dissertation, Pennsylvania State University, University Park.

Shinkle, A. (2001). *Interaction in distance education: A study of student-student and student-teacher interaction via an electronic distribution list.* Unpublished doctoral dissertation, University Of Wyoming, Laramie.

Stein, D. S., Wanstreet, C. E., Calvin, J., Overtoom, C., & Wheaton, J. E. (2005). Bridging the transactional distance gap in online learning environments. *The American Journal of Distance Education, 19*(2), 105–118.

Tait, A. (2003, April). Reflections on student support in open and distance learning. *International Review of Research in Open and Distance Learning.* Retrieved January 2, 2007, from http://www.irrodl.org/index.php/irrodl/article/view/134/214

Thompson, B. (1998). *An investigation of professional nurse autonomy and learner autonomy among female registered nurses enrolled in distance education and traditional baccalaureate programs.* Unpublished doctoral dissertation, Widener University School of Nursing, Chester.

Tough, A. M. (1971). The Adult's Learning Projecs. Toronto, The Ontario Institute for Studies in Education.

Williams, K. T. (2003). *Factors affecting student retention in an online graduate certificate program: A grounded theory study.* Unpublished doctoral dissertation, University Of Florida, Gainsville.

Vrasidas, C., & McIsaac, M. S. (1999). Factors influencing interaction in an online course. *The American Journal of Distance Education, 13*(3), 22–36.

Walker Fernandez, S. E. (1999). *Toward understanding the study experience of culturally sensitive graduate students in American distance education programs.* Unpublished doctoral dissertation, Florida International University, Miami.

Wedemeyer, C. A. (1971). Independent study. In Lee C. Deighton (Editor-in-Chief), *The Encyclopedia of Education*, Vol. 4 (p. 550). New York: The MacMillan Co.

Wheeler, S. (2002). Student perceptions of learning support in distance education. *Quarterly Review of Distance Education, 3*(4), 419–429.

Wikeley, F., & Muschamp, Y. (2004). Pedagogical implications of working with doctoral students at a distance. *Distance Education, 25(1)*, 125–142.

Witte, M. M. & Wolf, S. E. (2003). Infusing mentoring and technology within graduate courses: Reflections in practice. *Mentoring and Tutoring, 11*(1), 95–103.

Zhang, A. (2003). *Transactional distance in Web-based college learning environments: Toward measurement and theory construction*. Unpublished dissertation, Virginia Commonwealth University, Richmond.

II

LEARNERS, LEARNING, AND LEARNER SUPPORT

9

Independent Learning

Bill Anderson
Massey University, New Zealand

This chapter reviews the area of the independence of the learner in distance education. The term *independence* is used initially because of its connection to the beginnings of the modern practice and study of distance education through Wedemeyer's (1971) work on independent learning. However, this review will pull together threads of discussion from several related areas, each of which contributes in its own way to our understanding of the ways in which learners are seen as independent. Within distance education, and adult education, the field from which much of the early theoretical work in distance education was derived, three dominant descriptors can be discerned: self-directed learning (SDL), autonomous learning, and independent learning. These descriptors are often used with a considerable degree of equivalence. Tight (1996), for instance, suggests that the concepts of independent learning and SDL are so closely linked that they are essentially synonymous and Moore (1986), in describing educational transactions of a particular nature, described them by saying, "This is autonomous, or self-directed learning" (p. 12). These areas and the various concepts that have coalesced around each in relation to distance education form the basis of the literature from which this chapter draws.

In early work, Rogers (1969) and Boyd (1966) had identified personal autonomy and freedom of choice as key aspects of adult learning. For example, Boyd wrote the following:

> [Adult learners] approach subject matter directly without having an adult in a set of intervening roles between the learner and the subject matter. The adult knows his own standards and expectations. He no longer needs to be told, nor does he require the approval and reward from persons in authority. (p. 180)

In developing the concept of SDL, Tough's (1971) work on adult learning projects was seminal, and Knowles' (1975) engagement with and popularization of the notion of SDL supported the concept of andragogy that was at the core of his approach to adult education. These writers tended to focus on the design of learning activities, with Knowles writing that adult learners will take the lead "in diagnosing their learning needs, formulating learning goals, identifying human and material resources for learning, choosing and implementing appropriate learning strategies, and evaluating learning outcomes" (p. 18).

These developments occurred alongside Charles Wedemeyer's determination to move distance education from its strongly teacher- or institution-directed approach to one that gives more freedom and choice to learners. Wedemeyer (1971) chose to focus on the idea of independent learning, drawing his inspiration from the independent study system that had developed on some U.S. campuses for "superior students" who were on-campus. Moore (1972) provided the link between Wedemeyer's ideas and considerable authority in distance education, and the emerging ideas about self-direction in learning within the field of adult education, imbuing the field of distance education with a conceptual foundation that still has considerable influence.

In 1972, Moore set out an argument that independent study comprised two dimensions: distance teaching and learner autonomy. Distance teaching had two principal characteristics that Moore named "individualization" (later to be called "structure") and "dialogue." In explaining the second dimension, Moore (1972) cites Rogers (1969), Bruner (1966), Dewey (1966), and Thelen (1972) and describes the autonomous learner as one who has learned how to learn; as one who "knows how to proceed through each of the instructional processes" (p. 81). The autonomous learner is also a person who draws on a range of resources. When these resources include teachers, the autonomous learner is "surrendering temporarily some of his learner autonomy. . . . However, if he is a truly autonomous learner, he will not give up overall control of the learning processes" (p. 81). Moore (1980) notes that autonomous learners may at times be instrumentally dependent on teachers but they will not be emotionally dependent on them. The nature of autonomy in Moore's terms is best explored by considering the set of questions about distance programs that he suggests be used to determine the extent to which a learner is able to exercise autonomy (Moore, 1972, p. 82). Those questions tend to reflect the emphasis on design of learning activities that was noted previously in Knowles' (1975) work.

As conceptualizations of SDL slowly shifted in the field of adult education, so they changed in distance education. In the former field, work through the 1980s suggested a more complex picture of SDL than had been earlier developed. There was concern particularly for the need to capture learner characteristics internal to each individual and consideration of the social context in which learning occurs. In addition, in the distance education field, there was some concern that, in applying the early conceptualization of SDL, too great an emphasis was placed on learner autonomy. The concern is strongly evident in the work of Garrison (1987) and is also seen in Morgan's (1985) critique of independent learning. Morgan was particularly concerned about what he saw as the total nature of learner control in conceptualizations of SDL and the lack of consideration for a sharing of control between the student and the institution. Garrison's concerns centred on two main issues: the role of the teacher as a facilitator of learning, and the need to make SDL relevant to formal educational contexts. Moore (1980) had previously acknowledged that learners differed in their abilities to learn autonomously but he continued to advocate a strong version of learner autonomy. Moore (1986) argued that institutions should modify their teaching to give learners a chance to exercise their autonomy, citing, with emphasis, Ljosa and Sandvold's (1983) comment, "Through a long series of personal conscious choices the student will make his/her own course" (p. 21). Within this argument there was recognition that teachers would work as "joint enquirers" with students and each would act as a "resource person, a procedural specialist, and a co-inquirer" (Moore, 1986, p. 12). The key issue at this time was the balance of control between teacher and student. Where initially there was concern over the extensively directive approach of distance education institutions, a sense that the balance had swung too far beyond the notion of an educational transaction between teacher and learner was evident.

Candy's (1991) work on SDL in lifelong learning helped to highlight the dimensions of this issue. Candy differentiated between learner control and autodidaxy as two distinct domains of self-direction in learning. In the first, the learner maintained primary ownership of learning although "there is still a residue, albeit small, of teacher-control" (p. 18). In the second, no teacher is present and the learner might not even be aware that learning is occurring. The first of these domains—

recognising the role of the teacher, and implicitly the educational transaction that occurs between learner and teacher—has relevance to distance education, for, even if only through the presence of a voice within prepared study material, a teacher's part in the educational transaction is always evident, and learning is acknowledged as the purpose of student activity.

Alongside this assertion must be placed the argument that learners who are capable of and motivated to undertake SDL may choose at times not to do so. Knowles (1980) made this point, and the argument is supported by Candy (1991) and Brockett and Hiemstra (1991). Candy suggested that four major variables influence the extent to which a learner decides to engage in SDL: (a) commitment to learning at the current time, (b) sense of competence as a learner, (c) familiarity of the subject matter, and (d) technical skills related to the learning process. Even a learner who is capable of SDL to a considerable extent may choose to engage in a highly teacher-directed educational setting in, for example, the initial stages of a learning project, or for convenience. Responsibility for learning is something that is shared between teacher and learner although the orientation of this approach sees learners ceding control of the learning process and aspects of the design of learning activities as they wish, rather than fighting for them. The engagement of learner and teacher foregrounds the educational transaction that occurs between them.

Garrison's concern over what he regarded as the lack of conceptual clarity in the use of the term *independence* led to a further analysis of this concept in the attempt to account for the complexities of educational transactions. Garrison and Baynton (1987) suggested the use of the concept of learner control in order to achieve that end. "Control is concerned with the opportunity and ability to influence and direct a course of events. Control not only implies having choices and making decisions, but includes the capability to effect change" (Garrison, 1989, p. 27). Control is valuable in the educational process because "[w]ithout substantial control (i.e., information and communication) in the educational process learners are less likely to realize their potential" (p. 39).

Garrison and Baynton (1987) discussed the interrelationship between independence, support, and power as dimensions of control, and described control as a crucial and central concept in distance education. Garrison and Baynton note that it is "not the independence associated with the non-contiguous nature of the transaction" (p. 14) that is the most important attribute of distance education, but rather the education transaction itself. Their focus in relation to control was on the nature of the interaction between teacher and student, and linked control with communication. Garrison and Baynton wrote, "Clearly, communication is the process that makes an educational transaction possible. Two-way communication provides the means for negotiation and dialogue. This in turn determines the balance of control which will maximize educational development" (p. 14). More recently, Anderson and Garrison (1998) also suggested that the reciprocal component of educational communication, its two-way nature, moves the balance of control of the educational transaction toward the student. The major contribution here is that the proposal shifts the emphasis from an institution being the determinant of control in the learning situation to recognition of the role of learners. Control in the learning situation was a matter of negotiating the balance between institutional and personal factors.

Analysis of the concept of control in relation to educational transactions in distance education needed to be underpinned by a firmer and more coherent understanding of SDL that accounted for the transactional nature of education. Garrison (1997) proposed such a model based on three interconnected dimensions to account for both the external factors of learning (what, where, when, etc., to learn) and internal factors (cognitive, metacognitive, and motivational aspects). His approach also adopted a collaborative perspective that "has the individual taking responsibility for constructing meaning while including the participation of others in confirming worthwhile knowledge" (p. 19).

Garrison's (1997) proposed three dimensions were (a) self-management (task control), with a focus on the enactment of learning goals and the management of learning resources and support, (b) self-monitoring (cognitive responsibility), which addresses cognitive and metacognitive processes, and (c) motivation (entering and task), relating to initiation and maintenance of effort. The dimension of motivation was tied to the concept of control. Garrison argued that intrinsic motivation was necessary if students were to achieve quality educational outcomes, and that "to encourage intrinsically motivated learning, students must see opportunities to share control and to collaborate in the planning and implementation of the learning process" (p. 29). Motivation was also seen as having a mediating effect on the dimensions of self-management (task control) and self-monitoring (cognitive responsibility) which Garrison describes as "integral and reciprocal constructs" (p. 21) in this model of SDL. Versions of these two latter dimensions also appear central to Peters' (1998) discussion of autonomy.

Peters (1998), following Moore, writes that "distance education . . . consists fundamentally of the integration of instructive dialogues, structured learning and teaching programmes and activities covered by autonomous learning" (p. 33) and describes dialogue, structure, and autonomy as the three constitutive concepts of distance education. In his detailed discussion of autonomy he indicates there are two dimensions involved: a pedagogical dimension and a psychological dimension.

A key component of the pedagogical dimension is that a person is no longer "the *object* of educational guidance, influences, effects and obligations, but the *subject* of his or her own education" (p. 48). When learners "recognize their learning needs, formulate learning objectives, select contents, draw up learning strategies, procure teaching materials and media, identify additional human and physical resources and make use of them, and themselves organize, control, inspect and evaluate their own learning" (p. 48) they are autonomous in a pedagogical sense. This dimension has strong links with Moore's (1972) discussion of autonomy as related to a learner's skill in the preparation, execution and evaluation of learning. The second dimension Peters (1998) discusses, the psychological dimension, has a focus on metacognition. In this sense autonomy requires an awareness of one's knowledge and the ability to monitor and reflect on cognitive strategies used during learning. The capacity to critically reflect on the learning process is central here.

There is a high degree of correspondence between Peters' discussion of autonomy and Garrison's analysis of SDL. Peters' pedagogical and Garrison's self-management dimensions are clearly similar, as are Peters' psychological and Garrison's self-monitoring dimension. Both discussions recognize the importance of the social context of distance education and its transactional nature, and the requirement to consider within that social context the inter- and intrapersonal factors that impact learning. As noted previously, there is also close correspondence between Moore's description of learner autonomy, the pedagogical dimension of Peters, and the self-management of Garrison. With little further development of the concept of SDL since Garrison's 1997 article and this clear intersection of views, the two dimensions of self-management and self-monitoring, to use Garrison's terms, provide a starting point for investigation of empirical studies in this area.

The two sections that follow will consider these two dimensions more thoroughly through a review of empirical studies undertaken in distance education contexts. Because the first will be considered primarily by reviewing work that has been based on Moore's Theory of Transactional Distance, the term "learner autonomy" will often be used in the text to be largely consistent with the studies being reviewed. The second will be developed through a review of work that directly considers cognitive and metacognitive processes in relation to distance education students and will use the term "self-monitoring" from Garrison.

MANAGING EXTERNAL ACTIVITIES

Moore's attention to learner autonomy came through his classification of distance courses, on the basis of a combination of structure (originally the element of individualization) and dialogue, according to the extent to which learners could control and influence the learning. Moore (1980) called the combination of structure and dialogue "transactional distance." He considered that the courses would "vary in the extent to which they encourage learners to exercise autonomy" and that institutions would offer this range in "response to the demands of learners who are more or less autonomous in deciding what, when, where, and how they will learn" (p. 26). He developed the theory of transactional distance which hypothesized that students with a greater degree of autonomy as learners would be comfortable with courses in which transactional distance was greater; and students who were less autonomous in their learning would prefer courses in which the combination of structure and dialogue meant that transactional distance was less. Moore also conducted an empirical study that provided some evidence in support of this hypothesis, using field dependence/independence as the indicator of autonomy.

Since Moore's original work, a small number of studies have explicitly considered the nature of the variables involved in the transactional distance theory and their relationship to each other and to other relevant educational variables such as student satisfaction and course learning outcomes.

WHAT IS LEARNER AUTONOMY?

In Moore's original study the variable of field dependence/independence was used to indicate the level of autonomous learning. Rather than taking this cognitive style as the indicator of learning autonomy, three subsequent studies have used factor analysis as the basis for investigation of the nature of learner autonomy in distance education contexts.

The first of these, Baynton (1992), derives from an earlier collaboration with Garrison (Garrison & Baynton, 1987) that was discussed in the previous section. Their goal was to develop a concept of autonomy that took account of the relationship between the learner and the teacher in an educational transaction. They named that concept "control" and defined it as being "concerned with the opportunity and ability to influence, direct, and determine decisions related to the education process" (p. 5). Baynton undertook an empirical test of the model of learner control primarily using exploratory factor analysis of student responses to a questionnaire. Responses to a small number of open-ended questions were also gathered from the study participants to widen the scope of the analysis. When these responses were considered alongside the factor analysis, Baynton suggested that control could be conceptualized as the interaction of three categories or complexes of factors: (a) a predispositional category of factors that "predispose the learner and/or the teacher/tutor to enter the distance learning situation" (p. 26); (b) an operative category that relates to factors "that are interactive and operate within the context of communication . . . during the planning and instructional phase of learning" (p. 28); and (c) an environmental/contextual category of factors that "contribute to the enhancement or inhibition of the amount of control experienced by the learner" (p. 28). In addition, she indicated that the analysis reinforced the interdependence of student and teacher in the teaching-learning process.

Until 1999 no study focused specifically on Moore's Theory of Transactional Distance had attempted to empirically investigate the nature of learner autonomy. Such a study was conducted by Chen and Willits (1999) with students engaged in distance education in a videoconferencing environment using exploratory factor analysis. The analysis proceeded from a definition that described learner autonomy as "the learner's perception of both independent and interdependent participation in a learning activity and involves both the student's ability to learn individually/self-directedly and his or her preference or need for collaborative learning" (p. 48). In the study, independence referred to items such as the ability to develop a personal learning plan, to find resources for study, and to learn without lots of guidance; items related to interdependence referred to learning as a member of a team, preferring to learn in a group sharing effort, and sharing effort and responsibility with classmates.

A two-factor solution, in which students described themselves as both independent and interdependent learners, was generated. Noting that these characteristics are not intercorrelated, Chen and Willits added that the characteristics "were not contrasting poles of the same continuum but rather represented separate and distinct attributes" (Chen & Willits, 1999, p. 57) and that autonomy must thus be a combination of independence and interdependence, highlighting Baynton's (1992) emphasis on interdependence within the teaching-learning process.

The Chen and Willits (1999) factor-analytic study was replicated by Pruitt (2005) as part of a larger study. Pruitt used a slightly modified version of the Chen and Willits survey as the basis for his data collection and surveyed students in courses delivered by the Internet, telecourse, or compressed video. The results he obtained from an exploratory factor analysis supported the Chen and Willits study. Pruitt also obtained a two-factor solution for learner autonomy with the factors of independence and interdependence.

The use of factor analysis serves to summarize data by grouping together variables—in this case, survey items that are correlated. Interpretation is reliant on the conceptual framework and definitions that were used to develop the original items. Thus, since Chen and Willits and Pruitt built interdependence into their definition of learner autonomy from the outset, the finding that it emerged as a factor is not surprising. Moore (1994) appeared to separate learner autonomy from interdependence whilst recognizing their closeness. He defined learner autonomy as "the potential of distant learners to participate in the determination of their learning objectives, the implementation of their programs of study, and the evaluation of their learning" and wrote, with regard to his observation of a teleconference course, that "successful groups exhibit a high degree of interdependence among relatively autonomous individuals" (p. 3).

The inclusion of interdependence as an aspect of learner autonomy is consistent with an understanding of the individual as not "metaphysically independent of society" (Taylor, 1985; as cited in Wertsch, 1991). It reflects the view of education as a transactional practice, at the heart of which lies a process described by Mercer (1995) as "the guided construction of knowledge." Engagement with others is intrinsic to education and seems especially salient when distance education practice utilizes technologies that expand dialogic possibilities and may include software tools that enhance interaction in the service of learning. Perhaps, as Garrison (2003) suggests, *autonomy* is the wrong term. Whatever name it is given, the concept of learners managing external aspects of their learning activity must account for their ability to work with others in that activity.

The Relationship between Learner Autonomy and Outcomes for Students

Educational outcomes such as achievement and satisfaction are relevant to educational policymakers and administrators. Several relatively recent studies investigate the relationship between learner autonomy and such outcomes. Should we expect a direct relationship? In transactional distance theory, learner autonomy does not relate directly to outcomes. As noted previously, the theory proposes that different educational programs (courses) allow or expect learners to exercise different levels of autonomy; the gap, or transactional distance, between teacher and learner varies according to the nature of the program. The theory hypothesizes that there is a positive relationship between transactional distance and learner autonomy (Moore, 1972, p. 83). What does this relationship imply? Several possibilities present themselves. Perhaps students with greater autonomy as learners will be disproportionately represented in programs characterized by greater transactional distance because of the congruence between their skill as autonomous learners and the requirements of the program; although Willen (1988) disputes this possibility. Levels of student satisfaction with a program may be related to the match between measures of transactional distance and learner autonomy. Perhaps, indirectly through the degree of match between those measures, learning outcomes may also be affected. Transactional distance theory does not extend to hypotheses about the success of students in distance education, although Moore (1993) suggested there were "recognizable patterns of personality characteristics among student who preferred, or who succeeded in, teaching programmes that were more highly dialogic and less structured, compared with those who preferred, or succeeded in, less dialogic and more structured programmes" (p. 31). Other attempts to explore the theory in this regard have been made.

Pruitt (2005) and Chen and Willits (1998) used exploratory factor analysis to create variables representing the concepts of transactional distance theory (including autonomy with the factors of independence and interdependence), and both studies then used multiple regression techniques to determine the extent to which the variables predicted learning outcomes. Chen and Willits used a measure of perceived student learning in which students were asked to indicate how much they thought they had learned during the course, while Pruitt's study used instructor-assigned final course grades as the dependent variable in the regression analysis. Chen and Willits indicated that learner autonomy had neither direct nor indirect effect on perceived learning outcomes.

More recently, Pruitt (2005) noted interaction between independent variables in describing effect on grades. In particular he reported an interaction concerning the variable "learner autonomy-independence." When learner autonomy-independence was low, course grades improved if levels of in-class dialogue were high; when learner autonomy-independence was high, course grades dropped if levels of in-class dialogue were high. Within a given course structure, increasing the level of dialogue will decrease transactional distance (and vice versa); thus, Pruitt's finding provides some support for the possibility of successful attainment of course learning outcomes being correlated with the degree of fit between transactional distance and learner autonomy viewed as independence. Pruitt also reported two interaction effects for 'learner autonomy—interdependence'—one with number of distance courses taken, the other with mode of delivery. High levels of interdependence predict lower grades for students both in independence-demanding environments (as Pruitt describes the Internet-delivery option in his study), and when they have some experience (two or more courses) in distance education study. There is potential here to confuse delivery mode with the nature of the course and this should be resisted. But if we accept Pruitt's assertion that one type of delivery demanded greater independence of students, we see in that result additional support for a mediated relationship between autonomy and course outcomes.

DeTure (2004) used the cognitive-style variable field dependence/independence in her study of students undertaking Web-based general education distance courses. This variable was measured using the Group Embedded Figures Task and is of interest since this variable was used in Moore's original work. DeTure predicted that the cognitive style scores, representing the level of autonomy of learners, would predict student success as measured by grade-point average (GPA). A second predictor in the study was online technologies' self-efficacy. Neither variable was found to predict GPA. DeTure's work reported on results collapsed across five courses with clearly differing requirements for interaction and with different course structures. Unfortunately no attempt was made to examine GPA levels in relation to interactions between levels of autonomy and transactional distance.

Moving from a concern with learning outcomes, several studies suggest that learner autonomy, in some form, has an impact on other student outcomes. Drennan, Kennedy, and Pisarski (2005) investigated factors (including locus of control as a measure of autonomy) that affect student satisfaction with flexible online learning. Wheeler (2005) focused on perceptions of social presence as a dependent variable, arguing its importance in electronically mediated contexts, and used structural equation modelling to create path models that show the relationships between variables (including a measure of learner autonomy) used to predict the degree of social presence in four different learning modes: face-to-face, telephone, e-mail, and videoconference. In both cases, findings suggest a place for learner autonomy as an important variable in the prediction of the outcome being investigated.

These studies also point to a slightly tangential, but related and important, issue. Both studies present a somewhat technologically deterministic view, where there is potential for confusion of delivery type with nature of the course, of technology with pedagogy. The Drennan et al. (2005) findings implicate mode of delivery in an indirect relationship between autonomy and satisfaction, and Wheeler (2005) uses mode of delivery as the basis for developing different path models. I have noted elsewhere (Anderson, 2006) that technological determinism should be rejected. A caveat is that, because of the social origins of their design, all technologies bring their own affordances to their use, and these affordances will have an impact on the way technologies are used. Although both studies use mode of delivery as a variable, the subtext is that it is the nature of the course that is of interest. Drennan et al. refer to flexible learning as placing the onus on students to use study material and learning options as they deem suitable (p. 337), and Wheeler discusses telephone and e-mail modes of delivery in terms of dialogical possibilities. Equating delivery type with the nature of a course ignores the socially constructed nature of courses and the myriad, though not endless, possibilities for course design that such social construction brings. The important research variables must be those that characterize courses, not technologies.

Although the argument here is that the focus must not be directly on the technology, it is acknowledged that different technologies will bring different affordances to their use. This creates the likelihood that courses using a particular technology will have similar pedagogical characteristics (see, for example, Oliver and McLoughlin, 1997), and perhaps be markedly different pedagogically from those that take advantage of other technologies. Wheeler's (2005) work discusses the impact on outcomes of the role of learner autonomy in relation to the affordances of different technologies, especially with regard to their dialogic capability. This is an interesting line of research and worthy of further development.

Learner autonomy has also been suggested as a factor influencing student persistence in—or its obverse, dropout from—distance education. Following on from Moore's early work, Thompson (1984) suggested that field dependence should be investigated as an explanatory construct in explorations of distance education dropout, but this strand of investigation has never been pursued. Sweet (1986) and Parker (1999) both hypothesized locus of control as one predictor of dropout. Both studies suggest a direct effect of locus of control, but Sweet's path model predicts only 19% of the variance in dropout. However, Woodley (2004) is highly critical of research into dropout rates, citing the difficulty of adequately testing the general models of dropout that have been developed theoretically. In addition, models of dropout that might be considered at least relatively sophisticated (e.g., Billings, 1989; Kember, 1995; Tinto, 1993) employ a large number of potentially interacting variables highlighting the complexity of explanations. Woodley's suggestion that models of dropout may be "no less than a general theory of how people decide to take action and how they change their minds" (p. 61) implies that efforts that focus on determining the exact role of learner autonomy in distance education dropout rates may be misplaced.

DEVELOPING AUTONOMY

The potential for study by distance education to foster the development of independent or autonomous learners is of interest to distance educators. Such a link was proposed by Paul (1990), while Morgan (1993) also noted the challenge of developing in learners the self-knowledge and skills that are characteristic of the autonomous learner. The development of autonomous learners has been noted as a goal of the education of adults (Merriam & Caffarella, 1999, p. 290) either formally or incidentally. A small number of studies suggest that for students who learn in a distance education context, the ability to learn autonomously improves over time.

Ching (1998) reported the results of a study into changes in the level of field dependence/independence of students enrolled in a distance education nursing programme. The study involved both cross-sectional (data obtained from students new to a distance education program, and graduates of that program) and longitudinal (data obtained from new students at the beginning and end of the program) samples. Ching reported significant overall change toward field independence in both samples but noted especially that field-dependent students become more field independent as they progress through a course of distance study. McFerrin (1999) examined the incidental learning that occurs in a graduate-level asynchronous online distance education course, and noted the increase in time-management ability, self-directive behaviour, self-confidence, and self-discipline, while Anderson (1999) reported student perceptions that Internet-based courses facilitated learner autonomy. Rickwood and Goodwin (2000) and Vanijdee (2003) both develop a case for the growth in learner autonomy over time in distance education courses. This group of studies does not represent strong evidence of the link hypothesized by Paul (1990). Additional studies in a range of distance education contexts are needed to provide strong confirmatory support.

DISTANCE EDUCATION AND SELF-MONITORING

This section reviews work that directly considers cognitive processes and metacognition in relation to distance education students. Metacognition is a form of cognition which involves active control over one's cognitive processes, or, more briefly, a "person's cognition about cognition" (Wellman, 1985, p. 1). Research (Borkowski, Carr, & Pressley, 1987; Garner & Alexander, 1989; Pressley & Ghatala, 1990) indicates that metacognitively capable people are more likely to be successful in cognitive tasks. Zimmerman (1995) identified the importance of self-regulation in relation to metacognition, indicating that self-regulation "involves more than metacognitive knowledge and skill, it involves an underlying sense of self-efficacy and personal agency and the motivational and behavioral processes to put these self beliefs into effect" (p. 217). We see here the place of the third dimension of Garrison's (1997) model, although that dimension is not explored in this chapter. Importantly, we see that although it is not sufficient, the development of metacognitive ability is necessary for academic achievement and that, with this ability, students can develop control over their own learning.

The ongoing and proficient use of cognitive and metacognitive strategies would be characteristic of capability in Garrison's (1997) dimension of self-monitoring and Peters' (1998) psychological dimension of learner autonomy. Questions that could be considered here might ask about the extent to which distance students use cognitive and metacognitive strategies and whether that level of use differs from face-to-face students; whether use of cognitive and metacognitive strategies by distance students impacts on learning outcomes; and about whether and, if so, how distance education courses can be designed to foster the development of cognitive and metacognitive skills and knowledge.

Early work by Marland, Patching, and Putt (1992), Bernt and Bugbee (1993), and Koymen (1992) represented the first empirical exploration by distance educators of cognitive strategy use and metacognition. Marland et al. focused on determining study strategies of 17 students who were studying text and used a stimulated-recall interview technique to elicit information about the extent and nature of strategy use. The Bernt and Bugbee and Koymen studies reported that, although distance students do employ learning and study strategies, and high achievers report greater use of those strategies, there appeared to be no differences in strategy use between distance and face-to-face students.

The next major work in the area was by White (1995; 1997; 1999). White's thorough initial study was based on a large-scale questionnaire on learner strategies and a verbal report procedure with a smaller number of participants to gather accounts of cognitive and metacognitive strategy use. A second study used a similar verbal report procedure to obtain accounts of learners' metacognitive knowledge. The first study sought to compare strategy use by undergraduate foreign-language learners in distance and classroom learning contexts, the second to develop a more detailed picture of the nature of metacognitive knowledge of distance foreign-language learners and explore the role of metacognitive experiences in their learning.

Broadly, White's (1995; 1997) first study showed that distance learners made considerably greater use of metacognitive strategies than classroom learners, especially in the areas of monitoring and evaluation. In particular, the strategy of self-management was the most important strategy in differentiating between groups. The apparent importance of self-management that relies on learners' knowledge of how they learn best was the driver for White's (1999) second study. In this study she conceptualized metacognitive knowledge as comprising knowledge of self, task, strategies, and goals and found that knowledge about self and strategies was more influential than knowledge about task and goals. An additional finding related to the extent to which reports of metacognitive experiences were laden with affective elements, echoing Zimmerman's (1995) conceptualization of self-regulation in learning.

In contrast with White's conclusions, Jegede, Taplin, Fan, Chan, and Yum (1999) report that their study of 712 distance education students "did not show that the students engaged in meaningful metacognitive strategies to monitor, organise and reflect upon their information processing" (p. 268). They suggest this indicates a reliance on distance learning material as prepared, and this was supported in later interviews in which students indicated they rarely questioned ideas presented in the study material. Jegede et al. suggest that cultural or environmental factors may have come into play in determining this result. They do note, however, that there was evidence that high-achievers monitor, organise, and reflect on strategy use to a greater extent than low-achieving students.

The articles by White (1995, 1997, 1999) and Jegede et al. (1999) represent major studies of cognitive strategy use and metacognition in a distance education context, and separately and together give rise to a number of questions about this important aspect of learning. White's first study suggested that cognitive strategy use was related to language being studied. Does strategy use, cognitive, or metacognitive, also differ according to subject area, or level of study? In contrast with Jegede et al.'s suggestion that students rely on distance material as prepared and use it in an unproblematic way, White (1995) argues that student inability to regulate the degree of complexity of study material might well prompt them to make greater use of self-monitoring. The cultural background of students is suggested as an explanation of this difference. Work in the area of *Approaches to Study* by Richardson, Landbeck, and Mugler (1995), Richardson, Morgan, and Woodley (1999), and Smith and Smith (2000) has shown the importance of accounting for cultural background. Similar studies need to be conducted in the area of metacognition. Finally, the impact of mode of technology employed in a distance education context should be investigated.

White's studies were conducted with students who were undertaking study with little ongoing contact with other students. Students thus had little opportunity to have others help them monitor understanding of course material. Do the more socially interactive modes of technology used in distance education impact the extent to which metacognitive strategies are used?

The last study to be considered in relation to cognitive and metacognitive processes is interesting for its implications in a world that is increasingly moving to distance education using online communication, and to making some post-compulsory education in that manner a requirement. Smith (2000) undertook an investigation of the use of flexible online delivery for vocational education and training (VET) in Australia. Smith reports that a sample of over 1,200 VET learners had a strong preference for learning contexts in which instructors provide leadership of learning and it is clear what is to be learned and how. A small sample of students was interviewed; they identified restricted or rare use of the strategies of analysis and strategy planning and cognitive monitoring. Smith concluded that "apprentices are generally not ready for the self-directed learning demanded by flexible delivery. They do not have a preference for self-directed learning and they appear not to have developed the learning strategies needed."

Smith's study is valuable for the way it highlights two important factors. First is the notion that use of distance education methods, especially in an online form, is growing relative to classroom-based education. Second, as we have already noted, this brings an increasingly diverse range of students, including many more who may not wish or prefer to undertake study at a distance, and who do not bring with them the range or level of cognitive or metacognitive skills appropriate for distance study. Cognitive and metacognitive strategy training within distance education contexts can thus be seen to be essential. Such training goes beyond the use of support devices embedded in text as investigated by Martens, Valcke, Poelmans, and Daal (1996), and into a specific focus on cognitive and metacognitive strategy development as in the work outlined by McLoughlin and Hollingworth (2002). Metacognitive training for school-age students in face-to-face contexts has been researched reasonably extensively, but there is considerable scope to investigate the complexities of metacognitive strategy training across a range of subject matter for adult students in distance education contexts employing differing technologies.

These studies all suggest the importance of cognitive and metacognitive strategy use in distance education, but also allude to the difficulties that can arise when learners who are not self-directed undertake study in a mode that is not preferred or not consistent with cultural or environmental factors. Given the increasing prominence of courses delivered online, awareness of the cognitive and metacognitive strengths required of learners is essential. Additionally it will be important to ensure that course materials and interactions are consistent with and help to foster the goal of individual development in the use of study and metacognitive skills. When students have little or no choice but to study at a distance, supporting their development in this area is paramount.

REFERENCES

Anderson, B. (2006). Writing power into online discussion. *Composition and Computers, 23*(1), 108–124.
Anderson, D. S. (1999). Mathematics and distance education on the Internet: An investigation based on transactional distance theory. *Dissertation Abstracts International—A, 60/05,* 1488. (UMI No. 9930678)
Anderson, T., & Garrison, D. R. (1998). Learning in a networked world: New roles and responsibilities. In C. C. Gibson (Ed.), *Distance learners in higher education* (pp. 97–112). Madison, WI: Atwood.
Baynton, M. (1992). Dimensions of "control" in distance education: A factor analysis. *The American Journal of Distance Education, 6*(2), 17–31.

Bernt, F. M., & Bugbee, A. C. (1993). Study practices and attitudes related to academic success in a distance learning program. *Distance Education, 14*(1), 97–112.

Billings, D. M. (1989). A conceptual model of correspondence course completion. In M. G. Moore & G. C. Clark (Eds.), *Readings in distance learning and instruction, 2.* University Park, PA: American Center for the Study of Distance Education.

Borkowski, J., Carr, M., & Pressley, M. (1987). "Spontaneous" strategy use: Perspectives from metacognitive theory. *Intelligence, 11*, 61–75.

Boyd, R. (1966). A psychological definition of adult education. *Adult Leadership, 13*, 160–162.

Brockett, R. G., & Hiemstra, R. (1991). *Self-direction in adult learning: Perspectives on theory, research and practice.* New York: Routledge.

Candy, P. C. (1991). *Self-direction for lifelong learning: A comprehensive guide to theory and practice.* San Francisco: Jossey-Bass.

Chen, Y.-J., & Willits, F. K. (1998). A path analysis of the concepts in Moore's theory of transactional distance in a videoconferencing learning environment. *Journal of Distance Education, 13*(2), 51–65.

Chen, Y.-J., & Willits, F. K. (1999). Dimensions of educational transactions in a videoconferencing learning environment. *The American Journal of Distance Education, 13*(1), 45–59.

Ching, L. S. (1998). The influence of a distance learning environment on students' field dependence/independence [Online version]. *Journal of Experimental Education, 66*(2), 149–160.

DeTure, M. (2004). Cognitive style and self-efficacy: Predicting student success in online distance education. *The American Journal of Distance Education, 18*(1), 21–38.

Drennan, J., Kennedy, J., & Pisarski, A. (2005). Factors affecting student attitudes toward flexible online learning in management education. *Journal of Educational Research, 98*(6), 331–338.

Garner, R., & Alexander, P. A. (1989). Metacognition: Answered and unanswered questions. *Educational Psychologist, 24*(2), 143–158.

Garrison, D. R. (1987). Self-directed and distance learning: Facilitating self-directed learning beyond the institutional setting. *International Journal of Lifelong Education, 6*(4), 309–318.

Garrison, D. R. (1989). *Understanding distance education: A framework for the future.* London: Routledge.

Garrison, D. R. (1997). Self-directed learning: Toward a comprehensive model. *Adult Education Quarterly, 48*(1), 18–33.

Garrison, D. R. (2003). Self-directed learning and distance education. In M. G. Moore & W. G. Anderson (Eds.), *Handbook of distance education* (pp. 161–168). Mahwah, NJ: Lawrence Erlbaum Associates.

Garrison, D. R., & Baynton, M. (1987). Beyond independence in distance education: The concept of control. *The American Journal of Distance Education, 1*(3), 3–15.

Jegede, O., Taplin, M., Fan, R. Y. K., Chan, M. S. C., & Yum, J. (1999). Differences between low and high achieving distance learners in locus of control and metacognition. *Distance Education, 20*(2), 255–273.

Kember, D. (1995). *Open learning courses for adults.* Englewood Cliffs, NJ: Educational Technology Publications.

Knowles, M. (1975). *Self-directed learning: A guide for learners and teachers.* New York: Association Press.

Knowles, M. S. (1980). *The modern practice of adult education: From pedagogy to andragogy* (2nd ed.). New York: Cambridge Books.

Koymen, U. S. (1992). Comparison of learning and study strategies of traditional and open-learning-system students in Turkey. *Distance Education, 13*(1), 108–117.

McFerrin, K. M. (1999, February 28–March 4). *Incidental learning in a higher education online distance education course.* Paper presented at the 10th Society for Information Technology and Teacher Education International Conference, San Antonio, TX.

McLoughlin, C., & Hollingworth, R. (2002, June 24–29). *Bridge over troubled water: Creating effective online support for the metacognitive aspects of problem solving.* Paper presented at the ED-MEDIA 2002 World Conference on Educational Multimedia, Hypermedia & Telecommunications, Denver, CO.

Marland, P., Patching, W., & Putt, I. (1992). Thinking while studying: A process tracing study of distance learners. *Distance Education, 13*(2), 193–217.

Martens, R., Valcke, M., Poelmans, P., & Daal, M. (1996). Functions, use and effects of embedded support devices in printed distance learning materials. *Learning and Instruction, 6*(1), 77–93.

Mercer, N. (1995). *The guided construction of knowledge.* Clevedon, England: Multilingual Matters.

Merriam, S. B., & Caffarella, R. S. (1999). *Learning in adulthood* (2nd ed.). San Francisco: Jossey-Bass.

Moore, M. G. (1972). Learner autonomy: The second dimension of independent learning. *Convergence, 5*(2), 76–88.

Moore, M. G. (1980). Independent study. In R. Boyd & J. Apps (Eds.), *Redefining the discipline of adult education* (pp. 16–31). San Francisco: Jossey-Bass.

Moore, M. G. (1986). Self-directed learning and distance education [Online version]. *Journal of Distance Education, 1*(1), 7–24.

Moore, M. G. (1993). Theory of transactional distance. In D. Keegan (Ed.), *Theoretical principles of distance education* (pp. 22–38). London: Routledge.

Moore, M. G. (1994). Editorial. Autonomy and interdependence. *The American Journal of Distance Education, 8*(2), 1–5.

Morgan, A. (1985). What shall we do about independent learning? *Teaching at a Distance, 26,* 38–45.

Morgan, A. (1993). *Improving your students' learning: Reflections on the experiences of study.* London: Kogan Page.

Oliver, R., & McLoughlin, C. (1997). Interactions in audiographics teaching and learning environments. *The American Journal of Distance Education, 11*(1), 34–54.

Parker, A. (1999). A study of variables that predict dropout from distance education [Online version]. *International Journal of Educational Technology, 1*(2), 1–10.

Paul, R. (1990). Towards a new measure of success: Developing independent learners. *Open Learning, 5,* 31–38.

Peters, O. (1998). *Learning and teaching in distance education.* London: Kogan Page.

Pressley, M., & Ghatala, E. S. (1990). Self regulated learning: Monitoring learning from text. *Educational Psychologist, 25,* 19–23.

Pruitt, D. (2005). *Transactional distance and learner autonomy as predictors of student grades in distance learning courses delivered by three modalities.* Dissertation Abstracts International—A66/04, 1331. (UMI No. 3170380).

Richardson, J. T. E., Landbeck, R., & Mugler, F. (1995). Approaches to studying in higher education: a comparative study in the South Pacific. *Educational Psychology, 15,* 417–432.

Richardson, J. T. E., Morgan, A., & Woodley, A. (1999). Approaches to study in distance education. *Higher Education, 37,* 23–55.

Rickwood, P., & Goodwin, V. (2000). Travelers' tales: Reflections on the way to learner autonomy. *Open Learning, 15*(1), 47–56.

Rogers, C. (1969). *Freedom to learn.* Columbus, OH: Charles E. Merrill.

Smith, P. (2000, September 11–13). *Developing strategies for effective workplace use of flexible delivery for training.* Paper presented at the ICDE Conference "Distance education: An open question?", Adelaide, SA, Australia.

Smith, S. N., & Smith, P. J. (2000). Implications for distance education in the study approaches of different Chinese national groups [Online version]. *Journal of Distance Education, 15*(2), 71–84.

Sweet, R. (1986). Student dropout in distance education: an application of Tinto's model. *Distance Education, 7*(2), 201–213.

Thompson, G. (1984). The cognitive style of field-dependence as an explanatory construct in distance education drop-out. *Distance Education, 5*(2), 286–293.

Tight, M. (1996). *Key concepts in adult education and training.* London: Routledge.

Tinto, V. (1993). *Leaving college: rethinking the causes and cures of student attrition.* Chicago: University of Chicago Press.

Tough, A. (1971). *The adult's learning projects.* Toronto: Ontario Institute for Studies in Education.

Vanijdee, A. (2003). Thai distance language learners and learner autonomy. *Open Learning, 18*(1), 75–84.

Wedemeyer, C. (1971). Independent study. In R. Deighton (Ed.), *Encyclopedia of Education (Vol. 4)* (pp. 548–557). New York: MacMillan.

Wellman, H. (1985). The origins of metacognition. In D. L. Forrest-Pressley, G. E. MacKinnon, and T. G. Waller (Eds.), *Metacognition, Cognition, and Human Performance*, Volume 1—Theoretical perspectives (pp. 1–31). New York: Academic Press.

Wertsch, J. (1991). *Voices of the mind.* Cambridge, MA: Harvard University Press.

Wheeler, S. (2005, November 11). *Creating social presence in digital learning environments: A presence of mind?* Paper presented at the TAFE Conference, Queensland, Australia.

White, C. (1995). Autonomy and strategy use in distance foreign language learning: Research findings. *System, 23*(2), 207–221.

White, C. (1997). Effects of mode of study on foreign language learning. *Distance Education, 18*(1), 178–196.

White, C. (1999). The metacognitive knowledge of distance learners. *Open Learning, 13*(3), 37–46.

Willen, B. (1988). What happened to the Open University—in brief. *Distance Education, 9*(1), 71–83.

Woodley, A. (2004). Conceptualizing student dropout in part-time distance education: Pathologizing the normal? *Open Learning, 19*(1), 47–63.

Zimmerman, B. J. (1995). Self-regulation involves more than metacognition: A social cognitive perspective. *Educational Psychologist, 30*(4), 217–221.

10

Cognitive Perspectives on Technology-Enhanced Distance Learning Environments

Michael J. Hannafin and Janette R. Hill
The University of Georgia

Liyan Song
Towson University

Richard E. West
The University of Georgia

Beginning in the 1970s, cognitive psychology became a dominant influence in research, theory, and practice related to teaching and learning (see, for example, historical overviews by Shuell, 1986; Hannafin & Rieber, 1989). Cognitive psychological perspectives have since dominated a wide range of pedagogical frameworks and models for designing technology-mediated teaching and learning environments (see, e.g., Kozma, 1987; Salomon, 1979, 1986).

The application of advanced technologies in distance education has produced what we call technology-enhanced distance learning environments (TEDLEs), leading to a somewhat predictable debate among cognitive theorists and researchers. To what extent are existing cognitive principles generalizable to learning in TEDLEs? To what extent do the affordances of various technologies and contextual demands influence the applicability of cognitive principles? Do different cognitive perspectives warrant, or require, different approaches?

Some well-studied principles have already been applied to technology-enhanced learning (see, e.g., Hooper & Hannafin, 1991), suggesting that many cognitive constructs can be directly applied to TEDLEs. Others have adapted cognitive constructs (see, e.g., Fox's description of functional contextualism and design, 2006; and Iiyoshi, Hannafin, and Wang's use of technology-mediated cognitive tools to support individual processing functions, 2005), demonstrating that many cognitive constructs are applicable when modified based on the affordances of technology. Still others have suggested that significant research, theory, and practice issues related to the applicability of cognitive principles and constructs must be reconciled to psychologically and pedagogically ground TEDLEs (Hannafin, Kim, & Kim, 2004; Linn, 1998).

Yet, cognitive psychology does not provide a single, unitary framework; rather, it represents a collection of theories and perspectives that posit mental mediation as the means through which experiences are interpreted, knowledge is acquired, and meaning is ultimately defined. Considerable variation exists regarding the nature and locus of reality, underlying assumptions about the nature and mechanisms of cognition, and their associated implications for teaching and learning.

This chapter cannot address all possible variations within cognitive psychology. Rather, we focus on information-processing perspectives. The purposes of this chapter are to (a) briefly introduce background related to cognitive psychology and information-processing related constructs; (b) review and critically analyze research specific to TEDLEs; and (c) describe implications of cognitive perspectives for TEDLE research, theory, and practice.

INFORMATION PROCESSING PERSPECTIVES

Overview

Information processing perspectives are rooted in objectivist epistemology that assumes reality to be external to the human mind (Simon, 1979). Meaning, in effect, exists independent of the individual; individuals, in turn, acquire and comprehend this meaning in order to become knowledgeable, and productive with their knowledge. This stands in contrast to the views of many neo-cognitivists, who assert that reality lies in individual and shared constructions and does not (or cannot, among radical constructivists) exist independently of these constructions.

Collectively, information-processing models have been characterized as "mind as computer" (Atkinson & Shiffrin, 1968) and "microscopes of the mind" (Massaro & Cowan, 1993). The individual mediates what is valued, acted upon, remembered, recalled, and generalized based on unique prior knowledge, needs, and interests. Information processing, in effect, involves the exchange of signals between external stimuli and internal mental processes such as sensory registers, selective perception, short-term memory (STM), and long-term memory (LTM) (Shuell, 1986).

Schema theory has been used widely as the conceptual framework within which information is presumed to be processed. Donald Norman (1982) described the organized networks of prior knowledge as schemata—variables, "slots," and associations among knowledge which collectively define how a given individual knows or performs a task. As new knowledge is acquired, updated, and revised, the number and strength of associations and representations increases. The process of updating schema and retrieving representations in order to recall or perform is known as "spread of activation" (Anderson & Pirolli, 1984). The richer the network of representations, the better an individual can both recall existing knowledge and act under diverse conditions.

According to information-processing theory, sensory registers detect external stimuli, which are then selectively filtered (often with little or no conscious awareness). This culls the amount and type of information and signals information to be processed more deeply. Information initially perceived is processed temporarily in STM, where it is selectively regulated. Since STM, also referred to as "working memory," has limited capacity, much of the information is rapidly discarded while other information is retained and selectively further processed based on prior knowledge and the introduction of additional information.

Learning, then, involves the transfer of information from STM to LTM (permanent memory). Retrieval involves recalling "learned" knowledge from LTM to working, or short-term, memory where it assumes a production function (e.g., referenced with or to new information, or to make a decision). Precisely what is learned and how well it is retrieved depends on how knowledge is represented; the more richly knowledge is encoded initially or elaborated subsequently, the more likely it will be activated under appropriate conditions, retrieved (decoded), and applied or transferred to related situations.

ASSUMPTIONS

Prior Knowledge

Among cognitive psychologists, Ausubel (1968) was among the first to underscore the primacy of prior knowledge in learning. Prior knowledge provides both the conceptual foundation (schema) and the links or associations between and among "nodes" or discrete sets of ideas. The greater the depth and breadth and the richer the connections of prior knowledge, the more readily learners acquire new knowledge and integrate it with existing understanding. In effect, to the extent an individual has acquired knowledge about a to-be-learned concept—even if naïve or incomplete—a basis is established for selecting new stimuli, elaborating new with current knowledge, and refining existing conceptions. In addition, as prior knowledge and associations increase, the more capable and strategic learners become in seeking and evaluating new information and in monitoring their understanding.

Prior knowledge has played a significant role in learning and retention across a wide range of TEDLEs (see, e.g., Land & Hannafin, 1996). In Song's (2005) study of graduate students' online learning, for example, experienced learners tended to be more strategic in terms of managing time and soliciting support, such as raising questions during online chats to have the instructor address questions quickly. Experienced online learners also reported spending less time in bulletin-board discussions, focusing instead on their particular interests and discussions. In contrast, first-time online learners reported reading nearly all bulletin-board postings as they attempted to understand course content and avoid falling behind.

Prior system knowledge also appears to influence the manner in which TEDLE system affordances are accessed and used. In one study, prior system knowledge actually was found to have a stronger impact on performance than prior subject knowledge. Hill and Hannafin (1997) examined the decisions made by 15 current and future K-12 teachers enrolled in a "technology for teachers" course, who searched the Web to identify materials for a to-be-taught classroom topic of their choosing. Novice users were far more likely than experienced system users to become frustrated and disoriented in their attempts to locate resources, and thus less strategic and successful in their searches. In contrast, those with high system knowledge reported more confidence and persistence in their search strategy, and more success in their efforts to locate resources.

Prior experience with online learning also appears to influence perceptions about and use of TEDLE tools and resources. In distance education, for example, research has indicated that difference exists between first-time and experienced online learners. Whereas novices often struggle during their first online-learning course, experienced online learners tend to develop strategic knowledge about the use of system affordances, manifest greater metacognitive awareness of their distance learning strengths and needs, and persist in the face of confusion or frustration (Song, Singleton, Hill, & Koh, 2004).

Role of External Cues

Given the assumption of meaning, the nature, content, and structure of external cues become especially significant for information-processing purposes. External cues both represent to-be-learned concepts and provide the means though which internal mechanisms are invoked (selectively perceived), acted upon in STM, coded richly and appropriately, and transferred to LTM, and subsequently recalled and transferred as needed. Robert Gagne (1984), for example, developed his widely implemented *Events of Instruction* to account for and manage the exchange between external and internal events. Each external (instructional) event was keyed to a specific internal (cognitive) event in order to ensure a link between how external stimuli were organized and presented and the associated requisite cognitive processes. The co-mediation between external events and cognitive processes establishes a fundamental tenet of information-processing perspectives.

Acquiring and Retrieving

According to information-processing theory, encoding and retrieving are inextricably tied, and influenced by factors such as depth of processing, extensiveness of coding, and richness of association. Information that has been processed deeply in STM—for example, by comparing and contrasting with similar information, analyzing closely for similarities and differences, and relating to prior knowledge—tends to be encoded more richly, activated more readily, and retrieved more quickly and more completely than information processed shallowly (Anderson, Reder, & Lebiere, 1996).

Alan Paivio's (1971) dual-coding hypothesis posits that information coded in multiple ways (e.g., words and imagery) is better stored and retrieved than information coded via a single modality. This has been both intuitively and empirically validated. However, more stimulation does not necessarily improve learning, and often interferes. In a comprehensive review of numerous studies involving school-aged students using multiple representations (such as pictures accompanying text, or video with accompanying narration), Pressley (1977) found that combined verbal-visual representations improve learning when they are complimentary in nature, but interfere when they are not. Similar research findings have repeatedly supported the complementary versus competing potential of visual and verbal stimuli across ages, grade, and domains (Fleming, 1977). Cognitive resources are well-used and effective when complementary information is conveyed simultaneously, but become quickly overtaxed when learners attempt to simultaneously decode non-congruent information presented across modalities.

Knowledge Representation

A variety of explanations have been tendered as to how knowledge is ultimately represented (Rummelhart & Ortony, 1977). Among information-processing adherents, representation is commonly characterized in terms of propositions, productions, and associations. According to Hannafin and Rieber (1989), knowledge representations comprise simple propositions (knowing what) and productions (knowing what to do). Connections, both within and between types of knowledge, are established during initial encoding and modified through successive experience, creating associations of varied richness and depth based upon individual differences.

COGNITIVE CONSTRUCTS AND TEDLES

While all information-processing constructs cannot be addressed comprehensively, we will focus on three that have particular implications for TEDLEs: motivation, cognitive demands, and metacognition.

Motivation

According to cognitive perspectives, motivation involves initiating and sustaining a desirable behavior in accordance with defined goals (Driscoll, 2000; Schunk, 1990). Motivation is typically classified as being extrinsic and intrinsic. Course requirements often serve as extrinsic motivation for participation and performance by establishing an external incentive or goal to which the learner strives (Laszlo & Kupritz, 2003), while intrinsic motivation pertains to incentives and goals unique to the individual, such as individual interests (Lim & Kim, 2003).

Bures, Amundsen, and Abrami (2002) examined student motivation and computer conferencing (cc). During one study, they observed 167 students in 10 different courses who used varying levels of computer conferencing technology. They found that both intrinsic (personal task relevance and beliefs about the impact of computer conferencing on learning) as well as extrinsic elements (task attractiveness) predicted satisfaction. They further reported that students with a personal learning orientation (intrinsic motivation) participated more in CC activities, had higher grades, and benefited more from the CC environment than those without intrinsic interest.

Whipp and Chiarelli (2004) used naturalistic case methods to study the experiences of six graduate students using Lotus Notes/Learning Space during an instructional technology and assessment course. Based on their analysis of interview transcripts, course documents, and student reflective journals, the researchers reported that students' motivation for self-regulated navigation depended upon their successes in managing both technical and social environments of the course. Success in managing technical and social aspects proved critical. To the extent they were able to manage both, motivation to utilize the learning space increased. Although the sample size was small, this study suggests that personal and system-related aspects of experience may influence motivation in online environments and the effectiveness of self-regulated learning.

Some have suggested that emerging forms of technology can increase motivation in TEDLEs (Mei-Mei, 2005). Hee Jun and Johnson (2005) reported a significant difference in learners' motivation between video-based instruction and text-based instruction. In their quasi-experimental, posttest-only study, 16 participants enrolled in an online master's degree program were provided both video-based and traditional text-based instruction within an online module, then asked for perceptions of understanding and motivation for each type of instruction. Perceptions of retention were assessed via an electronic questionnaire using open-ended questions at the end of the semester. Results indicated a significant difference between the video-based instruction and traditional text-based instruction for perceived learning and motivation to attend to instruction. Participants reported that the video-based instruction was more appealing and memorable than the text-based instruction. While Clark's (1994) cautions concerning novelty effects must be heeded, these findings suggest that online, context-based videos may provide additional extrinsic motivation for students to engage online instruction.

Hsinyi, Chin-Chung, and Ying-Tien (2006) recently found gender-based differences in motivation, reporting that male undergraduates demonstrated more positive Internet attitudes than females. In addition, students who perceived the Internet as a leisure tool reported more positive attitudes and higher self-efficacy than students viewing the Internet in only a functional role. In effect, Hsinyi et al. suggest that fostering an informal, exploratory, and leisurely attitude towards the Internet may improve students' motivations toward learning in TEDLEs.

Others, however, have suggested motivation may actually decline following online learning. For example, Schrum, Burbank, Engle, Chambers, and Glassett (2005) studied the motivations and beliefs of 22 higher-education faculty from eight different colleges and universities enrolled in an online professional development course. After contrasting pre-course information on background and online experience with post-course data using open- and closed-ended questions, the researchers concluded that en-route difficulties sustaining the learning community and learning new technologies decreased learner morale. Schmeeckle (2003) also reported a significant negative impact on learner motivation in quantitative studies involving trainees who were divided into control (classroom) and experimental (online) groups. Following completion of the training, trainees in the classroom group reported both higher motivation and more positive feelings about learning than did the online group.

Findings such as these reinforce the conclusion that there is nothing inherently motivational about online learning. Indeed, evidence suggests that due to the increased technical and interpersonal complexity of many systems, motivation to engage may decline in many instances. Good, well-designed, and supported instruction will generally increase motivation to engage and learn, while cumbersome, problematic instruction will not. Consistent with general learning environment research, several more fundamental cognitive and design factors seem to influence student motivation (cf. Clark, 1994).

COGNITIVE DEMANDS

Cognitive load has been characterized as demands on a person's mental processing while he or she attempts to learn. Some attempts to measure cognitive load utilize post-treatment questionnaires, where learners self-report their mental effort (Paas, van Merrienboer, & Adam, 1994; Paas, Tuovinen, Tabbers, & Van Gerven, 2003) or rate the difficulty of the material they learned (Kalyuga, Chandler, & Sweller, 1999). However, Brunken, Plass, and Leutner (2003) argue for direct, objective measures of cognitive load. Thus far, few direct measures of cognitive load have been developed.

Total cognitive load has been conceptualized as comprising intrinsic, extraneous, and germane cognitive load (Gerjets & Scheiter, 2003; van Merrionboer & Ayres, 2005). *Intrinsic load*, the number of elements that need to be processed in working memory (STM), is influenced by expertise and task complexity and varies as a function of individually perceived difficulty inherent in to-be-learned material. For example, learning from a biology text may present a higher intrinsic load than reading a children's story to the everyday person, but not to a scientist (Pollock, Chandler, & Sweller, 2002). Since a great deal of to-be-learned knowledge and skill made available at a distance is designed for non-experts, intrinsic load is especially relevant to TEDLE.

Extraneous load is influenced by the mental resources required to engage a learning environment; well-organized information, instructions, and tools tend to minimize extraneous load, while poorly organized information and tools engender higher extraneous load. In effect, to the extent the learner must expend cognitive resources simply to locate and access content, extraneous load (and effort) increases. Extraneous load is evident in research documenting learner disorientation in online environments, and becoming "lost in hyperspace" while attempting to navigate ill-structured or poorly scaffolded TEDLEs.

Germane load is defined as the amount of working memory needed to create new or activate existing schemas to learn desired or required concepts (Gerjets & Scheiter, 2003; Renkl & Atkinson, 2003). Germane load involves the allocation of cognitive resources that are appropriate for and relevant to the processing task and requirements. Increasing germane load may help to promote efficiencies, while increasing extraneous load may prove inefficient, ineffective, and overwhelming (van Merrienboer, Schuurman, de Croock, & Paas, 2002).

Researchers have suggested that hyperlinking may increase extraneous load (Oliver & Hannafin, 2000). In a study of 39 undergraduate students in an educational computing course, Niederhauser, Reynolds, Salmen, and Skolmoski (2000) tested the impact of different navigational patterns on learning using hyperlinked text. They used surveys to assess students' reading ability, domain knowledge, and background using computers. Computer software was used to measure the time spent reading each screen and the navigation patterns, and a posttest questionnaire and essay assignment were employed to measure learning. As expected, they found that reading comprehension, background knowledge, and reading time were positively related to learning. They were surprised to learn, however, that using hyperlinked material to compare and contrast concepts had a negative influence on learning. The authors concluded that the hypertext environment's increased cognitive load negatively impacted student learning.

Similarly, Eveland and Dunwoody (2001) divided 219 students into five groups taught via different online materials. One group browsed a Web site using linear navigation buttons, while another group browsed a site with links embedded throughout the material to encourage students to explore the content nonlinearly. A third group used nonlinear links with linear navigational guides; the remaining students served as a paper-based and independent task control groups. All groups were given 15 minutes to study the material, and completed a posttest asking them to rate their motivation and Web expertise and the difficulty of learning. The paper-based control group outperformed two of the three Web-based groups, suggesting that Web-based hyperlinking, in the absence of advice, increased extraneous cognitive load associated with learning.

Consistent with Hill and Hannafin's (1997) finding related to prior system knowledge, limited technological familiarity may also increase extrinsic load. Clarke, Ayres, and Sweller (2005) assigned 24 Australian ninth-graders into four groups based on their experience using spreadsheets and mathematics abilities. They compared technology instruction prior to domain instruction with simultaneous instruction in both and measured student ability to perform math and spreadsheet problems and obtained subjective ratings of cognitive load. These researchers reported that initial technology instruction followed by domain instruction was most effective for students with low prior spreadsheet abilities, rather than teaching both concurrently. Concurrent instruction in technology and domain content apparently simultaneously increased extraneous, while decreasing germane, cognitive load.

Research on increasing germane load has flourished recently. Researchers report benefits from providing students with worked examples (problems showing an example along with the step-by-step solution process); likewise, self-explanation may help to increase schema creation (Gerjets, Scheiter, & Catrambone, 2004; Paas, 1992; Paas & van Merrienboer, 1994; Reed & Bolstad, 1991; Renkl, Atkinson, & Grosse, 2004; Renkl, Stark, Gruber, & Mandl, 1998; Sweller, 1988). Other methods for increasing germane load include the use of example elaboration and example comparison (Gerjets, Scheiter, & Catrambone, 2004), and fading procedures (Renkl & Atkinson, 2003; Renkl et al., 2004). As a result of highly developed mental models, students may better transfer learning (Paas & van Merrienboer, 1994). Since the goal is to minimize extraneous load while increasing germane load, these strategies hold considerable promise for organizing, structuring and supporting online learning.

Research on developing, instantiating, and inducing mental schemas further suggests the influence the cognitive load on to-be-learned concepts. In a study by Eveland, Cortese, Park, and Dunwoody (2004), two groups of participants (college students and nonstudents) explored for 20 minutes health-topic Web sites designed with either linear navigation or nonlinear navigation. They then post-tested participant understanding of factual information by distributing questionnaires and asking participants to list and rate relationships among concepts they remembered (knowledge structure density). Whereas participants learned factual information best from linear websites, nonlinear sites improved knowledge structure density which participants interpreted to be more transferable knowledge. The study also suggests that nonlinear websites may increase germane load (positive load); interestingly, in a previous study by the same researchers, nonlinear websites increased extraneous (negative) load (Eveland & Dunwoody, 2001).

While several studies examine extraneous load in TEDLEs, little research exists about intrinsic load. However, research from information-literacy studies may provide interesting insights. Jones, Ravid, and Rafaeli (2004) reported a trend towards high intrinsic load in informal online spaces based on an analysis of more than 2.65 million postings in over 600 Usenet newsgroups over a six-month period; the higher the intrinsic load, the lower the participation by the users. In addition to researching element-interactivity online, research on how varying levels of expertise impacts intrinsic load in TEDLEs could warrant more studies on the potential for adaptive learning in TEDLEs (Federico, 1999).

METACOGNITION

Metacognition refers to one's awareness of, and ability to manage, one's own cognitive processes (Flavell, 1977). Researchers and theorists tend to discuss metacognitive activity as involving the ability to anticipate, detect, and correct or "repair" understanding needs as they emerge (Schraw & Dennison, 1994). Like many cognitive phenomena, metacognitive awareness and skill are influenced by prior domain knowledge, experience, and expertise. As individuals become increasingly knowledgeable, experienced, and expert-like, their metacognitive awareness and skill increases.

Metacognitive awareness and skill may be especially relevant to learning from and during TEDLEs. Zion, Michalsky, and Mevarech (2005) argue that asynchronous learning networks (ALNs) allow students to review digital records of the learning that was constructed, enabling students to better monitor their learning and making cognition more visible while students develop metacognitive skills. The authors conducted a two-by-two experiment involving 407 Israeli tenth-grade microbiology students, and found that ALN students with metacognitive scaffolding performed significantly better than those in the face-to-face group with no scaffolding. No significant differences were found between the ALN students without metacognition help and the face-to-face group with the scaffolding, indicating that metacognition was the most effective method. This finding is in accord with authors such as Workman (2004), who suggested that the repetitive nature of self-paced computer-based education, where learners interact with material presented via CD-ROM and structured sequentially with multi-model instruction followed by review, provides cognitive cueing and supports metacognitive awareness "by prompting learners to reflect on their learning progress and allowing them to repeat material at critical junctures if needed" (p. 520).

Metacognitive proficiency in TEDLEs may be related to ability and prior knowledge. Oliver and Hannafin (2001), for example, reported that middle-school students lacked even basic metacognitive activity while attempting to solve science problems using Web-based resources. In their study, students aged 12–14 years of age relied on co-opted scaffolds to provide explicit direction rather than to induce metacognitive reflection as designed.

Smidt and Hegelheimer (2004) conducted a qualitative study of nine adult English as a second language (ESL) learners as part of a larger study on the use of Web-based video for a vocabulary- and listening-comprehension course. The researchers sampled high, middle, and low-performing ESL students in the course, and interviewed them regarding their learning strategies, which were categorized as either cognitive or metacognitive. Advanced learners exhibited both metacognitive and cognitive learning strategies, but intermediate and lower-level learners used mainly cognitive strategies suggesting greater metacognitive awareness and utilization among advanced students. They also reported that males were more likely to use metacognitive strategies, while females used more cognitive strategies in their learning.

Land and Greene (2000) found that metacognitive knowledge can sometimes compensate for limited system or domain knowledge. In their qualitative study, the authors studied undergraduate pre-service teachers working alone, in pairs, or in groups in an online instructional technology course. For two of the four cases studied, metacognitive knowledge seemed to build off of system and domain knowledge. However, for teachers who struggled with low domain/system knowledge, metacognitive knowledge compensated and helped them to complete tasks successfully. This suggests the importance of providing scaffolds to develop and regulate metacognitive knowledge and support ongoing reflection.

Schwartz, Andersen, Hong, Howard, and McGee (2004) suggested that individuals often fail to regulate meta-comprehension during online hypermedia learning because some mental resources must be used to interpret the material, thereby increasing extraneous cognitive load. They recruited 28 students between the ages of 9 and 17 to freely explore a science website in one of two formats: a conventional, linear outline format or a nonlinear format. Using the *Junior Metacognitive Awareness Inventory* and *How I Study Questionnaire*, they found that metacognitive skill was not a good predictor of retention for students using an outline structure, but it was for students using the nonlinear websites. The authors concluded that metacognitive skills are necessary but not sufficient for learning from hypermedia, and that well-designed TEDLEs need to provide familiar structures and conventions to reduce metacognitive demands.

In a study of 119 undergraduate students in educational psychology and child-development courses, Kaufman (2004) asked online learners to take notes using either a freeform method or strategically with the aid of a matrix. While taking notes, some students received prompts to reflect on their learning and note-taking. Students that received metacognitive prompts and took notes using a matrix performed significantly better on post-experiment achievement tests than did students in other groups; significantly, only three prompts per hour of note-taking yielded this improvement. Similarly, Bannert (2003) assigned 40 university students to experimental or control groups and asked them to study motivational psychology for 35 minutes via a Web-based learning environment. While the experimental group was prompted only three times to review their learning, those who received prompts performed better than non-prompted students on post-experiment performance assessments. These studies suggest that seemingly modest attempts to metacognitively scaffold TEDLEs can improve learning—especially for students who attempt to be strategic during their learning.

The World Wide Web, with its connecting nodes of information, has been characterized as a metaphor for human cognition (Mayer-Kress & Barczys, 1995); accordingly, TEDLEs might support the mapping and enactment of metacognitive scaffolding. Using a neural network model, Yeh and Lo (2005) developed a system for assessing students' metacognitive knowledge based on their Web-browsing abilities. They assigned 146 students enrolled in a freshman English course to participate in a Web-based learning activity. Prior to and following the activity, the researchers administered a metacognitive awareness inventory comprising 52 self-report items, thus providing a standardized measure of metacognitive knowledge. The researchers reported that their system accurately assessed metacognitive knowledge, which could potentially benefit students with language barriers or limitations, such as those learning language online, who might experience difficulties reporting their metacognitive knowledge through typical questionnaires. Though not yet tested on a significant scale, the capacity to identify and address metacognitive knowledge needs may prove helpful in mitigating problems associated with limited prior domain and system knowledge.

IMPLICATIONS

Research related to cognitive perspectives has several important implications for TEDLEs. First, it is apparent that motivational factors are as critical for online as for other learning environments. Importantly, both intrinsic and extrinsic aspects of motivation can be addressed in well-crafted TEDLEs. The initial, and to some extent continuing, assumption that technology provides inherent motivational benefits has been widely debunked. Individuals hold different values, draw from diverse backgrounds and experiences, and vary in their goals and expectations. Identifying individual differences across learners may well increase our capacity to accommodate diverse learner needs. Likewise, the affordances—available features, structures, and supports—will influence the extrinsic motivation potential of a TEDLE. Research clearly indicates that extrinsically-mediated motivation to engage and succeed increases as technical and navigation requirements decrease.

Next, theorists and researchers have underscored the need to assess and balance how cognitive resources are allocated. While the findings appear obvious, we rarely design or evaluate online learning environments based on processing requirements. Often, TEDLEs provide extensive sets of links, supplementary information, and tools presumed to support cognitive processing, but do they? Clearly, while learners have cognitive resources available, they are limited and they vary based on unique background and experiences. The cognitive load associated with online learning varies widely, and it can prove difficult to separate those loads that are relevant and necessary from those extraneous to a given individual's processing needs. Many structural organizers and scaffolds found helpful in text-based learning research have also proven valuable in mitigating extraneous load during online learning. Given wide variations in how online learning environments are organized and supported, the need to simultaneously maximize germane load and minimize extraneous load has particular import for TEDLEs.

Finally, while metacognition principles are perhaps the most intuitively relevant among TEDLE researchers, theorists, and practitioners, they are also among the least employed. Virtually all learning involves metacognitive regulation to some degree, but the cognitive demands associated with online learning can be especially formidable. Often, individuals decide what to study, judge the veracity of information they seek and encounter, determine when learning needs have been addressed, and otherwise manage their learning processes. Since metacognitive knowledge and skill are highly correlated with prior domain knowledge in a given lesson, and those lessons are generally intended for individuals without extensive domain knowledge, online learners are often in the dubious position of making metacognitive judgments for which they are ill-prepared. Research has indicated that online novice learners benefit from even occasional metacognitive prompts, suggesting that modest efforts to scaffold understanding may help to compensate for limited background as well as system knowledge.

CLOSING COMMENTS

We have advocated that design practices be grounded in defined epistemological and foundation roots and are consistent with research findings associated with those perspectives (see, e.g., Hannafin, Hannafin, Land, & Oliver, 1997; Hannafin & Hill, 2007; Kim & Hannafin, in press). Information-processing perspectives, while at odds with contemporary constructive perspectives, provide a well-articulated and richly studied knowledge base related to cognition, relationships between and among cognitive processes, methods to stimulate mental activity, and techniques to compensate for background and experiential differences among learners. We harbor no illusions as to the universality of information-processing principles for online learning; indeed, we encounter many circumstances in which TEDLEs cannot be effectively grounded in information-processing cognitive perspectives.

At the same time, we recognize the relevance of information processing perspectives to many individual cognitive dilemmas and design issues to be addressed. A great deal of knowledge and wisdom has been generated by cognitive psychologists. While this chapter represents a relatively narrow and selective sample of available research and theory, it is apparent that cognitive psychology has significant, though as yet largely untapped, potential to improve online learning.

REFERENCES

Anderson, J., & Pirolli, P. (1984). Spread of activation. *Journal of Experimental Psychology: Learning, Memory, and Cognition, 10*(4), 791–798.

Anderson, J., Reder, L., & Lebiere, C. (1996). Working memory: Activation limitations on retrieval. *Cognitive Psychology, 30*, 221–256.

Atkinson, R. C., & Shiffrin, R. M. (1968). Human memory: A proposed system and its control processes. In K. W. Spence & J. T. Spence (Eds.), *The psychology of learning and motivation: Advances in research and theory* (Vol. 2, pp. 89–195). New York: Academic Press.

Ausubel, D. P. (1968). *Educational psychology: A cognitive view*. New York: Holt, Rinehart and Winston.

Bannert, M. (2003). Effects of metacognitive help on knowledge acquisition in Web-based learning environments. *German Journal of Educational Psychology, 17*(1), 13–25.

Brunken, R., Plass, J., & Leutner, D. (2003). Direct measurement of cognitive load in multimedia learning. *Educational Psychologist, 38*(1), 53–61.

Bures, E. M., Amundsen, C. C., & Abrami, P. C. (2002). Motivation to learn via computer conferencing: Exploring how task-specific motivation and CC expectations are related to student acceptance of learning via CC. *Journal of Educational Computing Research, 27*(3), 249–264.

Clark, R. E. (1994). Media will never influence learning. *Educational Technology Research and Development, 42*(2), 21–29.

Clarke, T., Ayres, P., & Sweller, J. (2005). The impact of sequencing and prior knowledge on learning mathematics through spreadsheet applications. *Educational Technology Research and Development, 53*(3), 15–24.

Driscoll, M. P. (2000). *Psychology of learning for instruction* (2nd ed.). Boston: Allyn & Bacon.

Eveland, W. P., Cortese, J., Park, H., & Dunwoody, S. (2004). How Web site organization influences free recall, factual knowledge, and knowledge structure density. *Human Communication Research, 30*(2), 208–233.

Eveland, W. P., & Dunwoody, S. (2001). User control and structural isomorphism or disorientation and cognitive load? *Communication Research, 28*(1), 48.

Federico, P.-A. (1999). Hypermedia environments and adaptive instruction. *Computers in Human Behavior, 15*(6), 653–692.

Flavell, J. H. (1977). *Cognitive development*. Englewood Cliffs, NJ: Prentice-Hall.

Fleming, M. (1977). On pictures in educational research. *Instructional Science, 8*, 235–251.

Fox, E. J. (2006). Constructing a pragmatic science of learning and instruction with functional contextualism. *Educational Technology Research and Development, 54*(1), 5–36.

Gagne, R. (1984). *The conditions of learning and theory of instruction* (4th ed.). New York : Holt, Rinehart and Winston.

Gerjets, P., & Scheiter, K. (2003). Goal configurations and processing strategies as moderators between instructional design and cognitive load: Evidence from hypertext-based instruction. *Educational Psychologist, 38*(1), 33–41.

Gerjets, P., Scheiter, K., & Catrambone, R. (2004). Designing instructional examples to reduce intrinsic cognitive load: Molar versus modular presentation of solution procedures. *Instructional Science, 32*(1), 33–58.

Hannafin, M. J., Hannafin, K. M., Land, S., & Oliver, K. (1997). Grounded practice in the design of learning systems. *Educational Technology Research and Development, 45*(3), 101–117.

Hannafin, M. J., & Hill, J. R. (in press). Epistemology and the design of learning environments. In R. Reiser & J. Dempsey (Eds.), *Trends and issues in instructional design and technology* (2nd ed). Upper Saddle River, NJ: Merrill/Prentice-Hall.

Hannafin, M. J., Kim, M., & Kim, J. (2004). Reconciling research, theory and practice in Web-based teaching and learning. *Journal of Computing in Higher Education, 15*(2), 3–20.

Hannafin, M. J., & Rieber, L. P. (1989). Psychological foundations of instructional design for emerging computer-based instructional technologies: Part I & II. *Educational Technology Research and Development, 37*, 91–114.

Hee Jun, C., & Johnson, S. D. (2005). The effect of context-based video instruction on learning and motivation in online courses. *American Journal of Distance Education, 19*(4), 215–227.

Hill, J. R., & Hannafin, M. J. (1997). Cognitive strategies and learning from the World Wide Web. *Educational Technology Research and Development, 45*(4), 37–64.

Hooper, S., & Hannafin, M. J. (1991). Psychological perspectives on emerging instructional technologies: A critical analysis. *Educational Psychologist, 26*, 69–95.

Hsinyi, P., Chin-Chung, T., & Ying-Tien, W. (2006). University students' self-efficacy and their attitudes toward the Internet: The role of students' perceptions of the Internet. *Educational Studies, 32*(1), 73–86.

Iiyoshi, T., Hannafin, M. J., & Wang, F. (2005) Cognitive tools and student-centered learning: Rethinking tools, functions, and applications. *Educational Media International, 42*(4), 281–296.

Jones, Q., Ravid, G., & Rafaeli, S. (2004). Information overload and the message dynamics of online interaction spaces: A theoretical model and empirical exploration. *Information Systems Research, 15*(2), 194–210.

Kalyuga, S., Chandler, P., & Sweller, J. (1999). Managing split-attention and redundancy in multimedia instruction. *Applied Cognitive Psychology, 13*, 351–371.

Kaufman, D. F. (2004). Self-regulated learning in Web-based environments: Instructional tools designed to facilitate cognitive strategy use, metacognitive processing, and motivational beliefs. *Journal of Educational Computing Research, 30*(1 & 2): 139–161.

Kim, H., & Hannafin, M. J. (in press). Grounded design and Web-enhanced, case-based reasoning. *Educational Technology Research and Development.*

Kozma, R. (1987). The implications of cognitive psychology for computer-based learning tools. *Educational Technology, 27*(11), 20–25.

Land, S. M., & Greene, B. A. (2000). Project-based learning with the World Wide Web: A qualitative study of resource integration. *Educational Technology Research and Development, 48*(1), 45–67.

Land, S. M., & Hannafin, M. (1996). A conceptual framework for the development of theories-in-action with open-ended learning environments. *Educational Technology Research and Development, 44*(3), 37–53.

Laszlo, F., Jr., & Kupritz, V. W. (2003). The identification of online learning motives in use by undergraduate students. *Delta Pi Epsilon Journal, 45*(1), 63–72.

Lim, D. H., & Kim, H. (2003). Motivation and learner characteristics affecting online learning and learning application. *Journal of Educational Technology Systems, 31*(4), 423–439.

Linn, M. C. (1998). Cognition and distance learning. *Journal of the American Society for Information Science, 47*(11), 826–842

Massaro, D., & Cowan, N. (1993). Information processing models: Microscopes of the mind. *Annual Review of Psychology, 44*, 383–425.

Mayer-Kress, G., & Barczys, C. (1995). The global brain as an emergent structure from the worldwide computing network, and its implications for modeling. *The Information Society, 11*(1), 1–27.

Mei-Mei, C. (2005). Applying self-regulated learning strategies in a Web-based instruction: An investigation of motivation perception. *Computer Assisted Language Learning, 18*(3), 217–230.

Niederhauser, D. S., Reynolds, R. E., Salmen, D. J., & Skolmoski, P. (2000). The influence of cognitive load on learning from hypertext. *Journal of Educational Computing Research, 23*(3), 237–255.

Norman, D. (1982). *Learning and memory*. San Francisco: W.H. Freeman & Co.

Oliver, K., & Hannafin, M. J. (2000). Student management of Web-based hypermedia resources during open-ended problem solving. *Journal of Educational Research, 94*(2), 75–92.

Oliver, K., & Hannafin, M. J. (2001). Developing and refining mental models in open-ended learning environments: A case study. *Educational Technology Research and Development, 49*(4), 5–33.

Paas, F. G. W. C. (1992). Training strategies for attaining transfer of problem-solving skill in statistics: A cognitive-load approach. *Journal of Educational Psychology, 84*(4), 429–434.

Paas, F., Tuovinen, J., Tabbers, H., & Van Gerven, P. W. M. (2003). Cognitive load measurement as a means to advance cognitive load theory. *Educational Psychologist, 38*(1), 63–71.

Paas, F. G. W. C., & van Merrienboer, J. J. G. (1994). Variability of worked examples and transfer of geometrical problem-solving skills: A cognitive-load approach. *Journal of Educational Psychology, 86*, 122–133.

Paas, F. G. W. C., van Merrienboer, J. J. G., & Adam, J. J. (1994). Measurement of cognitive load in instructional research. *Perceptual and Motor Skills, 79*, 419–430.

Paivio, A. (1971). *Imagery and verbal processes.* New York: Holt, Rinehart and Winston.

Pollock, E., Chandler, P., & Sweller, J. (2002). Assimilating complex information. *Learning and Instruction, 12*(1), 61–86.

Pressley, M. (1977). Imagery and children's learning—Putting the picture in developmental perspective. *Review of Educational Research, 47*, 582–622.

Reed, S. K., & Bolstad, C. A. (1991). Use of examples and procedures in problem solving. *Journal of Experimental Psychology: Learning, Memory, and Cognition, 17*(4), 753–766.

Renkl, A., & Atkinson, R. K. (2003). Structuring the transition from example study to problem solving in cognitive skill acquisition: A cognitive load perspective. *Educational Psychologist, 38*(1), 15–22.

Renkl, A., Atkinson, R. K., & Grosse, C. S. (2004). How fading worked solution steps works: A cognitive load perspective. *Instructional Science, 32*(1), 59–82.

Renkl, A., Stark, R., Gruber, H., & Mandl, H. (1998). Learning from worked-out examples: The effects of example variability and elicited self-explanations. *Contemporary Educational Psychology, 23*, 90–108.

Rummelhart, D., & Ortony, A. (1977). The representation of knowledge in memory. In R. C. Anderson, R. J. Spiro, & W. E. Montague (Eds.), *Schooling and the acquisition of knowledge.* Hillsdale, NJ: Lawrence Erlbaum Associates.

Salomon, G. (1979). *Interaction of media, cognition and learning.* San Francisco: Jossey-Bass.

Salomon, G. (1986). Information technologies: What you see is not (always) what you get. *Educational Psychologist, 20*, 207–216.

Schmeeckle, J. M. (2003). Online training: An evaluation of the effectiveness and efficiency of training law enforcement personnel over the Internet. *Journal of Science Education and Technology, 12*(3), 205–260.

Schraw, G., & Dennison, R. S. (1994). Assessing metacognition. *Contemporary Educational Psychology, 19*, 460–475.

Schrum, L., Burbank, M. D., Engle, J., Chambers, J. A., & Glassett, K. F. (2005). Post-secondary educators' professional development: Investigation of an online approach to enhancing teaching and learning. *Internet and Higher Education, 8*(4), 279–289.

Schunk, D. H. (1990). Goal setting and self-efficacy during self-regulated learning. *Educational Psychologist, 25*, 71–86.

Schwartz, N. H., Andersen, C., Hong, N., Howard, B., & McGee, S. (2004). The influence of metacognitive skills on learners' memory information in a hypermedia environment. *Journal of Educational Computing Research, 31*(1), 77–93.

Shuell, T. (1986). Cognitive conceptions of learning. *Review of Educational Research, 56*(4), 411–436.

Simon, H. (1979). Information processing models of cognition. *Annual Review of Psychology, 30*, 363–396.

Smidt, E., & Hegelheimer, V. (2004). Effects of online academic lectures on ESL listening comprehension, incidental vocabulary acquisition, and strategy use. *Computer Assisted Language Learning, 17*(5), 517–556.

Song, L. (2005). *Adult learners' self-directed learning in online environments: Process, personal attribute, and context.* Unpublished dissertation, The University of Georgia, Athens, GA.

Song, L., Singleton, E. S., Hill, J. R., & Koh, M. H. (2004). Improving online learning: Student perceptions of useful and challenging characteristics. *Internet and Higher Education, 7*(1), 59–70.

Sweller, J. (1988). Cognitive load during problem solving. *Cognitive Science, 12*, 257–285.

van Merrienboer, J. J. G., Schuurman, J. G., de Croock, M. B. M., & Paas, F. G. W. C. (2002). Redirecting
learners' attention during training: Effects on cognitive load, transfer test performance and training efficiency. *Learning and Instruction, 12*(1), 11–37.

van Merrionboer, J. J. G., & Ayres, P. (2005). Research on cognitive load theory and its design implications
for e-learning. *Educational Technology Research and Development, 53*(3), 5–13.

Whipp, J. L., & Chiarelli, S. (2004). Self-regulation in a Web-based course: A case study. *Educational
Technology Research and Development, 52*(4), 5–22.

Workman, M. (2004). Performance and perceived effectiveness in computer-based and computer-aided education: Do cognitive styles make a difference? *Computers in Human Behavior, 20*(4), 517.

Yeh, S.-W., & Lo, J.-J. (2005). Assessing metacognitive knowledge in Web-based CALL: A neural network approach. *Computers & Education, 44*(2), 97–113.

Zion, M., Michalsky, T., & Mevarech, Z. (2005). The effects of metacognitive instruction embedded within
an asynchronous learning network on scientific inquiry skills. *International Journal of Science Education, 27*(8), 957–983.

11

Group Development in Online Distance Learning Groups

Kayleigh Carabajal

Central New Mexico Community College

Deborah LaPointe and Charlotte N. Gunawardena

The University of New Mexico

This chapter begins with a brief overview and review of group development models. The second section discusses the implications of a system's theory perspective that include tensions between individual identity and group identification, and complexity theory analyses. Research related to the technological, task, and psycho-social dimensions of group development in online learning groups (OLGs) is discussed in section three. The chapter concludes with recommendations for future research.

GROUP DEVELOPMENT MODELS

Loosely defined, groups consist of two or more individuals interacting in such a way that each person exerts influence on and is influenced by the other individuals in the group (Shaw, 1976). Groups are an integral part of society and, at the most basic level, all groups serve two main needs for members: to attain the defining goal or central task of the group (i.e., the purpose the group was formed to achieve) and to satisfy the social needs of the members. In the case of OLGs, the important task-related needs of the group center on the enhancement or achievement of learning goals. As group members organize themselves in pursuit of these goals, the content of their communication shifts from one need to the other. Conflicts then develop between task-oriented learning goals and the socio-emotional needs of the members. When one aspect of this ongoing conflict is resolved, the topic of communication can then advance. The more cohesive a group, the more likely the group will progress from one stage to the next. Achieving a balance in this interplay between emotional and task-oriented needs is the basis for a majority of group-development theories.

Group development is a characteristic ascribed to groups as they change over time; a function of both group structure and group process (Hare, Blumberg, Davies, & Kent, 1994; Ridgeway, 1983) and group development represents "the degree of maturity and cohesion that a group achieves over time as members interact, learn about one another, and structure relationships and roles within the group" (Mennecke, Hoffer, & Wynne, 1992, p. 526). Group-development models described elsewhere in more detail (Carabajal, LaPointe, & Gunawardena, 2003) may generally be classified into one of three categories: progressive, cyclical, or nonsequential models. Progressive and cyclical models focus on the sequential stages of group development; nonsequential models shift this focus to recognize that contingent factors may impact and alter the observed stages. The more dynamic nature of the nonsequential model descriptions is in direct contrast to the cyclical and progressive models that assume groups are closed systems that exhibit a somewhat static developmental pattern that is unresponsive to impacts exerted by the environment in which the group is embedded.

Progressive Models

Progressive models imply that groups exhibit an increasing degree of maturity and performance over time (Mennecke, et al., 1992). Bales' (1950) equilibrium model assumes that a group continually divides efforts between instrumental (task-related) needs and expressive (socio-emotional) needs and seeks to maintain this balance through three progressive phases: (a) orientation (exploration), (b) evaluation (seeking opinions), and (c) control (norms that guide action). Successful group outcomes are dependent on two factors: how well the group can solve the tasks facing it (task function), and how well the group can maintain member satisfaction (socio-emotional function). Tuckman's (1965; Tuckman & Jensen, 1977) *Team Development Model* assumes groups develop in a definite order of progression from one phase to the next: (a) forming (dependence and testing), (b) storming (conflict), (c) norming (structure and cohesion), (d) performing (goal attainment), and (e) adjournment (mourning). Similar to Bales' task-oriented and socio-emotional behaviors (Bales & Strodbeck, 1951), each of the stages contains two aspects: interpersonal relationships (group structure), and task behaviors.

Cyclical Models

Cyclical models may be either linear or recurring. A linear cyclical model assumes a sequence of life-cycle events but differs from the progressive models because of the emphasis placed on the terminal phase that either results in group dissolution or regeneration to another cycle (Mennecke et al., 1992). Recurring cyclical models assume groups oscillate between various issues that can never be resolved in more than a temporary way (Mann, Gibbard, & Hartmann, 1967) and phases emerge, recede, and re-emerge to be confronted later in greater depth (Sudweeks & Allbritton, 1996). Schutz's (1958) fundamental interpersonal relationships orientation (FIRO) model attempts to explain group development in response to three interpersonal needs: (a) inclusion of members in the group, (b) control of members' activities, and (c) affection between members. Schutz' theory maintains that interpersonal areas of need do not occur in mutually exclusive phases. All three areas are always present, each emphasized at different times. Every interpersonal relation is based upon a principle of group integration and group resolution, and group members will back out of the group using a sequence of behaviors opposite the sequence used as they entered the group.

Nonsequential Models

In contrast, nonsequential models do not emphasize sequential events; rather, occurring events are the result of contingent factors. These models suggest the possibility of differential developmental paths based on the interplay of group structure and group-process variables.

According to McGrath's (1990, 1991) *Time, Interaction, and Performance* (TIP) model, groups interact with and contribute to systems at three levels and perform three distinct functions: (a) production, (b) well-being, and (c) member-support functions. These functions are similar to the task-related and socio-emotional needs that Bales (1950) and others (Tuckman, 1965) have suggested. Groups realize these functions through several modes of group activity and group process: inception, problem solving, conflict resolution, and execution (performance). The TIP model also suggests that group process and development must be investigated both in terms of task-related behaviors and their socio-emotional behaviors. According to McGrath (1990, 1991) viewing groups on one dimension alone is insufficient for understanding how a group develops over time. Gersick (1988, 1989) proposed a punctuated equilibrium model that posits group development and change occur in a stepwise manner. Stable periods of "habitual routines" are altered by abrupt transitional periods. Groups hold on to current practices (an equilibrium position) until forced to alter those practices because of crises or temporal constraints (a state of disequilibrium). This model suggests group development behavior patterns vary according to the cues the group encounters as they process a task.

Consistent Themes across the Models

A number of consistent themes can be posited across the proposed models. First, almost all models possess similar stages. This is noteworthy because most models were developed in highly dissimilar settings, ranging from therapy groups to ad hoc experimental groups. It is not surprising that observers in such varying contexts recorded a variable number of stages and applied different labels to basically similar processes. This suggests each model likely represents one example of many different potential developmental paths as a consequence of variations in a number of variables: group structure, composition, context, group goals, physical and technological environment, task type, and other contingencies (McGrath, 1990, 1991; Poole & Roth, 1989; Mennecke et al., 1992).

Second, it is also likely that certain stages—found consistently throughout the models—are crucial for a group to achieve success as it develops, but that the actual sequencing may not be important, suggesting that, if the contingent factors warrant, at least some of the traditional phases will be observed as a group develops over time (McGrath, 1990, 1991).

Finally, newer models of group development assume a far more dynamic view of group development. Nonsequential models suggest groups are components of a larger system responding to inputs from and generating inputs for the environment; likewise, groups are composed of individuals who contribute resources but at the same time diminish resources from the group (Mennecke et al., 1992). These themes are consistent with an increased attention in the literature to the view that groups are social systems and must be examined from a system's perspective. Doing so presents a number of implications to group researchers.

SYSTEM'S THEORY PERSPECTIVE

Arrow, McGrath, and Berdahl (2000) argued for a system's perspective in the study of groups by positing that groups are complex, adaptive, and dynamic and must be studied holistically and unconstrained by an analytical-experimental paradigm. While former group-development models and research focused on member influence, patterns of interaction, or task performance, general system theory emphasizes the importance of examining the larger context in which the group exists, the nature of the whole group phenomena, the interactional events between the members, and the intrapsychic processes within each member. This view effectively expands the boundaries of substantive interest to researchers beyond a limited number of relevant variables and simulta-neously focuses attention on the psycho-social dimension of group development.

Complexity Theory

Complexity theory provides a new model for examining groups from this perspective. Complex-ity theory, emerging from general system theory, cybernetics and catastrophe theory (Berta-lanaffy, 1968), is concerned with the behavior of certain kinds of complex systems over time. The systems of interest to complexity theory are dynamic systems which, under certain circumstances, perform in predictable and regular ways; under other circumstances these systems—capable of changing over time—exhibit behavior in which regularity and predictability is lost. Growing applications of complexity theory to group development are found in the organizational man-agement literature (Campbell, Flynn, & Hay, 2002; McGrath, 1997).

Complexity theory suggests that systems behavior is divided into two zones, stable and unstable, plus the boundary between them. There is a stable, extremely predictable zone (order), where, if it is disturbed, the system returns to its initial state. There is also a zone of instability or extreme unpredictability (chaos), where a small disturbance leads to movement away from the starting point, and, in turn, generates further divergence. What is particularly interesting is that, under appropriate circumstances, systems may operate at the boundary between these zones, sometimes called a phase transition or the "region of complexity," where systems are most likely to adapt and evolve into higher-level systems (Campbell et al., 2002). Here the system exhibits a bounded instability—that is, unpredictability of specific behavior within a predictable general structure of behavior. It is within the "region of complexity" that creativity, innovation, and trans-formational learning can best occur. Social groups do seem to exhibit patterns of either being somewhat chaotic or somewhat orderly, or, at their most creative and complex, when they are in the region between.

According to Campbell et al. (2002), complexity theory can serve as an overlay to explain what is occurring across a number of group-development models. For example, in Tuckman and Jensen's (1977) model, forming corresponds to participants bringing in a history of order, storm-ing represents a pattern of chaos, norming signifies the introduction of simple rules which guide the transition from chaos to complexity, performing is what the groups do in the creative zone, and adjourning refers to transition back to the world of order. Similarly, the punctuated equilib-rium model emphasized the contrast between a period of relative stability, punctuated by initial and midpoint periods of instability, change, and even transformation (Arrow et al., 2000). Groups likely move between order and complexity, with the ever-present possibility that either external inputs (nonsequential models) or internal conflict (progressive and cyclical models) may push the group into chaos with the ever-present threat of dissolution. In this manner, complexity theory may literally and conceptually explain group-system patterns which are sometimes orderly, some-times chaotic, and sometimes complex, and may offer insight into the role of the learning facili-tator in enhancing these transitions.

Of importance to researchers, analyses such as this can inform practitioners by illuminating systems-centered practice and enhancing system potentiality. Beyond describing the mixture of order, chaos, and complexity, researchers in the field now seek to understand the conditions under which groups transition from one phase to the other. It then becomes critical to test whether using the phases of development to orient and direct instructor/learning facilitator interventions con-tributes to the group's effectiveness. Keeping groups fairly small or restricting the links between participants through the use of subgroups; allowing supportive comments while forbidding destructive, critical feedback; creating an environment in which participants are willing to work toward a common goal and move toward that goal collectively; and preparing the instructor to assume a role that supports direct internal feedback and weaving or connecting events with awareness may promote group activity in the region of complexity (Campbell et al., 2002).

Individual Identity Needs

Looking beyond the initial focus on task-related and social needs to include the impact of individual-identity needs is a third implication in adopting a system's perspective. In addition to group processes involved in group development, individual members face a paradoxical tension in shifting from an individual focus to group identification (Smith, 2005). Emotional tensions exist between the individual- and the group- (Smith & Berg, 1987) developmental processes. Success of the group is related to the active participation and the intrinsic/extrinsic goals and needs of the individual group members. A tension exists between wanting to be affiliated with a group and yet wanting to be seen as a contributing individual member, especially in a group that is functioning well and successfully accomplishing prescribed tasks. Emotional challenges surface when the group members engage in task-related work and narrow their focus to reach consensus toward group decisions and accomplishing the group task. According to Smith (2005), the back-and-forth movement toward the group and away from the group continues each time a group needs to achieve consensus. Periods of emotional challenge are followed by positive comments after the group task is completed and group members begin to reflect on their process and work. The cyclical process of moving to connect with the group and pulling away from the group to avoid a threat to individual members' sense of identity must also be factored into the study of group-development phases. Unless group members make the shift from individual to group, group members often fail to become a group and attain skills necessary to achieve group goals.

Linking Group Development and the Achievement of Learning Goals

The theories related to group development are intended to provide insight into the processes at work when individuals come together as a group for specific purposes. Group processes are composed of the constantly changing patterned behaviors or interactions through which groups progress toward a goal. Recent research attempts to link group-development and group-process models to collaborative learning outcomes for which group-development is a requisite. Two proposed group-process models are particularly well suited for illuminating group processes that promote online collaborative learning. One such model was elaborated by Gibb and Gibb (1967). The Trust-Level (TORI) framework reflects the manifestation of four group processes: Trust formation, Open communication, Realization of goals, and Interdependence. According to this theory, as groups develop, fears become superseded by trust. When trust is high, relative to fear, participants function well, whereas when the reverse is true, groups break down and do not develop. The growth of engaged participants, i.e., group development, occurs as a movement from fear towards increasing trust. According to Murphy and Laferriére (2005), these processes can be monitored and, it is expected, facilitated with the aim of orienting the group toward better levels of trust and open communication. Murphy (2004) proposes a six-stage group-process model that considers both interaction and collaboration in online learning groups. This sequential framework is built on a hierarchy of six stages: learners' (a) creating their social presence as real people to their classmates, (b) articulating their individual perspectives, (c) accommodating and reflecting back others' perspectives, (d) co-constructing new perspectives and meanings, (e) building shared goals and purposes, and (f) producing shared products. In this model, the first three stages are the prerequisites and foundations for the final three. Promoting collaboration can be facilitated and utilized to counteract participants' tendency to remain at the individual level rather than group or collaborative effort.

Groups, then, are composed of a set of patterned, dynamic relations among three types of elements: people who are the group's membership, the group tasks that make up the groups' projects, and the group's technology. Groups develop patterns of relations among these elements. "A group, therefore, can be described as a complex network of member-task-technology ties" (McGrath, 1997, p. 18). The network of these dimensions has a profound effect upon group structure, process, and development within OLGs.

ONLINE GROUP DIMENSIONS

Technological Dimension

Traditionally, face-to-face groups are associated with a place and location, leading members to associate a sense of group membership and shared purpose with the place. The sense of place suggests that group membership is perceived both structurally and psycho-socially (Porter, 2004). An online group uses networked telecommunications systems to create, exchange, and perceive information and engage in group activities. This adds a technological dimension to online group development. The structural component of the technological dimension provides the gathering place that reinforces the socio-psychological component—the group's purpose—and meets the group's needs (Kim, 2000). Research relating to the technological dimension indicates the choice of the CMC technology has important consequences for the successful accomplishment of group tasks and the successful maintenance of the group (Ahern & El-Hindi, 2000).

In 2003, when our chapter for the first edition of this *Handbook* was written, most online group communication and group development occurred through asynchronous modes. Today online groups increasingly operate in blended learning environments and use a variety of collaborative, synchronous technologies to communicate and accomplish their work. Baskin, Barker, and Woods (2005) call such an environment "ICT-rich." The technologies include Voice over Internet Protocol (VoIP), Instant Messaging (IM) with voice conferencing, browser sharing, document and application sharing, shared workspaces, presentations, whiteboards, Web casts, blogs, and wikis. Frequently these tools are contained within a learning-management system that also includes the original asynchronous forms of online communication.

Communicating and accomplishing work are no longer limited to text, the timing of work is no longer restricted to individuals working alone offline, and the speed of response from group members can be seconds rather than days, thereby creating more social cues and a greater sense of the group. Groups can select technologies and set the timing of work to better match the characteristics of the work and needs of group members. With a greater mix of tools available, selecting the right mix of tools as well as designing appropriate tasks to encourage group process and accomplishment of group tasks, create insight and understanding, and facilitate learning becomes a critical skill of the online facilitator (Fisher, Thompson, & Silverberg, 2004/2005) and group members.

The technological dimension has both a technical and a social component. The technology provides a mediated place where the social component and task accomplishment can occur. The effectiveness of the communication technology is largely dependent upon the tools and the degree to which those tools facilitate a shared dialogue (Gallini & Zhang, 1997). Also, the degree of the technology's fit to the richness of information that can be transmitted and the information richness requirements of the task (Hollingshead, McGrath, & O'Connor, 1993) determine the technology's effectiveness. The technology must allow group members to contribute private knowledge; provide scaffolded assistance and interaction tools needed for members to adequately relate concepts and experience; and offer a space for the group's working memory, long-term memory, and archives for the group's extended memory (Smith, 1994). The technological dimension determines what documents can be saved; how and when intermediate and finished products are saved; as well as whether work is searchable, shared, and reusable. The technology tracks individual and group actions, provides for both public and private exchanges, and helps the group monitor its progress, provide feedback, and celebrate specific benchmarks.

Blanchard (2004) suggests the technology provides group members with cues about where the interaction occurs, where group members are in the flow of conversations with other members, and how other members are present. These cues present the social component of the technology dimension, which refers to the degree to which the technology can be used to create a sense of social presence. Social presence is defined as the degree of salience of others in the interaction and the consequent salience of the interpersonal relationship (Gunawardena & Zittle, 1997). Social presence is both a factor of the medium as well as of the communicators and their presence (Gunawardena & Zittle, 1997). Social presence determines the degree to which collaborative partners perceive each other, moderates the communication that focuses on the socio-emotional communication, and maintains the group's well being. Collaborative, synchronous technologies provide more social cues, increase spontaneity, and add a richer sense of presence and fidelity to group communication. The perceived association with other group members and their ideas becomes the initial step in the development of group awareness, group skills, management of the group-work experience (Baskin, et al., 2005), and emergence of group roles (De Laat & Lally, 2004).

Task Dimension

A predominant finding in the literature is that CMC and face-to-face groups differ in the frequency and content of interaction with face-to-face groups generating more communication units than CMC. Research suggests only 40% of a face-to-face group process is spent on task-focused interactions, implying more than half of a group's communication is off-task (Huang & Wei, 2000). Guadagno and Cialdini (2002) found that CMC groups focused less attention on their partners and focused more attention on accomplishing the group's assigned task. Other researchers as well have found CMC groups exchange more task-oriented messages as a proportion of their total messages (Hillman, 1999; Kahai & Cooper, 1999). Palloff and Pratt (1999), however, reported that, similar to face-to-face groups, 42% of group online messages were directed toward group relationship rather than toward group task. Rose and Flowers (2003) found 41% of messages posted were of a cognitive nature while 36% were related to organizing the task. Rose and Flowers (2003) also found that assigning roles to groups involved in problem-solving learning situations influenced the function, level, and interconnectedness of the group interaction and decreased the time the group spent organizing and clarifying roles before initiating work on the task.

Valacich, Dennis, and Connolly's (1994) research suggested that when groups work online, anonymity and idea generation are increased. Individuals working in large online groups feel a greater sense of anonymity, are less inhibited, and feel freer to express their ideas. They also have a tendency to produce more unique ideas. The diversity of opinions generated, however, may be responsible for the fact that CMC groups experience more difficulty reaching consensus and exhibit more choice shift (defined as the degree to which team decisions differ from the initial opinions of the members). However, the productivity loss in CMC groups is overcome as more group members contributing to the group discussion maximize the group's potential (Olaniran, 1994; Hedlund, Ilgen, & Hollenbeck, 1998).

CMC groups quickly become overwhelmed with information overload. Information overload is a function of group size and social behavior rather than a characteristic of the technology. Optimal group size has been researched as an influential factor determining the number of messages exchanged and impacting the amount of opportunity for ideas to flow and develop. A group either too large or small restricts ideas and voices. Fisher, Thompson, and Silverberg (2004/2005) found online groups need at least 15 members to ensure a minimum of messages, 25 was best for student and instructor satisfaction, large groups worked well for conferences and discussions, and small groups of three to five members worked best for joint projects. More than 10 members are needed for collaborative dialogue (Paulus, 2005). Palloff and Pratt (1999) advise that synchronous meetings be small enough to allow full participation and prevent information overload, while an asynchronous meeting can have larger participation depending upon the skills of the facilitator (Fisher et al., 2004/2005).

In addition to group size, type of task assigned determines group performance. For a task with a few steps to perform, the group will perform at the level of its best group member. If a task has multiple parts and no one group member possesses all the information and skills necessary to solve it, the need for discussion is greater. The group will outperform the level of its best group members.

Paulus (2005) observed online groups performing either a synthesis task or an application task to determine if the groups performed their task by cooperating or collaborating. A cooperative task promotes division of labor, task specialization, and individual responsibility for part of the final product. In contrast, a collaborative task requires a dialogue with others to create awareness of one's thinking, clarify reasoning, and construct common meaning. Like other researchers, Paulus found 62% of messages were related to logistical issues, technical concerns, and social exchanges. After becoming organized, the synthesis group used collaboration while the application group used a cooperative approach to the task.

A precaution for designers of group tasks is that groups may focus more on completion of the task over learning, constructing new knowledge, or acquiring group skills to transfer to subsequent courses or the community of practice. Knowledge gain, effective group processes, and outcomes result from effectively designed group projects that provide the link between group behaviors and group effectiveness. Swigger and Brazile (1995) delineated effective group behaviors and monitored groups' processes via their actions in a computer-supported learning environment looking for evidence of effective and ineffective behaviors and then coaching members to become more effective group problem-solvers. The effective group behaviors were (a) establishing correct operating procedures, (b) analyzing problems, (c) establishing criteria, (d) generating alternative solutions, and (e) evaluating solutions as well as active exchange of information.

Psycho-Social Dimension

The purpose of every group discussion is two-fold: (a) to ensure group goal achievement and (b) to provide member satisfaction and keep the group together (Pavitt & Johnson, 1999). Although the technology usually garners most of the attention, it is social behavior that sustains the online group over time. Group task interactions involve interaction among multiple participants, who need to maintain some degree of mutual caring and understanding (Baker, Hansen, Joiner, & Traum, 1999). Graham (2003) believes that online groups can be taught to establish group norms which will later help them communicate and negotiate throughout the groups' life cycles. However, Michinov, Michinov, and Toczek-Capelle (2004) write that social identity is determined by the groups to which one belongs, and mere categorization of people into distinct groups is sufficient for group members to feel a sense of belonging and subsequently take on the known characteristics of the group, changing their individual behaviors.

The sense of membership is experienced by social processes of exchanging support, creating identities, building trust, and establishing group norms (Blanchard & Markus, 2002) rather than through the technological dimension. Group members establish their identities, tend to the tools, manage the files and work, follow established ground rules, keep group members' e-mail addresses up to date, and participate by generating messages, responding to messages, and creating and consuming content. When members fail to create relevant content, and read and respond to each other's postings, the group fails. Without group-maintenance activities, even the wide assortment of synchronous and asynchronous technologies cannot sustain the CMC group.

The group task may require group members to question and clarify their underlying assumptions. Group members will have to feel a certain level of caring and trust to disclose those assumptions. In a group, there is an implied promise to provide at least some of the evidence and reasons when a group member poses a belief. Therefore, the social aspect of CMC is an important element that contributes to the overall satisfaction of a task-oriented or academic computer conference (Gunawardena & Zittle, 1997). The low amount of off-task communication mentioned previously may hinder the computer-mediated group's ability to maintain group well-being and provide member support necessary for gaining and maintaining consensus and supporting the group decision or problem solution (McDonald & Gibson, 1998; Kahai & Cooper, 1999). Yet, positive interpersonal relationships develop in online groups (Brandon & Hollingshead, 1999). In fact, Walther found several instances wherein CMC groups surpassed the level of affection and emotion found in traditional face-to-face groups (Walther, 1996).

RECOMMENDATIONS FOR FUTURE RESEARCH

The increasing level of research related to the functional perspectives of online groups is encouraging. The research addresses the design of group tasks and even scaffolding group processes. In a parallel fashion, the literature on group development continues to grow. Despite the burgeoning literature, many challenges for online learning-group researchers remain. Research on effectual methods for developing groups and, more importantly, streamlining group formation within temporal constraints frequently imposed in online learning environments is scant at best. Methods to (a) recognize and incent group development in real time and thereby influence further development formatively, (b) shift the locus of learning from instructor-driven to group-developed, and (c) effectively evaluate group-based learning products, are largely anecdotal. Preeminently, the connection between group-development processes and collaborative learning remains largely unexplored.

Simply stated, social behavior does not have a technological solution. Providing the opportunity for technologically mediated, many-to-many, learner-to-learner interaction does not guarantee collaborative learning groups will develop online. We cannot assume that because a group of learners come together as a virtual community with similar individual learning-related intents and purposes that it will eventually develop fully and be able to achieve common goals and shared understandings. Creating this opportunity is but the first step. For collaborative learning to occur, we must address the challenges inherent in furthering our understanding of how to more explicitly and effectively counteract learners' tendency to remain at the level of individuals rather than engage as a group entity. Recent research demonstrates that group-development theories can be utilized to assist us in the process of helping online learners become more effective group members and fully potentiate the learning system's knowledge productivity.

REFERENCES

Ahern, T. C., & El-Hindi, A. E. (2000). Improving the instructional congruency of a computer-mediated small-group discussion: A case study in design and delivery. *Journal of Research on Computing in Education, 32*(3), 385–400.

Arrow, H., McGrath, J. E., & Berdahl, J. L. (2000). *Small groups as complex systems: Formation, coordination, development, and adaptation.* Thousand Oaks, CA: Sage.

Baker, M., Hansen, T., Joiner, R., & Traum, D. (1999). The role of grounding in collaborative learning tasks. In P. Dillenbourg (Ed.), *Collaborative learning: Cognitive and computational approaches* (pp. 31–63.) New York: Pergamon.

Bales, R. F. (1950). *Interaction process analysis.* Cambridge, MA: Addison-Wesley.

Bales, R. F., & Strodbeck, F. L. (1951). Phases in group problem solving. *Journal of Abnormal and Social Psychology, 46*, 485–495.

Baskin, C., Barker, M., & Woods, P. (2005). When group work leaves the classroom does group skills development also go out the window? *British Journal of Educational Technology, 36*(1), 19–31.

Bertalanaffy, L. (1968). *General system theory: Foundations, development, applications.* New York: G. Graziller.

Blanchard, A. (2004). Virtual behavior settings: An application of behavior setting theories to virtual communities. *Journal of Computer Mediated Communication, 9*(2). Retrieved December 9, 2004, from http://jcmc.indiana.edu/vol9/issue2/blanchard.html

Blanchard, A. L., & Markus, M. L. (2002). The experienced "sense" of a virtual community: Characteristics and processes. *The Data Base for Advances in Information Systems, 35*(1), 65–79.

Brandon, D. P., & Hollingshead, A. B. (1999). Collaborative learning and computer-supported groups. *Communication Education, 18*(2), 109–126.

Campbell, J., Flynn, D. J., & Hay, J. (2002, July). *The group development process seen through the lens of complexity theory.* Paper presented at the Fifteenth World Congress of Sociology in Brisbane, Australia.

Carabajal, K., LaPointe, D., & Gunawardena, C. (2003). Group development in online learning communities. In M. G. Moore & W. Anderson (Eds.), *Handbook of distance education.* Mahwah, NJ: Lawrence Erlbaum Associates.

De Laat, M., & Lally, V. (2004). It's not so easy: Researching the complexity of emergent participant roles and awareness in asynchronous networked learning discussions. *Journal of Computer Assisted Learning, 20*, 165–171.

Fisher, M., Thompson, G. S., & Silverberg, D. A. (2004/2005). Effective group dynamics in e-learning: Case study. *Journal of Educational Technology Systems, 33*(3), 205–222.

Gallini, J. K., & Zhang, Y. (1997). Socio-cognitive constructs and characteristics of classroom communities: An exploration of relationships. *Journal of Educational Computing Research, 17*(4), 321–339.

Gersick, C. J. G. (1988). Time and transition in work teams: Toward a new model of group development. *Academy of Management Journal, 31*, 941.

Gersick, C. J. G. (1989). Marking time: Predictable transitions in task groups. *Academy of Management Journal, 32*, 274–309.

Gibb, J., & Gibb, L. (1967). Humanistic elements in group growth. In J. Bugental (Ed.), *Challenges of humanistic psychology.* New York: McGraw-Hill.

Graham, C. R. (2003). A model of norm development for computer-mediated teamwork. *Small Group Research, 34*(3), 322–352.

Guadagno, R. E., & Cialdini, R. B. (2002). Online persuasion: An examination of gender differences in computer-mediated interpersonal influence. *Group Dynamics: Theory, Research, and Practice, 1*(6), 38–51.

Gunawardena, C. N., & Zittle, F. J. (1997). Social presence as a predictor within a computer-moderated conferencing environment. *The American Journal of Distance Education, 11*(3), 8–26.

Hare, A. P., Blumberg, H. H., Davies, M. F., & Kent, M. V. (1994). *Small group research: A handbook.* Norwood, NJ: Ablex Publishing Company.

Hedlund, J., Ilgen, D. R., & Hollenbeck, J. R. (1998). Decision accuracy in computer-mediated versus face-to-face decision-making teams. *Organizational Behavior and Human Decision Processes, 76*(2), 30–47.

Hillman, D. C. A. (1999). A new method for analyzing patterns of interaction. *The American Journal of Distance Education, 13*(2), 37–47.

Hollingshead, A., McGrath J., & O'Connor, K. (1993). Group task performance and communication technology: A longitudinal study of computer-mediated versus face-to-face work groups. *Small Group Research, 24*(3), 307–333.

Huang, W. H., & Wei, K. K. (2000). An empirical investigation of the effects of group support systems (GSS) and task type on group interactions from an influence perspective. *Journal of Management Information Systems, 17*(2), 181–206.

Kahai, S. S., & Cooper, R. B. (1999). The effect of computer-mediated communication on agreement and acceptance. *Journal of Management Information Systems, 16*(1), 165–189.

Kim, A. J. (2000). *Community building on the Web.* Berkeley, CA: Peachpit Press.

Mann, R. D., Gibbard, G. S., & Hartmann, J. J. (1967*). Interpersonal styles and group development.* New York: Wiley.

McGrath, J. E. (1990). Time matters in groups. In J. Galegher, R. E. Kraut, & C. Egido (Eds.), *Intellectual teamwork, social and technological foundations of cooperative work.* Hillsdale, NJ: Lawrence Erlbaum.

McGrath, J. E. (1991). Time, interaction, and performance (TIP): A theory of groups. *Small Group Research, 22*(2), 147–174.

McGrath, J. E. (1997). Small group research, that once and future field: An interpretation of the past with an eye to the future. *Group Dynamics, 1*(1), 7–27.

McDonald, J., & Gibson, C. C. (1998). Interpersonal dynamics and group development in computer conferencing. *The American Journal of Distance Education, 12*(1), 7–25.

Mennecke, B. E., Hoffer, J. A., & Wynne, B. E. (1992). The implications of group development and history for group support system theory and practice. *Small Group Research, 23*(4), 524–572.

Michinov, N., Michinov, E., & Toczek-Capelle, M.-C. (2004). Social identity, group processes, and performance in synchronous computer-mediated communication. *Group Dynamics: Theory, Research, and Practice 2004, 8*(1), 27–39.

Murphy, E. (2004). Recognizing and promoting collaboration in online asynchronous discussions. *British Journal of Educational Technology, 35*(4), 421–431.

Murphy, E., & Laferriére, T. (2005). Identifying and facilitating group development processes in virtual communities of teacher-learners. *International Journal of Instructional Technology and Distance Learning.* Retrieved January 24, 2006, from http://www.itdl.org/Journal/Apr_05/article03.htm

Olaniran, B. A. (1994). Group performance in computer mediated and face-to-face communication media. *Management Communication Quarterly, 7*(3), 256–281.

Palloff, R. M., & Pratt, K. (1999). *Building learning communities in cyberspace.* San Francisco: Jossey-Bass.

Paulus, T. M. (2005). Collaborative and cooperative: Approaches to online group work: The impact of task type. *Distance Education, 26*(2), 111–125.

Pavitt, C., & Johnson, K. K. (1999). An examination of the coherence of group discussions. *Communication Research, 26*(3), 303–321.

Poole, M. S., & Roth, M. S. (1989). Decision development in small groups V: Test of a contingency model. *Human Communications Research, 15*(4), 549–589.

Porter, C. E. (2004). A typology of virtual communities: A multi-disciplinary foundation for future research. *Journal of Computer-Mediated Communication (10).* Retrieved December 15, 2005, from http://jcmc.indiana.edu/vol10/issue1/porter.html

Ridgeway, C. L. (1983). *The dynamics of small groups.* New York: St. Martin's Press.

Rose, M. A., & Flowers, J. (2003, August). Assigning learning roles to promote critical discussions during problem-based learning. Proceedings of the 19th Annual Conference on Distance Teaching and Learning, Madison, WI.

Schutz, W. C. (1958). *FIRO: A three-dimensional theory of interpersonal behavior.* New York: Holt, Rinehart, & Winston.

Shaw, M. E. (1976). *Group dynamics* (2nd ed.). New Delhi, India: Tata McGraw Hill.

Smith, J. B. (1994). *Collective intelligence in computer-based collaboration.* Hillsdale, NJ: Lawrence Erlbaum Associates.

Smith, K. K., & Berg, D. N. (1987). *Paradoxes of group life: Understanding conflict, paralysis, and movement in group dynamics.* San Francisco: New Lexington Press.

Smith, R. O. (2005). Working with difference in online collaborative groups. *Adult Education Quarterly, 55*(3), 182–199.

Sudweeks, F., & Allbritton, M. (1996). Working together, working apart. In C. D. Keen, C. Urquhart, and J. Lamp (Eds.), *Proceedings of the 7th Australasian Conference of Information Systems (ACIS96), 2,* Department of Computer Science, Hobart: University of Tasmania, 701–712.

Swigger, K. M., & Brazile, R. (1995). Evaluating group effectiveness through a computer-supported cooperative training environment. *International Journal of Human-Computer Studies, 43*(4), 523–538.

Tuckman, B. W. (1965). Developmental sequence in small groups. *Psychological Bulletin, 63,* 384–399.

Tuckman, B. W., & Jensen, M. A. C. (1977). Stages in small group development revisited. *Group and Organizational Studies, 2,* 419–427.

Valacich, J. S., Dennis, A. R., & Connolly, T. (1994). Idea generation in computer-based groups: A new ending to an old story. *Organizational Behavior and Human Decision Processes, 57,* 448–467.

Walther, J. B. (1996). Computer-mediated communication: Impersonal, interpersonal and hyperpersonal interaction. *Communication Research, 23*(1), 3–43.

12

Literature of Satisfaction

Mike Allen, Nancy Burrell, and Erik Timmerman
University of Wisconsin–Milwaukee

John Bourhis
Missouri State University

Edward Mabry
University of Wisconsin–Milwaukee

This chapter considers the issue of student satisfaction with distance learning. Satisfaction constitutes an evaluation by students about the quality of the educational experience. The issues of student evaluation of the quality of instruction have received much attention from scholars over the years (see meta-analyses, Allen, 1996; Feldman, 1979, 1983, 1984, 1986, 1987). The growing use of new technological formats for implementing distance learning requires a reconsideration of these issues.

The profound impact that technological innovations are having in all facets of education focuses attention on assessing the changing practices of instruction. Understanding the impact of technologically driven differences between traditional classrooms and DL contexts is clearly appropriate (Althaus, 1997; Greene & Meek, 1998; McHenry & Bozik, 1995; Verduin & Clark, 1991; Whittington, 1987). Phipps and Merisotis (1999) have concluded that current research, while rapidly accumulating, generally lacks systematic comparisons of factors that differentiate traditional classroom and distance learning outcomes. This sentiment is present in the calls for more research on the consequences of using mediated communication technologies in instructional settings (Kuehn, 1994; Institute for Higher Education Policy, 2000). This chapter does not consider the issues of technology used in the face-to-face (f2f) classroom or computer-assisted instruction (for a meta-analytic review, see Timmerman & Kruepke, 2006a, 2006b). The available meta-analyses reviewed in this chapter do not include "blended" courses that combine f2f and DL approaches.

The value of distance education is still a controversial issue among educators. Hiltz (1986) demonstrated that computer-mediated communication (CMC) technologies supporting online courses were perceived by instructors as an effective mode of instruction. However, Mottet's (2000) assessment of interactive television instruction indicated teachers' preexisting positive attitudes and experiences produced positive impressions of distance teaching, but teachers still perceived distance instruction negatively (even among generally approving teachers) because of the diminished contact with students and a loss of control over the classroom environment caused by technological intrusiveness. Even training in technology use may not be entirely effective in diminishing that perception (Abou-Dagga & Herring, 1997). This reflects issues expressed in Tinto's (1975, 1982, 2004) model of student satisfaction in which the students' feeling of connectedness to the university could be reduced when the communication becomes mediated (Sweet, 1986). However, the morale and motivational impact on instructors remains an underresearched and necessary area for exploration. A central question is whether the students in a DL environment feel "connected" to the learning experience. The requirement and impact of the instructional immediacy requires consideration (Allen, Witt, & Wheeless, 2006; Hackman & Walker, 1990a, 1990b; Walker & Hackman, 1992; Witt, Wheeless, & Allen, 2004).

Besides the issue of instructor satisfaction, a pressing question of whether *students* are relatively satisfied with their experiences in distance education exists (Whittington, 1987). In an observation of an interactive television distance education class, McHenry and Bozik (1995) noted substantial variability in classroom climates which evolved at different instructional sites. However, the variability did not appear to undermine students' relatively positive orientation toward the class.

Other early research dealing with user impressions of rudimentary audio and video teleconferencing technologies did not show strong user satisfaction when compared to face-to-face communication (Fowler & Wackerbarth, 1980; Ryan, 1976; Williams, 1978). Yet, there were clear differences between these three modes of communication. Williams (1978), for example, noted that nearly 50% of the face-to-face meetings could be substituted for by using an audio or videoconference with little negative reactance from participants. Ryan (1976) found that both videoconferencing and face-to-face communication modes were perceived as more aesthetically positive than audio conferencing. Both mediums, video and audio conferencing, were perceived as more "potent" communication channels than face-to-face communication. Mediated channels in Ryan's (1976) study probably evoked a greater sense of social distance and formality (very common reactions to communication technology) even though they represented a somewhat narrower signal bandwidth than face-to-face communication.

Various human factors (e.g., personality, attitude, skill) emerge to influence user reactions to communication technologies in distance education. Early research on computer-mediated communication conferencing systems showed that user attitudes toward the technology, prior use experience, and skill positively affected user satisfaction with participation in computer conferencing (Kerr & Hiltz, 1982). Application of similar technologies to the university classroom (creating the so-called "virtual classroom") with more experienced and extensively oriented students produced strong relationships between evaluation attributes about the experience and learning outcomes (Hiltz, 1986). User experience played a similar role in Althaus's (1997) study of students involved in online e-mail discussion groups used in supporting traditional classroom instruction. Students with more computer experience were more likely to use the online discussion groups and perceive them as beneficial. Cody, Dunn, Hoppin, and Wendt (1999) reported a similar connection between the extent of mentoring experiences used in training and subsequent use of the Internet in a group of elderly adult learners. Scott and Rockwell (1997) noted opposite trends for self-reported likelihood of use of new communication technologies and both computer apprehension and communication-bound apprehension. Higher scores on the anxiety measures were negatively correlated with technology usage preferences.

Clearly, both user and technological efficacy are involved in the success of new communication technologies when they are applied in learning contexts. A critical question is whether DL opportunities can provide a consistent level of satisfaction for students. One theoretical approach to the issues surrounding the diverse set of communication channels that comprise new communication technologies (e.g., e-mail, telephone/audio, interactive video) is the perceived message *richness* (complexity of message stimuli) contained in a mode of communication that delivers an intact message.

Media-richness theorists (Fulk, Schmitz, & Steinfield, 1990) seek to explain the effectiveness and desire to communicate using particular channels on the basis of information and affect. Media-richness theory has been valuable in explaining the interplay between mediated messages and distance education effects (Timmerman & Kreupke, 2006a). The application to computer-mediated communication (CMC) indicates some issues deserving consideration in the context of DL. Essentially, persons will choose media to reflect the various needs for types and amounts of information. Media lacking that information may be evaluated as unsuitable or undesirable. For the practice of DL, the chosen means of delivery of materials should relate to the level of satisfaction with the experience in the course.

Many satisfaction issues operate before a student enrolls in a particular type of course. For example, students with computer apprehension or the need to have an instructor physically present remain unlikely to enroll in a course taught entirely online. Possibly, the impact of self-selection in the context of DL limits the amount of dissatisfaction by removing the persons most likely to have negative experiences with the course.

USING META-ANALYSIS TO UNDERSTAND
THE DL SATISFACTION LITERATURE

Meta-analysis provides a means of synthesizing vast amounts of literature using quantitative methods. Meta-analysis represents a method of quantitatively synthesizing results across a number of studies. The goal is to provide a general estimate across the data combined over a set of studies. What this permits is an understanding of what the entire body of literature provides for the estimation of any parameter. Meta-analysis provides a means of literature synthesis that is more systematic, comprehensive, and accurate than more traditional narrative reviews. Essentially, rather than reviewing the more than 100 empirical investigations of student satisfaction individually, meta-analysis permits summarization to represent the sample of studies more systematically.

The reason for this improved accuracy is a reduction in sampling error (combining sample sizes reduces the confidence interval), corrections for sources of bias and error (regression to the mean, attenuated measurement, dichotomization of continuous variables, restriction in range, halo effects, construct validity, etc.), as well as the evaluation of potential moderator variables (Hunter & Schmidt, 2004).

A series of meta-analyses exist that consider DL outcomes (Allen, Bourhis, et al., 2002; Allen et al., 2004; Allen, Timmerman, Bourhis, Mabry, & Burrell, 2002; Bernard et al., 2004; Machtmes & Asher, 2000). These reports consider the issues of DL student satisfaction compared with traditional face-to-face instruction, student performance comparing DL to face-to-face instruction, and finally the relationship of learning styles of a student to the reported level of satisfaction with DL. The reader should know that, due to space and other limitations, details of all analyses and methods are not presented. For additional analyses and details the reader is encouraged to obtain the original reports and examine the findings for additional details and further statistical analyses. Various compilations of existing literature served as a place to collect information for these reports (Russell, 1999; Stickell, 1963). The results from the various meta-analyses will report three basic statistical properties: (a) average effect measured in the metric of a correlation-positive correlation favors DL compared to f2f; (b) the number of studies or investigations contributing to the estimate, or k; and (c) the combined total sample size used to make the estimate, or N. The larger the number of studies and sample size, the less sampling error in the estimate of the population parameter.

RESULTS CONSIDERING STUDENT SATISFACTION

The overall analysis from Allen, Bourhis, et al., (2002) demonstrates that students only have a slight preference for a live course when compared to distance learning environments (*average r* = −.031, *k* = 25, *N* = 4,702), replicated by Bernard et al. (2004) (*average r* = −.045, *k* = 154, *N* = 21,047). The two meta-analyses essentially reach identical conclusions about the comparison of satisfaction between f2f and DL classrooms, namely that students exhibit slightly higher levels of satisfaction with a f2f environment.

One study (Köymen, 1992) functions as an outlier in Allen, Bourhis, et al. (2002) in which the effect favoring DL was large (*r* = −.239). (Bernard et al. (2004) did not perform an outlier analysis so no comparison between meta-analyses is possible). Köymen illustrates that while students do indicate a small preference for the live classroom, that preference can be mitigated or even reversed if the live environment is less than optimal (stuffy, crowded, lacking in technology, having poor technology). The findings should therefore not be interpreted as a blanket statement of preference for one setting over another, and indicate a general sense of preference that is subject to changes in circumstances.

Another consideration is the selection of the channels of communication (video, audio, and written). The Allen, Bourhis, et al. (2002) meta-analysis examined three distinct methods of delivery: video, audio, and written. However, there were not enough studies using strictly audio communication to form a separate group. This comparison was restricted to written and video channels. The comparison of f2f and DL courses using video channel only results in a small correlation favoring the DL course (*average r* = .006, *k* = 23, *N* = 4,277). The results indicate no difference between video DL and f2f courses in terms of student satisfaction. When comparing courses conducted entirely using a written channel, f2f courses demonstrate higher levels of satisfaction (*average r* = −.247, *k* = 4, *N* = 255). Not surprisingly, the addition of sensory information slightly increases the level of satisfaction reported. Students demonstrate a higher level of preference for video DL courses versus written courses compared to a f2f version of the same course. This finding provides support for those arguing that the level of sensory input is related to the level of student satisfaction with a particular course format.

One feature of DL courses is the degree to which interaction with the instructor is possible—interaction defined as synchronous message transmission (for example, a two-way audio/visual signal, telephone, or written interactive system). One question is whether employing and incorporating such feedback improves satisfaction with the course (Fulford & Zhang, 1993). The research must address whether the inclusion of some form of interaction provides a social, as opposed to a physical, presence that creates a better relationship between student and instructor (Gunawardena & Zittle, 1997). There were only enough studies to conduct this examination using courses with a combination of video and audio channels. The Allen, Bourhis, et al. (2002) meta-analysis divided the studies into three groups: (a) full and live interaction, in which the students and instructor could communicate immediately and simultaneously; (b) limited interaction, in which students and instructors could communicate either by a restricted means (telephone or computer) or were limited to a few times; and (c) where no direct interaction was provided for the course. The expectation would be that the most satisfying experience would be that with full interaction, followed by the limited interaction and then no-interaction conditions. Contrary to expectations, there is a slight trend indicating a greater difference between f2f and DL courses based on channel and availability of information. The fully interactive audio/visual course had the largest contrast effect favoring f2f (*average r* = −.078, *k* = 12, *N* = 2,476), followed by the limited interaction format (*average r* = −.049, *k* = 3, *N* = 421), and the no-interaction courses favor DL (*average r* = .029, *k* = 5, *N* = 674). This trend of effects indicates that the addition of information led to more favorable satisfaction with the f2f version of the course.

One possible explanation lies in what were probably the relatively primitive technological systems at the time of the study. Many studies using multi-channel instructional methods and setting used delivery systems that required the cobbling together of various methods of communication that were not integrated. The question is whether such differences will exist in future investigations as the technology improves.

The results reported by Bernard et al. (2004) provide a comparison for synchronous and asynchronous formats. The results reported by the authors replicate the earlier Allen, Bourhis, et al. (2002) findings. Synchronous format DL courses have a correlation favoring the f2f format (*average r* = −.092, *k* = 83, *N* = 9,483). However, comparing f2f to a DL course employing an asynchronous format reports the same level of satisfaction (*average r* = −.002, *k* = 71, *N* = 11,624). This indicates the analyses reported by Allen, Bourhis, et al. (2002) and Bernard et al. (2004) are in agreement.

Another aspect of the issue is the relationship of learning style to student satisfaction in the context of DL (the results of a meta-analysis reported in Allen, Timmerman, et al., 2002). The critical question is whether the level of satisfaction experience in a DL or f2f course is a consequence of student learning style. The findings indicate that students with a preference for social learning (learning with and in the presence of others) demonstrate greater satisfaction for f2f instruction (*average r* = −.148, *k* = 6, *N* = 1,166). Similarly, results demonstrate that students preferring the use of technology to learn were more satisfied with distance learning situations (*average r* = .221, *k* = 5, *N* = 872). This finding is not surprising since a preference for technology should be associated with the satisfaction with a comparable educational format.

CONCLUSIONS

The essential conclusions of the current meta-analyses comparing DL and f2f instructional contexts is that there exists little difference in outcomes when one considers levels of student satisfaction. The results associated with these meta-analyses demonstrate that the expectation that distance learning satisfaction outcomes differ from traditional education appears unwarranted. Two independent meta-analyses of the literature (Allen, Bourhis, et al., 2002; Bernard et al., 2004) report almost identical findings for the same literature. While the number of estimates exceeds 150 in the Bernard report and exceeds 50 in Allen, additional work is warranted in understanding a number of issues addressed below.

What is a bit surprising is that synchronous classrooms with simultaneous communication report less satisfaction than asynchronous approaches to DL. We believe that one possibility for this finding across the investigations involves expectations about how communication takes place. Technology is limited, uncertain, and sometimes difficult in a synchronous environment. The problem of failed expectations may result in slightly higher levels of frustration than in a conventional f2f classroom.

The most interesting finding about student satisfaction is the association of learning styles with the method of instruction. Not surprisingly, results indicate students report higher levels of satisfaction when the preferred learning style matches the attributes of a pedagogical structure. The same finding is true for measurements involving issues of performance (see Allen et al., 2004). Students perform better in educational environments where the structure of the instruction matches the preferred learning style. This finding is important to both DL and f2f instructional contexts. The finding implies that instructional environments may require modifications to accommodate learning styles, and tracking students into DL contexts may be one effective way to accomplish this outcome.

The findings of the meta-analyses reviewed do not indicate a broad preference favoring either DL or f2f instruction. A more fundamental understanding of how students learn in general is required. There exists some evidence to argue for a kind of student-context match such that the learning style of the student would be matched to the appropriate educational format to maximize student satisfaction. Future research should target an understanding of why formats which appear on the surface to be very different do not differ in student satisfaction.

The long-term implications of using DL education need to be addressed. Why do students stay in a program? Does DL instruction have higher levels of attrition (Fjortoft, 1995, 1996)? Most educational programs are not simply a single course but require the completion of an entire degree program to be considered fully successful. Bernard et al. (2004), indicate only slightly higher levels of attrition in DL formats (*average* $r = .028$, $k = 103$, $N = 3,735,050$). When separated by whether the DL format was synchronous (*average* $r = -.003$, $k = 17$, $N = 3,604$) or asynchronous (*average* $r = .047$, $k = 53$, $N = 10,435$), this finding indicates that synchronous communication does increase student retention, supporting the arguments about the impact of media richness. However, the differences are small and do not indicate a fundamental challenge to or preference for either format.

One consideration is the attitude of faculty towards the inclusion or substitution of DL. In most institutions faculty governance and participation is required for the success of any program. The attitudes of faculty that participate as well as those that do not participate in DL require monitoring and consideration (Clark, 1993). Training in the effective use of the technology, while essential, does not necessarily translate into adoption and use (Abou-Dagga & Herring, 1997). The potential for research to demonstrate the comparability, or even desirability, of DL formats underscores the need for and value of teacher programs. An educational innovation like DL that must gain acceptance across complete and diverse curriculums requires broad participation and acceptance by faculty.

Distance learning offers a challenge to ideas about educational formats and resources. This challenge is determining how best to incorporate new tools into the educational system. The problem of relying on a "one size fits all" philosophy for instruction may not be maximizing the potential of individual students. Instead, the need may exist for some diagnosis and matching of pedagogical formats to the abilities of students to achieve maximum instructional benefits. This new orientation provides an opportunity for DL approaches to be enlisted in fulfilling educational missions. The admonition is that most effective educational practice is going to require a combination of both f2f and DL approaches to maximize the potential of every student in higher education.

REFERENCES

Abou-Dagga, S., & Herring, M. (1997, June). Teachers' training in distance education and their willingness to use the technology after the completion of inservice training. In N. Maushak, M. Simonson, and K. Wright, K. (Eds.), *Encyclopedia of distance education research in Iowa* (2nd ed.) (pp. 15–22). Ames, IA: Teacher Education Alliance of the Iowa Distance Education Alliance, Iowa's Star Schools Project, Technology Research and Evaluation Group, Iowa State University. (ERIC ED 409 001)

Allen, M. (1996). Research productivity and positive teaching evaluations: Examining the relationship using meta-analysis. *Journal of the Association for Communication Administration, 7*, 77–97.

Allen, M., Bourhis, J., Burrell, N., Mabry, E., Emmers-Sommer, T., Titsworth, S., et al. (2002). Comparing student satisfaction with distance education to traditional classrooms in higher education: A meta-analysis. *The American Journal of Distance Education, 16*(2), 83–97.

Allen, M., Mabry, E., Mattrey, M., Bourhis, J., Titsworth, S., & Burrell, N. (2004). Evaluating the effectiveness of distance learning: A comparison using meta-analysis. *Journal of Communication, 54*(8), 402–420.

Allen, M., Timmerman, E., Bourhis, J., Mabry, E., & Burrell, N. (2002, November). *Distance education: A meta-analysis of how learning styles influence outcomes.* Paper presented at the National Communication Association Convention, New Orleans, LA.

Allen, M., Witt, P., & Wheeless, L. (2006). The role of teacher immediacy as a motivational factor in student learning: Using meta-analysis to test a causal model. *Communication Education, 55*, 21–31.

Althaus, S. L. (1997). Computer-mediated communication in the university classroom: An experiment with online discussion. *Communication Education, 46*, 158–174.

Bernard, R. M., Abrami, P. C., Lou, Y., Borokhovski, E., Wade, A., Wozney, L., et al. (2004). How does distance education compare with classroom instruction? A meta-analysis of empirical literature. *Review of Educational Research, 74*, 379–439.

Clark, T. (1993). Attitudes of higher education faculty toward distance education: A national survey. *The American Journal of Distance Education, 7*(2), 19–33.

Cody, M. J., Dunn, D., Hoppin, S., & Wendt, P. (1999). Silver surfers: Training and evaluating internet use among older adult learners. *Communication Education, 48*, 269–286.

Feldman, K. (1979). The significance of circumstances for college students' ratings of their teachers and courses. *Research in Higher Education, 10*, 49–172.

Feldman, K. (1983). Seniority and experience of college teachers as related to the evaluations they receive from students. *Research in Higher Education, 18*, 3–124.

Feldman, K. (1984). Class size and college students' evaluations of teachers and courses: A closer look. *Research in Higher Education, 21*, 45–116.

Feldman, K. (1986). The perceived instructional effectiveness of college teachers as related to their personality and attitudinal characteristics: A review and synthesis. *Research in Higher Education, 24*, 139–213.

Feldman, K. (1987). Research productivity and scholarly accomplishments of college teachers as related to their instructional effectiveness: A review and exploration. *Research in Higher Education, 26*, 227–298.

Fjortoft, N. (1995, October). *Predicting persistence in distance learning programs.* Paper presented at the Mid-Western Educational Research Meeting, Chicago. (ERIC ED 387 620)

Fjortoft, N. (1996). Persistence in a distance learning program: A case in pharmaceutical education. *The American Journal of Distance Education, 10*(3), 49–59.

Fowler, G. D., & Wackerbarth, M. E. (1980). Audio teleconferencing versus face-to-face conferencing: A synthesis of the literature. *Western Journal of Speech Communication, 44*, 236–252.

Fulford, C., & Zhang, S. (1993). Perceptions of interaction: The critical predictor in distance education. *American Journal of Distance Education, 7*(3), 8–21.

Fulk, J., Schmitz, J. A., & Steinfield, C. (1990). A social information model of technology use. In J. Fulk & C. Steinfield (Eds.), *Organizations and communication technology* (pp. 117–140). Newbury Park, CA: Sage.

Greene, B., & Meek, A. (1998). *Distance education in higher education institutions: Incidence, audiences, and plans to expand.* (Report no. NCES-98-132). Washington, DC: U.S. Government Printing Office.

Gunawardena, C. N., & Zittle, F. J. (1997). Social presence as a predictor of satisfaction within a computer-mediated conferencing environment. *The American Journal of Distance Education, 11*(3), 8–26.

Hackman, M., & Walker, K. (1990a, April). The impact of system design and instructional style on student reactions to distance education. *Research in Distance Education, 37*, 7–9.

Hackman, M., & Walker, K. (1990b). Instructional communication in the televised classroom: The effects of system design and teacher immediacy on student learning and satisfaction. *Communication Education, 39*, 196–206.

Hiltz, S. R. (1986). The "virtual classroom": Using computer-mediated communication for university teaching. *Journal of Communication, 36*, 95–104.

Hunter, J. E., & Schmidt, F. L. (2004). *Methods of meta-analysis: Correcting for error and bias in research findings.* 2nd ed. Thousand Oaks, CA: Sage.

Institute for Higher Education Policy, (2000). *Quality on the line: Benchmarks for success in Internet-based distance education.* Washington, DC: Institute for Higher Education Policy and National Education Association.

Kerr, E. B., & Hiltz, S. R. (1982). *Computer-mediated communication systems.* New York: Academic Press.

Köymen, U. (1992). Comparisons of learning and study strategies of traditional and open-learning-system students in Turkey. *Distance Education, 13*, 108–117.

Kuehn, S. A. (1994). Computer-mediated communication in instructional settings: A research agenda. *Communication Education, 43*, 171–183.

Machtmes, K., & Asher, J. W. (2000). A meta-analysis of the effectiveness of telecourses in distance education. *The American Journal of Distance Education, 14*(1), 27–46.

McHenry, L., & Bozik, M. (1995). Communicating at a distance: A study of interaction in a distance education classroom. *Communication Education, 44*, 362–371.

Mottet, T. P. (2000). Interactive television instructors' perceptions of students' nonverbal responsiveness and their influence on distance education. *Communication Education, 49*, 146–164.

Phipps, R. A., & Merisotis, J. P. (1999). *What's the difference? A review of contemporary research on the effectiveness of distance learning in higher education.* Washington, DC: American Federation of Teachers and National Education Association.

Russell, T. (1999). *The no significant difference phenomenon.* Raleigh: Instructional Telecommunications, North Carolina State University.

Ryan, M. G. (1976). The influence of teleconferencing medium and status on participants' perception of the aestheticism, evaluation, privacy, potency, and activity of the medium. *Human Communication Research, 2*, 255–261.

Scott, C. R., & Rockwell, S. C. (1997). The effects of communication, writing, and technology apprehension on likelihood to use new communication technologies. *Communication Education, 46*, 44–62.

Stickell, D. (1963). A critical review of the methodology and research comparing televised and face-to-face instruction. (Unpublished doctoral dissertation, The Pennsylvania State University, 1990).

Sweet, R. (1986). Student dropout in distance education: An application of Tinto's model. *Distance Education, 7*, 201–213.

Timmerman, C. E., & Kruepke, K. A. (2006a). Computer-assisted instruction, media richness, and college student performance. *Communication Education, 55*, 73–104.

Timmerman, C. E., & Kruepke, K. A. (2006b). Computer assisted instruction and student performance. In B. Gayle, R. Preiss, N. Burrell, & M. Allen, (Eds.), *Classroom communication and instructional practices: Advances through meta-analysis* (pp. 77–98). Mahwah, NJ: Lawrence Erlbaum Associates.

Tinto, V. (1975). Dropout from higher education: A theoretical synthesis of recent research. *Review of Education Research, 45*, 89–125.

Tinto, V. (1982). Limits of theory and practice in student attrition. *Journal of Higher Education, 53*, 687–700.

Tinto, V. (2004). *Student retention and graduation: Facing the truth, living with the consequences.* Retrieved January 12, 2006, from at http://www.pellinstitute.org

Verduin, J. R., & Clark, T. A. (1991). *Distance education: The foundations of effective practice.* San Francisco: Jossey-Bass.

Walker, K., & Hackman, M. (1992). Multiple predictors of perceived learning and satisfaction: The importance of information transfer and nonverbal immediacy in the televised course. *Distance Education, 13*, 81–92.

Whittington, N. (1987). Is instructional television educationally effective? A research review. *The American Journal of Distance Education, 1*(1), 47–57.

Williams, E. (1978). Teleconferencing: Social and psychological factors. *Journal of Communication, 28*, 125–131.

Witt, P., Wheeless, L., & Allen, M. (2004). A meta-analytical review of the relationship between teacher immediacy and student learning. *Communication Monographs, 71*, 161–183.

13

Student Achievement in Elementary and High School

Cathy Cavanaugh
University of North Florida

OVERVIEW OF K–12 ONLINE LEARNING

This chapter is a review of research on teaching and learning online by children in elementary and high schools, commonly referred to in the United States as K–12; that is, from kindergarten to high school graduation.

Online learning programs for K–12 students offer instruction and content in the form of synchronous or asynchronous Web-delivered courses, also known as virtual schools. About half of the U.S. states have statewide K–12 online learning programs, and online courses are offered by schools or districts in every state. Online schools have experienced growth rates of 50% to 100% each year since they began (Watson, 2005). The largest publicly funded virtual school programs enroll over 35,000 students. The predominant mode of delivery for K–12 distance learning courses is the Internet (Setzer, Lewis, & Green, 2005). While more than 10% of postsecondary students have enrolled in at least one online course (Snyder, Tan, & Hoffman, 2004), only about 1% of K–12 students have taken online courses (Watson, 2005).

A necessary characteristic for success as a distance learner is autonomy (see Chapter 9 in this *Handbook*), which is present at different levels in children and adults. Most adults have acquired a degree of autonomy in learning, whereas younger students require scaffolding in their distance education experience. Adult learners approach expertise in their learning and in their ability to learn independently, as a result of their extended experience with the concepts and with metacognition. In contrast, children are relative novices. Experts organize and interpret information differently from novices, and these differences affect learners' abilities to remember and solve problems (Bransford, Brown, & Cocking, 1999), and their ability to learn independently. Children develop metacognitive skills gradually and with guidance.

A second characteristic of successful distance learners that differentiates K–12 distance learners from adult learners is locus of control. Learners persist in an educational endeavor when they have developed an internal locus of control (Rotter, 1989). Older children have more internal locus of control than younger children (Gershaw, 1989).

EFFECTIVENESS OF K–12 ONLINE LEARNING

Meta-Analyses of Research in K–12 Online Learning

In recent years, five meta-analyses have included data from studies of K–12 distance education (Table 13.1). Cavanaugh's (2001) meta-analysis incorporated the full range of telecommunications technology in use for courses and supplemental educational programs in the 1980s and 1990s at the K–12 level. The small positive effect size fell within the confidence interval, resulting in a finding of no significant difference in academic achievement between distance and classroom programs. However, the few online programs included in the synthesis showed higher effect sizes than the audio and videoconferencing programs.

The Shachar and Neumann (2003) synthesis found a significant positive effect for distance education programs delivered between 1990 and 2002, noting that, "in two thirds of the cases, students taking courses by distance education outperformed their student counterparts enrolled in traditionally instructed courses" (n.p.). Detail about the ages of the students and the delivery systems used in the courses was not included in the meta-analysis, preventing conclusions about the relative effectiveness of online programs for K–12 students. In contrast, Ungerleider and Burns (2003) restricted their analysis to networked and online distance education programs. Two out of the 12 studies were conducted at the secondary level, and the others were conducted at the postsecondary level. No significant difference was reported for student achievement, and a small positive effect size was found for satisfaction in classroom courses.

The meta-analysis of 232 studies of online and video-based learning in K–12 and postsecondary students by Bernard et al. (2004) resulted in a small positive effect size for achievement in online learning, although online learners had lower retention rates. The single meta-analysis that focused solely on the K–12 online learning delivery systems in use in today's virtual schools

TABLE 13.1.
Meta-Analyses of K–12 Distance Education, 2001–2004

Author(s), Date	Focus	Delivery System	N of Studies	Effect Size; 95% CI
Cavanaugh (2001)	Academic achievement of K–12 students	Analog and digital	19	+0.015; −1.113 to 1.407
Shachar & Neumann (2003)	Student achievement of postsecondary and K–12 students	Online	86	+0.37; 0.33 to 0.40
Ungerleider & Burns (2003)	Networked and online learning in postsecondary and K–12 programs	Online	16	Near zero; NA
Bernard, Abrami, Lou, Borokhovski, Wade, Wozney, Wallet, Fiset, & Huang (2004)	Student achievement, attitude, retention of postsecondary and K–12 students	Online	232	+0.0128; −0.0068 to 0.0325
Cavanaugh, Gillan, Kromrey, Hess, & Blomeyer (2004)	Academic achievement of K–12 students	Online	14	−0.028; 0.060 to −0.116

was by Cavanaugh, Gillan, Kromrey, Hess, and Blomeyer (2004). This synthesis found an effect size near zero, and because it was limited to 14 studies, it did not differentiate achievement levels by student characteristics or course features.

The uniformity of the results across these meta-analyses and other distance education studies (Russell, 1999) suggests that as distance education is currently practiced, student learning on average in well-designed online elementary and secondary environments appears to be equivalent to learning in a well-designed classroom environment. Such broad syntheses may mask fine-grained trends and have to date offered illumination of the practices that contribute to student success. To begin to answer the question of what works in K–12 online learning, several studies of individual online programs have been published over the past five years. These studies will be examined in the following section.

Effects on K–12 Student Outcomes of the Features of Online Distance Education

The examination of the literature regarding the effects on K–12 student outcomes of online distance education is organized thematically to focus on student characteristics, course design, instructional strategies, technological approaches, administrative/management practices, and policy. The knowledge base in each theme serves to guide online program administrators, course designers, and instructors toward best practice, and it points policymakers and researchers toward developing initiatives that will move the field to better meet the needs of students.

Student Characteristics

Rates of successful completion of distance education courses have improved over time as course design, instructional practice, support services, and student screening have been refined. At the K–12 level, virtual schools have experienced increases in retention and completion rates in the past decade (Weiner, 2003; Zucker & Kozma, 2003). While each virtual course and program has unique features that intersect in different ways with different types of students, results research on the characteristics of successful virtual school learners suggest a common set of characteristics likely to result in successful virtual learning.

An evaluation of Canada's virtual secondary schools (Barker & Wendel, 2001) was one of the first reports to describe the bimodal nature of students opting for virtual courses. These students tended to be either students who were in accelerated programs in their schools and sought advanced or specialized courses not otherwise available to them, or students who had experienced failure and dissatisfaction in school and needed a slower pace, individualization, or "credit recovery." Barker and Wendel found in their two-year study of nine schools that the former group was more likely to find success in an online course, indicating that students who have developed strategies as learners in conventional settings can often apply them online.

A key to success for adolescents, both online and offline, appears to be motivation, according to a study of Oregon's CyberSchool (Weiner, 2003). The study used surveys, interviews, journals, and course reviews to identify success factors in high school courses by collecting data from 118 students. While identifying discipline and self-motivation as critical factors, Weiner emphasized that at the secondary level students are still learning how to learn and they were often able to develop responsibility and organization through participation in a structured online course.

Student learning styles were examined in a study of secondary students taking a driver education course taught traditionally, using virtual reality with guided exploration, or virtual reality using non-guided exploration (Chen, Toh, & Ismail, 2005). This study included a sample of 184 students in randomly chosen classes from randomly selected schools assigned randomly to experimental or control groups. Learning styles were determined using Kolb's Learning Style Inventory and were described as having either the "accommodator" style, preferring active experimentation and concrete experience, or the "assimilator" style, preferring abstract conceptualization and reflective observation. The results indicated that assimilators performed better than accommodators in traditional settings and using virtual reality with guided exploration. For both learning styles, increased learning was documented when students used virtual reality with guided exploration relative to the other settings. Student learning styles were the most frequently identified factor influencing the success of virtual schooling, as reported by teachers surveyed in the evaluation of Australia's virtual schools (Kapitzke & Pendergast, 2005).

These studies provide evidence that strong academic skills, motivation, discipline, and course structure compatible with one's learning style are conducive to success in K–12 online learning. Factors such as these have been accounted for in a student success prediction instrument developed specifically to identify secondary level students who are likely to succeed in virtual school courses. The Educational Success Prediction Instrument (ESPRI) was evaluated with 135 students in 13 virtual high schools, and "found to discriminate with high accuracy and reliability between groups of successful and unsuccessful students" (Roblyer & Marshall, 2003, p. 214). As tested, the ESPRI was a 70-item Likert-format instrument with additional items to collect data including age, prior experience with distance learning, work hours, and extra-curricular activities. ESPRI data was combined with course completion, course grade, and student performance assessment data to build a predictive model. The instrument predicted with 100% confidence students who would succeed, and with 95% confidence students who would fail. The factors that appeared to have the greatest effect on success were hours involved in out-of-school activities, study environment, computer confidence, achievement beliefs, responsibility, self-organization, and technology skill/access. A subsequent study with 202 students in online charter schools found that the ESPRI correctly classified 100% of the students and was significant in predicting course grades (Ferdig, DiPietro, & Papanastasiou, 2005).

Course Design Factors

Knowledge of factors that contribute to student success in virtual courses has implications for the types of support services provided to students, particularly counseling and study-skill development and course design. An online science program for deaf high school students in three schools was found to foster independent learning through a collaborative project-based design (Barman et al., 2002). Students worked in teams with peers from the other schools to develop a hypothesis, conduct Web-based literature searches, perform hands-on experiments, and critique the work of other teams. Students valued the models of portfolios and problem solving produced by other students for helping them develop their own science and technology abilities.

Weiner's (2003) study of cyber-school students found that structure in courses was critical to student success. Components of structured courses were clear expectations, concrete deadlines with some flexibility, outlines of course requirements, time sheets, and study guides. A meaningful curriculum was also cited as an important contributor to student success in a virtual course, as was the opportunity for rich interactive collaboration among students and teachers. In fact, students felt frustration and isolation when interaction was limited. Students advocated for a design that allowed them to complete course activities at the pace that was comfortable for them, with due dates that reduced procrastination, and that maximized communication among students working at the same pace.

Barker and Wendel (2001) reinforce the need for flexible timetables for students who select virtual schooling because these students need more control over the pace of their learning. Their report states that the combination of flexibility, independence, and experience with online tools resulted in improved critical thinking, research, and computer skills, as compared to learners in conventional schools when measured by standardized exams. Virtual school students also showed greater improvement in problem solving, creative thinking, decision making, and time management, had equivalent performance in reading and science, and exhibited lower performance in listening and speaking.

Virtual course designs have many strengths, but they have not so far compared well with traditional settings for auditory production and reception skills among other forms of performance. A study of an online instrumental music course in Australia (Bond, 2002) showed that distance between teacher and student had "negative effects on quality of performance, level of engagement, and development and refinement of skills and knowledge" (p. 5), even though the course design included audio, video, guided practice, and additional resources. Mathematics has been seen as a content area with its own challenges for online learners. The need to communicate using "formulae, diagrams, and specific positioning of information on a page" was especially problematic online (Haughey & Muirhead, 2004, p. 61), as shown in a study of online students in grades 6 and 9. In this case, fax machines were used to allow the transfer of handwritten material in a way that could now be accomplished using drawing tablets and journaling software.

After long-term study of virtual course design, Schnitz and Azbell (2004) propose the following guidelines for materials used in virtual schools.

Online materials must be visual and dynamic, downloadable and printer-friendly, randomly accessible and manipulable, conducive to production/interaction, documented to model appropriate permissions and copyright alignments, instructionally aware of and prepared for remote use, aware of the audience, assessable and accountable, easily updatable (p. 165).

Instructional Factors

It has been established that in elementary and secondary education, teacher quality is among the most important contributors to student achievement (Darling-Hammond, 2000). Because most K–12 online courses are moderated in part or in full by a teacher, teacher preparation, professional development, and instructional practices are significant elements of effective virtual courses.

On the basis that virtual students and practices differ from students and practices in conventional schools, Davis and Roblyer (2005) have planned a model to prepare virtual school teachers with the unique knowledge, skills, and dispositions they will need to become effective online teachers. Online, teachers need to work differently in time and space and they need to be able to engage students using communications technology. The proposed model uses guided observations, mentoring in K–12 online courses, and design of virtual course materials to prepare new teachers to transition to online teaching. This model ensures that new teachers will leave their teacher-preparation programs knowing whether they are suited for online teaching and possessing the skills to begin teaching online.

To meet their demand for online teachers, many virtual schools have developed their own professional-development programs. Professional development for online teachers has been shown to have an effect on teacher ability and on student perceptions. Virtual High School (VHS) created graduate-level courses for all of its teachers and implemented a Teachers Learning Conference (Zucker & Kozma, 2003). The courses teach comprehensive course design and instruction skills and were found to be "very effective in helping them to implement a VHS course" (p. 104). The VHS instructor preparation program was seen to have an effect on the participating teachers even after they returned to classroom teaching (Lowes, 2005). Of the VHS teachers surveyed, three-fourths reported a positive impact on their face-to-face teaching.

Student perceptions of their learning environment may be related to the amount of professional development their teachers receive in technology (Hughes, McLeod, Brown, Maeda, & Choi, 2005). In their study of online algebra students, Hughes et al. administered the What Is Happening in This Classroom (WIHIC) instrument and found that teacher professional development appeared to have a positive effect on students' perceptions of cohesiveness. Teacher technology skill was identified as a "significant factor affecting pedagogical success" (n.p.) in an evaluation of Australia's Virtual Schooling Service Pilot (Kapitzke & Pendergast, 2005).

How teachers enact their skills in the virtual classroom affects student satisfaction and achievement. A quasi-experimental study of online algebra classes in 31 Louisiana schools examined student performance and the role of the teacher (Kleiman, Carey, Bonifaz, Haisted, & O'Dwyer, 2005). In the Louisiana model an in-class coach works with the online students during the school day, while they complete the work assigned by the online teacher. The "frequency with which the in-class teacher worked with small groups of students and observed individual student work related positively to student achievement" (p. 39). Achievement also improved "when online and in-class teacher teams collaborated frequently on planning" (p. 39).

Middle-school science students using the Internet were found to have higher levels of reading comprehension and science concept knowledge but lower levels of science declarative knowledge, compared to the control group, which did not use the Internet (Leu, Castek, Hartman, Coiro, & Henry, 2005). In addition, when the Internet was fully integrated and accompanied by "consistent reading comprehension strategy instruction" (p. 30), students performed best.

Interaction is at the heart of online learning. Indeed, it is alternately named as the primary difference between online and face-to-face instruction (Muirhead, 2000), one of the major challenges in online instruction (Murphy & Coffin, 2003), and one of the most important aspects of the online setting (Weiner, 2003). In Muirhead's (2000) review of Alberta's virtual schools, teachers reported that their interactions with students, parents, and colleagues were more often focused on teaching and learning than they had been in the traditional setting, but the teachers expressed dissatisfaction about the difficulty of building relationships, while managing learning. Qualitative and quantitative dimensions of interaction emerge in virtual schools in that participants seek both deeper and stronger relationships, and also value frequent and timely responses to questions (Weiner, 2003). Communication with and feedback from instructors was identified as the most valuable aspect of online courses in a study of students with specific learning disabilities (SLD) and students with attention deficit hyperactivity disorder (ADHD) at the Florida Virtual School (Smouse, 2005).

The ways an online teacher uses interaction tools influence how students encounter and master concepts in a course. Murphy and Coffin's (2003) study of an online high school French class shows that "simultaneous use of a number of tools in combination" (p. 244) enables group collaboration, one-to-one coaching, oral practice, and other strategies that compensate for the lack of visual cues online.

Zucker (2005) focused on student-student interaction in a study of 282 students at the Virtual High School. The majority of students valued inter-student communication within courses. However, student satisfaction, amount of communication, persistence in the course, and course grade were not affected by more heavily weighting student postings to discussion boards in randomly selected classes.

Technological Approaches

New technologies and tools are adopted in virtual courses to decrease the constraints of the online environment and increase affordances for learning. Recent advances in K–12 online learning technology provide solutions to some of the most important and perplexing issues in K–12 education today: teaching core literacy skills to young learners, teaching complex math and science skills at advanced levels, and teaching problem solving in authentic contexts.

Teaching children to read is an intensive process, and teaching them to read online is particularly problematic. Popovici et al. (2004) have developed a distributed virtual reality environment in which teachers and students use avatars to work in reading groups on story reconstruction. Students are able to work in cross-cultural groups on cooperative games with a virtual tutor. The system has been used in primary schools in several countries, and has been found to provide immediate validation for student work and foster in children the sense that they are playing rather than working.

Teaching handwriting is the goal of a Web-based system developed by Leung and Komura (2006). The teacher's handwriting is captured by a pen-based device and transformed into an animated virtual teacher. Students practice handwriting exercises using the digital pen device and their work is automatically analyzed for immediate feedback. Results of student practice are sent to the teacher, who customizes feedback and further practice. A proposed extension to this work is the use of a glove for three-dimensional handwriting analysis, an innovation with potential applications in other psychomotor activities such as the arts and sports.

In the high-need fields of mathematics and science, the focus for advanced high school courses is teaching abstract concepts and problem solving. Symbolic representations of mathematical concepts can be made more concrete for students in online courses through the use of virtual manipulatives. A study of online algebra classes at the Florida Virtual School compared the performance on graphing linear equations of students who used online graphing tools to students who did not (Cavanaugh, Bosnick, Hess, Scott, & Gillan, 2005). Students using the tools showed larger gains between pretest and posttest scores, but the differences were not significant.

In learning advanced sciences, students must solve complex problems while accounting for numerous variables. Acquiring and demonstrating these abilities online may be supported by several new technological approaches. Hwang's (2005) study of data mining for diagnosing student learning problems in science shows that the teacher's work can be streamlined when the intelligent testing and diagnosis system identifies poorly learned and well-learned concepts. The system was tested with K–6 students in science and math. The system compares the students' concept-effect relationships to the teacher's representation of the concept, and then provides learning suggestions for each student in about half the time than without the system. After acquiring science concepts, students often apply them by performing experiments. In a study of physics students in 20 Brazilian high schools, an online simulation and tutoring system was evaluated (Schiel, Dassin, de Magalhaes, & Guerrini, 2002). The course failure rate among students using the system was significantly lower than students of the same teachers not using the system.

Just as students can feel isolated as online learners, online teachers also experience isolation as professionals. In addition, online teachers face challenges in networking with peers because the numbers of online K–12 teachers are still low. A technological approach to teacher collaboration was studied by Carroll, Neale, and Isenhour (2004). The Collaborative Critical Incident Tool was used with a group of virtual school teachers as a problem-and-solution database. Teachers who taught a similar curriculum joined in a focused online forum to report critical incidents in their teaching and threaded discussion of the critical incident reports among the teachers and others involved in the program. The tool was found to be effective "at evoking usability evaluation information, as well as reflective analysis of usability issues from diverse points of view" (p. 215).

Administrative Practices

Virtual school effectiveness is influenced by administrative practices from the school level to the individual student level. Recent state and district virtual school reports have cited the institutionalization of a range of student support services as considerable contributors to their increasing course completion rates (Clark, Lewis, Oyer, & Schreiber, 2002; Good, 2005; Harlow & Baenen, 2003). These public schools serve at-risk and remediation students who have benefited from mentors, on-site support staff, counseling, or technical support because decision makers recognized the need for services.

Dickson (2005) and his collaborators at Michigan Virtual School recognized the variability inherent in student ability and performance in virtual classes and examined the ways that fine-grained views of data can inform teaching practice. School staff organized data that had been collected in the school's course-management system, and then the data were analyzed and represented visually to illuminate relationships between activity in courses and student course grades. For example, it was found that the number of times a student clicks in a course discussion board is strongly, positively, and consistently correlated with the student's grade in the course.

Policy Studies in K–12 Online Distance Education

A series of reports sponsored by the North Central Regional Educational Laboratory provides an overview of state policy and practice in K–12 online learning. These descriptive studies, *Keeping Pace with K–12 Online Learning* (Watson, 2005; Watson, Winograd, & Kalmon, 2004), review the state of the U.S. states in the areas of funding, curriculum, teacher qualification and evaluation, accountability for student achievement, quality assurance, equity and access, and enabling policies. The 2005 report collected data from each state regarding its laws and policies that influence online learning, and its publicly supported statewide online-learning programs. Among the findings was that 16 states had a "significant level of policy activity" (p. 112) and four states prohibit cyber-charter schools. While over half of the states have public online schools, no states have developed curriculum standards that address online courses. Only two states require teacher preparation for teaching online. It appears that states are working to achieve an appropriate balance between permissiveness and restrictiveness in their policies that govern virtual schools. Some policies are adaptations of traditional educational policies that have not been fully adapted for the online setting.

Blomeyer and Dawson's (2005) descriptive study of online learning policy included a review of the organizations exploring policy and practice, and reported that several regional or national organizations have taken on the role of recommending policy over the past five years, but little progress has been made in addressing the issues and barriers.

The State Educational Technology Directors Association (SETDA) developed its 2005 toolkit document with an emphasis on K–12 e-learning after study of e-learning models and policy nationwide in the U.S. One goal of the toolkit was to "provide a framework for state directors as they address online learning legislation" (p. 81). The document lists critical components of e-learning courses and criteria for evaluating e-learning course quality, based on several course-quality-standards documents. The toolkit also includes a matrix of e-learning models as a step toward a common vocabulary in K–12 online learning. The identified legislative issues were the logistical issues of student demographics, enrollment priorities, class size, seat time, teacher qualifications; and the quality assurance issues of content and instructional design, student support, accountability for student achievement, funding, cyber-charter schools, equity, and access. Barriers to initiating and implementing online learning programs were described as "funding, leadership, effectively making the case, quality and legal issues surrounding eLearning programs and models" (p. 88).

RECOMMENDATIONS FOR RESEARCH, POLICY, AND PRACTICE

Even after a decade of exponential growth, little research has been conducted on K–12 online learning relative to adult online learning. The field has begun to learn, share, and implement best practice as the community of practitioners and researchers has grown, but much work remains. A critical step in moving the field forward is consensus on the goals of K–12 online learning. Without agreement on these goals, evaluation directed at assessing progress toward the goals cannot happen. If the primary goal is increasing educational equity and access to alternate learning opportunities, then it is likely that online courses judged as "as good as" classroom courses made available to large numbers of students will be sufficient for achieving the goal. If, however, the goal is to offer high-quality education using materials and practices that may not be possible in a classroom, then the desired outcomes will look very different from outcomes with no significant difference compared to traditional settings. In practice, the goals will vary depending on needs and resources, and the goals will evolve as media and our understating of learning evolve.

Student Characteristics

It is imperative that all decision makers in K–12 online learning better understand the students who take courses online, so the level of scaffolding can be adapted for "bimodal" student populations and to enable multiple pathways for students with different learning preferences. In particular, research should focus on the optimal combinations of student needs, course structure, and support services. Predictive instruments, diagnosis, and prescription of services and scaffolds could enhance every student's chance of success while increasing the efficiency of teachers. Advances in cognitive science can be important contributors to a multidisciplinary research agenda in K–12 online learning. An initiative that would benefit online and offline learners would be the development of programs or course modules that foster the abilities known to result in success: self-discipline, motivation, responsibility, and organization.

Course Design

Based on the recent research that has shown that online learning can strengthen K–12 students' teamwork skill, problem-solving abilities, creativity, decision-making proficiency, and higher-order thinking skills, virtual schools can design courses to highlight and evaluate these skills. By reporting success in these areas, virtual schools can distinguish themselves as vanguard institutions in education of citizens prepared for participation in a democracy. Long-term research in methods of promoting these skills online and tracking their effects will inform stakeholders and the public. Detailed study of the demands of the content areas will enable course designers to supplement auditory and performance-based courses with the appropriate media, synchronous tools, and offline materials. Such study should result in course design standards and job aids for designers that account for intended learning across domains.

Instructional Practices and Technology

State or Federal definitions for highly qualified online teachers should be articulated to higher education and professional-development providers. New online teachers require preparation with mentors and practice with the media and methods that work in an environment that they may not have experienced as learners. Study of the teacher preparation and professional development practices that produce exemplary teachers is needed, as are standards. Research is also needed to inform instructors about the most effective interaction types, tools, and frequency for the learners and tasks in a course. Online courses seem to work best for well-defined knowledge domains and pose greater challenge for ill-defined learning and complex skills. Research is needed to develop tools in psychomotor subjects and abstract, complex subjects.

Administration and Policy

Standards are needed for reporting outcomes of online learning programs. For the first time in education, immense amounts of detailed data are available in course-management systems, but standards do not exist that allow data to be shared, synthesized, and analyzed. A common descriptive system and metrics should be created and refined to ensure that outcomes from online programs can be accurately compared and combined. Such a system would streamline processes such as developing cost-benefit rubrics to determine course sustainability, the feasibility of developing in-house courses as compared to purchasing courses, and the most effective and efficient student-teacher ratios. Ultimately, knowledge resulting from standardized data will result in improvements in student success.

REFERENCES

Barker, K., & Wendel, T. (2001). E-learning: Studying Canada's virtual secondary schools. Kelowna, BC: Society for the Advancement of Excellence in Education.

Barman, C., Stockton, J., Ellsworth, M., Gonzales, C., Huckleberry, T., & Raymond, S. (2002). Evaluation of the soar-high project: A Web-based science program for deaf students. *American Annals of the Deaf, 147*(3), 5–10.

Bernard, R. M., Abrami, P. C., Lou, Y., Borokhovski, E., Wade, A., Wozney, L., Wallet, P. A., Fiset, M., & Huang, B. (2004). How does distance education compare with classroom instruction? A meta-analysis of the empirical literature. *Review of Educational Research, 74*(3), 379–439.

Blomeyer, B., & Dawson, M. (2005). Virtual schools: Policy and practice considerations. In Z. Berge & T. Clark (Eds.), *Virtual schools: Planning for success* (pp. 61–76). New York: Teachers College Press.

Bond, A. (2002). Learning music online: An accessible program for isolated students. Leabrook, SA: Australia National Training Authority.

Bransford, J., Brown, A., & Cocking, R. (Eds.). (1999). *How people learn.* Washington, DC: National Academies Press.

Carroll, J., Neale, D., & Isenhour, P. (2004). The collaborative critical incident tool: Supporting reflection and evaluation in a Web community. In C. Cavanaugh (Ed.), *Development and management of virtual schools* (pp. 216–243). Hershey, PA: Information Science.

Cavanaugh, C. (2001). The effectiveness of interactive distance education technologies in K–12 learning: A meta-analysis. *International Journal of Educational Telecommunications, 7*(1), 73–78.

Cavanaugh, C., Bosnick, J., Hess, M., Scott, H., & Gillan, K. (2005). *Succeeding at the gateway: Secondary algebra learning in the virtual school.* Unpublished manuscript.

Cavanaugh, C., Gillan, K., Kromrey, J., Hess, M., & Blomeyer, R. (2004). The effects of distance educa-tion on K–12 student outcomes: A meta-analysis. Naperville, IL, Learning Point Associates. http://www.ncrel.org/tech/distance/k12distance.pdf

Chen, C., Toh, S., & Ismail, W. (2005). Are learning styles relevant to virtual reality? *Journal of Research on Technology in Education, 38*(2), 123–140.

Clark, T., Lewis, E., Oyer, E., & Schreiber, J. (2002). Illinois Virtual High School Evaluation, 2001–2002. http://www.ivhs.org/index.learn?action = other#year1evaluation

Darling-Hammond, L. (2000). Teacher quality and student achievement: A review of state policy evidence. *Education Policy Analysis Archives, 8*(1). http://epaa.asu.edu/epaa/v8n1/

Davis, N., & Roblyer, M. (2005). Preparing teachers for the "schools that technology built": Evaluation of a program to train teachers for virtual schooling. *Journal of Research on Technology in Education, 37*(4), 399–409.

Dickson, W. (2005). Toward a deeper understanding of student performance in virtual high school courses: Using quantitative analyses and data visualization to inform decision making. In R. Smith, T. Clark, & B. Blomeyer, (Eds.), *A synthesis of new research in K–12 online learning* (pp. 21–23). Naperville, IL: Learning Point Associates.

Ferdig, R., DiPietro, M., & Papanastasiou, E. (2005). Teaching and learning in collaborative virtual high schools. In R. Smith, T. Clark, & B. Blomeyer, (Eds.), *A synthesis of new research in K–12 online learning* (pp. 31–33). Naperville, IL: Learning Point Associates.

Gershaw, D. (1989). *Line on life: Locus of control* http://virgil.azwestern.edu/~dag/lol/ControlLocus.html

Good, D. (2005). Colorado online learning final evaluation report, 2002–2005. http://www.col.k12.co.us/aboutus/evalreports/COLFinalRptYear3.pdf

Harlow, K., & Baenen, N. (2003). Novanet student outcomes. Eye on evaluation, E & R Report No. 02.15. http://www.wcpss.net/evaluation-research/reports/2002/0215_novanet.pdf

Haughey, M., & Muirhead, W. (2004). Managing virtual schools: The Canadian experience. In C. Cavanaugh (Ed.), *Development and management of virtual schools* (pp. 50–67). Hershey, PA: Information Science.

Hughes, J., McLeod, S., Brown, R., Maeda, Y., & Choi, J. (2005). Staff development and student percep-tion of the learning environment in virtual and traditional secondary schools. In R. Smith, T. Clark, & B. Blomeyer, (Eds.), *A synthesis of new research in K–12 online learning* (pp. 34–35). Naperville, IL: Learning Point Associates.

Hwang, G. (2005). A data mining approach to diagnosing student learning problems in science courses. *International Journal of Distance Education Technologies, 3*(4), 35–50.

Kapitzke, C., & Pendergast, D. (2005). Virtual schooling service: Productive pedagogies or pedagogical pos-sibilities? *Teachers College Record, 107*(8), 1626–1651.

Kleiman, G., Carey, R., Bonifaz, A., Haistead, E., & O'Dwyer, L. (2005). A study of the effectiveness of the Louisiana Algebra I Online Project. In R. Smith, T. Clark, & B. Blomeyer, (Eds.), *A synthesis of new research in K–12 online learning* (pp. 36–39). Naperville, IL: Learning Point Associates.

Leu, D., Castek, J., Hartman, D., Coiro, J., & Henry, L. (2005). Evaluating the development of scientific knowledge and new forms of reading comprehension during online learning. In R. Smith, T. Clark, & B. Blomeyer, (Eds.), *A synthesis of new research in K–12 online learning* (pp. 27–30). Naperville, IL: Learning Point Associates.

Leung, H., & Komura, T. (2006). Web-based handwriting education with animated virtual teacher. *International Journal of Distance Education Technologies, 4*(1), 71–80.

Lowes, S. (2005). Online teaching and classroom change: The impact of virtual high school on its teachers and their schools. In R. Smith, T. Clark, & B. Blomeyer, (Eds.), *A synthesis of new research in K–12 online learning* (pp. 24–26). Naperville, IL: Learning Point Associates.

Muirhead, W. (2000). Online education in schools. *The International Journal of Educational Management, 14*(7), 315–324.

Murphy, E., & Coffin, G. (2003). Synchronous communication in a Web-based senior high school course: Maximizing affordances and minimizing the constraints of the tool. *The American Journal of Distance Education, 17*(4), 235–246.

Popovici, D., Gerval, J., Chevaillier, P., Tisseau, J., Serbanati, L., & Gueguen, P. (2004). Educative distributed virtual environments for children. *International Journal of Distance Education Technologies, 2*(4), 18–40.

Roblyer, M., & Marshall, J. (2003). Predicting success of virtual high school students: Preliminary results from an educational success prediction instrument. *Journal of Research on Technology in Education, 35*(2), 241–255.

Rotter, J. B. (1989). Internal versus external control of reinforcement: A case history of a variable. *American Psychologist, 45,* 489–493.

Russell, T. (1999). *The No Significant Difference phenomenon.* Montgomery, AL: International Distance Education Certification Center.

Schiel, D., Dassin, J., de Magalhaes, M., & Guerrini, I. (2002). High school physics instruction by way of the World Wide Web: A Brazilian case study. *Journal of Interactive Learning Research, 12*(4), 293–309.

Schnitz, J., & Azbell, J. (2004). Instructional design factors and requirements of online courses and modules. In C. Cavanaugh (Ed.), *Development and management of virtual schools* (pp. 158–177). Hershey, PA: Information Science.

Setzer, J. C., Lewis, L., & Green, B. (2005). Distance education courses for public elementary and secondary school students: 2002–2003 (NCES 2005–010). Washington, DC: National Center for Educational Statistics. http://nces.ed.gov/pubs2005/2005010.pdf

Shachar, M., & Neumann, Y. (2003). Differences between traditional and distance education academic performances: A meta-analytic approach. *International* http://www.irrodl.org/index.php/irrodl/issue/view/16

Smouse, T. (2005). Students with either specific learning disabilities or attention deficit hyperactivity disorder: Perceptions of self as learning in online courses at Florida Virtual School and in the traditional learning environment. Unpublished dissertation, University of Central Florida, Orlando, FL.

Snyder, T. D., Tan, A. G., & Hoffman, C. M. (2004). Digest of educational statistics, 2003. (NCES 2005-025). Washington, DC: National Center for Educational Statistics. http://165.224.221.98/pubs2005/2005025a.pdf

State Educational Technology Directors Association. (2005). National Leadership Institute's Toolkit 2004–2005. http://www.setda.org/Toolkit2004/toolkit2005_entirekit.pdf

Ungerleider, C., & Burns, T. (2003). *A systematic review of the effectiveness and efficiency of networked ICT in education: A state of the field report. Council of Ministers Canada and Industry Canada.* Ottawa: Industry Canada.

Watson, J. (2005). *Keeping pace with K–12 online learning: A review of state-level policy and practice.* Naperville, IL: Learning Point Associates.

Watson, J., Winograd, K., & Kalmon, S. (2004). *Keeping pace with K–12 online learning: A snapshot of state-level policy and practice.* Naperville, IL: Learning Point Associates.

Weiner, C. (2003, July–September). Key ingredients to online learning: Adolescent students study in cyberspace., 44–50.

Zucker, A. (2005). A study of student interaction and collaboration in the virtual high school. In R. Smith, T. Clark, & B. Blomeyer (Eds.), *A synthesis of new research in K–12 online learning* (pp. 43–45). Naperville, IL: Learning Point Associates.

Zucker, A., & Kozma, R. (2003). *The virtual high school: Teaching generation V.* New York: Teachers College Press.

14

Gender Matters in Online Learning

Cheris Kramarae
University of Oregon

Gender matters. During the past several decades, a great deal of research has found significant gender disparity across many areas of computer technology use in educational contexts, including online education.

This review of the research and suggestions regarding some of the gender-related[1] issues that address problems and accountability has information for everyone involved in online education in countries where English is the primary language. The aim is to foster dialogue among diverse groups concerned with gender and education issues. The focus is on post-secondary education, because this is the focus of most distance education research. While the research on the online courses offered in preschool, elementary school, and middle-school students is rather limited, what is clear is that equity issues infuse all stages of all online course development and teaching, including preparing guidelines for recruitment and enrollment; attending to language and interaction patterns; creating a learning context that considers the race, gender, ethnicity, and disabilities of the students; and preparing instructional tools that meet the needs of all users (Kaser, 2004).

As we continue to assess equity in distance education, quite obviously we will need to learn much more about what's happening online for students at all levels and ages.

---

[1]"Gender" is used extensively in this article to refer to images, representations, expectations, beliefs and conventions attributed to the biological sexes, and to our subjective, but continuous and persistent, sense of ourselves as masculine or feminine. Gender is seen as not just a "binary" difference, but as a hierarchical difference, since in our culture men and women are so often in a power relationships, with men, as a class, dominant.

"Sex" in this article is usually used to refer to categories based on ascribed (i.e. born with) physical differences. Sex refers to biological differences: chromosomes, hormonal profiles, internal and external sex organs.

Increasingly we recognize that the terms sex and gender are not neatly differentiated. Sex, like gender, is regulated, constructed, and interpreted by traditions, practices and beliefs. It is therefore more common to use gender differences as a blanket term for sex and gender difference when speaking about people because you can't usually know that a difference is 100% biological, separate from a social environment.

WHO'S TAKING ONLINE COURSES AND WHY?

While women are generally under-represented in the design of software, hardware, networks, etc., and in traditional college teaching and administrative positions, they are key consumers of new technology-driven education.

Although national figures for online enrollment are difficult to find, most programs report more women than men are enrolled. One survey reporting that women have higher rates of participation in distance education than men indicates that older women with families and jobs are more likely to take undergraduate distance education programs than are members of other groups (Sikora, 2002). They take the courses primarily for convenience, not for ease, since the majority of students report that online instruction is more academically demanding than traditional classroom instruction. (See, for example, Wyatt, 2005.)

It's important to note that most studies of women's distance education experiences rely on the responses of those women who are likely the most organized, and, therefore, can find time to answer researchers' questions. We need to also keep in mind those "unheard" women, who are having the greatest difficulty with time and responsibility pressures, especially since more women are now single parents, and since recent economic and social policies have increased women's unpaid responsibility for the care of children, the elderly, and the disabled.

However, women taking online courses report that, while they experience many difficulties with the addition of course work to their employment and family responsibilities, they value the opportunity to take classes. One of the biggest benefits of online learning for women is that it eases the transition back to school; many women report feeling uncomfortable about returning to a classroom in which many of the students are much younger and have little or no work experience. Distance learning allows many women to pursue a degree and find intellectual satisfaction even when they do not have the time for, or interest in, the more social aspects of a traditional college program (Kramarae, 2001).

One of the reasons that women who have more to do (e.g., childcare) are enrolling in college courses is that they are trying to improve their economic and employment status with additional education. Paid work for women without a college degree is primarily found in the extremely low-wage professions, such as waitress, domestic servant, cashier, and home-health aide. Men have more chances to make a decent living with just a high-school diploma. A woman with a 2-year associate's degree earns approximately 34% more than a woman with a high school education, and a woman holding a bachelor's degree can expect to earn approximately 68% more per year than a woman who holds only a high school diploma (U.S. Census Bureau, 2000; Marx, 2002). Many of these women work full time and have relatively inflexible schedules at work and at home, so online courses are especially desirable, even if difficult to take, as the women strive to increase their income.

However, accessibility is not the only benefit of online education for women; educational effectiveness is also a benefit. In a study of the perceived learning reported by women and men in 12 online graduate education courses, the women rated their experience as socially richer and educationally more effective than did the men (Rovai & Baker, 2005). Yet for all their interest, participation, and perseverance, women still encounter a number of issues that impede their success.

WHAT'S ONLINE?

The Internet is often talked about as a place of information production, storage, exchange, and (in case of commerce and politics) manipulation. Discussions of "digital divides" reflect the concern by many that equal access to the Internet and to education does not occur automatically. Most of these discussions focus on who has what access, how often, and where, which are certainly critical issues. However, additionally, we need to discuss other kinds of deep empowerment differences, such as what information is highlighted online and what is left off, or suppressed.

Many students interviewed about their online experiences or plans (Kramarae, 2001) report that they cannot get the subject matter they want online. Not being able to find the particular course they want or need is not an unusual complaint; some students have always had difficulties getting the specific courses they want at the time they want them. But, of course, one of the supposed benefits of online education is that students can obtain what is needed, when it is needed. In the past, "geographical place" has often functioned as a prime barrier to access to higher education. It continues to be a factor in the online courses and programs that require some on-campus time.

In addition, many of the women Kramarae (2001) interviewed talked about the types of courses and programs that they cannot find at any time online. Most of the women taking online courses have done a lot of thinking about the kinds of careers they want. For example, they talk about wanting to enroll in art education programs designed for work with handicapped children and adults in institutions, about needing training to start independent businesses that cater to handicapped children, and about wanting to be able to write narrative computer programs for children and adults. We need to know more about women's lives and career plans to know what online programs are most useful.

Further, students may find that the material and assignments in available online courses have little to do with their lives. Using the problems, interests, and experiences of the students (e.g., connecting the learning with the everyday life of the students) is a generally acknowledged way of actively engaging students (Palloff & Pratt, 1999, pp. 116–118). Yet many teachers may know very little about their online students' lives, interests, knowledge, and experiences.

Further, while we often talk about all the information that is available through the powerful Internet (and, indeed, we are developing a means for reshaping human knowledge and education), there is little novelty and innovation in the online courses, which often seem designed to replicate traditional course tasks, using traditional materials (de Castell, Bryson, & Jenson, 2002, p. 5). Many education critics suggest that if learning, particularly adult learning, is to be successful and long-lasting, students must be actively and continually involved in the creation of knowledge.

Increasingly, the kind of knowledge associated with global education and computers is that of abstraction, rationality, theory, and a focus on "universal" methods of diagnosing problems and framing solutions. "High-status knowledge" is what is usually considered important to digitalize and disseminate as education. The kind of knowledge associated with local experience is considered "low-status knowledge" (Bowers, 2000, pp. 74–75), and is seldom digitalized as part of higher education materials. Women are, of course, most closely associated with experiential, local, and ecological knowledge. Their knowledge may become even more disregarded in this millennium than in the past (Kramarae & Zhang, 2002). Given that women have the greater responsibilities regarding family and household, they are more likely to be involved in community-level politics and services, acts that are often not even recognized in conventional political analyses (Stromquist, 2006, p. 146) or as educational backgrounds.

WHO PARTICIPATES ONLINE AND HOW ?

As Susan Herring's (2000; 2003; 2004) studies of discourse on the Internet show, computer-mediated communication is gendered, often producing male dominance. In online classes, men are prone to project a sense of agency and to occupy positions of power, often disrupting and controlling discourse even when their numbers are not large and their experiences aren't the topics of discussion.

Similar to what happens in face-to-face groups, online discussions of all-female groups have significantly more messages per student than do the male groups. The average number of messages written by women decline in groups containing men while the men tend to write more messages in mixed-sex groups (Bostock & Lizhi, 2005). Yet, when a professor, female or male, acts as a moderator, maintaining civility and focus for the interactions, female students often participate more than the male students (Herring, 2000; Rovai & Baker, 2005). When one group of online learning students was asked what is important to them in this context, the women, more than the men, indicated interest in interaction and inclusion. We often think about face-to-face interaction as being rich in social context cues, but online interaction as being comparatively stimulus-deprived. Yet, when given the chance, the women appear to want, and to help develop, a repertoire of social context cues for their online interaction (Baskin, Barker, & Woods, 2005). Aligned with an interest in discussions of connection, women have indicated more interest than men in having a discussions forum, or "home base," to provide a sense of belonging and involvement in their online classes (Ausburn, 2004).

Further, facilitators who model multiple models of discourse, including both challenge and connection, may motivate the participation of women more than those who model primarily challenge and argumentation (Paulus, 2006, p. 24). Patricia Miller (2005) suggests that, in a feminist approach to human interaction, we should pay more attention to how children use computers to communicate with friends over the Internet rather than focusing our attention on the computer games centered on conflict, individualism, and separation. In flexible online courses, people can coconstruct knowledge together, in negotiated and shared activity, sharing, building on, nurturing, and supporting the ideas of others. With encouragement of collaborative discussions can come an awareness of how our diverse experiences (formed by gender, race, class, sexual orientation, age, and geographical location, for example) contribute to our attitudes, beliefs, and behaviors. Girls and women, because of their gender socialization, may tend to choose more collaborative models of discussion. However, with encouragement and support, boys and men may also enjoy and benefit from problem-solving approaches that encourage attention to less traditional ways of thinking that are often encouraged in formal education.

WHO "OWNS" THE COMPUTERS IN THE HOME?

In general, for women, more so than for men, the home is a worksite. So, if a woman living with a family "retires" to use the computer for a few hours, other members may be worried about her "inactivity" in a space and time construed as her workplace. The decision of who has primary ownership of the computers and who decides where they are located/worked on is an expression of family dynamics. Students in a primarily online course in England reported differential access to the computers in their home. Almost half of the women stated that they didn't have equal access to the home computer, while none of the men students reported this (Gunn & McSporran, 2003). A study of the locations of computers in homes found that when women played a leading role in computer acquisition and use, the computers were often placed in a central location. In contrast, in other homes, the computers were located in a basement or other place where users could be relatively alone. Power differences in the family affect the acceptable time and space women have at the computer (Bakardjieva, 2005). Decision making regarding the zoning of time, space, and "ownership" of computers, whether explicit or implicit, may make it very difficult for some women to take distance education classes.

Researchers have found that income is correlated with a greater interest in taking online courses (Mossberger, Tolbert, & Stansbury, 2003); however, studies and discussions that focus only on *family* income and *family* access to the Internet may not address critical issues of who has access to the incomes and the computers.

Often gender and technology observations need to consider class issues as well, as is indicated by the study that found that male students from higher family income levels who had access to a computer at home before age 10 were more likely to use higher levels of a wide range of technologies such as computers, calculators, cell phones, scanners, and digital computers (Ching, Basham, & Jang, 2005). Just asking simple questions about who has access to a computer is not enough to sort out the needed ingredients for online student learning and achievement.

Preparation for Distance Education College Courses

In the past decade in Canada and the United States public schools have invested a great deal of financial resources to technology—in some cases, more than to any other area in their budgets. But since girls are under-represented in the labs and technology courses, they are not benefiting equally from the large financial investments in technology (Bryson, Petrina, & Braundy, 2003). The girls' under-involvement with technology equipment and classes in grade and secondary schools has implications not only for their K-12 years, but also for their post-secondary education and job possibilities. (See the work by Bryson, Petrina, Braundy, & de Castell, 2003.) Boys work with computers at home more often than girls; this seems to be true not only in the United States, but also in the Netherlands, Germany, Sweden, and Japan. (See the review of studies in Volman, van Eck, Heemskerk, & Kuiper, 2005.) In sum, boys use computers more than girls, both at home and at school (Lowe, 2003, p. 150), and girls and boys learn about gender-based "ownership" of computers in both places.

Another "head start" advantage for boys, in grade school and beyond, comes from their early involvement with computer-based gaming. Girls and women remain marginal participants in the gaming activities and wider game culture, despite the findings that show that girls have clear, strong ideas about the kinds of games they would design: games that include simulation, strategy, and interaction. These games, in fact, would likely appeal to a broad range of boys and girls alike (Commission on Technology, Gender, and Teacher Education, 2000). Video games can help players learn quickly. They hold the attention of many boys, while giving pleasure through gradated quests, tasks, and reward structures and give them a ready acquaintance with electronic equipment and software, which makes use of instructional technologies easier. However, while boys may become more adept at learning through using computers, they may have difficulties attending to the school-based assumptions of learning and intelligence when the presentation of the material isn't as flashy, and the rewards are not as immediate (de Castell & Jenson, 2004).

Students learn early what kinds of electronic communication are encouraged, permitted, and considered normal. Many students, especially girls and women, report experiences with cyber-harassment, which is the intentional use of e-mail, chat rooms, cell phones, instant messaging, pagers, or text messaging to inflict humiliation and fear. In a recent study, the majority of middle-school students studied reported being harassed and/or harassing their peers through electronic communication. The researchers suggest that such bullying may begin at school and then move into the home and community via electronic technology, or may start with bullying at a distance—by using computers and cell phones—and then may move to face-to-face bullying (Beran & Li, 2005, p. 271). Teachers, students, and parents admit that they are unprepared to deal with this new method of peer harassment (Strom & Strom, 2005). Teaching, expecting, and rewarding politeness and civility from all students, early-on, may lead to a reduction of the crude and aggressive behaviors that often characterize adult computer-mediated communication (CMC) (see Herring, 2003). Cyber-harassment is related to other crimes; however, courts have maintained a student's right to free speech in cases when a school presents a forum with no restrictions (Fitzer, Griffin, Kastor, & Kelsey, 2002). So, for administrators, teachers, and students, the value of setting guidelines for respectful online interaction seem obvious.

In writing about gender harassment in online classes, Mindy Machanic (1998) notes that if online learning is to be successful, participants need to be interacting with each other. She writes,

> For that to occur, all participants must feel safe. If women, gays, ethnic minorities, or others perceived as "different" do not feel safe, they will not interact fully in the online classroom, and less learning will occur, not only for those who do not feel safe, but for those who are deprived of hearing the different perspectives of those who are silenced. (p. 4)

Recently, there has been a lot of attention to boys' "underachievement" and a call for schools to pay more attention to what boys and men are interested in. At the elementary and secondary level, the disaffection of many males from school language and literacy programs has negative impacts both for their own learning and that of their classmates if the behavior of many uninterested boys disrupts classes. There are some initial indications that the frequently voiced solution of providing higher numbers of male teachers,or trying to make use of the types of gaming activities that boys favor, does not by itself appear to increase knowledge attainment or result in less disruptive behavior (Thornton & Brichenco, 2002). In single-sex classes, teachers may have a tendency to modify their methods to fit stereotypical ideas about boys' and girls' supposed orientations to learning (Martino, Mills, & Lingard, 2005; Arms, in press). What does seem to help all students is a disruption of conventional gendered attitudes, expectations, and behaviors in the classroom, not additional sex-specific remedies. That is, rather than assuming that boys, not girls, like computer programs, adventure, and sports, and then providing boys with more of the same, teachers would do better to make gendered associations problematic and changeable (Pickering 1997). Programs that give girls and boys equitable access to computers require a shifting of institutional practices and continual evaluations to sustain progress (Jenson, de Castell, & Bryson, 2003).

WHAT'S THE COST OF IT ALL?

Many people remain convinced that eventually distance learning will be a relatively inexpensive method of education. However, certainly for new programs, the costs for universities and students (in faculty development, implementation, delivery, and equipment) may be substantially higher than traditional education. A national survey in U.S. universities indicated that three-quarters of universities offering online learning courses charged the same tuition fees as the on-campus courses (National Education Association, 2000). Many women with difficult economic situations express keen interest in taking courses; however, at the moment, distance learning opportunities are disproportionately taken by those who already have access to needed resources.

The cost of education is a frequently discussed topic by the students or potential students who respond to questions about online education. Understanding the varying meaning of the costs of education also requires understanding the structural inequalities of power in families. For example, my interviews indicate that the cost of childcare is most often added to women's lists of expenses, but not to the men's cost of education. Successful students report that they have obtained the support of other family members. But many students report heavy demands put upon them at home, which often makes it difficult for them to take and complete distance education courses (Kramarae, 2001).

HOW TO DO IT ALL?

Most women taking distance education courses are juggling many activities. Researchers surveying nearly 600 women in online health and accounting professional programs found that the women were managing a mean of six other major responsibilities in addition to their class work. Ninety percent worked full time, most were married, 48% had dependent children, others had elder care responsibilities, and many had pet care (sometimes with animals as large and demanding as horses), and 21% reported participation in community work (Cragg, Andrusyszyn, & Fraser, 2005). Some students may need additional time for assignments when they have to deal with unexpected, time-consuming troubles in the family. A student who suddenly has a daughter with a cast on her broken leg may have to add hours to an already crowded schedule and that student may have to drop out of a class if time extensions are not allowed.

A decade ago many administrators were very concerned, if tight-lipped, about the rates of course completion and retention in online programs. Some women were disturbed that they were called "quitters" when they had to drop courses because of conflicting demands from family, work, and education commitments (Kramarae, 2001). Now there is more emphasis on student records of "persistence" and on what the providers of distance learning programs need to do in order to make it possible for students to continue their education (Yorke, 2004). This shift to looking at what the providers need to do to enhance student persistence makes the gender issues discussed here even more important to discussions of successful distance learning programs.

WHEN TO DO IT ALL?

Many women agree with the proponents of distance learning that it is a good option—or at least a compromise—for women with children and without much free time. In interviews and surveys some men also mentioned the value of distance learning for men with family responsibilities. But the discussion of time and family runs through most conversations (of both women and men) about women and distance learning, which is often posited as a remedy for the problems that women with children, in particular, have with time (Kramarae, 2001).

In one sense the reasons for the refrain of distance education being such a boon for women are simple. Most women enrolled in online courses have even less time to call their own than do most traditional students in face-to-face environments; in addition to taking their courses, many of the women in online courses serve as primary caretakers of family members and also work at jobs outside the home. Women, especially those with children, have less free time away from their family responsibilities and work. Distance education allows them to both stay at home and study, at least in the evenings or when off work, while still taking care of home duties and being available to others when needed. Men are more likely to have time that they can use more or less as they wish, both in or out of the home. (For discussions of research on housework, employment, and time, see Greenstein, 2000; Hersch & Stratton, 1997.)

Most of the student mothers mentioned devoting late evening or very early morning hours to study. Given that most of the women also had part- or full-time jobs, their preference for setting their own times for study does not seem surprising. However, late evening hours are not necessarily the only "natural" time for adults to study; researchers evaluating a graduate online course in the United Kingdom found that men were most likely to mention studying from 4 to 8 p.m. while the majority of the women studied later, fitting in their study times after fulfilling other commitments (Richardson & French, 2000, p. 305).

WHAT SUPPORT IS WANTED?

Women students rate support from tutors/teachers as most important, although they also report often not receiving adequate support (Furst-Bowe, 2002). Spouses were rated as the most important support in the home, as well as the most actually supportive group. However, about one-third of the women students think that their partners resent the time the women spent at their studies, and about one-third think that their relationship with their children has been negatively affected. Some students report receiving support from employers, while others meet opposition and roadblocks from supervisors, even when the credentials being earned are a workplace requirement or asset. Most of the women report frustrations and concerns about how their studies were adversely affecting family life (Cragg et al., 2005, pp. 30–31).

WHO'S TEACHING?

In most online programs, teachers are adjunct faculty. This saves money for administrators (who can pay by the course without paying benefits), and fills positions that full-time faculty members are often reluctant to take. Many of these teachers are women, who traditionally have lower-paying, temporary, nontenure track positions in education, and many teach for more than one university and also teach multiple courses. There is little pooled information on adjunct teachers—where they are teaching, what they are teaching, and at what wages. While some institutions try to avoid leaning heavily on adjunct professors to teach online courses by attempting to keep the proportion of adjuncts and permanent faculty members the same in online courses as in face-to-face ones (Carnavale, 2004), this practice is unusual. For example, at one Florida community college with yearly enrollment of more than 35,000 in the distance learning program, about 80% of the courses are taught by virtual adjuncts, about 30% of whom live outside the state (Puzziferro-Schnitzer, 2005).

In the many situations when adjuncts are not hired each term by the same institution, the adjuncts have little influence in determining the content of the courses they teach (Twigg, 2001). Canned courses are being used more frequently ("The Naked Truth about Distance Education," 2006), a situation that brings serious limitations for teachers who may want to introduce more diversity issues in courses across disciplines but who are not allowed to alter the syllabus. As administrators acknowledge the online education trends and reconsider the place of online students in their overall missions, they will need to make sure that the faculty members who participate in the creation and the teaching of the courses understand the backgrounds (including the age, class, race, sex, location, and experience) of the "nontraditional" students. For example, working-class women's voices and lives have been largely absent in academic texts and courses. Yet many working-class women are participating in adult education and are questioning and challenging their traditional role and status in society. Their education can only be liberating if it is linked to their experiences and knowledge. (See Merrill, 2005, for a discussion of the missing voices of working-class women.)

SOME RECOMMENDATIONS

The focus in this chapter has been on women's online education. Issues of gender inequities online cannot be considered independent of other factors such as race, ethnicity, class, learning styles, income, and educational background. However, gender needs to be addressed by everyone who wants to offer equal oppurtunities to all students in distance education. This chapter identifies and documents some of the online experiences that are gender-specific, and that pose problems and possibilities, and remedies that can be used for interventions. In addition, following are a few specific suggestions about how educators can help prepare and encourage more students in online courses:

Prepare the Environment

Provide a "home base" or "student lounge" for the course, to help provide learners with a sense of belonging and involvement. Create a distinctive online gathering place, and then encourage leadership from within the class (Ausburn, 2004; Palloff & Pratt, 1999, p. 24). Provide a range of support options (e.g., online tutorials) that are available without being requested; this may be of special interest for the men who may be less likely to ask for assistance (Gunn & McSporran, 2003).

If students give permission, provide email lists (or use programs with built-in email systems) to facilitate student interaction. Most students do not want to meet classmates in person for friendship (Furst-Bowe, 2002), but may need course-related support, especially if the teachers and administrators are not able to provide as much help as needed. Many students list strong support from tutors/instructors as most or highly important to success in online classes but indicate that contact with teachers and tutors is often difficult or unsatisfactory; thus, making it easy to contact fellow students can be helpful (Cragg et al., 2005, pp. 29–31). Clear explanations about how to contact teachers, expected turn-around time for responses (Kowslowski, 2004), and reminders about course deadlines and expectations (Hill, 2003) are also important.

Suggest to students that they negotiate expectations and responsibilities at home, so that all family members realize that family life will not be the same when a woman takes classes, and suggest that, if possible, they delegate or get rid of some traditional family activities (Cragg et al., 2005, p. 34).

Recognize the Diversity within the Class during the Course

Try to welcome different types of learners at multiple entry points, allowing learners to relate their personal experiences in a variety of ways (Whitehouse, 2002). While implementing practices that respect the years of experience that adult learners bring to class is a stated goal of many adult-education courses, sometimes the experiences that women bring to class are not seen as relevant as the experiences that men, as least in the professions, bring. (See the examples of how various learning approaches can be offered to students in every course in Hunter & Nebitt, 2003.)

Avoid required group assignments, because while students may enjoy them in theory, many women report disliking group work because of schedule and time differences. Women report having to manage their time very carefully to fit with their many other responsibilities; they need to be able to complete their work on their own schedule as much as possible (Cragg et al., 2005, p. 30; Kramarae, 2001).

Model appropriate discussion strategies, including not only a discourse of challenge and argumentation, but also of connection, agreement, acknowledgement of validity of other views, and uncertainty or the possibility that different views exist (Paulus, 2006). Providing opportunities for students to write of their own experiences may help them speak as a person of color, as a woman, as a person from a working-class family, as a person with a disability, situating individual experiences with wider social systems. Prepare students for analyzing their relations to others' posts. Discuss with students not only about what not to do, such as flaming, but also what to do, such as encouraging self-analysis of their individual and cultural positions in relation to, for example, race, gender, class, and disabilities (McKee, 2002).

Gender matters in preparing, teaching, and taking online courses. Working on equity in online education requires not expressing benign goodwill toward all, but acting deliberately to alter the current problems and work toward educational transformation.

REFERENCES

Arms, E. (2007). Gender equity in coeducational and single sex educational environments. In S. Klein (Ed.), *Handbook for achieving gender equity through education*. Hillsdale, N.J.: Lawrence Erlbaum, in press.

Ausburn, L. J. (2004). Course design elements most valued by adult learners in blended online education environments: An American perspective. *Educational Media International, 41*(4), 327–337.

Bakardjieva, M. (2005). *Internet society: The Internet in everyday life*. London and Thousand Oaks, CA: Sage.

Baskin, C., Barker, M., & Woods, P. (2005). When group work leaves the classroom does group skills development go out the window? *British Journal of Educational Technology, 36*(1), 19–31.

Beran, T., & Li, Q. (2005). Cyber-harassment: A study of a new method for an old behavior. *Journal of Educational Computing Research, 32*(3), 265–277.

Bostock, S. J., & Lizhi, W. (2005). Gender in student online discussions. *Innovations in Education and Teaching International, 42*(1), 73–85.

Bowers, C. A. (2000). *Let them eat data: How computers affect education, cultural diversity, and the prospects of ecological sustainability*. Athens: The University of Georgia Press.

Bryson, M., Petrina, S., & Braundy, M. (2003). Conditions for success? Gender in technology-intensive courses in British Columbia Secondary Schools. *Canadian Journal of Science, Mathematics and Technology Education, 3*(2), 185–192.

Bryson, M., Petrina, S., Braundy, M., & de Castell, S. (2003). "Conditions for success"? Sex-disaggregated analysis of performance and participation indicators in technology-intensive courses in B.C. secondary schools. *Canadian Journal of Science, Mathematics and Technology, 3*(2), 185–194.

Carnavale, D. (2004, April 30). For online adjuncts, a seller's market: Part-time professors, in demand, fill many distance education faculties. *Chronicle of Higher Education*. Retrieved December 20, 2006 at http://chronicle.com/free/v50/i34/34a03101.htm

Ching, C. C., Basham, J. D., & Jang, E. (2005). The legacy of the Digital Divide: Gender, Socioeconomic status, and early exposure as predictors of full-spectrum technology use in young adults. *Urban Education, 40*(4), 394–411.

Commission on Technology, Gender, and Teacher Education. (2000). *Tech-savvy: Educating girls in the new computer age*. Washington, DC: American Association of University Professors.

Cragg, C. E., Andrusyszyn, M., & Fraser, J. (2005). Sources of support for women taking professional programs by distance education. *Journal of Distance Education, 20*(1), 21–38.

de Castell, S., Bryson, M., & Jenson, J. (2002). Object lessons: Towards an educational theory of technology. *First Monday, 7*(1). Retrieved December 20, 2006 at http://www.firstmonday.org/issues/issue7_1/castell/index.html

de Castell, S., & Jenson, J. (2004). Paying attention to attention: New economies for learning. *Educational Theory, 54*(4), 381–397.

Fitzer, K., Griffin, L., Kastor, G., & Kelsey, Y. (2002). Addendum to the educator's guide to computer crime and technology misuse. Retrieved December 20, 2006 at http://lrs.ed.uiuc.edu/wp/crime/index.html

Furst-Bowe, J. (2002). Identifying the needs of adult women in distance learning programs. In R. M. Cervero, B. C. Courtenay, & C. H. Monaghan (Comps.), *The Cyril O. Houle Scholars in Adult and Continuing Education Program Global Research Perspectives: Vol. 2* (pp 82-89). Athens: University of Georgia.

Greenstein, T. N. (2000). Economic dependence, gender, and the division of labor in the home: A replication and extension. *Journal of Marriage and the Family, 62*, 322–335.

Gunn, C., & McSporran, M. (2003). Dominant or different? Gender issues in computer supported learning. *Journal of Asynchronous Learning Networks, 7*(1). Retrieved December 20, 2006 at http://www.sloan-c.org/publications/jaln/v7n1/pdf/v7n1_gunn.pdf

Herring, S. C. (2000). Gender differences in CMC: Findings and implications. *The CPSR Newsletter, 18*(1), 3–11.

Herring, S. C. (2003). Gender and power in online communication. In J. Holmes and M. Meyerhoff (Eds.), *The handbook of language and gender* (pp. 202–228). Oxford: Blackwell.

Herring, S. C. (2004). Gender equity issues in online learning: Considerations for discussion. Retrieved December 20, 2006 at http://mailman.edc.org/pipermail/diversityonline/20040719/000004.html

Hersch, J., & Stratton, L. S. (1997). Housework, fixed effects, and wages of married workers. *Journal of Human Resources, 32*(2), 285–307.

Hill, J. (2003). Where's the human element in online education. *Women in Higher Education, 12*(12), 42.

Hunter, L., & Nebitt, S. (2003). Assisting students with self-directed learning skills. In J. C. Moore (Ed.), *Elements of quality online education: Into the mainstream: Wisdom from the Sloan Consortium*, (pp. 87–93).

Jenson, J., de Castell, S., & Bryson, M. (2003). "Girl talk": Gender, equity, and identity discourses in a school-based computer culture. *Women's Studies International Forum, 26*(6), 561–573.

Kaser, J. S. (2004). Equity in online professional development: A guide to e-learning that works for everyone. Newton, Mass.: Education Development Center, Inc. Retrieved December 20, 2006 at http://www2.edc.org/gdi/publications_SR/equity6_04_FULLBOOK.pdf

Kowslowski, D. (2004). Factors for consideration in the development and implementation of an online RN-BSN course: Faculty and student perspectives. *CIN: Computers, Informatics, Nursing, 22*(1), 34–43.

Kramarae, C. (2001). *The third shift: Women learning online*. Washington, DC: American Association of University Women.

Kramarae, C., & Zhang, W. (2002). At home in education: The future of online learning for women. In C. Floyd, G. Kelkar, S. Klein-Franke, C. Kramarae, & C. Limpangog (Eds.), *Feminist challenges in the Information Age* (pp. 241–251). Opladen, Germany: Leske + Budrich.

Lowe, G. S. (2003). Influence of socioeconomic status and gender on high school seniors' use of computers at home and school. *The Alberta Journal of Educational Research, 69*(2), 138–154.

Machanic, M. (1998). Gender & power issues in online learning environments. Proceedings, First International Conference on the Social Impacts of Technology, ERIC No. ED442972.

Martino, W., Mills, M., & Lingard, B. (2005). Interrogating single-sex classes as strategy for addressing boys' educational and social needs. *Oxford Review of Education, 31*(2), 237–254.

Marx, F. (2002). Grassroots to graduation: Low-income women accessing higher education. Final report on the Evaluation of the Women in Community Development Program. Boston: Center for Research on Women. Wellesley College Center for Research on Women.

McKee, H. (2002). "YOUR VIEWS SHOWED TRUE IGNORANCE!!!": (Mis)communication in an online interracial discussion forum. *Computers and Composition, 19*, 411–434.

Merrill, B. (2005). Dialogical feminism: Other women and the challenge of adult education. *International Journal of Lifelong Education, 24*(1), 41–52.

Miller, P. H. (2005). Gender and information technology: Perspectives from human cognitive development. *Frontiers: A Journal of Women Studies, 26*(1), 148–167.

Mossberger, K., Tolbert, C. T., & Stansbury, M. (2003). Virtual inequality: Beyond the digital divide. Washington, DC: Georgetown University Press.

National Education Association. (2000). *Enrollment projections*. Retrieved December 20, 2006 at http://www2.nea.org/he/heupdate/images/vol6no5.pdf

Palloff, R. M., & Pratt, K. (1999). *Buiding learning communities in cyberspace: Effective strategies for the online classroom.* San Francisco: Jossey-Bass.

Paulus, T. M. (2006). Challenge or connect? Dialogue in online learning environments. *Journal of Computing in Higher Education, 18*(1), 3–29.

Pickering, J. (1997). *Raising boys' achievement.* Stafford, United Kingdom: Network Educational Press.

Puzziferro-Schnitzer, M. (2005). Managing virtual adjunct faculty: Applying the Seven Principles of Good Practice. *Online Journal of Distance Learning Administration, VIII*(II). Retrieved December 20, 2006 at http://www.westga.edu/~distance/ojdla/summer82/schnitzer82.htm

Richardson, H. J., & French, S. (2000). Education online: What's in it for women? In E. Balka & R. Smith (Eds.), *Women, work and computerization: Charting a course to the future*, (pp. 300–307). Boston: Kluwer Academic Publishers.

Rovai, A., & Baker, J. (2005). Gender differences in online learning: Sense of community, perceived learning, and interpersonal interactions. *The Quarterly Review of Distance Education, 6*(1), 31–44.

Sikora, A. C. (2002). A profile of participation in distance education: 1999–2000. *Education Statistics Quarterly, 4*(4). Retrieved December 20, 2006 at http://nces.ed.gov/programs/quarterly/vol_4/4_4/q4_3.asp

Strom, P., & Strom, R. D. (2005). Cyberbullying by adolescents: A preliminary assessment. *The Educational Forum*, fall. Retrieved December 20, 2006 at http://www.kdp.org/archives/files/edforum/ff05_21-32.pdf

Stromquist, N. P. (2006). Women's rights to adult education as a means to citizenship. *International Journal of Educational Development, 26*, 140–152.

The naked truth about distance education. (2006). *AdjunctNation.com*, January/February. Retrieved December 20, 2006 at https://www.adjunctnation.com/shop/product_info.php?products_id=164

Thornton, M., & Brichenco, P. (2002). Staff gender balance in primary schools. Paper presented at the British Educational Research Association Annual Conference, University of Exeter, 12–14 September.

Twigg, C. A. (2001). Innovations in online learning: Moving beyond no significant difference. Center for Academic Transformation, Rensselaer Polytechnic Institute.

U.S. Census Bureau. (2000). *Current population reports: Money income in the United States.* Washington, DC: U.S. Government Printing Office.

Volman, M., van Eck, E., Heemskerk, I., & Kuiper, E. (2005). New technologies, new differences: Gender and ethnic differences in pupils' use of ICT in primary and secondary education. *Computers & Education, 45*(1), 35–55.

Whitehouse, P. (2002). Women's studies online: An oxymoron? *Women's Studies Quarterly, 30*(3&4), 209–225.

Wyatt, G. (2005). Satisfaction, academic rigor and interaction: Perceptions of online instruction. *Education, 125*(3), 460–468.

Yorke, M. (2004). Retention, persistence and success in on-campus higher education, and their enhancement in open and distance learning. *Open Learning, 19*(1), 19–32.

15

Academic Advising in Degree Programs

Robert F. Curry and Phyllis D. Barham
Old Dominion University

A student's success in distance learning is often determined by the quality of academic advising and other student services (Miller, 1993; Wagner, 1993). Distance learners are usually returning students, at least 25 years old, and employed (Peterson's, 1998). As reported by Sloan and Wilmes (1989), an academic advisor may be the first and only institutional contact adult students have outside the classroom. This statement seems even more important for distant students, who may not have a classroom; if they do, it is away from the main campus.

Because few studies have been published, research on academic advising in distance education is not extensive. This review begins with the international research, followed with United States research by level of distance advising program studied: associate, baccalaureate, and other certificate or degree programs.

INTERNATIONAL PROGRAMS

Several international studies have relevance for distance advising in the United States. Potter (1998) surveyed students who had taken credit courses through distance education at one of three Canadian universities. The majority of these students were enrolled in undergraduate degree programs. Students rated the following support services as important or very important: information about specific programs, general information about distance education opportunities, advice about course selection, orientation to media/course delivery format, and help with the application process. When asked to rate the accessibility of the services, each service listed had a lower percentage of students considering it accessible than rated for importance.

In an open-ended question, students were asked to identify factors that caused difficulties in their academic progress. The most frequently mentioned issues were insufficient time because of multiple responsibilities, and difficulty in financing their education (Potter, 1998).

Lalande (1995) reported on psycho-educational workshops through audio teleconferencing; the audience was registered nurses enrolled in a bachelor's program at the University of

Calgary. Workshop topics included "Preparation for the Student Role," "Developing Independent Learning Skills: Information Selection and Evaluation," "Stress Management for the Multiple-Role Adult," and "Strategies for Career Planning for Nurses." According to student evaluations, the majority of students believed objectives of the workshop were somewhat or completely met. A qualitative analysis of the written comments indicated that participants found the workshops helpful and informative. Attendance was lower than desired, so a questionnaire was mailed to all students in the program. As their reasons for not attending the workshops, students most frequently mentioned having other commitments or being too busy. The author concluded that effective student services can be provided by teleconferencing technology.

In a study of students at the United Kingdom Open University in Scotland, Carr and Ledwith (1980) found that 63% of respondents considered valuable the advice that they received from an introductory advising session, an open house, and mailed written material before enrollment. Students indicated that information on courses, advice on time needed for study and preparatory work, and reassurance by institutional representatives were the most helpful activities. Nevertheless, 66% of respondents stated that they would have benefited from more advice, in particular on the level and pace of course work.

Bowser and Race (1991) evaluated the orientation program for new students in distance education programs at an institution in Australia. Students attended orientation sessions the week before the academic year began in 14 centers. Students ranked the opportunity to meet other students as the most important function of the session. Clarification of academic, administrative, and enrollment information was also rated high in importance.

Kemp (2002) did a correlational study to assess whether resilience, life events, and external commitments were predicators of persistence in distance learning. The population was undergraduate students at Athabasca University who were taking their first distance course and 30–45 years old. A random sample of 460 students was obtained. Of these, 124 completed two psychometric tests and a questionnaire.

Ten months after starting it, 47% of students in the study had finished the course.

The study found no significant differences in life events for persisters compared with those who dropped the course. Work commitment was the only predictor of the external commitments. For resilience, those successfully completing the course were more likely to develop and maintain healthy relationships, persist in working through difficulties, and have the confidence to make the most of bad situations (Kemp, 2002).

Bird and Morgan (2003) did a qualitative study on adult students' issues regarding enrollment and persistence. A purposeful sample of 20 on-campus and distant university students, aged 21–56, was chosen for diversity in discipline, enrollment patterns, family commitments, work commitments, and financial status. In 2 groups of 10, students were asked an open-ended question of how they decided to attend the university. Seven of the students, chosen largely because they were articulate in describing their academic journeys, participated in a second interview. This interview was more structured, confirming details from the first interview and probing into more detail. The researchers found that students with high motivation and commitment resolved many problems regarding family support, fear of failure, and financial issues.

The authors identified several issues to discuss with potential distance students: identifying and managing fears; building academic skills; developing computer skills; investigating degree programs of interest; exploring impact of study on family roles; considering work and financial commitments; and identifying support networks. Although providing rich qualitative data, a weakness of the study is that the data was not separated for distance learners versus traditional students (Bird & Morgan, 2003).

ASSOCIATE DEGREE PROGRAMS

From questionnaires sent to 59 two-year higher education institutions with distance education programs, Paneitz (1997) identified ten institutions for her research. This sample of ten was chosen based on the means of delivering student services. In addition to the requirement of having an associate degree program available at a distance, Paneitz sought a wide range of technology used in providing advising, counseling, and library/media services. Forty cover letters and questionnaires were sent to the contact person for each of the institutions. The contact persons distributed the questionnaires randomly to students enrolled in distance education degree programs. A total of 183 out of 400 questionnaires were returned, for a response rate of 46%.

For the study, Paneitz (1997) made the following distinction in level of technology:

1. No technology—Students must come to the main campus for advising.
2. Low technology—Advising is done with the assistance of a toll-free telephone number and/or a facsimile.
3. High technology—Students have access to a toll-free number and a facsimile for advising. In addition, technical assistance for advising includes at least one other means such as voice mail, email, computer bulletin, or videotapes.

Paneitz (1997) surveyed distance students on their use of academic advising. In high-technology institutions, the following percentages of students reported using academic advising for scheduling of classes (83%), initial degree planning (80%), referral to remedial/study skills (76%), and guidance on transfer to four-year schools (48%). These high percentages of use were also reported at no technology and low technology institutions. Paneitz concluded that the means of providing the advising service may not be important in getting students to use it, but that advising should be provided in some manner.

Students were also asked to rate their satisfaction with advising services. The majority of students were satisfied or very satisfied with the assistance in recommending remedial and study skills classes, assistance with initial degree planning, and assistance with transfer to four-year institutions. There were no significant differences in satisfaction based on level of technology in providing the services (Paneitz, 1997).

Students at low-technology institutions were less satisfied with the advising provided for class scheduling than those at institutions with either no or high technology. This no tech face-to-face advising was considered as desirable as high tech email or voice mail. Paneitz suggested that a low tech school upgrade technology to increase student satisfaction. She added, however, that face-to-face contact may also be helpful when feasible.

Academic advising was considered the most essential student service by distance students. Thirty-nine percent ranked it first, while 31% ranked it second in importance when compared with library/media services, career counseling, tutorial services, and personal counseling (Paneitz, 1997).

Paneitz concluded that academic advising is the most essential student service for distance students in two-year institutions. She also concluded that technology will play a larger role in future years in providing student services to distance students. She indicated, however, that having advising services in an efficient and consistent process is more important than spending resources on high-technology delivery systems.

The questionnaire sent by Paneitz (1997) to distance students provided valuable data on the use of advising services and student satisfaction with the services. A strength is that the survey was completed by students at multiple institutions, with varied delivery models for academic advising. Although the response rate was not very high, the randomness of the selection offsets this fact for a valid study. The comparisons based on level of technology, however, should be considered with caution. Other variables were not controlled and may have been factors in the differences in satisfaction noted.

Tallman (1994) studied students who had taken correspondence courses from Southeastern College, a private, religiously affiliated institution. He developed the Student Satisfaction Questionnaire (SSQ) for the study. The SSQ was mailed to 505 students, a proportionately stratified sample of students who had completed correspondence courses. The stratified sample was done so that there would be a proportional representation of all students by month of course completion; 311 students returned the study for a response rate of 61%. In addition, demographic characteristics of nonrespondents were analyzed and did not differ significantly from those of students who did respond. Sixty-eight percent of respondents were enrolled in an external degree program at Southeastern, with an additional 11.3% seeking a degree from another institution. It was not stated which degree respondents were pursuing, although a guide by Peterson's (1998) indicated the institution offered both associate and baccalaureate degree programs.

The admission process was the most influential factor in student satisfaction. Important components were helpfulness of admissions personnel, "user-friendliness" of admissions materials, and the orientation session (telephone or face-to-face). While admissions dealt with the preenrollment process, other variables involved satisfaction while attending. Of these variables during enrollment, assistance provided by the Continuing Education staff was the most significant factor in student satisfaction. In order of significance, this variable was followed by contact with advisors, feeling a part of the institution, promptly returned phone calls, and motivation inspired by advisors (Tallman, 1994).

Houle (2004) studied adult student persistence in Web-based education. The instrument was the Distance Education Student Progress Inventory (Kember, Murphy, Siaw, & Yuen, 1991) with questions eliminated that were not relevant to Web-based study. It was sent to all students enrolled in an online associate degree program in telecommunications. By the end of the term, 174 students (82.1%) successfully completed the course, 16 students (7.5%) did not successfully complete the course, and 22 (10.4%) had dropped out. The study found that

- Factors leading to success in asynchronous Web-based courses were having a location at home for study, work experience of 16 or more years, having a higher GPA, and motivation.
- Students who were not successful were more likely to study at work instead of home. Unsuccessful students had unexpected events such as a change in family circumstance, change in work, or illness.
- Primary caretakers of children or the household comprised 86.4% of students who dropped out of the program. These students also had little if any encouragement to enroll in the course from family, friends, and employer.

The author suggests that online students need enhanced communication and integration with the institution to increase persistence and success. Advisors need to give students encouragement to help them deal with stress and reduce the perceived barriers of distance education (Houle, 2004).

BACCALAUREATE DEGREE PROGRAMS

For a doctoral dissertation, Curry (1997) conducted a national survey of academic advising in distance education. Institutions selected for the sample had a least one baccalaureate degree program available at a distance, using primarily electronic means of instruction. While only 89 institutions met the study's sample criteria, 73 surveys were returned for a response rate of 82%. Results from the Academic Advising in Distance Education Survey were compared to data from American College Testing's (ACT) Fourth National Survey of Academic Advising (Habley, 1993). With these data, Curry compared and contrasted current goals and practices of distance education programs with those of institutions as a whole.

Academic practices were found to be similar for distance education and institutions as a whole in that faculty advisors were the most frequent deliverers of advising services. There were differences in other practices, with less utilization of group advising, institutional reference materials, and advising evaluation in distance education (Curry, 1997).

The advising goals of the National Academic Advising Association (NACADA) were listed on Curry's (1997) survey. Based on his results, distance education programs have greater achievement of NACADA's advising goals than do institutions as a whole. The mean of means for the advising goals in distance education was 3.97, compared with 3.31 for institutional advising programs. With a rating of 4 indicating satisfactorily achieving a goal, distance education programs were closer to that aggregate achievement level than institutions as a whole. In addition, mean achievement was higher for each of the eight advising goals in distance education programs (See Table 15.1). Results pertaining to goal achievement were subjective, reported by one survey respondent for institutional advising programs and distance education advising programs.

Although some respondents disagreed, the goals of distance education advising programs are largely consistent with NACADA's goals. The goal cited as not relevant most often was assisting students in developing decision-making skills. This goal still had 82% of institutions reporting it was relevant for distance education students (Curry, 1997).

Most respondents indicated it was likely that advisors and distance education students would develop personal relationships. In Fielstein's (1989) study, 83% of students indicated it was a priority advising activity that advisors be personally acquainted with their students. A respondent who reported that a personal relationship was likely qualified the answer with the statement, "if

TABLE 15.1.
Mean Achievement of Advising Goals by Survey Category

NACADA Advising Goal	Distance Education	ACT
Survey Category		
Assisting students in self-understanding and self-assistance	3.63	2.82
Assisting students in their consideration of life goals	3.87	3.12
Assisting students in developing an educational plan	4.23	3.48
Assisting students in developing decision-making skills	3.82	2.71
Providing accurate information about institutional policies	4.42	3.99
Making referrals to other support services	3.74	3.43
Assisting students in evaluation of progress toward established goals and educational plans	4.16	3.49
Providing information about students to the institution	3.94	3.47
Mean of means	3.97	3.31

Note. Data in column 2 are from Curry (1997). Data in column 3 are from Habley (1993).

indicating a satisfactory comfort level in their interactions as opposed to a social type relationship" (Curry, 1997).

From the dissertation results, an article was published focusing on academic advising practices specifically for distance education students (Curry, Baldwin, & Sharpe, 1998). The reported practices included means of communication and types of advisors for distance students. When asked about the top three means of communication between advisors and distance education students, institutions reported telephone conversations in real time most often (94%), followed by in-person (61%), written correspondence by mail (55%), telephone conversations through voice mail (33%), and computer conferencing out of real time such as electronic mail (33%).

Faculty advisors, academic department heads, full-time advisors, part-time advisors, paraprofessional advisors, and peer advisors were listed as possible advisor types on the survey. All were reported as used by some institutions in distance education. Although the academic advisor was most often reported as being based on the main campus, some institutions also reported the use of each advisor type based closer to distant students. In addition to the choices of advisors listed on the survey, respondents indicated other types. The other type of advisor most often mentioned was an individual connected to the distance education office such as a central administrator or site director (Curry et al., 1998).

A discriminant analysis statistical procedure was undertaken to determine the practices most consistent with achieving NACADA's advising goals. These practices were providing advisors with an academic advising handbook and having advising-oriented courses for students on the main campus. Although the statistical results were not conclusive, an advising handbook is certainly a helpful tool for those advising distance education students. Requiring students to visit campus may not be feasible or consistent with the goals of some distance education programs (Curry, 1997).

In addition to the advising handbook, Curry et al. (1998) gave several recommendations. These recommendations are: encouraging advisors to develop personal relationships with students, providing a campus referral directory for advisors, and evaluating advisors and advising programs.

The dissertation (Curry, 1997) and article based on it (Curry et al., 1998) represent the most comprehensive national data on academic advising in distance education currently available. The high response rate resulted in a valid study despite the small population at the time. Institutional representatives may have been overly favorable when reporting goal achievement, but the respondents did seem to have knowledge of advising practices. With the fast changing environment of distance education, however, the results can no longer be considered current. The percentage of institutions with advisors using electronic mail, for example, is likely much higher than reported through this research.

Workman and Stenard (1996) conducted interviews with 60 students enrolled in distance education programs at Eastern Oregon State College. The institution offers distance learning programs through external degrees, weekend college classes, independent study, and telecommunications. Results of interviews with students at the main campus and six regional centers were consistent in identifying five needs of students:

1. Clarity of program, policies, and procedures for consistency and assistance in student planning
2. Increasing self-esteem
3. Identification with institution
4. Developing interpersonal relationships with peers, faculty, and staff
5. Accessibility of student support services

All students interviewed reported that the center directors were their most important resource. Many students indicated they would have dropped out without the support and assistance of these personnel (Workman & Stenard, 1996).

The institution developed several programs to help meet the needs identified by students. One program is a "Back to School Night," broadcast to the off-campus audience. This interactive televised presentation is held for prospective students. Before this particular televised presentation, information packets were made available at regional centers. Each of the 50 students attending the session completed an evaluation form; 90% rated the student services presentations as "good" to "excellent" (Workman & Stenard, 1996).

The study by Workman and Stenard (1996) is valuable in its interviews with 60 students. A weakness is that the authors did not identify how students were selected for the interviews. In addition, the type of distance education program the students were participating in was not reported. Students taking classes through independent study, weekend college, and telecommunications may have different needs. These omissions in sample information make it difficult to generalize the results to other institutions.

Brown (2004) studied the differences between student service satisfaction for traditional versus distance learning students. The population was undergraduate and graduate students enrolled in a residential or distance program at two universities. Both universities were small, private institutions with a religious affiliation, located in the eastern United States. All students at both institutions were asked to participate; of a total of 17,685 students, 8,697 were traditional and 8,988 were distance. The request came by e-mail from the student's home institution, with a follow-up two weeks later. The instrument was the Student Satisfaction Inventory Version Two (SSI–2) by Noel Levitz. With 5,292 students completing the online survey instrument, the response rate was 29.9%. The majority of distance and traditional students who responded were undergraduates.

The distance learning students were more satisfied than traditional students in most student services, including the following: recruitment and financial aid, academic advising, registration, library services, tutoring, counseling, career services, and the new student program. Traditional students were more satisfied than distance students with campus services and spiritual activities. The researcher speculated that a higher level of satisfaction was attained because the distance learning student was more advanced developmentally, with an average age 10 years greater than the traditional students. However, there may be other factors in the students' lives that were not investigated. Brown (2004) encouraged student services personnel to question what services should be offered online and to whom, whether online services can meet the developmental needs of each students, and how community can be formed among online students.

The author acknowledged that the study has limited generalizability with the specialized institutions involved (Brown, 2004). For the population studied, additional insights could have been gained if the undergraduate and graduate student data had been separated.

OTHER DEGREE AND CERTIFICATE PROGRAMS

Beitz (1987) studied academic advising in distance graduate library science programs in the United States. She conducted a telephone survey of library administrators at all schools that offered off-campus courses. Most institutions were not using telecommunications to deliver courses and did not offer entire degree programs at a distance. The majority of programs had academic advising by telephone (61%), but students were encouraged to come to the main campus for advising sessions when possible.

Some schools had faculty members provide in-person advising services to students when faculty traveled to sites for teaching. Beitz reported that most of the library schools did not require advising. For students who took the time to seek advising, however, it was available and effective. She concluded that a planned program of advising services was essential for the success of distance education programs offered by professional schools.

Beitz's (1987) study was based on programs where only 20% of them used any telecommunications to deliver distance education. Consistent with the instruction, a very technical means of academic advising was not reported. All 18 programs offering off-campus courses were surveyed. The survey was valid for this specialization during this time period. It is also important to provide some data on the issue of advising graduate students at a distance.

Wang (1997) did a case study to assess Maine's statewide distance education network. This network offers distance education courses to homes, high schools, business, and other sites. Classes are televised with one or two way video. Through the distance education network, off-campus students can pursue associate, bachelor, and, master's degrees, and Certificates of Graduate Studies.

The methodology included interviews, survey questionnaires, and analysis of documents. The part of the study relevant to academic advising was a survey questionnaire to students.

A total of 1,400 survey questionnaires were distributed to students; only 248 questionnaires were returned for an 18% response rate. For a question on quality of academic advising, the study reported the following responses: excellent (22%), good (22%), acceptable (24%), not acceptable (10%), poor (2%), not applicable (15%), or left this section blank (7%). The researcher was concerned that 15% indicated academic advising was not relevant for them. She speculated that lack of time for academic advising and adults' independence could be factors in their avoidance of the services. She said academic advising should be considered useful given the length of time away from school for many distant adult learners, lack of choice in course selection, and probable need to take courses from multiple distance education centers (Wang, 1997).

Open-ended questions gave students opportunities to express any comments related to their distance education experiences. The researcher indicated that students in rural and remote areas appreciate access and convenience to distance education, but would prefer classes that are more traditional if given the choice. Distance students have often been out of school for some time and need "hand-holding" in the beginning to learn the use of electronic technologies. Once they learn the technology, however, they like it and want more (Wang, 1997).

The questionnaire results cannot be considered valid for the population because of a very low return rate. The researcher acknowledged that summer was not the best time to reach students. The questionnaire did not include what degree, if any, the student was pursuing. Perhaps the students who indicated that academic advising did not apply were taking a distance education course only for personal or professional interest. Categories based on degree level would have been valuable to distinguish differences among students who were pursuing associate, baccalaureate, or graduate degrees (Wang, 1997).

An online survey was included with the final exam for four Web-based courses at the University of Central Florida. Forty-eight students voluntarily responded, but the authors did not indicate the size of the population. These students were obtaining teacher certification in vocational education. For overall ratings of student support services, the respondents indicated never used (10%), poor (0%), average (42%), or above average (48%). For student services in the College of Education for majors, the respondents indicated never used (58%), poor (0%), average (20%), or above average (23%). The institution's student academic resource center has a Web site with self-help information in such areas as learner attitudes, reading and comprehension, skills, notetaking, and math study skills (Greer, Hundson, & Paugh, 1998).

From this study (Greer et al., 1998), we can learn that there is a potential for satisfaction with student support services, but they may not be used. This was a specialized study of students obtaining teacher certification. In addition to the unknown factor of volunteer response rate, the study has limited generalizability.

Ruth (2005) studied students taking online courses within the College of Nursing and Health Professions. All 691 students taking online courses in the spring semester of 2005 were asked to participate. After the initial request and one reminder, 99 students responded to the survey which was developed by faculty and program directors. The researcher also interviewed five faculty members who taught online courses and three administrators involved with the online offerings.

All programs offered completely online are graduate, but the results did not distinguish undergraduate versus graduate students. It was determined that 86% of students completing the survey were taking all online courses; there were no significant differences when compared with the other respondents. Library services, computer technical support, and academic advising were the services considered most essential, helpful, convenient, and enabling. A limitation for the study's generalizability is that only students within College of Nursing and Health Sciences were surveyed (Ruth, 2005). Validity for the population studied is also questionable with the low response rate of only 14%.

The researcher concluded that faculty and administrators involved with teaching and developing distance course and programs help students establish a sense of community and help them feel part of the university. Also, student affairs professionals need to provide services that are attractive and useful for distance students (Ruth, 2005).

RECOMMENDATIONS FOR FURTHER RESEARCH

While some knowledge of academic advising in distance education has been gained, the review of research demonstrates that voids in the literature exist. A study similar to Curry's (1997) should be done approximately every three years. Trends and new developments can be identified by periodically surveying administrators. Future national studies of academic advising in distance education should include associate and baccalaureate programs for consistency with NACADA's national surveys. This research will provide knowledge in comparing and contrasting advising goals and practices in distance education with institutions as a whole.

Workman and Stenard's (1996) study identified student needs at one institution. Brown (2004) studied student satisfaction at two institutions. For more comprehensive data, a national survey of distance education students should be conducted. This study of academic advising needs would provide quantitative data from the student perspective, including the mode of advising delivery that is consistent with the needs and types of students served. Associate, baccalaureate, and graduate students should be surveyed. Information based on solid research will help advisors develop appropriate advising services for distance students.

Retention is a difficult issue to study with any nontraditional student population. Studies similar to Kemp's (2002) should be done by many institutions. With follow up to increase response rate, these studies can be valid for their populations. Houle's (2004) study can also be a model for retention studies in distance programs. With several studies, advisors can begin to see trends that may be applicable to students at their institutions. They can provide students with tools and knowledge to increase the likelihood of their success.

Other sources of data such as Bird and Morgan's (2003) study can provide rich qualitative data on enrollment and persistence. To increase the insights gained specific to distant students, studies of this specific population should be performed.

For additional qualitative data, several case studies are recommended. One case study should be a comparison of advising for students in a professional degree program and a nonprofessional degree program. An institution with distance learning options for varied degree programs may need to provide very different services for the different student populations. An RN to BSN student, for example, will likely have very different advising needs than those of a liberal arts major.

A case study of academic advising at institutions with Web-based instruction should be done. This should include interviews of advisors and students. Questions would include how advising methods relate to instruction mode, use of Web discussion groups, and by what means rapport can be established when face-to-face contact is not involved in advising.

A case study focusing on students' perceptions of advising throughout their academic careers is needed. A longitudinal study would be ideal, but researchers can also study separate groups of students concurrently as long as some are beginning a program, taking courses about midway through the program, and nearing completion of the program. Graduates of the distance education program should also be included in this study. In-depth interviews of students and graduates would be the primary method of data collection.

Master's and doctoral students are often neglected in advising research. Although Wang (1997) and Ruth (2005) included graduate students in their studies, the data were not distinguished from the undergraduate students. A case study should focus specifically on advising issues of graduate students in distance education. While academic needs are very different from an undergraduate's, the more advanced students will still have issues related to pursuing a degree at a distance.

CONCLUSION

This chapter described practices in academic advising in distance education degree programs. Research is not extensive and does not provide definitive answers on best practices. As additional research is undertaken, information can be found to improve advising services.

It is important that attention be devoted to the issue of academic advising in distance education. Research by Paneitz (1997) found that academic advising was the most essential student service in associate degree programs available at a distance. Studies by Beitz (1987) and Curry (1997) also demonstrated the importance of academic advising for distance education students pursuing baccalaureate or graduate degrees.

A theme in the research is the advisor/student relationship. Curry's (1997) survey indicated that advisors were developing personal relationships with their distance education students. One way to help personalize the advising process is for advisors to have Web pages with pictures and biographical information. Another way is with friendliness and personalization of telephone and e-mail contacts. Concern with confidentiality can make this personalization difficult in group electronic discussions. Fornshell (1993) described the use of codes rather than names in identifying participants in an electronic advising session. If this were the student's only advising contact, it could be seen as making a reality of the students' worst nightmare: being treated "like a number." In the program Fornshell described, students visited the campus twice a year for in-person advising contacts. While Workman and Stenard (1996) and Barnett and Kline (1999) reported the importance of in person assistance, this contact may not be possible as students become more geographically dispersed. With any means of communications used, academic advisors should make every effort to treat each student as an individual.

With additional national and institutional studies, knowledge will continue to advance in the field of academic advising in distance education degree programs. While distance education programs and student services are diverse, some issues are relevant for academic advising of any student at a distance. Advising must be accessible, user-friendly, accurate, and consistent. As advisors examine knowledge in the field and practices that have been successful, they can choose the advising strategies that will be accessible and helpful to their own distance education students.

REFERENCES

The American College Testing Program (1993). *Fulfilling the promise? Final report: ACT fourth national survey of academic advising.* Iowa City, IA: Habley, W. R.

Barnett, E. M., & Kline, J. P. (1999). The role of site directors in faculty and student success. Distance Learning '99. Annual Conference on Distance Teaching and Learning. Proceedings. (ERIC Document Reproduction Service No. ED440287)

Beitz, N. C. (1987). Academic advisement for distance education students. *Journal of Education for Library and Information Science, 27,* 279–287.

Bird, J., & Morgan, C. (2003). Adults contemplating university study at a distance: Issues, themes, and concerns. *International Review of Research I Open and Distance Learning, 4*(1).

Bowser, D., & Race, K. (1991). Orientation for distance education students: What is it worth? *Distance Education, 12*(2), 109–122.

Brown, J. T. (2004). Student service satisfaction: Differences between traditional and distance learning students. Azusa Pacific University. *Masters Abstracts International, 43,* 1055.

Carr, R., & Ledwith, F. (1980). Helping disadvantaged students. *Teaching at a Distance, 18,* 77–85.

Curry, R. F. (1997). Academic advising in distance education. (Doctoral Dissertation, College of William and Mary, 1997). *Dissertation Abstracts International, 58–02 A,* 396.

Curry, R. F., Baldwin, R. G., & Sharpe, M. S. (1998). Academic advising in baccalaureate distance education programs. *The American Journal of Distance Education, 12*(3), 42–52.

Fielstein, L. L. (1989). Student priorities for academic advising: do they want a personal relationship? *NACADA Journal, 9*(1), 33–38.

Fornshell, G. K. (1993). Academic advisement for distance learners. *Journal of Instruction Delivery Systems, 7*(3), 17–19.

Greer, L. B., Hudson, L., & Paugh, R. (1998). Student support services and success factors for adult online learners. (ERIC Document Reproduction Service No. ED441155)

Houle, B. J. (2004). Adult student persistence in Web-based education. New York University. *Dissertation Abstracts International, 65–03 A,* 851.

Kember, D., Murphy, D., Siaw, I., & Yuen, K. S. (1991). Towards a causal model of student progress in distance education: Research in Hong Kong. *The American Journal of Distance Education, 5*(2), 3–15.

Kemp, W. C. (2002). Persistence of adult learners in distance education. *The American Journal of Distance Education, 16*(2), 65–81.

Lalande, V. (1995). Student support via audio teleconferencing: Psycho-educational workshops for post-bachelor nursing students. *The American Journal of Distance Education, 9*(3), 62–73.

Miller, G. E. (1993). Comparing distance education programs. In Peterson's Guides. (Ed.). *The electronic university: A guide to distance learning.* Princeton, NJ: Peterson's Guides.

Paneitz, B. (1997). [Community college students' perceptions of student services provided when enrolled in telecourses.] Unpublished raw data.

Peterson's. (1998). *Peterson's guide to distance learning programs.* Princeton, NJ: Peterson's Guides.

Potter, J. (1998). Beyond access: Student perspectives on support service needs in distance learning. *Canadian Journal of University Continuing Education, 24*(1), 59–82.

Ruth, D. A. (2005). An investigation into the need for co-curricular student services for distance education students. Drexel University. *Dissertation Abstracts International, A 66/03,* p. 923.

Sloan, D., & Wilmes, M. B. (1989). Advising adults from the commuter perspective. *NACADA Journal, 9*(2), 67–75.

Tallman, Frank D. (1994). Satisfaction and completion in correspondence study: The influence of instructional and student-support services. *The American Journal of Distance Education, 8*(2), 43–57.

Wagner, E. D. (1993, April). Variables affecting distance educational program success. *Educational Technology*, 28–32.

Wang, J. (1997). [Statewide collaboration in adult continuing education: A case study of distance education in Maine.] Unpublished raw data.

Workman, J. J., & Stenard, R. A. (1996). Student support services for distance learners. *DEOSNEWS, 6*(3). Retrieved from Distance Education Online Symposium on October 24, 2005 from http://www.ed.psu.edu/acsde/deos/deosnews/deosnews6_3.asp

16

Supporting the Disabled Student

Shelley Kinash and Susan Crichton
University of Calgary

French and Valdes (2002) indicated that one in five people has a disability. Cook and Gladhart (2002) stated that 10% to 15% of postsecondary students identify themselves as disabled. Classification as disabled includes those experiencing educational barriers due to physical, sensory, or cognitive impairments, as well as learning disabilities. For many of these learners, traditional education is largely inaccessible. The accessibility of computer-mediated information and the convenience of distance delivery have the potential to "level the playing field" for disabled students (Coombs & Banks, 2000), in large part because planned redundancy of modes (i.e., making equivalent content available via speech, text, and audiovisual) is possible and practical when using digital communication (Negroponte, 1995). Multimedia, defined by Mayer (2001) as the delivery of information in both words and pictures, also has the potential to enhance accessibility. Mayer wrote that the promise of multimedia presentation is the enhancement of learning. The benefits extend beyond students with disabilities to those with differential learning styles or simple situational preferences, such as the need to listen to a recorded lecture while in transit.

The gain in studying disabled distance learners extends well beyond a disability issue. O'Connor (2000) called disabled distance learners "early adopters," implying that they are taking advantage of technology-infused education and leading the way for other learners who are slower on the uptake. He predicted that this early adoption will move them from the fringes or "outer edge" to the "leading edge." Jacobs (2004) described 53 technologies used by the mainstream populace that were originally designed by and/or for disabled users. Examples include the telephone (1876) that was inspired by Alexander Graham Bell's opening of a school to train teachers for the deaf; e-mail (1972), developed by Vinton Cerf, who, being hard-of-hearing since birth, communicated with his deaf wife through text messaging; and the flatbed scanner (1972), designed by Ray Kurzweil, who is one of the primary inventors of technology for the blind.

Authors such as Jacobs (2004) and Coombs and Banks (2000) use the metaphor "electronic curb-cut." This is a reference to physical curb cuts, or the portion of the sidewalk that rests flush with the street, that were instituted for people in wheelchairs. However, curb-cuts are much more frequently used by parents with strollers, shoppers with carts, cyclists, and inline skaters. Coombs' and Banks' recommendations for distance education apply to all learners; all learners benefit if courses are interactive, accessible, and simple (intuitive interfaces). The formal term for developing for diversity is *universal design*. Universal design is "the design of products and environments to be usable by all people, to the greatest extent possible, without the need for adaptation or specialized design" (North Carolina State University, 1997, p. 1). Fichten and her colleagues (2000, 2001, 2003, 2005) highlighted three integral components. First, design that enhances accessibility for learners with disabling conditions enhances usability for all students. Second, interfaces are more accessible and cost-efficient when designed for all learners up front, rather than attempting retrofitting after the fact. Third, consultation with disabled students in the design phase substantially enhances accessibility. Opitz (2002) provided numerous examples of how designing a distance education course, such that it is accessible to students with disabilities, benefits all learners:

> Images can be effective in providing alternative examples or explanations of content. The addition of an alternative text tag to the image enables a screen reader used by a visually disabled person to read the textual description to the learner, describing the attributes of the image. Adding a title representative of a description of an image also allows learners without disabilities a more detailed explanation of the images. Sounds can also be used, but captions or alternative text benefits the deaf and those with hearing by providing a written script to follow and to refer back to at a late date. Easy-to-read content benefits all learners by "chunking" the information into blocks of important information that can be easily read and understood by an audience. (p. 12)

The literature has yet to embrace learners with disabilities as "leading edge." Many published works consider the notion of universal design as a retrofit to existing courses, modifying the norm for the perceived "abnormal."

LITERATURE CLASSIFICATION

A small number of publications are positioned at the overlap between distance education and disability. Of those, very few are research, and the source publications are largely conferences and journals within the field of disability studies rather than in mainstream educational technology. In a comprehensive search, we found 67 publications released between 2000 and 2006 that were situated at the intersection of distance education and disability. In this review, "publications" are defined as journal articles, government and newspaper reports, and full-article conference proceedings. Proceedings from the 2000–2006 Technology and Persons with Disabilities Conferences through California State University Northridge's (CSUN) Center on Disabilities comprise 39% of the publications. The number of CSUN presentations in the topic stream of distance education shows a steady rate of increase until 2003, with two presentations in 2000, three in 2001, nine in 2002, and eleven in 2003. In 2004 and 2005, presentation in this stream declined with two and three, respectively. Analysis of the conference proceedings enabled us to conduct a more lucrative search, expanding key search terms to contemporary constructs, such as "universal design," "assistive technologies," and "accessible learning;" conference presenters (e.g., Burgstahler) as publishing authors; and organizations' Web sites with links, such as Equal Access to Software and Information.

Of the 67 publications (see Table 16.1), 27 (40%) are didactic. They present guidelines and how-to information in regard to a single or combination of topics including accessibility, communication tools, instructional design, pedagogy, policy, teaching strategies, and universal design. The next highest category of publications (18, or 27%) is description of vendor products and/or educational programs (including postsecondary institutions and private industry). The lowest category can best be classified as editorials or opinion pieces at five articles (7%).

TABLE 16.1.
Four Classifications of 2000–2006 Literature on Distance Education and Disability

Didactic	Descriptive	Research	Opinion
Amtmann, Cook, & Johnson, 2003	Ashton, 2002	Asuncion, et al., 2006	Blaser, 2001
Banks & Banks, 2002	Babbitt, 2003	Cook & Gladhart, 2002	Fauth, 2002
Banks, Lazzaro, & Noble, 2003	Babbitt, Thoma, & Adamson, 2002	Fichten, et al., 2005	French, 2002
Barstow, 2003	Bauder & Sharon, 2002	Fichten, et al., 2003	Vanderwal, 2006
Burgstahler, 2005	Brown & Ritter, 2002	Fichten, et al., 2001	Watts, 2003
Burgstahler, 2003	Buys, Coombs, & Coombs, 2003	Fichten, et al., 2000	
Burgstahler, 2002a	Cohen, Kimball, Coombs, & Coombs, 2002	Kim-Rupnow & Burgstahler, 2004	
Burgstahler, 2002b	Enagandula, Juthani, Ramakirshnan, Rawal, & Vidyasagar, 2005	Kim-Rupnow, Dowrick, & Burke, 2001	
Burgstahler, 2002c	Freed, 2001	Kinash 2003	
Burgstahler, 2002d	Kennedy & Colwell, 2003	Kinash 2002	
Byzek, 2002	Merryman & Barber, 2003	Kinash, Crichton, & Kim-Rupnow, 2004	
Coombs & Banks, 2000	Merryman & Barber, 2004	Moisey 2004	
Draffan, 2004	Milchus, 2005	Muilenburg & Berge, 2005	
Edmonds, 2004	Mistrett, 2001	Richardson & Woodley, 2004	
Ferrell, Persichitte, & Lowell, 2000	Nevile, et al., 2005	Richardson, Long, & Foster, 2001	
French & Valdes, 2002	Porto 2001	Schmetzke 2001a	
Geoffroy, 2002	Rothberg, et al., 2005	Tobin, 2003	
IMS Global Learning Consortium, Inc., 2002	Sasser, 2002		
O'Connor, 2000			
Opitz, 2002			
Philpot, 2003			
Rehabilitation Services Administration, 2002			
Sax & Duke, 2003			
Schenker & Scadden, 2002			
Schmetzke, 2001b			
Urban & Burks, 2002			
White, Wepner, & Wetzel, 2003			

Seventeen articles (25%) can be counted as research. Even this small amount of research is a recent phenomenon; 12 of the articles have 2003 to 2006 as their publication dates. The total is amplified in that 11 of the 17 articles are written by four first-authors (Fichten, 4; Kim-Rupnow, 2; Kinash, 3; and Richardson, 2). Further, two of the Kinash articles and two of the Fichten articles are multiple depictions of the same research. To date, there is a small body of researchers producing a small body of research largely in their fields of concentration.

REVIEW OF EMPIRICAL RESEARCH

For the purposes of this chapter, seven of the research pieces are reviewed: Cook and Gladhart's (2002) "A Survey of Online Instructional Issues and Strategies for Postsecondary Students with Learning Disabilities"; Kim-Rupnow, Dowrick, and Burke's (2001) "Implications for Improving Access and Outcomes for Individuals with Disabilities in Postsecondary Distance Education"; and Asuncion et al.'s (2006) "Accessibility of eLearning in Postsecondary Education: Student and Faculty Perspectives"; Fichten et al.'s (2005) "Accessibility of eLearning in Canadian Postsecondary Education"; Fichten, Asuncion, Robillard, Fossey, and Barile's (2003) "Accessible Computer Technologies for Students with Disabilities in Canadian Higher Education"; Fichten et al.'s (2001) "Technology Integration for Students with Disabilities: Empirically based Recommendations for Faculty"; and Fichten, Asuncion, Barile, Fossey, and de Simone's (2000) "Access to Educational and Instructional Computer Technologies for Post-Secondary Students with Disabilities: Lessons from Three Empirical Studies." The first two articles have been selected for review because they adopt a survey approach, resulting in a breadth of inquiry that contributes to a macro-perspective on the phenomenon of online learning with respect to learners with disabilities. In the context of a paucity of research, such global perspective is a necessary predecessor of depth inquiry. The next set of five by Fichten and colleagues was selected due to its rigorous approach to empirical research, as yet unique within the field of accessible education.

Cook and Gladhart (2002)

Although the title and many of the examples within Cook and Gladhart's (2002) article are drawn from the context of "learning disabilities," their content applies to all types of disabilities. Beyond disability, within the first paragraph of their introduction, the authors state their philosophy: "When we encourage the use of adaptive technology in accommodating the needs of learners with disabilities, we also serendipitously make positive strides in addressing the diverse learning styles of students without disabilities as well" (Cook & Gladhart, 2002, p. 1).

This article flanks the categories of didacticism and research. As didactic, the article addresses distance education generally, differentiates between distance and traditional approaches to education, reviews educational technologies, and practically applies issues to guide accessible practices in instructional design and provision. In addition, the authors engaged in two modes of research: original and secondary. The authors described their first method as "an extensive search using half a dozen keyword combinations with major databases . . . various Web sites and software training manuals" (Cook & Gladhart, 2002, p. 2). The authors did not count, classify, or chart their results, as they only addressed them globally. They commented on the paucity of literature addressing the needs of postsecondary students with disabilities. They elaborated slightly, stating "there were few publications found which offered recommendations for accommodations and modifications for the electronic classroom, and certainly none that offered an overview of these considerations along with discussion of pedagogical techniques" (p. 2). The article includes 48 references. The majority of the citations inform either the issue of distance education or of disability, but do not consider the two in combination. For example, a number of the citations address assistive technology or accessible Web sites, and still others are mainstream distance education citations that do not take up disability issues.

The second research component in Cook and Gladhart's (2002) article is the 2000 *National Survey of Information Technology in Higher Education.* The first annual Campus Computing survey was published in 1989 (Green, 2000). Computing officials (typically the chief academic computing officer) of two- and four-year colleges and universities across the United States are surveyed in the fall of each year. The number of institutions submitting completed surveys ranges from 469 in 2000 (the report reviewed by Cook & Gladhart, 2002) to 650 in 1995. The Green (1995, 1999, 2000, 2001, 2002) reports do not mention disability. Some of the summary reports include short segments addressing distance education as one of the thematic topics. Examples of other thematic topics include e-commerce and other e-service issues such as online registration; purchase plans; and numbers of students with personal computers. The 2000 report indicates that "less than one-third [of surveyed higher education institutions] (29.3%) have a strategic plan for distance education" (Green, 2000, p. 3). Further, one-seventh use some type of "course management tool" such as WebCT or Blackboard for their online courses, and three-fifths have "established a single product standard" (p. 5). Cook and Gladhart briefly applied these survey results to accessibility issues. They wrote, "in many respects, these services provide increased access for all students, but access can be limited by the institution's lack of experience in how to use these resources to meet the needs of students, particularly students with disabilities." (Cook & Gladhart, 2002, p. 2).

Kim-Rupnow, Dowrick, and Burke (2001)

The question guiding Kim-Rupnow, Dowrick, and Burke's (2001) analysis of the literature was, "Do the increase in distance education programs and use of advanced technology indicate better access and better outcomes in higher education for persons with disabilities?" (p. 25). They answered positively, yet inconclusively due to the paucity of research. Using electronic data-bases of published journal articles and manual searches of the table of contents of distance education journals, Kim-Rupnow, Dowrick, and Burke derived ten articles. Each of the ten articles includes information about postsecondary students with disabilities enrolled in distance education courses. Most of the articles are written from the perspective of the postsecondary institution and include very brief descriptions of one or two students with disabilities.

Although not explicitly differentiated by the authors, some of the emerging themes resonate with issues for all postsecondary distance education support systems regardless of whether the respective students are disabled, whereas the others appear to be the contribution of technological advances for supporting postsecondary students with disabilities at a distance. The more general themes are students' prior experience with computers (this emerged as a common characteristic of the students depicted in the literature), university programs delivering distance education using a combination of several technologies (including multimedia and some interactive platforms), and varied use of synchronous and/or asynchronous communication tools for collaboration. The themes closely related to disabilities are: (a) availability of technical assistance to facilitate content accessibility (examples include transcribed text and interpretation), (b) formats that are not effectively translated by text readers (such as tables and graphics), (c) university supports extended to disabled students (such as access to home computers and assistive devices), and (d) existence of an individualized education (and/or accommodation) plan for disabled learners.

Kim-Rupnow, Dowrick, and Burke's (2001) article may be considered seminal at the intersection of disability and distance education. Not only is their article one of a mere handful of research initiatives in this area, but the authors have sought to establish a foundation, or a platform, from which to launch a more in-depth inquiry; however, the authors' commitment to including only research articles that documented the distance education experience of postsecondary learners with disabilities severely restricted their source documents. In addition, a large proportion of their source literature is dated before computer-mediation became an instrumental component of distance education. In other words, some of the literature addresses correspondence rather than distance learning. The thematic content of Kim-Rupnow, Dowrick, and Burke's article therefore fails to address some important contemporary concepts. Most notably, their article does not address universal design.

Fichten et al. (2000, 2001, 2003, 2005) and Asuncion et al. (2006)

Across five articles, Fichten et al. (2000, 2001, 2003, 2005) and Asuncion et al. (2006) described the results of six research projects in the domain of accessible education. While five of these studies are not focused specifically on distance education, the topic definition of computer technologies necessitated the inclusion of subject matter regarding disabled distance education students.

The first study was informed by questionnaires and interviews with 156 postsecondary personnel responsible for services to students with disabling conditions, across 91 institutions, including two that provide only distance education. The 40 participants in the second study were the same type of personnel from 34 Francophone two-year postsecondary preparatory institutions (CEGEP). Eighteen of the Study Two participants were also participants in Study One. Notable results were that among the 91 general postsecondary institutions and the 34 Francophone CEGEP institutions, the computer-related needs of students with disabling conditions were perceived by the personnel responsible for services to students with disabling conditions to be only moderately well met (mean of 4.3 in each case on a 6-point Likert scale). Most pertinent to this review, the overall perception of the postsecondary personnel was that Internet-based distance education was largely inaccessible. Accessibility of distance education was rated at an average of 2.8/6 among the institutions overall and 2.9 among the 18 respondents to this item from the CEGEPs.

The participants in the third through fifth studies were postsecondary students with disabling conditions, and in one study, their professors. The third study involved two focus groups: one comprised of 12 students and the other of five professors. The authors interpreted the content of both focus groups as indicating that "computers have tremendous potential but that they also can pose barriers" (Fichten et al., 2001, p. 192). One example of such a barrier was specific to distance education; a comment from the professor-comprised focus group was that participation in online dialogue requires fast typing which may not be possible for students with some types of disabling conditions. The fourth study was comprised of telephone interviews with 37 disabled postsecondary students. Two of the interviewees were enrolled in distance education institutions. The authors listed barriers categorized by types of disabling conditions, such as mobility and neuromuscular impairment, and visual impairment. The authors did not differentiate between face-to-face and distance education, nor provide any examples specific to online learning. The results of the fifth study are based on questionnaires returned by 725 disabled Canadian postsecondary students (11 of whom were distance education students) across 154 institutions. Ninety-five percent of the respondents indicated that they use a computer and 87% indicated use of the Internet; it was not indicated whether or not their use is for distance education purposes. Consistent with the discussion of universal design above, the most common technologies used to ensure accessibility were mainstream rather than disability-specific applications. "The most popular computer technologies were sophisticated or adapted versions of mainstream equipment which students felt they needed to accommodate their disabilities" (Fichten et al., 2000, p. 191). The top two cited technologies used by disabled students were spelling/grammar checkers and scanners.

The sixth study focused on distance education. The 22 participants in structured telephone interviews were Canadians in the context of accessible postsecondary education. The participants were members of five groups: (a) disabled students, (b) postsecondary personnel responsible for services to students with disabling conditions, (c) professors experienced in facilitating distance education with disabled learners, (d) postsecondary leaders with respect to disabled student participation in distance education, and (e) e-publishers. The research showed that the most popular distance education interfaces were through learning management systems such as WebCT™ and Blackboard, and next, online presentation through such software as PowerPoint; and these interfaces were generally accessible to students with disabling conditions. However the researchers documented formats that were problematic to learners with specific disabling conditions, such as (a) students with visual impairments reporting challenges with online presentations that their screen reading technologies could not decipher (e.g., scanned-in presentations manifesting as an image); (b) students with learning disabilities and some types of neuromuscular impairments experiencing difficulty navigating the simultaneous tasks of typing and reading within online text-based chats; and (c) learners with hearing impairments were unable to participate in audio-based chat sessions. The authors concluded that it is the responsibility of course developers and instructors to consider learners with diverse needs in the upfront design of learning environments to plan for all students.

CONCLUSION

At least one subset of the student population—disabled adults—does not seem to be well-served by the postsecondary system. Students with disabilities are underrepresented. An estimated six percent of 1995–1996 undergraduates in the United States reported a disability (U.S. Department of Education, National Center for Education Statistics, 1999). The low proportion of postsecondary students with disabilities is alarming considering that graduates appear to be hired into positions equivalent to their non-disabled colleagues (U.S. Department of Education, National Center for Education Statistics, 1999). The small amount of literature that informs what it is like to be a disabled postsecondary student indicates an unwillingness to make courses accessible to disabled learners, and/or to accommodate particular support needs (when these emerge).

A techno-structuralist view of distance education balances the optimism of the potential of distance education to meet the needs of students with disabilities, with provisos and cautions. Full accessibility does not appear to be experienced by learners with disabilities (McGrane, 2000). The question remains as to whether the dominance of text-heavy, visual interfaces can and will be balanced with auditory options. There is also a question as to whether an increase in online options for students with disabilities might set off a reactive decrease in traditional options. In short, will instructors and administrators bother to make traditional course content and communication accessible, if the distance education alternative exists (Blaser, 2001)?

Although our analysis of the 2000–2006 literature positioned at the intersection of distance education and disability somewhat elaborates the debates, the questions posed by Kim-Rupnow, Dowrick, and Burke (2001) remain unresolved. We pose these questions once again, urging further study: Is the prevalence of distance education increasing postsecondary access to students with disabilities? What services are most important in supporting postsecondary distance learners? What are the long-term outcomes of distance learners with disabilities? And what "standard accommodations" and innovations "especially encourage diverse learners" (Kim-Rupnow, Dowrick, & Burke, 2001, p. 37)? To these, we add this question: How can we promote universal design of the distance education environment, with particular emphasis on complementing the visual, text dependency with the auditory interface? The answer to these questions lies, we believe, in the intersection of the promise afforded by distance education technology, and the needs of learners and teachers with disabilities, recognizing the potential of multimedia to support multiple learning styles and needs.

REFERENCES

Amtmann, D., Cook, D., & Johnson, K. (2003, March). *Online learning management systems: Accessibility of tools for synchronous communication.* Retrieved September 15, 2006 from Cal State University at Northride, Center on Disabilities, Technology and Persons with Disabilities Conference Web site: http://www.csun.edu/cod/conf/2003/proceedings/168.htm

Ashton, T. (2002, March). *The development of a new tool for online teaching: www.merlot.org.* Retrieved from California State University at Northridge, Center on Disabilities, Technology and Persons with Disabilities Conference Web site: http://www.csun.edu/cod/conf/2002/proceedings/9.htm

Asuncion, J., Fichten, C., Wolforth, J., Hewlett, M., Klomp, R., & Barile, M. (2006, March). *Accessibility of eLearning in postsecondary education: Student and faculty perspectives.* Retrieved from California State University at Northridge, Center on Disabilities, Technology and Persons with Disabilities Conference Web site: http://www.csun.edu/codconf2006/proceedings/3061.htm

Babbitt, B. C. (2003). *Features of effective graduate degree training in assistive technology at a distance.* Retrieved from California State University at Northridge, Center on Disabilities, Technology and Persons with Disabilities Conference Web site http://www.csun.edu/cod/conf/2003/proceedings/142.htm

Babbitt, B., Thoma, C., & Adamson, G. (2002, March). *University training programs in assistive technology via distance education.* Retrieved from California State University at Northridge, Center on Disabilities, Technology and Persons with Disabilities Conference Web site http://www.csun.edu/cod/conf/2002/proceedings/116.htm

Banks, R., & Banks, G. (2002, March). *Virtual presentations: Using Internet multimedia to simulate online presentations in e-learning.* Retrieved from California State University at Northridge, Center on Disabilities, Technology and Persons with Disabilities Conference Web site http://www.csun.edu/cod/conf/2002/proceedings/229.htm

Banks, R., Lazzaro, J. J., & Noble, S. (2003, March). *Accessible e-learning: Policy and practice.* Retrieved from California State University at Northridge, Center on Disabilities, Technology and Persons with Disabilities Conference Web site http://www.csun.edu/cod/conf/2003/proceedings/139.htm

Barstow, C. (2003). *Making online learning accessible: Update on activities of the IMS accessibility working group.* Retrieved from California State University at Northridge, Center on Disabilities, Technology and Persons with Disabilities Conference Web site http://www.csun.edu/cod/conf/2003/proceedings/138.htm

Bauder, D. K., & Sharon, D. (2002, March). *Online assistive technology training: Making it do-able for all.* Retrieved from California State University at Northridge, Center on Disabilities, Technology and Persons with Disabilities Conference Web site http://www.csun.edu/cod/conf/2002/proceedings/225.htm

Blaser, A. (2001, September 5). Distance learning—Boon or bane? *Ragged Edge Online.* Retrieved from http://www.raggededgemagazine.com/0901/0901ft1.htm

Brown, R., & Ritter, G. (2002, March). *Blackboard & WebAIM: Building an accessible e-education platform.* Retrieved from California State University at Northridge, Center on Disabilities, Technology and Persons with Disabilities Conference Web site http://www.csun.edu/cod/conf/2002/proceedings/233.htm

Burgstahler, S. (2002a). Distance learning, universal design, universal access. *Association for the Advancement of Computing in Education, 10*(1). Retrieved from http://www.aace.org/pubs/etr/issue2/burgstahler.cfm/framePage.htm

Burgstahler, S. (2002b). Real connections: Making distance learning accessible to everyone. In Do-It, University of Washington.

Burgstahler, S. (2002c). Universal design of distance learning. *Information Technology and Disabilities,—*(1). Retrieved from http://www.rit.edu/~easi/itd/itdv08n1/burgstah.htm

Burgstahler, S. (2002d). Universal design of instruction. In Do-It, University of Washington.

Burgstahler, S. (2003, March). *Developing policy for making distance learning programs accessible to everyone.* Retrieved from California State University at Northridge, Center on Disabilities, Technology and Persons with Disabilities Conference Web site http://www.csun.edu/cod/conf/2003/proceedings/137.htm

Burgstahler, S. (2005). Steps toward making distance learning accessible to students and instructors with disabilities. *Information Technology and Disabilities, 11*(1). Retrieved from http://www.rit.edu/%7Eeasi/itd/itdv11n1/brgstler.htm

Buys, G., Coombs, E., & Coombs, N. (2003). *Enhancing distance learning with online interactive voice conferencing.* Retrieved from California State University at Northridge, Center on Disabilities, Technology and Persons with Disabilities Conference Web site http://www.csun.edu/cod/conf/2003/proceedings/134.htm

Byzek, J. (2002). Internet education. *New Mobility, May.* Retrieved from http://www.newmobility.com/review_article.cfm?id=544&action=browse

Cohen, L., Kimball, W., Coombs, E., Coombs, N. (2002, March). *Two online certificate programs in assistive technology and accessible information technology.* Retrieved from California State University at Northridge, Center on Disabilities, Technology and Persons with Disabilities Conference Web site http://www.csun.edu/cod/conf/2002/proceedings/232.htm

Cook, R. A., & Gladhart, M. A. (2002). A survey of online instructional issues and strategies for postsecondary students with learning disabilities. *Information Technology and Disabilities, 8*(1). Retrieved from http://www.rit.edu/~easi/itd/itdv08n1/gladhart.htm

Coombs, N., & Banks, R. (2000, March). *Distance learning and students with disabilities: Easy tips for teachers.* Retrieved from California State University at Northridge, Center on Disabilities. Technology and Persons with Disabilities Conference Web site http://www.csun.edu/cod/conf/2000/proceedings/0119Coombs.htm

Draffan, E. A. (2004). *Dyslexia, e-learning and e-skills.* Retrieved from California State University at Northridge, Center on Disabilities, Technology and Persons with Disabilities Conference Web site http://www.csun.edu/cod/conf/2004/proceedings/214.htm

Edmonds, C. D. (2004). Providing access to students with disabilities in online distance education: Legal and technical concerns for higher education. *The American Journal of Distance Education, 18*(1): 51–62.

Enagandula, V., Juthani, N., Ramakirshnan, I. V., Rawal, D., & Vidyasagar, R. (2005, October). BlackboardNV: A system for enabling non-visual access to the Blackboard course management system. In proceedings for The Seventh International ACM SIGACCESS Conference on Computers and Accessibility, Baltimore.

Fauth, L. (2002). Distance education: Is it for you? *Alberta Vision, 23*(2): 1–2.

Ferrell, K. A., Persichitte, K. A., & Lowell, N. L. (2000, March). *Distance learning technologies for blind and visually impaired students.* Retrieved from California State University at Northridge, Center on Disabilities, Technology for Persons with Disabilities Conference Web site: http://www.csun.edu/cod/conf/2000/proceedings/0055Ferrell.htm

Fichten, C. S., Asuncion, J. V., Alapin, I., Barile, M., Gaulin, C., Guimont, J. P., et al. (2005, June). Accessibility of eLearning in Canadian postsecondary education. Presentation at the Canadian Psychological Association Annual Convention, Montreal, Quebec.

Fichten, C. S., Asuncion, J. V., Barile, M., Fossey, M., & de Simone, C. (2000). Access to educational and instructional computer technologies for post-secondary students with disabilities: Lessons from three empirical studies. *Journal of Educational Media, 25*(3): 179–201.

Fichten, C. S., Asuncion, J. V., Barile, M., Généreux, C., Fossey, M., Judd, D., et al. (2001). Technology integration for students with disabilities: Empirically based recommendations for faculty. *Educational Research and Evaluation, 7*(2–3): 185–221.

Fichten, C. S., Asuncion, J. V., Robillard, C., Fossey, M. E., & Barile, M. (2003). Accessible computer technologies for students with disabilities in Canadian higher education. *Canadian Journal of Learning and Technology, 29*(2): 5–33.

Freed, G. (2001, March). *Distance learning projects at NCAM.* Retrieved from California State University at Northridge, Center on Disabilities, Technology and Persons with Disabilities Conference Web site http://www.csun.edu/cod/conf/2001/proceedings/0174freed.htm

French], D. (2002). Editorial: Accessibility . . . an integral part of online learning. *Educational Technology Review, 10*(1).

202 KINASH AND CRICHTON

French, D., & Valdes, L. (2002). Electronic accessibility: United States and International Perspectives. *Educational Technology Review, 10*(1).

Geoffroy, C. (2002, March). *E-learning: The challenge for the blind and visually impaired.* Retrieved from California State University at Northridge, Center on Disabilities, Technology and Persons with Disabilities Conference Web site http://www.csun.edu/cod/conf/2002/proceedings/132.htm

Green, K. (1995). *The 1995 national survey of information technology in U.S. higher education.* Available online at http://www.campuscomputing.net

Green, K. (1999). *The 1999 national survey of information technology in U.S. higher education.* Retrieved from http://www.campuscomputing.net

Green, K. (2000). *The 2000 national survey of information technology in U.S. higher education.* Retrieved from http://www.campuscomputing.net

Green, K. (2001). *The 2001 national survey of information technology in U.S. higher education.* Retrieved from http://www.campuscomputing.net

Green, K. (2002). *The 2002 national survey of information technology in U.S. higher education.* Retrieved from http://www.campuscomputing.net

Jacobs, S. (2004). *The electronic curbcut effect.* Information technology technical assistance and training center (ITTATC). Retrieved from http://ideal-group.org/articles/ECC_1_6.htm

Kennedy, H., & Colwell, C. (2003). *Accessible online learning at the Open University UK, using XML and Java.* Retrieved from California State University at Northridge, Center on Disabilities, Technology and Persons with Disabilities Conference Web site http://www.csun.edu/cod/conf/2003/proceedings/315.htm

Kim-Rupnow, W. S., & Burgstahler, S. (2004). Perceptions of students with disabilities regarding the value of technology-based support activities on postsecondary education and employment. *Journal of Special Education Technology, 19*(2): 43–56.

Kim-Rupnow, W. S., Dowrick, P. W., & Burke, L. S. (2001). Implications for improving access and outcomes for individuals with disabilities in postsecondary distance education. *The American Journal of Distance Education, 15*(1): 25–40.

Kinash, S. (2002, June). Online education in disability studies, and interactive interviewing online as research methodology. Conference Paper, 2nd Annual Second City Conference on Disability Studies and Education: Education, Social Action, and the Politics of Disability. Chicago.

Kinash, S. (2003, March). *Questioning online learning for blind post-secondary students.* Retrieved from California State University at Northridge, Center on Disabilities, Technology and Persons with Disabilities Conference Web site http://www.csun.edu/cod/conf/2003/proceedings/152.htm

Kinash, S., Crichton, S., & Kim-Rupnow, W. S. (2004). A review of 2000–2003 literature at the intersection of online learning and disability. *The American Journal of Distance Education, 18*(1): 5–19.

Mayer, R. E. (2001). *Multimedia Learning.* New York: Cambridge.

McGrane, S. (2000). CNET Special reports: Is the Web truly accessible to the disabled? Retrieved from http://www.cnet.com/specialreports/0-6014-7-1530073.html

Merryman, L., & Barber, M. (2003, March). *Assist online: Distance learning computer training for blind and visually impaired individuals.* Retrieved from California State University at Northridge, Center on Disabilities, Technology and Persons with Disabilities Conference Web site http://www.csun.edu/cod/conf/2003/proceedings/155.htm

Merryman, L., & Barber, M. (2004, March). *Assist online: Distance learning computer training for blind and visually impaired individuals.* California State University at Northridge, Center on Disabilities, Technology and Persons with Disabilities Conference Web site http://www.csun.edu/cod/conf/2004/proceedings/85.htm

Milchus, K. (2005, March). *Web-based continuing education on workplace accommodations.* Retrieved from California State University at Northridge, Center on Disabilities, Technology and Persons with Disabilities Conference Web site http://www.csun.edu/cod/conf/2005/proceedings/2254.htm

Mistrett, S. (2001, March). *Web-based learning: Assistive technology training online project.* Retrieved from California State University at Northridge, Center on Disabilities, Technology and Persons with Disabilities Conference Web site http://www.csun.edu/cod/conf/2001/proceedings/0206mistrett.htm

Moisey, S. (2004). Students with disabilities in distance education: Characteristics, course enrollment and completion, and support services. *Journal of Distance Education, 19*(1): 73–91.

Muilenburg, L. Y., & Berge, Z. L. (2005). *Distance Education, 26*(1): 29–48.

Negroponte, N. (1995). *Being digital.* New York: Vintage.

Nevile, M., Graham, C., Carr, M., Milford, T., Ethier, E., & Mailhot, E. (2005, March). *Anytime, anyplace: Technology-supported distance education program for students with special needs.* Retrieved from California State University at Northridge, Center on Disabilities, Technology and Persons with Disabilities Conference Web site http://www.csun.edu/cod/conf/2005/proceedings/2171.htm

North Carolina State University, Center for Universal Design. (1997). *About universal design.* Retrieved from http://www.design.ncsu.edu/cud/about_ud/about_ud.htm

O'Connor, B. (2000, March). E-learning and students with disabilities: From outer edge to leading edge. Keynote address for NETWorking 2000 Conference, Flexible Learning, Australia. Retrieved from http://www.flexiblelearning.net.au/nw2000/main/key04.htm

Opitz, C. (2002). Online course accessibility: A call for responsibility and necessity. *Educational Technology Review, 10*(1). Retrieved from http://www.aace.org/dl/index.cfm?fuseaction=Print&paperid=11564

Philpot, J. (2003, March). *Applying assistive technology in the transformation of face-to-face courses into online formats.* Retrieved from California State University at Northridge, Center on Disabilities, Technology and Persons with Disabilities Conference Web site http://www.csun.edu/cod/conf/2003/proceedings/256.htm

Porto, P. (2001, March). *Ohio's AT distance learning project.* Retrieved from California State University at Northridge, Center on Disabilities, Technology and Persons with Disabilities Conference Web site http://www.csun.edu/cod/conf/2001/proceedings/0056porto.htm

Rehabilitation Services Administration, U.S. Department of Education, The Council of State Administrators of Vocational Rehabilitation, & The George Washington University Rehabilitation Continuing Education Program. (2002). 28th Institute on Rehabilitation Issues: Distance Education: Opportunities and Issues for Public Vocational Rehabilitation Programs.

Richardson, J. T. E., Long, G. L., & Foster, S. B. (2004). Academic engagement in students with a hearing loss in distance education. *Journal of Deaf Studies and Deaf Education, 9*(1): 68–85.

Richardson, J. T. E., & Woodley, A. (2001). Approaches to studying and communication preferences among deaf students in distance education. *Higher Education, 42*: 61–83.

Rothberg, M., Almasy, E., Bower, R., Cheetham, A., Kirkpatrick, A., & Treviranus, J. (2005, March). *Accessible e-learning demonstrations using IMS accessibility specifications.* Retrieved from California State University at Northridge, Center on Disabilities, Technology and Persons with Disabilities Conference Web site http://www.csun.edu/cod/conf/2005/proceedings/2328.htm

Sasser, S. (2002, March). *Distance-learning computer certification training program for blind and visually impaired individuals.* Retrieved from California State University at Northridge, Center on Disabilities, Technology and Persons with Disabilities Conference Web site http://www.csun.edu/cod/conf/2002/proceedings/335.htm

Sax, C. L., & Duke, S. (2003, March). *Distance education: Strategies for teaching and learning.* Retrieved from California State University at Northridge, Center on Disabilities, Technology and Persons with Disabilities Conference Web site http://www.csun.edu/cod/conf/2003/proceedings/254.htm

Schenker, K. T., & Scadden, L. A. (2002). The design of accessible distance education environments that use collaborative learning. *Information Technology and Disabilities, 8*(1). Retrieved from http://www.rit.edu/~easi/itd/itdv08n1/scadden.htm

Schmetzke, A. (2001a, March). Distance education, Web-resources design, and compliance with the Americans with Disabilities Act. General sessions proceedings for ACRL Tenth National Conference, Denver, CO.

Schmetzke, A. (2001b). Online distance education—"Anytime, anywhere" but not for everyone. *Information Technology and Disabilities E-Journal, 7*(2). Retrieved from http://www.rit.edu/~easi/itd/itdv07n2/axel.htm

Tobin, T. J. (2003). Issues in preparing visually disabled instructors to teach online: A case study. *Information Technology and Disability, 8*(1). Retrieved from http://www.rit.edu/~easi/itd/itdv08n1/tobin.htm

U.S. Department of Education. (1999). *Students with disabilities in postsecondary education: A profile of preparation, participation, and outcomes,* NCES 1999–187. Washington, DC: Horn, L., Berktold, J., & Bobbitt, L.

Urban, M., & Burks, M. (2002, March). *Challenges in creating software and content for distance learning.* Retrieved from California State University at Northridge, Center on Disabilities, Technology and Persons with Disabilities Conference Web site http://www.csun.edu/cod/conf/2002/proceedings/231.htm

Vanderwal, R. (2006, January 24). Boman overcomes obstacles with masters degree. *Ponoka News.*

Watts, S. (2003). What color is that comment: The mechanics of online collaboration from a blind student's perspective. *Information Technology and Disability, 9*(1). Retrieved from http://www.rit.edu/%7Eeasi/itd/itdv09n1/watts.htm

White, E. A., Wepner, S. B., & Wetzel, D. C. (2003). Accessible education through assistive technology. *THE Journal Online.* Retrieved from http://www.thejournal.com/articles/16270/

17

The Role of Academic Libraries

Stephen H. Dew
University of North Carolina–Greensboro

With distance learning alternatives growing in popularity worldwide and academic courses being taught in a wide variety of formats and locations, librarians are constantly being challenged to provide resources and services to students and faculty who are frequently far removed from the main campus. The literature concerning this increasingly important field of library and information services is very broad, and in recent years, articles concerning distance learning library services have appeared in a wide range of journals, books, and other resources covering librarianship, information science, and related fields.

PROFESSIONAL RESOURCES

For librarians and others looking for information about the provision of library services to distance education students, there are several resources that are immensely valuable. Four of the best databases available are (a) *Library Literature and Information Science Full Text* (a commercial *WilsonWeb* database), (b) *Library, Information Science & Technology Abstracts* (a free *EBSCO host* database), (c) *ERIC* (The *Education Resources Information Center*, a commercial database sponsored by the Institute of Education Sciences in the United States Department of Education), and (d) *Education Full Text* (a commercial *WilsonWeb* database). Possibly the best free resource for such information, however, is *Library Services for Distance Learning: The Fourth Bibliography*, a Web-based resource originally created and edited by Alexander Slade (2004); in 2005, however, the editorial responsibility for the *Library Services for Distance Learning* Web site was transferred to the Distance Learning Section of the Association of College and Research Libraries (ACRL). Slade is currently the executive director of the Council of Prairie and Pacific University Libraries (COPPUL)—a consortium of 20 university libraries located in Manitoba, Saskatchewan, Alberta, and British Columbia—and he is an internationally recognized leader in distance education librarianship. In addition to creating and developing the *Library Services for Distance Learning* Web-based bibliography, Slade was also the editor of the first three printed editions of the bibliography and the author of numerous articles, including "Research on Library Services for Distance Learning: An International Perspective" (Slade, 2004).

There are two very important international conferences focusing on distance education library services: (a) the "Libraries Without Walls" conferences, sponsored by the Centre for

Research in Library and Information Management (CERLIM, 2005), which is located at the Manchester Metropolitan University in the United Kingdom, and (b) the "Off-Campus Library Services" conferences, sponsored by Central Michigan University (2005), in the United States. The proceedings produced from both conferences are extremely valuable sources of information about library resources and services supporting distance education programs.

In North America, the Distance Learning Section of ACRL is the most prominent professional organization providing leadership and direction in the area of distance learning library services, including all higher-education programs designated as off-campus, extended campus, distance education, or distributed education. The Section facilitates the development and sharing of expertise, practice, resources and research in distance learning library services through its creation and development of the *Guidelines for Distance Learning Library Services*; its supervision of the popular Listserv, OFFCAMP; its editorial development of the *Library Services for Distance Learning* Web site; its conference programs; and its many other projects and publications. Linda Frederiksen (2004) published the first thorough history of the Distance Learning Section, tracing the organization's development from its beginnings as an ACRL discussion group, through its creation as a section (originally the Extended Campus Library Services Section), detailing the dynamic nature of the organization, one of the fastest growing sections within ACRL (currently, just over 1,500 members).

The most significant contribution that the Distance Learning Section has made to the profession probably has been the creation and development of ACRL's *Guidelines for Distance Learning Library Services*. As more institutions have provided nontraditional avenues for college degree course work, the need to provide direction and guidance to academic libraries dealing with the challenges of distance learning has grown immensely. The *Guidelines* have developed into an extremely important and influential document, providing a description of the scope and quality of library resources and services that are necessary to adequately support distance learning students and faculty. Importantly, librarians, academic administrators, and accrediting agencies use the document to help measure the adequacy and equity of distance learning library services (Caspers, Fritts, & Gover, 2001; Frederiksen, 2003).

The Distance Learning Section was also instrumental in the initial publication of the first commercial journal devoted to distance learning librarianship. For the distance learning library community, 2003 was a hallmark year, when the charter issue of the *Journal of Library & Information Services in Distance Learning* was released—a notable groundbreaking experience and the culmination of a tremendous amount of work done by many individuals over the span of several years. Although many publications have contributed to the literature on distance learning librarianship, until 2003, no journal provided a primary focus on the subject of library and information services in distance learning. The *Journal of Library & Information Services in Distance Learning* is the first commercially published journal to specifically address the issues and concerns of librarians and information specialists in this rapidly growing field. The journal is a peer-reviewed quarterly publication, providing readers with substantive articles, essays, reviews, and research reports. The journal has a large and inclusive scope. It covers programs and innovations throughout the international community, and the content includes articles covering the vast array of subjects involved in library and information services in distance learning. Taking the journal from "idea" to "fruition" was a long and arduous task involving many individuals. For several years, members of the Distance Learning Section of ACRL worked to find a publisher that would be willing to take a risk with such a publication. Harvey Gover, Jack Fritts, and others were instrumental in approaching Haworth Press, Inc. about the idea, and Haworth, a publisher of over 35 journals related to library and information services, decided to take the idea from "possibility" to "reality."

In addition to the Distance Learning Section, there are other professional organizations that can be very valuable for librarians and others interested in the issues related to distance learning librarianship. The Distance Learning Interest Group of the Library and Information Technology Association (LITA) focuses on leading edge technology and applications for distance education librarians and other information providers. The Group sponsors programs, workshops, and institutes reaching across many levels of experience, from absolute beginners to high-tech professionals. Distance education librarians interested in instructional issues frequently use the guidelines, listserv, and other resources provided by the Instruction Section of ACRL, as well as the resources provided by *LOEX* (Library Orientation Exchange), a self-supporting, non-profit educational clearinghouse for library instruction and information literacy. In addition, two discussion groups within ACRL (the Electronic Reserves Discussion Group and the Regional Campuses Discussion Group) provide venues for exchanging information about topics important to distance education librarians.

For librarians who are new to distance education, one book that proved to be very useful for information on the wide range of issues confronting distance education librarianship. Carol Goodson's (2001) *Providing Library Services for Distance Education Students: A How-to-Do-It Manual* is a bit dated now, but it is still the best one-volume work available on the subject, providing a great deal of useful information, especially for North American librarians.

LIBRARY INSTRUCTION & REFERENCE SERVICES

According to the *Guidelines for Distance Learning Library Services*, it is "essential" that each institution provide distance education students with services and resources "equivalent" to those provided on-campus students, including the provision of a "program of library user instruction designed to instill independent and effective information literacy skills." How academic institutions provide services and resources vary widely depending on the personnel, facilities, and technology employed by the individual institution. In some cases, librarians are located at various satellite or remote sites, where they provide access to resources and services, meet face-to-face with students, and assist them in using library resources and services—the traditional method of instruction and reference prevalent throughout the last half of the 20th century. In an ever-increasing number of situations, however, librarians are using the interactive capabilities of new technologies—especially the Web, television, and videoconferencing—to communicate simultaneously with students who can be located at many different sites. In addition, a great deal of library instruction is being conducted asynchronously through online tutorials, course management systems, and other software. With resources and clientele varying greatly among academic institutions, pedagogical practices for distance learning librarians also vary greatly, and frequently for large institutions, depending upon the nature of the particular program or course being supported, practices may vary within the institution.

To meet a growing demand for distance education, colleges and universities have increased their course and degree offerings by utilizing a wide variety of teaching methods, formats, and technologies. Although some distance education classes continue to conform to the traditional correspondence-course format, others are conducted entirely over the Internet, or entirely by videoconferencing or videotape. Probably most distance education classes involve some level of live interaction between faculty and students. For some courses, faculty members travel to classrooms located at various sites throughout the state or region, where they lecture, hold class, and interact with students. In an ever-increasing number of situations, faculty members use the interactive capabilities of television or videoconferencing, and they conduct their classes while communicating simultaneously with students who can be located at several different sites.

Undoubtedly, most academic libraries try to support the informational, research, and instructional needs of all of their distance education students and faculty, regardless of course format or location. The promotion of library resources and services can be an important key to a successful program. In many cases, in an attempt to promote their services, prior to the start of each semester, distance education librarians attempt to contact all distance education faculty members at their institutions, offering the faculty formal face-to-face instruction for their students when appropriate, as well as other instructional services, including reference assistance (by e-mail and toll-free telephone) and course-specific chat communications through course-management systems. Probably for most librarians, the preferred method of instruction and reference assistance remains the face-to-face alternative, especially when each student has access to a computer with an Internet connection, providing the best advantage of the hands-on experience and active learning, taking each student through the research process of using library resources and services, while highlighting information literacy components.

INFORMATION LITERACY & ACTIVE LEARNING

According to ACRL, information literacy is the "set of skills needed to find, retrieve, analyze, and use information," and in order to guide instruction librarians interested in promoting information literacy skills, ACRL published the *Information Literacy Competency Standards for Higher Education* (ACRL, 2000). Building upon this, ACRL's Distance Learning Section developed a SPEC (Systems and Procedures Exchange Center) Kit for the Association of Research Libraries entitled *Collaboration for Distance Learning Information Literacy Instruction* (ACRL, 2005), and in its study, the committee observed,

> The ability to utilize a variety of tools and technologies, from face-to-face instruction to synchronous and asynchronous online assistance, appears to be a trend for libraries that are taking the lead in distance information literacy instruction. . . . Many of those libraries that are engaged in the distance information literacy instruction appear to be approaching the unique challenges of the distance learning environment dynamically and creatively. (ACRL, 2005, p. 18)

Debbie Orr and Margie Wallin also recognized the need for creativity—that the "individualistic" information literacy needs and learning styles of off-campus students require a realignment of traditional services and flexible delivery of instruction (Orr & Wallin, 2001). During the last four years, the Off-Campus Library Services Conference and a number of journals have produced a good deal of scholarship concerning the creative development of information literacy programs for distance education students (Buchanan, Luck, & Jones, 2002; D'Angelo & Maid, 2004; Dewald, Scholz-Crane, & Booth, 2000; Heller-Ross & Kiple, 2000; Holmes, 2002; Kearley & Phillips, 2002; Kelley, Orr, & Houck, 2001; Lockerby, Lynch, Sherman, & Nelson, 2004; McFarland & Chandler, 2002; Manuel, 2001; Mulherrin, Kelley, & Fishman, 2004; Reynolds, 2001; Walsh, 2002).

LEARNING STYLES

In order to connect with as many students as possible, distance education librarians must be aware of the wide variety of student learning styles, especially when their instruction involves new technology. For example, Yunfei Du (2004) noted that, for online courses, students with "concrete" learning styles are naturally more satisfied with the learning experience, so instructors may increase overall student satisfaction by including more active/reflective dimensions for "abstract" learners (pp. 60–61). Christopher Brown-Syed, Denice Adkins, and Hui-Hsien Tsai (2005) discovered that, although "visual and intuitive learners may gravitate to the Web with ease," sequential and aural learners may have problems. To help alleviate such problems, they concluded, "Just as with classroom presentations, distance education programming demands the employment of a variety of teaching methods to accommodate a variety of learning styles" (p. 22). Katherine Holmes (2002) also emphasized the need to better understand the variety of learning styles among distance education students, concluding, "When we offer a diversity of learning approaches, we enable all students to choose the best environment (possibly multiple environments) for their learning" (p. 376).

VIDEOCONFERENCING

For joint videoconferencing with on-campus and off-campus courses, academic institutions may employ a wide variety of technologies and software; nevertheless, for librarians involved in instruction, the teaching and learning issues remain the same. As Cheryl McCarthy (2004) at the University of Rhode Island has observed, a positive attitude about learning through the medium of videoconferencing can be increased by interactivity and the active participation of distant students, and as she concluded, "The benefits of interactive video far outweigh the barriers" (p. 25). At Nova Southeastern University, Mou Chakraborty and Shelley Victor were involved in an innovative delivery method for library instruction to graduate students using compressed video, and in a study presented at the Eleventh Off-Campus Library Services Conference, they highlighted the many challenges confronting instructors using videoconferencing. Chakraborty and Victor (2004) emphasized the need to incorporate active learning techniques whenever possible, and they concluded that each remote site needs to be set up to be "conducive to a positive learning process," with access to computers for hands-on experience at the sites being the ideal (p. 111). In addition, several other studies have emphasized the positive aspects of reaching distance education students through the use of videoconferencing technology (Dunlap, 2002; Ronayne & Rogenmoser, 2002; Ruttenberg, & Housewright, 2002).

COURSE MANAGEMENT SYSTEMS & ONLINE COURSES

A variety of course management systems are currently in use in North American colleges and universities; however, the three most widely used systems are probably *Blackboard*™, *WebCT*™, and *Desire2Learn*™. For many distance education librarians, working with faculty using course management systems involves such activities as the creation of special resource pages, the development of mini-tutorials, the provision of electronic reserves, and the provision of course-specific chat reference, in addition to other services. In order to take greater advantage of the courseware, librarians work with and collaborate with teaching faculty to determine current and potential uses of the courseware, with the goal being to find the particular arrangement of resources and services for each class that provides the best service for each particular group of students.

North American academic institutions have taken advantage of online courses and course management systems in a wide variety of ways. For instance, librarians at Central Missouri State University used *Blackboard*™ to create a "pseudo course" that was designed to provide library instruction, research assistance, and communication to all of the institution's nursing students (Dinwiddie & Winters, 2004). Librarians at the University of Kentucky have developed faculty/librarian co-instructor teams for online courses, allowing students to work with the course librarian throughout the entire life of a research project or course, thus providing greater continuity in their projects and alleviating the need for constant re-explanation (Lillard, 2003, pp. 209–210; Lillard, Wilson, & Baird, 2004). Several institutions have used courseware to develop for-credit courses in information literacy and library instruction, including the Open University (Needham, 2004; Parker, 2003), Royal Roads University (McFarland & Chandler, 2002), Austin Peay State University (Buchanan, Luck, & Jones, 2002), Louisiana State University (Wittkopf, 2003), Purdue University (Reynolds, 2001), Texas Tech University (Hufford, 2004), Washington State University (Lindsay, 2004), Rollins College (Zhang, 2002); Regent University (Lee & Yaegle, 2005), California State University, Chico (Blakeslee & Johnson, 2002), California State University, Hayward (Manuel, 2001), University of Texas at Austin (Ardis, 2003), and University of Maryland, University College (Kelley, Orr, & Houck, 2001; Mulherrin, Kelley, & Fishman, 2004). Librarians at the Houston Community College System have expanded upon the concept of the online course by having embedded librarians in the online classes, and they have creatively used a blog, available through links in all of the online classes, to serve as an instructional and communication tool with large numbers of students (Drumm & Havens, 2005).

WEB-BASED TUTORIALS

During the last decade, as the Internet has continued to expand as an enormously powerful tool for providing services and resources to distance education students, significant numbers of libraries have turned to Web-based tutorials to provide instruction and promote information literacy skills. Although some institutions still utilize CDs as an option for reaching a certain segment of distance learners, there is an overwhelming trend to transition from CD to Web access (Arnold, Sias, & Zhang, 2002; Jones, 2004). Web-based tutorials, many of which are in-house creations, can work effectively, especially for introductory information, but they do vary greatly in quality, and those lacking active learning components appear to be the least effective (Viggiano, 2004). According to Paul Hrycaj (2005), almost 60% libraries in the Association of Research Libraries (ARL) have created their own tutorials, and in addition, approximately 60% have active learning components—a learning process involving the gathering of information, critical thinking, and problem solving. The *TILT* (Texas Information Literacy Tutorial), developed by the University of Texas, is probably the best known of the Web-based tutorials, and many institutions have developed tutorials around that model (Fowler & Dupuis, 2000; Orme, 2004). A significant number of institutions have developed effective, interactive tutorials for distance education students and other remote users, including Western Michigan University (Behr, 2004), Deakin University (Churkovich & Oughtred, 2002), Shippensburg State University (Cook, 2002), University of Wyoming (Kearley & Phillips, 2002), and the Resource Discovery Network in the United Kingdom (Place & Dawson, 2002). A trend seems to be shifting toward the use of mini-tutorials or short-tutorials, focusing on particular subjects or research techniques, so that students do not have to go through long tutorials containing information superfluous to their particular needs. In addition to the use of Web-based tutorials, the University of Calgary has utilized Web-based worksheets for instruction, so that students can follow along interactively during hands-on instruction, or they can use the worksheet later asynchronously after the session (MacMillian, 2004).

ELECTRONIC RESERVE

Over the last decade, with ever-increasing numbers of distance education students gaining Internet access, more and more information being published in full-text, and scanning technology constantly improving, many academic libraries have developed electronic reserve services, providing easy online access to class readings for distance education courses. Each nation has its own copyright laws that librarians must abide by, and in the United States, two recent acts—the Digital Millennium Copyright Act (DMCA) of 1998 and the Technology, Education, and Copyright Harmonization (TEACH) Act of 2001—have helped to clarify the rights and limits that American libraries have in scanning materials and providing electronic access to copyrighted material (Dames, 2005; Strickland, 2004). Although there are a number of Web sites and other sources of information on the two acts, probably the best Web sites for information on the acts are available through the Association of Research Libraries.

In the United States, librarians have famously touted the "fair use" provisions of copyright law, which allows libraries to provide electronic access to copyrighted works that are owned by the library, as long as the works are password protected and accessible to only students in each particular class, and the works are taken down at the end of the semester. Whenever the material is available in full text, most libraries make persistent links to the full text of the article or document, but when the materials are originally available only in print, libraries can scan the works into PDF format to make them available for one semester before taking down the images. When libraries wish to make unowned copyrighted works available electronically or when they wish to make copyrighted works available electronically for a period of time longer than a semester, they must get permission from the publisher or copyright holder, which can be accomplished by either contacting the publisher or working through an agency or company, such as the Copyright Clearance Center (Wilson, 2003). A permission for copyright clearance usually involves the payment of a fee for each work. Canadian copyright is a little more restrictive than American copyright. Instead of "fair use," Canadian law recognizes "fair dealing," which requires permission from the copyright holder to scan material, even in a secure environment and even if the material is to be made available for just one semester (Magusin & Johnson, 2004; Pival & Johnson, 2004).

Even with the restrictions to "fair use" and "fair dealing," electronic reserves will be an increasingly important service that academic libraries provide to distance education students and faculty.

SURVEYS & ASSESSMENT

In order to have a successful library program for distance education students, librarians must understand who their students are, as well as what their students want and need. Of course, the best way to get this information is to ask the students. ACRL's *Guidelines for Distance Learning Library Services* emphasize this point, encouraging librarians to regularly survey students involved in distance education and off-campus programs. A review of the literature on user surveys shows that, as a tool to assess quality of service and customer satisfaction, key indicators of an organization's performance, user surveys are increasingly popular in many institutions, especially academic libraries supporting distance education programs. A substantial body of literature has recently been developing on library surveys, especially the use of surveys for distance education (Boadi & Letsolo, 2004; Kelley & Orr, 2003; Liu & Yang, 2004; Mabawonku,

2004; McLean & Dew, 2004; Shaffer, Finkelstein, & Woelfl, 2004). The qualitative and quantitative data secured periodically from such surveys allows distance education librarians to keep current about client issues and concerns.

CONCLUSION

The particular delivery method used to provide library resources and services is usually mirrored by (or determined by) the nature of the particular program or course being supported. When institutions offer courses in a variety of formats utilizing a variety of technologies, resources and services are necessarily offered in a variety of modalities, and they should include a full array of options, from high-tech to low-tech. Librarians must be flexible; they must understand the variety of learning styles, and they should provide instruction and reference assistance to distance education students through a variety of learning environments. According to Holly Heller-Ross and Julia Kiple (2000, p. 196), "Instruction formats are usually closely connected to the technology and format of the other academic course offerings." Heller-Ross and Kiple also noted "every possible format is currently in use somewhere . . . (but no particular one) is any better than the others. They have developed from the practical experiences and philosophical ideas of the librarians who shaped them and represent different institutional profiles in terms of size and types of degrees offered" (Heller-Ross & Kiple, 2000, pp. 196–197). Johanna Tunon reinforced the conclusions of Heller-Ross and Kiple when she observed that no particular technique or format is a "silver bullet," offering the perfect solution. Offering flexibility and variety to support distance education programs are the keys to success, but Tunon also noted a political campus reality: "Decisions about whether to offer library training online or in a face-to-face format often are made by academic programs, and are based on the administrative and political constraints of those academic programs and curricula rather than fundamental pedagogical considerations" (pp. 525–526).

Distance education programs vary widely throughout academia, with great varieties found across regions of the world and within individual nations and states. Although there can be great differences in their programs, institutions are using many of the same techniques and technologies to provide library resources and services to their distance learners. All colleges and universities with distance learning programs must support the informational, research, and instructional needs of all of their off-campus students and faculty, regardless of course format or location. The Internet has revolutionized many of the ways that academic libraries serve their off-campus clientele. Nevertheless, face-to-face instruction and reference service continues to be a very important and very effective method of supporting distance education programs, but increasingly, new technologies are providing important and useful alternatives for reaching many distance learners who would otherwise not receive assistance. The challenge to each distance learning librarian is how to use funding, staff time, and technology to provide a particular variety of resources and services that best fits his/her institution's course offerings and student needs.

REFERENCES

Ardis, S. B. (2003). A tale of two classes: Teaching science and technology reference sources both traditionally and through distance education. *Issues in Science & Technology Librarianship, 37,* 1092–1206.

Arnold, J., Sias, J., & Zhang, J. (2002). Bringing the library to the students: Using technology to deliver instruction and resources for research. *Journal of Library Administration, 37,* 27–37.

Association of College and Research Libraries. (2005). *Collaboration for distance learning information literacy instruction: SPEC kit 286.* Washington, DC: Association of Research Libraries, Office of Leadership and Management Services.

Association of College and Research Libraries. (2000). Information literacy competency standards for higher education. Retrieved September 22, 2005, from http://www.ala.org/ala/acrl/acrlstandards/informationliteracycompetency.htm

Behr, M. D. (2004). On ramp to research: creation of a multimedia library instruction presentation for off-campus students. *Journal of Library Administration, 41*, 19–30.

Blakeslee, S., & Johnson, K. (2002). Using *HorizonLive* to deliver library instruction to distance and online students. *Reference Services Review, 30*, 324–9.

Boadi, B. Y., & Letsolo, P. (2004). Information needs and information seeking behaviour of distance learners at the Institute of Extra-Mural Studies in Lesotho. *Information Development, 20*, 189–99.

Brown-Syed, C., Adkins, D., & Tsai, H. (2005). LIS student learning styles and web-based instruction methods. *Journal of Library and Information Services in Distance Learning, 2*, 5–25.

Buchanan, L., Luck, D., & Jones, T. (2002). Integrating information literacy into the virtual university: A course model. *Library Trends, 51*, 144–66.

Caspers, J. S., Fritts, J., & Gover, H. (2001). Beyond the rhetoric: A study of the impact of the ACRL *Guidelines for Distance Learning Library Services* on selected distance learning programs in higher education. *Journal of Library Administration, 31*, 127–48.

Central Michigan University. (2005). "Thirteenth off campus library services conference." Retrieved December 22, 2006, from http://ocls.cmich.edu/conference/index.html

Centre for Research in Library and Information Management (CERLIM). (2005). "Conferences and events." Retrieved December 22, 2006, fron http://www.cerlim.oc.uk/conf/index.php

Central Michigan University. (2005). Off Campus Library Services Conference. Homepage. http://ocls.cmich.edu/conference/index.html

Centre for Research in Library and Information Management (CERLIM). (2005) Homepage. http://www.cerlim.ac.uk/index.php

Chakraborty, M., & Victor, S. (2004). Do's and don'ts of simultaneous instruction to on-campus and distance students via videoconferencing. *Journal of Library Administration, 41*, 97–112.

Churkovich, M., & Oughtred, C. (2002). Can an online tutorial pass the test for library instruction? An evaluation and comparison of library skills instruction methods for first year students at Deakin University. *Australian Academic & Research Libraries, 33*, 25–38.

Cook, D. L. (2002). Ship to shore: An online information literacy tutorial using *BlackBoard* distance education software. *Journal of Library Administration, 37*, 177–87.

Dames, K. M. (2005). Copyright clearances: Navigating the TEACH Act. *Online, 29*, 25–29.

D'Angelo, B., & Maid, B. (2004). Beyond instruction: Integrating library service in support of information literacy. *Internet Reference Services Quarterly, 9*, 55–63.

Dewald, N., Scholz-Crane, A., & Booth, A. (2000). Information literacy at a distance: Instructional design issues. *The Journal of Academic Librarianship, 26*, 33–44.

Dinwiddie, M., & Winters, J. (2004). Two-stepping with technology: An instructor/librarian collaboration in health promotion for baccalaureate nursing students. *Journal of Library and Information Services in Distance Learning, 1*, 33–45.

Drumm, M., & Havens, B. (2005) A foot in the door: Experiments with integrating library services into the online classroom. *Journal of Library and Information Services in Distance Learning, 2*(3), 25–32.

Du, Y. (2004). Exploring the difference of "concrete" and "abstract": Learning styles in LIS distance education. *Journal of Library and Information Services in Distance Learning, 1*, 51–64.

Dunlap, S. (2002). Watch for the little red light: Delivery of bibliographic instruction by unconventional means. *Journal of Library Administration, 37*, 279–285.

Fowler, C. S., & Dupuis, E. A. (2000). What have we done? TILT's impact on our instruction program. *Reference Services Review, 28*, 343–8.

Frederiksen, L. (2004). Beyond the extended campus library: A brief history of the Distance Learning Section, ACRL. *Journal of Library and Information Services in Distance Learning, 1*, 45–54.

Frederiksen, L. (2003). Grading ourselves: Using the ACRL *Guidelines for distance learning library services* to develop assessment strategies. *Journal of Library Administration, 37*, 333–9.

Goodson, C. (2001). *Providing library services for distance education students: a how-to-do-it manual.* New York: Neal-Schuman.

Heller-Ross, H., & Kiple, J. (2000). Information literacy for interactive distance learners. In T. Jacobson & H. Williams (Eds.) *Teaching the new library to today's users* (pp. 191–219). New York: Neal-Schuman.

Holmes, K. E. (2002). A kaleidoscope of learning styles: Instructional supports that meet the diverse needs of distant learners. *Journal of Library Administration, 37,* 367–378.

Hrycaj, P. L. (2005). Elements of active learning in the online tutorials of ARL members. *Reference Services Review, 33,* 210–18.

Hufford, J. R. (2004). User instruction for distance students: Texas Tech University system's main campus library reaches out to students at satellite campuses. *Journal of Library Administration, 41,* 153–65.

Jones, M. F. (2004). Creating a library CD for off-campus students. *Journal of Library Administration, 41,* 185–202.

Kearley, J., & Phillips, L. (2002). Distilling the information literacy standards: Less is more. *Journal of Library Administration, 37,* 411–424.

Kelley, K., Orr, G., & Houck, J. (2001). Library instruction for the next millennium: Two web-based courses to teach distant students information literacy. *Journal of Library Administration, 32,* 281–94.

Kelley, K. B., & Orr, G. J. (2003). Trends in distant student use of electronic resources: A survey. *College & Research Libraries, 64,* 176–91.

Lee, M., & Yaegle, S. (2005). Information literacy at an academic library: Development of a library course in an online environment. *Journal of Library and Information Services in Distance Learning, 2,* 33–44.

Lillard, L. L. (2003). Personalized instruction and assistance services for distance learners: Cultivating a research relationship. *Research Strategies, 19,* 204–12.

Lillard, L., Wilson, P., & Baird, C. (2004). Progressive partnering: Expanding student and faculty access to information services. *Journal of Library Administration, 41,* 227–242.

Lindsay, E. B. (2004). Distance teaching: Comparing two online information literacy courses. *The Journal of Academic Librarianship, 30,* 482–7.

Liu, Z., & Yang, Z. Y. (2004). Factors influencing distance-education graduate students' use of information sources: A user study. *The Journal of Academic Librarianship, 30,* 24–35.

Lockerby, R., Lynch, D., Sherman, J., & Nelson, E. (2004). Collaboration and Information Literacy: Challenges of Meeting Standards when Working with Remote Faculty. *Journal of Library Administration, 41,* 243–253.

LOEX (Library Orientation Exchange). (2005). "Instruction resources." Retrieved December 22, 2006, from http://www.emich.edu/public/loex/resources.html

Mabawonku, I. (2004). Library use in distance learning: a survey of undergraduates in three Nigerian universities. *African Journal of Library, Archives & Information Science, 14,* 151–65.

MacMillian, D. (2004). Web-based worksheets in the classroom. *Journal of Library and Information Services in Distance Learning, 1,* 43–51.

Magusin, E., & Johnson, K. (2004). Collaborating on electronic course reserves to support student success. *Journal of Library Administration, 41,* 255–64.

Manuel, K. (2001). Teaching an online information literacy course. *Reference Services Review, 29,* 219–28.

McCarthy, C. A. (2004). Interactive video technology for distance learning: An assessment of interactive video technology as a tool. *Journal of Library and Information Services in Distance Learning, 1,* 5–27.

McFarland, D., & Chandler, S. (2002). "Plug and play" in context: Reflections on a distance information literacy unit. *Journal of Business & Finance Librarianship, 7,* 115–29.

McLean, E., & Dew, S. H. (2004). Assessing the Library Needs and Preferences of Off-Campus Students: Surveying Distance-Education Students, from the Midwest to the West Indies. *Journal of Library Administration, 41,* 265–302.

Mulherrin, E., Kelley, K., & Fishman, D. (2004). Information literacy and the distant student: One university's experience developing, delivering, and maintaining an online, required information literacy course. *Internet Reference Services Quarterly, 9,* 21–36.

Needham, G. (2004). Information literacy-who needs it? In Brophy, P., Fisher, S., & Craven, J. (Eds.), *Libraries without walls 5: The distributed delivery of library and information services* (pp. 109–119). London: Facet Publishing.

Orme, W. A. (2004). A Study of the residual impact of the Texas information literacy tutorial on the information-seeking ability of first year college students. *College & Research Libraries, 65*, 205–15.

Orr, D., & Wallin, M. (2001). Information literacy and flexible delivery: Are we meeting student needs? *Australian Academic & Research Libraries, 32*, 192–203.

Parker, J. (2003). Putting the pieces together: Information literacy at The Open University. *Library Management, 24*, 223–228.

Pival, P., & Johnson, K. (2004). Tri-institutional library support: a lesson in forced collaboration. *Journal of Library Administration, 41*, 345–54.

Place, E., & Dawson, H. (2002). Building the RDN virtual training suite to teach Internet information skills via the Web. In P. Brophy, S. Fisher, & Z. Clarks (Eds.) *Libraries without walls 4: The delivery of library services to distant users* (pp. 161–172). London: Facet Publishing.

Reynolds, L. J. (2001). Model for a web-based information literacy course: Design, conversion and experiences. *Science & Technology Libraries, 19*, 165–78.

Ronayne, B., & Rogenmoser D. (2002). Library research instruction for distance learners: an interactive, multimedia approach. In P. Brophy, S. Fisher, & Z. Clarks (Eds.) *Libraries without walls 4: the delivery of library services to distant users* (pp. 187–196). London: Facet Publishing.

Ruttenberg, J., & Housewright, E. (2002). Assessing library instruction for distance learners: a case study of nursing students. In J. Nims and E. Owen (Eds.), *Managing library instruction programs in academic libraries: Selected papers presented at the 29th national LOEX library instruction conference*: Vol. 33. Library Orientation Series (pp. 137–148). Ann Arbor, MI: Pierian Press.

Shaffer, J., Finkelstein, K., & Woelfl, N. (2004). A systematic approach to assessing the needs of distance faculty. *Journal of Library Administration, 41*, 413–28.

Slade, A. L. (2004). Research on library services for distance learning: An international perspective. *Journal of Library and Information Services in Distance Learning, 1*, 5–43.

Strickland, L. S. (2004). Copyright's digital dilemma today: fair use or unfair constraints?: The DMCA, the TEACH Act and other e-copying considerations. *Bulletin of the American Society for Information Science and Technology, 30*, 18–23.

Tunon, J. (2002). Creating a research literacy course for education doctoral students: design issues and political realities of developing online and face-to-face instruction. *Journal of Library Administration, 37*, 515–27.

Viggiano, R. G. (2004). Online tutorials as instruction for distance students. *Internet Reference Services Quarterly, 9*, 37–54

Walsh, R. (2002). Information literacy at Ulster County Community College: Going the distance. *The Reference Librarian, 77*, 89–105.

Wilson, P. (2003). The ins and outs of providing electronic reserves for distance learning classes. *Journal of Library Administration, 37*, 537–48.

Wittkopf, B. (2003). Recreating the credit course in an online environment: Issues and concerns. *Reference and User Services Quarterly, 43*, 18–25.

Zhang, W. (2002). Developing web-enhanced learning for information literacy. *Reference & User Services Quarterly, 41*, 356–363.

III

DESIGN AND TEACHING

18

Instructional Design and the Technologies: An Overview

Rick Shearer
The Pennsylvania State University

When thinking about how to discuss instructional design in distance education, several alternatives can come to mind. One could discuss the subject in terms of technologies, types of interactions, learner autonomy, and learner control; or in a multitude of other ways, including an emphasis on costs. In truth, all of these elements are part of the formula that defines the design and development of a course to be offered at a distance; however, in all of these approaches there is an underlying acknowledgement or understanding that a particular technology is being utilized to bridge the distance between the student, the instructor, and learning organization. Key to any one of the technologies chosen is how it allows or does not allow the other elements of the course to behave in a systems environment where all of the elements or variables interact.

In distance education, we have, in many ways, several critical factors that must be reviewed prior to even considering how the course will be presented and how it will function. These include (a) the audience characteristics, (b) geographic dispersion of the audience, (c) the technologies available to the audience, (d) the goals of the learners, (e) the goals and missions of the learning organization, (f) the costs that must be recovered, (g) the costs of delivery, (h) the political environment at the time for the learning organization, (i) faculty compensation, and (j) market competition. All of these factors come into play in determining the design of a course before we even look at its learning goals and objectives. In many instances, these factors will dictate the technologies we use. While discussing technology at the beginning of the design process can appear backwards to classic instructional design, it tends to surface early in discussions in distance education.

Single-mode and dual-mode institutions of distance education have striven for years to integrate the latest technologies into their courses in an effort to provide the student at a distance a richer learning experience and a feeling of connectedness to the education enterprise and instructors. The field has used and experimented with education radio, educational television, audiographics, two-way interactive teleconferencing, computer-based education, learning centers, the telephone, the fax, and now the Internet. Each of these technologies has had its pluses and minuses in terms of impact on factors that go into designing and delivering a course at a distance. Some have added immediacy of presentation and instructor feedback, and others have provided cost economy of scale for the education institutions, while other technologies have simply provided needed access for the learners. As the Internet and online learning began to evolve in the 1990s, we saw many publications espousing online learning as a panacea; however, as we have witnessed once again, no single technology addresses all the needs of learners or the results expected by the constituents involved in the distance education enterprise. The current adoption of broadband, the integration of reach media (e.g., Flash), and the ability for synchronous sessions with VoIP (voice over Internet protocol) has again provided a blending of media in our designs. As we look across the broad spectrum of distance education courses being offered today, we see there is no single best technological solution.

In any field of study, it is often important to take a step back and look at how the field has conducted its business in the past. With regard to distance education, a reflective look back at older technologies may help us examine how we are trying to use the Internet in today's distance education courses. It is important to look at how these earlier technologies not only provided access, but provided learner autonomy, learner control, teacher-student interaction, structure in the learning experiences, and a multitude of other factors. Further, we should look at how these constructs are tied to the theories in the field.

THEORETICAL FRAMEWORK: TRANSACTIONAL DISTANCE

Without going into a full review of the theory on transactional distance it needs to be discussed in order to form a framework for the key design factors that will be reviewed in the chapter. Moore's (1980) theory on transactional distance remains one of the central theories to the field of distance education and has a profound impact on instructional design for distance education courses.

As Moore explored his ideas for the theory of transactional distance throughout the 1970s, he examined numerous distance education courses and proposed a systems linkage between three key variables: (a) dialogue, (b) structure, and (c) learner autonomy. Transactional distance was the resultant of the interplay between these variables. Dialogue, at the time the theory was introduced, was viewed as a subset of the communications between the student and the instructor that led to the construction of knowledge or advanced a student's understanding of the material being studied. Structure was viewed as the amount of freedom a program gives the student in determining pace, sequence, learning objectives and outcomes, and assessment strategies; learner autonomy, which can sometimes be viewed as a subset of structure, looked at the degree of interplay the student needed with the learning organization or learning environment.

In general, the theory looks at the interaction between these three variables. On one dimension, it looks at how structure and dialogue interact. As diagrammed by Saba (1989), in a systems model, as dialogue increased, transactional distance—or the psychological separation of the learner from the instructor—decreased. What was not represented in Saba's work, however, was how the idea of learner autonomy interacted with the dialogue/structure plane. Moore's (1983) work depicted the interplay between the three key variables in a three dimensional cube. The cube showed how you could have high learner autonomy and low dialogue, and in his analysis he suggested what this meant to transactional distance and to the type of learning program involved based on who set the objectives, who decided on the learning materials, and who dictated the type of evaluation or assessment. Here Moore derived his thinking about learner autonomy from the work done on learner dependence and independence.

DESIGN FACTOR: LEARNER AUTONOMY/LEARNER CONTROL

Learner autonomy and learner control are very important in a distance education learning environment. Students involved in distance education are often isolated geographically from the instructor and institution, and must behave in a more autonomous manner in order to meet their learning goals and those of the institution. The amount of control that the design of a distance education course provides these learners is critical to their successful completion. If we provide too much structure within pacing, sequencing, and timing of assessment, then the learner, with competing life demands, may be forced to drop out. If we provide too little structure, then the learner may feel cut off and flounder through the course. Also, the type of control referred to here is not simply the control over how one interacts with the course and the instructor, but as Garrison and Baynton (1989) argue, control is a dynamic balance between independence, power, and support. Where power can be viewed as a psychological dimension of the learner and involves the learner's motivation, cognitive style, emotional maturity, and attitude, and support refers to the support of family, financial support, the administrative processes of the institution, and so forth.

In relation to the theory of transactional distance, we have two of the key variables in play—structure and learner autonomy—when we consider learner control. One must question whether these two variables are negatively correlated or positively correlated; however, if we assume that they are negatively correlated, then as learner autonomy increases, structure decreases. Thus, as we think about our course design, we need to think about the students we are trying to serve. Are they independent adult learners who are highly autonomous, or are they more traditional, aged students? Or are we trying to design a course to meet multiple audiences? which is never an easy task. In Moore's (1983) work on the theory of transactional distance, he developed a table that examined the types of programs in relation to the idea of learner autonomy and dependence or independence. In the table, he looked at who determined the learning objective, who decided what material to use, and who set the assessment strategies. He also depicted a learner as being in less control of the learning environment if all three of these aspects of dependence or independence were set by the teacher or learning institution. While this construct of learner control may seem subtle, it is vital to reflect on it in terms of how we design courses for distance education. When thinking about how courses are structured in higher education, how many leave it up to the student to determine objectives, material, and assessment? The answer is few, which leads one to consider that even if our audience is one of highly autonomous learners, we have traditionally taken away the ability for them to act in an independent fashion. (See also Chapter 9 in this *Handbook*.)

Therefore, good course design, in consideration of the institution's policies and goals, must build in, whenever possible, time for students to catch up on work and assignments, as well as provide alternative periods of assessment and alternative ways of being assessed. The course design should also provide, where possible, adequate levels of self-assessment and alternative representation of concepts to account for different cognitive styles. Further, do we consider different levels of interaction or dialogue based on what an individual student feels necessary to meet the stated learning outcomes? These types of control variables for the autonomous/self-directed learner are essential to providing a positive learning experience.

The question of who sets learning outcomes is a difficult one, as within coherent curricula, we must assure that students meet stated objectives in our courses in order to perform well at the next level. Thus, it is unlikely that we will see many courses constructed so the student can determine the learning objectives. If a course was conceived in a manner where structure was very low, in terms of the setting of objectives, one would likely not even have a traditionally designed educational event, as the instructional designers would not know what to include or how to assess the material that is included in the design. (See also Chapter 21 in this *Handbook*.)

DESIGN FACTOR: INTERACTION

When we think of interaction, we often think in terms of verbal communications between two individuals or a group; however, there are several forms of interaction—some verbal and some nonverbal. Moore (1989) has discussed interaction for distance education in terms of learner-instructor, learner-learner, and learner-content. Hillman, Willis, and Gunawardena (1994) have discussed interaction in terms of learner-interface, while Moore (1980) and Saba and Shearer (1994) have discussed interaction in terms of dialog. In essence, all of these forms of interaction come into play during a distance education course, including interaction with the learning organization. How we accommodate and provide for these different forms of interaction is a function of the technology chosen to deliver the course to the distant student. The amount of interaction we provide in a distance learning environment also contributes to the degree of isolation a student may feel, or the amount of transactional distance that exists between the learner and the instructor.

Over the years, much has been written in the fields of computer-aided instruction (CAI) and computer-based education (CBE) in terms of interface design and the need for a user-friendly and intuitive interface. This body of literature has primarily dealt with the navigational aspects of self-contained courses and the ease with which an end user can navigate through the program and understand what is to be accomplished to meet the learning objectives. There is also now a body of literature concerning the interface design for Web-based courses. While this aspect of course design is extremely important for assisting the student in navigating through the course and the course requirements, the three levels of interaction described by Moore (1989) are perhaps more central to what we view as interaction in a distance education course.

Also, the interaction between the learner and the content goes beyond pure navigational and directional concerns and implies what Holmberg (1981) discusses as the guided didactic conversation. This type of conversation or interaction between the student and the content can occur whether the content is in print or electronic form. It refers to the way the author writes to the student when describing the intricacies of the subject matter, the way that examples are presented and discussed and how the author may write to the student in the first person. For students in a traditional print-based correspondence course, this type of interaction is essential, as it is through the printed word that they hear the authors's or instructor's voice. Not unlike a well written novel where the author speaks to you through the characters and not simply at you, it is this conversational form in the distance education course where the author brings himself into the course and goes beyond the simple presentation of content. As Bates (1995) states, "A text is not a neutral object; its meaning depends on the interpretation of the reader. . . . If the reader is to obtain meaning from a text, there has to be an interaction. What differentiates distance learning texts from other kinds of printed material is a deliberate attempt to structure explicitly a student's response to the material" (p. 120).

For many distance education students, who are studying in an asynchronous mode, the learner-content interaction is the primary voice they hear through their studies. Even when coupled with other forms of interaction, this guided didactic conversation is the course element that they often rely on to get them through the course.

Learner-content interaction can also be seen in video and audio lectures where well written scripts have the presenter or instructor having a conversation with the learner about the content.

Here the content is not simply presented and discussed as if giving a lecture to someone, but the program script has the presenter pose questions and provide insights. As one can imagine, writing in this style, whether for print, educational television, or radio, is not something that comes easily to many, and it is in the development of these guided didactic discussions that the design team's editorial staff and production staff can contribute greatly to the effort.

Moore's other categories, learner-learner interaction and learner-instructor interaction, may be more familiar especially in today's world, as much has been written about the use of e-mail, bulletin boards, Listservs, and message boards in providing the opportunity for discussion between learners and the instructor. These categories, however, have existed in many forms prior to the Internet. Interaction between the learners and the learner-instructor has occurred through the postal service, by means of the telephone, by means of learning centers, and synchronously for students enrolled in two-way interactive video courses, or audiographics courses. What has become key to the idea of interaction between learners and the instructor is timely interaction.

This idea of timely interaction or dialogue ties into Moore's (1980) concept of transactional distance; however, what we must strive to understand is what counts as dialogue. Some like Neff (1998) have argued that in the asynchronous online world, dialogue only exists if a message or posting is responded to in a timely fashion. Further, Hillman (1999) states that if a posting on a message board does not have a logical sequence of post–respond—conclude, then it is open-ended and not dialogue. Therefore, while no one will likely argue that dialogue—whether guided didactic, synchronous or asynchronous—is important, we must understand what should be considered as dialogue and when it should be used. Saba and Shearer (1994) conducted a study using a prototype desktop computer video system to explore this idea. They proposed a typography of interaction categories in order to examine speech acts that occurred during a 30-minute lesson. Categories such as classroom management, passive, active, direct, and indirect emerged. What is important in this study is the attempt to separate conversation and classroom management discussions from instructional dialogue; however, much more work needs to be done in this area. Also, as discussed by Hirumi (2002), it is important that we analyze how each required interaction or dialogical sequence will lend support to the obtainment of the stated learning outcomes. To have discussion for discussion's sake is not good instructional design. The discussions within an online distance education course must be well orchestrated to enable the leaner to meet the learning outcomes.

As Shearer (2003) discussed, interaction in online courses is as complex as in face-to-face courses. While the original thinking was that the Internet was going to be the great leveling influence between all who participated, research now shows that the same cultural, gender, and class issues we witness in face-to-face classes still exist online; therefore, we must know our course audiences and help the authors of our courses understand the complexities of a diverse audience participating in the courses.

Thus learner-learner interaction and learner-instructor interaction needs to be examined not only for how it occurs, but also for the frequency of occurrence, timeliness of interactions, and in terms of type of interaction (conversation, questions, elaboration, etc.). We also need to examine how we account for passive observation of dialog and interaction and for cultural influences. This type of analysis will help in answering the ongoing question posed by instructors of online courses: What is the appropriate level of interaction to include in a course? These questions all tie back to the idea of transactional distance and how interaction/dialogue should be woven into our course designs in support of helping the students feel connected and in assisting them in meeting the stated learning outcomes.

DESIGN FACTOR: ACCESS

Access has been one of the cornerstones of distance education since the first correspondence course. Making learning opportunities available to the disenfranchised has been a primary goal of distance educators and adult educators for over a century; however, access has many attributes. In today's literature, there is no shortage of articles and news stories on the technology aspect of the digital divide. But this is just one way of looking at the concept of access. Access issues in education can be viewed in terms of gender, culture, financial, geographic, supply and demand, disabilities, preparedness (entrance exam qualifications), motivational (self-esteem), language, and a number of other ways. To view access strictly as a concern of geographic separation, or simply as a concern of technology access, when we design courses is too limiting a view. To design distance education courses and curriculums of study without acknowledging the variety of access issues that the intended audience may face can lead to the exclusion of many who may otherwise be interested in or need the course of study.

Traditionally in distance education, we have thought of access primarily as an issue of geographic separation of the learner and the instructor. In many ways, the technologies we have employed in the delivery of courses have been used to address this concern; however, technologies such as print, radio, and TV (with closed captioning) have also addressed a range of disabilities, as well as cultural and financial issues of access. These are technologies that can reach broad audiences, are relatively inexpensive to receive, are often readily available in most countries, and can address the needs of those who have special visual or auditory needs.

It is extremely important that those in the field are aware of issues of access as we witness how the Internet and the World Wide Web are integrated into distance education courses. In the United States, as indicated in the Pew Internet & American Life Project Report "Digital Division" (Fox, 2005), 68% of American adults now use the Internet. The categories of use, however, are no longer simply the haves and the have-nots. In today's society, the division is now three tiered: (a) those with broadband access, (b) those with dial up or moderate access, and (c) those who truly do not have access. This new differentiation is important to our designs and to who we see as our audience for distance education courses. The findings of the study indicate that the educated and those in the higher socioeconomic classes are the ones most likely to have high-speed access. Thus, as we add technologies like Macromedia Flash and synchronous tools, we must be aware that we are now disenfranchising not only those without Internet access, but those that have only moderate access to the Internet.

Internationally, a report by WRI Research (Wired Digital Inc., 2000) indicated that 80% of the world population is being left out of the global communications system, and a report by the Commonwealth of Learning (2005) stated that "millions of children in commonwealth countries lack access to basic education. An estimated 100 million children are still out of school worldwide" (p. 8). William Ruckelshaus, the chairman of WRI, pointed out in 2000 that 4 billion people in the world make $5 a day or less and another 1.5 billion have incomes between $1,500 and $20,000 annually.

National and international statistics are critical to consider when we design and develop courses to be offered at a distance. We need to know our institutional mission, the audience(s) we intend to serve, and their access to technologies. When we integrate various technologies into distance education courses, we are knowingly disenfranchising a large portion of the population. It can also be argued that the integration of technologies increases the cost of education to the student not only through the need for information technology access, but due to the fact that the cost of developing technology-rich courses will be much greater, thus driving up the fee or tuition structure for technology-rich courses. Further, it is important to consider issues of access related to disabilities, as well as supply and demand for education when we integrate the Internet and other computer technologies.

DESIGN FACTOR: COSTS

The phrase "economy of scale" is a benchmark in the literature of distance education. It is one of the main cornerstones many of the mega distance education universities have relied upon in order to fulfill their mission of making education opportunities more broadly available to the general public. Costs for designing and developing courses for distance education have normally been associated with high fixed costs of development and low delivery (variable) costs to the students. In this way, as the number of students taking any one course increased, the development costs were spread across a large student body, thus lowering the development cost per student. This has essentially been the rationale behind the high costs that distance education providers have put into the production of education television and radio broadcasts, as well as traditional print correspondence courses; however, each technology used in delivering a distance education courses has its own unique cost structure.

When designing courses for a distance education audience, it is important to understand the unique cost implications for each technology. As we add technology to a course, we not only drive up the costs of development, but we potentially drive up the costs to the students for delivery. If we look at some of the cost analysis that has been conducted at the Open University of the UK and other distance education institutions (Hülsmann, 1999), we see that the benchmark media that all other distance education courses are measured against is print. This is not surprising, as print can have a relatively low cost for production per hour of study usage, and duplication and distribution of print-based courses tend to be low. Also, courses developed in this medium tend to have a long shelf life before they need to be revised. Once we move up the technology continuum we add development costs, as we are now changing the printed narrative of the course authors into audio, video, or a host of other interactive technologies. In looking at the studies presented by Hülsmann (1999) where they have used a measure of "development cost per student learning hour by medium," other technology costs are measured in terms of a ratio to print. Here we see that development for Educational Television is roughly 180 times that of print, CD-ROM 40 times that of print, and audio (cassette tapes) is 34 times that of print. What is important to note here is that all these technology forms are canned productions meant to have long shelf lives and to be accessible by a large student population.

The concept of long shelf life and large student audience is what allows for economies of scale. What is unclear since the adoption of the Internet technologies and World Wide Web is whether one can design a course which will have a long shelf life and be available to a large number of students. Many distance education institutions now incorporate the Internet into their courses in order to provide a greater sense of connectedness between the learners and the instructor and institution. This is hoped to provide a greater sense of community and timeliness of feedback; however, what is not clear is to what extent this limits the number of students who can enroll in a single section of a course. For once we as designers add greater interactivity between the student and the instructor, we limit the number of students a faculty member can effectively interact with. For institutions that have moved to semester-based online distance education courses, this aspect of connectedness can be quite limiting in terms of the number of students who can take an individual section of a course; and obviously, the more individual course sections an institution needs, the greater the variable costs in terms of instructor salaries. While increased interactivity may seem like a positive in terms of transactional distance, it may have negative consequences in regard to costs.

In Shearer's (2004) report "The Distance Education Balance Sheet," he presents a series of tables that illustrate the impact on a course's bottom line when class size is altered, or yearly revisions are required, when compared to a traditional rolling enrollment course. This analysis highlights how the mission of the institution and how an institution implements distance education can impact a unit's or organization's return on investment (ROI).

The idea of course shelf life and ROI must be examined when we as designers integrate technologies, especially highly interactive technologies, into distance education courses. Learning management tools like *Angel,*™ *Blackboard,*™ *Desire2Learn*™ and others allow faculty and authors a great degree of flexibility in terms of updating and revising courses. With this flexibility and ability to make minor revisions each time the course runs, we lose a degree of shelf life that will dramatically impact the economies of scale. If we are constantly revising courses, then additional development costs are incurred which reduce even the positive monetary impact of a large student audience. This logic, however, assumes that a traditional relationship between the design team and the faculty author continues to exist after the initial development of the course. If after the initial development, the task of maintaining the course and integrating changes falls to the individual faculty, then the ROI equation changes depending on faculty pay model. In a scenario like this, the added faculty time might not be captured as an ongoing cost, and the impact of the constant tweaks and revisions will be viewed as minimal to the unit's or organization's bottom line.

As designers, we need to take into consideration the ROI goals of the institution or unit of distance education. If the model is one where the design team handles all initial development and revisions, and the institution is looking for a strong ROI, then we want to strive for content presentation that can be stable for three to five years to ensure a certain degree of shelf life. The degree of shelf life one can achieve will depend on establishing a balance between the desire for continuous improvement of academic quality and the need for the course to have economies of scale. Therefore, a decision needs to be made between what content can exist in a fixed form for three to five years and what aspects of the course can to be updated each semester or year through means of electronic postings to bulletin boards or through the use of asynchronous tools like Centra or Elluminate Live™. Further, we must weigh the impact of high levels of interaction between the students and the teacher on the ROI. The more interactive the course, the lower the number of students a faculty member can effectively communicate with. Even the addition of the Internet technologies into open enrollment courses will add some limitations in terms of level of instructor-learner interaction that a single instructor or tutor can handle.

The analysis of costs associated with delivering courses at a distance is complex, as demonstrated by Keegan (1996), where he examines several formula based approaches to the topic. There are several factors in the cost equation, and each must be viewed in a systemic manner, as there is no simply cause-effect relationship. For designers, it is important to be cognizant of how decisions about distance education course design impact both development and delivery costs—which affects both the students' and the unit's or organization's bottom line.

TECHNOLOGY OPTIONS IN DISTANCE EDUCATION

How have we used technologies in the design of distance education courses to address the four factors outlined above? To some extent, we have already talked about print and the Internet as we discussed learner autonomy, interaction, access, and costs. To further examine the question of how we as a field have used technologies in distance education, however, we will take a brief look at how print, educational television, two-way interactive teleconferencing, and the Internet provide for or diminish these four design factors.

Print

For many designers and distance education institutions, print (non-electronic text) is still the most versatile medium for the delivery of course content. It is user-friendly, easily transported, can be marked up readily—and most everyone knows how to use the medium. In terms of learner autonomy and learner control, print provides each learner the opportunity to move through the content in a linear fashion, or in a self-designated pattern where they may browse, jump ahead, or read the conclusions for each section first. Of course, print provides no more control over pace than many other media, as much of the pace and structured sequence is often determined by the instructor or learning institution. Print also has its drawbacks in that we are limited in our expression of ideas. Print alone cannot provide alternative forms for expressing concepts. It is not a visual or auditory medium, and it limits us in this regard. Also, as a stand-alone medium, it must be coupled with other technologies (postal service, fax, telephone, or Internet) to provide for interactions with the instructor or tutor and institution. The type of technology coupled with the printed learning material will also determine the timeliness of interactions between the learners and the instructor and institution.

While print has its limitations, it does generally provide the greatest degree of access and cost efficiencies in terms of

- Individuals who know how to use the medium.
- Ease of distribution nationally through the postal systems.
- Adaptability to address several disabilities.
- Fairly inexpensive to duplicate.
- Tends to have a long shelf life.
- Production costs are low (excludes aspect of author payment which can be the same for any course independent of media).
- No additional equipment needed by the learners.

These aspects of access and costs can change for print when the distance education institution begins to consider access by students beyond the geographic bounds of one's country. Once distance education providers start to think of access as a global issue, they are faced with language decisions, cost of distribution to and within other countries, and changes in forms of interaction. In cases where institutions are addressing the learning needs of an international audience, they may end up with a course product that is similar but different, and that has its own cost structure in terms of the fixed and variable costs associated with course development and delivery.

Today print continues to be a part of almost every distance education course regardless of the primary delivery technology. For almost every course there tends to be a print package that accompanies other course materials. It may be in the form of reading packets, case studies, or most commonly, a study guide or student handbook that describes how to get started, how to interact with the instructor and educational institution, and how to use the other media. Therefore, as Bates (1995) stated, "Print is, and will remain, a most important technology for open and distance teaching" (p. 137). We may, however, see traditional print morph into electronic forms such as PDF files, where the cost of printing is passed along to the student.

Educational Television

For distance education, there also seems to be an inverse correlation between educational television's ability to increase access and learner autonomy or learner control, and interaction. Broadcast television or satellite feeds are in general push type technologies in that they are only one way, meaning they do not allow for any real immediacy of interaction, nor do they allow for a great deal of learner control. Educational programs in general were often prerecorded and scheduled to air at a set time. Until the adoption of the VCR, learners had to tune in to broadcasts at given times each day and then complete follow-up lessons, which were generally delivered through print in a study guide or resource notebook. Thus, the learning experience was highly structured and allowed very little control over how the learner interacted with the media. Also, interaction with the instructor or institution was generally by the postal service or telephone. In terms of Moore's (1980) model of transactional distance, learners who were participating in educational television courses were at a great psychological distance from the instructors.

This is not to say that these limitations to educational television inhibited its value. Television and video provide us with a visual medium that has the ability to portray concepts and emotions in a way few other media can. How we use television and/or video in the design of courses to assist learners in visualizing concepts can have a dramatic impact on learning; however, as designers, we must always be cognizant of the costs of production, the shelf life of the programming, and how we couple this technology with others to provide for interaction—and to some degree, aspects of learner control.

Two-Way Interactive Video Teleconferencing

Two-way interactive video, in the early 1990s, relied on high-speed telephone lines and sophisticated bridging technologies; thus, it was not only expensive to set up, but expensive to deliver. In the early 1990s institutions spent from $50,000 and up to purchase and set up two-way interactive video systems and rooms. It also cost roughly $.50 per minute per ISDN line or switched 56 circuit to carry the live video signals. Though the technology basically provided us the ability to extend the traditional classroom, the numbers of sites that received the broadcast was usually limited to five with no more that 75–100 students total. Any more than this number and the level of interaction dropped dramatically to the point where the advantages of the technology were diminished. Learners also had to travel to the locations that had the equipment installed.

Therefore, the cost structure, limited audience, and need for sophisticated telephony technologies greatly limited the impact of the technology on increasing access to educational opportunities. Additionally, the technology did not provide for a great deal of learner autonomy or control any different than we witness in a traditional classroom—the pace, sequence, and the time of day for participation was set—with no way of recording the class at a later time. Therefore, as a distance education technology, two-way interactive video quickly receded from the spotlight as the Internet and World Wide Web became more prevalent in society. By the end of the 1990s, as is noted in Schreiber and Berge's (1998) book, two-way interactive video teleconferencing was used primarily by corporations for training where groups of employees could gather at corporate locations to participate in short courses and just-in-time learning modules.

However, with the move to voice-over-IP (VoIP) and video-over-IP (Internet protocol), we have seen a resurgence of the technology and new implementations. The equipment price for interactive video has dropped sharply, and with transmission of the signal over IP, the cost of distribution and delivery has dropped to almost nothing. Further, synchronous tools like Centra™, Elluminate Live™, and Polycoms™ own systems which now bring two-way interactive video to the desktop with full collaboration features. These new systems are very effective with small groups and for students needing to collaborate on group projects. We must be cautious, however, when integrating these technologies into our online courses. To use these tools as a form of lecture presentation defeats the strength they bring to course environment, for they are best suited for collaboration, and if we as designers are looking to use them for pure presentation of content, then it is likely that there are better tools for that purpose.

As designers of distance education courses, it is important to understand the strengths and weaknesses of large group interactive video systems and newer collaborative interactive systems. As the technology and bandwidth continue to improve and the subscription costs for the newer collaborative technologies drops, it is only a matter of time until designers are faced with deciding how or how not to integrate aspects of two-way interactive video into distance education courses.

The Internet and the World Wide Web

The Internet and the World Wide Web have elevated public awareness of the field of distance education in a way not previously seen. This increased awareness has lead to a reexamination of the field, and to the chagrin of many, a public mindset that views distance education only in terms of the Internet and the World Wide Web. Unfortunately, this view of distance education tends to ignore the vast amount of existing research that has been conducted in the field and in the other related fields such as CAI and CBE. Also, in the rush to use the new Internet technologies, issues of access, cost to students and learner autonomy have not been widely addressed in the literature.

Institutions, and in many regards, designers, continue to be caught up in the ability to present information online and to build elaborate communication environments, sometimes with little thought about how the technologies will impact students and instructors. While there is no doubt that the Internet has improved our capability for more immediacy of feedback, assessment, and collaboration, it has, at the same time, limited access due to technology requirements and development costs.

As discussed in the sections on access and costs, the Internet can have a tremendous negative impact on the accessibility by individuals to distance education courses. Even within the United States, where 68% of the adult population is now connected to the Internet, an institution can significantly narrow its reach by adding higher-end computer requirements and higher-bandwidth Internet applications like streaming media. Distance education institutions that deliver their courses over the Internet not only require that individuals have access to the necessary infrastructure, but that they pay for some sort of access to these technologies. If the reach of the institution is to be global in scope, then the Internet and computer technologies can pose an even greater barrier.

One must also consider the issues of comfort with technology and the ability to use technology that come into play when we incorporate computers and the Internet into distance education courses. Further, student expectations must be considered in our new technologically connected world. If a distance education provider sees itself serving a younger audience, then maybe it needs to examine how the new mobile technologies like smart phones, Sony's new paperback-size e-book (eWEEK, 2006), and gaming systems are used in our designs. But if we are targeting a traditional adult market or a global audience, then our move to new technologies in our designs should be tempered by the knowledge of our audience's technology access and literacy; however, the continued evolution of wireless and handheld devices will eventually make it possible to deliver education to broad audiences, where the instruction is convenient in time, flexible, and cost-effective for students.

The aspects of learner autonomy and learner control should also be examined as we design courses that use the Internet and the World Wide Web. Many institutions have attempted to model their distance education offerings after the traditional campus-based semester system. While this fits well within existing policies and within the normal faculty contract timeframes, it may not work well for the independent learner. The question remains whether this structure assists students in completing their course work or adds to drop out. The inability of some adult students to work in such a structured environment which competes for their time with work, family, and other social commitments needs to be considered. In many ways we may be establishing pace, sequence, interaction requirements, and technology requirements that eliminate the ideas of anytime and anyplace. Aspects of pacing, sequence, and meeting times of semester based distance education courses may resemble the traditional classroom model so closely that we have in fact negated, to a large degree, any feelings of independence and learner control. A key question to be answered by many distance education providers is what audience they are attempting to address when they develop courses to be delivered online. Some may argue that we are designing distance education courses to fit within the policies and procedures of the traditional university structure and not to address the unique needs of learners at a distance. This is especially true of institutions moving to a hybrid course format in order to meet flexibility requirements of resident students and to capitalize on physical plant usage. This new focus on hybrid courses may require that we, as designers, must now develop courses to meet both the needs of true distance education students and resident instruction students who are looking for more flexibility in their course scheduling to allow time to work part time.

CONCLUSION

As instructional designers of distance education courses and programs, we make a series of conscious choices each time we design and develop a course to be delivered to distant students. In some cases, the decisions we make are for pedagogical reasons, at other times the decisions are made for access reasons, and yet at other times the design decisions we make are based on costs. Each time we decide to use a particular technology or combination of technologies, we need to be very clear on why we are using the chosen technology, and for what purpose. Knowing and understanding the strengths of each technology at our disposal, whether the latest Internet tool or an old faithful such as print, is critical to defending and implementing our design decisions.

All too often we witness designs that latch onto the latest technology tool in the hope that the technology will finally solve the multitude of problems encountered in delivering a course at a distance; however, this is often done without careful consideration or understanding of how the new technology will impact learner autonomy, access, end-user costs, or transactional distance. To develop a better mousetrap should not always be the goal for distance education. Understanding the specific attributes that each technology, whether old or new, brings to the design table is essential in helping the learner meet their educational goals. It is critical that we take a systems view of how the technologies we choose impact all the components of a distance education delivery system. While a new technology may sometimes appear to address a particular problem— for example, animated demonstrations of a difficult topic—the cost of supporting the student in the use of the new tool may outweigh the benefits.

In the development of distance education courses there is no one best technology and it is usually a combination of technologies that produces the best course in terms of meeting the learners' educational objectives. In many ways print is still the most dependable means for the delivery of content. This media, when combined with others like the Internet or CD-ROM, can produce a powerful learner experience. Delivery and production costs must also be in the forefront of our decisions, for if as designers, the design decisions are driven by the goal of reduced delivery costs to an international audience, then one may decide to provide the study guide or content by means of a downloadable PDF (portable document format) file. Here we are passing on the printing costs and delivery costs to the students, but may in the long run save the student very expensive postal costs or connectivity fees.

It is essential, therefore, that designers of instructional material for distance education courses understand the strengths and weaknesses of a vast array of technologies and how the older technologies have been deployed in the past to address the multitude of design factors. Returning to the question posed at the beginning of the chapter, why do we strive to replicate the classroom environment? Is this counter intuitive to good design? The answer is, it depends. If we simply replicate the lecture mode online, then this may be poor design. If, however, we visually enhance the material presented and then build upon the interactive moments that occur in traditional classroom environments through well-orchestrated discussions, then we have taken the best of both worlds and have created a strong learning environment for the learners and the instructors. How and why we integrate certain technologies into our designs is the key to the success of our distance education courses and institutions.

REFERENCES

Bates, A. W. (1995). *Technology, open learning, and distance education*. London: Routledge.

Commonwealth of Learning. (2005). ODl for teacher and school development. *Connections, 10*(2), 8. Retrieved July 1, 2006, from http://www.col.org/colweb/site/pid/3040

eWEEK. (2006). *Electronic publishing: Sony envisions new chapter in e-book story*. Retrieved January 29, 2006, from http://www.eweek.com

Fox, S. (2005). *Digital divisions*. Pew Internet and American Life Project. Washington, DC.

Garrison, D. R., & Baynton, M. (1989). Beyond independence in distance education: The concept of control. In M. G. Moore & G. C. Clark (Eds.), *Readings in principles of distance education* (pp. 16–28). University Park, PA: American Center for the Study of Distance Education.

Hillman, D. C. A. (1999). A new method for analyzing patterns of interaction. *The American Journal of Distance Education, 13*(2), 37–47.

Hillman, D. C. A., Willis, D. J., & Gunawardena, C. N. (1994). Learner—interface interaction in distance education: An extension of contemporary models and strategies for practitioners. *The American Journal of Distance Education, 8*(2), 30–42.

Hirumi, A. (2002). A framework for analyzing, designing, and sequencing planned e-learning interactions. *The Quarterly Review of Distance Education, 3*(2), 141–160.

Holmberg, B. (1981). *Status and trends of distance education*. London: Kogan Page.

Hülsmann, T. (1999). The costs of distance education. In K. Harry (Ed.), *Higher education through open and distance learning* (pp. 72–84). New York: Routledge.

Keegan, D. (1996). *Foundations of distance education* (3rd ed.). London: Routledge.

Moore, M. G. (1980). Independent study. In R. Boyd, J. Apps, & associates (Eds.), *Refining the discipline of adult education* (pp. 16–31). San Francisco: Jossey-Bass.

Moore, M. G. (1983). On a theory of independent study. In D. Stewart, D. Keegan, & B. Holmberg (Eds.), *Distance education: International perspectives* (pp. 68–94). New York: Croom Helm.

Moore, M. G. (1989). Three types of interaction. *Readings in principles of distance education* (pp. 100–105). University Park, PA: American Center for the Study of Distance Education.

Neff, B. D. (1998). Harmonizing global relations: A speech act theory analysis of PRForum. *Public Relations Review, 24*(3), 351–376.

Saba, F. (1989). Integrated telecommunications systems and instructional transaction. In M. G. Moore & G. C. Clark (Eds.), *Readings in principles of distance education.* (pp. 29–36). University Park, PA: American Center for the Study of Distance Education.

Saba, F., & Shearer, R. L. (1994). Verifying key theoretical concepts in a dynamic model of distance education. *The American Journal of Distance Education, 8*(1), 36–59.

Schreiber, D. A., & Berge, Z. L. (1998). *Distance training: How innovative organizations are using technology to maximize learning and meet business objectives.* San Francisco: Jossey-Bass.

Shearer, R. L. (2003). *Interaction in distance education.* Special report, 2(1). Madison, WI: Distance Educator.com and Atwood.

Shearer, R. L. (2004). *The Distance Education Balance Sheet: What are the measures of success for institutions and students?* Special Report, 2(2). Madison, WI: Distance Educator.com and Atwood.

Wired Digital Inc. 2000. *On creating digital dividends.* Retrieved March 21, 2001, from http://www.wired.com/news/technology/

19

Frameworks for Design and Instruction

Curtis J. Bonk
Indiana University

Vanessa P. Dennen
Florida State University

As technological innovations bring about not just another wave of education and training possibilities, but a transformation of higher education as we know it, there is heightened need to research, articulate, share, and harness the principles of effective online pedagogy. What is quite noticeable in all this transformation is that those in the midst of it need frameworks, models, advice, and other guidance related to technology integration, learner motivation, instructor roles, and learner-centered instruction. In response, in this chapter, we provide such Web-based teaching frameworks and discuss the pedagogical strategies and tools instructors can use to exploit the Web more fully.

ONLINE LEARNING FRAMEWORKS

Frameworks provide a useful way to examine possibilities. The ones we share here were developed based on a series of research studies (Bonk & King, 1998) and course experiments (e.g., Bonk, 1998; Bonk, Hara, Dennen, Malikowski, & Supplee, 2000). Some of these studies explored the forms of learning assistance and mentoring found in online learning environments (Bonk & Sugar, 1998; Kirkley, Savery, & Grabner-Hagen, 1998) and the structure of online tasks (Dennen, 2000). Others have investigated online case creation and mentoring with preservice teachers (Bonk, Daytner, Daytner, Dennen, & Malikowski, 2001; Bonk, Hara, et al., 2000; Bonk, Malikowski, Angeli, & East, 1998; Bonk, Malikowski, Angeli, & Supplee, 1998). More recently, some of these frameworks and ideas have been tested and expanded in a highly reputable and fast-growing online MBA program (Liu, Bonk, Magjuka, Lee, & Su, 2005; Su, Bonk, Magjuka, Liu, & Lee, 2005). Using much of this research as a base, we have outlined five Web-based instruction frameworks relating to (1) psychological justification of online learning; (2) participant interaction; (3) levels of technology integration; (4) instructor and student roles; and (5) pedagogical strategies. When combined, these five factors address issues pertaining to the overall learning environment and sense of community present in online courses. They can be used to plan, design, teach, and evaluate online courses. These general frameworks also lead to five practical initiatives presented later: (1) focused programs of research in e-learning; (2) tool-development efforts; (3) instructional-design benchmarks for e-learning; (4) instructor training programs; and (5) teaching tips and guidelines.

Table 19.1 demonstrates how each framework impacts and influences each practical initiative.

Framework #1: Psychological justification for online learning.   The first area of the model considers how use of the Web relates to current psychology theory. For instance, Bonk and Cummings (1998) linked 14 learner-centered psychological principles (LCPs) from the American Psychological Association (1993, 1997) to a dozen guidelines for using the Web in instruction. The LCPs, which are based on a meta-analysis of hundreds of psychological studies (Alexander & Murphy, 1994), highlight the importance of helping learners construct meaning, represent knowledge, link new information to old, monitor their own critical and creative thinking thoughts, and achieve complex learning goals. These principles also focus on how to foster student curiosity and intrinsic motivation, confront students with appropriately high and challenging standards, recognize individual differences in learning, and nurture social interaction and interper-

TABLE 19.1.
Framework of the Effects of Instructional Frameworks for the Web
on Practical Online Learning Initiatives

Instructional Frameworks for the Web	Online Learning Initiatives				
	1. Research Agendas	*2. Tool Development Initiatives*	*3. Instructional Design Benchmarks*	*4. Instructor Training Programs*	*5. Pedagogical Guidelines, Reports, Resources, and Materials*
1. Psychological Justification	Guides research	Justifies tool design	Provides benchmark criteria	Use as theoretical basis in training	Guides pedagogy
2. Participant Interaction	Variable as well as outcome of research	Influences tool design	Embedded in benchmarks	Provides training content	Generates activity ideas
3. Level of Web Integration	Provides classification system				
4. Student and Instructor Roles	Variable as well as outcome of research	Influences tool design	Embedded in benchmarks	Provides training content	Generates activity ideas
5. Pedagogical Strategies	Variable as well as outcome of research; focuses research funding	Establishes goals for tool design and funding sponsorship	Provides benchmark criteria	Provides training content	Generates activity ideas

sonal reasoning. As such, the LCPs are especially relevant to adult distance education settings, since they tend to attract adult learners who want personally meaningful activities (Wagner & McCombs, 1995) as well as instructors who are willing to experiment with and employ a variety of instructional techniques to accommodate individual student needs (Bonk 2001, 2002). Bonk and Cummings specifically linked each of their 12 practical guidelines to one or more of the APA principles:

1. Establish a safe environment and a sense of community;
2. Exploit the potential of the medium for deeper student engagement;
3. Let there be choice;
4. Facilitate, don't dictate;
5. Use public and private forms of feedback;
6. Vary the forms of electronic mentoring and apprenticeship;
7. Explore recursive assignments that build from personal knowledge;
8. Vary the forms of electronic writing, reflection, and other pedagogical activities;
9. Use student Web explorations to enhance course content;
10. Provide clear expectations and prompt task structuring;
11. Embed thinking skill and portfolio assessment as an integral part of Web assignments;
12. Look for ways to enhance the Web experience.

Each of these 12 guidelines were linked to more than one of the 14 LCPs. For instance, the third recommendation on allowing students choice is related to fostering student intrinsic motivation to learn, natural curiosity, and creativity (LCP #8). It also is related to the effects of motivation and guided learning on effort (LCP #9) and addresses individual differences in learning (LCP #12).

An additional psychological framework offered by Bonk and Cunningham (1998) documented collaborative learning tools from three theoretical perspectives. More specifically, Bonk and Cunningham explicated the learner-centered, constructivist, and sociocultural beliefs, principles, and approaches that inform the use of electronic conferencing and collaborative media. These theoretical perspectives have grown in their popularity as an underpinning for online class discussion as instructors have seen the discussion tools as a way to hear multiple voices and give students practice with articulation and argumentation. The development of shared responsibility for maintaining a dialogue and intersubjectivity amongst discussants are outcomes resulting from this approach (Bober & Dennen, 2001; Master & Oberprieler, 2004).

Framework #2: Participant interaction.   This second framework offers a means to reflect on the types of interaction structures that the Web affords as well as the possible players or participants in typical online learning situations (Cummings, Bonk, & Jacobs, 2002). As noted in Table 19.2, Cummings, et al. (2002) document how online interactions among three key participants—instructors, students, and practitioners—should be investigated and made more explicit through the use of different media. Listed in Table 19.2 are some of the interactions mentioned in their matrix.

To evaluate the types of interactions found in higher-education courses, Cummings, et al. (2002) evaluated a number of education syllabi posted to the World Lecture Hall (see http://www.utexas.edu/world/lecture/) for indicators of learning interaction. This framework opens up discussion on the types of interactions and information exchanges that are important in learning. For instance, in this study, there was minimal practitioner involvement in one's courses.

TABLE 19.2.
E-Learning Communication Flow among Instructors, Students, and Experts/Practitioners

	To Students	*To Instructors*	*To Practitioners/Experts*
From Instructors	Syllabus, schedule, profiles, tasks and tests, lecture notes and slides, feedback and email, resources, course changes	Course resources, syllabi, lecture notes and activities, electronic forums, teaching stories and ideas, commentary	Tutorials, online articles listservs, electronic conferences, learning communities, news from discipline/field, products to apply in field
From Students	Models or samples of prior work, course discussions and virtual debate information, introductions and profiles, link sharing, personal portfolios, peer commenting or evaluation	Class voting and polling, completed online quizzes and tests, minute papers, course evaluations and session feedback, reflection logs, sample student work	Resumes and professional links, Web page links, field reflections and commentary
From Practitioners/ Experts	Web teleapprenticeships, online commentary and feedback, e-fieldtrips, internship and job announcements	Survey opinion information, course feedback, online mentoring, listservs	Discussion forums, listservs, virtual professional development team explorations and communities

This matrix provides an opportunity to examine how online learning tools can be used to engage different participants. As such, it widens one's views on the range of online participants, the forms of online instruction, the degree and type of interactions online, and the online environments that may soon be common. This is just one view of online interaction. For instance, Bonk, Medury, and Reynolds (1994) developed a similar framework to understand the levels of interaction fostered by synchronous and asynchronous computer conferencing and collaborative writing tools.[1] Collectively, such frameworks are powerful aides in tool selection and instructional-design processes as well as in reflection on instructional options and challenges where minimal guidelines exist.

Framework 3: Level of web or technology integration.   A third model highlights 10 distinctive levels of Web integration (Bonk, Cummings, Hara, Fischler, & Lee, 2000). These levels range from syllabus sharing to posting course materials on the Web, to having online discussions, to placing an entire course on the Web, to coordinating an entire program on the Web. In effect, such levels afford a useful way of examining how fully a particular course uses the Web, and demonstrate a future path of integration that an instructor might work toward. Rather than simply referring to a course as a Web course or acknowledging that it has a Web presence, these levels, which have been expanded from 10 to 12 levels since the first edition of this *Handbook* (see Table 19.3), provide a way of being more specific in categorizing a Web-based course.

The first five levels largely represent informational or resource repository uses of the Web, whereas the next five levels require a significantly greater time commitment on the part of students and instructors. The final two levels are more institutional in nature. Once at Level 6, where graded activities typically begin, there is more reliance on student interaction and instruc-

---

[1]Note that more than 30 synchronous and asynchronous tools were reviewed in that particular study.

TABLE 19.3.
A Continuum of Web Integration in College Courses
(Bonk, Cummings, et al., 2000; Bonk & Dennen, 1999; Rowley, Lujan, & Dolence, 1998)

Levels of Web Integration	Description
1. Marketing/Syllabi via the Web	Instructors use the Web to promote course and teaching ideas via electronic fliers and syllabi.
2. Student Exploration of Web Resources	Students use the Web to explore pre-existing resources, both in and outside of class.
3. Student-Generated Resources Published on the Web	Students use the Web to generate resources and exemplary products for the class.
4. Course Resources on Web	Instructors use the Web to create and present class resources such as handouts, prior student work, class notes and PowerPoint presentations.
5. Repurpose Web Resources	Instructors take Web resources and course activities from one course and, making some adjustments, use them in another.
6. Substantive and Graded Web Activities	Students participate with classmates in Web-based activities such as weekly article reactions or debates as a graded part of their course requirements.
7. Course Activities Extending Beyond Class	Students are required to work or communicate with peers, practitioners, teachers, and/or experts outside of their course, typically via computer conferencing.
8. Web as Alternate Delivery System for Resident Students	Local students with scheduling or other conflicts use the Web as a primary means of course participation, with the possibility of a few live course meetings.
9. Entire Course on the Web for Students Located Anywhere	Students from any location around the world may participate in a course offered entirely on the Web.
10. Course Fits Within Larger Programmatic Web Initiative	Instructors and administrators embed Web-based course development within larger programmatic initiatives of their institution (e.g., a master's degree, certificate program, or a doctoral degree).
11. Web as an Environment for the Entire Organization or Institution	The university or institution exists entirely or almost entirely online. Online courses, therefore, are the expectation—for example, Jones International University (Pease, 2006), Capella University (Offerman & Tassava, 2006), etc.
12. Consortia of Universities for Online Program or Degrees	There are a consortium of colleges, universities, or organizations working together to offer degree programs—for example, the Canadian Virtual University, the Global Virtual University (GVU), Iowa Regents Institutions Distance Education (IRIDE).

tor facilitation for online learning success. In fact, at Levels 8–12 of Web integration, the Web becomes the primary delivery platform for the course or program. This framework is often used for online instructor training, since, in Bonk, Cummings, et al. (2000), not only are the first 10 levels described with examples and key issues, but student issues and instructional design guidelines are detailed in each level (for a earlier draft, see http://php.indiana.edu/~cjbonk/paper/edmdia99.html).

This framework was designed to help educators think more deeply about the level of Web integration. Each decision about course design has long-term implications for student attitudes, social interaction, and overall learning. Reflecting on the levels of Web integration or technology use is yet another way for instructors as well as instructional designers to grasp the range of options for their online course- and tool-development efforts. Once a decision has been made regarding the level of Web integration, an instructor might investigate and select instructional strategies that make the Web effective at that level.

Framework #4: Instructor and student roles.   The fourth framework concerns the roles of instructors and students in online learning environments. Web-based tools such as asynchronous discussion forums can be used to alter traditional instructor-led discussion formats and promote student interaction, critique, and collaboration activities based on constructivist learning theories. As with face-to-face instruction, instructor guidance is necessary throughout the online teaching and learning process. One cannot expect students to simply engage in discussion on their own without any guidance or facilitation from an instructor. Aligning the activity with assessments and providing reinforcement also may be helpful (Blass & Davis, 2003; Dennen, 2005). Thus, instructors must determine what types of roles they wish to take in the class and to purposefully maintain such roles in the design of the course and throughout course activities and learner interactions.

Students may be broken into small discussion groups, each simultaneously monitored but not necessarily run by the instructor, in which they might assume roles such as coordinator/leader, starter or resource investigator, summarizer, secretary or scribe, advocate or encourager, specialist, implementer, and reviewer or editor of results (Bonk, Wisher, & Lee, 2003). In addition to functional roles, students might take thematic or historical roles. Such an activity can help spark student interest in written documents and may provide some authenticity they might be seeking (Kolloff & Rahimzadeh, 2004; Oliver, Herrington, & Reeves, 2006). Role play is sometimes difficult for students at first, but they tend to learn more from taking responsibility for their own learning.

While student roles may be assigned at the activity level, the online instructor must constantly shift between instructional, facilitator, and consultant roles. Mason (1991) advocated three key roles of the online instructor: (1) organizational, (2) social, and (3) intellectual. The organizational role entails setting the agenda, objectives, timetable, and procedural rules for posting and interaction. In contrast, the social role involves sending welcoming messages, thank-you notices, prompt feedback on student inputs, and a generally friendly, positive, and responsive tone. Of the three roles Mason describes, the intellectual role is the most crucial since it includes probing responses, asking questions, and refocusing discussion. It also entails setting goals, explaining tasks and overlooked information, weaving disparate comments, synthesizing key points raised and identifying unifying themes, directing discussion, and generally setting and raising the intellectual climate of the course or seminar. In effect, Mason's framework allows teachers an opportunity to reflect on the multiple roles or hats of the instructor in online courses.

In expanding on Mason's framework, both Berge (1995) and Ashton, Roberts, and Teles (1999) provide a slightly different framework to document the social, managerial, and technological actions that instructors can use to enhance their online courses. Berge (1995) elaborates on these 4 instructional roles or actions to make suggestions for instructors. For instance, his pedagogical recommendations include presenting conflicting opinions and finding unifying threads. In contrast, the social recommendations include using introductions and accepting lurkers. Whereas Berge's managerial recommendations include being clear and avoiding informational or task overloads, his technical recommendations include using technical support and providing time to learn new software features.

These frameworks have since been used to describe the various components of online courses in our own research (Bonk, Kirkley, Hara, & Dennen, 2001). Liu, et al. (2005) found that instructors in an online MBA program were most adept at the pedagogical role (e.g., course designer, profession inspirer, feedback giver, and interaction facilitator) and least savvy with social roles. As such, there was a perceived need to raise instructor awareness of the importance of the social role in creating a more rich and engaging learning environment or community of learners. While a deep sense of community is difficult due to the brief duration of online courses (Wilson, Ludwidg-Hardman, Thornam, & Dunlap, 2004), there are many tasks and tools that the online instructor can use to have students feel more socially supported and connected. Research on this framework such as that by Liu, et al. (2005) and Bonk, Kirkley, et al. (2001) can lead to more effective training support for instructors as well as for students.

As is clear from Table 19.4, there are many ways to teach online courses. In Bonk, Kirkley, et al. (2001) as well as in Liu, et al. (2005), the framework is elaborated upon and more ideas are provided from interviewing and observing online instructors and students in a range of settings within higher education. By understanding how instructors can use the Web to design and enhance student social interaction, knowledge building, higher-order thinking, and reflection, we can improve learning in all types of educational environments.

TABLE 19.4.
Summary of the Pedagogical, Social, Managerial, and Technological Roles of the Online Instructor (Ashton, et al., 1999; Berge, 1995, Bonk, Kirkley, et al., 2001; Mason, 1991).

	General Components and Questions	*Examples, Features, and Strategies*
1. Pedagogical Role	Assume facilitator or moderator role and ask questions, encourage student knowledge building, design a variety of instructional activities, elicit reflection, weave or summarize discussions, identify themes in discussions, offer constructive criticism, push to articulate ideas and explore resources, and provide explanations and elaborations where necessary	Problem-based learning tasks, peer feedback tools, electronic cases, team activities, discussion forums, role play, constructive controversy, field reflections, Web site and resource evaluations, and online debates
2. Social Role	Create a friendly and nurturing environment or community feel, exhibit a generally positive tone, foster some humor, personalize in messages, display empathy and interpersonal outreach, and create community feel	Cafes, digitized class pictures, online guests and visitors, jokes, and online stories or anecdotes
3. Managerial Role	Coordinate assignments with set due dates and extensions, assign groups and partners, clear expectations, set office hours, grading and feedback, and overall course structuring	Online chats, detailed syllabus, course FAQs, online grade book and portfolios, login data, and calendar of events
4. Technological Role	Assist participants with technology issues, clarify problems encountered, and notify when the server is down	Orientation tasks, help systems, tutorials, and vote on preferred technologies

Framework #5: Pedagogical strategies.   As the growth in this area of teaching explodes, it becomes important to understand various types of learning activities that can be effectively used to enhance the quality of online teaching. Such activities include problem-based learning or inquiry-based learning (Dennen, 2000; Duffy & Kirkley, 2004; Gunawardena, 2004; Koschmann, 1996; Zhang, Hung, & Peng, 2005; Zhang & Peck, 2003), peer-feedback activities (Dennen & Jones, 2006), online case learning (DeLacey & Leonard, 2002), and online debates (Jeong, 2004; Pilkington & Walker, 2003; Salmon, 2002). Each of these pushes the environment from mindless content dumping to a more engaging and interactive learning environment that is based on what we know about how people learn (Bransford, Brown, & Cocking, 1999; Carmean & Haefner, 2002).

Beyond just learning activities, there also are pedagogical strategies that might be used across learning activities to help support learner performance. Oliver and his colleagues (Oliver & Herrington, 2000; Oliver & McLoughlin, 1999; Oliver et al., 2006) offer frameworks for thinking about instructional strategies that one might use for online teaching and learning. Their experimentation bridges technology and psychological theory by providing thinking-related templates for online tool development. For instance, they focus on how Web tools can foster student articulation, collaboration, intentional learning, and goal setting. They also connect these constructivist principles to Web-based resources such as bulletin boards, asynchronous conferencing, concept mapping, and survey tools that might be employed for student debates, reflection, cooperative group situations, and online discussions. More recently, they offer advice for developing online and blended courses rich in authentic learning situations and problems (Oliver et al., 2006).

Bonk and Reynolds (1997) designed a similar framework in detailing a set of instructional strategies for the Web and relating them to the relevant creativity, critical thinking, cooperative-learning literature, and, more recently, motivation. For instance, role play, "what if" activities, online journals, and brainstorming tasks were linked to creative thinking; idea ranking, flow-

TABLE 19.5.
Online Learning Pedagogical Activities by Thinking and Learning Model
(Bonk & Reynolds, 1997; Dennen & Bonk, 2007)

Motivational and Ice Breaking Activities	Creative Thinking Activities
1. 8 Noun Introductions	1. Brainstorming
2. Coffee House Expectations	2. Role Play
3. Scavenger Hunts	3. Topical Discussions
4. Two Truths, One Lie	4. Web-Based Explorations and Readings
5. Public Commitments	5. Recursive Tasks
6. Share-A-Link	6. Electronic Séances
Critical Thinking Activities	Collaborative Learning Activities
1. Electronic Voting and Polling	1. Starter-Wrapper Discussions
2. Delphi Technique	2. Structured Controversy
3. Reading Reactions	3. Symposia or Expert Panels
4. Summary Writing and Minute Papers	4. Electronic Mentors and Guests
5. Field Reflections	5. Round-robin Activities
6. Online Case Analyses	6. Jigsaw and Group Problem Solving
7. Evaluating Web Resources	7. Gallery Tours and Publishing Work
8. Instructor as well as Student Generated Virtual Debates	8. E-mail Pals/Web Buddies and Critical/Constructive Friends

charting, comparison and contrast, critiques and rebuttals, summary writing, and case analyses were deemed to foster critical thinking; and group investigations, "round robins," project-based learning, "Web buddy tasks," asynchronous conferencing, and panel discussions and symposia were examples of cooperative-learning tasks for the Web. Bonk and Reynolds also noted how such instructional approaches and activities can foster a cognitive apprenticeship.

As is shown by this table, there are many pedagogically and instructionally interesting activities available for online-learning environments. For example, the Web offers a unique forum for classroom discussion, role-play, case-based discussion, brainstorming, special guest appearances, and collaborative learning. In effect, such activities can be embedded into existing course-management systems for deeper learning opportunities rich with collaboration, apprenticeship, and knowledge construction and sharing (Carmean & Haefner, 2002; Herrington & Oliver, 1999).

As noted in Table 19.6, some of these pedagogical strategies heavily employ reading and writing. One popular and effective reading and writing strategy is the starter-wrapper technique (Hara, Bonk, & Angeli, 2000). In this method, the starter summarizes the chapter ideas and issues for a particular week. The starter also provides questions meant to jumpstart discussion. In the wrapper role, students reflect on issues and themes discussed during the week or unit as well as the issues that remain open. In effect, students are the teachers here. The instructor might respond within this discussion as a second wrapper by pointing out what topic and issues were accurately portrayed and what issues still need further discussion and clarification. He or she weaves discussion fragments, while directly teaching content only when necessary. Those who are not starters or wrappers might take on various roles such as devil's advocate, pessimist, or optimist.

Of course, there are many other reading and writing techniques for online environments. For instance, students might respond to articles online in small groups or individually. They might also comment on the confusing as well as the clear aspects of a class in a weekly minute or muddiest point paper. Such formative feedback will help the instructor make weekly shifts in class.

Various forms of instructor facilitation can help support learner success within these activities. For example, models can be used to help increase learner understandings of instructor expectations (Dennen & Bonk, 2007). Rubrics based on Bloom's Taxonomy can help encourage learners to keep their participation focused on appropriate cognitive tasks for meeting the stated learning objectives (Christopher, Thomas, & Tallent-Runnels, 2004). Although the burden of facilitation will be on instructors, some students may take on a leadership role and engage in strategies that will help support their peers in online social groups (e.g., see Butler, Sproull, Kiesler, & Kraut, in press).

Online discussion is a vital part of e-learning courses. Instructors can assume many roles here. Typically a conversational or informal role allows for more student participation and dialogue (Weedman, 1999). Formal or directive statements indicate an authoritative model of instruction. When online instructors are more informal and spontaneous in their commenting, students become more interactive with each other (Ahern, Peck, & Laycock, 1992). In effect, responding to teacher questions or statements online is simply an extension of the recitation method—the more teacher-centered the environment, the less student exploration, engagement, and interaction. As Tharp and Gallimore (1988) demonstrated with their highly acclaimed "instructional-conversation" method, students need to be invited into the discourse through complex interactions of instructor and peer assistance.

What about motivation? The permanency of this electronic text, however brief, and ability to comment on or revisit it are motivating aspects of online learning. Also motivating are cooperative-learning techniques such jigsaw; wherein learners might divide or subdivide their learning quests and responsibilities. In addition, learners might be sorted in pro and con groups on controversial topics for online debates. They might vote on topics or articles for these discussions or

TABLE 19.6.
Online Reading and Writing Techniques (Bonk, 1998; Bonk & Reynolds, 1997;
Oliver, Omari, & Herrington, 1998; Paulsen, 1995)

1. Starter-Wrapper (Hara, Bonk, & Angeli, 2000)
   a. Starter-Wrapper Conventional: Starter reads ahead and starts discussion and wrapper (and perhaps the teacher) summarizes what was discussed; others participate.
   b. Starter-Wrapper with Roles: Same as #1 but include roles for other participants (optimist, pessimist, devil's advocate, coach, questioner, mediator, connector, commentator, bloodletter, etc.).
2. Article Discussions
   a. Reading Reactions with No Choice: Students post critiques or reactions to a small set of preassigned articles and react to posts of a certain number of peers.
   b. Reading Reactions with Extensive Choice: List all the articles in their reading packet within an online discussion tool. Next, assign students to reply to a set number of those articles. They decide which articles they want to discuss and reply to, however.
3. Jigsaw
   a. Research Article Jigsaw: Assign research articles to groups and then segment article or set of articles within groups (e.g., member #1 reads introduction and literature review; #2 reads the methods section, #3 reads the findings, #4 reads the conclusions and implications, etc.). In each group, students summarize the research flaws and confounds in an electronic discussion and share what learned.
4. Web Explorations and Readings
   a. Evaluate Existing Articles: Students search for electronic articles on a topic and summarize, categorize, and/or react to them.
   b. Generate Reading Packet: Students find a set of similar articles on a topic and create an electronic reading packet.
5. Field Observations Reactions
   a. Individual Observations: Students observe situations in their field or discipline during internship or job experiences and reflect on how these experiences relate to current course material. Instructors post issues or questions for student reaction.
   b. Private Online Diaries or Blogs: Students reflect on field or internship observations in a private online journal (with or without instructor feedback).
6. Structured Controversy
   a. Assigned Roles: Assign two students a pro side and two students a con side and debate an issue electronically and then switch roles and come to compromise; perhaps later post a reflection on the compromise positions of 1–2 other groups.
   b. Chosen Roles: Same as in "A" above, but students select their own roles.
7. Topical Discussions
   a. List possible topics for discussion and have students vote on them and sign up to take the lead on one or more weeks.
8. Cases
   a. Instructor Generated Cases: Place set number of cases on the Web and link to a bulletin board system or conferencing tool for students to discuss. These cases can be used as collaborative quizzes that instructors and students from other universities or institutions can use.
   b. Student Generated Cases: Have students generate a set number of cases during semester based on field experiences or job related experiences and respond to a set number of peer cases.
9. Debates
   a. Reading Reactions as Debates with Free Choice: Assign a set number of articles to read, but student reactions on one or more of these must be in the form of a debate.
10. Minute or muddiest point papers
    a. Individual Minute Papers: Have students send the instructor 1–2 minute reflections via e-mail perhaps to recap a class or to summarize things that remain unclear.

As alluded to above, the initial pedagogical framework from Bonk and Reynolds (1997) was later extended to include motivational techniques and principles. Dennen and Bonk (2007) outline a set of 10 motivational principles related to tone or climate, feedback, engagement, meaningfulness, choice, variety, curiosity, tension, interactivity and collaboration, and goal setting. They link each of these principles to specific pedagogical activities for online environments. For instance, cases entail opportunities for obtaining instructor as well as student feedback, more authentic and meaningful learning, high learner engagement in the activity, cognitive dissonance or tension concerning the appropriate case resolution, peer interaction both within a class as well as across classes, goals in the form of needed solutions, and choice among several case solution options as well as case formats if more than one case is offered. As online instructors begin to use such a motivational framework in their class preparation and delivery, they can address student learning needs as well as begin to reach the possibilities of the Web for interactive and engaging learning. When this happens, student retention rates, which are presently under a microscope at colleges, universities, and corporate training organizations around the world, should significantly rise.

post cases or topics of importance based on internship experiences. Student posting of cases, instead of instructor or prepackaged problems, adds to the authenticity and currency of the online classroom. As these examples indicate, no matter what the online course, there are likely many opportunities to embed reading and writing activities.[2]

FINAL THOUGHTS

The e-learning frameworks outlined in this chapter play a vital role in helping instructors, administrators, and policy makers reflect on their decisions concerning the theoretical perspectives, tools, activities, interaction patterns, roles, and instructional strategies pertinent to online learning. Frameworks can also lead to more focused research agendas, enhanced tool and courseware designs, prominent course and program comparison benchmarks, well-planned instructor training programs, accessible pedagogical materials and reports, and better overall online teaching and learning environments. As online learning continues to be a growth area, it is expected that these frameworks, perspectives, and models will further develop and new ones will arise, all in the interest of improving Web-based teaching and learning. Let's make it so.

REFERENCES

Ahern, T. C., Peck, K., & Laycock, M. (1992). The effects of teacher discourse in computer-mediated discussion. *Journal of Educational Computing Research, 8*(3), 291–309.

Alexander, P. A., & Murphy, P. K. (1994, April). *The research base for APA's learner-centered psychological principles*. Paper presented at the annual meeting of the American Educational Research Association New Orleans, LA.

American Psychological Association. (1993). *Learner-centered psychological principles: Guidelines for school reform and restructuring*. Washington, DC: American Psychological Association and the Mid-Continent Regional Educational Laboratory.

American Psychological Association. (1997). *Learner-centered psychological principles: A framework for school redesign and reform,* Washington, DC: American Psychological Association.

Ashton, S., Roberts, T., & Teles, L. (1999, December). *Investigation the role of the instructor in collaborative online environments*. Poster session presented at the CSCL '99 Conference, Palo Alto, CA.

Berge, Z. L. (1995). Facilitating computer conferencing: Recommendations from the field. *Educational Technology, 35*(1), 22–30.

Blass, E., & Davis, A. (2003). Building on solid foundations: Establishing criteria for e-learning development. *Journal of Further and Higher Education, 27*(3), 227–245.

Bober, M. J., & Dennen, V. P. (2001). Intersubjectivity: Facilitating knowledge construction in online environments. *Educational Media International, 38*(4), 241–250.

Bonk, C. J. (1998, April). *Pedagogical activities on the "Smartweb": Electronically mentoring undergraduate educational psychology students*. Paper presented at the annual convention of the American Educational Research Association, San Diego, CA.

Bonk, C. J. (2001). *Online teaching in an online world*. Bloomington, IN: CourseShare.com. Retrieved December 29, 2006, from http://mypage.iu.edu/~cjbonk/faculty_survey_report.pdf

Bonk, C. J. (2002, January). *Executive summary of "Online teaching in an online world."* United States Distance Learning Association (USDLA). Retrieved December 29, 2006, from http://www.usdla.org/html/journal/JAN02_Issue/article02.html

---

[2]See our Table 23.6 and 23.7 in the earlier edition of the *Handbook of Distance Education* for many more pedagogical strategies that might be used online.

Bonk, C. J., & Cummings, J. A. (1998). A dozen recommendations for placing the student at the centre of Web-based learning. *Educational Media International, 35*(2), 82–89.

Bonk, C. J., Cummings, J. A., Hara, N., Fischler, R., & Lee, S. M. (2000). A ten level Web integration continuum for higher education. In B. Abbey (Ed.), *Instructional and cognitive impacts of Web-based education* (pp. 56–77). Hershey, PA: Idea Group.

Bonk, C. J., & Cunningham, D. J. (1998). Searching for learner-centered, constructivist, and sociocultural components of collaborative educational learning tools. In C. J. Bonk & K. S. King (Eds.), *Electronic collaborators: Learner-centered technologies for literacy, apprenticeship, and discourse* (pp. 25–50). Mahwah, NJ: Lawrence Erlbaum Associates.

Bonk, C. J., Daytner, K., Daytner, G., Dennen, V., & Malikowski, S. (2001). Using Web-based cases to enhance, extend, and transform preservice teacher training: Two years in review. *Computers in the Schools, 18*(1), 189–211.

Bonk, C. J., & Dennen, V. P. (1999). Teaching on the Web: With a little help from my pedagogical friends. *Journal of Computing in Higher Education, 11*(1), 3–28.

Bonk, C. J., Hara, H., Dennen, V., Malikowski, S., & Supplee, L. (2000). We're in TITLE to dream: Envisioning a community of practice, "The Intraplanetary Teacher Learning Exchange." *CyberPsychology and Behavior, 3*(1), 25–39.

Bonk, C. J., & King, K. S. (Eds.). (1998). *Electronic collaborators: Learner-centered technologies for literacy, apprenticeship, and discourse.* Mahwah, NJ: Lawrence Erlbaum Associates.

Bonk, C. J., Kirkley, J. R., Hara, N., & Dennen, V. (2001). Finding the instructor in post-secondary online learning: Pedagogical, social, managerial, and technological locations. In J. Stephenson (Ed.*), Teaching and learning online: New pedagogies for new technologies.* London: Kogan Page.

Bonk, C. J., Malikowski, S., Angeli, C., & East, J. (1998). Case-based conferencing for preservice teacher education: Electronic discourse from the field. *Journal of Educational Computing Research, 19*(3), 269–306.

Bonk, C. J., Malikowski, S., Angeli, C., & Supplee, L. (1998, April). *Holy COW: Scaffolding case-based "Conferencing on the Web" with preservice teachers.* Paper presented at the annual convention of the American Educational Research Association, San Diego, CA.

Bonk, C. J., Medury, P. V., & Reynolds, T. H. (1994). Cooperative hypermedia: The marriage of collaborative writing and mediated environments. *Computers in the Schools, 10*(1/2), 79–124.

Bonk, C. J., & Reynolds, T. H. (1997). Learner-centered Web instruction for higher-order thinking, teamwork, and apprenticeship. In B. H. Khan (Ed.). *Web-based instruction* (pp. 167–178). Englewood Cliffs, NJ: Educational Technology.

Bonk, C. J., & Sugar, W. A. (1998). Student role play in the World Forum: Analyses of an Arctic learning apprenticeship. *Interactive Learning Environments, 6*(1–2), 1–29.

Bonk, C. J., Wisher, R. A., & Lee, J. (2003). Moderating learner-centered e-learning: Problems and solutions, benefits and implications. In T. S. Roberts (Ed.), *Online collaborative learning: Theory and practice* (pp. 54–85). Hershey, PA: Idea Group.

Bransford, J. D., Brown, A. L., & Cocking, R. (Eds.). (1999). *How people learn: Mind, experience, and school.* Washington, DC: National Academy Press.

Butler, B., Sproull, L., Kiesler, S., & Kraut, R. (in press). Community effort in online groups: Who does the work and why? In S. Weisband, & L. Atwater (Eds.), *Leadership at a distance.* Mahwah, NJ: Lawrence Erlbaum Associates.

Carmean, C., & Haefner, J. (2002, November/December). Mind over matter: Transforming course management systems into effective learning environments. *EDUCAUSE Review, 37*(6), 27–34.

Christopher, M. M., Thomas J. A., & Tallent-Runnels, M. K. (2004). Raising the bar: Encouraging high level thinking in online discussion forums. *Roeper Review, 26*(3), 166–172.

Cummings, J. A., Bonk, C. J., & Jacobs, F. R. (2002). Twenty-first century college syllabi: Options for online communication and interactivity. *Internet and Higher Education, 5*(1), 1–19.

DeLacey, B., & Leonard, D. (2002). Case study on technology and distance in education at the Harvard Business School. *Educational Technology & Society, 5*(2). Retrieved December 29, 2006, from http://ifets.ieee.org/periodical/vol_2_2002/delacey.html

Dennen, V. (2000). Task structuring for online problem based learning: A case study. *Educational Technology and Society, 3*(3), 329–336.

Dennen, V. P. (2005). From message posting to learning dialogues: Factors affecting learner participation in asynchronous discussion. *Distance Education, 26*(1), 125–146.

Dennen, V. P., & Bonk, C. J. (2007). We'll leave a light on for you: Keeping learners motivated in online courses. In B. H. Khan (Ed.), *Flexible learning in an information society* (pp. 64–67). Hershey, PA: The Idea Group Inc.

Dennen, V. P., & Jones, G. (2006). How's my writing? Using online peer feedback to improve performance in the composition classroom. In T. S. Roberts (Ed.), *Self, peer and group assessment in e-learning*. Hershey, PA: Idea Group.

Duffy, T. M., & Kirkley, J. R. (Eds.). (2004). *Learner-centered theory and practice in distance education: Cases from higher education*. Mahwah, NJ: Lawrence Erlbaum Associates.

Gunawardena, C. N. (2004). The challenge of designing inquiry-based online learning environments: Theory into practice. In T. M. Duffy and J. R. Kirkley (Eds.), *Learner-centered theory and practice in distance education: Cases from higher education* (pp. 143–158). Mahwah, NJ: Lawrence Erlbaum Associates.

Hara, N., Bonk, C. J., & Angeli, C. (2000). Content analyses of online discussion in an applied educational psychology course. *Instructional Science, 28*(2), 115–152.

Herrington, J., & Oliver, R. (1999). Using situated learning and multimedia to investigate higher-order thinking. *Journal of Educational Multimedia and Hypermedia, 8*(4), 401–421.

Jeong, A. (2004). The combined effects of response time and message content on growth patterns of discussion threads in computer-supported collaborative argumentation. *Journal of Distance Education, 19*(1), 36–53.

Kirkley, S. E., Savery, J. R., & Grabner-Hagen, M. M. (1998). Electronic teaching: Extending classroom dialogue and assistance through email communication. In C. J. Bonk & K. S. King (Eds.), *Electronic collaborators: Learner-centered technologies for literacy, apprenticeship, and discourse* (pp. 209–232). Mahwah, NJ: Lawrence Erlbaum Associates.

Kolloff, M., & Rahimzadeh, K. (2004). Role play as a distance learning strategy. In C. Crawford et al. (Eds.), *Proceedings of Society for Information Technology and Teacher Education International Conference 2004* (pp. 3911–3916). Chesapeake, VA: AACE.

Koschmann, T. D. (Ed.). (1996). *CSCL: Theory and practice of an emerging paradigm*. Mahwah, NJ: Lawrence Erlbaum Associates.

Liu, X., Bonk, C. J., Magjuka, R. J., Lee, S. H., & Su, B. (2005). Exploring four dimensions of online instructor roles: A program level case study. *Journal of Asynchronous Learning Networks, 9*(4). Retrieved December 29, 2006, from http://www.sloan-c.org/publications/jaln/v9n4/v9n4_liu.asp

Mason, R. (1991). Moderating educational computer conferencing. *DEOSNEWS, 1*(19). Retrieved December 29, 2006, from http://www.ed.psu.edu/acsde/deos/deosnews/deosnews1_19.asp

Master, K., & Oberprieler, G. (2004). Encouraging equitable online participation through curriculum articulation. *Computers and Education, 42*, 319–332.

Offerman, M., & Tassava, C. (2006). A different perspective on blended learning: Asserting the efficacy of online learning at Capella University. In C. J. Bonk & C. R. Graham (Eds.). *Handbook of blended learning: Global Perspectives, local designs* (pp. 235–244). San Francisco: Pfeiffer.

Oliver, R., & Herrington, J. (2000). Using situated learning as a design strategy for Web-based learning. In B. Abbey (Ed.), *Instructional and cognitive impacts of Web-based education* (pp. 178–191). Hershey, PA: Idea Group.

Oliver, R., Herrington, J., & Reeves, T. C. (2006). Creating authentic learning environments through blended learning approaches. In C. J. Bonk & C. R. Graham (Eds.), *Handbook of blended learning: Global perspectives, local designs* (pp. 502–515). San Francisco: Pfeiffer.

Oliver, R., & McLoughlin, C. (1999). Curriculum and learning-resources issues arising from the use of Web-based course support systems. *International Journal of Educational Telecommunications, 5*(4), 419–436.

Oliver, R., Omari, A., & Herrington, J. (1998). Exploring student interactions in collaborative World Wide Web computer-based learning environments. *Journal of Educational Multimedia and Hypermedia, 7*(2/3), 263–287.

Paulsen, M. F. (1995). Moderating educational computer conferences. In Z. Berge & M. Collins (Eds.), *Computer-mediated communication and the online classroom in distance education*. Cresskill, NJ: Hampton Press.

Pease, P. (2006). Blended learning goes totally virtual by design: The case of a for-profit, online university. In C. J. Bonk & C. R. Graham (Eds.). *Handbook of blended learning: Global Perspectives, local designs* (pp. 245–259). San Francisco: Pfeiffer.

Pilkington, R., & Walker, A. (2003). Discussion skills in higher education: Developing constructive argument in an online community. *Instructional Science, 31*, 41–63.

Rowley, D. J., Lujan, H. D., & Dolence, M. G. (1998). *Strategic choices for the academy: How demand for lifelong learning will re-create higher education*. San Francisco: Jossey-Bass.

Salmon, G. (2002). *E-tivities: The key to active online learning*. Sterling, VA: Stylus.

Su, B., Bonk, C. J., Magjuka, R., Liu, X., & Lee, S. H. (2005, summer). The importance of interaction in Web-based education: A program-level case study of online MBA courses. *Journal of Interactive Online Learning, 4*(1). Retrieved December 29, 2006, from http://www.ncolr.org/jiol/issues/PDF/4.1.1.pdf

Tharp, R., & Gallimore, R. (1988). *Rousing minds to life: Teaching, learning, and schooling in a social context*. Cambridge, MA: Cambridge University Press.

Wagner, E. D., & McCombs, B. L. (1995). Learner centered psychological principles in practice: Designs for distance education. *Educational Technology, 35*(2), 32–35.

Weedman, J. (1999). Conversation and community: The potential of electronic conferences for creating intellectual proximity in distributed learning environments. *Journal of the American Society for Information Science, 50*(10), 907–928.

Wilson, B., Ludwidg-Hardman, S., Thornam C. L., & Dunlap J. C. (2004, April). *Bounded community: Designing and facilitating learning communities in formal courses*. Paper presented at the meeting of the American Educational Research Association, San Diego, CA.

Zhang, K., Hung, J., & Peng, S. (2005, October). *Moderating online collaborations during various tasks in a project-base learning environment*. Paper presented at the annual meeting of the Association for Educational Communications and Technology, Orlando, FL.

Zhang, K., & Peck, K. L. (2003). The effects of peer-controlled or moderated online collaboration on group problem solving and related attitudes. *Canadian Journal of Learning and Technology, 29*(3), 93–112.

20

Instructional Designs for Optimal Learning

Som Naidu
The University of Melbourne, Australia

Distance education is widely known for spearheading and refocusing our attention on several aspects of teaching and learning. The most pervasive of them all, perhaps, is the recognition of the important role and function of instructional design. Others include the role and function of publishing and distribution of study materials, use of alternative and non-contiguous delivery technologies in teaching and learning (i.e., alternative to face-to-face instruction), asynchronous communication among participants in learning and teaching, and ownership of intellectual property and copyright.

In conventional face-to-face educational settings, what passes for instructional design was and still is, rightly or wrongly, the sole responsibility of the teacher-in-charge. This situation changed with the advent of distance teaching and learning practices. Teachers-in-charge, largely as subject matter experts, could no longer be held responsible for the entire teaching and learning transaction. The development of printed and other types of study materials for self study by distance learners required a team effort with significant input in the educational process from instructional designers and media producers. This brought into the educational process the need for specialized skills in instructional design, media production, and in supporting learning in non-contiguous learning and teaching environments.

GROWTH OF INSTRUCTIONAL DESIGN IN DISTANCE EDUCATION

The critical role of instructional design in distance education perhaps received greatest prominence from the development of the team approach to course development at the United Kingdom Open University (UKOU). This team approach to course development comprised the participation of a group of specialists in the design and development of courses for distance education. These specialists would include subject matter experts, media producers, and instructional designers (Kelly, 1994). They would bring to the course design and development process specialist knowledge in the design of a range of study materials for distance education, including printed materials, audio and video, and television programs.

The focus of instructional design knowledge in this process was on a range of learning and teaching issues. These included (a) analyzing and understanding learners and their learning context; (b) developing goals and learning outcomes; (c) analyzing, sequencing, and synthesizing subject matter content; (d) activating learning and engaging learners with the subject matter; (e) supporting learning with socialization and interaction among learners; (f) selecting appropriate media; (g) assessing learning outcomes and providing feedback; and (h) evaluating the learning and teaching process.

In most educational settings, very little attention is paid to analyzing and understanding learners and their learning context before any learning and teaching occurs. A great deal about learner characteristics, their learning styles, and approaches to study is quite often presumed. This is especially true in classroom-based educational settings; however, distance education, with its policy of open access, opens up opportunities for a wide range of learners from young and old, to those in full- or part-time employment, and those with families to support and with little or no prerequisites (Moore, 1987). This meant that the distance education course design and development process needed to pay particular attention to distance learners, their styles and approaches to studying, and their special learning contexts (Kember & Harper, 1987; Richardson, 2000).

Generally, in most educational settings, the development of instructional goals and learning outcomes is considered a chore, as neither teachers nor students give it much attention, and also because these goals and outcomes are not closely aligned with the learning and assessment activities. In distance education settings specifically, carefully designed instructional goals and learning outcomes can serve a critical role for learners who are studying on their own, independently and without a great deal of opportunity to interact with their peers and tutors (Garrison & Baynton, 1987; Mager, 1984).

In both distance education and conventional classroom-based educational settings, selecting, analyzing, sequencing, and synthesizing subject matter content is where much of the thinking about learning and teaching has generally begun. This process comprises selecting the relevant subject matter content, analyzing and representing it in a suitable form (Jonassen, Hannum, & Tessmer, 1989; Scott, Clayton, & Gibson, 1991), and then presenting it to the learner to enable an efficient and effective learning process (Reigeluth, 1983; Van Patten, Chao, & Reigeluth, 1986). Failure to effectively carry out this critical design task makes the learning task very difficult for the distance learner and causes problems such as lack of motivation and attrition. For this reason, there has been growing interest in approaches to representing subject matter content that is more goal-directed, problem-oriented, and embedded in the context of the subject matter content. (See also Barrows & Tamblyn, 1980; Brown, Collins, & Duguid, 1989; The Cognition and Technology Group at Vanderbilt, 1990, 1993; Schank, 1997).

Engaging learners with the subject matter content and their learning activities involves the selective use of learning and instructional strategies to activate and support learning (Lockwood, 1998; Rigney, 1978). In the distance education context, these strategies include a range of self-assessment activities embedded within the study materials that serve to scaffold and assist learning (Bernard & Naidu, 1992; Bernard, Naidu, & Amundsen, 1991; Jonassen, 1988; Naidu, 1994; Naidu & Bernard, 1992).

Learners can be also kept engaged with the subject matter and their learning activities with a range of collaborative and cooperative learning techniques to support learning and socialization (Koschmann, Kelson, Feltovich, & Barrows, 1996; Slavin, 1990, 1994). In distance education contexts, many of these cognitive supports can be made available through face-to-face meetings at local or regional study centers, and increasingly now, via computer-mediated communications technologies such as e-mail, bulletin boards, and mailing lists (Bernard & Naidu, 1990; Naidu, 1989; Salmon, 2002, 2004).

A critical instructional design task is the selection of appropriate media or delivery system for the teaching and learning of a particular body of subject matter content or skill. A great deal of care and consideration needs to be given to selecting the media that will enable the achievement of the intended learning outcomes and at an affordable price. The most current and fashionable—or the cheapest—media may not necessarily offer the best match for the subject matter, the learners, the intended learning outcomes, and the context, especially in distance education settings.

There has been a great deal of discussion on the instructional effects of media on learning. Thomas Edison, for instance, claimed that the use of the moving image for teaching and learning would make schools more attractive and motivating for students (Heinich, Molenda, & Russell, 1993). Marshall McLuhan saw media as extensions of humans that allow them to affect other people who are not in face-to-face contact with them. This view later led McLuhan to claim that the "medium is the message" (McLuhan, 1964). In making this claim, McLuhan was referring to the societal impacts of electronic media such as television, film, and telephone on the lives of people (Campbell, 2000).

Neither Edison's nor McLuhan's premonitions were realized as they had been projected. Moreover, more recently, Clark (1983, 1994) argued that instructional media do not influence learning achievement. He suggested that media are like vehicles that deliver instruction, and they cannot influence learning achievement any more than the truck that delivers our groceries can cause changes in our nutrition. While Clark's view on the role of media in learning achievement remains contentious, the main point of his argument is that it is the instructional method (i.e., the pedagogical approach) and not media that is mostly responsible for learning achievement. He argues that the selection of appropriate media for learning and teaching needs to be based on the intended learning outcomes, the nature of the subject matter, and the learning context (Reiser & Gagné, 1983). In distance education settings, the learning context takes on a special significance in the choice of appropriate instructional media.

The assessment of learning achievement is foremost in the minds of both the teachers and the students in any educational setting. The teachers are concerned about how best to ascertain if their students have acquired the desired level of knowledge and capability in the subject matter, and the extent to which they have accomplished the intended learning outcomes. Students, on the other hand, are concerned about how, when, where, and against what criteria their learning achievement will be assessed. They would also be very eager to know what opportunities there are for receiving feedback and advice on their work. The flexibility and openness afforded by distance education contexts further complicates procedures and processes for all of these issues. Instructional designers and teachers have to be particularly vigilant about assessment of learning achievement in the most valid, reliable, equitable, and secure manner (Grondlund, 1985). They also need to ensure that there is ample opportunity for students to receive appropriate amounts of feedback in a timely manner (Bangert-Drowns, Kulik, Kulik, & Morgan, 1991; Kulhavy, 1977; Kulik & Kulik, 1988; Schimmel, 1983).

A systematic approach to the instructional design and development process also comprises evaluation of the efficacy of the process as well as the impacts of the learning and teaching processes (Dick & Carey, 1994; Gagne, Briggs, & Wager, 1992; Smith & Ragan, 1993); however, despite the importance of gathering data on the instructional design, development and implementation processes, evaluation is often poorly carried out or completely neglected from most educational settings. To ensure a high quality of learning and teaching experience, it is critical that evaluation is considered as an integral component of the instructional design, development, and implementation process (Flagg, 1990; Guba & Lincoln, 1989; Kirkpatrick, 1994). Moreover, it is important that evaluation is considered proactively and not as something that is carried out at the end of the entire process (Sims, Dobbs, & Hand, 2002). In addition, a range of approaches and data gathering instruments ought to be used to gather various types of evaluation data (Patton, 1990; Shulman, 1988).

RECONSIDERING INSTRUCTIONAL DESIGNS
FOR DISTANCE LEARNING

There is growing evidence which suggests that delivery media (including print) offer tremendous opportunities for building rich, resourceful, and highly interactive learning environments (Dede, 2000; Edelson & O'Neill, 1994; Lockwood, 1998; Pea, 1994; Schank, 1997). It has been also suggested, however, that media alone can have little impact on the quality of teaching and learning (Clark, 1983; Kozma, 1991). As such careful attention must be paid foremost to the instructional method (i.e., the *pedagogy* of the learning and teaching transaction). This is especially critical in distance education settings where a greater degree of independence is required from learners due to their separation in time and place from their teachers or educational organization.

Paying attention to the instructional method or pedagogy means looking after the "design architecture" of the learning and teaching environment which incorporates, inter alia, definition of the learning outcomes, what the learners will do, how learning will be supported with the available media and resources, what will comprise formative and summative assessment, and how feedback will be provided to the learners. In distance education contexts, these considerations take on an added degree of complexity due to the asynchronous nature of much of the learning and teaching transaction.

Careful integration of the instructional media and the instructional method (i.e., the pedagogy) is a core instructional design function. It requires careful reconsideration of our approaches to teaching and learning to ensure that we are making the most of the delivery technologies that are accessible to us (Burgess & Robertson, 1999; French, Hale, Johnson, & Farr, 1999). This incorporates shifting the role of the classroom teacher from one of being a "sage on the stage" to a "guide on the side." It also includes a more "student-directed" or "student-centered" focus on learning.

Contemporary information and communications technologies, which are able to place a great deal of resources within easy reach of teachers and students, have a significant role to play in supporting these foreshadowed changes in the nature of teaching and learning (French et al., 1999). They are also critical in promoting learning and teaching environments that are resource- and activity-based, in which learners are allowed and expected to develop understanding by engaging in authentic learning tasks. These are called "situated learning environments," as they are grounded in the context and culture of the learning environment (Brown et al., 1989).

Situated learning environments are based on constructivist learning principles (Wilson, 1996). They are less heavily dependent on the acquisition of subject matter knowledge and more on "learning by doing" (The Cognition and Technology Group at Vanderbilt, 1991; Schank & Cleary, 1995; Schank, 1997). The concept of learning by doing is at the heart of pedagogical designs that have the potential to engage students in the learning process better and retain their interest and motivation in learning. These pedagogical designs are better suited for distance education settings as they focus more heavily on the learning activities and less so on the declarative subject matter content. They include designs such as scenario- and problem-based learning, case study-based learning, role play-based learning, and design-based learning (see also Naidu,

2002). Their common trait and strength is their learner-centered focus and the greater degree of attention to learner engagement in the learning and teaching process (Hmelo, 1998; Williams & Hmelo, 1998).

For a fuller discussion of a range of strategies for learning through problem solving, readers are encouraged to consult *The Journal of the Learning Sciences*: Special Issue: Learning through Problem Solving (Volume 7, Numbers 3 and 4, 1998), guest editors Susan M. Williams and Cindy E. Hmelo.

INSTRUCTIONAL DESIGNS FOR OPTIMIZING DISTANCE LEARNING

The following is a selection of instructional designs that stand to optimize the opportunities and challenges posed by distance education settings and contemporary information and communications technologies. They are grounded in the principles of situated learning and constructivist learning theory, and promote a resource- and an activity-based approach to student-centered learning.

Scenario-Based Learning

Scenario-based learning is a pedagogical design in which an authentic or contrived scenario forms the basis of all learning, teaching and assessment activities (Naidu, Menon, Gunawardena, Lekamge, & Karunanayaka, 2005). The best scenarios are those that are extracted from real-life settings as they are likely to contain the complexity that is needed to address the full range of skills and knowledge that needs to be covered. An effective learning scenario looks like a good story (Naidu, 2004a). It will have a context and characters. However, the important thing about a good learning scenario is that it will have a "precipitating event" and a "goal" for the learner to pursue in order to address the precipitating event (Schank, 1990, 1997).

A "precipitating event" is a trigger for a chain of events. A good example of a precipitating event is as follows. A patient is brought into a hospital where you are working. The patient needs immediate attention and care. Your goal in this contrived situation is to deal with this case and resolve it, hopefully with the best results. In order to do this, you will need to follow hospital procedures and consult with your colleagues. The aim of putting you through this activity is to enable you to acquire the knowledge and skills for managing such cases (Naidu, Oliver, & Koronios, 1999) in real life. It is designed to be inherently motivating and also able to afford you the opportunity to learn by doing. Such a learning scenario is organized around "performance" skills, and the result is a student who can perform the specified task (Schank & Cleary, 1995). This contrived, but authentic, learning scenario offers students an opportunity to also learn by making mistakes in a safe environment, as mistakes offer real opportunities for learning when these are accompanied by timely and potent feedback.

Problem-Based Learning

Problem-based learning is a pedagogical design in which a contrived but authentic problem provides the anchor for all learning, teaching, and assessment activities (Barrows, 1994; Barrows & Tamblyn, 1980; Schmidt, 1983). It is different from scenario-based learning in that in problem-based learning (PBL), a problem situation is used to contextualize and anchor all learning activities (Naidu, Oliver, & Koronios, 1999). In scenario-based learning, the anchor for all learning, teaching and assessment activities need not be a problem situation. It could be an event, such as a visit to your school by a parent or an official. It could be a legislation, such as one that requires you to deal with some aspect of curriculum reform in a school where you are teaching (Naidu et al., 2005).

Beyond this essential difference, PBL is very similar to scenario-based learning in the remainder of its operation. It also incorporates a "precipitating event" or "trigger" and a "goal," which learners are expected to pursue in order to address the problem at hand. Learners work in groups and also individually over a defined period of time to address the presenting problem (Evensen & Hmelo, 2000). Many of these small group and individual activities can take place either face-to-face in situ, or in distributed settings via computer-mediated communications technologies (Dede, 1991, 1996, 2000; Naidu & Oliver, 1996).

Critical Incident-Based Learning

This is a pedagogical design in which a *critical incident* provides the anchor for all learning, teaching, and assessment activities (Naidu & Oliver, 1999). It is different from scenario-based learning and problem-based learning essentially in the nature of the event or incident that is used to contextualize all learning and teaching activities. Beyond that essential difference, it is similar to scenario-based learning and PBL.

A hallmark feature of critical incident-based learning is its use of reflection on and in action (Schon, 1983, 1987). Unlike in PBL and scenario-based learning, in critical incident-based learning, learners are required to identify a critical incident from their life or workplace. A typical critical incident is a significant event that has caused someone to rethink or change their perceptions and/or behavior about something and in some way. Practitioners regularly encounter such situations in their workplace which present them with learning opportunities (Naidu & Oliver, 1999); however, many of these learning opportunities are passed by unnoticed. The aim of this pedagogical design is to teach learners how to recognize these critical incidences as learning opportunities, and how to reflect on them critically while in action (Naidu & Oliver, 1999; Wilson, 1996).

Design-Based Learning

In design-based learning, the *design task* serves as the essential scaffold and anchor for all learning, teaching, and assessment activities (Hmelo, Holton, & Kolodner, 2000). A design task comprises a number of cognitive tasks. These include information gathering, problem identification, constraint setting, idea generation, modeling, prototyping and evaluating (Newstetter, 2000). The design task is widely used for skill development and knowledge acquisition in practice-based disciplines such as engineering and architecture.

Like the scenario, problem, or critical incident, the design task offers the learner an opportunity to learn by doing. In order to be able to afford that, a good design task is one that closely resembles real-life tasks in the field. Such a design task seeks to engage and immerse the learner in the complexity and culture of the targeted skill and subject matter content (Naidu, Anderson, & Riddle, 2000). Depending on the subject matter and the skill that is being taught, design tasks may involve a range of critical learning activities including periods of collaborative group work and individualized self-study. The complexity of carefully articulated design activities makes them excellent vehicles for learning and teaching.

CHALLENGES AND DIRECTIONS FOR FURTHER RESEARCH

Despite the promises and potential of distance education, contemporary information and communications technologies, and situated cognitive approaches to meaningful learning, distance education practices in many parts have continued to promote a very content-driven and teacher-directed approach to learning and teaching (Willems, 2005). Evidence of this is all around us in the form of distance education study course materials that do little more than summarize or reproduce content from published text books, media that are often inaccessible, and in the case of online distance education, course Web sites that contain little more than the course schedule, an outline of the subject matter content, lecturer's slides and notes, and sample examination papers (Boshier et al., 1997).

Instead of making the most of the potential and unique attributes of distance education and contemporary information and communications technologies, such practices have promoted a model of teaching that is a very poor imitation of conventional classroom practices; therefore, regardless of our awareness of the important role of instructional design in distance education, a lot of it continues to be teacher-directed and delivery-mode-centered. Rarely have we paused to think about what we are using to teach, why we are teaching the way we teach, and if our instructional approaches are based on sound educational principles of learning.

This kind of instructional practice has led to a great deal of frustration for both the learners and the teachers, many of whom have grown increasingly skeptical about the educational benefits of the newer delivery technologies (Kirkwood, 2000; Rumble, 2000; Schellens & Valcke, 2000). The source of much of this frustration has to do with the failure of instructional designers to come up with instructional and learning designs that best match the type of the learning and teaching context, the subject matter, and the needs of their learners within the constraints of their learning environments.

The goal of this chapter is to point out the relevant literature and knowledge that is necessary for the design and development of effective distance education environments, or for that matter, any kind of an educational environment. The instructional designs that are described and promoted in this chapter are based on proven principles of human learning, including "learning by doing," "learning by experimentation and failure in a safe learning and teaching environment," and on the role of "context" and "learning scaffolds" in learning and teaching. They are good for both distance education and other forms of educational practice. The challenge is for instructional designers to assert that these are the fundamental principles that must guide learning and teaching practices, and that these principles stand to make most of the opportunities afforded by distance education, and information and communications technologies, in supporting student learning.

Toward a Proactive Approach to Student Support

Student support in conventional distance education settings often comprises assistance that is provided to the learner beyond what is available in their study materials (Tait & Mills, 2003). This kind of support normally comes by way of local center and tutorial support, and increasingly now online via contemporary information and communications technologies. A major disadvantage of this disposition toward student support is that it is a regressive approach because it approaches student support as an afterthought and as something that needs to be taken care of because of an endemic problem with the existing instructional system. The argument that is proffered in this chapter promotes a proactive approach to student support by emphasizing the need to conceptualize all learning and teaching support activities as part of the instructional design process (see also Naidu, 2004b).

Instructional designs such as scenario-based learning, problem-based learning, and so forth are embedded with ample opportunities for feedback and intervention throughout the student learning process (Brown et al., 1989; Collins, Brown, & Holum, 1991). In doing so, they are much better able to scaffold and support students' learning activities leading to better learning outcomes.

A learning scaffold is a transitional student support strategy. It provides learners with supports that they are unable to afford on their own or without assistance (Pea, 2004). It comprises carefully targeted support for a range of learning activities such as learning of the subject matter content and also learning how to learn (Azevedo & Hadwin, 2005). Effective learning scaffolds are those that are accessible to the learner at the time, place, and pace it is most needed, and those that are appropriately matched to, and directed at, the task or problem at hand.

The provision of this kind of scaffolding is a very complex task. A good place to start integrating this kind of scaffolding is to begin with the intended learning outcomes of the subject. The learning outcomes will help determine the kinds of learning activities that learners will be required to undertake as part of their learning and assessment activities in the subject. Once these are developed, it will become abundantly clear what kinds of tools and cognitive supports learners will need to accomplish these tasks. For instance, in a study of a school curriculum, if learners are required to survey teacher's perceptions of an aspect of the school curriculum, they will need tools to ascertain that. In this case, the tool for ascertaining teacher's perceptions serves as an essential scaffold. Will this tool need to be available in print form, or in electronic form, online or offline? Answers to these questions will determine the exact nature of this tool, and where, when, and how it will need to be provided to the learners (see, e.g., Naidu et al., 2005).

There has been considerable work on developing and integrating learning scaffolds in computer-based learning materials for conventional educational settings (Azevedo & Hadwin, 2005). With the growth of online distance education across all sectors of education, many of these computer-based learning materials will soon enter the self-paced and self-instructional online distance education environment. With a different set of learner and learning needs in online distance education settings, several of these learning scaffolds are quite likely to be found not as effective because they had not been developed to cater for the needs of online distance learners. There will be a need to develop learning scaffolds that can address the unique needs of online distance learning. The obvious opportunities for these would be when incorporating information and communications technologies and collaborative learning with problem-based learning (Kirschner, Kreijns, Beers, & Strijbos, 2005; Koschmann et al., 1996). Other opportunities for scaffolding learning in online distance education settings would be in moderating computer conferencing and other forms of online discussions (Salmon, 2002, 2004).

For a fuller discussion of a whole range of issues to do with scaffolding learning, the readers of this chapter are strongly encouraged to consult two very reputable journals in the field of learning and instructional sciences which have recently produced two Special Issues of their journals on the subject of scaffolding. These are *Instructional Science: An International Journal of Learning and Cognition*. Special Issue: Scaffolding self-regulated learning and metacognition: Implications for the design of computer-based scaffolds (Volume 33, Numbers 5–6, November 2005; Guest Editors: Roger Azevedo and Allyson Hadwin). The other is *The Journal of the Learning Sciences*. Special Issue: Scaffolding (Volume 13, Number 3, 2004; Guest Editors: Elizabeth Davis and Naomi Miyake).

ACKNOWLEDGEMENT

The instructional design models that are described in this chapter have been developed in collaboration with several colleagues, and the author of this chapter is grateful for their contribution to the development and implementation of these models. These include: *Scenario-based learning* (Som Naidu, Mohan Menon, Chandra Gunawardena, Dayalata Lekamge, Shironica Karunanayaka), with funding support from Commonwealth of Learning and the Open University of Sri Lanka; *Problem-based learning; Critical incident-based learning* (Andy Koronios and Mary Oliver), with funding support from the Committee for University Teaching and Staff Development, Australia; and *Design-based learning* (Jaynie Anderson and Mathew Riddle), with funding support from the University of Melbourne.

REFERENCES

Azevedo, R., & Hadwin, A. F. (2005). Scaffolding self-regulated learning and metacognition—Implications for the design of computer-based scaffolds. *Instructional Science, 33*(5–6), 367–379.

Bangert-Drowns, R. L., Kulik, C.-L. C., Kulik, J. A., & Morgan, M. T. (1991). The instructional effects of feedback in test-like events. *Review of Educational Research, 61*, 213–238.

Barrows, H. S. (1994). *Problem-based learning applied to medical education.* Springfield, IL: Southern Illinois University School of Medicine.

Barrows, H. S., & Tamblyn, R. (1980). *Problem-based learning: An approach to medical education.* New York: Springer.

Bernard, R. M., & Naidu, S. (1990). Enhancing interpersonal communication in distance education: Can "voice-mail" help? *Educational and Training Technology International, 27*(3), 293–300.

Bernard, R. M., & Naidu, S. (1992). Post-questioning, concept mapping and feedback: A distance education field experiment. *British Journal of Educational Technology, 23*(1), 48–60.

Bernard, R. M., Naidu, S., & Amundsen, C. L. (1991). Choosing instructional variables to enhance learning in distance education. *Media and Technology for Human Resource Development: Journal of Educational Technology, 4*(1), pp. 3–13.

Boshier, R., Mohapi, M., Moulton, G., Qayyum, A., Sadownik, L., & Wilson, M. (1997). Best and worst dressed Web courses: Strutting into the 21st century in comfort and style. *Distance Education, 18*(2), 327–349.

Brown, J. S., Collins, A., & Duguid, P. (1989). Situated cognition and the culture of learning. *Educational Researcher, 18*(1), 32–42.

Burgess, B., & Robertson, P. (1999). *Collaboration: How to find, design and implement collaborative Internet projects.* Saratoga, CA: BonusPoint, Inc.

Campbell, R. J. (2000, September/October). Descending into the maelstrom of the 21st century with Marshall McLuhan. *Educational Technology, 40*(5), 18–27.

Clark, R. E. (1983). Reconsidering research on learning from media. *Review of Educational Research, 53*(4), 445–460.

Clark, R. E. (1994). Media will never influence learning. *Educational Technology Research and Development, 53*(2), 21–30.

The Cognition and Technology Group at Vanderbilt. (1990). Anchored instruction and its relationship to situated cognition. *Educational Researcher, 19*(6), 2–10.

The Cognition and Technology Group at Vanderbilt. (1991). Technology and the design of generative learning environments. *Educational Technology, 31*(5), 34–40.

The Cognition and Technology Group at Vanderbilt. (1993). Designing learning environments that support thinking. In T. M. Duffy, J. Lowyck, & D. H. Jonassen (Eds.), *Designing environments for constructivist learning* (pp. 9–36). New York: Springer-Verlag.

Collins, A., Brown, J. S., & Holum, A. (1991). Cognitive apprenticeship: Making thinking visible. *American Educator, 15*(3), 6–11, 38–39.

Dede, C. (1991). The evolution of constructivist learning environments: Immersion in distributed, virtual worlds. In B. G. Wilson (Ed.), *Constructivist learning environments: Case studies in instructional design* (pp. 165–175). Englewood Cliffs, NJ: Educational Technology Publications.

Dede, C. (1996). The evolution of distance education: Emerging technologies and distributed learning. *The American Journal of Distance Education, 10*(2), 4–36.

Dede, C. (2000). Emerging technologies and distributed learning in higher education. In D. Hanna (Ed.), *Higher education in an era of digital competition: Choices and challenges*. New York: Atwood.

Dick, W., & Carey, L. (1994). *The systematic design of instruction* (3rd edition). London: Scott, Foresman and Company.

Edelson, D. C., & O'Neill, D. K. (1994). The CoVis collaboratory notebook: Supporting collaborative scientific inquiry. In *Recreating the revolution: Proceedings of the National Educational Computing Conference* (pp. 146–152). Eugene, OR: International Society of Technology in Education.

Evensen, D. H., & Hmelo, C. E. (Eds.). (2000). *Problem-based learning: A research perspective on learning interactions*. Mahwah, NJ: Lawrence Erlbaum Associates.

Flagg, B. N. (1990). *Formative evaluation for educational technologies*. Hillsdale, NJ: Lawrence Erlbaum Associates.

French, D., Hale, C., Johnson, C., & Farr, G. (1999). *Internet based learning: An introduction and framework for higher education and business*. London: Kogan Page.

Gagné, R. M., Briggs, L. J., & Wager, W. W. (1992). *Principles of instructional design* (4th edition). New York: Harcourt Brace Jovanovich College.

Garrison, D. R., & Baynton, M. (1987). Beyond independence in distance education: The concept of control. *The American Journal of Distance Education, 1*(3), 3–15.

Grondlund, N. E. (1985). *Measurement and evaluation in teaching* (5th edition). New York: Macmillan.

Guba, E. G., & Lincoln, Y. S. (1989). *Fourth generation evaluation*. Newbury Park, CA: Sage.

Heinich, R., Molenda, M., & Russell, J. D. (1993). *Instructional media and the new technologies of instruction*. New York: Macmillan.

Hmelo, C. E. (1998). Problem-based learning: Effects on early acquisition of cognitive skill in medicine. *The Journal of the Learning Sciences, 7*, 173–208.

Hmelo, C. E., Holton, D. L., & Kolodner, J. L. (2000). Designing to learn about complex tasks. *The Journal of the Learning Sciences, 9*(3), 243–246.

Jonassen, D. H. (1988). Integrating learning strategies into courseware to facilitate deeper processing. In D. H. Jonassen (Ed.), *Instructional designs for microcomputer courseware* (pp. 151–181). Hillsdale, NJ: Lawrence Erlbaum Associates.

Jonassen, D. H., Hannum, W. H., & Tessmer, M. (1989). *Handbook of task analysis procedures*. New York: Praeger.

Kelly, M. (1994). Course creation issues in distance education. In R. Garrison and D. Shale, (Eds.), *Education at a distance: From issues to practice* (pp. 93–94). Malabar, FL: Kreiger.

Kember, D., & Harper, G. (1987). Implications for instruction arising from the relationship between approaches to studying and academic outcomes. *Instructional Science, 16*, 35–46.

Kirkpatrick, D. L. (1994). *Evaluating training programs: The four levels*. San Francisco: Berrett-Koehler.

Kirkwood, A. (2000). Learning at home with information and communications technologies. *Distance Education, 21*(2), 248–259.

Kirschner, P. A., Kreijns, K., Beers, P. J., & Strijbos, J.-W. (2005). Designing electronic tools for collaborative learning. *Educational Technology, 45*(5), 48–52.

Koschmann, T., Kelson, A. C., Feltovich, P. J., & Barrows, H. S. (1996). Computer-supported problem-based learning: A principled approach to the use of computers in collaborative learning. In T. Koschmann (Ed.), *CSCL: Theory & practice in an emerging paradigm* (pp. 83–124). Mahwah, NJ: Lawrence Erlbaum Associates.

Kozma, R. B. (1991). Learning with media. *Review of Educational Research, 61*(2), 179–211.

Kulhavy, R. W. (1977). Feedback in written instruction. *Review of Educational Research, 47*, 211–232.

Kulik, J. A., & Kulik, C.-L. C. (1988). Timing of feedback and verbal learning. *Review of Educational Research, 58,* 79–97.

Lockwood, F. (1998). *The design and production of self instructional materials.* London: Kogan Page.

Mager, R. F. (1984). *Preparing instructional objectives* (2nd ed.). Belmont, CA: Lake.

McLuhan, M. (1964). *Understanding media: The extensions of man.* New York: McGraw-Hill.

Moore, M. G. (1987). Learners and learning at a distance: Computer conferencing in distance education. *International Council of Distance Education Bulletin, 14,* 59–65.

Naidu, S. (1989). Computer conferencing in distance education. *International Council of Distance Education Bulletin, 20,* 39–46.

Naidu, S. (1994). Applying learning and instructional strategies in open and distance learning. *Distance Education, 15*(1), 23–41.

Naidu, S. (2002). Designing and evaluating instruction for e-learning. In P. L. Rodgers (Ed.), *Designing instruction for technology-enhanced learning* (pp. 134–159). Hershey, PA: Idea Group.

Naidu, S. (2004a). *Learning design as an indicator of quality in teacher education.* Paper presented at NAAC-COL Roundtable on Innovations in Teacher Education, Bangalore, India.

Naidu, S. (2004b). Supporting learning with creative learning and instructional designs. In J. E. Brindley, C. Walti, and O. Zawacki-Richter (Eds.), *Learner support in open, distance and online learning environments, ASF series: Vol. 9* (pages 109–111). Oldenburg, Germany: Bibliotheks- und Informationssystem der Universität Oldenburg.

Naidu, S., & Bernard, R. M. (1992). Enhancing academic achievement in distance education with concept mapping and inserted questions. *Distance Education, 23*(1), 218–233.

Naidu, S., & Oliver, M. (1996). Computer supported collaborative problem-based learning (CSC-PBL): An instructional design architecture for virtual learning in nursing education. *Journal of Distance Education, XI*(2), 1–22.

Naidu, S., & Oliver, M. (1999). Critical incident-based computer supported collaborative learning. *Instructional Science: An International Journal of Learning and Cognition, 27*(5), 329–354.

Naidu, S., Anderson, J., & Riddle, M. (2000). The virtual print exhibition: A case of learning by designing. In R. Sims, M. O'Reilly, & S. Hawkins (Eds.), *Learning to choose: Choosing to learn (short papers and works in progress)* (pp. 109–114). Lismore, New South Wales, Australia: Southern Cross University Press.

Naidu, S., Menon, M., Gunawardena, C., Lekamge, D., & Karunanayaka, S. (2005, November 9–11). *Quality teaching and learning in the Master of Arts in Teacher Education program at the Open University of Sri Lanka.* Paper presented at the biennial conference of the Open and Distance Learning Association of Australia, Adelaide, South Australia, Australia.

Naidu, S., Oliver, M., & Koronios, A. (1999). Approaching clinical decision-making in nursing practice with interactive multimedia and case-based reasoning. *The Interactive Multimedia Electronic Journal of Computer Enhanced Learning* volume 1(2), October 1999. Retrieved December 15, 2006, from http://imej.wfu.edu/

Newstetter, W. C. (2000). Guest editor's introduction. *The Journal of the Learning Sciences, 9*(3), 247–298.

Patton, M. Q. (1990). *Qualitative evaluation and research methods* (2nd ed.). Newbury Park, CA: Sage.

Pea, R. (2004). The social and technological dimensions of scaffolding and related theoretical concepts for learning, education, and human activity. *The Journal of Learning Sciences, 13*(3), 423–451.

Pea, R. D. (1994). Seeing what we build together: Distributed multimedia learning environments for transformative communications. *The Journal of the Learning Sciences, 3*(3), 285–299.

Reigeluth, C. M. (Ed.). (1983). *Instructional design theories and models: An overview of their current status.* Hillsdale, NJ: Erlbaum.

Reiser, R. A., & Gagné, R. M. (1983). *Selecting media for instruction.* Englewood Cliffs, NJ: Educational Technology.

Richardson, J. T. E. (2000). *Researching student learning: Approaches to studying in campus-based and distance education.* Philadelphia: Open University Press.

Rigney, J. W. (1978). Learning strategies: A theoretical perspective. In H. F. O'Neil, Jr. (Ed.), *Learning strategies* (pp. 165–205). New York: Academic Press.

Rumble, G. (2000). Student support in distance education in the 21st century: Learning from service management. *Distance Education, 21*(2), 216–235.

Salmon, G. (2002). *E-tivities: The key to active online learning*. London: Kogan Page.

Salmon, G. (2004). *E-moderating: The key to teaching and learning online*. London: Kogan Page.

Schank, R. C. (1990). *Tell me a story*. Evanston, IL: Northwestern University Press.

Schank, R. C. (1997). *Virtual learning: A revolutionary approach to building a highly skilled workforce.* New York: McGraw-Hill.

Schank, R. C., & Cleary, C. (1995). *Engines for education*. Hillsdale, NJ: Lawrence Erlbaum Associates.

Schellens, T., & Valcke, M. (2000). Re-engineering conventional university education: Implications for students' learning styles. *Distance Education, 21*(2), 361–384.

Schimmel, B. J. (1983). *A meta-analysis of feedback to learners in computerized and programmed instruction.* Montreal, Quebec, Canada: American Educational Research Association. (ERIC Document Reproduction Service No. 233 708).

Schmidt, H. G. (1983). Foundations of problem-based learning: Some explanatory notes. *Medical Education, 27*, 11–16.

Schon, D. A. (1983). *The reflective practitioner*. New York: Basic Books.

Schon, D. A. (1987). *Educating the reflective practitioner*. San Francisco: Jossey-Bass.

Scott, A. C., Clayton, J. E., & Gibson, E. L. (1991). *A practical guide to knowledge acquisition.* New York: Addison-Wesley.

Shulman, L. S. (1988). Disciplines of inquiry in education: An overview. In R. M. Jaeger (Ed.), *Complementary methods for research in education* (pp. 3–17). Washington, DC: AERA.

Sims, R., Dobbs, G., & Hand, T. (2002). Enhancing quality in online learning: Scaffolding planning and design through proactive evaluation. *Distance Education, 23*(2), 135–148.

Slavin, R. E. (1990). *Cooperative learning: Theory, research and practice*. Englewood Cliffs, NJ: Prentice-Hall.

Slavin, R. E. (1994). Student teams-achievement divisions. In S. Sharan (Ed.), *Handbook of cooperative learning* (pp. 3–19). Westport, CT: Greenwood Press.

Smith, P. L., and Ragan, T. J. (1993). *Instructional design*. New York: Merrill McMillan.

Tait, A., & Mills, R. (2003). *Rethinking learner support in distance education: Change and continuity in an international context*. London: RoutledgeFalmer.

Van Patten, J., Chao, C., & Reigeluth. C. M. (1986). A review of strategies for sequencing and synthesizing instruction. *Review of Educational Research, 56*(4), 437–471.

Willems, J. (2005). Flexible learning: Implications of "when-ever", "where-ever" and "what-ever." *Distance Education, 26*(3), 429–435.

Williams, S. M., & Hmelo, C. E. (1998). Guest editors' introduction. *The Journal of the Learning Sciences, 7*(3&4), 265–270.

Wilson, B. G. (Ed.). (1996). *Constructivist learning environments: Case studies in instructional design.* Englewood Cliffs, NJ: Educational Technology.

21

Teaching and Learning in Directed Environments

Priya Sharma
The Pennsylvania State University

Kevin M. Oliver
North Carolina State University

Michael J. Hannafin
The University of Georgia

Technology-enhanced distance learning environments (TEDLEs) comprise both online and hybrid courses that utilize various network technologies to structure learning interactions for students who are geographically or temporally dispersed. The epistemological roots, design strategies, and course affordances employed vary widely. This chapter focuses on the epistemic roots and components related to distance learning environments in which learning is "directed" as contrasted with "negotiated" or "informal." (For a discussion of informal and negotiated distance learning, see chapter 22 in this *Handbook*.)

DIRECTED DISTANCE LEARNING ENVIRONMENTS

Directed distance learning environments (DDLEs) typically emphasize the acquisition of specified knowledge with aligned assessment, and are often designed to disseminate similar (or identical) instruction across multiple sites and learners. DDLEs are commonly used in corporate training or content-based continuing education programs, as well as in traditional learning environments (i.e., K-12, higher education), and often emphasize acquiring foundational knowledge through focused content presentation and directed assessment (Martindale, Pearson, Curda, & Pilcher, 2005; Myers & Nelson, 2004).

Theoretical and Epistemological Foundations

In contrast to growing interest in applying constructivist epistemology to distance learning, DDLEs are rooted in objectivist models of knowledge acquisition, where external information is organized and strategies are developed to ensure consistent acquisition of knowledge and skill. In DDLEs, the locus of learning goals and authority is external: an expert establishes learning goals and means in accordance with the norms and practices of a specific discipline or community. DDLEs are often created using well-established instructional design models, designed to systematically engineer specific learning outcomes (see, e.g., Streibel, 1995). Some DDLEs, for example, mimic programmed instruction wherein learners study specified content with follow-up testing and feedback through input-output loops (McDonald, Yanchar, & Osguthorpe, 2005). Other designs reflect cognitive learning and information-processing theory, specifying the content to be learned as well as interactions to enhance retention and transfer of course material. (For a detailed analysis of information-processing research, see *Cognitive Perspectives* chapter 10 in this *Handbook*.)

The FCAT Explorer (http://www.fcatexplorer.com), for example, is a Web-based, self-paced instructional program designed to provide extended practice in core math and reading skills found on the Florida Comprehensive Assessment Test (FCAT) (Martindale et al., 2005). Rich graphic displays provide age-appropriate scenarios, along with practice items designed to reinforce knowledge and skills to be tested at key grade levels. Consistent with objectivist epistemology and associated behavioral theory, correct answers are reinforced as "right" while answers considered "wrong" are followed by corrective feedback to help students understand why they missed an item and to increase the likelihood of a subsequent correct response.

The University of South Africa (Pretorius, 2004) undergraduate degree program in environmental management, designed for nontraditional students, consists of several core geography modules, specialization modules, and a practical/project module. The program is "outcomes-based" with explicitly stated learning outcomes for modules and study units. Embedded activities allow students to practice skills while self-tests allow them to demonstrate mastery of material. In another initiative, North Carolina's Center for Public Health Preparedness (NCCPHP) developed more than 100 training modules for working public-health professionals on topics such as bioterrorism and disease agents (Horney, MacDonald, Rothney, & Alexander, 2005). The online modules include lectures with streaming audio and PowerPoint slides, downloadable scripts, and follow-up testing.

Typically, DDLEs that emphasize learning of core material have less student-student interaction than other TEDLE models. Although limited interaction has been noted as a concern among trainers (Welsh, Wanberg, Brown, & Simmering, 2003), DDLEs may be especially useful in addressing other associated logistical problems, such as limited opportunities for practice, difficulty convening a dispersed group, and a need to widely and rapidly disseminate timely information.

Components

Learning from Interactions

Learners interact with various DDLE components to achieve their learning goals. During content interaction, learners interact with domain content in textbooks, Web sites, and course syllabi (Moore, 1989). In DDLEs, content is largely externally bounded and pre-specified to identify explicitly the scope of knowledge or skills to be learned. The instructor, as external agent, identifies, evaluates, and modifies content to make it accessible for student learning. DDLEs tend to emphasize expert-sanctioned interactions—that is, specific strategies deemed to be most effective across students.

While early DDLEs were likened to "page-turners" that provided static, online content and tested students on their knowledge of the content, recent efforts have focused on situating learning within authentic problem- or case-based contexts (see, e.g., Chanlin & Chan, 2004; Cheung & Hew, 2004; Ellis, Marcus, & Taylor, 2005; Lou & MacGregor, 2004) and enhancing learning by promoting student interaction with peers and instructors using asynchronous and synchronous tools (see, e.g., Davies & Graff, 2005; de Bruyn, 2004; Dennen, 2005; McAlister, Ravenscroft, & Scanlon, 2004). In these directed, authentically-structured environments, learning results from interactions with content, instructor, and peers.

Content interaction.   In DDLEs, instructional content is typically prescribed, organized, and sequenced to support learning benchmarks presumed to ensure breadth and depth of knowledge and skill related to established learning goals. Chanlin and Chan (2004) designed a Web-enhanced, problem-based learning (PBL) activity for pre-service student dieticians. The instruction was designed to familiarize students with the most common drug and nutrient interactions. The 108 students were divided into groups of five or six members to develop a final project using two alternate content presentations. In one form, students were provided a list of project topics on a Web site, on which each topic was linked to a variety of resources and related instructional content. The remaining groups were provided the same list, but topics were situated within a specific-problem context. To access resources, students first needed to engage the problem and explore potential solutions using available resources. The researchers found that the structured PBL groups tended to discuss more topics, use more cases to frame their contribution within discussions, analyze the problem from multiple perspectives, and share and discuss resources. PBL groups also demonstrated higher levels of peer assessment and satisfaction with the learning experience. Thus, authentic, problem-based contexts may be more meaningful and improve the quality and quantity of student dialogue, peer-to-peer assessment, and student satisfaction with learning.

Student learning may also be enhanced when content presentation is accompanied by clarification of the learning activity's purpose and structure. Providing domain-specific knowledge, clarifying accompanying disciplinary practices, and emphasizing the use of disciplinary tools and strategies (see, e.g., Walton & Archer, 2004) may enhance student interaction with content. One system, AcademicTalk (McAlister et al., 2004), is a chat tool designed to foster and structure educational argumentation in distance courses. AcademicTalk offers specific sentence openers derived from research on peer collaboration and dialogue and engages students in a structured debate. For example, students first compare and elaborate issues, then consider their positions, and finally take sides on specific issues. Discourse analysis of dialogue of regular chat and AcademicTalk transcripts on the same topic indicated that students who used AcademicTalk rarely engaged in off-topic discussion, used twice as many arguments, offered more rebuttals and reasoned claims, and were five times more likely to engage in direct disagreement with peers than students who used a normal chat window. Thus, integrating domain-specific strategies within the chat tool as well as staging introductions to the purpose of the activity helped students to identify and develop more appropriate academic argumentation.

In drawing parallels between programmed instruction and online learning, McDonald et al. (2005) caution against designs that assume that instructional materials, per se, will cultivate learning; rather learner interactions with content enable students to extract meaning. It is critical, therefore, that students interact with to-be-learned content in order to select, process, and encode, as well as to personalize their knowledge.

Instructor Interaction.   In DDLEs, the instructor supports student learning by clarifying content, providing feedback, and adapting ongoing support. In traditional classrooms, the instructor's immediate verbal and nonverbal interactions with students have influenced student learning. Arbaugh (2001) surveyed student satisfaction and learning as a result of instructor immediacy, which refers to (1) textual communication including chat and discussion boards involving use of personal examples, humor, encouragement of student ideas and discussion, and, (2) name recognition, referring to the use of the instructor's name by students, and vice versa. In looking across 25 Web-based courses, 390 student respondents (out of 502) indicated that the immediacy of instructor interaction was a significant predictor of both student learning and attitudes toward the course.

Immediacy of interaction is closely related to perceived social presence. Wise, Chang, Duffy, and Del Valle (2004) explored the perceptions of social presence of 20 graduate students enrolled in a professional development course on communicating appropriate designs for integrating technology into curricula. The students worked with two instructors who provided comparable feedback and information to all students, but manipulated social-presence cues to suggest high or low social presence. Social presence cues included using humor, disclosing emotions, providing support and agreement, addressing people by name, and alluding to physical presence. Wise et al. reported that, although social presence affected perceptions of the atmosphere of the course and of the instructor, it did not significantly affect learning outcomes, engagement, or student perceptions of learning and satisfaction. They suggested that a minimum amount of presence is necessary, but that further differences are unlikely when additional social-presence cues are provided.

In DDLEs, online discussion is a primary mechanism for gauging student sense-making, clarification, and learning. Meskill and Anthony (2004) summarized three roles of the instructor within a discussion as "sage on the stage," "guide on the side," and "ghost in the wings." As the sage on the stage, the instructor is an active participant in all discussions and directs all activities, including offering feedback, establishing rules of engagement and criteria of evaluation, and modeling appropriate behaviors and responses. As ghost in the wings, the instructor is not highly visible but provides help when asked, and is mostly outside of the discussion forums with the understanding that students are primarily responsible for the task.

Whether as an active participant or observer, the instructor shapes online discussion through specific activities and facilitation to direct student participation. For example, Dennen (2005) conducted a multiple case study of online asynchronous discussions, and found that when instructors established regular requirements and deadlines, students engaged in more and better-quality discussions. Instructors who provided ongoing prompts and provided discussion feedback encouraged more discourse among students. High-quality discussions resulted from the use of specific instructor strategies, such as when instructors provided detailed expectations about the format and quantity of discussion, or when instructors modeled the type of dialogue expected from students. In addition, when instructors clarified the link between discussion topics and the final product, significant increases in dialog were evident. Similarly, Hoskins and van Hooff (2005) found that active discussants were more likely than passive participants to perform better on assessments of understanding. Passive readers scored lower than non-active readers and were exposed to conceptual misunderstandings and confusion.

Consistent with DDLE epistemology, asynchronous discussions offer opportunities for instructors to reinforce learning and provide feedback. The pause afforded by asynchronous discussions may provide opportunities for both students and instructors to notice, reflect on, and react to feedback. Meskill and Anthony (2004) examined the strategies of language teachers in an online session and noted that experienced instructors offered students multiple opportunities to observe concepts in richly contextualized, meaningful, generative, and interactive contexts. Intermediate language learners learned sophisticated forms of the target language as a result of the reinforcement and feedback.

Peer interaction.   Although research on the influence of peer interaction on individual learning is largely inconclusive (see, e.g., Ge & Land, 2003), students often work in groups to develop teamwork and communication skills to address authentic problems (McLoughlin & Luca, 2002). Guided cooperative or collaborative interactions may help learners to both engage in group processes and develop consensus-building and reasoning strategies. A cooperative approach involves providing groups with necessary task structure and roles to engage in high levels of discussion and problem-solving, while collaborative approaches tend to favor critical dialogue in which group members negotiate perspectives and meanings to solve problems. Rose (2004) studied cooperative and collaborative student teams that engaged in a problem with specified goals, context, and deliverables. Overall, Rose reported that both groups exhibited very high levels of interaction on the discussion board and appropriate cognitive and organizational strategies to deal with the problem. While the cooperative groups demonstrated higher initial levels of interaction than the collaborative groups during the six-week project, interaction numbers became comparable during successive weeks. Findings also indicated no differences between cooperative and collaborative groups for interaction quality or problem-solving strategies. Thus, both cooperative and collaborative learning activities can facilitate interaction and strategic problem-solving.

Lou (2004) suggests that structured between-group discussions may facilitate student learning about the group process. Between-group discussions allow students to clarify and understand group processes, to see how they can be instantiated, and to identify problems in group performance and strategies. In addition, between-group discussions may improve project performance as they allow students to compare the strengths and limitations of each project and identify common challenges.

Explicit direction regarding the utility and form of interaction may be needed for students to engage effectively in cooperative or collaborative activities. Munzer (2003) integrated brief, synchronous interactions in individual online learning sessions to deepen participant knowledge of specific content. Four chat sessions were convened at specific times and participants were invited to engage in a cooperative learning venture to deepen knowledge gained in the individual sessions. In general, poorly designed interaction led to negative reviews and high variations in individual performance in the cooperative activity. Participants were more likely to benefit when a tutor directed the activities or when specific instructions on the use of activities to support learning were provided.

Resources

Resources, ranging from complete Web sites to individual learning objects in the form of multimedia, video, sound, and text, have been categorized as static or dynamic (Hill & Hannafin, 2001). Static resources, such as published articles and presentations, are fixed in nature and provide stable, reliable source information such as historical documentation and expert knowledge. Dynamic resources, such as simulations and databases, can change based on both natural, ongoing events (e.g., changes in weather databases from day to day) and how the resource is used (e.g., entering weekly weight while dieting). Both static and dynamic resources are employed in DDLEs, but their functions are to support specific, defined learning outcomes.

DDLE resources vary widely in format, and include lecture notes and slides, media artifacts (audio, video, graphics) to supplement or enhance content, hyperlinks to online resources, and "e-tivities" (Salmon, 2002). In a blended undergraduate chemistry DDLE, lecture slides made available online served as study-aids to anchor student learning (Harley, Maher, Henke, & Lawrence, 2003). Additionally, allowing students to complete homework assignments and pre-lab assignments online increased student-teacher interaction and discussion during lab sessions. Newnham, Mather, Grattan, Holmes, and Gardner (1998), upon providing a set of text, image, and discussion board resources in an undergraduate geography course, found that students tended to perform better on their coursework compared with students who were not given these additional resources. Students indicated that the additional resources gave them a broad view of the topic and made their coursework motivating and enjoyable.

Various media resources have been integrated to enhance or supplement course content. In Choi and Johnson's (2005) study, students noted that video examples and non-examples reinforced their understanding of video-based instruction and were more motivating and memorable due to their realistic, authentic nature. Christel (1994) used multiple versions of an interactive, digital video course to help students understand the importance of software quality, the utility of code inspections in improving quality of software, and the dynamic processes inherent in code inspection. In this study, 64 students were randomly assigned to a treatment containing motion video and audio or still images and audio. Students with the motion video treatment recalled significantly more information than non-video students, and were also more likely to readily recall the opinions and content present in the video. Similarly, Pavey and Garland (2004) provided animated feedback and interactive Web pages to support college students learning about cardiovascular physiology. Most students indicated that they found the animations and interactive pages useful, since animations allowed them to visualize processes. In addition, students commented that they found it easier to learn facts when they engaged in the content, rather than simply read materials.

Tools

A range of tools have been applied in DDLEs, ranging from communication tools to manipulation tools to representation tools. According to Iiyoshi, Hannafin, and Wang (2005), tools help in seeking or presenting information, as well as in organizing, integrating, and generating knowledge. Consistent with the external locus of authority, DDLE tools support the learner in attaining externally-established goals.

Communication tools such as bulletin boards and chat tools are commonly used in DDLE online-learning contexts. Each tool offers distinct advantages for learning; bulletin boards can facilitate asynchronous discussion, useful for encouraging descriptive, thoughtful writing, while chat tools simulate "face-to-face" interactivity, thus enabling synchronous communication and real-time feedback. For example, online synchronous discussions proved effective in improving eating habits and body-image among college-age women (Zabinski, Wilfley, Calfas, Winzelberg, & Taylor, 2004). Sixty at-risk women were recruited from a university based on their score on a Weight Concerns Scale and assigned to either an intervention group with a chat room or a control group without chat. Women who participated in hour-long facilitated chats to discuss issues related to eating and bodyweight showed significant improvements in their eating behavior and self-esteem compared to participants who did not, as measured by several online assessment scales 10 weeks following the program. Thus, synchronous tools may enable dynamic, customized, and flexible support needed for therapeutic or diagnostic interventions.

In other DDLE contexts, asynchronous tools provided a flexible space for reflective, descriptive writing in reaching a specific learning goal (Cheung & Hew, 2004). Liu and Lee (2005) investigated the role of discussion boards in helping student peers to reach compatible-construct definitions about database components that were closely aligned with the construct definitions proposed by the instructor. By using specific trigger questions designed to encourage student elaboration, differentiation, and refinement of conceptual understanding, the discussion board promoted reconciliation and negotiation between peer understanding of concepts, which also closely approximated the understanding of the instructor. Based on follow-up discussion, the researchers reported that concept distance had been reduced by almost two-thirds between student pairs.

DDLEs tools have also been used to support manipulation of data and representation. Carver, Evans, and Kingston (2004) created a Web-based geographical information system (GIS) using pre-selected datasets with specific representational and manipulation options. Students used these tools to understand and solve problems (e.g., the best location for a nuclear waste facility). Online case studies allowed students to research information on the Web, explore geographical information through provided maps, experiment with solutions through various comparative options, and identify and justify their solutions using available data. Log files were used to track student choices as they investigated case studies, and students exhibited active use of the maps and manipulation tools to reach solutions. Following the case studies, students also indicated that the tools enabled them to both better understand and appreciate the problems introduced as well as to understand GIS theory, concepts, and applications.

Scaffolds

Scaffolds assist learners in accomplishing tasks that they would not be able to achieve on their own (Wood, Bruner, & Ross, 1976). Scaffold types also vary according to the assumptions underlying the distance learning context (see, e.g., Hill & Hannafin, 2001, for more detail). Procedural and strategic scaffolds, for example, support task performance by cueing appropriate sequence and decisions. Metacognitive and conceptual scaffolds support reflection on and understanding of to-be-learned concepts and content. Based on a comprehensive analysis of online research and practice, Sharma and Hannafin (2006) concluded that "hard" (fixed technology support) and "soft" (dynamic human support) scaffolds are needed to address cognitive and representational aspects of learning. Both may be blended to balance the scaffolding needed to account for individual differences and the type of learning supported in the TEDLE.

In DDLEs, scaffolds refer to planned strategies and content structures that assist the learner in more efficiently and effectively processing and internalizing course materials. In a study of hypertext architectures (linear, hierarchical, and relational), Graff (2005) confirmed prior research results suggesting that matching student cognitive style with hypertext structure can facilitate recall. Fifty-five undergraduate computer-science students were randomly assigned to one of three hypertext conditions, and then given 20 minutes to read text and answer 10 follow-up questions to determine recall. Intuitive (or global) learners were most successful at recalling from the linear hypertext condition that cumulatively represented whole ideas, while analytic reasoners were the most successful at recalling from hierarchical texts that enabled an organized investigation of discrete parts. Intermediates were the most successful at recalling from relational hypertext that required qualities of both intuitives and analytics.

Another content-specific scaffold relates to information added to course materials. Wallen, Plass, and Brunken (2005) developed a 650-word text on cell phones that was supplemented with three different types of annotations: selection annotations pointing out key concepts and words, organization annotations further defining or contextualizing ideas across a number of words, and integration annotations explicating connections between different ideas. In all, 98 college students were divided across a control group and six treatment groups that used one or a combination of two annotation types. By comparing scores on recognition, comprehension, and transfer tests following student reading, the researchers were able to show that selection and organization annotations improved student scores on all three measures while integration annotations improved transfer performance. However, combining annotation types increased cognitive load and degraded the overall effect.

Similarly, Lee and Calandra (2004) studied the effect of conceptual annotations on student responses to Web-based problems in two high-school history classes. One class was provided with Web-based text with annotations, and the other with only Web-based text. Functional annotations that helped to explain concepts provided assistance to students in constructing written responses to problems, as 84% of students in the annotation treatment responded to an impeachment question correctly, while none in the non-annotation group provided a correct answer.

A final content-specific scaffold focuses on suggesting strategies and techniques to organize information during learning activities. In one study, two fifth-grade classes of 26 students each worked on a Webquest about endangered species with a culminating product (MacGregor & Lou, 2004–2005). All students were directed to extract key information (e.g., habitat) from online resources using a study guide, but only one-half of each class was provided with a concept map template that suggested connections between study guide items and major concepts that could be applied to their project. Significant differences were noted between the concept map and non-map groups on their ability to list "what I learned" on a free-recall assessment, and on their content and organization scores from the project multimedia product.

Given that DDLEs focus on externally-specified learning goals, it is important to consider how instructors support unique learning requirements. Selinger (2004), while developing the Web-based Cisco Networking Academy, cited the importance of local tutors who adapted instructional strategies to address their students' culture and pedagogical needs (i.e., structured versus open-ended learning, limited choices versus complexity, task-focus versus conceptual development, etc.). In France, for example, instructors tended to follow their tradition of *didactique* (Selinger, 2004, p. 232) in summarizing the program for students, with little group work. In South Africa, limited Internet access has necessitated that students read online curriculum during class, thus limiting time available for out-of-class exercises. Instructor scaffolds that prescribe alternative instructional strategies and allow for the flexible use of core content across different activities may help to ensure learning across diverse audiences and barriers.

Assessment

In DDLEs, assessments are used to document attainment of specified goals for each learner. The instructor or expert defines a standard form and implementation of assessment for all students. The type of assessment for delivering and supporting assessment ranges from quizzes, exams, and tests to individual or group projects and electronic portfolios (Mason, Pegler, & Weller, 2004). Garrett and Vogt (2003) noted the influence of outcomes-based evaluation in e-learning, citing decreased emphasis on factors such as course completion rates. Automated testing and scoring allows agencies to track learner progress and mastery of outcomes required for continuing education or certification credit. For example, researchers tested the feasibility of evaluating a sample of 30 continuing medical education (CME) courses by assessing criterion knowledge and skills prior to, at the conclusion of, and four weeks following online CME courses (Casebeer et al., 2004). Six-question tests were individualized for each course in the sample and repeated at pre, post, and follow-up. Significant knowledge gains were noted for 89 physicians who completed all three tests, with an effect size of .30 from pretest to follow-up. While the study demonstrated that standardized templates were feasible across courses from different providers, designers must address potential disagreements from providers regarding the most important concepts to test using generic instruments.

Peat and Franklin (2002) described the integration of alternative assessment exercises in, and student reactions to, a blended first-year biology course at the University of Sydney. The switch from paper- to computer-based quizzes was cited positively by a majority of students, who preferred its ability to provide instant scores/feedback, illustrative diagrams, and related materials in question stems. A Web-based mock examination provided students with feedback on their understanding of course concepts as a precursor to possible needed remedial action. A third assessment type, the "self-assessment module" or SAM, required students to respond to questions that integrate material laterally across class sessions, which assisted in promoting complex thinking. Students reported that the SAMs helped them to understand course material, to identify details not provided by textbooks and linkages between them, and to identify personal improvements needed.

According to Benson (2003), the potential for academic dishonesty on traditional assessments has been a challenge for DDLEs where mastery of course concepts is important. Alternative assessment strategies, such as discussion, concept maps, portfolios, writing, reflection on field experience, projects, and peer critique, may enable students to demonstrate understanding while minimizing the possibility of cheating. Pretorius (2004) integrated practical exercises as part of an environmental management distance degree program to promote real-world problem-solving and team work skills. Case studies were incorporated into some modules for analysis, with students contacting instructors to clarify questions.

Russell (2004) described a method for assessing nurse participation in continuing education courses that meets American Nurses Credentialing Center requirements to document course completion without the need for traditional multiple-choice tests. Two short essay items of a subjective nature were used to describe something learned and how it would be applied it to practice. A content analysis of nurse responses illustrated their ability to extract key information from journal articles and identify implications for their own practice.

Implications

DDLEs support individual learning and achievement of identified goals by providing specific content, practice, and follow-up. Although learning goals are prescribed and content is predefined, research indicates that situating content in authentic contexts may contribute to in-depth student learning and analysis (Chanlin & Chan, 2004). Authentic contexts may use situations or problems likely to be encountered within a specific community and may include sanctioned forms of discourse within a community. Exposing students to authentic discourse structures augments their ability to reason and learn within authentic contexts (see, e.g., McAlister et al., 2004).

In DDLEs, the instructor often provides information, support, clarification, and feedback. Student learning is affected by the instructor's social actions, as well as the instructor's ability to reinforce and facilitate desired learning. Instructor immediacy—communication and ability to encourage discussion and provide feedback—was a significant predictor of student learning. However, Wise et al.'s (2004) research indicates that social presence may not always be correlated with student learning. Thus, the instructor may prompt, model, and provide directed feedback to individuals and groups during discussions. Instructors who provide specific guidelines for format, quality, and expectations of discussion are more likely to engage students in in-depth, objective-oriented discourse. Learning may be particularly enhanced when instructors provide multiple opportunities to situate information in rich, meaningful, and generative a contexts (see, e.g., Meskill & Anthony, 2004).

While research on the effects of peer interactions is emerging, initial work indicates that cooperative and collaborative peer groups may help to engage students in high-level discussion and problem-solving, especially when scaffolded with explicit task structures and dialogue formats. Engaging students in cooperative or collaborative DDLE activities requires explicit directions about the utility and form of interaction, without which students may fail to engage in appropriate learning interactions with peers.

Students encounter a variety of environmental influences during learning. For example, diverse media and resources provide multiple interpretations of to-be-learned content. DDLE tools can facilitate learning opportunities, such as using chat rooms to customize learning (Zabinski et al., 2004) and discussion boards to direct student reflection. Students may be better able to explore information in different ways and to manipulate problem-and-solution sets, thereby improving conceptual understanding and awareness of everyday applications (Carver et al., 2004).

Scaffolds such as embedded annotations and visual maps have been shown to help students to understand and organize concepts. However, excessive or poorly designed scaffolds may increase cognitive load rather than help students to allocate cognitive resources. In DDLEs, where learning objectives and course materials, tools, and resources are determined externally, assessment needs to confirm the extent to which criteria for learning have been attained, and to provide further support as needed where attainment has not been demonstrated. Traditional assessments such as quizzes and exams are commonly used, but can be augmented with immediate feedback and remedial information. Alternative assessments such as discussions, projects, and portfolios can also be used to evaluate student performance provided they include clear, unambiguous indicators of the criteria defined for learning.

Tallent-Runnels et al. (2006) suggested that well designed and well implemented courses are more likely to engender student learning, but little research exists clarifying how tools should be structured to support specific DDLE interactions. How should interactions be designed and managed to foster specific learning outcomes? What types of online discussion tools or structures facilitate specific types of thinking and learning skills?

Finally, DDLE students have indicated that access to course notes, lecture materials, and study aids enhanced their content knowledge (Newnham et al., 1998). However, research is needed to clarify which resources are vital versus supplementary, as well as which resources are used effectively by students. Research on the process of evaluating, selecting, and using resources is needed to determine how they should be structured and administered to minimize cognitive overload and confusion.

REFERENCES

Arbaugh, J. B. (2001). How instructor immediacy behaviors affect student satisfaction and learning in Web-based courses. *Business Communication Quarterly, 64*(4), 42–54.

Benson, A. D. (2003). Assessing participant learning in online environments. *New Directions for Adult and Continuing Education, 100*, 69–78.

Carver, S., Evans, A., & Kingston, R. (2004). Developing and testing an online tool for teaching GIS concepts applied to spatial decision-making. *Journal of Geography in Higher Education, 28*(3), 425–438.

Casebeer, L., Kristofco, R. E., Strasser, S., Reilly, M., Krishnamoorthy, P., Rabin, A., et al. (2004). Standardizing evaluation of online continuing medical education: Physician knowledge, attitudes, and reflection on practice. *Journal of Continuing Education in the Health Professions, 24*(2), 68–75.

Chanlin, L.-J., & Chan, K.-C. (2004). Assessment of PBL design approach in a dietetic Web-based instruction. *Journal of Educational Computing Research, 31*(4), 437–452.

Cheung, W. S., & Hew, K. F. (2004). Evaluating the extent of ill-structured problem solving process among pre-service teachers in an asynchronous online discussion and reflection log learning environment. *Journal of Educational Computing Research, 30*(3), 197–227.

Choi, H. J., & Johnson, S. D. (2005). The effect of context-based video instruction on learning and motivation in online courses. *The American Journal of Distance Education, 19*(4), 215–227.

Christel, M. G. (1994). The role of visual fidelity in computer-based instruction. *Human-Computer Interaction, 9*(2), 183–223.

Davies, J., & Graff, M. (2005). Performance in e-learning: Online participation and student grades. *British Journal of Educational Technology, 36*(4), 657–663.

de Bruyn, L. L. (2004). Monitoring online communication: Can the development of convergence and social presence indicate an interactive learning environment? *Distance Education, 25*(1), 67–81.

Dennen, V. P. (2005). From message posting to learning dialogues: Factors affecting learner participation in asynchronous discussion. *Distance Education, 26*(1), 127–148.

Ellis, R. A., Marcus, G., & Taylor, R. (2005). Learning through inquiry: Student difficulties with online course-based material. *Journal of Computer Assisted Learning, 21*(4), 239–252.

Garrett, L. A., & Vogt, C. L. (2003). Meeting the needs of consumers: Lessons from business and industry. *New Directions for Adult and Continuing Education, 100*, 89–101.

Ge, X., & Land, S. M. (2003). Scaffolding students' problem-solving processes in an ill-structured task using question prompts and peer interactions. *Educational Technology Research and Development, 51*(1), 21–38.

Graff, M. (2005). Differences in concept mapping, hypertext architecture, and the analyst-intuition dimension of cognitive style. *Educational Psychology, 25*(4), 409–422.

Harley, D., Maher, M., Henke, J., & Lawrence, S. (2003). An analysis of technology enhancements in a large lecture course. *EDUCAUSE Quarterly, 26*(3), 26–33.

Hill, J. R., & Hannafin, M. J. (2001). Teaching and learning in digital environments: The resurgence of resource-based learning environments. *Educational Technology Research and Development, 49*(3), 37–52.

Horney, J. A., MacDonald, P. D. M., Rothney, E. E., & Alexander, L. K. (2005). User patterns and satisfaction with online trainings completed on the North Carolina Center for Public Health Preparedness training Web site. *Journal of Public Health Management Practice, 11*(November/December 2005 Suppl.), 90–94.

Hoskins, S. L., & van Hooff, J. C. (2005). Motivation and ability: Which students use online learning and what influence does it have on their achievement? *British Journal of Educational Technology, 36*(2), 177–192.

Iiyoshi, T., Hannafin, M. J., & Wang, F. (2005). Cognitive tools and student-centered learning: Rethinking tools, functions, and applications. *Educational Media International, 42*(4), 281–296.

Lee, J. K., & Calandra, B. (2004). Can embedded annotations help high school students perform problem solving tasks using a Web-based historical document? *Journal of Research on Technology in Education, 37*(1), 65–84.

Liu, C.-C., & Lee, J.-H. (2005). Prompting conceptual understanding with computer-mediated peer discourse and knowledge acquisition techniques. *British Journal of Educational Technology, 36*(5), 821–837.

Lou, Y. (2004). Learning to solve complex problems through between-group collaboration in project-based online courses. *Distance Education, 25*(1), 49–66.

Lou, Y., & MacGregor, S. K. (2004). Enhancing project-based learning through online between-group collaboration. *Educational Research and Evaluation, 10*(4–6), 419–440.

MacGregor, S. K., & Lou, Y. (2004–2005). Web-based learning: How task scaffolding and Web site design support knowledge acquisition. *Journal of Research on Technology in Education, 37*(2), 161–175.

Martindale, T., Pearson, C., Curda, L. K., & Pilcher, J. (2005). Effects of an online instructional application on reading and mathematics standardized test scores. *Journal of Research on Technology in Education, 37*(4), 349–360.

Mason, R., Pegler, C., & Weller, M. (2004). E-portfolios: An assessment tool for online courses. *British Journal of Educational Technology, 35*(6), 717–727.

McAlister, S., Ravenscroft, A., & Scanlon, E. (2004). Combining interaction and context design to support collaborative argumentation using a tool for synchronous CMC. *Journal of Computer Assisted Learning, 20*(3), 194–204.

McDonald, J. K., Yanchar, S. C., & Osguthorpe, R. T. (2005). Learning from programmed instruction: Examining implications for modern instructional technology. *Educational Technology Research and Development, 53*(2), 84–98.

McLoughlin, C., & Luca, J. (2002). A learner-centred approach to developing team skills through Web-based learning and assessment. *British Journal of Educational Technology, 33*(5), 571–582.

Meskill, C., & Anthony, N. (2004). Teaching and learning with telecommunications: Instructional discourse in a hybrid Russian class. *Journal of Educational Technology Systems, 33*(2), 103–119.

Moore, M. G. (1989). Three types of interaction. *The American Journal of Distance Education, 3*(2), 1–6.

Munzer, S. (2003). An evaluation of synchronous co-operative distance learning in the field: The importance of instructional design. *Educational Media International, 40*(1–2), 91–99.

Myers, S. C., & Nelson, M. A. (2004, January). *Do online students in a mastery-based principles course analyze, synthesize, and evaluate better than face-to-face students? Preliminary evidence.* Paper presented at the annual conference of the National Association of Economics Educators, National Council for Economics Education Sessions, ASSA Meetings, San Diego, CA.

Newnham, R., Mather, A., Grattan, J., Holmes, A., & Gardner, A. (1998). An evaluation of the use of Internet sources as a basis for geography coursework. *Journal of Geography in Higher Education, 22*(1), 19–34.

Pavey, J., & Garland, S. W. (2004). The integration and implementation of a range of "e-tivities" to enhance students' interaction and learning. *Innovations in Education and Teaching International, 41*(3), 305–315.

Peat, M., & Franklin, S. (2002). Supporting student learning: The use of computer-based formative assessment modules. *British Journal of Educational Technology, 33*(5), 515–523.

Pretorius, R. W. (2004). An environmental management qualification through distance education. *International Journal of Sustainability in Higher Education, 5*(1), 63–80.

Rose, M. A. (2004). Comparing productive online dialogue in two group styles: Cooperative and collaborative. *American Journal of Distance Education, 18*(2), 73–88.

Russell, S. S. (2004). Evaluation of a new method to verify CE completion. *Urologic Nursing, 24*(6), 509–512.

Salmon, G. (2002). *E-tivities: The key to active online learning.* London: Kogan Page.

Selinger, M. (2004). Cultural and pedagogical implications of a global e-learning programme. *Cambridge Journal of Education, 34*(2), 223–239.

Sharma, P., & Hannafin, M. J. (2006). *Scaffolding in technology-enhanced learning environments.* Manuscript submitted for publication.

Streibel, M. J. (1995). Instructional plans and situated learning: The challenge of Suchman's theory of situated action for instructional designers and instructional systems. In G. J. Anglin (Ed.), *Instructional technology: Past, present, and future* (pp. 117–132). Englewood, CO: Libraries Unlimited.

Tallent-Runnels, M. K., Thomas, J. A., Lan, W. Y., Cooper, S., Ahern, T. C., Shaw, S. M., et al. (2006). Teaching courses online: A review of the research. *Review of Educational Research, 76*(1), 93–135.

Wallen, E., Plass, J. L., & Brunken, R. (2005). The function of annotations in the comprehension of scientific texts: Cognitive load effects and the impact of verbal ability. *Educational Technology Research and Development, 53*(3), 59–72.

Walton, M., & Archer, A. (2004). The Web and information literacy: Scaffolding the use of Web sources in a project-based curriculum. *British Journal of Educational Technology, 35*(2), 173–186.

Welsh, E. T., Wanberg, C. R., Brown, K. G., & Simmering, M. J. (2003). E-learning: Emerging uses, empirical results and future directions. *International Journal of Training and Development, 7*(4), 245–258.

Wise, A., Chang, J., Duffy, T., & Del Valle, R. (2004). The effects of teacher social presence on student satisfaction, engagement, and learning. *Journal of Educational Computing Research, 31*(3), 247–271.

Wood, D., Bruner, J., & Ross, G. (1976). The role of tutoring in problem solving. *Journal of Child Psychology and Psychiatry and Allied Disciplines, 17*, 89–100.

Zabinski, M. F., Wilfley, D. E., Calfas, K. J., Winzelberg, A. J., & Taylor, C. B. (2004). An interactive psychoeducational intervention for women at risk of developing an eating disorder. *Journal of Consulting and Clinical Psychology, 72*(5), 914–919.

22

Teaching and Learning in Negotiated and Informal Environments

Janette R. Hill, Denise P. Domizi,
and Michael J. Hannafin
The University of Georgia

Minchi C. Kim
New York University

Hyeonjin Kim
Korea Education & Research Information Service

In negotiated distance learning environments (NDLEs), learning goals and means are jointly determined, balancing individual with externally established priorities. In informal distance learning environments (IDLEs), learners identify the learning goals, deploy individual learning approaches, and assume responsibility for assessing their learning. While each has unique theoretical foundations and assumptions, they share common environmental components, including interaction strategies, resources, tools, scaffolds, and assessment strategies. Each is enacted according to its unique epistemological foundations and associated learning goals and contexts.

NEGOTIATED DISTANCE LEARNING ENVIRONMENTS (NDLES)

Negotiated distance learning environments (NDLEs) support learner-, instructor-, and curriculum-generated goals. NDLE components provide a variety of options, and are designed to facilitate negotiation of learning goals and promote learner autonomy.

THEORETICAL AND EPISTEMOLOGICAL FOUNDATIONS

NDLEs typically manifest constructivist epistemology in that learners construct knowledge by actively engaging in learning activities and meaning making (Piaget, 1972). In contrast to directed learning environments, scaffolding facilitates individual meaning-making and goal-setting. Constructivist pedagogical models (e.g., problem-based learning, project-based learning, and anchored instruction) support NDLEs in that they focus on student-centered reasoning and knowledge construction as individuals negotiate which components to use and how to use them. Negotiation generally occurs between and among learners, instructors and/or peers (virtual, live), affordances of the environments, and constraints and limitations in available resources and tools. Negotiation also occurs as students establish their learning goals, select and adapt resources to their learning goals, discuss emergent understandings, and reflect on their learning processes. Typically, learners attempt to reconcile their interpretations—and sometimes misconceptions— with the socially shared meanings of the community.

Guidance helps learners to practice and develop autonomous learning processes. For example, individuals often become disoriented—lost in hyperspace—while navigating resources in complex learning contexts (Clark, 2003) and need guidance through discourse, driving questions, worksheets, and examples. For example, ESTEPWeb guides preservice teachers in their study of learning sciences using modified problem-based learning (Derry & the STEP Team, 2004). Procedural guidance and opportunities for collaboration are afforded through a variety of tools including Group Whiteboard, My Notebooks, and Discussion Board. Online problem-based scaffolds provide steps that guide students' design work (e.g., step 2, initial proposal), including due dates, guidelines, and templates for writing and submitting ideas (i.e., My Notebook). Online facilitation provides monitoring and formative assessment of individual and group progress by collecting and displaying student performance data while offline facilitation, designed to guide discussions and submissions, is provided by teaching assistants. The preservice teachers involved in ESTEPWeb reported that both the individual and collaborative activities were useful for their future lesson planning.

NDLE components vary according to learner type, learning style, preferences, and motivation. Individuals use and adapt various components, such as exploration tools, scaffolding questions, and discussion boards based on their needs. For example, WebQuests (Dodge, 1995, 2001) have been used for diverse subjects and various levels of learners in both online and face-to-face contexts, including K-through-higher education classes in social studies, mathematics, and sciences (see examples, http://webquest.org.). Consistent with NDLE epistemology, WebQuest's six phases (i.e., introduction, task, information sources, description of process, guidance, and conclusion) are aligned with constructivist, inquiry-based, and project-based learning.

NDLE COMPONENTS

Learning from Interactions

Because of the constructive nature of NDLEs, interactions often promote problem-solving and self-regulation skills. This shift is apparent in Web-based distance learning environments, where management systems (e.g., WebCT, Blackboard) are designed to help students effectively act on *their* learning goals (e.g., Kim & Hannafin, 2004; Kitsantas & Dabbagh, 2004; Whipp & Chiarelli, 2004). Dabbagh and Kitsantas (2005) explored student interaction using a learning management system to facilitate instructional design, conceptual understanding, and self-regulation.

The 65 students enrolled in three college courses interacted with various technological functions in WebCT (e.g., administrative, collaborative and communication, content creation and delivery, and assessment) during exploratory, dialogical, and collaborative learning projects involving software evaluations, course content discussions, in-class group activities, case studies, and instructional design projects. The results indicated that use of WebCT features helped students to develop self-regulation design skills. Content development and delivery experience supported individual goal setting, time management, and help-seeking behavior, while technological functions enabled students to pace completion of course assignments.

Learners may also engage with instructors and peers in NDLEs. The instructor participates but does not dominate discussions, asking provocative questions, suggesting alternatives, encouraging discourse, and modeling the practices of their specific community. In discovery learning, for example, instructor planning and structuring promotes problem-solving and interpretation, while unplanned, unstructured activities engenders misunderstandings (Tallent-Runnels, et al., 2006). The instructor also affects student perceptions of online learning. Positive student experiences have been reported when instructors provide personalized and immediate feedback to students, engage in the discussions as a coach and facilitator, and use strategies to increase group-based and collaborative work (McIsaac, Blocher, Mahes, & Vrasidas, 1999).

Instructor interactions are reified as learners read text, find Web resources, and use asynchronous discussion boards (e.g., Garrison & Cleveland-Innes, 2005; Gerber, Scott, & Clements, 2005). Conversations with the instructor help to bridge gaps between the state of an individual's knowledge and skills and desired knowledge and skills. For example, students who negotiated and clarified understandings through asynchronous Socratic dialog with an instructor (clarifying students' comments and probing students' assumptions, reasons, and evidence) demonstrated advanced critical-thinking skills in their discourse. In Yang, Newby, and Bill's (2005) study, some undergraduate students participated in Socratic questioning during the first half of a semester, while the remaining students negotiated Socratically during the second half. Students provided with questions in the first half only sustained critical-thinking skills throughout the semester, while those who interacted Socratically during the second half demonstrated critical thinking only during the latter half of the semester, indicating both that questioning helped students develop and sustain critical-thinking skills.

Uribe, Klein, and Sullivan (2003) investigated online collaboration's influence on student performance, time on task, and attitudes during ill-structured problem solving. Using a 2×2 (individual vs. computer-mediated collaboration; low vs. high ability) mixed factor design, 59 students were engaged in a four-step problem-solving process either as a member of an online collaborative dyad or alone using a posttest only. In addition, communication transcripts were collected and analyzed to explore interactions between dyad members. The results indicated that both collaboration groups reported positive attitudes toward collaborative learning, the program, and transfer of problem-solving skills. However, collaborative dyads solved ill-defined problem scenarios better and spent significantly more time on task by sharing via discussion board.

Resources

Resources are used in various NDLE contexts, including resource-based learning (Armatas, Holt, & Rice, 2003; Macdonald, Heap, & Mason, 2001), problem-based learning (Derry & the STEP Team, 2004), case-based learning (Kim, Hannafin, & Kim, 2005), inquiry-based learning (Dodge, 1995), and information seeking (Hill & Hannafin, 1997). In online case-based learning, a variety of resources are available, including Web-based cases, lesson plans, lesson materials, textbooks, and related references. Kim, Hannafin, and Kim (2005) found that preservice teachers used resources in a primary or supplementary capacity by evaluating each for their individual lesson goals and designs.

Researchers have reported that learners develop and refine both critical-thinking (Dodge, 2001) and metacognitive and self-regulation skills (Hill & Hannafin, 1997; Macdonald et al., 2001) when they seek and use diverse resources to negotiate meaning. However, the benefits of NDLE resources vary according to learners' abilities and strategies (Macdonald et al., 2001). Hill and Hannafin (1997) explored adult learners' strategies, while seeking information on the Internet. Using a case-study methodology, data were collected from 14 participants in a graduate-level technology integration course via surveys, observations, and interviews. Participants with high metacognitive knowledge, prior knowledge of content and technology systems, and self-efficacy were best able to refine their searching actions and recognize their orientation within the system. In contrast, browsing and searching among learners with low metacognitive knowledge became readily disoriented and engaged in random searching.

Oliver and Hannafin (2001) reported that learners often failed to use resources in the absence of procedural and metacognitive support. Twelve eighth-grade students were asked to find, frame, and solve open-ended scientific problems via the online tools as they reviewed resources using peers, teacher, and online scaffolds. Students whose searching was scaffolded (e.g., through the use of advance organizers) sought information relevant to the problem, while those without scaffolds tended to find little problem-related information, sought information randomly, and did not use keywords effectively. Instructor guidance is critical when using various resources in an environment with high learner autonomy.

Tools

With the proliferation of Web sites and search engines (e.g., Google, Yahoo), concerns over non-validated Web resources, limited classroom time for students to navigate, and age-inappropriate sites have grown (Soloway & Wallace, 1997). Web site-filtering (Recker, Walker, & Lawless, 2003) and online library systems have become increasingly important as educators seek to support students in finding, filtering, and utilizing learning resources.

Through the Michigan Digital Library Project, Wallace, Kupperman, Krajcik, and Soloway (2000) studied pairs of sixth-graders as they sought and used Web-based resources to support inquiry-oriented ecology activities. Video and audio captures of student activities during the six-day activities indicated that students' information seeking involves "asking and refining questions, exploring, gathering, and evaluating information" (p. 87). Although the goal was to enhance students' interest and understanding of ecology through Web-based research, the students focused on finding information and completing the assignments quickly. Students tended to seek the correct answers rather than exploring, which was described as an intermediate stage between seeking information and answer generation. The researchers concluded that the cognitive complexity involved in seeking and exploring resources requires meta-knowledge and navigation skills to access and use online sources. Metacognitive scaffolds embedded in the exploration tools, for example, can be used to structure and support learning activities hierarchically.

To facilitate resource navigation, tools can provide structure and meta-context in which students identify, investigate, and solve authentic problems. For example, in web-based inquiry science environments (WISE), students collect scientific evidence from reliable sources (e.g., scientists and government agencies) in order to confront controversial or naïve scientific theories, construct their own queries, and warrant conclusions (Linn, Clark, & Slotta, 2003). Using embedded scaffolds, students learn science in personally meaningful ways, exchange help with peers, and continuously expand their interest in everyday science.

Representation tools may help learners to present their knowledge, receive feedback, and reflect on their learning processes. In Jonassen and Kwon's (2001) study, 18 undergraduate engineering students collaboratively solved problems through face-to-face group meetings and asynchronous computer-mediated communication (CMC). Data were collected from student questionnaires and conversations. Using tools to support analyzing problems, developing solutions, and reflecting on the process, CMC students demonstrated superior problem-solving and richer task-oriented patterns. The researchers attributed improvements to flexibility in learning time and space, which allowed CMC students to spend more time reflecting and thinking critically.

Similarly, Daroszewski, Kinser, and Lloyd (2004) found that nursing students who posted weekly online journals demonstrated superior critical thinking, mentoring, and socialization about their practical clinical experiences. Graduate nursing students were directed to write a minimum of three weekly journal entries, which included one original entry and two responses to colleagues' journal entries. Journal entries were analyzed for content, and students completed a 10-item questionnaire. Journal entries indicated that students were building shared understanding and meaning of their peers' clinical settings, while the surveys indicated that students appreciated the opportunity to share and compare experiences and learn more about the different practical settings. In this instance, the opportunity to engage in discourse allowed nursing students to learn from and contribute to a shared pool of experiences.

Harasim (2002) reported success in sharing expertise and co-constructing knowledge through the Global Educators' Network. International scholars from over 60 countries contributed to seminars and discussion on online teaching and learning. Data from interviews, surveys, e-mail communications, and participants' comments were analyzed. The findings revealed that participants generated and linked initial ideas through "intellectual convergence," which enabled them to cooperatively refine, revise, and develop their perspectives. Harasim concluded that the social and friendly nature of the community, which encouraged intellectual and social discourse, contributed to successful knowledge sharing and generating observed.

Scaffolds

NDLE scaffolds help to "problematize" (Reiser, 2004) ideas and beliefs and corroborate or revise individual knowledge (e.g., conceptual scaffolds, Hill & Hannafin, 2001), enable learners to conduct formative progress assessments and clarify or adjust goals and tasks (e.g., metacognitive and procedural scaffolds), and encourage alternative views and perspectives to accommodate knowledge (e.g., strategic scaffolds).

Technology-based scaffolds may augment or supplant mentoring traditionally provided by live instructors. For example, online expert cases provided exemplars for students to relate their own experience to the learning contexts (Kim et al., 2005). Likewise, embedded prompts can facilitate learners' thinking about learning processes and problem-solving strategies. Ge and Land (2003) studied the effects of peer interaction and question prompts on the problem-solving of 117 undergraduate students enrolled in introductory information sciences and technology classes. Students were randomly assigned to a peer-question, peer-control, individual-question, and individual-control group. The researchers reported a significant relationship between question prompts and problem-solving performance, which they attributed to conceptual and metacognitive scaffolds that helped students identify relevant information, organize plans, generate arguments based upon the information, and evaluate solutions.

Instructor facilitation may include feedback assistance and prompts that foster critical thinking. Hill (2002) reported that could-should-must (CSM) messages functioned as procedural scaffolds and outlined necessary activities. Weekly CSM messages were sent to remind students of what they could be, should be, and must be doing related to class activities. Hill reported that CSM strategies helped distant learners build "structural habits" (p. 77), remain on-task, and overcome limited numbers of communication and face-to-face meetings.

Whipp (2003) studied preservice teachers' use of electronic discussion tools to share ideas and experiences in urban education settings. "Tailored questioning" scaffolds cued critical reflection through online discussion. For example, students posted more descriptive and reasoned e-mail responses to the instructor's question regarding whether white teachers could teach African American students effectively. When the instructor employed specific, thought-provoking questions tailored to students' interests and their teaching context (e.g., socioeconomic issues), students were better able to contemplate multiple perspectives and express critical ideas.

Researchers have explored various peer scaffolds in distance education. Hoadley and Linn (2000) examined how eighth-graders debated and developed scientific understanding about colors using an asynchronous, online discussion board to examine: "How do the paint chips look different under different lighting?" (p. 844). The authors suggested that performance improved because students shared perspectives through peer discussion. While such studies provide initial evidence of the power of peer scaffolding, research is needed to promote meaningful interaction among peers in NDLEs.

Assessment

NDLE assessment is formative, dynamic, interactive, and negotiated between instructors and learners. Broad learning goals, defined by the instructional authority, guide students by framing individual objectives and tasks; the negotiation of assessment varies accordingly. Likewise, formats for delivering and supporting assessment range from quizzes, exams, and tests to individual or group projects or electronic portfolios (Mason, Pegler, & Weller, 2004).

Gulikers, Bastiaens, and Kirschner (2004) argue that authentic assessment requires careful consideration of associated dimensions—authentic tasks, physical or virtual context, social context, assessment result, and criteria and standards (p. 73). NDLE interest has emerged in tools that address lifelong learning, student self-direction, and reflection and revision of one's work. Mason et al. (2004) studied electronic portfolio assessment in student-centered, online graduate courses. Students' e-portfolios contained selected resources and projects from different courses (e.g., writings, PowerPoint slides, and online discussion messages). Mason et al. reported that students integrated experiences from various courses and built authentic, meaningful artifacts in their e-portfolios, and advised instructors to offer explicit guidelines regarding e-portfolio design. Alternative evidence and assessments provided opportunities to focus on personally meaningful topics and to develop strategies for student-centered learning.

Using a Web-based peer-assessment system (*NetPeas*) with undergraduate students, Lin, Liu, and Yuan (2001) examined the relationship between feedback mode (specific and holistic) and thinking patterns (high executive and low executive). They reported that students with high-executive thinking patterns improved significantly using peer assessments, but students with low-executive thinking patterns did not. Predictably, high-executive thinkers tended to offer better quality comments, while low-executive thinkers benefited most from specific than generic feedback.

IMPLICATIONS

NDLEs emphasize active student roles in generating and revising learning goals, selecting tools and resources, and conducting self-assessment. However, comparatively little research exists regarding what or how guidance enhances different capabilities. Different scaffolding strategies (e.g., teachers, peers, and online) can enhance or hamper students' use of resources and learning. Research is needed to identify guidance types and functions and how guidance interacts with other NDLE components as well as the guidance needed to support quality interactions between instructors and peers. Finally, research is needed to balance structured, explicit and open-ended, implicit guidance to support online learning. Alternative assessments have gained widespread interests, but further study is needed to examine their validity for negotiated learning goals involving self-regulation and collaboration.

INFORMAL DISTANCE LEARNING ENVIRONMENTS (IDLES)

According to Dierking (1991), learning is "strongly influenced by setting, social interaction, and individual beliefs, knowledge, and attitudes" (p. 4). Thus, while a given setting can be formal or informal based on its initial design, we use Coombs and Ahmed's (1974) characterization of informal learning:

> The lifelong process by which every individual acquires and accumulates knowledge, skills, attitudes and insights from daily experiences and exposure to the environment—at home, at work, at play; from the example and attitude of families and friends; from travel, reading newspapers and books; or by listening to the radio or viewing films or television. Generally informal education is unorganized, unsystematic and even unintentional at times, yet accounts for the great bulk of any person's total lifetime learning—including that of a highly "schooled" person (p. 8).

Conscious choice or *free-choice* learning is "self-directed, voluntary, and guided by an individual's needs and interests" (http://www.ilinet.org/freechoicelearning.html), and occurs when an individual or group engages in an activity with the intent to learn. While the setting can influence structures (informal vs. formal), free-choice learning is based on individual motivation, interest, and intent. For example, an individual interested in sea life might watch a public television program about aquariums. This program might inspire the viewer to seek additional information about aquariums, to visit Web sites highlighted in the program, or to visit an aquarium in person. Each individual seeks and engages resources based on his or her particular motivation, prior knowledge, and goals for the visit. These differences are at the heart of free-choice learning; each individual guides the experience based on his or her interests.

In contrast, incidental learning as "a byproduct of some other activity, such as task accomplishment, interpersonal interaction, sensing the organizational culture, trial-and-error experimentation, or even formal learning" (Marsick & Watkins, 1991, p. 12). Incidental learning is spontaneous; often the learner is unaware of their learning. For example, an individual who visits the Holocaust Museum Web site searching for information on Hitler's rise to power may incidentally learn about the formation of Axis governments during pre–World War II.

THEORETICAL AND EPISTEMOLOGICAL FOUNDATIONS

Falk, Scott, Dierking, Rennie, and Cohen Jones (2004) described learning as "shifts in attitudes, values, and beliefs; aesthetic understandings; psychomotor skills, such as discovering how it feels to turn a pot or play an instrument; social/cultural dimensions such as learning about someone in your family; and process skills such as thinking critically and refining one's learning skills, or perhaps even learning more about how to use a museum for lifelong learning" (p. 172). Interplay between and among the individual, IDLE affordances, and others in the environment, as well as the motivations, interests, and needs of the learners themselves, are important considerations for learning.

From a sociocultural perspective, IDLE learning emphasizes the importance of culture and context in understanding; social knowledge constructions reflect this understanding (Derry, 1999; McMahon, 1997). Learning can be construed as an individual's ability to engage in ". . . meaningful tasks and solve meaningful problems in an environment that reflects their own personal interests as well as the multiple purposes to which their knowledge will be put in the future" (Collins, Brown, & Newman, 1989, p. 487). There is both an emphasis on the needs of the individual, and a view toward the community in which the individual will be situated.

IDLE LEARNING AFFORDANCES

Given the emergent nature of IDLEs, research has only recently begun to emerge from the perspective of community formation and social interaction.

Collaboration and Interaction

IDLEs provide opportunities to interact and collaborate to promote shared understanding. Various tools, resources, and technologies are used to support learner collaboration and engagement. For example, the Mote Aquarium's SeaTrek Distance Learning Project uses highly interactive videoconferences. Participants interact with educational staff, a presenter, and a technology coordinator during virtual visits, using a combination of live-feed and prerecorded videos of scientists and animals, PowerPoint slides, the Internet, sound effects, and music. Participants can also engage in activities with knowledgeable affiliates (e.g., scientists) to ask questions and explore concepts.

Recently, researchers have studied the impact of the SeaTrek program on students' perceptions and the usability of the program in schools. Ba and Keisch (2004) observed school-based classrooms and videoconferences from the SeaTrek studio, and interviewed project staff and SeaTrek teams in the schools. They also conducted focus groups and administered online surveys. Students and teachers reported improved content knowledge as well as incidental increases in curiosity about science-related professions, use of multimedia technology, and use of video as an educational tool.

On-demand Resources Support Individual Learning

In order to address diverse learner needs, IDLE resources often vary in form and may represent multiple perspectives (Hill, Hannafin, & Domizi, 2005). For example, the online Exploratorium (http://www.exploratorium.edu) both supplements and works independently of the physical museum in California. The Exploratorium is a widely recognized, resource-rich informal learning environment. The Exploratorium Web site is a rich repository, both in number and variety of resources available on the site (see www.exploratorium.edu/educate/dl.html), including images, activities, movies, and audio files. During Webcasts, learners observe and hear experts discuss a variety of topics (e.g., space exploration), and interact via a dynamic e-mail system enabled during the broadcast. This enables real-time access to different resources and expert knowledge that can be pursued according to individual interests.

Ford Motor Company's Learning Network (FLN) also uses static resources extensively. FLN contains more than 400,000 titles, including online courses, e-books, articles, Web sites, and thousands of 20-minute learning objects. Consistent with IDLE principles, resources are designed to support learning when and where needed. Although evaluation data have not yet published publicly, Ford representatives suggest that FLN is both positively received and useful for learning (Sosbe, 2003).

Since resources can vary in number and form, IDLEs may require guidance in the appropriate use resources. Libraries, for example, now employ "virtual reference desks" to assist learners in using online resources. Initially, librarians used e-mail or chat rooms to provide support, but with limited success. Advances in Web-contact center software have enabled reference librarians to provide services that approximate the experience at a call center (e.g., calling for technical assistance at Apple) (Coffman, 2001). Technologies such as *Virtual Reference Desk* enable librarians to provide the just-in-time assistance when working in a virtual library space.

Varied Tools

IDLE tools must be sufficiently robust to support a range of goals and applications per individual goals and needs. Several dynamic tools were used in LEVERAGE (LEarn from Video Extensive Real ATM Gigabit Experiment) to explore the learning of language online. Twenty-six postsecondary participants learned English, French, or Spanish. Videoconferencing was used to connect learners with more knowledgeable others (native speakers), while editing and chat tools were used to provide just-in-time knowledge. Results indicated that students preferred the videoconferencing tool followed by chat to facilitate language learning. Most importantly, use of videoconferencing and chat tools helped learners develop communication skills incidental to the context (e.g., cooperation, flexibility). The dynamic nature of the tools enabled the learners to extend their experience in ways that enabled learning beyond what might have been expected or anticipated.

Manipulation. Tools enabling user manipulation are important for self-study. For example, by using a database learners can gather, explore, and manipulate information gathered during the informal experience. The CancerHelp UK Web site has been studied in terms of how individuals learn about cancer, cancer treatment, and cancer recovery, and how it meets individually defined needs and goals (Tweddle, James, & Daniels, 2000). Using the database, individuals capture unique data for their personal needs, enabling customized analysis and application in real time.

In a two-phase pilot study, Tweddle et al. (2000) interviewed a total of 23 patients and relatives to assess attitudes toward their Web site. During phase one, 14 participants were invited to use the site while being observed, while during the second phase 9 participants representing a mix of gender, age (21–80), and computer experience used the site independently. Results indicated that those who used the site (phase two) independently to search and retrieve information as needed/desired reported positive cognitive and affective outcomes. The authors concluded that manner of site use has important implications for how medical information should be organized and conveyed. By enabling individuals to address personal needs and dynamic questions related to cancer, initial results indicate that CancerHelp met highly situated needs driven by the individual's motivation and need to learn.

Representation. Discussion boards, typically considered a communication tool, can also be used to represent artifacts of understanding. Unlike word processors, they can document the emergence of both individual and shared understanding by reviewing the conversations and reflecting on what has been shared. Gustafson, et al. (2001) demonstrated the power of a computer-based patient communication support system with younger women (under the age of 60) with breast cancer, particularly for disadvantaged groups (e.g., African American women, women without insurance). Using a controlled experiment ($n = 246$), breast cancer patients in the experimental group ($n = 147$) were given access to CHESS (Comprehensive Health Enhancement Support System) to assist with information provision, decision making and emotional support. Results indicated that the experimental group reported better information competence and social support, and the disadvantaged group benefited most.

Community Scaffolds

In IDLEs, human resources scaffold the development of knowledge and understanding using communication tools (e.g., bulletin boards, chat rooms). CENTERS (CollaborativE INformal InTERaction System) was developed to create opportunities for interaction in an online environment (Contreras-Castillo, Favela, Pérez-Fragoso, & Santamaría-del-Angel, 2004). Participants came from two Mexican universities and included 15 graduate students, 28 undergraduate students, and four teachers enrolled in one of four asynchronous, online courses. Mexican students and their teachers were able to identify other participants logged in to the CENTERS system and interact with them through chat and instant messaging. The researchers reported that the system satisfied the students' need to interact, increased collaboration, helped students learn content knowledge, and helped build social relationships between classmates and their instructors, thereby reducing feelings of isolation.

The CENTERS interface was designed to allow users just-in-time interactions with their peers and instructor. When students were confused, they could send a message to another user logged in to the system. If that student was also confused, they could discuss the issue in a chat room and ultimately ask their teacher for help using those same communication tools. The researchers suggested that the exchanges helped the learners strengthen relationships with classmates and the instructor and improve understanding of the course material.

Several online mentoring communities scaffold learning informally. MentorNet (www .mentornet.net) is designed to link female students with working professionals in science and math. A 2003 evaluation involved over 2,000 matched mentors and mentees who completed a survey, with a subset completing interviews (see full report at http://www.mentornet.net/documents/files/WomenofColorFinalReportMay2004.pdf). According to Barsion (2004), the vast majority of the participants reported a positive experience with MentorNet for informal learning, including information on careers and fields of study. Participants also reported that mentor support and encouragement was important for their educational experiences. Like CENTERS, MentorNet enables multiples levels of interaction between less and more knowledgeable others.

Individual Assessment

While assessment is important, individual accountability is the primary focus of IDLE assessment. Fundamentally, the uniquely individual goals and aims of participants frame the assessment; each individual determines the extent to which his or her goals and aims have been addressed. Such assessments, however, can prove difficult to identify or validate. Rennert-Ariev (2005) identified several challenges with self-assessment, including the myriad of highly personal and individualized perspectives that influence the assessment. Halliday and Hager (2002) suggested that context should be considered when judging formal of informal learning processes; context varies with the individual situations and circumstances of individuals.

In IDLEs, learners have reported difficulty identifying their unplanned or incidental learning outcomes. McFerrin (1999) studied a group of 22 students in a graduate-level asynchronous online distance education class, and reported that incidental learning, including personal development, time management, self-directed behaviors, self-confidence, and self-regulation, resulted from the use of the technology itself. These skills were not included in the course objectives, but resulted from activities related to participation. McFerrin found that the students did not differentiate between these incidental outcomes and those that were intended in the course design.

IMPLICATIONS

IDLEs have become increasingly prevalent in the workplace, community, science centers, and museums. It is paradoxical, therefore, that research remains so sparse. In many ways, IDLEs remain in their infancy. We need to expand our understanding of how people learn informally at a distance, particularly what people use, how they use it, and what they want to get out of it (see Imel, 2003, for an overview of issues). Of particular interest is the role of individual interaction with different resources, scaffolds, and peers and how these interactions might lead to learning. Given that IDLEs support different interests and goals, individual tool and resource use may appear idiosyncratic. Many interactions may prove to be uniquely metacognitive and reflective in nature.

However, individuals also interact with materials and others who explore the IDLE. For designers to understand how to support learning in such environments, rich descriptions of individual use of tools are needed. In addition, we need to better understand the preferences of different types of learners so that appropriate tools, resources, and interactions can be made available. While self-assessment may prove difficult, Gerber, Marek, and Cavallo (2001) developed a tool to guide assessment of informal learning in a more systematic fashion. Initial results are encouraging, but work is needed to refine and extend the use of the tool.

FUTURE DIRECTIONS FOR NDLEs AND IDLEs

Communication tools are central to both NDLEs and IDLEs where negotiation of ideas and exploration of individual resources are at a premium. While research has examined the affordances of different tools for communication and established student preference for each tool in specific contexts (Davidson-Shivers, Muilenburg, & Tanner, 2001), little research exists describing how tools should be structured to support specific learning and thinking interactions (Tallent-Runnels et al., 2006). Continued context-specific research (i.e., NDLE, IDLE) will help facilitate answers to these questions. For example, Thomas (2002) identified that a variety of factors (e.g., familiarity with content and discussion technologies) can influence the level of student engagement in high-level thinking. He also indicated that discussion boards do not necessarily support engagement in conversational learning or shared knowledge building. Thus, one avenue of research is to examine how the interface and structure of communication tools can support student engagement in true learning dialogue.

The impact of cultural and informal interactions on learning in the online environment requires further study. For example, peer support plays an important role in NDLEs and IDLEs.

Discourse and conversation cues (e.g., emoticons) may help to acculturate students to the culture of, improve their performance in, and enable community building in online learning environments (Bielman, Putney, & Strudler, 2003). Thus, it is important to examine how peers and community establish, communicate, and refine discourse and how community affiliation and belonging affect learning.

A final recommendation is related to the structure of these environments. Students have indicated that access to multiple resources (e.g., course notes, lecture materials, and study aids) enhanced their content knowledge (Newnham, Mather, Grattan, Holmes, & Gardner, 1998). In NDLEs, multiple options enabled learners to assess, select, and use resources based on need and suitability (Kim et al., 2005). Research on the process of evaluating, selecting, and using resources for individual goals in NDLEs and IDLEs is needed to determine how resources should be structured and administered while minimizing cognitive overload and confusion.

REFERENCES

Armatas, C., Holt, D., & Rice, M. (2003). Impacts of an online-supported, resource-based learning environment: Does one size fit all? *Distance Education, 24*(2), 141–158.

Ba, H., & Keisch, D. (2004, May). *Bridging the gap between formal and informal learning: Evaluating the SeaTrek Distance Learning Project*: Center for Children and Technology.

Barsion, S. J. (2004). MentorNet: 2002–2003 program evaluation. New York: SJB Research Consulting.

Bielman, V. A., Putney, L. G., & Strudler, N. (2003). Constructing community in a postsecondary virtual classroom. *Journal of Educational Computing Research, 29*(1), 119–144.

Clark, R. E. (2003). Research on Web-based learning: A half-full glass. In R. Bruning, C. A. Horn, & L. M. PytlikZillig (Eds.), *Web-base learning: What do we know? Where do we go?* (pp. 1–22). Greenwich, CT: Information Age.

Coffman, S. (2001). Distance education and virtual reference: Where are we headed? *Computers in Libraries, 21*(4). Retrieved December 15, 2006, from http://www.infotoday.com/cilmag/apr01/coffman.htm

Collins, A., Brown, J. S., & Newman, S. E. (1989). Cognitive apprenticeship: Teaching the crafts of reading, writing, and mathematics. In L. B. Resnick (Ed.), *Knowing, learning, and instruction* (pp. 453–494). Hillsdale, NJ: Lawrence Erlbaum Associates.

Contreras-Castillo, J., Favela, J., Pérez-Fragoso, C., & Santamaría-del-Angel, E. (2004). Informal interactions and their implications for online courses. *Computers & Education, 42*(2), 149–168.

Coombs, P. H., & Ahmed, M. (1974). *Attacking rural poverty: How nonformal education can help*. Baltimore: Johns Hopkins University Press.

Dabbagh, N., & Kitsantas, A. (2005). Using Web-based pedagogical tools as scaffolds for self-regulated learning. *Instructional Science, 33*(5–6), 513–540.

Daroszewski, E. B., Kinser, A. G., & Lloyd, S. L. (2004). Online, directed journaling in community health advanced practice nursing clinical education. *Journal of Nursing Education, 43*(4), 175–181.

Davidson-Shivers, G. V., Muilenburg, L. Y., & Tanner, E. J. (2001). How do students participate in synchronous and asynchronous online discussions? *Journal of Educational Computing Research, 25*(4), 351–366.

Derry, S. J. (1999). A Fish called peer learning: Searching for common themes. In A. M. O'Donnell & A. King (Eds.), *Cognitive perspectives on peer learning* (pp. 197–211). Mahwah, NJ: Lawrence Erlbaum Associates.

Derry, S. J., & the STEP Team. (2004). Estepweb.Org: A case of theory-based Web course design. In A. O'Donnell & C. Hmelo (Eds.), *Collaboration, reasoning and technology*. Mahwah, NJ: Lawrence Erlbaum Associates.

Dierking, L. D. (1991). Learning theory and learning styles: An overview. *Journal of Museum Education, 16*(1), 4–6.

Dodge, B. (1995). WebQuests: A technique for Internet-based learning. *Distance Educator, 1*(2), 10–13.

Dodge, B. (2001). Focus: Five rules for writing a great Webquest. *Learning and Leading with Technology, 28*(8), 6–9, 58.

Falk, J. H., Scott, C., Dierking, L., Rennie, L., & Cohen Jones, M. (2004). Interactives and visitor learning. *Curator, 47*(2), 171–198.

Garrison, D. R., & Cleveland-Innes, M. (2005). Facilitating cognitive presence in online learning: Interaction is not enough. *The American Journal of Distance Education, 19*(3), 133–148.

Ge, X., & Land, S. M. (2003). Scaffolding students' problem-solving processes in an ill-structured task using question prompts and peer interactions. *Educational Technology Research and Development, 51*(1), 21–38.

Gerber, B. L., Marek, E. A., & Cavallo, A. M. L. (2001). Development of an informal learning opportunities assay. *International Journal of Science Education, 23*(6), 569–583.

Gerber, S., Scott, L., & Clements, D. H. (2005). Instructor influence on reasoned argument in discussion boards. *Educational Technology Research and Development, 53*(2), 25–39.

Gulikers, J. T. M., Bastiaens, T. J., & Kirschner, P. A. (2004). A five-dimensional framework for authentic assessment. *Educational Technology Research and Development, 52*(3), 67–86.

Gustafson, D. H., Hawkins, R., Pingree, S., McTavish, F., Arora, N. K., Mendenhall, J., et al. (2001). Effect of computer support on younger women with breast cancer. *Journal of General Internal Medicine, 16*(7), 435–445.

Halliday, J., & Hager, P. (2002). Context, judgment and learning. *Educational Theory, 52*(4), 429–443.

Harasim, L. (2002). *What makes online learning communities successful? The role of collaborative learning in social and intellectual development.* Greenwich, CT: Information Age.

Hill, J. R. (2002). Overcoming obstacles and creating connections: Community building in Web-based learning environments. *Journal of Computing in Higher Education, 14*(1), 67–86.

Hill, J. R., & Hannafin, M. J. (1997). Cognitive strategies and learning from the World Wide Web. *Educational Technology Research and Development, 45*(4), 37–64.

Hill, J. R., & Hannafin, M. J. (2001). Teaching and learning in digital environments: The resurgence of resource-based learning environments. *Educational Technology Research and Development, 49*(3), 37–52.

Hill, J. R., Hannafin, M. J., & Domizi, D. P. (2005). Resource-based learning and informal learning environments: Prospects and challenges. In L. T. W. Hin & R. Subramaniam (Eds.), *E-learning and virtual science centers* (pp. 110–125). Hershey, PA: Information Science.

Hoadley, C. M., & Linn, M. C. (2000). Teaching science through online, peer discussions: Speakeasy in the knowledge integration environment. *International Journal of Science Education, 22*(8), 839–857.

Imel, S. (2003). Informal adult learning and the Internet. Trends and issues alert. *ERIC Clearinghouse: Adult, Career, and Vocational Education.*

Jonassen, D. H., & Kwon, H., II. (2001). Communication patterns in computer mediated versus face-to-face group problem solving. *Educational Technology Research and Development, 49*(1), 35–51.

Kim, H., Hannafin, M. J., & Kim, M. C. (2005). Online case-based learning: Components, applications, and assessment. *Distance Learning, 1*(5), 23–31.

Kim, M. C., & Hannafin, M. J. (2004). Designing online learning environments to support scientific inquiry. *Quarterly Review of Distance Education, 5*(1), 1–10.

Kitsantas, A., & Dabbagh, N. (2004). Promoting self-regulation in distributed learning environments with Web-based pedagogical tools: An exploratory study. *Journal on Excellence in College Teaching, 15*(1/2), 119–142.

Lin, S. S. J., Liu, E. Z. F., & Yuan, S. M. (2001). Web-based peer assessment: Feedback for students with various thinking-styles. *Journal of Computer Assisted Learning, 17*(4), 420–432.

Linn, M. C., Clark, D., & Slotta, J. D. (2003). WISE design for knowledge integration. *Science Education, 87*(4), 517–538.

Macdonald, J., Heap, N., & Mason, R. (2001). "Have I learnt it?" Evaluating skills for resource-based study using electronic resources. *British Journal of Educational Technology, 32*(4), 419–433.

Marsick, V. J., & Watkins, K. E. (1991). *Informal and incidental learning in the workplace.* London, New York: Routledge.

Mason, R., Pegler, C., & Weller, M. (2004). E-portfolios: An assessment tool for online courses. *British Journal of Educational Technology, 35*(6), 717–727.

McFerrin, K. M. (1999, March). *Incidental learning in a higher education asynchronous online distance education course*. Paper presented at the SITE99: Society for Information Technology and Teacher Education International Conference, San Antonio, TX.

McIsaac, M. S., Blocher, J. M., Mahes, V., & Vrasidas, C. (1999). Student and teacher perceptions of interaction in online computer-mediated communication. *Educational Media International, 36*(2), 121–131.

McMahon, M. (1997, December). *Social constructivism and the World Wide Web—A paradigm for learning*. Paper presented at the ASCILITE Conference, Perth, Australia.

Newnham, R., Mather, A., Grattan, J., Holmes, A., & Gardner, A. (1998). An evaluation of the use of Internet sources as a basis for geography coursework. *Journal of Geography in Higher Education, 22*(1), 19–34.

Oliver, K., & Hannafin, M. J. (2001). Developing and refining mental models in open-ended learning environments: A case study. *Educational Technology Research and Development, 49*(4), 5–32.

Piaget, J. (1972). *The psychology of the child*. New York: Basic Books.

Recker, M. M., Walker, A., & Lawless, K. (2003). What do you recommend? Implementation and analyses of collaborative information filtering of Web resources for education. *Instructional Science, 31*(4–5), 299–316.

Reiser, B. J. (2004). Scaffolding complex learning: The mechanisms of structuring and problematizing student work. *Journal of the Learning Sciences, 13*(3), 273–304.

Rennert-Ariev, P. (2005). A theoretical model for the authentic assessment of teaching. *Practical Assessment, Research & Evaluation, 10*(2). Retrieved December 15, 2006, from http://www.pareonline.net/pdf/v10n2.pdf

Soloway, E., & Wallace, R. (1997). Does the Internet support student inquiry? Don't ask. *Communications of the ACM, 40*(5), 11–12.

Sosbe, T. (2003, May). Ed Sketch: Ford's drive toward quality education. *Chief Learning Officer.* Retrieved December 15, 2006, from http://www.clomedia.com/content/templates/clo_article.asp?articleid=180&zoneid=4

Tallent-Runnels, M. K., Thomas, J. A., Lan, W. Y., Cooper, S., Ahern, T. C., Shaw, S. M., et al. (2006). Teaching courses online: A review of the research. *Review of Educational Research, 76*(1), 93–135.

Thomas, M. J. W. (2002). Learning within incoherent structures: The space of online discussion forums. *Journal of Computer Assisted Learning, 18*(3), 351–366.

Tweddle, S., James, C., & Daniels, H. (2000). Use of a Web site for learning about cancer. *Computers & Education, 35*(4), 309–325.

Uribe, D., Klein, J. D., & Sullivan, H. (2003). The effect of computer-mediated collaborative learning on solving ill-defined problems. *Educational Technology Research and Development, 51*(1), 5–19.

Wallace, R. M., Kupperman, J., Krajcik, J., & Soloway, E. (2000). Science on the Web: Students online in a sixth-grade classroom. *Journal of the Learning Sciences, 9*(1), 75–104.

Whipp, J. L. (2003). Scaffolding critical reflection in online discussions—helping prospective teachers think deeply about field experiences in urban schools. *Journal of Teacher Education, 54*(4), 321–333.

Whipp, J. L., & Chiarelli, S. (2004). Self-regulation in a Web-based course: A case study. *Educational Technology Research and Development, 52*(4), 5–22.

Yang, Y.-T. C., Newby, T. J., & Bill, R. L. (2005). Using Socratic questioning to promote critical thinking skills through asynchronous discussion forums in distance learning environments. *The American Journal of Distance Education, 19*(3), 163–181.

23

Developing Text for Web-Based Instruction

Diane J. Davis
University of Pittsburgh

In the years since the first volume of this *Handbook* was published, the World Wide Web has evolved from an emerging to an essential phenomenon in American distance education as educators have capitalized upon its potential for interactivity. The adoption of course-management systems has accelerated Web-based instruction in our colleges and universities for both distance and distributed learning. At the University of Pittsburgh, for example, use of the Blackboard system expanded by an average of 33% each year following its adoption in 1998 and this growth rate is not atypical. As Web-based courses grow in number, so does use of electronic text as faculty routinely write, post, or link to readings that are an integral part of their courses. Although use of multimedia in Web-based courses is growing, faculty still rely upon textbook chapters, journal articles, and instructor-authored explanations of content. Strategies for the effective integration and use of text in Web-based courses will be useful to course developers.

DEFINITION AND SCOPE

The term *online text,* as used in this chapter, refers to electronic text which often includes embedded Internet links, multimedia, and instructional aids, and which is generally intended to be read and studied in a linear, sequential manner for purposeful learning. This kind of text appears in online journals and Web-based courses. A course designer can develop various degrees of linearity in the instructional sequence from instructor-planned and controlled at one end of the continuum to a completely unstructured environment at the other. Unstructured environments seem to be more suited to learners with substantial prior knowledge or expertise, while the more structured, teacher-directed sequencing is appropriate for developing initial knowledge (Jonassen, Mayes, & McAleese, 1993).

This chapter is concerned with instructional text delivered via the Web. Although devices and appliances have emerged to facilitate the reading of digital text, some of which even offer a "read aloud" button that provides synthetic speech (Brown, 2001), and iPods offer audio and video that is portable and convenient to use, the focus here is on text that is embedded within the Web-based course.

Finally, the chapter does not focus on technical elements of Web page design, such as typeface, layout, and use of color, or on the design of navigation systems, although both are relevant to the design of good instructional hypertext. A significant body of literature is evolving on these topics, including Muter's (1996) comprehensive review of research on interface-design techniques to optimize the reading of continuous text. Also useful are the online *User Interface Design Newsletter*, which publishes an annual summary of user interface research findings, and *Usability News*.

BACKGROUND

Much has happened since 1987 when Hartley cautioned, "It may take years for people to become as familiar with electronic text as they are with printed text" (p. 14) and even since 1997 when Shneiderman observed that the Web was "still in the Model T stage of development" (p. 27). Some of the obstacles to reading on the Web, such as eye strain and screen size, have been addressed by advancements in technology, and others, such as typeface and line length, by advancements in research and practice. See, for example, the work on Visual Syntactic Text Formatting, which uses a cascading format to reveal syntax in text (*LiveInk*, 2005).

In the past decade, we also have learned more about the idea that "how" we read online is related to "why" we are reading (O'Hara, 1996; Unz & Hesse, 1999), and we recognize that Web-based instruction must take advantage of the special capabilities of the Web in order to reflect established learning theories and proven instructional design practices (Frizell & Hübscher, 2002). This chapter draws upon research about reading and electronic text to argue the importance of purpose, structure, and interactivity in online instructional hypertext. It includes a review of comprehension strategies used by competent readers and discusses how they can be facilitated in an online course. The goal of the chapter is to provide faculty and other course designers with some guidelines and ideas for the effective use of text in online courses.

READING ONLINE

One message that has a fair amount of research support is that learners do not read lengthy text online. Ward and Newlands (1998), for example, in a study on use of Web-based lectures, found that two-thirds of their students immediately printed the online lectures and most of the others read first at the computer, then printed the lectures. Other studies support this observation of learner behavior (Oliver, Omari, & Herrington, 1998; De Groote & Dorsch, 2001; Kurniawan & Zaphiris, 2001). There also is evidence to suggest that online reading is problematic for students. While earlier studies comparing online with print reading have indicated that people read electronic text more slowly (Gould et al., 1987; Gray & Shasha, 1989), and that it is more tiring than reading from print (Cushman, 1986; Wilkinson & Robinshaw, 1987), Lacroix (1999) suggests that modern technology has eliminated many of the problems that contributed to slower and more tiring reading of computer screens, and there are even some indications that screen reading now can be as fast as reading from printed text. The introduction and rapid development of the graphical user interface and computer graphics cards for displaying higher resolutions, movement to flat panel displays, and new screen materials and technologies continue to improve the online reading experience. With time and experience, students' expectations, along with increasingly effective Web-learning strategies, are likely to evolve to accommodate more sustained use of electronic text for learning.

Just as students are not yet fully accustomed to learning from online text, faculties are not yet experienced in its development. There were so many examples of early faculty attempts to duplicate their printed materials online that the term "shovelware" evolved to describe the phenomenon. These early materials failed to take advantage of the interactivity of the Web and it is not surprising that students merely printed them to read offline. As faculty become more experienced in the design and use of online hypertext, they are developing course materials that optimize use of the Web as an instructional tool and thereby creating incentives for student use.

INTERPRETATIONS OF RESEARCH:
FURTHER CAUTIONS

A fair amount of the inquiry and observation supporting today's "common knowledge" about authoring online text is focused not on use of the Web for instruction, but rather on its use for commercial and recreational purposes. Many of the best guides for writing on the Web, both online and in print, are intended for the design of attractive and effective commercial Web sites. The oft-cited works of Morkes and Nielson (1997) and Nielson (2000) are examples. Even the highly referenced *Yale Style Guide* (Lynch & Horton, 1997) refers readers to Sun Microsystems' *Guide to Web Style* and the *Ameritech Web Page User Interface and Design Guidelines*. Information about the design of good Web sites is useful and important, but its ability to be generalized to the design of good Web courses is limited, not in the least because of the difference in purpose. Purpose, or the task at hand—and most notably the complexity of that task—has proven to be a critical factor in research on the efficacy of hypertext. Chen and Rada (1996) addressed task complexity in their meta-analysis of experimental studies on interacting with hypertext. The fact that so much more is known about creating good Web *sites* than is known about creating good Web *courses* probably reflects the reality that there are more good sites than good courses to study. That this reality is changing, however, is evidenced by Campbell (2000) in her review of theory-based architectures and frameworks for Web design, and in the examples of good practice she provides.

Another problem of overgeneralization is the failure to distinguish between research and observation about different types of computer-based text. Some of the best articles on the use of electronic text (Gillingham, 1993; van Nimwegen, Pouw, & van Oostendorp, 1999; Unz & Hesse, 1999, for example) were based on hypertext systems designed for searching. Hyperbase research typically has focused on the system's "searchability," and when used for instruction, on students' ability to locate answers to specific questions, while online instructional text is intended for reading and comprehension. Just as caution is warranted in generalizing from research on printed text to electronic text (Hartley, 1987; Muter, 1996), so should caution be used in applying the conclusions of research on one form of hypertext to the design and use of another form. Unz and Hesse (1999) call for the development of a classification scheme for hypertext systems for just this reason: the difficulty of comparing and generalizing results from hypertext research.

Overgeneralization should not discourage us from trying to develop, evaluate, and improve instructional text for Web-based courses. To this end, the next section of this chapter focuses on three broad, fundamental text-design concepts: purpose, structure, and interactivity.

THE IMPORTANCE OF PURPOSE

We seem to learn more effectively and efficiently when we approach the learning activity with specific purposes in mind. We need to understand why we are reading a particular text, for example, and what kind of information we should be looking for as we read. Given the greater potential for distraction, via links or scrolling for example, this principle is particularly important for online text. Unz and Hesse (1999) pointed to the lack of identified purpose, such as locating information, reading comprehension, or recall, as a shortcoming in many studies they reviewed on the use of hypertext for learning.

Therefore, well-designed instructional text should begin with a rationale explaining the function of the text and what the instructor expects the student to learn from it. This is not to suggest that students will fail to learn other things from a text, but rather that they are more likely to learn what the instructor intends them to learn from it if those expectations are explicit. Some instructional text authors communicate purpose by including specific objectives at the beginning of text. Such objectives are more effective—and more likely to be read—if they are linguistically interesting and embedded in the natural flow of the text (Bernard & Lundgren, 1994). Additional strategies for communicating purpose in online text are discussed below.

THE IMPORTANCE OF STRUCTURE

One of the most pervasive themes in literature on electronic text is the importance of structure. Structure may be even more important in electronic text because of the lack of physical cues regarding the length of the document and its parts (Piolat, Roussey, & Thunin, 1997). If the text includes links to other texts with differing structures, this adds complexity to the naturally ill-structured nature of some hypertext (Gillingham, 1993). In their discussion of text design for distance education, Bernard and Lundgren (1994) emphasize the importance of clear, concise writing for text comprehension, regardless of medium. Thuring, Hannemann, and Haake (1995) add to the argument for structure by citing research showing that a readers' ability to understand and remember a text, to construct a "mental model" of it, depends upon its coherence, which is facilitated by a well-defined structure. Both Bernard and Lundgren (1994) and Parlangeli, Marchigiani, and Bagnara (1999) recognize the value of structure in reducing cognitive load—clear, consistent structure enables the reader to focus more mental effort on reading and comprehending text content than on trying to figure out its logic. Lacroix's (1999) experiments support the notion that text comprehension involves global as well as local levels of processing and uses whole text structure as input.

Strategies for providing structure in electronic documents include use of tables of contents, overviews, headings and subheadings, graphical maps, and stable screen layout. Readers seem to respond to global structure indicators, such as headings, menu order, and underlining, when they are reading complex expository text to synthesize information, a task common in college-level courses (Lacroix, 1999). Continuity overviews, showing the relationship between previous and new reading assignments, also can be useful (Bernard & Lundgren, 1994).

Navigation and screen design, while not explored at length in this chapter, have particular importance for the structure and coherence of electronic text and the amount of cognitive load required for its use. For example, use of the page format, as opposed to scrolling, has been shown to enable users to develop a better "sense of text" (Piolat, Roussey, & Thunin, 1997). Stable screen layout, visualization of structure, and descriptive links increase document coherence and reduce cognitive load (Thuring et al., 1995). Use of embedded "closed" screens (information nodes that open and close within a document, but do not exit the document) helps prevent reader disorientation and retains the text's structural coherence.

Metaphors—such as file cabinets, bookshelves, and shopping malls—also have been used successfully for structuring hyperbases (Trumbull, Gay, & Mazur, 1992; Shneiderman, 1997; Streitz, 1988) and may also have application for more linear instructional text, particularly for organizing multiple readings in a section or across an entire course. One could easily imagine how content-relevant metaphors, such as a museum display for a history or an anthropology course or a street scene for a course in social psychology, could be used to add structure to academic readings. Metaphors have the advantage of providing opportunities for students to activate prior knowledge and relate it to current learning as they consider how the metaphor relates to the new information. Having students create their own structure for information also is a valuable learning aid. This technique is used as a synthesizing task after the student has read the content.

Regardless of the strategies selected for achieving it, clarity in document structure should be of paramount importance in the design of online instructional text. Great care should be taken to explicate and reinforce that structure in order to reduce cognitive load and facilitate learner comprehension.

THE IMPORTANCE OF INTERACTIVITY

Probably the greatest advantage of electronic text over printed materials is its capacity for interactivity. Students studying online can access related information through links, visualize through dynamic applets, and receive immediate feedback on quizzes. Instructors can enhance student motivation and learning through use of multimedia, and they can increase the powerful educational effects of active learning (The National Reading Research Center, 1994; Campbell, 2000). Moore (1989) describes three types of interaction in distance education: learner-content interaction, learner-instructor interaction, and learner-learner interaction. Each is relevant to the discussion of Web-based course design, but the emphasis here is on learner-content interaction as affected by the design of online text. It is interesting, although not surprising, that some experienced distance education instructors rated *asynchronous learner-material interaction* as more important for learning than either *synchronous teacher-learner* or *synchronous learner-learner interaction* in distance education courses (Soo & Bonk, 1998).

COMPREHENSION

Pearson, Roehler, Dole, and Duffy (1992) synthesized current knowledge about reading comprehension to identify seven strategies consistently used by successful readers. They also proposed general "rules of thumb" for reading instruction. The reading strategies they identified are reviewed here within the context of online instruction, and used to suggest techniques that can be used by instructors and designers to enhance comprehension of Web-based instructional text.

STRATEGIES AND TECHNIQUES

Pearson et al. (1992) identified seven strategies used by active, thoughtful, expert readers and used these strategies to develop guidelines for a reading comprehension curriculum. Web-based text can be constructed to teach, encourage, and reinforce these seven strategies.

1. Use Existing Knowledge to Make Sense of Text

Comprehension improves when a reader relates the topics and information in the reading to what he or she already knows. Good readers recognize familiar concepts and ideas and draw accurate inferences about their importance in the reading. Pretests or prereading questions can prompt the reader to activate relevant prior knowledge, as can explicit prompts, such as:

- *Review the title and major headings of this reading.*
- *How would you define [the main concept of the reading]?*
- *What have you already studied about this topic in this course? In other courses?*
- *Why do you think this reading has been assigned at this point in the course and what do you expect to learn from it?*

In a Web-based course, instructors can enhance the use of questions and prompts by creating teams or pairs of students to encourage interaction and feedback in responding to questions. The Web makes it relatively easy for students to compare answers or experiences with a teammate or within a small group.

Knowledge about the structure of the text and the purpose of the reading, discussed earlier, also facilitate the reader's ability to identify and integrate prior learning. Well-crafted instructional text provides:

- a rationale and goals for the reading
- an introduction that describes structure and organization
- additional organizational cues, such as an outline, table of contents, or concept map
- specific statements of objectives

The instructor in an online environment can use this strategy to enhance immediacy by developing an audio-recorded introduction, overview, or rationale for readings. This added social presence may also encourage dialogue and provide motivation for students, and is likely to increase perceived achievement and course satisfaction (Richardson & Swan, 2003).

Good readers activate and use prior knowledge not just at the beginning, but throughout the reading assignment. This is encouraged through occasional, explicit opportunities for reflection, such as embedded questions asking students specifically to relate what they are reading to previous content in the course or in the reading itself. Links to definitions or ideas studied previously may create less distraction when placed within such questions and, therefore, be more effective than in the reading itself.

2. Monitor Comprehension Throughout the Text

Reading for comprehension is an active endeavor and its purpose is to make sense of the content of the text. In addition to relating new ideas in the reading to prior knowledge, students who read effectively pause at key points to review, reflect on what was read, and try to summarize or restate ideas in their own words. They monitor their progress and often stop to reread when they lose focus or feel they have not fully understood the passage. These activities help readers to monitor their comprehension and to recognize when they are having difficulty.

Self-monitoring of comprehension can be encouraged in readings through the use of occasional, explicit opportunities for reflection, such as embedded questions that require students to stop and reflect on the meaning of what they are reading or to summarize the content encountered thus far. Students should be encouraged to pause more frequently when reading complex or difficult text.

Within online electronic text, it is relatively easy to insert specific directions and cues to encourage the metacognitive task of monitoring comprehension. The online environment also facilitates comprehension-monitoring quizzes to help readers to more quickly identify misunderstandings and receive corrective feedback.

3. Repair Comprehension When it Goes Awry

Good readers use a variety of strategies to regulate and repair errors or failures in comprehension. They read more slowly when they encounter difficult text, they reread or refer back to sections or ideas in the text, they ask themselves questions about the text, and they try to draw inferences and relate those inferences to one another to strive for meaning and consistency. In a Web environment, course developers can facilitate comprehension repair by inserting cues to encourage careful reading or rereading of difficult text, or by using questions that include feedback and explanations that help to correct misunderstandings. If a student answers a question incorrectly, the instructor can embed links to easily refer the student back to the relevant section of text. Guiding questions can direct the focus of rereading, discussion boards can provide students with opportunities to interact about the ideas they've read, and small-group assignments can enable collaboration to create meaning and shared understanding. For collaborative strategies, controls must be designed to elicit individual as well as group comprehension-monitoring and repair activities.

4. Determine What's Important in the Text

Comprehending what we read, particularly in academic text, requires us to distinguish important ideas and relate them to one another and to the supportive material provided. Good readers do not memorize what they read. Instead, they develop an organized mental representation and understanding of the information provided in the reading. Pearson et al. (1992) cite research demonstrating that readers use the purpose established for the reading to determine what is important in the text. As noted above, establishing purpose is particularly important for Web-based courses in which scrolling or embedded links can so easily distract the reader. Even though good readers are more adept at identifying or developing a purpose for a given reading, this information should be provided or elicited as part of the instructional process.

In addition to relying upon the overall purpose or goals for reading text, good readers reflect on what they read to identify the author's main points and to make sure they understand those points. They are aware of cues such as key words, headings, and summarizing statements, and use them to confirm central ideas. Such microstrategies occur, of course, within the context of broader background knowledge, such as the purpose of the course, the priorities of the instructor, and the biases toward or past experiences with the text's author.

In online text, instructors can embed cues into the text to alert students to important ideas. They can use quizzes, discussion questions, and assignments that require the application and synthesis of important ideas. Some online courses rely on quizzes to motivate students to complete assigned readings. Therefore, items used for this purpose must be carefully constructed to avoid misdirecting students by focusing on supporting details rather than the main ideas of a reading. Successful students are able to distinguish between the overall goals and objectives of a course or module and the detailed information that is provided to help them achieve those broader aims.

5. Synthesize Information from Readings

In general, analysis is defined as the procedure by which we break down an intellectual or substantial whole into parts or components. Synthesis is defined as the opposite procedure: to combine separate elements or components in order to form a coherent whole. (Ritchey, 1996)

Developing summaries is a primary strategy used to synthesize information because it requires readers to bring together the ideas of the reading into one or more coherent and accurate statements. Good readers seek and verbalize key ideas, thus carrying out tasks of analysis and synthesis throughout their reading. They ask questions of themselves to clarify the central ideas in a paragraph or section, and they try to verbalize to themselves how those ideas relate to ideas in earlier parts of the reading or other readings they've already completed.

Instructors can facilitate the synthesis process by requiring students to summarize central ideas from their readings and then encouraging teams or groups of students to share their perceptions about which ideas are central and how they relate. Individually or in teams, students in online courses can be given assignments that involve creating a paragraph, a timeline, a concept map, or a table to show ideas and relationships within and across readings.

6. Draw Inferences During and After Reading

Thoughtful, effective readers continually draw inferences from their reading and even predict what will come next. Higher-level text, like that used in online university courses, rarely provides every detail that readers need to comprehend it; rather, readers must draw upon their existing knowledge to develop a hypothesis about the author's message and then must use the information in the text to confirm or adapt that hypothesis. For example, the phrase that clarifies *higher-level learning* in the previous sentence could have been omitted under the assumption readers would infer it to be the kind of text used in online university courses since that is the topic of this chapter. Instructors can embed questions into their online readings that encourage students to consider the implications of a given passage, rather than relying solely on the printed words. Students also can be asked to make inferences about the author's point of view and potential biases, based on the text and their knowledge of its author.

7. Ask Questions

Pearson et al. (1992) cite theorists who propose that the very process of generating questions leads to deeper processing and better comprehension and learning. They also report that there seems to be a benefit to teaching readers to ask good questions, particularly higher-order questions. In an online course, students could work in teams to develop test questions for one another based on their reading. They could submit their best questions and answers to the instructor or to another team for feedback and grading, along with any questions they were unable to answer on their own. Online help could provide just-in-time guidance to teach students about levels of learning, to establish expectations for the kinds of questions they should create, and to provide good models for those questions.

CONCLUSIONS

Developers of online courses should pay particular attention to the design of online text. They will facilitate student learning if they explicate the purpose and structure of online readings, and if they maintain interactivity. Furthermore, online text can be designed to encourage students' routine use and mastery of strategies that are proven to enhance reading comprehension. The kinds of strategies outlined by Pearson and his colleagues for improved comprehension are a good starting point.

Interestingly, Mokhtari and Reichard (2002) have developed a self-report instrument to assess adolescents' and adults' metacognitive awareness and perceived use of reading strategies. Their synthesis of 30 specific strategies represents global reading, support reading, and problem solving. The instrument could help students become more aware of the kinds of activities that may facilitate their own reading comprehension.

REFERENCES

Bernard, R. M., & Lundgren, K. M. (1994). Learner assessment and text design strategies for distance education. *Canadian Journal of Educational Communication, 23*(2), 133–152.

Brown, G. J. (2001). Beyond print: Reading digitally. *Library Hi Tech, 19*(4), 390–399.

Campbell, K. (1999). *The Web: Design for active learning.* Retrieved December 21, 2006. from University of Alberta, Academic Technologies for Learning Website: http://www.atl.ualberta.ca/documents/articles/activeLearning001.htm

Chen, C., & Rada, R. (1996). Interacting with hypertext: A meta-analysis of experimental studies. *Human Computer Interaction, 11*(2), 125–156.

Cushman, W. H. (1986). Reading from microfiche, VDT and the printed page: Subjective fatigue and performance. *Human Factors, 28*(1), 63–73.

De Groote, S. L., & Dorsch, J. L. (2001). Online journals: Impact on print journal usage. *Bulletin of the Medical Library Association, 89*, 372–8.

Gillingham, M. G. (1993). Effects of question complexity and reader strategies on adults' hypertext comprehension. *Journal of Research on Computing in Education, 26*(1), 1–15.

Gould, J. D., Alfaro, L., Barnes, V., Finn, R., Grischkowsky, N., & Minuto, A. (1987). Reading is slower from CRT displays than from paper: Attempts to isolate a single variable explanation. *Human Factors, 29*(3), 269–299.

Gray, S. H., & Shasha, D. (1989). To link or not to link? Empirical guidance for the design of nonlinear text systems. *Behavior Research Methods, Instruments, & Computers, 21*(2), 326–333.

Hartley, J. (1987). Designing electronic text: The role of print-based research. *Educational Communication and Technology, 35*(1), 3–17.

Hübscher, R., & Frizell, S. (2002). Aligning theory and web-based instructional design practice with design patterns. *World Conference on E-Learning in Corp., Govt., Health., & Higher Ed. 2002*(1), 298–304. [Online]. Available: http://dl.aace.org/9377

Jonassen, D., Mayes, T., & McAleese, R. (1993). A manifesto for a constructivist approach to uses of technology in higher education. In T. Duffy, J. Lowyck, & D. Jonassen (Eds.), *Designing Environments for Constructivist Learning* (pp. 231–247). Berlin, Heidelberg, Germany: Springer-Verlag.

Kurniawan, S. H., & Zaphiris, P. (2001). Reading online or on paper: Which is faster? *Abridged Proceedings of the 9th International Conference on Human Computer Interaction, 2001* (pp. 220–222), August 5–10, New Orleans, LA.

Lacroix, N. (1999). Macrostructure construction and organization in the processing of multiple text passages. *Instructional Science, 27*, 221–233.

LiveInk. (2001–2005). Walker Reading Technologies, Inc. Retrieved May 17, 2006, from http://www.liveink.com

Lynch, P. J., & Horton, S. (1997). *Web style guide,* 2nd ed. Retrieved May 17, 2006, from http://www.webstyleguide.com/index.html

Mokhtari, K., & Reichard, C. (2002). Assessing students' metacognitive awareness of reading strategies. *Journal of Educational Psychology, 94*(2), pp. 249–259.

Moore, M. G. (1989). Three types of interaction. *The American Journal of Distance Education, 3*(2), 1–6.

Morkes, J., & Nielson, J. (1997). *Concise, scannable, and objective: How to write for the Web*. Retrieved May 17, 2006, from http://www.useit.com/papers/webwriting/writing.html

Muter, P. (1996). Interface design and optimization of reading of continuous text. In H. van Oostendorp & S. de Mul (Eds.), *Cognitive Aspects of Electronic Text Processing*. Norwood, NJ: Ablex.

The National Reading Research Center (1994). Electronic literacy (Perspective Series No. 1-PS-N-07). Athens, GA and College Park, MD: Reinking, D.

Nielson, J. (2000). *Designing web usability: The Practice of Simplicity*. Indianapolis, IN: New Riders.

O'Hara, K. (1996). *Towards a typology of reading goals*. (Technical Report EPC-1996-107). Retrieved December 21, 2006, from http://www.xrce.xerox.com/Publications/Attachments//1996-107/EPC-1996-107.pdf

Oliver, R., Omari, A., & Herrington, J. (1998). Investigating implementation strategies for WWW-based learning environments. *International Journal of Instructional Media, 25*(1), 121.

Parlangeli, O., Marchigiani, E., & Bagnara, S. (1999). Multimedia systems in distance education: Effects of usability on learning. *Interacting with Computers, 12*(1), 37–49.

Pearson, P. D., Roehler, L. R., Dole, J. A., & Duffy, G. G. (1992). Developing expertise in reading comprehension. In S. Samuels, S. Jay, and A. E. Farstrup (Eds.) Newark, DE: International Reading Association, pp. 145–199.

Piolat, A., Roussey, J., & Thunin, O. (1997). Effects of screen presentation on text reading and revising. *International Journal Human-Computer Studies, 47*, 565–589.

Richardson, J., & Swan, K. (2003). Examining social presence in online courses in relation to students' perceived learning and satisfaction. *Journal of Asynchronous Learning Networks, 7*(1), pp. 68–81.

Ritchie, T. (1996). Analysis and synthesis: *On scientific method-based on a study by Bernhard Riemann*. Retrieved May 17, 2006, from http://www.swemorph.com/pdf/anaeng-r.pdf

Shneiderman, B. (1997). Designing information-abundant web sites: Issues and recommendations. *International Journal of Human-Computer Studies, 47*, 5–29.

Soo, K., & Bonk, C. J. (1998). Interaction: What does it mean in online distance education? In *Ed-Media/Ed-Telecom 98 World Conference on Educational Multimedia and Hypermedia & World Conference on Educational Telecommunications. Proceedings* (10th), Freiburg, Germany. (ERIC Document Reproduction Service No. ED428 724).

Streitz, N.A. (1988). Mental models and metaphors: Implications for the design of adaptive user-system interfaces. In H. Mandl & A. Lesgold (Eds.), *Learning issues for intelligent tutoring systems* (pp. 164–186). New York: Springer-Verlag.

Thuring, M., Hannemann, J., & Haake, J. M. (1995). Hypermedia and cognition: Designing for comprehension. *Communications of the ACM, 38*(8), 57–66.

Trumbull, D., Gay, G., & Mazur, J. (1992). Students' actual and perceived use of navigational and guidance tools in a hypermedia program. *Journal of Research on Computing in Education, 24*(3), 315–328.

Unz, D. C., & Hesse, F. W. (1999). The use of hypertext for learning. *Journal of Educational Computing Research, 20*(3), 279–295.

van Nimwegen, C., Pouw, M., & van Oostendorp, H. (1999). The influence of structure and reading-manipulation on usability of hypertexts. *Interacting with Computers, 12*, 7–21.

Ward, M., & Newlands, D. (1998). Use of the Web in undergraduate teaching. *Computers & Education, 31*, 171–184.

Wilkinson, R. T., & Robinshaw, H. M. (1987). Proof-reading: VDU and paper text compared for speed, accuracy, and fatigue. *Behaviour & Information Technology, 6*, 125–133.

24

Modes of Interaction

Terry Anderson
Athabasca University

Alex Kuskis
University of Toronto

This chapter reviews six types of interaction and suggests areas and approaches to research that will expand our understanding and competence in using these new and traditional distance education tools, pedagogy, and technologies.

LEARNER-TEACHER
AND LEARNER-INSTITUTION INTERACTION

Much has been written about the importance of interaction between students and instructors, beginning with Plato and Socrates and continuing with later educators, notably John Dewey; however, while the literature of online facilitation is extensive, studies that focus specifically on learner-teacher interaction are less evident. Many of the pedagogical benefits of learner-teacher interaction, especially those related to motivation (Wlodkowski, 1985) and feedback (Laurillard, 1997, 2000) are equally relevant in classroom-based and distance education. Studies of audio (Hampel & Hauck, 2004) and videoconferencing (Katz, 2000; Hearnshaw, 2000; Wang, 2004) show that effective learner-teacher interaction can take place at a distance, but that these synchronous media, in themselves, seem to have little direct impact on educational outcomes (Russell, 2005). As with related studies of the effects of educational media, the impact of the instructional design or application of the technology seems to be a far greater determinant of learning outcomes than the use of any given medium per se (Clark, 1994). Recent work has extended the study of learner-teacher interaction in the text-based, distance context (Garrison, Anderson, & Archer, 2000; Shea, Pickett, & Pelz, 2003; Moore & Kearsley, 2005) and confirms that quality learner-teacher interaction does take place, even in the "lean" context of a text-based medium.

A major concern for both teachers and administrators is the perception of high workloads, with resulting increased costs associated with learner-teacher interaction in distance education.

From an administration perspective, Daniel and Marquis (1988) noted that the costs of human interaction "tend to increase in direct proportion to the number of students" (p. 342). From the perspective of over 1,000 American distance education teachers, Berge and Muilenburg (2000) report survey results that identify concerns with increased time requirements as the largest barrier associated with adoption of networked forms of distance teaching. Is this perception a function of media unfamiliarity and uncertainties of appropriate instructional design, or is it an implicit attribute of interaction in an environment that can take place "anywhere/anytime"? There has now been some research involving measurement of teacher time that suggests that increased workload for online courses is not generally supported (Lesh, 2000; DiBiase, 2000; Lazarus, 2003; Hislop & Ellis, 2004; McLain, 2005)—at least once the learning curve for competent use of the technology is surmounted; however, concerns with the high cost of modern forms of e-learning continue, and the challenges of measuring and compensating teachers appropriately for time spent in teacher-learner interaction remain (Fielden, 2002). Moore's (2000) advice is sensible: it should not be a question of more or less work than in the classroom, but rather "getting better quality out of the same effort" (p. 5).

Interaction must provide "relative advantage" (Rogers, 2003) to teachers who have become accustomed to a system that supports temporal restriction on teacher-learner interaction. It is difficult to imagine a distance education teacher telling students he or she will respond to e-mail only during regular office hours from Tuesday afternoon between 2:00 p.m. and 4:00 p.m.! Learner-teacher interaction is enabled by a sense of social presence and of teacher immediacy perceived by all participants. Social presence is defined as "the degree to which a person is perceived as a 'real person' in a mediated situation" (McIsaac & Gunawardena, 1996, p. 427). For teachers, social presence is purposeful and is perceived mainly as "teaching presence," which Anderson, Rourke, Garrison, and Archer (2001) define as "design, facilitation, and direction of cognitive and social processes for the purpose of realizing personally meaningful and educationally worthwhile learning outcomes." The result of meaningful teaching presence should be "greater positive affect and higher perceived cognition than students taught by less immediate instructors" (Baker, 2004, p. 1).

We have updated Figure 24.1 in this edition to note the important role of learner-institution interaction in formal distance education. This interaction is often mediated by the teacher, but extends beyond this interaction to a variety of learner support interactions (Tait & Mills, 2003). Anderson (2004) noted the pervasive impact of the Web on provision of student services and argues that the potential for automation will increasingly move learner-institution interaction from a focus on the teacher as primary "interactor" to portals containing customized views of institutional resources, expectations, and services available to learners.

LEARNER-LEARNER INTERACTION

The rich educational value of collaborative and cooperative learning was not available to students involved in first generation forms of distance education—i.e., correspondence study. Work on the social construction of knowledge (Rogoff, 1990; Brown & Duguid, 2000), communities of practice (Wenger, 2000; Wenger et al., 2002), situated learning (Lave, 1988), and the applications of these theories to education have resulted in a rich and growing body of knowledge related to student-student interaction and collaborative learning (Brown, 2001; Johnson, Johnson, & Smith, 1991; Slavin, 1995). Most of this research has focused on classroom-based delivery, largely with school-age children; however, adult and especially professional learners have also been shown to benefit from interaction with others with common professional concerns and aspirations (Brookfield, 1987; Schön, 1991). Damon (1984) noted that "intellectual accomplishments flour-

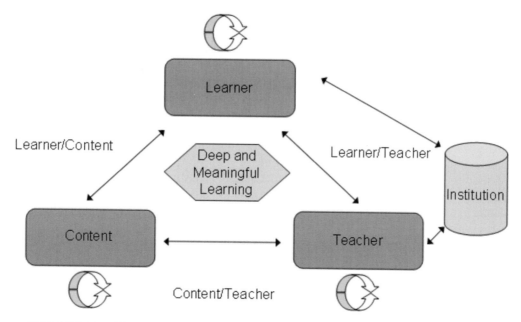

FIGURE 24.1.   Modes of Interaction in Distance Education from Anderson and Garrison (1998)

ish best under conditions of highly motivated discovery, the free exchange of ideas and the reciprocal feedback between mutually respected individuals" (p. 340).

The applications of a new medium usually begin by imitating older media that serve as their content (McLuhan, 1964). Online distance education was initially adapted the "virtual classroom" collaborative, and learning community techniques that were originally developed for campus classrooms; however, online distance education has gone beyond this imitation stage and is developing unique forms of learner-learner interaction—some of which are not possible in place-bound contexts (Downes, 2005).

The act of engaging in learner-learner interaction forces learners to construct or formulate ideas in a deep learning sense. John Dewey predated and influenced modern constructivist theorists when he describe this formulating process as "getting outside of it, seeing it as another would see it, considering what points of contact it has with the life of another so that it may be got into such form that he can appreciate its meaning" (Dewey, 1916).

Weigel (2002) attributes deep learning to communities of inquiry and defines it as learning that promotes the development of conditionalized knowledge that "specifies the contexts in which it is useful" (p. 6) and metacognition through communities of inquiry. This most social component of the online distance education process is what allows it to move beyond independent study and be re-conceptualized as "education at a distance," rather than distance education (Shale, 1990).

Learner-learner collaboration via computer networks is far from being a new idea. There have been practitioners and advocates of it for classroom groups prior to the advent of online distance education. As Johnson et al. (1991) wrote, "Throughout human history, it has been those individuals who could organize and coordinate their efforts to achieve a common purpose that have been most successful in virtually any human endeavor" (p. 13). Smith and MacGregor (1998) define collaborative learning as an umbrella term for educational approaches that involve joint intellectual effort by learners, or learners working with teachers together. Typical collaborative learning situations involve students working in groups of two or more, together seeking understanding, solutions, and meanings, or creating a joint intellectual product, such as an essay, report, or Web site.

Collaborative learning is based on at least five assumptions: (a) that learning is an active process of creating something; (b) that it depends upon rich contexts; (c) that it is inherently social; (d) that it has both affective and subjective dimensions; and (e) that learners bring diverse skills and experiences to bear (Smith & MacGregor, 1998). Kennedy and Duffy (2004) contextualize these assumptions for successful online collaborative learning: (a) learners must be prepared for it by course providers; (b) technical support is essential, especially at the start; (c) teachers must be proficient in supporting it; and (d) the institutions themselves must openly support it. Finally, since collaborative learning depends on interaction, motivators or incentives (either external or internal to the student) must be available. Fung (2004) reported that nonparticipation is a function of student's expressed lack of time and preferences for independent study, rather than engagement in discussions. It could be equally true, however, that many online activities lack sufficient intrinsic value to the learner to sustain learner engagement. The inference is that collaborative learning must be made integral to courses through effective and compelling design and facilitation; otherwise, students will simply spend their time reading or on other individual activities.

Interaction with peers is a critical component of the formal curriculum in many disciplines. The capacity to participate effectively in teams and within professional communities of practice, communicate effectively with colleagues and clients, and generally demonstrate highly developed communication skills is critical to both vocational and personal success. Learning a discipline usually involves becoming a member of a community of practice and requires the learning of its methods, language and culture (Brown & Duguid, 2000). As Brown and Duguid wrote, "Become a member of a community, engage in its practices, and you can acquire and make use of its knowledge and information. Remain an outsider, and these will remain indigestible" (p. 126). Wenger et al. (2002) define communities of practice as "groups of people who share a concern, a set of problems, or a passion about a topic, and who deepen their understanding and knowledge of this area by interacting on an ongoing basis" (p. 4). Online professional programs, such as master's programs in business, education, nursing, engineering, and computer science, can benefit from being designed as communities of practice, with learners adopting and developing the discourse, research, and knowledge sharing techniques of working practitioners. Thus, online communications skills are both taught and practiced as major objectives of most higher education programming and are integral to the training process in many professional programs.

Distance education courses, lacking the shared competencies of professional disciplines that characterize communities of practice, still share knowledge domains and can be organized as communities of inquiry. Moller (1998) proposed that community in distance learning performs two functions: (a) social reinforcement, through shared identity based on shared values, norms and preferences, resulting in more group cohesion and less attrition; and (b) information exchange, through collaboration and knowledge building. Swan et al. (2000) emphasized that three factors contribute to the success of online courses by supporting the growth of knowledge building communities: "a transparent interface, an instructor who interacts frequently and constructively with students, and a valued and dynamic discussion" (p. 379). Rovai (2002) found that online learners who develop a strong sense of community and experience greater cognitive learning feel less isolated and have greater satisfaction with their academic programs, possibly resulting in fewer dropouts. And McInnerney and Roberts (2004) propose three protocols that can be built into online courses to enable a sense of community and productive social interaction: (a) greater use of synchronous communication, in addition to asynchronous; (b) inclusion of a community "forming" stage, or warm-up period; and (c) greater emphasis on the use of guidelines for successful online communication. To these we add the competent use of new social software tools such as syndicated blogs, podcasts, and wikis that are becoming the communication and knowledge aggregation media of choice for many courses and professional organizations.

Despite the many pedagogical benefits of learner-learner interaction, it is known that some students purposely select distance education formats that support independent study, free from the contact and temporal restraints associated with interactive forms of learning (Pagney, 1988; Daniel & Marquis, 1988). Arnold (1999) argued that by focusing on individual learning designs, distance education can be more customized and "be closer to the content of the learning process and closer to the comprehension and grasp of the problems by individual learners" (p. 5). There is contentious debate between those who value independent versus collaborative forms of distance education (Garrison, 1999), and some have even argued for a basic learning equivalence among the various interaction modalities (Anderson, 2003). It is clear that we can no longer assume that distance education is, by definition, either an individual or a collaborative process. When we build in learner-learner interaction in our distance education programming, we should ensure that our instructional designs promote interactions that are pedagogically grounded and produce enough learning to justify the restrictions on student's temporal independence. Further, the diversity of distance education compels us to be explicit in our promotion of distance education programming, so that students can make informed choices that meet their individual needs and desires.

In addition to studies focusing on collaborative learning and learning in online communities, which impact notions of learner-learner interaction, there are numerous studies specifically on various aspects of learner-learner interaction. Indeed, this whole category appears to have been researched far more than the other types of learning interactions. While this might be appropriate for a constructivist, learner-centered paradigm, it does suggest the need for more research on the other learning interaction types. For example, Lobel, Neubauer and Swedberg (2002) detect four distinct stages of interaction in online courses: greeting, gathering, activity, and conclusion. Furthermore, each activity stage also has four distinct phases: (a) adding knowledge to the group, (b) facilitation, (c) building on the knowledge of others, and (d) reporting back to the group. This kind of detailed theoretical understanding can aid in the instructional design of learning interaction activities. Molinari (2004) discovers the important role that social communication plays in online group problem-solving courses, where learners employed self-revelation, "tying," and etiquette to construct a foundation for collaborative work. The implication is that instructors need to provide time and space for social discourse as an enabler of learning-specific communications. Finally, Garrison and Cleveland-Innes (2005) determined that "interaction is not enough," and that teaching presence is necessary to provide "the structure (design) and leadership (facilitation/direction) to establish social and cognitive presence (i.e., community of inquiry)" (p. 144).

We next turn to a discussion of the first of three forms of interaction that include non-human entities.

LEARNER-CONTENT INTERACTION

The majority of student time, in all forms of adult education, is consumed by interactions with a variety of educational content. In traditional distance education, this has meant study with texts and other electronic resources, often supplemented by faculty-created study guides.

Current technologies provide a wide variety of media alternatives with which to create content for student interaction. Tuovinen (2000) classified these media into five basic categories—

sound, text, graphics, video, and virtual reality—paying particular attention to combinations that include sound with any of the other media. He argued that sound and visual images are processed by different parts of the brain and thus combinations of sound with other media are less likely to produce cognitive overload than other combinations.

Learner-content interactivity in educational contexts can take many forms and serve a variety of functions. Sims (1997) reviewed taxonomies of student-media interactions and proposed a "developers classification" that includes object, linear, support, update, construct, reflective, simulation, hyperlinked, immersive, and non-immersive virtual forms of interactivity. In a study of the benefits of interactivity within an educational Web site, Brady (2004) found that learner-content interactivity positively influenced learning outcomes, satisfaction, and learner time-on-task. Tuovinen (2000) added "multimedia creation" as a separate, more constructive form of student-content interactivity. Benefits of this creation of content are attributed to learning acquired through development of the structure, strategies, and skills needed for effective content creation (Dunlop, 1999).

It is beyond the scope of this paper to review the 30 years of experimental study related to learner-content interaction (see Moore & Thompson, 1997). It is, however, probably safe to say that results have not been as conclusive as desired by either proponents or opponents of the use of mediated learner-content interaction. The classic debate between Clark (1994) and Kozma (1994) related to the extent (if any) that media influences learning has served to inform, but hardly resolves this issue. All would agree that the challenge of conducting research in situ that meaningfully isolates the confounding variables of design, media, content, context, learners, and measurement is an extremely challenging task.

Clark (2000) has suggested that any evaluation of learner-content interaction must recognize that every distance education context consists of two distinct levels of interaction: the first dealing with attributes of the media that support the interaction, and the second with the "technology" of the learning or instructional design. Confounding these two separate types of learner-content interaction, according to Clark, is at the root of many of the terminology and research problems debated in the literature. Although it is conceptually useful to differentiate and even measure these interactions as distinct events, Marshall McLuhan's (1964) famous aphorism that "the medium is the message" reminds us that simple reductionism often fails to identify sympathetic reactions between variables. For example, Diaz (2000) made a convincing argument that research designs informed from an "instructivist worldview" are not likely to inform learner-centered and constructivist forms of learning, in which relationships and communication far outweigh the effect of the media that support educational transactions. Research methods that illuminate differences within applications of particular sets of learners or instructional designs are likely to be more productive than those that are designed to compare effect of interactions across different media and instructional designs.

The capacity of the Internet to store, catalog, and deliver such content, supplemented with the capacity of computers to support a rich variety of computer-assisted instruction, simulations, and presentation creation tools, is significantly altering the context of learner-content interaction. In particular, work with the development, cataloging and distribution of learning objects (Downes, 2003; Richards, McGreal, Hatala, & Friesen, 2002; McGreal, 2004), provides educators and learners with an expanded set of student-content interaction resources. The pioneering work of the MERLOT consortium (http://www.merlot.org) in augmenting learning objects with metatags, peer reviews, learning activities, and user comments, and the free provision of these value-added resources, is an example of the way in which educators need to collaboratively disseminate materials for learner-content interaction. The initial exuberance over the potential of reusable learning objects has been tempered by realization that learning is locally and culturally contextualized and that the object's efficacy is dependent upon its use in effective learning designs

(Koper, 2001). Further, the challenges of accurate and complete tagging, versioning, and intellectual property management have slowed the development and deployment of learning objects. Nonetheless, the Internet has become the first place to look for activities and tools designed to enhance learner-content interaction by both teachers and learners.

Theroux and Kilbane (2004) described an innovative use of a real-time business case distributed via the Internet to business classes at four universities in the United States and Canada in 2001. A case writer, stationed full-time at the subject company, published weekly case installments on the Internet, allowing students to view real-time corporate operational data in unprecedented depth and detail. In addition, students shared their analyses and best thinking with company management, influencing the corporate decision-making process. The Internet enables such learner interaction with dynamic, real-world content.

A variety of new network services allow students to direct and automate their interaction with content. Most pervasive of the technologies used are various forms of syndication (RSS, *Atom*, etc.). Syndication provides real-time notifications (in machine readable format) of new additions to a Web-enabled resource or collection such as maintained by a publishing house, discussion group, or personal blog space. These syndicated notices can be searched, sorted, and aggregated by individuals or groups of learners or teachers to create customized and personal views of emerging content. Further development of autonomous agents will provide learners with increasingly powerful tools to search, evaluate, select, and "interact" with networked-based learning content. These interactions are not restricted to text-based media. For example, most of the general purpose as well as specialty search engines such as http://www.findsounds.com allow for searching and selection of thousands of hours of podcast, radio, and video content, while *Ditto* (http://www.ditto.com) and *Google Images* (http://images.google.com) contain searchable indexes to millions of images.

Content may also be programmed to interact with learners at various levels of sophistication and support. The goal of these "adaptive" systems is to customize interaction for individual student needs, including the "ability to set the level of the lesson closely to the student's current and changing level of understanding, to alter instructional strategies and provide remedial tutoring as required, to respond to student input at various levels from keystroke to the overall plan of the solution to the problem, and finally to detect and analyze mistakes in terms of conceptual errors" (Eklund, 1995). Research determining how content can best be programmed to interact with the unique cognitive attributes of individual learners is the subject of much human-computer interaction study (Hedberg and Perry, 1985). Content can also be programmed to act as independent agents, undertaking tasks such as notification, note taking, summarizing, and other clerical and administrative tasks for learning groups or individuals (Whatley, Beer, Staniford, & Scown, 1999; Negatu & Franklin, 1999; Lieberman, 2002). Early research has shown that this form of automated, always available assistance "holds promise for improving completion rates, learner satisfaction, and motivation" (Thaiupathump, Bourne, & Campbell, 1999); however, programming such "intelligent software" is expensive and research related to cost effectiveness and actual use and performance is necessary to guide ongoing development of this kind of learner-content interaction. There is no doubt that learner-content interaction can perform some functions of the educational transaction formerly accomplished exclusively through teacher-learner interaction. The appropriate amount, efficiency, and efficacy of this substitution of technology for human labor will dominate learner-content research for the foreseeable future. It is interesting to speculate if and when intelligent content agents will routinely pass the equivalent of an "Educational Turing Test" in which students will be unable to determine if they are interacting with human or non-human teachers.

A final comment on learner-content interaction relates to the phenomenal growth in interest and use of content formatted as education games or simulations. In an insightful academic review of the impact on literacy and learning with videogames, Gee (2003) argued that it is not that "what people are learning when they are playing video games is always good. But rather that what they are doing when they are playing video games is often good" (p. 198). In a more formal higher education context, Oblinger (2004) overviewed the match between the needs of learners raised on networked learning tools and the pedagogical, motivational, and flow attributes of games as learning environments (Prensky, 2001).

In a Net-infused distance education context, it is not only learners but also teachers who continuously interact with content—the focus of the following section.

TEACHER-CONTENT INTERACTION

The first of three less discussed forms of interaction initially highlighted by Anderson and Garrison (1998) is interaction between teachers and content. As noted above, the selection, development, and application of content learning objects has become an increasingly important component of the teacher's role in both distance and classroom-based education. The Internet provides opportunities for teachers to create learning objects that can easily, and in some cases automatically, be updated by publications, data, and other research-based artifacts. For example, objects can be created that display and then calculate trends from real time data sources such as economic indicators, climate monitors, or other sensory data. Teachers will interact with content through use of adaptable search engines that will learn from previous teacher behavior to effectively and periodically search the networks for relevant information and data. We are also seeing the early results of teacher use of online labs in which results and even student manipulations of remote scientific instruments are integrated into distance teaching programs (Kennepohl, Baran, Connors, Quigley, & Currie, 2005).

The role of teacher-content interaction is focused in the instructional design process. Teachers and developers create and re-purpose research results and other discipline-related information in the process of creating content. Easier tools for creation of content, from simple presentation and illustration packages to complex authoring environments, allow teachers to create content more directly than in earlier eras when instructional designers and programmers performed much of this work. For example, lectures, guest speakers, and debates are easily captured and digitized to create podcasts and video-casts that are retrievable by learners. Although some have argued for the pedagogical and administrative superiority of content produced by teams of experts, as opposed to "Lone Rangers" (Bates, 1995)—that is, independent teacher-designers—the recent explosion of largely instructor-created content, produced with the aid of authoring and delivery systems such as *Dreamweaver®*, *Moodle*, and *Blackboard®*, illustrates that teachers can (either alone, or with minimal consultative assistance) produce effective and acceptable content.

One often overlooked advantage of such "homegrown" content is that it allows instructors to continually update and annotate content throughout the course. This allows the instructional design process to continue throughout the learning sequence and does not confine design to the time before learner-content interaction takes place, as is necessitated in the various forms of "canned" instruction (Tuovinen, 2000). Finally, we can expect these authoring and distribution systems to become more comprehensive, functional and "user-friendly," as they evolve in both commercial and "open source" production models. Forms of teacher-content interaction will become more automated as "intelligent agents" and "wizards" are incorporated into course creation packages, making maintenance and updating of content easier and less time-consuming. Where more work is needed is in the development of more sophisticated pedagogical tools for teacher-content interaction; tools are needed that assist teachers in designing, supporting, and administrating courses based on a wide variety of pedagogical theories and offering a diversity of learning activities.

Our hope is that the combination of object repositories and better pedagogically driven development and delivery tools will create opportunities for more significant teacher-content interaction. This, in turn, will lead to the development of more sophisticated, powerful, and cost-effective teacher-created learning environments and enhanced interaction in all modes (Trafford, 2005).

In summary, teacher-content interaction tools support the production of increasingly sophisticated teacher-produced content and courses, thus keeping alive the tradition of instructor-developed forms of "little distance education" (Garrison & Anderson, 1999). It is unclear whether these tools will ever be powerful enough, or if instructors will ever have the skills needed to produce programming of "Disney" quality. Teachers using these tools, however, are increasingly able to create powerful distance learning programming that supports high levels of critical teacher-learner, learner-learner, and learner-content interaction.

Despite these optimistic projections for teacher-content interaction, it is clear that administration and management concerns must be addressed that measure both the cost and benefit of teacher creation and interaction with content. Thus, the major research issues related to teacher-content interaction revolve around workload, changing skill sets, copyright, and the contentious relationship between teaching and research, especially in the university context (Brand, 2000).

TEACHER-TEACHER INTERACTION

The pervasive existence of the Internet is providing unprecedented opportunities for teacher-teacher interaction. Such interactive networking is increasingly being exploited by teachers to take advantage of developments in both their own disciplines and in distance teaching pedagogy. This interaction between teachers forms the basis of networked scholarly communities of practice within formal education institutions, as well as scholarly societies, or "invisible colleges" (Genoni, Merrick, & Willson, 2005; Wellman, Koku, & Hunsinger, 2005). Anderson, Varnhagen, and Campbell (1998) found that the first and most important source of assistance in both technical and pedagogical challenges comes not from technical or pedagogical experts, but from colleagues at hand. Such colleagues need no longer be at the same institution and can now be readily accessed through e-mail and networked scholarly communities of practice (Koku & Wellman, 2004). Koku and Wellman (2004) note that computer-mediated communication provides a technological platform for new kinds of "spatially-based, loosely bounded, networks of scholars that are more connected than the fitful, amorphous relationships of the past and less physically proximate and bureaucratically structured than contemporary universities" (p. 301). Rapid computer-mediated communications allow distant scholars to initiate contacts, stay in touch, and collaborate on research, as well as teaching. Experience with network-based professional development (Williams, 1997; Anderson & Mason, 1993) illustrates that this form of teacher-teacher interaction has tremendous cost savings and is the basis for online distance educator communities of practice.

We are currently seeing the emergence of first-generation distance teaching "portals" in which resources, experiences, tools, and forums for teacher-teacher exchange are gathered in a single Web location. These portals provide a form of collaborative knowledge management that supports distance education teachers and researchers. These portals are supported by professional distance education publishers (i.e., http://Distance-Educator.com), commercial educational software vendors (i.e., http://www.blackboard.com), postsecondary institutions (i.e. http://www.uwex .edu/disted/home.html; http://www.umuc.edu/ide/), and nonprofit professional research and development organizations (i.e. http://tappedin.org/tappedin/; http://cider.athabascau.ca; http://www.digitallearning.org/about.htm). Some of these sources will likely consolidate as the distance education "industry" matures, leaving a limited number of high-quality, full-service distance education portals in support of teacher-teacher interaction.

CONTENT-CONTENT INTERACTION

Computer scientists and educators are creating "intelligent" programs or agents that "differ from conventional software in that they are long-lived, semi-autonomous, proactive, and adaptive" (Massachusetts Institute of Technology [MIT], 2000). We are seeing early examples of programs written to retrieve information, operate other programs, make decisions, and monitor resources on networks. An education example of such an agent might be designed by an Agriculture Economics instructor teaching a lesson on futures marketing. An agent would regularly update the lesson by retrieving information from online future quotations, alerting the teacher or learners of any unusal activity taking place. The lesson, thus, becomes "ever green" and gains in relevance as it displays dynamic real information from today's marketplace.

Internet search engines provide other examples of intelligent agents interacting with each other as they continuously scour the Web, sending the results of their discoveries back to central databases. Next-generation systems will use intelligent agents to search multiple Web indices and support selective winnowing of results (Kapur & Zhang, 2000). In the near future, teachers will create and use learning resources that continuously improve themselves through their interaction with other intelligent agents. Segal (2000) has projected that "the Web will slowly disappear into devices and into the environment around us. This means the browser is not a pointer, but an active collector, retriever, connisseur, extractor and store of all our information" (p. 12). The integration of blogging tools and syndication into browser applications also illustrates the ways in which customized views of content are created and continuously updated by new content. Research in this mode is exploding across the Web. It will focus on both development and testing of agents designed to undertake a variety of educational tasks (Yau, Ngai, & Cheng, 2005). This research is by definition multi-disciplinary, calling on the resources of computer scientists, linguists, educators, and others.

CONCLUSION

To summarize, although learner-learner interaction has been studied the most, each of the six modes of interaction in distance education needs systematic and rigorous theoretical and empirical research using a variety of research tools and methodologies. Greg Kearsley (1995) provided a list of eight questions related to interaction, the answers to which are critical to our development of effective distance education programming. These questions relate to the effects of frequency of interaction, types of learners, subject matter, and learning objectives to which interaction is most critical, as well as the effects of interaction on learner satisfaction. These questions must be answered with reference to all six forms of interaction. Additional questions related to cost, time requirements, and other workload implications are critical in an expanding era of distance education programming. Unfortunately, the answers to most of these questions remain largely unanswered eleven years after Kearsley posed them to the community of distance education researchers.

The search for single-faceted solutions that generalize to the many diverse contexts of distance education is likely a quixotic quest. We are developing a growing mosaic of distance education technologies and practices, with no single "best way" to use interaction. Each institution, discipline, region, and user group will develop unique cultural practices and expectations related to its need for and use of interaction; however, this is not to say that all applications are equally effective or efficient. Too much of our practice in distance education is not "evidence-based," and our actions and instructional designs are often grounded on untested assumptions about the value (or lack of) of all modes of interaction. Thus, the research opportunities that focus on interaction in all its forms are boundless and critically important.

Daniel and Marquis' (1988) seminal challenge to distance educators was to "get the mixture right" between independence (learner-content interaction) and interaction (mainly learner-teacher interaction). In the 21st century, we are still challenged to get the mixture right—only now we must consider combinations of all six modes of interaction to try to decide which combinations are optimal in different situations (Anderson, 2003). Appropriate mixtures will result in increased learning and exiting new educational opportunities; inappropriate combinations will be expensive, exclusive, and exigent. Our responsibility as professional distance educators remains to ensure that the modes of interaction we practice and prescribe maximize the attainment of all educational objectives and increase motivation for deep and meaningful learning. Further, we are challenged to do all of this at expenditure rates that are affordable to both providers and consumers.

We conclude with the words of John Dewey, who noted that "every expansive era in the history of mankind has coincided with the operation of factors which have tended to eliminate distance between peoples and classes previously hemmed off from one another" (Dewey, 1916, p. 100). As distance educators, we follow this noble tradition of using our most technologically "expansive" era to reduce the social, political, technical, economic, and geographic distances that separate us from one another.

REFERENCES

Anderson, T. (2003). Getting the Mix Right: An updated and theoretical rational for interaction. *International Review of Research in Open and Distance Learning, 4*(2). Retrieved October 30, 2003, from http://www.irrodl.org/index.php/irrodl/article/view/149/230

Anderson, T. (2004). Student services in a networked world. In J. Brindley, C. Walti, & O. Zawacki-Richter (Eds.) *Learner Support in Open, Distance and Online Learning Environments* (pp. 95–108). Oldenburg Germany: Bibliotheks- und Informationssystem der Universität Oldenburg.

Anderson, T., & Garrison, D. R. (1998). Learning in a networked world: New roles and responsibilities. In C. Gibson (Ed.), *Distance Learners in Higher Education* (pp. 97–112). Madison, WI: Atwood Publishing.

Anderson, T., & Mason, R. (1993). The Bangkok Project: New tool for professional development. *American Journal of Distance Education, 7*(2), 5–18.

Anderson, T., Rourke, L., Garrison, D. R., & Archer, W. (2001). Assessing teaching presence in a computer conferencing context. *Journal of Asynchronous Learning Networks, 5*(2). Retrieved December 14, 2005, from http://www.sloan-c.org/publications/jaln/v5n2/v5n2_anderson.asp.

Anderson, T., Varnhagen, S., & Campbell, K. (1998). Faculty Adoption of Teaching and Learning Technologies: Contrasting earlier adopters and mainstream faculty. *Canadian Journal of Higher Education, 28*(2,3), 71–98.

Arnold, R. (1999). Will distance disappear in distance education? *Journal of Distance Education, 14*(2), 1–9.

Baker, J. D. (2004). An investigation of relationships among instructor immediacy and affective and cognitive learning in the online classroom. *The Internet and Higher Education, 7*(1) 1–13.

Bates, T. (1995). *Technology, Open Learning and Distance Education.* London: Routledge.

Berge, Z., & Muilenburg, L. (2000). Barriers to Distance Education as Perceived by Managers and Administrators: Results of a survey. In M. Grey (Ed.) *Distance Learning Administration Annual 2000*. Retrieved January 20, 2006, from http://www.emoderators.com/barriers/man_admin.shtml

Brady, L. (2004). The role of interactivity in web-based educational material. *Usability News, 6*(2). Retrieved November 20, 2005, from http://psychology.wichita.edu/surl/usabilitynews/62/interactivity.htm

Brand, M. (2000). Changing Faculty Roles in Research Universities: Using the Pathways Strategy. *Change, 32*(6), 42–45.

Brookfield, S. (1987). Recognizing Critical Thinking. In S. Brookfield (Ed.), *Developing Critical Thinkers* (pp. 15–34). Oxford, UK: Jossey-Bass.

Brown, J. S., & Duguid, P. (2000). *Social Life of Information*. Cambridge, MA: Harvard Business School Press.

Brown, R. E. (2001). The process of community-building in distance learning classes. *Journal of Asynchronous Learning Networks, 5*(2). Retrieved April 30, 2004, from http://www.sloan-c.org/publications/jaln/v5n2/v5n2_brown.asp

Clark, R. (1994). Media will never influence learning. *Educational Technology Research & Development, 42*(3), 21–29.

Clark, R. (2000). Evaluating Distance Education: Strategies and cautions. *Quarterly Review of Distance Education, 1*(1), 3–16.

Damon, W. (1984). Peer Interaction: The untapped potential. *Journal of Applied Developmental Psychology, 5*, 331–343.

Daniel, J., & Marquis, C. (1988). Interaction and Independence: Getting the mix right. In D. Sewart, D. Keegan, & B. Holmberg (Eds.) *Distance Education: International Perspectives* (pp. 339–359). London: Routledge.

Dede, C. (1996). The Evolution of Distance Education: Emerging technologies and distributed learning. *American Journal of Distance Education, 10*(2), 4–36.

Dewey, J. (1916). *Democracy and Education*. New York: Macmillan.

Diaz, D. (2000). Carving a new path for distance education research. *Commentary: March/April*. Retrieved May 21, 2001, from http://horizon.unc.edu/TS/commentary/2000-03a.asp

DiBiase, D. (2000). Is distance teaching more work or less work? *American Journal of Distance Education, 14*(3), 6–20.

Downes, S. (2003). Learning Objects: Resources for Distance Education Worldwide. *International Review of Research on Open and Distance Learning, 2*(1). Retrieved October 25, 2005, from http://www.irrodl.org/content/v2.1/

Downes, S. (2005). E-learning 2.0. *eLearn Magazine*. Retrieved October 17, 2005, from http://elearnmag.org/subpage.cfm?section=articles&article=29–1

Dunlop, J. (1999). Developing web-based performance support systems to encourage lifelong learning in the workplace . *WebNet Journal, 1*(2) 40–48.

Eklund, J. (1995). Adaptive Learning Environments: The future for tutorial software. *Australian Educational Computing, 10*(1), 10–14. Retrieved May 21, 2001, from http://nabil.vuse.vanderbilt.edu/nabil/Adaptive_Learning.htm

Fielden, J. (2002). Costing e-Learning: is it worth trying or should we ignore the figures? London: The Observatory on Borderless Higher Education. Retrieved Sept. 2005 from http://www.obhe.ac.uk/products/reports/pdf/August2002.pdf.

Fung, Y. Y. H. (2004). Collaborative Online Learning: Interaction patterns and limiting factors. *Open Learning, 19*(2), 136–149.

Garrison, D. R., & Cleveland-Innes, M. (2005). Facilitating cognitive presence in online learning: Interaction is not enough. *American Journal of Distance Education, 19*(3), 133–148.

Garrison, D. R. (1999). Will distance disappear in distance education? A reaction. *Journal of Distance Education, 14*(2), 10–13.

Garrison, R., & Anderson, T. (1999). Avoiding the Industrialization of Research Universities: Big and little distance education. *American Journal of Distance Education, 13*(2), 48–63.

Garrison, R., Anderson, T., & Archer, W. (2000). Critical Inquiry in Text-based Environment: Computer conferencing in higher education. *The Internet and Higher Education, 2*(2–3), 87–105.

Gee, J. (2003). *What video games have to teach us about learning and literacy.* New York: Palgrave MacMillan.

Genoni, P., Merrick, H., & Willson, M. (2005). The use of the Internet to activate latent ties in scholarly communities. *First Monday, 10*(12). Retrieved December 14, 2005, from http://firstmonday.org/issues/issue10_12/genoni/index.html

Hampel, R., & Hauck, M. (2004). Towards an effective use of audio-conferencing in distance language courses. *Language Learning and Technology, 8*(1), 66–82. Retrieved January 20, 2006, from: http://llt.msu.edu/vol8num1/pdf/hampel.pdf

Hearnshaw, D. (2000). Effective desktop videoconferencing with minimal network demands. *British Journal of Educational Technology, 31*(3), 221–227.

Hedberg, J., & Perry, N. (1985). Human-Computer Interaction and CAI: A review and research prospectus. *Australian Journal of Educational Technology, 1*(1), 12–20. Retrieved May 21, 2001, from http://cleo.murdoch.edu.au/gen/aset/ajet/ajet1/win85p12.html

Hislop, G. W., & Ellis, H. J. C. (2004). A study of faculty effort in online teaching. *The Internet and Higher Education, 7*(1), 15–31.

Johnson, D., Johnson, R., & Smith, K. (1991). *Active learning cooperation in the college classroom.* Edina, MN: Interaction Book Co.

Kearsley, G. (1995). The nature and values of interaction in distance education. In Third Distance Education Research Symposium. College Park, PA: American Center for the Study of Distance Education.

Katz, Y. (2000). The comparative suitability of three ICT distance learning methodologies for college level instruction. *Education Media International, 37*(1), 25–30

Kennedy, D., & Duffy, T. (2004). Collaboration—a key principle in distance education. *Open Learning, 19*(2), 203–211.

Kennepohl, D., Baran, B., Connors, M., Quigley, K., & Currie, R. (2005). Remote access to instrumental analysis for distance education in science. *International Review of Research in Open and Distance Learning, 6*(3). Retrieved January 20, 2006, from http://www.irrodl.org/content/v6.3/kennepohl.html

Koku, E., & Wellman, B. (2004). Scholarly Networks as Learning Communities: The case of TechNet. In S. Barab, R. Kling & J. H. Gray (Eds.) *Designing virtual communities in the service of learning* (pp. 299–337) Cambridge, UK: Cambridge University Press.

Koper, R. (2001). Modeling Units of Study from a Pedagogical Perspective: The pedagogical meta-model behind EML Heerlen. Open University of the Netherlands. Retrieved June 28, 2002, from http://eml.ou.nl/introduction/docs/ped-metamodel.pdf

Kozma, R. (1994). Will Media Influence Learning? Reframing the debate. *Educational Technology Research & Development, 42*(2), 7–19.

Lave, J. (1988). *Cognition in Practice: Mind, mathematics, and culture in everyday life.* Cambridge, UK: Cambridge University Press.

Laurillard, D. (1997). *Rethinking university teaching: A framework for the effective use of educational technology.* (ed.). London: Routledge.

Laurillard, D. (2000). New technologies and the curriculum. In Scott. P. (Ed.), *Higher Education Re-formed.* (pp. 133–153). London: Falmer Press.

Lazarus, B. L. (2003). Teaching courses online: How much time does it take? *Journal of Asynchronous Learning Networks, 7*(3). Retrieved December 3, 2005, from, http://www.sloan-c.org/publications/jaln/v7n3/v7n3_lazarus.asp

Lesh, S. (2000, November). Asynchronous versus Synchronous Learning: *A comparative investigation of the effectiveness of learner achievement and faculty time demands. In Presentations of the 6th Asynchronous Learning Network.* Philadelphia. Retrieved Jan. 2007 from www.sloan-c.org/conference/proceedings/2000/ppt/00_lesh.ppt

Lobel, M., Neubauer, M., & Swedburg, R. (2002). The eClassroom used as a teacher's training laboratory to measure the impact of group facilitation on attending, participation, interaction, and involvement. *International Review of Research in Open and Distance Learning, 3*(2). Retrieved December 12, 2005, from http://www.irrodl.org/content/v3.2/lns.html

McGreal, R. (2004). *Online Education Using Learning Objects.* London: Routledge-Falmer.

McInnerney, J. M., & Roberts, T. S. (2004). Online Learning: Social Interaction and the Creation of a Sense of Community. *Educational Technology and Society, 7*(3), 73–81

McIsaac, M. S., & Gunawardena, C. N. (1996). Distance education. In D. H. Jonassen (Ed.) *Handbook of Research for Educational Communications and Technology: A project of the association for educational communications and technology* (pp. 403–437). New York: Simon & Schuster. Retrieved December 23, 2005, from http://seamonkey.ed.asu.edu/~mcisaac/dechapter/

McLain, B. P. (2005). Estimating faculty and student workload for interaction in online graduate music courses. *Journal of Asynchronous Learning Networks, 9*(3). Retrieved December 7, 2005, from http://www.sloan-c.org/publications/jaln/v9n3/v9n3_mclain.asp

McLuhan, M. (1964). *Understanding Media: The extensions of man.* Toronto: McGraw-Hill.

MIT (2000). *Software Agents Group.* Retrieved May 21, 2001, from http://mevard.www.media.mit.edu/groups/agents/.

Molinari, D. L. (2004). The role of social comments in problem-solving groups in an online class. *American Journal of Distance Education, 18*(2), 89–101.

Moller, L. (1998). Designing communities of learners for asynchronous distance education. *Educational Technology Research and Development, 46*(4), 115–122.

Moore, M., & Kearsley, G. (2005). *Distance Education: A Systems View.* Belmont, CA: Thompson Wadsworth

Moore, M., & Thompson, M. (1997). *The effects of distance learning.* University Park, PA: American Center for the Study of Distance Education, The Pennsylvania State University.

Moore, M.G. (2000). Is distance learning more work or less? *American Journal of Distance Education, 14*(3), 1–5.

Negatu, A., & Franklin, S. (1999). Behavioral learning for adaptive software agents. In International Society for Computers and Their Applications. Proceedings of the ISCA 5th International Conference. Raleigh NC: International Society for Computers and Their Applications. Retrieved May 21, 2001, from http://www.msci.memphis.edu/~franklin/behaviorLearning.html

O'Reilly, T. (2005). What is Web 2.0: Design patterns and business models for the next generation of software. Retrieved October 7, 2005, from http://www.oreillynet.com/pub/a/oreilly/tim/news/2005/09/30/what-is-web-20.html.

Oblinger, D. (2004, May). The next generation of educational engagement. *Journal of Interactive Media in Education, 1.* Retrieved April 24, 2004, from http://www-jime.open.ac.uk/2004/8

Pagney, B. (1988). What advantages can conventional education derive from correspondence education? In D. Sewart, D. Keegan, & B. Holmberg (Eds.) *Distance education: International perspectives* (pp. 157–164). London: Routledge.

Prensky, M. (2001). *Digital game-based learning.* New York: McGraw Hill

Richards, G., McGreal, R., Hatala, M., & Friesen, N. (2002). The Evolution of Learning Object Repository Technologies: Portals for on-line objects for learning. *Journal of Distance Education, 17*(3), 67–79.

Rogers, E. (2003). *Diffusion of Innovations.* (5th ed.). New York: Free Press.

Rogoff, B. (1990). *Apprenticeship in Thinking: Cognitive development in social context.* New York: Oxford University Press.

Rovai, A. (2002). Sense of community, perceived cognitive learning, and persistence in asynchronous learning networks. *The Internet and Higher Education, 5*(4), 319–332

Russell, T. L. (2005). *No Significant Difference Phenomenon.* Retrieved December 22, 2005, from http://www.nosignificantdifference.org/

Schön, D. (1991). *The Reflective Practitioner: How Professionals Think in Action.* Avebury UK: Ashgate Publishing.

Segal, B. (2000). Who said What: Quotable quotes from Information Highway 2000. *Information Highway, 7*(12)

Shale, D. (1990). Toward a reconceptualization of distance education. In Moore. M. (Ed.) *Contemporary Issues in American Distance Education* (pp. 333–343). Oxford, UK: Pergamon Press.

Shea, P., Pickett, A., & Pelt, W. (2003). A follow-up investigation of teaching presence in the SUNY Learning Network. *Journal of the Asychronous Learning Network, 7*(2). Retrieved September 17, 2003, from http://www.aln.org/publications/jaln/v7n2/v7n2_shea.asp#shea4

Sims, R. (1997). *Interactivity: A Forgotten Art?* Retrieved January 20, 2006 from: http://www.gsu.edu/~lwwwitr/docs/interact/

Slavin, R. (1995). *Cooperative learning theory, research, and practice.* Boston, MA: Allyn and Bacon.

Smith, B. L., & MacGregor, J. T. (1998). What is collaborative learning? In A. Goodsell, M. Maher, V. Tinto, B. L. Smith, & J. MacGregor (Eds.) *Collaborative learning: A sourcebook for higher education* (pp. 9–22). University Park, PA: Pennsylvania State University Press.

Swan, K., Shea, P., Fredericksen, E., Pickett, A., Pelz, W., & Maher, G. (2000). Building knowledge building communities: Consistency, contact and communication in the virtual classroom. *Journal of Educational Computing Research, 23*(4), 359–383.

Tait, A., & Mills, R. (2003). *Rethinking learner support in distance education: Change and continuity in an international context.* London: Routledge.

Thaiupathump, C., Bourne, J., & Campbell, O. (1999). Intelligent agents for online learning. *Journal of the Asynchronous Learning Network, 3*(2). Retrieved May 21, 2001, from http://www.aln.org/alnweb/journal/Vol3_issue2/Choon2.htm

Theroux, J., & Kilbane, C. (2004). Experimental Online Case Study for a Breakthrough in Student Engagement: Description and results. *Journal of Asynchronous Learning Networks, 8*(4). Retrieved December 10, 2005, from, http://www.sloan-c.org/publications/jaln/v8n4/v8n4_theroux.asp

Trafford, P. (2005, July). Mobile Blogs, Personal Reflections and Learning Environments. *Ariadne Magazine, 44*. Retrieved January 20, 2006, from http://www.ariadne.ac.uk/issue44/trafford/

Tuovinen, J. (2000). Multimedia distance education interactions. *Education Media International, 37*(1), 16–24.

Wang, Y. (2004). Supporting synchronous distance language learning with desktop videoconferencing. *Language Learning and Technology, 8*(3), 1–37. Retrieved January 20, 2006, from llt.msu.edu/vol8num3/pdf/wang.pd

Weigel, V. B. (2002). *Deep learning for a digital age: Technology's untapped potential to enrich higher education.* San Francisco, CA: Jossey-Bass.

Wenger, E. (2000). Communities of practice and social learning systems. *Organization, 7*(2), 225–246. Retrieved Jan. 2007 from http://dissertation.martinaspeli.net/papers/communities-of-practice/wenger-2000-communities-of-practice-and-social-learning-systems/wenger-cop.pdf

Wenger, E., McDermott, R., & Snyder, W. (2002). *Cultivating communities of practice: A guide to managing knowledge.* Cambridge: Harvard Business School Press.

Wellman, B., Koku, E., & Hunsinger, J. (2005). Networked scholarship. In J. Weiss, J. Nolan & J. Hunsinger (Eds.), *International handbook of virtual learning environments* (pp. 1399–1417), Amsterdam: Springer.

Whatley, J., Beer, M., Staniford, G., & Scown, P. (1999, Sept./Oct.). Group project support agents for helping students work online. *Education Technology.* Retrieved January 20, 2006, from http://www.isi.salford.ac.uk/staff/jw/HCII99.htm

Williams, M. (1997). Connecting Teachers: A professional development model in a distance education context. In T. Muldner & Reeves T. (Eds.), *Educational Multimedia, Hypertext and Telecommunications Vol. 2: Association for the Advancement of Computing in Education.* Retrieved January 20, 2006, from http://www.home.gil.com.au/~shellyw/mid_calgery.htm

Wlodkowski, R. (1985). *Enhancing Adult Motivation to Learn.* San Francisco, CA: Jossey-Bass.

Yau, H., Ngai, E., & Cheng, T. (2005). Conceptual framework and architecture for agent-orientated knowledge management supported e-learning systems. *Journal of Distance Education Technologies, 3*(2), 48–67.

25

Collaborative Interaction

Morris Sammons
University of Kentucky

In this chapter, literature and research on collaboration are reviewed. The primary topics are the descriptions and explanations of what constitutes collaboration and of what can be done to prompt and facilitate it in distance education settings. Questions about these descriptions and explanations and their implications for distance teaching and learning will be considered briefly in the concluding paragraphs.

There is no concise definition of the concept of collaboration common to all of the literature and research reviewed here. This is due in part to the fact that collaboration is a dynamic and context contingent process. In a given teaching and learning situation, it is dependent on elements in the situation, particularly the character of the learners, the learning activities involved, and the teaching strategies employed (Sims, 2003). The literature and research do include descriptions of learners' actions and their attitudes when they are collaborating and of the social context resulting from their actions and attitudes. There are also descriptions and explanations of what is not collaboration.

The implicit position of the scholars and researchers whose work is reviewed here is that collaboration can occur in settings where learners and teachers are not face to face. This literature and research is primarily concerned with describing and explicating collaboration in terms of the actions, perceptions, and attitudes of learners and teachers and with explaining how these characteristics can be prompted and facilitated in a distance learning setting. Unless otherwise noted, this literature and research is about computer-mediated, asynchronous communications among learners in distance education settings.

DESCRIPTIONS OF COLLABORATION

To begin the report of their research on collaboration, Aviv, Erlich, Ravid, and Geva (2001), cited the earlier work of Gunawardena, Lowe, and Anderson (1997), who used an interaction analysis model to study learners' actions. The study found that collaborating learners go through five phases of actions: (1) sharing and comparing existing knowledge related to the problem situation they are considering; (2) discovering and exploring the problem situation; (3) negotiating a synthesis of what ideas have been gathered; (4) testing and modifying what has been synthesized against the facts, beliefs, and theories that are already held; and (5) reaching an agreement and, if needed, changing what is understood as known.

These actions parallel studies of collaboration in face-to-face settings. In their work, Curtis and Lawson (2001) refer to some of these studies. Among others, they mention that Johnson and Johnson (1996) described collaboration in terms of behaviors of social interdependence. These include receiving and giving assistance to each other, sharing information and sources of information, exchanging feedback with each other, challenging each other to persist, offering encouragement to each other, and sharing reflections on each other's activities.

With the earlier research of Gunawardena et al. (1997) as a starting point, Aviv et al. (2001) used the methods of social network analysis (SNL) in an asynchronous learning situation to show that members of the group exhibit cohesion, or shared ideas and behaviors. They assume this cohesion influences the distribution of roles and power within the group and contributes to the social negotiation from which knowledge is constructed. Earlier research by Aviv (2000) indicated that collaborating learners sought to involve non-participating members (bridging activity) and to stimulate discussion during periods when communications waned (triggering activity). Using these behaviors, learners build cohesion among themselves.

Hathorn and Ingram (2002) set about to define collaboration operationally and to describe what happens in groups when members are collaborating. They based their operational definition on three characteristics of collaboration they considered prominent in the literature: (1) interdependence in the communication patterns of the learners; (2) syntheses of what is known with the result that new ideas are formed; and (3) independence from the teacher as they work out a synthesis among themselves. They used this construct to develop a coding scheme with which they analyzed threaded discussions among learners in three different groups. The results of the analysis supported their contention that all three characteristics have to be present for collaboration to occur.

In the discussion of their work, Hathorn and Ingram (2002) state several important points about collaboration. They stated that there is a distinction between learners cooperating and learners collaborating. Learners can cooperate to produce a specified outcome, and this may or may not involve collaboration. Also, cooperation may be successful for some outcomes and collaboration may not be, but in cases when it is not, learner satisfaction with the groups' interactions is less.

Hathorn and Ingram (2002) emphasized that while communication among all learners of the group is essential, more has to occur than just communicating well. Lots of ideas have to be presented for discussion, and the discussion must be reciprocating. That is, the participants go back and forth with each other about the ideas a great deal. Reciprocating discussions are more likely to happen, Hathorn and Ingram stress, when learners are explicitly encouraged to collaborate by the teacher. Without encouragement, these types of discussions are not likely to occur even when there is asynchronous interaction among learners.

The research of Jung, Choi, Lim, and Leem (2002) supports the conclusions of Hathorn and Ingram (2002). It also extends the analysis of collaboration. Jung et al., studied differences in the patterns of interaction of three groups of learners in separate distance education settings. They based their research on earlier investigations by Kanuka and Anderson (1998), McDonald and Gibson (1998), Moller (1998), and Adelskold, Alklett, Axelsson, and Blomgren (1999). The learners were in separate settings, but in a course with the same content and required assignments.

In each setting, learners were given different information and instructions about how they were to interact asynchronously. One group could only interact with online resources and with the instructor about matters directly related to the content of the course. Members of the second group, the collaborative-interaction group, were told they should share ideas and collaborate on topics they selected from a list. Members of the third group, the social-interaction group, were given a great deal of interpersonal and social feedback from the instructor, and the social presence of the instructor was made a prominent feature of interactions. The two groups in which interaction occurred among the learners were given interaction strategies and training on using them. Questionnaires designed to indicate the level of satisfaction with the activities of the course were administered, and scores on the required work were compared.

Jung et al. (2002) concluded from analyzing the research results that collaborative learning and social integration have a positive affect on learning outcomes and on learner satisfaction. In their study, social interaction was more closely connected to positive learning outcomes than to learner satisfaction. Collaboration was more closely correlated with learner satisfaction than to learning outcomes. Both social interaction and collaboration, however, were correlated with higher levels of learning motivation.

Jung et al. (2002) also found that active participation in interaction, whether social or collaborative, does not simply happen because the means to communicate are present. It must be intentionally built into the teaching and learning situation. This conclusion was also reached by Kreijns, Kirschner, and Jochems (2002) and in earlier research, specifically that of King and Doerfert (1996) and Berge (1999). According to Jung et al., this conclusion is also supported by the findings of Anderson and Harris (1997), Gunawardena and Zittle (1997), Murphy and Collins (1997), Hillman (1999), and Salmon (1999).

The preceding review of literature and research describes and clarifies what learners do when they collaborate. It also describes learners' and teachers' actions, perceptions, and attitudes associated with collaboration. The literature and research makes it clear that collaboration has to be built into the teaching and learning situation. Learners should be encouraged to collaborate; the teaching/learning situation should explicitly involve a great deal of interaction. The teaching/learning situation must be set up to elicit interaction among the learners, and most importantly, the learners must be given a reason and an opportunity to interact among themselves. For them to collaborate, their interaction must be independent of the teacher. Further review of the literature and research will show how these conditions can be met.

PROMPTING AND FACILITATING COLLABORATIVE ACTIVITIES

When compared to face-to-face situations, the severely limited social dimensions of distance learning situations are often cited as a major weakness. When interpersonal communication occurs mostly with the teacher, and when all communication is mediated, it is difficult if not impossible for learners to feel they are a part of a group. Learners in distance education setting who are not motivated often drop out. If social and collaborative interaction facilitates and enhances learning and motivation, then building these into teaching and learning situations will keep learners in the course or program. This is another reason why building social interaction and collaboration into the distance learning setting is important.

In their research study, Kreijns et al. (2002) argue that if social interaction is built in, learners will be more willing to engage in collaboration. When learners are anxious about the distance teaching and learning situation they are in, they are more likely to be defensive and unwilling to take risks (Rourke, Anderson, Garrison, & Archer, 2001). On the other hand, being comfortable interacting socially in the situation has a positive influence on the instructional goals of the situation (Liaw & Huang, 2000). Hill (2001) describes the situation when there is both social and collaborative interaction as a community of learners.

The literature and research suggests, then, that getting learners to be comfortable and actively engaged in social interaction with each other should facilitate collaboration. In other words, getting learners to be comfortable and actively engaged can bridge the transactional distance that exists in a distance education setting. The literature and research on what to do to build in conditions for social interaction in a distance teaching/learning situation leaves little doubt that the major responsibility for this is the person or persons who guide the teaching/learning activities, i.e., the teachers or the tutors/instructors.

Scaffolding

The literature and research includes a concept that explains what teachers do to promote social interaction and facilitate collaboration. This concept comes right out of constructivist-learning theory; it is scaffolding. In constructivist-learning theory, scaffolding is when the teacher provides assistance and support to a learner at such a time that it helps the learner to understand something that had been difficult for the learner to grasp. This intervention enables learning to proceed. Scaffolding is the term Vygotsky used to describe the timely assistance provided by the teacher. It was used originally in reference to what teachers did in face-to-face settings. According to Vygotsky (1931), what the teacher does, or how the teacher provides support, in these situations varies in form, substance, and complexity depending on the context.

The concept of scaffolding has been adapted to distance learning situations. Literature and research studies indicate that the concept is generally understood as teachers' actions and activities that support collaborative learning. Muirhead and Juwah (2004) categorize scaffolding as conceptual, metacognition, procedural, and strategic. Scaffolding can be an explicit action taken by the teacher to assist learners attaining a level of understanding that in the teacher's judgment, the learners would not have been able to attain otherwise. Scaffolding, however, can also be an implicit element or condition the teacher builds or designs into the teaching/learning situation to elicit collaboration.

These explicit and implicit actions can be part of any dimension of the teaching/learning situation, i.e., the technological, pedagogical, social, and psychological. The teacher's explicit and implicit activities these situations can prompt and facilitate learners' collaboration. Though they are not always labeled as scaffolding activities, the literature and research studies reviewed have many examples of activities of this type.

Examples of scaffolding activities involve the social dimension of the teaching/learning situation and the importance of learners' perceptions that they are interacting with others in genuine and substantive ways. In mediated teaching/learning situations, teachers can do a great deal to facilitate a social presence for themselves and for the individual learners.

Social Presence

According to Richardson and Swan (2003), the concept of social presence comes from communications theory. For computer-based communications, it means the extent to which the person to whom an individual is communicating through the mediating interface is considered to be real. In their research, Richardson and Swan found that learners in distance learning settings who perceived significant social presence in their communications with other learners and teachers believed they learned more, were more satisfied with their teachers, and were more satisfied with their course than learners who perceived less social presence in their course related communications. Richardson and Swan concluded that learners' perception of others' presence in the learning setting and learners' perception of the teacher's presence in the learning setting were essential parts of the learning experience.

To introduce their own work, Swan and Shih (2005) reviewed a number of research studies on social presence (Gunawardena & Zittle, 1997; Richardson & Swan, 2003; Rourke, Anderson,

Garrison, & Archer, 2001). This research indicated that it is important that learners project themselves into the social interaction. Learners should perceive that they have a social presence in the setting themselves in addition to perceiving that others in the setting, including the teachers, have social presence. Rourke et al., found that social presence is indicated in social interaction by responses that include individual expressions of emotion, values, beliefs, and feelings; communicative acts that build and sustain the sense of a cohesive group such as greetings and references to the group and individuals within the group; and communicative acts that demonstrate other members of the group are listening such as indicators of agreeing and disagreeing and approving and disapproving.

Transactional Presence

Expanding the concept of social presence, Shin (2003) develops the notion of transactional presence. She defines this idea as the extent learners in a distance learning setting perceive others in the setting being connected and available. A learner's perception of others' availability is indicated by the extent to which the learner believes requested needs and desires will be provided. Others' connectedness is indicated by the extent to which the learner believes or feels she/he has a reciprocal relationship with at least two others in the group.

Teachers can prompt and facilitate social interaction by promoting social/transactional presence in the setting. They can do this form of scaffolding in two primary ways. They can model projecting a social/transactional presence in their own communications with learners and they can set up conditions that encourage learners to project a social/transactional presence for themselves. Modeling the projecting of social/transactional presence can be done by demonstrating one's humanness.

Here are a few examples of modeling actions that are more implicit forms of scaffolding. Teachers can provide introductions for themselves and for each of the learners; use a colloquial style; reveal personality traits; offer information from past personal experiences; respond quickly to requests and inquiries; use a friendly and polite tone; express respect for all members of the group and their points of view; demonstrate interest, support, sincerity, understanding, and trust; and draw connections among learners (Brown, 2001; McFadzean & McKenzie, 2001; Verbeeten, 2001). In an implicit way, each of these activities supports interaction among the learners in general and collaborative interaction in particular.

Other Scaffolding Activities

In addition to modeling activities, teachers can set up conditions in the learning situation that encourage learners to project a social presence. These actions are more explicit forms of scaffolding. Examples of these actions are stating the importance of cooperating and collaborating; stating that collaborating is a significant element of the learning activities; making the work groups or teams of learners working together small; have members of the group share responsibilities for facilitating collaboration; changing the makeup of the work groups or teams from time to time; setting up groups according to shared interests; setting explicit ground rules for communications; requiring that the members of a team learn about each other; formally establishing a mechanism by which members of a team can communicate with each other individually and individually with the teacher; requiring timely responses to questions and feedback on each others claims; and providing sufficient time for group discussions (Brown, 2001; McFadzean & McKenzie, 2001; Verbeeten, 2001).

Much of the scaffolding teachers can do that concerns the technological dimension is implicit. Teachers can scaffold the situation for learners by structuring and organizing the Web resources of the teaching/learning situation including the communication systems so that learners can easily and clearly understand how to access the resources and how to use the systems (McLoughlin, 2002). Teachers can make arrangements so learners can study, present, and work with information in multimedia forms. Teachers can set up a wide array of types and means of communication and make helpful resources available. Teachers should be alert to technical problems that arise and be prepared to manage them. If technical problems occur, either for an individual or for the whole group, the teacher needs to respond quickly, and, whenever possible, provide assistance, suggest solutions, and direct students to system support resources (Bonk & Reynolds, 1997).

In the psychological dimension, scaffolding tends to be explicit. It is important for the teacher to provide personalized support when interventions are needed to assist a learner with a difficulty (Fahy, 2003). For example, teachers can tailor motivational feedback to the needs of specific learners. Also, specific individual learning difficulties should be managed as much as possible (Tait, 2000). Teachers should explicitly recognize and affirm learners' efforts and the results they attain (Oren, Mioduser, & Nachmias, 2002). Similarly, teachers should emphasize the importance of credibility and of building trust among the learners. It is important for teachers to encourage harmony among the learners and facilitate compromises when needed (Rovai, 2002).

In a teaching/learning situation, a great deal of scaffolding activity by teachers concerns the pedagogical dimension. These activities can be both implicit and explicit. Making expectations as clear and precise as possible early on implicitly sets the learning parameters for learners (Verbeeten, 2001). Similarly, setting the guidelines for participation informs learners about the conditions of the teaching/learning situation (Ehrlich, 2002). It is most important to provide information on how individuals' participation in collaborative group work will be evaluated. The standards for collaborative work should be clear and fair to all learners. Most of all the standards need to be applied consistently (Verbeeten, 2001). These actions are among those that teachers can build into the situation to prompt learners to move from passive to more active roles in the situation. They are part of the ongoing negotiation between the instructional expectations of teachers' and learners' expectations for the learning experience.

Some of the most important scaffolding activities in the pedagogical area are those involving teachers giving feedback to learners. There should be many instances of formative assessment to inform learners what they can do to improve their performance. In conjunction with this assessment, teachers should be sensitive to different learning styles and recommend alternative approaches when a learner comprehends in a way that is different from others (Verbeeten, 2001).

Using indirect interventions, teachers can guide learners to accurate interpretations of material and of others' ideas when the direction of understanding is wrong. This can be done by posting summaries of discussions of divergent views for everyone to examine (Smith & Winking-Diaz, 2004), prompting for clarifications, and suggesting participants assume reciprocal perspectives and work toward formulating mutually held perspectives (Spatariu, Hartley, & Bendixen, 2004). In these cases, teachers should encourage and facilitate the interdependence of the group and move its members toward independently collaborating on differences that occur.

To facilitate learners' collaborative activities, teachers can ask lots of questions as a way of getting learners to reveal what they know. Teachers can add to what ideas learners have by providing heuristic resources, making outside expertise available, and providing many examples and parallel cases. They can also coach individual learners to participate, elicit learners' articulation of their current understanding, and present and illustrate alternative perspectives.

Teachers' judgments on what scaffolding is needed and whether to explicitly provide an intervention or design in an implicit one are critically important to generating and maintaining collaborative activities. If teachers' interventions are too explicit and frequent, distance is created among learners and between the teachers and the learners. Learners will become passive. On the other hand, if teachers' interventions are too causal and infrequent, then collaborative activities break down. The teaching/learning situation becomes mainly a depersonalized, technological arrangement. The transactional distance between the teacher and the learners is expanded.

This brief review of the forms of scaffolding leaves no doubt that scaffolding activities are complex, diverse, and contingent on the conditions and circumstances of the situation. Whatever form they take, scaffolding activities are primarily functions of the teachers' judgment. One of the major goals in generating and facilitating collaborative interaction among learners, however, is to generate conditions for them to become so actively engaged in the teaching/learning situation that they provide scaffolding for each other.

When learners genuinely provide scaffolding for each other, they are illustrating the characteristics of collaborative activity. They are engaged and interacting socially with some degree of comfort. They are projecting a transactional presence and acknowledging the importance of reciprocity in the setting. They are doing more than encouraging cooperation; they are assisting another learner to come to a greater level of understanding. They are demonstrating their interdependence with other learners, and they are demonstrating their independence from the teacher.

CONCLUSION

Reviewing the literature and research on collaboration has provided a detailed and complex description of what is involved when collaboration occurs and what is involved in prompting and facilitating it. Adopting the constructivist conception in distance education practice presents a way to utilize the power of Web-based technology for communicating at a distance and a way to actively engage students in learning. There's no doubt, however, that responsibility for setting up, fostering, and maintaining the conditions for collaborative activity in a teaching/learning situation rests on the teacher. Certainly, the role of the teacher is much different in the context of collaborative activity from the traditional role of the content expert who dispenses knowledge to learners through lectures with points that are to be passively absorbed and recapitulated.

The descriptions indicate that adopting the learner-centered, constructivist approach to teaching and learning activities in distance education practice does require major changes in the thought and action of teachers accustomed to the traditional, teacher-centered conception of teaching and learning activities. Becoming effective at prompting and facilitating collaboration will require much effort to develop the needed skills. Most of all, it will require time and practice to gain the experience needed to acquire the powers of judgment needed to effectively facilitate and maintain a collaborative learning environment.

It should also be noted that the idea of collaborative learning is certainly not without problems. There is much to investigate and examine. Many of the specific concepts of constructivist-learning theory are not settled, and this undercuts the theoretical foundation. Scholars and researchers of learning theory are still following the ideas of Piaget (1962, 1969) over Vygotsky (1930, 1931) and debating the degree to which learning is an individual versus a social activity. There are followers of constructivist theory who argue that genuine collaborative interaction can only occur when learners are confronted with real problems and when learners work under the real circumstances found in the context or setting of the problem. In other words, according to their point of view, genuine collaboration cannot occur in a distance learning setting.

Independent of those theoretical problems, however, a brief critical look at the descriptions of collaboration reviewed in distance education literature and research reveals difficulties. In general, some of the ideas are not clear conceptually. Though collaboration itself is sharply delineated conceptually in the abstract, it's difficult to see how that sharpness carries over to the context of practice. For example, though there are conceptual differences between collaborating and cooperating, it's not clear how obvious the differences would be in a case of learners working together. In that kind of situation, the precise meaning and intent of recorded comments by learners would be difficult to discern.

This same conceptual looseness affects most of the concepts involved. As another example, consider the idea of social presence. This idea seems to operate more as a metaphor than as a concept that can be clearly explained. Certainly, whether or not a learner is interacting with other learners can be easily determined; however, whether the learner perceives the social presence of the teacher or the other learners is not so easy to figure out even if that learner is asked. What exactly is it that the learner is to perceive?

Perhaps the most difficult idea to grasp firmly for distance learning practice is scaffolding. The notion of providing support is clear, and making the judgment of when and where an intervention is needed to provide assistance to learners' cognitive processing is easy to understand. Scaffolding is so broad, though, that it seems to cover everything a teacher might do, and because everything is included, the concept ends up with no distinguishing substance.

There are also practical difficulties involved in emphasizing collaboration and in structuring and organizing teaching/learning activities to prompt and facilitate collaborative activities. One of the difficulties is more minor. It's troublesome, but not insurmountable. This difficulty is that of evaluating collaborative activity when that activity is defined mostly by concepts related to an individual's motives and intentions. Specific behavioral expectations and standards can be stipulated, and as long as they are fair for all learners and used consistently, they can work. It's difficult, nevertheless, to conceive of stipulated behavioral expectations that relate meaningfully to a learner's intentions with validity and reliability.

The other major difficulty involved is the relationship of the evaluations used in a teaching/learning setting emphasizing collaborative learning to accountability, which is so significant in the field of education today. Collaborative-learning settings do not lend themselves easily to objective accountability standards. If standards were formulated to fit a particular collaborative-learning setting, their application would come as an explicit mandate from an authority or agency outside the context of the setting. According to constructivist-learning theory, this intervention would detract from the naturalness of the learning that the setting was designed to prompt. The literature and research in distance learning suggests that such impositions of authority expand the transactional distance among the learners and the teacher.

Even though there are difficulties with some of the concepts involved in the collaborative-learning approach, actively engaging learners in interactive, collaborative activities that have been designed to advance learners' knowledge and understanding offers opportunities that other approaches lack. This is particularly true for the application of collaborative learning to distance learning. Research has shown that learners in collaborative-learning settings that include support for social, collaborative, and communicative interaction are more satisfied with their distance learning experience and are less likely to drop out (Aviv et al., 2001; Fisher, Silverberg, & Thompson, 2005; Jung et al., 2002; Richardson & Swan, 2003; Swan & Shih, 2005). Learners in these types of settings have reported that they developed a sense of camaraderie and cohesion with the other learners and had a sense of participating on an equal level with them. These are positive qualities that should not be easily dismissed.

The preceding review of literature and research indicates that because of the value of the collaborative-learning approach for distance learning, much more analysis and research is needed. The concepts of the collaborative-learning approach should be refined. Research should aim for providing solid social scientific bases, which are valid and reliable. Research is also needed on how the opportunities that come from the wider availability of increased bandwidth and increased computer power can be used to enhance collaborative activities. Research is also needed on how virtual-reality games (Branigan, 2002; Brumfield, 2005) and multi-user virtual environments, or MUVEs (Dede, 2003) can be used in collaborative activities. Most importantly, because of the increasing pressures to measure the outcomes of teaching and learning activities, it is crucial to investigate whether the outcomes of learning activities of the collaborative approach can be evaluated without generating conditions that inhibit collaboration. Clearly, there is a continuing need in distance learning for more research and analysis of collaboration and strategies for prompting and facilitating collaborative activities.

REFERENCES

Adelskold, G., Alklett, K., Axelsson, R., & Blomgren, G. (1999). Problem-based distance learning of energy issues via computer network. *Distance Education, 20*(1). Retrieved November 17, 2005, from the World Wide Web: http://taylorandfrancis.metapress.com/(hz1b24453khsfbbfpg4yxwyn)/app/home/content.asp?referrer=contribution&format=3&page=1&pagecount=18

Anderson, S. E., & Harris, J. B. (1997). Factors associated with amount of use and benefits obtained by users of a statewide Educational Telecomputing Network. *Educational Technology Research and Development, 45*(1), 19–50.

Aviv, R. (2000). Educational performance of ALN via content analysis. *Journal of Asynchronous Learning Networks, 4*(2). Retrieved November 28, 2005, from the World Wide Web: http://www.sloan-c.org/publicaitons/jaln/v4n2/v4n2_aviv.asp

Aviv, R., Erlich, Z., Ravid, G., & Geva, A. (2001). Network analysis of knowledge construction in asynchronous learning networks. *Journal of Asynchronous Learning Networks, 7*(3). Retrieved November 28, 2005, from the World Wide Web: http://www.sloan-c.org/publications/jaln/v7n3/v7n3_aviv.asp

Berge, Z. L. (1999). Interaction in post-secondary Web-based learning. *Educational Technology, 39*(1), 5–11.

Bonk, C. J., & Reynolds, T. H. (1997). Learner-centered web instruction for higher order thinking, teamwork, and apprenticeship. In Khan, B. H. (Ed.), *Web-based instruction* (pp. 167–178). Englewood Cliffs, NJ: Educational Technology Publications.

Branigan, C. (2002). Students design virtual-reality games. *eSchool Newsonline*, November 1, 2003. Retrieved November 1, 2005, from the World Wide Web: http://www.eschoolnews.com/news/PFshowstory.cfm?ArticleID=4042

Brown, R. E. (2001). The process of community-building in distance learning classes. *Journal of Asynchronous Learning Networks, 5*(2). Retrieved November 28, 2005, from the World Wide Web: http://www.sloan-c.org/publications/jaln/v5n2/v5n2_brown.asp

Brumfield, R. (2005, November 8). Educators take serious look at video gaming. *eSchool Newsonline*, November 8, 2005. Retrieved November 9, 2005, from the World Wide Web: http://www.eschoolnews.com/news/showstoryts.cfm?Articleid=5965

Curtis, D. D., & Lawson, M. J. (2001). Exploring collaborative online learning. *Journal of Asynchronous Learning Networks, 5*(1). Retrieved November 28, 2005, from the World Wide Web: http://www.sloan-c.org/publications/jaln/v5n1/v5n1_curtis.asp

Dede, C. (2003). Multi-user virtual environments. *EDUCAUSE Review, 38*(3), 60–61.

Ehrlich, D. B. (2002). Establishing connections: Interactivity factors for a distance education course. *Educational Technology & Society, 5*(1). Retrieved November 10, 2005, from the World Wide Web: http://ifets.ieee.org/periodical/vol_1_2002/ehrlich.html

Fahy, P. J. (2003). Indicators of support in online interaction. *International Review of Research in Open and Distance Learning, 4*(1). Retrieved November 2, 2005, from the World Wide Web: http://www.irrodl.org/content/v4.1/fahy.html

Fisher, M., Silverberg, D. A., & Thompson, G. S. (2004–2005). Effective group dynamics in e-learning: Case study. *Journal of Educational Technology Systems, 33*(2), 205–222.

Gunawardena, C. N., Lowe, C. A., & Anderson, T. A. (1997). Analysis of a global online debate and the development of an international analysis model for examining social construction of knowledge in computer conferencing. *Journal of Educational Computing Research, 17*(4), 397–431.

Gunawardena, C. N., & Zittle, F. J. (1997). Social presence as a predictor of satisfaction within a computer-mediated conferencing environment. *American Journal of Distance Education, 11*(3), 8–26.

Hathorn, L. G., & Ingram, A. L. (2002). Cooperation and collaboration using computer-mediated communication. *Journal of Educational Computing Research, 26*(3), 325–347.

Hill, J. (2001). Building community in Web-based learning environments: Strategies and techniques. In A. Treloar & A. Ellis (Eds.) *AusWeb01: The Seventh Australian World Wide Web Conference,* (pp. 157–169). Coffs Harbour, New South Wales, Australia: Southern Cross University Press.

Hillman, D. C. A. (1999). A new method for analyzing patterns of interaction. *The American Journal of Distance Education, 13*(2), 37–47.

Johnson, D. W., & Johnson, R. T. (1996). Cooperation and the use of technology. In D. H. Johanssen (Ed.), *Handbook of research for educational communications and technology* (1017–1044). New York: Simon and Schuster Macmillan.

Jung, I., Choi, S., Lim, C., & Leem, J. (2002). Effects of different types of interaction on learning achievement, satisfaction and participation in Web-based instruction. *Innovations in Education and Teaching International, 39*(2). Available online at http://www.tandf.co.uk/journals

Kanuka, H., & Anderson, T. (1998). Online social interchange, discord, and knowledge construction. *Journal of Distance Education, 13*(1), 57–74.

King, J. C., & Doerfert, D. L. (1996). *Interaction in the distance education setting.* Retrieved November 1, 2005, from the World Wide Web: http://www.ssu.missouri.edu/ssu/AgEd/NAERM/s-e-4.htm

Kreijns, K., Kirschner, P. A., & Jochems, W. (2002). The sociability of computer-supported collaborative learning environments. *Educational Technology & Society, 5*(1), 8–22.

Liaw, S., & Huang, H. (2000). Enhancing interactivity in Web-based instruction: A review of the literature. *Educational Technology, 40*(3), 41–45.

McDonald, J., & Gibson, C. C. (1998). Interpersonal dynamics and group development in computer conferencing. *American Journal of Distance Education, 12*(1), 7–25.

McFadzean, E., & McKenzie, J. (2001). Facilitating virtual learning groups: A practical approach. *Journal of Management Development, 20*(6), 470–494.

McLoughlin, C. (2002). Learner support in distance and networked learning environments: Ten dimensions for successful design. *Distance Education, 23*(2), 149–162.

Moller, L. (1998). Designing communities of learners for asynchronous distance education. *Educational Technology Research and Development, 46*(4), 115–122.

Muirhead, G., & Juwah, C. (2004). Interactivity in computer-mediated college and university education: A recent review of the literature. *Educational Technology & Society, 7*(1), 12–20.

Murphy, K. L., & Collins, M. P. (1997). Development of communication conventions in instructional electronic chats. *Journal of Distance Education, 12*(1/2), 177–200.

Oren, A., Mioduser, D., & Nachmias, R. (2002). The development of social climate in virtual learning discussion groups. *International Review of Research in Open and Distance Learning, 3*(1). Retrieved November 17, 2005, from the World Wide Web: http://www.irrodl.org/content/v3.1/mioduser.html

Piaget, J. (1962). *Comments on Vygotsky's critical remarks concerning "The Language and Thought of the Child" and "Judgment and Reasoning in the Child."* Retrieved November 30, 2005, from the World Wide Web: http://www.marxists.org/archive/vygotsky/works/comment/piaget.htm

Piaget, J. (1969). *Science of education and the psychology of the child.* New York: Grossman Publishers.

Richardson, J. C., & Swan, K. (2003). Examining social presence in online courses in relation to students' perceived learning and satisfaction. *Journal of Asynchronous Learning Networks, 7*(1). Retrieved November 1, 2005, from the World Wide Web: http://sloan-c.org/publications/jaln/vv7n1/v7n1_richardson.asp

Rourke, L., Anderson, T., Garrison, D. R., & Archer, W. (2001). Assessing social presence in asynchronous text-based computer conferencing. *Journal of Distance Education, 14*(2). Retrieved November 5, 2005, from the World Wide Web: http://cade.icaap.org/vol14.2/rourke_et_ al.html

Rovai, A. P. (2002). Building sense of community at a distance. *International Review of Research in Open and Distance Learning 3*(1). Retrieved November 5, 2005, from the World Wide Web: http://www .irrodl.org/content/v3.1/rovai.html

Salmon, G. (1999). Computer mediated conferencing in large scale management education. *Open Learning, 14*(2), 34–43.

Shin, N. (2003). Transactional presence as a critical predictor of success in distance learning. *Distance Learning, 24*(1). Retrieved November 28, 2005, from the World Wide Web: http://taylorandfrancis .metapress.com/(hz1b24453khsfbbfpg4yxwyn)/app/home/content.asp?referrer=contribution&format =3&page=1&pagecount=18

Sims, R. (2003). Promises of interactivity: Aligning learner perceptions and expectations with strategies for flexible and online learning. *Distance Learning, 24*(1). Retrieved November 17, 2005, from the World Wide Web: http://taylorandfrancis.metapress.com/(3psmdu553nrnv3mtrc0prv55)/app/home/ contribution.asp?referrer=parent&backto=issue,2,8;journal,8,9;linkingpublicationresults,1:300226,1

Smith, M. C., & Winking-Diaz, A. (2004). Increasing students' interactivity in an online course. *Journal of Interactive Online Learning, 2*(3). Retrieved November 1, 2005, from the World Wide Web:http://www .ncolr.org/jiol/issues/PDF/2.3.3.pdf

Spatariu, A., Hartley, K., & Bendixen, L. D. (2004). Defining and measuring quality in online discussions. *Journal of Interactive Online Learning, 2*(4). Retrieved November 1, 2005, from the World Wide Web: http://www.ncolr.org/jiol/issues/PDF/2.4.2.pdf

Swan, K., & Shih, L. F. (2005). On the nature and development of social presence in online course discussions. *Journal of Asynchronous Learning Networks, 9*(3). Retrieved November 10, 2005, from the World Wide Web: http://sloan-c..org/publications/jaln/v9n3/v9n3_swan.asp

Tam, M. (2000). Constructivism, instructional design and technology: Implications for transferring distance learning. *Educational Technology & Society, 3*(2). Retrieved December 1, 2005, from the World Wide Web: http://ifets.icce.org/periodical/vol_2_2000/tam.html

Tait, A. (2000). Planning student support for open and distance learning. *Open Learning, 15*(3), 287–299.

Verbeeten, M. J. (2001). Learner-centered? It's just a click away . . . *Journal of Educational Technolgy Systems, 30*(2), 159–170.

Vygotsky, L. S. (1930). *Mind and society.* Retrieved November 30, 2005, from the World Wide Web: http://www.marxists.org/archive/vygotsky/works/mind/index.htm

Vygotsky, L. S. (1931). *The development of thinking and concept formation in adolescence.* Retrieved November 30, 2005, from the World Wide Web: http://www.marxists.org/archive/vygotsky/works/ 1931/adolescent/

26

Fulfilling the Promise of Learning Objects

Susan Moisey and Mohamed Ally
Athabasca University

With the advent of e-learning and online instruction, learning objects have emerged as a promising means of achieving efficiencies and enhanced flexibility in instructional design and course development. Learning objects—reusable, digital resources designed to facilitate learning—are the product of three diverse disciplines:

1. instructional design, which provides the methodology and means whereby instructional materials are created (e.g., Dick, Carey, & Carey, 2001);
2. computer science, which offers the concept of "objects," parts of program code that can be constructed, assembled, and shared to serve different purposes (Whitten, Bentley, & Dittman, 2001); and
3. library science, which provides the concept of cataloging and using labels or "tags" to allow materials to be easily identified or located.

The idea of sharing and reusing educational resources is not new. In the past, educators commonly reused learning materials in the same or in different courses, and shared both non-digital and digital learning materials with other instructors and with students. Until recently, however, there was no formal or systematic way to share learning materials widely, particularly digital learning materials, or to revise, adapt, and reuse them as needed. But learning objects have changed this situation. By taking digital materials and cataloguing and housing them in repositories, an abundance of instructional resources is becoming increasingly available to educators and learners worldwide.

Learning objects hold great promise for distance education and e-learning, providing the potential for "mass customization" of individualized instructional materials (McGreal, 2004, p. 3), reducing wasted resources associated with duplicate and redundant learning materials, and providing educators and learners with access to high-quality, instructionally effective learning materials (Downes, 2001). The vision is bold and exciting—educators and learners alike would have anytime, anyplace access to repositories containing vast stores of high-quality, proven-effective learning objects that meet an array of training and educational needs. Instructors could assemble selected learning objects, customizing them according to student needs and characteristics, and deliver them using adaptive learner management systems that allow students to tailor activities to meet their personal preferences and individual learning styles. Learners' formal and informal learning needs alike could be served by learning object repositories, providing ubiquitous access to resources for lifelong learning and enhancing educational opportunities and success. To realize this vision, however, careful research and development is required. As the review below will show, there are challenges to be met, barriers to be overcome, and insights to be gained to fulfill the promise that learning objects offer.

WHAT IS A LEARNING OBJECT?

Although learning objects first appeared on the educational and training scene in the mid–1990s, there is still no commonly accepted definition of what precisely constitutes a learning object. Moreover, imprecise nomenclature is also a problem as learning objects have been variously termed "information objects," "content objects," "learning resources," and "knowledge objects," among others (McGreal, 2004). At issue, too, is the term "learning object" itself (Friesen, 2004). Lack of a clear definition and an inconsistent lexicon creates misunderstanding and confusion; hinders the growth and development of learning objects; and hampers a shared understanding of the concept essential for grounding research in this area.

The Institute of Electrical and Electronic Engineers (IEEE), in its Learning Objects Metadata (LOM) standard document (IEEE, 2002) defined a learning object as "any entity, digital or non-digital, which can be used, re-used or referenced during technology supported learning." McGreal (2004, p. 9) referred to this definition as including "anything and everything," contending that its expansiveness makes it of little use in directing research and practice. Wiley (2002) narrowed the definition somewhat to include only digital resources, defining a learning object as "any digital resource that can be reused to support learning" (p. 7). Further refinements have been proposed (e.g., Hamel & Ryan-Jones, 2002; Sosteric & Hesemeier, 2002), including Polsani (2003), who added more detail, defining a learning object as "an independent and self-standing unit of learning content that is predisposed to reuse in multiple instructional contexts" (section 2.2, para. 4). Noting the shortcomings of previous definitions, Sicilia and Garcia (2003) added two other characteristics: (a) that learning objects are "digital entities," and (b) that they possess a related "metadata record" describing the potential contexts in which they may be used. Ally (2004) added yet another facet to the definition—that of learning outcomes—proposing a more specific definition of a learning object as "any digital resource that can be re-used to achieve a specific learning outcome" (p. 87), and contending that learning objects must be tied to learning outcomes so that suitable content and assessment can be included and the appropriate delivery medium identified.

Review of the various definitions proposed in the literature shows that despite the differences, there appear to be three commonly agreed-upon characteristics of learning objects: they are *digital*, they support *learning,* and they are *reusable.*

Given the above characteristics, learning objects can take many forms, the most common being digital text and graphic presentations on specific topics, interactive multi-media activities, streaming audio and video productions, and assessment tools and test item banks. Adherents to the more encompassing definitions (see, e.g., Downes, 2001) argue that non-digital resources such as a library book, a hands-on activity, or even an instructor could be considered a learning object.

Things that present information digitally, but that are not tied to a specific learning outcome (such as photographs, pictures, maps, articles, applets, etc.), are often considered learning objects, although others would consider them more appropriately termed information objects. The small size or granularity of such objects requires them to be aggregated into a larger size learning object—what Dalsgaard (2005) calls a learning framework—to be useful in instructional situations. Similarly, Williams (2004) describes learning objects as combinations of elements or granules, which may include photographs, text, animations, graphics, workshop exercises, assessment questions, articles, video and audio clips, and substantial case studies.

USES OF LEARNING OBJECTS

Learning objects must be in a digital format to facilitate storage in a repository so they can be searched and retrieved electronically over the Internet and used in different instructional situations. Repositories may house the objects themselves and/or provide links to materials located elsewhere. Growing numbers of repositories are being established (Table 26.1), so many so that "meta-repositories," or referatory sites, are emerging that allow users to search many repositories simultaneously in order to obtain a complete and comprehensive list of resources (Hart & Albrecht, 2004).

Both the content and the process of a learning object may be reused. Usually, learning objects are selected for the content they contain and the learning outcomes they elicit. But learning objects can also be reused for their processes, that is, the underlying code or structure is reused, but the content area is changed.

Various metaphors have been advanced to describe the use of learning objects. Early metaphors like LEGO® block assemblies, which suggested a somewhat random selection of

TABLE 26.1.
Common Learning Object Repositories and Referatories

Repositories	Location
MERLOT (Multimedia Educational Resources for Learning and Online Teaching)	http://www.merlot.org
CAREO (Campus Alberta Reusable Educational Objects)	http://www.careo.org
Canada's SchoolNet	http://www.schoolnet.ca
MarcoPolo	http://marcopolo.worldcom.com
CLOE (Cooperative Learning Object Exchange)	http://cloe.on.ca
Wisc-Online (University of Wisconsin)	http://www.wisc-online.com
XanEdu	http://www.xanedu.com
AEShareNet	http://www.aesharenet.com.au
Referatories	
EduResources Portal	http://sage.eou.edu/spt
Web Tools for Learning (Hong Kong University)	http://www.tools.cityu.edu.hk

components, later progressed to that of atom-molecular structures (Wiley, 2002), where objects were aggregated according to their internal structures and potentiality to combine with other objects. Deeming this latter metaphor better, but still insufficient, Paquette and Rosca (2002) posited an "organic" metaphor akin to the cellular structures and processes of the human body, where an ideal learning object "behaves like a complete organism when alone or as a well-integrated being when aggregated as a part. It must have its own autonomy, the connectivity potential to combine physically or through communication, an encapsulation capability through an interface that concentrate its external relationships and some plasticity, that is the ability to adapt to the evolution of the aggregate" (pp. 12–13).

The organic metaphor is unique from its predecessors by the inclusion of communication or interaction as an element. In the organic model, the "whole is more than the sum of the parts," and the result is a dynamic, adaptive, self-organizing structure, unlike the more static models proposed earlier. In the organic model, learning objects are selected and placed within a learning environment that not only promotes learning, but also has the potential to foster a sense of community among learners (Moller, Prestera, Harvey, Downs-Keller, & McCausland, 2002). In their organic, knowledge-building learning environment, learning objects (or "knowledge objects," as they are termed by the authors) are interrelated with three other elements: scaffolds, discourse action communities, and facilitation. "These components are used in concert with the individual's context to create a rich and open environment that is alive with opportunities, exploration, and meaning-making" (Moller et al., 2002, p. 49). Similarly, Wiley and Edwards (2002) described an online, self-organizing social system with the capacity to solve problems and accomplish specific goals. In this social system, learning objects are "digital tools used to mediate learning" (p. 38), and members of the community evaluate and choose the most appropriate one(s) to access.

BENEFITS OF LEARNING OBJECTS

Digital learning materials have the advantage of being able to be used widely in distance education, where they can be shared and accessed anytime, anyplace. The increasing excitement and interest in the use of learning objects in instruction stems from several factors. Because learning objects are standalone entities, they can be revised or retired without affecting other learning objects. Instructors can draw from a broad range of learning objects, thus allowing flexible assembly of lessons and ease of updating and revisions. Moreover, they may be used in a broad range of instructional approaches, (e.g., problem-based learning, collaborative learning) due to the "pedagogically neutral" nature of learning objects, although as Friesen (2002, p. 64) noted, this latter point has engendered considerable debate.

From an organizational point of view, learning objects allow for efficiencies, avoiding duplication of effort between instructors and among educational institutions, and promoting more consistent instruction within and between courses. Access to learning objects frees instructors from the time-consuming task of content development, providing more opportunity to spend time with students promoting success and supporting learning, in their role as tutors and facilitators of learning (Ally, 2004).

Learning objects also benefit learners, who can search repositories for resources to help achieve specific learning outcomes or for personal interest. The ability to search and access large stores of digital learning materials facilitates lifelong learning for those who have access to learning object repositories. As well, students' use of learning objects increases achievement and promotes success (Bradley & Boyle, 2004), and may facilitate other educational endeavors, such as special education and home schooling.

Similar, and possibly even greater, benefits exist for business, industry, and the military sector. Learning objects can be used to train staff and support professional development, providing businesses and other organizations with resources to foster a more skilled and educated workforce. Learning objects can easily serve as resources for uses such as just-in-time training or updating product knowledge. Concomitant economic benefits, such as greater marketability and increased competitiveness, may result from the use of learning objects for staff training and development. The potential of learning objects for the military sector has prompted extensive research and development efforts such as those associated with the SCORM initiative (Shareable Courseware Object Reference Model), which is directed toward developing a "collection of standards and specifications adapted from multiple sources to provide a comprehensive suite of e-learning capabilities that enable interoperability, accessibility and reusability of Web-based learning content" (Advanced Distributed Learning, 2004, section SCORM, para. 1).

BARRIERS AFFECTING THE USE OF LEARNING OBJECTS

To realize the benefits of learning objects, barriers associated with their use need to be recognized and overcome. Metros (2005) identified several reasons why learning objects have not fulfilled their promise: (a) ambiguous definition of what constitutes a learning object; (b) requirement of special expertise and release time for instructors; (c) instructors' discomfort with sharing and reusing course materials; (d) lack of indexing standards; and (e) limited proof that learning objects benefit education.

Moisey, Ally, and Spencer (2006) investigated the barriers and facilitating factors associated with the development and use of learning objects in a graduate-level course on instructional design. They identified similar barriers to those found by Metros (2005) and added several others, including: difficult-to-navigate repositories; lack of learning objects in some disciplines; poor quality learning objects; inappropriate granularity; lack of a common system and skills for creating metadata; copyright and intellectual property concerns; and attitudinal barriers, particularly lack of confidence in the scholarly and instructional adequacy of the created learning materials and an unwillingness to share them. Similar findings were reported by Collis and Strijker (2003) based on a survey and interviews with instructors. They found that copyright and intellectual property concerns were a major reason why instructors were hesitant to develop and use learning objects, as was the concern that using others' materials might reflect a lack of expertise on the part of the instructor. Release time, recognition, financial remuneration, specialized authoring software, and technical support were identified as ways to promote the use and development of learning objects.

ISSUES ASSOCIATED WITH THE USE
OF LEARNING OBJECTS

Several issues, including granularity, contextualization, and lack of organizational support, affect the development and use of learning objects. As the discussion below shows, the situation is complex and involves many interrelated factors.

Granularity

When a course or a lesson is broken down to create a set of stand-alone, independent learning objects, how large should these segments be? When creating a learning object to provide students with specific skills or knowledge, how long should it take them to complete the learning activity and achieve the intended outcomes? These questions raise the important issue of granularity.

In terms of granularity of learning objects, the literature suggests an inverse relationship between size and reusability (Littlejohn, 2003; Sicilia & Garcia, 2003; Wiley et al., 2004). The finer the granularity, the greater the potential to reuse a learning object in different situations; while on the other hand, smaller learning objects tend to have less educational value and result in less and/or lower-level learning.

The metric for granularity varies, including instructional time, amount of learning achieved, and amount of content covered. Practically speaking, learning objects should be neither so large that they require an inordinate amount of learner completion time, nor so small that they lack meaning or a sense of connectedness. Attempts have been made to specify what constitutes the optimal granularity of a learning object. For example, Polsani (2003) recommended that granularity be limited to a single concept or a small number of related concepts; Hamel and Ryan-Jones (2002) recommended limiting the granularity of a learning object to a single educational objective. To specify the desirable size of a learning object for its repository (http://www.wisc-online.com), the University of Wisconsin included granularity as a special condition (McGreal, 2004) in its definition of a learning object, indicating that a learning object should take approximately 15 minutes to complete; however, designations of granularity based on time have been criticized as being subjective and arbitrary (Polsani, 2003). At present, it would appear that granularity is idiosyncratic, and that the requirements of the situation or preference of the author are the primary determinants of the size of a learning object.

Contextualization

A major criticism of learning objects is that they decontextualize learning. To promote reusability, situational information is removed in order to make the learning object as generic and non-specific as possible. Wiley et al. (2004) discussed the current trend toward the decontextualization of learning objects, noting the inverse relationship between the internal context (and hence, size) of a learning object and its reusability. In other words, a less specific learning object will fit into more instructional contexts, whereas a more specific one will fit fewer instructional contexts. As Robson (2004) pointed out, however, information depends on context to maximize its meaning. He asserted, "the greater the contextual match between a LO and the learner, the more effective it is likely to be" (p. 161). Consequently, he recommended preserving context, citing the high cost of (re)contextualization.

In addition to revising or expanding upon a decontextualized learning object, another way of introducing context is to develop additional learning objects so learners can transfer what they learn to their own particular situation. In this way, generic learning objects are developed for maximum reuse, accompanied by additional learning objects to address the contexts in which the learning may be applied.

Organizational Support

As noted earlier, lack of organizational support is a barrier affecting the development and use of learning objects. For the most part, educational institutions are not yet ready for wide-scale development and implementation of learning objects. Some of the immediate challenges organizations are facing include

1.   development of learning objects to be delivered using different media and technology
2.   management of learning objects
3.   version control of learning objects
4.   updating of learning objects
5.   conversion of existing learning materials into learning objects

For a variety of reasons, faculty members are reluctant to develop and use learning objects. Intellectual property concerns, attitudinal barriers, lack of time and expertise, and unmet needs for technical support and proper development tools—these are but a few of the reasons why faculty have not embraced learning objects as a means of developing and delivering instruction. Hart and Albrecht (2004) recommended that organizations consider the following key questions to promote the acceptance and use of learning objects:

- What are the points of resistance in the use of learning objects?
- What support is available for the development and use of learning objects?
- Are the right tools to develop and access learning objects available to staff?
- How will learning objects from repositories integrate with existing courses?

Above all, they emphasize that instructors' attitudes will have to change, and that support is required to facilitate the development and use of learning objects.

DEVELOPMENT AND USE OF LEARNING OBJECTS

As with the development of any learning materials, proper instructional design techniques and learning theories must be adhered to in order to ensure that learning objects are high quality, learner-centered, and tied to specified learning outcomes (Ally, 2004; Sosteric & Hesemeier, 2002; Wiley, 2000). They must add value to the learning experience so that learners and instructors alike will choose to use learning objects and be satisfied with their experience. Therefore, the development of learning objects should keep learners and instructors in the forefront throughout the development process (Richards, 2002).

Debate exists over the requirement for an underlying learning theory or instructional strategy in the design of a learning object. Many theorists emphasize the importance of developing learning objects from a learning theory base (see, e.g., Ally, 2004; Wiley, 2002), whereas others contend that learning objects should be "pedagogically neutral," allowing instructors to fit them to the learning strategy of their choice.

Baruque and Melo (2004) proposed an eclectic learning theory approach for designing electronic learning materials. Integrating the behaviorist, cognitivist, and constructivist schools of learning, they recommend an iterative process for developing modules using learning objects, in a manner similar to the standard ADDIE instructional design model (e.g., Dick, Carey, & Carey, 2001). In the first phase—analysis—specific learning problems are determined, learner characteristics identified, and existing learning objects sought. In the next phase—design—content is determined, task and content analyses are conducted, and the learning object interface is developed. In the third phase—development—learning objects are created and stored in repositories.

This is followed by the implementation phase where the instruction is delivered to learners, and the final phase, evaluation, where formative and summative evaluations are conducted.

GUIDELINES FOR LEARNING OBJECT DEVELOPMENT

Solid instructional design is a must when developing learning objects to ensure their effectiveness and reusability. Learning objects should be based on a learning strategy, and be active, revisable, and adaptive to allow for learner differences such as learning style, background, interest, and competency level (Ally, 2004; Lee & Su, 2006). They should be able to be used in different instructional settings, for a variety of purposes including achieving learning outcomes, remediation, just-in-time learning, as a job aid, or for enrichment. They should be designed for and tested with multiple users before placed in a repository.

Ally (2004) focused on "learning" in learning objects, emphasizing that students should learn as a result of interacting with the object—that is, that a change in behavior, knowledge, or attitude should occur. To assure learning, he recommends that a learning object have at least three components, as described below:

1. a pre-learning strategy, such as a learning outcome, pre-assessment, advance organizer, or overview, to prepare the learner for the learning situation.
2. a presentation strategy, which includes the content, materials, and activities to achieve the outcome for the learning object. Content may include facts, concepts, principles, and procedures in the form of text, audio, graphic, pictures, video, simulations, and animation. A combination of active and passive activities may be used.
3. a post-learning strategy in the form of a summary or a post-assessment to check for achievement of the learning outcome and provide a sense of completion.

As Hamel and Ryan-Jones (2002) noted, emerging standards do not yet provide specific guidance for designers on how to plan for or to create learning objects. Reviewing open literature on learning object development, they provide a set of five principles to serve as guidelines for authors:

1. Learning objects must be units of instruction that stand alone.
2. Learning objects should follow a standard instructional format.
3. Learning objects should be relatively small.
4. A sequence of learning objects must have a context.
5. Learning objects must be tagged and managed.

Similar to the principles presented above, Longmire (2000) provided the following set of practical suggestions to guide the development of learning objects:

- Use consistent language and terminology.
- Present information in easily accessible and comprehensible formats.
- Present information for onscreen viewing.
- Avoid sequential information across objects (i.e., no backward-forward referencing across objects).

- Use uniform editorial tone across objects.
- Use keywords in searchable elements.
- Use language and content appropriate for a broad audience.

Jones (2004) emphasized that a learning object should have the following properties to ensure maximum reuse: (a) it should be cohesive, focusing on one topic only; (b) it should be decoupled, having no dependencies on other learning objects; and (c) it should be context-free. To ensure optimum reusability, the readability level and language of a learning object should be appropriate for different audiences, and information presentations and learning activities suitable for students with different learning styles. Expanding upon the technical writing considerations for learning objects, Bartz (2002) provided practical guidelines for developing the content of learning objects, noting again that learning objects should be independent and not make reference to other learning objects.

AGGREGATING LEARNING OBJECTS

Although learning objects are developed to be usable as independent entities, they should also be linkable. Learning objects should be constructed so they are able to function independently, yet also able to be linked seamlessly forming a coherent module, lesson, or course, allowing learners to achieve the desired learning outcomes. They should be assembled so that a single learning object may be revised without affecting other objects (Wiley, 2000). Some common ways for linking learning objects are described below:

1. *Specific to General.* The specific learning objects are presented first, and are then followed by more general learning objects. In some cases, a general learning object can be used as an overview for the lesson.
2. *Simple to Complex.* Simple learning objects are completed to set the stage for more complex learning objects. From a learning theory perspective, learners attain basic knowledge and skills they need before they can apply it in real-life situations.
3. *Known to Unknown.* Learners use what they already know to learn new materials. From a learning point of view, learners access familiar learning objects to activate existing cognitive structures, making them better prepared to learn the new materials.
4. *Spiral.* A learning object with a low-level activity can be introduced initially, and the same learning object with a higher level activity presented at a later time. The spiral structure can be used to help contextualize learning; for example, a generic learning object presented early in the lesson is followed by a practical application learning object with a higher level learning activity that contextualizes the information.

Proposing an organic approach for learning object assembly, Paquette and Rosca (2002) described several models of aggregation including fusion or juxtaposition; composition through referencing; control and filtering; scripting; and coordination. All but the last are directed toward the assembly of learning objects for a single user. The last model, coordination, describes an aggregation model involving multiple learners where communication and cooperation structures the collection of learning objects.

Learning styles or learner preferences may also play a role in the aggregation of learning objects. When assembling learning objects to create a larger entity (e.g., a lesson, module, or course), a variety of learning objects should be available to accommodate learners with different learning styles or preferences. For example, a "buffet" approach may be used where students self-select the objects they prefer from an array of choices, or a more prescriptive approach may be taken where suitable objects are presented via a learner management system (LMS) after determination of the students' learning style.

REPURPOSING EXISTING MATERIALS

Many educational institutions and organizations are interested in converting existing learning materials into the form of learning objects. Doorten, Giesbers, Janssen, Daniels, and Koper (2004) outlined the beginning steps for converting existing materials to learning objects, as follows:

1. Determine what material is in demand for reuse.
2. Check availability of selected material, including copyright clearances.
3. Check whether original format matches the agreed-upon interoperable format.
4. Analyze selected material and categorize according to content, activities, a combination of both, or test object.
5. Check possible side effects.
6. Determine beginning and end of smallest meaningful part (modularity).

There are some examples of projects where learning objects are being instituted on an organization-wide scale. South and Monson (2000) described an initiative at Brigham Young University involving a university-wide system for sharing learning objects. Lasseter and Rogers (2004) described a project at the University of Georgia where courses were converted into reusable learning objects to provide more flexibility in course delivery. They concluded that instructors were able to develop better courses more efficiently using learning objects, and provided the following recommendations:

1. Develop a good plan for the project.
2. Change faculty attitude by describing the benefits of learning objects.
3. Specify the granularity of the learning objects at the start.
4. Use good instructional design techniques.
5. Label the learning objects properly.
6. Ensure that there is a need for specific learning objects prior to development.

TOOLS FOR LEARNING OBJECT DEVELOPMENT AND USE

The creation of technology and software tools to assist the development and use of learning objects is at an early stage of development. Schaffer and Douglas (2004) noted that learning and content management systems are becoming increasingly object-oriented, making it easier to develop learning objects and build repositories for different types of learning objects. They foresaw that the newer object-oriented systems will allow the integration of knowledge, performance, and learning, where learners and designers are able to access different learning objects as needed. Similarly, Lee and Su (2006) proposed the use of object-oriented distributed and heterogeneous data and application systems, which store individual pieces of information that can be assembled into learning objects. Richards (2002) noted that as the use of learning objects increases and the field matures, intelligent agents will be developed within the learning object system to match and adapt learning objects to meet individual learner needs during the learning process.

STUDENTS' USE OF LEARNING OBJECTS

While considerable work has been done on the technical attributes, characteristics, and standards for learning objects, comparatively less emphasis has been placed on students' use of and experience with learning objects and how they affect achievement. Ally, Cleveland-Innes, Larwill, and Boskic (in press) investigated learners' experience and satisfaction with learning objects. They concluded that students' selection of repositories and learning objects was based on personal learner needs and expectations for satisfying specific learning outcomes.

Research on the effect of learning objects on achievement is also limited. Review of the literature revealed only a single study in this area. Bradley and Boyle (2004) examined the use of learning objects in multiple sections of a computer science course. They found that students used learning objects primarily for review and for studying before assessments and exams. Results showed that 12% to 23% more students using the learning objects received a passing grade on the course modules in comparison to those who did not use the learning objects.

LEARNING OBJECT METADATA

Learning objects can only be used if they are able to be easily located and retrieved from the repositories in which they are housed. Hence, proper labeling or "tagging" is essential to create metadata—"data about data"—to allow instructors, instructional designers, and learners to locate the learning object(s) that best meet their particular needs (McGreal & Roberts, 2001); however, to date, there is no consensus on the content of metadata and the form in which it should be represented.

Metadata is comprised of domain-specific elements and qualifiers. It functions like an entry or card in a library catalogue, and includes searchable "access points" such as title, author, date, location, and subject (Friesen, Roberts, & Fisher, 2002). Metadata also contains information on areas such as object life cycle, copyright, technical requirements, and intended audience, among others. Carey, Swallow, and Oldfield (2002) propose the inclusion of instructional strategy information in metadata, suggesting the use of metadata tags such as the following to explicitly describe the instructional strategy inherent in the learning object: anchor new knowledge in authentic contexts (Anchor); apply theory in practice (Apply); employ multiple styles of learning (Styles); engage in expository or teaching activities (Teach); use trial and error to discover something new (Discover). To supplement the descriptions in metadata records, Koper (2001) proposed the use of Educational Modeling Language (EML) to provide further detail of the content and processes contained in learning objects. A subset of EML has since been integrated into the Instructional Management Systems (IMS) Learning Design Specification, an occurrence that Paquette (2004) describes as "the most important initiative to date to integrate instructional design into the standards movement" (p. 332).

Since the mid-1990s, several projects have been geared toward the cataloguing of digital objects and the development of systems or "standards" for their identification. The first standard, Dublin Core, was so named as it resulted from a meeting in Dublin, Ohio, which established the Dublin Core Metadata Initiative (http://dublincore.org). Notable projects followed, like the IMS initiative (http://www.imsproject.org) in North America and the Alliance of Remote Instructional Authoring & Distribution Networks for Europe (ARIADNE; http://www.ariadne.unil.ch), which were geared toward the development of a common system for cataloguing learning objects. In 1998, these consortia made a proposal to the IEEE, which resulted in the Learning Object Metadata (LOM) standard, the only officially approved standard for learning object metadata to date (Friesen et al., 2002; IEEE, 2002). At about the same time, a Canadian initiative resulted in the CanCore metadata standard (http://www.cancore.ca), and the U.S. Department of Defense adopted the Sharable Courseware Object Reference Model (SCORM, http://www.adlnet.org/scorm/index.cfm) metadata standard.

Several standards for tagging learning objects have been proposed. Most conform to the Learning Objects Metadata (LOM) standard (IEEE, 2002); however, the standard proposed by the IMS Global Consortium (http://www.imsglobal.org) provides a larger, more comprehensive collection of specifications. One of the simplest standards is the CanCore profiling system which consists of 8 main categories, 15 sub-categories, and 36 elements. CanCore is a subset of the IEEE LOM standard (which includes 76 data elements) and is easier to implement, making it more suitable for educators (Friesen et al., 2002).

Two schools of thought exist regarding how metadata should be obtained. Supporters of "internal referencing" believe that the creators of learning objects should also provide the metadata. Advocates of "external referencing" contend that metadata is a job for professionals and that only librarians or information specialists should create metadata (McGreal & Roberts, 2001).

Inter-rater reliability is a concern in creating metadata, that is, the consistency with which different "meta-taggers" will assign the same value or label to an attribute of a learning object. Consistency is important for ensuring maximum reuse of learning objects and maintaining the quality of repositories. Kabel, De Hoog, Wielinga, and Anjewierden (2004) studied the reliability of using indexing vocabularies to annotate fragments of instruction. They found a 75% rate of similarity between the annotations of a group of 28 "inexperienced indexers" with those of an expert, with more agreement on tangible rather than abstract attributes.

The metadata record is in many ways as important as the learning object itself, and its development should be approached with the same diligence and skill. Hamel and Ryan-Jones (2002) recommended developing the metadata as the learning object itself is being developed. Sicilia and Garcia (2003) emphasized the importance of a complete metadata record to ensure the maximum reusability of a learning object—the more complete the metadata, the more likely it will be located in a search, and therefore, the greater its likelihood for reuse.

EVALUATING LEARNING OBJECTS

Assuring the quality of learning objects is another major concern identified in the literature (see, e.g., Collis & Strijker, 2003; Metros, 2005). Li, Nesbit, and Richards (2006) provided a review of different tools for evaluating learning objects, emphasizing that learning objects should be evaluated before they are placed in repositories, and then should be continually evaluated thereafter to ensure their continued relevance and effectiveness.

A unique characteristic of the MERLOT learning object repository is its peer review system for evaluating the quality of the learning objects it contains. MERLOT contains 14 discipline-specific communities, each with an editorial board guiding peer review policies and practices. Each review is conducted by at least two higher education faculty members who compose a composite review that is posted to the MERLOT web site. Learning objects are evaluated on three dimensions: quality of content; potential effectiveness as a teaching tool; and ease of use. Each dimension is evaluated separately. In addition to a written review, a 1- to 5-star rating (5 being highest) is given on each of the three dimensions. An object must average three stars to be posted to the MERLOT site (MERLOT, 2006).

One commonly used tool for evaluating the quality of learning objects is the Learning Object Review Instrument (LORI), which uses the following dimensions to evaluate the quality of learning objects: content quality, learning goal alignment, feedback and adaptation, motivation, presentation design, interaction usability, accessibility, reusability, and standards compliance (Nesbit, Belfer, & Leacock, 2003).

Nesbit, Belfer, and Vargo (2002) proposed a convergent participation model for evaluation of learning objects with eight goals: (a) aid for searching and selecting, (b) guidance for use, (c) formative evaluation, (d) influence on design practices, (e) professional development and student learning, (f) community building, (g) social recognition, and (h) economic exchange. Their evaluation process utilizes a panel of members from different stakeholder groups who conduct the evaluation independently and then meet as a group, with a facilitator, to compare their assessments and make adjustments to obtain consensus.

CONCLUSION

The potential of learning objects is yet to be realized. Proponents tout the benefits of learning objects—reusability, flexibility, efficiency, and cost savings, among others. But to realize these benefits, there are challenges to be overcome. More and better quality learning objects are needed. A critical mass of learning objects is not, as yet, available to meet the needs of educators to fulfill the promise of learning objects (Metros & Bennett, 2004). Learning objects must be learner-focused and instructionally sound. Repositories need to be better coordinated and more accessible, with a common and reliable system for meta-tagging. Agreed-upon standards are required for all aspects of the learning object development process. More research is needed to develop an underlying theoretical framework, to clarify definitions and nomenclature, to provide a foundation for the use of learning objects, and to investigate learners' and educators' experiences with learning objects.

Learning objects have the potential to change the way instruction is produced and delivered on a worldwide scale. If the use of learning objects is to become widespread and have a major impact, however, then both organizations and educators alike must believe in, advocate for, and develop and use learning objects.

REFERENCES

Advanced Distributed Learning (ADL). (2004). *Sharable Content Object Reference Model (SCORM) 2004*. Retrieved December 10, 2005, from http://www.adlnet.org/scorm

Ally, M. (2004). Designing effective learning objects for distance education. In R. McGreal (Ed.), *Online education using learning objects* (pp. 87–97). London: RoutledgeFalmer.

Ally, M., Cleveland-Innes, M., Larwill, S., & Boskic, N. (in press). Learner use of learning objects. *Journal of Distance Education*.

Baruque, L. B. & Melo, R. N. (2004). Learning theory and instructional design using learning objects. *Journal of Educational Multimedia and Hypermedia, 1*, 343–361.

Bartz, J. (2002). Great idea, but how do I do it? A practical example of learning object creation using SGML/XML. *Canadian Journal of Learning and Technology, 28*(3), 73–89.

Bradley, C., & Boyle, T. (2004). The design, development, and use of multimedia learning objects. *Journal of Educational Multimedia and Hypermedia, 13*(4), 371–390.

Carey, T., Swallow, J., & Oldfield, W. (2002). Educational rationale for learning objects. *Canadian Journal of Learning and Technology, 28*(3), 55–71.

Collis, B., & Strijker, A. (2003). Re-usable learning objects in context. *International Journal of E-learning, 2*(4), 5–17.

Dalsgaard, C. (2005, November, 3). *New ways to think about and use learning objects.* Online presentation at the Canadian Institute for Distance Education Research (CIDER), Athabasca University. Athabasca, Alberta, Canada. Retrieved November 21, 2005, from http://cider.athabascau.ca/CIDERSessions/sessionarchive

Dick, W., Carey, L., & Carey, J. (2001). *The systematic design of instruction* (5th ed.). New York: Addison-Wesley.

Doorten, M., Giesbers, B., Janssen, J., Daniels, J., & Koper, R. (2004). Transforming existing content into reusable learning objects. In R. McGreal (Ed.), *Online education using learning objects* (pp. 116–127). London: RoutledgeFalmer.

Downes, S. (2001, July). Learning objects: Resources for distance education worldwide. *International Review of Research in Open and Distance Learning.* Retrieved January 10, 2006, from http://www.irrodl.org/content/v2.1/downes.html

Friesen, N. (2004). Three objections to learning objects. In R. McGreal (Ed.), *Online education using learning objects* (pp. 59–70). London: RoutledgeFalmer.

Friesen, N., Roberts, A., & Fisher, S. (2002). CanCore: Metadata for learning objects. *Canadian Journal of Learning and Technology, 28*(3), 43–53.

Hamel, C., & Ryan-Jones, D. (2002). Designing instruction with learning objects. *International Journal of Educational Technology, 3*(1). Retrieved November 23, 2005, from http://www.ao.uiuc.edu/ijet/v3n1/hamel

Hart, J., & Albrecht, B. (2004). Instructional repositories and referatories. *Educause Research Bulletin, 5,* 1–12.

Institute of Electrical and Electronic Engineers (IEEE). (2002). *The learning object metadata standard.* Retrieved December 10, 2005, from http://ieeeltsc.org/wg12LOM

Jones, R. (2004). Designing adaptable learning resources with learning object patterns. *Journal of Digital Information, 6*(1), Article No. 305. Retrieved January 15, 2006 from http://www.jodi.tamu.ed/Articles/v06/i01/Jones.

Kabel, S., De Hoog, R., Wielinga, B., & Anjewierden, A. (2004). Indexing learning objects: Vocabularies and empirical investigation of consistency. *Journal of Educational Multimedia and Hypermedia, 13*(4), 405–426.

Koper, R. (2001). *Modelling units of study from a pedagogical perspective. The pedagogical meta-model behind EML.* Retrieved January 15, 2006, from http://eml.ou.nl/introduction/articles.htm

Lasseter, M., & Rogers, M. (2004). Creating flexible e-learning through the use of learning objects. *Educause Quarterly, 27*(4), 1–4.

Lee, G., & Su, S. (2006). Learning object models and an e-learning service infrastructure. *Journal of Distance Education Technologies, 4*(1), 1–16.

Li, J., Nesbit, J., & Richards, G. (2006). Evaluating learning objects across boundaries: The semantics of localization. *Journal of Distance Education Technologies, 4*(1), 17–30.

Littlejohn, A. (2003). Issues in reusing online resources. *Journal of Interactive Media in Education, 2003,* 1. Retrieved January 10, 2006, from http://www.jime.open.ac.uk/2003/1

Longmire, W. (2000, March). A primer on learning objects. *ASTD Learning Circuits.* Retrieved November 8, 2005, from http://www.learningcircuits.org/2000/mar2000/Longmire.htm

McGreal, R. (2004). Introduction. In R. McGreal (Ed.), *Online education using learning objects* (pp. 1–16). London: RoutledgeFalmer.

McGreal, R., & Roberts, T. (2001). *A primer on metadata standards.* Retrieved November 21, 2005, fromhttp://www.campussaskatchewan.ca/pdf.asp?pdf=primer-learning%20objects.pdf

MERLOT. (2006). *MERLOT peer review.* Retrieved November 16, 2005, fromhttp://www.merlot.org

Metros, S. E. (2005). Learning Objects: A rose by any other name. *Educause Review, 40*(4), 12–13.

Metros, S., & Bennett, K. (2004). Learning objects in higher education: The sequel. *Educause Research Bulletin, 11,* 1–13.

Moisey, S. D., Ally, M., & Spencer, B. (2006). Factors affecting the development and use of learning objects. *The American Journal of Distance Education, 20*(3), 143–161.

Moller, L., Prestera, G., Harvey, D., Downs-Keller, M., & McCausland, J. (2002). Creating an organic building environment within an asynchronous distributed learning context. *Quarterly Review of Distance Education, 3*(1), 47–58.

Nesbit, J. C., Belfer, K., & Leacock, T. (2003). *E-learning research and assessment network.* Learning object review instrument (LORI). Retrieved December 10, 2005, from http://www.elera.net/eLera/Articles/LORI%20.15.pdf

Nesbit, J. C., Belfer, K., & Vargo, J. (2002). A convergent participation model for evaluation of learning objects. *Canadian Journal of Learning and Technology, 28*(3), 105–120.

Paquette, G. (2004). Educational modeling languages from an instructional engineering perspective. In R. McGreal (Ed.), *Online education using learning objects* (pp. 331–346). London: RoutledgeFalmer.

Paquette, G., & Rosca, I. (2002). Organic aggregation of knowledge objects in educational systems. *Canadian Journal of Learning and Technology, 28*(3), 11–26.

Polsani, P. (2003). Use and abuse of reusable learning objects. *Journal of Digital information, 3*(4). Retrieved November 21, 2005, from http://jodi.ecs.soton.ac.uk/Articles/v03/i04/Polsani

Richards, G. (2002). The challenges of the learning object paradigm. *Canadian Journal of Learning and Technology,* 28 (3), 3–9.

Robson, R. (2004). Context and the role of standards in increasing the value of learning objects. In R. McGreal (Ed.), *Online education using learning objects* (pp. 159–167). London: RoutledgeFalmer.

Schaffer, S. P., & Douglas, I. (2004). Integrating knowledge performance and learning objects. *Quarterly Review of Distance Education, 5*(1), 11–19.

Sicilia, M., & García, E. (2003). On the concepts of usability and reusability of learning objects. *International Review of Research in Open and Distance Learning, 4*(2). Retrieved January 10, 2006, from http://www.irrodl.org/content/v4.2/sicilia-garcia.html

Sosteric, M., & Hesemeier, S. (2002). When is a learning object not an object: A first step towards a theory of learning objects. *International Review of Research in Open and Distance Learning Journal, 3*(2). Retrieved January 16, 2006, from, http://www.irrodl.org/content/v3.2/soc-hes.html

South, J., & Monson, D. (2000). A university-wide system for creating, capturing, and delivering learning objects. In D. A. Wiley (Ed.), *The Instructional Use of Learning Objects* [Electronic Version]. Retrieved January 15, 2006, from http://reusability.org/read/chapters/south.doc

Whitten, J., Bentley, D., & Dittman, K. (2001). *Systems analysis and design methods.* Burr Ridge, IL: Irwin/McGraw-Hill.

Wiley, D. (2000). *Learning object design and sequencing theory.* Unpublished doctoral dissertation, Brigham Young University, Utah.

Wiley, D. (2002). Connecting learning objects to instructional design theory: A definition, a metaphor, and a taxonomy. In D.A. Wiley (Ed.), *The Instructional Use of Learning Objects* (pp. 1–35). Bloomington, IN: Agency for Instructional Technology.

Wiley, D., & Edwards, E. (2002). Online self-organizing social systems: The decentralized future of online learning. *Quarterly Review of Distance Education, 3*(1), 33–46.

Wiley, D., Waters, S., Dawson, D., Lambert, B., Barclay, M., Wade, D., et al. (2004). Overcoming the limitations of learning objects. *Journal of Educational Multimedia and Hypermedia, 13*(4), 507–522.

Williams, R. (2004). Context, content and commodities: e-Learning objects. *Electronic Journal of e-Learning, 2*(2), 305–312.

27

Media-Based Learning Styles

Chris Dede, Edward Dieterle, Jody Clarke,
and Diane Jass Ketelhut
Harvard Graduate School of Education

Brian Nelson
Arizona State University

Learning styles are defined as "cognitive, affective, and physiological behaviors that serve as relatively stable indicators of how learners perceive, interact with, and respond to the learning environment" (Keefe, 1979). Just as the varied modalities for learning—such as hearing, seeing, and doing—influence and shape cognition, so too do frequent behaviors and skills that result from media-based experiences influence and shape the activities individuals find most valuable for learning. Outside of academic settings, many students today are highly engaged and expert in multiple forms of informal, online learning that involve "mediated" interaction and expression. For example, people of all ages form virtual communities based around favorite video games, television shows, movies, anime, or fan-fiction, using media such as instant messaging, multi-user virtual environments, and cell phones that can exchange text and images.

This chapter describes how and why people of all ages develop learning styles and strengths based on their informal use of these media, and what this means for education. For many students, media-based patterns of information-seeking, communication, expression, and meaning-making affect their perceptions of learning in academic settings. As a result of these new learning patterns and strengths, many students accustomed to mediated interaction do not see face-to-face learning as the gold standard for education. Instead, they often "find their voice" in virtual settings of various types (Ketelhut, Dede, Clarke, Nelson, & Bowman, forthcoming). Their participation in multifaceted, distributed, and mediated learning experiences outside of classrooms and courses causes them to see more traditional school learning as rather mundane because it is based solely on face-to-face learning. How do we as educators, designers, and researchers expect these media-based learning styles and strengths to evolve over the next decade, and what are the implications of this evolution for distance education?

MILLENNIALS' LEARNING STYLES

Millennials and Access to Media

"Millennials" comprise those students born after 1982. During their formative years, millennials in the United States have had unprecedented access to a broad range of media. Table 27.1 captures the percentages of U.S. 8–18 year olds with various media devices in their homes (Roberts, Foehr, & Rideout, 2005).

As this data indicate, almost *all* 8–18 year olds in the United States have at least one television in their homes, and more than 7 in 10 have at least three. This trend is consistent from 1999 to 2004. More interesting are the gains in access to interactive media (i.e., video game consoles, computers, the Internet), especially the increase in the number of households that now own three or more of a particular device, and concomitant increases in usage of information and communication technologies (e.g., instant messaging). Complementing household access, teens engage such media at school, work, public places (e.g., the library), and family and friends' houses. Such ubiquitous access has led a variety of scholars to describe the millennial cohort as having an information-age mindset, classifying them as millennials or members of the Net Generation (Howe & Strauss, 2000; Oblinger, 2003; Tapscott, 1998).

Seeking, Sieving, and Synthesizing

Pervasive availability of interactive media has contributed to nearly 9 in 10 U.S. teens accessing the Internet and to more than half going online daily (Lenhart, Madden, & Hitlin, 2005). More interesting than access is what millennials do once they go online. Of those who access the Internet, four out of five play online games, three out of four gather news, and just under one out of three seek out health information (Lenhart, et al., 2005). By its nature, the Web rewards users for comparing multiple sources of information, as each is individually incomplete and possibly biased, while collectively they are inconsistent. This induces a characteristic of millennials' learning based on seeking, sieving, and synthesizing multiple sources of information, rather than on assimilating a single "validated" source of knowledge from books, television, or a professor's lectures.

Multi-Tasking

Millennials are adept not just with stand-alone computers; they have grown up with fast, portable devices that are networked and allow for a sense of "connectedness" and fluency in multiple forms of media and communication (Lenhart et al., 2005). Modern digital media and human computer interfaces encourage multi-tasking, another learning style commonly exhibited by

TABLE 27.1.
Percentages of U.S. 8–18 Year Olds with Various Media Devices in Their Homes

Medium	1 or more		3 or more	
	2004	*1999*	*2004*	*1999*
Television	99	99	73	70
Video Game	83	81	31	24
Computer	86	73	15	8
Internet	74	47		
Instant Messenger	60			

millennials. The majority of U.S. adolescents use multiple media at any given time (Roberts et al., 2005); for example, many teenagers "do their homework" by simultaneously reading a textbook, listening to an MP3 player, writing e-mail, utilizing a web browser, and dialoguing with class-mates via instant messaging. Roberts et al.'s (2005) research finds that more than half of seventh to twelfth graders report accessing at least one additional medium either "most of the time" or "some of the time" when watching TV (53%), reading (58%), listening to music (63%), or using a computer (65%). In contrast to this emphasis on multi-tasking, "the proportion of kids who say they 'never' use other media in response to these questions ranges from a low of 12% when listening to music to a high of 19% when watching TV" (p. 36).

Napsterism

A third illustration of a millennial learning style is "Napsterism": the recombining of others' designs to individual, personally tailored configurations (Mitchell, 2003). This is evident, for example, in the acquiring and playing of music. Online music providers have diminished the prac-tice of purchasing music as prepackaged albums; in February 2006, Apple Computer issued its one-billionth iTune download of an individual piece of music (Garrity, 2006). Music consumers of all ages now mix and tailor their own sequences of artists and songs into individualized play lists. A second example of Napsterism is the production and repurposing of media through the Internet. Instead of passively consuming information from the Internet, Lenhart and Madden (2005) report that nearly three out of five U.S. teenagers contribute to the content of the Internet by creating blogs and Web pages (e.g., MySpace); posting original artwork, stories, and photos; and remixing existent content in novel ways. In addition, phenomena such as machinima—modifying computer games to be played on users' own terms and creating short videos and movies from videogame play—are emerging and shaping students' learning preferences towards individually tailored and customizable configurations.

MILLENNIAL LEARNING STYLES BEYOND
THE MILLENNIAL AGE COHORT

The technology and media used or ignored by children during their formative years certainly have an influence on their methods of communication, expression, and understanding. However, pun-dits often oversimplify their portrayal of generational learning styles by treating age cohorts as the principal factor shaping learning styles; yet adults who intensively use current media also develop learning styles similar to those of the Net Generation. In other words, the media-based learning styles some have characterized to define the Net Generation are evident in all generational cohorts and not necessarily specific to, or always found in, those born after 1982. Effective instructional designs for distance education, therefore, must consider that millennial learning styles are present to varying degrees in students of all ages. Also, while computers and telecommunications have incul-cated pervasive patterns in how many students seek information, master knowledge, and establish intellectual and social bonds with others, this is not a quality present in every student. Although pupils bring many commonalties into the classroom, they also bring essential, individual differences.

The Development of Media that Shape Thinking,
Learning, and Doing

By mindfully establishing learning conditions for students that build on their media-based learning styles, we can begin preparing for neomillennial learning styles—those attributes resulting from mediated interaction with next-generation technologies that go beyond the information/communications capabilities that have led to millennial learning styles. For example, cell phones are a medium widely used by kids, poised to evolve, and likely to lead to new types of learning styles and strengths as their capabilities increase. In its recent report *Wireless Industry Indices: 1985–2005*, the Cellular Telecommunications Industry Association (2005) demonstrates the pervasive nature of cell phones. In June 1985, the United States accounted for an estimated 200,000 wireless subscribers. In 10 years time, the number of subscribers increased to just over 28 million. In June 2005, wireless subscriptions continued to rise exponentially to just under 195 million. Stated another way, approximately six out of ten U.S. citizens now hold a cellular telephone subscription. Among U.S. teens, as Lenhart, Madden, and Hitlin (2005) have found, almost half (45%) report owning a cell phone, with a greater percentage of older teens owning a phone (nearly three out of five teens aged 15–17) than younger teens (nearly one out of three teens aged 12–14). Similar growth trends in cell phone pervasiveness are taking place globally and in some instances, more so than in the United States. In Italy, the United Kingdom, and Taiwan, the ratio of activated cell phones to residents is greater than one-to-one (International Telecommunication Union, 2005).

Driven by advances in software, hardware, and networking, what was once defined as a hand-held mobile telephone has moved beyond single-purpose functionality to evolve into a new generation of mobile wireless devices (MWDs), which hybridize the affordances of personal information managers, telephony, wireless Internet connectivity, and global positioning systems. Although MWDs such as cell phones, personal digital assistants, and handheld gaming devices retain their primary functionality, convergence has resulted in each device taking on characteristics of the others (e.g., cell phones that take digital pictures, and handheld gaming devices that connect to the Internet).

MWDs and cell phones in particular have profoundly changed the culture of how, when, and for what purpose people communicate over distance (Rheingold, 2002). With these devices carried with users at all times, calls and text messages are placed and received at the users' convenience, regardless of location. Users no longer need to know the location of the parties they wish to communicate with in order to get in touch with them. Premeditation has been replaced with the ability to establish or alter plans in action—the micro-coordination of activities (Ling & Haddon, 2003).

Through convergence in general, the Internet, digital television, and MWDs interweave sophisticated infrastructures that support many media, including such disparate applications as "groupware" for virtual collaboration, asynchronous threaded discussions, massively multiplayer online games, videoconferencing, and mobile, location-aware wireless devices such as personal digital assistants (PDAs) with embedded Global Positioning System (GPS) capabilities. As these new media are evolved and implemented for education, research indicates that each fosters particular types of interactions that enable—and undercut—various learning styles (Dede, Brown-L'Bahy, Ketelhut, & Whitehouse, 2004). This constant cycle of evolution makes understanding the effect of media on teaching and learning more complex.

THE LIKELY EVOLUTION OF MEDIA-BASED LEARNING STYLES

Over the next decade, three complementary interfaces will shape how people learn:

- **World to the Desktop.** Workstations and laptops provide access to distant experts and archives and enable collaborations, mentoring relationships, and virtual communities of practice.

- **Multi-user virtual environments (MUVEs).** Participants' avatars (self-created digital characters) interact with other's avatars, computer-based agents and digital artifacts in virtual contexts.
- **Ubiquitous Computing.** Mobile wireless devices of varying sizes and functions engage virtual resources as we move through the real world, creating "augmented realities."

Generational theorists describe media-based learning styles—what we refer to above as "millennial learning styles"—as driven primarily by the world-to-the-desktop interface. As discussed later, however, the growing prevalence of interfaces to virtual environments and augmented realities is beginning to foster so-called "neomillennial" learning styles in users of all ages (Dede, 2005).

Immersion

As the world-to-the-desktop interface prevalent today is increasingly complemented and even partially supplanted by virtual environments and augmented realities, the millennial media-based learning styles described above will inevitably evolve to a neomillennial style. What will change in these new technologies to foster this evolution? Psychological immersion is posited as the crucial factor leading to the augmentation of millennial learning styles with neomillennial characteristics, as the world-to-the-desktop interface is not psychologically immersive, while in contrast virtual environments and augmented realities induce a strong sense of "presence" (Dede, 2005). Immersion is the subjective impression that one is participating in a comprehensive, realistic experience (Heeter, 1992; Witmer & Singer, 1998). As an example, when watching a *Lord of the Rings* movie, the plot and characters coupled with visual and auditory input produce a sense of psychological immersion: the audience does not focus on the sensations of sitting in a theater seat, but instead on being present in a magical "world," observing a fascinating series of events. Immersion therefore involves the willing suspension of disbelief. The immersion induced by a medium is even stronger when participants move beyond observing an experience to interactively shaping it, as in video games about *Lord of the Rings*. This is a key feature of virtual environments and augmented realities.

Massively Multiplayer Online Games

Many students now experience this type of immersion in MUVEs that facilitate multiplayer online gaming. As Steinkuehler (2004) noted:

> Massively multiplayer online games (MMOGs) are highly graphical 2- or 3-D videogames played online, allowing individuals, through their self-created digital characters, or "avatars," to interact not only with the gaming software (the designed environment of the game and the computer-controlled characters within it) but with other players' avatars as well. These virtual worlds are persistent social and material worlds, loosely structured by open-ended (fantasy) narratives, where players are largely free to do as they please—slay ogres, siege castles, barter goods in town, or shake the fruit out of trees.

Through the Internet, hundreds—in some cases thousands—of users collectively and simultaneously interact in the same MMOG, establishing authentic qualities of community and culture. As Steinkuehler (2004) continues:

> Thanks to out-of-game trading of in-game items, Norrath, the virtual setting of the MMOG EverQuest, is the seventy-seventh largest economy in the real world, with a GNP per capita

between that of Russia and Bulgaria. One platinum piece, the unit of currency in Norrath, trades on real world exchange markets higher than both the Yen and the Lira (Castronova, 2001).

Black (2004) indicated that players of all ages are involved in many different MMOGs and in ancillary activities such as fan-fiction Web sites, where people enamored with a particular game or book can add to its genre with their own writing. While the content of these games and activities seldom inculcates knowledge useful in the real world, the process of mediated, collaborative gaming fosters rich types of learning and identity formation.

One attribute that makes mediated immersion in virtual environments different and powerful is the ability to access information resources and psychosocial community distributed across distance and time, broadening and deepening participants' experiences. A second important attribute is the ability to create interactions and activities in mediated experience not possible in the real world, such as teleporting within a virtual environment, enabling a distant person to see a real-time image of your local environment, or interacting with a (simulated) chemical spill in a busy public setting. A multiuser virtual environment for learning developed by the authors illustrates these attributes.

Immersion in Educational Multiuser Virtual Environments

Instead of "slash and slay" activities, the MUVE interface can be used for more substantive purposes. The River City MUVE, for example, is centered on skills of hypothesis formation and experimental design, as well as on content related to national standards and assessments in biology and ecology (Ketelhut et al., forthcoming). We are demonstrating how students can gain this knowledge through immersive simulations, interactive virtual museum exhibits, and "participatory" historical situations. Students learn to think and behave as scientists while they collaboratively identify problems through observation and inference, form and test hypotheses, and deduce evidence-based conclusions about underlying causes.

The River City virtual world (http://muve.gse.harvard.edu/rivercityproject/) consists of a city with a river running through it; different forms of terrain that influence water runoff; and various neighborhoods, industries, and institutions, such as a hospital and a university. Through egocentric perspectives, the learners themselves populate the city, along with computer-based agents, digital objects that can include audio or video clips, and the avatars of instructors. River City is typical of the United States in the late 19th century; a window on the Web site depicts how we use museum artifacts to illustrate building exteriors and street scenes from that historical period. In addition, throughout the world students encounter residents of River City and "overhear" their conversations with one another. These computer-based "agents" disclose information and provide indirect clues about what is going on in River City.

Dialogue is shown in a text box. To aid their interactions, participants also have access to one-click interface features that enable the avatar to express, through stylized postures and gestures, emotions such as happiness, sadness, and anger. These interface features also allow looking upward or downward, as well as seeing the world from a first-person perspective or from behind one's own body in a third-person viewpoint. In addition, learners can interact with digital artifacts and tools, such as a virtual microscope in which the image from the microscope slide appears in the right-hand interface window. Through data gathering, students observe the patterns that emerge and wrestle with questions such as "Why are many more poor people getting sick than rich people?" Multiple causal factors are involved, including polluted water runoff to low-lying areas, insect vectors in swampy areas, overcrowding, and the cost of access to medical care.

Multiple teams of students can access the MUVE simultaneously, each individual manipulating an avatar which is "sent back in time" to this virtual environment. Students must collaborate to share the data each team collects. Although students see the avatars of other users participating in the simulation, they are purposefully constrained by the technology to communicate only with members of their team and citizens of River City. Beyond textual conversation, students can project to each other "snapshots" of their current individual point of view (when someone has discovered an item of general interest) and also can "teleport" to join anyone on their team for joint investigation. Each time a team reenters the world, several months have passed in River City, so learners can track the dynamic evolution of local problems.

Three strands of illness in River City (waterborne, airborne, and insect-borne) are integrated with historical, social, and geographical content to allow students to experience the realities of disentangling multi-causal problems embedded within a complex environment. After working through various preliminary activities (e.g., learning to use the tools of scientists), students devise an experiment that tests their ideas about why people are getting sick in River City. They begin by entering a control world and selecting the independent variable the team has agreed to investigate. By focusing on data that will help them test their hypothesis, students learn that not all information is relevant. Afterward, students enter an experimental world in which all factors are identical to the control world, except for the independent variable they chose to investigate. By collecting data from the same sources in the control and experimental worlds, students are equipped with a dataset they can bring to bear on their hypothesis, formulating conclusions based on empirical data. As in real world situations, not all teams of students will formulate the same hypotheses, collect the same data, or arrive at the same conclusions. Variations among conclusions do not suggest that one team is right while another is wrong. Instead, students begin to learn that the world is a complex place in which multiple perspectives exist and "truth" is often a matter of interpretation and point-of-view.

To illustrate River City as an immersive learning environment, we are developing case studies that demonstrate the power of immersion in virtual environments for learning. How immersion fosters learning in River City is best illustrated through the experience of "Marie," a female student in eighth grade. Marie, when interviewed prior to using River City, claimed she did not enjoy science class and found it "boring." Yet, when describing her experience in River City, she talks as if she is part of the world:

> We get to move and go places . . . traveling through the city . . . I am trying to figure out what is causing this sickness and we are using like we are talking to different people and we're like going places and we also had to test, yesterday, we had microscopes and had to test the water for bacteria and stuff. And we usually don't get to do that in regular science class. Like in class we are usually taking notes and doing work from the book.

For Marie, River City becomes a physical place that she has visited. This example indicates how immersion in a MUVE enables learning that is situated in an authentic context and activity (Brown, Collins, & Duguid, 1989; Greeno, 1997; Lave & Wenger, 1991) in which students are able to move from passive observers of scientific content to shapers of a scientific experience.

In our research on this educational MUVE based on situated learning, we are studying usability, student motivation, student learning, and classroom implementation issues. The results thus far are promising:

- All learners are highly motivated, including students typically unengaged in classroom settings.

- All students build fluency in distributed modes of communication and expression and value using multiple media because each empowers different types of communication, activities, experiences, and expressions.
- Even typically low-performing students can master complex inquiry skills and sophisticated content.
- Shifts in the pedagogy within the MUVE alter the pattern of student performance.

We are now conducting large-scale studies to assess the strengths and limits of this educational approach, in particular how MUVEs shape students' learning styles (Nelson, Ketelhut, Clarke, Bowman, & Dede, 2005). Other researchers who study educational MUVEs designed for young people, such as *Quest Atlantis* (Barab, Thomas, Dodge, Carteaux, & Tuzun, 2006) and *Whyville* (Kafai, 2006), also are assessing how immersive virtual environments influence their participants' learning styles. These studies are documenting how storyline and players' progression through various levels of capability/power enhance motivation and integrate content and skills, as well as how mediated identity-play complements and extends learning.

Immersion in Educational Augmented Realities

An emerging interface that complements the Alice-in-Wonderland immersion of MUVEs is augmented reality via ubiquitous computing, in which MWDs immerse participants in virtual resources as they move through the real world. AR handheld-computer simulations, like the ones described below, embed students inside lifelike situations, which are otherwise impossible or impractical to interact with, and help them understand the complex scientific and social dynamics underlying challenges involving the environment, community, and public health. Participants in these distributed simulations use location-aware handheld computers, allowing them to physically move throughout a real-world location while collecting simulated field data, interviewing virtual characters, and collaboratively investigating simulated scenarios.

Klopfer and colleagues' AR simulation, *Environmental Detectives*, the first in a series they have developed, engaged high-school and university students in an authentic environmental consulting scenario to which most learners normally do not have access (Klopfer, Squire, & Jenkins, 2002). Students role-play as environmental scientists investigating a rash of health concerns on campus linked to the release of toxins in the water supply. Working in teams, players attempt to identify the contaminant, chart its path through the environment, and devise possible plans for remediation if necessary. As students physically move about campus, their handheld devices respond to their location, allowing them to collect simulated field data from the water and soil, interview virtual characters in location, and perform desktop research using mini-webs of data. At the end of the exercise, teams compile their data and synthesize their findings.

Initial research on prototype AR simulations (Klopfer & Squire, 2004; in press) demonstrates that this technology can effectively engage students in critical thinking about authentic scenarios. Students participating in these simulations indicated that they felt invested in the situations and were motivated to solve the problem. As they collected data from virtual scientific instruments and accounts from virtual experts and witnesses, students moved nearly seamlessly between the real world and the information presented to them on handheld computers. While this approach has tremendous potential, further research is necessary to improve this technology and to understand its benefits and limits for learning.

NEOMILLENNIAL LEARNING STYLES BASED
ON MEDIATED IMMERSION

How might distributed, immersive media be designed specifically for distance education, and what neomillennial learning styles might they induce? Emerging devices, tools, media, and virtual environments offer opportunities for creating new types of learning communities for students and teachers. Bielaczyc and Collins (1999) indicated that:

> The defining quality of a learning community is that there is a culture of learning, in which everyone is involved in a collective effort of understanding. There are four characteristics that such a culture must have: (1) diversity of expertise among its members, who are valued for their contributions and given support to develop, (2) a shared objective of continually advancing the collective knowledge and skills, (3) an emphasis on learning how to learn, and (4) mechanisms for sharing what is learned. If a learning community is presented with a problem, then the learning community can bring its collective knowledge to bear on the problem. It is not necessary that each member assimilate everything that the community knows, but each should know who within the community has relevant expertise to address any problem. This is a radical departure from the traditional view of schooling, with its emphasis on individual knowledge and performance, and the expectation that students will acquire the same body of knowledge at the same time.

Mediated immersion creates distributed learning communities, which have different strengths and limitations than location-bound learning communities confined to classroom settings and centered on the teacher and archival materials. In particular, distributed learning communities infuse education throughout students' lives, orchestrating the contributions of many knowledge sources embedded in real-world settings outside of schooling and fostering neomillennial learning styles.

The benefits of learning styles enhanced by mediated immersion in distributed learning communities are illustrated in Table 27.2.

These ideas are admittedly speculative rather than based on detailed evidence, but, in distance education, a future similar to this is more probable than a future much like the present.

How Emerging Media Are Fostering Mediated
Immersion Throughout Life

Quite apart from educational innovation based on emerging media, people's daily use of new devices is shifting their lifestyles toward frequent mediated immersion, which in turn is shaping their learning styles toward neomillennial characteristics (Dede, 2005). Prognosticators such as Howard Rheingold (2002) and William Mitchell (2003) have speculated about the impacts on individuals and civilization as new digital media pervade every aspect of life. For example, Rheingold depicted a future based on geographically distributed processes of information-seeking, personal expression, and communication—as contrasted with the historic pattern of lifestyles centered on face-to-face groups interacting primarily with local resources. Now, people of similar ages living in the same college dormitory may have non-overlapping personal communities of geographically remote participants that serve as their major sources of sociability, support, information, a sense of belonging, and social identity. He sees these distributed communities, created through mediated immersion, as far-flung, loosely bounded, sparsely knit, and fragmentary.

Rheingold's forecasts draw on lifestyles seen at present among millennials who are intensive users of new media, as well as the projections of scholars and marketers developing products and services based on virtual environments and ubiquitous computing. In the future world

TABLE 27.2.
Neomillennial Versus Millennial Learning Styles

Neomillennial Learning	*Millennial Learning*
Fluency in multiple media, values each for the types of communication, activities, experiences, and expressions it empowers	Centers on working within a single medium best suited to an individual's style and preferences
Learning based on collectively seeking, sieving, and synthesizing experiences rather than individually locating and absorbing information from some single best source; prefers communal learning in diverse, tacit, situated experiences; values knowledge distributed across a community and a context, as well as within an individual	Solo integration of divergent, explicit information sources
Active learning based on experience (real and simulated) that includes frequent opportunities for embedded reflection (for example, infusing experiences in the Virtual University simulation <http://www.virtual-u.org/> in a course on university leadership); values bicentric, immersive frames of reference that infuse guidance and reflection into learning-by-doing	Learning experiences that separate action and experience into different phases
Expression through nonlinear, associational webs of representations rather than linear stories (for example, authoring a simulation and a Web page to express understanding rather than writing a paper); uses representations involving richly associated, situated simulations	Uses branching, but largely hierarchical, multimedia
Co-design of learning experiences personalized to individual needs and preferences	Emphasizes selecting a precustomized variant from a range of services offered

Rheingold envisages, composed of high-end users with access to these new products and services, the following types of experiences would pervade people's lifestyles:

- MWDs, such as gaming devices, cell phones, digital music players, and PDAs would access media that are virtually connected to locations (such as street signs linked to online maps), objects (such as books linked to online reviews), and services (such as restaurants linked to ratings by their customers).

- MWDs would access every type of data service anywhere (such as banking and stock market information, weather, tickets and reservations, and transport schedules).

- MWDs would locate strangers nearby who have identified themselves as having common interests (such as people interested in dating and matched on desired attributes; friends of friends; fellow gamers; or fans of a certain sports team, actor, or author).

- Rather than having their core identities defined through a local set of roles and relationships, people would express varied aspects of their multifaceted identities through alternate extended experiences in distributed virtual environments and augmented realities.

Rheingold paints a largely positive picture of this "social revolution" while articulating some concerns about privacy, quality of life, and loss of humanity.

Mitchell's forecasts are similar to Rheingold's in many respects. He too envisions largely tribal lifestyles distributed across dispersed, fragmented, fluctuating habitats: electronic nomads wandering among virtual campfires. Mitchell expounds, "The relationships of mobile bodies to sedentary structures have loosened and destabilized; inhabitation is less about doing what some designer or manager explicitly intended in a space and more about imaginative, ad hoc appropriation for unanticipated purposes." Learning outside of schools, Mitchell continues, has led to café tables serving as library reading rooms, a quiet place under a tree becoming a design studio, and a subway car becoming a place to watch movies. People's senses and physical agency are extended outward and into the intangible, at considerable cost to individual privacy. Individual identity is continuously reformed via an ever-shifting series of networks with others and with tools. People express themselves through nonlinear, associational webs of representations rather than linear "stories," and through co-design services rather than by selecting a pre-customized variant from a menu of possibilities.

That these forecasts of extreme shifts in society are fully accurate is unlikely. Probably, some people will choose the distributed immersive lifestyles Rheingold and Mitchell portray, while others will have less intensive interactions with new media that do not lead to dramatic changes in their activities or identity. More and more, though, people of all ages will have lifestyles involving frequent immersion in both virtual and augmented reality.

IMPLICATIONS OF NEOMILLENNIAL LEARNING STYLES FOR DISTANCE EDUCATION

If we accept much of the analysis above, four implications for investments in physical and technological infrastructure are apparent:

- **Universal networking**—provides total coverage; allows users to capture, process, send, and receive information through multiple devices anytime and anywhere
- **Multipurpose habitats**—create layered/blended/personalizable places which value connectivity, power resources, and ergonomics rather than specialized locations (such as computer labs)
- **Augmented reality**—experiments with smart objects and intelligent contexts (via GPS and RFID tags and transceivers)
- **"Mirroring"**—experiments with virtual environments that not only replicate physical settings, objects, and people, but also offer "magical" capabilities for immersive experience

This is not to imply that all academic settings should immediately undertake massive shifts toward these four themes, but rather that students of all ages with increasingly neomillennial learning styles will be drawn to distance education providers that have these capabilities.

Professional Development for Neomillennial Learning Styles

Four implications for investments in professional development also are apparent. Instructors at all levels of education will increasingly need capabilities in:

- **Co-design**—developing learning experiences students can personalize
- **Co-instruction**—using knowledge-sharing among students as a major source of content and pedagogy

- **Guided social constructivist and situated-learning pedagogies**—infusing case-based participatory simulations into presentational/assimilative instruction
- **Assessment beyond tests and papers**—evaluating collaborative, nonlinear, associational webs of representations; using peer-developed and peer-rated forms of assessment; employing student assessments to provide formative feedback on faculty effectiveness

Some of these shifts are controversial for many instructors; all involve "unlearning" almost unconscious beliefs, assumptions, and values about the nature of teaching, learning, and schooling. Professional development that requires unlearning necessitates high levels of emotional/social support in addition to mastering the intellectual/technical dimensions involved. The ideal form for this type of professional development is distributed-learning communities so that the learning process is consistent with the knowledge and culture to be acquired. In other words, instructors must themselves experience-mediated immersion and develop neomillennial learning styles to continue teaching across distance effectively as the nature of students alters.

CONCLUSION

While generational depictions of learning styles based on emerging media can be useful, they also oversimplify. Differences among individuals are greater than dissimilarities between groups, so students in any age cohort will present a mixture of neomillennial, millennial, and traditional learning styles. Predictions of the future also carry risk. The technologies discussed are emerging rather than mature, so their final form and influences on users are not fully understood. A substantial number of educators will likely dismiss and resist some of the ideas and recommendations presented here, as they have with other innovations that run counter to an established school culture (Cuban, 1986).

However, widespread discussion among members of the distance education community about the trends delineated above is important, regardless of whether at the end of that dialogue those involved agree with these speculative conclusions. Further, to the extent that some of these ideas about neomillennial learning styles are accurate, educational institutions that make strategic investments in physical plant, technical infrastructure, and professional development along the dimensions suggested will gain a considerable competitive advantage in both recruiting top students and teaching them effectively.

REFERENCES

Barab, S., Thomas, M., Dodge, T., Carteaux, R., & Tuzun, H. (2006). Making learning fun: Quest Atlantis, a game without guns. *Educational Technology Research and Development, 53*(1), 86–107.

Bielaczyc, K., & Collins, A. (1999). Learning communities in classrooms: A reconceptualization of educational practice. In C. M. Reigeluth (Ed.), *Instructional-design theories and models: A new paradigm of instructional theory* (Vol. 2, pp. 269–292). Hillsdale, NJ: Lawrence Erlbaum Associates.

Black, R. (2004). *Access and affiliation: The literacy and composition practices of English language learners in an online fanfiction community.* Paper presented at the 2004 National Conference of the American Educational Research Association, San Diego, CA.

Brown, J. S., Collins, A., & Duguid, P. (1989). Situated cognition and the culture of learning. *Educational Researcher, 18*(1), 32–42.

Castronova, E. (2001). Virtual worlds: A first-hand account of market and society on the cyberian frontier. *The Gruter Institute Working Papers on Law, Economics, and Evolutionary Biology, 2*(1).

Cellular Telecommunications Industry Association. (2005). *Wireless industry indices: 1985–2005.* Washington, DC: Cellular Telecommunications Industry Association.

Cuban, L. (1986). *Teachers and machines: The classroom use of technology since 1920.* New York: Teachers College Press.

Dede, C. (2005). Planning for "neomillennial" learning styles: Implications for investments in technology and faculty. In J. Oblinger & D. Oblinger (Eds.), *Educating the net generation* (pp. 226–247). Boulder, CO: EDUCAUSE Publishers.

Dede, C., Brown-L'Bahy, T., Ketelhut, D., & Whitehouse, P. (2004). Distance learning (virtual learning). In H. Bidgoli (Ed.), *The Internet encyclopedia* (pp. 549–560). Hoboken, NJ: John Wiley & Sons.

Garrity, B. (2006). Apple's MP3 lead faces legal, technical challenges. Retrieved from http://today.reuters.co .uk/news/newsArticle.aspx?type=entertainmentNews&storyID=2006-03-06T001943Z_01_N05400506_ RTRUKOC_0_UK-APPLE.xml

Greeno, J. G. (1997). On claims that answer the wrong questions. *Educational Researcher, 26*(1), 5–17.

Heeter, C. (1992). Being there: The subjective experience of presence. *Presence: Teleoperators and Virtual Environments, 1*(2), 262–271.

Howe, N., & Strauss, W. (2000). *Millennials rising: The next great generation.* New York: Vintage Books.

International Telecommunication Union. (2005). *The Internet of things.* Geneva, Switzerland: International Telecommunication Union.

Kafai, Y. B. (2006). Playing and making games for learning: Instructionist and constructionist perspectives for game studies. *Games and Culture, 1*(1), 36–40.

Keefe, J. W. (1979). Learning style: An overview. In *NASSP's Student learning styles: Diagnosing and prescribing programs* (pp. 1–17). Reston, VA: National Association of Secondary School Principals.

Ketelhut, D., Dede, C., Clarke, J., Nelson, B., & Bowman, C. (in press). Studying situated learning in a multi-user virtual environment. In E. Baker, J. Dickieson, W. Wulfeck, & H. O'Neil (Eds.), *Assessment of problem solving using simulations.* Mahwah, NJ: Lawrence Erlbaum Associates. Manuscript in preparation.

Klopfer, E., & Squire, K. (2004). Getting your socks wet: Augmented reality environmental science. In Y. B. Kafai, N. Enyedy, W. A. Sandoval, A. S. Nixon, & F. Herrera (Eds.), *Proceedings of the Sixth International Conference of the Learning Sciences: Embracing Diversity in the Learning Sciences* (pp. 614–621). Mahwah, NJ: Lawrence Erlbaum Associates.

Klopfer, E., & Squire, K. (in press). Environmental Detectives: The development of an augmented reality platform for environmental simulations. *Educational Technology Research and Development.*

Klopfer, E., Squire, K., & Jenkins, H. (2002). *Environmental detectives PDAs as a window into a virtual simulated world.* Paper presented at the International Workshop on Wireless and Mobile Technologies in Education, Växjö, Sweden.

Lave, J., & Wenger, E. (1991). *Situated learning: Legitimate peripheral participation.* Cambridge, UK: Cambridge University Press.

Lenhart, A., & Madden, M. (2005). *Teens content creators and consumers.* Washington, DC: Pew Internet & American Life Project.

Lenhart, A., Madden, M., & Hitlin, P. (2005). *Teens and technology: Youth are leading the transition to a fully wired and mobile nation.* Washington, DC: Pew Internet & American Life Project.

Ling, R., & Haddon, L. (2003). Mobile telephony, mobility, and the coordination of everyday life. In J. E. Katz (Ed.), *Machines that become us: The social context of personal communication technology* (pp. 245–265). New Brunswick, NJ: Transaction Publishers.

Mitchell, W. J. (2003). *Me++: The cyborg self and the networked city.* Cambridge, MA: MIT Press.

Nelson, B., Ketelhut, D., Clarke, J., Bowman, C., & Dede, C. (2005). Design-based research strategies for developing a scientific inquiry curriculum in a multi-user virtual environment. *Educational Technology, 45*(1), 21–27.

Oblinger, D. (2003). Boomers, gen-Xers, and millennials: Understanding the "new students." *EDUCAUSE Review, 38*(4), 37–47.

Rheingold, H. (2002). *Smart mobs: The next social revolution.* Cambridge, MA: Perseus.

Roberts, D. F., Foehr, U. G., & Rideout, V. (2005). *Generation M: Media in the lives of 8–18 year-olds.* Washington, DC: Henry J. Kaiser Family Foundation.

Steinkuehler, C. A. (2004). Learning in massively multiplayer online games. In Y. B. Kafai, N. Enyedy, W. A. Sandoval, A. S. Nixon, & F. Herrera (Eds.), *Proceedings of the Sixth International Conference of the Learning Sciences: Embracing Diversity in the Learning Sciences* (pp. 521–528). Mahwah, NJ: Lawrence Erlbaum Associates.

Tapscott, D. (1998). *Growing up digital: The rise of the net generation.* New York: McGraw-Hill.

Witmer, B. G., & Singer, M. J. (1998). Measuring presence in virtual environments: A presence questionnaire. *Presence: Teleoperators and Virtual Environments, 7*(3), 225–240.

IV

POLICIES, ADMINISTRATION, AND MANAGEMENT

28

Institutional Policy Issues

Michael Simonson
Nova Southeastern University

Policy is defined as a written course of action, such as a statute, procedure, rule, or regulation, that is adopted to facilitate program development (King, Nugent, Eich, Mlinek, & Russell, 2000; King, Nugent, Russell, Eich, & Lacy, 2000b). Distance education policy is the written course of action adopted by institutions to facilitate the development of distance education programs.

Depending on the size of the organization, the leader may independently establish policies and then disseminate them to the organization. In larger institutions, policies are developed by committees of users and stakeholders. In universities, the curriculum committee may set policies for distance education. In schools, policies are often set by ad hoc committees of administrators and teachers and approved by the school board. In the private sector, policies are most often developed by staff and approved by executive teams.

This chapter will review previous work related to distance education policies, and will present a framework for the development of policies by educational organizations, especially K–12 institutions. Private organizations with distance education programs should find this information useful also.

IMPORTANCE OF POLICY

Policies provide a framework for the operation of distance education. They form a set of agreed-on rules that explain roles and responsibilities. Policies can be compared to laws of navigation, rules of the road, or language syntax. They provide a standard method of operation, such as "no-wake zone," "keep to the right," or "subject and verb must match." Policies give structure to unstructured events and are a natural step in the adoption of an innovation, such as distance education. The institutionalization of a new idea includes the development of rules and regulations (policies) for the use of the innovation (Rogers, 2003). One key indicator that distance education is moving into the mainstream is the increased emphasis on the need for policies to guide its effective growth.

Berge (1998) and Gellman-Danley and Fetzner (1998) have proposed models for distance education policy. These models have been reported and evaluated a number of times in literature

(King, Nugent, Eich, et al., 2000; King, Nugent, Russell, et al., 2000; King, Lacy, McMillian, Bartels, & Fredilino, 1998), and seem to provide a useful framework for an investigation of distance education policy.

POLICY CATEGORIES

For this discussion, policies for distance education are divided into seven categories (King, Nugent, Eich, et al., 2000; King, Nugent, Russell, et al., 2000; Gellman-Danley & Fetzner, 1998). Key issues related to each of these seven categories are explained and then examples and sample policies are offered.

   Policy Area #1: Academic—The key issues in this area deal with academic calendars, accreditation of programs, course quality, course and program evaluation, Carnegie units, grading, admission, and curriculum review and approval processes.

   Policy Area #2: Fiscal, Geographic, Governance—The key issues in this area deal with tuition rates, special fees, full-time equivalencies, state-mandated regulations related to funding, service-area limitations, out-of-district versus in-district relationships, consortia agreements, contracts with collaborating organizations, board oversight, administration cost, and tuition disbursement.

   Policy Area #3: Faculty—The key issues in this area deal with compensation and workloads, design and development incentives, staff development, faculty support, faculty evaluation, intellectual freedom, and union contracts.

   Policy Area #4: Legal—The key issues in this area deal with intellectual property agreements, copyright, and faculty/student/institutional liability.

   Policy Area #5: Student—The key issues in this area deal with student support, academic advising, counseling, library services, student training, financial aid, testing and assessment, access to resources, equipment requirements, and privacy.

   Policy Area #6: Technical—The key issues in this area deal with system reliability, connectivity, technical support, hardware/software, and access.

   Policy Area #7: Philosophical—The key issues in this area deal with the acceptance of distance education based on a clear understanding of the approach, organizational values and mission, and visions statements.

Academic Policies

Academic issues are in many respects at the heart of why policies are critical. Academic issues deal with the overall integrity of the course. They deal with students, instruction, curriculum, and program. They probably have the longest and most widespread impact, as students take courses, earn diplomas, and move to other schools or higher education. Policies help insure that institutional integrity is maintained.

   A theme that is increasingly being applied to distance education policy development is referred to as an *integrated approach*. This approach advocates using the same procedures for distance education as for other academic issues. Instead of developing new structures and policies for distance education, the intent is to modify existing structures, regulations, rules, and policies to integrate a distance education approach. Flexibility is a necessary ingredient of an integrated approach. Teachers, administrators, and policy-makers should recognize that changes do not reflect a weakening, or that modification is not a threat to integrity. Rather, policy changes necessitated by the development of a distance education program merely demonstrate a natural process and evolution of a school, district, or state to accommodate technology-based instruction. Watkins and Schlosser (2000) discuss Carnegie units and explain processes for demonstrating how distance education courses can be compared to traditional face-to-face classes in which "seat time" is measured.

First, once an institutional commitment to distance education is made, academic policies should be reviewed and distance education requirements should be integrated into regulations. Specifically, the following academic issues are examples of those to be considered:

- Course schedules and academic calendars, especially for synchronous learning experiences
- Event, course, and program approval and evaluation
- Student admission
- Grading and assessment of students
- Grade record-keeping and reporting
- Accreditation

Fiscal, Geographic, and Governance Policies

The central issue behind most fiscal, geographic, and governance (FGG) polices is one of ownership—ownership of the course, the student, and the curriculum. Ownership is defined in this context as the institution that has ultimate responsibility, and whose decisions are final.

Most of the time, the school offering the unit, course, or program has ownership, but, if a student is taking only one course as part of a locally offered diploma, in most respects the diploma-granting school is the responsible institution. Most often several policy statements need to be in place that relate to various situations in which courses are delivered or received.

With ownership comes the question of costs. Certainly the school offering a unit, course, or program has considerable expenses, but so does the receiving school and even the student. In sharing relationships the hope is that costs will average out over a period of time. In other words, if three schools enter into a relationship to share courses, and do so uniformly, the costs of offering and receiving courses will be fairly equal for the three schools. Conversely, if one school does most of the offering of units, courses, or programs then that school will have disproportionate expenses. Policies are needed to clarify how situations such as this are dealt with.

Other fiscal policies for schools offering instruction include those related to tuition, network fees, room and equipment expenses, administration of student files and records, and troubleshooting. Schools receiving courses have costs for room maintenance, library and media support, reception equipment, and student support. Technology fees are often levied to support distance education costs. If fees are implemented, policies need to be in place to determine who collects and distributes this money, and how expenditures are monitored.

Finally, agreements to regularly review costs and to share revenues are important. Often it is difficult to anticipate costs, so if agreements can be made in good faith to yearly or quarterly review expenses and income, it is easier to establish working consortia.

Geographic service areas are also difficult administrative issues. Traditionally, schools served clearly designated areas, such as districts, counties, or regions. With electronic distribution of instruction, these boundaries are invisible. Regulations that set particular geographic limits for schools may need to be clarified or altered when distance education programs are started.

Governance is closely related to finances and geography. What school board is responsible for courses delivered at a distance—the receiving or the sending board? Policies need to clarify this issue before problems in need of resolution emerge.

Faculty Issues

Faculty, or labor-management, issues can easily be the most difficult for policy developers, especially if teachers are unionized. Increasingly, existing labor-management policies are being used to cover distance education. Clearly, faculty need to be recognized for their efforts and expertise in working with distant learners, and until distance education becomes mainstream and expected of all teachers, policies need to be in place that clarify distance teaching responsibilities.

Key issues include class size, compensation, design and development incentives, recognition of intellectual property of faculty, office hours, staff development for teachers, and other workload issues. Many recommend that labor-management issues be kept flexible since many are difficult to anticipate (Gellman-Danley & Fetzner, 1998). However, faculty issues should be resolved early on in order to avoid critical problems later. Once again, the concept of integration is important. Integrating distance education faculty policy with traditional labor-management policy seems to most often be the best strategy.

Legal Issues

Many faculties and administrators are quite naïve about the legal issues involved in distance education. Policies about copyright and fair use; liability, especially for inappropriate use of telecommunications networks; and intellectual property are important to resolve. When units, courses, and programs are offered at a distance, they are easily scrutinized and violations are very apparent. In addition to developing clear policies related to these issues, many institutions are developing comprehensive staff development/training experiences for faculty that deal with copyright and liability.

Ownership of intellectual property is an important issue for distance education. When courses or portions of courses are packaged for delivery to the distant learner, the question of who owns the "package" becomes an obvious issue, more obvious than when students entered a classroom in a traditional school. On one side of the issue are those that emphasize the *property* side of the intellectual property equation. This group argues that the school is the owner of any works produced during working hours, using school resources, by faculty. At the other extreme are those that feel the contribution of knowledgeable faculty, the *intellectual* component of "intellectual property," is most important. This camp advocates course ownership by faculty.

Most would agree that both elements are necessary and that neither extreme best serves the school. Often, policies that share profits after expenses with faculty that develop instruction for distant learners are best. The exact split for this sharing should be negotiated, and policies developed, before courses are offered.

Student Policies

Student services should be integrated. In other words, policies related to students learning at a distance should be reflected by general student policies. However, regular policies may need to be modified to accommodate the distant learner. Specifically, if asynchronous instruction is being offered, then support services will need to be available when students need them. For example, if a school offers courses such as Advanced Placement calculus to students in other schools, then distant students may need to be able to access support services outside of regular school hours. Homework "hotlines" may need to be established and be available to all students, not just distant learners. Library/media center resources should be available to everyone, and computer laboratories should be of equal quality. Polices related to students and their needs are often overlooked, but become more critical in a distance education environment.

Student-support policies should be clear, flexible, and widely understood, not only by students but also by faculty. Policies related to feedback from instructors should be monitored and special requirements of distance learners, such as mailing of assignments, use of e-mail, access to Web sites, and proctoring of exams should be clear and designed to assist the student in becoming a successful distant learner.

Technical Policies

Usually, some organization owns the network used for distance education, or is responsible for its reliability. If a private-sector business is the provider, then clear expectations must be in place, and all members of a consortium should be part of the relationship. If a public agency such as a state education department or education organization is the telecommunications service provider, then very clear chain-of-command responsibilities should be in place. Often, telecommunications policies are not the same as other policies related to the distance education enterprise since they are not related to the educational mission of the organizations involved and often they are mandated by the private or public provider of services. However, telecommunications procedures should be understood by all people involved with managing distance education.

Policies related to student and faculty technical needs, such as the quality of personal computers needed by students who learn at home, should be established. Hardware, software, and connectivity minimum requirements should be clearly explained.

Philosophical Issues

Often overlooked when policies are developed are those which relate to vision, mission, and understanding of distance education. Many advocate that, when an educational organization decides to become involved in offering or receiving distance education, its vision and mission statements should reflect this commitment.

Of more direct importance to the success of distance education is the recognition that this approach is credible, high quality, and appropriate. Distance education is an innovation, new to most, and misunderstood by many (Rogers, 2003). Training, administrator support, publicity, and attention to quality are important components of a successful and accepted distance education program. Organizational policies related to these issues should include distance education.

SAMPLE POLICIES

Next, sample policy statements in each of the seven areas will be listed. These samples are to provide examples of issues that are often included in state and district distance education policy statements.

Academic

- **Title 92—Nebraska Department of Education Chapter 10**—". . . to be an accredited high school in Nebraska, the school must provide access to 400 instructional units for each student each school year . . . schools provide required instructional units on sit or through a combination of local and distance learning programs . . . up to 100 instructional units of the 400 unit instructional program requirements of the high school may be met through the use of courses presented primarily through one or more forms of distance learning technologies, such as satellite, regional course sharing, or other audio-video distance learning. . ."

- "each course is shown on the high school class schedule . . . at least one student is enrolled and participating in each course to be counted . . . each student enrolled in a course is assigned to a local certificated teacher who monitors student progress and general appropriateness of the course . . ."
- ". . . off-site courses are made available to all students at the school's expense."
- ". . . at least one student enrolled in each course used towards compliance with the instructional program requirement."
- ". . . class is scheduled . . . each day that school is in session with a certificated teacher present (one teacher may supervise several courses within a single class period)"
- ". . . the distance education class must be shown on the high school class schedule."
- ". . . Carnegie class time equivalents will be the same for television courses as for any course."

Fiscal

- "students pay the same fees for distance education classes as for classes delivered on-site."

Faculty

- "Instructors must meet the standards and procedures used by the institutions for regular instructors."
- "Instructors teaching on interactive distance education will be compensated at the rate of $500 per remote site."
- "Instructor training, including system use and suggested teaching procedures, shall be a requisite prior to teaching a course via the distance learning system."
- "The school will provide 12 clock hours of formal training, including at least 8 hours using the network."

Legal

- ". . . course materials will be reviewed by appropriate school officials to insure copyright regulations are strictly adhered to . . ."
- ". . . course materials developed locally will be the property of the originating school, unless special arrangements are made in writing."

Student

- "students . . . must have the same services, the same options for continuing education, and the same choices of delivery methods as the traditional on-site students."

Technical

- ". . . students must remain in sight of the video camera."
- ". . . students must respect the equipment."
- ". . . three violations and students are dismissed from the distance education class."
- ". . . classes missed because of technical problems will be rescheduled and required. . ."

Philosophical

- ". . . is the mission of . . . school district . . . using electronic or other technologies to provide high quality educational experiences."
- ". . . courses delivered to distant learners are considered equivalent to those offered traditionally."
- "Each student, prior to graduation, will enroll and complete at least one course delivered using distance education technologies."

SUMMARY

Integrated policies for distance education are preferred (King et al., 1998). In other words, policies that provide guidance and direction to the educational systems should seamlessly include and incorporate the concept of distant delivery of instruction. Students should be defined by their enrollment in a course or program, not by whether they are distant or local learners (Simonson, Smaldino, Albright, & Zvacek, 2006). Initially, distance education policies will probably need to be infused with existing policies. Ultimately, they should be integrated to indicate that distance education is a routine and regularly occurring component of the educational enterprise. Policies are merely tools to facilitate program integrity.

In order to plow straight rows, the farmer does not look down at the ground, but at the end of the field.

REFERENCES

Berge, Z. (1998). Barriers to online teaching in post-secondary institutions: Can policy changes fix it? *Online Journal of Distance Learning Administration, 1*(2). Retrieved July 24, 2006, from http://www.westga.edu/~distance/Berge12.html

Gellman-Danley, B., & Fetzner, M. (1998). Asking the really tough questions: Policy issues for distance learning. *Online Journal of Distance Learning Administration, 1*(1). Retrieved July 24, 2006, from http://www.westga.edu/~distance/danley11.html

King, J., Lacy, D., McMillian, J., Bartels, K., & Fredilino, M. (1998, November). *The policy perspective in distance education: A futures landscape/panorama.* Invited paper presented at the 1998 Nebraska Distance Education Conference, Lincoln, NE.

King, J., Nugent, G. Eich, J. Mlinek, D., & Russell, E. (2000). A policy framework for distance education: A case study and model. *DEOSNEWS, 10*(10). Retrieved July 24, 2006, from http://www.ed.psu.edu/acsde/deos/deosnews/deosnews10_10.asp

King, J., Nugent, G., Russell, E., Eich, J., & Lacy, D. (2000). Policy frameworks for distance education: Implications for decision makers. *Online Journal of Distance Learning Administration, 3*(2). Retrieved July 24, 2006, from http://www.westga.edu/~distance/king32.html

Rogers, E. (2003). Diffusion of innovations (5th ed.). New York: Free Press.

Simonson, M., Smaldino. S., Albright, M., & Zvacek, S. (2006). *Teaching and learning at a distance: Foundations of distance education* (3rd ed.). Upper Saddle, NJ: Prentice-Hall.

Watkins, R., & Schlosser, C. (2000). Capabilities-based educational equivalency units: Beginning a professional dialogue. *The American Journal of Distance Education, 14*(3), 34–47.

29

Strategic Planning

Ryan Watkins
The George Washington University

Roger Kaufman
Florida State University and Sonora Institute of Technology

Too often when professors, instructors, trainers, instructional designers, managers, and other education professionals hear "we need a distance education program" their first impulse is to search through course curriculums. They quickly try to decide which courses will easily be transformed into online, video, audio, or other digital formats; rarely questioning the requirement and/or usefulness of distance education in the first place. "All too often those charged with setting up a distance education system are not given the choice to recommend against it" (Rumble, 1986). Successful strategic planning for distance education challenges this immediate and premature call for solutions. Instead, pragmatic planning starts with a close examination of what results should be accomplished based on who are the primary clients and beneficiaries of whatever is delivered (Watkins, 2006).

Rumble (1986) urged educators to understand that just because there are education problems that may be satisfied by distance education methods, this does not necessarily mean that distance education is the best choice for addressing them. Fortunately, educators today have a wide variety of tools available to them that reduce the possibilities of implementing distance education solutions for inappropriate institutional opportunities or problems. Devoting time to a rigorous needs assessment, for example, is a valuable method for justifying all actions that follow the request for distance education—or any other solution in search of a problem (Kaufman, 2000; 2006).

Before your institution elects to invest resources of time and money in a distance education program, a rigorous needs assessment may justify the decision and prepare you to make the difficult decisions that follow (Kaufman, 2006; Kaufman & Watkins, 2000; Watkins, 2006). Today's educators all too often feel pressure to implement solutions prior to justifying their actions based on adding value to all stakeholders (such as learners, faculty, administrative staff, employers, and the shared society). As in corporate settings, educational institutions frequently leave few incentives for the educators to step back and analyze all the necessary information before making complex decisions. The lack of effective strategic planning and aligned front-end assessment is unfortunate because often by the time the impact of a possibly ineffective intervention (e.g., distance education) is known, the institution has sustained damage and/or the ideal time for addressing the problem or opportunity has passed.

NEEDS ASSESSMENT: A MODEL FROM THE LITERATURE THAT GUIDES STRATEGIC PLANNING

A systemic-needs assessment can identify, prioritize, and justify the closure of societal, institutional, and individual needs (e.g., gaps in results) in support of effective strategic planning.[1] While there are many models for conducting a needs assessment, arguably the most fashionable models include those of Rossett (1987),[2] Robinson and Robinson (1995), Mager and Pipe (1997), and Kaufman (1992, 1998, 2000, 2006).[3] Each of these models can be of value, providing educators with insights otherwise missing from the strategic planning and decision-making processes. The Kaufman framework, however, provides a rigorous process that aligns strategic planning, tactical decision-making, operational planning, and needs-assessment processes with a focus on societal, organizational, and individual results. These alignments, we suggest, are of great advantage when making and justifying difficult decisions regarding the future of distance education in any institution. As a consequence, the needs-assessment procedures suggested below represent a blend of strengths from a variety of assessment models, yet remain structured within a results-focused framework. In addition, the performance criteria generated by an appropriate needs assessment provides the bases for design, development, implementation, and continual improvement.

For effective strategic planning, assessment, and decision making, the needs assessment framework we propose is based on three fundamental concepts:

Distance Learning Is a Means, Not an End

Needs assessments that differentiate between ends and means can guide strategic decision-making. Ends are the results of all that your institution does and delivers. Means are the ways in which results are obtained (Kaufman, 1992, 2000, 2006). Distance learning is, as a consequence, a means for achieving institutional results. We should first focus on the ends required by the institution for long-term success (based on contributions to both the organization and the external partners) before we make the decision that distance learning is the most effective and efficient means for achieving these results.

Not All Results Are the Same

All institutional results should be differentiated depending upon their primary client and beneficiary. While many institutions are proficient at analyzing their inputs and processes, most have

---

[1]See Kaufman, 1992; 1998; 2000; 2006.

[2]There have been serious challenges to "training needs assessments" on the basis that they will, because of their target organizational level, be wrong 80–90% of the time. See Clark and Estes, 2002; Stolovich, 2000.

[3]See Watkins, Leigh, Platt, and Kaufman (1998) for a comparison of alternative-needs assessment models in terms of what they deliver in scope and content.

spent far less time differentiating the results that they contribute. By differentiating among related results we can assure that all institutional *products* and *outputs* are aligned with the desired contributions (*outcomes*) of the institution to its external clients and community. Institutions should seek to link the *products* they produce (for example, learners with a defined set of competencies) and the *outputs* they deliver (for example, graduates with a bachelors, masters, or doctoral degree) with the *outcomes* that result (for example, alumni who add value to employers, community groups, and shared society); thus aligning Micro, Macro, and Mega level results (Kaufman, 2000, 2006; Kaufman, Watkins, and Leigh, 2001).

For Effective Strategic Planning and Needs Assessment, "Need" Is a Noun and Not a Verb

In the context of a needs assessment this differentiation in vocabulary is vital. By electing to refer to needs as gaps in institutional results (nouns) you can avoid the alluring selection of solutions, such as distance learning, prematurely. Being able to identify, prioritize, and justify interventions and expenditures on the basis of gaps in results (rather than desired programs or initiatives) is the reward for this slight adjustment to your vocabulary. From those individuals who insist on using need as a verb, you will undeniably hear comments like "we *need* a distance learning program" long before the difference in desired and current results has been identified.

Built on these fundamental concepts are the strategic planning processes and procedures for effectively determining if and when a distance education program may be an appropriate option for your institution. The steps that follow will help justify a distance education or alternative effort when appropriate for achieving useful results, as well as define the desired results which those initiatives should be designed to accomplish.

STEP ONE: IDENTIFY AND ALIGN THE INSTITUTION'S VISION AND MISSION

Step One often is (but shouldn't be) an "additional task" for many educational institutions. While most institutions today have multiple mission statements (such as goals, values, principles, and visions) to include in their strategic plan, rarely are these the useful documents they could be for directing decision-making (Watkins, 2004). In addition, departments and units often have their own missions, which may or may not be in alignment with the vision used by the institution to define its future and its contribution to internal and external stakeholders. This alignment is essential, however, for providing direction to programs and initiatives that seek to contribute valuable results.

A typical challenge for educators is to also ensure that all of the missions (including those of the program, department, school, or college, for example) are aligned and contribute to the success of the institution and society. Covey (1996) tells us that "total organizational alignment means that within the realities of the surrounding environment, all components of your organization—including your mission, vision, values, strategy, structure, systems, individual styles and skills, and especially the minds and hearts of your people—support and work together effectively for maximum performance" (p. 1). For institutions conducting a needs assessment, these alignments are essential for defining the desired and/or required results to be achieved (as well as optimal process efficiency and effectiveness). The societal value-added focus that we call "Mega Thinking and Planning" is now becoming increasingly recognized and required by for-profit organizations as well (Davis, 2005).

If any institutional mission (or even the objective of a distance learning program) does not move toward the achievement of the overall vision (best set in measurable yet ideal terms), then this mission should be revised before any interventions are implemented. Interventions not linked to the aligned institutional Ideal Vision and Mission Objective may lead to the achievement of inappropriate and/or damaging results (Kaufman 1998, 2000, 2006). The implementation of a distance learning program must contribute to the achievement of value-added results for learners and the community. This alignment is what links programs to the attainment of institutional objectives and assures that they are not merely implementing solutions to unknown problems (Kaufman, 1995).

An institution may be lacking a vision and/or related mission that set measurable performance criteria for success.[4] If so, then it is imperative for effective decision-making that these be established so that all educational programs clearly define where they are going and how to tell when they have arrived. Often institutional and program objectives are not written with measurement criteria. These measurement standards will also be essential in the third step of the needs assessment in which needs are prioritized, selected for closure, and integrated into the institution's strategic plans.

STEP TWO: IDENTIFY THE NEEDS

Needs are discrepancies between current results and results required for the accomplishment of the institution's vision, mission, program objectives, and individual/team objectives. Identifying needs requires both the information obtained in Step One as well as the collection of additional data regarding the current performance and results of the institution. It is common for a needs assessment to utilize both institutional data available in existing files, accreditation reports, and other resources, as well as opinion data from interviews, questionnaires, focus groups, or other procedures to supplement the findings (Kaufman, Watkins, & Leigh, 2001; Willis, 1992, 1994). The combination of both "hard" and "soft" data, as well as qualitative and quantitative data, is essential in determining if distance education is right for your institution (see Table 29.1).

The Organizational Elements Model (OEM) can be a useful tool for organizing the information you collect. The OEM differentiates five levels of institutional planning and assessment:

Mega—planning and assessment with the primary client and beneficiary being society, and results termed as Outcomes.

Macro—planning and assessment with the primary client and beneficiary being the institution, and results termed as Outputs.

Micro—planning and assessment with the primary client and beneficiary being the individuals and teams within the institution, and results termed as Products.

Process—planning and assessment with the primary focus on institutional processes and activities.

Inputs—planning and assessment with the primary focus on resources and assets.

Based on the OEM, institutional data should be collected that reflects each of the interdependent levels (see Table 29.2 for examples).

---

[4]See Abrahams, 1995; Covey, 1996; Byars and Neil, 1987; Garratt, 1995; Senge, 1990; and Nanus, 1992.

TABLE 29.1.
Example Data Collections Tools and Techniques for Each Data Type

	Hard	*Soft*
Quantitative	• Performance data • Budgets	• Likert-type scale surveys* • Performance ratings
Qualitative	• Focus groups • Analysis of professional list serve • Multi-source performance observations	• Opinion surveys • Individual interviews • Single source performance observations

*The results of Likert-type scale surveys are often mistakenly thought of as hard data since they result in quantifiable data. This is a good example of why we should consider data on both dimensions (hard-soft and quantitative-qualitative) since a single dimension may lead to confusion and the use of inappropriate statistical techniques and related conclusions.

The Mega level of the OEM adds a stakeholder—society—that has traditionally been forgotten or assumed in the development of distance education programs (Kaufman, 2000; Kaufman, Watkins, & Leigh, 2001). Society, as a whole, is not only a beneficiary of that which an institution does and delivers, but for many institutions (especially K–12 schools and universities) society is a primary financial supporter for their efforts. The application of this strategic approach assures that societal contributions are not forgotten in the needs assessment, strategic plans, and/or the possible implementation of a distance learning program.

Many needs-assessment approaches suggest that institutions only collect data regarding current processes and achievements, thus relying on the assumptions that desired results are known, agreed upon, and similarly evaluated throughout the institution and among its partners.

TABLE 29.2.
Examples of Hard and Soft Data in Relation to the OEM

Level	Hard Data	Soft Data
Mega (societal value added)	• Ideal Vision • Student and faculty safety	• Student quality of life • Continuing taxpayer satisfaction with education resulting in funding
Macro (organizational pay-offs)	• Mission objective accomplished	• Executive management satisfaction and perceptions of value
Micro (individual and team results)	• Operating costs • Individual/team performance	• Individual/team morale and perceptions of value • Learning/learner mastery gains • Student satisfaction with what they learn
Process (Methods and means)	• Cycle time • Length of time taken on a course topic • Number of overheads used in instruction • Use of computer-driven instruction.	• Learner "attendance" and participation • Learner satisfaction with the learning processes
Input (Resources and pre-requisites)	• Resource availability • Resource functionality	• Resource adequacy • Resource timeliness

By collecting data on both current (i.e., What Is) and desired (i.e., What Should Be) results, a needs assessment can inform decision-making without relying on an assumption that desired performance is well defined and measured. Utilizing both What Is (WI) and What Should Be (WSB) data, you can identify gaps or discrepancies between What Is and What Should Be (Gap = WSB − WI). Using a consistent scale of measurement (e.g., interval or ratio), these gaps can illustrate real and/or perceived differences between current individual, organizational, and societal performance (WI) and the desired or required performance that necessary for individual, organization, and societal success (WSB).[5]

Examination and participation in all five elements of the OEM (inputs, processes, products, outputs, and outcomes) allow educators to gain a systems view of their institution, external clients, and their societal context and realities. By applying the OEM, decision-makers are not limited to a Macro view (organization-wide) or a Micro view (sections and/or departments) of their organization.

STEP THREE: PRIORITIZE AND SELECT NEED(S) TO BE ADDRESSED

Prioritizing and selecting the needs to be closed is essential to the success of any institution (Watkins, 2006). In this step of the assessment process, collected data will drive the decision-making, while comparing the cost of closing the gaps and the cost of not closing the gaps will be the basis of this analysis. The extent to which data is collected and analyzed will have two effects on the quality of the needs assessment: (a) an extended period of data collection can negate the timeliness of the assessment, and (b) not enough supporting data can invalidate the results of the assessment. The context of the performance problem (i.e., the reason why distance education is being considered) within your institution should facilitate the balancing of these two variables.

The cost of not closing the gaps is essential to this third step in the assessment process and unfortunately it is often left out during application. A costs analysis can, nonetheless, keep you from enacting a $10,000 distance learning solution to a $500 problem. Economies of scale can complicate this issue, and determining procedures for this analysis is difficult due to the context of each institution. A smart starting place for the analysis of the cost of not closing the gaps is the elements previously used to complete the OEM in Step Two (Kaufman, Watkins, & Sims, 1997). It will be worth your time to at least estimate the costs of each gap between What Is and What Should Be (see Figure 29.1).

A Cost-Consequences Analysis (Kaufman, Watkins, & Sims, 1997; Muir, Watkins, Kaufman, & Leigh, 1998) is a tool that provides educators with a coarse-grain examination of the cost of closing the gaps, and keeps the needs assessment within the context of the OEM (see Table 29.3). The Cost-Consequences Analysis incorporates, as suggested by Rumble (1986), the cost-efficiency, cost-effectiveness, and cost-benefit analyses.

As opposed to estimating the cost of not addressing a need, approximating the cost of closing the gaps is more familiar to most educators and administrators. To complete this analysis, however, we must enter Step Four in order to assign estimated costs for potential solutions (such as distance education) that could be used to address needs.

---

[5]See Watkins, 2006.

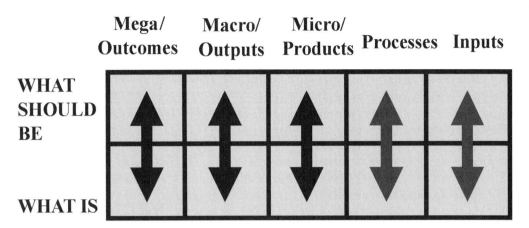

FIGURE 29.1.   The Organizational Elements Model as it related to needs assessment (Kaufman, 1992, 1998, 2000, 2006; Kaufman, Watkins, and Leigh, 2001).

STEP FOUR: IDENTIFY SOLUTION REQUIREMENTS AND ALTERNATIVE SOLUTIONS

Before leaping forward to the identification of alternative solutions—unfortunately the conventional place where most programs begin—it is useful to define the solution requirements. These requirements will establish the criteria by which each alternative solution will be judged and later evaluated for successful implementation. Specific solution requirements will facilitate the listing of alternative solutions and the selection of the "best" solution(s). Solution requirements should include time, costs, available resources, and accomplishment of necessary results.

At least two or three alternatives (i.e., ways and means for meeting identified needs) should be identified for each need (i.e., gap in results) since most problems and opportunities have more than one possible solution. A distance education program is only one feasible solution for most institutions, but other alternatives exist and should be sought out. Now is the time to get creative and innovative. Alternative solutions should even be identified in spite of limitations that may bar them from being selected for implementation.

One should also identify the pros, cons, and costs for each possible solution. Creating an extensive list of alternative solutions is a process that allows the most effective and efficient solution. The effort put into thoroughly analyzing all the possible solutions for any problem will pay off when making decisions and when searching for justification for those decisions (Watkins, 2006).

STEP FIVE: SELECTING THE SOLUTION(S) FROM AMONG ALTERNATIVES

Based on the analyses in Steps Three and Four, and assuring alignment with Steps One and Two, it is now time to decide which distance education or other alternatives will be valuable tools for accomplishing the results that now define your institution's strategic plans. Deciding upon a single solution may or may not be advisable. For most any problem or opportunity a combination of solutions will typically yield the best results (Watkins, 2006). Costs (such as money or

TABLE 29.3.
The Questions Posed by CCA and Conventional ROI Frameworks in Relation
to Their Level of Planning and Decision Making

Level of Planning and Decision Making	Cost-Consequences Questions	Conventional ROI Questions
Mega	Cost to achieve Outcomes vs. Cost of not getting Outcomes? (*cost-utility*)	What did we give vs. What utility of Outcomes did we get?
Macro	Cost to achieve Outputs vs. Cost of not getting Outputs? (*cost-benefit*)	What did we give vs. What benefit of Outputs did we get?
Micro	Cost to achieve Products vs. Cost of not getting Products? (*cost-effectiveness*)	What did we give vs. What effectiveness of Products did we get?
Process	Cost of efficient Processes vs. cost of inefficient Processes? (*cost-efficiency*)	What did we give vs. What efficiency of Processes did we get?
Input	Cost of the quality Inputs vs. Cost of inferior Inputs? (*accounting or auditing*)	What did we give vs. What audited Inputs did we get?

time) and/or political pressures (for instance, from those saying "we *need* a distance learning program") should not, however, be drivers of these decisions. The data from the needs assessment should provide you with the essential information for identifying the "right" solutions for your institution. Having systematically implemented a needs-assessment process will add validity, usefulness, and confidence to your decisions.

This needs-assessment process offers several distinct advantages for institutions that implement it with rigor:

1. Strategic plans can be driven by results-focused needs-assessment data rather than knee-jerk responses to current or projected trends in education.
2. Decisions are based on accomplishing measurable results for individuals, the institution, and the society/community. The selection of means and methods may be made on the basis of the costs to meet the needs as compared to the costs to ignore the needs.
3. The rigor of the process can be adjusted for differing context and constraints of the institution.
4. Information from the assessment will define both performance and evaluation criteria.
5. The process leads toward alignment of all that the institution uses, does, produces, and delivers with contributions to students and others in the community.

Since educators are increasingly being held accountable for the results of their efforts, time should be taken to assess any performance solution before implementation. These advantages are invaluable, especially when a distance education solution has been prematurely prescribed for you.

In the end, distance education programs or initiatives might be justified when the strategic plans and needs assessment are complete. The accessibility and reduced long-term costs typically associated with well-planned distance education programs can make them viable options for meeting many institutional objectives. In these cases, the rigorous needs-assessment process can provide a level of assurance that distance education will meet its objectives at the Micro, Macro,

TABLE 29.4.
Change Creation and Change Management (based on Kaufman and Lick, 2000).

Change Creation	Change Management
Proactive	Reactive
Being pursued	Catching up
Setting the standard	Trying to be competitive
Leading	Following
Long-term focus	Short-term focus (quick fixes)
Vision-driven to add value to all stakeholders	Driven by external events
Internal planning for a better future	Externally imposed disruptions
Change-adaptable or Change-inviting mind-set: A learning organization	Responsive mind-set
Strategic	Tactical
Focuses on all of the institution plus external clients and society	Focus on parts of the institution
A "system" approach	A "systems approach"
Future-creating organization	Responsive and resilient organization
Synergy and co-mentoring	Collaboration
Learning organization	Organizational learning
Works to reinvent a new corporate culture	Works within the current corporate culture

and Mega levels. Afterwards, there are many useful resources for how to complete the tactical planning that leads to the successful implementation of the new distance education program.[6]

PROACTIVE CHANGE

The institutions that will lead distance education in the future will not address the changing realities of education from a reactive perspective. The tactic of waiting to respond to the actions of your competitors, although common in many of today's educational institutions or corporations, can be a death sentence in today's educational market place (Kaufman & Lick, 2000).[7] And yet predicting the future is not a science. So how will leaders in distance education ensure a useful and successful future? They will create it!

Proactive change creation moves institutional strategic planning and needs assessment away from a responsive mindset, to one focused on adaptability and creation (see Table 29.4). This change in perspective is essential for determining if and/or when distance education (or any new educational program) may be appropriate for an institution.

Success in the future is likely to be dependent on this ability of an institution to create the future they want as opposed to reacting to that produced by others. Those institutions that can create the market they want have a definite competitive advantage. In higher education we can identify a similar trend with institutions such as the University of Phoenix, Nova Southeastern University, and others creating markets for distance education, and then finding success in meeting the desires of those markets.

---

[6]See Berge, this Handbook; Pfeiffer, Goodstein, and Nolan, 1989; Mitroff, Mason, and Pearson, 1994; Hamel and Prahalad, 1994.

[7]See Haeckel, 1999.

TABLE 29.5.
An Analysis of Distance Education Delivery Systems
(Kaufman and Watkins, 2000)

	Conventional Instruction	Classic/ Historic DL	Current DL	Future DL
Is it learner, teacher, organizationally, or societal focused?	Teacher/ organizational	Learner	Learner/ organizational	Societal/ organizational/ learner
Is it content driven or usefulness of what is learned-driven?	Content	Content	Content delivery (see Saba, 1999)	Usefulness
Are needs identified? Are needs assessed? Are needs assessed as gaps in result?	Assumed needs	Assumed needs	Assumed needs	Formally determined as gaps in results
Are the courses/programs linked to external usefulness? Are courses/ programs linked with other learning opportunities?	Assumed	Assumed	Assumed	Linked to external value added
Are the courses/programs delivered at an institution or at a remote site, including one's home or workplace?	Institution	Remote site/home	Remote site/home (see Matthews, 1999)	All possible (see Welsh, 1999; Moore and Kearsley, 1996)
Are the courses delivered using conventional, telephone, books, and/or workbooks, video, computer, web-based means? What are the degrees of freedom for the delivery?	Conventional with some audio visual support (see Duning, 1987)	Video, telephone, correspondence materials/boos and workbooks (see Matthews, 1999; Moore and Kearsley, 1996)	Computer, web-based, some video	All used
Is the content of the courses/programs designed by using a performance system/instruction—system process?	Rarely	Rarely	Some of the time	Always
Is there open interactivity between learner and instructor/deliverer? Does the learner get immediate feedback concerning performance?	Some of the time	Rarely	Some of the time	Always when appropriate
Are the courses/programs evaluated for return-on investment for: a. the learners b. the designers/deliverers c. the institution, d. the society?	Assumed	Assumed	For learners and, sometimes, the organization (see Moore and Kearsley, 1996)	For all

FUTURE RESEARCH IN PLANNING
FOR DISTANCE EDUCATION

The recent growth and prosperity of distance education is unlikely to continue in the future if educational institutions are not focused on adding value to lives of learners and communities (Kaufman & Watkins, 2000). By continuing to focus on achieving results at Micro and Macro levels (at best), institutions are not planning for the competitive future when others will be focused on the required skills and knowledge for learners to attain long-term success and quality of life. Yet, for institutional planning to be prepared for these new requirements, the educational paradigms that have brought success in the past must be reconsidered for their effectiveness today and tomorrow.

The transformation of future planning in distance education should be considered within the context of the history of distance education (see Table 29.5). While some trends are more evident in the literature than others, a composite of planning and assessment within distance education provides us with several arenas for future research. These include

1. the determination of what constitutes a useful distance education program;
2. the determination of what constitutes an effective distance education course/degree;
3. how institutions validate decisions made regarding the implementation of distance education;
4. how educational institutions can maintain their adaptability—responsive and responsible—and create the future they and their community desire;
5. what happens to distance education programs when the technologies drive the decision-making rather than learner value added;
6. why distance education is determined to be the "best" solution for an institution;
7. how effective and efficient systems can be designed;
8. how effective and efficient distance education systems are managed; and
9. how we can prove that our distance education program and curriculum adds value, measurably, to internal and external clients and how we can continually improve the value we add for all stakeholders.

In conclusion, many opportunities exists for researchers to investigate the effective planning of distance education programs.

REFERENCES

Abrahams, J. (1995). *The mission statement book: 301 corporate mission statements form America's top companies.* Berkeley, CA: Ten Speed Press.
Byars, L., & Neil, T. (1987, July/August). Organizational philosophy and mission statements. *Planning Review, 15*(4), 32–36.
Clark, R., & Estes, F. (2002). Turning research into results: A guide to selecting the right performance solutions. Atlanta, GA: The Center for Effective Performance.
Covey, S. (1996). Principle-centered leadership: Organizational alignment. *Quality Digest,* 21. Retrieved December 19, 2006, from http://www.qualitydigest.com/mar/covey.html
Davis, I. (2005, May 26). The biggest contract. *The Economist, 375*(8428), 87.

Duning, B. (1987). Independent study in higher education: A captive of legendary resilience? *The American Journal of Distance Education, 1*(1), 37–46.

Garratt, B., Edit. (1995). *Developing strategic thought: Rediscovering the art of direction-giving.* London: McGraw-Hill.

Haeckel, S. (1999). *Adaptive enterprise: Creating and leading dense-and-respond organizations.* Boston: Harvard Business School Press.

Hamel, G., & Prahalad, C. K. (1994). *Competing for the future: Breakthrough strategies for seizing control of your industry and creating the markets of tomorrow.* Boston: Harvard Business School Press.

Kaufman, R. (1992). *Strategic planning plus: An organizational guide* (Rev. ed.). Newbury Park, CA: Sage.

Kaufman, R. (1995). If distance learning is the solution, what's the problem: Beyond DDSS. *DEOSNEWS,*

Kaufman, R. (1998). *Strategic thinking: A guide to identifying and solving problems* (Rev. ed.). Arlington, VA. & Washington, DC: American Society for Training & Development/International Society for Performance Improvement.

Kaufman, R. (2000). *Mega planning: Practical tools for organizational success.* Thousand Oaks, CA: Sage.

Kaufman, R. (2006). *Change, choices, and consequences: A guide to mega thinking and planning.* Amherst, MA: HRD Press.

Kaufman, R., & Lick, D. (2000). Technology-driven planning: Principles to practice. In J. Boettcher, M. Doyle, & R. Jensen (Eds.), *Mega-level strategic planning: Beyond conventional wisdom.* Ann Arbor, MI. Society for College and University Planning.

Kaufman, R., & Watkins, R. (2000). Assuring the future of distance learning. *The Quarterly Review of Distance Education, 1*(1), 59–67.

Kaufman, R., Watkins, R., & Leigh, D. (2001). *Useful educational results: Defining, prioritizing and achieving.* Lancaster, PA: Proactive Publishing.

Kaufman, R., Watkins, R., & Sims, L. (1997). Cost-consequences analysis: A case study. *Performance Improvement Quarterly, 10*(2), 7–21.

Mager, R. F., & Pipe, P. (1997). *Analyzing performance problems.* (3rd ed.) Atlanta, GA: The Center for Effective Performance.

Matthews, D. (1999, September). The origins of distance education and its use in the United States. *T.H.E. Journal, 27*(2), 54–67.

Mitroff, I., Mason, R. O., & Pearson, C. M. (1994). Radical surgery: What will tomorrow's organizations look like? *Academy of Management Executives, 8*(2), 11–21.

Muir, M., Watkins, R., Kaufman, R., & Leigh, D. (1998). Costs-consequences analysis: A primer. *Performance improvement, 37*(4), 8–17.

Moore, M.G., & Kearsley, G. (1996). Distance education: A systems view. Belmont, CA: Wadsworth.

Nanus, B. (1992). *Visionary leadership.* San Francisco: Jossey-Bass.

Pfeiffer, J. W., Goodstein, L. D., & Nolan, T. M. (1989). *Shaping strategic planning: Frogs, bees, and turkey tails.* Glenview, Ill: Scott, Foresman & Co.

Robinson, D. G., & Robinson, J. C. (1995). *Performance consulting: Moving beyond training.* San Francisco: Berrett-Koehler.

Rossett, A. (1987). *Training needs assessment.* Englewood Cliffs, NJ: Educational Technology Publications.

Rumble, G. (1986). *The planning and management of distance education.* New York: St. Martin's Press.

Saba, F. (1999). Planning for distance education: Too much focus on delivery systems? *Distance Education Report, 3*(4), 5.

Senge, P. M. (1990). *The fifth discipline: The art & practice of the learning organization.* New York: Doubleday-Currency.

Stolovich, H. (2002). Front-end analysis, implementation planning, and evaluation: Breaking out of the Pamela syndrome. *Performance Improvement, 41*(4), 5–7.

Watkins, R. (2004). Ends and means: Aligning e-learning with strategic plans. *Distance Learning Magazine, 1*(5), 33–34.

Watkins, R. (2006). *Performance by design: The systematic selection, design, and development of performance technologies that accomplish useful results.* Amherst, MA: HRD Press.

Watkins, R., Leigh, D., Platt, W., & Kaufman, R. (1998). Needs assessment: A digest, review, and comparison of needs assessment literature. *Performance Improvement, 37*(7), 40–53.

Welsh, T. (1999). Implications of distributed learning for instructional designers: How will the future affect the practice? *Educational Technology Magazine, 39*(2), 41–45.

Willis, B. (1992). *Effective distance education: A primer for faculty and administrators.* Fairbanks, Alaska: University of Alaska.

Willis, B. (1994). *Distance education strategies and tools.* Englewood Cliffs, CA: Educational Technologies Publications.

30

Faculty Participation: Motivations, Incentives, and Rewards

Linda L. Wolcott
Utah State University

Kay Shattuck
Carroll Community College

This review builds on the foundation laid by Dillon and Walsh's (1992) review of faculty issues, and examines pertinent works published since 1992. Works identified for review are limited to those that (a) are empirical—that is, based on the collection of data and reporting the results of data analysis either qualitative or quantitative in nature, (b) address higher education in the United States and involve faculty members who teach courses in distance education programs that used synchronous or asynchronous learning networks including online delivery, and (c) focus on higher education faculty and their reasons to participate or not participate in distance education, as well as barriers to and incentives and rewards for participation. The review synthesizes research aimed at answering the following questions about higher education faculty and their involvement in distance education: Why do faculty members get involved? What enables them to participate (or hinders them)? What encourages or discourages them? What do they get out of it?

WHY DO FACULTY PARTICIPATE IN DISTANCE EDUCATION?

Psychological definitions identify two types of motivation: intrinsic and extrinsic motivation. The former has an internal origin; an individual derives satisfaction from performing or being associated with a particular activity because it appeals to his/her values or fulfills a personal need or drive (i.e., motive). In other words, engaging in the activity is reward in itself. Extrinsic motives, on the other hand, are associated with benefits received from a source other than the activity itself. The individual is moved to action in response to the prospect of an externally derived benefit or reward. The majority of research on faculty participation has focused on why faculty do or do not participate and factors that encourage or discourage them.

Intrinsic Motives

Intrinsic motives are closely associated with the activity of distance teaching where a particular attribute or set of properties holds an inherent appeal for the faculty member. Wolcott and Betts (1999) classified five types of intrinsic motives: (a) personal or socially derived satisfactions, (b) personal or professional growth, (c) personal challenge, (d) altruistic, and (e) career-enhancing. Factor analyses conducted by Schifter (2002) and Cook (2003) produced similar sets of motives. Four groups of personal motivations for online teaching emerged from faculty narratives collected by Suter (2002): (a) wonder, (b) convenience, (c) professional growth and renewal, and (d) esprit de corps.

Intrinsic motives have consistently been at the top of the list of factors most influential in faculty decisions to participate in distance education. For example, as reported by participants in Betts' (1998) study, the most frequently cited reasons were intrinsic: to reach new audiences, to develop new ideas, to use new technologies, intellectual challenge, and overall job satisfaction. In subsequently modifying and administering Betts' survey at different institutions, other researchers (Cook, 2003; Gupton, 2004; Hebert, 2003; O'Quinn, 2002; and Schifter, 2000a, 2002) observed the same primary motivators. The majority of factors that were found by these studies to have motivated participators or had the potential to motivate them were intrinsic factors.

Results are similar across a variety of disciplines and institutions. Often, the motives relate to the faculty members' self-improvement or professional development. Faculty studied by Rockwell, Schauer, Fritz, and Marx (1999) and Myers, Bennett, Brown, and Henderson (2004) identified similar personal motives: providing innovative instruction, developing and applying new teaching techniques and skills, keeping abreast of new technologies, and fulfilling a personal desire to teach. Community college faculty rated self-fulfillment, the enjoyment of teaching, and professional challenge as their most motivating factors (Miller & Husmann, 1999). Likewise, the central motivation among faculty studied by Tastle, White, and Shackleton (2005) was clearly personal in nature and related to teaching.

Interest in promoting the goals and programs of their department or college is another category of frequently cited intrinsic motives. Developing distance education courses and programs presented an effective way to reach larger audiences and provided the opportunity to increase public interest and meet public requests for information (Jackson, 1994) while also increasing enrollments (Ndahi, 1999).

Cook (2003) concluded that "faculty motivation and distance education participation are closely aligned with faculty being intrinsically motivated to help students" (p. 238), especially those who were underserved or geographically disadvantaged. Making courses more accessible (Bebko, 1998; Kirk & Shoemaker, 1999; Ndahi, 1999) and helping students (Christo-Baker, 2004; Halfhill, 1998; Keen, 2001; Lin, 2002; Montgomery, 1999; Wilson, 2002) were oft-cited examples of student-centered factors that motivated the faculty.

Extrinsic Motives

In contrast to factors that are intrinsically or personally motivating, other factors stem from external sources of influences. For example, Schifter (2000a) identified a group of extrinsic motives that included (a) the expectation or requirement by the university or department that the faculty participate in distance teaching, and (b) support and encouragement from individual departments and institutions. However, none of these factors was included as strong motivators identified by the faculty. In fact, few reasons to participate have been attributed to extrinsic motives.

That is not to say that extrinsic motives do not play a role in faculty decisions to participate in distance education. Some evidence of extrinsic motivation was found among the community college faculty studied by Kirk and Shoemaker (1999), who reported that the prospect of being extrinsically rewarded with more money, equipment, or release time figured as a strong motivator in influencing them to participate, as did chances of being promoted and receiving public recognition by one's supervisor. Similarly, Lin (2002) found faculty to be motivated by monetary support and encouragement from the university and their supervisors. In a replication of Betts' study, Cook (2003) found faculty to be extrinsically motivated by incentives that included course release, tenure considerations, and additional financial considerations.

However, the preponderance of evidence such as that reported initially by Wolcott (1997), Betts (1998), and Wolcott and Betts (1999) asserts that faculty members who are involved in distance teaching are not extrinsically motivated and, especially, are not, in it for the money. Least motivating among factors, extrinsic reasons typically tend to be at the bottom of the lists of motives. For example, the anticipation of reward such as merit pay, tenure, and promotion credit (Miller & Husmann, 1999) or financial gain (Myers et al., 2004; O'Quinn & Corry, 2004; Wilson, 2002) were rated low by the faculty surveyed.

Unlike the faculty in research universities, the community college teachers surveyed by Miller and Husmann (1999) saw distance teaching as part of their jobs, hence mitigating the influence of external pressures. Kirk and Shoemaker (1999) further observed that motives of community college faculty members varied with their personal and demographic characteristics such as career stage, age, and prior experience. Specifically, "extrinsic rewards tended to be a greater motivator for younger versus older instructors" (Kirk & Shoemaker, 1999, p. 315), and instructors with prior experience teaching online were more motivated than were the inexperienced instructors by the challenge of online teaching, their interest in computers, and making courses more accessible to students. Similarly, Rockwell et al. (1999) reported that faculty members, having taught at a distance, were more likely to be motivated by a personal desire to teach and by self-gratification than were their non-distance-teaching colleagues. Gender factored into motivation for the faculty surveyed by Lin (2002), who concluded that female faculty members were much more likely to be motivated to teach distance education courses than were males. While Gupton (2004) also documented significant differences with respect to gender, as well as four other variables—(a) age, (b) tenure status, (c) years teaching in higher education, and (d) position—others such as Hebert (2003) and Schifter (2002) found no statistically significant relationship among the same variables and participation.

The research also reveals differences between faculty motives to participate and what administrators believed motivates or would motivate their faculty. Although faculty participators in Betts' (1998) and Gupton's (2004) studies cited intrinsic reasons, the deans attributed extrinsic motives to faculty decisions about participation. They speculated that faculty would participate if offered monetary support, increase in salary, credit toward tenure and promotion, and release time. For their part, faculty (whether distance education participants or non-participants) in Schifter's (2000a) study did not include extrinsic motives in the resulting list of their top five motivators. Administrators, however, believed that "faculty were more likely to be motivated by factors that included additional money, credit toward promotion and tenure, and release time" (Schifter, 2000a, p. 43). Hebert (2003), Isham (2004), Keen (2001), O'Quinn and Corry (2004), and Rockwell et al. (1999) also report a disparity in perceptions between faculty and administrators concerning motives for participation.

Several studies, notably Betts (1998) and those who replicated her work (Cook, 2003; Gupton, 2004; O'Quinn & Corry, 2004; Schifter, 2000a, 2002) illuminate differences between faculty members who participate in distance education and those who do not with respect to what motivates or would motivate them. Consistently, participators were intrinsically motivated and non-participators speculated that extrinsic motives such as increase in salary and monetary support in the form of overload pay or a stipend would influence their decision to participate. Edwards (2001) recorded a significant difference between participators and non-participators in this regard.

WHAT ENCOURAGES PARTICIPATION?

An incentive is "an external stimulus which energizes behavior and/or gives it direction" (Ramachandran, 1994, p. 213). In the context of this review, incentives are factors that have the effect of lowering perceived barriers and stimulating interest because they enhance the attraction of distance teaching or otherwise appeal to a particular goal or personal need. Incentives that have been identified with respect to distance education are of several types, including (a) enhancers present in the environment or institutional climate, and (b) inducements offered by the institution expressly to entice faculty to participate.

Enhancers

Certain characteristics of the institutional climate or aspects of the work environment encourage some faculty to become involved in distance education programs by heightening the attraction of distance teaching. These faculty members perceive such enhancers as creating favorable circumstances for participation. This set of incentives typically relates to institutional support services or reflects institutional or administrative commitment.

The availability of services designed to support both the activities of distance teaching and learning is widely reported as an incentive that underlies faculty members' decisions to participate in distance education. Services that have been found to serve as enhancers include: training in the skills of using distance education technology (Iken, 2000; Keen, 2001); technical support (Keeton, 2000; Martin, 2003; Tastle et al., 2005); instructional support, such as assistance in instructional design and pedagogy (Lee, 2001); and student support services (Keen, 2001; Keeton, 2000). Bebko (1998), for example, identified "strong enhancers," which include the availability of "technology training and technical assistance for students, a framework for student to student support systems, [and] student-friendly student services" (p. 95).

Faculty, though intrinsically motivated, value and desire support services. Ricci (2002) found that support for faculty to develop Web courses was identified as a priority by over 80% of the community college faculty in his study. Other studies (e.g., Donovan, 2004; Pina, 2005; Schoats, 2002) highlight faculty perceptions regarding the importance of and need for support services and a support infrastructure.

Evidence is prevalent that there is a relationship between enhancers and motivation. Faculty appear to respond to the motivational boost that enhancers offer. Lee (2001) and Lin (2002) posited that motivation increases with the availability of institutional support mechanisms that help faculty meet their instructional needs. Lee noted that motivation, satisfaction, and commitment were stronger among faculty who felt well-supported by their institutions. Along the same lines, Shea, Pickett, and Li (2005) found a link with satisfaction where faculty learning and technical support were predictors of satisfaction in online teaching.

Further evidence of the importance of institutional support as an incentive is offered by Owusu-Ansah (2001) who discovered that well-established support systems—those in effective operation for at least three years—reduced faculty concerns and motivated them to participate. Likewise, having support services in place had the highest correlation with faculty member's willingness to deploy distance education technology (Keen, 2001). And Hebert (2003) identified a statistically significant relationship between faculty participation in distance education and whether faculty members had participated in training.

A common theme among faculty is that institutions could do more to encourage participation in distance education. Faculty studied by Betts (1998) wanted their institutions to provide more information about distance education and to offer technical training and support. Other studies documented the lack of pedagogical training (Lee, 2002; Lindquist, 2004), the lack of support in using distance education technology (Nelson, 2003), and the lack of faculty development (Kaml, 2001).

Neither Lee (2000) nor Wolcott and Haderlie (1995) found evidence that institutional support services were widely available to promote professional growth and the improvement of instruction specifically for distance education faculty. The most widely available support services were workshops and seminars, instructional consultation, and materials production. Occasional support was found in the form of site facilitators, instructional designers, teaching assistants, and graders. Rhoads (2005) found some evidence of mentoring, but no statistically significant relationship between institutional size and the presence of mentoring networks. Similarly, Hagovsky (2002), Kambutu (1998), Lee (2002), and Poe (2000) documented the lack of institutional support incentives for distance teaching.

Yet Ricci (2002) found that a majority of one state's community colleges provided a wide variety of technical support incentives for not only developing Web-based courses, but also subsequent to it. He inferred a commitment to distance education: "The cumulative effect of the support processes, procedures, and instructional design, and technical support developments identified in this study would seem to indicate a cultural acceptance and institutional readiness of Web courses" (Ricci, 2002, p. 120). In examining strategies to encourage participation, French (2001) also observed differences in climate between two- and four-year institutions, concluding that, "faculty participation in distance education may be increased more easily within community colleges than within four-year residential institutions" (p. 140).

As with motives for participation, faculty and administrators do not always share the same perceptions regarding institutional support. The faculty participating in Hagovsky's (2002) study felt they were "going it alone" and "operating . . . in a support vacuum" (p. 103), while the administrators thought they were adequately supporting faculty. French (2001) noted that both faculty and administrators viewed instructional support as an important strategy for encouraging online teaching. They differed, however, based on the type of institution: the faculty and administrators at community colleges perceived that their leaders had been more effective in implementing a variety of strategies than did those respondents representing four-year residential campuses. Further, "faculty and administrators at the four-year residential institutions were more likely than those at the community colleges to identify problems with the level of instructional support available to faculty who teach on-line, as well as a more general lack of support from their college or university administration" (French, 2001, p. 143). Specific problems relating to communication and knowing what support services were available and how to access them were identified by Lee (2002) and Lindquist (2004), and by Donovan (2004) and (Lee, 2002), respectively.

In addition to institutional support services, the degree of institutional commitment that faculty members perceive is shown to distance education has an influence on their decisions. Having a supportive department head proved to be a factor that enabled participation (Halfhill, 1998; Wolcott, 1997), as did the involvement of respected faculty, the commitment of one's department (Wolcott & Haderlie, 1995), and the support of one's peers (Keen, 2001). Keen also found a strong association between faculty members' belief that there was an organizational climate supportive of distance education and their willingness to use distance education.

Inducements

Institutions traditionally offer inducements to encourage a particular behavior or activity valued by the organization. A high proportion of incentives for distance education relates to the issues of workload and salary. Wolcott and Haderlie (1995) found that workload inducements can take several forms, including modification or reduction of the teaching assignment (e.g., release time), and the opportunity to teach a distance education course as part of one's assigned teaching load rather than as an overload. Workload considerations were important to the faculty studied by Christo-Baker (2004), Iken (2000), and Martin (2003), and an important faculty issue for deans (Schwer, 2001) and department chairs (Mlinek, 2002). Other inducements identified in the research include the availability of course development funds (Jackson, 1994; Ricci, 2002; Wolcott & Haderlie, 1995); travel, equipment, or discretionary funds (Schifter, 2000b, 2004; Wolcott & Haderlie, 1995); training grants (Christo-Baker, 2004; Iken, 2000); and staff support and time to plan (Jackson, 1994). Indeed, having the time to develop distance education courses, especially through release from some portion of one's teaching assignment, was a highly valued incentive for faculty (Ellis, 2000; Keen, 2001; Keeton, 2000; Martin, 2003; Ricci, 2002), but one that was not necessarily provided (Nelson, 2003).

As previously noted, the prospect of financial gain is a low motivator for faculty, yet overload stipends are common among monetary incentives. Supplemental compensation, for example, was one of the most frequently offered incentives identified by Kambutu (1998). He found, however, that over 50% of the institutions he surveyed did not offer incentives such as release time, extra compensation, and favorable workload policies. Lee (2002) reported similar findings, and Lindquist (2004) observed a preference for release time over stipends. Looking at compensation practices and incentives for both developing distance education courses and teaching them, Schifter (2000b, 2004) concluded that practices vary widely among institutions, and that "compensation and incentives are only marginally better for developing a distance education course than for teaching one" (2000b, p. 11).

Support for offering incentives for distance teaching has been widely noted among both faculty and administrators. Jones and Moller (2002/2003) found that additional compensation, technical support, and release time were "the primary resources needed to teach distance education courses" as identified by faculty. There is a widespread perception among administrators, as well, that incentives are important and should be provided. Faculty issues including incentives were prominent among issues that impacted department chairs in the implementation of distance education (Mlinek, 2002; Schauer, 2002). Ndahi (1999), however, found that "86% of the respondents would like their institution to provide more incentives for teaching a distance class" (p. 29). Studies also suggest that the faculty desires greater clarity in the criteria for promotion and tenure with respect to distance education. As an example, faculty thought that revising the definition of scholarship could encourage the development of online courses if doing so would mean credit toward promotion and tenure (Lindquist, 2004).

Others (e.g., Edwards, 2001; Hagovsky, 2002; Poe, 2000; Whicker, 2004) have likewise noted the lack of incentives for participating in distance education. As recently as 2005, Pina reported that offering incentives was the factor rated least successfully implemented in higher education—an indicator, he concluded, of the lack of institutionalization of distance education. Colagross' (2000) findings are illuminating in this regard. Although the majority of upper- and division-level administrators felt that incentives should be offered, more than half of the presidents, vice presidents, and deans responded that faculty should be expected to undertake distance teaching without incentives. He concluded: "The highest level administrators are willing to provide the necessary funds for faculty to be trained how to develop distance education courses, but they tend to be in agreement that faculty should develop these courses without extra monetary incentives in addition to their regular salaries" (Colagross, 2000, p. 88).

WHAT DISCOURAGES PARTICIPATION?

Evidence provided by the research suggests that if the presence of a factor acts as an incentive, its absence may present an obstacle or barrier to participation. Research on factors that discourage or hinder faculty participation in distance education is abundant. Clark (1993) categorized barriers as "administrative, technical, economic, and student support obstacles to distance teaching" (p. 30). Berge, Muilenburg, and Haneghan (2002) outlined an expanded list in which barriers to distance teaching and learning were categorized as situational, epistemological, philosophical, psychological, pedagogical, technical, social, and/or cultural. For the purpose of this review, we focus on those factors found in the environment or institutional context, what Olcott and Wright (1995) referred to as "institutionally embedded disincentives" (p. 8).

Contextual Barriers

Contextual barriers are those deterrents associated with the institutional setting typically outside of the control of the individual. While not necessarily intentional or institutionally imposed, common contextual barriers involve the inadequacy or absence of some supportive structure, policy, or practice. Five contextual barriers are consistently cited as influencing faculty decisions to participate in distance education: (a) lack of time, (b) lack of compensation, (c) lack of incentives and/or rewards, (d) lack of policies, and (e) lack of institutional support.

Not only is it widely contended that distance teaching takes more preparation time, but faculty and many administrators also perceive that institutions fail to provide time for course development and management apart from more traditional teaching responsibilities. The lack of administratively provided time, especially release time, was a highly-ranked barrier (Christo-Baker, 2004; Curbelo-Ruiz, 2002; Ellis, 2000; Gupton, 2004; O'Quinn, 2002). Lack of monetary support such as a stipend rated highest among deterrents for distance education faculty and division chairs in community colleges surveyed by O'Quinn (2002). Both time and compensation ranked as the greatest obstacles at all stages of organizational maturity in distance education, as determined by Berge and Muilenburg (2001).

Faculty participation frequently hinges on the availability of incentives and rewards for one's involvement. Studies not only note that incentives stimulate participation, but that the lack of incentives and/or rewards works against it (Bolduc, 1993; Ellis, 2000; Curbelo-Ruiz, 2002; French, 2001; Halfhill, 1998; Jackson, 1994; Montgomery, 1999; Ndahi, 1999; Nelson, 2003). The lack of adequate rewards (French, 2001; U. S. Department of Education, 1997) and associated policies (Dooley & Murphrey, 2000; Meyer, 2002) have been cited as barriers to institutional development in distance education. The same appears to be true of institutional support where the lack of administrative or technical support services emerges as an important category of barriers affecting adoption of distance education (Bader, 2004; Bebko, 1998; Ndahi, 1999), as well as participation in it (Berge & Muilenburg, 2001; Betts, 1998; Halfhill, 1998; Montgomery, 1999; Rockwell et al., 1999; Schifter, 2000a; Wolcott & Haderlie, 1995). More than a barrier to the participation of individual faculty members, the lack of support is a barrier to the incorporation of distance education within the institution, concluded Nelson (2003).

Other contextual barriers reported in the literature include the lack of adequate information (Montgomery, 1999; Ndahi, 1999); inadequacy or lack of training (Lin, 2002; Ndahi, 1999;

Schifter, 2000a; Zirkle, 2004), lack of funding for materials and other associated expenses (Curbelo-Ruiz, 2002), and lack of clear commitment to or policy on distance education (Bebko, 1998; Halfhill, 1998; Ndahi, 1999; Sumrall, 2002). In regard to the latter, findings led Porter (2003) to suggest that the prevailing climate and "rigid processes" deter rather than motivate.

Disincentives

Here, disincentives are defined as those deterrents associated with the activity of distance teaching and are related to the costs and benefits perceived to derive from participation. Wolcott and Betts (1999) divided disincentives into two categories, inhibitors and demotivators, both of which function to reduce personal motivation and, thus, pose a barrier to participation. They defined inhibitors as "those aspects or characteristics of distance teaching that relate to the cost of involvement," and demotivators as "factors that represent the lack of benefit perceived to result from involvement" (Wolcott & Betts, 1999, p. 43).

One of the most common inhibitors is time commitment. Almost universally, faculty expressed the concern that distance teaching costs them too much time. Specifically, time requirements associated with preparing courses (Halfhill, 1998; Jackson, 1994; Ndahi, 1999; Rockwell et al., 1999; Tastle et al., 2005; Wolcott & Betts, 1999) and learning new teaching or technological skills (Betts, 1998; Halfhill, 1998; Ndahi, 1999; Wolcott & Haderlie, 1995) surfaced as major disincentives.

Rockwell et al. (1999) observed differences between tenured and nontenured faculty: time taken from research, training requirements, assistance or support needs, and developing effective technology skills posed fewer obstacles for nontenured faculty members than for those who were tenured. Indeed, Wolcott (1997) described the risk to junior faculty when distance teaching robs them of the time needed for research and publishing activities that are more highly valued and rewarded.

Closely associated with time commitment, faculty concerns about workload surface as a major disincentive. Martin (2003) found significant agreement among faculty irrespective of experience, rank, and tenure status regarding the conviction that online and classroom courses be accorded the same weight in assigning faculty workload. Typically, however, policies regarding workload issues are a source of dissatisfaction (Iken, 2000) and inhibit faculty decisions to teach distance education courses (Betts, 1998; Curbelo-Ruiz, 2002; Halfhill, 1998; Lin, 2002; Wolcott & Haderlie, 1995). There is support from several studies (French, 2001; Gupton, 2004; Schwer, 2001) that administrators as well as the faculty rank workload issues among the major barriers to faculty participation. Workload was the highest rated factor that either did influence or would influence the decision of faculty and division chairs participating in O'Quinn's (2002) study to not participate in distance education.

In addition to issues of time and workload, the faculty in a number of studies cited other costs among the factors that either did or would inhibit them from participating. These inhibitors included the perceived lack of quality or academic rigor in distance education courses (Curbelo-Ruiz, 2002; Lin, 2002; Nelson, 2003; Tastle et al., 2005), the absence or loss of student interaction (Betts, 1998; Halfhill, 1998; Lin, 2002; Nelson, 2003), and the perceived restrictive nature of the medium relative to course content and objectives (Nelson, 2003; Sumrall, 2002). Concerns about quality was the top inhibitor identified by Gupton (2004) and others, especially for faculty who had chosen not to participate (O'Quinn, 2002; Schifter, 2000a). Underscoring the influence of such concerns, French (2001) cited compatibility issues which include faculty interest, perceived need for a course, and concerns about quality as "some of the most serious obstacles to increasing faculty participation in on-line distance education at the institutions studied" (p. 142).

Another group of disincentives relates to the perceived lack of benefit from participating in distance education. One such demotivator was the lack of consideration accorded distance teaching in annual and promotion/tenure reviews (Curbelo-Ruiz, 2002; Schauer, 2002; Wolcott, 1997). [See more at discussion of extrinsic rewards.]

WHAT DO FACULTY GET OUT OF PARTICIPATING?

Rewards can be defined as return on one's investment. The term typically calls to mind some tangible return provided by the institution to acknowledge good performance. Rewards, however, neither have to be material, large, nor come from an external source to be valued. Individuals may draw considerable satisfaction from their involvement in activities that return a valued outcome despite its size or origin. As with motives, rewards can be both intrinsic and extrinsic in nature.

Intrinsic Rewards

Intrinsic rewards are the personally valued outcomes received for participation. For many, teaching is its own reward. The anticipation of getting back something of value that satisfied their professional growth or career development was one type of outcome that functioned both as an incentive and reward. For example, faculty were enticed by the opportunities to enhance their own professional development, and found distance education instrumental in improving their teaching and technology skills, and adding resources to their classroom instruction (Hagovsky, 2002; Wolcott & Haderlie, 1995). Other faculty members found that participation in distance education afforded them the opportunity to make industry contacts and increased their visibility and reputation in their field (Wolcott & Betts, 1999). The faculty they studied also drew satisfaction from the opportunity to boost their department's enrollments, to extend its influence, and to reach a particular segment of the student population such as adult learners.

Extrinsic Rewards

Whether formal or informal recognition, extrinsic rewards serve as the means through which institutions acknowledge employees for their efforts. Informal recognition can come in a number of forms, ranging from pats on the back to more formal acknowledgements such as awards. Faculty members reported that a casual "atta boy" or token of appreciation were welcome forms of informal recognition (Wolcott, 1997). Keen (2001) found a high correlation between personal recognition and faculty willingness to become involved in distance education.

In examining institutional practices, researchers have noted few instances of formal rewards and recognition. Noticeably absent is evidence that those who developed and taught distance education courses were accorded recognition in the promotion and tenure process or in earning merit pay. Wolcott (1997) examined the relationship between distance teaching and the institutional reward system. She described a culture in which distance education held a marginal status, was not highly valued, well rewarded, or highly correlated with the tenure and promotion process. Rewards were dependent on the commitment of the academic unit and its head. Asking how reward processes such as tenure and promotion accommodated distance teaching in institutions that traditionally emphasized research, she found that faculty received little credit for teaching and developing distance education courses, that the support of the institution and department head was critical, and that participation in distance education posed a risk the junior, nontenured faculty.

As the ultimate extrinsic reward at research institutions, tenure is the holy grail of an academic career, and as the nursing faculty studied by Bodenbender (1998) urged, participation in distance education is deserving of professional recognition and needs to be a consideration in the promotion and tenure process. Yet Kambutu (1998) noted that among the majority of administrators, distance teaching did not receive consideration during promotion and tenure decisions, and was not recognized by departments and senior faculty members, nor did administrators think it important to do so. He concluded that "distance instruction is not instrumental in attaining some of the extrinsic rewards valued by faculty such as workload policies that recognize distance teaching, career promotion, tenure, and status in the institution" (Kambutu, 1998, p. 146). Iken (2000) also noted faculty dissatisfaction with workload policies and with distance education's lack of fit with tenure and promotion policies.

Hagovsky (2002) attributes the disparity to a communication breakdown between faculty and administrators. Lacking written policies, the deans and department chairs he surveyed did not communicate with faculty on issues relative to time, workload, and credit toward merit, promotion, or tenure. For their part, the faculty did not ask. Consequently, neither understood how participation in distance education affected faculty careers. Lindquist's (2004) study offers additional evidence that the answer may lie in reforming the institutional reward system. Study participants believed that revising the definition of scholarship might encourage greater participation of faculty if designing and teaching online courses received credit toward promotion and tenure.

The lack of policies regarding distance education and its relation to the promotion and tenure process is widely noted (e.g., Dooley & Murphrey, 2000; Iken, 2000; Meyer, 2002). Rhoads (2005), for example, found that two thirds of the 93 institutions she surveyed did not have distance education policies in place. Similar findings led Hagovsky (2002) to conclude that "distance education has not become a salient factor in the promotion process" (p. 117). Research, such as that by Porter (2003), continues to point to promotion and tenure practices as inhibiting the integration of distance education into the higher education culture.

From a personal perspective, is distance teaching worth it? Betts (1998) found that the majority of faculty members and deans saw little or no career advantage for distance teaching. Her conclusion is echoed by Hagovsky (2002), Keeton (2000), and Schoats (2002), whose subjects concluded that there was no real benefit to teaching distance education courses. Particularly when considering the extra work involved in developing distance education courses, the faculty did not perceive it to be as worth the effort. Moreover, citing "minimal overt rewards," the faculty in Hagovsky's study (2002) perceived that any personal growth associated with distance teaching "[came] at a cost to their time and energy towards on site classes, and although many were positive about the gains, there [seemed] to be a consequential loss in the energy of teaching" (p. 107).

One of the keys to successful distance education continues to be the participation of the institution's best faculty. Research tells us that faculty participation hinges on their being intrinsically motivated and equitably rewarded for their efforts. To realize the promise of distance education, we must understand faculty motivation, and that means understanding the culture in which faculty work.

REFERENCES

Bader, J. R. (2004). Faculty perception of issues affecting the utilization of distance education technology: The case of New Mexico State University's College of Agriculture and Home Economics. *Dissertation Abstracts International, 65*(12), 4405A. (UMI No. AAT 3155970)

Bebko, P. R. (1998). Influences upon higher education faculty use of distance education technology. *Dissertation Abstracts International, 59*(02), 0427A. (UMI No. AAT 9823277)

Berge, Z. L., & Muilenburg, L. (2001, July/August). Obstacles faced at various stages of capability regarding distance education in institutions of higher education. *TechTrends, 45*, 40–45.

Berge, Z. L., Muilenburg, L. Y., & Haneghan, J. V. (2002). Barriers to distance education and training. *Quarterly Review of Distance Education, 3*(4), 409–418.

Betts, K. S. (1998). Factors influencing faculty participation in distance education in postsecondary education in the United States: An institutional study. *Dissertation Abstracts International, 59*(07), 2376A. (UMI No. AAM 9900013)

Bodenbender, K. D. (1998). Baccalaureate and graduate nursing faculty attitudes towards and perceptions of interactive television teaching. *Dissertation Abstracts International, 59*(09), 3413A. (UMI No. AAT 9904279)

Bolduc, W. J. (1993). The diffusion of digital compressed video-interactive in a university environment, 1988–92: A case study. *Dissertation Abstracts International, 54*(12), 4294A. (UMI No. AAC 9413272)

Christo-Baker, E. A. H. B. (2004). College and university faculty attitudes, incentives and barriers toward distance education. *Dissertation Abstracts International, 65*(09), 3297A. (UMI No. AAT 3146740)

Clark, T. (1993). Attitudes of higher education faculty toward distance education: A national survey. *The American Journal of Distance Education, 7*(2), 19–33.

Colagross, J. T. (2000). Perceptions of administrators on issues related to distance education in two-year colleges in Alabama. *Dissertation Abstracts International, 61*(12), 4653A. (UMI No. AAT 9996467)

Cook, R. G. (2003). Factors that motivate or inhibit faculty participation in distance education: An exploratory study. *Dissertation Abstracts International, 64*(06), 1953A. (UMI No. AAT 3094001)

Curbelo-Ruiz, A. M. (2002). Factors influencing faculty participation in Web-based distance education technologies. *Dissertation Abstracts International, 63*(04), 1227A. (UMI No. AAT 3049007)

Dillon, C. L., & Walsh, S. M. (1992). Faculty: The neglected resource in distance education. *The American Journal of Distance Education, 6*(3), 5–21.

Dooley, K. E., & Murphrey, T. P. (2000, Winter). How the perspectives of administrators, faculty, and support units impact the rate of distance education adoption. *Online Journal of Distance Learning Administration, 3*(4). Retrieved January 23, 2006, from http://www.westga.edu/~distance/ojdla/winter34/dooley34.html

Donovan, P. R. (2004). Faculty in online distance education: An exploration of four faculty members' experience. *Dissertation Abstracts International, 65*(08), 2957A. (UMI No. ATT NQ93511)

Edwards, Y. V. (2001). Rehabilitation education faculty motivation toward distance education: A national study of CORE rehabilitation faculty. *Dissertation Abstracts International, 62*(06), 2035A. (UMI No. AAT 3018573)

Ellis, E. M. (2000). Faculty participation in the Pennsylvania State University World Campus: Identifying barriers to success. *Open Learning, 15*(3), 233–242.

French, R. C. (2001). Encouraging faculty participation in college and university distance education programs. *Dissertation Abstracts International, 61*(12), 4690A. (UMI No. AAT 9997946)

Gupton, K. L. (2004). Factors that affect faculty participation in distance education: An institutional study. *Dissertation Abstracts International, 65*(12), 4488A. (UMI No. AAT 3158437)

Hagovsky, T. C. (2002). Factors affecting the implementation of distance education initiatives in the Indiana Partnership for Statewide Education. *Dissertation Abstracts International, 64*(08), 2802A. (UMI No. AAT 3099152)

Halfhill, C. S. (1998). An investigation into factors influencing faculty behavior concerning distance learning instruction using the theory of planned behavior. *Dissertation Abstracts International, 59*(11), 4113A. (UMI No. AAT 9910797)

Hebert, J. G. (2003). Perceived barriers to faculty participation in distance education at a 4-year university. *Dissertation Abstracts International, 64*(09), 3257A. (UMI No. AAT 3106885)

Iken, M. B. T. (2000). Faculty attitudes toward computer-mediated distance education. *Dissertation Abstracts International, 61*(10), 3917A. (UMI No. AAT 9991647)

Isham, E. K. (2004). Faculty and administrators' beliefs about, experience with, and willingness to utilize distance education technologies in medium-sized New Mexico community colleges. *Dissertation Abstracts International, 65*(04), 1224A. (UMI No. AAT 3129894)

Jackson, G. (1994, February). Incentives for planning and delivering agricultural distance education. *Agriculture Education Magazine, 66,* 15–16.

Jones, A. E., & Moller, L. (Fall 2002/Winter 2003). A comparison of continuing education and resident faculty attitudes toward using distance education in a higher education institution in Pennsylvania. *College and University Media Review, 9,* 11–37.

Kambutu, J. N. (1998). A study of selected administrators' self-perceptions concerning the available support services and extrinsic rewards for distance education at the 67 land-grant institutions in the United States. *Dissertation Abstracts International, 59*(09), 3318A. (UMI No. AAT 9904677)

Kaml, C. A. (2001). Faculty development efforts in support of Web-based distance education among the University of North Carolina schools of education. *Dissertation Abstracts International, 62*(10), 3312A. (UMI No. AAT 3029871)

Keen, M. A. (2001). Attitudes and beliefs of faculties and administrators in the Ivy Tech State College System on the deployment of technology-mediated, interactive distance education. *Dissertation Abstracts International, 62*(02), 436A. (UMI No. AAT 3004751)

Keeton, C. L. (2000). Institutional structures that influence faculty to participate in distance education. *Dissertation Abstracts International, 61*(10), 3840A. (UMI No. AAT 9993226)

Kirk, J. J., & Shoemaker, H. (1999). Motivating community college instructors to teach on-line: An exploration of selected motivators. In *Academy of Human Resource Development (AHRD) Conference Proceedings* (pp. 311–317). (ERIC Document Reproduction Service No. ED 431942).

Lee, J. (2000). Institutional support for distance education among higher education institutions. *Dissertation Abstracts International, 61*(12), 4742A. (UMI No. AAT9999102)

Lee, J. (2001). Institutional support for distance education and faculty motivation, commitment, satisfaction. *British Journal of Educational Technology, 32*(2), 153–160.

Lee, J. (2002). Faculty and administrator perceptions of instructional support for distance education. *International Journal of Instructional Media, 29*(1), 27–45.

Lin, H. P. (2002). Motivating and inhibiting factors that affect faculty participation in distance education at Idaho State University. *Dissertation Abstracts International, 63*(05), 1799A. (UMI No. AAT 3052734)

Lindquist, S. L. (2004). With a map and compass: Planning for the online journey. *Dissertation Abstracts International, 65* (11), 4129A. (UMI No. AAT 3154782)

Martin, M. H. (2003). Factors influencing faculty adoption of Web-based courses in teacher education programs within the State University of New York. *Dissertation Abstracts International, 64*(04), 1223A. (UMI No. AAT 3089087)

Meyer, K. A. (2002, Winter). Does policy make a difference? An exploration into policies for distance education. *Online Journal of Distance Learning Administration, 5*(4). Retrieved January 23, 2006, from http://www.westga.edu/~distance/ojdla/winter54/Meyer_policy_54.htm

Miller, M. T., & Husmann, D. E. (1999). Faculty incentives to participate in distance education. *Michigan Community College Journal, 5*(2), 35–42.

Mlinek, D. D. (2002). Differences in the reasons and issues impacting the implementation of technology-based distance education courses and programs as identified by department chairs using the Biglan Model. *Dissertation Abstracts International, 63*(03), 878A. (UMI No. AAT 3045526)

Montgomery, C. J. (1999). Faculty attitudes toward technology-based distance education at the University of Nevada, Las Vegas. *Dissertation Abstracts International, 60*(09), 3222A. (UMI No. AAT 9946518)

Myers, C. B., Bennett, D., Brown, G., & Henderson, T. (2004). Emerging online learning environments and student learning: An analysis of faculty perceptions. *Educational Technology and Society, 7*(1), 78–86.

Ndahi, H. B. (1999). Utilization of distance learning technology among industrial and technical teacher education faculty. *Journal of Industrial Teacher Education, 36*(4), 21–37.

Nelson, S. J. (2003). Perceptions of agricultural education teacher preparation programs toward distance education. *Dissertation Abstracts International, 64*(07), 2452A. (UMI No. AAT 3098434)

Olcott, D., & Wright, S. J. (1995). An institutional support framework for increasing faculty participation in postsecondary distance education. *The American Journal of Distance Education, 9*(3), 5–17.

O'Quinn, L. R. (2002). Factors that influence community college faculty participation in distance education. *Dissertation Abstracts International, 63*(03), 879A. (UMI No. AAT 3045485)

O'Quinn, L. R., & Corry, M. (2004). Factors which motivate community college faculty to participate in distance education. *International Journal of E-Learning, 3*(1), 19–30.

Owusu-Ansah, A. O. (2001). Institutional support of technology-based distance education, faculty views, and participation. *Dissertation Abstracts International, 62*(12), 4016A. (UMI No. AAT 3038693)

Pina, A. A. (2005). Distance learning: The importance and implementation of factors affecting its institutionalization. *Dissertation Abstracts International, 66*(03), 970A. (UMI No. AAT 3168540)

Poe, M. E. C. (2000). Selected factors affecting attitudes of graduate faculty toward use of two-way audio/two-way video as a primary instructional delivery system. *Dissertation Abstracts International, 61*(07), 2672A. (UMI No. AAT 9980204)

Porter, R. D. (2003). Internet-based distance educators address major distance education barriers in large postsecondary institutions. *Dissertation Abstracts International, 65*(04), 1278A. (UMI No. AAT 3130048)

Ramachandran, V. S. (Ed.). (1994). *Encyclopedia of Human Behavior*. San Diego: Academic Press.

Rhoads, S. B. (2005). Teaching and developing distance education courses: Issues associated with university faculty benefits. *Dissertation Abstracts International, 66*(05), 1671A. (UMI No. AAT 3176518)

Ricci, G. A. (2002). System infrastructure needs for Web course delivery: A survey of online courses in Florida community colleges. *Dissertation Abstracts International, 63*(02), 569A. (UMI No. AAT 3042973)

Rockwell, S. K., Schauer, J., Fritz, S. M., & Marx, D. B. (1999). Incentives and obstacles influencing higher education faculty and administrators to teach via distance. *Online Journal of Distance Learning Administration, 2*(4). Retrieved April 11, 2000, from http://www.westga.edu/~distance/rockwell24.htm

Schauer, J. A. (2002). Role of the department chair in implementing distance education in colleges of agriculture in land-grant institutions. *Dissertation Abstracts International, 63*(03), 840A. (UMI No. AAT 3045534)

Schifter, C. C. (2000a, March/April). Faculty motivators and inhibitors for participation in distance education. *Educational Technology, 40*, 43–46.

Schifter, C. C. (2000b, June). *Distance education faculty incentives and compensation: An exploratory study*. Paper presented at the meeting of the National University Teleconferencing Consortium, Toronto, Ontario, Canada.

Schifter, C. C. (2002, Spring). Perception differences about participating in distance education. *Online Journal of Distance Learning Administration, 5*(1). Retrieved January 23, 2006, from http://www.westga.edu/%7Edistance/ojdla/spring51/schifter51.html

Schifter, C. C. (2004, Spring). Compensation models in distance education: National survey questionnaire revisited. *Online Journal of Distance Learning Administration, 7*(1). Retrieved January 23, 2006, from http://www.westga.edu/%7Edistance/ojdla/spring71/schifter71.html

Schoats, J. L. (2002). Distance education: The attitudes and perceptions of OSU-Tulsa faculty. *Dissertation Abstracts International, 63*(10), 3451A. (UMI No. AAT 3066192)

Schwer, A. D. (2001). Role of the department chair in the delivery of distance education programs. *Dissertation Abstracts International, 62*(08), 2651A. (UMI No. AAT 3022664)

Shea, P., Pickett, A., & Li, C. S. (2005, July). Increasing access to higher education: A study of the diffusion of online teaching among 913 college faculty. *International Review of Research in Open and Distance Learning, 6*(2). Retrieved December 2, 2005, from http://www.irrodl.org/content/v6.2/shea.html

Sumrall, J. G. (2002). Factors which influence faculty attitudes and perceptions of distance education in analytical subject areas. *Dissertation Abstracts International, 65*(06), 2081A. (UMI No. AAT 3135309)

Suter, M. C. (2002). College faculty's transition to online teaching: From classroom space to virtual place. *Dissertation Abstracts International, 62*(12), 4091A. (UMI No. AAT 3037368)

Tastle, W. J., White, B. A., & Shackleton, P. (2005). E-learning in higher education: The challenge, effort, and return on investment. *International Journal of E-Learning, 4*(2), 241–251.

U.S. Department of Education. National Center for Educational Statistics. (1997). *Distance education in higher education institutions* (NCES 98-062). Washington, DC: Author.

Whicker, T. R. (2004). Critical issues in Internet-based distance learning in community colleges: Perceptions of problems and strategies for solving those problems. *Dissertation Abstracts International, 65*(04), 1209A. (UMI No. AAT 3129911)

Wilson, W. M. (2002). Faculty and administrator attitudes and perceptions toward distance learning in Southern Baptist-related educational institutions. *Dissertation Abstracts International, 63*(04), 1277A. (UMI No. AAT 3050702)

Wolcott, L. L. (1997). Tenure, promotion, and distance education: Examining the culture of faculty rewards. *The American Journal of Distance Education, 11*(2), 3–18.

Wolcott, L. L., & Betts, K. S. (1999). What's in it for me? Incentives for faculty participation in distance education. *Journal of Distance Education, 14*(2), 34–49.

Wolcott, L. L., & Haderlie, S. (1995, August). The myth of dangling carrots: Incentives and rewards for teaching at a distance. In *Proceedings of the 11th Annual Conference on Teaching and Learning at a Distance* (pp. 307–312). Madison, WI: University of Wisconsin–Madison.

Zirkle, C. (2004). Distance education programming barriers in career and technical teacher education in Ohio. *Journal of Vocational Education Research, 29*(3), 157–179.

31

Institutional Leadership

Michael F. Beaudoin
University of New England

A new role for the professoriate in the new millennium has emerged and evolved, especially as technology-assisted instruction has proliferated and changed the way teachers and students interact, as well as the manner in which educational entities must now do business to meet the demands of a digitized society. Faculties in most institutions have been encouraged to be more receptive and adaptive to opportunities for playing exciting new roles in the distance education arena.

But have we yet paid adequate attention to new roles required of leaders within those institutions and in other education/training venues? Schools and colleges in the new millennium need leaders who have reflected on their experiences and internalized understandings about their own capacity to lead. The intended purpose here is to better understand the role and impact of leadership in distance education settings; examine recent research and writing in this area, and identify research lacunae needing further investigation; offer insights and suggestions for "Best Practices" to those involved in, or aspiring to, leadership roles; and generate increased interest in the study of distance education leadership.

For purposes of this appraisal, leadership in distance education, as distinct from managerial functions in a variety of settings, is defined as a set of attitudes and behaviors which create conditions for innovative change, which enable individuals and organizations to share a vision and move in its direction, and which contribute to the operationalization of ideas that advance distance education initiatives. This leadership role is not only limited to experts in the field; a university president or elected public official who endorses, articulates, and facilitates distance education goals crafted by others can have widespread impact. It is also important to note here that effective leadership practice is not confined to those in administrative roles; indeed, there are leaders without portfolio who, as influential thinkers, have significantly impacted their organizations and the field.

However persuasive the arguments might be that fundamental changes are occurring in the digital age that will profoundly impact the academic workplace, many skeptics still believe that educational innovators are alarmists who insist that the teaching/learning environment must be dramatically restructured; they point out that the academy has been educating the citizenry in essentially the same fashion throughout other significant periods of change. But the issues to be addressed in order to remain competitive today are not quite so simple anymore. Institutional decision-makers need to be informed and enlightened enough to ask fundamental questions that could well influence their institution's future viability. How many faculty will we be needed in 10 years? Will the notion of classrooms survive? Is the present infrastructure of the institution viable? Will teachers and students need to meet on campus anymore? Can the organization's decision-makers respond to new competitors?

The changing context of education and the aggressive encroachment into its domain by the powerful forces of digital commerce makes it impossible to ignore these questions. The confluence of competition, cost, technology, and new consumer demands have insinuated new rules of engagement into a historically placid environment that has derived its strength from tradition rather than change. This new set of circumstances is going to force all academic enterprises to rethink their place and purpose, not just in philosophical terms, but in very pragmatic ways as well. Indecision and immobility during these tumultuous times could prove fatal to a number of institutions, and it is the presence of effective distance education leadership in such an uncertain milieu that could well make the difference between success, failure, or even survival.

Whether or not it fully embraces the trend, the academy is shifting from a campus-centric to a distributed-education model, and while the administrative and instructional infrastructures that presently characterize most of our institutions won't necessarily disappear, they will be utilized in different ways. Those who dismiss this as a passing phase perhaps do not recognize how pervasive these changes already are even within their own institutions, however mainstream they may still appear to be. In increasing numbers, students now simply want access to learning resources and an accepted credential to verify their learning, both commodities that have typically been aggregated and self-contained on a campus. But because distance education technologies now make it possible for students to get what they need while geographically separated from a fixed location, and with less human mediation, educational administrators continue to carry the burden of a bureaucratic infrastructure and physical plant that are becoming increasingly vestigial and costly.

Thus, as the boundaries and distinctions between traditional and so-called "non-traditional" education are blurring, there is need for leaders able to function effectively in both contexts, and because many distance educators are among the few who have already moved within these overlapping circles, they are well positioned to play key roles. Many, having succeeded to some extent in "institutionalizing" open and distance education, are now able to move from the margins to the mainstream of their organizations, and assume new roles. However, for those now willing to enter, or who are thrust, into this milieu, is it readily apparent what attitudes are best suited to manage these distance education endeavors, what techniques are effective in directing this burgeoning phenomenon, and what type of leadership might be most appropriate to move the field to its next phase? It seems that we have yet to offer much guidance to educational administrators about how they can best contribute to this inexorable shift in their midst.

Certainly, we have chronicled the activities and accomplishments of several early pioneers as correspondence study was incorporated into the extension units of a few institutions, and we have recognized and recorded the efforts of a few influential activists, such as Lord Perry of Walton and Charles Wedermeyer, who both advanced the notion of this new form of educational practice. Eventually, some of those who began teaching in this mode, and who directed the first distance education units being established at a few bold institutions, reflected on those early experiences, and began to articulate ideas and ideologies around the practice of teaching and learning at a distance. Based on their observations and experiences, a new body of literature gradually took form, mostly around pedagogical issues.

As the field took shape in the form of a separate and distinct area of academic activity and inquiry, and more programs began to emerge, experientially based accounts of program activities and accomplishments proliferated. Great efforts were made during this era to legitimize distance education by offering evidence that it was comparable to classroom-based instruction. As new technologies rapidly emerged to facilitate delivery through a variety of media, increased attention was given to analyses of which delivery system was most effective in aiding teachers to teach, and learners to learn, and to the impact of certain delivery systems on the nature of the interaction between teachers, students, and the medium they utilized. Some attention was also given to case studies of various approaches to planning and management of selected programs, both successful and unsuccessful ones, and to evaluation methods appropriate to measure the outcomes and efficacy of these ventures. Yet, largely absent throughout this period of research and writing in this emerging field was any focused consideration of the dimension of leadership and its impact on the obvious growth and apparent success of distance education at literally hundreds of institutions worldwide.

Although educational structures may appear to be relatively static, they do gradually accommodate selected change, often in response to external factors that eventually force decision-makers to consider new strategic initiatives. Few institutional leaders today would not acknowledge that technological innovation is perhaps the single most compelling factor driving them toward new organizational arrangements and, for many, it represents the most significant change since their institution was established. Despite its seemingly inherent resistance to change, and an historical unwillingness to keep pace with corporate innovations, higher education has itself entered an industrialized phase, and the resulting changes in structure and systems will demand compatible leadership styles, including approaches that have not typically characterized educational management.

Otto Peters (1994), one of the first to make important contributions to distance education theory, believes this industrialization is nowhere more evident than in this field. He has written extensively on how distance education practitioners have necessarily incorporated entrepreneurial elements such as division of labor, marketing, quality control, and other measures that are more akin to operating a business than overseeing an academic enterprise. To be sure, such characteristics exist in many educational organizations, but they are far less evident there than in most distance education environments. Indeed, some educational planners have often chosen to establish entirely new and distinct distance education entities based on an industrial model, such as the British Open University, rather than attempt to transform existing institutions. Roy McTarnaghan, founding president of Florida Gulf Coast University, speaks insightfully in an interview by *The American Journal of Distance Education* (Beaudoin, 1998) of establishing that institution as a distance education entity in 1997, noting that such large-scale endeavors must create a distinctive culture with a clearly articulated mission that is shared by all stakeholders, especially faculty, if they are to succeed.

James Hall (1998) offers a thoughtful analysis of what new, emerging institutional structures will look like, and how leaders within them will be required to function. As traditional and distance education institutions converge, leaders who have been dealing with separate and distinct programs identified with their institutions will now have to manage networked institutions in which proprietary lines between programs and students are merging, and participants shift among multiple formal and informal learning venues, with no single institution as a point of reference. As alliances develop and networks expand to increasingly include for-profit entities, the mega-university is evolving toward what Hall defines as the "meta-university." He argues that bold and creative leadership is required to manage as well as evaluate these emerging new structures, driven in large measure by networking technology.

Typically, those suggesting ways to attract and develop new leadership into distance education might encourage mentoring by senior administrators, attendance at professional meetings, seeking out relevant graduate courses, and keeping current with literature in the field. But this latter suggestion, of consulting the literature as a source of guidance for aspiring leaders, presumes that there is a worthwhile body of work available. In the early 1990s, Duning (1990) undertook an in-depth review of the literature on managerial leadership in distance education. At that point, she asserted that this area had attracted far less attention than other dimensions of the field. While there had been descriptions of program-planning processes, little examination had occurred of leadership, however defined, within a larger distance education context. Thus, at that point, Duning and others assessing the status of scholarly inquiry into the area of distance education management concluded that the field lacked a theoretical framework to guide our understanding of distance education practices, and that of all the areas of study in distance education, management still appeared to be the most neglected. We now undertake the task of re-examining the status of this vacuum to determine if it has been filled; to ask, if not, why, and, if so, whether it a useful contribution to theory and practice in the field.

This author dutifully reviewed selected literature in the field in the last 10 years by conducting a content analysis of titles and abstracts of articles appearing in two American publications from 1996 to 1999: *The American Journal of Distance Education* (*AJDE*) and *DEOSNEWS*, an electronic journal, both published by the American Center for the Study of Distance Education at The Pennsylvania State University. Also examined were the 1998 and 1999 issues of a European journal, *Open Learning*, edited by Greville Rumble, and the contents, from 1997 through 1999, of *Distance Education*, an international journal published by the Open and Distance Learning Association of Australia. Volumes 10 through 13 of *AJDE* revealed that, with the conspicuous exception of one issue (Summer 1998) which was devoted entirely to distance education leadership (and edited by this author), no other authors wrote specifically about activities and outcomes that seemed to have any obvious connection to leadership. Volumes 6 through 10 of *DEOSNEWS* contain only two titles that have any leadership connotations. It is of some interest to note that one issue contained a review of literature classified as "administration and organization," offering the possibility that leadership would be addressed, even if only tangentially, but this was not the case. Although the titles in the European and Australian journals included several articles related to staff development and the economics of distance education, no articles appeared on the specific topic being searched. Thus, we conclude that over a four-year period, several widely read sources of research and writing in distance education theory and practice offered us very little indeed on the topic of leadership.

We did optimistically note, however, a new journal introduced in January 1999, the *International Journal of Leadership in Education: Theory and Practice*, published by the Taylor-Francis Group (London), and edited by Duncan Waite. Although the early volumes seem to favor school-leadership issues, it nonetheless provides a promising forum wherein distance education practitioners and researchers may now make contributions in a professional publication dedicated entirely to educational leadership. Perhaps even more encouraging is the emergence and success of the *Online Journal of Distance Learning Administration* (*OJDLA*), published by West Georgia State University. This appears to be a flourishing electronic medium for research and writing, almost entirely focused on issues relevant to distance education managers. The editors receive many manuscripts, and published pieces are frequently cited.

Another useful device for gauging how popular a specific topic seems to be at a given moment is to conduct a content analysis of presentations at major national and international distance education conferences. A number of these papers eventually find their way into the published literature in the field, and can thus serve as indicators of what topics are currently in vogue. This activity was undertaken through an examination of titles and abstracts of papers presented at the European Distance Education Network, Bologna, Italy (1998); the distance education conference sponsored by the University of South Australia (2000); and the ICDE World Conference on Open Learning and Distance Education in Duesseldorf, Germany (April 2001).

Not unexpectedly, the interest and attention focused on the general theme of distance education management in general and leadership in particular, was conspicuously thin. The Bologna conference offered 137 papers and workshops on a wide range of topics, including several under the category of Organization and Policy. Although several of these referred to various approaches used to plan and implement particular projects, none directly addressed matters concerning leadership per se. The Australia conference program listed 133 presentations. Again, of these, not one, based on a reading of the abstracts, appeared to address issues related to leadership. One keynote address discussed technology-driven change in education and did contain a few comments germane to distance education leaders. The world conference in Germany received a total of 624 proposals for presentations. From this enormous body of work, it could be presumed that certainly a few authors would likely contribute to the leadership theme as their area of special interest. Several of these proposals were placed in the categories of Strategies and Policies, and Management and Logistics; no doubt, a reading of full texts would reveal some content related to the leadership theme, yet only one session dealt specifically with this subject. In the conference arena, West Georgia State University again distinguishes itself as sponsoring the only national professional meeting that attempts to focus on distance education administration. Though presentations unrelated to administration are sometimes included in the proceedings, this conference has certainly hosted more presentations and papers devoted to leadership related topics than any other.

Finally, with respect to the current body of written work, there is an increasingly steady supply of new books on distance education, many offering a chapter or two on aspects of administration and organization. For example, Moore and Kearsley's (2005) volume presenting a systems approach to distance education does contain a chapter, "Management, Administration and Policy," with brief but useful discussions on such topics as staffing and planning, but nothing specifically on leadership. An examination of new books on open and distance learning reviewed and/or received by the journals noted above yielded no titles that dealt primarily with organizing and leading distance education activities. Also, the subject indexes of 10 prominent books on open and distance education published since 1993 were reviewed; none contained any listings under the subject of leadership, and only two listed administration or management. Thus, if the literature on the broader topic of management in distance education is relatively thin, we can hardly be sanguine about the prospect of finding much on the more specific aspects of leadership in this field. Yet, it is encouraging to observe that there are now occasional volumes appearing which focus more exclusively on topics that flirt with the leadership theme. A review of the database on Open and Distance Education publications, edited by Keith Harry of the British Open University, listed several book titles devoted to open and distance education leadership and management. And while these works are mainly intended to offer strategies for developing and directing open-learning initiatives, rather than formulating more theoretical constructs, this material will nonetheless certainly help close the gap in the literature on leadership.

At least three other books are worth noting briefly here. One, of course, is this ambitious volume, the *Handbook of Distance Education*, with a substantial section titled "Policies, Administration and Management." Though the eleven chapters include a wide range of topics from planning to accreditation, all have implications for those responsible for leading distance education programs. Hanna and Latchem's (2001) *Leadership and Management in Open and Flexible Learning* is an especially insightful book offering interesting perspectives on leadership presented through case studies and interviews. This author's own work, *Reflections on Research, Faculty and Leadership in Distance Education* (Beaudoin, 2004) contains several essays on distance education leadership, relating to both research and practice.

In summing up this brief review of research, writing, and presentations on leadership, it should be acknowledged that, within the body of work receiving this cursory examination, there may well be more attention given to the leadership theme than we were able to discern, and no doubt some authors would protest that their contributions do address, at least by implication, some dimension of leadership. We suspect that this may be a legitimate claim, yet it can be stated that much of the work reviewed and noted here, in both conference and publication venues, is largely descriptive in nature (e.g., case studies) of specific programs. It must be asked, then, how useful this reportage is in contributing to the body of work on leadership theory and practice or, in truth, to any other important aspects of distance education.

It should also be asked at this juncture if the paucity of scholarly material related to leadership in distance education is compensated for, to some extent, by the availability of material in other areas of educational theory and practice. It is within the area most closely aligned with distance education (i.e., adult and continuing education) that we can find a somewhat promising answer. As with distance education, there is a long and impressive history in continuing education, but in this particular area, we find a considerably well developed and quite impressive portfolio relating not only to the planning and management of continuing education activities, but also some attention to the area of leadership. Simerly (1987) has contributed a number of worthwhile studies which can be quite useful to distance educators until there is a more fully articulated body of work on distance education leadership. It will be interesting to observe if some contributors to the literature on continuing education will now offer similar insights in distance education where these endeavors intersect. This is quite possible, since many distance education initiatives are spawned within continuing education units where there is often a spirit for entrepreneurial and innovative practices.

One is tempted to conclude, from this review, that the subject of leadership in distance education is being actively avoided, in favor of the usual fare: reports and case studies of specific projects and programs that go into excessive detail about the life (and sometimes death) of particular initiatives at selected institutions. Unfortunately, the typical treatment of these accounts seldom offer any useful insights about distance education practice that might be generalized for possible relevance and application in other similar settings, and almost never is there any thoughtful analysis about the impact of leadership, or the lack of it, in affecting the outcomes chronicled in these studies.

What might be some plausible explanations for this minimal interest in an area of study that, until now, seems to be largely neglected while, in other organizational settings (most notably the for-profit corporate sector) there is enormous interest in topics related to organizational leadership, as seen in best-selling books and high-priced seminars? First, those researching and writing in the field of distance education may just now be getting beyond the phase in its history where there has been an inordinate amount of interest focused on analyses of how distance instruction compares with more conventional methods and, as new technologies were rapidly deployed, how effectively these various learning environments worked compared to one another. A related factor may be that most who have written in the field thus far have themselves been academics who preferred to devote their writing to pedagogical issues rather than administrative matters.

Second, there has been, in fact, a reasonable amount of attention given to the planning and administration of distance education programs for quite some time. And although most of this work to date has been confined to accounts of specific case histories, this treatment has perhaps been considered adequate enough without getting involved in the more esoteric domain of leadership. Related to this is the fact that the concept of "leadership" is not widely recognized as a separate and distinct element of administrative practice or study. This is especially so outside of the United States. In European literature, for example, leadership is seldom alluded to, at least not in the field of education. Prominent European theorists such as Otto Peters and Börje Holmberg have made notable contributions to the organization of distance education, but they and others have not identified leadership as a discrete topic for analysis.

Third, there are those who simply dismiss the concept as one that is not especially useful for advancing the study or the practice of distance education. It is seen as an elusive idea that does not readily lend itself to reliable analysis, or to a universal set of desirable behaviors safely applicable to the particulars of each situation. Further, just as some argue that there are no characteristics attributable to distance education that are uniquely its own within the field, they likewise believe the question of leadership within distance education merits no special scrutiny or analysis as a distinct area of study.

What, ultimately, is the usefulness of the body of work accumulated thus far on the subject of distance education leadership? Although most of the work which does exist is largely confined to an occasional book chapter, conference presentation, journal article, or "Principles of Good Practice" lists, perhaps it can be stated with some confidence that distance education practitioners currently in, or moving toward, leadership roles do have a variety of growing resources available to guide their practice. Assuming that there may be some value in the field of distance education if there is increased attention to leadership issues, what can be done to generate more interest in the topic? At the very least, those planning publications and meetings related to distance education could actively solicit contributions on the subject, and dedicate entire conferences, journal issues, or books to leadership in distance education.

Beyond some useful literature in continuing education, as previously noted, are there resources from other areas of study that could compensate for this void we allege still persists in distance education? We suggest that Donald Schon's (1983) important study of reflective practice has significant implications for distance educators, no less so than for the several professions Schon uses to illustrate his theories. He makes a provocative case for developing mature practitioners by insisting that they actively engage in a process of ongoing systematic reflection of their work during their practice, rather than at a later point when they may no longer be able to make appropriate interventions to enhance their effectiveness. This seems an especially worthwhile process for an entire generation of distance education practitioners who now have substantial personal and institutional experience, and are still highly active. By engaging in "reflection in action," these veterans have the opportunity, as Schon aptly describes it, to define new truths, not only for their own benefit but for the entire profession as well. This effort and its results have the potential to make important new contributions to the field and offer insights into its leadership.

Is there, in fact, any value in attempting to craft, if not a bona fide theoretical framework for leadership practice that is unique to distance education, at least a set of guiding principles that, at this moment in which distance education has evolved to a new role and status, can well serve its providers and consumers? Those responsible for mapping new directions in which to move distance education practice to the next stage of its development might be somewhat heartened by the recent attempts by several groups, including professional associations and accrediting bodies, to define so-called "Principles of Good Practice." The New England Association of Schools and Colleges (1998), for example, has developed and promulgated a "policy for the accreditation of academic degree and certificate programs offered through distance education." These standards for quality are useful in providing suggested criteria by which we can plan new programs, measure what we are doing in such areas as matching technology with needs, providing appropriate student support, implementing evaluation measures, and the like. In the absence of a more precise theoretical framework, such principles do offer, at least, some insights about what constitutes effective leadership practice, and how it ultimately impacts the success or failure of our efforts. But producing checklists of helpful hints about what to do and what not to do hardly seems adequate to face the tasks ahead.

While the most common mode of assessing progress in the development of a body of knowledge in an area of study is the usual review of the literature, it is possible that a brief survey of other activities related to distance education leadership may yield some useful information that could compensate for the apparent lack of any substantial corpus of written work thus far on the subject. For example, there are a number of centers for distance education housed at colleges and universities (e.g., the American Center for the Study of Distance Education at The Pennsylvania State University) which sponsor symposia, workshops, publications, and programs of study which, while not necessarily activities focused entirely on leadership, do contribute to greater awareness and understanding of distance education practice. Also, professional development sessions on distance education administration are increasingly evident. Several institutions now offer summer institutes that do, in fact, specifically address distance education leadership (e.g., the Institute for the Management of Distance Education, offered by the Western Cooperative for Educational Telecommunications; see http://www.wiche.edu/telecom/Events/). These, presumably, are serving a useful purpose in providing experienced and aspiring leaders with insights and guidance. More importantly, a number of institutions, particularly in the United States, now offer certificate- and graduate-level programs of study with curricula in distance education, including courses specifically designed to prepare leaders for the field. Just one example of this emerging field of study is a Master of Distance Education offered online by the University of Maryland University College, which also offers related graduate-level certificate programs in collaboration with Oldenburg University's Center for Distance Education (Germany). This degree program is attracting an international cohort of students, and has recently won two national awards for "Best Online Program" since its inception. (See http://www.umuc.edu/mde).

It is interesting to speculate on what impact these curricula might eventually have in creating a distinct body of work that offers a more theoretical approach regarding leadership, rather than the prevailing emphasis on practical applications of administrative techniques. Preparing candidates for careers specifically in distance education through professional education programs has potentially significant implications as, for the first time, the field will acquire a new generation of individuals in leadership roles who did not "come up through the ranks" during a period when the field was just emerging as a recognizable and viable area of professional practice. In addition to introducing new leadership styles and strategies in their chosen field, this cohort might contribute important new theoretical perspectives as well.

Having now entered a new millennium in which the promise of ever-advancing technologies is likely to present provocative new challenges as well as opportunities, it is tempting to ask if there is perhaps a leadership style that is most appropriate for distance education. While it may be too bold to suggest a single best approach, it might be useful to at least identify those situations in which distance education leaders are most likely to find themselves in the near-term, and consider those strategic perspectives that might be most compatible and productive in those settings. These include more collaborative partnerships, such as alliance building with for-profit companies more typically seen as competitors; more meta-university arrangements, in which networking structures make parochial interests a handicap; more expansive markets requiring a truly global view well beyond one's usual environs; more freestanding virtual entities utilizing asynchronous formats; and more exclusively online delivery systems rather than mixed-media approaches. These would seem to be a few of the venues in which there will be need for high-performing leaders.

While we should perhaps avoid committing to any particular leadership style as the most suitable, certainly the concept of transformative leadership advocated by Bennis and Nanus (1985) remains a particularly compelling model for distance education leaders today. This is so because organizational practices long entrenched in educational entities urgently require reshaping to adapt to environmental changes, most notably the emergence of a worldwide market for students, but also an exponential increase in potential competitors for those students. Transformational leaders in education must be capable of helping stakeholders (e.g., administrators, faculty, students, and trustees), and recognizing that there are obvious benefits in doing business in new ways, and that they can no longer afford the luxury of adopting new ways of teaching and learning in an incremental fashion to which academics are so accustomed and comfortable in doing. To be sure, there are no facile formulae that can be matched with particular settings that will ensure infallible leadership performance; ultimately, a sense of vision, resoluteness, and the ability to operationalize concepts are requisite to succeed.

Advocates and initiators of distance education no longer need be seen, or to view themselves, as mavericks on the fringes of their institutions, but rather as contributors who can play a key role in bringing their institution to the next stage of its development. This new status among those responsible for "alternative" programs is now more common, as institutional decision-makers become more aware, often with some alarm, that they may not be as relevant and responsive as their competition is to the demands of diverse new market segments seeking access to learning opportunities. Leaders can capitalize on their institution's growing need to remain competitive in a broader arena by demonstrating how distance education offerings, once relegated to the margins, can now be central to an institution's strategic planning for success and, in some cases, even survival in the new global marketplace. And while some might object to the notion of appealing to an organization's self-interest as a means of advancing distance education, the fact is that an innovative new idea very often succeeds, not because it is noble, but because it can serve a useful purpose, both for the larger system as well as for its proponents.

Leaders must create conditions conducive to energy, initiative, and innovation in their particular milieu, and bring others along, both above and below them in the organizational hierarchy. This requires, in addition to transformational leadership, what Hersey, Johnson, and Blanchard (2001) call "situational" leadership, with its ability to diagnose the organization at that moment and determine its stakeholders' readiness for moving in a new direction. In fusing these two approaches, the leader diagnoses the unique situation in the immediate environment, and then transforms it as far along the change continuum as necessary, through a collaborative style. In this way, a climate less resistant and more receptive toward distance education is created, often in an incremental fashion as the situation is gradually transformed.

Since few distance educators have the opportunity to create entirely new free-standing entities exclusively designed for online or other delivery systems, but rather labor within institutions positioned somewhere along the continuum between conventional and alternative infrastructures—what might be called a "hybrid model"—most eventually face the conundrum of whether or not to promote the notion of a central unit to coordinate distance education activities, or at least to foster new initiatives. One argument is that, in the absence of a focal point for such endeavors, individual faculty will likely tinker indefinitely and inefficiently on their own with a variety of instructional-technology options intended to augment their classroom-based courses, but this approach will not ultimately result in a system-wide adoption of distance education in any comprehensive and cost-effective manner. And those institutions that do incorporate small-scale distance education initiatives but contract out many specialized functions that allow them to retain their existing infrastructure are often suspect because they can conveniently tout their involvement in distance education without any real institutional shift in its direction.

Another view is that this incremental process of individual initiatives becoming increasingly prevalent within an institution is what will eventually lead to a critical mass of participation that ultimately creates the demand for more institutional commitment and support. Proponents of this latter strategy maintain that it is the pattern that typifies most institutions' progression toward distance education today, and that premature, administratively driven initiatives will only generate further faculty resistance and impede any prospects for longer-term change. Bernath provides interesting insights into this dilemma, using various European models to illustrate the positive and negative forces at play when attempting to integrate distance education into conventional universities (1996). For opinion leaders in distance education, this particular issue can be one of the most critical, and their insights and advice on the best option will test their credibility and influence within their organizations.

To succeed in any of these contexts, a macro view is critical. Distance education leaders must not be overly preoccupied with nurturing their own existing programs, and providing the horsepower for only their initiatives; they must also work their way into the academic mainstream and the inner circle of decision-makers responsible for bringing the entire organization to a new place. Distance educators should no longer see themselves as protectors and survivors of isolated programs for which they have labored mightily, but rather as valued strategic partners who can enable the larger institution, often long seen as the enemy, to catch up with them and emulate their practices and successes. In short, distance education managers must see themselves, and be seen, as educational leaders who, through less directing and more motivating, facilitate the articulation, development, implementation, and stewardship of a vision of learning that is shared and supported by a wider academic community.

But leaders must disabuse themselves of the idea that their programs, however more widely accepted and adopted within their institutions than in the past, are now seen as more legitimate (i.e., more equivalent to classroom-based instruction). It is more likely that, in most instances, these alternative delivery methods are now more widely recognized as effective means of capturing a larger market share of prospective consumers and generating additional revenues. Distance education activists can be convincing advocates because colleges and universities, as in the past, must still plan their futures in a continuing context of uncertainty. Since much of that uncertainty in this era has been brought about by the rapid emergence of instructional technology, this phenomenon allows experienced open-learning practitioners to be far more influential in shaping a strategic agenda for the digital decades than was usually the case in the past.

The challenges facing higher education and its most experienced leaders are formidable indeed, as organizations remain stubbornly resistant to change, even when exciting opportunities present themselves. For example, despite its accessibility to the world's lucrative foreign-student market, most universities remain oblivious to or complacent about huge cross-border enrollments. This missed chance for significant growth is likely to especially affect American institutions, which already suffer from the federal government's misguided measures at impeding foreign students' entry into the country. American universities' continuing infatuation with the campus-centric growth model will further cede this new worldwide market to competitors elsewhere.

If their institutions still remain unresponsive, then distance education planners must diligently seek opportunities to convey a sense of urgency that what they currently are doing, perhaps somewhat unnoticed and serving a relatively small proportion of overall enrollments, nonetheless represents a model for replication elsewhere if further institutional growth and success is to be realized. But this requires that past successes be touted. By doing so, distance education can now, more convincingly than ever before, be cast as an activity to be emulated elsewhere in the organization. This is already happening in the area of instructional design, where many faculties may be unaware of just how much learning from a distance is taking place through their own institution, and who couldn't perhaps care less about it, but are nonetheless eager to acquire new technology tools and training to augment their classroom-based courses.

Much of higher education is still characterized by "Old Millennium" thinking that has functioned for a long time in an old economy in which decisions are made regarding the number of sections required for a particular course to optimize faculty workloads. In the new economy, where information is the product to be delivered to a broader market in less time and at lower cost, distance education activists must help their organizations ask the right questions and see that both the institution and its teaching personnel can thrive if they are willing to find their appropriate niche through "New Millennium" strategic thinking. In an earlier era, distance educators typically assumed a warrior mentality to advance their cause; today, they can be more effective as brokers facilitating the expansion or replication of programs and services they championed during more contentious times.

Although effective distance education leadership requires presence and participation in a wider arena, playing a role in the macro environment cannot be at the expense of attending to the details of this complex enterprise. The tasks to be overseen by managers of both small and large, as well as both new and established, distance education projects represent a formidable repertoire of skills which need constant attention and refinement. To identify but a few areas: needs assessment, market analysis, strategic planning, fitting technology to needs, operationalizing ideas, resource mobilization, introducing online infrastructure, policy formulation, training and support for faculty, collaborating with partners, program evaluation and accreditation, and mentoring the next generation of leaders—all are tasks requiring vigilance and guidance.

The presumed dominance of online teaching-learning environments for the foreseeable future raises a further question: Are there particular leadership roles that are more appropriate than others, and are there any "best practices" for leading distance education initiatives and activities in the online domain? Are some of the complex roles exercised by the previous generation of leaders less relevant now than in earlier periods of the movement? Regardless of the medium in use, it would seem that the roles of conceptualizer, implementor, and evaluator are still viable ones to play. Perhaps less critical in the repertoire of today's leaders are the roles of advocate, reformer, and technician that occupied so much time in the past. Too often, those presiding in decision-making forums engage in deliberations long on complex technological options and bereft of fundamental pedagogical issues. The distance education leader, whatever other roles he or she may assume, must always maintain the essential role of educator. This is not to suggest, however, that the distance education leader does not need to be attentive to the technological side of the enterprise. Indeed, keen attention to the medium is critical, but as Neil Postman (1996) so insightfully points out, it is not so much knowledge of how technology works, as it is how technology impacts its users. Every new technological innovation applied to education at a distance changes things. These changes may be in the intellectual, social, political, economic, or ecological domain, and the effective leader cannot afford to be ignorant of the advantages and also the possible disadvantages of what such technology creates.

A final caution is perhaps appropriate for those who may feel best equipped to provide the creative new leadership the field warrants. Paradoxically, it seems that the past experience and longevity of some distance educators actually works against them in providing leadership for a new age of learning. Ever more powerful interactive technology has resulted in the diminution of distance, and it has reduced the decision-making window demanded of institutions to respond to a new class of educational consumers who are willing to spend money to save time. Yet many who may have pioneered distance education at their institutions may still be preoccupied with bridging the distance gap which effectively no longer exists. Distance education advocates who, in the past, put their energy into debating the virtues of out-of-classroom learning must now play a more valuable role in facilitating discussions and decisions of much wider scope and more profound consequences for the future of their institutions. There must now be a shift in leaders' focus from the micro issues around technology and its impact on learners to a more macro view of institutions and the impact of technology in this larger context. Thoughtful attention to issues in this broader arena will contribute to appropriate action that will ultimately impact the teaching-learning process, institution-wide, regardless of what technology is utilized.

It is essential that veteran as well as emerging leaders be prepared for these new roles, not just by relying on instinct derived from past experience, but also from new insights acquired through greater attention to leadership as a discreet area of study and practice for the important work ahead. The potential contribution of distance educators in a widening sphere of influence is too significant at this juncture to relegate to the periphery of others' thinking, or to obscure our vision of where we want to go and where we want to lead others.

REFERENCES

Beaudoin, M. (ed.). (1998). Interview: Speaking personally with Roy McTarnaghan. *The American Journal of Distance Education, 12*(2), 73–78.

Beaudoin, M. (2004). *Reflections on research, faculty and leadership in distance education*. Oldenburg, Germany: Oldenburg University Press.

Bennis, W., & Nanus, B. (1985). *Leaders: The strategies for taking charge*. New York: Harper and Row.

Bernath, U. (1996). Distance education in mainstream higher education: A strategic issue at conventional universities. In M. Thompson (Ed.), *Internationalism in distance education: A vision for higher education*. (ACSDE Research Monograph No. 10, pp. 45–51). University Park: The Pennsylvania State University.

Duning, B. (1990). The literature of management. In M. Moore (Ed.), *Contemporary issues in American distance education*. Oxford: Pergamon Press.

Hall, J. W. (1998). Leadership in accreditation and networked learning. *The American Journal of Distance Education, 12*(2), 5–15.

Hanna, D., & Latchem, C. (2001). *Leadership and management in open and flexible learning*. London: Kogan Page.

Hersey, P., Johnson, D., & Blanchard, K. (2001). *Management of organizational behavior: Leading human resources*. Englewood Cliffs, NJ: Prentice Hall.

Moore, M., & Kearsley, G. (2005). *Distance education: A systems view* (2nd ed.). Belmont, CA: Wadsworth.

New England Association of Schools and Colleges, Commission on Institutions of Higher Education. (1998). *Policy for the accreditation of academic degree and certificate programs offered through distance education*. Bedford, MA: New England Association of Schools and Colleges.

Peters, O. (1994). Otto Peters on distance education: The industrialization of teaching and learning. In D. Keegan (Ed.), *Foundations of distance education* (pp. 77–88). London, New York: Routledge.

Postman, N. (1996). *The ends of education*. New York: Vintage Books.

Schon, D. (1983). *The reflective practitioner: How professionals think in action*. London: Temple Smith.

Simerly, R. G. (1987). *Strategic planning and leadership in continuing education*. San Francisco: Jossey-Bass.

32

Accreditation: Quality Control in Higher Distance Education

Amy Kirle Lezberg

Associate Director (ret), Commission on Institutions of Higher Education
New England Association of Schools and Colleges

HISTORICAL BACKGROUND

Unlike most other countries in the world, the United States has never had a Ministry of Higher Education directly regulating the quality of its postsecondary institutions of learning; such control is not among the powers granted to the federal government by the U.S. Constitution. Instead, in order to operate legally, academic institutions must, like other businesses, be licensed by one of the fifty states, each of which sets individual rules governing entities incorporated within its borders. Rooted in the differing political philosophies of these states, these rules range from the almost nonexistent to the quite stringent (Bear & Bear, 1998). For the most part, such rules describe the minimal inputs necessary for initiating an institution of higher education rather than set any criteria for the effectiveness of their educational outcomes. Because of the variety of these requirements, private accreditation associations, devoted to both the evaluation of current performance and the encouragement of continuing improvement, have, for more than 100 years, provided the primary mechanism for assuring employers, governments, and, most importantly, students and their families, that degree-granting institutions are offering acceptable levels of education (Young, Chambers, & Kells, 1983).

INVOLVEMENT OF THE REGIONAL ACCREDITING ASSOCIATIONS

The most widely accepted and respected of these bodies in the United States are the following six regional associations: (a) the Middle States Association of Colleges and Schools, (b) the New England Association of Schools and Colleges (NEASC), (c) the North Central Association of Colleges and Schools, (d) the Southern Association of Schools and Colleges, Northwest Commission on Colleges and Universities, and (e) the Western Association of Schools and Colleges (see http://www.chea.org for detailed information about these associations, including their geographic scope, standards, processes, and personnel). These currently accredit approximately 3,500 institutions of higher education, including those offering academic degrees ranging in level from associate to doctoral degrees. The range of institutions encompasses public and private institutions (both non-profit and for-profit); research universities and community technical colleges; secular and religious schools; those with exclusively on-site or cyberspace offerings, and such independent members as Harvard, Princeton, Duke, and Wellesley, as well as the state-supported or state-assisted public institution of virtually every state and territory in the nation.

The specific regional association by which an institution is recognized is generally determined by the geographic location in which it is chartered, the 50 states having been divided up for historical reasons into regions that in some instances correspond with common usage (e.g., the New England Association accredits institutions in the six New England States) but in others do not (e.g., the North Central Association accredits institutions in 19 states, ranging from West Virginia to Arizona and North Dakota). By common agreement, a satellite campus of an institution accredited by a region other than that in which the satellite is located conforms to the standards of the region of the home campus, although a representative of the accrediting body responsible for the region in which that satellite is located is included on the team which visits it for an accreditation review. Further, five of the regional accrediting associations now extend membership (i.e., accreditation) to a growing number of site-based (but not Web-based) institutions outside the geographical borders of the United States, both public and private.

Of course, even throughout the 20th century, not all instruction has taken place in geographically distinct locations. In response to an increase in distance education offerings, criteria and standards for the acceptability of such programs were established by three major groups: (a) in 1955, by the Distance Education and Training Council (DETC; http://www.detc.org), an accrediting body devoted solely to non-site-based education; (b) throughout the last quarter of the century by the American Council on Education, which offered equivalency credit for certain accepted programs; and (c) more recently by various consortia such as the Western Interstate Commission for Higher Education, whose members were regionally accredited institutions. By the end of the century, however, the regional accrediting associations and their commissions on higher education recognized that there was a need for them to at least provide guidelines in the area of distance and Web-based education, and they acted, first individually and then as a unified group, to establish regulations that would allow their members to include distance education offerings within their overall institutional accreditation.

As early as 1986, the North Central Association of Schools and Colleges, the largest of the regional associations, had evaluated and bestowed membership upon National Technological University, which offers degrees in engineering to working professionals through courses designed and delivered by faculty with full-time appointments at institutions that are themselves accredited both institutionally by the appropriate regional accrediting association and programmatically by the American Board of Engineering Technology (ABET). In so acting, the North Central Association established the importance of focusing on the effectiveness with which an entity delivers education rather than on the physical location at which the credits are earned. Consequently, when the number and variety of courses, programs, and complete degrees offered through electronically mediated technology began to proliferate in the last decade of the 20th century, the regional accrediting associations had experience and precedent to draw on as they considered the ways in which such offerings conformed to the overriding set of four nationally accepted accreditation criteria, as well as to the specific standards of the relevant accrediting association. That is, even without the impetus provided by expressions of concern raised by the federal government as to the legitimacy of such offerings being represented as "higher education," the six regional associations had begun to consider whether they could expand and explicate their standards in order to include such offerings within the accreditation of their member institutions, whether existing and site-based or newly developed entities, both non-profit and for-profit.

What was being confronted reflected the changes in the academy brought about by distance education, which has transformed the ways in which professors teach, students learn, and researchers collaborate. Amidst such changes, it is not at all surprising that the regional accrediting associations faced and wrestled with the question of whether regionalism, although it had served the country so well and for so long, was now, in fact, obsolete, as argued by Perley and Tanguay (1999) and the responses to their article in *The Chronicle of Higher Education.* Certainly, definitions of regionalism become complicated when called upon to address such situations as the campus of Cornell Weill Medical School located and with students in Doha, Qatar, where on-site teaching alternates with video-conferencing involving students in the Persian Gulf and faculty in New York.

In addition to formulating rules for the quality control of these varied offerings, the regionals were aware that they also had to carefully consider the identification and training of those would who enforce such regulations, both as on-site visitors and as members of their central decision-making bodies. Although the cohort from whom they drew was at first quite limited, by the beginning of the 21st century, none had any problem in finding sufficient numbers of appropriately experienced people to review their standards, staff their visiting teams, and participate on their central commissions. And, indeed, more than half their teams visited institutions that included distance learning among their offerings.

From the outset, the associations were aware that questions would arise about the meaning of regional boundaries when dealing with education in which the instructor might be in one state (or country) while the learner was in another. It quickly became evident that because new entities were in a position to seek a charter, and therefore accreditation, from more than one association, it would be necessary to ensure that accreditation standards made accreditation shopping—that is, looking for the easiest association by which to be accredited—impossible, or at least difficult.

Among the issues that had to be addressed by the regional accrediting associations was the fact that, although they do pay some attention to graduate study and research, they traditionally have taken as their model the residential liberal arts college, and therefore focus primarily on undergraduate education. Consequently, the standards set by regional accrediting associations not only address the qualifications of faculty and general expectations for curricular offerings but also attend to library and information resources, and such cocurricular activities as student services (including athletics, counseling, and residence halls), and the organizational and administrative format of the institution. In addition, the pragmatic cast of American higher education meant that a general, if usually unspoken, assumption was that education is more than the transfer of cognitive knowledge, but also involves the behavioral and cognitive domains of learning. An associated assumption was that the success of education depends upon its taking place at certain times and in certain places where both the faculty member and his or her students are present in a locale appropriate for learning and have immediate access to a properly staffed library in which information resources can be located. Indeed, so pervasive was this belief that for many years most traditional colleges and universities did not assign correspondence courses (as they were then universally known)—the first form of distance education and usually delivered by pen, paper, and the U.S. Postal Service—the same academic credit as site-based courses. Often, such offerings were, at best, granted continuing education credit. The great majority of these institutions, whether publicly supported or in the independent sector, were accredited by one of the regional associations and offered credentials that were generally accepted in transfer by other regionally accredited institutions and established eligibility for certain forms of financial aid and employment.

THE DISTANCE EDUCATION AND TRAINING COUNCIL

Technically, off-campus learning was included in an institution's regional accreditation, since accreditation is never partial, and if an institution is accredited, all of its offerings are included in that accreditation. Nevertheless, for the first three fourths of the 20th century, the regional accrediting associations concentrated almost exclusively on quality control of the site-based education offered by their members. There were, however, non-traditional institutions that did grant degrees through correspondence, including some that had no campus at all on which instruction could take place. That is, during the period when the regional accrediting bodies were focusing on the quality control of education delivered at sites where students, faculty, and resources could all be found in the same place at the same time, organizations were arising that offered instruction to those who attended such institutions. As it had with site-based education, the growth of such programs was followed by recognition of the need to distinguish those that actually delivered education from those that merely supplied credentials. In 1926, owing to the proliferation of various entities that were offering credentials to students who completed a course of study while not physically at the institution offering it but through the mail, the Home Study Council was formed. Its stated purpose was "to promote sound educational standards and ethical business practices within the correspondence school field" (DETC, 1998, p. 7). Having established standards for membership, the Council, in 1955, was recognized by the U.S. Department of Education as an accrediting organization, membership in which was a reliable guarantee of quality. Four years later, in response to the growing variety of modes for delivering education, the council changed its name to the Distance Education and Training Council (DETC), promoting itself as the only accrediting association devoted entirely to institutions offering distance education.

Recognition of DETC as an accrediting body made it possible for consumers to have some assurance as to the legitimacy of certain correspondence schools, even when unaware of what such recognition entailed. In fact, in order for an accreditation association to be listed by the U.S. Government as a reliable judge of institutional quality, it must undergo a review by the U.S. Department of Education every five years. Although the exact tone and wording of the standards of each accrediting body, whether DETC or any national or regional association, may be quite distinctive and reflect its individual character, each applies its standards to ensure that every member institution has a mission and purposes appropriate to higher education has the resources available to accomplish its mission and purposes; is currently meeting its mission and purposes; and seems likely to continue meeting its mission and purposes.

However, despite its recognition by the U.S. Department of Education, its membership in the Council on Postsecondary Accreditation (COPA), and its successors, the Commission on Recognition of Postsecondary Education (CORPA) and the Council for Higher Education Accreditation (CHEA), the umbrella organizations for institutional and programmatic accreditation, DETC is still not able to assure students enrolled in its member programs and institutions that they will have their credentials recognized by certain employers or governments (municipal, state, or national) or transfer their credits to regionally accredited institutions, which include the majority of mainstream institutions currently operating in the United States. To some extent, this reflects the fact that although certain DETC programs may offer advanced academic degrees, others are postsecondary, but not necessarily appropriate, to higher education. Indeed, although the Council currently accredits more than 55 degree-granting distance programs (as well as others not offering any academic degrees), some offer programs lasting only four weeks. In addition, since accreditation is voluntary and membership-based, the refusal of many regionally accredited institutions to automatically accept credits earned from DETC-accredited institutions may reflect an attitude that its membership, which not only establishes, but also interprets and applies the specific standards of an accrediting body, may interpret their standards not as stringently as those set by the regionals (e.g., some may give humanities credit for Business English, which is not considered college-level by regionally accredited institutions). Similar concerns are often expressed as the reason that regionally accredited institutions will not transfer credits from entities accredited by other nationally recognized associations, such as the Accrediting Council for Independent Colleges and Schools (ACICS), which accredits postsecondary rather than higher-educational institutions, and which allows its members to offer distance education programs internationally, both one-quarter of which may be in languages other than English and none of which need undergo separate accreditation review.

QUALITY ASSURANCE IN DISTANCE EDUCATION— THE NINETIES

By 1995, a U.S. Department of Education survey had revealed that distance education courses— and in some cases, whole programs—were being offered by more than 90% of the institutions that enroll more than 10,000 students, and by 85% of institutions that enroll between 3,000 and 10,000 students. By 1997–98, according to the National Center for Education Statistics, the number of offerings using electronically mediated instruction rather than traditional correspondence course methodologies had more than doubled, with 44% of two- and four-year higher education institutions offering distance education, up from 33% in 1995 (American Council on Education, 2000); and, according to an article in *The Chronicle of Higher Education* (July 8, 2005, *51*(44), A29), Eduventures, a research and consulting company, in "Online Distance Education Market Update 2005: Growth in the Age of Competition," reported that "about 937,000 students were enrolled in all-online education programs at the end of 2004. By the end of 2005, Eduventures expects more than 1.2 million students to be taking such courses, making up about 7 percent of the 17 million students enrolled at degree-granting institutions."

That is, although even today some offerings are still using the old-fashioned pen, pencil, and post-office approach to learning, an increasing number of institutions were delivering education through various communication technologies—fax machines (especially for the delivery of exams and journal articles from on-site libraries); telephone lines (for language lab assignments); chat rooms and threaded conversations (for the student-to-student interaction required for regional accreditation); CD-ROMS (especially for overseas offerings); one-way video; and interactive TV (which allows geographically separated students and instructors to interact with each other in real time).

Many programs combined two or more of these technologies to give reality to the idea of instruction on an anytime, anyplace basis.

As they began to institute their extended menu of distance education offerings, institutions, although understandably loath to add yet another specialized accrediting association to those already active on their campuses, wanted the assurance of external quality control mechanisms.

Consequently, throughout the last decade of the twentieth century, they sought guidance from their regional accrediting associations about quality control of such offerings. Meanwhile, as electronically mediated instruction became more prevalent and requests for guidance from member institutions became more pervasive, a number of organizations to which these institutions also belonged and which were interested in preserving the quality of higher education offerings, developed sets of rules and guidelines to assist members in their activities. Some, like the Western Interstate Commission on Higher Education (WICHE), established a separate body—for example, such programs as the Western Cooperative for Educational Telecommunication (1966)—devoted to the development of guiding principles and consultation on mediated instruction. Others, however, such as the American Council on Education, developed suggested procedures as just one of the many services they offered their members.

THE MOVE FROM STRICT REGIONALISM
TO NATIONAL COOPERATION

The regionals, however, were slowly coming to understand that even within the constraints of regionalism, certain national standards had to be agreed upon. In discussing and determining the standards they adopted to measure quality in distance education programs, they entered into fairly new territory, for never before had these accrediting associations been willing to yield their regional sovereignty to achieve a nationwide consensus. As a group, the regional associations had already subscribed to the WICHE guidelines as they then were, and several of the associations had adopted rules and regulations governing their own membership. Others were well along in adopting such standards before 1993, when it became clear that what was needed was a joint statement of expectations to which any institution seeking regional accreditation would have to conform. A task force was therefore formed, composed of staff representatives of the six regional associations, with an observer from CHEA, their umbrella organization. Before adopting encompassing standards, its first task was to review all existing relevant documents from both the regional accreditors and other organizations. Looking for any standards that might make the inclusion of distance education offerings within regional accreditation either impossible or difficult, it discovered that the mission-driven, qualitative nature of the great majority of existing standards already allowed for the accreditation of such disparate entities as Harvard University and Quinsigamond Community College. Reviewing documents from outside organizations, the task force further concluded that, although suitable as a starting point for their work, the existing guidelines were too broad for the regionals' purpose of limiting their accreditation to those entities offering academic degrees, as they applied equally to degree-granting and non-degree-granting programs. The task force eventually suggested a set of expanded criteria, which, after consideration by the members of each association, were accepted with minor linguistic changes by all eight commissions for whom they were relevant (six commissions on higher education plus two devoted to postsecondary technical and vocational offerings). In adopting such policies, they were, of course, following the long tradition of adapting to changing social needs that had allowed them over time to include within their membership community colleges, teachers colleges, and single-purpose graduate programs, all of which had originally been excluded from the associations. The new policies were quickly distributed to and accepted by members (see, e.g., NEASC's Policy on the Accreditation of Academic Degrees and Certificate Programs Offered Through Distance Education at http://www.neasc.org/cihe/disted2.htm, adopted March 6, 1998).

INSTITUTIONAL CONCERNS

Prior to the meeting of their joint committee, the accrediting bodies had surveyed their members to discover what specific problems they were concerned with (New England Association of Schools and Colleges [NEASC], 1994). Most frequently mentioned were the following:

First and foremost was the need to be assured of the integrity of the degree, by which respondents meant not only that the person receiving the degree was the one who had done the work toward it, but that the requirements for online credit were similar to those for on-site instruction, as both would grant similar credentials;

Next, institutions were concerned about cost and accessibility for both students and institutions;

Third, there was a concern about student-student and student-faculty interaction absent from face-to-face involvement and shared classrooms;

Fourth, many administrators were concerned about faculty development, so great a part of higher education in the United States, in programs set up with many of the faculty both part-time and distant from any but a virtual campus;

Fifth, faculty wanted to know how posting their syllabi and notes on the Internet might impact their compensation, workloads, and intellectual property rights;

Sixth, because on-site higher education is much more than cognitive information shared in a classroom, all respondents were concerned about students having access to academic support services and adequate information resources.

Finally, it was generally agreed that both student and faculty members would need specialized guidance and training in order to gain and benefit from appropriate technological expertise.

ADAPTING REGIONAL STANDARDS TO INCORPORATE DISTANCE EDUCATION

With theses concerns in mind, the task force decided that the regional accrediting bodies could expand their existing standards to include distance education within institutional accreditation for two main reasons. First, the existing standards within the various regional accrediting associations emphasized educational outcomes and required that institutions command the resources (both human and other) for their effective achievement. Indeed, the assessment of educational outcomes, which had long been established as an indicator of institutional quality, was receiving increased attention as higher education, more expensive than ever, found itself increasingly consumer- and market-driven. In adjusting to that reality, the regional associations had already adopted standards of appropriate flexibility to evaluate entities where they could focus more on the quality of those who designed and delivered the courses than on their employment status (full-time, part-time, or adjunct).

Nevertheless, examining the standards already applied to site-based institutions, the accreditors recognized that they would have to make some adaptations to accommodate the particular necessities of distance education. For example, although accrediting standards require institutions to admit those students who can benefit from the programs offered, they do allow an institution to have an open admission policy if it supplies appropriate remediation for those who need help in order to work at the collegiate level. For distance education, this rule had to be extended to include the technological expertise needed by the graduate in order to complete a program. The requirements for library and information resource personnel likewise had to be expanded to mandate student access to a help desk.

In addition to specific issues to be dealt with at individual institutions, there were also questions about the meaning of regional boundaries when dealing with educational entities in which the instructor might be in one state while the learners in her "class" were in different states or even countries.

Although the individual accrediting associations ascribed to the general principles contained in the joint guidelines, the actual wording adopted by each reflected the language and approach characteristic of the individual association. The issue of institutions without a regional base became prominent with the establishment and eventual accreditation in 2000 of Western Governors University, which catered to students in three (later expanded to five) of the six accrediting regions. In response to its founding, a separate commission, the Interregional Accrediting Commission, was set up, and the rules promulgated for that one institution are now in place as precedents for any others which transcend regional boundaries.

THE CURRENT REGULATIONS

As the number and complexity of distance education programs continued to increase, the regional commissions realized that they had to rewrite their policy yet again to develop one document to which all could ascribe without modification. In August, 2000, they published a draft of the "Statement of Regional Accrediting Commissions on the Evaluation of Electronically Offered Degrees and Certificate Programs." Renamed "The Statement of Commitment by the Regional Accrediting Commissions for the Evaluation of Electronically Offered Degree and Certificate Programs," this document currently places technologically mediated instruction squarely within the context of regional accreditation and was prepared under a contract by CRAC, the Council of Regional Accrediting Commissions group within CHEA) by WICHE. It marks the first time the regional commissions have jointly issued a set of rules rather than developing guidelines to be restated in terms suitable for each region. Recognizing that they have to strike a balance between accountability and imaginative experimentation, the accrediting associations saw this as very much a work in progress, a set of regulations that might need to be rethought and further developed as new methodologies evolve that allow for delivery of education of the same quality as in traditional in site-based education.

They first note that the regional commissions use mission-driven standards to define institutional quality. "The college or university that has purposes appropriate to higher education, the resources necessary to achieve those purposes, demonstrates that it is achieving them and has the ability to continue to do so, is one worthy of the distinction of being regionally accredited. This implicitly flexible paradigm is particularly appropriate for the assessment of new forms of distance education as well as technologically-spawned innovations in educational practice on campuses" (see, for example, http://www.neasc.org/cihe/commitment_electronically_offered_degree.htm).

As a preamble, the statement sets forth several values and principles that will guide this and future documents:

1. Education is best experienced within a community of learning where competent professionals are actively and cooperatively involved with creating, providing, and improving the instructional program.

2. Learning is dynamic and interactive, regardless of the setting in which it occurs.
3. Instructional programs leading to degrees having integrity are organized around substantive and coherent curricula that define expected learning outcomes.
4. Institutions accept the obligation to address student needs related to, and to provide the resources necessary for, their academic success.
5. Institutions are responsible for the education provided in their name.
6. Institutions undertake the assessment and improvement of their quality, giving particular emphasis to student learning.
7. Institutions voluntarily subject themselves to peer review.

Although the regional commissions limit their scope to degree-granting institutions, they are aware that "their field of view increasingly includes educational entities and configurations which test conventional ideas as to what constitutes and institution of higher learning." They understand that the new technologies allow for numerous forms of collaboration between accredited institutions and entities outside the academy, but they consider it essential "that accountability be clearly fixed within the accredited entity and that reasonable guarantees are provided to assure the continued availability of necessary resources outside the institution's control." In addition, noting that distance education may extend the scope of their member institutions beyond regional and national boundaries, they pledge to ensure the quality of such offerings through the application of an evaluative framework utilizing peer review common to all the regions:

1. The first-time development of distance education programming leading to a degree designated for students off-campus will be subject to careful prior review.
2. Institutional effectiveness in providing education at a distance will be an explicitly and rigorously appraised as a part of the regular evaluation of colleges and universities such as the comprehensive visit and the interim report.
3. An essential element in all evaluative processes will be institutional self-evaluation for the purpose of enhancing quality.
4. In cases where deficiencies are identified and/or concerns regarding integrity, remediation will be expected and aggressively monitored.
5. Appropriate action will be taken in keeping with individual commission policy and procedure in those cases where an institution is found to be demonstrably incapable of effectively offering distance education programming.

This general statement of joint principles is, in the case of each of the accrediting associations, supplemented by a statement of "Best Practices for Electronically Offered Degree and Certificate Programs" (see, for example, http://www.neasc.org/cihe/best_practices_electronically_offered_degree.htm). These "Best Practices" are divided into five separate components, each of which addresses a particular area of institutional activity relevant to distance education. Each component begins with a general statement followed by individual numbered paragraphs addressing specific matters describing those elements essential to quality distance education programming. These, in turn, are followed by protocols in the form of questions designed to assist in determining the existence of those elements when reviewing either internally or externally distance education activities.

The five areas and a sample of their related protocols and questions, all of which can be found on the Internet (see http://www.neasc.org/cihe/commission_policies.htm), follow:

1. Institutional Context and Commitment: Electronically offered programs both support and extend the roles of educational institutions. Increasingly they are integral to academic organization, with growing implications for institutional infrastructure.

1a. In its content, purposes, organization, and enrollment history if applicable, the program is consistent with the institution's role and mission.
   - What is the evidence that the program is consistent with the role and mission of the institution including its goals with regard to student access?
   - Is the institution fulfilling its stated role as it offers the program to students at a distance, or is the role being changed?

1e. The internal organizational structure which enables the development, coordination, support, and oversight of electronically offered programs will vary from institution to institution. Ordinarily, however, this will include capability to:
   - facilitate the associated instructional and technical support relationships
   - provide (or draw upon) the required information technologies and related support services
   - develop and implement a marketing plan that takes into account the target student population, the technologies available, and the factors required to meet institutional goals
   - provide training and support to participating instructors and students
   - assure compliance with copyright law
   - contract for products and outsourced services
   - assess and assign priorities to potential future projects
   - assure that electronically offered programs and courses meet institution-wide standards, both to provide consistent quality and to provide a coherent framework for students who may enroll in both electronically offered and traditional on-campus courses
   - maintain appropriate academic oversight
   - maintain consistency with the institution's academic planning and oversight functions, to assure congruence with the institution's mission and allocation of required resources
   - assure the integrity of student work and faculty instruction

Organizational structure varies greatly, but it is fundamental to the success of an institution's programs. The previous points can be evaluated by variations of the following procedure and inquiries:

- Is there a clear, well-understood process by which an electronically offered program evolves from conception to administrative authorization to implementation? How is the need for the program determined? How is it assigned a priority among the other potential programs? Has the development of the program incorporated appropriate internal consultation and integration with existing planning efforts?
- Track the history of a representative project from idea through implementation, noting the links among the participants including those responsible for curriculum, those responsible for deciding to offer the program electronically, those responsible for program/ course design, those responsible for the technologies applied, those responsible for faculty

and student support, those responsible for marketing, those responsible for legal issues, those responsible for budgeting, those responsible for administrative and student services, and those responsible for program evaluation. Does this review reveal a coherent set of relationships?

- In the institution's organizational documentation, is there a clear and integral relationship between those responsible for electronically offered programs and the mainstream academic structure?
- How is the organizational structure reflected in the institution's overall budget?
- How are the integrity, reliability, and security of outsourced services assured?
- Are training and technical support programs considered adequate by those for whom they are intended?
- What are the policies and procedures concerning compliance with copyright law?
- How does program evaluation relate to this organizational and decision-making structure?

2. Curriculum and Instruction. Methods change, but standards of quality endure. The important issues are not technical but curriculum-driven and pedagogical. Decisions about such matters are made by qualified professionals and focus on learning outcomes for an increasingly diverse student population

2a. As with all curriculum development and review, the institution assures that each program of study results in collegiate level learning outcomes appropriate to the rigor and breadth of the degree or certificate awarded by the institution, that the electronically offered degree or certificate program is coherent and complete, and that such programs leading to undergraduate degrees include general education requirements.
   - What process resulted in the decision to offer the program?
   - By what process was the program developed? Were academically qualified persons responsible for curricular decisions?
   - How were "learning outcomes appropriate to the rigor and breadth of the degree or certificate awarded" established? Does the program design involve the demonstration of such skills as analysis, comprehension, communication, and effective research?
   - Is the program "coherent and complete?"
   - Are related instructional materials appropriate and readily accessible to students?

2b. Academically qualified persons participate fully in the decisions concerning program curricula and program oversight. It is recognized that traditional faculty roles may be unbundled and/or supplemented as electronically offered programs are developed and presented, but the substance of the program, including its presentation, management, and assessment are the responsibility of people with appropriate academic qualifications.
   - What were the academic qualifications of those responsible for curricular decisions, assessment, and program oversight?
   - What are the academic qualifications of those presenting and managing the program?
   - If the principal instructor is assisted by tutors or student mentors, what are their qualifications?
   - Are these qualifications considered appropriate to the responsibilities of these persons?

2c. In designing an electronically offered degree or certificate program, the institution provides a coherent plan for the student to access all courses necessary to complete the program, or clearly notifies students of requirements not included in the electronic offering. Hybrid programs or courses, mixing electronic and on-campus elements, are designed to assure that all students have access to appropriate services. (See also 2d below, concerning program elements from consortia or contract services.)

- How are students notified of program requirements?
- If the institution relies on other providers to offer program-related courses, what is the process by which students learn of these courses?
- Is the total program realistically available to students for whom it is intended? For example, is the chosen technology likely to be accessible by the target student population? Can target students meet the parameters of program scheduling?

2d. Although important elements of a program may be supplied by consortial partners or outsourced to other organizations, including contractors who may not be accredited, the responsibility for performance remains with the institution awarding the degree or certificate. It is the institution in which the student is enrolled, not its suppliers or partners, that has a contract with the student. Therefore, the criteria for selecting consortial partners and contractors, and the means to monitor and evaluate their work, are important aspects of the program plan. In considering consortial agreements, attention is given to issues such as assuring that enhancing service to students is a primary consideration and that incentives do not compromise the integrity of the institution or of the educational program. Consideration is also given to the effect of administrative arrangements and cost-sharing on an institution's decision-making regarding curriculum.

Current examples of consortial and contractual relationships include:

- Faculty qualifications and support.
- Course material:
  - Courses or course elements acquired or licensed from other institutions.
  - Courses or course elements provided by partner institutions in a consortium.
  - Curricular elements from recognized industry sources, e.g., Microsoft or Novell certification programs.
  - Commercially produced course materials ranging from textbooks to packaged courses or course elements.
- Course management and delivery:
  - WebCT, Blackboard, College, etc.
- Library-related services:
  - Remote access to library services, resources, and policies.
  - Provision of library resources and services, e.g., online reference services, document delivery, print resources, etc.
- Bookstore services.
- Services providing information to students concerning the institution and its programs and courses.
- Technical services:
  - Server capacity.
  - Technical support services, including help desk services for students and faculty.

- Administrative services:
  - Registration, student records, etc.
- Services related to advising, counseling, or tutoring.
- Online payment arrangements.
- Student privacy considerations.

3. Faculty Support. As indicated above, faculty roles are becoming increasingly diverse and reorganized. For example, the same person may not perform both the tasks of course development and direct instruction to students. Regardless of who performs which of these tasks, important issues are involved.

3a. In the development of an electronically offered program, the institution and its participating faculty have considered issues of workload, compensation, ownership of intellectual property resulting from the program, and the implications of program participation for the faculty member's professional evaluation processes. This mutual understanding is based on policies and agreements adopted by the parties.

- Have decisions regarding these matters been made in accordance with institutional or system processes customarily used to address comparable issues?

3b. The institution provides an ongoing program of appropriate technical, design, and production support for participating faculty members.

4. Student Support. Colleges and universities have learned that the twenty-first century student is different, both demographically and geographically, from students of previous generations. These differences affect everything from admissions policy to library services. Reaching these students, and serving them appropriately, are major challenges to today's institutions.

4b. Prior to admitting a student to the program, the institution:

1. Ascertains by a review of pertinent records and/or personal review that the student is qualified by prior education or equivalent experience to be admitted to that program, including in the case of international students, English language skills.
2. Informs the prospective student concerning required access to technologies used in the program.
3. Informs the prospective student concerning technical competence required of students in the program.
4. Informs the prospective student concerning estimated or average program costs (including costs of information access) and associated payment and refund policies.
5. Informs the prospective student concerning curriculum design and the time frame in which courses are offered, and assists the student in understanding the nature of the learning objectives.
6. Informs the prospective student of library and other learning services available to support learning and the skills necessary to access them.
7. Informs the prospective student concerning the full array of other support services available from the institution.
8. Informs the prospective student about arrangements for interaction with the faculty and fellow students.
9. Assists the prospective student in understanding independent learning expectations as well as the nature and potential challenges of learning in the program's technology-based environment.

    10.   Informs the prospective student about the estimated time for program completion.

    To evaluate this important component of admission and retention, it is appropriate to pursue the following:

- How do potential students learn about the electronically offered program? Is the information provided sufficient, fair, and accurate?
- How are students informed about technology requirements and required technical competence?
- How are students informed about costs and administrative arrangements?
- What information and/or advice do students receive about the nature of learning and the personal discipline required in an anytime/anywhere environment?
- What criteria are used to determine the student's eligibility for admission to the program?
- What steps are taken to retain students in the program?
- What is the history of student retention in this program?

5.   Evaluation and Assessment. Both the assessment of student achievement and evaluation of the overall program take on added importance as new techniques evolve. For example, in asynchronous programs the element of seat time is essentially removed from the equation. For these reasons, the institution conducts sustained, evidence-based and participatory inquiry as to whether distance learning programs are achieving objectives. The results of such inquiry are used to guide curriculum design and delivery, pedagogy, and educational processes, and may affect future policy and budgets perhaps have implications for the institution's roles and mission

5f.   Institutional evaluation of electronically offered programs takes place in the context of the regular evaluation of all academic programs.

- What are the administrative and procedural links between the evaluation of electronically offered programs and the ongoing evaluation of all academic programs?
- How are the respective characteristics of campus-based and electronically offered programs taken into account?

    In implementing the guidelines and regulations indicated in these documents, the regional accrediting associations have become ever more specific in their expectations of university responses to their expectations. At the same time, an increasing number of institutions have implemented distance education programs. As a result, the associations, such as NEASC, make available on their Web site the forms and guidelines for specifically reporting the activities their members are undertaking in this area. Yet, even as quality assurance mechanisms developed for distance education become ever more specific and reliable, the number of "accreditation mills"— privately formed groups not recognized by either the Department of Education or the Council on Higher Education Accreditation—proliferate and are referenced by members seeking to convince the unsuspecting that distance education entities are not eligible for regional accreditation because it lacks a campus, full-time faculty, or a bricks-and-mortar library and set of classrooms. A good reference to what is acceptable in various states is found on the CHEA Web site (http://www.chea.org/degreemills/frmStates.htm). Because of the suspicions aroused by the existence of such non-recognized associations, certain foreign governments will not accept any distance education credits—a situation which may be alleviated as the stringency of both the requirements and practices of evaluation by the regional accrediting agencies from the United States becomes better known. Certainly, after several years of experience in evaluating distance education programs at both traditional and new entities, the regional associations feel confident that as new forms of distributed education arise, they will have both the expertise and adaptability to continue ensuring that American higher education, no matter how it is delivered, meets the same standards of quality that traditional site-based institutions have already achieved.

REFERENCES

American Council on Education. (2000). Higher education and national affairs. Retrieved from http://www
    .acenet.edu/
Bear, J. B., & Bear, M. P. (1998). *Bear's guide to earning degrees nontraditionally.* El Cerrito, CA: Ten
    Speed Press.
Distance Education and Training Council. (1998). *Accreditation handbook.* Washington, DC: Author.
New England Association of School and Colleges. (1994). *Survey on distance education activities.* Bedford,
    MA: Author.
Perley, J., & Tanguay, D. M. (1999, October 29). Accrediting on-line institutions diminishes higher educa-
    tion. *The Chronicle of Higher Education.* (See also ensuing colloquy retrieved October 29 issue from
    Chronicle on-line: http://chronicle.com/weekly/v46/i13/13b00501.htm)
Young, K. E., Chambers, C. M., & Kells, H. R. (1983). *Understanding accreditation.* San Francisco:
    Jossey-Bass.

33

Evaluating Distance Education Programs

Melody M. Thompson
The Pennsylvania State University

Modupe E. Irele
Key Learning Solutions

Evaluation is an important component of distance education activities. Monitoring the value and effectiveness of programs is necessary to (a) justify initial investment of resources, (b) ensure that goals are being met, (c) guide improvement of both processes and outcomes, and (d) provide a basis for decisions to continue, expand, or discontinue programs. Unfortunately, evaluation of distance education programming is too often poorly designed and/or underfunded; it is more of an afterthought than an integral part of planning and implementation. Responsible stewardship of ever-tightening resources as well as responsiveness to increased demands for accountability argue for well-planned and adequately supported evaluation activities.

I. WHY EVALUATE?

The global educational context is changing rapidly. Programs, institutions, and societies must make significant decisions as to how they wish to influence or shape these changes, and/or be shaped by them. Intentional, planned, and thoughtful responses, however, depend on the availability of sufficient actionable information. Evaluation activities are a vital source of such information.

Distance Education Past: Evaluation as the Basis for Acceptance

In the past, the impact of distance education programming on the institutional system as a whole was small (although the impact on individual lives was often great). The level of resources devoted to monitoring and evaluating distance education programming was correspondingly small; evaluation was of interest to the parent institution only as a means of ensuring that distance education programs did not detract from the reputation enjoyed by its traditional programming.

For this reason, decades of evaluation studies focused on demonstrating that distance education programs were "as good"—that is, that students learned as much in them—as resident instruction programs. The primary approach used was the media-comparison study, in which the learning outcomes of classroom-based students were compared to those of students receiving technologically mediated instruction. Although findings of comparable outcomes (Moore & Thompson, 1997) and "no significant difference" (Russell, 1999) were reported in hundreds of such studies, evaluators continued to face questions of credibility from entities that undervalued all forms of nontraditional education. Thus, until recently, the evaluation of distance education programs has been defensively focused on presenting data that would allow their continued existence, if only on the margins.

Distance Education Present: Evaluation of a Transformative Phenomenon

The situation has changed dramatically during the last decade. Thanks to the power and reach of the World Wide Web, distance education has been "discovered." Recast first as "online learning," and then as "e-learning," it has moved from the margins into the mainstream.

No longer tolerated as long as it conforms to and defers to the "real thing"—that is, resident instruction—and no longer an alternative primarily for nontraditional students, distance education is now being touted for its potential to transform traditional resident instruction as well. This new image of promise, however, is not without its skeptics. There are some in the academy who view "e-learning," or at least the unexamined acceptance of e-learning, as a threat to the quality of traditional educational programming. It is through evaluation that institutions can determine whether particular programs can, as some predict, contribute to a positive transformation of education, or will, as others fear, compromise traditional educational quality.

Judith Eaton, president of the Council for Higher Education Accreditation (CHEA), reinforced this point when she stated that distance education, "however unintentionally," challenges the "core academic values . . . central to the history and tradition of higher education" (Eaton, 2000, p. 1). While a challenge to tradition may have either negative or positive results, the extent of the current challenge underlines its potential impact: The most recent report from the U.S. Department of Education's National Center for Education Statistics (NCES, 2003) reported that in the 12-month 2000–2001 academic year, there were an estimated 2,876,000 enrollments in college-level, credit-granting distance education courses (with all forms of distance education counting in this number), and enrollments have soared since that report was published. A 2005 study sponsored by the Sloan Consortium reported that in 2004, approximately 2.35 million higher-education students took *online* distance education courses, up 18.2% over the previous year. This growth rate is over 10 times higher than the NCES projected for the general postsecondary population, and 74.8% of the over 1,000 schools surveyed reported that they expected their online enrollments to continue increasing (Allen & Seaman, 2005).

Given this increasing prominence and the potentially transformative effects of new forms of distance education on the existing educational enterprise, the need for rigorous evaluation and research studies has become imperative. As Bates (2000) pointed out, because of

> the rapid speed with which new technologies for teaching are infiltrating even the most cautious and conservative of universities, and the lack of experience in the use and management of such technologies, the case for researching and evaluating the applications of these new technologies is obvious. (p. 198)

However, even more important than doing evaluation is doing evaluation right—that is, asking the right questions and then using the answers appropriately. Ehrmann (1997b, p. 1) noted that it "takes just as much effort to answer a useless question as a useful one," but institutions cannot afford to be asking useless questions. Only thoughtful and focused examination of distance education programming, especially in its newest forms, will reveal whether, and under what conditions, the adoption of these innovations will be the fulfillment of the transformative promise or the threat to educational quality.

Although the current headlong rush to move this little-understood but potentially transformative educational phenomenon into the mainstream is resulting in increased, often impatient, demands for evaluation information, it is imperative that evaluation studies be rigorously planned and executed, rather than being merely an unconsidered adoption of past approaches to evaluating either traditional or distance programs. Only in this way can studies provide the information necessary to ensure that whatever transformation occurs is intentional rather than accidental, directed rather than haphazard.

II. WHAT IS EVALUATION?

The terms *evaluation, assessment*, and *research* are often used interchangeably, but each has a different meaning, function, and value in understanding the operations and outcomes of distance education programs. Both assessment and evaluation are focused on practical examination of programs to discover what works and what needs to be improved as the basis for effective management and planning decisions (Bates, 2000; Lockee, Burton, & Cross, 1999; Rovai, 2003). Research studies, on the other hand, are intended to develop a deep understanding of particular aspects of a phenomenon through rigorous examination of relevant variables. This present chapter focuses on evaluation rather than research.

Evaluation and Assessment

Stufflebeam (1999), in his treatment of educational program evaluation, defined evaluation as "a study designed and conducted to assist some audience to measure an object's merit and worth" (p. 3). In educational contexts, evaluation studies are implemented to examine and report on the strengths and weaknesses of programs, policies, personnel, processes, products/outcomes, and organizations to improve their effectiveness (American Evaluation Association, cited in Saba 2000, 1). Evaluation encompasses both expected and unexpected occurrences and involves making judgments about their merit and worth (Institute for Higher Education Policy, 1999; Rowntree, 1992; Stufflebeam, 1999; Thorpe, 1996). Thus, the focus of evaluation is always on the "value" of some aspect of programming to a group or groups of stakeholders: society, institutions, students, employers, and so forth.

Assessment, on the other hand, attempts to determine the objective level of some variable of interest: test scores, interaction levels, response time, and so forth (Joint Committee on Standards for Educational Evaluation, 1994). Assessments, with their focus on measuring "what is," are a subset of evaluation (Rowntree, 1992). They are valuable tools in the larger evaluation activity, which has as its focus comparison to some previously determined standard: "What should be." Assessment asks "How much?", while evaluation asks "Is it good enough?" and "If not, why not?"

Some activities conducted in the name of evaluation are lacking the focus on merit or value. Stufflebeam (1999) characterized those activities that are motivated by a desire to project a specific view of a program, regardless of its actual worth, as pseudo-evaluations. Practices such as using biased surveys or releasing only positive findings may advance particular agendas by seeming to support the claims of excellence necessary to secure sponsor support, but these practices are not evaluation. Not only do they mislead stakeholders, but they also make the information gathered useless in making planning decisions or program improvements.

Purposes of Evaluation

Evaluative studies are conducted to answer questions of interest to stakeholders, who "may include learners, instructors, staff, administrators, policy makers, boards, vendors, consultants, community groups, accrediting agencies, government organizations, businesses, and employers" (Rovai, 2003, p. 113). Thus, the focus of an evaluation will vary with the informational needs of each stakeholder or stakeholder group, although most evaluation activities have more than one purpose. Common purposes include (a) justifying the investment of resources, (b) examining issues of quality and effectiveness, (c) measuring progress toward program goals, (d) establishing a basis for improvement of both program processes and outcomes, and (e) providing a basis for strategic decision making.

Justification of investment.   The monetary and staff resources necessary to develop high quality distance learning programs—especially those designed and delivered with high levels of technical, instructional, and student-service support—are extensive. Although such programs may not in themselves be more expensive than traditional instruction—indeed, when "brick and mortar" costs (for buildings and grounds) and convenience benefits are factored in, distance learning programs may be comparably or less expensive (Bates, 2000; Thompson, 1994; Whalen & Wright, 1999)—they do in most cases represent new costs that ultimately must be justified.

Such is particularly the case when distance programs are "grafted" onto a traditional educational institution where the standard for both format and effectiveness is resident instruction and where competition for resources is almost always fierce. In this environment, evaluative measures that provide cost-benefit or return-on-investment information offer a basis for choosing between alternatives with different costs (Ehrmann, 2002), as well as for judging the program's productivity or value to the institution in economic terms (Stufflebeam, 1999).

Measuring progress toward program objectives.   Probably the most prevalent motivation for conducting evaluation activities is to gather information about the extent to which program objectives are being met. Demonstrating that objectives have been meet can be important in justifying program costs and establishing credibility for distance education within the larger institution or educational system, particularly when these goals are important to or reflect the mission of the larger system.

As M. G. Moore (1999) noted, within an educational system, the most important of these goals is learning outcomes; however, other goals such as maintaining cost-effectiveness or increasing educational access also are legitimate foci for monitoring and evaluation.

The value of objectives-focused evaluations is dependent on both the clarity of program objectives and the flexibility with which the evaluation is designed and implemented. According to Cyrs (2001), "without the specification of objectives, there are no criteria on which to base an evaluation" (p. 1). M. G. Moore (1999) took the argument even further, stating that "whether or not evaluators can show that the project was effective will ultimately depend on how well the objectives of the project have been stated" (p. 2).

Clearly stated objectives are a necessary, but not sufficient, criterion for effective evaluation, however. A too-narrow focus on stated objectives can "lead to terminal information that is of little use in improving a program" or for judging the program's merit or value; it also runs the risk of crediting objectives that in themselves have little merit or value (Stufflebeam, 1999, p. 12).

These limitations can be overcome by broadening the focus to include an assessment of the correspondence between program objectives and participants' assessed needs; a search for unanticipated side effects; and an examination of the program processes as well as its outcomes (Stufflebeam, 1999). To count as evaluation rather than merely monitoring or assessment, there must be an attempt to go beyond the question "Did the program do what it set out to do?" to "Did achieving the programs' objectives give value to the stakeholders?"

Measuring "quality" and/or "effectiveness."   Measuring "quality" and "effectiveness" is another commonly stated purpose. The term "quality" is generally used to refer to program characteristics and processes (technological infrastructure, student services, etc.), while "effectiveness" more usually refers to outcomes (learning outcomes, participant satisfaction, etc.). The appropriate overarching question for a distance education program is not "Is this a quality program?" or "Is this an effective program?", but rather "Does this program meet accepted and articulated standards of quality?" and "Is the program effective in particular ways in meeting specific goals of stakeholders?" For this reason, Rovai (2003) recommended program-specific criteria, as opposed to comparisons to uniform standards of quality.

Until recently, few standardized criteria for distance education quality or effectiveness existed. In the context of institutional demands for evidence of parity with traditional educational programs, the term "quality distance education program" generally referred to programs that replicated as closely as possible the institution-specific features, services, and assumed outcomes of traditional resident programs (Chambers, 1995; Ehrmann, 1997b; O'Shea, Bearman, & Downes, 1996). However, a better understanding of the potential for online education to offer not only the same benefits as traditional education, but totally new benefits as well, means that improvement can encompass both better outcomes and new outcomes (Ehrmann, 2002), all of which should be the target of evaluation studies.

The past decade, however, has seen the development of distance education program standards that are purportedly applicable across institutional contexts. Examples of such standards, intended to focus and rationalize distance education evaluation, will be discussed in section four.

Providing a basis for improvement.   Closely related to both tracking progress toward goals and measuring quality and/or effectiveness is the focus on improving programs. Both activities are built on the implied assumption that any gaps discovered by evaluation activities between program performance and desired goals or standards will trigger efforts toward improvement.

The component of action is inherent in the concept of evaluation and follows naturally from assessment or "monitoring" activities: "Evaluation . . . is the process of analyzing the feedback data gathered by monitoring, reviewing it, and making decisions" that will lead to improved materials, methods, processes, and outcomes (M. G. Moore, 1999, p. 1). *When* the improvement takes place is a function of the type and timing of evaluation.

Formative evaluation, conducted during the planning and development stage of a program, provides information necessary to make "up-front" improvements to products, programs, and activities before they are actually offered to students. Lockee, Moore, and Burton (2002) identified instructional design and interface design issues as the two primary categories of formative evaluation and suggest a six-stage process of formative review that involves course designers, content experts, instructors, and representatives of the target population.

Summative evaluation, on the other hand, "takes places at the end of a course or program. These data are used to redesign a course or program. This type of evaluation includes attitudes toward the course or program, as well as learning outcomes. In addition, summative evaluation would include administration of the program/course" (Cyrs, 2001, Section C, #2).

Formative and summative evaluation approaches can be combined effectively to provide the basis for program improvement in a number of areas.

Informing institutional strategic planning and decision making.   As noted in section one, distance education is no longer on the margins of higher education. Rather, it is converging with traditional education in ways that have the potential to be transformative for both. As Bers (1999) pointed out, however, to date "[strategic] planning for distance education is taking place as a separate process from more comprehensive or traditional planning" (p. 73).

The changing internal and external factors affecting higher education today suggest that successful and rewarding institutional "mainstreaming" of distance education will result not from its conformity to the dominant and established direction of the current mainstream, but rather from the new and the established entities together "dredging a new mainstream" (Miller, 1990, p. 211)—that is, a more flexible and powerful extension of the knowledge and teaching resources of educational institutions to meet the lifelong learning needs of individuals, regardless of time or place. Approaches such as Elloumi's (2004) value chain analysis can help institutions strategically negotiate and evaluate the changes precipitated and enabled by this mainstreaming.

Watkins and Kaufman (2003, p. 507) cited Barker's contention that "when a paradigm shifts, everyone (even those who have been extremely successful in the past) goes back to zero." In deciding how to most effectively incorporate the power and promise of distance education into long-term plans on either an institutional or societal level everyone may begin at zero, but those with the right kind of information—actionable data from evaluation and research—will have the tools to move intentionally and confidently into the future.

Evaluation studies that focus on issues of access, equity, learning effectiveness, and organizational impact can provide the basis for assessing the ability of distance education programs to forward the values and vision of the institution. When the information from these studies is combined with that gained from more long-term research studies that rigorously examine the effect of this innovation on all parts of the educational system—learners, faculty, institution, and society—distance education initiatives can be purposefully integrated into strategic plans to promote the intended goals of the institution.

III. THE EVALUATION PROCESS

Following we present an overview of selected literature on the process of evaluating distance education programs. We draw on both face-to-face education and distance education resources that provide a foundation for evaluation best practices.

Making Evaluation Choices

An evaluator is faced with a number of choices in planning and implementing an evaluation project. He or she must clarify the purpose of the evaluation in meeting stakeholders' information needs and what specifically will be evaluated; choose the most appropriate data collection methods and tools; and write an evaluation report that gets the right information into the right hands.

Clarify the purpose and focus of the evaluation.   To obtain reliable, valid evaluation information, evaluators must begin with a clear understanding of the purpose and focus of the evaluation. They must begin with questions such as "Who are the stakeholders?" "What do they need to know?" and "How will the data be used?" (Cyrs, 2001). Probably the most common mistakes made by evaluators are to try to answer too many questions with one evaluation activity, or to try to answer very general questions. Ehrmann (1997a) suggested that "the most difficult challenge in [thinking] about doing a study is the process of figuring out what to study" (p. 6). As part of the planning phase, the evaluator should gather the feedback from stakeholders necessary to clarify the purpose and focus of a particular evaluation activity based on program and institutional priorities.

Choosing evaluation data collection methods and tools.   Matching the purpose and focus to the appropriate approach or tools is the evaluator's second challenge. M. G. Moore and Kearsley (1996) identified a range of data-collection methods including participant observations, questionnaires, interviews, online monitoring of responses, and advance prototyping or pilot testing. Cyrs (2001) added to this list surveys, student personal diaries, learning assessment instruments (tests, essay questions, portfolios, etc.), and product assessment criteria.

Reeves and Hedberg (2003) offered a variety of evaluation tools keyed to the design, development, and implementation of interactive learning systems or products such as multimedia DVDs, Web-based training, electronic performance support systems, and e-learning solutions. These tools provide both novice and experienced evaluators with guidance in the planning, implementation, and reporting of evaluation activities. The following tools are available for downloading from http://evaluateitnow.com/Downloads/Downloads.htm:

Evaluation Plan	Evaluation Plan Checklist
Evaluation Matrix	Evaluation Status Report
Evaluation Sign-Off Form	Anecdotal Record Form
Expert Review Checklist	Focus Group Protocol
Interview Protocol	Questionnaire
Formative Review Log	Implementation Log
User Interface Rating Form	Web Site Evaluation Form
Evaluation Report Sample	Heuristic Evaluation Instrument
Evaluation Report Checklist	

Write an evaluation report.   Just as evaluators make choices about the process of evaluation, they also need to make decisions about the final product of the evaluation activity: the evaluation report. The Program Evaluation Standards (Joint Committee on Standards for Educational Evaluation, 1994) suggests criteria relating to several aspects of evaluation reporting:

- Report Clarity—Evaluation reports should clearly describe the program being evaluated, including context, purposes, procedures, and findings, so that essential information is provided and easily understood.

- Report Timeliness and Dissemination—Significant interim findings should be disseminated to allow timely use.

- Disclosure of Findings—The full set of evaluation findings, along with pertinent limitations, should be made accessible to the persons affected by the evaluation and those with expressed legal rights to receive the results.

- Impartial Reporting—Reporting procedures should fairly reflect the findings, avoiding distortion caused by personal feelings or biases.

The AEA "Guiding Principles for Evaluators" further notes that, although "evaluations often will negatively affect the interests of some stakeholders, evaluators should . . . communicate [their] results in a way that clearly respects stakeholders' dignity and self-worth" (American Evaluation Association, 1995, p. 7).

Reeves and Hedberg (2003) suggested that the long reports written by many evaluators are seldom read. To increase the likelihood that an evaluation report will ultimately have an impact on institutional decision-making, they suggested formatting the report in easy-to-consume "chunks" of information in four sections: (a) an attention-getting headline, (b) a description of the major issues related to the headline, (c) a presentation of data related to the issues, and (d) a bottom-line recommendation or summary of the findings.

Distance Education Evaluation Models

Over the years, a number of experienced distance educators have developed evaluation approaches with an exclusive focus on distance education contexts. The work done by Duning, Van Kekerix, and Zaborowski (1993); Ehrmann (1997b, 1999, 2001); Bates (2000); Lockee et al. (2002); and Rovai (2003) in this area is representative.

Duning et al. (1993) approached the evaluation of distance education from the perspective of "assessing and maintaining quality" (p. 187). They began their discussion with a myth and its corresponding reality:

> *Myth:* Quality in telecommunications-based education is a matter of combining traditional instructional standards with assessments of technical accessibility, reliability, and interactivity.
>
> *Reality:* The potential reach and instructional impact of educational telecommunications systems require measures of quality that speak to values underlying new relationships with the learner. (p. 187)

Thus, these authors neatly integrate the concepts of needing new and well-articulated standards in distance education with the concept of value (and values) inherent in any evaluation activity.

Duning et al. (1993) suggested that distance learning systems can and should be evaluated at three levels: (a) the functional, (b) the managerial, and (c) the instructional or ethical. They identify the functional level with the technical-design activities involving equipment requirements and specifications, as well as the technical support staff. The managerial level focuses on the extent of success in fostering and managing necessary relationships within and outside the organizational structure of the program. These relationships may be with other organizational units, or with faculty, learners, or others crucial to the implementation of the program. Finally, the ethical level is focused on program outcomes. The ethical dimension of this level is reflected in the choices that are made in deciding what to measure and in what these decisions illustrate about the values of the institution; as the authors put it, "We become what we measure" (p. 197).

Ehrmann (1997, 1997b, 1999, 2001) has contributed extensively to the literature on distance education evaluation. As the director of the Flashlight Project, a program of the American Association of Higher Education's Teaching, Learning, and Technology (TLT) Group, he has spearheaded investigation of evaluation issues from a variety of perspectives and has led in developing a comprehensive "Tool Kit" to guide evaluators of distance education programs.

Ehrmann (1999) built his evaluation approach around the idea that distance education has and enables general goals that can be isolated and closely studied:

- enabling important new content to be taught
- changing who can learn

- improving teaching and learning activities
- lowering or controlling the costs of teaching and learning activities

Using the metaphor of a flashlight, which illumines a small area brightly, he suggested that evaluators begin with their general, usually "almost incoherent," question of interest or importance in one of these areas and then transform it from formless "blob" to focused evaluative "triad." Ehrmann used the term "triad" to refer to a focused question or set of questions crafted to examine (a) a particular technology or method (e-mail, paced instruction, etc.) in relation to (b) a particular practice enabled by that technology or method and (c) a desired program outcome.

The next step in the process is to ask questions in five related areas: (a) about the technology per se; (b) about the use of the technology for the activity; (c) about the activity per se; (d) about whether and how the activity is contributing to the desired outcome; and (e) about the outcome per se.

The Flashlight Project has developed a number of services and tools to help evaluators implement their own focused evaluation studies. An overview of Flashlight resources is available at http://www.tltgroup.org/resources/index.html.

Bates (2000) began with the assumption that past approaches to and questions about distance education evaluation are no longer relevant to the current context. From his perspective, a continued focus on the relative effectiveness of distance delivery compared to face-to-face instruction is "frankly a waste of time" (p. 198). Like Duning et al. (1993) and Ehrmann (1997b), he challenged evaluators to focus not on similarities to traditional education, but rather on differences, particularly on different or new learning outcomes enabled by technology-mediated distance education.

Bates' (2000) ACTIONS model focuses attention on "a wider range of factors than the ability of technology to replicate classroom teaching" (p. 200). The acronym ACTIONS represents seven factors to be considered in evaluating the effectiveness of different instructional technologies:

1. **A**ccess and flexibility
2. **C**osts
3. **T**eaching and learning
4. **I**nteractivity and user friendliness
5. **O**rganizational issues
6. **N**ovelty
7. **S**peed

For each of these factors Bates suggests appropriate evaluation and research questions.

Lockee et al. (2002) offered an "incremental" model based on the stages of program development and delivery and data collection methods appropriate for each stage. Within two broad categories, formative evaluation and summative evaluation, they suggest specific strategies for ensuring the quality of distance programs. Formative evaluation proceeds in six stages: (a) design review, (b) expert review, (c) one-on-one review, (d) small-group reviews, (e) field trials, and (f) ongoing reviews. Together the activities in these stages address issues of quality and effectiveness *before* the release of courses in a program. Summative evaluation activities gather information *after* a course or program has been completed. Lockee et al. (2002) identified the "definitive steps" (p. 23) of a summative evaluation:

1. Delineate the general areas of concern and develop questions focused on those areas.
2. Choose data-gathering techniques.

3. Implement the data-gathering process.
4. Analyze data.

These authors identified as the five common areas of concern (a) program inputs, (b) performance outcomes, (c) attitude outcomes, (d) programmatic outcomes, and (e) implementation concerns. Their "sample evaluation scenario" provides readers with an example of how these proposed strategies can be effectively implemented.

Rovai (2003) suggested an evaluation approach based in a systems model as "a departure from, and refinement of, the view of categorizing evaluations as formative or summative" (p. 113). Including as it does a focus on internal and external factors that affect a program's success, such an approach provides information useful for strategic decision making. It also builds in opportunities for feedback from multiple stakeholder groups, which is essential for program improvement. Within this model, evaluations are categorized by type and strategic orientation. Types include input evaluation, process evaluation, output evaluation, and impact evaluation. Strategic orientations include objectives-oriented, management oriented, consumer-oriented, expertise-oriented, adversary-oriented, and participant oriented. Rovai offered a number of potential evaluation questions synthesized from literature on common distance education program challenges.

Focusing on costs.   The models above provide the basis for evaluating the multifaceted activity that we call distance education. Some authors, however, have focused more narrowly on one specific element of distance education—cost—and have proposed models specifically for evaluating the costs related to distance education.

The cost structures of distance education are more complex than those of face-to-face instruction because they derive from a wider range and combination of factors. Beyond simple analyses of monetary cost, other considerations such as learning outcomes and their expected value for learner, employer, and other stakeholders need to be taken into account (M. G. Moore & Thompson, 1997; Rowntree, 1992). Because of this complexity, many distance education evaluators have adopted a cost-benefit approach when evaluating the costs of distance education programs.

Distance education costs are driven by fixed and variable costs, the technologies used, the production and delivery systems employed, the number of students served, and the length of time the teaching materials can be used (Bates, 1995). Benefits may be categorized into three groups: (a) those that are performance driven (e.g., learning outcomes), (b) those that are value driven (e.g., access, flexibility, or ease of use), and (c) those that are societal/value-added benefits (e.g., decreased unemployment and potential for new markets; Bates, 1999; Chute, Thompson, & Hancock, 1999).

A clear understanding of costs relative to benefits requires understanding of the relative importance of each cost variable on decision making. Ehrmann (2002) noted that cost and benefits are generally evaluated separately, primarily because of the difficulty in evaluating benefits. The unfortunate result is that "the cheaper program option will automatically be considered better" (p. 7).

Evaluators attempting to tie costs and benefits closely together will ask questions such as "Will the cost of achieving superior learning gains negatively impact students' access?" Answers to such questions are likely to reveal wide variability in the strategies used by organizations to achieve their objectives. For example, an organization with the objective of collaborative learning in a live environment may integrate technologies that allow for socializing, such as interactive satellite, rather than limit itself to less-expensive asynchronous technologies or media, such as e-mail.

Inglis (1999) questioned the emphasis on the cost-benefit approach in a distance education environment that is now so heavily influenced by the World Wide Web, with its associated high development costs. With Rumble (1997), he argued that an activity-based costing approach, in which costs of discrete educational activities are evaluated separately, allows a focus on those variables that have the greatest impact on costs.

The *Flashlight™ Cost Analysis Handbook*, developed by the TLT Group of the American Association of Higher Education (AAHE), uses activity-based costing to analyze how educational uses of technology consume a variety of resources, including time, money, and space. The intent of the model is to provide a basis on which institutions can improve how current activities use resources, forecast resource needs of proposed new activities, or report total costs (TLT Group, 2007, ¶ 1).

The Technology Costing Methodology (TCM) Project, conducted jointly by the Western Interstate Commission for Higher Education and the National Center for Higher Education Management Systems (NCHEMS), offers a tool for analyzing the costs of instruction that makes significant use of technology and comparing costs for different instructional approaches. Although not focused exclusively on distance education programs, the project provides a useful approach to cost (but not cost-benefit) analysis. The Project's BRIDGE model supports simulation and analysis of different institutional scenarios representing different mixes of instructional design and delivery strategies by adjusting factors such as "initial development costs, the marginal costs of offering a course, the technologies used, the number of students served, the number of partners developing the course(s), and other factors" to come up with a projected "break-even point" between technology-mediated and face-to-face instruction (WCET, 2007; BRIDGE Model History ¶ 1).

V. CURRENT AND FUTURE TRENDS IN DISTANCE EDUCATION EVALUATION

Development of Standards for Distance Education

> "How can a teaching/learning process that deviates so markedly from what has been practiced for hundreds of years embody quality education?"
>
> —*Quality on the Line: Benchmarks for Success in Internet-Based Distance Education*
> (Institute for Higher Education Policy, 1999, p. 7)

Trying to convincingly answer the question above has been the goal of distance education evaluators for decades. The attempt has also been the source of considerable frustration. Conducting meaningful evaluations in the absence of appropriate and clearly articulated standards for distance education programs and processes is an understandably daunting task. This situation has been exacerbated by the fact that distance education has generally been compared and asked to "measure up" to resident instruction, itself an activity "too easily satisfied with surrogate measures of its performance" (Pew Higher Education Research Report, cited in Duning et al., 1993, p. 188).

Quality guidelines, standards, and best practices.   Over the past decade, a number of organizations have worked to meet this need by developing standards for distance education practice to guide the development, delivery, and evaluation of distance education programs and processes in a rapidly changing educational environment. Examples include

- *Distance Learning Evaluation Guide* (American Council on Education, 1996)
- *An Emerging Set of Guiding Principles and Practices for the Design and Development of Distance Education* (The Pennsylvania State University, 1998)

- *ADEC Guiding Principles for Distance Teaching and Learning* (American Distance Education Consortium, 2000)
- *Elements of Quality: The Sloan-C™ Framework* (J. Moore, 2002)
- *Principles of Good Practice for Electronically Offered Academic Degree and Certificate Programs* (Western Cooperative for Educational Telecommunications, 1999)

These guidelines are generally quite consistent in their focus on issues related to course design; learning outcomes; technology; learner and faculty support; institutional commitment; and assessment and evaluation; however, the question remains as to the ultimate impact such documents will have on distance education practice and evaluation.

Putting standards into practice.   Encouraging evidence of the future impact of these emerging standards on distance education evaluation is reflected in the fact that one set of guidelines, *Principles of Good Practice in Electronically Offered Academic Degree and Certificate Programs* (Western Cooperative for Educational Telecommunications, 1999), has been refined for incorporation into the evaluation guide used by all eight regional accrediting agencies for higher education institutions. The resulting document, *Best Practices for Electronically Offered Degree and Certificate Programs* (Regional Accrediting Commissions, 2001a), is being used as the basis for "a consistent approach to the evaluation of distance education informed through collaboration with others" (Regional Accrediting Commissions, 2001b, p. 1).

Perhaps of even greater importance in terms of both current practice and future impact is the statement made within the guide that reflects a new and significant awareness of the changing place of distance education in American higher education:

> Electronically offered programs both support and extend the roles of educational institutions. Increasingly they are integral to academic organizations, with growing implications for institutional infrastructure. (Regional Accrediting Commissions, 2001a, p. 3)

This recognition, and its articulation in a document that will guide distance education program evaluation throughout American higher education, will perforce have a profound impact on distance education practice and evaluation in the years to come. This impact will be intensified through the interest shown by the U.S. Department of Education (2006) in working with accrediting agencies and institutions to develop means for the "consistent and thorough assessment of distance education programs, including developing evaluative components for holding schools accountable for such outcomes" (p. 1). One outcome of this interest is a recent report from the Department's Office of Secondary Education that identifies indicators of quality in distance education programs ("good practices") and indicators of potential problems ("red flags") in relation to institutional mission, curriculum and instruction, faculty support, student and academic services, strategic planning, and evaluation and assessment (U.S. Department of Education, 2006).

Articulation and implementation of quality standards in an important contribution to improving the quality of evaluation activities focused on distance education programs. However, as Frydenberg (2002) noted, the quality context in the United States differs greatly from that in other countries, since "all 50 states have chosen to allow tertiary education to be largely self-governing and self-policing, similar to those organizational models used by the medieval guilds" (p. 1). As a result, only some of the groups with a stake in program quality are involved in the development of standards used for evaluating programs. She identifies three main stakeholder groups that influence the quality of higher education programs in general, and distance education programs in particular: (a) faculty associations, (b) regional accrediting agencies, and (c) university faculty and administrators. Although students are routinely surveyed as to their satisfaction with courses and programs, the absence of the student or consumer perspective in the development of quality standards used as the basis for evaluation limits institutions' ability to conduct truly comprehensive evaluations. Research into end-user perceptions of standards and the integration of these with more traditional, institutionally focused concerns is necessary to provide an assurance of quality to all stakeholder groups (Frydenberg, 2002).

Research on Evaluation and Quality

Given the relatively short history of distance education evaluation and the only-recent development of standards on which such evaluation can be based, it is not surprising that research on the evaluation function itself is comparatively scarce. Additionally, to date, most researchers who have focused on evaluation have done so at the course rather than program level. Calls for program-level evaluation research, however, are becoming more prominent, which is promising development. For now, we report on several research studies with a focus on quality and its evaluation.

Recent studies.   The research report *Quality on the Line* (Institute for Higher Education Policy, 2000) begins with the published benchmarks or quality indicators developed by a variety of organizations involved in distance education and asks, among other questions, "Are the benchmarks viewed as essential to [high] quality on-line education by faculty, students, and administrators?" and "To what extent are the benchmarks being implemented in educational institutions?"

The study examined these questions with a case-study approach involving six institutions. Benchmarks were grouped into seven categories:

1. Institutional support
2. Course development
3. Teaching/learning process
4. Course structure
5. Student support
6. Faculty support
7. Evaluation and assessment

The subsequent report notes that "quality benchmarks were considered with great care and embraced by every institution that participated" (Institute for Higher Education Policy, 2000, p. 13). Of the 45 benchmarks originally identified from the literature, 13 were omitted from the subsequent list of recommended benchmarks because of the low importance ratings given them by the study respondents. The study also identified several benchmarks that generally were rated as very important, but scored relatively low in terms of actual implementation. These include

- A documented institutional technology plan
- Faculty incentives and institutional rewards
- Specific time expectations for students and faculty
- Technical assistance and training for students
- Technical assistance and training for faculty
- Evaluation and assessment

The findings of *Quality on the Line* indicate that distance educators and higher education institutions are taking guidelines and standards for high-quality distance education seriously, and are in most cases incorporating them into their distance education programs. The few disparities between reported importance and level of implementation are themselves useful in identifying areas for future examination and improvement.

Frydenberg (2002) analyzed published standards of quality in the U.S. higher education context and organized them into a nine-cell matrix that highlights areas of concern and institutional focus:

1. Institutional commitment
2. Technology
3. Student services
4. Instructional design and course development
5. Instruction and instructors
6. Delivery
7. Finances
8. Regulatory and legal compliance
9. Evaluation

On the basis of her analysis, Frydenberg identified current issues in each domain and suggested relevant research to answer outstanding questions related to program quality and evaluation.

Mariasingam (2005) conducted a Delphi study on quality criteria as a basis for developing a comprehensive framework for assessing the quality of online degree programs. Thirty-five international experts participated in a two-stage process to answer questions that included the following:

1. What are the relevant criteria for assessing the quality of online degree programs?
2. Of the relevant criteria in (1), which ones form a core set that should be used by all institutions?
3. What is the current extent of institutions' use of the criteria?

The study resulted in a framework of 67 criteria—24 of which were identified as core—in the categories of (a) institutional requirements, (b) learner requirements, (c) faculty requirements, (d) employer requirements, (e) society requirements, and (f) government requirements. What sets this framework apart from earlier standards and guidelines is the incorporation of threshold, modal, and best benchmark anchors for each criterion.

New directions for research on quality and evaluation.   A number of researchers have pointed out that the affordances of today's powerful information and communications technologies argue for research that goes beyond questions appropriate for traditional face-to-face education. This is particularly true in the area of research on evaluation and quality.

Most evaluations today are conducted either to comprehensively examine all aspects of a program, as in regional institutional evaluations, or to examine one or more elements in depth, as in most of the formative or summative evaluations conducted by programs themselves. What is missing, Ewell (1998, p. 4) noted, is "attention to how disparate aspects of the institution or program actually fit together," a focus on the relationships among "various functions in light of their intended and actual contributions" toward intended goals. In order to integrate a focus on quality, research on evaluation might focus on questions such as the following:

- How are institutions defining quality in relation to e-learning? Are definitions structurally process- or outcomes-based?
- Do quality definitions go beyond parity with traditional programs?
- Are approaches to quality based on generalities or specific performance indicators?
- Is there congruence between institutional strategic goals and the foci of quality assessment activities?
- Is quality being viewed from the perspective of maintaining an acceptable status quo of educational value or about gradually raising minimum standards?

Also needed is research focused on evaluating other levels of distance education systems including the institutional level, the national level, and even the international level. Given the globalization of the distance education enterprise, "Evaluations "of single institutions operating in isolation from one another are increasingly problematic" as learning resources and processes become "de-institutionalized."

An important related research focus is on how to evaluate the collaborations that are an integral part of the new distance education environment. Technology-based collaborations between and among students, faculty, staff, administrators, and researchers are operating at the course, program, institutional, national, and international levels (Worldwide Universities Network, 2003–2005). Research-based evaluation of the effectiveness of different types and levels of collaboration will be crucial in building, maintaining, and improving collaborative relationships. In this effort we can benefit greatly from interdisciplinary approaches that build on and incorporate work done in other fields (Edgelab, 2004).

CONCLUSION

The convergence of distance education and traditional education is at once the educational community's most exciting possibility and its biggest challenge. The excitement comes from the opportunity to extend knowledge and teaching resources to new populations of learners regardless of time and/or place, while at the same time revitalizing and enhancing those resources through the new pedagogical approaches enabled by powerful communications and data technologies. The challenge comes in melding an innovative, rapidly changing area of practice with complex and firmly established structures built on "traditional institutional hallmarks" of quality (Regional Accrediting Commissions, 2001b, p. 1).

This challenge is reflected clearly in the area of evaluation. If, as Duning et al. (1993) suggested, "We become what we measure" (p. 7), we must ask ourselves as individual educators, institutions, and the educational community as a whole, "What do we want to become?" Answering this question will guide us in structuring evaluations in the service of these goals.

REFERENCES

Allen, I., & Seaman, J. (2005). Growing by degrees: Online education in the United States. Retrieved January 16, 2006, from http://www.sloan-c.org/resources/survey.asp

American Council on Education. (1996). *Distance learning evaluation guide*. Washington, DC: American Council on Education.

American Distance Education Consortium. (2000). *ADEC Guiding principles for distance teaching and learning*. Retrieved March 5, 2005, from http://www.adec.edu/admin/papers/distance-teaching_principles.html

American Evaluation Association. (1995). Guiding principles for evaluators. *New Directions for Evaluation, 66*, 19–26.

Bates, A. W. (1995). *Technology, open learning and distance education*. London: Routledge.

Bates, A. W. (1999). *Developing and applying a cost-benefit model for assessing telelearning* (NCE-Telelearning Project No. 2.3). Retrieved December 10, 2005, from http://research.cstudies.ubc.ca

Bates, A. W. (2000). *Managing technological change. Strategies for college and university leaders*. San Francisco: Jossey-Bass.

Bers, T. (1999). The impact of distance education on institutional research. *New directions for institutional research, 103*, 61–78.

Chambers, E. (1995). Course evaluation and academic quality. In F. Lockwood (Ed.), *Open and distance learning today* (pp. 342–343). London: Routledge.

Chute, A., Thompson, M., & Hancock, B. (1999). *The McGraw-Hill handbook of distance learning. An implementation guide for trainers & human resources professionals*. New York: McGraw-Hill.

Cyrs, T. E. (2001). *Evaluating distance learning programs and courses*. Retrieved March 20, 2005, from http://www.zianet.com/edacyrs/tips/evaluate_dl.htm

Duning, B. S., Van Kekerix, M. J., & Zaborowski, L. M. (1993). *Reaching learners through telecommunications*. San Francisco: Jossey-Bass.

Eaton, J. S. (2000). *Core academic values, quality, and regional accreditation: The challenge of distance learning*. Washington, DC: Council for Higher Education Accreditation.

Edgelab. (2004). *Computer Supported Collaborative Work (CSCW) 2004 workshop: Methodologies for evaluating collaboration in co-located environments*. Retrieved December 29, 2005, from http://www.edgelab.ca/CSCW/Workshop2004/

Ehrmann, S. C. (1997a). *The Flashlight Program: Spotting an elephant in the dark*. Flashlight Program. Retrieved March 7, 2005, from http://www.tltgroup.org/programs/elephant.html

Ehrmann, S. C. (1997b). *What does research tell us about technology and higher learning*. Flashlight Program. Retrieved March 7, 2005, from http://www.learner.org/edtech/rscheval/rightquestion.html

Ehrmann, S. C. (1999). *Studying teaching, learning and technology: A tool kit from the Flashlight Program*. Flashlight Program. Retrieved March 7, 2005, from http://www.tltgroup.org/resources/fstudtool.html

Ehrmann, S. C. (2002, December). *Evaluating (and improving) benefits of educational uses of technology*. A paper prepared for WCET through the Technology Costing Methodology Project Initiative. http://www.wcet.info/projects/tcm/whitepapers.asp

Elloumi, F. (2004). Value chain analysis: A strategic approach to online learning. In T. Anderson & F. Elloumi (Eds.), *Theory and practice of online learning* (pp. 61–92). Athabasca, AB, Canada: Athabasca University.

Ewell, P. (1998). *Examining a brave new world: How accreditation might be different*. Council for Higher Education Accreditation. Retrieved March 1, 2005, from http://www.chea.org/Events/Usefulness/98May_05Ewell.html

Frydenberg, J. (2002). Quality standards in elearning: A matrix of analysis. *International Review of Research in Open and Distance Learning, 3*(2). Retrieved October 1, 2005, from http://www.irrodl.org/index.php/irrodl/article/view/109/551

Inglis, A. (1999). Is online delivery less costly than print and is it meaningful to ask? *Distance Education, 20*(2), 220–239.

Institute for Higher Education Policy. (1999). *What's the difference? A review of contemporary research on the effectiveness of distance learning in higher education*. Washington, DC: Institute for Higher Education Policy.

Institute for Higher Education Policy. (2000). *Quality on the line. Benchmarks for success in Internet-based distance education*. Washington, DC: Institute for Higher Education Policy.

Joint Committee on Standards for Educational Evaluation. (1994). *The program evaluation standards. How to assess evaluations of educational programs.* Thousand Oaks, CA: Sage.

Lockee, B. B., Burton, J. K., & Cross, L. H. (1999). No comparison: Distance education finds a new use for "no significant difference." *Educational Technology, Research & Development, 47*(3), 33–44.

Lockee, B., Moore, M., & Burton, J. (2002). Measuring success: Evaluation strategies for distance education. *EDUCAUSE Quarterly, 25*(1), 20–26.

Mariasingam, M. (2005). Findings of the Delphi Study on quality criteria and benchmarks for online degree programs. Retrieved October 10, 2005, from http://www.odlaa.org/resources/DelphistudyResults Summary.pdf

Miller, G. E. (1990). Distance education and the curriculum: Dredging a new mainstream. In M. G. Moore (Ed.), *Contemporary issues in American distance education* (pp. 211–220). Oxford, United Kingdom: Pergamon Press.

Moore, J. (2002). Elements of quality: The Sloan-C framework. *Learning Abstracts, 5*(12). Retrieved September 12, 2005, from http://www.league.org/publication/abstracts/learning/lelabs0212.html

Moore, M. G. (1999). Monitoring and evaluation. *The American Journal of distance education, 13*(2), 1–5.

Moore, M. G., & Kearsley, G. (1996). *Distance education: A systems view.* Belmont, CA: Wadsworth.

Moore, M. G., & Thompson, M. M. (1997). *The effects of distance learning* (Rev. ed.). University Park, PA: American Center for the Study of Distance Education.

National Center for Education Statistics (NCES). (2003). *Distance education at degree granting postsecondary institutions: 2000–2001,* NCES 2003-017. Washington, DC: Waits, T., Lewis, L., & Greene, B. Retrieved November 4, 2005, from http://nces.ed.gov/pubs2003/2003017.pdf

O'Shea, T., Bearman, S., & Downes, A. (1996). Quality assurance and assessment in distance learning. In R. Mills & A. Tait (Eds.), *Supporting the learner in open and distance learning* (pp. 193–205). London: Pitman.

The Pennsylvania State University. (1998). *An emerging set of guiding principles and practices for the design and development of distance education.* University Park, PA: Author.

Reeves, T., & Hedberg, J. (2003). *Interactive learning systems evaluation.* Englewood Cliffs, NJ: Educational Technology Publication.

Regional Accrediting Commissions. (2001a). *Best practices for electronically offered degree and certificate programs.* Retrieved October 6, 2005, from http://www.wcet.info/resources/accreditation/Accrediting% 20-%20Best%20Practices.pdf

Regional Accrediting Commissions. (2001b). *Statement of commitment by the Regional Accrediting Commissions for the evaluation of electronically offered degree and certificate programs.* Retrieved October 6, 2005, from http://www.wcet.info/resources/accreditation/Accrediting%20-%20Commitment.pdf

Rovai, A. (2003). A practical framework for evaluating online distance education programs. *Internet and Higher Education Programs, 6,* 109–124.

Rowntree, D. (1992). *Exploring open and distance learning.* London: Kogan.

Rumble, G. G. (1997). *The costs and economics of open and distance learning.* London: Kogan Page.

Russell, T. L. (1999). *The no significant difference phenomenon as reported in 355 research reports, summaries and papers. A comparative research annotated bibliography on technology for distance education.* Raleigh, NC: Office of Instructional Telecommunications, North Carolina State University.

Saba, F. (2000). Evaluating distance education programs. *Distance education report, 4*(4), 1.

Stufflebeam, D. L. (1999). *Foundational models for 21st century program evaluation.* Kalamazoo, MI: The Evaluation Center, Western Michigan University.

Thompson, M. M. (1994). Speaking personally with Alan G. Chute. *The American Journal of Distance Education, 8*(1), 72–77.

Thorpe, M. (1996). Issues of evaluation. In R. Mills & A. Tait (Eds.), *Supporting the learner in open and distance learning* (pp. 222–234). London: Pitman.

TLT Group (2005). Articles: Flashlight and other relevant assessment and evaluation topics. Studies of costs. Retrieved January 13, 2005, from http://www.tltgroup.org/resources/farticles.html

U.S. Department of Education. (2006). *Evidence of quality in distance education programs drawn from interviews with the accreditation community.* Retrieved May 21, 2006, from http://www.itcnetwork.org/Accreditation-EvidenceofQualityinDEPrograms.pdf

Watkins, R., & Kaufman, R. (2003). Strategic planning for distance education. In M. G. Moore & W. G. Anderson (Eds.), *Handbook of Distance Education* (pp. 507–517). Mahwah, NJ: Lawrence Erlbaum Associates.

WCET (2007). About TCM: BRIDGE model history, ¶ 1. Retrieved January 14, 2007, from http://www.wcet.info/services/tcm/about.asp

Western Cooperative for Educational Telecommunications. (1999). Principles of good practice for electronically offered academic degree and certificate programs. Retrieved January 13, 2007, from http://www.wcet.info/services/publications/balancing/principles.asp

Whalen, T., & Wright, D. (1999). Methodology for cost-benefit analysis of Web-based tele-learning: Case study of the Bell Online Institute. *The American Journal of Distance Education, 13*(1), 24–44.

Worldwide Universities Network (WUN). (2003–2005). *Models of elearning collaboration.* Retrieved January 10, 2005, from http://www.wun.ac.uk/view.php?id=1344

34

Comparing Costs of Alternative Delivery Methods

Alistair Inglis
Victoria University

When online learning first became a major focus of interest for educational institutions, it was widely believed that delivering courses online offered a major opportunity to reduce costs. The belief that online learning offered a panacea for an institution's spiralling budget was reflected in a large number of studies at the institutional level and within the sector examining the impact of costs (Bacsich et al., 1999; Bartolic-Zlomislic & Bates, 1999a, 1999b; Hülsmann, 2003; Inglis, 1999; Jewett, 1998; Morgan, 2000; Oslington, 2004).

The subsequent experience of institutions' attempts to reap the economic benefits of moving to teaching online showed that in many cases the savings that had been predicted were illusory (Hülsmann, 2003; Shaw & Young, 2003). Following from that recognition, senior managers in institutions have turned their attention from promoting the more rapid uptake of online learning to looking into ways of managing the costs of online learning that are consistent with maintaining the quality of student learning.

The proportion of courses that are taught entirely online is still comparatively low. While the number is growing, it is much more common for a blend of delivery methods to be used. Thus, through achieving an understanding of the factors that impact costs, it is possible to anticipate how particular changes in a delivery model are likely to affect the costs of delivery and therefore the viability of programs.

THE DRIVE FOR INCREASED PRODUCTIVITY

The importance that educational institutions are placing on developments in areas of online learning, at least at the higher education level, is indicated by the degree of interest that has been shown in the National Learning Infrastructure Initiative (NLII) that has been sponsored and promoted by EDUCAUSE (formerly EDUCOM). The rationale for the NLII was initially set out in a white paper that explained the necessity for taking a more system-wide approach to use of new learning technologies in terms of the economic imperatives facing educational authorities (Twigg, 1994).

The case that Twigg (1994) made for shifting to new learning technologies was based on the need for future governments to achieve economies in the provision of postsecondary education. Twigg argued that the growth in population plus the disappearance of old jobs and the creation of new jobs would lead to a substantial growth in lifelong learning. This increase in demand for post-school education would place so much economic pressure on governments that they would be forced to respond by looking for ways to cut the cost of education. The National Learning Infrastructure Initiative (NLII) was put forward as the answer to achieving more with less.

TWIGG'S MODEL

Twigg (1994) argued that the ways to reduce costs were to reduce the need for direct faculty intervention, and to make savings in buildings and plants. Both of these outcomes could be achieved, she said, by increasing students' abilities to locate and use learning resources. Twigg argued that, when implemented, the NLII would 'increase access (via the network), improve quality (through the availability of individualised interactive learning materials), and contain costs (by reducing labor intensity in instruction)' (Twigg, 1994).

The means by which Twigg (1994) saw savings being achieved was not, therefore, simply through a shift from face-to-face to online learning, but more particularly through a shift from classroom-based to resource-based learning. The argument that Twigg mounted for the NLII was, in essence, the same that had been made two decades earlier by the champions of the Open University model.

THE DISTINCTION BETWEEN CLASSROOM-BASED
AND RESOURCE-BASED MODELS OF COURSE DELIVERY

Inglis, Ling, and Joosten (2002) pointed out that distance education programs, including those delivered online, differ according to whether they adopt a classroom-based or resource-based model of delivery. Classroom-based learning is learning that takes place through dialogic interaction between student and tutor and student and student. Resource-based learning is learning that takes place through interaction between the student and self-paced instructional materials (see Table 34.1). Most examples of distance education programs combine elements of both classroom-based and resource-based learning; however, it is the manner in which these types of learning are combined that determines the model of delivery that is used. In the case of the classroom-based model, learning is based on group activities. Such resource materials serve the purpose of supporting and extending those group activities. In the case of the resource-based model, learning occurs through interaction between the learner and the learning materials.

The reason for drawing this distinction between classroom-based and resource-based models of delivery is that the differences between these two models are critical to the economics of distance education delivery. It helps in understanding the economics of online delivery if one first has a grasp of the way in which the economics of teaching at a distance have served to shape the earlier history of distance education.

TABLE 34.1.
Examples of Delivery Methods

	Classroom-Based	*Resource-Based*
On-campus	Tutorials Seminars	Computer-assisted instruction Computer-managed learning
Traditional delivery	Audio teleconferences Videoconferences	Print-based self-instructional packages
Online delivery	Asynchronous learning networks	Web-based delivery Multimedia packages

THE IMPORTANCE OF ECONOMIES OF SCALE

The successful establishment of the U.K. Open University marked a watershed in the development of higher education. Prior to the establishment of the Open University, distance education programs had been characterised by high failure and dropout rates.

The Open University was founded on a vision of offering mature-aged adults from lower socio-economic groups, who had been deprived of the opportunity of gaining a university education, a second chance. The Open University used a mode of teaching that was heavily resource-based. The model that the University adopted combined the use of correspondence material, television and radio broadcasts, face-to-face tutoring at local study centres, and residential schools. This model was chosen because the students to whom the University would be catering were expected to be working while they were studying and therefore would not be able to attend daytime classes. However, the use of broadcast television and high-quality print packages involved substantial development costs. Nevertheless, the University recognised that its resource-based delivery model also offered considerable potential for economies of scale and that these economies were capable of yielding considerable savings in recurrent costs for the University compared with conventional universities (Wagner, 1972).

THE IMPORTANCE OF ECONOMIES OF SCALE

The costs of any productive activity may be subdivided into costs that do not increase with the unit of output, and costs that do. The former are termed *fixed* costs and the latter *variable* costs. In education, examples of fixed costs include the costs of institutional infrastructure, such as buildings and plants, while examples of variable costs include the costs of labor.

Economies of scale are obtained by spreading the fixed costs over a larger student intake. Ashenden (1987) pointed out that opportunities for obtaining economies of scale arise at two levels. At the course level, economies of scale can be obtained by spreading the fixed costs associated with the design and development of learning packages over a larger course intake. At the institutional level, economies of scale are obtained by spreading the costs of institutional infrastructure needed for delivery of programs across a larger distance education cohort. While Ashenden was referring specifically to the type of print-based distance education practised in Australia, the principles he described apply to all types of resource-based online delivery. Thus, in online learning, economies of scale can be obtained by spreading the fixed costs of design and development of Web-delivered resource materials across a larger course intake and the costs of the information and communications technology infrastructure needed to support online delivery across a large total online cohort.

ALTERNATIVE DELIVERY MODELS

The immediate success of the U.K. Open University led to many other countries around the world establishing national distance education universities based on the Open University model. However, two countries that stand out as not having followed this trend are Australia and the United States.

In Australia, a well-developed system of off-campus education was already in existence at the time that the Open University was established. Even so, a major government inquiry was launched to assess whether an open university should be established in Australia (Committee on Open University to the Universities Commission, 1974). This inquiry recommended against the establishment of an open university and recommended instead the establishment of a national institute for a new regional university with special responsibility for distance education. Due to the economic conditions that developed shortly afterwards, neither was established. This outcome left the way open for the newly established colleges of advanced education in Australia's dual-sector higher education system to fill the gap in the market. By the early 1980s more than 40 institutions were operating in distance education, and there was widespread duplication of courses. Most institutions were unable to capture a sufficient portion of the market to operate efficiently.

Recognition by the statutory authority that was then responsible for overseeing the funding of the higher education sector, the Commonwealth Tertiary Education Commission, of the inefficiencies that such a dispersed system created led to a decade of research into the costs of distance education. At the end of this period, the Australian government legislated to rationalize distance education. It did not reduce the number of providers to one, however. Ashenden (1987) had demonstrated that by adhering to the production values that were accepted in Australia, institutions could operate cost-effectively with average course intakes of 50–150 and average total intakes of 3,000. The government therefore designated eight Distance Education Centres, covering a total of 11 universities.

In the United States, the fact that a high proportion of residential-school leavers move away from home to begin higher education meant that there was not the level of unmet demand for higher education places that had driven the expansion of distance education elsewhere in the world. When educational institutions in the United States began to move into distance education, they did so not by adopting the resource-based learning model that had been adopted, but by extending the classroom-based model beyond the walls of the institutions, using the power of the communications media. They created a "remote classroom" model based on two-way video conferencing, and one-way audio/two-way video. Because of the strong U.S. economy, institutions were not faced with such cost constraints as universities elsewhere. Institutions took advantage of economies of scale to recoup the substantial investment costs needed to implement distance education by this mode. Most did not take the second step, however, of trying to reap economies of scale through a shift to resource-based learning.

Twigg's (1994) argument has carried such weight in the U.S. context because of the difference described between characteristics of the U.S. higher-education system and the higher-education systems in other countries. Twigg was not, however, the first person to campaign for the adoption of online delivery on economic grounds. A much earlier proponent of technology was Murray Turoff.

In 1982, Turoff proposed the establishment of a new institution that would teach online, and developed a costing model to demonstrate the viability of the proposal; he has updated the model since (Turoff, 1996). Given Turoff's longstanding advocacy of the role of computer conferencing in business and education, it is only to be expected that the type of virtual classroom he would advocate is one based on the classroom-based model.

In view of what has been said above about the way in which economies of scale are obtained, one would not expect substantial savings to be generated through the adoption of Turoff's (1996) model, and indeed Turoff makes no such claims. In setting out his costing, Turoff was not trying to show that it was possible to make substantial savings through making the shift from campus-based to online delivery, but that it was possible to deliver programs online at a cost commensurate with delivering the same programs face-to-face. Turoff (1996) believed that the purpose of using technology in the delivery of programs in higher education should not be to enable larger class sizes to be supported, nor to increase efficiency, but rather to improve the effectiveness of teaching. Turoff did not seek to achieve savings by such means as relegating teaching to low-paid instructors nor by limiting the extent of instructor contact. To ensure that the quality of faculty would be on average higher than in existing institutions, he proposed that instructors be paid generously in comparison with the pay offered by traditional universities.

Where savings are achieved in Turoff's (1996) model is in the institutional infrastructure. Computer and communications costs are kept low, principally by requiring students to accept most of these costs. Turoff argued that the US$15–20 cost of unlimited network access compared favourably with the cost of travel to a college over a significant distance or the cost of room and board to live on campus.

Interestingly, Turoff's decision to shift the use of funds from the physical plant to faculty also largely eliminates any opportunities that might otherwise have existed for obtaining economies of scale.

THE EDUCATIONAL MERIT OF ALTERNATIVE MODELS

The models proposed by Twigg (1994) and Turoff (1996) represent the opposite ends of a continuum which ranges across various combinations of classroom-based and resource-based components. In considering how these two complementary approaches to delivery might be best applied, it is necessary to take into account the educational rationales for choosing one or other approach, or a combination of the two.

Turoff argues that in this fast-paced world, by the time that subject matter is sufficiently well understood that it can be presented in the form of learning packages, it is too out-of-date to be relevant at university level (Turoff, 1997).

Many distance educators would not agree with Turoff's assessment of the limitations of learning packages. The pace at which disciplinary knowledge is expanding varies greatly from discipline to discipline. Even in those disciplines where progress is rapid, distance education providers have found ways of keeping up with development through implementing just-in-time methods of production. Twigg (1994) argued that what students need to learn is the means by which disciplinary knowledge is accessed. If that is accepted, then the pace at which what students need to learn is changing is by no means as rapid as Turoff has claimed, even in disciplines such as computing and law. Nevertheless, it is important to be aware of the philosophical assumptions Turoff makes in order to understand the basis upon which his costing model is derived.

Feenberg (1999) characterized the difference between these two alternative models of online distance education as being between "automating and informating" (p. 2). In describing the difference in this way, Feenberg tries to accentuate the difference between an emphasis on costs and an emphasis on quality. Feenberg acknowledges the opportunity that exists with what he terms an "automated" system to obtain economies of scale but argues that courses produced by a live teacher, which have the advantage of enabling learners to engage actively in dialogue, will be designed in relatively simple and flexible formats.

In portraying the resource-based learning model as an automated model is something of a shibboleth, however. Almost never has implementation of the resource-based model been seen to obviate the need for student interaction. Local study groups and residential schools have always been key features of the U.K. Open University model, while in Australia, teletutorials, weekend residential schools, or residential schools have traditionally been widely used. Similar opportunities for interaction may be provided in the case of courses offered online. However, the availability of synchronous and asynchronous communication tools makes the incorporation of opportunities for interaction much easier. Feenberg (1999) acknowledged that pre-packaged computer-based materials will supplement the teacher. In acknowledging the legitimacy of the use of these materials, Feenberg accepted that there will be components of either delivery model in which the potential for economies of scale will exist and can be exploited.

DIFFICULTIES IN MAKING COMPARISONS ON THE BASIS OF ACTUAL COSTS

While it is usual to base comparisons of different modes of delivery on actual costs, this approach runs into difficulties when addressing an international arena.

Actual costs vary considerably from country to country but they don't vary consistently; for example, labor costs are much higher in First-World countries than in Third-World countries. The costs of technology and telecommunications, however, are generally higher in Third-World countries than in First-World countries. Furthermore, relative costs are not stable, being subject to exchange-rate variations that at times can be quite large.

In coming to understand the way in which the costs of different delivery methods compare, it is more important to appreciate the relative impact that different variables have on costs and the way in which they have an impact on costs than to have a detailed knowledge of the actual costs themselves.

In analysing the costs of two alternative ways of going about a process, it is generally of little value to compare the costs of inputs without comparing the value of outputs. Comparing inputs, while at the same time not comparing outputs, carries the tacit assumption that the outputs are the same or equivalent. In the case of delivery of educational programs, this equivalence is seldom if ever the case.

Cost-effectiveness analysis compares costs with outcomes, whether or not those outcomes can be measured in financial terms. Cost-benefit analysis compares costs with benefits expressed in economic terms (Moonen, 1997).

One of the most important ways in which outputs can be compared is in terms of the quality of the learning that results. Cukier (1997) has pointed out that many published cost-benefit studies examine costs but not benefits. Consequently, such studies are of limited value in establishing the "big picture." However, it is often the case that before and after conditions are often so different when courses are moved online that finding suitable outcome measures is often quite difficult. In the studies that Cukier reviewed, the types of benefits that were identified included cost savings, opportunity costs, or learning outcomes. Bartolic-Zlomislic and Bates (1999a), drawing on the work of Cukier, assessed the benefits flowing from a joint-venture development involving the University of British Columbia and the Monterrey Institute of Technology using a range of outcome measures. These included measures of performance-driven benefits such as student/instructor satisfaction, learning outcomes, and return on investment; measures of value-added benefits such as increased access, flexibility, and ease of use; and measures of value-added benefits including the potential for new markets.

Bates (1995) pointed out that the basis on which costs are compared should take into account the purpose for which they are being compared. If this purpose is to decide whether or not to use a particular technology or if there is a fixed, overall budget, then it may be more appropriate to use the total cost over the whole of life of the project; if the purpose is to maximise the investment in the production of the resource, then the marginal cost of increasing the amount of resource material may be the best measure; if the purpose is to recover the costs of delivery through student fees, then the marginal cost of adding an additional student may be the most appropriate measure; and if the purpose is to compare different technologies, then the average cost per student hour is probably the best measure.

An alternative approach to using actual costs for comparing costs of alternative methods of delivery is to use break-even analysis (Markowitz, 1987) in which the comparison is made on the basis of the time taken to recover the initial investment. This approach is most appropriate for use in situations where all of the initial investment is being recovered through course fees and it is important to know whether investment in the initial development of the course is justified.

WHICH COSTS SHOULD BE COMPARED?

The costs of delivery of distance education programs can be divided up in a variety of ways. Bates (1995), for example, divided them into capital and recurrent costs, into fixed and variable costs, and into development and delivery costs. However, what is more important than being able to place costs into their appropriate categories is understanding how the different types of costs interrelate. For it is the ways in which costs interrelate that determines whether, in a particular set of circumstances, one mode of delivery will be less costly than another.

However, even understanding the relationship between different cost components is not, on its own, sufficient because the relationship between different types of costs depends on the measure that is used—whether costs are compared on the basis of overall costs, costs per student per workload hour, costs per student per contact hour, or some other measure. Each of these bases of comparison has the potential to produce a different result. Given this situation, the aim in comparing costs should not be to determine which is the best measure of costs but to decide which is the best measure for the purpose at hand.

THE IMPORTANCE OF COMPARING LIKE WITH LIKE

If costs are compared without also comparing benefits, a tacit assumption is made that the delivery methods being compared yield the same or similar benefits. However, the more two delivery methods differ, the less it is likely that the benefits will be equivalent.

It is not difficult to imagine how existing courses delivered in alternative modes might be directly translated into online versions. For most institutions that are currently heavily involved in distance education, direct translation of existing courses is the obvious and probably preferred first step to moving into this medium. However, simple translation of courses into the online medium is often deprecated because it makes no attempt to take advantage of the particular attributes of the media (Oliver, 1999).

Moving into the online environment offers options that are not available, or are not available at acceptable cost, via alternative media (for example, animation, streaming audio, streaming video, and full colour). Advantage can be taken of some of these options, such as colour, without appreciably increasing cost. However, in other cases, such as interactive multimedia, the costs of enhancement of the learning environment are typically much higher than the costs of direct translation. The development costs of interactive multimedia products are many times higher than the development costs of print materials designed to support attainment of the same learning outcomes (Bates, 1995). If more traditional methods of delivery are to be compared with augmented forms of online delivery, then any improvement in the effectiveness with which students learn should be treated as an additional benefit, and some attempt should be made to measure the economic value of this improvement.

The decision to shift to online delivery may provide the trigger for initiating a major course revision. However, the staff time involved in regular revision ought not to be regarded as an additional cost. Regular revision of courses is an accepted aspect of good practice in the resource-based learning model of distance education. If the timing of the redesign effort is altered by virtue of moving a course online, then only that portion of the development cost attributable to the cycle time of redevelopment ought to be considered an additional cost.

THE CONFOUNDING EFFECTS OF HIDDEN COSTS

A difficulty that arises in trying to compare the costs of online delivery with the costs of other forms of delivery is that there are invariably some costs that remain unaccounted for. These "hidden" costs can distort the basis of comparison. The costs of long-established methods of delivery are usually well understood, whereas the costs of emerging methods of delivery are often not all known. Comparisons of this type therefore tend to understate the costs of newer methods of delivery while fully accounting for the costs of existing methods. The effect is to place new methods of delivery in a more favourable light.

The work of Paul Bacsich and his colleagues has helped to identify the contribution to overall costs of hidden costs (Bacsich et al., 1999). Bacsich subdivides hidden costs into three separate categories: institutional costs, costs to staff, and costs to students. Institutional costs are the costs born by the institution. Bacsich includes amongst these the costs of costing, the costs of collaboration, the costs of monitoring informal staff-student contact and the costs of copyright compliance. Staff costs are the costs born by the staff, even though in some cases they ought in principle to be born by the institution. Amongst the staff costs, Bacsich includes the costs of time spent out-of-hours in development of learning materials and the costs of use of privately-purchased computers and consumables. Amongst the costs to students, he points to the costs of ink-jet cartridges needed to print out learning materials.

Bacsich and his colleagues concluded that there is a pressing need for institutions to track the costs of online delivery while acknowledging that there are a number of quite serious difficulties in trying to do this costing; academics, management, and administrators are reluctant to consider the use of any form of time sheet to track the extent of the investment of staff time in these activities; institutions are reluctant to acknowledge that staff work overtime; and there is inconsistency and non-granularity of internal accounting of costs within institutions (Bacsich et al., 1999).

Researchers differ on what should be regarded as "hidden" costs. For example, Morgan (2000) includes as hidden costs the costs of maintaining the central administrative services, such as the central finance office and the president's office; the costs of construction and maintenance of Web sites; and the costs of evaluation, even though these costs are usually readily quantifiable.

SHIFTING COSTS FROM THE PROVIDER TO THE LEARNER

A special case of hidden costs occurs where costs are shifted from the provider to the learner. Moonen (1994) argued that, for costs to be reduced in the long run, some must be passed on to the student.

As has already been pointed out, Turoff's (1996) costing model assumed that students would provide their own computer and would accept the costs of communication. Rumble (1999) gave examples that suggested that institutions are moving in the direction of requiring students to assume responsibility for communication charges. Inglis (1999) also found that in comparing the actual costs of offering a print-based course with the expected costs of offering the same course online, communication represented a significant proportion of costs. However, advances in technology are quickly diminishing the significance of this shift. With the accelerating uptake of unlimited-access ADSL broadband plans for entertainment, or at least in areas where such services are available, growing numbers of learners are able to obtain online access to educational institutions at no additional cost. Although that is not yet the case in many rural areas, and it is certainly not the case in developing countries, the situation is rapidly improving.

OTHER COSTS THAT NEED TO BE CONSIDERED IN A TRAINING CONTEXT

Most of the published research into the costs of delivery of distance education programs has been related to the delivery of programs in higher education. In higher education, costs are born by the student or the state or both, while in a training environment the cost is more commonly born by the employer. When the focus is shifted to the training environment an additional set of cost factors has to be taken into account. For an employer, the costs of training include not only the costs of the training itself but also the costs of any travel and accommodations required to participate in the training and the cost of the loss of the trainee's time (Moonen, 1997). The savings that may result from reductions in the time and travel costs involved by replacing face-to-face training with online training may be considerable (Ravet & Layte, 1997). Whether such ancillary costs ought to be taken into account in making any cost comparison depends on the standpoint from which costs are being compared. If one is comparing costs from the viewpoint of the training provider, then the costs of travel, accommodation, and lost working time are not relevant. However, if one is comparing the costs from the perspective of the employer, then the magnitude of these ancillary costs tip the balance between online delivery and face-to-face delivery when choosing between training. It is therefore obviously important for the employer to take into account these costs.

COMPARISON OF THE COSTS OF DELIVERY IN A BUSINESS CONTEXT

Online delivery is assuming growing importance in corporate training because of its synergistic relationship with e-business. In making decisions on investments, businesses are more interested in the benefits that the investment can generate than just the magnitude of the investment. Return on investment (ROI) is the metric most commonly used to assess the value of a training investment (Cukier, 1997). ROI may be expressed as the annual profit from an investment after taking into account taxation, expressed as the percentage of the original investment, or the number of months or years for the cash-flow generated by the investment to recover the initial investment.

While ROI can be calculated for an individual investment decision, it is more common for the ROI for different alternatives to be compared. The way that the expected return is measured is obviously of critical importance in such comparisons. Training managers are apt to measure return in terms of the attainment of training outcomes. However, as Cross (2001) has argued, business unit managers, who are generally the clients of training providers, judge the worth of training in terms of the improvements in business outcomes that can be attributed to the training investment; astute training managers will therefore estimate returns in business terms.

The returns that can be expected from an investment in training are highly dependent on the nature and state of the business and the relationship of the particular training to the activities of the business. The costs of staff time and travel costs involved in training will depend on the location of a business. It is therefore difficult to generalize about how the costs of alternative delivery methods compare in a business context.

WHAT CONCLUSIONS CAN WE DRAW?

Rumble (1999), in reviewing the findings of the small number of studies that had by then attempted to measure the actual costs of delivering courses online, highlighted the great disparity in the findings. However, given what has been said here about the impact of economies of scale, the great differences in development costs for different types of delivery options, and the importance of the delivery model, this should not be surprising. However, from an understanding of the way these and other factors impinge on fixed and variable costs it is possible to predict how costs are likely to be impacted by changes in delivery methods, and the results of such studies as have been undertaken do broadly correspond with these predictions.

Shifting from a remote classroom to a virtual classroom model is likely to result in some increases in overall costs. There is limited scope for obtaining economies of scale at the course level by moving from on-campus to online delivery. Because even though classroom-based delivery uses institutional infrastructure there is still scope for obtaining economies of scale. However, variable costs are likely to increase because of the additional time taken to communicate in the written, rather than the spoken, word. Fixed costs are likely to increase because of the additional investment in infrastructure and support services.

Shifting from print-based delivery to an online RBL model is unlikely to result in appreciable savings. In this case also, additional investment in infrastructure and support services will be required compared with existing methods of delivery.

In both of the above cases, there is also likely to be an additional cost to the student of moving online. However, this additional cost will probably not be distributed evenly across the student body. For students who already have access to a computer and a broadband connection in the home, the additional cost is likely to be negligible. However, students who are not yet equipped to access the Internet could find that the cost is substantial. The students most likely to face additional costs will be those in rural and remote regions or from disadvantaged backgrounds. This will also be a major factor in developing countries.

In workplace training, the costs of staff time, travel, and accommodation need to be taken into account in comparing online delivery with other methods of delivery. However, these factors will affect the relativities between online delivery and face-to-face delivery much more than the relativities between online delivery and other methods of distance education delivery. In all cases, there will be a substantial impact initially from the start-up costs associated with the establishment of new infrastructure, the development of new procedures, and the creation of new organisational structures for student and staff support.

WHAT MORE WOULD IT BE USEFUL TO KNOW ABOUT THE RELATIVE COSTS OF ONLINE LEARNING?

The question that managers now want answered is not "Which method of delivery is less costly?" but "How can the costs of delivery best be managed?" In other words, given that the decision has been taken to go online, it is important to determine how the quality of courses and programs can be maintained or increased, without at the same time escalating costs.

In times of rapid change, the ways in which institutions conduct their operations and deploy staff and resources are generally more dependent on political rather than on economic factors. It is only once the new ways of operating have become more stable and predictable that costs begin to play a more decisive role in determining the choices that managers make. The phenomenon that Cross (2001) alludes to in relation to workplace training of managers relying more on intuition in making their decisions in relation to the implementation of online delivery probably applies more generally, if for no other reason than that the paucity of dependable information leaves them with no other choice.

What has been argued here is that effective management of costs is more readily achieved if the delivery of courses and programs is conceived of in terms of delivery models rather than in terms of delivery-systems components, and that, when considered in these terms, maintenance of the quality of programs and courses is most easily achieved through a blending of resource-based and classroom-based approaches.

Because productivity and costs are likely to become increasingly important issues in education and training, providers in the United States are likely to move more and more towards resource-based learning in order to take greater advantage of the economies of scale. At the same time, distance education providers elsewhere in the world will take advantage of the conferencing capabilities of networked learning in order to decrease the isolation of distance learners and improve the quality of their learning experiences. The combined effects of these trends will be to bring the practice of distance education in the United States into alignment with the practice of distance education elsewhere in the world. From a situation in which it is readily possible to distinguish two quite different, and often competing, approaches of distance education delivery, we will move to a situation in which two complementary approaches to distance education delivery are melded into a single hybrid approach.

This phenomenon is likely to start to bring to the surface new costing issues such as:

- How can the melding of classroom-based and resource-based learning optimise the trade-off between costs and quality?
- How can resources best be deployed to take advantage of economies of scale while not adversely affecting the quality of the student's learning experience?
- What are the most effective ways of supporting student-student and student-instructor interaction without at the same time increasing costs?
- What possibilities exist for using the potential of information technologies to reduce the variable costs associated with student support?

- In what ways can improvements in the management of start-up of projects help to contain the initial investment in infrastructure, institutional reorganization, and staff development required to shift from existing methods of delivery to online delivery?

- How are course-completion rates and student-satisfaction measures impacted by the balance struck between the use of self-instructional courseware and virtual classroom group interaction?

REFERENCES

Ashenden, D. (1987). *Costs and cost structure in external studies: A discussion of issues and possibilities in Australian higher education*, ACT, Australia: Australian Government Publishing Service.

Bacsich, P., Ash, C., Boniwell, K., Kaplan, L., Mardell, J., & Carvon-Atach, A. (1999). *The costs of networked learning*. Sheffield: Sheffield Hallam University.

Bartolic-Zlomislic, S., & Bates, A. W. (1999a). Assessing the costs and benefits of telelearning: A case study from the University of British Columbia, United Kingdom.

Bartolic-Zlomislic, S., & Bates, A. W. (1999b). Investing in online learning: potential benefits and limitations. *Canadian Journal of Communication, 24*, 349–366.

Bates, A. W. (1995). *Technology, open learning and distance education*. London: Routledge.

Committee on Open University to the Universities Commission. (1974). *Open Tertiary Education in Australia*. ACT, Australia: Australian Government Publishing Service.

Cross, J. (2001). A fresh look at ROI, *Learning Circuits*, American Society for Training and Development. Retrieved May 12, 2001, from http://www.learningcircuits.org/2001/jan2001/cross.html

Cukier, J. (1997). Cost-benefit analysis of telelearning: Developing a methodology framework. *Distance Education, 18*(1), 137–152.

Feenberg, A. (1999). Whither educational technology, *Peer Review, 1*(4). Retrieved March 3, 2001, from http://www.rohan.sdsu.edu/faculty/feenberg/peer4.html

Hülsmann, T. (2003). A cost-analysis of Oldenburg University's two Graduate Certificate programs offered as part of the Online Master of Distance Education (MDE)—A case study. In U. Bernath & E. Rubin (Eds.), *Reflections on teaching and learning in an online masters program. A case study* (pp. 167–226). Oldenburg, Germany: Bibliotheks- und Informationssystems der universitat.

Inglis, A. (1999). Is online delivery less costly than print and is it meaningful to ask? *Distance Education, 20*, 220–239.

Inglis, A., Ling, P., & Joosten, V. (2002). *Delivering digitally: Managing the transition to the knowledge media* (2nd ed.). London: Kogan Page.

Jewett, F. (1998). A simulation model for comparing the costs of expanding a campus using distributed instruction versus classroom instruction (BRIDGE) California State University. Retrieved March 3, 2001, from http://www.calstate.edu/special report1/mediated.instr/

Markowitz, H. Jr. (1987). Financial decision making—Calculating the costs of distance education. *Distance Education, 18*(2), 147–61.

Moonen, J. (1994). How to do more with less? In K. Beattie, C. McNaught, & S. Wills (Eds.), *Interactive multimedia in university education: Designing for change in teaching and learning*. Amsterdam: Elsevier.

Moonen, J. (1997). The efficiency of telelearning. *Journal of Asynchronous Learning Networks, 1*(2), 68–77.

Morgan, B. M. (2000). *Is distance learning worth it? Helping determine the costs of online courses*. Unpublished master's thesis, Huntington, West Virginia, USA.

Oliver, R. (1999). Exploring strategies for online teaching and learning. *Distance Education, 20*(2), 240–254.

Oslington, P. (2004). The impact of uncertainty and irreversibility on investments in online learning. *Distance Education, 25*(2), 233–242.

Ravet, S., & Layte, M. (1997). *Technology-based training. A comprehensive guide to choosing, implementing and developing new technologies in training*. London: Kogan Page.

Rumble, G. (1999). The costs of networked learning: what have we learnt? Papers from the Conference on Flexible Learning and the Information Superhighway. Retrieved May 12, 2001, from http://www.shu.ac.uk/flish/rumblp.htm

Shaw, D., & Young, S. (2003). Costs to instructors in delivering equated online and on-campus courses, *The Journal of Interactive Online Learning, 1*(4).

Turoff, M. (1996). Costs of the development of a virtual university. *Journal of Asynchronous Learning Networks, 1*(2), 17–27. Retrieved August 16, 1997, from http://www.aln.org

Turoff, M. (1997, April). Alternative futures for distance teaching: The force and the darkside. Invited Keynote Presentation, UNESCO/Open University International Colloquiem, Virtual Learning Environments and the Role of the Teacher, Milton Keynes, United Kingdom.

Twigg, C. A. (1994). The need for a National Learning Infrastructure, *EDUCOM Review, 29*, Nos 4, 5, 6. Retrieved August 2, 1997, from http://www.educause/nlii/keydocs/monograph.html

Wagner, L. (1972). The economics of the Open University, *Higher Education, 1*, 159–183.

35

Legal Issues in the Development and Use of Copyrighted Material

Tomas A. Lipinski
University of Wisconsin–Milwaukee

The expansion of education into digital web and other environments is forcing participants—educators, institutions, students, and proprietors (copyright owners)—to reexamine the nature of ownership and use rights. Recent case law and legislation reflect this reexamination. While the developing legal environment accommodates the expansion of distance education, this expansion does not occur without some cost measurable in terms of new obligations that the educator and institution must undertake before advantage of those provisions can be made. These obligations are dubbed "compliance-oriented" by the author, as the goal expressed in the legislative history of the new provisions is to promote a more compliant environment in terms of the copyright law. In the midst of these initiatives, controversy over the ownership and control of faculty-created or enhanced educational materials in support of the distance education curriculum continues to be unresolved.

FACULTY AND INSTITUTIONAL OWNERSHIP ISSUES

In the development of instructional or curricular-related materials, the issue of ownership under the copyright law arises. There are three legal factors that impact or underlie any discussion. First, understanding the legal significance of instruction undertaken in a "work made for hire" scenario versus instruction in an independent contractor setting is necessary. In addition, whether such legal result can be altered by unilateral action such as an institutional policy, employee handbook, etc., is explored. Second, the teaching or "lecture-note" exception to the work-for-hire doctrine as it has been developed in relevant appellate court precedent must be considered. Finally, the application of faculty or "scholarly" ownership concepts to Web-based environments should be addressed. Understanding the relationship between these factors is also important. These issues should be addressed as instructors or faculty members are sure to raise these, or related, concerns as distance and Web-based instructional modes expand. (Note: This discussion updates material from the first edition; for a full discussion, see Lipinski, 2003.)

Institutional Policy Formation and the Work-for-Hire Doctrine

If the work-for-hire doctrine truly vests the copyright ownership of employee work-product, including that of faculty, with the institution (the author however is unwilling to resign to this legal result!), the statutory presumption of employer author-ownership is not subject to unilateral action. This is so because the plain meaning of the section 201 indicates:

> In the case of a work made for hire, the employer or other person for whom the work was prepared is considered the author for purposes of this title, and, *unless* the parties have *expressly agreed* otherwise in a written instrument signed by them, owns all of the rights comprised in the copyright (17 U.S.C. § 201(b)).

As a result, the only effective way to alter the ownership ordering of the work-for-hire doctrine would be either by court-created exception to the work-for-hire rule at the outset and as discussed below, or by an express written instrument signed by both parties agreeing to the transfer. As the district court observed in *Foraste v. Brown University*: "It would defy that intention [to safeguard employers' authorship and ownership rights] to accept the claim that an employer could transfer copyright ownership in a work made for hire to an employee without complying with the strict requirements of section 201(b)'s 'unless' clause" (*Foraste v. Brown University*, 2003, 290 F. Supp. 2d at 239). Another district court made a similar observation regarding the legal impact of such an ownership statement in the college's Policy Manual:

> Here, even if this court agreed with Plaintiff that the language of the copyright policy was sufficient to create an implied contract, it would not help Plaintiff. An agreement altering the statutory presumption [of employer ownership] under the Copyright Act must be *express*. . . . This court concludes that the parties did not expressly agree to rebut the statutory presumption that the employer owns the copyright in a work made for hire. Accordingly, Parkland College owns the copyright in the photographs and is entitled to judgment as a matter of law (*Manning v. Board of Trustees of Community College District No. 505* [*Parkland College*], 2000, 109 F. Supp. 2d at 981 [citations omitted]).

The technical requirements of the statute must be met for a transfer of copyright to occur. "Unwritten understandings or writings not containing the signatures of both parties are insufficient to rebut the presumption [of the vesting of ownership rights with the employer]" (*Manning v. Board of Trustees of Community College District No. 505* [*Parkland College*], 2000, 109 F. Supp. 2d at 981 [citations omitted]). The transfer must be in writing ("written instrument"); it must be express ("expressly agreed")—i.e., transfer of ownership cannot occur as a matter of practice, but must identify each work; and finally, both parties—institution-transferor and faculty-transferee—must sign the document ("signed by them"). Obviously, as the distance environment increases the portability of faculty scholarly and curricular work-product, articulations of such transfer must conform to the statutory requirements in order to be valid.

Teaching Materials and the Development
of a Faculty Ownership Right

If a faculty member is in fact an "employee," whereby the institution-employer by operation of the work-for-hire doctrine owns his or her copyrighted work-product, then precedent (particularly strong in the 7th Circuit) suggests that there is a recognized "teaching" exception for faculty at institutions of higher education. (See *Weinstein v. University of Illinois*, 1987; *Hays v. Sony Corporation of America*, 1988; Kulkarni, 1995; Lape, 1992; Contra, *University of Colorado v. Amer-*

ican Cyanamid, 1995; *Vanderhurst v. Colorado Mountain College District*, 1998.) Under the academic or teaching exception to the work for hire, the faculty, not the university, would hold the copyright associated with faculty-produced material. Two commentators believe that this exception might also extend to the K–12 environment (see Nimmer & Nimmer, 2000, § 5.03(B)(1)(b)(I) n. 31, at 5-17–5-18). However, recent appellate case law suggests the contrary result:

> Without denigrating in any way the time and effort devoted by Shaul in fulfilling his teaching duties, we hold that his ownership of the tests, quizzes, homework problems, and other teaching materials in his former classroom is precluded by the work-for-hire doctrine. Because the teaching materials at issue were owned by the School District . . . (*Shaul v. Cherry Valley-Springfield Central School District*, 2004, 363 F.3d at 186).

While students are not employed to teach and research in quite the same capacity as are faculty (see Patel, 1996), a similar path of analysis can be made for ownership vesting with the graduate student so situated, though such analysis would not apply with respect to other (non-employee) students, as no employment relationship exists between these students and the institution.

The issue of the existence of a teaching or scholarship (see discussion below) exception to the work-for-hire doctrine is by no means settled. Case law supporting the exception appears only in one federal appellate circuit (covering the states of Wisconsin, Illinois, and Indiana). Furthermore, recognizing the exception is in contrast to the plain language of the statute and is based on tradition and public policy. In *University of Colorado v. American Cyanamid* the district court observed that the

> [p]laintiffs maintain the Regents "are quite obviously the owner, because the article is a 'work made for hire' by the coauthors done within the scope of their employment" (footnote to 17 U.S.C. § 201 omitted; Pls.' citing Reply Br. Supp. Mot. Partial Summ. J. at 29 n.55). Plaintiffs argue Cyanamid has offered no evidence to rebut such ownership. I agree (*University of Colorado v. American Cyanamid*, 1995, 880 F. Supp. at 1400).

Subsequently, the same district court in *Vanderhurst v. Colorado Mountain College District* interpreted the "scope" of the work-for-hire doctrine:

> It is undisputed that Vanderhurst prepared the Outline on his own time with his own materials. However, there is no genuine dispute that Vanderhurst's creation of the Outline was connected directly with the work for which he was employed to do and was fairly and reasonably incidental to his employment. Further, creation of the Outline may be regarded fairly as one method of carrying out the objectives of his employment. [citation omitted] I conclude, therefore, that pursuant to the "work for hire" doctrine, as of 1995, any copyright remaining in the Outline did not belong to Vanderhurst. Thus, I will grant defendants' motion for summary judgment on claim eight (*Vanderhurst v. Colorado Mountain College District*, 1998, 16 F. Supp. 2d at 1307).

It should be noted that, while these cases represent more recent precedent, the cases are from a district court and if this issue arose in another circuit, the appellate decisions from the Seventh Circuit might have greater weight though both series of cases would represent mere persuasive precedent.

A "Second" Copyright in the Performance of Teaching Material

A faculty member does have a right to deliver course content in a manner of his or her own choosing. This creates a distinction between what is taught and how it is taught. In other words, even if the institution owns the lesson plans and other teaching materials faculty create, it can be argued that the delivery of the those plans (in copyright parlance, the "performance" of that copyright-content) would rest in the performer, the faculty or graduate teaching assistant (see, *Williams v. Weisser*, 1969). Once the performance is fixed in a tangible medium (i.e., a recording of a performance is made) a new copyrighted is created and, likewise, ownership rights in that work should be of concern to faculty.

This issue has not been addressed in the courts and a strict application of the work-for-hire doctrine might also lead a court to conclude that any recording of that performance of the employer's copyrighted content (assuming that the lesson plan, lecture notes, outlines, etc., are indeed under the institution's copyright) likewise belongs to the employer in the form of a "derivative" work (again, using the proper term from the copyright law). In the same sense that a "sound recording" made by Andy Williams of "Moon River" is derivative of the original work, the Henry Mancini song (a "musical work"); likewise, a recorded lecture (whether by audio, video with sound, transcription, etc.) is also derivative of the lesson plan, lecture notes, outline, Power Points presentations, etc., on which it is based. (Of course the lecture could be completely extemporaneous as well, and therefore, while not "derivative," would still raise the same unresolved ownership issue.) As a result, the faculty (or the employer, depending upon whose legal argument one prefers) has a copyrightable interest in the fixed expressions of particular expressions of teaching. (Some commentators, including the present author, believe faculty ownership extends to the expression, the performance, as well as the underlying content. (See, Nimmer & Nimmer, 2000, § 5.03 [footnotes omitted]: "Thus, if a professor elects to reduce his lectures to writing, the professor, and not the institution employing him, owns the copyright in such lectures.")) This would by implication include, for example, the recording or other fixation of faculty performances (lectures) by a commercial note-taking service. (See also *Williams v. Weisser*, 1969, 273 Cal. App. 2d at 732, 78 Cal. Rptr. at 544: "We are, however, convinced that in the absence of evidence the teacher, rather than the university, owns the common law copyright in his lectures.")

Turning to distance education scenarios, this would by logic extend to situations in which lectures are routinely recorded as a part of the delivery of course content, e.g., simultaneous recordation during a distance education broadcast or live Web stream (see discussion of 17 U.S.C. § 112(b) below), or it could include the preparation of prerecorded lectures created in order to facilitate 24-7 learning by students. Since the original and creative content of either recorded broadcast lectures or Internet Web-based instruction involves the fixation of teaching expression, the requirements for a valid copyrightable work are met, i.e., it is a work of authorship fixed in a tangible medium. (See, 17 U.S.C. § 102: "Copyright protection subsists, in accordance with this title, in original works of authorship fixed in any tangible medium of expression, now known or later developed.") The fact is that if a broadcast, streamed, or pre-recorded lecture is recorded and stored on institutional facilities, a copyrighted work has been created. As a result, it is argued that the ownership of that work, under the "teaching" exception to the work-for-hire doctrine, belongs to the faculty, and that storage of the work on institutional facility along with control over its subsequent use should be at the direction or under the control of the faculty member.

Faculty Ownership of Scholarly Work Product: The Academic Exception

It should also be pointed out that many universities have a copyright policy in place, similar to the one at issue in *Weinstein*, which defines conditions under which faculty output would be considered a work for hire and when it would be considered to belong to the faculty. Typically such a copyright policy is considered part of the employment contract with the university. In fact, for public institutions it may be part of the state's administrative code. In *Weinstein*, an Illinois faculty member retained the copyright to his or her scholarly output unless the work fell into one of three categories:

> (1) The terms of a University agreement with an external party require the University to hold or transfer ownership in the copyrightable work, or (2) Works expressly commissioned in writing by the University, or (3) Works created as a specific requirement of employment or as an assigned University duty. Such requirements or duties may be contained in a job description or an employment agreement which designates the content of the employee's University work. If such requirements or duties are not so specified, such works will be those for which the topic or content is determined by the author's employment duties and/or which are prepared at the University's instance and expense, that is, when the University is the motivating factor in the preparation of the work (*Weinstein v. University of Illinois*, 1987, 811 F.2d at 1094).

The third prong of the policy is consistent with the case law in determining when work is considered to belong to the institution. In spite of the "publish or perish" atmosphere of the university setting (with scholarly writing a condition of employment vis-à-vis the tenure, promotion, and merit processes), the Seventh Circuit observed that the University of Illinois' policy appeared to apply "more naturally" to administrative reports, documentation created through campus services, etc., than to journal articles or other scholarly output (*Weinstein v. University of Illinois*, 1987, 811 F.2d at 1094–1095). Therefore, there is some legal support for the argument that faculty scholarly output (even when it is employment-dependant vis-à-vis tenure, promotion, merit, etc., requirements) is not within "employment duties" nor prepared at "the University's instance and expense," at least not according to the Seventh Circuit. For faculty at institutions with similar policy language, such a policy would at least not stand in the way of ownership rights vesting in the faculty.

In the most recent discussion of the issue, a state court concluded that the work-for-hire doctrine did not per se vest ownership of faculty scholarship with the university. If the subject of intellectual-property rights were a condition of employment then the ownership issue would properly be subject to Kansas state collective bargaining laws, i.e., a matter subject to mandatory negotiation between the parties as opposed to a management prerogative. By logic, if the faculty scholarship were outside the conditions of employment, and (as suggested by the *Weinstein* court) beyond the reach of the work-for-hire doctrine, then by logic the university should not be able to unilaterally command disposition of the ownership right faculty would possess outright. The Kansas Supreme Court did not proceed that far in the analysis, making mere comment on the possibility of faculty ownership:

> While it is far from clear that there is an absolute teacher exception to the work-for-hire doctrine . . . [the Regent's] argument on this point goes too far in the opposite direction . . . all intellectual properties created by the faculty in the form of scholarly works or creative endeavors are works for hire . . . [with] all rights to any intellectual property created by PSU faculty [owned by the Regents]. That is too big a leap. Even if PSU faculty are employees . . . that does not end the analysis for purposes of determining whether the works they create are works for hire. . . .This will necessarily involve not just a case-by-case evaluation, but potentially a task-by-task evaluation. Accordingly, the Court of Appeals, the hearing officer, and PERB erred in assuming that the work-for-hire doctrine would apply to any intellectual property created by PSU faculty simply because those faculty are employees of PSU (*Pittsburg State University/Kansas National Education Association v. Kansas Board of Regents/Pittsburg State University*, 2005, 122 P.3d at 346–347 [citation omitted]).

The issue of faculty versus institutional ownership rights will continue to arise until the issue is resolved either by federal legislative reform or adjudication by the Supreme Court.

LIABILITY ISSUES IN THE USE OF COPYRIGHTED MATERIAL IN DISTANCE EDUCATION

Appreciating the importance of immunity (section 504) and damage reduction (section 512) cannot be undertaken unless the concept of liability in copyright law is first understood. Liability in copyright law has three parts: direct, contributory, and vicarious. Thus, in a case of illegal downloading by a student that was commanded by a faculty member, each of the three forms of liability might operate to impose liability on the student, faculty member, and institution, respectively.

Direct Copyright Infringement

Establishing a claim of direct infringement is important to the copyright owner, as direct infringement must occur before a finding of contributory or vicarious infringement can be made. Violate one of the exclusive rights of the copyright owner (to reproduce the work; to make public display, public performance, or public distribution (transmission) of the work; or to make a derivative work) and a claim of direct infringement is possible, as when a faculty member posts—implicating the rights of reproduction, and public display and distribution—another's copyrighted text-based material without permission onto a course Web site in excess of any fair use or other statutory limits. Various provisions of the copyright law offer defense to claims of infringement, such as fair use under section 107 or section 110 designed to offer additional rights of performance and display to educators. These defenses operate as a sort of privilege to infringe.

Direct Infringement in Online Networks: Lessons from the Fair Use Cases

Non-profits as well as individuals can be the target of direct infringement claims. A tax-exempt trade organization that uploaded several volumes of the plaintiff's clip art onto its Web site without permission violated not only the right of reproduction but also the right of display (*Marobie-F v. National Association of Firefighter Equipment Distributors*, 1997). A recent decision from the Seventh Circuit like the P2P cases before it confirmed that downloading and retaining music (or other copyrighted material for that matter) even if the use is not in conjunction with any commercial enterprise per se, i.e., but is a personal use, is nonetheless not a fair use (see, *BMG Music v. Gonzalez*, 2005). First, the court rejected the so-called "time shift argument" often forwarded by defendants in P2P cases: "The premise of *Betamax* is that the broadcast was licensed for one transmission and thus one viewing. . . . Time-shifting by an authorized recipient this is not" (*BMG Music v. Gonzalez*, 2005, at 890). In commenting on the fair-use defense, in particular, the first factor that looks to the nature of the use the court commented that "Gonzalez was not engaged in a nonprofit use; she downloaded (and kept) whole copyrighted songs" (*BMG Music v. Gonzalez*, 2005, at 890). Rather courts will characterize efforts to avoid payment as commercial. Thus an instructor who uploads a copy of a workbook to a distance education course site so students or the institution need not purchase the required copies, even though the instructor does not sell or otherwise make direct profit from the act, will nonetheless garner a conclusion that the character of the use is indeed commercial, since it saved students or the school district the cost of purchasing the material.

Educators should also be wary of excessive rationalizations of conduct. It is obvious that everything an instructor does is in furtherance of the lofty goal of education. Yet educational markets are arguably more limited than general consumer or entertainment markets and, thus, lost revenues can be more injurious (market harm is the fourth fair-use factor; the second is the nature of the work and the third is "the amount and substantiality of the portion used in relation to the copyrighted work as a whole.") For example, in *BMG Music v. Gonzalez*, the court rejected a so-called try-it before you buy-it defense, as there is negative market impact: "Many radio stations stream their content over the Internet, paying a fee for the right to do so. Gonzalez could have listened to this streaming music to sample songs for purchase; had she done so, the authors would have received royalties from the broadcasters and reduced the risk that files saved to disk would diminish the urge to pay for the music in the end." (*BMG Music v. Gonzalez*, 2005, at 891). As a result, educational institutions may wish to rethink practices built upon the erroneous assumption that all personal or educational uses are fair uses.

Proceeding to the four-part fair-use test, the Ninth Circuit in *A&M Records, Inc. v. Napster, Inc.*, found that, while individuals engage in the file sharing, it is nonetheless commercial. "Direct economic benefit is not required to demonstrate a commercial use. Rather, repeated and exploitative copying of copyrighted works, even if the copies are not offered for sale, may constitute a commercial use" (*A&M Records, Inc. v. Napster, Inc.*, 2001, 239 F.3d at 1015). This was true for two reasons: first, the scale of the MP3 file-sharing using Naptser technology makes it a non-private use, and second, unlike a case where one might make a copy for a friend, Napster transfers are made to an "anonymous requester." The second and third factors, again like the *MP3* case, weigh against a finding of fair use as the works are creative (second factor) and 100% of the works are typically taken (third factor). Finally, various studies demonstrated a negative impact on the market. In addition, the widespread use of Napster created a market barrier to the entry by legitimate players into the Internet file-sharing arena. Using the same four-part fair-use test, the Southern District of New York found the MP3 defendant liable for similar reasons. (See *UMG Recordings v. MP3, Inc.*, 2000.)

Contributory Copyright Infringement

Contributory copyright infringement occurs when someone induces, causes, or materially contributes to the infringement of another and possesses knowledge or awareness of the infringing nature of the conduct. What if a faculty member referred students to a site where "illegal" copies of Cliffs Notes or some other educational support material could be obtained for free? This "referral" might take the form of a link on a course Web site, or a non-active URL could be listed or directions provided in an online syllabus, or even assistance in locating the material online during a computer lab session. The scenarios raise the issue of how much "contribution" by the educational institution will trigger liability for contributory copyright infringement.

A disturbing development with application to Web environments is presented in the *Intellectual Reserve, Inc. v. Utah Lighthouse Ministry, Inc.* litigation. In that case the defendants initially posted copyrighted material without permission on their Web site (about 17 pages, or about 5% of a 330-page, two-volume handbook). A temporary restraining order was issued to the defendants to cease display of the pages on their Web site. Undaunted in their quest to publicize the inner workings of the Church of Latter Day Saints, the defendants placed a note on their Web site that the handbook was still online. The note included a description of how viewers of their site could locate three other sites from which the full text of the handbook could be obtained. The defendants also included the text of several e-mails that encouraged subsequent browsing of the handbook by their viewers and urged viewers once at one of the three full-text sites to download and send the handbook to others. The court believed that actions of the defendants went beyond any sense of passive awareness or that of a mere informational or directory service. The court also referred to one incident in particular: "[I]n response to an e-mail stating that the sender had unsuccessfully tried to browse a website that contained the Handbook, defendants gave further instructions on how to browse the material" (*Intellectual Reserve, Inc. v. Utah Lighthouse Ministry, Inc.*, 1999, 75 F. Supp. at 1295). The defendants were thus found to have materially contributed (contributory infringement) to the infringement by the subsequent visitors (direct infringement) to the three other Web sites on which the plaintiff's work was posted.

The message is clear: do not steer students to a source or site of infringing material, nor encourage students to visit and download the material from the infringing sites. The factor for an educational institution may be one of reasonableness. For example, is it reasonable to suppose that a link from a course Web page or online library catalog record to a particular Web site containing over 1,000 textbooks downloadable for free would be a link to an infringing site? This represents a sort of "red flag" test and is incorporated into the section 512 standards as well, discussed below. The lesson for educational institutions is clear, because the acts of students using MP3/Napster or MP3/Napster-like copying and file-sharing technology is direct infringement, and the institution or its employees should not do anything to "induce or cause, or materially contribute to infringement" by its students.

Contributory infringement in online networks: Lessons from Grokster.   In June of 2005, the United States Supreme Court, in a unanimous decision, held "that one who distributes a device with the object of promoting its use to infringe copyright, as shown by clear expression or other affirmative steps taken to foster infringement, is liable for the resulting acts of infringement by third parties" (*Metro-Goldwyn-Mayer Studios Inc. v. Grokster, Ltd.*, 2005, 125 S.Ct. at 2770). The Court created a new way for an intermediary to be liable—infringement by inducement, another form of contributory infringement. Educational entities that make "devices" available to students that can be put to infringing uses should take note of the safe harbor the court offered, lest an aggressive copyright owner claim the institution contributed to the infringement by inducing such conduct. First, what is the context? Does the device and its having been supplied by the institution aim to "satisfy a known source of demand for copyright infringement," evidenced by a similarity of product name, similar program functionality, or attempts to divert interest to its domain (*Metro-Goldwyn-Mayer Studios Inc. v. Grokster, Ltd.*, 2005, 125 S.Ct. at 2781–2782)? This factor recognizes a reality that for some content and for some technologies there is, for better or for worse, a culture of infringement. Is the institution aware of this; is it exploiting this proclivity? Second, what is the response? The Court observed the absence of any attempt by defendants to "develop filtering tools or other mechanisms to diminish the infringing activity using their software" (*Metro-Goldwyn-Mayer Studios Inc. v. Grokster, Ltd.*, 2005, 125 S.Ct. at 2781). It is not clear whether this now requires institutions to take affirmative steps to prevent infringement, such as inserting its own safety mechanisms or switches into such systems, i.e., a "content governor" or tracking protocol. The question is whether such measures have become standard industry practice, wherein suspicion would arise if the institution refused to institute or enable such protocols, or deactivated the protection mechanism contained within products it acquires. Third, is there the financial benefit present? In *Grokster* there was a positive relationship between the infringing use and revenue generated from advertisements, a main source of income for Groskter and StreamCast (*Metro-Goldwyn-Mayer Studios Inc. v. Grokster, Ltd.*, 2005, 125 S.Ct. at 2781–2782). Fee structures that depend on the amount of infringing activity versus those that treat infringing and non-infringing users alike generally satisfy the required direct-financial-interest element there. Are students assessed an annual technology fee or is a service fee charged by the download or by the server space used? Where the more students download (potentially infringing material), the more revenue the institution stands to make from the infringing activity. As with the second factor, this factor alone is insufficient to infer "unlawful intent" or "unlawful objective."

Vicarious copyright infringement.   Vicarious infringement is found when one has the "right and ability to supervise the infringing activity and also has a direct financial interest in such activities" (*Fonovisa, Inc. v. Cherry Auction, Inc.*, 1996, 76 F.3d at 262). Vicarious liability is imputed from employee to employer—i.e., the employer is responsible for acts of its employee, but not vice-versa. Vicarious liability is grounded in the tort concept of respondeat superior (a concept from agency law that translates as "let the superior respond" or answer for the acts of its agent), whereas contributory infringement is founded in the tort concept of enterprise liability. (See, *Demetriades v. Kaufmann*, 1988, 690 F. Supp. at 293 ["Benefit and control are the signposts of vicarious liability, (whereas) knowledge and participation (are) the touchstones of contributory infringement."]) Vicarious liability in employment settings does not require knowledge of the infringement by the vicarious defendant. (See, Hazard, 2004, ¶ 7.08, at 7-72–7-75.) It is also applicable in independent-contractor settings—i.e., the acts of the independent contractor are imputed to the contracting institution. (See, *Southern Bell Telephone and Telegraph v. Associated Telephone Directory*, 1985.) However, an employment setting is not always required, as was the case in *Fonovisa* where a swap-meet purveyor was held liable for acts of infringement by booth renters who bought and sold bootleg tapes, or in *Columbia Pictures Industries v. Redd House* (1984), in which a shop-owner who allowed customers to view copyrighted video cassettes was liable for the infringing acts of its customers. The significant lesson for the educational institution is that employers are strictly liable for any copyright infringement in which its employees engage. This makes imperative the design of risk-management mechanisms that uncover and respond to potential infringing conduct and do so early.

DAMAGE ENHANCEMENT AND REMISSION PROVISIONS OF 17 U.S.C. § 504

Several provisions of the copyright law may operate to lessen the sting that a successful infringement suit may bring to the institution by reducing the damages that may be awarded or by eliminating altogether the monetary relief of the plaintiff. Under section 504(c)(2):

> The court shall remit statutory damages in any case where an infringer believed and had reasonable grounds for believing that his or her use of the copyrighted work was a fair use under section 107, if the infringer was: (i) an employee or agent of a nonprofit educational institution, library, or archives acting within the scope of his or her employment who, or such institution, library, or archives itself, which infringed by reproducing the work in copies or phonorecords . . . (17 U.S.C. § 504).

This immunity applies to both the employee as well as the institution. Once the immunity applies, all statutory damages must be remitted; statutory damages can range from $750 to $30,000. However, the immunity does not operate to remit attorney's fees or other costs! The alternative remedy for the copyright plaintiff is for actual damages. Compare the protection awarded to an infringing educational institution under section 504 with the defendants in the *UMG Recordings* litigation cited above. Suppose a university with a music program loaded, and made available to students, approximately 4,700 CDs on its server (the same approximate number as the defendants MP3, Inc. in the *UMG Recordings* case); at a value of $15 per CD that would be approximately $70,500, a far cry from the estimated $17.5 million the *UMG Recordings* court hypothesized might be awarded under a statutory damages scheme (in which the court set statutory damages in the amount of $25,000 per work infringed). However, the section 504(c)(2) remission mechanism requires that the distance educator demonstrate a "reasonable belief" that the use was fair. As the legal landscape in digital environments develops, and as compliance programs in educational institutions become more widespread and effective, convincing a court as to the reasonableness of persistent uploading, downloading, or the facilitation of those acts by faculty and students is less and less likely.

Recall that intent is not an element of a claim of direct copyright infringement. However, if the infringement is proved to be "willful" (the burden of proof is on the plaintiff-copyright owner), the court may increase damages further: "In a case where the copyright owner sustains the burden of proving, and the court finds, that infringement was committed willfully, the court in its discretion may increase the award of statutory damages to sum of not more than $150,000" (17 U.S.C. § 504(c)(2)). In copyright law, willfulness "exists where there is a deliberate act of infringement, knowledge that an act constitutes infringement, or intentionally disregards of warnings that infringement is taking place" (Hazard, 2004, § 7:49, at 7–115). The standard "connotes wantonness," (Nimmer & Nimmer, 2000, § 14.04c(B)(3)) a belief so unsupportable in law that a court would, in fact, consider it unreasonable. The point is that excessive, repeated uploading, downloading, posting, pasting, and so forth in the educational environment to an extent clear and far in excess of fair use may not only fail to qualify for the mandatory damage remission, but also trigger a damage enhancement for willfulness. For example, in a case where there is evidence of customary knowledge of a plaintiff's copyright, such as in the television industry, the Ninth Circuit observed that a defendant "who nonetheless continued to air the series in question until well into the course of this litigation [ ] is sufficient to support a finding of willfulness" (*Columbia Pictures Television, Inc. v. Krypton Broadcasting of Birmingham, Inc.*, 2001, 259 F.3d at 1195). Such a scenario might occur when a faculty member continues the infringing behavior of sensitive (in terms of harm to the market for the work) curricular materials such as standardized test prep materials that admonish users on the cover "DO NOT REPRODUCE."

THE SECTION 512 SAFE HARBOR:
COMPLETE MONETARY DAMAGE REDUCTION

As part of the Digital Millennium Copyright Act (DMCA), Pub. L. No. 105-304, 112 Stat. 2860 (1998), Congress created a new provision dealing with the "limitations on liability relating to material online." The subsections of section 512 indicate those circumstances in which a "service provider" (which could be an institution of higher education) will not be held responsible for the infringing acts of third parties. Immunity is never complete under section 512—liability is established but remedy limited to statutorily prescribed forms of injunctive relief in subsection (j)—but unlike the section 504 damage remission, section 512 eliminates all monetary award including costs and attorneys' fees. The provisions are complex and an only a brief overview is presented here. (See Lipinski, 2006, for a thorough review.)

Unlike remission under section 504 applying in cases of infringement by reproduction, section 512 damage limitation may operate where any of the exclusive rights of the copyright owner are implicated. However, the infringing content must be digital and online:

> The Committee, however, has tweaked the definition . . . to ensure that it captures offerings over the Internet and other on-line media. Thus, the new definition . . . not only includes 'the offering

of transmission, routing or providing of connections,' but also requires that the service provider be providing such services for communications that are both 'digital' *and* 'on-line.' By 'on-line' communications, the Committee means communications over interactive computer networks, such as the Internet." As a result, even if the communication is digital, "over-the-air broadcasting," cable, satellite, and so forth would be excluded from obtaining the protection of the safe harbor as these are not "communications over interactive computer networks" (H.R. Rep. No. 105-551, 1998, Part 2, at 63; S. Rep. No. 105-190, 1998, at 54).

Second, the monetary damage immunity would protect a school, college, or university only from the liability that might arise from the infringing conduct of third parties such as students, not employees (except for the special rules affecting institutions of higher education in section 512(e) discussed below).

Third, the activity must fall into one of four service provider functions: (a) transmitting, routing, and providing connections to infringing material (the "transitory digital network communications" or store and forward limitation of 17 U.S.C. § 512(a)); (b) system caching (17 U.S.C. § 512(b)); (c) information stored by a user (the "user storage" limitation of 17 U.S.C. § 512(c)); and (d) linking or referring users to infringing material (the "information location tools" limitation of 17 U.S.C. § 512(d)). The first two provisions, transitory store and forward and caching are acts that happen automatically. The posting (third party "storage") and linking are not temporary or transient acts. Moreover, these latter two provisions concern visible acts (posting and linking) and thus "by their nature allow service providers to intervene" (Dratler, 2004, § 6.01, at 6–11). As a result, elaborate take down and counter notification provisions accompany the posting and linking subsections of Section 512. There is additional immunity for as well as additional obligations when disabling access to, or removing in good faith, allegedly infringing material (the take-down provisions of 17 U.S.C. § 512(g)).

Setting the Stage for Intervention: Policy Adoption and Enforcement

In order to seek the refuge of immunity, the institution must first fulfill various threshold obligations. For example, the educational institution "service provider" must have "adopted and reasonably implemented" a policy providing that it will terminate repeat infringers (17 U.S.C. § 512(i)(1)(A)). Several courts have commented on the policy adoption and enforcement obligation. In *Corbis Corp. v. Amazon.com, Inc.*, the court offered a three-step compliance effort: "A service provider must: 1) adopt a policy that provides for the termination of service access for repeat copyright infringers in appropriate circumstances; 2) inform users of the service policy; and 3) implement the policy in a reasonable manner" (*Corbis Corp. v. Amazon.com, Inc.*, 2004, 351 F. Supp. 2d at 1100). But what is reasonable? It is suggested that such policy be enforced in a manner consistent with other policies relating to student affairs and conduct. In *Perfect 10, Inc. v. Cybernet Ventures, Inc.*, the court offered:

> When confronted with 'appropriate circumstances,' however, such service providers should reasonably implement termination. [Citation omitted.] These circumstances would appear to cover, at a minimum, instances where a service provider is given sufficient evidence to create actual knowledge of blatant, repeat infringement by particular users, particularly infringement of a willful and commercial nature. (*Perfect 10, Inc. v. Cybernet Ventures, Inc.*, 2002, 213 F. Supp. 2d at 1177).

Considering the reality of some campus computing environments it is reasonable to expect that some students will indeed have their network access terminated. This can, of course, prove disastrous to the student but illustrates the heavy-handed nature of the many response mechanisms built into section 512.

It would be logical to conclude that a policy that had little chance of being enforced was not "reasonably implemented" under the section 512(i)(1)(A) requirement. At a minimum, educational institutions, after adopting a copyright compliance policy, should make every effort to publicize the copyright policy and provide employees with basic education on the copyright law. This might include postings on all faculty, staff, and student-accessible Web pages, documentation and training programs, and some acknowledgement on the part of faculty, staff, and students of their responsibility to comply with the copyright law.

Implementing the Intervention: The Role of the Registered Agent

In order to take advantage of the section 512(c) (posting) monetary limitation, the service provider must also designate an agent to receive complaints of infringement from copyright owners and coordinate compliance measures. The registered agent serves as point person, receiving complaints from copyright owners or their representative and coordinating statutory responses. The use of an agent is not required of the store and forward limitation of section 512(a), and while not required for subsections (b) and (d) (the cache and link provisions, respectively), it is recommended (Dratler, 2004, § 6.01, at 6–13). This is so because section 512(b)(2)(E), section 512(c)(1)(C), and section 512(d)(1)(C) all require the service provider to "respond[ ] expeditiously to remove, or disable access to, the material that is claimed to be infringing or to be the subject of infringing activity." The registered agent (required in post settings and optional but recommended for cache and linking scenarios) coordinates this response mechanism, and therefore must be entrusted with the authority to respond, i.e., order removal or disabling within the institutional network environment and ensure that the response is expeditious. Participating in the "registered agent" provisions increases the administrative oversight required and the cost of meeting the safe harbor obligation required by the educational institution.

The duty does not end there. While the notice must conform to the specific statutory requirements (a written communication that includes a physical or electronic signature, identification of the copyrighted work, identification of the material that is claimed to be infringing, sufficient contact information, an attestation statement of good faith that the use of the material in the manner complained of is not authorized, and an attestation statement subject to perjury that the complaining party is authorized to act on behalf of the owner), a failed notice may nonetheless trigger a second, or "general," removal or disabling obligation in post and link scenarios.

Section 512(c)(1)(a) and section 512(d)(1) indicate that in order for the monetary damage limitation to apply, the service provider must not possess actual knowledge that the material or an activity using the material on the system or network is infringing or in the absence of such actual knowledge, not be aware of facts or circumstances from which infringing activity is apparent or upon obtaining such knowledge or awareness, acts expeditiously to remove, or disable access to, the material. Section 512(c)(3)(B)(i) indicates that an imperfect notice from the copyright owner or representative does not now trigger this second and more general disabling or removal obligation. However, if the failed notice does at least "substantially" identify the work claimed to be infringed, the material claimed to be infringing, and sufficient contact information, then this information can trigger the second removal and disabling requirement under subsections (c)(1)(A) and (d)(1) *unless* the service provider through its registered agent attempts to contact the person who sent the initial notice and offer opportunity to perfect that notice. If perfection of the notice occurs, then the specific (and formal) disabling and removal obligation is triggered.

When might the general awareness of infringement be triggered such that removal or disabling is also required? Note that unlike the specific notice provision in which information is received from the copyright owner or his or her representative, this general awareness could come from anyone within the institution and is based on the "subjective awareness of the service provider," which is then assessed by an objective standard (i.e., "whether infringing activity would have been apparent to a reasonable person operating under the same or similar circumstances") (H.R. Rep. No. 105-551, 1998, at pt. 2, 53; S. Rep. No. 105-190, 1998, 44). The legislative history offers two examples to clarify: (a) **No Red Flag** of awareness, "a directory provider would not be similarly aware merely because it saw one or more well known photographs of a celebrity at a site devoted to that person," and (b) **Red Flag** of awareness, "pirate directories refer Internet users to sites that are obviously infringing because they typically use words such as 'pirate,' 'bootleg,' or slang terms in their illegal purpose obvious to the pirate directories and other Internet users" (H.R. Rep. No. 105-551, 1998, at pt. 2, 58; S. Rep. No. 105-190, 1998, 48).

Obligation to Respond to Subpoenas under Section 512(h)

The institution is also obligated to respond to subpoenas it receives under section 512 for subscriber (faculty, staff, and students) identification. A copyright owner or his or her representative would desire such information so that he or she could name the person believed to be engaging in direct infringing conduct in a lawsuit. Since monetary remedy is foreclosed to copyright plaintiffs under section 512, from the institutional service provider, the only recoverable subject is the direct infringer (i.e., the faculty, staff, or student). Upon receipt of a subpoena meeting the statutory requirements (see 17 U.S.C. § 512 (h)(1)–(3)), the service provider must "expeditiously disclose to the copyright owner or person authorized by the copyright owner the information required by the subpoena" (17 U.S.C. § 512 (h)(5)). Universities that have tried to challenge attempts to obtain identifying student information have not met with success in the courts. (See, e.g., *Atlantic Recording Corp. v. Does 1–3*, 2005 [The Rochester Institute of Technology]; *Electra Entertainment Group, Inc. v. Does 1–9*, 2004 [New York University.])

Additional Benefits and Obligations in Higher Education

Additional safe harbor is provided for institutions of higher education. Section 512(e) allows institutions of higher education to treat faculty and graduate students as third parties in order for the general provisions of section 512 (monetary damage limitation) to be more widely applicable. (Recall, section 512 does not apply to the conduct of employees.) There are several conditions as well as obligations. First, it applies only to faculty or graduate student employees when "performing a teaching or research function." Concepts of academic freedom and the nature of the tertiary work environment suggest that the institution of higher education be held less accountable for the acts of its employees. Thus, a strict application of respondeat superior (vicarious liability) should not operate. For purposes of 512 (a) and (b) (transitory "store and forward" communication and system caching), the institution may refuge in the immunity of those subsections because section 512(e)(1) commands that the "faculty member or graduate student shall be considered to be a person other than the institution." As a result, an employee's infringing acts are not imputed to the employer (i.e., the institution). For purposes of 512 (c) and (d) (storage and information location tools), the knowledge or awareness of a post or link by a faculty member or graduate student is not imputed to the institution from that faculty member or graduate student. "[T]hat determination must be made on the basis of the knowledge or awareness of other employees of the institution, such as administrators and paid professional staff" (Dratler, 2004, § 6.06, at 6–142).

   In order for the imputation or attribution not to occur and the liability limitation to protect an institution of higher education, three conditions must exist. First, within the preceding three years the institution must not have more than two notices of infringement (according to the notice provisions of 512(c)(3)) by the faculty member or graduate student. Second, the institution must be engaged in a compliance program that "provides to all users of its system or network informational material that accurately describe, and promote compliance with the laws of the United States relating to copyright." Finally, the infringing activities must not "involve the provision of online access to instructional materials that are or were required or recommended, within the preceding 3-year period, for a course taught at the institution by the faculty member or graduate student" (17 U.S.C. § 512(e)(1)(A)–(C)). "The reference to 'providing online access' to instructional materials includes the use of e-mail for that purpose. The phrase 'required or recommended' is intended to refer to instructional materials that have been formally and specifically identified in a list of course materials that is provided to all students enrolled in the course for credit; it is not intended, however, to refer to the other materials which, from time to time, the faculty member or graduate student may incidentally and informally bring to the attention of students for their consideration during the course of instruction" (H.R. [Conference] Rep. No. 105-796, 1998, 74–75). In other words, the posting of infringing reading lists, e-reserves, or specifically created digital libraries in support of a particular course will not fulfill the condition with the result that the acts of the faculty member or graduate student employee would still be imputed to their employer under agency principles, and the institution would share liability as a contributory or vicarious infringer, subject to the general safe harbor rules of section 512(c) (posting).

As with all of the section 512 defenses, the limitation on liability for monetary relief is complete. In addition, 512(e) limits the types of injunctive relief available to plaintiffs under 512(j). However, the quid pro quo for this means that injunctive relief aimed at an infringing non-profit educational institution might go "beyond disabling access to particular material on a specified site . . . [and i]n a proper case, the nonprofit educational institution might even be subject to structural relief designed to correct a chronic or persistent tendency to infringe copyrights" (Dratler, 2004, § 6.06, at 6–146). An example would be a remedial order commanding the faculty to take a class involving instruction in copyright law taught by the resident campus expert.

REVISION OF SECTION 110(2):
PERFORMANCE AND DISPLAY RIGHTS

As amended by the Technology, Education and Copyright Harmonization [TEACH] Act (Pub. L. No. 107-273, 116 Stat. 1758, tit. III, subtitle C, sec. 13301), section 110(2) grants additional display and performance rights to qualifying educational institutions (i.e., those that are nonprofit and accredited). (See Lipinski, 2005, for a detailed study of the new provisions.) There is limit on the amount of material that can qualify for the section 110(2) performance and display right. (Recall that fair use is always available, as well as the secure of such rights by license or permission.) Revised section 110 improves, though continues, a bifurcated approach to teaching: face-to-face performances and displays governed by section 110(1) versus section 110(2), applying to distance education, or to use the phrasing of the copyright statute, teaching that is made "by or in the course of a transmission." The obvious practical complication that the amended law failed to address is a "hybrid" situation where some instruction occurs in the "live" classroom while remaining components are completed by students online, for example, through computing facilities and a Web site. As a result, copyrighted material may be subject to two different sets of rules within the same course. Moreover, it maybe that an "on-campus" class that uses Web-based delivery mechanisms is, in the eyes of the copyright law, a distance education course (i.e., "a transmission governed by the rules of section 110(2)).

With respect to the performance of nondramatic literary (text) or musical works (sheet music), there is no limitation on the portion of the copyrighted work that can be used. All other performances are limited to a reasonable and limited portion of the work. What is reasonable in a given circumstance depends on "both the nature of the market for that type of work and the pedagogical purposes of the performance" (H.R. [Conference] Rep. No. 107-685, 2002, 227). However, the use of the conditional "reasonable and *limited* portions" phrasing clearly imposes some restriction on the amount of the work falling into this category. The legislative history also makes clear that the amount is less than the entire work even though this might contradict the logic of a pedagogical purpose, for example, the statute does not authorize the performance in its entirety of an audiovisual aid that demonstrates a complex medical procedure. Any display of copyrighted material in the distance education environment is limited to "an amount comparable to that which is typically displayed in the course of a live classroom session" (17 U.S.C. § 110(2)).

Material Excluded from the Section 110(2) Performance and Display Right

Certain material is excluded from the performance and display rights of section 110(2). The opening clause of section 110(2) excludes a certain category of statutory defined curricular materials: "a work produced or marketed primarily for performance or display as part of mediated instructional activities [MIA] transmitted via digital networks." The legislative history explains that "[t]he exclusion is not intended to apply generally to all educational material or to all materials having educational value [but] limited to material whose primary market is the digital network environment, not instructional materials developed and marketed for use in the physical classroom" (H.R. [Conference] Rep. No. 107-685, 2002, 227). Why the exclusion of material designed explicitly for online instruction from a provision of the copyright law articulating the boundaries of educators' use of copyrighted material? One possibility is that Congress desired to create the requisite statutory breathing room for the nascent online instructional materials industry to develop. A second significant exclusion is for what might best be called instructional support material: "The amended exemption is not intended to address other uses of copyrighted works in the course of digital distance education, including student use of supplemental or research materials in digital form, such as electronic course-packs, e-reserves, and digital library resources. Such activities do not involve uses analogous to the performance and displays currently addressed in section 110(2)" (H.R. [Conference] Rep. No. 107-685, 2002, 229). The concept beyond the revised section 110(2) is to limit use of materials in actual online instruction, whether synchronous or asynchronous, pertinent to actual instruction, and not background or supporting material.

Finally, copyrighted material cannot be used if the "accredited nonprofit education institution knew or had reason to believe [that the material] was not [a] lawfully made and acquired" copy or phonorecord. Since "educational institutions" cannot actually know anything, as each is made up of the sum of its parts—its faculty, staff, and administrators—any knowledge on their part is imputed to the institution, creating a sort of institutional scienter for the purposes of section 110(2) eligibility.

Section 110(2)(C)(i) requires that "to the extent technologically feasible the reception of such transmission is limited to . . . students officially enrolled in the course for which the transmission is made." This is not an absolute test, but allows some technological leakage, as a result of a qualification on the reception limitation, the "to the extent technologically feasible" language. Use of password or other mechanisms appears contemplated.

Compliance Obligations Before Advantage
of the Right Can be Sought

Several compliance obligations are also incorporated into amended section 110(2); an initial set applies whether the transmission of the distance education session is analog or digital while a second set of obligations applies only in case of digital transmissions.

First, the statute requires that the "transmitting . . . institution institutes policies regarding copyright" (17 U.S.C. § 110(2)(D)(i)). The legislative history does not provide detail as to the contents of the policies but the statute uses the plural to suggest multiple policy statements or documents. It would be broader than the single "repeat infringer" policy requirement of section 512(i)(1)(A) discussed previously and does not relegate policies to those concerning distance education and copyright alone, but commands the institution of "policies regarding copyright" in general.

Second, and similar to section 512(e)(1)(C), but also in an expanded articulation, the institution must "provide[] informational materials to faculty, students, and relevant staff members that accurately describe and promote compliance with, the laws of the United States relating to copyright" (17 U.S.C. § 110(2)(D)(i)). The section 512(e) command only required that the "institution provides to all users of its system or network informational material that accurately describe, and promote compliance with the laws of the United States relating to copyright." Unlike section 512, under section 110(2) there is no limitation to "users of its system or network" alone, but the information must proceed to reach all "faculty, students, and relevant staff members" whether or not "connected" or whether or not involved in education, online or otherwise. Third, the institution must "provide[] notice to students that materials used in connection with *the course* may be subject to copyright protection (17 U.S.C. § 110(2)(D)(i)).

A second set of obligations apply to transmissions that are digital. First, under section 110(2)(D)(ii)(I)(aa), the educational institution must use technology to prevent "retention of the work in accessible form by recipients of the transmission from the transmitting body or institution for longer than the class session." While the legislative history suggests a flexible definition of "class session" designed to accommodate current notions of 24-7 distance education, it does not envision unlimited access to content throughout the semester or academic year: "It does not mean the duration of a particular course (i.e., a semester or term), but rather is intended to describe the equivalent of an actual face-to-face mediated class session" (H.R. [Conference] Rep. No. 105-796, 1998, 231). In addition, section 110(2)(D)(ii)(I)(bb) requires the use of technology to "reasonably prevent" the "unauthorized further dissemination of the work in accessible form by such recipients to others." The legislative history again softens the apparent harsh language of the statute: "the technological protection measure in subparagraph (2)(D)(ii) refers only to retention of a copy or phonorecord *in the computer of the recipient* of a transmission" (H.R. [Conference] Rep. No. 107-685, 2002, 231 [emphasis added]). Further, the "in accessible form" language contemplates the use of encrypted files for which accessibility beyond the class session can be controlled. This would suggest at least periodic monitoring to determine if the technological measures used by the institution are reasonably effective in accomplishing this control. "Examples of technological protection measures that exist today and would reasonably prevent retention and further dissemination, include measures used in connection with streaming to prevent the copying of streamed material, such as the Real Player 'Secret Handshake/Copy Switch' technology discussed in *Real Networks v. Streambox*, 2000 WL 127311 [(W.D. Wash. 2000)] or digital rights management systems that limit access to or use encrypted material downloaded onto a computer" (H.R. [Conference] Rep. No. 107-685, 2002, 232).

A final proviso related to the use of technological measures in digital distance education is found in section 110(2)(D)(II) and admonishes the institution not to "engage in conduct that could reasonably be expected to interfere with technological measures used by copyright owners to prevent such retention or unauthorized further dissemination." Unfortunately, there is no definition of the sorts of technological measures. The provision creates no new liability (in contrast to the prohibition against circumventing access control measures or trafficking in devices that can circumvent such access or use in section 1201). However, the prohibition operates to disqualify the educator from using section 110(2) in a broader set of circumstances, i.e., where conduct though not actually interfering with a technical measure can nonetheless be found to reasonably expect to interfere. Even if such interference never occurs, such conduct can disqualify the institution.

LIMITED RECORDING RIGHTS IN SECTION 112
FOR DISTANCE EDUCATION

As amended by TEACH, an additional provision relating to distance education was created in section 112(f). Distance educators might desire to record their teaching session (e.g., a video broadcast, a web-stream, etc.) for later review by students. That recording might also record not only the teacher's performance of the content (i.e., the lecture) but also the copyright content as well (e.g., pages from a text book, an illustration or a map, a video clip to which the instructor offers explanation, etc.). The recording then also reproduces copyrighted material of others. Since the reproduction of works in these circumstances (the by-product of what is assumed to be an otherwise authorized performance or display of those copyrighted works) is incidental to a legitimate use of the material, the reproduction is said to be ephemeral. The pre-TEACH law accommodated this in section 112(b), allowing a qualifying section 110(2) entity ("nonprofit education organization entitled to transmit a performance or display of a work, under section 110(2) or under the limitations on exclusive rights in sound recordings specified by section 114(a)") to make "no more than thirty copies or phonorecords of a particular transmission program embodying the performance or display," provided that (a) "no further copies or phonorecords are reproduced from the copies or phonorecords made under this clause (i.e., ephemeral recordings under section 112(b))," and (b) all copies or phonorecords are "destroyed within seven years from the date the transmission program was first transmitted to the public." The exception to this rule allowed the retention of one copy "preserved exclusively for archival purposes."

Today, there may be circumstances when an instructor desires to record content in anticipation of an online learning event. (Recall the enhanced definition of class session under amended section 110(2).) In other words, an instructor would like to record his or her lectures ahead of time, making the class session available to students 24-7. The lecture might also include copyrighted content, such as several pages from a text book, illustrations or maps, or a video clip (a "reasonable and limited portion") to which the instructor offers explanation. This, therefore, is a before-the-session reproduction of copyrighted material and the exclusive reproduction right of the copyright owner is implicated. Section 110 offers no assistance as that provision related to performance and display rights alone. Appeal to fair use in every case would be time-consuming or otherwise burdensome, so TEACH also created section 112(f).

Section 112(f) allows educators to make such ephemeral recording of copies of works that are already in digital form ("to make copies or phonorecords of a work that is in digital form") as well as to convert from analog to digital, subject to certain conditions. First, the ephemeral recording can be "retained and used solely by the institution" (no lending to another school district) and can be used only in teaching sessions "authorized under section 110(2)" (i.e., the material cannot also be used for e-reserve or for a face-to-face section 110(1) teaching session). Second, if conversion is sought (analog-to-digital), then additional requirements are imposed. The only portion that may be digitized is that which is authorized by the section 110(2) right discussed above (see previous discussion 6.0) and no more. Conversion can occur only when one of the following two conditions exist: either (a) "no digital version of the work is available" or (b) "the digital version of the work that is available to the institution is subject to technological protection measures that prevent its use for section 110(2)." Considering the market driven nature of the copyright law, "available" should be interpreted to mean available for purchase, rental, lease, and so forth.

CONCLUSION

This chapter has provided an overview of some the issues involved in the development and use of copyrighted material in Web-based distance education environments. The ever-changing nature of the legal landscape requires constant vigilance of the various issues. It is hoped that this chapter has provided the basis for a sound evaluation of those issues as new legal developments occur.

CASES

A&M Records, Inc. v. Napster, Inc., 239 F.3d 1004 (9th Cir. 2001).
Atlantic Recording Corp. v. Does 1–3, 371 F. Supp. 2d 377 (W.D. N.Y. 2005).
BMG Music v. Gonzalez, 430 F.3d 88 (7th Cir. 2005).
Columbia Pictures Television, Inc. v. Krypton Broadcasting of Birmingham, Inc., 259 F.3d 1186 (9th Cir. 2001), cert. denied, 534 U.S. 1127 (2002).
Columbia Pictures Industries v. Redd House, 749 F.2d 154 (3rd Cir. 1984).
Corbis Corp. v. Amazon.com, Inc., 351 F. Supp. 2d 1090 (W.D. Wash. 2004).
Demetriades v. Kaufmann, 690 F. Supp. 289 (S.D. N.Y. 1988).
Electra Entertainment Group, Inc. v. Does 1–9, 2004 WL 2095581 (S.D. N.Y. 2004).
Fonovisa, Inc. v. Cherry Auction, Inc., 76 F.3d 259 (9th Cir. 1996).
Foraste v. Brown University, 290 F. Supp. 2d 234 (D. R.I. 2003).
Hays v. Sony Corporation of America, 847 F.2d 412 (7th Cir, 1988).
Intellectual Reserve, Inc. v. Utah Lighthouse Ministry, Inc., 75 F. Supp. 2d 1290 (Dist. Utah 1999).
Manning v. Board of Trustees of Community College District No. 505 (Parkland College), 109 F. Supp. 2d 976 (C.D. Ill. 2000).
Marobie-F v. National Association of Firefighter Equipment Distributors, 983 F. Supp. 1167 (N.D. Ill. 1997).
Metro-Goldwyn-Mayer Studios Inc. v. Grokster, Ltd., 125 S.Ct. 2764 (2005).
Real Networks v. Streambox, 2000 WL 127311 [(W.D. Wash. 2000)].
Perfect 10, Inc. v. Cybernet Ventures, Inc., 213 F. Supp. 2d 1146 (C.D. Cal. 2002).
Pittsburg State University/Kansas National Education Association v. Kansas Board of Regents/Pittsburg State University, 122 P.3d 336 (Kan. 2005).
Shaul v. Cherry Valley-Springfield Central School District, 363 F.3d 177 (2d Cir. 2004).
Sony Corporation of America v. Universal Studios, Inc., 464 U.S. 417 (1984).
Southern Bell Telephone and Telegraph v. Associated Telephone Directory, 756 F.2d 801 (11th Cir. 1985).
UMG Recordings v. MP3, Inc., 92 F. Supp. 2d 349 (S.D. N.Y. 2000) (determining liability).
   UMG Recordings v. MP3, Inc., 2000 U.S. Dist. LEXIS 13293 (S.D. N.Y. 2000) (determining damages).
University of Colorado v. American Cyanamid, 880 F. Supp. 1387 (D. Colo. 1995).
Vanderhurst v. Colorado Mountain College District, 16 F. Supp. 2d 1297 (D. Colo. 1998).
Weinstein v. University of Illinois, 81 F.2d 1091 (7th Cir. 1987).
Williams v. Weisser, 273 Cal. App. 2d 726, 78 Cal. Rptr. 542 (1969).

REFERENCES

Dratler, J., Jr. (2004). *Cyberlaw: Intellectual property in the digital millennium.* St. Paul, MN: West Group.

Hazard, J. W., Jr. (2004). *Copyright law in business and practice.* St. Paul, MN: West Group.

Kulkarni, S. R. (1995). All professors create equally: why faculty should have complete control over the intellectual property rights in their creations. *Hastings Law Journal, 47,* 221–256.

Lape, L. G. (1992). Ownership of copyrightable works of university professors: the interplay between the copyright act and university copyright policies. *Villanova Law Review, 37,* 223–271.

Lipinski, T. A. (2003). Legal issues in the development and use of copyrighted material in Web-based distance education. In M. G. Moore and W. G. Anderson (Eds.), *Handbook of American distance education* (pp. 481–505). Hillsdale, NJ: Lawrence Erlbaum Associates.

Lipinski, T. A. (2005). *Copyright law and the distance education classroom.* Lanham, MD: Scarecrow Press, Inc.

Lipinski, T. A. (2006). *The complete copyright liability handbook for librarians and educators.* New York: Neal-Schuman Publishers, Inc.

Nimmer, M. B., & Nimmer, D. (2000). *Nimmer on copyright.* Albany, NY: Matthew Bender.

Patel, S. H. (1996). Graduate students' ownership and attribution rights in intellectual property. *Indiana University Indiana Law Journal, 71,* 481–512.

Simon, T. F. (1982–1983). Faculty writings: are they "works made for hire" under the 1976 copyright act? *Journal of College & University Law, 9,* 485–513.

LEGISLATIVE SOURCES

H.R. (Conference) Rep. No. 107-685 (2002).

H.R. (Conference) Rep. No. 105-796 (1998).

S. Rep. No. 105-190 (1998).

H.R. Rep. No. 105-551 Part 2 (1998).

Digital Millenium Copyright Act (DMCA), Pub. L. No. 105-304, 112 Stat. 2860 (1998).

Technology, Education and Copyright Harmonization Act [TEACH], Pub. L. No. 107-273, 116 Stat. 1758, Title III, Subtitle C, § 13301.

V

AUDIENCES AND PROVIDERS

36

Virtual and Distance Education in North American Schools

Tom Clark
TA Consulting

In the United States, education of students between the ages of 5 and 18 usually occurs in early elementary or primary schools, middle- or upper-elementary schools, and at the secondary level in high schools. Together these schools are referred to as K–12 schools. Over 53 million students were enrolled in public or private K–12 schools in the United States in 2004 (U.S. Department of Education, 2005a). Public and private education is primarily regulated at the state level, with each of the 50 states having its own system. The organization of K–12 education is similar in the 13 provinces and territories of Canada. However, Canada does not have a federal department of education. Passage of the No Child Left Behind (NCLB) Act in 2001 had a major impact on U.S. public education. NCLB imposes federal standards for academic outcomes, assistance to disadvantaged students, school improvement, and teacher quality. Under NCLB, public schools must show academic progress annually, including for underserved students. If they cannot, their district must fund alternative-schooling options for students after two years, called Educational Choice, and provide supplemental-educational services after three years.

FROM INDEPENDENT STUDY TO VIRTUAL LEARNING

Distance education for North American elementary and secondary students is an evolving phenomenon. Distance education courses and supplemental instruction for K–12 learners incorporate print, audio, video, multi-media, and online technologies. The primary purpose of K–12 distance education, expanding access to curriculum and providing educational choices, has changed little over time. In Chapter 13, Cavanaugh discusses research, policy, and practice in K–12 online learning. In the present chapter, the focus is on describing the evolution of K–12 distance education and providing an overview of research on other distance education methods.

Clark (2001) defined a virtual school as "an educational organization that offers K–12 courses through Internet- or Web-based methods" (p. 1). Virtual schooling is a form of distance education, or formal study, in which teacher and learners are separate in time or space. While online learning is currently in the spotlight, other distance education methods such as independent study and video conferencing continue to see significant use. The virtual-school movement of today is in many ways an outgrowth of the independent-study high-school movement that began in the 1920s. At least five independent-study high schools in the United States offer all essential courses in their online high-school-diploma program (Clark, 2001). The learning and support infrastructures of these program's online learning efforts build directly upon their long experience operating independent-study high-school programs.

Video-based distance education also has a long history. Iowa can claim both the first educational television broadcast in 1933 (Kurtz, 1959) and the most extensive network of two-way full-motion video rooms in North America—if not the world—the Iowa Communications Network, which served 781 sites in 2006 (www.icn.com). About 40% of K–12 unit schools, typically the smallest and most rural districts, reported use of satellite television in 1999 (Howley & Harmon, 2000). Video-based courses are still a major source of K–12 distance education opportunities today. The U.S. Department of Education (2005d) surveyed districts nationwide, finding video technologies were used as frequently as online technologies to deliver K–12 distance education.

Independent study at Nebraska.   The role of independent-study programs as the forerunner of virtual schools is nowhere more apparent than at the University of Nebraska-Lincoln. The university began a supervised correspondence study program in 1929. Its Independent Study High School won state accreditation for its diploma program in 1967 and regional accreditation through the North Central Association in 1978 (Young & McMahon, 1991). In spring 1996, the university was the first organization to obtain federal funding to build a virtual high school through its CLASS Project. The university used a $2.5 million proof of concept funding from the U.S. General Services Administration and a five-year, $17.5 million U.S. Department of Education Star Schools Program grant to develop custom software and build a complete Web-based high-school curriculum. In 1999, the university built on its experience in spinning off private companies from its research-and-development efforts to create Class.com, now an independent for-profit provider of virtual courses for K–12 learners. The university continues to offer a full print and online high-school curriculum via University of Nebraska High School today (http://nebraskahs.unl.edu).

Many years earlier, Nebraska's supervised correspondence study effort appears to have been the first federally funded K–12 distance education program. In 1932 Nebraska received a $5,000 grant from the Carnegie Foundation for curriculum enrichment in small high schools through its supervised study method (Broady, 1932). Pilot funding from Carnegie led to what was an enormous federal grant at the time for an educational program—$100,000 a year for 10 years from the federal Works Progress Administration (WPA) (Young & McMahon, 1991).

Supervised study model.   From the beginning, a key way high-school independent study differed from postsecondary study was in the use of supervision. The Nebraska plan for enriching the curriculum of small high schools through a supervised extension service has become the model for much of Nebraska's subsequent work in independent study. In supervised correspondence study, "the local high school secures the lessons, provides periods in the regular school day for study, supervises the pupils' work, and returns the lessons to the correspondence study center," which prepares and grades the lessons (Broady, Platt & Bell, 1931, p. 9).

This plan had its basis in an earlier experiment. Superintendent Sydney C. Mitchell devised the Benton Harbor Plan for supervised vocational correspondence study in 1923 (Mitchell, 1923). As evidenced by the title of his groundbreaking 1923 article, Mitchell conceived it as a method "For the Ninety Percent" who were at risk of not finishing high school. He saw expanding vocational curricula during the school day as a way of reaching these at-risk learners. The plan required local adult supervision throughout the course of study and other support structures intended to help guarantee high completion and retention rates. From 1923 to 1930, over 100 U.S. high schools started supervised correspondence study programs (Harding, 1944). Prior to 1929, Mitchell's Benton Harbor Plan and most other high-school programs relied primarily on vocational programs from for-profit proprietary correspondence study firms. These proprietary schools had introduced independent study for secondary-level diplomas early in the century (Edelson and Pittman, 2001). In 1929, the University of Nebraska became the first university to offer supervised high-school correspondence study, using a mix of vocational and academic courses from its university correspondence-study department.

Independent study programs.   Independent study is the term commonly used by universities since the 1960s to describe their style of correspondence study. The University Continuing Education Association (UCEA), founded in 1915 as the National University Extension Association (NUEA), represents mainly colleges and universities with outreach functions including independent study for K–12, college, and noncredit audiences. As of 2001, the sole member institution offering high school but not college courses by independent study was the North Dakota Division of Independent study, part of the state department of education. Six other states had non-university-based K–12 independent-study divisions. Most UCEA member institutions also belong to the American Association for Collegiate Independent Study (AACIS). Vocational institutions use the term *home study* to describe their type of independent study (Moore & Kearsley, 1996). The Distance Education and Training Council (DETC), formerly the Home Study Council, acts mainly as a clearinghouse and accrediting body for distance education providers. Eight of the 12 private high-school programs accredited by DETC in 2006 offered full diploma programs (www.detc.org).

Some colleges and universities began K–12 distance-learning efforts outside their independent-study units. The Education Program for Gifted Youth at Stanford University is a research unit that offers advanced computer-based and online coursework for gifted and talented students. Many higher-education institutions participate in satellite-based or two-way video networks to deliver dual or concurrent enrollment courses, discussed in a later section.

There has been limited experimentation with elementary-level correspondence study through the years. Montana's department of education used it during the World War II gasoline shortage (Haight, 1944). Many independent-study high-school programs grant limited admission to their programs for junior-high students. Independent study has continued to make quiet contributions to K–12 distance learning. The Portable Assisted Study Sequence (PASS) Program is a good example. Begun in 1978 by Parlier High School in California, PASS used competency-based credits and portable learning (independent study) packets to help migrant students complete high school. By the mid–1980s, PASS had been adopted in 13 states, enrolling over 4,000 students in nearly 7,000 courses and allowing them to earn over 1,000 semester credits, with 806 achieving high-school graduation (Morse, Haro & Herron, 1986). The workbook-based PASS is still a component of many migrant-education programs across the nation.

ESTIMATING THE SCOPE OF K–12 DISTANCE EDUCATION

Based on a survey of a stratified random sample of districts nationwide, the U.S. Department of Education (2005) estimated 328,000 enrollments in electronic distance-education courses through U.S. public schools in 2002–2003. About one-third of all school districts sampled reported enrollments. An estimated 68% of enrollments reported were at the high-school level, and about 14% were in Advanced Placement or college-level courses. Online and video-based enrollments were not counted separately, and the study was limited to students enrolled via public schools. However, it helps demonstrate the extent of electronic distance education taking place in K–12 schools.

Non-electronic distance education was until recently the mainstay of independent study, which has been tracked for many years. Figure 36.1 shows the growth of U. S. K–12 independent study over 70 years. The NUEA began tracking academic high-school study by correspondence in its member institutions in 1929. Bittner and Mallory (1933) bemoan the "difficulty of securing uniformity in methods of counting students and enrollments" (p. 270). The first numbers graphed in Figure 36.1 are for 1934–1935, when 75% of enrollments were at the University of Nebraska-Lincoln. The steady growth of supervised correspondence study continued during World War II, when a teacher shortage and early enlistment spurred a jump in high-school enrollments. The U.S. Armed Forces Institute (USAFI), affiliated with the University of Wisconsin, acted as a broker for high-school completion and other independent-study educational opportunities for soldiers from 1942 through 1974 (Gooch, 1998). After the war, high-school enrollments in NUEA institutions dropped until the mid-1950s, when they resumed a steady upward trend. The NUEA continued to track enrollments, as it became the National University Continuing Education Association (NUCEA) in the 1960s, then the UCEA in the 1990s. After slower growth in the 1970s, enrollments increased 40% in the 1980s (NUCEA, 1991) then flattened out in the 1990s, when a majority of programs were seeing high-school enrollment declines offset by enrollment increases in the largest programs. Some universities phased out or downsized their high-school programs. The American Association for Collegiate Independent Study (AACIS) continued the documentation of K–12 independent study enrollments in 2000–2001. Enrollments rebounded to an all-time high of 175,000 in 2004–2005 (D. Gearhart, personal communication, March 31, 2006). About 45% of enrollments were online, double the percentage four years earlier. A majority of independent-study programs expected online enrollments to exceed print enrollments by 2009–2010 (University Continuing Education Association, 2002).

Clearly online learning is a growing part of the K–12 distance education mix. There were about 300,000 K–12 online-learning enrollments in public and private schools in 2002–2003 (Newman, Stein, & Trask, 2003), up from an estimated 40–50,000 in 2000–2001 (Clark, 2001).

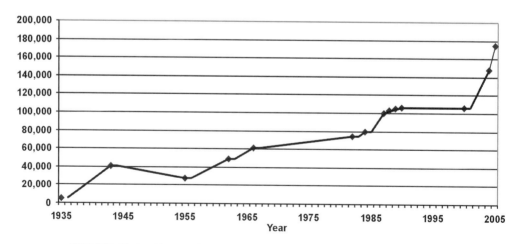

FIGURE 36.1. K–12 Independent Study Course Enrollments, 1935–2005.

K–12 is an emerging market for online learning, while higher education is a maturing one. In fall 2003, about 81% of colleges and universities offered online courses, one in three offered degree programs online, and over 1.6 million students enrolled in an online course. By fall 2005, nearly 2 million college students were taking a course online (Allen & Seaman, 2005).

EMERGENCE OF THE VIRTUAL SCHOOL

The emergence of virtual schools for K–12 learners in the late 1990s represents the latest in an ever-accelerating series of technological advances in the field of K–12 distance education. Clark (2001) identified and surveyed a "peer group" of 44 regionally accredited or state approved U.S. K–12 schools that offered Web-based instruction in 2000–2001, achieving a 73% response rate. Here a virtual school was defined as a regionally accredited or state-approved school offering one or more Web or Internet-based K–12 courses. Identifying the total universe of virtual schools is complicated by the fact that many schools offer a course or two through a consortium or from an external provider, granting credit locally. For example, the VHS consortium reported over 5,000 enrollments in 154 online courses at 207 schools in 2003–2004, with many participating schools contributing an online course (Virtual High School, 2004).

Virtual high schools have given way to virtual schools, as online learning expanded to include elementary as well as secondary education. Of the schools responding to the Clark's 2001 survey, all reported offering high-school courses online in 2000–2001, and a surprising 51% said they offered middle-school courses as well. A majority developed at least some of their own courses. Providers such as Connections Academy and K12, Inc. have emerged to provide online learning focuses on the elementary grades.

Virtual K–12 schools may be classified in many ways (Clark, 2001). As seen in the previous section, they may be part of or an outgrowth of independent-study high-school programs at universities. Some are sponsored or sanctioned as statewide by state entities, while others are virtual charter schools with a statewide reach. Numerous local and regional-education agencies have developed online schools, mainly to supplement local course options. Private for-profit and nonprofit schools have developed online courses and programs to serve academic and vocational curricula. Virtual schools developed by public and private consortia and nonprofit organizations have also had a national impact. Course, content, and platform providers, many of them for-profit corporations, also play a critical role in virtual school development.

Some authors made prescient statements about virtual schools during the "pre-Web" era. In December 1987, Morten Paulsen, a Norwegian distance education expert, penned an article titled, "In Search of a Virtual School." Referring to both K–12 and postsecondary education, Paulsen asserted, "the virtual school will dominate future distance education. It is possible to create a virtual school around a computer-based information system . . . at present, computer conferencing is the only technology that can serve as a basis for creating a 'virtual school' (pp. 71–73)." Paulsen believed that in contrast to previous distance learning systems, computer-conferencing systems had the capability to handle the professional, didactic, administrative, and social tasks necessary to run a virtual school. Other authors expressed similar ideas, but the technology was not ready.

In the 1980s and 1990s, many schools used computer-based or computer-aided instruction methods for supplemental drill and practice and individualized instruction. Computer conferencing emerged, in which computer users could exchange information by e-mail or interact in real time. During the 1990s, the main focus in U.S. K–12 schools was getting on the Internet. Berge and Collins (1998) compiled descriptions from the field of the supplemental use of Internet technologies in a wide variety of K–12 "online classroom" contexts. They characterized these K–12 activities as a form of computer-mediated communication (CMC). Computer networking at the school building, district, regional, and statewide level has been used to integrate technology into the curriculum, perform administrative tasks, and provide online resources and supplemental distance learning activities for students and teachers since the late 1980s (Eisenberg, 1992). Multi-media tools emerged in the 1980s and 1990s that could be used to create interactive, engaging content and instructional methods in computer-based environments. All of these technologies and approaches helped set the stage for the virtual-school movement.

By 1994, there were already several virtual-school experiments underway. Many of the early virtual schools combined Internet tools such as e-mail, chat, and FTP with computer-aided instruction techniques to deliver mainly text-based online instruction. The Utah Electronic High School began in 1994 as a broker for a blend of technology-delivered high-school courses from in-state and out-of-state providers. It was housed in the state department of education, an approach subsequently used by many statewide virtual schools.

Federal and state funding has played a major role in the growth of the virtual-school movement. The University of Nebraska-Lincoln CLASS Project was federally funded in 1996, as was the Hawaii e-School later that year, and Concord Consortium's Virtual High School in 1997. The Utah Department of Education began its Electronic High School as an internal initiative in 1994, while the Florida Virtual School began in 1997 as a cooperative effort between two Florida school districts funded through a state grant. A second wave of virtual schools began appearing in 2000. Just as the Western Governors University jump-started interest in virtual universities, these high-profile projects helped raise similar interest in virtual schools.

State-level virtual schools.   By 2005, at least 18 U. S. states had virtual schools in operation that were officially recognized by the governor, legislature, or state education agency as the statewide virtual school (Clark, 2002; Watson, 2005; see Table 36.1), an increase of four states since 2002. Florida and Michigan have a freestanding statewide virtual school funded through a legislative line item, but other statewide schools typically are operated by the state education agency or by a consortium that includes this agency. Some, such as Wisconsin Virtual School, are operated as a statewide program by a regional education agency with state recognition. The New Mexico Virtual School ceased operations during this period. Several other online initiatives are not state-recognized as the statewide virtual school, but provide learning services statewide. Most notable of these are the University of California College Prep initiative, begun in 1999, and online Advanced Placement schools in Iowa, Kentucky, and Virginia.

TABLE 36.1.
State-Sanctioned State-Level Virtual Schools: Operating Agency and Year Founded

Free-Standing School	Operated by a Consortium, State Education Agency a Partner	Primarily Operated by a Unit within State Education Agency	
Florida (1997)	Arkansas (2000)	Utah (1994)	Wisconsin (2000)
Michigan (2000)	Alabama (2000)	Hawaii (1996)	Mississippi (2002)
	Illinois (2001)	Kentucky (2000)	Idaho (2002)
	Oklahoma (2002)	Louisiana (2000)	Maryland (2003)
	Colorado (2003)	North Dakota (2000)	Iowa (2004)
		West Virginia (2000)	

Virtual charter schools.   In 2004–2005, there were about 31,000 students enrolled in 86 virtual charter schools in 16 states (Center for Education Reform, 2005). Virtual charter schools, also called cyber-charters, are one type of charter school, a tuition-free public school operated independently by a state-approved entity. The costs of attending are usually paid by the district in which a student resides, directly or via reduced student aid. Most virtual charter schools are operated by or through local or regional education agencies, such as the Basehor-Linwood Virtual Charter School, established by a Kansas public school district in 1997. Some states allow operation by non-profits, such as eCOT, the Electronic Classroom of Tomorrow, Ohio's largest charter school, with about 6,000 enrollments. For-profit entities, such as K12, Inc. and Connections Academy, often provide educational services on behalf of the charter entity. Virtual charter schools may be better known to the American public than supplemental programs, but they probably enroll one-tenth as many students. Based upon available figures, virtual charter schools enroll about 3% of charter-school students (Center for Education Reform, 2005), and a similar percentage of home-schoolers (U.S. Department of Education, 2004).

Local school programs.   Many local education agencies use online learning programs to provide alternative or supplemental education for in-district students and to reach out to home-schoolers in their states, without seeking charter-school designation. Cumberland County Schools in North Carolina mainly serves students from other districts through its Web Academy, while Houston ISD in Texas provides a full middle-school curriculum in addition to high-school courses. Some offer online summer school courses for the district's students, such as FCPS Online in Fairfax County, Virginia. Nevada's Clark County School District started its Virtual High School in 1998 as a district initiative, but the large majority of the state's K–12 learners reside in its service area.

Virtual private schools.   A wide range of private K–12 schools have also entered the virtual education market. Virtual private schools serve home-schoolers, but also act as online learning providers to public schools. A growing number have achieved regional or transregional accreditation within the last few years. Doing so helps them establish the equivalency of their diplomas for students seeking employment or university admission. Accredited virtual private schools include the Keystone Virtual High School, part of Keystone National High School, one of the oldest proprietary high schools in the nation, AMDG, which offers middle- and high-school curricula and workforce preparation courses, and the non-profit Christa McAuliffe Academy, which emphasizes individualized instruction via courseware delivered over the Internet, with personal mentoring and weekly cohort classes online. Another accredited provider is the University of Miami Online High School, which has continued the online private Sagemont Virtual School, while adding a separate credit-recovery program for public school entities.

Virtual learning consortia.   Consortia are also playing an important role in the growth of virtual schooling. The best known of these is the Virtual High School (VHS, Inc.), founded in 1997 by the Hudson (Massachusetts) Public Schools and the Concord Consortium. The nonprofit VHS, Inc.® is a unique cooperative in whose basic model schools contribute a "netcourse" and trained staff and in return received 20 student enrollments in courses offered by consortium member schools. Based on the success of the VHS model, other virtual schools such as the Colorado Online School Consortium have adopted similar approaches. Many consortia are extending existing "P–16" dual-credit partnerships with online courses. Consortia of state governments, such as AP Nexus, seek to expand access to Advanced Placement (AP) online courses in member states.

e-Learning service providers.   Course, content, and platform providers, many of them for-profits, also play a critical role in the growth of the virtual-school movement. Many virtual schools today are basically "portals" that obtain their Web-based courses from vendors or other virtual schools, but a majority use external provider software and delivery platforms to develop their own courses, or codevelop courses with external providers or other schools. Course providers such as the for-profits Class.com and Apex Learning and the nonprofit Florida Virtual School have become builders and operators of virtual schools, working with local districts. Some for-profit providers of course development and delivery platforms have added a focus on K–12 to their primary focus on postsecondary education markets.

VIRTUAL SCHOOLING IN CANADA

Canada, like the United States, has considerable virtual schooling underway. Given a relatively open border and shared language and educational traditions, this is probably not surprising. Examples of well-established virtual schools operated by public-school districts include Durham Virtual School in Ontario and Fraser Valley Distance Education School in British Columbia. Virtual schools may act as home-school providers under supervision of a public or private-school board in Alberta. Examples include School of Hope, a Catholic online school, and Rocky View Virtual School, operated by a public-school district. These home-based schools appear to play a role similar to cyber-charter schools in the United States. Other nations with a history of K–12 distance education, such as Australia and England, have a limited number of online learning programs at the elementary and secondary levels. For example, A School Without Walls, or ASW2, opened in London in 2003, offers 6 Level A subjects and 6 International Baccalaureate subjects online on a supplemental basis for students enrolled in other schools, and the Virtual School for the Gifted, founded in Melbourne in 1997, provides online-enrichment courses.

The high levels of access and use of networked computers on the Internet in the United States and Canada are often given as an explanation for the growth in virtual schooling in these nations. Canada's SchoolNet (www.schoolnet.ca) was the first network to connect public schools and libraries to the Internet across an entire nation, in 1999. In addition to the high penetration of the Internet in U.S. schools, 35 states in the U.S. have joined the Internet 2 K–20 initiative established to share high-bandwidth educational projects (www.internet2.edu). However, information and communication technology (ICT) is part of the compulsory minimum curriculum of pupils in Europe, where almost two-thirds of 15-year-olds reported using computers regularly in school in 2000 (Eurydice, 2004). This raises the question, why is virtual schooling largely a North-American phenomenon? Some factors in the growth of K–12 distance and virtual learning are presented in a later section.

AUDIO-BASED K–12 DISTANCE EDUCATION

The first major electronic media used in distance education, educational radio, saw limited use in U.S. K–12 education, especially in the 1920s and 1930s. It was used mainly for supplemental instruction. Gordon (1931) conducted music instruction by radio for Wisconsin schools and in 1930 conducted a simple comparative study of 25 music classes receiving instruction by radio versus an equal number studying conventionally, with the same materials. Barresi (1987) notes that while the study would not withstand "the rigorous scrutiny of today's researchers" (p. 266), it gave Gordon the opportunity to test K–12 instructional materials designed for radio. Radio still has many supplemental uses in U.S. K–12 education, mainly as an object of study rather than an instructional-delivery method (Ninno, 2000). Educational telephone has also had limited applications in K–12 education. Statewide educational telephone networks such as Wisconsin's ETN began to appear in the late 1970s, serving mainly continuing- and community-education purposes. Some universities experimented with audio-conferencing, supplemented by video tape or other media, for K–12 instruction. Schmidt, Sullivan, and Hardy (1994) report the use of audio conferencing by the UT Telelearning Center to successfully teach an Algebra I course for remedial purposes to migrant students at a growing number of sites. The audio conferencing portion of the Learn Alaska Network was its only successful component, provided programming for K–12 and other audiences in remote areas (Bramble, 1988). Audio conferencing and computer conferencing led into a variety of low-bandwidth networking technologies in the 1980s, such as freeze-frame video, audio graphics, and Videotex (Hudson & Boyd, 1984). For example, the Northeastern Utah Telelearning Project used audio graphics to deliver high-school courses among five rural high schools (Miller, 1989). Contact North built an audio conferencing network in Northern Ontario, with a focus on providing college-preparatory courses (McGreal & Simand, 1992). Audio conferencing was used as a key component in later technologies with widespread applications in K–12 education, such as satellite and network-based video conferencing.

VIDEO-BASED K–12 DISTANCE EDUCATION

A variety of video-based media have been used for distance education in schools. Through its Sixth Report and Order in 1952, the Federal Communications Commission reserved television channels for educational use, facilitating the creation of a national network of educational stations. Later rulings reserved space for education on cable television and direct-to-home satellite systems. The Communications Act of 1934, establishing the FCC, did not reserve educational frequencies for radio.

K–12 educational television programming began in 1933 at the University of Iowa over Experimental Visual Broadcasting Station W9XK, with supplemental 15-minute evening broadcasts to groups of children, such as Boy Scouts seeking to meet merit-badge requirements. About 389 such telecasts were broadcast between 1932 and 1939 (Kurtz, 1959). This early tradition of out-of-school educational broadcasting for children was continued through popular programs such as *Sesame Street* and *3–2–1 Contact* on Public Broadcasting Service stations beginning in the 1970s. Supplemental in-school experiences have also been a major focus. In 1998, about 80% of U.S. public television stations provided educational services to elementary or secondary schools (Corporation for Pubic Broadcasting, 1999). In general, the use of educational broadcast television in the United States for full courses designed for K–12 learners has been rare. In Canada, provincial networks have provided both supplemental broadcasting and full courses for K–12 learners. Kuplowska (1987) evaluates four K–12 courses offered by TVOntario.

Satellite video conferencing.   Satellite video conferencing also emerged in the mid–1980s, as a method of providing high-quality video-based instruction without the use of terrestrial transmitters. It represented an evolution from airplane-based transmitters, such as the Midwest Program on Airborne Television Instruction, launched in 1961 by Purdue University to provide supplemental telecasts to K–12 learners in six Midwestern states (Smith, 1961). Ten years after the first satellite was placed in a stationary geosynchronous orbit around the earth, the Applications Technology Satellite F (ATS-F) series was used in 1973 to telecast pilot programs for K–12 educators (Grayson, Norwood, & Wigren, 1973). In 1985, the first national satellite network created to serve K–12 education was founded. The TI-IN Network was privately oper-ated and delivered courses and staff-development programming developed at Education Ser-vice Center 20 in San Antonio, Texas. By 1986, it had 150 receive sites in 12 states and offered 18 high-school courses and staff-development opportunities (Pease & Tinsley, 1986). Similar networks operated by universities, state-education agencies and consortia were developed to serve national and state-level audiences. In 1988, these educational satellite networks began to receive federal funding to support their programming through the U.S. Department of Educa-tion's Star Schools Program, which may be considered the first modern-day federal funding for K–12 distance education (Kirby, 1998). Small and rural school districts have shown the great-est continuing interest in these curriculum-expanding opportunities, as evidenced by figures pre-sented previously.

The emergence in 1989 of the for-profit Channel One led to controversy similar to that over virtual charter schools today. A commercial satellite provider that offers a video news magazine for grades 6–12 via dedicated satellite receivers in schools, Channel One interlaced advertising with content. However, studies did appear to indicate positive impact, as detailed later in this chapter. In the late 1990s, as satellite direct-to-home commercial TV systems emerged to compete with cable TV systems for television viewers, they forged partnerships similar to Cable in the Classroom, an initiative begun by the cable TV industry in 1989. These partnerships allow com-mercial cable and satellite providers to fulfill FCC requirements through public-interest pro-gramming channels and free access to copyright-cleared content for schools. Some satellite edu-cation networks are providing programming for these new satellite-based public-interest channels offered by commercial providers. New technologies allow the use of satellite networks as Inter-net backbones, linking directly into school networks and allowing applications such as high-quality video streaming and video on demand. Doubtless new K–12 applications will emerge from these innovative uses of a "mature" technology.

From 1987 through 1999, Hezel Associates annually documented distance learning activities in all 50 states. Their last report (Hezel Associates, 1998) is probably the best overall descriptive source on networking activity at all educational levels, including terrestrial and satellite networks. Beginning in the 1980s, terrestrial video-conferencing networks were established with a succes-sion of technologies. Closed-circuit educational telecommunications networks using compressed or full-motion video-conferencing systems for two-way video, two-way audio emerged in the early 1990s and began replacing systems based on microwave closed-circuit telecasts and Instruc-tional Television-Fixed Service microwave broadcasts. Hundreds of small video-conferencing networks appeared at the K–12 level, linking schools at the district, regional, and state level, and consortia of all levels of educational institutions. These networks are used for distance educa-tion and supplemental learning, in-service training, and meetings (Bosak, 2000). Planning for statewide networks can be traced at least to the mid–1970s. Most statewide networking efforts have involved separate or bundled services for voice, video, and data and include computer net-works linking K–12 schools.

Early educational networks, such as the Education Network of Maine in 1989, combined two-way video via microwave with microwave broadcasts (ITFS) or compressed video to outly-ing sites. The Utah Education Network, serving both K–12 and higher education, came online in 1991 using a microwave backbone and compressed video to other sites. Oregon's EDNET, begun in 1989, consisted of satellite, compressed video, and computer networks. Later networks used fiber-optic technologies. The Iowa Communications Network is the most extensive and unique example. This state-owned and financed network connects hundreds of full-motion video class-rooms in K–12 schools and other mainly nonprofit facilities, and also provides data and telephony services. Sites must use compatible equipment and follow a central-network design. Costs of network use are subsidized. Similar statewide networks were built in the mid–1990s, usually with private financing and ownership by the regional telephone company, such as the Maryland Information Highway and the North Carolina Information Highway. The Georgia Statewide Academic and Medical System was financed in 1992 through legislation applying overcharges by the regional telephone company to network construction. Later regional and statewide networks, such as the Illinois Century Network, have been overlays of existing regional or local videoconferencing networks.

There has been declining interest in adding new capacity to educational networks in recent years. Subsidies for local schools are decreasing and transmission costs increasing. Many satellite education networks have transitioned to online. For example, Oklahoma State University's Advanced Placement Physics by Satellite left the air in 1997 due to rising costs (Oklahoma State University, 2001), as did the United Star Distance Learning Consortium five years later (Clark, 2004). Both continue to offer K–12 courses and staff development online.

DISTANCE AND VIRTUAL PROFESSIONAL DEVELOPMENT FOR K–12 EDUCATORS

In addition to providing direct K–12 instruction, distance learning systems from independent study to the Internet have played an important role in the provision of professional-development programming for K–12 educators (Schmidt & Faulkner, 1989). Schrum (1992) provides one of the earliest references to online professional development, describing an early Internet-based professional-development course designed to introduce teachers to technology and distance learning methods. Distance learning for preservice teacher education and in-service professional development has a long history in the United States. The first teachers or normal college to offer correspondence study for teachers appears to have been Western State Normal School (later Western Michigan University) in Kalamazoo, Michigan, beginning in 1905 (Bittner & Mallory, 1933). Maul (1929, in Perlham, 1936) identified 59 of 157 teacher's colleges and normal schools responding to a 1928 survey as offering college courses by correspondence. Today hundreds of postsecondary institutions offer courses via distance learning for K–12 educators, and some offer online-degree programs in education. These courses and programs are applicable toward initial and special certification, recertification, administrative certifications, and advanced degrees in education or teaching content areas. The use of video-taped or live broadcasts of "best practice" classrooms to instruct preservice educators in teaching techniques (for example, Merkley & Hoy, 1985) is an example of the supplemental use of distance education methods in preservice educator training. Today virtual classroom observations are more likely to occur via streaming video to the desktop.

K–12 educators must hold appropriate licensure to teach in a state's schools, within a grade range or content area. Many states are creating new competency-based certification requirements as part of education reform to replace approaches that merely require the accumulation of university credits. In addition, many local districts have policies for tying increased pay to advanced degrees or certificates. Shortages of certified teachers and more recently the Highly Qualified Teachers provisions of No Child Left Behind have led to a focus on online-learning programs for the alternative certification for educators. At least 32 alternative teacher-certification programs were available via online learning or a blend of online and conventional methods in 2005 (DANTES, 2006). One of the first was CalStateTeach, originally developed by California State University to provide online courses for alternative certification of K–8 teachers with emergency credentials (Shaker, 2000).

Online learning has emerged as an important strategy for meeting the Highly Qualified Teachers (HQT) provisions of No Child Left Behind, not only through alternate teacher-certification programs, but through online teaching by highly qualified teachers. Some initiatives combine online teaching and local-capacity building. Through the Louisiana Algebra 1 Online Program, a teacher certified in high-school mathematics teaches online, while a local teacher working toward the same certification acts as a mentor to the local students (Kleiman, 2005). The Educational Technology Cooperative provides resources for online professional development in southeastern U.S. states, including provider links and standards that build upon National Staff Development Council guidelines (Southern Regional Education Board, 2006).

Online staff development can compliment data-driven assessment and support teachers in their individualized professional-development portfolios. For online professional-development providers to be successful they must build on existing staff-development activities and networks, with a focus on improving teaching and learning, not on the technology (Killion, 2000). External providers supplement the efforts of staff-development infrastructures within local and regional education agencies. Regional universities are the traditional providers of college-credit courses applicable to re-certification, but distance and virtual learning allows access to new providers.

FACTORS IN THE CURRENT STATE OF K–12 DISTANCE AND VIRTUAL LEARNING

Some of the factors affecting the current state of K–12 virtual and distance education include demographic factors, attitudes in society and schools, education market forces, access and equity issues, and federal and state support and policies.

Demographic factors.   As noted earlier, participation in K–12 distance education courses delivered by satellite appear highest in rural and small schools. Over half of the schools participating in the Virtual High School collaborative in 1999 had enrollments under 800 students (U.S. Department of Education, 2000a). K–12 student populations have continued to grow in many states, taxing conventional school facilities and resources. However, it is not clear that distance learning has been an important factor in directly addressing shortages of educational facilities in these states. Conventional K–12 schools play an important role by supervising children as their parents work, a role that virtual schools cannot play. Most students in Web-based and video-based courses offered by state-approved or regionally accredited schools appear to be taking their courses as part of regular instruction within a public school (Clark, 2001). Instead of replacing conventional schools, virtual schools have expanded curricular options and extended teaching resources for students in those schools, while also expanding options for home-schooled or special-needs students.

Attitudes in society and schools.   The attitudes of parents and community members play an important role in determining K–12 student participation in distance and virtual learning. As Iowa developed its statewide education network in the mid–1990s, an important goal was to obtain community support through public relations efforts and a focus on network use in K–12 education (Sorensen & Sweeney, 1994). These efforts may help explain the continuing financial support of Iowans in building what became the largest statewide video-conferencing network. A national Phi Delta Kappa poll of 1,108 adults in (Rose & Gallup, 2001) showed that 30% of respondents approved allowing students to earn high-school credits over the Internet without attending a regular school, compared with 41% who approved of home-schooling. The authors felt that this showed that the public "is less willing to embrace cyberspace instruction" than home-schooling (p. 42). However, those surveyed were not asked about students earning credits over the Internet while attending a regular school, which appears to be a more common arrangement in practice. Schools are responsive to local public demands for education reforms like integrating the latest technology into education, but slow to institutionalize such changes. Only reforms with deep-rooted constituencies tend to persist. Cuban (1998) has long noted the limited and unimaginative use of available technology by classroom teachers. Teachers are mainly concerned with using instructional methods they see as practical and effective within traditional school structures. These structures often work against interdisciplinary, distributed uses of technology and provide limited technology support for teachers.

Education market forces.   As described earlier in this chapter, many for-profit vendors are participating in the development of virtual schools. For these for-profit companies, distance and virtual learning is part of a multibillion-dollar education market in which the interests of venture capitalists and shareholders must be weighed along with those of students, parents, and local communities. A significant portion of the technology investments in schools has come through in-kind donations from technology vendors. These for-profit organizations work closely with state and local education agencies and play a role in public policy-making and planning.

Access and equity issues.   Access to distance education and educational technology has been seen by states and the federal government as a way in which schools can address important equity issues. Coupled with issues of curriculum equity and equitable support structures for distance learners, these inequities in technology access and use have serious implications for those seeking to provide equal access to virtual schooling via the Internet.

Support for technology infrastructure building at the local, regional, and state levels is one way policy-makers have sought to equalize educational opportunities. By 2003, 99% of U.S. public schools had access to the Internet, and over 9 in 10 instructional rooms were connected. Classroom connectivity in high-poverty schools rose from 60% in 2000 to 90% in 2003, close to the national average of 93% (U.S. Department of Education, 2005c). This rapid rise can be attributed in part to the Education rate (E-rate) program, a federal program to develop Internet infrastructure in schools and libraries. Since 1998, it has funded $13 billion in connectivity services for E-rate applicants.

However, poor children, minority students, girls, low achievers, students learning to speak English, children with disabilities, and youngsters who live in rural or central city areas may not benefit equally from computer access (*Education Week*, 2001). Support structures for K–12 distance learners in multiple-site courses can also vary considerably in rural or high-need schools. For example, Moore, Burton, and Dodl (1991) found considerable variability in local standards and qualifications for satellite education facilitators in a statewide project. Some researchers have studied technology access for special populations, such as the compliance of distance learning systems with the Americans with Disabilities Act (Meyen, Lian & Tangen, 1998) and barriers to technology access for K–12 learners with disabilities (U.S. Department of Education, 2000b). White (2004) found that ill, home-bound children were as likely to participate actively with their classmates in a Canadian school when participating in class via two-way video with robotic assistance or using desktop video-conferencing software.

Curriculum equity has become a rallying point for those seeking to redress historical inequities in education (Hill, 2000). The virtual school movement has been fueled in part by a lawsuit against the state of California over access to Advanced Placement high-school courses that can increase college opportunities for K–12 learners. A number of state departments of education have used a portion of their federal AP funding to purchase services from virtual school AP providers and incorporated these AP courses into their statewide virtual schools in part to address curriculum equity issues. Tushnet and Fleming-McCormick (1995) reported on an evaluation of projects funded through the Star Schools Program that found participating rural schools more likely to achieve equity objectives through satellite-based distance learning than high-minority and low-income urban schools. Urban high-need schools face challenges in making effective use of distance education. The TEAMS project of the Los Angeles County Office of Education, funded through the federal Star Schools Program, is frequently cited as an example of supplemental distance learning successful with urban K–12 learners (Majdalany & Guiney, 1999).

Another curriculum equity issue is the use of distance learning in academic tracking. In a 1984 survey, only 25% of school counselors at small high schools in Texas reported recommending correspondence study to students needing additional credits, and most correspondence students they referred were D and F students (Barker & Petersen, 1984). On the other hand, a later survey of principals at small Texas schools showed that 80% limited enrollment in satellite video-conferencing courses to A and B students (Barker, 1987). However, vocationally oriented high-school correspondence study has been shown to reduce dropout rates and increase GED completion for school leavers (Bucks County Public Schools, 1972). In the 1980s, computer-based drill and practice became a common tool in working with at-risk learners, and Internet-based alternative schools have emerged as a strand in the virtual school movement.

Federal and state support and policies.   The National Education Technology Plan (U.S. Department of Education, 2005b) encourages states and education agencies to "support e-Learning and virtual schools" as a strategy for meeting No Child Left Behind and other goals. In Chapter 13, Cavanaugh summarizes the findings of policy studies in K–12 online learning.

The federal government has traditionally seen educational technology and distance learning as tools for use in education reform and school-improvement efforts. In the United States, K–12 education is locally controlled but governed at the state level with some federal assistance (Clark & Else, 1998a). Canadian K–12 education is similarly governed at the provincial or territorial level (MacKeracher, 1984). A number of federal grant programs have supported the development of K–12 and virtual learning in the United States, as is evident in projects described earlier in this chapter. States have provided "pass-through" grants through federal education reform programs used for widespread experimentation at the local and regional level and have developed state-level initiatives for education networks and technology in support of educational reform. Federal grants spurred the development of the first large-scale uses of supervised independent study and virtual or online study. Future federal support for such innovations may be targeted more directly to high-need school districts. The educational technology programs of the U.S. Department of Education are proposed for consolidation into state block grants by the Bush administration, with formula application to districts serving low-income populations replacing competitive grant proposals.

The first federal policy document to focus on K–12 distance learning in the United States was *Linking for Learning* (Office of Technology Assessment, 1987), which contained case studies, contractor reports and analyses of technological and policy options. Defining distance education in terms of electronically delivered instructional activities, including supplemental classroom experiences via telecommunications, the authors concluded its use in K–12 education had increased dramatically over the past five years. They noted that state education agencies could act both as gatekeepers and catalysts and that government regulation has significantly affected the development of distance education. The report called for supportive policies, more research and evaluation to show effectiveness, stronger dissemination efforts, expansion of infrastructures, and support for teachers involved in distance education. The report of the Web Based Education

Commission (2000) made similar recommendations across all education levels, with a focus on expanding access to Internet technologies.

State mandates on the compulsory nature of K–12 education and seat-time requirements for state aid to local districts have helped sustain the supervised independent-study method, and other distance learning methods such as group-based videoconference courses, to the present day. State departments of education provide state-level approval of programs and diplomas, sometimes applying requirements that private or university-based virtual schools cannot meet. Distance education teacher certification is a continuing issue. Moore and Kearsley (1996) cite England (1991), who found that only 37% of state education agencies responding to a survey allowed out-of-state K–12 teachers to teach distance students in their state without obtaining in-state certification. While no recent state-by-state distance teacher certification studies are apparent in the literature, some states have developed certification reciprocity agreements applicable to distance learning. However, many distance education providers continue to work around this issue by assigning a local teacher as supervisor who becomes the teacher of record or training in-state teachers to teach sections of their courses.

Several researchers have attempted state-by-state reviews of K–12 distance education policies and practices, mostly in the 1980s and early 1990s. Moore and Kearsley (1996) cite a number of state-level inventories or other resource studies leading to recommendations for policies or regulations supporting the statewide development of distance learning systems. They state that "eventually, statewide systems will have to be created" (p. 185) due to the advantages of economies of scale. However, while some states sought to create unified "one-stop" access to their various distance learning infrastructures, the components continue to be operated by different agencies. With few exceptions, states that have begun state-level virtual schools have done so as parallel efforts, unconnected to existing video-based or independent study distance learning programs. Thomas (2000) reviews policy issues related to virtual high-school courses and offers questions for discussion by policymakers. The Educational Technology Cooperative of the Southern Regional Education Board (2000) has provided a list of *Essential Principles of Quality for Web-Based Courses for Middle and High Schools*.

Virtual and distance education occurs through a variety of technologies and methods in schools today. The emergence of the virtual school provides new options for student learning while online learning expands continuing education opportunities for educators. If policy issues can be effectively addressed, distance and virtual learning has a bright future in K–12 education.

REFERENCES

Allen, I. E., & Seaman, J. (2005). *Growing by degrees: Online education in the United States, 2005*. Needham, MA: The Sloan Consortium.

Barker, B. O. (1987, January). *An evaluation of interactive satellite television as a delivery system for high school instruction.* Paper presented at the annual meeting of the Southwest Educational Research Association, Dallas, TX. (ERIC Document Reproduction Service No. ED277534)

Barker, B. O., & Petersen, P. D. (1984). *A research report of small high schools in the United States in regards to curricular offerings, micro-computer usage, and correspondence courses.* Salt Lake City, Utah: Brigham Young University, Division of Continuing Education. (ERIC Document Reproduction Service No. ED239825)

Barresi, A. L. (1987), Edgar P. Gordon: a pioneer in media music education. *Journal of Research in Music Education, 35*(4), 259–274.

Berge, Z. L., & Collins, M. P. (Eds.). (1998). *Wired together: the online classroom in K–12*. Cresskill, N.J.: Hampton Press.

Bittner, W. S., & Mallory, H. F. (1933). *University teaching by mail; a survey of correspondence instruction conducted by American universities*. New York: The Macmillan Company.

Bosak, S. (2000). Videoconferencing comes of age. *American School Board Journal, 187*(6), 48–50.

Bramble, W. J. (1988, Winter). Distance learning in Alaska's rural schools. *Learning Tomorrow, 4,* 241–256. (ERIC Document Reproduction Service No. ED302210)

Broady, K. O. (1932, February). Supervised correspondence study given new impetus. *Nebraska Education Journal.* Abstracted in Perlham, P. D. B., *Teaching by correspondence: an annotated bibliography* (p. 13). Sacramento: California State Department of Education, 1936.

Broady, K. O., Platt, E. T., & Bell, M. D. (1931). *Practical procedures for enriching the curriculums of small schools.* Lincoln: University of Nebraska.

Bucks County Public Schools. (1972). *Supervised independent study program. Annual report.* Doylestown, PA: Bucks County Public Schools. (ERIC Document Reproduction Service No. ED072213)

Center for Education Reform. (2005). *National charter school directory.* Washington, DC: Author.

Childs, G. B. (1966). Review of research in correspondence study. In C. A. Wedemeyer (1966), *The Brandenburg memorial essays on correspondence instruction: II* (pp. 126–140). Madison, WI: University of Wisconsin Extension.

Clark, T. (2001). *Virtual schools: status and trends.* Phoenix, AZ: WestEd. Retrieved June 1, 2005, from http://www.wested.org/online_pubs/virtualschools.pdf

Clark, T. (2002). Virtual and distance education in American schools. In M. G. Moore & W. A. Anderson, *Handbook of Distance Education,* pp. 673–699. Mahwah, NJ: Lawrence Erlbaum.

Clark, T. (2004). *STAR Project evaluation report, year 3.* Macomb: Western Illinois University/United Star Distance Learning Consortium.

Clark, T., & Else, D. (1998a). *Distance education, electronic networking, and school policy.* Fastback 441. Bloomington, IN: Phi Delta Kappa. (ERIC Document Reproduction Service No. ED 425 711).

Corporation for Public Broadcasting. (1999). Elementary and secondary educational services of public television grantees: highlights from the 1998 station activities survey. *CPB Research Notes,* No. 116. (ERIC Document Reproduction Service No. ED 428 746).

Cuban, L. (1998, Winter). High-tech schools and low-tech teaching: a commentary. *Journal of Computing in Teacher Education, 14*(2), 6–7.

DANTES. (2006). Alternative teacher certification programs. Retrieved April 19, 2006, from http://www.dantes.doded.mil/dantes_Web/troopstoteachers/altcert/tco.htm

Edelson, P. J., & Pittman, V. V. (2001). E-Learning in the United States: New directions and opportunities for university continuing education. *Global E-Journal of Open, Flexible & Distance Education, 1*(1), 71–83.

Education Week. (2001, May 10). *Technology counts 2001: The new divides.* Special Report.

Eisenberg, M. B. (1992). *Networking: K–12. ERIC digest.* Syracuse, NY: ERIC Clearinghouse on Information Resources. (ERIC Document Reproduction Service No. ED354903)

England, R. (1991). A survey of state-level involvement in distance education at the elementary and secondary levels. *Research Monograph Number, 3.* State College: Pennsylvania State University, American Center for the Study of Distance Education.

Eurydice, European Commission. (2004). *Key data on information and communication technology in schools in Europe.* (2004). Brussels, Belgium: Author. Retrieved April 19, 2006, from http://www.eurydice.org/Documents/KDICT/en/FrameSet.htm

Gooch, J. (1998). *They blazed the trail for distance education.* Madison: University of Wisconsin Extension. Retrieved April 19, 2006, from the Distance Education Clearinghose Web site http://bluto.uwex.edu/disted/gooch.htm

Gordon, E. B. (1931, February). An experiment in radio education by radio broadcasting. *School Life,* 104–105.

Grayson, L. P., Norwood, F. W., & Wigren, H. E. (1973). *Man-made moons: satellite communications for schools.* Washington, DC: National Education Association.

Haight, R. C. (1944). Elementary education by correspondence. *School Management, 13,* 307.

Harding, L. W. (1944, May). Correspondence instruction. *Education Digest, 9,* 8–11.

Hezel Associates. (1998). *Educational telecommunications and distance learning: the state-by-state analysis, 1998–99.* Syracuse, NY: Hezel Associates.

Hill, D. (2000). Test case. *Education Week, 19*(25), 34–38.

Howley, C. B., & Harmon, H. L. (2000). K–12 unit schooling in rural America: a first description. *Rural Educator, 22*(1), 10–18.

Hudson, H. E., & Boyd, C. H. (1984). Distance learning: A review for educators. Austin, TX: Southwest Educational Development Laboratory. (ERIC Document Reproduction Service No. ED246872).

Killion, J. (2000, Summer). Log on to learn. *Journal of Staff Development, 21*(3), 48–53.

Kirby, E. (1998). Administrative issues for high school distance education. *Online Journal of Distance Learning Administration, 1*(2). Internet-only journal. Retrieved April 19, 2006, from http://www.westga.edu/~distance/jmain11.html

Kleiman, G. M. (2005). Meeting the need for high quality teachers: e-learning solutions. (White Paper). No Child Left Behind Leadership Summit (Orlando, FL, July 12–13).

Kuplowska, O. (1987). Distance education activities at TVOntario: Evaluation results. *Media in Education and Development, 20*(3), 88–90.

Kurtz, B. E. (1959). *Pioneering in educational television, 1932–1939.* Iowa City: State University of Iowa.

MacKeracher, D. (1984). An Overview of the Educational System in Canada. Toronto, Ontario, Canada: TVOntario, Office of Development Research. (ERIC Document Reproduction Service No. ED 323 970).

Majdalany, G., & Guiney, S. (1999). *Implementing distance learning in urban schools.* ERIC/CUE Digest, No.150. New York: ERIC Clearinghouse on Urban Education. (ERIC Document Reproduction Service No. ED438338)

Maul, C. (1929). Administrative practices in correspondence study departments of teachers colleges and normal schools. Unpublished masters thesis, University of Kansas, Lawrence.

McGreal, R., & Simand, B. (1992). Problems in introducing distance education into Northern Ontario secondary schools. *American Journal of Distance Education, 6*(1), 51–61.

Merkley, D., & Hoy, M. P. (1985). Teacher-on-television: a new mode of preservice classroom observation. *Phi Delta Kappan, 66*(5), 373–74.

Meyen, E. L., Lian, C. H. T., & Tangen, P. (1998). Issues associated with the design and delivery of online instruction. *Focus on Autism and Other Developmental Disabilities, 13*(1), 53–60.

Miller, G. T. W. (1989). Using high technology in education—The Northeastern Utah Telelearning Project. *Rural Special Education Quarterly, 9*(4), 33–36.

Mitchell, S. C. (1923, June). For the 90 per cent. *School Review,* pp. 439–444.

Moore, D. M., Burton, J. K., & Dodl, N. R. (1991). The role of facilitators in Virginia's electronic classroom project. *The American Journal of Distance Education, 5*(3), 29–39.

Moore, M. G., & Kearsley, G. (1996). *Distance education: a systems view.* Belmont, CA: Wadsworth Publishing.

Morse, S. C., Haro, L., & Herron, P. (1986). *The P.A.S.S. program.* San Diego, CA: Interstate Migrant Secondary Team Project. (ERIC Document Reproduction Service No. ED269193)

National University Continuing Education Association. (1991). *Independent study program profiles 1989– 1990. Final report.* Washington, DC: NUCEA, Research and Evaluation Committee. (ERIC Document Reproduction Service No. ED328723)

Newman, A., Stein, M., & Trask, E. (2003, September). *What can virtual learning do for your school?* Boston; Eduventures.

Ninno, A. (2000). Radios in the classroom: curriculum integration and communication skills. *Educational Media and Technology Yearbook 2000, 25,* 70–73.

Office of Technology Assessment. (1987). *Linking for learning: a new course for education.* Washington, DC: OTA, U.S. Congress.

Oklahoma State University. (2001). *K–12 distance learning academy.* Retrieved April 19, 2006, from the Oklahoma State Extension Web site http://extension.okstate.edu/k12.htm

Paulsen, M. F. (1987, December/January). In search of a virtual school. *T. H.E. Journal,* pp. 71–76.

Pease, P. S., & Tinsley, P. J. (1986, October). *Reaching rural schools using an interactive satellite based educational network.* Paper presented at the annual conference of the National Rural and Small Schools Consortium in Bellingham, WA. (ERIC Document Reproduction Service No. ED281681)

Rose, L. C., & Gallup, G. (2001, September). The 33rd annual Phi Delta Kappa/Gallup poll of the public's attitudes toward public schools. *Phi Delta Kappan,* pp. 41–58.

Schmidt, B. J., & Faulkner, S. L. (1989, Fall). Staff development through distance education. *Journal of Staff Development, 10*(4), 2–7.

Schmidt, K. J., Sullivan, M. I., & Hardy, D. W. (1994). Teaching migrant students algebra by audio-iconference. *American Journal of Distance Education, 8*(3), 51–63.

Schrum, L. (1992, April). *Information age innovations: a case study of online professional development.* Paper presented at the annual conference of the American Educational Research Association in San Francisco. (ERIC Document Reproduction Service No. ED346849)

Shaker, P. (2000, February). *CalStateTEACH: The origins and emergence of a state university distributed learning teacher education program.* Paper presented at the annual meeting of the American Association of Colleges for Teacher Education in Chicago. (ERIC Document Reproduction Service No. ED440062)

Smith, M. H., Ed. (1961). *Using television in the classroom: Midwest program on airborne television instruction.* New York: McGraw-Hill.

Smith, R. E. (1990). Effectiveness of the interactive satellite method in the teaching of first-year German: A look at selected high schools in Arkansas and Mississippi (Doctoral dissertation, University of Mississippi, 1990). *Dissertation Abstracts International, 52*(2), 0517A.

Sorenson, C., & Sweeney, J. (1994). *Iowa Distance Education Alliance. Final evaluation report. Abbreviated version.* Ames: Iowa State University, Research Institute for Studies in Education. (ERIC Document Reproduction Service No. ED389060)

Southern Regional Education Board. (2000, August). *Essential principles of quality: guidelines for Web-based courses for middle and high schools.* Atlanta, GA: Educational Technology Cooperative, Southern Regional Education Board. Retrieved April 19, 2006 from http://www.sreb.org/programs/edtech/webbased/srebpubs.asp

Southern Regional Education Board. (2006). *Multi-state online professional development.* Retrieved April 19, 2006, from http://www.sreb.org/programs/EdTech/MOPD/about.asp

Thomas, W. R. (2000). *Web courses for high school students: potential and issues.* Atlanta, GA: Southern Regional Education Board. Retrieved February 28, 2006, from http://www.sreb.org/programs/edtech/webbased/srebpubs.asp

Tushnet, N. C., & Fleming-McCormick, T. (1995). Equity issues in the Star Schools Distance Learning Program. *Journal of Educational Computing Research, 13*(2), 173–83.

University Continuing Education Association. (2002). *1999–00 Independent study program profiles. Final report, February 2002.* Retrieved February 28, 2006, from www.ucea.edu/pages/surveyreport.pdf

U.S. Department of Education. (2000a). *e-learning: putting a world class education at the fingertips of all children.* Washington, DC: U.S. Department of Education, Office of Educational Research and Improvement.

U.S. Department of Education. (2000b). *What are the barriers to the use of advanced telecommunications for students with disabilities in public schools?* (National Center for Education Statistics No. 2000-042). Washington, DC: Author.

U.S. Department of Education. (2001b). *Internet access in U.S. public schools and classrooms: 1994–2000.* Washington, DC: U.S. Department of Education, National Center for Education Statistics (NCES 2001-071).

U.S. Department of Education. (2004). *1.1 million homeschooled students in the United States in 2003.* (National Center for Education Statistics No. 2004115). (Issue Brief). Washington, DC: Princiotta, D., Bielick, S., & Chapman, C.

U.S. Department of Education. (2005a). *Condition of education 2005.* (National Center for Education Statistics No. 2005-094). Washington, DC: Author.

U.S. Department of Education, Office of Educational Technology. (2005b). *National educational technology plan.* Washington, DC: Author.

U.S. Department of Education. (2005c). *Internet access in U.S. public schools and classrooms: 1994–2003.* (National Center for Education Statistics No. 2005-015). Washington, DC: Parsad, B. and Jones, J.

U.S. Department of Education. (2005d). *Distance education courses for public elementary and secondary school students: 2002–03.* (National Center for Education Statistics No. 2005-010). Washington, DC: Setzer, J. C., & Lewis, L.

Virtual High School, Inc. (2004). *Virtual High School program evaluation 2003–2004.* Maynard, MA: Author.

Watson, J. (2005). *Keeping pace with online learning 2005. A review of state-level policy and practice.* Naperville, IL: Learning Point Associates.

Web Based Education Commission. (2000). *Report of the Web Based Education Commission to the President and the Congress of the United States.* Washington, DC: The Commission.

White, R. E. (2004). Telepresence goes to school: An evaluation of the PEBBLES™ videoconferencing system for ill children (Master's thesis, Carleton University, 2003). *Masters Abstracts International, 42*(5), 1895.

Young, R. G., & McMahon, M. (1991). University-sponsored high school independent study. In B. L. Watkins & S. J. Wright (Eds.), *The foundations of American distance education: A century of collegiate correspondence study* (pp. 93–108). Dubuque, IA: Kendall/Hunt.

37

Community Colleges

Christine Mullins
Instructional Technology Council

Community colleges have led the way in the adoption of distance education for good reason. Distance learning technologies have allowed them to serve the educational needs of their core constituency—older, more disciplined students who work full time and attend college part time (National Center for Education Statistics, 2002). The average age of the 11.6 million students who attended 1,158 community colleges across the country in 2005 is 29. Fifty-eight percent are women, 43% work full time while enrolled, 16% are single parents, and 62% attend college part time (Phillippe & Patton, 2005). The U.S. Department of Education reinforced this connection when it reported in 2002 that undergraduate distance learning students tend to be older than 24 years, work full time, be financially independent and/or married, have dependent children, and attend college part time (National Center for Education Statistics, 2002).

Distance learning allows community colleges to expand their reach: to employees who need to enhance their job skills, but cannot attend a "traditional" face-to-face class during their work hours; to mothers who want to earn their college degree while caring for their children or an elderly parent at home; to students in rural areas, where geography prevents them from traveling to and from campus within a reasonable timeframe. High-school students who want to take advanced placement courses offered by a community college during school hours, military personnel who are stationed overseas, international students who cannot obtain a visa to travel to the United States, prisoners who want to earn their GED, so they can find a job when they are released, disabled students who cannot physically attend class on campus—all take advantage of the wide variety of courses offered by community colleges at a distance.

Since the early 1970s, community colleges have offered their students distance education opportunities for a variety of reasons. In addition to responding to increasing student demand and a desire to serve new audiences, technology allows them to fulfill their philosophical mission to provide affordable "open access" to higher education to all students, regardless of their educational, financial, or ethnic background. Others see self-preservation as a motive—they realize that if they don't respond to the needs and wishes of this new "client" base, potential students will "vote" with their computer mouse, rather than their feet, and go to another college that caters to them. Students are no longer limited to choosing from the courses offered by their local college or university to meet their educational goals—the Internet opens the door to educational opportunities offered by institutions of higher learning from around the world, including for-profit institutions like the University of Phoenix and corporate training facilities like Motorola University.

The National Center for Education Statistics (2003) reported that 90% of public two-year, and 89% of public four-year, higher education institutions offered distance learning courses in the 2000–2001 academic year, an increase from 62% and 78% respectively from 1997–98. Public two-year institutions had the greatest number of enrollments in distance education courses, with 1,472,000 out of 3,077,000, or 48% of the total enrollments in distance education. Public four-year institutions had 945,000 enrollments (31% of the total), and private four-year institutions had 589,000 enrollments (19% of the total).

Community colleges have traditionally worked as partners with business and industry to provide training for their employees through degree, certificate, and non-credit training programs. In the past five years, community colleges have rapidly expanded their online distance learning course offerings to include a broader selection of courses, including more technical and vocational courses. "Community colleges are the primary providers of education for workers in career fields in highest demand locally and nationally. Among these fields are nursing, and other allied-health fields, law enforcement, and computer technologies." Now that most community colleges have developed their core course offerings at a distance, they are expanding their programs to include more vocational options. However, many will admit that at a distance "the availability of programs and the level of service vary enormously from one community to the next." (Dubois, 2002, p. 8).

A LITTLE HISTORY

Since the mid-1970s, community colleges have offered students telecourses, or high-quality preproduced video programs. Students learn asynchronously from a series of twenty-six 30-minute video segments. In the past, colleges often contracted with their local PBS or cable access channel to broadcast the programs, so students could watch the course material live or tape the segments on their VHS recorders for later viewing. Increasingly, most colleges have found it easier to just make the tapes available in the college library, so students can check them out or rent them from a local video store. Other colleges mail students a complete set of the tapes and retrieve them at the end of the semester. The college assigns an instructor to guide the students though the course material. A textbook and detailed study guide usually accompanies the program and students communicate regularly with the professor via phone, audiobridge or increasingly by e-mail. Depending on the course, students might meet on-campus for face-to-face study sessions with the professor or fellow classmates, or to complete science lab assignments. Most colleges require students to come to campus or go to a designated testing center to take a proctored mid-term and final exams.

Telecourses remain an important, and sometimes the only, distance learning option available for many community college students—particularly for those who lack the high-speed Internet connections that are required to take some online courses or those who cannot afford to have a computer at home. For example, Kevin Eason, assistant director of distance learning for Tarrant Community College District in Fort Worth, Texas, says that 2,726 students, or 27% of their entire distance learning enrollments, took traditional telecourses in spring 2006. Eason does mention, however, that the number of traditional telecourse enrollments is steadily decreasing—his students tend to gravitate toward the college's online offerings, which fill up very quickly and before the telecourse-based classes.

As more students come online, as high-end computers and high-speed Internet connections become more affordable, many instructors have enhanced their asynchronous video-taped
courses with online functionalities, such as a course Web site where instructors post their course
syllabus, additional information about the subject, and links to pertinent Web sites to make the
course material or discussion topics more timely. Instructors also use e-mail and Web discussion
boards to communicate with their students and offer activities that encourage student-to-student
interaction.

In response to a new demand from instructors who want to incorporate bits and pieces of
course material from a variety of sources and media, many of the traditional telecourse producers,
such as Dallas TeleLearning, have reformatted their video tape inventory, so instructors can easily use portions of their videos, rather than have to pay for licensing the entire course. At the same
time, other community colleges use video and audio streaming technologies to deliver the entire
telecourse, multi-media segments and video clips to a student's desktop or laptop computer,
PDA or iPod. The bottom line is that instructors want to have the flexibility to use this powerful
instructional video material in different ways, depending on the learning outcomes they wish
to achieve.

A second form of distance learning that has been popular at community colleges since the
early 1970s is live interactive television in which colleges use broadcast technologies, such as
ITFS, to teach students at remote locations in real time. These courses have been popular at colleges located in rural settings where small groups of students attend classes at branch campuses
and participate in the live interactive video courses—they watch the instructor present in real time
on video monitors using compressed or full-motion video from a central hub or location and
usually communicate with him or her via a telephone line. The courses are virtually the same as
face-to-face classes, since they take place live and they are usually highly interactive.

ONLINE COURSES

The Internet revolutionized distance learning in the mid-1990s. Many community colleges rushed
to produce and offer their students online courses as soon as the prices for computers came down
for both the college and students, who study from their home, dorm room, workplace or anywhere
else. Easy-to-use online course management software, such as that offered by Blackboard or
WebCT, became affordable and made it easier for colleges to teach their faculty to develop customized online courses. Community colleges have taken advantage of this medium that encourages asynchronous communication among students, teachers and their peers via e-mail, bulletin
boards, and course chat rooms.

Distance learning faculty often go to great lengths to make sure that their students do not
have to travel to campus to achieve the same learning outcomes as their face-to-face counterparts.
For example, every semester Jennifer Herzog, assistant professor of biology at Herkimer County
Community College, painstakingly creates and mails each student a science lab kit that includes,
among other things, a microscope, a preserved starfish and grasshopper, glass beakers, a Petri
dish, dried peas and iodine, so her students can conduct biology experiments at home using common household products and the items in the lab kits. Herzog's students write reports, draw
illustrations, and provide digital pictures and movies to show her the techniques they used while
conducting their experiments.

Jan Ballantine at St. Petersburg College, provides another example of innovative teaching.
She uses fairly inexpensive Web-conferencing software and digital cameras to teach speech
online, a course which many have argued is impossible to conduct in an online environment. In

addition to participating in online lectures and chat rooms, students are required to make three short speeches to the instructor and six fellow classmates who they can see and interact with live on their computer. Students must also videotape three short speeches they present before at least eight adults during the semester which they send to Ballantine, attend and write reports on three Toastmasters club meetings, and, attend and write a rhetorical analysis/critique on a live speech given in the community, college, or workplace.

QUALITY ASSURANCE

In early 2000, as distance learning became more commonplace at colleges and universities across the country, the eight regional accrediting commissions[1] endorsed the *Best Practices for Electronically Offered Degree and Certificate Programs* (Council of Regional Accrediting Commissions, 2001), a systematic approach to applying "well-established essentials of institutional quality to distance learning." These guidelines were designed to help institutions plan for distance learning activities and provide a self-assessment framework for those colleges that are already offering, or planning to offer, distance learning courses. "For the regional accrediting associations they constitute a common understanding of those elements that reflect quality distance education programming. They are intended to inform and facilitate the evaluation policies and processes of each region."

In many ways these best practice guidelines should convince distance learning skeptics that colleges are applying the same rigorous pedagogical scrutiny to their distance learning programs as they are to their traditional face-to-face course offerings. Maintaining regional accreditation status is of vital importance to higher-education institutions—not only is the college's reputation at stake, but the institution must be accredited to offer students federal financial aid and/or receive government grants.

The guidelines state that the distance learning program must be consistent with the college's educational role or mission. The curriculum must be faculty-driven and the college must provide appropriate staffing and technical assistance to ensure the course is top notch. There should be an appropriate amount of synchronous or asynchronous interaction among the students and instructor to ensure the desired educational outcomes are realized. Consequently, there should be a correlation between the number of students and the amount of interaction educators and students expect to receive. The guidelines also ask colleges to provide distance learning students with the corresponding student services they need to help them succeed in their educational program.

Ensuring consistent quality in all of their distance learning course offerings has become a central concern for most community colleges. A poll which the Instructional Technology Council (ITC) recently conducted of its members in Fall 2005 (Instructional Technology Council, 2005) pointed to several practices community colleges are implementing to ensure course quality and the academic integrity of the program.

---

[1]Commission on Higher Education, Middle States Association of Colleges and Schools—info@msache.org; Commission on Institutions of Higher Education, New England Association of Schools and Colleges—cihe@neasc.org; Commission on Technical and Career Institutions, New England Association of Schools and Colleges—rmandeville@neasc.org; Commission on Institutions of Higher Education, North Central Association of Colleges and Schools—info@ncacihe.org; Commission on Colleges, The Northwest Association of Schools and Colleges—pjarnold@cocnasc.org; Commission on Colleges, Southern Association of Schools and Colleges—webmaster@saccoc.org; Accrediting Commission for Community and Junior Colleges, Western Association of Schools and Colleges—accjc@aol.com; Accrediting Commission for Senior Colleges and Universities, Western Association of Schools and Colleges—wascsr@wascsenior.org.

Most community colleges limit online course enrollment to 20 to 30 students to make sure faculty are able to devote the proper attention to each student in the class. Many faculty report that they interact much more frequently with their online students because they encourage them to send e-mail to respond to the course material or ask questions. Although most instructors relish this increased level of student interaction, they have to take extra steps to manage their time because they can quickly become inundated and overwhelmed. Many colleges limit the number of distance learning classes a faculty member can teach to one or two courses each semester, particularly for those instructors who are new to teaching online.

Many college administrators and policy makers are extremely concerned about proper evaluation and testing procedures for distance learning students. How can you be sure that the person who takes a test or writes a paper online is the same student who enrolled in the class? How can you make sure he or she is not looking up the answers while taking his or her test?

Most community colleges require their distance learning students to travel to campus or to a designated location such as a college or high school that is more accessible to the student, to take their mid-term and final exams in a proctored testing center. Distance educators often take extra steps to get to know their students, through e-mail communications, writing assignments, or quizzes offered throughout the term, to gage a student's writing style or knowledge base. This enables them to ascertain a student's progress throughout the course and determine what he or she has learned. Most course management systems give instructors some control by allowing them to time the tests or quizzes they offer.

FACULTY TRAINING

To teach quality, pedagogically sound distance education courses, faculty need to know how to use the appropriate technology to incorporate different types of learning media to create a complete educational package that makes sense to their students. At the simplest level, instructors need to know how to use e-mail to communicate with their students or post their syllabi to a course Web site. More experienced distance learning instructors enhance their Web sites with photographs, charts, animations and video clips to illustrate ideas, or use chatrooms to create class discussions or facilitate student-to-student interaction.

Most community colleges with quality distance education programs have created systematic, coordinated training programs for their distance learning faculty—which they offer online or face-to-face to faculty throughout the school year and during the summer. Many employ full-time instructional designers to help those who are uncomfortable using new and ever-changing technologies. They teach faculty—who are new to or old hands at distance learning—how to incorporate new and proven pedagogical techniques into their distance learning courses to teach students in a completely different way. An often-used saying in the distance education world is that the instructor is no longer a "sage on the stage," but a "guide on the side," or mentor and coach who often communicates one-on-one with his or her students who learn at their own pace, according to their unique learning styles in an asynchronous environment.

Kristen Betts (1998) did an extensive survey of 1,001 faculty at George Washington University and found that the lack of release time, lack of technical support from their institution, and concern about workload prevented many instructors from getting involved in distance learning. It is unreasonable to expect faculty to take on new initiatives without a high level of institutional support. The need for colleges to offer their teachers enhanced training in educational technologies will only expand as student demand for online courses increases and distance learning becomes a mainstream teaching tool.

"Will New Teachers Be Prepared to Teach in a Digital Age?," a study funded by the Milken Family Foundation (1999) and conducted by the International Society for Technology in Education, found that teacher preparation programs at most four-year colleges of teacher education, "while well-intentioned, are not providing the kind of training and exposure teachers need if they are to be proficient and comfortable integrating technology with their teaching."

Community colleges have increasingly been involved in training preservice K–12 and post-secondary-level teachers to use technology tools in their face-to-face and distance learning classrooms. Many teachers attend classes at community colleges and transfer to four-year institutions to complete their education degrees. In Illinois, 67.4% of public university graduates who received a bachelor's degree in education in 1997 took more than half of their classes at a community college.[2]

STUDENT SUPPORT SERVICES

The regional accrediting bodies recognize that to be successful, quality distance learning programs must offer comprehensive support services to students at a distance so they can complete administrative tasks and take advantage of other educational services that colleges make available to their on-campus students (Western Interstate Commission for Higher Education, 2004). Today's Internet-savvy students expect to be able to register, choose their classes, and purchase books in an online environment.

Research has also shown that student retention and academic program completion increase as access to integrated student services "are visible, accessible, and responsive via the instructional medium by which a student learns" (McCracken, 2004). Sandra Miller, director of the Learning Assistance Center and Support at Atlantic Cape Community College, wrote in her chapter on online tutoring in "Quality Enhancing Practices in Distance Education: Student Services," that "alienated, isolated students tend to drop out of their classes. Many educators have studied the issues and possible causes for attrition. Several have applied Tinto's (1975) theory of cognitive affiliation, which emphasizes the importance of integrating distance learning students both academically and socially (Sweet, 1986). Collective affiliation is more likely developed by sustained contact with an individual than by a succession of short contacts with diverse people (Dalziel & Payne, 2001)." For example, personal e-mails from an online instructor, tutor, or counselor can strongly contribute to a distance learning student's feeling of integration within the academic community and put him or her on the path toward success.

In the fall of 2005 the Instructional Technology Council asked its members what types of services they are offering their students online (ITC, 2005). Here were the responses.

- Helpdesk and technical support for distance education students—87%
- Admission to institution—77%
- Registration for classes—86%
- Payment of tuition and fees—77%
- Textbox sales—70%
- Student orientation for distance education classes (or orientation CD)—75%
- Library services and resources—98%

---

[2]University/Community College Shared Data Files.

- Tutoring assistance—44%
- Counseling/advising services—49%

Every student needs to have adequate technical expertise to successfully complete a distance learning course. As online courses become more mainstream, administrators find students from a variety of educational and technical backgrounds are interested in taking courses at a distance. Students need to know how to use the network properly, how to install and operate any necessary software or computer hardware, and how to send and receive e-mail messages. Many colleges have 24-hour help desks (with answers provided by e-mail or phone) to accommodate questions from students.

Most colleges require their distance learning students to take an online or face-to-face orientation session to make sure they know how to use the technologies that will be used during the course, can work independently, and are not just looking for an "easy A" to enhance their grade-point average. Many distance learning administrators attribute the higher student drop-out rate many distance learning programs experience to students who do not realize what they are getting into. They fail for the same reasons they signed up to take a course at a distance in the first place—they lead busy lives and their many work and family commitments prevent them from completing the course. A good orientation will explain how much time and work students should set aside to succeed in their coursework so they don't become frustrated and stymied by a bad educational experience.

Most colleges provide some sort of online library services to their distance learning students. The online environment makes it easier for colleges and universities to collaborate and/or combine their resources, so they can offer their online and on-campus students access to more complete collections and services. Many libraries provide a variety online services so their students can: renew or order books, documents or other materials online; submit a question to a reference librarian; order books via interlibrary loan; and, access electronic reserves, online databases, electronic books, full-text journals and relevant Web sites. Often the online college library provides a portal for other student services, such as counseling, academic advising, and tutoring.

Examples of statewide college and university partnerships include OhioLink; the Portland Area Library System, PORTALS, in Portland, Oregon; the Louisiana Library Network, LOUIS; and, the Missouri Bibliographic Information User System, MOBIUS.

STATEWIDE VIRTUAL NETWORKS OR COLLABORATION

Most states have created statewide virtual networks or collaborations where students can find all of the distance learning course offerings in their state, listed on one Web site (for a list of these statewide collaborations, see http://www.itcnetwork.org.). These networks take on various sizes, distance learning delivery formats and student service options.

For example, two- and four-year institutions participate in the Illinois Virtual Campus (see http://www.ivc.illinois.edu), while only two-year technical colleges belong to the Georgia Virtual Technical Institute (http://www.gvti.org). The Electronic Campus of Virginia (http://www.vacec .bev.net) offers a variety of distance learning course delivery options while, as its name implies, Colorado Community College Online (http://www.ccconline.org) includes only online courses.

Collaborations exist at all levels. For example, the colleges within the Virtual College of Texas have developed articulation agreements, so students can sign up with a home institution and automatically receive credit for the courses they take from another college in the network. The colleges in the Michigan Community College Virtual Learning Collaborative (http://www.mccvlc.org)

follow a similar home/provider college model, but they also pool their resources and receive mini-grants from the Kellogg Foundation to develop courses and programs that will be offered on their network.

For example, in 2003 the Michigan colleges were able to offer their students a RN from LPN program online by combining pre-requisite and required courses that were already offered online by colleges across the state. To complete the full degree offering, the colleges needed to create three new online courses—pharmacology, nursing assessment, and nursing leadership. Offering this type of online-degree program requires a great deal of cooperation and coordination among the colleges—since they must market the program to students, offer student services, and administer the clinical requirements to the students who enroll, regardless of their location.

These statewide consortia are involved in other projects that the individual colleges would not have been able to complete on their own. For example, in 2003 the U.S. Department of Education Fund for the Improvement of Post-Secondary Education (FIPSE) awarded a three-year grant to MarylandOnline, a statewide consortium of 19 Maryland community colleges and universities, to develop a faculty-centered, consortium-wide, peer-review process for identifying, assessing, and insuring quality in online courses. Their assessment process and peer course review rubric have become a model for quality assurance for colleges across the country.

Depending on the services they will provide, the administrators of these statewide networks face many challenges, including finding the necessary funding to sustain themselves, deciding how the network will be structured and governed, developing common forms and articulation agreements, formulating course assessment procedures, determining how the network will deliver student services, coordinating program and curriculum development, and arranging for common faculty training programs.

PRESENT AND FUTURE CHALLENGES

Educators face many challenges when offering courses to students at a distance. In its November 2005 poll, ITC asked its members to list some of their greatest challenges (ITC, 2005). These included recruiting and training faculty, finding adequate support staff for training and technical assistance, providing adequate student services for distance learning students, maintaining adequate operating and equipment budgets, and offering certain courses such as those that *seem to* require a hands-on or face-to-face element, such as science labs, clinical nursing, speech, mathematics, languages.

Distance educators face a continual need to keep abreast of the latest technologies so they can take advantage of the latest software and hardware developments and offer their students courses using the technologies with which they are familiar. The cost of technology is high and many distance learning administrators struggle with the need to convince their college administration to spend the necessary funds to implement and maintain an innovative and current program. For example, many distance educators are concerned with the recent steep increases in the annual cost to license the most popularly-used course management systems (CMS) or learning-management systems (LMS), Blackboard and WebCT. Distance educators who have committed to using these systems are concerned that the fees could further increase after the recent Blackboard/WebCT merger announced in late 2005.

Licensing proprietary course management systems like Blackboard or WebCT can speed a college's online course development and delivery because the systems make it easier for small colleges to offer comprehensive online courses without the need for great technical expertise. These programs influence design, delivery, and provide basic services, such as chat rooms, e-mail lists, and places to link Web pages. However, many colleges just cannot afford the fees Blackboard and WebCT are demanding. For example, in 2005 Truckee Meadows Community College in Reno, Nevada, faced an annual increase from $28,000 to $60,000 per year to license WebCT Vista. These colleges are looking to smaller CMS vendors, such as Angel and Desire2Learn, and to open source solutions, such as Moodle and Sakai, to quell their sticker-shock woes and provide greater flexibility to online faculty.

In fall 2005, 30% of ITC members said they are considering switching to another CMS in the next couple of years (ITC, 2005). This is a high percentage when one considers everything that is involved in changing an entire distance learning program to a new operating system—a monumental task that few educators want to undertake. Such a move involves the time-consuming task of retrofitting every course to a different learning platform, re-training the entire distance learning faculty and administration, and familiarizing students to a different program. Choosing an open source solution will probably require hiring the necessary technical support staff to run the systems, but this option might be cheaper than paying an ever-increasing annual licensing fee—many colleges will not have a choice.

CONCLUSION

Distance education will continue to be an increasingly popular option for many community college students. Seventy percent of the distance learning administrators who responded to ITC's fall 2005 survey said that student demand for their distance learning courses exceeds their current offerings (ITC, 2005). Our new generation of students who have grown up with, and who expect to use the Internet and other technologies to learn, will only push this trend further. They will refuse to be limited to the face-to-face courses offered by their local college or university at a time or location that is too inconvenient or impossible for them to attend given their other school, work, or personal commitments. They will use technology to go elsewhere to fulfill their educational and vocational goals and those colleges who refuse to cater to the needs and wishes of this new student "cliental," will lose to the other non-profit and for-profit colleges that do.

To be sure, some students will always need to learn in a face-to-face environment. There are many reasons high-school students should leave home after they graduate at age 18—to experience the independence, diversity, and free flow of ideas a college-campus environment provides. However, many community college educators have long realized that technology can give educational opportunities to those students who prefer to learn on their own time, at their one place, or who have no other choice, but to learn at a distance.

REFERENCES

Betts, K. (1998). *Factors influencing faculty participation in distance education in postsecondary education in the United States: An institutional study.* Unpublished doctoral dissertation, The George Washington University. UMI Dissertation Services, Report #9900013.

Council of Regional Accrediting Commissions. (2001). Best practices for electronically offered degree and certificate programs. Retrieved February 16, 2007, from http://wcet.info/services/publications/accreditation/Accrediting_BestPractices.pdf

Dalziel, C., & Payne, M. (Eds.). (2001). *Quality enhancing practices in distance education: Student services.* Washington, DC: Instructional Technology Council.

Dubois, J. H. (2002, February). The role of distance learning in vocational education. Cocoa Beach, FL: Synergy Plus, Inc. Retrieved February 16, 2007, from http://www.itcnetwork.org/DuboisVocEdFeb2002.pdf

Instructional Technology Council. (2005, February). Second annual survey on distance education. Retrieved February 16, 2007, from http://www.itcnetwork.org/ITCAnnualSurveyFeb2006Results.pdf

McCracken, H. (2004). Extending virtual access: Promoting engagement and retention through integrated support systems. *Online Journal of Distance Learning Administration, 7*(1). Retrieved February 16, 2007, from http://www.westga.edu/%7Edistance/ojdla/spring71/mccracken71.html

Milken Family Foundation. (1999). Will new teachers be prepared to teach in a digital age? Retrieved February 16, 2007, from http://www.mff.org/publications/publications.taf?page=154

National Center for Education Statistics. (2002, November). *A profile of participation in distance education: 1999–2000*. Washington, DC: Department of Education.

National Center for Education Statistics. (2003). *Distance education at degree-granting postsecondary institutions: 2000–2001*. Washington, DC: Department of Education.

Phillippe, K. A., & Patton, M. (2005). *National profile of community colleges: Trends and statistics* (4th ed.). Washington, DC: Community College Press, American Association of Community Colleges.

Sweet, R. (1986). Student drop-out in distance education: An application of Tinto's model. *Distance Education, 7*(2), 201–213.

Tinto, V. (1975). Dropout from higher education: A theoretical synthesis of recent research. *Review of Educational Research, 45*, 89–125.

Western Interstate Commission for Higher Education. (2004). Beyond the administrative core: Creating Web-based student services for online learners. Retrieved February 16, 2007, from http://www.wcet.info/services/studentservices/beyond/

38

Organizational Change in Higher Distance Education

Donald E. Hanna
University of Wisconsin-Extension

Distance education in the current educational environment is inevitably about changing existing organizational practices through the development of new structural, pedagogical, and technological models. This has always been true as distance education programs and processes departed from those used in more traditional instructional settings; however, until recently, the changes that distance education brought were not transformational changes in universities, but rather procedural and process changes designed to deliver existing programs, courses, and services.

Schlechty (1997) described three basic forms of organizational change:

1. procedural change that has to do with altering how organizational tasks are accomplished
2. technological change that consists of changing the means by which the job is done
3. structural and cultural (systemic change) that consists of changing the nature of the work itself, reorienting its purpose, and refocusing its intent.

This chapter will address emerging distance education organizational models in relation to each of these forms in ways that elucidate future directions in the field.

There are many reasons why the move toward distance education is inextricably linked with changing organization processes and procedures as well as the development of emerging organizational models. Demand for learning across the globe is escalating as national economies increasingly are based around knowledge and a pace of technological change that is unprecedented. Rapidly growing and increasingly youthful populations in many areas of the world are also fueling pressures on higher education institutions to respond in new and creative ways. In all countries, continuous learning for adults is becoming essential as jobs change, entire career tracks are eliminated, and new ones are developed. Access to education—from any location, at any time, for any age, and in many ways—is critical for individual, community, economic, and collective well-being. Democratization also requires an educated populace, providing further pressure upon governments to increase educational opportunity for all. Clearly, global educational access, at all levels and in all contexts, is more important than ever before, and it is no exaggeration to suggest that it is an element of strategic global positioning within societies and economies.

Corresponding with this elevated importance is increasing pressure on traditional universities to be creative and innovative in providing the maximum access possible, as well as to provide this access as efficiently as possible. In the United States, and in many other countries, public budgets are severely constrained, and this has placed considerable stress on funding for higher education. Projections from the National Council on Higher Education Management Systems (NCHEMS) for 2006–2013 indicate that the trend of reduced public support for higher education in the United States is accelerating (NCHEMS, 2005). According to Lyall and Sell (2005), the result has been a gradual privatization of public higher education, with much less public support being provided per student served, and with an increasing burden placed on students to cover the costs of their educations, whether in public or in private institutions. Globally, this same trend is observed, although the causes in many countries are more complex and include dramatically growing young populations (in many parts of the world), growing economies resulting in burgeoning demand for and access to learning (in China, India, and Southeast Asia), poor economies resulting in reduced funding capacity of government (in parts of Africa and other developing regions). The result of these trends is that many countries are unable to keep up with demand and provide affordable higher education. Daniel (1996) illustrated this impending crisis by suggesting that simply to keep up with the participation rates worldwide in higher education at the time, there would need to be one new residential university of 20,000 students built each week through the year 2025. Clearly, that is a goal that we are not achieving.

This crisis of access and funding has led to increasing pressure to adopt alternative methods such as distance and online learning, and has forced even traditional universities to search for new ways of organizing and paying for their instructional programs that depend upon new organizational assumptions, models, and strategies for providing not only distance learning, but also campus-based learning.

CHANGING ORGANIZATIONAL CONTEXTS, STRATEGIES, AND TACTICS

Schlechty (1997) first order changes are those that allow the institution to continue in its original role, form, and context, and to accomplish its goals using new strategies and tactics even as the context in which it operates dramatically. Much of the change outlined in this first section of this chapter involves first-order changes. These changes are not transformational, as in Schlechty's third-order changes, nor are they necessarily dependent upon advanced technologies for their direction, as in second-order changes.

Clearly, the distinction between what is on-campus learning and what is distance learning has blurred significantly during the past decade. Campuses are wired (and are also wireless), access to the Internet is ubiquitous, courses are routinely offered online simultaneously to both on- and off-campus students, and blended formats for learning are routinely provided as options to more and more students. Allen and Seaman (2005) reported in a national institutional survey of online learning that almost two thirds of reporting institutions offer graduate and undergraduate courses online, and almost half of those offering programs at the masters degree level also offer graduate programs online; among institutions offering graduate business degrees, more than 40% offer online business degree programs. Dramatic, first-order change has occurred, and these changes are accelerating with the integration of technology into the core of universities, but they are only beginning to create opportunities for and examples of third-order or transformational change.

Several of these first-order procedural, strategic, and tactical changes are described in the following sections, followed by an in-depth analysis of how learning models are evolving to accommodate these changes.

THE EXTENDED TRADITIONAL UNIVERSITY

Recent trends and studies in the United States show that learners, especially adults, expect institutions of higher education to be responsive to their individual needs, which increasingly means providing course schedules and formats that are convenient, easily accessed, and independent of a fixed times and locations (Allen & Seaman, 2004; Primary Research Group, 2004). Where distance learning programs in past decades were operated largely at the margins of traditional universities, and were focused almost exclusively on meeting the needs of adult students, the changing context for learning has forced rethinking of institutional strategies even among traditional universities. Universities have developed increasingly sophisticated units charged with leading change in order to address new needs and new markets. It is now unclear whether the changes that are occurring are resulting in distance education being mainstreamed, or, as Allen and Seaman (2004) suggested, whether mainstream universities are being transformed by changing society demands, rapid technological change, and new competition. Recent changes in all sectors of higher education, in the United States and in many other countries around the world, have been highly entrepreneurial, market-oriented, and responsive to these growing clienteles. A variety of programming strategies have been tested, including duplication, replication, diversification, niche programming and technologies, and aggregation (Hanna, 2000b).

THE DISTANCE EDUCATION/
TECHNOLOGY-BASED UNIVERSITIES

With the rapidly changing circumstances described above, the environment for higher education across the globe is increasingly competitive, turbulent, and unsettled. Hannan and Freeman (1989) indicate that uncertain, volatile environments will support diverse organizational forms. Kaufman (1991) indicated that the increase in diversity of organizational forms is, in and of itself, a critical factor adding further to the complexity of the environment over time. Indeed, over the past 30 years, several new and rapidly growing institutional forms of higher education have emerged. These range from smaller national universities formed in many countries around independent or distance education teaching strategies to mega-universities (United Kingdom Open University, the China TV University System, the Indira Ghandhi Open University in India, and others) with enrollments of more than 100,000 students learning at a distance (see Daniel, 1996, chapter 1). In many countries around the world, these large-scale "mega-universities" organized around distance learning are a fundamental component of national economic development and educational strategies.

Smaller institutions of this type in the United States include Empire State College, Thomas Edison State University in New Jersey, and the College of Lifelong Learning in New Hampshire. Hanna (2000c) described these new universities under the framework of distance education/technology-based universities, and these are but one of the organizational forms that have emerged in response to new and expanded needs, and new opportunities. In this context, Kaufman suggested that, just as nature abhors a vacuum, organizations abhor uncertainty. The new programming opportunities of this volatile environment result in ever-increasing forms of competition while at the same time producing responses from existing universities that attempt to minimize the uncertainty created by new and emerging models. In this way, the door has opened to an entirely new form of university, one that operates in the business world with representation on Wall Street.

FOR-PROFIT UNIVERSITIES

During the past several decades, a small number of for-profit universities (e.g., the University of Phoenix, DeVry University, Strayer University, Capella University, Argosy University, and Walden University) have been established in the United States in order to take advantage of lucrative "high-end" learning "markets" created by the accelerating pace of change, and the changing structure of the global economy (Hanna, 2000d). These for-profit universities are generally founded by entrepreneurial leaders (see Sperling, 2000), often frustrated by a lack of responsiveness and change in traditional universities, and motivated in part by the opportunity to generate revenue.

Most of the for-profit universities have added online programs, and these online programs have grown substantially as the market has expanded. Several for-profit universities—for example, Jones International University, Concord University, and Cardean University—have been organized exclusively around making programs available only online. While enrollments in these online universities are still relatively modest, they represent a dramatically growing segment of higher education.

STRATEGIC ALLIANCES

Collaborations or strategic partnerships that bring together two or more universities are increasingly a means of enhancing the competitive positions of existing universities. In many cases, university-business strategic alliances are being formed to build organizational capacity to deliver new services and programs and to reach new audiences. These new collaborations and alliances exhibit many elements and forms, and involve blending organizational missions, goals, programs, capabilities, and personnel to create new learning strategies and opportunities. Kaufman (1991) suggested that alliances are effective in times of complexity and competition in at least three ways. First, they spread risk; second, they enable the organization to incorporate new ideas; and third, they help the organization to bypass cultural prohibitions against previously heretical ideas or practices.

These formal strategic alliances in distance learning began rather modestly in the early 1980s in the United States, and were generally formed between organizations (university to university or university to business) in a single country. National Technological University in the United States, founded in 1982 as a separate degree-granting institution working in partnership with other major institutions to offer degrees in engineering, is an excellent early example of this type of alliance.

Such alliances are now becoming global in nature. One example is the World Universities Network (WUN; http://www.wun.ac.uk), an alliance of leading universities from China, North American, Europe, Australia, and the United Kingdom. This consortium was originally formed to share investments in emerging scientific research areas, but quickly expanded to include e-learning research, program collaboration in online programs, and technology development. A second example is Universitas 21 (http://www.universitas21.com/), another worldwide consortium that was formed in 1999 for the purpose of facilitating collaboration and cooperation between the member universities and creating entrepreneurial opportunities on a scale that no individual member would be able to achieve operating independently or through traditional bilateral alliances. While these types of international alliances appear impressive on the surface, most have yet to actually organize full-scale collaborative degree programs beyond those provided by their members. A major challenge is whether they can overcome the significant cultural differences, operational understandings, and educational practices among their members and arrive at a common vision, mission, and direction.

Western Governors University (WGU; http://www.wgu.edu) in the United States is another example of a strategic alliance designed to gain market advantage and serve students more effectively. Originally formed by the western states governors in 1996 around the concept of becoming a clearinghouse and marketing vehicle for distance learning courses for universities throughout the West, WGU leaders quickly learned that something more was needed to attract both partners and students, and as a result, they have selected as a core programmatic feature the concept of competency-based degrees, which require measures of competencies for each degree to be developed. This has enabled WGU to occupy a relatively unfilled (but very likely to grow in the future) programming niche in distance learning.

Another example of a strategic alliance that is becoming prevalent is the business-university alliance, such as Cardean Learning Group (http://www.unext.com), a business that has developed its own university, Cardean University, and established partnerships with a number of universities to offer online degree programs in business to adult students. Also, universities and companies have developed alliances and agreements where the university provides online course content and the company provides the online Web-based platforms for computer conferencing, course management, and content delivery. These platforms have been developed with many different features, and they relieve universities of significant development and implementation costs.

In this competitive environment—with the pace of change accelerating, with learners becoming more knowledgeable and sophisticated, with greater diversity and numbers of organizations coming into existence, and with the high cost of investing in new technologies—strategic planning and careful organizational development in distance education is increasingly critical, and an understanding of learning models and pedagogical choices, as well as the academic, financial, and marketing implications of the choices, is essential.

EVOLVING LEARNING MODELS AND CONCEPTS
OF DISTANCE EDUCATION

Until just a few years ago, distance education was a first-order change designed to provide the same learning opportunities available in on-campus settings to individual students separated from the campus by distance. Distance education was conceptualized as involving a teacher (T) interacting asynchronously (A) with a single student (S). Separated by distance, the teacher and student engaged in a structured two-way exchange (Keegan, 1988, 1993; Moore, 1973; Moore & Kearsley, 1996; Peters & Keegan, 1994) mediated by print and electronic technologies ($T:A:S:1>1$). Wedemeyer (1981) emphasized the independence of learner action within this model, and Keegan (1990, p. 44) specifically excluded the learning group as a primary context for distance education learning and teaching, although he acknowledged the possibility of "occasional meetings for didactic and social purposes." This model of learning was adopted in university correspondence or independent learning courses in the United States at the turn of the 20th century, and was expanded dramatically with the development of open universities in the latter half of the century. In the United Kingdom, Europe, Australia, and New Zealand, as well as many other countries, print-based materials, audiocassettes, and other learning resources were used to create a common framework for the learner to access university courses and degree programs at times and schedules convenient to them.

Over the past two decades, a large number of countries—especially those with higher education systems unable to meet the burgeoning demand created by rapidly growing populations and economic circumstances—have created open universities based upon the independent learner model, primarily to deal with this explosion in demand. As already noted, many of these universities have very large enrollments, in the hundreds of thousands (Daniel, 1996). This development led Otto Peters to suggest that distance education could be described as an industrial form of education, where mass distribution, standardization, division of labor, and assembly-line procedures were defining characteristics (Peters & Keegan, 1994). Referring to the development of national open universities, Evans (1999) referred to these focused efforts as "single-mode" distance teaching universities, as contrasted with "single-mode" campus-based universities, or the mixed-mode universities described by Rumble (1986).

In the United States, Thomas Edison State University (New Jersey) and Empire State College (New York) were created based upon the concept of offering degrees using the $T:A:S:1>1$ model. Until the past decade or two, other more established universities in the United States were limited to offering courses but usually not full degrees using this model. Much earlier in Australia and New Zealand, many campus-based universities also offered full degree programs at a distance using the $T:A:S:1>1$ model; these universities were known as dual-mode institutions, reflecting the fact that they offered degrees both on-campus and at a distance. The term *dual-mode* has gradually been supplanted in Australia by the concept of flexible learning. For example, the University of Wollengong defines flexible learning as allowing duration and intensity, place, method, and delivery medium to reflect the learning objectives, the needs of the student, the subject and course requirements, and the judgment of the teacher (see http://cedir.uow.edu.au/NCODE/info/definitions.html#flexdef); however, the structures have changed remarkably little (Evans, 1999). From a policy perspective, this model fit well within traditional universities in that it involved little change in curriculum, minimal demands on faculty, and could be budgeted in such a way as to be self-sufficient. The model relies upon intrinsic, independent learner motivation for success (Holmberg, 1989, p. 189; Sewart, Keegan, & Holmberg, 1983, p. 168). Course completion rates for this model have consistently been quite low, and from the individual learner's perspective, this represents a serious disadvantage. Some scholars have argued that low completion rates occur because adults have targeted learning goals other than course and degree completion (Wedemeyer, 1981, p. 556). It is also the case, however, that, from a program financial perspective, low course completion rates have resulted in greater institutional profit per student served, and such financial reinforcement of negative outcomes has served as an unfortunate disincentive to program leaders hoping to improve on this weakness of the model.

More recent definitions of distance education programs have included the extension of traditional classrooms to new locations where a teacher (T) is connected synchronously (S) with students (S^2) in classrooms ($T:S:S^2:1>S^2$). Widely utilized in the United States, the most common form of this definition has been the connection of off-campus learners via audio conferencing, video conferencing, or computer conferencing at scheduled times. Very often, especially when utilizing video connections, students may still travel to a central location, such as a community site or an educational center, to access the technology and to meet with other students. Yet this requirement is rapidly changing as systems become more robust in their connective capabilities and technology access in homes and businesses improves. Both of these traditionally structured and institutionally framed definitions of distance education, and the resulting pedagogical strategies, are heavily dependent upon teacher-directed instructional goals and activities, and have become quite limiting as the Internet and the World Wide Web have developed. As such, they still largely represent Schlechty's (1997) first dimension of change, that of the adoption of procedural changes that alter how the task of teaching is accomplished. While the $T:S:S^2:1>S^2$ model has been effective in addressing the issues of completion rates and course comparability well, its requirement for students to meet together in real time presents a serious impediment for many busy adult students.

A third set of emerging new models is rapidly developing, where students are dynamically connected through the Internet and other advanced technologies—with each other, with faculty mentors, and with institutional academic support structures—in ways not imagined just a few years ago; and where choices regarding pedagogy, technology, culture, and strategy are increasingly complex and blurred (Hanna, 2000a). Students are provided with continuous and regular opportunities to interact with each other and with the teacher, but to do so asynchronously. The teacher (T) is connected asynchronously (A) with students (S^2) who are able to interact with both the teacher and with other students around collaborative discussions, assignments, and team projects ($T:A:S^2:1>S^2$). The Sloan Foundation in the United States has provided millions of dollars of financing of Web-based online instruction to almost 50 universities and colleges in the past 10 years; it is worth noting, however, that the Foundation has traditionally funded only those online programs that do not require synchronous interaction among students, still a relatively small percentage of online courses and programs that are campus-based. In these emerging models, what is on-campus and what is off-campus in most traditional institutions is growing more difficult to discern, and independent learning is increasingly mixed with collaborative learning (Hanna, 2000c). Technologies are also rapidly converging, so that video, audio, and print are all coming together through the Web in support of learning, and access to these advanced technologies is growing. Even today, however, the question of whether or not learners in online Web-based courses are required to interact only with their instructors, or also with other learners, is a point of distinction among instructors, and among organizational models that are in place or under development at many universities (Hanna, Glowacki-Dudka, & Conceição-Runlee, 2000). In fact, this difference may emerge as a singular point of distinction among degree programs and courses offered at a distance, which otherwise will likely become more and more similar from one institution to another in the areas of technology employed, modes of access, services provided, and content delivered.

These new pedagogical frameworks and organizational models have come into prominence in concert with the development and application of constructivist learning theory in higher education. Constructivist learning theory suggests that

- knowledge and beliefs are formed within the learner
- learners personally imbue experiences with meaning
- learning activities should enable learners to gain access to their experiences, knowledge, and beliefs
- learning is a social activity that is enhanced by shared inquiry
- reflection and metacognition are essential aspects of constructing knowledge and meaning
- the outcomes of the learning process are varied and often unpredictable
- learning occurs when "students generate knowledge from within, not when they receive information from outside." (Lambert et al., 1995, pp. 17–18.)

What these principles suggest is a very different focus for the creation of effective learning environments, from an environment that focuses upon the knowledge, teaching performance, and competence of the teacher first and foremost, to one that emphasizes the engagement of the student with both the content and with other students; the systematic creation of opportunities within and outside of the "classroom," both to learn and to demonstrate or model what has been learned; and assessment strategies that enable the growth and development of the learner in more personally meaningful and measurable ways. In a sense, learning changes from being the product of an "industrial process of mass distribution of knowledge" to becoming a process whereby learners' needs for knowledge are addressed through customized and highly personal strategies that are initiated by the learner with assistance from and in consultation with the teacher.

TECHNOLOGICAL MODELS

Schlecty's (1997) second major process for change involves changing the means by which work is accomplished. In this context, the changes in distance education practice have been dramatic, if not profound. For most of the 20th century, distance education involved the technologies of pen and pencil, paper, the typewriter, and the postal service, which provided the sole link between the individual instructor and the individual student. Electronic technologies have increasingly changed this interaction. With the development of radio and then television, it became possible to transmit educational courses, programs, and content widely using these mass media distribution channels. More recently, satellite distribution enabled even broader access to university courses, and the emergence of teleconferencing software, allowing many people to be connected together simultaneously by audio, added to the power of these technologies by enabling interaction between and among students and teachers. Some universities developed an electronic technological framework for their distance education programs, investing heavily in expensive satellite equipment, audio conferencing equipment, the electronic blackboard, and computers. It is now possible to go to the most remote areas of countries throughout the world and visit schools fueled by solar power and generators that are connected by satellite with universities, and they are also able to connect to the World Wide Web. In many cases, the technologies available have advanced far more rapidly that the capacity to use them to full potential, resulting in costly investments in technology and programs that have not met expectations in student learning or in numbers of enrollments. Very often, maintenance of equipment in difficult environments is an afterthought, weather difficulties still interfere with signals, the confidence to use technology in new ways is not present within the learner or the teacher, and motivation wanes after the initial excitement. One of the important lessons of implementing technology wisely is that providing 24-hour technology support and help, even for experienced users, is essential.

While access to electronic learning technologies has increased dramatically, none of these technologies have fundamentally challenged basic learning models of universities. Instead, technologies have been used to enable universities to do what they were already doing, but more expansively and more efficiently, rather than being the catalyst to radically change either the content or the instructional processes employed. Even when two-way interactive video was developed, the first models, such as those employed at Ohio University and at Washington State University in the United States in the mid-1980s, were organized around the principle of not requiring the faculty member to adjust his or her teaching in any way. The model was intended simply to extend what the faculty member was already doing to new sites and to more students. More recent video systems enable or sometimes require the faculty member to manage the technology, but rely essentially on the faculty member as content distributor in the same way the traditional lecture does.

The rapid deployment of the Internet radically altered previous technological environments for distance learning, opening up many new possibilities for connecting learners and teachers, as noted in the previous section. The Internet has made possible the World Wide Web, with powerful and very rapidly expanding means of distributing and sharing knowledge on a global basis. As just one example, Google, Google Scholar, and Google Earth (http://www.google.com) are three knowledge seeking and sharing services that have been available less than 10 years, but they have impacted our ways of accessing, storing, and sharing information in profound ways. There are also new and inexpensive ways of creating virtual interactions among people across international borders. Skype (http://www.skype.com), for example, enables worldwide audio, text, and video interactions between online users at a fraction of the cost of previous interactive technologies. It is now literally possible to be a learner or a teacher in universities without being present at the university, and still be connected to one's colleagues or to other learners on a daily real-time way. While there is considerable debate about whether or not the Internet is a "disruptive" technology regarding higher education (see Armstrong, 2000), or a sustaining one, there is little disagreement that its arrival has opened up many new possibilities for delivering education.

During the past two decades, new universities have been established and existing universities have made adaptations to take advantage of computer-mediated conferencing systems and the emergence of the World Wide Web to enable asynchronous and synchronous interaction among students and the teacher. The goal of these technology-based approaches to learning is to minimize the physical and psychological separation of the learner from the instructor. Growing experience with online Web-based platforms in distance education and in campus-based programs are changing the strategies for learning at a distance to be more group oriented and interactive. Early adopters are also attempting to document or demonstrate the financial advantages of online instruction. During the past decade, the Sloan Foundation has funded numerous venues for discussion of the challenge of "scaling up," or serving more students at less cost (than through face-to-face courses), and has funded a number of universities with the goal of demonstrating this greater efficiency of online instruction. Unfortunately, this focus on cost-efficiency is often directly counter to the opportunities for a greater range of human interaction made possible by emerging pedagogical models and technologies designed to link faculty with students more interactively in the construction of knowledge. Today, being connected is within the realm of possibility for learners separated by distance, and the connection with others and to increasingly sophisticated sources of content is becoming central to the learning process.

It is important to note that learning technologies are often interjected into the learning process even as it makes the connection between the student and the teacher possible across distance. Whether audio, video, text, or a combination of all three basic means of communication, the technology chosen continues to influence to a great extent what can and cannot be done in the learning environment among students and the instructor. New technologies include the pocket PC, the omnipresent cell phone, videostreaming and storage technologies, and worldwide low cost audio such as that provided by companies such as Skype and Yahoo. The presence of these technologies is always a "fourth force" in the "classroom"; the other three forces being the content to be learned, the teacher, and the learner. Until recently and for many reasons, this fourth force of technology has been employed primarily to extend the teacher rather than to empower the student, a concept that is transformational and involves radically changing assumptions about learning and teaching.

TRANSFORMATIONAL CHANGE
AND ORGANIZATIONAL MODELS

Understanding the complex dynamics of cultural values, conflict, and organizational change in universities is critical to building a framework for analyzing issues in distance education. Transformational change, according to Schlechty (1997), involves changing the nature of the work of the university, reorienting its purpose, and refocusing its intent, and involves deep changes in the culture of the organization. It is not clear whether transformational change in universities, and specifically with distance education, is occurring or not, but there are some signals that dramatic changes may be underway. For example, will the university continue to focus on producing academic degrees and credits as its primary measure of learning, or will other measures become prominent? Will its activities continue to be concentrated in campuses, conveying the idea that the "university is a place," or will its focus increasingly be "independent of place" and focused on the widest possible forms of knowledge sharing and discovery? How will the productivity of the university of the future be measured, and will its distance education efforts gradually become its most prominent future? These possibilities are clearly in the future, but if realized, they would clearly be transformational in nature.

Bergquist (1992), writing about traditional campus-based universities, characterizes most academic environments as involving a mix of four primary internal cultures interacting with each other in different ways depending upon the mission, programs, and historical framework of the specific institution. The four internal cultures described by Bergquist include:

- the managerial culture, which finds meaning in the organization of work, and which conceives of the institution's enterprise as the inculcation of specific knowledge, skills, and attitudes in students who will become successful and responsible citizens;
- the developmental culture, which finds meaning in furthering the personal and professional growth of all members of the collegiate community, primarily defined as existing within the campus environment;
- the negotiating culture, which is concerned with and responsible for establishing and executing equitable and egalitarian policies and procedures for the distribution of resources and benefits in the institution; and
- the collegial culture, which is the core of most institutions, sustained primarily by faculty members, and finding meaning in academic disciplines; valuing faculty research, scholarship, teaching, and governance; and holding sway over the institution's most important assets—its curriculum and its faculty.

In adapting Bergquist's work to be more applicable to emerging organizational models and university cultures, Hanna (2000c) introduced a fifth important culture that is emerging as a powerful force in universities worldwide—the *entrepreneurial culture*. The entrepreneurial culture values the ability to change, and to change quickly; to respond to market forces; to connect with and generate support from external audiences and constituencies; and to introduce new ideas, programs, delivery mechanisms, and goals and purposes into the other four cultures described by Bergquist.

McNay (1995) framed organizational options differently, suggesting that four dominant cultures within universities have been in major transition over the past decade. These four cul-

TABLE 38.1.
Evolution of Organizational Models in the Academy

Organizational Model	Key Words	Dominant Values
Collegium	Freedom	Permissive
Bureaucracy	Regulation	Equity
Corporation	Power	Loyalty
Enterprise	Client	Competence

Adapted from: McNay (1995), Summary characteristics of four organizational models, p. 109

tures—the (a) collegium, (b) bureaucracy, (c) corporation, and (d) enterprise—are all present in most universities, but McNay noted in many universities a general evolution toward the enterprise model. He suggested key words associated with each model, as noted in Table 38.1.

As these examples illustrate, dramatic changes in higher education are underway and distance education programs and technologies are very often major drivers of this change. These changes are more than simple procedural changes or ways of conducting business; they represent fundamental shifts in values, assumptions, and missions, and will result in new cultural assumptions and understandings over time. Already, many universities are becoming more focused around what the student is experiencing, and less centered around the internal organizational framework of the university. To put it another way, more attention is being paid to the experience of the client, and the nature of the academy is likely to change dramatically over time as a result. As just one example of this evolving culture, institutional accreditation processes, long an instrument for maintaining and preserving higher education standards and practice, are moving away from measuring inputs and program elements such as faculty, library books, and administrative and governance processes, and toward the measurement of student learning outcomes and benefits. An example of how these processes are changing is the Academic Quality Improvement Project (AQIP) sponsored by the North Central Association Commission on Higher Learning, the largest of the regional accrediting associations (North Central Association Higher Learning Commission, 2001). This project is focused around change, improvement, and processes related to the student experience.

Table 38.2 are some of the ways that changing values and mission may change decision making and leadership in the future.

Of particular note is the culture's orientation to change. Musselwhite (2000) developed an instrument called the Change Style Indicator,[1] which measures individual preferences toward change. The Change Style Indicator provides feedback to individuals using a continuum from Conserver to Pragmatist to Originator. While no clear assignment to organizational models or culture can be established yet, data collected thus far suggests that individuals in enterprises (businesses, manufacturing, and for-profit organizations) tend to be stronger originators than those in government, education, and non-profit organizations. As universities develop enterprise orientations, their comfort in originating new institutional directions, programs, and innovations should grow.

---

[1]See also Discovery Learning Web site, http://www.discoverylearning.net

TABLE 38.2.
The Changing Cultures of Higher Education*

	Collegium	Bureaucracy	Enterprise
Orientation to change	Conservers	Pragmatists	Originators
Leadership	Stewardship	Preservation	Visionary
Values	Faculty/program	Administrative efficiency	Client-oriented
Decision-making	Restricted/shared internal	Vertical/Top-down	Horizontal/shared with stakeholders
Support structures	Program-driven	Rule-focused	Learner-focused
Key messages	Quality	Efficiency	Market-driven
Communication strategies	Internal	Vertical/formal	External/internal horizontal informal
Systems and resources	Duplicated according to need	Stable, efficient, and pre-organized	Evolving "as needed"
Key messages	Stick together	Don't rock the boat	Seize the day
Alliances	Value not easily recognized	Unnecessary	Sought out and implemented
Organizational features	Specialized	Segmented and vertical	Integrated and cross-functional
Budgets	Stable/priority programs	Tightly controlled	Fluid/opportunity seeking
Actions	Evolutionary	Targeted	Revolutionary
New Programs	Complement existing programs	Fit existing structures	Make new markets/force new structures
Competition	Avoid competition	Minimize competition through regulation	Exploit competitive advantage
Strategies	Improve quality	Improve efficiency	Establish new market "niches"
Faculty and Staff Value	Independence	Authority and predictability	Collaboration
Rewards	Individual	Functional	Organizational

*For purposes of this discussion, the corporation structure described by McNay is omitted. A case can be made for its inclusion, based upon the growing presence of for-profit universities. Yet, given the relatively recent arrival of these new forms of universities, the enterprise definition seems more appropriate at this stage of development.

CONCLUSION

Higher education in general has been primarily concerned with the education of young adults in residential settings rather than with distance learning programs primarily organized through stable correspondence programs. In both of these contexts, however, educational life has been relatively predictable. Change was viewed, as Schwahn and Spady (1998) suggested, as a destination, an event that, while episodic in nature, was quite predictable. Major change has been viewed within the academy as either unnecessary or risky, but this orientation is likely to change as the environment for education has become more volatile.

Schlechty (1997) stated

> Until recently, structural and cultural change has been viewed by many as largely beyond the direct control of leaders and planners. Therefore, rather than asking, How can organizations be reoriented

so that they do new things and serve new ends? leaders and planners have asked, How can organizations be made to serve the ends they now serve more efficiently? and, How can organizations do the jobs they now do better? Given these latter questions, culture and structure are likely to be viewed as impediments to change, rather than as the content that must be changed. (p. 220)

And from another perspective more critical to change in the current culture and structure of higher education, emerging organizational, pedagogical, and technological models of distance education will continue to be threatening to the core of higher education.

Universities with active distance learning programs are now operating in a more competitive and businesslike environment than ever before. In many cases, the distance learning program is charged with providing leadership for new ideas, approaches, and models and for leading organizational change. The leaders of these programs are much more likely to view change as a journey, and to plan processes into the institution that assist in assessing options and implementing new program directions. According to Schwahn and Spady (1998), change is a continuous process, highly chaotic in nature, but necessary for organizational renewal and even survival. Even when change is viewed as "disruptive to the existing order," as David Noble and others have argued (Armstrong, 2000; Noble, 1998; Winner, 1998), there is no question that distance learning has the potential to radically change and transform educational practice in higher education.

REFERENCES

Allen, E. I., & Seaman, J. (2004). *Entering the mainstream: The quality and extent of online education in the United States, 2003 and 2004*. Wellesley, MA: The Sloan Consortium

Allen, E. I., & Seaman, J. (2005). *Growing by degrees: Online education in the United States, 2005*. Wellesley, MA: The Sloan Consortium.

Armstrong, L. (2000). Distance learning: An academic leader's perspective on a disruptive product. *Change, 32*(6), 20–27.

Bergquist, W. H. (1992). *The four cultures of the academy: Insights and strategies for improving leadership in collegiate organizations* (1st ed.). San Francisco: Jossey-Bass.

Daniel, S. J. (1996). *Mega-universities and knowledge media: Technology strategies for higher education*. London: Biddles Ltd.

Evans, T. (1999). From dual-mode to flexible delivery: Paradoxical transitions in Australian open and distance education. *Performance Improvement Quarterly, 12*(2), 84–95.

Hanna, D. E. (2000a). Approaches to learning in collegiate classrooms. In D. E. Hanna (Ed.), *Higher education in an era of digital competition: Choices and challenges* (pp. 45–70). Madison, WI: Atwood.

Hanna, D. E. (2000b). Emerging organizational models: The extended traditional university. In D. E. Hanna (Ed.), *Higher education in an era of digital competition: Choices and challenges* (pp. 92–113). Madison, WI: Atwood.

Hanna, D. E. (Ed.). (2000c). *Higher education in an era of digital competition: Choices and challenges*. Madison, WI: Atwood.

Hanna, D. E. (2000d). New players on the block: For-profit, corporate, and competency-based learning universities. In D. E. Hanna (Ed.), *Higher education in an era of digital competition: Choices and challenges* (pp. 139–164). Madison, WI: Atwood.

Hanna, D. E., Glowacki-Dudka, M., & Conceição-Runlee, S. (2000). *147 practical tips for teaching online groups: Essentials of Web-based education*. Madison, WI: Atwood.

Hannan, M. T., & Freeman, J. (1989). *Organizational ecology*. Cambridge, MA: Harvard University Press.

Holmberg, B. (1989). *Theory and practice of distance education*. London, New York: Routledge.

Kaufman, H. (1991). *Time, chance, and organizations: Natural selection in a perilous environment* (2nd ed.). Chatham, NJ: Chatham House.

Keegan, D. (1988). On defining distance education. In D. Sewart, D. Keegan, & B. Holmberg (Eds.), *Distance education: International perspectives*. New York: Routledge, Chapman & Hall, Inc.

Keegan, D. (1990). *Foundations of distance education*. (2nd ed.). London, New York: Routledge.

Keegan, D. (1993). *Theoretical principles of distance education*. London, New York: Routledge.

Lambert, L., Walker, D., Zimmerman, D. P., Cooper, J. E., Lambert, M. D., Gardner, M. E., et al. (Eds.). (1995). *The constructivist leader*. New York: Teachers College Press.

Lyall, K. C., & Sell, K. R. (2005). *The true genius of America at risk: The de facto privatization of public higher education*. Westport, Connecticut: Praeger/Greenwood.

McNay, I. (1995). From the collegial academy to corporate enterprise: The changing cultures of universities. In T. Schuller (Ed.), *The changing university?* (pp. 105–115). Buckingham, England; Bristol, PA: Society for Research into Higher Education; Open University Press.

Moore, M. G. (1973). Toward a theory of independent learning and teaching. *Journal of Higher Education, 44*, 661–679.

Moore, M. G., & Kearsley, G. (1996). *Distance education: A systems view*. Belmont, CA: Wadsworth.

Musselwhite, W. C. (2000). *Change style indicator: Research and development report*. Greensboro, NC: Discovery Learning Press.

National Center for Higher Education Management Systems (NCHEMS). (2005). *NCHEMS News*. Retrieved January 22, 2006, from http://www.nchems.org/News/NCHEMS%20News%20June2005.pdf

Noble, D. (1998). *Digital diploma mills*. Retrieved January 22, 2006, from http://www.firstmonday.dk/issues/issue3_1/noble/index.html

North Central Association Higher Learning Commission. (2006). *Academic quality improvement project*. Retrieved January 22, 2006, from http://www.aqip.org/

Peters, O., & Keegan, D. (1994). *Otto Peters on distance education: The industrialization of teaching and learning*. London, New York: Routledge.

Primary Research Group. (2004). *The survey of distance learning programs in higher education*. New York: Primary Research Group.

Rumble, G. (1986). *The planning and management of distance education*. London: Croom Helm.

Schlechty, P. C. (1997). *Inventing better schools: An action plan for educational reform*. San Francisco: Jossey-Bass.

Schwahn, C. J., & Spady, W. G. (1998). *Total leaders: Applying the best future-focused change strategies to education*. Arlington, VA: American Association of School Administrators.

Sewart, D., Keegan, D., & Holmberg, B. (1983). *Distance education: International perspectives*. London, New York: Croom Helm; St. Martin's Press.

Sperling, J. G. (2000). *Rebel with a cause: The entrepreneur who created the University of Phoenix and the for-profit revolution in higher education*. New York: Wiley.

Wedemeyer, C. A. (1981). *Learning at the back door: Reflections on non-traditional learning in the lifespan*. Madison: University of Wisconsin Press.

Winner, L. (1998). *Report from the digital diploma mills conference*. Chatham Center for Advanced Study. Retrieved January 22, 2006, from http://www.oreilly.com/people/staff/stevet/netfuture/1998/Jun0298_72.html#3.

39

Training in the Corporate Sector

Zane L. Berge
University of Maryland, Baltimore County

One way to view management's role is that managers must constantly align and realign the strategic plan of the organization so that mission-critical functions match the core capabilities and core competencies of the enterprise.

If we begin to analyze the above statement, we find several concepts that need to be explored: strategic plan, mission-critical functions, core capabilities, and core competencies. Distance education forces managers to think of each of these in new ways. Even how strategic planning is accomplished successfully in the global economy of the 21st century is different from in the past.

Managers and leaders who are charged with distance training and education functions decide on what courses and programs to produce and what media/infrastructure will be used to implement these programs. Their decisions are guided by organizational mission and business needs, usually determined by market research or policy (Berge, 2001; Berge & Kearsley, 2003). This means aligning projects and programs that involve distance training and education activities with strategic plans. Said simply, managers are using distance training and education to solve business problems through managing and planning (Berge & Smith, 2000). That having been said, we are only beginning to identify in useful ways what the capabilities and competencies are that are needed in distance training and education.

GLOBAL ECONOMY IS CHANGING HOW WE DO BUSINESS

Our global society is moving into the Knowledge Age, where technology dictates that we will live, work, and learn differently than we did during the Industrial Age. These changes demand more skills, knowledge, learning, and relearning. What is mission-critical to an organization often changes, because what is important in today's society seems ever-changing. The transition from an industrial economy to a knowledge-based economy has companies competing to control intellectual assets, not physical assets (McCrea, Gay, & Bacon, 2000). With the increased rate at which the amount of information is doubling, it becomes important that the right information reaches the right people when it is needed (Ruttenbur, Spickler, & Lurie, 2000, p. 10).

Many changes have to do with philosophy and, in turn, organizational culture. For instance, it used to be that university students could, for the most part, in four years or four years plus graduate work, expect to gain the skills and knowledge necessary to prepare them for a lifetime of work in their chosen field. Of course, today's university educators do not harbor any illusions. Each professor knows that it is increasingly important to teach students how to learn, so that the effects of the ever-decreasing half-life of knowledge can be ameliorated with life-long learning as a goal. The same is true of learners in the workplace.

A consideration of training at a distance forces a re-examination about the ways people learn and are trained (Albright & Post, 1993). Corporate employees in the future will need to take control of their own growth and development, demanding training time and money as part of their rewards for supplying their services. Adult-education principles of self-directed and life-long learning will become a major part of compensation packages. Collective-bargaining agreements in the future will probably require levels of training for employees that do not exist today. Companies desiring a competitive advantage will "jump on the band wagon" and establish policies and procedures to take advantage of distance learning to deliver these services. . . . The rapidly changing workplace of the future will demand that trainers move toward this vision with a spirit of adventure. Training professionals at all levels will need considerable imagination, common sense, and creativity to cope with the changes that undoubtedly await us. Corporate success depends upon having and keeping talented people. The shortage of such people is widely accepted, and training (including distance education), at long last, is beginning to be recognized as part of the solution (Dooley, Dooley, & Byrom, 1998, p. 353).

Along with these changes in how training and education is perceived are cultural changes throughout the organization and the people associated with it. For instance, as more employees have technology systems at home and as pressure increases for individuals to take control of their own learning throughout their lifetime, there can be a blurring of the distinction between what is learning and what is work (Berge et al., 2005; Takiya, Archbold, & Berge, 2005).

Employees know that they must continuously learn; otherwise they will personally be at a competitive disadvantage in the marketplace, and, therefore, they must demand the organization support their learning. McCrea et al. (2000) state that management's mission is to develop an "enterprise-wide process of continuous and globally distributed learning that directly links business goals and individual learning outcomes" (p. 16). While the concept of "just enough" training may be useful (Zielinski, 2000), there is no such thing as "just enough" learning.

BUSINESS NEEDS FOR DISTANCE EDUCATION
AND TRAINING

Training resources need to be used to accomplish the organization's strategic objectives. The usual approach, however, is for the various areas of an organization to look at the training function *after* the goals, objectives, and plans are in place. Essentially, business units or departments place their "orders" for training. This approach often leaves the training function scrambling for time and resources. This situation almost always results in a training function that cannot provide all the services requested of it, with those services that are supplied often being ineffective. Thus, training must provide its support with the constraints of a budget that has little relationship to need (Brace & Berge, in press).

Having a strategy that links distance training and education to the organization's business goals is important (Galagan, 2000; Watkins & Kaufman, this volume). There are compelling reasons for distance training and education in the workplace. Needs for which organizations are turning to distance training to help solve include a more widespread exposure to nationally and internationally recognized experts; reductions in costs such as time to market, travel expenditures, time spent in training; and lower opportunity costs of lost productivity that directly affect the productivity, quality, and access of employees in the organization.

SIGNIFICANT BUSINESS NEEDS

Essentially, one can view distance training serving three significant business needs:

1. meeting the challenge of uncommon organizational change
2. sustaining competitive advantage
3. achieving organizational goals

It can not be emphasized too strongly that in the global economy today, distance training, and education must solve critical business needs for it to be sustainable in the organization.

Meeting the Challenge of Uncommon Organizational Change

Short of bankruptcy, there may be no business event that serves as a more imperative catalyst for change than a corporate merger. The cultural context in which people work is made clear when a merger juxtaposes different cultures and challenges everyone to change and grow. For example, Friend and Hepple (2001) described the merging of SBC Communication's (now AT&T) regional telecom training centers:

> Working across time zones with widely varying systems, practices, and cultures challenged the merged SBC. Eliminating redundancies resulted in savings for the CFL and its SBC internal clients. However, staffing varied continuously through restructuring, job changes, outsourcing, and new hiring. As employee experience levels fluctuated, the need for faster, more effective, and flexible training had never been greater. (p. 52)

Another type of tumultuous change can come from a mandate, whether from a government authority or from the organization's chief executive. The cultural and organizational changes necessary to deal with these events are one of the principal reasons distance education has found success in meeting training and educational needs within many organizations.

Sustaining Competitive Advantage

We have entered the Knowledge Age, in which the new economy requires a continuously learning workforce (Walker, 2001). Rapid technological change and a core of knowledge workers who must stay abreast of these changes are considered key to sustaining a competitive advantage in the workplace. As organizations invest in building learning systems that serve the individual and the corporation for success in our new economy, distance training and education help meet the challenge of their competition and set the standards in the marketplace.

Achieving Organizational Goals

As the global economy changes the way business is transacted and as technology is a contributing factor to change, the competition for markets and customers continues to be a significant challenge. Distance training and education is looked upon as a way of investing in people throughout the organization, thereby adding value in the achievement of organizational goals.

KEY BUSINESS DRIVERS

The key drivers affecting the business unit using distance training and education include 1) cost to the employer, 2) lack of time for trainees and trainers, 3) the fast-paced and quickly changing industries, with rapid development-to-delivery cycles, which does not allow a window for training, 4) developing training for high volumes of employees 5) training for employees who are spread across a geographically diverse area, 6) reduced training budgets (in times of increased training needs), and, 7) the need to become a learning organization.

Cost to Employer

Many times, there are high costs to the organization associated with having a majority of training delivered in the traditional classroom. If trainers are not on-site, line managers must fund travel budgets and assume the loss of productivity for travel time for participants. With traditional training methods, companies generally spend more money, up to two-thirds of the training expenses, on transporting and housing trainees than on actual training programs (Mottl, 2000; Urdan & Weggen, 2000). Alternatives include outsourcing or having a trainer travel to each site. Other alternatives include having trainers travel to participants and, therefore, potentially reduce the overall corporation's training cost. The impact on the trainers, however, is often too great (Howard, 2001; Latten, Davis, & Stallings, 2001).

Lack of Time for Trainees

While cost is a major issue for the organization, the lack of time is a critical factor for the employees. Time to attend to personal technical skill development, while concurrently needing to attend to business deliverables that are on rapid development-to-delivery cycles, often seems impossible to everyone concerned (Branch, Lyon, & Porten, 2001).

Rapid Development-to-Delivery Cycles

By the time training is designed, developed, and scheduled, the employee no longer needs it! As competition and demand in today's society cause more rapid development-to-delivery cycles, there is a smaller window for training to occur with each of those products and services (Bersin, 2005; Dobbs, 2000). Latten et al. (2001) explained,

> Our client base was quickly surpassing the existing training infrastructure. Mergers and organizational changes were creating an environment where key business decisions were being made faster than ever. The result, an increased demand for training as a result of new business strategies and processes. The need for training to reach growing numbers of participants, faster and in their place of business was at an all time high. We knew that traditional classroom training was not a possible solution for meeting the current business challenges. Both cost and reduced cycle times were obstacles that traditional classroom training could not easily address. (p. 164)

In many cases, learning opportunities have to be modular, just-in-time, and highly relevant to compete with other tasks and opportunities that are critical to the success of the organization (Rogers & Becker, 2001). Many organizations face mergers, mandates, and increased business from other sources to the point that new initiatives occur faster than ever. As project timelines accelerate to meet the growing demands, the impact on training is that there is less time to build trainer expertise and less time to reach larger numbers of participants (Latten et al., 2001).

High Volumes of Employees

Large organizations are especially challenged in providing training, in trying to reduce costs with limited resources, and in providing a consistent message. Training at national or regional facilities becomes impossible when thousands or hundreds of thousands of employees need to be trained uniformly very quickly (Wankel, 2001).

Training Employees Who Are Spread Across a Geographically Diverse Area

When there are a great number of employees to train, and especially when they are dispersed geographically, equitable training delivery is difficult and costly.

Distance training and education usually makes economic sense, and can also make sense in these cases by making training content available in convenient, adult-sized bites, rather than in week-long sessions at remote locations. Persons charged with training can target specific audiences regardless of geographic location, or make subject matter experts available based on need rather than ease of access to location (Dessinger & Conley, 2001; Walker, 1998).

Reduced Training Budgets at a Time When More Training Is Needed

Budgets continue to be squeezed and managers are required to do more with less. Payne and Payne (1998) described such a scenario at the Federal Aviation Administration:

> The FAA's technical training budget was cut by Congress from over $135M in 1992 to just over $77M in 1996, a 43% decline (Federal Aviation Administration, 1997). This dramatic reduction in the training budget resulted in the number of FAA students receiving technical training declining from over 28,000 to just over 16,000, a corresponding drop of 41% (Federal Aviation Administration, 1997). A congressional mandate during this same period caused the FAA to go through a downsizing activity that reduced the size of the agency by 11%. This downsizing asked fewer FAA employees to do more during an era of a severely constrained and a continually declining training budget as the mission of the Agency did not change. The problem the FAA faced was finding ways to reduce the overall cost of providing training while increasing the training opportunities for employees. The FAA needed to solve this problem in a manner that was not prohibitively expensive in its start-up costs and that could begin to show a return on the investment almost immediately. (p. 202)

This type of phenomenon is more common each day.

Need to Become a Learning Organization

As mentioned earlier, university professors know they can not teach all that students will need to know in a field for a lifetime. Workplace organizations are starting to understand that the same thing is true about training. This is why Peter Senge's work regarding becoming a "learning organization" resonated as it has (Senge, 1990; Zemke, 1999). At the heart of the learning organization is a change in philosophy from instruction and training to learning—and a key element in distance training is the students' taking responsibility for their own learning. Workers who neglect to invest in their own intellectual capital do so at their own risk, given they can no longer rely on a single set of skills for a lifetime of work (Ruttenbur et al., 2000). So, employees today demand that organizations make a continuous investment in their professional development (McCrea et al., 2000, p. 11). All this significantly changes the roles and functions of both instructors and learners.

PLANNING AND MANAGING DISTANCE TRAINING AND EDUCATION

The challenge of planning and implementing distance education programs includes both pedagogical changes and organizational issues. The management team must systematically analyze organizational needs. It must include at least one person with high enough rank at the level in the organization that matches the strategic goals for the business unit to champion technology-enhanced learning. The team must also have a person or persons in charge of infrastructure and support services, and other managers and staff with a stake in promoting successful technology-enhanced learning. The charge to this management team may include the following:

- identify the business purposes and goals of initiating and supporting a distance learning program;
- collect and summarize information on current distance education programs and the strategic plans of various business units considering the use of distance training and education;
- evaluate strategies and technologies for delivering distance education programs (advantages, disadvantages, costs) and reach agreement on which strategies and technologies will be proposed;
- define what is needed to deliver technology-enhanced learning programs effectively including equipment and facilities; competencies and training; policy development and culture change;
- investigate successful models at other organizations;
- specify needs and incentives for instructors, designers, and developers who become involved in developing and implementing technology-enhanced learning;
- estimate costs and resource commitments;
- identify potential barriers to successful implementation of the recommended strategies and technologies and suggest how to manage these;
- establish a process for at least annual review of new technologies and other aspects of the distance programs to assess their potential for improving the delivery of distance training and reducing associated costs;
- report findings and recommendations to senior decision makers;
- define needs for particular academic programs (University of Kansas Medical Center, 1996).

OBSTACLES TO DISTANCE TRAINING AND EDUCATION

There are many individual barriers to distance training and education (Berge & Kendrick, 2005). Based on survey responses, a subsequent factor analysis clustered the 64 barriers into the following 10 factors: (1) administrative structure, (2) organizational change, (3) technical expertise, (4) social interaction and quality, (5) faculty compensation and time, (6) threatened by technology, (7) legal issues, (8) evaluation/effectiveness, (9) access, and, (10) student-support services (Muilenburg & Berge, 2001).

Administrative Structure

Lack of credibility for distance education within a particular administrative structure and lack of money can be problems for distance education. Competing with, or using, new business models can cause difficulties, too. When partnerships are formed among different units within an organization, or among different organizations, lack of agreement concerning such issues as revenue sharing, regulations, tuition and fees, as well as scheduling, full-time equivalents (FTEs), and issuance of credits can become obstacles to distance education.

Organizational Change

Most organizations are resistant to change. Without a shared vision for distance learning, a strategic plan, and key players within the organization who are knowledgeable and supportive of distance learning, implementing a distance learning program is a slow and difficult process. Difficulty in convincing stakeholders of the benefits of distance learning, the often slow pace of implementation, or the lack of an identifiable business need are all barriers to distance education.

The difficulty is not in converting training materials into an electronic format, but in trying to change corporate tradition and attitudes (Dooley et al., 1998, p. 353).

Technical Expertise, Support, and Infrastructure

It is difficult to keep up with the fast pace of technological change. Many instructors lack the knowledge and skills to design and teach distance learning courses, yet their organizations lack support staff to assist with technical problems, to develop distance learning course materials, or to provide distance learning training. The technology-enhanced classrooms or laboratories and the infrastructure required to use them may not be available.

Social Interaction and Quality

Participants in distance learning courses can feel isolated due to lack of person-to-person contact. Some educators and students are uncomfortable with the use of student-centered and collaborative-learning activities on philosophical grounds, or because these methods are usually a change from the traditional social structure of the classroom. There are concerns about the quality of distance learning courses, programs, the possible lack of prerequisite skills and knowledge of students, and student learning. The outcomes of student learning in distance education, as well as the testing and assessment of student outcomes are concerns.

Faculty Compensation and Time

In all stages of design, development, and evaluation, distance education courses almost always require a greater time commitment than the same instructional objectives or goals when using an in-person classroom. Therefore, instructor compensation, incentives, and workload become important issues if the system in use assumes traditional, in-person classrooms.

Threatened by Technology

Some people fear that an increase in the use of distance learning technologies may decrease the need for teaching instructors. Feeling intimidated by technology may also threaten an instructor's sense of competence or authority. Either or both of these psychological factors may lead a person to feel that his or her job security is threatened.

Trainers (line evaluators, contractors, and institute staff) perceived their classroom days were over. They had relished the role of "sage on the stage" and were reluctant to relinquish that gratifying identity. With technology perceived as the "enemy" in human interaction and spontaneity, many felt the joys of interacting with peers and colleagues would rapidly decline in this new medium reminiscent of the "high-tech, low-touch" theory. They struggled to envision the possibilities of building positive educational relationships online or through video conferencing (Longnecker, 2001).

Legal Issues

The increasing use of the Internet to deliver distance learning raises concerns about copyright, fair-use policies, intellectual property rights, and other legal issues such as piracy, problems with hackers, and viruses.

Evaluation/Effectiveness

There is concern over a lack of research supporting the effectiveness of distance learning as well as a lack of effective evaluation methods for distance learning courses and programs.

Access

Many students lack access or have concerns over equal access to courses offered via newer technologies such as Web-based instruction. Instructors also lack access to the necessary equipment and courses.

Student-Support Services

Provision of student services such as advisement, library services, and registration is a critical facet of any distance learning program. There are also concerns about how to monitor the identity of distance learning students.

STAGES OF ORGANIZATIONAL CAPABILITY

When considering the distance delivery of training and education and viewing the organization collectively, it is useful to think of the "stage" that the enterprise is at. As with any innovation, the process usually looks like two steps forward and one step back.

The promise of distance learning remains unfulfilled in many organizations. In spite of many good intentions, extensive pilots and trials, and a great deal of perception-building efforts, these organizations fail to recognize some key planning and implementation steps that can make the difference in sustaining distance learning (Howard, 2001, p. 270).

A brief model that described stages of organizational maturity, or capabilities, with regard to the delivery of distance training and education (Schreiber, 1998) was presented:

- Stage 1: Separate or sporadic distance learning events occur in the organization.
- Stage 2: The organization's technological capability and infrastructure can support distance learning events. When distance education events occur, they are replicated through an interdisciplinary team, which responds to staff and management needs and makes recommendations regarding the organization and management of distance learning among the workforce.
- Stage 3: The organization has established a distance learning policy, procedures are in place, and planning occurs. This means that a stable and predictable process is in place to facilitate the identification and selection of content and of technology to deliver distance training.
- Stage 4: Distance training and education has been institutionalized in the organization as characterized by policy, communication, and practice that are aligned so that business objectives are being addressed. The business unit has established a distance education identity and conducts systematic assessment of distance training events from an organizational perspective.

Of course, these stages represent points along a continuum; the capability stages an organization moves through, if planning to institutionalize distance training and education, are neither linear nor discrete. While it is convenient to describe an organization as generally being at a particular stage, this does not mean the absence of all elements from earlier stages, nor does it mean that all units within the organization are at that same stage.

In general, success early in Stage 1 is characterized by the use of effective project-management processes. Later, in late Stage 1 and in Stage 2, the emphasis shifts to *program* management. In late Stage 2 and Stage 3, along with the continuation of program management, a good amount of organizational development and cultural change efforts are necessary to sustain distance training and education implementation and use at the organizational level. Stage 4 in an organization's distance delivery capability relies on effective strategic planning to guide cultural change and resource reallocation for success and on the ability to link program planning and perspectives to organizational strategic planning and perspectives. Keep in mind that there are often two levels of analyses. There are activities, processes, and work at the program level, such as evaluation and marketing. There are also these same functions at a higher, organizational level.

Excessive problems arise when the implementation of distance education exceeds the level of organizational core capabilities and core competencies to support those activities—that is, when there is lack of strategic and tactical planning.

SUMMARY OF THE STAGES OF ORGANIZATIONAL CAPACITY

Not all organizations, perhaps not even most organizations, should consistently strive toward a goal of achieving a higher stage of technology use or the highest stage of integrating distance education as part of the way business is conducted. There is nothing wrong with an organization's distance training and education being a series of events or one or more separate programs. Program implementation initially relies on sound project management, and regardless of whether the organization changes to a more integrated stage of distance training or not, solid program planning and management will always continue to be a key to effective and efficient program presentation. What matters most is that the appropriate level of capability for distance education is strategically planned for at the respective organizational level, and that the allocation of resources matches that level of capability.

LINKING THE ORGANIZATIONAL PERSPECTIVVE
WITH DISTANCE TRAINING PROGRAMS

Strategic planning consists of all of the means that an organization can use to redefine itself and realize a plan. Since the fundamental objective of a strategic plan is to chart a course from where the organization is now to where it wants to be at an agreed point in the future (i.e., at the end of the planning cycle), knowing a particular stage of organizational capability would be useful to identify common barriers to implementation of distance training and education at that level along the continuum.

The overarching goal of strategic planning is to cause a common vision of the desired future within the organization, with performance objectives integrated into operations and strategies, and with training, providing those involved with the skills to contribute (Watkins & Callahan, 1998). One way to view such planning is as a systematic means of identifying and capitalizing on the strengths within the enterprise. At the same time, planning is done to identify and provide for the needs of the organization, and a part of this is overcoming barriers that are obstacles to the organization. Serious consideration must be given to the critical issues (core competencies and core capabilities) and barriers (both perceived and real) that will be confronted when implementing distance training and education within the organization.

There are a variety of strategic planning models that have been described for business, non-profit, and educational organizations (see, e.g., Bean, 1993; Burkhart & Reuss, 1993; Cafferella, 1994; Goodstein, Nolan, & Pfeiffer, 1992). Regardless of the particular model or process an organization uses for such planning, major issues that must be planned for include educational process, student recruitment and enrolment management, higher-education development and student-development services, human resources, research, information, physical planning and development, financial management and planning, development, national role, collaboration, and institutional culture (Pienaar, Brink, & Barsby, 1999). Strategic planning is not defined by a methodology, a process or a system, but from the entire context and system in which strategic planning occurs.

Strategic planning could be considered a concerted effort to achieve an ensemble of decisions and actions which form and guide an organization to be what it is, to do what it does, and to know why it does it (Bean, 1993). By utilizing a future-looking approach, strategic planning emphasizes the future implications of decisions made in the present (Hache, 1998).

With a clear vision of the future of the organization, strategic planning is used to create and define the environment—with its boundaries and parameters—in which distance training and organizational learning will take place. The idea is to create a mission and objectives, gather extensive data, analyze and diagnose information regarding the internal and external environment, and decide on the strategies, actions, and evaluations that have as high a possibility of success in implementation, while avoiding expensive pitfalls (Albrecht & Bardsley, 1994).

The tools used to link strategic planning to program management include communication systems and management of those systems, budgeting, infrastructure, workforce development, and revisions to policies and procedures.

COMMUNICATION

Distance training and education depends on the marriage of computer- and communication *systems*. It should be managed as a system, in which the communication aspect of the technologies is emphasized. The technologies most often associated with distance learning include print, audio conferencing, audio graphic teleconferencing, interactive compressed video teleconferencing, computer-mediated conferencing and video teleconferencing using satellite, broadcast, cable, and fiber-transmission media. The technologies typically used in corporate, distance learning settings emphasize "conferencing capabilities," which underscores the communication dynamic that is typically encountered in classroom settings (Wagner, 2000).

ESTABLISHING A BUDGET

The organization must decide what equipment and resources are considered infrastructure and what are considered operational expenses. A review of cost analyses for all distance training programs may show that a program will appear to lose money if technology infrastructure costs are included in the program budget. Still, a program budget, to give a true indication of costs, must cover all areas including support services (e.g., instructional development; registration; materials development), infrastructure, and instructor training and development (Berge & Schrum, 1998). Essentially, the budget and resource allocation issues in distance training and education involve course design or course purchase, course development and delivery, learner support, and administration costs of the program.

DETERMINING FUNCTIONAL INFRASTRUCTURE

Some infrastructure resources and functions should be common across all distance training, and others are more useful when decentralized across business units or location. While decentralization may appear to unnecessarily duplicate efforts and costs, it may more closely align expertise with program needs. Centralization of services may allow managers of all distance training and education programs more direct access to top decision makers and encourage a more efficient use of resources. The risk is in overburdening specific programs with bureaucracy and overhead, while not meeting specific program needs. Generally, centralization is favored for the following functions: marketing, instructional design and development support, technology help desk and infrastructure, professional/faculty development, evaluation, promotion and incentive structures, and registration.

WORKFORCE DEVELOPMENT

It is hard to imagine anything more important to program implementation than recruiting and retaining expert trainers and support staff. Are all instructors equally suited to teach in distance training and education programs? The answer is generally, "No." Would it be wise to begin with a small cohort of willing trainers? If time and energy are spent in training this cohort, and it is given support for its development and implementation, its successes will often inspire others.

In some organizations an initial group of enthusiastic instructors have been trained in effective distance teaching methods, and the individuals comprising the group then become mentors for the next group of instructors. Ongoing support is given to these instructors through workshops, online discussion groups, and strategic feedback. Occasionally, an instructor works as an apprentice to a practitioner who is teaching a distance course, and the following term is mentored as he or she practices what was learned.

A timeline is helpful to new distance training instructors as they begin to conceptualize their tasks. Answers to the following questions, and the availability of specific training as needed, will go a long way toward retaining new distance instructors. What business needs are being targeted? At what point should the syllabus be in place? What materials need to be developed and tested? Is the hardware and software already in place and functional? What are the options when something goes wrong?

REVISING POLICIES AND PROCEDURES

The management team can provide leadership in policy revision and remove barriers to the mainstreaming of distance training and education. Each incentive or disincentive, the reporting and accountability structures, and the determination of major resource allocations have a role in changing the organizational culture. Leadership is required to effectively interpret changes in the social, political, economic, and training/educational environment. Several critical issues unique to program planning for distance training emerge.

Policies and procedures are normally framed within organizational policies or outside mandates. Such policies are tools for leading an organization in ways that are thought by management to be useful—either in defining a vision or orchestrating cultural change within the organization. A key to ensuring that mandates or missions are carried out and that organizational policies are implemented is the development of a strategic plan. This plan becomes one of the primary instruments of organizational policy and provides the framework for allocating and managing resources and accommodating organizational change and development (World Bank, n.d.).

CONCLUSIONS

In the global economy of the 21st century, learning organizations are under increasing pressure to demonstrate that training and development are directly contributing to the profitability of the organization. This must be done at a time when employees are often scattered around the world, and when the expense of bringing learners to a central location and keeping them from their job for extended periods of time is no longer an option, either from a cost perspective or from a time-to-market standpoint. This chapter focused on the organizational perspective with a few hints of dramatic changes to the roles and functions of instructors and learners.

Distance training and education—that is, what *organizations do*—is an important part of increasing performance in the workplace. To remain competitive, more emphasis will have to be placed on distance learning. It is through sound management and planning that distance training and education can effectively and efficiently meet business needs of the organization.

REFERENCES

Albrecht, R., & Bardsley, G. (1994). Strategic planning and academic planning for distance education. In Barry Willis (Ed.), *Distance education: Strategies and tools* (pp. 67–86). Englewood Cliffs, NJ: Educational Technology.

Albright, R. C., & Post, P. E. (1993). The challenges of electronic learning. *Training and Development, 47*(8), 27–29.

Bean, W. (1993). *Strategic planning that makes things happen.* Amherst, MA: HRD Press.

Berge, Z. L. (Ed.). (2001). *Sustaining distance training: Integrating learning technologies into the fabric of the enterprise.* San Francisco: Jossey-Bass.

Berge, Z. L., Bichy, C., Grayson, C., Johnson, A., Macadoff, S., & Nee, K. (2005). Where does work end and home life begin? In P. Rogers, C. Howard, J. Boettcher, L. Justice, K. Schenk, & G. Berg (Eds.), *Encyclopedia of distance learning* (pp. 2038–2043). Hershey, PA: Idea Group.

Berge, Z. L., & Kearsley, G. (2003, November/December). The sustainability of distance training: Follow-up to case studies. *The Technology Source.* Retrieved December 20, 2006, from http://www.technology source.org/article/sustainability_of_distance_training/

Berge, Z. L., & Kendrick, A. A. (2005, February). Can interest in distance training be sustained in corporate organizations? *International Journal of Instructional Technology & Distance Learning, 2*(2). Retrieved December 20, 2006, from http://www.itdl.org/Journal/Feb_05/article05.htm

Berge, Z. L., & Schrum, L. (1998). Strategic planning linked with program implementation for distance education. *CAUSE/EFFECT, 21*(3), 31–38.

Berge, Z. L., & Smith, D. (2000). Implementing corporate distance training using change management, strategic planning, and project management. In L. Lau (Ed.), *Distance learning technologies: Issues, trends and opportunities* (pp. 39–51). Hershey, PA: Idea Group.

Bersin, J. (2005, July). Making rapid e-learning work. *Chief Learning Officer.* Retrieved December 20, 2006, from http://www.clomedia.com/content/templates/clo_article.asp?articleid=1008&zoneid=62

Brace, T., & Berge, Z. L. (in press). Distance training at the strategic planning table. In M. Khosrow-Pour (Ed.), *Encyclopedia of e-commerce, e-government and mobile commerce.* Hershey, PA: Idea Group.

Branch, A., Lyon, A., & Porten, S. (2001). Hewlett-Packard's Regional Training Center—Site Information & Learning Centers (SILC). In Z. L. Berge (Ed.), *Sustaining distance training: Integrating learning technologies into the fabric of the enterprise* (pp. 235–254). San Francisco: Jossey-Bass..

Burkhart, P. J., & Reuss, S. (1993). *Successful strategic planning: A guide to nonprofit agencies and organizations.* Newbury Park, CA: Sage.

Cafferella, R. S. (1994). *Planning programs for adult learners: A practical guide for educators, trainers and staff developers.* San Francisco: Jossey-Bass.

Dessinger, J., & Conley, L. (2001). Beyond the sizzle: Sustaining distance training at Ford Motor Company dealerships. In Z. L. Berge (Ed.), *Sustaining distance training: Integrating learning technologies into the fabric of the enterprise* (pp. 178–198). San Francisco: Jossey-Bass.

Dobbs, K. (2000, June). Who's in charge of e-learning? *Training, 37*(6), 54–58.

Dooley, L. M., Dooley, K. E., & Byrom, K. (1998). Distance training under construction at H. B. Zachry Company. In D. A. Schreiber & Z. L. Berge (Eds.), *Distance training: How innovative organizations are using technology to maximize learning and meet business objectives* (pp. 351–368). San Francisco: Jossey-Bass.

Federal Aviation Administration. (1997, September). *Survey of educational technology.* Training Program Office, AHR-14 USA: Department of Transportation.

Friend, N., & Hepple, T. (2001). Lessons from merging SBC's Regional Telecom Learning Centers. In Z. L. Berge (Ed.), *Sustaining distance training: Integrating learning technologies into the fabric of the enterprise* (pp. 48–69). San Francisco: Jossey-Bass.

Galagan, P. A. (2000, May). Getting started with e-learning: An interview with Dell Computer's John Cone about pulling the big lever. *Training & Development, 54*(5), 62–64.

Goodstein, L. D., Nolan, T. M., & Pfeiffer, J. W. (1992). *Applied strategic planning: A comprehensive guide.* San Diego: Pfeiffer & Company.

Haché, D. (1998, Summer). Strategic planning of distance education in the age of teleinformatics. *Online Journal of Distance Learning Administration, 1*(2). Retrieved from State University of West Georgia, Distance Education Center. Retrieved December 20, 2006, from http://www.westga.edu/~distance/Hache12.html

Howard, B. (2001). Supporting an enterprise distance learning program at NYNEX. In Z. L. Berge (Ed.), *Sustaining distance training: Integrating learning technologies into the fabric of the enterprise* (pp. 270–290). San Francisco: Jossey-Bass.

Latten, S., Davis, M., & Stallings, N. (2001). Sustaining distance education and training at First Union: Transitioning from the classroom. In Z. L. Berge (Ed.), *Sustaining distance training: Integrating learning technologies into the fabric of the enterprise* (pp. 164–177). San Francisco: Jossey-Bass.

Longnecker, J. L. (2001). Attracting, training, and retaining instructors for distance learning at the U.S. General Accounting Office. In Z. L. Berge (Ed.), *Sustaining distance training: Integrating learning technologies into the fabric of the enterprise* (pp. 85–105). San Francisco: Jossey-Bass.

McCrea, F., Gay, R. K., & Bacon, R. (2000, January 18). *Riding the big waves: A white paper on the B2B e*learning industry.* Thomas Weisel Partners. San Francisco.

Mottl, J. N. (2000, January 3). Learn at a distance: Online learning is poised to become the new standard. *InformationWeek Online.* Available online at http://www.informationweek.com/767/learn.htm

Muilenburg, L., & Berge, Z. L. (2001). Barriers to distance education: A factor-analytic study. *The American Journal of Distance Education, 15*(2), 7–22.

Payne, L. W., & Payne, H. E. (1998). Interactive video teletraining in the Federal Aviation Administration. In D. A. Schreiber & Z. L. Berge (Eds.), *Distance training: How innovative organizations are using technology to maximize learning and meet business objectives* (pp. 201–222). San Francisco: Jossey-Bass.

Pienaar, H., Brink, C., & Barsby, T. (1999). Strategic planning framework 1997–2000. (Unpublished). Coordination Unit for Strategic Planning, University of Cape Town.

Rogers, N. E., & Becker, S. L. (2001). From training enhancement to organizational learning: The migration of distance learning at the American Red Cross. In Z. L. Berge (Ed.), *Sustaining distance training: Integrating learning technologies into the fabric of the enterprise* (pp. 329–350). San Francisco: Jossey-Bass.

Ruttenbur, B. W., Spickler, G., & Lurie, S. (2000, July 6). *E-learning: The engine of the knowledge economy.* Morgan Keegan & Co. Inc. Retrieved December 20, 2006, from http://www.masie.com/masie/research reports/elearning0700nate2.pdf

Schreiber, D. A. (1998). Organizational technology and its impact on distance training. In D. A. Schreiber & Z. L. Berge (Eds.), *Distance training: How innovative organizations are using technology to maximize learning and meet business objectives* (pp. 3–18). San Francisco: Jossey-Bass.

Senge, P. M. (1990). *The fifth discipline: The art and practice of the learning organization.* New York: Doubleday.

Takiya, S., Archbold, J., & Berge, Z. L. (2005, April). Flexible training's intrusion on work/life balance. *The Turkish Online Journal of Distance Education, 6*(2). Retrieved December 20, 2006, from http://tojde.anadolu.edu.tr/tojde18/articles/article5.htm

University of Kansas Medical Center. (1996, January). *Teaching with Technologies at KU Medical Center: Report of the Distance Education Strategies and Technologies.* Retrieved June 10, 1998, from http://www.kumc.edu/de_strategies/final_report.html#comparing

Urdan, T. A., & Weggen, C. C. (2000). *Corporate e-learning: Exploring a new frontier.* W. R. Hambrect and Company. Retrieved December 20, 2006, from http://www.spectrainteractive.com/pdfs/Corporate ELearningHamrecht.pdf

Wagner, E. D. (2000, Fall). Emerging technology trends in elearning. *Line Zine.* Retrieved December 20, 2006, from http://www.linezine.com/2.1/features/ewette.htm

Walker, D. M. (2001). *Human capital: Building the information technology workforce to achieve results.* Testimony before the Subcommittee on Technology and Procurement Policy Committee on Government Reform, U.S. House of Representatives. Washington, DC: GAO. Retrieved December 20, 2006, from http://www.gao.gov/new.items/d011007t.pdf

Walker, S. (1998). Online training costs and evaluation. In D. A. Schreiber & Z. L. Berge (Eds.), *Distance training: How innovative organizations are using technology to maximize learning and meet business objectives* (pp. 270–286). San Francisco: Jossey-Bass.

Wankel, M. J. (2001). The United States Postal Service's integration of distance training and education initiatives to meet organizational goals. In Z. L. Berge (Ed.), *Sustaining distance training: Integrating learning technologies into the fabric of the enterprise* (pp. 291–311). San Francisco: Jossey-Bass.

Watkins, K., & Callahan, M. (1998). Return on knowledge assets: Rethinking investments in educational technology. *Educational Technology, 38*(4), 33–40.

World Bank. (n.d.). Management: Benefits and costs. *Global Distance Educationet*. Retrieved December 20, 2006, from http://www1.worldbank.org/disted/Management/Benefits/benefits.html

Zemke, R. (1999, September). Why organizations still aren't learning. *Training, 36*(9), 40–49.

Zielinski, D. (2000, March). Can you keep learners online? *Training, 17*(3), 64–75.

40

Continuing Professional Education

Gary W. Kuhne
The Pennsylvania State University

George E. Krauss

Participating in continuing professional education (CPE) enables practitioners in the professions to achieve a number of important occupational aims including keeping abreast of changing knowledge and skills, maintaining and enhancing their competence, assisting their progress from novice to expert practitioners, and advancing their careers through promotion and other job changes.

Deciding which occupations actually fit under the term "profession," and thus qualify as a legitimate focus for CPE, remains a source of debate. The various views form a continuum running from those occupations recognized as possessing professional knowledge bases, scientific-research foundations, and general-public recognition of status (such as law, medicine, and clergy) to nearly any occupation committed to professionalizing processes (Houle, 1980). These professionalizing processes involve making consistent efforts to improve the competency and proficiency of their members, as well as developing meaningful quality-control mechanisms to police the occupation and maintain proficiency in the eyes of the general public. Despite the lack of consensus regarding the exact extent of professional occupations, most current CPE literature tends to be toward the more inclusive end of the continuum and regards groups as diverse as accountants, allied-health professionals, social workers, and realtors as falling within the professional domain. Using this broader definition of "profession," more than 25% of the U.S. workforce could be viewed as proper recipients of CPE (Cervero, 2000). Although no precise data is available, based upon the more inclusive view of CPE, most knowledgeable observers estimate that billions of dollars are spent annually by professionals and their employing organizations on CPE.

The significant growth of CPE in recent years has been fostered by a number of factors (Cervero & Azzaretto, 1990; Nowlen, 1988; Queeney & English, 1994). Certainly the inherently changing nature of professional knowledge is a major factor. Professional knowledge quickly becomes obsolete, requiring continuous updating. In many fields the "half-life" of knowledge is less than five years (Cervero, 2000). Beyond the changing nature of knowledge, the professions themselves are inclined to foster CPE as a way to both maintain excellence and increase competitive advantage. The scope of educational programming within CPE is further expanded by the fact that most professions accept and enforce the importance of CPE by mandating continuing-education requirements. Society also expects (and often mandates) that professionals engage in CPE throughout their working lives. Thus, calls for professional accountability from the general public, professional associations, consumer-advocacy groups, and state legislatures also help foster CPE. Closely related to professional accountability concerns are increased concerns for public health and safety, as well as the growing threats of malpractice litigation—all of these increase the pressure for CPE. Underlying all of these factors is a public confidence that CPE is the best answer for maintaining the competency needed by professionals (Nowlen, 1988). The issue of whether such confidence is justified is a major area of debate within CPE and beyond the focus of this chapter.

A wide variety of educational providers are attracted to the CPE market as an outgrowth of the billions being spent to meet these expectations and mandates (Queeeney, 2000; Cervero, 2000; Curry, Wergin, & Associates, 1993). The educational providers competing for CPE dollars include scholarly societies, professional associations, regulatory agencies, government agencies, employers, private entrepreneurs, universities and colleges, foundations, and proprietary schools (Houle, 1980; Queeney, 2000).

The various providers of CPE generally draw upon one of three strategies (or some combination of the three) when designing CPE programming for a professional group: updating knowledge and skills, increasing professional competencies, or improving personal performance assessment abilities (Nowlen, 1988). The content of CPE programs reflecting the update model prioritize keeping professionals up to date in their practices by addressing gaps in professional knowledge and skills. The content of CPE programs reflecting the competence model combines the removal of knowledge and skill gaps with the development of soft skills such as critical thinking. The content of CPE programs reflecting the performance model go beyond knowledge/skill gaps and soft skills to focus upon such things self-assessment and critical reflection upon the complex professional practice context.

DISTANCE EDUCATION USE WITHIN CPE CONTEXTS

Regardless of the design strategy chosen, the content chosen for CPE must be delivered in some format or mode. The debate about the proper delivery mode for CPE has been an important issue within contemporary CPE (Cervero, 1988; 2000). Cost factors play heavily in the consideration of delivery formats. Professionals cannot calculate the cost of attending CPE solely on the basis of travel expenses and conference fees. For many professionals, the time they spend away from the practice for education and training is time unable to be "billed" for professional services. Thus, the true costs must include such lost income for CPE. One important result of this cost reality has the increasing use of distance education as a delivery method of choice in CPE. In fact, Cervero (1998; 2001) suggests that one of the most significant trends changing the field of CPE is the growth of distance education as a preferred delivery format. Distance education within CPE is offered in a variety of forms, including video conferencing, computer conferencing, and Web-based design and delivery. The distance education option is permitting programs to be delivered at the worksite of the professional. Since many such programs are asynchronous, the training can fit more easily into the actual schedules of professionals, thus reducing costs associated with CPE.

Since the focus of this chapter is on distance education use within CPE, the remainder of this chapter will provide a synopsis of the current literature on the actual state of distance education-based CPE. While distance education is being used in a wide variety of professions, a representative picture of the uses, results, and issues with distance education-based CPE will be gained by examining the current use of distance education within three professional groups: medicine, nursing, and accounting. An examination of these three professions will be followed by a synopsis of distance education finding from a variety of other professions.

Distance Education Use Within Continuing Medical Education

The American Medical Society (AMS) defines continuing medical education (CME) as those educational activities serving to maintain, develop, or increase the knowledge, skills, professional performance, and relationships that comprise the services offered by a physician to the public (American Medical Association, 1993). Medical schools in the United States began offering CME in the late 1920s, with mandatory CME program beginning in 1934 (National Library of Medicine Online, 2004). Mandatory CME became widespread by the end of the 1960s with 41 states currently mandating some form of continuing medical education for re-licensure. There are some 2,500 CME providers in the United States (Pijanowski, 1998).

Not all forms of continuing education undertaken by doctors are accepted for re-licensing requirements. The American Medical Association (AMA) specifies that CME must take the form of formal educational programs (normally face-to-face), offered by traditional CME providers in a format consisting of a series of programs lasting up to five days (Davis, Lindsay, & Mazmanian, 1994). In addition to satisfying mandated requirements, Pijanowski (1998) suggests that CME is being driven by physicians seeking ways to address stress and pressure caused by the continued shift to managed health care and to reduce practice tensions caused by the increased threat of lawsuits, changes in ethnic and demographic composition of patients, and technological changes. The need of many doctors to address bioethical challenges in their practice is also driving a portion of contemporary CME (Wentz, Jackson, Raichle, & Davis, 2003).

Whether driven by mandatory re-certification requirements, or the contemporary practice demands outlined above, contemporary CME utilizes a variety of program formats to assist the practicing physician to address these needs. While traditional face-to-face formats still dominate the market, research reveals that medical online research, just-in-time patient information, medical record integration, telemedicine, and distance education are growing in importance as program delivery formats (Pijanowski, 1998). In fact, Manning and DeBakey (2001) suggest a paradigm shift is occurring within CME, a shift in which CME is refocusing on the individual needs of physicians in their everyday practice setting. The program emphasis within this paradigm shift in CME emphasizes learner-centered adult-learning orientations, personal-needs assessments, elaboration of physician competencies, identification of learning style preferences, the use of learning contracts, learning journals, reflective learning, and practiced-based learning. Even the term "hours" in CME has been replaced with the term "credits" to eliminate the static and negative concept of "seat time" or "hours" equating to learning. Such a paradigm shift has even led the AMA to change the name of its Division of Continuing Medical Education (CME) to the Division of Continuing Physician Professional Development (CPPD).

Predictably, as CME moves into a more learner-centered, technology-based, individualized approach, the use of distance education delivery modes is also increasing (Wentz et al., 2003). Distance delivery methods are changing the landscape of CME. Internet and Web-based CME hold great promise for assisting physicians in developing self-directedness and recognizing their own educational needs. Harden (2005) suggests that the rapid growth of the Internet and e-learning is altering the very nature of CME as program designers make increased use of reusable learning objects, virtual practice with virtual patients, learning-outcomes frameworks, self-assessments, guided-learning resources, and collaborative or peer-to-peer learning. Harden further suggests that online learning opportunities provide a bridge between the cutting edge òf CME and often out-dated education procedures embedded in institutions and professional organizations. Barnes and Jackson (2003) suggest the effective use of online learning approaches in CME could even facili-tate fuller integration of education and clinical care. The use of such an integrated practice-learn-ing environment strategy could provide ongoing demonstration of competency, reduction of med-ical errors and evidence-based decision making. Manning and DeBakey (2001) also believe online approaches hold great promise for fostering a more individualized CME that draws upon per-sonal clinical data, targeted reading of evidence-based information and focused discussions with collegial experts. They suggest Web-based CME designs hold promise to facilitate the shift to more practice-linked and self-directed programming.

Despite this growing evidence, physicians still tend to be a conservative group and their attitudes toward distance education-based CME and non-traditional approaches to CME change slowly. Carriere and Harvey (2001) examined the current state of distance continuing medical education in North America with three surveys of members of the Alliance of Continuing Med-ical Education. While their study revealed considerable interest in distance education, the major-ity (68%) of recognized CME providers had not yet developed any distance education program-ming. Ironically, while physician interest was found to be growing for future distance education offerings, most CME providers found limited medical faculty support for distance education Another study of physicians' attitudes toward distance education-based CME compared the pref-erences of Texas physicians who participated in a CME program that was offered in three differ-ent formats: live lecture, Web based, and video (Stancic, Mullen, Prokhorov, Frankowski, & McAlister, 2003). While the study concluded that physicians preferred the live-lecture format, a major weakness of the study was that none of those completing the online course actually com-pleted evaluation forms. Interestingly, while research suggests that lecture results in the lowest level of behavioral change, live lecture continues to be the preferred format of CME for physi-cians (Nowlen, 1988; Cervero, 2000). The conservative nature of physicians approaching CME was further highlighted by a study on the use of several different online CME programs within three different groups of California physicians. The study found that physicians who used online CME courses tended to be younger than average and more likely to be female (Harris, Novalis-Marine, & Harris, 2003).

In addition to studies of distance education use in CME, research studies have also examined learning outcomes and learner satisfaction with distance education in CME. Wutoh, Boren, and Balab (2004) examined 16 research studies on online learning in CME in terms physician per-formance and health care outcomes. Six of the studies confirmed positive changes in participant knowledge over traditional formats, while three studies showed a positive change in practices. The remainder of the studies showed no difference in knowledge levels between Internet-based interventions and traditional formats of CME. The results affirmed that online CME programs are at least as effective as traditional formats. Curran and Fleet (2005) also reviewed evaluation out-comes of Web-based medical education and concluded that while learner satisfaction was high, limited studies were available for actual impacts on practice change and health outcomes. While such studies of practice impact may be desirable, the reality is that few such studies have been done for more traditional formats of CPE.

Sargent, et al. (2004) investigated interactive online continuing medical education from the vantage point of physicians' satisfaction with interpersonal interaction in online CME. Because they highly valued interpersonal interaction with peers during face-to face CME, physicians tended to critique online CME in terms of their experience of such interactions. Most physicians indicated they had equally rich discussions with peers within the online environment, although they noted that such interactions were influenced by the quality of the programs and the presence of skilled facilitators. They also affirmed their satisfaction with online CME in terms of the degree of self-pacing possible and the opportunity for self-reflection prior to interaction. Prior experience with online learning was a strong influence over perception of effectiveness—in other words, those with no prior experience with online programs were reluctant to trust that mediated interaction could be as satisfying as face-to-face CME.

One final note: When drawing conclusions from the research, it is important to recognize that CME is offered in a variety of distance education formats. The literature tends to draw conclusions on effectiveness of distance education in CME without defining the specific format employed (a live video conference is very different from an asynchronous online course). Even studies using the same format studies (i.e., comparing online courses) do not necessarily compare apples to apples. A well-designed, interactive online course would have very different learning outcomes from an online course that is little more than lecture notes and readings scanned into a Web page. In other words, a well-designed distance education program is going to provide different learning outcomes than a poorly designed program. Understanding this limitation, Olson and Shershneva (2004) suggest the need to develop quality standards for each form of distance education employed. When considering Web-based designs in CME, they suggest drawing upon the standards already adopted by such groups as American Federation of Teachers, Distance Education and Training Council (DETC), Institute for Higher Education Policy, Alfred P. Sloan Foundation, and the Western Cooperative for Educational Telecommunications (WCET).

Distance Education Use Within Continuing Nursing Education

Continuing Nursing Education (CNE) is defined as ongoing, continuing professional education in which nurses learn new knowledge, skills, and attitudes, and assistance in knowing how to integrate these into their nursing practices (Bell, Chelf, & Geerdes, 2000; Farrah, 1998; Mamary & Charles, 2000). Nurses as a profession have historically demonstrated openness to new delivery modes. CNE even made use of distance education (correspondence courses) as far back as the late 19th century (Armstrong, Gessner, & Cooper, 2000; Stein, 1998). By the second half of the 20th century, telephone audio courses became common in CNE, with video conferencing soon added. By the late 1970s computers began to be used, particularly at Ohio State University (Chumley-Jones, Dobbie, & Alford, 2002). The transition from onsite to online formats in CNE has accelerated during the past decade (Ali, Hodson-Carlton, & Ryan, 2002; Bothel, 2001; Mueller, 2002).

In a literature review of 17 research articles focused on the evaluation of online CNE, Cobb (2004) found that while face-to-face CNE remained the most frequent and popular choice, online CNE was gaining in popularity. Most CNE online participants found the experience rewarding and an effective learning format. The value of developing online alternatives for CNE was further confirmed by a study of rural nurses in Pennsylvania (Beatty, 2001). Most of the rural nurses faced a variety of obstacles in seeking face-to-face CNE, including travel distance, time, fear of traveling alone in a city, navigating city traffic, family concerns, weather, late night classes, and no experience with professional networks. Online CNE was presented as a viable way resolve most of these barriers. Similarly, Piernik-Yoder (2004) examined the use of distance education to meet continuing education requirements by allied health care professionals in the state of Texas. While the study found that overall allied professionals' use of distance education to meet CE requirements was low, the perception of distance education-based CNE was very positive among those who had previously experienced using distance education to meet CE requirements.

Andrusyszyn, Cragg, and Humbert (2005) surveyed nurse practitioners in Canada concerning attitudes toward multiple delivery methods, concluding the preferred method to learn was print-based and the least preferred was audio conferencing. Convenience, self-direction, and timing of learning were found to be more important than delivery method or learning style, findings which bode well for further development of distance education-based CNE. Another study examined the use of Webcasting (technology used to deliver audio and video presentations via the Internet, usually in a synchronous format) for graduate nursing education at West Virginia University School of Nursing (DiMaria-Ghalili, Ostrow, & Rodney, 2005). This approach was tried because it offered a more cost-effective way to deliver quality distance education than previously employed interactive teleconferencing strategies. Because the classes were live (or synchronous), students were able to ask for immediate clarification of concepts; and faculty could provide immediate feedback. Both students and faculty viewed the program favorably and within eight months, and Webcasting, as a delivery format, was integrated throughout the nursing program.

A number of studies within CNE have examined Web-based programs in terms of knowledge gains. Prows, Hetteberg, Hopkin, Latta, and Powers (2004) found statistically significant improvements in posttest scores for similar courses offered in Web-based versus face-to-face formats. Jeffries (2005) measured knowledge gains in online CNE courses and found that 100% of the learners passed the required exams, successfully completed the online course, and demonstrated acceptable levels of knowledge gain. Atack and Rankin (2002) found that nurses' posttest scores for a specific CNE course offered in both residential and distance formats were not significantly different for the Web and paper version of the course. They further found that participation in the Web-based version of the course enhanced the nurses' computer skills, an important learning outcome, since so much of nursing practice and health care is becoming computerized. Olson, Stedman-Smith, and Fredrickson (2005) examined 70 nurse practitioners in a Web-based CNE program concerning environmental health core concepts. Changes in learning from pretest to posttest demonstrated acceptable knowledge gains and 91% of the nurses felt the course content helped them to gain further professional knowledge concerning environmental health. Nearly 86% felt the online course helped them to improve their ability to conduct environmental exposure histories. Finally, Phillips (2005) found that learning outcomes in online CNE were improved by the use of active learning strategies such as asynchronous discussions and the use of case studies. Phillips also found that feedback from peers, educators, and technology greatly influenced learner satisfaction.

One issue impacting the move toward online CNE is the computer literacy of nurses. Hegge, Powers, Hendrickx, and Vinson (2002) studied registered nurses in South Dakota, finding that 75% of nurses had computers at home while 76% had computers at work, yet fewer than 20% used computers for nursing CE. They suggested one key to increased participation in online CNE is better orientation of nurses to use new technology. One final study examined the needs of nursing faculty as CNE transitioned from traditional classroom instruction to an online community of learning (Ali et al., 2005). They found that faculty development in online education is a critical component of effective CNE and that redesigning and rethinking faculty roles must become a priority in order to improve the value of distance-based CNE.

Distance Education Use Within CPE for Accountants

Formal accounting education began in 1890 with the formation of the American Association of Professional Accountants (AAPA). American Association of Professional Accountants (AAPA) was subsequently renamed the American Institute of Certified Public Accountants (AICPA) and became the primary source of continuing professional education to its 334,000 members (AICPA Online, 2004). Mandatory continuing education within accounting was first suggested in 1967, with Iowa becoming the first state to require CPE as a requirement for re-licensure in 1971. Currently 52 of the 54 legal jurisdictions that issue CPA licenses require mandate continuing professional education for re-licensure. CPA re-licensure certification requires 40 hours of CPE per year with annual, biennial or tri-annual renewal periods depending upon state jurisdiction (Streer, Clark, & Holt, 1995; American Institute of Certified Public Accountants, 2000). The mandating of continuing professional education for CPAs has encouraged CPE providers to consider a variety of formats and delivery strategies, including distance education approaches (Perdue & Valentine, 1998).

According to Thomas and Harper (2001), traditional continuing professional education in the accounting field has taken the form of participants being awarded credit for attending a requisite number of session hours in face-to-face education programs. Such credit is granted for attendance, regardless of whether any learning takes place. AICPA president Barry Melancon suggested this approach to CPE should be changed to an outcome-based CPE (Stevens, 1999). Today, the AICPA advocates a competency-based model and recommends credit be awarded for programming beyond traditional classroom time, such as teaching or authoring courses, and self-directed learning activities such as reading professional journals, leadership in professional organizations, research on professional topics, and mentoring activities. Under this new paradigm, CPAs use learning logs or self-designed portfolios to document learning activities.

Research indicates that CPAs feel overwhelmed in managing their day-to-day practices and that meeting the mandated continuing professional education contributes further to the problem (Kahan, 1998). Many practitioners specifically choose continuing professional education courses to correspond to a perceived need or a suspected business niche opportunity. Others indicate that they limit CPE to courses that are germane to their practice and approved for CPE credit. Still others used alternative methods to educate their employees including conducting in-house CPE programs, subscribing to a video series education or having college professors provide annual CPE updates.

The use of distance education with accounting is growing. One empirical study conducted for the Georgia Society of Certified Public Accountants found that respondents believe distance education, including use of the Internet, is an effective way to learn (Perdue and Valentine, 1998). The study also found that the majority of respondents reported having adequate access to the technology necessary for participation in a variety of distance education activities. However, with the exception of text-based distance education, the percentage of respondents actually using distance education for CPE was minimal. In another study of distance education use for CPE within accounting, Ernst and Young (Kahan, 1998) found that programs delivered via the Internet, audio and video tapes, and CD-ROM have been favorably received by practitioners. Practitioners who took courses on interactive, multi-media continuing professional education products performed far better on-the-job than those attending seminars and conferences and finished their work at a faster pace. One obstacle to the growing use of distance education within CPE in accounting was the requirement of the American Institute of Certified Public Accountants (AICPA) and the National Association of State Boards of Accountancy (NASBA) that two hours of self-study receive only one hour of continuing professional education credit (American Institute of Certified Public Accountants & National Association of State Boards of Accountancy, 1998). Some resolution of this problem emerged when the AICPA agreed to permit one hour of self-study on an interactive self-study course (such as an online course) to count for one hour of credit.

Finally, Nacinovich (1998) found that organizations offering distance education-based continuing professional education courses to CPAs tended to find poor market reception, although the research was limited to self-study forms of distance education and not interactive online courses. In a similar study, Foy (1998) found limited acceptance of many self-study forms of continuing professional education such as CD-ROMs or audio tapes. Despite such documented resistance to distance education, Gagne and Shepherd (2001) compared a distance education and a traditional graduate accounting class and found the performance of distance education students similar to residential students. The course evaluations were also similar, although the distance-learning students were less satisfied with the accessibility to the instructor.

Distance Education in a Variety of Other Professional Contexts

This next section draws upon literature from a variety of other professions to gain a sense of the state of distance education-based CPE in a number of different practice settings. This potpourri of research provides a representative sense of the growing use and perspective on distance education within CPE. The findings summarized below are presented in no particular order of priority.

Distance education alternatives for CPE are slowly growing for insurance agents. A survey of insurance agents and brokers in the states of California, Oregon, and Washington as to their attitudes on distance education indicated that only one percent of insurance agents took an online course (CPCU 2001). The study indicated that the low interest in Internet training was due to the networking and personal interaction opportunities in a classroom setting. Although current online learning was low, 22% of respondents indicated that they would take online courses in the future. A recent study by the Independent Insurance Agents and Brokers of America (IIABA) indicated that 95% of the agents surveyed believed cost-savings and not losing time from work were good reasons to consider taking CPE online (Ruquet, 2004). As the opportunity for online CPE grows, Ruquet warns insurance agents of the importance to choose distance education-based CPE options carefully, due to lack of quality of some providers.

Umble and Dooley (2004) surveyed a number of professions and HRD settings regarding the use of educational technologies and distance education. They concluded many programs lack quality and often are limited in extent because they are designed in ways that are ultimately unsustainable. There seemed to be limited use of program planning models and very little effort to take into account the needs of all internal and external stakeholders. Hyer, Taylor, and Nanni (2004) discuss the problem of satisfying regulator requirements based upon fixed-hour curriculums and the use of online learning formats within geriatric risk-management settings. While broad understanding of the need for other evaluation strategies beyond time-based formats is increasingly being acknowledged, consensus on acceptable alternatives is slow in developing. In a study of Canadian rehabilitation professionals utilizing distance education for CPE, Liu, Cook, Varnhagen, and Miyazaki (2004) found the majority were very satisfied with programs offered in such formats as satellite, video conferencing, and online. Online CPE programming for social workers in the United States has grown in popularity to the point that further development of online CPE threatens to fundamentally alter the marketplace for CPE away from traditional face-to-face providers (Dezendorf, Green, & Krul, 2004). Styra (2004) found that psychiatrists in Canada have embraced many aspects of the Internet for health care information, online journals, and e-mail, although they are slow to fully accept online CME offerings. Winters (1998) suggested distance education-based CPE offers hope for overcoming the isolated nature of pastoral ministry.

The use of distance education-based CPE alternatives is developing among lawyers. In states mandating continuing legal education, lawyers are required to complete between 12 and 15 hours per year (including 3 hours of ethics) of continuing professional education credits for re-licensure (ABA Online, 2004). In 2001, the American Bar Association (ABA) endorsed the inclusion of new technologies (computer-based training, Web-based training) for approval in continuing legal education. The ABA's position is that lawyers have different learning styles, and as such, should have the option to undertake continuing legal education based upon their own individual needs. The ABA also emphasizes that learning should be self-directed and learner-centered. According to the ABA, over 50% of the states with continuing legal education requirements now approve learner-centered and self-directed computer-based and Web-based CPE. Today, some states have gone even further, advancing a holistic approach to continuing legal education rather than the traditional didactic-content driven courses. According to Keeva (2004), Minnesota has approved "soft-skill" type courses in the areas of self-reflection, stress, resiliency, and career satisfaction for continuing legal education.

In summary, regardless of the profession studied, the use of distance education-based CPE is growing in both professional acceptance and numbers of course offerings. Growing research confirms the value of distance education within CPE in terms of learning outcomes, practice change, and cost-effectiveness.

SOME FINAL THOUGHTS ON THE FUTURE OF DISTANCE EDUCATION WITHIN CPE

Certainly Cervero's (1998; 2001) earlier prediction, that one of the most significant trends in CPE is the growth of distance education as a preferred delivery format, will continue to prove accurate. Perdue (2003) suggests that globalization will be effecting the integration of distance education and CPE in the future because its emphasis on life-long learning and global labor markets will increase the number of providers seeking a piece of the CPE market. Many such providers will choose the use of distance education formats to offer programs to expanding professions within the under-developed world. Perdue further suggests that influx of younger workers will change the composition of the workforce as increasing numbers of professionals will have a digital back-ground and prefer an interactive, Web-based learning environment over traditional face-to-face learning formats. Such a change should accelerate the move toward Web-based learning in the professions.

Harden (2005) suggests that Web-based distance education will continue to grow in impor-tance within continuing medical education, although the future is likely to take the form of blended learning initiatives that incorporate the best of face-to-face and mediated learning approaches. Wutoh et al. (2004) agree, although they also suggest that more quantitative research is needed to discover if Web-based learning alternatives are changing physician behavior in the practice setting. The call for more research into actual learning outcomes is likely to grow within all forms of CPE, although such calls have not previously been successful in fostering much research into such outcomes within traditional forms of CPE. Certainly the call for establish-ment of quality standards for Web-based CPE will continue to be heard in most professions (Olson & Shershneva, 2004; Armstrong et al., 2000; Chumley-Jones et al., 2002).

The next five years should produce a growing body of CPE research within a variety of pro-fessions on the best practices, course design issues, learning outcomes, and viability of distance education-based CPE. Hopefully, the professions will decide to draw upon such research findings across professions rather than maintain the isolated focus that has plagued much of the history of modern CPE. The synthesis of multi-discipline research in distance education promises a bright future for the application of distance education to the professions. Distance education could soon become the preferred way of enabling professionals to keep abreast of changing profession-specific knowledge and skills, maintain and enhance their professional competence, assist their progress from novice to expert practitioners, and advance their careers through promotion and other job changes.

REFERENCES

ABA Online. (2004). *ABA Online. American Bar Association*. Retrieved from http://www.abanet.org

AICPA Online. (2004). *AICPA Online. American Institute of Certificated Public Accountants*. Retrieved from http://www.aicpa.org/members/index.htm

Ali, N. S., Hodson-Carlton, K., & Ryan, M. (2002). Web-based professional education for advanced practice nursing: A consumer guide for program selection. *The Journal of Continuing Education in Nursing, 33*, 33–38.

Ali, N. S., Hodson-Carlton, K., Ryan, M., Flowers, J., Rose, M. A., & Wayda, V. (2005). Online education: Needs assessment for faculty development. *The Journal of Continuing Education in Nursing, 36*(1), 32–38.

American Institute of Certified Public Accountants. (2000). *Statement of standards for continuing professional education (CPE)*. New York: American Institute of Certified Public Accountants.

American Institute of Certified Public Accountants, & National Association of State Boards of Accountancy. (1998). *Digest of state accountancy laws and state board regulations*. New York: American Institute of Certified Public Accountants.

American Medical Association. (1993). *The Physician's Recognition Award: 1993 information booklet*. Chicago: American Medical Association.

Andrusyszyn, M., Cragg, C. E., & Humbert, J. (2005). Nurse practitioner preferences for distance education methods related to learning style, course content, and achievement. *Journal of Nursing Education, 40*, 163–170.

Armstrong, M. L., Gessner, B. A., & Cooper, S. S. (2000). Pots, pans, and pearls: The nursing profession's rich history with distance education for a new century of nursing. *The Journal of Continuing Education in Nursing, 31*, 63–70.

Atack, L., & Rankin, J. (2002). A descriptive study of registered nurses' experiences with Web-based learning. *Journal of Advanced Nursing, 40*(4), 457–465.

Barnes, B. E., & Jackson, C. P. (2003). Using technology in continuing professional development. In D. Davis, B. Barnes, & R. Fox (Eds.), *The continuing professional development of physicians: From research to practice* (pp. 205–219). New York: AMA Press.

Beatty, R. M. (2001). Continuing professional education, organizational support, and professional competence: Dilemmas of rural nurses. *The Journal of Continuing Education in Nursing, 32*, 203–209.

Bell, D. F., Chelf, J. H., & Geerdes, P. (2000, May/June). An outcomes model prototype: Integrating continuing education learning into practice. *Journal of Continuing Education in Nursing, 31*(3), 111–115.

Bothel, R. (2001, Spring). Bringing it all together. *Online Journal of Distance Education Administration, 4*(1). Retrieved from http://www.westgate.edu/%Edistance/ojdia/spring41/spring41.html

Carriere, M. F., & Harvey, D. (2001). Current state of distance continuing medical education in North America. *The Journal of Continuing Education in Health Professions, 21*, 150–157.

Cervero, R. M. (1988). *Continuing learning in the professions*. San Francisco: Jossey-Bass.

Cervero, R. M. (1998). Forward. In W. H. Young (Ed.), *Continuing professional education in transition: Visions for the professions and new strategies for lifelong learning*. Malabar, FL: Kreiger.

Cervero, R. M. (2000). Trends and issues in continuing professional education. In V. W. Mott & B. J. Daley (Eds.), *Charting a course for continuing professional education: Reframing professional practice*. San Francisco: Jossey-Bass.

Cervero, R. M. (2001). Continuing professional education in transition, 1981–2000. *International Journal of Lifelong Education, 20*(1–2), 16–30.

Cervero, R. M., Azzaretto, J. F., & Associates. (1990). Renewing and redirecting continuing professional education. In R. M. Cervero, J. F. Azzaretto, & Associates (Eds.), *Visions in the future of continuing professional education* (pp. 183–208). Athens: The University of Georgia.

Chumley-Jones, H. S., Dobbie, A., & Alford, C. L. (2002, October). Web-based learning: Sound educational method or hype? A review of the evaluation literature. *Academic Medicine, 77*(10), S86–S93.

Cobb, S. C. (2004). Internet continuing education for health care professionals: An integrative review. *Journal of Continuing Education in the Health Professions, 24,* 171–180.

CPCU Society's Pacific Northwest and Lake Washington Chapters. (2001). The Internet: CE choice for the future? *CPCU Journal, 54,* 19–29.

Curran, V., & Fleet, L. (2005). A review of evaluation outcomes of Web-based continuing medical education. *Medical Education, 39*(6), 561–567.

Curry, L., Wergin, J. F., & Associates (Eds.). (1993). *Educating professionals. Responding to new expectations for competence and accountability.* San Francisco: Jossey-Bass.

Davis, D., Lindsay, E., & Mazmanian, P. (1994). The effectiveness of CME interventions. In D. A. Davis & R. A. Fox (Eds.), *The physician as learner: Linking research to practice.* Chicago: American Medical Association.

Dezendorf, P., Green, R., & Krul, R. (2004). CE online: Use it or lose it. *Professional Development: The International Journal of Continuing Social Work Education, 7*(1), 24–34.

DiMaria-Ghalili, R. A., Ostrow, L., & Rodney, K. (2005). Webcasting: A new instructional technology in distance graduate nursing education. *Journal of Nursing Education, 44,* 11–18.

Farrah, S. J. (1998). Variables influencing the likelihood of practice change after continuing nursing education participation. (Doctoral dissertation, University of Missouri-Columbia, 1998). *Dissertation Abstracts International, 60,* 1598.

Foy, N. F. (1998). *Continuing professional education needs of NYNEX Certified Management Accountants and implications for the Institute of Certified Management Accountants' mandates.* New York: Columbia Teachers College.

Gagne, M., & Shepherd, M. (2001). Distance learning in accounting. *T.H.E. Journal, 28,* 58–64.

Harden, R. M., (2005). A new vision for distance learning and continuing medical education. *The Journal of Continuing Education in Health Professions, 25,* 43–51.

Harris, J. M., Novalis-Marine, C., & Harris, R. B. (2003). Women physicians are early adopters of online continuing education. *The Journal of Continuing Education in Health Professions, 23,* 221–228.

Hegge, M., Powers, P., Hendrickx, L., & Vinson, J. (2002). Competence, continuing education, and computers. *The Journal of Continuing Education in Nursing, 33,* 24–32.

Houle. C. O. (1980). *Continuing learning in the professions.* San Francisco: Jossey-Bass.

Hyer, K., Taylor, H., & Nanni, K. (2004). Designing health care risk management online: Meeting regulators' concerns for fixed-hour curriculum. *Gerontology and Geriatrics Education, 24*(4), 77–94.

Jeffries, P. R. (2005, August). Development and testing of a hyperlearning model for design of an online critical care course. *Journal of Nursing Education, 44*(8), 366–372.

Kahan, S. (1998). Using CPE to bring in business. *The Practical Account, 31,* 1.

Keeva, S. (2004). CLE for the whole person. *ABA Journal, 90,* 76.

Liu, L., Cook, A., Varnhagen, S., & Miyazaki, M. (2004). Rehabilitative professionals' satisfaction with continuing education delivered at a distance using different technologies. *Assistive Technology. Special Issue: Distance Learning, 16*(2), 104–115.

Mamary, E. M., & Charles, P. (2000). On-site to online: Barriers to the use of computers for continuing education. *Journal of Continuing Education in the Health Professions, 20*(3), 171–175.

Manning, P. R., & DeBakey, L. (2001). Continuing medical education: The paradigm is changing. *The Journal of Continuing Education in Health Care Professions, 21,* 46–54.

Mueller, C. L. (2002). Teaching at a distance via the Web. *Excellence in Nursing Education Research, 3*(2), 1–4.

Nacinovich, M. (1998). CPE: Lights, camera, action? *Accounting Technology, 14*(3), 38–43.

National Library of Medicine Online. (2004). History of continuing medical education. Retrieved from http://www.ncbi.nlm.nih.gov

Nowlen, P. M. (1988). *A new approach to continuing education for business and the professions: The performance model.* New York: Macmillan.

Olson, C. A., & Shershneva, S. B. (2004). Setting quality standards for Web-based continuing medical education. *The Journal of Continuing Education in Health Professions, 24,* 100–111.

Olson, D., Stedman-Smith, M., & Fredrickson, A. (2005, August). Environmental health and nursing: Piloting a technology-enhanced distance learning module. *AAOHN Journal, 53*(8), 353–359.

Perdue, K. J. (2003). Web-based continuing professional education: Uses, motivations, and deterrents to participation. In M. G. Moore & W. G. Anderson (Eds.), *Handbook of Distance Education* (pp. 615–630). Mahwah, N.J.: Lawrence Erlbaum Associates.

Perdue, K. J., & Valentine, T. (1998). Beliefs of certified public accountants toward distance education: A statewide Georgia survey. *The American Journal of Distance Education, 12*(3), 29–41.

Phillips, J. M. (2005). Strategies for active learning in online continuing education. *The Journal of Continuing Education in Nursing, 36,* 77–83.

Piernik-Yoder, B. (2004). The use of distance education to meet continuing education requirements by allied health professionals in the state of Texas. *Dissertation Abstracts International.* (UMI No. 3141864)

Pijanowski, K. (1998). Waring, P. J. S., (1998). Continuing medical education in transition: The evolution of a new paradigm. In W. H. Young (Ed.), *Continuing professional education in transition: Visions for the professions and new strategies for lifelong learning* (pp. 143–169). Malabar, FL: Kreiger.

Prows, C. A., Hetteberg, C., Hopkin, R. J., Latta, K. K., & Powers, S. M. (2004, September/October). Development of a Web-based genetics institute for a nursing audience. *Journal of Continuing Education in Nursing, 35*(5), 223–231.

Queeney, D. S. (2000). Continuing professional education. In A. L. Wilson & Hayes, E. R. (Eds.), *Handbook of Adult and Continuing Education* (pp. 375–391). San Francisco: Jossey-Bass.

Queeney, D. S., & English, J. K. (1994). *Mandatory continuing education: A status report.* Columbus, OH. ERIC Clearinghouse on Adult, Career, and Vocational Education. (ERIC Document Reproduction Service No. XXXX)

Ruquet, M. E. (2004). Agents warned to avoid CE mills for training. *National Underwriter Company, 108,* 25.

Sargent, J., Curran, V., Jarvis-Selinger, S., Ferrier, S., Allen, M., Kriby, F., et al (2004). Interactive online continuing medical education: Physicians' perceptions and experiences. *The Journal of Continuing Education in Health Professions, 24,* 227–236.

Stancic, N., Mullen, P. D., Prokhorov, A. V., Frankowski, R. F., & McAlister, A. L. (2003). Continuing medical education: What delivery format do physicians prefer? *The Journal of Continuing Education in Health Professions, 23,* 162–167.

Stein, A. M. (1998, November/December). History of continuing nursing education in the United States. *Journal of Continuing Education in Nursing, 29*(6), 245–252.

Stevens, M. G. (1999). Changing the direction of CPE. *The Practical Accountant, 32,* 1.

Streer, P. J., Clark, R. L., & Holt, M. E. (1995). Assessing the utility of continuing professional education for certified public accountants. *Research in Accounting Regulation, 9,* 211–222.

Styra, R. (2004). The Internet's impact on the practice of psychiatry. *Canadian Journal of Psychiatry, 49*(1), 5–11.

Thomas, P. B., & Harper, B. S. (2001). CPE: Changing with the profession. *The CPA Journal, 71,* 2.

Umble, K. E., & Dooley, L. M. (2004). Planning human resource development and continuing professional education programs that use educational technologies: Voices that must be heard. *Advances in Developing Human Resources. Special Issue: Boundary Spanning: Expanding Frames of Reference for Human Resource Development and Continuing Professional Education, 6*(1), 86–100.

Wentz, D. K., Jackson, J. J., Raichle, L., & Davis, A. (2003). Forces for change in the landscape of CME, CPD, and health systems-linked education. In D. Davis, B. Barnes, & R. Fox (Eds.), *The continuing professional development of physicians: From research to practice* (pp. 25–48). New York: AMA Press.

Winters, M. L. (1998). The ministry: A concert of concerns. In W. H. Young (Ed.), *Continuing professional education in transition: Visions for the professions and new strategies for lifelong learning.* Malabar, FL: Kreiger.

Wutoh, R., Boren, S. A., & Balab, E. A. (2004). E-learning: A review of Internet-based continuing medical education. *The Journal of Continuing Education in Health Professions, 24,* 20–30.

41

Distance Education in the Armed Forces: Air Force

Philip J.-L. Westfall

*Air Force Institute for Advanced Distributed Learning,
Department of the Air Force*

The U.S. Air Force has used distance learning since 1950. The need to leverage new instructional technologies and to expand the use of distance learning to meet readiness requirements and keep training and education costs down has led to the independent development of a variety of distance learning programs. While the Air Force has a mature paper-based distance learning program, the last 10 years have seen a rapid expansion of distance learning programs using interactive television (ITV), computer-based instruction (CBI), and online courses. Each school within the Air Force developed most of its distance learning courses independently, with no central management. With distance learning receiving increased attention from the leadership in the Department of Defense (DOD), in 1995 the Air Force formed the Air Force Distance Learning Office (AFDLO). Its mission was to serve as the focal point for implementation of distance learning policy and emerging distance learning technology. In this capacity, it coordinated and facilitated distance learning across the Air Force, and developed a distance learning roadmap for the future. As a result of this roadmap and the 2000 Reorganization of HQ Air University, the Air Force greatly expanded AFDLO's responsibilities. In February 2000, the AFDLO merged with the Extension Course Institute and became the Air Force Institute for Advanced Distributed Learning (AFIADL). The AFIADL is located in Montgomery, Alabama, at the Gunter Annex of Maxwell Air Force Base, and is part of the Air University, a Directorate of the Air Education and Training Command (AETC). The AFIADL brought three separate distance learning mission areas into one organization: (a) the Extension Course Institute, (b) the Air Technology Network Program Office, and (c) the Air Force implementation of the Advanced Distributed Learning Initiative (ADLI) and emerging distance learning technology.

PROGRAMS AND INITIATIVES

Extension Course Institute

The Extension Course Institute (ECI) was established in 1950 as the Air Force's only correspondence school. The institute's original mission was to provide voluntary non-resident courses for both active duty and reserve Air Force personnel. Since 1950, more than 13 million airmen have taken these distance learning courses, furthering their careers while acquiring critical job knowledge and skills. Today, with a staff of both civilian and military personnel, the institute supports formal training and educational programs of the Air Force, Air National Guard, and Air Force Reserve. The institute provides over 450 career-broadening courses (at the low cost of $42 per student) to people throughout the Department of Defense (DOD) and to civil-service employees in all federal agencies. This translates to more than 255,000 course offerings every year. These courses are known for their instructional excellence and have always exceeded the standards of both the Distance Education and Training Council (DETC) and the American Council on Education (ACE). Over the years, the institute's mission has undergone several major changes. In 1963, the institute became an essential and mandatory part of a large number of on-the-job-training programs when it started providing self-study materials for the specialty knowledge portion of the Air Force's official upgrade training program. In 1969, the Extension Course Institute (ECI) was given the additional mission of providing study reference materials used in preparation for specialty knowledge testing for the enlisted personnel promotion system. In February, the institute was brought under the management of the AFIADL, and continues essentially intact as the Extension Course Program (ECP).

The ECP operates in a fully automated environment. Course development, production, distribution, the registrar, and student administration functions are managed on a sophisticated system consisting of nearly 400 personal computers and a mainframe. To profit from rapidly growing technological capabilities, the ECP is enhancing its efficiency and productivity by procuring advanced computer systems and software. The new equipment and software should greatly enhance AFIADL's ability to meet the needs of the Air Force for better training at a better price. Students will experience better service and enjoy lessons that are more current. All of these ECP improvements will contribute to increased Air Force readiness.

The quality of ECP's correspondence courses is maintained through internal efforts, of course, but additionally, the DETC has traditionally accredited the program, and it undergoes periodic review by the Air University Board of Visitors. The American Council on Education (ACE) also evaluates the ECP courses for credit recommendations in upper baccalaureate, lower baccalaureate, and vocational areas. This program assists graduates of these courses to continue their education and pursue degrees at non-DOD institutions.

Since 1993, the ECP has incorporated the CBI into its curricula. The trend is to convert more paper courses to multi-media where more interactivity is required. The CBI programs are forwarded to the students in the form of disks or CDs with supplementary hard copy of printed reference materials.

Air Technology Network

Using interactive television (one-way video over satellite with multi-point audio conferencing) for distance learning began in 1991. The Secretary of the Air Force for Acquisition gave funding that year to the Air Force Institute of Technology (AFIT—also a school within the Air University) at Wright-Patterson Air Force Base to quickly reduce the backlog of students that required courses for certification on the then newly designed career-field progression. Located near Dayton, Ohio, AFIT is the Air Force's graduate engineering school. It also offers professional continuing education in acquisition and civil engineering. It was the acquisition program, however, that brought satellite to the rest of the Air Force and led to the creation of the Air Technology Network (ATN) (http://atn.afit.edu). A Center for Distance Education (CDE) was created, and there, the planning for the development of a digital video satellite network was patterned after the pioneering efforts in digital technology of the National Technological University of Fort Collins, Colorado. The CDE took the idea one step further by conceiving and developing a network that would be interoperable across the Federal Government; it was dubbed the "Government Education and Training Network" (GETN) (http://getn.govdl.org). CDE collaborated with the Army Logistics Management College (ALMC) at Fort Lee, Virginia, to use the same satellite service provider to establish the first multi-service, distance learning network. The Army had been using an analog network for several years, but saw the promise of digital technology, so ALMC agreed to have its existing satellite network retrofit to the same digital technology the Air Force was adopting. Through use of government-wide contract vehicles provided by the Federal Government's General Services Administration, GETN has grown from these first two broadcast centers (at AFIT and ALMC) in 1993 to 12 digital-Ku-band satellite uplink broadcast centers, with 13 video channels available, reaching over 2400 downlink sites located throughout the continental United States (CONUS), Alaska, Hawaii, and Puerto Rico. GETN currently broadcasts approximately 9,000 hours per year. Within the DOD, the other agencies using GETN are the Air National Guard (ANG), the Air Force Reserve, the Defense Equal Opportunity Management Institute (DEOMI), the Defense Logistics Agency (DLA), and the U.S. Navy. The following civilian government agencies currently use GETN: the Federal Aviation Agency (FAA), the Department of Energy (DOE), the Federal Bureau of Investigation (FBI), U.S. Courts, the Department of Justice, the U.S. Coast Guard, the U.S. Fish and Wildlife Service, and the National Parks Service.

The advantages of a single network are obvious: GETN allows the various user agencies to share distance learning programs and use common facilities. Additionally, the Army National Guard provides a listing of other satellite programs that may be of interest to the government community, but that are on other satellites that are analog. These programs are rebroadcast on GETN, adding even more distance learning programs to the community of users.

As for the ATN, it has grown to a network of six broadcast centers and 270 ITV classrooms. The Air Force's ATN can broadcast any GETN program to a total of 15 sites in Germany, England, Italy, Guam, Korea, and Japan, and will soon add six sites in southwest Asia. Additionally, this year, 2006, AFIADL will begin employing a dedicated 24-7 channel for broadcasting medical training to sites across the DOD, in partnership with the Veterans Health Administration (VA). ATN now broadcasts over 3,500 hours per year, and is used to accomplish over 260,000 student-hours of training per year. These interactive television courses range from a few days to a few weeks in length, and cover subjects such as contracting and acquisition management, environmental management, safeguards and security, aircraft maintenance and repair, professional military education, professional continuing education, parenting courses, communication courses, air-traffic control and related courses, diversity courses, equal opportunity training, legal, medical, chaplain, and management and leadership courses.

ATN is very cost effective. With respect to out-of-pocket costs for putting a course on the air, there are usually no development costs. The time to convert an existing lecture-based course to "on-the-air" can be as little as three months. Delivery costs vary somewhat from school to school, but using actual costs for one of ATN's biggest users, the AFIT, reveals that cost avoidance or savings can be as much as 95%. On average, AFIT current in-residence cost for a typical 40-hour course is $121,500 for 100 students. By satellite, it is only about $5,250—that is under 5% of the costs of in-residence. More important is the total cost to the Air Force of doing business over satellite. If the costs of personnel and other overhead are added to these out-of-pocket costs, and then one compares ATN's total costs with only the per diem and travel of temporary duty (TDY), it is still remarkably favorable: $318 per student day in residence compared to just $41 per student day using ATN. That means that training using ITV can be done for only 13% of the cost of in-residence. For 2005, the cost avoidance estimate for all courses combined was over $11.5 million.

Today, the ATN and its Program Management Office are part of AFIADL. Its operation,

- meets a vast number of educational objectives
- preserves academic quality
- is cost effective
- is geographically unconstrained
- is interactive
- is responsive to frequent changes
- offers ten-fold increase in student throughput
- permits interoperability with other Government agencies

A few agencies using GETN now have the capacity to store-and-forward digital video programs as well as datacast Internet Protocol courseware to servers across the world. GETN, therefore, not only offers its traditional ITV courses, but is becoming the bypass technology to the public Internet to offer distance learning *anytime, anywhere, anyway*.

The Advanced Distributed Learning Initiative

The Office of the Secretary of Defense (OSD) is leading the effort known as the Advanced Distributed Learning Initiative (ADLI). The ADLI is a structured, adaptive, collaborative effort between the public and private sectors to develop the standards, tools, and learning content for the future distance learning environment. The effort seeks to make distance learning available "anytime, anywhere" through the use of the Internet. The ADLI envisions high-quality, cost-effective, network-centric, asynchronous instruction. It primarily consists of a learning-management system and a reference model for the development of shareable content. The sharable content object reference model (SCORM), which is still in its developmental stages, sets the standards for the development and sharing of instructional modules in a networked environment. The Air Force is an active participant in OSD's vision, which is captured in the *DOD Strategic Plan for Advanced Distributed Learning, 1999*. As distance learning technologies mature and become cost effective, eligible Air Force courses will be converted to ADLI format to exploit positive return on investment (AETC, 2000).

The AFIADL strategy is to: (a) pursue emerging network-based technologies; (b) create common standards that will enable reuse and interoperability of learning content; (c) lower development costs; promote widespread collaboration that can satisfy common needs; (d) enhance performance with next-generation learning technologies; (e) work closely with industry to influence the commercial-off-the-shelf product development cycle; (f) and establish a coordinated implementation process. The ADLI is designed to deliver efficient and effective high-quality learning continuously to DOD personnel "anytime-anywhere." The ADLI end-state envisions universal use of instructional components that are characterized by,

- *accessibility* from any location, remote or local
- *interoperability* between all ADLI instructional platforms, media, and tools
- *durability* to withstand base technology changes without significant recoding or redesign
- *reusability* between applications, platforms, and tools
- *cost effectiveness* to provide significant increases in learning and readiness per net increment in time or cost

AFIADL TODAY

The Air Force Institute for Advanced Distributed Learning's (AFIADL) entire focus is distance learning. According to DOD Instruction 1322.26, "Distance Learning is structured learning that does not require the physical presence of an instructor." AFIADL's mission is to "promote, deliver, and manage distance learning for our aerospace forces." AFIADL functions to create an Air Force environment that recognizes the value of distance learning. It works with OSD and sister services to review best practices in industry and academia (HQ USAF, 2003).

It is generally known in the distance learning community that the DOD's strategy is to focus on Web-based instruction through its ADLI. Although AFIADL is focusing on the ADLI as its flagship strategy of the future, AFIADL's programs are currently being delivered by CBI, ITV, and print. Through its distance education programs (the Extension Course Program and the Air Technology Network), AFIADL delivers education at a distance by developing, publishing, and distributing or broadcasting over 400 courses for professional military education, professional continuing education, career-development programs, and specialized courses to Air Force war fighters and war fighting support personnel worldwide. AFIADL also distributes study materials to eligible Air Force enlisted personnel in support of the Weighted Airman Promotion System (WAPS). The four major content areas are briefly described here.

Professional Military Education Courses

The professional military education courses are taken by both commissioned and non-commissioned officers. These courses, of which there are currently 36, teach leadership, management principles, techniques of effective communication, problem solving, analysis of professional reading materials, international relations, national decision making, and defense management. The courses give students the broad skills and knowledge needed to be effective leaders at various stages in their careers. AFIADL offers PME via print, CD-ROM and Internet media.

Professional Continuing Education Courses

These courses meet the professional continuing educational (PCE) needs primarily of two career fields in the Air Force: civil engineering and law. There are currently 52 courses that vary in length from few days to a few weeks. The primary audience is composed of officers and middle-management civil-service employees. These courses are developed by Air University schools outside of AFIADL, but those that are developed for interactive television are provided through the Air Technology Network (ATN). These courses, therefore, come under the accreditation guidelines of the DETC.

Career Development Courses

Career development courses (CDC) constitute the largest portion of the institute's curricula. There are currently 394 courses and are primarily print based. These self-study courses help enlisted personnel complete the specialty knowledge portion of their on-the-job-training program. Enlisted personnel must complete CDCs successfully at various stages to advance in their careers. CDCs are also available on a voluntary basis to others for career broadening. The institute offers CDCs in a very wide variety of career fields. Students enroll individually through their Base Education Services Office.

Specialized Courses

These courses provide valuable information and career-broadening knowledge to individuals in a variety of career fields. Today, AFIADL offers 27 specialized courses in such areas as aircrew operations, general military training, medical, nursing, civil engineering, security police, contract law, finances, logistics plans, supervisor safety, public affairs, weather, and chaplain programs.

AFIADL AND THE FUTURE OF DL MEDIA

The focus on distance learning does not mean the end of the traditional classroom. The Air Force will still have traditional classrooms for courses that should not be converted to distance learning formats. Whereas the requirement for traditional classrooms may be reduced, traditional methods will still play a vital role in necessary categories such as Basic Military Training. The end result is that the Air Force will add value to the total education and training system by providing more courses to a greater number of students.

Print. Print will continue to be used extensively. Whereas there is a DOD drive to convert as many courses as possible to online, AFIADL will not select media that are less than optimal to reach its many learning objectives. Print still offers the most effective way for students to read large amounts of text. Those using online or CBI media for reading report a decrease in reading speed and retention. Additionally, it is truly the only "anytime-anywhere" medium. DOD firewalls, cost of development of personal computer-based courses and lack of bandwidth assures this medium a long future in distance learning. It will continue to be used as a supporting medium for most courses, whether they are ITV, audio conferencing, CBI, or online. As soon as technology and quality-control permits, some text materials will be delivered electronically for onsite printing and binding.

Satellite. The use of ITV is growing due to increasing availability and ease of converting classroom programs to distance learning. All development is done quickly and in-house, which makes ITV an attractive and cost-effective medium. The VHA-DOD medical training initiative, which is beginning this year, will double the satellite broadcast hours of ATN—bringing together a variety of medical training providers on a single network. Satellite has been used exclusively for ITV so far, but with the advancement of digital technologies, the bandwidth once used for synchronous video will be used as a bypass technology to the Internet. Current firewall restrictions within the DOD, and the current bandwidth limitations on terrestrial networks, make the use of satellite for data-casting an attractive alternative. Additionally, there is a DOD initiative to distribute asynchronous video content across military installations to avoid transportation of celluloid films. AFIADL is working with the DOD to use its ATN to distribute digitally converted films to any military installation that uses the GETN. Use of satellite technology for distance learning in the Federal Government is currently in a state of growth (less than dramatic, however), so it continues to have a future as a viable distance learning medium, at least for the near term (this decade). The cost of satellite delivery, however, will very likely continue to grow from year to year, and bandwidth may become less available. Add to the equation an expanding terrestrial infrastructure with reduced usage charges, and the use geosynchronous satellites may not be as attractive tomorrow as it is today.

CBI.   The AFIADL's CD-ROM/DVD courses will continue to be used due to the number of courses already developed. CBT offers richer multi-media and interaction than (asynchronous) online courses. CBI is very portable, and courses that exclusively used paper have been supplemented by CD-ROMs for added interactivity. With the development of data-casting, many of these courses will be available for delivery by satellite to local servers without having to modify them to meet the constraints of public Internet delivery. It is expected, however, that with time and funding, many of these legacy CD-ROM courses will migrate to SCORM standards.

Advanced distributed learning initiative.   The AFIADL has begun piloting SCORM-compliant courses. It is anticipated across the DOD that Internet delivery will be the distance learning medium that will experience the most extensive growth. As increased funding becomes available, the AFIADL will work closely with its ADLI partners to develop courses in conformity with SCORM standards. As these standards are being adopted throughout the industry, it seems to have a secure future. Internet-based courses will be more efficiently developed and shared across the DOD; but they are not a panacea. While they offer interchangeability and availability, there are still significant hurdles to overcome, and many questions not yet answered. "Granulating" all instruction, as the SCORM requires, may result in many, if not most, learning objects having to be extensively retooled to be usefully integrated in any given course. While the focus is on "sharability," the author has never received a satisfactory answer to the question of how much course content needs to be shared. Intelligent tutoring will be a facet of Internet-based instruction, but costs and development time will continue to be substantial despite the expected cost efficiency of the SCORM. Courses that require synchronous video instruction, or require the reading of large amounts of text, may not be suitable for online delivery in the near term.

CONCLUDING REMARKS

AFIADL has developed a strategic plan (AFIADL, 2005) and is marshalling the resources necessary to expand its programs to enhance the Air Force's readiness by leveraging the latest and existing technologies in a cost-effective blend of distance learning media. In a nutshell, AFIADL supports a blended media approach. Its fundamental principle in distance learning is that learning objectives and cost drive media selection. It is axiomatic at AFIADL that no single distance learning medium is a panacea. Its vision statement below includes a qualifier to the popular mantra, "anytime, anywhere":

Excellence in Advanced Distributed Learning . . . Right Way, *Any Time, Any Where*

REFERENCES

Air Education & Training Command. (2000, Aug). *AETC ADL Implementation Plan.* Available with limitations from AETC/DOS, Randolph AFB, TX 78150-4321.

Air Force Institute for Advanced Distributed Learning. (2005). *The AFIADL Strategic Plan.* Available with limitations from AFIADL/XR, Maxwell AFB—Gunter Annex, AL 36118-5643.

Department of Defense Instruction 1322.26 (2006, June). Available with limitations from USD (P&R), Pentagon, Arlington, VA: Author.

Department of Defense Strategic Plan for Advanced Distributed Learning (1999, April). Available from ODUSD(R), Pentagon, Arlington, VA: Author.

Headquarters United States Air Force. (2003, January). Air Force Strategic Plan for Advanced Distributed Learning. Available with limitations from AF/DPL, Pentagon, Arlington, VA: Author.

DISCLAIMER

Whereas descriptions of AFIADL's programs were drawn directly from available documents published by AFIADL, the views expressed in this article are those of the author and do not reflect the official policy or position of the United States Air Force, Department of Defense, or the US Government. This chapter, however, has been reviewed for factual accuracy by the AFIADL and the Air University Public Affairs Office.

42

Distance Education
in the Armed Forces: Army

Walter R. Schumm and Farrell J. Webb
Kansas State University

David E. Turek and Glenn E. Ballard
U.S. Army Reserve

THE ARMY'S LEGACY SYSTEM OF EDUCATION

Freeman (2003) reviewed distance learning in the U.S. Army, describing the pitfalls of the legacy system of education, in which soldiers would try to enroll in courses well ahead of time in hopes that they might have the right training in a few months for their most likely future assignments. Sometimes, enrollment might be denied or delayed. Sometimes, even if enrollment was accepted, the soldiers would have to cancel their "seat" because of personal emergencies or unit priorities. Most training involved travel, which meant costs to the military and time away from family and friends for the soldier.

Many professional development leader courses were full of information that might be needed someday, somewhere—but there was often only a remote connection between real-world missions and the training programs that might have been developed years previously. What information was learned was often subject to considerable "skill decay" because it was either never used or only used a long while after the initial learning experience. Course material was often outdated. Soldiers also needed to improve their civilian education for personal development and for increased promotion opportunities (and, it was hoped, higher retention rates), but it was difficult for them to attend college classes regularly, without absences due to field training, short Army schools on post, or short training deployments.

Reserve Component Soldiers in the Army Reserve or the Army National Guard faced similar obstacles, but their training windows were more limited, to approximately 12 weekends a year and one period of two weeks' annual training, normally during the summer timeframe. Despite contrary ideals, the reality in the Reserve Component was that training organizations wanted to shift travel costs to students (you send your students at your cost to where we have instructors) whereas the units wanted to shift travel costs to the training organizations (you send your instructors to where our soldiers are, at your expense).

There had been a long-standing mail distance education program in the Army, operated through regular postal services and paper-based correspondence courses. The courses were free, fairly easy to access, and easy to complete. There were essentially no restrictions on which courses a soldier could request. One danger, however, was that unethical soldiers could order a correspondence course and then hire other soldiers to complete the course's examination for them. Moreover, because most correspondence courses had no hands-on component or difficult practical exercises, their educational validity was often questioned. Clearly, improvements were needed. Here, electronic distance education was to begin playing a major role.

ELECTRONIC DISTANCE EDUCATION IN THE ARMY

Proposed Advantages

As Freeman (2003) observed, electronic distance education (also known as "distance learning" or "e-learning") arrived on the scene in the 1990s with potential for correcting many of these training challenges. It was hoped that electronic distance education would allow training to be delivered to the right soldier (and more soldiers) at the right place at the right time, exactly when needed by his or her unit(s). The right place might be the soldier's home, a field work site, the unit office at an installation, the armory or reserve training center, or an austere overseas location. It was hoped that such distance learning would reduce travel expenses and often training expenses, too. The increased costs of multiple overseas Army missions and of in-residence training needed offsets. One goal was to allow soldiers and marines to stay home to train rather than having to leave their families for residence schools (Jones, Mally, Blevins, & Munroe, 2003). It was hoped that electronic distance learning would also provide equal or better learning than traditional methods, especially if soldiers could be exposed to the world's best subject-matter experts.

Army Initiatives

In 1995, the Office of the Secretary of Defense directed the Army to develop a program for training by exploiting information technology (IITRI/AB Tech Group, 2002, p. 9). Subsequently, the U.S. Army Training and Doctrine Command (TRADOC) developed the Army Distance Learning Program (TADLP), implementation being directed by the Chief of Staff of the Army (CSA) in 1996. The CSA, General Dennis J. Reimer, predicted at that time that, eventually, all leader professional education would involve a combination of resident training and distance learning (DL) or would be by DL alone (IITRI/AB Tech Group, 2002, p. 9). In April 2002, TADLP was renamed The Army Distributed Learning Program. Distributed learning is broader than distance education, including the use of new methodologies to create more effective training (knowledge webs, interactions in virtual worlds, synthetic environments, and sensory immersion) (Howard, 1997, p. 14). TADLP has had several goals, among them harnessing the power of emerging technologies, providing anytime/anywhere access to Army training, and improving Army readiness. Furthermore, the Army's secure internet site, Army Knowledge Online (AKO), had more than six trillion documents in 2003, one of the largest examples of knowledge management (KM) operations in the world, clearly a critical adjunct to the Army's distance learning programs.

Most Recent DL Policy

In February 2006, the Army promulgated a message, *Subject: Army Distributed Learning Policy*, that defined distributed learning as "the delivery of standardized individual, collective, and self-development training to Soldiers and units at the right place and right time, using multiple means and technologies, with synchronous and asynchronous student-instructor interaction." Multiple means can include print, audio, video, computer-mediated conferencing, and computer-based training, whether delivered via the Internet or through more traditional distance education pathways. The message notes that the Army has in place digital training facilities (DTFs; over 700 such classrooms to be established), Army National Guard DL classrooms, and Classroom XXI high-tech classrooms to support distributed learning. TADLP addresses operational training needs, institutional training requirements, and self-development. DL will allow schools to share their instructors, reduce the time needed for resident training, and hopefully reduce personnel tempo by reducing travel to distant-training sites. TADLP does not include most entry-level classes that feature extensive hands-on soldierization training (e.g., basic training (Initial Entry Training), high-risk training (Ranger, Airborne, and Special Forces), Officer Basic Courses, Warrant Officer Basic Courses, and Officer Pre-Commissioning Training). Since Freeman (2003) wrote about Army DL, the Army has directed, as of November 2004, the use of the Army Learning Management System (ALMS) throughout the Army, to, among other things, register students in courses, track their progress and individual skill development electronically via what is called "skills-gap analysis," and record and report relevant data to students, course managers, and personnel records (TRADOC, 2001, p. D-1). Commanders are now required to make time available during duty hours to soldiers for DA-directed training and for related homework, although soldiers must use personal time for most self-development training. DL-based training may not be identified as such on official student records or transcripts, to preclude resident courses or courses taught at active component schools from being considered more favorably than other courses. The Army is also enhancing opportunities for soldiers to earn college credits by DL via the Army University Access Online (AUAO) or Electronic Army University (eArmyU), an online portal, whereby they can access 28 higher education institutions and 144 college degree programs via the Internet and the related online education system, eArmyU.com. Laptop computers, printers, and internet service accounts are provided free to soldier users. However, as of April 2006, as this chapter went to press, the Army was launching a new way to get tuition assistance and to enroll for college credits at the www.GoArmyEd.com Web site, which will replace eArmyU.com. GoArmyEd, an online portal that automates many of the paper-based processes previously conducted with Army Education counselors, will be the soldier's new one-stop location for managing their college education and using tuition assistance benefits. Through GoArmyEd, soldiers will be able to request tuition assistance, enroll in college courses, register for classes, and check the status of their programs of study, all online. They will also be able to review their tuition-assistance balance, class grades, and current course enrollments at any time. A toll-free phone number (800-817-9990) is also available to provide assistance for soldiers within the continental United States.

Caveats

Some were not so sure that distance education would provide high-quality education (Macy, Rooney, Hollister, & Freddolino, 2001) even if accessibility was improved. Some research suggests the students with lower grade-point averages do better with live instruction (Macy et al., 2001). Indeed, as Freeman (2003) noted, there were problems. The earliest stages of implementation of The Army Distance Learning Program (TADLP), initiated in April 1996, did not include e-mail access, used only legacy learning management tools, and were restricted to central locations, of limited number, that had the requisite equipment. Because few soldiers could afford the expensive laptop computers and software to support distance learning, most early efforts provided, at no small expense, soldiers with such equipment at no cost (pending their completion of training). With respect to making college courses available to soldiers online, Noble (2001) has criticized the military's potential effect on university curricula and its professorate—will the demands of the huge military customer create a standardized curriculum free of critical thought and taught by low-paid adjunct professors?

Abell (2003) raised a number of challenges for distributed learning. She (p. 5) described reports by Joyce, Weil, and Calhoun (2000, p. 400) who found that teachers had to see new techniques "demonstrated up to 20 times" and to practice them "approximately 12 times" before attaining proficiency. Instructors may need "train-the-trainer" assistance to avoid poor performance at initial attempts to deliver distributed learning. It would be easy for distance learning to try to replicate ordinary lectures or to assume that now students must motivate themselves. Rather, she contends, instructors must make motivation part of their lesson plans and consider affective as well as psychomotor and cognitive-learning objectives. Students must be helped to find personal meaning in distance education content and ways must be found to reduce their anxiety so that it does not hinder learning but instead promotes learning.

Regardless of such caveats, Wisher, Sabol, and Moses (2002, p. 20) observed, "Given current trends, it seems that distance education will be playing a key role in Army training efforts for the foreseeable future." TRADOC's (2001, p. xiv) TADLP Campaign Plan at one point projected that at least one-half of soldier and leader training would be provided through distance education while at another point it expected distance learning to satisfy "between 30–65 percent of the quota-managed training load (pp. 1–3)." Those may be understatements; one recent document stated, "Distributed learning will become the primary method of training except when resident training is justified" (IITRI/AB Tech Group, 2002, p. 1). The "way ahead" in the TADLP Campaign Plan (TRADOC, 2001, p. ix) has DL centers for units between 1998 and 2004, students engaged in DL in their homes between 2000 and 2005, and DL reaching soldiers in their vehicles between 2005 and 2010.

EFFECTIVENESS OF DISTANCE EDUCATION IN THE ARMY

Initial Outcomes

Early analyses of the research literature found support for the effectiveness of distance learning in the military (Barry & Runyon, 1995; Howard, 1997). It did appear that distance education required, at least initially, more preparation time by the instructor. Howard (1997, p. 11) found that many students preferred face-to-face learning, even if learning outcomes were similar. As early as 1997, the U.S. Army Research Institute (ARI) signed an agreement with the Training and Doctrine Command (TRADOC) to support distance learning research. In Special Report 49 (Wisher et al., 2002), ARI reported that 41% of soldiers believed that traditional classroom instruction was more effective than DL, compared to 9% who believed DL was more effective, or about the same (26%). Clearly, some soldiers question the ability of DL instruction to handle complex subjects. However, ARI's review of the literature indicates that research shows no difference in effectiveness between DL and traditional methods. However, ARI also found that dropout rates were higher for DL-based learning and that satisfaction rates were lower, even though satisfaction rates were not correlated with actual learning outcomes. DL requires more student self-motivation, which can be discouraging to students used to depending upon instructors for motivation. As timely contact between the instructor and the student increases, satisfaction with DL increases. ARI concluded that DL did save money. High dropout rates have been observed in DL courses (Phipps & Merisotis, 1999), including military courses (Bonk, Olson, Wisher, & Orvis, 2002), but are not well understood. At the same time, it is possible that by bringing the school to the student, improved access to training could increase retention while differences between active and reserve component curricula could be reduced (IITRI/AB Tech Group, 2002, p. 7). An interesting observation from the Army National Guard (IITRI/AB Tech Group, 2002, p. 3) is that DL could save lives given that automobile accidents on mission-related travel are the leading cause of ARNG fatalities.

Later Research

More recent research has continued to vindicate the use of DL in the military (Stapp, 2001; Wisher, Curnow, & Seidel, 2001). Bernard et al. (2004, p. 399) found in their meta-analyses that business and military subjects were suited for distance education but that math, science, and engineering subjects fared better in classroom settings, which may explain an apparently lesser emphasis on distance education in the U.S. Air Force, which was planning on converting only 120 of 1,500 in-residence courses to DL (Westfall, 2003, p. 637). Perhaps the same reasoning, applied to the complexity of medical training, led DeLorenzo (2005) to recommend distance education as only one component of improved methods for future military medical training. Overall, with respect to achievement, distance education was slightly better than classroom instruction, but asynchronous distance education was somewhat better while synchronous distance education was somewhat less effective than classroom instruction (Bernard et al., 2004). Bernard et al. (2004) did find that classroom instruction yielded more positive student attitudes than did distance education, and greater retention. Zhao, Lei, Yan, Lai, and Tan (2005, p. 1859) found that military students appeared to benefit from distance education relative to traditional forms of education, even though military content per se was more weakly (positively but not significantly) associated with distance education gains.

Of particular relevance to military distance education, Zhao et al. (2005) found that greater instructor involvement; students having a high-school diploma (versus a college degree); topics including business, computer science, medical science or multiple areas; and undergraduate (as opposed to graduate) instruction were associated with gains for distance education relative to other approaches. In contrast to Bernard et al. (2004), they also found that purely asynchronous distance education did not fare well although combinations of asynchronous and synchronous were favorable for distance learning gains.

INDEPENDENT RESEARCH ON ARMY DISTANCE EDUCATION

Background

The command leadership of the Sixth Brigade, 95th Division, engaged in evaluation of a variety of methods of instruction (Schumm & Turek, 2003; Schumm, Turek, & Jones, 2003; Schumm, Turek, Jones, & Carlton, 2004; Schumm, Turek, & McCarthy, 2003; Schumm, Webb, Turek, Jones, & Ballard, 2006), but here our focus will be on our evaluations of distance education as it was introduced in 2001 and 2002 for the Combined Arms Services Staff School (CAS3) Course, taught under the 12th Battalion (CAS3). Indeed, Rosenberg (2006, pp. 316–317) has highlighted the importance of evaluation of distance education, noting, "You may have a problem if you have no significant review process to determine if the e-learning[1] you are about to deploy is accurate, authentic, instructionally valid, and easy to use." We were concerned about a number of outcomes, beyond mere user satisfaction. Would DL students be able to bond as well as traditional classroom students, as some doubted that bonding could occur very well in an online environment (Meyer, 2005, p. 1609)? How much time would DL save the Army student? Would DL training be received as favorably as traditional training? Would students look forward to taking future Army courses by DL? Would DL training yield positive training outcomes?

First DL CAS3 Training

As promised by the TADLP Campaign Plan (TRADOC, 2001, pp. 2–4) for the Reserve Components, the first DL CAS3 classes were initiated in the 2001 academic year, one DL class per each of three regional areas. On the initiative of the TASS brigade's leadership, the DL classes were evaluated in the summer of 2001 (Schumm & Turek, 2003). Traditional classroom students were more likely (73%) to rate their CAS3 training as superior to their previous military training than were CAS3 DL students (12%) ($p < .0001$). Slightly more traditional students rated their staff officers' abilities as improved (94%) than did DL students (88%) ($p < .04$). DL training reduced travel time ($p < .001$) but required more classroom activity ($p < .01$) for a net change of nearly zero (31.96 hours per month for traditional classroom CAS3 versus 32.08 hours per month for DL CAS3). CAS3 study and training time was reported by 69% of both groups to interfere with personal or family time, but fewer DL students (36%) reported hearing complaints from family or friends about being away from home too often than did traditional CAS3 students (52%). In terms of psychological absence from home, 57% of traditional students and 64% of DL students reported hearing such complaints from family or friends. All of the DL students reported that they would do DL again for CAS3, compared to only 11.5% of the traditional students who said they would prefer DL. Most (78%) DL students reported their plan to take Command and General Staff College (CGSC) by DL compared to 14–25% of the traditional students ($p < .001$). One problem shared by our data with previous studies (Stapp, 2001, p. 5) is that the DL instructors were handpicked to be among the best we had, whereas the comparison group of traditional classrooms included a range of instructor experience and skill, as reflected in student ratings. It is possible that the equivalence of DL instruction with possibly low-quality traditional education means no more than that good DL is as good as poor traditional educational methods.

Later Research

More recently, we evaluated satisfaction with critical-thinking skills taught in both CAS3 and Command and General Staff College (CGSC) during the summer of 2002 and found that overall outcomes for both groups were strongly related to critical-thinking outcomes, for both DL and traditional methods (Schumm et al., 2006). For our summer 2002 research, there were initially 174 students who attended the two-week annual training phase (2B) of CAS3 at Fort Leavenworth, but one student returned home prematurely. Of the 173 students remaining, 162 agreed to participate in the research. There were 13 responses in which reported training times were less

---

[1]Rosenberg (2006) defines e-learning as "the use of internet technologies to create and deliver rich learning environment that includes a broad array of instruction and information resources and solutions, the goal of which is to enhance individual and organizational performance" (p. 72).

than 12 hours a month; because of questionable validity, those responses were not included in our following statistical analyses. Most of the CAS3 students were males (79%), married (83.2%), had children under the age of 21 living with them at home (78.7%), and had taken phase 2A of CAS3 by IDT (weekend) training (90.1%). None of the students had taken phase 2A of CAS3 on two weeks of active duty, but 9.9% had taken that first phase by distance learning (two separate classes for DL in 2002 compared to one class in 2001). Twenty of the married students had no children while 13 of the unmarried students did have children. Most of the students were from the Army National Guard (53%), with others from the Army Reserve (35%), the Active Guard/Reserve (AGR) (10%), or the Regular Army (3%). Distance learning students were slightly less likely to be female (19% vs. 21%) than traditional classroom students, slightly more likely to be married (94% vs. 82%), and slightly less likely to have children (75% vs. 79%), but none of those differences were statistically significant by chi-square tests. A significant difference was found in that distance learning students were more likely to be Army National Guard (69% vs. 51%) or AGR (31% vs. 7%) while none of the DL students were Army Reserve (0% vs. 39%) or Active Army (0% vs. 3%), with chi-square (df = 3) of 15.6 ($p < .01$). The only notable differences in demographic characteristics between our 2001 CAS3 students (Schumm & Turek, 2003) and the 2002 CAS3 class was that the 2002 DL students were more likely to be married (94% vs. 76%) while a small percentage (3.5%) of the 2001 students had taken phase 2A of CAS3 on a two-week period of active duty.

SPECIFIC INDEPENDENT RESEARCH OUTCOMES

Travel

As expected, our 16 DL students saved travel time since their actual travel time was zero and the average travel time for the 133 traditional CAS3 students was 4.20 hours (SD = 4.71) with $t_{132} = 10.29$ ($p < .001$). We also asked the CAS3 DL students how much time it would have taken them to travel to their nearest traditional CAS3 class for phase 2A. Leaving the travel times the same for the traditional students, the DL students reported an average of 2.25 hours (SD = 1.53), yielding a $t_{60.07} = 3.49$ ($p < .002$). Our results suggest that CAS3 DL students did not choose DL because of travel time saved, because their average travel times would have been less than for the average traditional student. Nevertheless, it is quite clear that DL did save CAS3 students significant amounts of travel time.

Computer Work

We asked the CAS3 students how much time per month on average they spent in phase 2A trying to learn how to use a computer or related software needed for CAS3. The traditional students averaged 5.11 hours (SD = 6.42) compared to 1.81 hours (SD = 1.17) for the DL students, with $t_{128.7} = 5.22$ ($p < .001$). We also asked the CAS3 students how much time per month on average they spent in phase 2A trying to resolve computer, software, or distance learning-related problems associated with CAS3. The traditional students averaged 2.54 hours (SD = 3.35) compared to 2.88 hours (SD = 2.22) for the DL students, with $t_{146} = -0.39$ (n.s.). Thus, we found no significant difference for computer or software problems. Combining the two types of computer issues, the traditional students averaged 7.64 hours (SD = 8.69) compared to 4.69 (SD = 2.94) for the DL students, with $t_{56.46} = 2.80$ ($p < .01$). Overall, the DL CAS3 students spent less time learning about or resolving computer issues. It is possible that DL CAS3 students self-selected themselves on the basis of familiarity with computers or distance education skills. However, either way, computer issues represented a substantial investment of time for both groups of CAS3 students.

Studying and Class Time

Students were asked how much time during phase 2A they spent per month on average studying or preparing for CAS3 and how much time they spent in actual classroom or DL sessions with the instructor and other students. Traditional students averaged 7.95 hours (SD = 5.42) for studying compared to 14.13 hours (SD = 7.38) for DL students, with $t_{146} = 4.13$ ($p < .001$). For class time, traditional students averaged 15.09 hours (SD = 3.80) compared to 13.19 hours (SD = 2.64) for DL students, with $t_{147} = 1.94$ ($p < .06$). Thus, class times were roughly equivalent but DL appeared to require more preparation time. Averaging together travel time, study time, preparation time, and computer-issues times yielded a total average of 34.88 hours per month (SD = 13.90) for the traditional CAS3 students and 32.00 hours (SD = 9.95) for the DL students, a non-significant difference. Altogether, DL students appeared to save nearly three hours per month of time, but the difference was not statistically significant.

Future Preferences

When asked which format they would prefer if they had to take phase 2A of CAS3 again, most of the DL students said DL (62.5%), with 37.5% citing use of annual training whereas most of the traditional students cited the traditional IDT approach (58.3%), with others citing AT (28.8%) or DL (12.9%). The differences were significant by chi-square (df = 2) test of 29.0 ($p < .001$). In our 2001 research we had asked students how they would prefer to take Command and General Staff College but we did not ask that question of the 2002 CAS3 students.

Satisfaction

We asked the CAS3 students a number of questions pertaining to their satisfaction with phase 2A of CAS3, specifically, "Overall, how satisfied were you with the following issues for phase 2A?" Items included: (a) "Overall, with the phase you just completed," (b) "with how well the phase met your expectations," (c) "the extent to which you've been able to use what you've learned in CAS3 so far," (d) "how well the instructors took advantage of the diversity of student experience and background in the class to improve the learning experience," (e) "how well the instructors promoted critical thinking within the class among the majority of students," and (f) "how well the instructors stimulated discussion among the class members." Responses ranged in five levels from very satisfied, generally satisfied, neither satisfied nor dissatisfied, and generally dissatisfied to very dissatisfied, coded from 1 to 5, with highest satisfaction represented by the lowest score.

There were no significant differences between DL and traditional students with respect to overall phase 2A satisfaction, the extent to which they had used what they had learned in CAS3, or the extent to which discussion had been promoted. With respect to meeting expectations, the DL students were more satisfied (1.50, SD = 0.52) compared to the traditional students (1.92, SD = 0.73), with $t_{146} = 2.26$ ($p < .03$). With respect to critical thinking, the DL students were more satisfied (1.19, SD = 0.40) compared to the traditional students (1.64, SD = 0.81), with

$t_{32.46} = 3.71$ ($p < .002$). With respect to use of student diversity, the DL students were more satisfied (1.25, SD = 0.45) compared to the traditional students (1.59, SD = 0.75), with $t_{26.66} = 2.63$ ($p < .02$). The DL instructors were rated very highly by their students, with 84% of the reports being that their instructors were exceptionally well prepared and exceptionally effective in their delivery of instruction. When we restricted the comparisons to students who had rated their traditional classroom instructors as highly as the DL instructors had been rated (at least 75% of the reports being in the exceptional categories), we had 40 student reports and none of the satisfaction (or bonding) comparisons were statistically significant. However, the trends favored the traditional classroom, with overall phase 2A satisfaction being 1.56 for DL students and 1.33 for traditional students ($p < .08$, two-tailed) and bonding being 1.81 for DL students and 1.46 for the traditional students ($p < .09$, two-tailed).

Bonding

Students were asked how well they thought they had bonded with their classmates during the first phase (2A) of CAS3, responses of very well, fairly well, not sure, fairly poorly, and very poorly, coded from 1 to 5, respectively. While the DL students reported levels of bonding (1.81, SD = 0.83) not quite as good as those of traditional students (1.61, SD = 0.59), the difference was not significant statistically.

Overall Staff Training

The CAS3 students were asked how well the overall CAS3 course (both phases) had improved their staff-officer abilities, with responses from very great extent, great extent, some extent, minimal extent, and not at all or decreased my abilities, coded from 1 to 5, respectively. The DL students reported slightly better outcomes (1.69, SD = 0.79) compared to the traditional students (2.06, SD = 0.79) but the difference was not quite significant, with $t_{145} = 1.78$ ($p < .08$, two-tailed test).

Compensation

While 62.5% of the DL students had not received any compensation for their class training (other than the free loan of their computers and software), only 15.9% of the traditional CAS3 students had not received at least some compensation (e.g., retirement points or pay), a difference significant by chi-square (df = 1) test of 18.7 ($p < .001$).

Conflicts

Substantial percentages of the 2002 CAS3 students said that work-related requirements seriously interfered ("often," "very often," or "seemed like all the time") with their ability to spend evening or weekend time with their friends or family: civilian/AGR job (42.8%), USAR/ARNG part-time job (45.6%), CAS3 study and preparation (46.2%), CAS3 travel time (27.1%—lower because the DL students had no travel time), and CAS3 time in class or online with DL (51.0%). CAS3 DL students, as expected, cited far fewer conflicts over travel time for their CAS3 training than did traditional CAS3 students, but in all the other categories of conflicts, there were no significant differences between the DL and traditional CAS3 students.

PERSISTENT DISTANCE LEARNING ISSUES

The Army's DL "Push"

The Army is persuaded that DL is effective. The TADLP Campaign Plan (TRADOC, 2001, pp. 2–15) argued, "The evidence is overwhelming that DL works. It is effective for a variety of training needs required by Soldiers and their leaders. . . . DL can be used to deliver academically demanding training." Wisher and Freeman (2006, p. 93) have recently argued, "The use of technologies such as ADL for training the reserve component should be included in any contemporary training strategy." Wisher & Freeman (2006, p. 93) are particularly pleased with the more than "350 specially designed multimedia classrooms" of the National Guard that are "linked by a high-bandwidth network," which can help for preparation with deployments, as well as regular training or training for families.

Accordingly, there is a strong drive from Army leadership to market DL. "Agreement among Army leaders that DL is a viable way to train is essential to program success. It is imperative to overcome any remaining cultural prejudices impeding its acceptance and implementation" (TRADOC, 2001, pp. ix–x). The campaign plan for DL admitted that there were "cultural implications of shifting the training emphasis away from the training institution to the individual" (TRADOC, 2001, pp. 1–1). In other words, the motto used to be "if the student didn't learn, the teacher didn't teach." With DL, it might have to change to "if the student didn't learn, they weren't motivated, and it's the student's fault."

The campaign plan further noted that effectiveness of DL must be demonstrated: "Overcome resistance to change by demonstrating through studies and achievements that DL provides effective training" (TRADOC, 2001, pp. 1–2), and that it must be marketed effectively and resistance "that tends to sustain the status quo" eliminated. At one point in the campaign plan, a critical success indicator was "[e]ffective training. Commanders and senior leaders at unit level embrace DL as an effective means to train their Soldiers and maintain unit readiness" (pp. 1–3), whereas at another it was "DL is accepted throughout the force" (pp. 1–10). A message matrix was presented as Appendix F-1 (TRADOC, 2001, pp. F-8/9) as part of the TADLP Campaign Plan; for example, Congress is to be given the message that "DL improves readiness" and that it is "cost and training effective" via Department of Defense (DoD) reports to Congress, testimony on the Hill, visits to DL facilities, and use of the Congressional Liaison Office, so that TADLP support from Congress will be generated.

Managing Change

Resistance to change with respect to using DL has been a concern in other services as well (Jones et al., 2003). However, Rosenberg (2006, p. 7) warns us that technology is "the highway, but not the destination." It is all too easy to rely too much upon technology. At the same time, change must be managed and e-learning is part of that change (Rosenberg, 2006, p. 26). Rosenberg (2006, p. 2) observes that organizations may go through three phases in instituting e-learning. First, they build the technology infrastructure and go about putting out a substantial number of classes by distance learning. The second phase involves improving the quality of distance education, keeping the best products and cutting back on ineffective ones, while getting the most "bang for the buck." The final phase involves the adaptation of e-learning to the entire organization's information operations, with a focus on ultimate outcomes (e.g., organizational productivity, stakeholder satisfaction, and performance enhancement). In this final, third phase, knowledge is viewed as residing throughout the organization, not just at the training source, and e-learning is used in multiple directions rather than merely top-down (Rosenberg, 2006, p. 53). Clearly, the U.S. Army has cleared phase one, but it may not be clear how well-developed phases two and three are within the Army, even though Web sites such as PlatoonLeader.army.mil or Company .Command.com are excellent attempts to diffuse critical knowledge in multiple directions (Rosenberg, 2006, p. 162). With respect to the second phase, there may be a risk in the emphasis placed in Army DL on saving money and time to overlook the issue that high-quality instruction, regardless of method, takes money and time. In the rush to make as many courses as possible DL, it may be easy to overlook the fact that some classes may best be taught under traditional settings, as noted by Rosenberg (2006, p. 5). In fact, a balance of distance and traditional learning may be most effective in terms of cost and outcomes (Rosenberg, 2006, p. 69). It may sound great to allow soldiers to meet career educational requirements at home during the evening, but what if the main computer is clearly the spouse's, who resents the Army requiring the soldier to use it at any time? Furthermore, it is not clear to us that spouses will be looking forward to the soldier spending ten hours a day at work and then coming home at night or on the weekends, only to spend another four hours on mandatory DL training. On the other hand, if they can get DL training done while "off duty" in Iraq, that may not be much of an issue, if the logistical requirements can be maintained.

Other Concerns

We also wonder what the latent message is when soldiers are told that we cannot afford resident training—does that mean that they are not all that important? Especially if soldiers should see millions of dollars being wasted on contractor costs overseas and DL appears to be the way to "make up" for such waste, that might not be a surprising conclusion. We are concerned about the messages being sent to officers as professionals. In the Army, it used to be the thought that an officer was a generalist, equipped to some extent to do a wide range of activities. Resident training was designed to build one's identity as an officer, not a person who would be trained "just in time" for a particular job to be done. In part, resident training was a "vacation" from the rigors of line duty, even combat. Sure, some classes might finish before five o'clock some days but was losing a few hours such a price to pay for soldiers who had been operating 24/7 in combat for months on end? Are we going to "pay back" soldiers coming home from 18 months in Iraq with 12-hour workdays, eight hours on the job and then four more hours at home doing DL? When the senior author visited a distance learning facility at Fort Riley in March 2006, he was told that some of the battle-staff NCO classes involved 12-hour days in order to reduce the length of the courses.

Reserve Component Issues

More importantly, perhaps, let us consider "part-time" Reservists. It used to be that if they needed to complete a course, they could do it by correspondence or in residence. Either way they were compensated with retirement points or pay and allowances. If they were working a correspondence course, they could take the booklets wherever they wanted and work on them as time permitted. With DL, as shown in our CAS3 research (Schumm & Turek, 2003; Schumm, Webb, Turek, Jones, & Ballard, 2006; and this chapter), they are now often expected to do the same thing for free, not even for retirement-point credit. Unless they have access to a computer and the Internet, too bad, "no can do." And if someone wants to read their materials in hardcopy, guess who has to pay for the paper and the printer cartridges? Not the Army—it is saving money on its printing budget by passing the costs to the soldier! In other words, DL could become a cover for the Army doing less and the soldier doing more for less. To the extent that such a situation results in a soldier being under-benefited, the net result, according to social exchange theory, will be an angry soldier who is more likely to leave the Army, forcing the Army to, at far greater expense than a few mass-produced printing costs, find, hire, and retrain a replacement!

Ethical Education

A final caution: There are certain aspects of being an officer that are not easily imbued. For example, if a soldier is ordered to abuse enemy prisoners, how will an officer who comes upon the situation respond? Will he or she be able to sift through the rationalizations that will no doubt be offered as excuses? Will they have the courage to defy even a memorandum from a three-star flag officer? Suppose such a flag officer (Sanchez, 2003, p. 1, para B) prepares a memorandum in which he authorizes the withholding of the Koran or the Bible from prisoners while admitting at the same time in the same memorandum, "Other nations that believe detainees are entitled to EPW protections may consider that provision and retention of religious items (e.g., the Koran) are protected under international law (see, Geneva III, Article 34)." Will officers visit their commands and inspire soldiers to report violations before they get out of control rather than waiting until they have become an international incident? Can DL accomplish this type of ethical training? Or is DL a way to train the soldier in just enough to do his narrow little job without having training time for questioning the bigger picture? Is DL a way of ensuring a ready supply of "yes men" who know enough to "do their job" but not enough to question whether they are doing the ethically right job in the ethically right way in the first place? We hope not, but we are not entirely optimistic. Rosenberg (2006, p. 21) argues that almost any content can be taught online but admits that the classroom may be best for "providing an environment where collaborative teams can discover, invent, or otherwise solve complex problems."

CONCLUSIONS

The U.S. Army has made major strides in the development of both its distance learning and knowledge-management systems since 2003. Research indicates that distance learning is as effective in most cases as traditional classroom instruction, though more complex subjects, including ethical issues, may be best addressed in the environment of the traditional classroom. However, because most research has failed to control for instructor quality, it is possible that the effectiveness of distance education in the U.S. Army has been overestimated. Once we controlled for instructor quality in our assessment of distance learning in CAS3, we found results that were less supportive of distance learning relative to traditional classroom learning. There are a number of issues that we have discussed that are involved with distance learning in the military. We must be careful to avoid allowing distance learning to become a way for the military to save itself time and money at the soldier's expense. We found in our own research that distance learning students were far less likely to be reimbursed in any way for their training time than were traditional students, and that time saved in travel was lost, to a large extent, to other activities associated with distance learning. While it appeared that families appreciated having the soldier at home more often, they also were concerned about the soldier being psychologically absent during his or her hours dedicated to distance learning. In conclusion, distance learning will remain an important and evolving approach to improving soldier performance and the Army's combat readiness, but it is not a panacea. Its limitations must be discussed, and improvement in its development and applications must be continuous.

REFERENCES

Abell, M. (2003, December). *Deepening distributed learning: Motivating soldiers to learn, grow, and achieve.* Paper presented at the Interservice/Industry Training, Simulation, and Education Conference, Orlando, FL. Available as FILE_OT_10000314.doc from http://www.spider.bpc.navy.mil, downloaded 14 December 2006.

Barry, M., & Runyan, G. B. (1995). A review of distance-learning studies in the U.S. military. *The American Journal of Distance Education, 9*(3), 37–47.

Bernard, R. M., Abrami, P. C., Lou, Y., Borokhovski, E., Wade, A., Wozney, L., et al. (2004). How does distance education compare with classroom instruction? A meta-analysis of the empirical literature. *Review of Educational Research, 74*(3), 379–439.

Bonk, C. J., Olson, T. M., Wisher, R. A., & Orvis, K. L. (2002). Learning from focus groups: An examination of blended learning. *Journal of Distance Education, 17*(3), 97–118.

DeLorenzo, R. A. (2005). How shall we train? *Military Medicine, 170*, 824–830.

Freeman, M. W. (2003). Distance learning in the U.S. Army: Meeting the readiness needs of transformation. In M. G. Moore & W. G. Anderson (Eds.), *Handbook of distance education* (pp. 655–661). Mahwah, NJ: Lawrence Erlbaum Associates.

Howard, F. S. (1997). Distance learning annotated bibliography (TRAC-WSMR-TR-97-015). White Sands Missile Range, NM: TRADOC Analysis Center-White Sands Missile Range (TRAC-WSMR).

IITRI/AB Tech Group. (2002). Army National Guard distributed learning field guide. Alexandria, VA: Author.

Jones, S. M., Mally, W., Blevins, L. A., & Munroe, J. E. (2003). The U.S. Marine Corps distance learning program. In M. G. Moore & W. G. Anderson (Eds.), *Handbook of distance education* (pp. 641–654). Mahwah, NJ: Lawrence Erlbaum Associates.

Joyce, B., Weil, M., with Calhoun, E. (2000). *Models of teaching* (6th ed.). Boston: Allyn & Bacon.

Macy, J. A., Rooney, R. H., Hollister, C. D., & Freddolino, P. P. (2001). Evaluation of distance education programs in social work. *Journal of Technology in Human Services, 18*(3/4), 63–84.

Meyer, K. A. (2005). Common metaphors and their impact on distance education: What they tell us and what they hide. *Teachers College Record, 107*(8), 1601–1625.

Noble, D. F. (2001). Digital diploma mills: The automation of higher education. New York: Monthly Review Press.

Phipps, R. A., & Merisotis, J. P. (1999). What's the difference? A review of contemporary education on the effectiveness of distance learning in higher education. Washington, DC: The Institute for Higher Education Policy. http://www.ihep.org/Pubs/PDF/Difference.pdf (downloaded 14 December 2006)

Rosenberg, M. J. (2006) *Beyond e-learning: Approaches and technologies to enhance organizational knowledge, learning, and performance.* San Francisco: Wiley & Sons, Inc.

Sanchez, R. S. (2003). CJTF-7 interrogation and counter-resistance policy. (Enclosure 1, Memorandum for C2, CJTF-7, Baghdad, Iraq 09335; C3, CJTF-7, Baghdad, Iraq 09335; Commander, 205th Military Intelligence Brigade, Baghdad, Iraq 09335, 14 September). Baghdad Iraq: Headquarters, Combined Joint Task Force Seven.

Schumm, W. R., & Turek, D. E. (2003). Distance-learning: First CAS3 outcomes. *Military Review, LXXXIII*(5), 66–70.

Schumm, W. R., Turek, D. E., & Jones, K. D. (2003). Comparing learning environments in U.S. military officer educational settings: A field test. *Psychological Reports, 92*, 1131–1132.

Schumm, W. R., Turek, D. E., Jones, K. D., & Carlton, A. B. (2004). Comparing learning environments in U.S. military officer education: A brief replication. *Psychological Reports, 95*, 604–608.

Schumm, W. R., Turek, D. E., & McCarthy, D. (2003). Evaluating an all-ranks military staff ride. *Psychological Reports, 93*, 1156–1158.

Schumm, W. R., Webb, F. J., Turek, D. E., Jones, K. D., & Ballard, G. E. (2006). A comparison of methods for teaching critical thinking skills for U.S. Army officers. *The American Journal of Distance Education, 20*(1), 39–50.

Stapp, K. M. (2001). *Benefits and costs of distance learning: A perspective from the distance learning literature since 1995.* (TRAC-WSMR-AB-01-025). White Sands Missile Range, NM: TRADOC Analysis Center-White Sands Missile Range (TRAC-WSMR).

TRADOC (United States Training and Doctrine Command). (2001). *The Army distance learning program (TADLP) campaign plan.* Fort Monroe, VA: Deputy Chief of Staff for Training.

Westfall, P. J. L. (2003). Distance education in the U.S. Air Force. In M. G. Moore & W. G. Anderson (Eds.), *Handbook of distance education* (pp. 631–639). Mahwah, NJ: Lawrence Erlbaum Associates.

Wisher, R. A., Curnow, C. K., & Seidel, R. J. (2001). Knowledge retention as a latent outcome measure in distance learning. *The American Journal of Distance Education, 15*(3), 20–35.

Wisher, R. A., & Freeman, M. W. (2006). The U.S. Reserve Component: Training strategies for adapting to deployment. In T. W. Britt, A. B. Adler, & C. A. Castro (Eds.). *Military life: The psychology of serving in peace and combat (Volume 4: Military culture)* (pp. 81–96). Westport, CT: Praeger Security International.

Wisher, R. A., Sabol, M. A., & Moses, F. L. (2002). *Distance learning: The soldier's perspective* (pp. 1–24). (Special Report 49). Alexandria, VA: U.S. Army Research Institute for the Behavioral and Social Sciences.

Zhao, Y., Lei, J. Yan, B., Lai, C., & Tan, H. S. (2005). What makes a difference? A practical analysis of research on the effectiveness of distance education. *Teachers College Record, 107*, 1836–1884.

43

Network and Virtual Forms of Distance Education

Andrew Woudstra
Athabasca University

Marco Adria
University of Alberta

The network continues to constitute the single most important structural and organizing principle in the short history of distance education. Yet it remains largely un-theorized in the distance education literature and unrecognized within the practices and processes of distance education. Theorists and practitioners outside of distance education have used the principles of the network to develop approaches to e-commerce, community development, and e-government that have transformed entire industries. In this chapter, we argue that by drawing on the research in business and management information systems, distance education institutions may build larger, denser, and more responsive networks of learners.

DISTANCE EDUCATION AND THE EMERGING NETWORK ORGANIZATION

Although there is growing interest in the influence of the Internet on learning, and more research on how online courses may be presented, there continues to be a dearth of literature—descriptive, prescriptive, or analytical—on organizing for distance education. Rumble (1986) provided the earliest attempt to map the territory of organizing for distance education, identifying three macro-administrative designs possible for distance education organizations:

1. Single mode, in which distance education is the "core business" of the organization
2. Mixed mode, in which both traditional teaching and distance education take place within the same organization
3. Consortium, in which resources, especially teaching resources such as course materials and communications technology hardware, are shared within a region or nation

More recently, an emerging picture of the convergence of these three modes has been depicted. Dunning (1990) speculated on the integration of campus and distance education. Holt and Thompson examined the effects of information technology on distance learning institutions using a case study (1995) and a strategic framework (1998). Dede (1996) explored the effects of emerging technologies on both distance education and campus-based, face-to-face education and developed a three-part conceptual framework encompassing knowledge webs, virtual communities, and shared synthetic environments for enabling distributed learning. Bates (1997) postulated that the Internet and its increasing broadband capacity would encourage the convergence of campus-based organizations and distance education organizations as interactive network-based technologies begin to be used extensively in both.

At the same time, the capability of administrative systems to respond to and shape the convergence of campus-based and distance education initiatives has been questioned. Rumble (1981) examined the economics of distance education and some of the key cost structures found in distance education organizations, suggesting that management across academic and production departments would need to be focused and relatively strong in comparison to that found in traditional educational organizations. Murgatroyd and Woudstra (1989) distinguished between strategic planning, which they saw as a relatively common exercise, and strategic management focused on competencies needed to cope with uncertainty, which they claimed was a more important yet rarer process. Woudstra and Powell (1989) examined the use of value chain analysis in analyzing work processes at a single-mode distance education institution. Finally, Woudstra and Murgatroyd (1992) proposed a design process for distance education organizational structures using concepts based on Handy's (1989) shamrock organization and scenario-planning techniques (Schwartz, 1991; Wack, 1985a, 1985b). The model featured a dedicated core of academic and professional staff, combined with a collaborative network of part-time and contracted academics, professionals, and related organizations.

Over the past decade, the model described in Woudstra and Murgatroyd (1992) was largely implemented in the Athabasca University School of Business. A distinct strategic business unit, the Centre for Innovative Management (CIM), was created in 1993 to offer a for-profit MBA program. Professors in the management studies area at the university had persuaded the CIM's founding director, Dr. Stephen Murgatroyd, that a new online degree offered from a new organization could be successful given advances in information technology. A relatively small core of academic and professional staff would be responsible for developing and delivering an MBA, contracting to suppliers of services as required. Separate from the rest of Athabasca University, CIM was not hindered by legacy systems of administration or learning technology. The defining pedagogical feature of the Athabasca MBA has been its use of the students' workplace as a source of discussion, assignment, and case material. Students in the program have consistently rated highly the opportunity to use their workplace as a setting for projects and the ability to interact with students from other workplaces for online comment and discussion. The Athabasca University MBA program is a success story. It serves over 1,000 registered students and consistently ranks very high in student satisfaction surveys.

Meanwhile, the undergraduate business program, which remained on the main Athabasca University campus, extensively redesigned its operational model to serve more students more effectively, using financial resources that have increased more slowly than the enrollment rate. Using a Domino/Notes server platform parallel to the one used for the MBA, a call-center model serves over 6,000 students per year. A network of course assistants, academics, markers, and learning facilitators deals with student queries as a team (Adria & Woudstra, 2001).

TRANSACTIONS AND THE NETWORK ORGANIZATION

For faculty, staff, and managers of distance education organizations, there remains the underlying question of what it is about the organizational structure of a network that offers a competitive advantage. The network organization may be considered as one of three generic models of economic organization (Williamson, 1994). The "market model" of economic organization seeks an exchange relationship with the external environment directly. Transactions in the market model are founded on price. Price provides the basis for establishing the preference of a buyer for a particular seller. The cost of economic transactions can be low as long as the information required to make a transaction is easy to obtain.

The "hierarchy model," in contrast, is established to facilitate transactions that, if carried out in a market, would carry a higher cost. As Powell (1990) pointed out, "Transactions are moved out of markets into hierarchies as knowledge specific to the transaction (asset specificity) builds up" (p. 297). An organization that has implemented the hierarchy model allows the generic transaction of the market to take place in a more differentiated and specific context. As indicated at the beginning of this chapter, the Internet can reduce the cost of transactions by making richer, more complex, and more up-to-date information available to a larger group of people. It therefore reduces, though does not eliminate, the economic imperative for organizational boundaries. Organizations can become smaller and more focused on core activities while arranging for other organizations to perform peripheral, noncore tasks.

The "network model" is designed to establish transactions among organizational partners that form neither a market nor a hierarchy. Network models "entail more enduring and diffuse connections than markets but more reciprocal and egalitarian arrangements than hierarchies" (Scott, 1998, p. 276). Network transactions possess a different communication tone: "In markets the standard strategy is to drive the hardest possible bargain in the immediate exchange. In networks, the preferred option is use of creating indebtedness and reliance over the long haul" (p. 302). Table 43.1 shows the three models of economic organization, along with their salient characteristics.

The Internet can make the organization, and by extension the network, more transparent. More organizational members can see a truer picture of what the organization's management or leadership is doing. Individuals can access the network resources from any location at any time. In relation to both its members and its clients, the network organization must create the resources and knowledge repositories that will create and develop loyalty. It must add the extra value for its membership that will bind their loyalty. If it fails to add this value, members may quickly leave or the network itself may collapse. Members will also desert if there is a mismatch of values.

The transactions carried out historically by distance education organizations have been accomplished through both the hierarchy and market models of organization. The interactions within the hierarchy of the distance education organization have mainly been for the purpose of achieving a division of labor different from that of the conventional university or school.

This new division of labor was necessary for obtaining resources, realizing development and production capabilities, negotiating contracts with academic staff, and so forth. Distance education organizations have been heavily dependent on a production model. This has meant a more direct recourse to hierarchical structures and ultimately more power for managers than would typ-

TABLE 43.1.
Three Models of Economic Organization

Key Factors	Models		
	Market	*Hierarchy*	*Network*
Normative basis	Contract—Property rights	Employment relationship	Complementary strengths
Means of communication	Prices	Routines	Relational
Mode of conflict resolution	Haggling—Resort to courts for enforcement	Administrative fiat— supervision	Norm of reciprocity— Reputational concerns
Degree of flexibility	High	Low	Medium
Amount of commitment among parties	Low	Medium to high	Medium to high
Tone or climate	Precision and/or suspicion	Formal/bureaucratic	Open-ended, mutual benefits
Actor preference or choices	Independent	Dependent	Interdependent

Note. From "Neither Market Nor Hierarchy: Network Forms of Organization," by W. W. Powell, 1990, in B. M. Staw and L. L. Cummings, *Research in Organizational Behavior* (p. 300), Greenwich, CT: JAI Press. Copyright 1990 by JAI Press Inc. Adapted with permission.

ically be the case in an educational organization. Rumble's (1986) corollary remains valid, but only partially, in relation to the experience of a decade and a half ago:

> Management [of distance education] . . . needs to ensure integrated decision making across a range of functionally distinct areas. This can be achieved through joint decision making processes which involve both academics and operational and administrative staff. It is also most likely to be achieved by rational and possibly hierarchical approaches to management, rather than by approaches which tolerate collegiality, politicization and organised anarchy. This does not mean that these latter models are not found in distance education systems. They may be present, but the overall management of the institution must be both stronger and more rationally orientated than is necessarily the case in conventional educational institutions. (p. 181)

These imperatives are fading with the Internet's development as the communications platform and knowledge storehouse for all education organizations. Harrison's (1994) account of the network organization should ring true for many members of distance education organizations, with its description of "core" and "peripheral" jobs and functions:

> According to a central tenet of best-practice flexible production, managers first divide permanent ("core") from contingent ("peripheral") jobs. The size of the core is then cut to the bone, which, along with the minimization of inventory holding, is why "flexible" firms are often described as practicing "lean" production. These activities, and the employees who perform them, are then located as much as possible in different parts of the company or network, even in different geographical locations. . . . [T]he practice of lean production (the principle applies as much to the service sector as to manufacturing) involves the explicit reinforcement or creation *de novo* of sectors of low-wage, "contingent" workers, frequently housed with small business suppliers and subcontractors. (p. 11)

Network organizations in production industries may be considered to fall into four classes: (a) craft industry organizations, (b) industrial districts, (c) strategic alliances, and (d) vertically disaggregated organizations (Harrison, 1994). These classes are of varying relevance to distance education organizations because of the varying degree to which production principles are applied in these organizations. For example, in "craft industries" such as the construction, publishing, and film and recording industries, projects are the primary mode of production. Each product is unique, and suppliers and subcontractors are in a relationship of personal trust with the contractor.

The *industrial district* is characteristic of German textile firms and the Emilian model of production in Italy. Companies choose to locate in an area because of the "existence of a dense, overlapping cluster of firms, skilled laborers and an institutional infrastructure" (Powell, 1990, p. 309). The districts may be led either by small firms or by a smaller number of large firms.

In a *strategic alliance*, all participants provide technological expertise, managerial expertise, and capital. The strategic alliance model underlies the new distance education. In production industries, strategic alliances have been the domain of big-ticket production companies such as airline manufacturers. Partners enter such alliances in order to respond to technological constraints (i.e., they desire to share the large costs of developing new technologies) and to financial demands (i.e., they desire to reduce the risks of entering new markets). Although strategic alliances are common within the distance education field, the actual sharing of resources has not been in evidence in the alliances established to date. For example, Global University Alliance and the Canadian Virtual University market existing courses and programs for their member institutions as did Fathom before it ceased operations.

Finally, *vertical disaggregation* has been used by large organizations to keep pace with shorter product life cycles and rapid technological change. The U.S. automobile industry, for example, has used it as part of a process of "downsizing." Suppliers now compete to provide smaller components of the final product. Vertically disaggregated organizations may be expected to eventually develop in the distance education field, although, as noted above, the strategic alliance model has been the preferred choice to date. Vertical disaggregation is associated with a shortening of the life cycle of products (including, perhaps, products such as courses and course-development and course-production methods) and with keeping up with rapid and continuous change in information and communications technologies. Traditional campus-based universities are network-based organizations in which a strong administrative structure has been used to create some order and predictability among academics, especially in terms of their patterns of work, and to recruit and organize students. Although academics have come to see the university as a secure "employer," employment security was not among its original goals. Rather, the university was intended to be a safe haven in which discussion and dissent could be freely undertaken and the advancement of knowledge could be pursued in an unhindered manner. Historically, academics have been much more entrepreneurial and more prepared to venture than they are now. That could again be the case if vertical disaggregation continues to occur in both traditional universities and distance education institutions.

The virtual network (which can have a mix of "clicks and bricks") is a type of vertically disaggregated network but may also evolve further to allow even more rapid and flexible adjustment in knowledge-based industries such as education. Virtual organizing, according to Venkatraman and Henderson (1998), can result in a living organization that is multi-organizational in scope and contains customer (student) communities, resource coalitions, and professional communities of practice. Sustained innovation and growth are made possible by virtual organizing. Table 43.2 analyzes virtual organizing across three vectors: virtual encounters, virtual sourcing,

TABLE 43.2.
Virtual Organizing: Three Vectors and Three Stages

	Stage 1	Stage 2	Stage 3
Virtual Encounters	Remote experience of products and services	Dynamic customization	Customer communities
	Textbook publishers are creating supplementary web site links to connect students and professors throughout a course.	In place of standard textbooks, instructors now assemble textbooks that suit their styles and objectives. Textbook publishers move to create an organization that can deliver educational solutions for its customers.	User communities. Students and academic groups form and are incorporated and recognized as part of the value delivery system (e.g., Amazon's community of readers, Harley owners group).
Virtual Sourcing	Sourcing modules	Process interdependence	Resource coalitions
	The web is pushing the ability to source standard products, linking suppliers and customers and creating savings of 20% to 50%.	Companies assign responsibilities for functions such as customer service and logistics across organizational boundaries to outside organizations.	Organizations become a portfolio of capabilities and relationships. One firm does not dominate all others in the virtual integration network. Each participant balances its leadership position relative to one set of resources with secondary roles in complementary resource.
Knowledge Leverage	Work unit expertise	Corporate asset	Professional community expertise
	An organization's ability to make processes effective is supported by groupware, intranets, and communications technology. Case reasoning tools, neural nets, and the Web allow capture and leveraging of knowledge on a global scale.	Across work units knowledge collection, sharing, and creation is systematically managed. Virtual teamwork programs access expertise remotely to problem solve in real time.	This community is well beyond a focal organization. It leverages the experience and knowledge of professionals, researchers, students, teachers, and practitioners in a comprehensive virtual electronic network.
Target Locus	Task units	Organization	Interorganizational

Note. From "Real Strategies for Virtual Organizing," by N. Venkatraman and J. C. Henderson, 1998, *Sloan Management Review, 40*(1), p. 34. Copyright 1998 by the Sloan Management Review Association. Adapted with permission.

and knowledge leverage. It also depicts its progression through three stages of development. Meeting the challenges of moving toward stage 3 will require action in a number of key areas.

Distance education organizations have been more hierarchical than other educational organizations because of the production function. The differentiation of production processes that characterizes distance education organizations has resulted in a more highly differentiated division of labor. In this sense, distance education organizations have been developing the network form of organization both explicitly and implicitly for some time—explicitly through consortia and implicitly through the differentiation of production processes. These organizations must now bind their peripheral suppliers as well as their student groups more closely through the use of virtual organizing practices capable of creating loyalty. The increase in competition in the field of distance education, coupled with continued deployment of new technologies, will encourage a further development of the network model using virtual learning communities.

TOWARD THE STRATEGIC DEVELOPMENT OF THE NETWORK ORGANIZATION IN DISTANCE EDUCATION: COMMUNICATION IN VIRTUAL LEARNING COMMUNITIES

The critical components of networks are know-how, speed, and trust. By considering the economic basis for transactions and the means by which the costs of these transactions are reduced in the network form of organization, we have reviewed the means by which know-how and speed are given central importance in the network. The *economic* basis for network organizations has thus been described as a shift in the site for transactions. The *social* basis for network organizations is a shift in the way relationships between organizations are established and maintained. Personal ties and referrals by friends and associates are typical of network organizations. Communication systems and practices underlie these components. Referrals and ties emphasize the personal nature of a true network, because it is only a personal relationship, as opposed to a hierarchical relationship, that can lead to trust. Trust is the basis for not only network organizations but also online communities.

Handy (1989) and Kanter (1983, 1989, 2001) theorized about the shape of the emerging organization. Kanter, in particular, has studied the nature of innovation in large firms. There is also a growing literature on the virtual organization and its effective organization and management (Davenport & Pearlson, 1998; Drucker, 1985; Townsend, DeMarie, & Hendrickson, 1998; Venkatraman & Henderson, 1998; Williams & Cothrel, 2000). Markus, Manville, and Agres (2000) have examined the factors that make a virtual organization successful. Using the open source movement as a base for study, they looked at a variety of open source models and their methods for considering input, making decisions, and resolving disputes. They argue that virtual organizations tend to be successful when they are characterized by the following:

- Mutually reinforcing motivations, with a share or "ownership" for individuals in collective success.
- Self-governance, including membership management, rules, and institutions adaptable to individual needs.
- The ability to monitor and sanction members' behavior.
- Reputation as a motivator, along with control mechanisms and a shared culture.
- Effective work structures and processes.
- Effective technology for communication and coordination, with norms for its use.

This list of factors is echoed by McWilliam (2000) and Williams and Cothrel (2000). Williams and Cothrel studied four online communities, including About.com, a network of Web sites consolidated under one banner. About.com uses "guides" recruited initially by offering Web site creators a small fee to bring their site under the About.com banner. Guides receive a small share of advertising revenues. They are geographically dispersed and are not About.com employees. The "Community of Guides" is a forum that allows guides to interact with each other and with About.com staff. It is almost entirely virtual and includes e-mail, chats, and bulletin boards. There are training sessions, newsletters, and an ongoing stream of communication from About.com to the guides. Rookie guides are offered peer mentoring. All press releases are circulated to guides before they are distributed to the media. The community features a virtual lounge or water cooler where announcements are posted and where important resources such as contracts, promotional packages, stationery, and archived newsletters can be found. Guides help each other; About.com helps them to do that. Between 25% and 30% of the conversation on the bulletin boards consists of guides helping one another. E-mentoring, a form of online helping, has been shown to be a useful means of tapping the expertise and goodwill of a learning community (Bierema & Merriam, 2002).

The potential for distance education organizations to learn from operations such as About.com seems obvious. *Harvard Business Review* provided an example of a well-developed concept for an online community. The review created a discussion forum for its readers in which discussions could take place related to individual articles. Authors were encouraged to provide a note to lead off the discussion. After that, people commented on and questioned the ideas presented in the article. Future research in the pedagogy of distance education should be devoted to developing concepts similar to this one. It is toward the ideal of a committed, decentralized, and dynamic community of scholars and students that the network distance education organization is progressing.

In the hierarchy form of economic organization, a species of trust is enforced by fiat. Information is provided on demand. However, the kind of information and knowledge that is characteristic of network organizations is available only in situations in which the identity of the two participants is a critical factor in making the exchange possible. Communication in the network organization is characterized by trust.

Stokes and Logan (2004) point to two key conditions for collaboration in the virtual network. The first is the Internet or browser-based system which becomes linked to email, groupware, and data warehouses. This condition is often the focus of initial system design, but it is not enough. The second is the development of trust, teamwork, and collaboration—the "soft issues":

> The more complex and sophisticated technology, the more important are the human behavioral issues of attitude, cooperation, and motivation, as well as the training, education, and learning of all members of the organization. (Stokes & Logan, 2004, p. 4)

Researchers have found an association between calculative, competence, and relational interpersonal trust and performance. The different types of trust are necessary if virtual collaborative relationships are to result in positive performance (Paul & McDaniel, 2004). The virtual environment requires a different communication mode. Behavioral control in virtual relationships such as virtual teams must be used carefully. When the vigilance of team members increases, failures to fulfill obligations will be detected more often, and trust will decline.

Uzzi's (1996) study of network organizations in the New York garment district revealed that trust was not considered by CEOs as a nebulous or unimportant characteristic. Instead, they mentioned it frequently. Referring to other partners, one CEO said, for example, "They're part of the family" (p. 677). Trust in the network is the condition under which partners are willing to exchange *valuable* information and knowledge. Communication in networks shifts, as Powell has observed, from a market emphasis on prices and the hierarchical concern with routines to a focus on relational communication:

> Within hierarchies, communication and exchange is shaped by concerns with career mobility—in this sense, exchange is bound up with consideration of personal advancement. At the same time, intra-organizational communication takes place among parties who generally know one another, have a history of previous interactions, and possess a good deal of firm-specific knowledge; thus there is considerable interdependence among the parties. In a market context, it is clear to everyone concerned when a debt has been discharged, but such matters are not nearly as obvious in networks or hierarchies. (p. 302)

Urban, Sultan, and Qualls (2000) noted that, for the Internet organization, "Trust is built in a three-stage cumulative process that establishes (1) trust in the Internet and the specific Web site, (2) trust in the information displayed and (3) trust in the delivery fulfillment and service" (p. 40). In order to develop trust, individuals must provide information in an unbiased and complete manner, promises must be kept, and help, either in the form of software agents or human resources, must be accessible easily and with no or little delay. Privacy must be assured, and operations should be as transparent to the user as possible. Again, creation of communities of users can be very helpful in building trust. We have noted how effective communities have been for About.com. Communities of customers have been surprisingly valuable to companies such as Harley Davidson. The Harley Owners Group (hog.com) is housed at the Harley Davidson Web site and has been a valuable link for the company. For established organizations with brand recognition, transferring brand equity to the new medium can be an effective means of maintaining and building market share.

Trust of the type considered here is different from the variety discussed in the literature on hierarchical organizations (Graen & Uhl-Bien, 1995). Hierarchical organizations establish trust relationships vertically within the organization, whereas the network organization must establish such relationships horizontally. Horizontal relationships across organizations are much more difficult to establish than vertical relationships within the organization. Shared goals and organizational culture, along with financial incentives, encourage trust within the organization. In a network, a relationship of trust must be established progressively, using personal references and contacts, and it must be maintained through processes that encourage formal and informal communication at all levels of the organization.

PRACTICAL AND THEORETICAL IMPLICATIONS OF THE NEW DISTANCE EDUCATION

We turn finally to the likely challenges faced by practitioners in and theorists of the emerging network distance education organization. In his well-known concept of the learning community, Etienne Wenger described learning as social participation. In such a view, individuals engage in and contribute to the practices of their communities. Communities have a stake in fostering learning. Learning practices are thereby refined and the viability of the community is ensured. Organizations become more valuable by nurturing their communities of practice that are threaded through the organization. Wenger's view of the importance of technology in shaping learning communities and networks is described in terms that are invaluable for distance education practitioners:

> [C]ommunication technologies have changed the time and space constraints of identification. The success of worldwide computer networks, for instance, is due not only to the access to infor-

mation that they afford but also the possibility of connecting with people who share an interest in developing, in the process, relations of identification with people all over the world. Thus our identities are expanded, spreading (so to speak) along the tentacles of all these wires and taking, through imagination, planetary dimensions. (Wenger, 1998, p. 194)

The uncertain environment and rapid technological change are creating a new interest in planning and strategy models, as evidenced in recent literature. From general articles on theories of change (Beer & Nohria, 2000) through a survey on models of strategy formation (Mintzberg & Lampel, 1999) to specific prescriptions for strategy formation (Abell, 1999; Beinhocker, 1999; Pascale, 1999), recognition of increasing uncertainty and the need to cope with it flow through the management literature. Drucker (1985) noted that resistance to change or entrepreneurial innovation is especially strong in service organizations such as government agencies, labor unions, churches, hospitals, schools, and universities. In the most successful strategic changes, strategy follows structure (Chandler, 1962), but in practice there is most often an existing organizational structure that must adjust to change (Abell, 1999). In these cases, structure will often limit the implementation of a new strategy, causing the implementation to be suboptimal or to fail. The managers of existing organizations wishing to engage in e-education face strong barriers. The tendency of their organizations will be to limit strategic redirection in order to minimize structural change.

The task for managers and advocates of virtual distance education is to devise organizational and management processes that will encourage change and allow it to be measured (Garvin, 1998). Woudstra and Powell (1989) examined the workflow processes in a uni-modal distance education university through the value-chain model. Woudstra and Murgatroyd (1992) postulated factors required to initiate change toward a new organizational format. The "balanced scorecard" (Kaplan & Norton, 1992; Kaplan, 1996) provides an excellent framework for assessing performance and implementing strategies applicable to the education industry (O'Neil, Bensimon, Diamond, & Moore, 1999). Abell (1999) advocated dual-strategy paths for today and tomorrow. Beinhocker (1999) suggested the nurturing of multiple strategies and maintaining options until it becomes clearer which will be successful. Beinhocker used Microsoft as an example, noting that in 1988 Microsoft had initiatives in four operating systems. It eventually focused on Windows, which became the predominant personal computer operating system. However, in 1988 it was far from certain which operating system architecture would prevail, and Bill Gates kept Microsoft's options open.

An organization must be prepared to make a substantial commitment of resources and time if it is serious about learning enough about its portfolio to make future choices. Without commitment, there can be little learning and little development of trust between the organization and internal or external community partners. The organization must also take steps to communicate details of its projects and their success and failure to its members so that they become receptive to innovative change. An existing university—dual mode, single-mode distance, or single-mode traditional—will be best served by developing a portfolio of projects in virtual e-education. Some of these projects might be internal and others might be external. At Athabasca University, a small institution, there are at a minimum three departments with initiatives in online Web-enhanced course delivery. The university joined two university consortia in distance education and then left one of them, and the Canadian Virtual University is headquartered on its campus. It has numerous one-on-one collaborations domestically and internationally. There will come a point, however, when Athabasca University, like Bill Gates, will have to make some hard decisions about which initiatives to continue.

Beinhocker (1999) and Pascale (1999) both noted that the key to success in an uncertain environment is to be adaptive by diversifying strategic options and creating adaptive systems. Pascale (1999) and De Geus (1997) supported a view of the organization as a living system that, if allowed, will adapt to survive and prosper through experimentation, learning, and seizing the momentum of success. This concept of the living organization is compatible with Ghoshal, Bartlett, and Moran's (1999) new management model, in which facilitating cooperation among people has precedence over enforcing compliance and initiative is valued more than obedience.

Meeting the current challenges of distance education requires new patterns of communication between distance educators and their students. We would point to the following strategies as potentially helpful for distance educators who are considering organizing or reorganizing their operations with the intention of creating a network organization, virtual organization, or virtual community.

First, complementary strengths must be identified and developed cooperatively by partners. Examples of strengths that may be brought to a network by a partner include the disciplinary specific intellectual capital held by faculty and coded in learning materials, know-how that is specific to the tier, and structural capabilities such as the capacity to produce course materials or deliver courses continuously. Some distance education organizations have libraries. Others rely on students to use the libraries in their place of residence. Those who have developed libraries have a significant asset that should be identified as a strength. Those who have developed a significant body of courseware should also identify this as a strength. An open-handed, gain-sharing process must be used to create incentives for contributors to participate. Publishing companies (e.g., Thomson Learning) that are moving further into the curriculum process understand this. However, the entire network will have to adopt gain-sharing in some form as participants become more aware of their ability to generate returns from their intellectual capital.

Second, communication methods and practices should be assessed and, if appropriate, changed. Distance education operations that seek exchanges with one another must identify channels of communication that are available most of the time and communication processes that emphasize the relational nature of the network. Because distance education organizations have expertise in establishing communication pathways for their students, they should be able to establish similar pathways for communicating with their partners. Virtual communities use a variety of means, including e-mail, discussion forums, conferences, newsletters, knowledge storehouses, calendars, and shared network storage. The transfer of "fine-grained information" makes the network valuable to the partners. Fine-grained information encompasses both tacit and proprietary knowledge. Tacit knowledge is "know-how" that is generally not codified, that is, published or even expressed verbally (Abrahamson & Fairchild, 1999; Crossan, Lane, & White, 1999; Hirschorn, 1998; Pfeffer & Sutton, 1999). Tacit knowledge must be tapped and members must have a reason to provide it. It is not clear if information systems can codify tacit knowledge, but some organizations are trying to codify it (e.g., fathom.com). A member will contribute or exchange proprietary information if there is seen to be a net benefit from the exchange: "Social relations make information credible and interpretable, imbuing it with qualities and value beyond what is at hand" (Uzzi, 1996, p. 678).

Third, processes of conflict resolution must be given continuing attention. The network organization relies on what Powell (1990) calls "norms of reciprocity" (p. 304). Rather than seeking redress for damages suffered, the network organization attempts to (a) minimize and manage damages and (b) "trade" damages. Minimizing and managing damages involves communication to ensure that the resources of the network are deployed to reduce the scope and extent of damages where they occur and to avoid them in the future. Trading damages means recognizing that the network bestows advantages and that these should be set against the disadvantages of membership. In a well-functioning virtual community, the members participate in making and changing the rules, and the rules they adopt fit their unique needs. They need a set of procedures for discussing and voting on important issues (Markus et al., 2000). In a distance education network, these groups need to be respected throughout the organization's levels. Rules should not be hierarchically imposed. Joint problem-solving arrangements are required to ensure not only that damages do not spread but also that trust and the continuous exchange of information are maintained: "[F]irms that are linked through embedded ties work through problems and get direct feedback—increasing learning and the discovery of new combinations" (Uzzi, 1996, p. 679). Joint problem-solving must be initiated "just in time," overcoming the barriers of geography and organizational hierarchies. Virtual teams are emerging as a method of creating task forces "on the fly" (Boudreau, Loch, Robey, & Straub, 1998; Townsend et al., 1998). These may be used across organizations to ensure that problem solving, damage control, and trust are preserved.

Fourth, flexibility, commitment, an open-ended climate, and interdependence should become common values. Flexibility should be emphasized. However, managers and academics in network distance education organizations should accept that they will have less flexibility in making decisions in relationship to the market. This is because decisions of this kind will now be coordinated with partners and student-customers and freelance or volunteer contributors. Network members or participants should be aware of the need to contribute to the partnership. The degree of commitment is higher than it is outside of the network. A long-term perspective should be adopted toward benefits of membership in the network, along with a flexible approach to operations in the short term. Decisions in the network will have implications for other members. Unilateral actions will not only create the risk of damage to another partner but also will likely decrease the level of trust among partners.

Fifth, leadership and governance policies must create a system of checks and balances to distribute power throughout the network. A good example is the U.S. Constitution, with its division of power among the legislative, executive, and judicial branches. Checks and balances keep one branch from overtaking the others. De Geus (1997) advocates creating decision-making impediments that make it difficult to move decisions upward in the organization. If it is obvious that decisions must be made at the appropriate level and attempts to move the decision upward will hurt the organizational member's future in the organization, agreements to make a decision will be more forthcoming.

Sixth, entrepreneurial initiative and innovation should be natural and expected in the network organization. Learning by accommodation (De Geus, 1997), or making internal changes to fit a changing world, is critical to sustaining a healthy, thriving organization. Allowing and encouraging diversity helps accommodation. Use of techniques such as scenario planning helps the organization view possible futures and allows an assessment of their probabilities and the actions necessary to accommodate them.

Seventh, the network organization must systematically evaluate its progress and measure effectiveness. The balanced scorecard is winning wide acceptance in both production and service organizations as an effective framework for capturing the key factors of an organization's success. O'Neil et al. (1999) discussed the adaptation of the balanced scorecard in a major U.S. university.

Researchers considering the likely trajectory of the network organization in distance education should hold an explicit set of assumptions about the conditions under which the network is a preferred model of organizing. Powell (1990) stated that the establishment of a network organization is a response to a situation in which the following is true:

- Sustained cooperation is needed.
- Incentives are required for learning and circulation of information, leading to the quick translation of ideas into action.
- Resources are variable and environments uncertain.
- Means are needed to utilize and enhance intangible assets such as tacit knowledge and technological innovation. (p. 322)

These conditions of existence raise questions about how and why the network organization will continue to be the dominant mode of organizing in the field of distance education. We conclude with some further questions for research.

FUTURE RESEARCH

The trajectory of the network organization is toward "concentration without centralization" (Harrison, 1994). That is, power remains within the largest institutions, while the development of new technologies occurs in smaller organizations, and the risk of entering new markets is shared. Yet most alliances that have developed in distance education have involved partners in the same "tier" (i.e., similar in prestige, size, and technological capability). For example, the Canadian Virtual University seeks to create a network of *like* distance education organizations. These organizations are also exclusively Canadian institutions, although we would argue that geographical or national location will increasingly become irrelevant within a given network tier. The core-ring model, in which a dominant organization seeks to establish a disaggregated relationship with organizations that will compete with one another as suppliers, has not yet been realized, although the Open University, as noted earlier, may be seeking such a structure. A question that researchers should therefore consider as these alliances develop is whether a true alliance of equal partners is likely to emerge or whether, as Harrison (1994) suggests is the more common case, a core-ring structure will be formed.

Studies in organization theory and political economy have often considered networks in production industries. The question of how such networks emerge in service industries has been given less attention. Distance education network organizations may be characterized as hybrids of production and service. Even in the age of online learning, the production of course materials retains aspects of the industrial mode of book publishing. Indeed, printed materials remain at the center of most online courses and programs. However, as online, Web-enabled course development and delivery gains acceptability, we will see publishing companies moving further into the curriculum creation and delivery process. Printed materials will be accessed electronically rather than in hard-copy form. A distance education organization's services are provided to students, of course, but also to internal organizational groups. Which aspects of a network form of organization are most appropriately applied to the production activities of the distance education organization and which are best used in relationship to service activities? To what extent will the organization outsource the curriculum development process to publishing companies or similar groups?

Network organizations are not a new phenomenon in distance education or in the educational field generally. Educational organizations have traditionally combined their resources and shared knowledge. However, the distance education field has been characterized by more competition than has been the case in other types of education. So, what is really different about the network organization? What boundaries have shifted? What boundaries remain the same? How will virtual organizing affect the nature of the network? Will the distinctions blur between competition and cooperation among network participants?

Distance education organizations have conventionally considered their proprietary knowledge (knowledge that they wholly own) and their tacit knowledge (implicit in their practices) to be worth protecting at almost any cost. In the network organization, "new connections and new meanings are generated, debated, and evaluated" (Powell, 1990, p. 325). Ongoing personal relationships of trust are required to establish and maintain a web of relational connections whose purpose is the sharing of strategic and operational information and knowledge.

In the new distance education, knowledge will become embedded within a virtual network of organizations, individuals, information-sharing forums, and virtual knowledge storehouses.

REFERENCES

Abell, D. F. (1999). Competing today while preparing for tomorrow. *Sloan Management Review, 40*(3), 73–81.

Abrahamson, E., & Fairchild, G. (1999). Management fashion: Lifecycles, triggers, and collective learning processes. *Administrative Science Quarterly, 44*, 708–740.

Adria, M., & Woudstra, A. (2001). Who's on the line? Managing student interactions in distance learning using a one-window approach. *Open Learning, 16*(3), 249–261.

Bates, A. W. (1997). The impact of technological change on open and distance learning. *Distance Education, 18*(1), 93–109.

Beer, M., & Nohria, N. (2000, May/June). Cracking the code of change. *Harvard Business Review, 78*(3), 133–141.

Beinhocker, E. D. (1999). Robust adaptive strategies. *Sloan Management Review, 40*(3), 95–106.

Bierema, L., & Merriam, S. (2002). E-mentoring: Using computer-mediated communication to enhance the mentoring process. *Innovative Higher Education, 26*(3), 211–227.

Boudreau, M. C., Loch, K. D., Robey, D., & Straub, D. (1998). Going global: Using Information technology to advance the competitiveness of the virtual transnational organization. *Academy of Management Executive, 12*(4), 120–28.

Chandler, A. (1962). *Strategy and structure: Chapters in the history of the industrial enterprise.* Cambridge, MA: MIT Press.

Crossan, M., Lane, H., & White, R. (1999). An organizational learning framework: From intuition to institution. *Academy of Management Review, 24*, 522–537.

Davenport, T. H., & Pearlson, K. (1998). Two cheers for the virtual office. *Sloan Business Review, 39*(4), 51–65.

Dede, C. (1996). The evolution of distance education: Emerging technologies and distributed learning. *American Journal of Distance Education, 10*(2), 4–36.

De Geus, A. (1997). *The living company.* Boston: Harvard Business School Press.

Drucker, P. F. (1973). *Management: Tasks, responsibilities, practices.* New York: Harper & Row.

Drucker, P. F. (1985). *Innovation and entrepreneurship: Practice and principles.* New York: Harper & Row.

Dunning, B. (1990). The literature of management. In Moore, M. G. (Ed.), *Contemporary issues in American distance education* (pp. 30–41). New York: Pergamon Press.

Garvin, D. A. (1998). The processes of organization and management. *Sloan Management Review, 39*(4), 33–50.

Ghoshal, S., Bartlett, C. A., & Moran, P. (1999). A new manifesto for management. *Sloan Management Review, 40*(3), 9–20.

Graen, G. B., & Uhl-Bien, M. (1995). Relationship-based approach to leadership: Development of leader-member exchange (LMX) theory of leadership over 25 years: Applying a multi-level multi-domain perspective. *Leadership Quarterly, 6*(2), 219–247.

Handy, C. T. (1989). *The age of unreason.* London: Arrow Books.

Harrison, B. (1994). *Lean and mean: The changing landscape of corporate power in the age of flexibility.* New York: Basic Books.

Holt, D. M., & Thompson, D. J. (1995). Responding to the technological imperative: The experience of an open and distance institution. *Distance Education, 16*(1), 43–64.

Holt, D. M., & Thompson, D. J. (1998). Managing information technology in open and distance higher education. *Distance Education, 19*(2), 197–227.

Hirschorn, L. (1998). *The workplace within.* Cambridge, MA: MIT Press.

Kanter, R. (1983). *The change masters: Innovation and entrepreneurship in the American corporation.* New York: Simon & Schuster.

Kanter, R. (1989). *When giants learn to dance: Mastering the challenge of strategy, management, and careers in the 1990s.* New York: Simon & Schuster.

Kanter, R. (2001). *Evolve! Succeeding in the digital culture of tomorrow.* Boston: Harvard Business School Press.

Kaplan, R. (1996). *The balanced scorecard: Translating strategy into action.* Boston: Harvard Business School Press.

Kaplan, R., & Norton, D. (1992, January/February). The balanced scorecard: Measures that drive performance. *Harvard Business Review, 70*(1), 71–79.

Markus, M. L., Manville, B., & Agres, C. E. (2000). What makes a virtual organization work? *Sloan Management Review, 42*(1), 13–26.

McWilliam, G. (2000). Building stronger brand through online communities. *Sloan Management Review, 41*(3), 43–54.

Mintzberg, H., & Lampel, J. (1999). Reflecting on the strategy process. *Sloan Management Review, 40*(3), 21–30.

Murgatroyd, S., & Woudstra, A. (1989). Issues in the management of distance education. *American Journal of Distance Education, 3*(1), 4–19.

O'Neil, H., Bensimon, E., Diamond, M., & Moore, M. (1999). Designing and implementing an academic scorecard. *Change: The Magazine of Higher Learning, 31*(6), 32–40.

Pascale, R. T. (1999). Surfing the edge of chaos. *Sloan Management Review, 40*(3), 83–94.

Paul, D., & McDaniel, R. (2004). A field study of the effect of interpersonal trust on virtual collaborative relationship performance. *MIS Quarterly, 28*(2), 183–227.

Pfeffer, J., & Sutton, R. (1999). Knowing "what" to do is not enough: Turning knowledge into action. *California Management Review, 42*(1), 83–108.

Powell, W. W. (1990). Neither market nor hierarchy: Network forms of organization. In B. M. Staw & L. L. Cummings (Eds.), *Research in organizational behavior* (pp. 295–336). Greenwich, CT: JAI Press.

Rumble, G. (1981). Economic and cost structures. In A. Kaye & G. Rumble (Eds.), *Distance teaching for higher and adult education* (pp. 220–234). London: Croom Helm.

Rumble, G. (1986). *The planning and management of distance education.* London: Croom Helm.

Schwartz, P. (1991). *The art of the long view.* New York: Double Currency.

Scott, W. R. (1998). *Organizations: Rational, natural, and open systems* (4th ed.). Upper Saddle River, NJ: Prentice-Hall.

Stokes, L., & Logan, R. (2004). *Collaborate to compete.* Toronto: Wiley.

Thomson Learning partners with Universitas 21 to develop global e-university [Press release]. (2000, November 20). Retrieved November 28, 2000, from http://www.thomsonlearning.com/press/

Townsend, A. M., DeMarie, S. M., & Hendrickson, A. P. (1998). Virtual teams: Technology and workplace of the future. *Academy of Management Executive, 12*(3), 17–29.

Universitas 21 Global joins hands with the NSRCEL of Indian Institute of Management Bangalore. (2005, December 22). Retrieved January 12, 2006, from http://www.u21global.edu.sg/portal/corporate/html/press-2005-12-22.htm.

Urban, G. L., Sultan, F., & Qualls, W. J. (2000). Placing trust at the center of your Internet strategy. *Sloan Management Review, 42*(1), 39–48.

Uzzi, B. (1996). The sources and consequences of embeddedness for the economic performance of organizations: The network effect. *American Sociological Review, 61,* 674–698.

Venkatraman, N., & Henderson, J. C. (1998). Real strategies for virtual organizing. *Sloan Management Review, 40*(1), 33–48.

Wack, P. (1985a, September/October). Scenarios: Uncharted waters ahead. *Harvard Business Review, 63*(5), 72–89.

Wack, P. (1985b, November/December). Scenarios: Shooting the rapids. *Harvard Business Review, 63*(6), 139–150.

Wenger, E. (1998). *Communities of practice: Learning, meaning, and identity.* Cambridge: Cambridge University Press.

Williams, R. L., & Cothrel, J. (2000). Four smart ways to run online communities. *Sloan Management Review, 41*(4), 81–91.

Williamson, O. E. (1994). Transaction cost economics and organization theory. In N. J. Smelser & R. Swedberg (Eds.), *The handbook of economic sociology* (pp. 77–107). Princeton, NJ: Princeton University Press; Russell Sage Foundation.

Woudstra, A., & Murgatroyd, S. (1992). *Responding to change: Designing a flexible learning organization for distance education* (ACSDE Research Monograph No. 4). University Park: American Center for the Study of Distance Education, College of Education, Pennsylvania State University.

Woudstra, A., & Powell, R. (1989). Value chain analysis: A framework for management of distance education. *The American Journal of Distance Education, 3*(3), 7–21.

VI

GLOBAL PERSPECTIVES

44

Internationalizing Education

Robin Mason
The British Open University

Internationalization as applied to higher education has many guises; it also has different names: cross-border activity, borderless education, globalized education, even trade in education. Whatever the term used, it conjures up different practices amongst different stakeholders. In developing countries it might imply a threat that developed countries will undermine indigenous education, attract the best students out of the country or set up diploma mills which give all higher education a bad name. In developed countries, internationalization might mean access to new markets, more students paying higher fees to subsidize ailing programs at home or the opportunity to attract the best academics and researchers. To suppliers of educational resources such as testing or information technology (IT) support, it represents freedom to operate globally; to universities with a social mission, it represents a means of offering higher education to the vast numbers of people who currently have no access. It is an evolving, contentious and ill-researched area.

The university is in some ways the most international, and the best positioned, institution to promote genuine globalization. And yet, it is still not clear what it would mean to call for a new kind of engagement with the idea of a global university. Universities in the West need to come to grips with what it would mean not just for "us" to study "them," but for developing new forms of knowledge, and new institutional structures, that will facilitate our understanding of and participation in a world that is far more interdependent than ever before (Dirks, 2005, p. 3).

Internationalizing education includes all the activities involving cross border movements. These can be divided into four modes:

1. Materials moving e.g. distance education and e-learning
2. Students moving e.g. to universities abroad
3. Services moving e.g. commercial or university providers establishing a facility abroad
4. Staff moving e.g. academics teaching abroad.

These are the categories at the heart of the General Agreement on Trade in Services (GATS), which will have a profound impact on international education over the coming years.

The introduction of GATS serves as the catalyst for the education sector to move more deliberately into examining how trade rules may influence higher education policy, and determining whether the necessary national, regional, and international education frameworks are in place to deal with the implications of increased cross-border education, including commercial trade (Knight, 2003, p. 2).

The fact is that universities all over the world compete in a global market, not only for students, but for staff, research funding, and prestige. The scale of this competition is now of an altogether different order than even a decade ago.

A range of studies during the dot-com boom of the late 1990s confidently predicted vast market potential in online higher education and governments rushed to commission studies (e.g. Cunningham et al., 1998; Committee of Vice-Chancellors and Principals of the Universities of the U.K. (CVCP), 2000) in order to ascertain the national opportunity or threat. Numerous initiatives were established, often well funded by either public or private monies. Examples include Fathom, Cardean, NYU Online, Pensare, Melbourne University Private, Scottish Knowledge, U.K. e-University (UKeU), and United States Open University (USOU). All have floundered, consolidated, or shut down. Analyses, studies, reports, and blogs have been written at great length to understand this rise and fall, and to glean the lessons to be learned (e.g., Brown, 2005; Garrett, 2004; Meyer, 2003). One comprehensive list of the causes of failure comes from the president of a successful global university, Gerald Heeger of University of Maryland University College (UMUC). They were:

- Lack of brand recognition
- Lack of accreditation
- Unrealistic assessment of start-up costs and payback
- Inadequate infrastructure or technology base
- Minimal training and support for faculty
- Lack of full understanding of the range of online services required to educate students virtually
- The e-learning enterprise was marginalized and under-funded
- Not tying the e-learning operation to the institution's mission (Khan, 2005)

Despite the failures, no one predicts that e-learning is going to go away or that international education is dead in the water:

> The market forces that created the initial rush to dot-coms and virtual universities could well reappear in the future. . . . Perhaps after this rough spell, any new forms will be better planned and based on fewer misconceptions. (Meyer, 2003, p. 7)

WHAT ARE THE ISSUES?

There is a much more subdued climate for international education following the heady days of the dot-com era, yet the issues remain remarkably consistent:

- Access
- Accreditation and quality assurance
- Student readiness
- University's role and values
- Cultural diversity

Access

Without a doubt, the issue about globalized education which arouses most concern and discussion is access. Those who believe that education is a basic right think that commercialization carries acute risks.

They argue that education must not only train workers, but also citizens and responsible individuals; therefore, they question not only the effects liberalization will have—which would lead to discrimination against the most disadvantaged countries, groups, and individuals, but also the impact a commercial approach will have on the spread of "common values" or respect for the indispensable diversity of learning content and methods, which take into account the language, culture and teaching traditions of the people for whom they are intended (Hallak, 2000, p. 17).

There are two aspects to the concern about access:

- that those without an IT infrastructure will be disenfranchised, putting higher education even further out of reach
- that in countries, cities and wealthy enclaves where access to global online courses is possible, the status of degrees from prestigious Western universities will undermine local and national universities.

Accreditation and Quality Assurance

One area in which educational globalization lags behind economic globalization is that of cross-border regulations. While economic globalization is supported by increasing deregulation of financial markets and reductions in tariffs allowing an easy flow of goods and services, the educational counterpart of this—credit transfer—is undeveloped even at a national level in most countries outside the United States, let alone at an international level. If an international system of transferring credit from one university to another were in place, the full floodgates of global higher education would be opened.

What is more likely is that the monopoly on accreditation which universities have enjoyed for centuries will simply be sidestepped by organizations offering courses, information, resources, and educational opportunities that the market is demanding. This is already the case in the area of IT accreditation, where Microsoft certification is valued more highly than a BSc in computing.

The question of quality assurance in international education is vitally important to the long-term health of the process. Students, employers, parents, and the public at large need to have confidence in the value of a qualification. Knight (2003) stated, "A fundamental question is whether countries have the capacity and political will to establish and monitor quality systems for both incoming and outgoing education programs given the diversity of providers and delivery methods" (p. 14).

Student Readiness

We know that the technologies are already in place to manage teaching on a global scale—at least for those who have access to electricity, computers, and the Internet; however, the social and psychological fabric needed to underpin education online lags much further behind mere technical provision. Are the potential students of global education ready to be self-directed, self-motivated, and resourceful e-learners?

While this is questionable enough amongst American students, it is a much more complex issue when considering students from other countries. There are many variables: age, academic level, previous study, style of learning, and access to the technology of delivery. Early indications are that students who are older, studying at postgraduate level with easy access to a PC, self-confident, and willing to interact with their peers online, will be much more successful on global courses than those who begin without these advantages (Macdonald & Mason, 1998). While many local and national online courses have some provision for face-to-face tutorials, courses offered to students all over the world rarely do. Even real-time events online are difficult for a global student body.

University's Role and Values

The growth of international initiatives in higher education, the commercialization of education, and the reduction in public funding of universities are worldwide phenomena that are focusing debate on the role of universities and their contribution to society.

The trinity of teaching/learning, research, and service to society has traditionally guided the evolution of universities. Is the combination of these roles still valid, or can they be disaggregated and rendered by different providers? Values that have traditionally underpinned public education, such as academic freedom and institutional autonomy, are under scrutiny in many countries. Is education still considered to be a public good in the sense of contributing to the development of society, or is it now perceived as more of a private good for consumption by individuals? Some believe that these traditional values are even more relevant and important in today's environment; others argue for a shift away from these traditional values in light of globalization, and still others argue that if higher education is to fulfill its role as a "public good," then it will need to move away from its traditional public funding sources in favor of more market-based approaches (Knight, 2003, p. 16).

Others worry about the very language which has crept into educational debate: the student has become a customer, education has become a service to be traded, and knowledge has become a commodity. This undermining of the traditional value of learning is the result of larger forces than globalization; however, there is little doubt that the internationalization of education and the whole GATS process has hastened these changes.

Cultural Diversity

Another issue identified by the early pioneers of cross-border e-learning involves the cultural differences that inevitably arise in online courses with students from many countries, educational backgrounds, and mother tongues. While cultural differences are not unique to global courses or even to online courses, they are much more evident and more difficult to address without the benefit of face-to-face interaction. Two American researchers who have begun to investigate the affect of global courses on students from other cultures are Gayol and Schied (1997). They note:

> Content selection, visual design, central planning, language, teaching-learning routines, accreditation, academic prestige of the originating site, are all centralized textualities which might work together as an assimilationist or exclusionary pedagogy. (p. 12)

Edwards and Usher's book (2000) *Globalisation and Pedagogy* establishes a firm research base for the study of the significance of globalizing processes for education and pedagogy:

> At a time when learners are themselves subject to great changes in their sense of identity under the influence of economic, political and cultural change, there is therefore a question as to whether, for instance, the humanistic notions of learner-centredness provides us with the categories to "make sense" of learners. As with learners, so with learning. If identity is becoming subject to different forms of experiencing with the influence of globalising processes, then the ways in which learners are engaged may also need re-evaluating. (p. 53)

At a national level, some believe that internationalization of education will lead to the eroding of cultural identity, to westernization and worldwide cultural homogeneity. Others contend that new technology and movement of people, ideas and culture across borders provide new opportunities to promote indigenous cultures.

WHAT IS CURRENT PRACTICE?

Despite the failure of so many virtual universities, new programs are still being initiated. One of these is the "Virtual University for Small States in the Commonwealth" (VUSSC). The 32 small states in the Commonwealth comprise three quarters of all small countries in the world. The Commonwealth of Learning will coordinate some of the processes, but essentially this project will be run by the countries themselves and the "university" will exist where cooperation takes place. Initially, the focus is on producing, adapting, and using course materials that would be difficult for one small country to develop on its own. In short, this is a bottom-up approach. One element already agreed for the VUSSC is that people without formal secondary qualifications will be admitted, and selection will be based on whether the program of study the prospective student has chosen will benefit that student's country.

A project with several years of successful practice is the ArabOU (AOU). Following a feasibility study and a subsequent standing collaboration with the U.K. Open University, the AOU was established as a private Arab institution of higher education with special status. With headquarters in Kuwait, the AOU has branches in five Arab countries—Jordan, Lebanon, Bahrain, Egypt, and Saudi Arabia—and more are planned. U.K. Open University course materials are appropriately modified to adhere to Muslim values and to AOU's mission and philosophy of education. Initial courses include English Language and Literature, Information Technology and Computer Studies, and Business Studies. All courses are taught in English. Quality assurance processes are carried out by the U.K. Open University. A blended approach to course delivery has been adopted, with 25% of the total student study hours being devoted to face-to-face tutorials. The remaining hours are made up of a combination of distance teaching materials, online learning, and various media such as broadcast TV, CD-ROMs, and cassettes.

A different kind of internationalizing initiative involves consortia, networks, or associations amongst an international group of universities. Examples include the Circumpolar Universities Association, Association of Pacific Rim Universities, Universitas 21, the IDEA League, Worldwide Universities Network, and Academic Consortium 21. To this list can be added a new venture announced in 2006, The International Alliance of Research Universities (IARU), formed by ten prominent "research-intensive" universities in Australia, the United Kingdom, the United States,

Switzerland, Singapore, China, Japan, and Denmark. The primary activities of these networks are usually student and staff exchanges and collaborative research. Multilateral cooperation between universities is not a new phenomenon, but the increasing emphasis on internationalization of education has fuelled the growth of these groupings.

A different sort of initiative that is highly relevant to international education is that of Open-CourseWare, modeled on the idea of open source software. Sometimes called Open Educational Resources (OER), this initiative involves the open provision of teaching material, courses, and educational resources—through the means of information and communication technologies—for consultation, use, and adaptation for noncommercial purposes by educators, students, and self-learners. UNESCO sponsored an Internet forum during the last months of 2005 in which 410 participants from 81 countries took part. Many key issues were raised about the difficulties of making available even free content for developing countries:

- language problems
- cultural inappropriateness
- threat to indigenous scholarship
- one-sided knowledge sharing by developed countries
- lack of access to the materials

Translation and adaptation of the materials were considered to be partial solutions, and collaborative development of materials was deemed preferable to delivery entirely by developed countries. Challenges also exist for faculty in finding the time and incentive to make their educational materials available online. Nevertheless, this initiative is gathering strength following MIT's initial commitment to make its courseware available, and other institutions are beginning to see benefits in terms of public good and brand image.

The internationalization of education will eventually be profoundly affected by the GATS process, which is ongoing and highly significant. Its general purpose is to reduce or eliminate barriers to the free flow of educational provision, resources, and people across national boundaries. Most countries continue to regard it with suspicion and seem reluctant to engage in the process of deciding what limits to place on the process in their own country and what barriers in other countries are currently limiting activities they might wish to exploit. The few academics who have made their views known are largely negative: "From the point of view of the academics, the most serious consequence of GATS is that it has led to the 'commodification' of education. . . . In the case of the Indian higher education system, commodification is bound to affect access and equity, funding and quality" (Powar, 2002, pp. 11–18).

Four areas of concern stand out and are largely familiar issues:

1. The fear that domestic provision of higher education will be undermined by foreign competition
2. The focus on the economic aspect of education will increase the commercialization and commodification of higher education
3. The effect of increased trade on the quality of higher education, whether that be accreditation, standards or mutual recognition of degrees
4. The impact of trade on culture, brain drain and support for local developments.

As with globalization of trade in other sectors, there are countries which seek to create barriers to free access in their own domain, but demand free access in other countries. Knight (2003,

p. 10) noted that self-interest appears to be the strongest motivator for trade in education, even when there are seen to be benefits for all parties involved.

BLENDED LEARNING

The growth of blended learning is an important indicator for international education, and perhaps explains some of the virtual university failures, as the need for a local, face-to-face instructor seems to be indispensable for many learners.

> All the evidence from the three initiatives I have worked on . . . [in developing countries] has led me to believe that however many educational resources are made available on the Web and however much animation and simulation is employed in whatever new and engaging ways, students still need support and scaffolding for their learning. I have learned that when people work together, whatever the resources and the level of detail, the classroom situation provides a focal point to channel student thinking and help them focus on the subject they are studying (Selinger, 2006, pp. 441–442).

In fact, there are many forms of international education which are blended. Print or online materials supplied by the host institution are supplemented with visits by the instructor or tutor for short periods; alternatively, the face-to-face element might be supplied by local tutors in partnership with the host institution. These initiatives tend to be single programs and single arrangements between institutions in two countries. Australian universities have many such practices with a range of Asian countries, for example. Although there are many successful examples of this form of international education, this kind of arrangement does not scale very well to numerous countries or to large numbers of students.

WHAT FURTHER RESEARCH IS NEEDED?

The issues surrounding the internationalization of education have received very little research, mainly because they are relatively new, relatively complex, and represent something of a moving target. Any of the issues raised in this chapter so far would be worthy of research; two are highlighted here.

One area which has already been mentioned is student readiness for e-learning, especially for totally online programs. Trials and experiments in how to help students become more self-directed as learners are needed. What works for different types of learners/mentoring, preparatory material, computer-based self-testing exercises, carefully scaffolded learning materials, or combinations of these? Studies need to be carried out across a range of curriculum areas. Students from science backgrounds have different skills, approaches to learning, and habits of studying by the time they reach university level than their fellow students who have pursued arts subjects. This may mean they have different levels of readiness to engage in online interaction, collaboration, and group work, or to sustain motivation without any face-to-face support. The conclusions of one European study on this subject are:

> The skills for learning are not necessarily innate, and in particular, the skills for learning with technology need to be recognised and made more explicit. Of course these skills cannot be learned in isolation from the disciplines in which they are exercised and different approaches are required for different disciplines. However, regardless of discipline, the development of preparatory courses

for students to equip them with the skills for elearning is essential if maximum benefit is to be garnered from the potential of this exciting means of teaching and learning. (Lorenzi, MacKeogh, & Fox, 2004)

A very different topic worthy of research is that of the benefits or impacts of the import/export of education services. The study by Larsen and Vincent-Lancrin (2002) is one of very few on the subject and is equivocal in its conclusion: the authors cannot decide whether international education is basically positive or negative. They note that the particularly vulnerable countries are those in the medium income category where there has been a tradition of limited state funding for education, and where there is a relatively solvent middle class. Another commentator on the GATS process calls for more research in order to understand the positives and negatives:

> The picture is certainly not entirely negative, but a balanced perspective requires a careful analysis to prepare the education sector to move toward a global future. It is often argued that education at all levels is not simply a commodity to be bought and sold in the marketplace. An education system provides the skills needed for economic success, but it also builds the underpinnings of a civil society and of national participation. An understanding of the past, of culture, and of democratic values, among other things, is part of education, and these elements cannot be subsumed in global marketplace. They are integral to any society, and are part of the individual growth of people. (Ranjan, 2005, p. 2)

We need to understand from the pioneers in international education what are the effects on national provision, indigenous culture, brain drain, and quality and accreditation. This topic is potentially vast, but could be broken down by country or by type of education; it could be a snap-shot in time, or a longitudinal study.

A particularly useful resource for researchers on any of these topics is the Observatory on Borderless Education (http://www.obhe.ac.uk/). It provides a range of scholarly reports, briefings, critical analysis, and topical news, making it a leading authority on the internationalization of education.

CONCLUSION

The issues surrounding the practice of cross-border movements in education are complex, evolving, and under-researched. Virtual universities have been set up for an international market which has failed to materialize. Fully online learning seemed to be the only realistic means to increase access to tertiary education for developing countries with huge cohorts of young people and too small an academic workforce to meet their large, unmet demand; however, cultural differences and the unfamiliarity of the online learning environment have shown the theory to be lacking. Meantime, blended approaches to learning in higher education have become mainstream in the West.

In the face of the many concerns about the negative effects of internationalizing education, Couturier (2003) made the following plea:

> If current trends continue, higher education could accelerate the transfer of wealth from developing to developed countries and the stratification of the world into the affluent and the desperately poor. Higher education has the opportunity to stop and think about how to globalize with a conscience, avoiding many of the pitfalls and the loss of public purpose that have created the resentment and cynicism that have erupted into violent protests the world over. Before academia plants

another flag on foreign soil, its leaders should step back and reaffirm higher education's mission of serving the public good. Given the enormous public subsidies that most universities and colleges enjoy (public and private alike—financial aid, tax exemptions, etc.), it is higher education's responsibility to recognize that just as commercial interests now transcend borders, so do social interests (p. 24).

REFERENCES

Brown, G. (2005). *Three 'controversial' virtual universities: Lessons from the Australian experience.* London: The Observatory on Borderless Higher Education.

Committee of Vice Chancellors and Principals of the Universities of the U.K. (2000). *The business of borderless education: UK perspectives.* London: Higher Education Funding Council.

Couturier, L. (2003). *Globalizing with a conscience: The Implications of privatization in higher education.* Paper for the Markets, Profits and the Future of Higher Education Conference, Teachers College, Columbia University, New York. Retrieved December 12, 2006, from www.ncspe.org/publications_files/Couturier.pdf

Cunningham, S., Tapsall, S., Ryan, Y., Stedman, L., Bagdon, K., & Flew, T. (1998). *New media and borderless education: A review of the convergence between global media networks and higher education provisions, 97/22.* Canberra, Australian Capital Territory, Australia: Department of Education, Training and Youth Affairs.

Dirks, N. (2005, Winter). First thoughts: Columbia as a global university. *Columbia Magazine*, Retrived October 22, 2006, from http://www.columbia.edu/cu/alumni/Magazine/Winter2005/firstthoughts

Edwards, R., & Usher, R. (2000). *Globalisation and Pedagogy. Space, place and identity.* London: Routledge/ Falmer.

Garrett, R. (2004). The real story behind the failure of U.K.eUniversity. *Educause Quarterly, 27*(4), 1–3 .

Gayol, Y., & Schied, F. (1997, June 2–6). Cultural imperialism in the virtual classroom: Critical pedagogy in transnational distance education. Paper presented at the 18th International Council for Distance Education World Conference, Pennsylvania State University, US.

Hallak, J. (2000, November). Guarding the common interest, education: The last frontier for profit. *The Unesco Courier.*

Khan, B. (2005, July/August). Interview with Gerald Heeger. *Educational Technology, 45*(4), 60–62.

Knight, J. (2003). *GATS, trade and higher education: Perspective 2003—Where are we?* London: The Observatory on Borderless Higher Education. Retrieved December 22, 2006 from http://www.obhe .ac.uk/products/reports/publicaccessed.pdf

Larsen, K., & Vincent-Lancrin, S. (2002). International trade in education services: Good or bad?, *Higher Education and Management Policy, 14*(3), 9–45

Macdonald, J., & Mason, R. (1998). Information handling skills and resource based learning. *Open Learning, 13*(1), 38–42.

Lorenzi, F., MacKeogh, K., & Fox, S. (2004). *Preparing students for learning in an online world: An evaluation of the student passport to elearning (SPEL) model, EURODL.* Retrieved December 22, 2006, from http://www.eurodl.org/materials/contrib/2004/Lorenzi_MacKeogh_Fox.htm

Meyer, K. (2003). The rule of the marketplace. *EDUCAUSE Quarterly, 26*(2), 3–7.

Powar, K. (2002). *Internationalization of higher education.* New Delhi: Association of Indian Universities.

Ranjan, N. (2005). Changing role of education in the era of trade liberalization and globalization. *OneWorld South Asia.* Retrieved December 12, 2006, from http://southasia.oneworld.net/article/view/124546/1/78

Selinger, M. (2006). Developing an understanding of blended learning: A personal journey across Africa and the Middle East. In C. Bonk & C. Graham (Eds.), *The handbook of blended learning* (pp. 432–443). San Francisco: John Wiley & Sons.

45

Cultural Dynamics of Online Learning

Charlotte N. Gunawardena
and Deborah LaPointe
The University of New Mexico

Rogers (1995) has argued that the adoption of technological innovations has failed because the diffusion process did not take into account the cultural beliefs of the local communities. "An important factor regarding the adoption rate of an innovation is its compatibility with the values, beliefs, and past experiences of individuals in the social system" (p. 4).

Moore (2006) addressed the challenges and privileges that face distance educators within this context. Rather than addressing international students who have removed themselves from their own culture to be in the culture of the teacher, distance educators are now addressing students who remain physically and socially within their own culture, a culture that is foreign to, and mostly unknown to, the teacher. The educational culture that is transmitted can be very different from the educational culture that adopts the program and can become a dominating force. Whose ideas are being shared or incorporated into the local culture or frame of reference? How will this incorporation affect the local culture? Moore (2006) asked additional questions, such as: How does the instructor react to the student at a personal level, and how does the instructor integrate the student into the dominant culture of the online class? Or, how do we design courses to induce the different forms of understanding that lie in the culture represented by each student, to the greater benefit of the whole class? Global universities are faced with the choice between continuing to expect all students to adjust to traditional English-western academic values and uses of language, or changing their processes to accommodate others (Pincas, 2001).

For the purpose of this chapter, we would like to adopt the definition of culture put forward by Matsumoto (1996), who perceives culture as "the set of attitudes, values, beliefs, and behaviors shared by a group of people, but different for each individual, communicated from one generation to the next" (p. 16). As Matsumoto noted, this definition suggests that culture is as much an individual, psychological construct as it is a social construct. "Individual differences in culture can be observed among people in the degree to which they adopt and engage in the attitudes, values, beliefs, and behaviors that, by consensus, constitute their culture" (Matsumoto, 1996, p. 18).

As Rogers and Steinfatt (1999) observed, not only do nationalities and ethnic groups have cultures, but so do communities, organizations, and other systems. In the online environment, we are increasingly observing the emergence of networked learning communities, or "cybercommunities" bound by areas of interest, transcending time and space (Jones, 1995, 1997). These communities develop their own conventions for interaction and for what is acceptable and not acceptable behavior online (Baym, 1995).

CULTURE IS COMMUNICATION

Hall (1998) claimed that culture is communication. "The essence of any culture is primarily a system for creating, sending, storing, and processing information. Communication underlies everything" (p. 53). In the online context that communication takes place through a computer-mediated environment, by which people create, exchange, and perceive information using networked telecommunications systems that facilitate encoding, transmitting, and decoding messages. Most of the messages are text based.

The comparative anonymity provided by the text-based system has shown to create interpersonal distance that allows less vocal or introverted participants "space" and opportunity to contribute, resulting in an equalizing effect of participation (Hartman et al., 1995; Olaniran 1994). A cross-cultural study we conducted on group development and group process (Gunawardena et al., 2001) found that the text-based system equalized status differences in a high power-distance society such as Mexico. Because of the premium on text-based communication, however, those who felt that they were not good writers or for whom the language of the conference was not their native language, often felt disinclined to participate.

In a study that examined the impact of a global e-mail debate on intercultural communication, Chen (2000) noted that differences in thinking patterns and expression styles among participants affected their perception and utilization of e-mail and intercultural sensitivity. In a debate that took place between American college students studying business and their counterparts in Denmark, France, Germany, Hong Kong, and Turkey, Chen observed that the debate format immediately caused problems for some of the participants. The "debate" itself is a product of low-context culture that requires a direct expression of one's argument by using logical reasoning. American, Danish, and German students participating in the project did not show any difficulty in conducting the e-mail debate, while students in France, Hong Kong, and Turkey were confused by the format. The confusion led to two outcomes. First, students resisted or were reluctant to conduct the communication. Second, when they were required to conduct the e-mail debate, they tried to match their American counterparts by abandoning their own expression styles. In order to improve the format problem in future global e-mail communication, Chen (2000) suggested that a format suitable for both high- and low-context cultures be designed. He suggested that a regular exchange of information regarding one or several course related topics could be used to replace the debate format. Students should be encouraged to freely share their ideas and opinions from their cultural perspective without being confined by rigid communication formats.

Discussing his experience teaching international online courses, Bates (2001) pointed out the challenges of grading online discussions:

> In our online courses there appears to be major differences between ethnic groups in their willingness to participate in online forums, and these differences seem to be independent of skill in conversing in a foreign language. We reward through grades students who participate actively and work collaboratively through discussion forums, and this will seriously disadvantage students

for whom this is an alien or difficult approach to take, even for those willing to work in this way. I therefore find myself wondering to what extent I should impose "Western" approaches to learning on students coming from other cultures, while acknowledging on the other hand that this "new" or different approach may have attracted them to the courses in the first place. (p. 129)

Kaplan's (1966) study shed light on the differences in thinking patterns reflected in five different language systems—English, Semitic, Oriental, Romance, and Russian—that will affect online communication. Ishii (1985) illustrated this point by showing the differences in thought patterns that exist between Americans and the Japanese. He cited a Japanese work by Shigehiko Toyama, who contended that Anglo-Americans think in "lines" while Japanese think in "dots." Along these same lines, Ishii suggested that the concepts of the American "bridge" and the Japanese "stepping stone" reflect the patterns of thought characteristic of each culture. Using the American "bridge" model, the speaker or writer organizes his or her ideas and tries to send them explicitly and directly, as if building a bridge from point A to point B. Using the Japanese "stepping stone" approach, the speaker or writer organizes his or her ideas and sends them implicitly and indirectly, as if arranging stepping stones from point A to point B. Sometimes the arrangement itself is not clear, and the listener or reader must infer or surmise the intended meaning. Ishii observed that the distinction between these two rhetorical patterns may be supported by Hall's discussion of high-context and low-context cultures. The Japanese "stepping stone" pattern is an example of high-context communication, while the "bridge" pattern is an example of low-context communication.

These issues are considerations that we need to keep in mind as we begin to address cultural diversity in our online courses. Designing for diversity also means the need to design the social environment which supports online interaction, discussed in the following section.

Cultural Perceptions of Social Presence

Few studies have begun to examine cultural perceptions of social presence. Tu (2001) conducted a study of how Chinese perceive social presence in an online environment. In a cross-cultural study of group process and development in online conferences in the United States (U.S.) and Mexico, Gunawardena et al. (2001) found that social presence emerged as a theme addressed by both U.S. and Mexican focus group participants. U.S. participants felt that social presence is important to the smooth functioning of the group, to provide a sense that the members of the group are real people. Social presence can build trust and lead to self-disclosure, and building relationships certainly enhances civility online. The Mexican focus group participants, on the other hand, felt that having personal information about the participants was not important. For these participants, the way interaction works online and how participants contribute to the conference is far more important than knowing personal information about other participants. There were differences in the way that U.S. participants and Mexican participants perceived social presence, and some of these differences could be attributed to cultural differences.

Gunawardena, Bouachrine, Idrissi Alami, and Jayatilleke (2006) undertook a study to generate a theoretical model of social presence from the perspective of two sociocultural contexts, Moroccan and Sri Lankan, by examining the communication conventions and processes employed by Internet chat users who develop online relationships with people they do not know.

Employing qualitative ethnographic analysis and grounded theory building, this study explored cultural perspectives on "social presence" and properties related to the construct "social presence" in online communication in the Moroccan and Sri Lankan sociocultural contexts. Results indicate that social presence emerged as a central phenomenon in the communication patterns of Internet chat users. Properties associated with social presence in both cultural contexts include self disclosure, building trust, expression of identity, conflict resolution, interpretation of silence, and the innovation of language forms to generate immediacy. Theoretical propositions were as follows:

- Social presence is a key factor in building online relationships.
- There is a relationship between social presence and disclosure of private life. Participants tend to expect chatters to tell them about their problems, because that makes them "real." Self disclosure enhances social presence.
- Anonymity increases the ability to self-disclose and generates a heightened sense of social presence.
- Social presence is closely linked to building trust. When trust is established, there is an increased sense of social presence.
- Attempts to resolve conflict depends on the strength of the relationship that has been built.
- Silence is often expressed as "no presence."
- Chatters have devised means to communicate in the native language, or short forms of the native language using a Latin keyboard to increase social presence and the connection with each other.

In this study, the expression of identity in the informal communication medium of chat was markedly different from the more academic expression of identity in asynchronous conferences. In chat sessions, identity is expressed by asking for the communicator's Age, Sex, and Location (ASL). Depending on the situation, chatters either reveal their true identity, create a different identity, or communicate their identity in an ID that expresses their true or imagined character. The chatter uses this information to create an image about his/her interlocutor.

Sociocultural factors both affect online communication and are affected by communication in cyberspace and virtual environments. If we take into consideration the high-context nature (Hall 1976, 1984) of Moroccan culture—in which communication depends on information drawn from interaction, background, and surroundings—it can be assumed that it is much more difficult for a Moroccan to convey identity and social presence in the world of cyberspace. It seems that group identity, however, becomes central in computer-mediated communication, since the communicators could call on traits and profiles that they associate with certain groups and categories to establish their sense of presence. This method accords with theorizing that favors the social identity approach and which argues that "an absence of social cues to interpersonal contact does not necessarily imply an absence of social cues per se (Spears and Lea, 1992)" (Rogers & Lea, 2005, p. 153). IDs and account names can communicate ample information about the person involved in online conversation. Most of this information can be used to paint a picture of the person in the light of group identity or general category, such as race, ethnicity, and/or gender. One of the participants complained about the way in which many sessions end before he or she has hardly started after the chatter asks about ASL. This implies that the communicator uses the information of the ID to determine an image about his or her interlocutor, which is similar to the construction of identity through stereotyping.

Culture and Conflict Resolution

The Gunawardena et al. (2006) study showed that the nature of the relationship determines reactions to insults and the resolution of conflict. Chatters will close the window if the relationship is weak and employ a variety of techniques to resolve conflict if the relationship is stronger. Generally, they first seek an explanation and then decide on other courses of action, such as shutting down the communication, ignoring the person, insulting back, or asking for an apology. E-mail is resorted to in order to clarify the situation, settle misunderstandings, and present apologies. E-mail is preferable if the relationship has been going on for a long time and if the insulted person thinks that it is not intentional, but a result of a misunderstanding.

In Morocco, communication patterns are more high-context and less direct than in the United States. There are many taboos—lots of "hchouma"—that can be translated as shameful. Many questions do not get answered because Moroccans cannot be very direct and tell it to the face of the other. This opens up room for interpretation and sometimes miscommunication. Anonymity is a factor in the attempt to resolve conflict. If the person who insults is a stranger (and anonymous), either he will be ignored or insulted back. Cultural perceptions and social status seem to influence the way insults are handled. Insults in Morocco are associated with ill-mannered people, low social status, vulgarism, and lack of control; therefore, some will switch to French because "insulting is more acceptable" in French. French seems more "neutral" and "less vulgar." Switching to French in order to insult prevents one from losing his or her social status and manners.

Attempts to resolve conflict depend on the strength of the relationship that has been built and the reality of the other. Face-saving strategies are adopted when there is a bond and when there is an interest in maintaining the relationship. If not, in the real-time world of chat, the general tendency is to close the window and forget the person.

In an exploratory study that examined cultural perceptions of face negotiation in asynchronous online discussions by conducting interviews with 16 participants from six cultural groups, Gunawardena et al. (2002) found that cultural differences do exist in presentation and negotiation of "face" in the online learning environment. With regard to conflict behavior, responses were mixed and indicated cultural as well as individual differences. Members from all six cultures represented in the study would have posted a message in reply, saying that they had been misunderstood or that their discussion had been misinterpreted. Then they would have given further explanations to clarify the message. These studies have shown that attempts to resolve conflict were different in synchronous and asynchronous environments.

Culture and Group Process

To study the impact of culture on group dynamics, Chan (2005) gave the Myers-Briggs Type Indicator (MBTI) and the Chinese Personality Assessment Inventory (CPAI) to 59 tutors at the Open University of Hong Kong and their 1,106 students. Only one dimension on the MBTI—extraversion—was connected with group effectiveness in the classroom; however, four dimensions from the CPAI—Renqing, Face, Harmony, and Leadership—promoted group effectiveness. "Renqing" refers to a "humanized obligation," carrying with it a continued expectation for mutual favor exchanges with a sentimental touch. Tutors who brought face and saved face were considered more effective in creating harmony and balance in relationships. Tutors with a high concern for harmony subordinated personal needs and accepted group norms over their own norms. Tutors who were rated high on leadership were motivated, interacted well with their students, and made effective presentations. Chan's study emphasizes the social obligation to help others within the social group.

Sanchez and Gunawardena (1998), in a study using nine instruments, analyzed Hispanic learners on three elements that correspond with group process and accomplishment of group tasks. Those elements were (a) motivational maintenance, (b) task engagement, and (c) cognitive processing. "Motivational maintenance" refers to specific elements learners require in the learning environment. For motivational maintenance, Hispanic learners highly preferred frequent feedback and active participation in concrete, collaborative activities. "Task engagement" refers to the interaction between learner motivation and active processing required by the learning task. On task engagement, Hispanic learners preferred fact retention, use of imagery, and elaborate verbal processing to interrelate new and old information in practical applications. "Cognitive processing" refers to cognitive processing habits and controls system the learner brings to the learning situation. In terms of cognitive processing, Hispanic learners preferred using a thinking or feeling process plus reflection rather than a sensing or intuitive process.

Culture and the Meaning of Silence

The meaning of silence closely corresponds with cultural orientations towards time. For cultures focused on doing in the present in preparation for the future, time carries a monetary value. The choice to be silent can represent not doing, rudeness, inattention, uncertainty (Matthewson & Thaman, 1998), anger, lack of interest, and a waste of time. As silence is difficult to interpret, it becomes frustrating for Americans and Western Europeans. For Asian and Pacific Island cultures, silence is comfortable, indicates respect, and is understood as a precious asset, offering time for integration and consensus of diverse perspectives into a future workable solution (Brislin, 2000). Silence allows people to anticipate and collect thoughts, think carefully, listen to others, and reflect.

In a study of American instructors and Chinese learners enrolled in a class using Voice over Internet Protocol (VoIP), Burniske (2003) found that both American instructors and Chinese learners experienced discomfort over silence. The American instructors, uncomfortable with silence, expected the Chinese learners to speak at will and were initially uncomfortable with the long, reflective pauses of the Chinese students. In contrast, the cultural respect for authority and teachers conditioned some Chinese participants to remain silent and await an explicit invitation to speak at a time chosen by the instructor rather than make the impolite gesture of raising a question at any time (Burniske, 2003).

Feenberg (1993) described his experience with silence in the Western world during an initial online course offered by the Western Behavioral Sciences Institute to students scattered between Caracas, Philadelphia, and San Francisco:

> One teacher offered elaborate presentations that resembled written lectures. While interesting, these had the undesirable effect of reducing the participants to silence. In a face-to-face classroom teachers can determine from subtle clues whether students' silence signifies fascination or daydreaming. But silence on a computer network is unfathomable; it is intensely disturbing to address the electronic void. Hence the "communication anxiety" of conferencing participants, especially those with leadership roles. . . . Later we understood that it takes far more nerve to admit confusion and ask for clarification in a written medium than face-to-face. The lack of tacit cues such as raised eyebrows or puzzled looks proved fatal to this teaching style in the online environment. (p. 191)

When the teacher established a communication model, laid down explicit ground rules for discussion, posed problems, and asked questions illustrated by examples, the students started talking. Without a reassuring communication model, participants are fearful of writing the wrong thing and withdraw into the perfect silence of a blank screen. Feenberg (1993) argued that most online groups need a familiar framework adapted to their culture and tasks, otherwise "they are repelled by what might be called contextual deprivation" (p. 194). Social rules and conventions of communication are vital to understanding the norms according to which we carry out conversations and judge others. For instance, cultural variations in the use of silence might well lie behind some lack of participation in online discussions. As Ishii and Bruneau (1994) have pointed out, the Japanese culture nurtures silence, reserve, and formality, whereas Western cultures place more value on speech, self-assertion, and informality. They conclude that whereas verbal communication plays a very important role in promoting intercultural as well as interpersonal understanding, we should recognize that the ultimate goal-stage of communication—interpersonally or interculturally—may be communication through silence.

Culture and Help-Seeking Behaviors

Seeking help for a problem is a natural process that people frequently engage in each day. Cultures differ, however, in problem recognition, the problems for which help is sought, and attitudes and readiness to seek help. In the academic setting, "help-seeking" refers to learning strategies that solve problems through the combination of cognition and social interaction (Ryan, Gheen, & Midgley, 1998). Help-seeking behavior results in part from a cultural perspective and attitudes that view others as resources available to cope with the uncertainty and difficulty encountered in the learning process. Cultures determine the proper contact for problems; some cultures prefer traditional and culturally based healers and helpers—for instance, shamans, santeros, and curanderos—for specific problems. Whether a resource or help-seeking behavior is adaptive or maladaptive, behavior is viewed within the context of cultural and social expectations regarding success and failure (Al-Bahrani, 2004). Help-seeking behavior, its timing, and results, therefore, are judged by the learners themselves and by others with whom learners interact.

Cultures vary in the duties expected of teachers and impact the type of help teachers are expected to provide. American teachers are expected to perform academic instruction duties and are evaluated according to their teaching competence. Generally, they are not concerned about students' behaviors and problems outside of the school environment and are not contacted for such advice (Biggs & Watkins, 2001). American students infrequently contact instructors outside of the classroom. When American students do communicate with their instructors outside of class, they frequently do so through e-mail (Zhang, 2006); however, American students more frequently contact their peers for help with academic work.

Zhang (2006) studied 276 Chinese students enrolled in an urban university in central China and 145 U.S. students enrolled in a large urban university in the Southwest and found that Chinese students not only seek academic help from their instructors, but frequently communicate with their teachers outside of class, seeking guidance not only for academic concerns, but also for personal and family problems. Chinese culture views teaching as a holistic activity, requiring teachers to assume both instructional and pastoral roles (Biggs & Watkins, 2001), for teaching involves educating the whole person instructionally, cognitively, affectively, and morally. Traditionally, teachers and parents work harmoniously toward the mutual goal of preparing learners (Hu, 2004) for rigorous national examinations and contributing to the country's economic development. The teacher's, parents', and communities' mutual goal of preparing learners also exists in Arab countries.

Studies conducted with Asian American (of Chinese, Indian, Korean, Philippine, and Taiwanese descent) college students found females were more likely to seek help for academic concerns than males (Solberg, Ritsma, Davis, Tata, & Jolly, 1994). Asian American ethnic groups, however, did not differ from one another in their help-seeking attitudes. Mexican American female college students expressed more positive help-seeking attitudes than their male counterparts (Ramos-Sanchez, 2001).

CULTURE, LANGUAGE, AND DISCOURSE

Language represents a different way of thinking, as well as a different way of speaking, and cognition is mediated and influenced by language (Gudykunst & Asante, 1989; Pincas, 2001). Matsumoto (1996) noted that culture influences the structure and functional use of language, and as such language can be thought of as the result or manifestation of culture. Language also influences and reinforces our cultural values and worldview. "The cyclical nature of the relationship between culture and language suggests that no complete understanding of culture can be obtained without understanding the language, and vice versa" (Matsumoto, 1996, p. 266). Matsumoto demonstrated how one aspect of language, self-referents, exemplifies the cyclical relationship between language and culture. In American English, we generally use one of two words, and their derivatives, to describe ourselves when talking to others—"I" and "we." In Japanese, what you call yourself and others is totally dependent on the relationship between you and the other person, and often it is dependent on the status differential between the two people. Matsumoto explained that, "by using the complex system of self—and other—referents in the Japanese language, a person's system of thought and behavior becomes structured over time to reflect the culture" (p. 270).

The Sapir-Whorf hypothesis postulates that language shapes our thinking, beliefs, and attitudes. Whorf (1998) observed that the grammar of each language is not merely a reproducing instrument for voicing ideas, but rather is itself the shaper of ideas, the program and guide for people's mental activity—for their analysis of impressions, for their synthesis of their mental stock in trade, and so forth. The categories and types that we isolate from the world of phenomena are organized by our minds, and this means largely by the linguistic systems in our minds. As an example, he pointed out that the Eskimo language has three words for "snow," while the English language contains a single word.

Martin and Nakayama (2003) distinguished language from discourse. Language refers to a method of communication. Discourse refers to how language is used by particular groups of people, in particular contexts, and for particular purposes.

Consequently, using English as a second language (ESL) to learn and gain knowledge rather than using one's native language places ESL learners enrolled in online courses offered by American universities at a disadvantage. Visser and West (2005) pointed out that English is frequently an online learner's third or fourth language, and he or she may feel uncomfortable communicating in English, hindered by his or her unfamiliarity with English idioms, writing styles, and the hosts of beliefs and attitudes that accompany the English language. Many ESL learners feel shy and have a basic fear of writing and speaking English with native speakers (Kim & Bonk, 2002); they fear both that they may be unable to understand others and that others will be unable to understand them. They face concerns about being perceived as a competent learner and rebuilding their confidence of their own learning ability (Lin & Schwartz, 2003).

Additionally, entering English words on a computer keyboard one character at a time and frequently checking online dictionaries for spelling and usage accuracy become a struggle for most ESL learners. This struggle is intensified for learners from Asia and the Middle East, who are used to typing characters or ideograms.

The online learning environment does provide a safe place to speak and learn that most students, particularly adults, seek. The Internet provides that safe space through the removal of visual cues, as well as allowing learners to be in their homes with their families. Learners have reported that they are more willing to try to speak English when they can neither (a) see other students whom they perceive to be better English speakers, nor (b) sense their teacher's dismay as they are speaking. In Asia, home is increasingly becoming the location for getting online (Jiang, 2005).

Often learners from collectivist cultures have family members and friends nearby in their physical environment at home or in a cybercafe as they interact online with their teachers and classmates, providing support and encouragement.

ESL learners' fears are exaggerated when learning with people they do not know. Kim and Bonk (2002) stressed the importance of providing discussions to encourage relationships among the learners, so learners do not remain strangers. They also suggest that ESL learners have the opportunity to share their concerns about communicating through English with their classmates. As online participants have to initiate and sustain successful working relations with others and maintain the group, interaction and conversation are needed to develop trust, establish individual reliability, and signify the quality of future individual contributions. Getting to know each other, however, usually requires a high emphasis on writing and reading. Additionally, learners from collectivist countries may refrain from sharing concerns in order to avoid tension and disagreement and maintain interpersonal harmony (Hu, 2005). Some collectivist countries like Japan encourage the use of decoding rules, which are norms that inhibit understanding emotion when acknowledging and understanding would disrupt the social harmony (Elfenbein & Ambady, 2003). Learners from all cultures generally use display rules or norms to diminish, neutralize, or mask emotions that would be produced automatically (Elfenbein & Ambady, 2003).

Sharing the concerns, however, provides critical cultural awareness for native English-speaking classmates. Smith (2005) found that a lack of awareness to cultural differences and generalizations about others who use English as a second language may cause learners from dominant cultures to unknowingly de-authorize group members by using group coping strategies that, though well intended, limit opportunities for discussion. Groups assign minimal responsibilities to nonnative English speaking members because they felt these learners had faced unusual challenges of adapting to the United States and completing their studies. Nonnative English speakers, however, felt uncomfortable and unproductive, which maintained the recognition of nonnative speakers as "others" and created unsafe learning spaces (Smith, 2005). Attempting to "help" ESL learners ultimately took away psychological access (the potential to be motivated to use the technology and overcome anxiety) (Simpson, 2005) and silenced their voices.

Brew and Cairns (2004) found a convergence of the direct and indirect communication styles in a study of 49 Australian expatriates and 53 East Asian host nationals working for five Western organizations in Singapore and Bangkok. Australians modified their communicative behavior, being less direct and more diplomatic, especially when dealing with an Asian superior. Host nationals and expatriates reacted to the urgency of the situation, choosing more direct communication strategies depending upon the situation. Host nationals were more likely to react to the status of the other than were expatriates. Choosing a direct or indirect style according to the situation may reflect that communication strategy is more situational than strictly cultural. Brew and Cairns (2004) also suggested that the convergence in styles may be due to an evolving "third culture," which is becoming more common in our increasingly networked world.

ESL students recognize that they will study content through learning resources from the target culture. Those learning resources carry cultural values and practices (Lin & Schwartz, 2003). When ESL learners have no prior experience with the content and topics of the materials, they feel as if they cannot participate in online discussions. Learners from collectivist cultures express their experience in terms beyond themselves personally. Their life experiences include the experiences of their ancestors and their family members. For example, a Taiwanese learner relayed that when neither he nor his family has prior knowledge about a topic, the "topic is too far away," and he finds engaging in a conversation difficult (LaPointe & Barrett, 2005). Such distant topics may not produce the intended level of content familiarity and critical thinking the instructor intended.

Those from oral cultures may not embrace written communication (Burniske, 2003) and abstract group discussion, which permeate Western discourse. Learners from cultures rich in oral tradition, such as the Maori, desire intimate connections between the teacher and learner and a way to apply knowledge according to Maori customs (Anderson, 2005). Malaysia, like many other oral cultures, uses storytelling as a way of making sense of the world while teaching history, culture, and moral values (Norhayati & Siew, 2004). The storytelling uses the power of emotion to make lessons memorable. Sanchez (1996) also found Hispanic learners express a strong preference for frequent interaction and adequate feedback from the instructor.

Those from visual and oral cultures and nations have expectations that learning resources will be offered in media beyond mere text (Jiang, 2005). China has long promoted multimedia instructional design, online video games, digital entertainment, streaming media, and developing e-learning content. The Chinese written language has no alphabet. Instead, it consists of thousands of different pictographic and ideographic characters. Each word consists of one to three characters and carries sounds and visions of tradition and culture (Hu, 2004), both always present. Korean, Japanese, and Chinese students are holistic and visual. They like to read and obtain a great deal of detail and visual stimulation (Zhenhui, 2001).

Turkey's culture and oral traditions emphasize the sacredness of the text, honor the responsibility of the professor to interpret the text, and expect the students to memorize the professor's words (Gursoy, 2005). The storytelling of African-American traditions emphasizes the rhythm of the language and repetition of short phrases to make stories easier to understand and remember. For cultures embracing a strong connection with land, water, animals, plants, and other people, such as the Indigenous Australians, knowledge and cultural heritage are expressed through performance, song, and visual arts. This expression is learned through cultural teachers, self-teaching, and through university and college courses, and provides connection and is central to identity, place, and a sense of belonging (Janke, 2002).

Limiting online learning to text-based expression restricts the voices and the richness that can be brought to the online classroom. Interactive learning environments and Web casts supplemented by audio cassettes, videos, and CD-ROMs providing visual and oral content, materials, and support in context are, therefore, essential in areas of the world struggling with insufficient digital information and communication technologies (Mackintosh, 2005). Limiting oral communication to seminar discussions using premise and syllogisms restricts participation and dampens emotion in interaction. In contrast, Chinese culture emphasizes beauty, tradition, poems, and politeness in social interaction. The Chinese literate person memorizes characters, idioms, wise sayings, classics, literary allusions and memorizes the accepted patterns of expression. Ideas are expressed in a human context that keeps social harmony and maintains hierarchy (Hu, 2004).

Multimedia and synchronous forms of communication provide the potential to meet such learner needs. In African nations, radios are the portable, popular technology for connecting learners with the instructor and for oral communication of content in context (Shalyefu & Nakakuwa, 2005). As well, learners benefit from content provided in a variety of formats—written lectures, audio recordings, concept maps, and digital multimedia—with opportunity for localization of content and delivery (Sharma, 2005).

Culture and Non-Verbal Communication

Verbal language is just one aspect of communication. Another large and important part of communication is nonverbal communication, including facial expressions, tone of voice, posture, dress, and so forth. Just as spoken language differs from one culture to another, so does nonverbal behaviors. Matsumoto (1996) noted that the challenge in intercultural communication is that these nonverbal languages are silent. This challenge is further exacerbated in the online text-based medium which requires communicants to use other means such as emoticons (icons that express emotion such as a smiley face ☺) and meta-linguistic cues such as "hmmm" and "yuk" to express nonverbal cues in written form.

This chapter has discussed many cultural ways of life to consider when designing courses for delivery across national boundaries. The following section presents basic principles for designing online learning environments that incorporate cultural beliefs.

IMPLICATIONS FOR DESIGNING ONLINE DISTANCE LEARNING

The design of online distance learning must reflect cultural inclusivity, including multiple cultural ways of learning and teaching, enabling learners to access learning resources and activities congruent with their values, beliefs and styles of learning, contextualize their learning, reflect the multicultural realities of society, and promote equity of learning outcomes (McLoughlin & Oliver, 2000). Some principles are listed below.

1. Presentation of Content
   a. Recognize that learning is environmentally and culturally situated
   b. Explore shared cultural expectations
   c. Use a variety of presentation methods—for example, lecture notes, storytelling, videos, audio, CDs, Webcasts, and so forth
   d. Ensure content includes a variety of perspectives
2. Transfer
   a. Humanize cultural contact so people will be receptive to each other and reflect on their experiences
   b. Create authentic learning activities and tasks
   c. Create reflective activities that target educational goals
   d. Design tasks so learners can determine goals, learning resources, and assessment appropriate to their culture
   e. Discuss barriers of applying learning under one cultural perspective to another culture
3. Assessment and Evaluation
   a. Provide flexibility in learning goals, learning outcomes, and assessment
   b. Provide opportunity for application
   c. Examine the importance of strict due dates and timelines
4. Learner Support
   a. Provide opportunity to empower learners and honor diversity
   b. Provide a network of support for academic as well personal and family problems
5. Interaction with Instructor, Tutors, Mentors, and Learners
   a. Provide access to the instructor with frequent and regular feedback
   b. Promote learners entering into dialogue with each other through multiple channels
   c. Provide a communication model
   d. Ensure support from the families and communities through tutors and mentors
   e. Use formats appropriate for both high- and low-context cultures

6. Development of "Third Culture" Community of Learners
    a. Learners reflect on, share, and present their cultures' answers to the five universal problems through their chosen means—for example, photos and videos, drawings, story telling, animation, song, scholarly text, poetry, and so forth
    b. Learners share concerns of interacting with classmates from other cultures online
    c. Learners work in small groups to complete assigned task and reflect on the experience
    d. Learners share and describe an important personal artifact
    e. Incorporate emotion as well as cognition

CONCLUSION

What counts as sound educational practice for online environments in all likelihood presents a form of cultural bias on the part of the person promoting the educational practice. Inevitably, cultural differences influence the learning process in myriad ways. Simply requesting active online participation in written English may seriously disadvantage learners from an oral tradition, those for whom English is a second or third language, and those from nations who have promoted the use of high-quality digital multimedia. Course design issues such as these must be addressed with cultural awareness.

ACKNOWLEDGMENTS

We would like to thank Penne Wilson and Ana Nolla, who contributed to the earlier version of this chapter in the first edition of the *Handbook of Distance Education*.

REFERENCES

Al-Bahrani, M. A. (2004). *An investigation of the help-seeking process among Omani students at Sultan Qaboos University.* Unpublished dissertation, Ohio University, Columbus. Retrieved January 22, 2006, from http://www.ohiolink.edu/etd/send-pdf.cgi?ohiou1089747209

Anderson, B. (2005). New Zealand: Is online education a highway to the future? In A. A. Carr-Chellman (Ed.), *Global perspectives on e-learning: Rhetoric and realities* (pp. 163–178). Thousand Oaks, CA: Sage.

Bates, T. (2001). International distance education: Cultural and ethical issues. *Distance Education, 22*(1), 122–136.

Baym, N. K. (1995). The emergence of community in computer-mediated communication. In S. G. Jones (Ed.), *Cybersociety* (pp. 138–163). Thousand Oaks, CA: Sage.

Biggs, J. B., & Watkins, D. A. (2001). Insights into teaching the Chinese learner. In D. A. Watkins & J. B. Biggs (Eds.), *The Chinese learner: Cultural, psychological and contextual influences* (pp. 269–286). Hong Kong: Comparative Education Research Center.

Brew, F. P., & Cairns, D. R. (2004). Do culture or situational constraints determine choice of direct or indirect styles in intercultural workplace conflicts? *International Journal of Intercultural Relations, 28,* 331–352.

Brislin, R. (2000). *Understanding culture's influence on behavior* (2nd ed). Fort Worth, TX: Harcourt.

Burniske, R. W. (2003). East Africa meets West Africa: Fostering an online community of inquiry for educators in Ghana and Uganda. *Educational Technology Research and Development, 51*(4), 105–113.

Chan, B. (2005). From West to East: The impact of culture on personality and group dynamics. *Cross Cultural Management, 12*(1), 31–43.

Chen, G. M. (2000). Global communication via Internet: An educational application. In G. M. Chen & W. J. Starosta (Eds.), *Communication and global society* (pp. 143–157). New York: Peter Lang.

Elfenbein, H. A., & Ambady, N. (2003). Universals and cultural differences in recognizing emotions. *Current Directions in Psychological Science, 12*(5), 159–164.

Feenberg, A. (1993). Building a global network: The WBSI experience. In L. M. Harasim (Ed.), *Global networks: Computers and international communication* (pp. 185–197). Cambridge, MA: The MIT Press.

Gudykunst, W., & Asante, M. (1989). *Handbook of international and intercultural communication.* Newbury Park, CA: Sage.

Gunawardena, C. N., Bouachrine, F., Idrissi Alami, A., & Jayatilleke, G. (2006, April). Cultural perspectives on social presence: A study of online chatting in Morocco and Sri Lanka. Paper presented at the annual meeting of the American Educational Research Association, San Francisco, CA.

Gunawardena, C. N., Nolla, A. C., Wilson, P. L., López-Islas, J. R., Ramírez-Angel, N., & Megchun-Alpízar, R. M. (2001). A cross-cultural study of group process and development in online conferences. *Distance Education, 22*(1), 122–136.

Gunawardena, C. N., Walsh, S. L., Reddinger, L., Gregory, E., Lake, Y., Davies, A. (2002). Negotiating "face" in a non-face-to-face learning environment. In F. Sudweeks & C. Ess (Eds.), *Proceedings of cultural attitudes towards communication and technology, 2002* (pp. 89–106). Quebec, Canada: University of Montreal.

Gursoy, H. (2005). A critical look at distance education in Turkey. In A. A. Carr-Chellman (Ed.), *Global perspectives on e-learning: Rhetoric and realities* (pp. 35–51). Thousand Oaks, CA: Sage.

Hall, E. T. (1976). *Beyond culture.* Garden City, NY: Doubleday.

Hall, E. T. (1984). *The dance of life: The other dimension of time.* Garden City, NY: Anchor Press.

Hall, E. T. (1998). The power of hidden differences. In M. J. Bennett (Ed.), *Basic concepts of intercultural communication: Selected readings* (pp. 53–67). Yarmouth, ME: Intercultural Press.

Hartman, K., Neuwirth, C. M., Kiesler, S., Sproull, L., Cochran, C., Palmquist, M., et al. (1995). Patterns of social interaction and learning to write: Some effects of network technologies. In M. Collins & Z. Berge (Eds.), *Computer mediated communication and the online classroom: Volume II* (pp. 47–78). Cresskill, NJ: Hampton Press.

Hu, G. (2005). Using peer review with Chinese ESL student writers. *Language Teaching Research, 9*(3), 321–342.

Hu, Y. (2004). The cultural significance of reading instruction in China. *The Reading Teacher, 57*(7), 632–639.

Ishii, S. (1985). Thought patterns as modes of rhetoric: The United States and Japan. In L. A. Samovar & R. E. Porter (Eds.), *Intercultural communication: A reader* (4th ed., pp. 97–102). Belmont, CA: Wadsworth.

Ishii, S., & Bruneau, T. (1994). Silence and silences in cross-cultural perspective: Japan and the United States. In L. A. Samovar & R. E. Porter (Eds.), *Intercultural communication: A reader* (7th. ed., pp. 246–251). Belmont, CA: Wadsworth.

Janke, T. (2002). *Indigenous arts certification mark WIPO case study.* Available Retrieved January 26, 2006, from http://www.caslon.com.au/indigenousmarknote.htm

Jiang, J. Q. (2005). The gap between e-learning availability and e-learning industry development in Taiwan. In A. A. Carr-Chellman (Ed.), *Global perspectives on e-learning: Rhetoric and realities* (pp. 35–51). Thousand Oaks, CA: Sage.

Jones, S. G. (1995). *Cybersociety: Computer-mediated communication and community.* Thousand Oaks, CA: Sage.

Jones, S. G. (Ed.). (1997). *Virtual culture: Identity and communication in cybersociety.* London: Sage.

Kaplan, R. B. (1966). Cultural thought pattern in inter-cultural education. *Language Learning, 16*, 1–20.

Kim, K.-J., & Bonk, C. J. (2002). Cross-cultural comparisons of online collaboration. *Journal of Computer-Mediated Communication, 8*(1). Retrieved March 16, 2006, from http://jcmc.indiana.edu/vol8/issue1/kimandbonk.html

LaPointe, D., & Barrett, K. (2005, June). *Language learning in a virtual classroom: Synchronous methods, cultural exchanges.* Paper presented at the meeting of Computer-Supported Collaborative Learning, Taipei, Taiwan.

Lin, X., & Schwartz, D. L. (2003). Reflection at the crossroads of culture. *Mind, Culture, and Activity, 10*(1), 9–25.

Mackintosh, W. (2005). Can you lead from behind? Critical reflections on the rhetoric of e-learning, open distance learning, and ICTs for development in Sub-Saharan Africa (SSA). In A. A. Carr-Chellman (Ed.), *Global perspectives on e-learning: Rhetoric and realities* (pp. 223–239). Thousand Oaks, CA: Sage.

Martin, J. N., & Nakayama, T. K. (2003). *Intercultural communication in contexts* (3rd ed.). New York: McGraw-Hill.

Matsumoto, D. (1996). *Culture and psychology.* Pacific Grove, CA: Brooks/Cole.

Matthewson, C., & Thaman, K. H. (1998). Designing the *rebbelib*: Staff development in a Pacific multicultural environment. In C. Latchem & F. Lockwood (Eds.), *Staff development in open and flexible learning.* New York: Routledge.

McLoughlin, C., & Oliver, R. (2000). Designing learning environments for cultural inclusivity: A case study of indigenous online learning at tertiary level. *Australian Journal of Educational Technology, 16*(1), 58–72.

Moore, M. G. (2006). Editorial: Questions of culture. *The American Journal of Distance Education, 20*(1), 1–5.

Norhayati, A. M., & Siew, P. H. (2004). Malaysian perspective: Designing interactive multimedia learning environment for moral values education. *Educational Technology & Society, 7*(4), 143–152.

Olaniran, B. A. (1994, February). Group performance in computer-mediated and face-to-face communication media. *Management and Communication Quarterly, 7*(3), 256–281.

Pincas, A. (2001). Culture, cognition and communication in global education. *Distance Education, 22*(1), 30.

Ramos-Sanchez, L. (2001). The relationship between acculturation, specific cultural values, gender, and Mexican Americans' help-seeking intentions. *Dissertation Abstracts International: B. The Physical Sciences and Engineering, 62*(3), 1595 (ISSN: 0419-4217)

Rogers, E. M. (1995). *Diffusion of innovations* (4th ed.). New York: The Free Press.

Rogers, P., & Lea, M. (2005). Social presence in distributed group environments: The role of social identity. *Behavior and Information Technology, 24*(2), 151–158.

Rogers, E. M., & Steinfatt, T. M. (1999). *Intercultural communication.* Prospect Heights, IL: Waveland Press.

Ryan, A. M., Gheen, M. H., & Midgley, C. (1998). Why do some students avoid asking for help? An examination of the interplay among students' academic efficacy, teachers' social-emotional role, and the classroom goal structure. *Journal of Educational Psychology, 90*(3), 528–535.

Sanchez, I. M. (1996). *An analysis of learning style constructs and the development of a profile of Hispanic adult learners.* Unpublished doctoral dissertation, The University of New Mexico, Albuquerque.

Sanchez, I., & Gunawardena, C. N. (1998). Understanding and supporting the culturally diverse distance learner. In C. C. Gibson (Ed.), *Distance learners in higher education: Institutional responses for quality outcomes* (pp. 47–64). Madison, WI: Atwood.

Shalyefu, R. K., & Nakakuwa, H. (2005). Development and democracy in Namibia: The contribution of information and communication technologies (ICTs). In A. A. Carr-Chellman (Ed.), *Global perspectives on e-learning: Rhetoric and realities* (pp. 205–221). Thousand Oaks, CA: Sage.

Sharma, P. (2005). Distance education and online technologies in India. In A. A. Carr-Chellman (Ed.), *Global perspectives on e-learning: Rhetoric and realities* (pp. 52–65). Thousand Oaks, CA: Sage.

Simpson, O. (2005). E-learning, democracy, and social exclusion: Issues of access and retention in the United Kingdom. In A. A. Carr-Chellman (Ed.), *Global perspectives on e-learning: Rhetoric and realities* (pp. 52–65). Thousand Oaks, CA: Sage.

Smith, R. O. (2005). Working with difference in online collaborative groups. *Adult Education Quarterly, 55*(3), 182–199.

Solberg, V. S., Ritsma, S., Davis, B. J., Tata, S. P., & Jolly, A. (1994). Asian-American students' severity of problems and willingness to seek help from university counseling centers: Role of previous counseling experience, gender, and ethnicity. *Journal of Counseling Psychology, 41*(3), 275–279.

Spears, R., & Lea, M. (1992). Social influence and the influence of the "social" in computer-mediated communication. In M. Lea (Ed.), *Contexts of computer-mediated communication* (pp. 30–65). New York: Harvester Wheatsheaf.

Tu, C. H. (2001). How Chinese perceive social presence: An examination of interaction in online learning environment. *Education Media International, 38*(1), 45–60.

Visser, L., & West, P. (2005). The promise of m-learning for distance education in South Africa and other developing nations. In Y. L. Visser, L. Visser, M. Simonson, & R. Armirault (Eds.), *Trends and issues in distance education: International perspectives.* Greenwich, CT: Information Age.

Whorf, B. L. (1998). Science and linguistics. In M. J. Bennett (Ed.), *Basic concepts of intercultural communication: Selected readings* (pp. 85–95). Yarmouth, ME: Intercultural Press.

Zhang, Q. (2006). Immediacy and out-of-class communication: A cross-cultural comparison. *International Journal of Intercultural Relations, 30*, 33–50.

Zhenhui, R. (2001). Matching teaching styles with learning styles in East Asian contexts. *The Internet TESL Journal, 7*(7). Retrieved January 17, 2006, from http://iteslj.org/

46

The Mega-University Response to the Moral Challenge of Our Age

John Daniel
UNESCO

Wayne Mackintosh
Commonwealth of Learning

William C. Diehl
The Pennsylvania State University

The achievements of higher education in general and distance learning in particular, with regards to opening opportunities and widening access to tertiary education, have been impressive. Less than half a century ago, access to university level education "was regarded in most parts of the world as a privilege to which ordinary families could not aspire" (UNESCO, 2000a, p. 69). Global access to tertiary education has grown from 6.5 million enrollments in 1950 to 88.2 million enrollments in 1997 (UNESCO, 2000a, p. 67) and to over 110 million in 2004 (UNESCO, 2006a). This represents a growth of more than 1500% in less than one generation. Although increases in the absolute capacity of higher-education provision can partly be ascribed to population expansion, clearly there has also been a philosophical shift from "class to mass" (World Bank, 2000, p. 19).

It is disconcerting to note, however, that while a few industrialized countries report a gross enrollment ratio in excess of 65% (New Zealand, Norway, Sweden, Republic of Korea, and the United States); and while the number of countries in the developed world with enrollment in excess of 45% has risen over the past decade, two-thirds of countries in the developing world have a gross enrollment ratio below 15% (UNESCO, 2004). The average for Sub-Saharan Africa in 2005 was distressingly low at 5% (UNESCO, 2006a). Using demographic projections of the 18- to 23-year-old cohort, Saint (1999, p. 2) pointed out that at least 16 countries in Sub-Saharan Africa would need to *double* tertiary enrollments within the following decade just to maintain the existing and unacceptably low gross enrollment ratio.

What is more frightening is that the dismal performance of higher education in many parts of the developing world is limited to the traditional age cohort of tertiary education. For the majority of people, the contemporary prerequisites for lifelong learning in the modern economy are an unattainable aspiration. Furthermore,

- over 771 million adults on our planet still suffer from the bane of illiteracy and may never have the privilege of a tertiary education (UNESCO, 2006b);
- "More than one-third of the world's adults have no access to the printed knowledge, new skills and technologies that could improve the quality of their lives and help them shape, and adapt to, social and cultural change" (UNESCO, 2006b);
- 250 million children in the world are excluded from the fundamental right of learning and will not receive or complete their basic education—over 100 million children have no access to school at all. These children are destined to be barred from access to a tertiary education which is generally regarded as a prerequisite condition for gainful employment in our emerging knowledge economy (UNESCO, 2006b).

Harnessing the forces of the global-knowledge economy to ensure that all people of the world get a decent education is the greatest moral challenge of our age. In an ideal world, the university as institution, combined with its traditional values concerning the well-being of society, should be well positioned to assist in tackling the "Education for All" challenge that was articulated at UNESCO's World Education Forum in Dakar in April 2000 (UNESCO, 2000b). The essence of the "Education for All" challenge is to work towards the eradication of abject poverty throughout our world and to ensure that countries committed to education for all will not be impaired "in their achievement of this goal by lack of resources" (UNESCO, 2000c, para. 48).

Around the world today we need the equivalent of one large new university to open every week just to keep participation rates in higher-education constant. However, in the real world, universities face the perplexing task of balancing the tensions of the eternal triangle—that is, improving quality, cutting costs, and serving more and more students. Most of the world can't afford the campus model we know and love.

WHAT ARE THE MEGA-UNIVERSITIES?

The mega-universities are large distance teaching universities (usually called "open universities") found in various parts of the world, which report enrollments of more than 100,000 students each. In 1999, there were over 11 such institutions enrolling approximately 3 million students between them (Daniel, 1999, p. 30) and less than a decade later, the number of mega-universities has likely grown and, collectively, they account for over 6 million students.

The 100,000 enrollment criterion is an arbitrary cutoff classification. However, the interesting characteristic of these institutions is not primarily their size, but rather the fact that they are all single-mode distance education institutions. In other words, the mega-universities *were not able to achieve these levels of access and provision using the traditional campus model*. Hence, the pursuit of scale requires the establishment of a learning system. Furthermore, it is not surprising that the largest student numbers and majority of mega-university institutions are working in the developing world, particularly when assessed against the moral challenge facing higher education referred to in this chapter.

TABLE 46.1.
TABLE 46.1.
Mega-Universities of the World

Institution	Country	Number DE Students	Number of Full-time Academic Staff	Number of Part-time Academic Staff	Number of Administrative Staff
Allama Iqbal Open University[1]	Pakistan	456,126	145	23,000 (tutors)	1,426
Anadolu University[1]	Turkey	884,081	1,729	653 (tutors) 300 (lecturers)	1,763
Centre National d'Enseignement a Distance[2]	France	350,000	n/a	n/a	n/a
China Central Radio and TV University[1]	China	2,300,000	52,600	31,500 (tutors)	16,500
Dr. B.R. Ambedkar Open University[7]	India	450,000	n/a	n/a	n/a
Indira Gandhi National Open University[1]	India	1,013,631	339	35	1,337
Korea National Open University[1]	Korea	196,402	271	108 (tutors)	546
Open University[1]	UK	203,744	1,169	7,995 (Associate) lecturers	1,434 (academic-related staff) 2,139 (Secretarial, clerical, and television staff)
Payame Noor University[3]	Iran	467,000	n/a	n/a	n/a
Shanghi TV University[1]	China	101,218	n/a	n/a	n/a
Sukhothai Thammathirat Open University[1]	Thailand	181,372	375	n/a	904
Universidad Nacional de Educación a Distancia[4]	Spain	110,000	n/a	n/a	n/a
University of Phoenix Online[6]	USA	143,846	n/a	n/a	n/a
University of South Africa[5]	South Africa	250,000	1305	17	2931
Universitas Terbuka[1]	Indonesia	222,068	762	3,600 (tutors)	730
Yashwantrao Chavan Maharashtra Open University[8]	India	932,500	n/a	n/a	n/a

Notes:
1. (Jung, 2005)
2. (Centre National d'Enseignement a Distance, 2006)
3. (Payame Noor University, 2006)
4. (Daniel, 1999, pp. 30 & 31)
5. (University of South Africa—UNISA, 2006)
6. (Bacsich, P., 2005)
7. (Dr. B. R. Ambedkar Open University, 2006)
8. (Yashwantrao Chavan Maharashtra Open University, 2006)

THE DRIVERS UNDERPINNING THE SUCCESS
OF THE MEGA-UNIVERSITIES

The mega-university systems, as one of the most important innovations in higher education of the 20th century, have successfully combined the challenges of access and quality in an approach that can be scaled up in ways that reduce cost without compromising the core social values of the university (for example, promoting the development of the systematic skepticism and intellectual independence of its learners).

The distinguishing pedagogical feature of the mega-universities is that they have developed sophisticated learning systems based on innovative divisions of labor wherein the responsibility for teaching is carried collectively. The radical differentiating feature of the large distance learning systems is that the institution teaches, whereas in conventional forms of delivery, an individual teaches (Keegan, 1980, p. 19). By breaking the traditional lecturer-student bond and designing a total teaching system wherein the functions of teaching are divided into a range of specializations, the mega-universities have been able to scale up the delivery of quality teaching to levels that are simply not possible in conventional campus-based or dual-mode models.

What Explains Success of the Mega-University?

First, the innovation associated with division of labor and teaching through the course team. The idea of teamwork in teaching outside the mega-university context is not widespread in university practice, even though many universities may purport to support the ideals of teamwork. Although the traditions of the academy espouse a collegial model, faculty members tend to work independently and institutional reward and incentive practices tend to promote individual scholarship. Perhaps this is one of the reasons why Web-based teaching is being received so warmly by individual faculty—because the perception is that it facilitates online teaching by academics working alone. However, the course team is one of the critical success factors of the open universities. When Lord Perry, the founding vice chancellor of the United Kingdom Open University (UKOU), was asked what he considers to be the key innovation of the organization's success, he would unhesitatingly reply, "the course team."

Successfully carrying out distance education at scale is not merely a technological accomplishment. The innovation associated with proper implementation of the scholarship of course-team development has meant that the mega-university is capable of better-quality teaching than conventional universities on both academic and pedagogical grounds.

These levels of academic and pedagogical quality require a huge investment, particularly in terms of expensive academic time, and the mega-universities seek to spread this substantial investment over large numbers of students. Some have criticized this continued mass-production model at a time when the world is moving towards becoming a more individualistic society, often citing selected bytes from some quarters of business thinking that "small is better." But the significant levels of investment to maintain the quality described here cannot be sustained unless economies of scale can be generated, and furthermore, it is important to remember the moral aspects relating to the fact that the open universities, despite mass-production, provide a quality tertiary education to millions of people who otherwise may never have had the opportunity to study at a university. In China, for example, because of a "shortage of educational resources, only about 10 per cent of school-leavers can be enrolled in colleges or universities . . . and consequently there is intense competition for university places" (Xinfu, Xiaoqing, & Zhiting, 2005).

This brings us to the second element responsible for success in open-learning systems: the provision of individualized student support by means of a distributed tutor system to mediate the students' study of the materials and to provide individualized comments on students' progress. Student support refers to "the range of services both for individuals and for students in groups which complement the course materials or learning resources that are uniform for all learners" (Tait, 2000, p. 289). Student support covers the cognitive, affective, and administrative needs of the student.

It must be emphasized that the concept of "student support," as used here, refers to individualized customization for a learner, over and above the teaching contained in the mass-produced materials. For example, at the UKOU, students receive strong personal support through extensive use of part-time faculty. Every 20–25 learners are assigned to a dedicated tutor who is personally responsible for the progress of each student, and who maintains personal contact, grades assignments, and mediates the individual learning experience. As in the case of good universities, tutors are not engaged to feed students with answers, but to support them in asking good questions and to promote autonomous learning by supporting the search for finding and evaluating the answers to these questions.

The third element underpinning the success of the mega-universities is that these huge learning systems rely on good logistics and administration. Visitors from conventional universities are astounded by the magnitude and efficiency required of logistics and administration in the mega-university context. The logistics and administration are of industrial proportions and necessitate division of labor and specialized industrial equipment. In a recent survey, the OKOU rated highest in student satisfaction, ahead of all conventional universities in the United Kingdom (O'Leary, 2006). Good logistics and administration relate directly to the levels and quality of service provided to students, and as we move forward into the digital era, successful e-services will depend on getting the "services" as well as the "e" right.

Finally, in order to maintain intellectual excitement in teaching materials, it is important that faculty remain active in research. Research is a distinguishing feature of the university, as institution through academic research is expensive, and given its nature, it is difficult to quantify in terms of its contribution to "bottom-line" in the case of "for-profit" institutions.

Measuring Success in Terms of the Eternal Triangle

We have suggested that the perpetual challenge for universities is to effectively manage the tensions of the eternal triangle: widening access, improving quality, and lowering costs.

On the access dimension of the triangle, the mega-universities have performed extremely well. The UKOU provided leadership by becoming the first university of considerable size to waive the traditional academic prerequisites for undergraduate study. Although some mega-universities still apply prerequisite requirements (very often dictated by stipulations of the respective ministries of education for subsidy purposes) this opening of access constitutes a huge step forward in deconstructing controlled elitism in higher education.

The enrollment figures of the mega-universities speak for themselves. More than 6 million learners are studying through approximately a dozen institutions—numbers that would require upwards of 200 large campus-based institutions. What mega-university statistics do not show is the fact that there are more than 30 open university systems spread across the globe that do not meet the 100,000 enrollment threshold, and more often than not, these national open-learning institutions are sizeable when measured against the norms of campus-based institutions. The foundation of many of these open learning universities was assisted directly by the UKOU, or was modeled on the systems pioneered by the mega-universities, and these global institutions have demonstrated the capacity to transcend national boundaries in the provision of tertiary education. Their continued experiences of dealing with cultural diversity across national boundaries will become a significant resource as we address the global tertiary education crisis.

On the quality dimension we have explained that, by adopting the course-team approach, the mega-universities are capable of better and more consistent quality of teaching than conventional universities on both academic and pedagogical grounds. Quality is an illusive concept, and is best judged using independent assessments. The United Kingdom has a fierce but comprehensive state-run assessment system for universities.

In terms of research, the OKOU ranks in the top third of all U.K. universities and some of its research is world-leading. In teaching, the UKOU ranks in the top 10%. This list contains the elite of U.K. universities in which most programs are rated as excellent.

We accept that these ratings do not mean that all the mega-universities of the world can be rated among the top academic institutions. Furthermore the nature of distance education makes it easier for unscrupulous providers to ply their trade over the short term, and this is why in the previous era of correspondence education—and in recent years, the emergence of online diploma mills—distance education has received a bad reputation. However, the important point here is that, independently rated, the mega-universities seem to be capable of providing quality teaching and research comparable with the best in the world. There are simply no grounds to argue that DL is necessarily second-rate education. The mega-universities, in particular the UKOU, have succeeded in breaking the historic—and insidious—link between quality and exclusivity in higher education.

The third dimension of the eternal triangle, the objective of cutting costs in higher education, is another area of achievement by the mega-universities. Cutting costs is, first, a result of the values underpinning open learning systems, and second, a consequence of the strategy of operating at economies of scale. The core value of open universities is to be open to people, and the culture is such that, when faced with escalating expenses, these organizations seek innovative solutions which do not pass along the costs to students and thus do not discriminate against the economically disadvantaged. Second, operating at scale, the mega-universities are able to teach at much lower costs than conventional universities.

But operating at scale does not necessarily mean that the absolute costs of mass-provision are insignificant. In fact, the absolute cost of designing, developing, and teaching a quality distance education course with adequate levels of student support is considerable. However, by capitalizing on economies-of-scale and efficiencies achieved by the division of labor, the mega-universities have achieved considerable cost advantages. The low costs are partly possible because in open-learning systems, most of the money goes directly into teaching and learning. In the United Kingdom, the UKOU has saved government the capital cost of building about 10 new campuses. Likewise, in South Africa, the state allocation of public funding to the University of South Africa (UNISA) is less than 10% of the total allocation to the entire University sector, yet UNISA provides teaching for 32% of the total number of University students in South Africa (W. Diehl, personal communication, June 15, 2006).

Despite the impressive cost savings, it is important to emphasize that success is determined by the interplay among all the dimensions of the eternal triangle. This is particularly important for policy-makers in higher education to note; although distance education is an attractive policy alternative because it can provide teaching at lower cost, unless quality and access are increased in parallel, the strategy will not succeed. Plainly, in the mega-university context, the three dimensions of the triangle are not discrete variables.

LEADING ODL FUTURES

From the perspective of the mega-university experience, we make four observations which we believe are critical for the future success of distance learning at the university.

First, traditional university campuses will remain in demand. They create a protected environment where young people can come to terms with life while acquiring the disciplines of scholarship and a critical disposition. Digital ICTs will provide opportunities for enriching the quality of the learning experience in ways that were previously not possible. Arguably such a system may still be criticized as being elitist but will still fulfill an important function in society. However, this is not the core market focus of the mega-university.

Therefore, it is reasonable to anticipate that the way in which the application of digital ICTs at campus-based institutions has developed is likely to be different from how the large open-learning systems will implement digital technologies in the future. Certainly, campus-based systems will continue to utilize distance-teaching methods to a far greater extent because of the inherent capabilities of digital ICTs to overcome geographical barriers of distance. However, providing learning at scale is fundamentally different from conventional models of delivery. The popular belief that distance education and conventional face-to-face provision are converging because of the new technologies is difficult to justify.

The mega-universities practice a form of delivery that is, per definition, technology-mediated learning. As a result, they have already had to develop new pedagogical structures and corresponding organizational structures to cater for the specific divisions of labor associated with providing learning at scale. Consequently, the challenges of the mega-universities with regards to digital ICTs are fundamentally different. For example, the mega-universities are not faced with questions of how to integrate traditional university structures and conventional pedagogy with emerging forms of distance education practice. Their challenges, rather, concern how best to integrate the power of digital ICTs when operating at scale. This is a different question.

Second, entrepreneurial and corporate forces will place increasing pressures on the university to manage the eternal triangle more effectively. Drucker's (1997, p. 745) predictions concerning the demise of the university as we know it are based on the analysis that student demand will not continue to support the increasing costs of conventional campus-based provision and that corporate providers will be able to do a better job in terms of value-for-money in the higher-education market. The success of The University of Phoenix—and other players in this changing field (corporate universities, independents (like Jones International University), and strategic business partnerships between conventional universities and the private sector (for example, Universitas 21)—could be early signs justifying Drucker's prediction.

However, the university has survived, and in many respects has thrived. In his insightful work, *The University in Ruins*, Readings (1996) provides his readers with a critical but well-founded debate of how economic globalization and the collapse of the nation-state have resulted in the university becoming a transnational bureaucratic corporation. In general, higher education has responded to the societal challenges of globalization by adopting what could loosely be termed as an "entrepreneurial approach" driven by the objectives associated with the commodification of excellence and packaged quality. In many respects, this is a disappointing response to the challenges of our transforming society. The entrepreneurial approach is more about retaining the essence of the classical university, using criteria of economic sustainability rather than transforming our practice in response to the needs and development of society. The problem is that our noble intentions with quality in education—a concept which on its own has no internal meaning or universal external referent—may easily become an idol that is commodified. Such a commodification of quality would be nothing more than a symptom of an inappropriate response to fundamental and revolutionary changes in society.

For example, what should the university of the future—driven by entrepreneurial objectives of economic sustainability—do about those areas of the curriculum which are not directly employment-related and thus unlikely to be direct contributors to the so-called "profit" of the organization? The problem is likely to exacerbate, if for example, "for-profit" universities succeed in drawing larger numbers of students away from the conventional institutions specifically in the subject areas that are traditionally used to cross-subsidize the non-employment-related subjects. Thus, the more conventional universities restrict themselves to a work-related curriculum, the more the open universities, because of their values, should offer a broader curriculum that can excite the human spirit.

Third, the mega-university experience is founded on technology-mediated learning, and, based on our experience, we have found that it is far more important to concentrate on getting the "soft" technologies of people, institutional structures and processes right, because the "hard" technologies will inevitably change before they are perfected within the system. In other words, university-wide technology strategies should be defined in terms of fundamental pedagogical processes with a clear understanding of how emerging technologies can support these processes. Having said this, we concede that the implementation of technology in higher education is a complicated business.

A considerable component of this complexity can be attributed to the question of whether the emerging digital ICTs have the power to radically transform the landscape of educational provision. When speculating about the impact of each new technology on education, we find no clear-cut answers and we hesitate to provide a definitive answer. Rather, we would prefer to approach this question from the perspectives of both the skeptics and the radicals.

The skeptics argue that throughout history there have been major technological innovations that were destined to revolutionize education. These include radio, motion pictures, overhead projectors, television, and more recently, video conferencing, the computer, and computer-assisted learning. But compared with the invention of the printing press and universal postal services, none of these technologies has resulted in the predicted revolution in education. Why should the new digital ICTs be any different in changing the traditions of university provision?

The radicals argue that the convergence of computing and telecommunications technology, plus the dynamic skills and demands of the knowledge economy, will radically transform the landscape of higher education provision in the world. They argue that digital ICTs now offer the capabilities to do things that were never possible before and that the university system is too inflexible to respond to the market needs of the economy. These radicals point out that the corporate world has realized the potential market opportunities and will significantly reduce the traditional market share of the university to provide students value-for-money learning that may ultimately contribute to the demise of the university as institution.

The research work of Clayton Christensen should provide useful insights into resolving some of the tensions between the skeptics and the radicals regarding whether or not digital ICTs will revolutionize education. Christensen (2000, pp. xv–xvii) reveals that new technologies come in two types.

First, there are sustaining technologies which improve current practice in an incremental way. Second, there are disruptive technologies, which are innovations that initially result in worse product performance, but ultimately change the market in fundamental ways to become new mainstream markets. For example, IBM dominated the mainframe computer market but missed the minicomputer market by years. Disruptive technologies therefore create new markets that did not exist before. What is interesting about the failure of many large corporations, as a result of disruptive technologies, is that they are often regarded as the best-managed companies in the world. The paradox is that these successful companies fail despite applying the best management principles when faced with disruptive technologies. This is the innovators' dilemma—namely, that when faced with disruptive technologies, "the logical, competent decisions of management that are critical to the success of their companies are also the reasons why they lose their positions of leadership" (Christensen, 2000, p. xiii).

Disruptive technologies cannot be integrated into current operations in a straightforward way. They also require a different organizational structure to become successful. However, if they do flourish, they can transform the enterprise as well as the marketplace. This distinction raises some interesting questions insofar as technology and distance education are concerned. If campus-based institutions aim to provide distance education at scale using digital technologies, then the mega-university experience proves that this application would be a disruptive technology.

Considering the existing practice of the mega-universities, currently operating at scale, the new digital technologies are sustaining in some areas, and potentially disruptive in others. They are sustaining where they reduce costs of open-learning systems, (for example, improved on-line administration) or where they improve quality of the distance learning experience (for example, improved communication and online learning resources). In other respects, the digital ICTs are potentially disruptive because they could permit distance learning systems to be reconceived from scratch. At this juncture of our experience, we do not have conclusive examples of a reconceived distance learning system, although we recognize that it is perfectly possible. After all, the large open-learning systems were created in response to the disruptive technology of the combined effects of open learning and the provision of quality learning at scale.

Finally, the discussion of digital ICTs and the future of distance education may appear to be somewhat removed from the realities of the higher education crisis in developing society contexts. While about a third of the population of Europe and the Americas is online, only 2.6% of Africans are online (United Nations ICT Task Force, 2005), and even this 2.6% figure is deceptive because uneven distribution remains a major issue, as basic infrastructure, let alone reliable ICT infrastructure, is still virtually nonexistent in most countries of Sub-Saharan Africa—and this infrastructure issue applies to much of the developing world.

When we analyze access figures to various communications technologies in the developing world, it is understandable why many distance education policy advisors recommend that future distance education strategies should be based on first-generation correspondence study.

TABLE 46.2.
Information and Communications Technology Indicators by Region

	Africa	Oceania	Asia	Europe	Americas
Estimated main telephone lines per 100 inhabitants (2005)	3.22	42.39	15.76	40.97	33.97
Growth rates in fixed telephone lines (1994–2004)	6.1%	1.1%	11.5%	2.5%	2.0%
Estimated cellular subscribers per 100 inhabitants (2005)	11.29	68.51	22.24	84.42	51.51
World Distribution % of 3G subscribers (2004)	.2%	1.1%	48.6%*	5.5%	44.6%
Distribution of Broadband subscribers (2004)	.1%	.8%	41%	27.7%	30.5%
Cable subscribers as % of TV households (2004)	1.6%	18.7%	30.2%	21.2%	44.3%
Satellite antennas as % of TV households (2004)	29.4%	11.9%	13.5%	13.8%	17.6%
Share of telecommunication investment (2004)	4%	3%	37%	33%	23%

Source: (ITU, 2006)
*(CDMA (2000): 40.1% and WCDMA: 8.5%)

But promoting first-generation correspondence study in developing society contexts is problematic for a number of reasons.

First, we have already explained that the provision of individualized tutorial support is a critical success factor for ensuring the success of open-learning systems. However, because of considerable geographical distances and the shortage of suitably qualified tutors in remote locations where the majority of the population of the developing world reside, correspondence study will not be able to achieve the successes reported by the UKOU. Conversely, digital ICTs provide the potential of effectively overcoming the problems associated with providing local tutors.

Second, ODL materials that were developed in the traditions of correspondence study limit distribution alternatives in terms of carrier technology and furthermore will not embed the power of multi-mode, multi-media teaching. The practical realities of limited connectivity in developing countries is a seductive policy trap because the magnitude of the problem blinds the vision concerning how the inherent power of digital ICTs can be used to overcome the chasm between restricted access and generating sufficient demand for rolling out sustainable connectivity.

Third, Braga (1998) points out that technological developments "are rapidly eroding economic and technical barriers to entry into communication networks. Developing countries can, for example, leapfrog stages of development by investing into fully digitized networks rather than continuing to expand their outdated analog-based infrastructure" (Braga, 1998). There is evidence that, with government commitment and determination at policy level, developing countries can achieve the ideals of leapfrogging. Spending on ICTs grew more rapidly in developing regions than in high-income countries during the 1992–1997 period (Braga, 1998). Yunus (1998), for example, reports on the success of the "wireless women" initiative in Bangladesh. Rural women given $350 loans from the Grameen Bank to purchase cellular telephones and to cover the costs of training and repair services have been able to earn profits of $700 per annum as mobile telephone operators, which is significantly more than the average $250 annual per capita income in Bangladesh. In 1999, with support from UNESCO, COHCIT and the government, the isolated community of San Ramon, Honduras, became the first solar-energy village in Latin America, and, for the first time, a year later, classrooms wired for Internet connectivity became available to the citizens. As a result of this success, other villages that can benefit from these technologies are being identified (Verdisco, Melara de Fanconi, & Velásquez, 2005).

Fourth, developing societies should adopt a demand-push strategy by creating the demand for broad bandwidth applications. Infrastructure will then follow because it can now be sustained by the large demand. The implicit capabilities and advantages of digital ICTs for distance learning should be used as a point of departure to ensure that sufficient demand is generated by the ODL applications of these technologies. In this way, sustainability of the new technologies can be promoted because of the economy-of-scale potential associated with mass-demand, rather than waiting for acceptable levels of connectivity before transforming the practice of distance education in these societies.

The critical point here is that the problems experienced in the developing society are significantly different from the experiences of the industrialized world. From the outside, it is very easy to misinterpret the potential for digital solutions in distance education when analyzing absolute statistics. Using these approaches, it is very easy to miss pockets of indigenous innovation, which collectively may provide the foundation for culturally relevant solutions in the future. Global best-practice must be interpreted within the contexts of local relevance.

In conclusion, we have stated that we regard the mega-universities as being the most significant innovation in higher education of the 20th century, and that current and future organizations can use the mega-university model as a resource in a world that is confronting a tertiary educational crisis. If UNESCO and the U.N. Millennium Group successfully realize their goals of halving extreme poverty and of providing primary-school education for all by 2015 (and then continue to succeed), it follows that in the coming decades, tens of millions more adults will be equipped to seek tertiary educational opportunities—and the numbers will only continue to increase.

We agree with Brown's (1998, p. 25) experience that to be effective, invention is not enough, and pioneering work requires invention-plus-implementation. In other words, innovation is invention successfully implemented. The inventions associated with digital ICTs have the potential of radically transforming higher-education provision. However, this will require creative solutions, and by "creativity" we mean the art of designing within the constraints of the eternal triangle. The mega-university experience may provide strategists with a model that is capable of implementing the innovations associated with digital ICTs, but also of scaling-up their implementation so as to capitalize on further gains from successfully managing the tensions of the eternal triangle.

REFERENCES

Bacsich, P. (Ed.). (2005). *Report 08. University of Phoenix Online*. The Higher Education Academy. UK eUniversities Worldwide Limited. Available online at http://www.heacademy.ac.uk/documents/r08-phoenix.doc

Braga, C. A. P. (1998, December). Inclusion or exclusion? Will the networked economy widen or narrow the gap between developing and industrialized countries? *UNESCO Courier.* Available online at http://www.unesco.org/courier/1998_12/uk/dossier/txt21.htm

Brown, J. S. (1998). Seeing differently: A role for pioneering research. *Research Technology Management, 41*(3), 24–34.

Christensen, C. M. (2000). *The innovator's dilemma: When new technologies cause great firms to fail.* New York: HarperBusiness. (Reprinted from Harvard Business School Press edition, 1997)

Centre National d'Enseignement a Distance. (2006). Online: http://www.cned.fr/en/

Daniel, J. S. (1999). *Mega-universities and knowledge media: Technology strategies for higher education* (Rev. ed.). London: Kogan Page.

Dr. B. R. Ambedkar Open University. (2006). Online: http://www.braou.ac.in

Drucker, P. A., and Holden, C. (1997). Untitled. *Science, 275*(5307), 1745.

ITU. (2006). World Telecommunication/ICT Development Report. Measuring ICT for Social and Economic Development. Geneva: International Telecommunication Union.

Jung, I. 2005. Quality Assurance Survey Of Mega Universities. In McIntosh, C. (Ed.) *Perspectives on Distance Education. Lifelong Learning & Higher Education.* Vancouver & Paris: Commonwealth of Learning/UNESCO Publishing.

Keegan, D. (1980). On defining distance education. *Distance Education, 1*(1), 13–36.

O'Leary, J. (2006). Good university Q & A. Retrieved July 10, 2006, from http://www.timesonline.co.uk/article/0,,716-2208313,00.html

Payame Noor Univesity. (2006). Available online at http://www.pnu.ac.ir/engilish/htm/about.htm

Readings, B. (1996). *The university in ruins.* Cambridge, MA; London: Harvard University Press.

Saint, W. (1999). *Tertiary distance education and technology in Sub-Saharan Africa.* Washington, DC: Working group on Higher Education, Association for the Development of Education in Africa, The World Bank.

Tait, A. (2000). Planning student support for open and distance learning. *Open Learning, 15*(3), 287–299.

UNESCO. (2000a). *World education report 2000.* Paris: Author.

UNESCO. (2000b). The Dakar framework for action. Education for All: Meeting our collective commitments. [Text adopted by the World Education Forum Dakar, Senegal, 26–28 April 2000]. Retrieved June 12, 2006, from http://www2.unesco.org/wef/en-leadup/dakfram.shtm

UNESCO. (2000c). Expanded commentary on the Dakar framework for action. 23 May 2000. Paris: Author.. Retrieved June 12, 2006, from http://www2.unesco.org/wef/en-leadup/dakfram.shtm

UNESCO. (2004). EFA Global Monitoring Report 2003/4. Retrieved June 12, 2006, from http://www.efareport.unesco.org/

UNESCO. (2006a). Institute for Statistics. Retrieved June 12, 2006, from http://www.uis.unesco.org

UNESCO. (2006b). Literacy Portal. Retrieved June 12, 2006, from http://portal.unesco.org/education/

United Nations ICT Task Force. (2005). *Measuring ICT: the global status of ICT indicators: Partnership on measuring ICT for development*. New York: Author.

Verdisco, A., Melara de Fanconi, A., & Velásquez, C. (2005). Honduras: Loading technologies in isolated communities-lessons to learn. In W. Haddad & A. Draxler (Eds.), *Technologies for education: Potentials, parameters, and prospects* (pp. 180–185). Paris; Washington, DC: UNESCO; Academy for Educational Development.

World Bank. (2000). Higher education in developing countries: Peril and promise. Washington, DC: Author.

Xingfu, D., Xiaoqing, G., & Zhiting, Z. (2005). The Chinese approach. In McIntosh, C. (Ed.), *Perspectives on distance education: Lifelong learning & higher education*. Vancouver, British Columbia, Canada; Paris: Commonwealth of Learning; UNESCO.

Yashwantrao Chavan Maharashtra Open University. (2006). Online: http://www.ycmou.com/

Yunus, M. (1998). Alleviating poverty through technology. *Science, 282*(5388), 409–410.

47

A World Bank Initiative in Distance Education for Development

Michael Foley
The World Bank

This is the story of an evolution in thinking on the impact that knowledge sharing, distance learning, and communications technologies can have on the development agenda. It is a story of learning by doing, of how, by leveraging systems that already existed for one purpose and using them for another as a value added, a whole new way of doing business could be discovered. In the eight years since the initiative was first conceptualized and implemented, more lessons were learned and the emphasis has shifted from it being a training delivery mechanism to it being a process for partnership and engagement with development practitioners for knowledge sharing. Let us start at the beginning.

In a videoconference in June, 1998, Jim Wolfensohn, president of the World Bank, remarked, "As we look at the challenges of poverty, it is very clear that money alone is not what is needed. We need colleagues who can learn and share experience with each other. Distance learning, obviously is the tool that will enable this and benefit us all" (Wolfensohn, 1998).

This statement matched with the wide recognition that the emerging communications technologies were causing a revolution in the world economy, where knowledge was the new currency, and where economically advanced countries were moving from being industrial economies to becoming knowledge economies. The concepts of "information highway" an information society, a knowledge society, were evolving from this revolution. Among development practitioners, the role that knowledge and knowledge sharing had in development took on greater importance, to the point that it was seen as the key to development, maybe even more important than finance, grants, or lending.

The World Bank Institute (WBI) was founded over 50 years ago as the Economic Development Institute (EDI), with the mandate to offer a number of knowledge services—including courses, seminars, and policy dialogs—to client countries of the World Bank, which include

This material has been prepared by the staff of the World Bank. Any findings, interpretations, and conclusions, are entirely those of the authors and not necessarily those of the World Bank, its affiliated organizations, or the members of its Board of Executive Directors or the governments they represent.

almost all developing countries. It delivered these services in a traditional face-to-face manner, either in Washington, DC or in a region. This was an expensive process, involving much long-distance travel and hotel costs; therefore, it made sense to explore the potential of communications technologies and distance learning to improve the cost-effectiveness of the service. The problem was that the telecommunications infrastructures in the Bank's client countries were at a very low level of development. In a study carried out by the Academy for Educational Development (AED) in February 1997, it was concluded that approximately $40 million would be needed to build a distance learning network with a global reach, clearly not an option at that time.

Because the Bank had offices in almost 100 developing countries, however, it had its own needs, for operational and business purposes, for a more robust communications system than the local infrastructures could support. Over the years, the Information Solutions Group (ISG) of the Bank had built a global communications network based on VSAT technology to connect its worldwide offices to headquarters in Washington, DC, and to each other. By 1997, that network was providing fully interactive video, voice, and data services, and Jim Wolfensohn suggested in a meeting that it could be used to deliver some of the courses from Washington, using the local World Bank offices as venues at which the participants could attend. Things moved rapidly at that point. A distance learning unit was formed and staffed in WBI, studios were built in the main building of the Bank, and in September 1998 the World Bank Learning Network (WBLN) was launched.

The shortcomings of a learning network based in World Bank offices were apparent from the beginning. The local country offices were not equipped, or staffed, to be learning centers. All of the computers in the offices were networked inside the firewall of the Bank's intranet, and so they could only be used by staff of the World Bank; therefore, only the videoconferencing facility could be used for courses aimed at external clients, a big drawback for courses using a Web element. Besides, using the name "World Bank Learning Network" and using only offices of the World Bank as venues inhibited the growth of the network as a worldwide partnership of program partners, donors, and governments. It was clear that what was needed was an independent network of centers, connected still through the Bank's global satellite infrastructure, at least until a critical mass of centers was built that could support an independent sustainable network. Resources were mobilized within the Bank to set about working with client governments and donors in order to build the Global Distance Learning Network (GDLN). The name was changed later to Global Development Learning Network in order to put the emphasis on the mission rather than the means of the network, and without changing the acronym GDLN. A target was set by the president to get 10 distance learning centers (DLCs) established in the first year. The target was met, and in June 2000, the official launch of the GDLN took place with 14 centers taking part. By March, 2006, that number had grown to over 100.

DESIGN OF THE SYSTEM

At the outset of the project, the issue was to design an approach—based on adult learning principles and on the appropriate use of technology—that at least would be as effective as the traditional face-to-face model employed heretofore, but that would be more cost effective; reach a wider audience; and provide content from a wider circle of providers. The question then was to design a pedagogical scenario with a technology platform that would achieve the objectives desired, with the target audience concerned, and that was cost effective in the circumstances.

There are general principles of good design that can be applied to all distance learning activities, but in practice the specific pedagogical design employed in a particular course will be influenced by

- the target audience of the activity
- the content or subject matter to be delivered
- the outcomes or objectives desired

There are other considerations that affect the design of a delivery system for distance learning that will have profound effects on the design of the learning activities. They are primarily

- the cost effectiveness of the system
- the opportunity costs of alternative systems and methods
- the availability of technology to the provider and to the learners
- the geographical location of the learners
- the comfort level of the learners with any technology that is used

Each of these factors can be applied to a particular target audience, be they children, postsecondary students, or adults. The resulting criteria of quality design may be very different for each group as we move from pedagogy for children to andragogy (Knowles, 1970) for adults. The design requirements and sociopsychological conditions are quite different for each group, so at this stage there is a need to describe the group that is the focus of this initiative. There is also a need to define what the specific content areas are, and what outcomes are set for the activities.

TARGET AUDIENCE

The GDLN has as its target group a range that includes decision makers and midlevel career personnel in government, government agencies, NGOs, academia, civil society, and the private sector, the majority of whom are in developing countries. The following is known about these learners in terms of their resources and constraints:

- Participants tend to be mid-career professionals, i.e., adult learners.
- Participants are not computer savvy and they do not have ready access to technology such as computers and the Internet outside of these centers.
- Participants are traditionally educated, albeit not experienced with self-directed learning.
- Participants are juggling both family and work commitments with professional development activities.

CONTENT

The content area consists primarily of policy issues in the development agenda of the client countries and the related skill sets that would be needed to inform policy—for example, data collection and measurement, statistical analysis, project management, and economic forecasting.

The sharing of technical knowledge in the implementation of reform programs across a spectrum of development themes such as health, education, fiscal management, infrastructure, rural development, micro-credit, and so forth constitutes a major portion of the program of activities in the calendar.

OUTCOMES

In regard to the desired outcomes, while the ultimate objective is the alleviation of poverty and economic and social development, the outcome of learning activities themselves can be the same as those for face-to-face activities—that is, increased knowledge on a particular development topic. With the appropriate application of adult learning theory into the design of the learning activities, and with an appropriate use of a range of technologies, the bar can be raised on the level of outcomes achieved. In the early stages of the GDLN, much of the debate was centered around the effectiveness or otherwise of distance education compared to face-to-face activities. As with any radical organizational change, there was quite a bit of resistance to the move to distance learning, but, as will be described later in the chapter, that resistance is now largely overcome.

APPLYING ADULT LEARNING THEORY
TO THE SYSTEM DESIGN

In designing the pedagogical approaches for GDLN, the results of more than 30 years of research on adult learning was applied to the distance learning programs. They have the following criteria:

1. They are based on clearly established learning needs and built around succinct statements of outcome.
2. They are based on a variety of teaching and learning strategies and methods that are activity-based, such as simulations, case studies, and problem-solving exercises.
3. Effective distance learning materials are experiential; they address the learner's life experiences as a point of departure for the learning program and as a continuous reference throughout the process.
4. Quality distance learning programs are participatory in that they emphasize the involvement of the learner in all facets of program development and delivery.
5. Successful distance learning programs are interactive and allow for frequent opportunities for participants to engage in a dialogue with subject matter experts and other learners.
6. Learner support systems are an integral part of any successful distance learning program.

PLATFORM/TECHNOLOGY CHOICE

When it comes to technology or platform choice, any one technology may be able to deliver a quality distance learning experience, but the ideal delivery system will rarely be based on a single platform or technology; rather, it will be an integrated mix of methods, technologies, and networks, with their appropriate educational benefits and learner support services. This approach came to be called "blended" learning, a current buzzword in the distance education field.

The actual availability or cost of a particular technology or technologies to the target audience may be one of the primary criteria for media choice, but it is useful to be platform agnostic regarding cost and availability at the outset of designing a delivery system. The system can be designed for maximum pedagogical effectiveness, and it can then be modified by applying the cost and availability criteria. In actual practice, of course, all of the elements—cost, effectiveness, and availability—are considered at the same time. It is a classic "chicken and egg" situation.

THE GDLN TECHNICAL PLATFORM

Given that the GDLN has a target group as defined above, and content aimed at producing good governance and high-quality policymaking in developing countries, plus the skill sets to achieve these aims, a technological platform combined with a pedagogical approach designed for quality adult learning was developed. The fact that this technological platform was to a large extent already available through the World Bank's Global Communications Network was crucial to implementing this design. It would have been almost impossible to develop the infrastructure from scratch. This is what makes the network unique; a platform of technologies that was suitable for incremental growth without a large initial investment. What was available was a global VSAT network, which allowed for interactive video, voice, and data to be used for learning activities, as well as for the operational and business purposes for which it was designed. If a secondary network could grow as an added value to the existing network until it reached a critical mass, then it could be spun off when it was mature, but be protected in its early growth stages. The potential for two-way interactive video, high-speed Internet access, and voice communications, all independent of local telecom conditions through special licensing arrangements and with low-cost tariffs based on UN rates with Intelsat, gave a freedom to design a distance learning system that was unavailable to most providers. The critical mass for the bandwidth requirements was already met by the World Bank's usage. DLCs could be added with incremental purchase of more bandwidth without a large new investment.

The constraints of the availability of the technology and the learners' access to it were removed. Pedagogical scenarios could be developed according to best practice of adult learning if local Centers could be established and equipped to support the technologies and the requirements of adult distance learning. The centers were designed to support synchronous videoconferencing, data conferencing, and asynchronous Internet access, in two rooms dedicated to these functions. The added bonus of two-way videoconferencing and data conferencing was that one could deliver content from any center in the network to any other center. It was not a centralized distribution model, but an exchange model. Experience and expertise could be exchanged between centers.

The protocols for communication and user interface were standard protocols; H320 and T.120 for the synchronous side, and TCP/IP and HTML for the asynchronous side. Any program provider with a Web server and an ISDN/T1/Fiber or satellite connection to the videoconferencing bridges in the World Bank headquarters in Washington DC for videoconferencing could be a program partner. In the intervening years since the network was launched, the possibility of videoconferencing over Internet Protocol (IP) became a reality. The World Bank's Information Solutions Group (ISG) worked closely with Cisco engineers in their early work to build routers that would guarantee Quality of Service (QoS) in a satellite environment, and the Bank's satellite network was converted to IP in 2003. This opened the way for a more flexible H323 based videoconferencing, which allowed universities to participate in videoconferences by IP at no extra cost per minute, that had being paying through ISDN connectivity. In turn, this prompted the

World Bank to affiliate with the Internet2 organization in the United States, and to link into the Abilene academic backbone (described later in the chapter).

A standard design template was produced for institutions that wanted to build a DLC from scratch; but, as experience was gained, these templates became more flexible, and the current technical requirements to affiliate to GDLN have a fairly basic minimum technical specification. They are described in the GDLN Business Policies document as follows.

METHODS, MEDIA, AND FUNCTIONALITY

GDLN promotes the use of what is called "blended" learning methods—that is, a mix of methods and media that can be configured according to the learning styles of the target audience and to the desired outcomes and objectives of the activities. Therefore, a participating GDLN center needs to offer space and facilities for

1. Group videoconferencing with simultaneous display of video and data.
2. Recording and playback of videoconferencing sessions and videotapes.
3. Multimedia access to the Internet at reasonable speeds and to CD-ROM-based resources.
4. Breakout sessions and small group discussions and activities.
5. Printing and copying of learning materials.

Depending on the size of the center, all of these facilities may be contained either in one room, or, more appropriately, in separate rooms. A typical GDLN center provides space for at least 30 participants in each type of activity. Some centers, especially those in countries that do not speak the three main languages of GDLN—that is, English, Spanish, and French—may need to provide facilities for simultaneous interpretation.

CONNECTIVITY

An affiliate GDLN center will be able to connect to the videoconferencing Network Operations Center video bridges in Washington, DC or Paris at speeds of 256Kbps, through ISDN, IP over optic fiber, leased line, or by VSAT (Very Small Aperture Terminal) antenna. The VSAT option can only be adopted by connecting to the World Bank's Global Communications network. Connecting through IP through Internet 2 (the academic peer national education and research networks) is now an option. Connection through the commercial Internet for videoconferencing is not recommended, and the Information Solutions Group (ISG) of the World Bank cannot take responsibility for poor-quality connections using this method and may refuse to certify the affiliate GDLN center.

EQUIPMENT AND FUNCTIONALITY

The typical GDLN has two technology rooms, offering what can be called (a) synchronous communications, or live group videoconferencing, with Internet access on a least one PC/laptop, and, (b) asynchronous communications, or Internet e-mail, Web, and multimedia applications at individual workstations. Smaller centers may accommodate both functions in one room. In some countries where Internet access is readily available, there may not be the need for this second room or facility for groups of people.

In cases where Internet access is scarce, it is advisable for a GDLN center to provide facilities such that each participant in an event can access Internet and Web resources. It is recommended that each GDLN center in this situation provides a bank of PCs that are networked in a LAN internally and to the external Internet at sufficient speed to allow multiple access to learning resources online. A 768 Kbps bandwidth allows simultaneous operation of videoconferencing and multiple internet access at a reasonable speed. The computing facility does not have to be owned by the GDLN center, but participants in GDLN events must have easy access to these resources.

Since electricity is essential for operating a GDLN Event, it is recommended that each GDLN center has secured power supply in case of electricity failure (UPS or power generator).

CONNECTIVITY OPTIONS AND NATIONAL RESEARCH AND EDUCATION NETWORKS

While the GDLN, as a telecommunications network, was originally conceived as running on additional capacity of the World Bank's own global satellite network, it very rapidly evolved as a hybrid system of connectivity options. By partnering with other distance learning networks on a global, a regional, or a national level, and by interconnecting them technically, the mutual benefit to each network is significant, both in terms of the extended reach to wider audiences and in terms of the richness of content that can be shared.

The first partnering of GDLN with a regional network was with the Monterrey Institute of Technology (ITESM) in Mexico in 1999. By linking their satellite system in Monterrey with the World Bank Institute's studios in Washington, DC by a fiber connection, courses from WBI were broadcast "live," with interaction by e-mail, to over 100 centers in Mexico and Latin America. Another example of a regional partnership was with the Asociación de Televisión Educativa Iberoamericana (ATEI).

At the national level there are a growing number of examples of the GDLN center in the capital city being connected to an internal national network of the country. The early example of this arrangement was with Globatel in Ecuador, who have a 50-site satellite network for one-way video two-way audio. The latest example is where a GDLN Center can connect to the bridge of the National Informatics (NIC) Center in New Delhi and be linked to a choice of over 450 two-way videoconferencing sites throughout India on NIC's satellite network.

The greatest potential for the growth of GDLN, however, is with the National Research and Education Networks (NRENs). The early versions of these networks in the Untied States and Europe constituted what was the Internet twenty years ago, before the development of the commercial, or commodity, Internet. To avoid the congestion of the commodity Internet and to build sufficient capacity to carry the large amounts of data that are required in scientific research, these national networks are building high-speed, backbone infrastructures of 10 Gigabit per second. By an arrangement of "peering," these networks are interlinking to form a global, high-speed, academic infrastructure that is shaping the next generation of Internet. Hence, the association that is coordinating this work in the United States calls itself "Internet2" (http://www.internet2.edu) and its network, "Abilene." Similar organizations exist in other regions—for example, DANTE (for GÉANT network) in Europe, CANARIE in Canada, CERNET in China, and AARNET in Australia, and so forth.

In order to capitalize on these possibilities, the World Bank, as a recognized key player in knowledge for development, affiliated in January 2004 to the Internet2 organization as a corporate member with collaboration status, and the videoconferencing bridges in Washington, DC are now linked by fiber-optic cable to the mid-Atlantic GigaPoP of Abilene, Internet2's backbone. This interconnection brings great opportunities to GDLN Centers in poor countries (where no NREN exists), giving them access to the major universities of the world. In middle-income countries, where the existing NRENs are often being upgraded to higher capacity, the universities can join in the partnership of GDLN, and play a more immediate role in their own country's economic and social development.

EFFECTIVENESS OF THE SYSTEM

As mentioned earlier in this chapter, there was some initial resistance to the move to distance learning based on, among other factors, doubts about is effectiveness compared to a face-to-face model. Regardless of the fact that countless studies have demonstrated the "no significant differ-ence" syndrome, it was thought necessary to test the hypothesis with the client group concerned.

A study conducted by WBI (then, EDI) demonstrated that a distance learning version of a course on Economic and Business Journalism was as effective as the face-to-face versions of the same course, at least as measured by the participants' satisfaction with the course, its methodol-ogy, and its contribution to their professional skills (Bardini, 1998). The course experienced a "dropin" rate as distinct from a "dropout" rate, which is usual with distance learning courses—that is, the reputation and popularity of the course spread rapidly and there were more participants at the end of the course than at the beginning.

Some aspects of this course, with its delivery spread over a number of weeks to participants who did not have to leave their workplace for more than a half day a week and whose assignments were the actual articles that they were writing for their newspapers, indicated that there was more potential in distance learning than simple knowledge transfer—that is, that it could have direct results in professional performance and that, therefore, to compare it to face-to-face as a measure of its success was perhaps aiming too low.

MOVING BEYOND THE COURSE DELIVERY PARADIGM

With the target group of the GDLN as defined above, early measurements indicate that using DL methods are proving more cost-effective to deliver the same course to the same clients than by traditional methods. In other words, the same learning gains were achieved with a greater number of participants for less cost than a face-to-face version of the same content to a similar client group. But is this selling the technology and the pedagogy short? Can more be achieved in terms of impact than just successful course delivery?

An early example of how distance learning can move us from course delivery to a more com-prehensive technology enabled development paradigm was the Controlling Corruption "course." It is described below by the senior instructional designer on the course team, Don MacDonald.

CONTROLLING CORRUPTION:
TECHNOLOGY ENABLED DEVELOPMENT IN ACTION

Corruption is a serious problem in developing countries, a systemic impediment to sustained eco-nomic growth. There is a substantial body of empirical data that shows clear correlations between the growth indicators of impoverished countries (or lack thereof) and indices related to corruption. Previous World Bank attempts to address this issue focused on the regulatory, with strict attention to accountability and transparency policies and practices. These strategies, however, did not address fundamental cause and effects related to corruption: how to build an accountable, transparent, and self-regulating infrastructure in a developing country that will control corruption.

The emphasis turned to training, capacity building, and technical assistance approaches. These programs were targeted to high-level ministry officials from around the world who were brought to World Bank headquarters for a 10-day program. The course agenda was built around a daily nine hours of lectures and discussion covering a variety of topics related to consequences of corruption in developing economies. But these instructor-led, lecture-based programs did not achieve expected results. A new approach was tested at the World Bank, where a more learner-centered curriculum that used a blend of learning methodologies and technologies was developed. After protracted discussions with distance learning and adult learning specialists, however, course subject matter experts were persuaded to entirely rethink their approach to the delivery of this program.

The new curriculum consisted of the following attributes:

1. A move to a more learner-centered and action-oriented curriculum. Course designers and subject matter experts were asked to think not in terms of the information that needed to be transmitted in order to understand corruption, but rather, what individuals working in government ministries needed to know in order to actually control corruption. The program agenda focused on actions that need to be implemented in order to control corruption and the skills that participants need to learn in order to take these actions.

2. Instead of a global focus, with a broad invitation to all client governments of the World Bank to attend a conference-like setting, it was decided to instead focus on select countries. The initial program was targeted to seven countries in Sub-Saharan Africa: Benin, Ethiopia, Ghana, Kenya, Malawi, Tanzania, and Uganda. Invitations were sent to key ministerial personnel in these countries, who were asked to attend and to participate in the program as a team, with a mandate to address corruption issues in their respective countries.

3. The overall goal of the program was to enable each country team to develop a comprehensive action plan to control corruption in their respective countries. The specific objectives and program agenda focused on the skills required by the country teams to design, develop, and implement a country action strategy to control corruption.

4. Finally, the curriculum was delivered using a blended approach that included a combination of a traditional, face-to-face workshop approach, followed by a regular series of seminars convened by videoconferencing technology. There was also a substantial amount of print materials developed to support country teamwork, and over the course of time, e-mail communications were added to support the preparation of the strategy paper for Durban.

The blended and technology assisted aspects of this course offer critical "lessons learned" for related development learning projects.

- The face-to-face encounter is valuable in terms of building a sense of team among participants.
- Videoconferencing sessions allow participants to return to their respective countries, but still continue with the learning. Twice a week sessions over a month, which address topics introduced at the face-to-face session, allow participants to test and apply new concepts within the contexts of their own countries and at the same time, share experiences with

other country teams. The videoconferencing sessions also allow for participation by other members of a country ministry who were unable to attend the face-to-face sessions. In addition, videoconferences facilitated the preparation of a common strategy paper representing the views of the participating country teams.

- Internet approaches (Web sites, Listservs, discussion forums, e-mail) are being developed to support future roll outs of the program, which will further strengthen the intra-country collaboration that seems a critical feature of success for this curriculum. (MacDonald, 1999)

LINKING LEARNING WITH DEVELOPMENT AID

One of the major inhibiting factors in the effectiveness of development aid over the last half century has been a lack of capacity in the implementing agencies and institutions. The result has often been a significant waste of resources and an increase in poor country debt. The syndrome has been called the "challenge of implementation," which arises from a combination of poor policy making at the decision making tiers of government, and low level of skills among mid-level civil servants and others in civil society who are attempting to implement the reforms or development projects. The response of the donor community has been to provide capacity-building programs in the form of policy dialogues, technical assistance, and training. We could ask what has been the impact of these training efforts. Have they been effective? Have they targeted the right people? Have they been relevant, and have they been timely? Without being too critical of past endeavors in capacity building, it would be generally accepted that the answer to these questions would not be highly favorable.

In the light of recent experiences such as described above, it is emerging that the new information and communications technologies (ICTs), and the new approach to designing learning programs, is helping us move beyond purely learning objectives. In fact, it is helping us achieve the very behavioral and performance outcomes that the training was designed to bring about in the first place. This is especially true in cases where there is a need for access to international expertise and experience in national reform and development programs.

IS THE TRADITIONAL TRAINING PARADIGM EFFECTIVE?

The traditional approach to capacity building adopted by the lending and development agencies has been to offer training courses and workshops to small groups of individuals, who often had to travel long distances to centers of expertise in other countries, and to be absent from their work for concentrated periods of time. The travel, subsistence, and opportunity costs were significant and the impact of the training on job performance has been difficult to measure.

The fact that these courses were offered to individuals from many different countries meant that, firstly, the content was often too generic in nature and therefore not fully relevant to every country, and secondly, due to costs, it would be possible to invite only one or two people from each country. The training might have been good for the individuals concerned, but the impact of those individuals in the workplace on returning home could be insignificant. The team members that the persons worked with had not shared in the same experience, and therefore they would tend to be slow to change behavior, if at all. Hence, very low impact on the development of the country.

THE POTENTIAL OF DISTANCE LEARNING;
JUST-IN-TIME ACTION LEARNING FOR TEAMS

By using a blend of distance learning methods, such as a combination of face-to-face meetings with group videoconferencing and Internet resources, these same learning opportunities can be provided for full teams of people who are working together on projects in their home countries. They can be delivered over a period of time, which allows the teams to work on practical assignments related to their work (action learning). What's more, they can be offered "just-in-time," at the very point when the teams are grappling with implementation issues. If one normally uses case-study techniques in training programs, then by using distance learning, the participants themselves and their project can become the case in point. There is no need to simulate hypothetical cases, nor is the discussion of historical cases restricted to reading the cases from handouts. The participants can talk directly by videoconferencing to the people who are the subjects of the cases in the framework of what is called "electronic field visits."

The objectives of these types of learning activities can be based on practical outcomes and achievements of the teams and not just on learning gains for the individual participants. In this way the whole nature of learning programs can change from being abstract and general to being pragmatic and focused. This approach breaks down the perceived separation between learning and doing by creating an environment whereby learning is part of the doing and vice versa.

FROM A TRAINING MODEL TO
A KNOWLEDGE SHARING MODEL

The experience gained in the last few years within GDLN has shown that, with these approaches, it—and networks like it—can be used to support development in ways that go well beyond traditional ideas of "training." The change amounts to a paradigm shift in the approach to training and professional development. It marks a shift from the concept of knowledge *transfer* to the concept of knowledge *sharing*, an interactive approach that takes account of the experience of practitioners, as well as the knowledge of experts. Above all, it provides an opportunity to bring the people who are about to implement a program together with people who have experience in the area or who have already completed such a program. For example, teams in country A that are working on a higher education development project would value the opportunity to speak with their counterparts and others in countries X, Y, and Z, where similar programs were or are being enacted. These kinds of exchanges are very often more valuable than formal training courses (which many of these practitioners would say they do not want or need).

To put it succinctly, in many poor countries the primary goal of GDLN is *aid effectiveness*. In middle-income countries, where much development is government or private sector financed, GDLN's role is to improve the effectiveness of the development programs. The centers are located in a variety of institutions such as civil service training colleges, universities, or management training institutions, which have a mandate for the promotion of knowledge sharing for development. As a network of centers, GDLN puts emphasis on the idea of team learning in groups, and institutional capacity enhancement over purely individual professional development. It is ideally suited to support governments and aid agencies that are implementing reform programs, by integrating capacity-enhancement activities directly into the implementation process itself, and not separating learning from practice.

This approach overcomes the problem that besets the supply-driven model of training; which is often not based on real demand. In the GDLN model, the demand can create its own supply. The very people who are attempting to implement a program—that is, the managers and their teams in cooperation with development agencies—together know their knowledge needs, and in many cases, they know where to satisfy those needs. Time and again it has been stated by operational managers of development programs that what their counterparts in developing countries want is not training per se, but that they want to meet and speak with similar people around the world who have some experience in doing the same thing. Very often it is not training courses that they are looking for, but an opportunity to share experiences with, and ask questions of people who have tackled the same issues that they are currently addressing; and very often the people that they want to talk to are the civil servants and others in civil society, who were the implementers of the programs, not academic researchers in universities. These people are generally very open to sharing their experiences free of charge because they are proud of what they have achieved. They like to talk to their counterparts in other countries, keeping up to date with each other and forming what are called "communities of practice." Sharing stories and exchanging experience is the essence of Knowledge Management, and a so-called "south-south" dialogue is often much more valuable than a training course from a university academic or donor agency in the "north."

APPLYING THE MODEL TO TRAINING ACTIVITIES

This is not to say that the traditional courses and training model should be abandoned. It does, however, strongly suggest that we need to revisit the design of these training offerings. Too often the move to distance learning has merely been to offer the same content, with the same limited objectives, but now through technologies such as the Internet or videoconferencing. While research has shown that distance learning offers the equivalent quality as traditional approaches, the "no significant difference syndrome," if we only use this methodology to gain greater reach or to be more cost effective (which it does achieve), then we are missing out on the huge potential that the new technologies offer us. It is not a question of *converting* a face-to-face course to a distance learning version; it is a question of reevaluating how much further we can take the learners in being effective in their professional performance, and of designing a program of activities around that goal. This is where the paradigm shift lies. We can move from concentrating on achieving learning objectives to being more adventurous by attempting to achieve project implementation objectives, the ultimate reason for the "training" in the first place.

A needs-driven, just-in-time model of knowledge sharing like this can be used by development practitioners in government departments, development agencies, and NGOs as a way of doing business. This would help link capacity enhancement activities directly to reform and reconstruction programs, thereby ensuring their successful implementation. Even after project completion, the knowledge sharing can go on. By using the same communications tools as were used in the learning activities, the participants can form support networks as communities of practice, sharing their knowledge and issues on a continuing basis. The power of this type of peer learning is currently unappreciated by many training agencies, unlike technology vendors who, as part of their customer support, are setting up discussion forums on their Web sites, another form of communities of practice. This is peer learning at its best, and, as they are to a large extent self-moderated, they are inexpensive to support.

In such a demand-driven capacity enhancement program, the main players are in a client/service provider relationship. On the one hand, the client is a combination of the implementing agency of the development program itself (government department, NGO, or contractor) and the financier of the program, whether it is the government from its own funds, or a lending/aid agency. On the other, the service providers are the partners who make the knowledge-sharing activities happen. In the case of GDLN, this would be a partnership of the local GDLN center and other GDLN centers and knowledge institutes worldwide, wherever the expertise is residing. Together these parties would plan a series of activities that would bring the *right knowledge*, at the *right time*, to the *right people*. The activities would typically range from a series of knowledge sharing seminars, technical assistance consultancies delivered in a blend of face-to-face and distance learning fashion, to training courses specific to the needs of the implementing teams. Because this aims at team learning, and not merely at personal professional development alone, then different members of the teams would participate in different activities that would comple- ment each other in developing the project. An ideal learning plan for a development project would have a timeline for the duration of the project with intermediate milestones, but the detailed planning would only take place as the project rolled out. It is only as the project evolved that the learning needs would emerge, possibly as capacity road blocks to further progress. A learning intervention would then be organized to bring "just-in-time" knowledge to the problem. In this scenario, it is the project implementers that are setting the agenda, planning the activities, and seeking out the expertise. A network such as GDLN would be providing the enabling infrastruc- ture, the access and the support that these development clients required, and the individual cen- ters would be paid for their services out of project funds.

CONCLUSION

The right way forward will always be open to debate, but let me suggest a few initial ideas for dis- cussion on some steps and approaches that could be taken to realize the potential of the use of the new technologies for development impact:

- Focus programs on aid effectiveness, with outcome and impact objectives
- Include a learning plan/program into development projects
- Embed the learning activities into the operational implementation of development projects/ programs
- Apply what we know about adult learning and design programs appropriately
- Take learning design seriously
- Training does not ensure learning and learning does not have to involve training
- Knowledge sharing is not the same as instruction, so design appropriately
- Meet the learner before designing the learning program and design together
- Design for performance outcomes
- Evaluate outcomes and not just participant satisfaction and learning
- End the dichotomy between distance learning and face to face methods—adopt a blended approach for all activities
- Employ distance learning methods in technical assistance programs and advisory services

The future of technology is uncertain, but what is certain is that technology will be more and more a part of our lives, with more and more functionality, and it will be more and more avail- able. How it will affect our way of working and learning is also uncertain, but no doubt it will impact on us, and in a fundamental way. Now is the time to integrate its use into development programs, not as an add-on, but as a way of getting things done, cheaper, faster, and above all, better.

REFERENCES

Bardini, M. D. (1998). *Economics and business journalism: Kenya distance learning course.* (EDI Evaluation Studies No. ES99-19). Report to the World Bank. Retrieved from http://www.worldbank.org/wbi/evaluation/journalism.pdf

Knowles, M. S. (1970). *The modern practice of adult education: Andragogy versus pedagogy.* New York: Association Press.

MacDonald, D. (1999). Internal report to WBI Management on "Controlling Corruption" course.

Wolfensohn, J. D. (1998, June). [Videoconference] World Bank.

48

Learning in a Global Society

Jan Visser
Learning Development Institute

The development of distance education globally, particularly in the developing world, has largely been driven by the desire to overcome the shortcomings of established schooling practices. The literature of the period when distance education started to position itself as a serious alternative to, or complement of, school-based offerings would often contrast distance education—or, as it used to be called, "correspondence education," and, in some other cases, radio or TV education—with so-called "traditional" or "conventional" education (e.g., Edström, Erdos, & Prosser, 1970; Erdos, 1967; Faure et al., 1972; Perraton, 1976; Young, Perraton, Jenkins, & Dodds, 1980).

Various considerations motivated the emergence of distance education as a significant alternative. Chief among them was—and still is (e.g., Creed & Perraton, 2001)—the growing concern that a large proportion of the world's population remained deprived of opportunities to learn, while those same opportunities were commonly available to others.

At the same time there was the expectation that "new media" would usher in an era of until-then unimagined possibilities to overcome the barriers of the past. In an address to the State Department on August 20, 1971, Arthur C. Clarke expressed it this way: "The emerging countries of what is called the Third World may need rockets and satellites much more desperately than the advanced nations which built them. Swords into ploughshares is an obsolete metaphor; we can now turn missiles into blackboards" (Clarke, 1992, p. 208).

Hope and vision were accompanied by the desire to gather evidence in support of the claims that media, and the instructional design principles underlying their use, could indeed help to overcome the formidable obstacles faced by educational leaders and planners in developing countries. Most notable perhaps was a worldwide research project undertaken by the United Nations Educational, Scientific and Cultural Organization's (UNESCO) International Institute for Educational Planning in 1965 and 1966 under the leadership of Wilbur Schramm, resulting in the landmark publication of three volumes of *New Media in Action: Case Studies for Planners* and a companion volume, *The New Media: Memo to Educational Planners* (UNESCO, 1967a, 1967b). Other prominent sources reflecting the thinking of that time regarding the educational use of media are Schramm's (1977) *Big Media, Little Media*, Jamison and McAnany's (1978) *Radio for Education and Development*, and Jamison, Klees, and Wells's (1978) *The Costs of Educational Media: Guidelines for Planning and Evaluation*.

During the same period the instructional design field was coming of age with such classics as Gagné's *The Conditions of Learning* (1985) and Gagné and Briggs's *Principles of Instructional Design* (1974), giving confidence that the process of making people learn, and ensuring that their learning achievements would match their originally identified learning needs, could not only be controlled but also managed within a considerably wider range of parameters than those traditionally considered. Particularly, it became clear that such a process was not necessarily or exclusively dependent on the physical presence of a human facilitator.

The above factors taken together provided a powerful reason to search for the solution of the world's educational problems in settings beyond those of the conventional schooling practice. Naturally, it also raised questions about the quality of the contemplated alternatives as compared to the traditional practices they were supposed to replace or complement.

Two inadequacies of traditional education are usually highlighted in such sources as mentioned above. Then as well as now, traditional schooling systems cater to only a limited part of the audience they are supposed to serve. This results in great inequity globally regarding people's chances to become active participants in a world that is larger than their immediate environment. It led Julian Huxley, Executive Secretary of the Preparatory Commission for UNESCO in 1946, later UNESCO's first Director-General, to consider, "Where half the people of the world are denied the elementary freedom which consists in the ability to read and write, there lacks something of the basic unity and basic justice which the United Nations are pledged together to further" (UNESCO, 2000, p. 27). While Huxley recognized that various factors are responsible for such inequity, he saw what was then called "Fundamental Education" as essential to "the wider and fuller human understanding to which UNESCO is dedicated" (p. 27). The problem is far from over. According to current UNESCO statistics, nearly one in seven people in the world cannot read or write (Sharma, 2003). Moreover, a just-released report by the UNESCO Institute of Statistics (2006), combining the statistical data-gathering and analysis techniques of UNESCO and UNICEF, puts the number of children in the primary-school-age not going to school at 115 million, i.e., almost one in five of this age group worldwide. Both illiteracy and school exclusion affect females more than males.

However, access to learning opportunities was, and is, not the only problem. The other major shortcoming of the schooling system, recognized in at least part of the literature cited earlier (e.g., Faure et al., 1972; Young, Perraton, Jenkins, & Dodds, 1980), had and has to do with the schooling tradition itself, particularly the kind of learning it instills in students, the social consequences of expectations it generates, and the often poor relevance of what is being taught for those who learn and their surrounding development context.

The former of the two deficits constitutes a violation of the fundamental human right to education. That right is specified in Article 26 of the Universal Declaration of Human Rights. The World Education Report 2000 (UNESCO, 2000) gives ample coverage of how that right and its implications have been perceived and discussed since the Declaration was adopted and proclaimed by the General Assembly of the United Nations on December 10, 1948. The continuation of that debate and associated discourse is reflected in the current declared commitment by the international community to the Millennium Development Goals (MDG), adopted by the U.N. General Assembly in September 2000 (United Nations, 2005). While there are obvious advantages associated with benchmarking the kind of change intended by the MDG, making their degree of implementation measurable, some analysts, such as Amin (2006), argue that setting and adopting goals such as the MDG without engaging in deeper reflection on the causes of what is wrong and what must thus be done to make the world more just is an exercise in legitimizing the status quo of the dominant economic and political interests.

It is important for our discussion that the Universal Declaration of Human Rights links education to "the full development of the human personality and to the strengthening of respect for human rights and fundamental freedoms" (UNESCO, 2000, p. 16). Education, in the view of the Declaration, thus transcends the mere concern with the acquisition of particular skills and pieces of knowledge. Instead, it relates it to the ability to live in harmony with oneself, one's environment, and one's fellow human beings. Consequently, the deficit of the school system should not be interpreted solely in terms of the lack of opportunity to acquire such competencies as the ability to read and write, but rather in terms of how such, and other, abilities "promote understanding, tolerance and friendship among all nations, racial and religious groups, . . . and the maintenance of peace" (p. 16).

Insofar as distance education strives to overcome the shortcomings of the school systems, it should be judged by the above standards. The primary question to be asked is not how the development of distance education has improved access to and participation in education, and at what cost, but rather: Does distance education contribute to a better world? Put this way, the question also includes concerns about the second major area identified above, the one that motivated the distance education field to see itself as an opportunity not only to open up possibilities for learning to the as-yet unreached, but equally to do so in ways that would be responsive to questions about the purposes of education, the meaning of learning, and the critique of the existing schooling tradition.

MEANS OR END?

Article 26 of the Universal Declaration of Human Rights represents a rare instance in the development of international discourse about educational policy in which an unequivocal reference is made to the purposes of education beyond the scope of particular content concerns. It advances the perspective that education is not an end in itself, but rather a means towards how we, humans, collectively shape the ways in which we socially organize ourselves, live together, and share the resources of our planet. The terms in which that perspective is formulated reflect the post-World War II concerns of the time when the Declaration was drafted. The ensuing debate and subsequent international frameworks developed over the past half-century have consolidated, strengthened, and expanded the original vision of Article 26, allowing it to evolve and become responsive to currently felt global concerns. Sustainable development and poverty eradication are but two of the global concerns that were not explicitly expressed in the original formulation of Article 26, which are now felt to be essential for a stable and harmonious world order.

ARTICLE 26

1) Everyone has a right to education. Education shall be free, at least in the elementary and fundamental stages. Elementary education shall be compulsory. Technical and professional education shall be made generally available and higher education shall be equally accessible to all on the basis of merit.
2) Education shall be directed to the full development of the human personality and to the strengthening of respect for human rights and fundamental freedoms. It shall promote understanding, tolerance and friendship among all nations, racial or religious groups, and shall further the activities of the United Nations for the maintenance of peace.
3) Parents have a prior right to choose the kind of education that shall be given to their children.

From: Universal Declaration of Human Rights (1948; cited in UNESCO, 2000)

Particularly the last decade of the past century has seen heightened interest in discussing the purposes of education in the light of global issues and concerns. Those issues and concerns have to do with such matters as our fragile environment; the growth of the world population; our ability to interfere technologically and scientifically with who we are; the depletion of the world's resources; the advancement of peace, not as the mere absence of war, but as a culture, a set of values, attitudes, traditions, modes of behavior, and ways of life (United Nations, 1999); and the impact of pandemic diseases. An impressive range of world conferences—the World Education Report 2000 (UNESCO, 2000) mentions 15 of them, starting with the World Conference on Education for All in Jomtien, Thailand, in 1990 and ending with the World Science Conference in Budapest, Hungary, in 1999—has helped to put the crucial issues of our time on the agenda of the international community, while seeking to understand how education can contribute to addressing them. Two major UNESCO reports produced during the 1990s—*Education: The Treasure Within* (Delors et al., 1996) and *Our Creative Diversity* (Pérez de Cuéllar et al., 1996)—should be seen in the same light.

This renewed attention to the overriding purposes of education should come as no surprise. For the first time in several million years of hominid development, the human species faces challenges of a magnitude it has never had to deal with before. I have argued elsewhere (J. Visser, 2001), drawing also on the views of authors such as Koestler (1989/1967), Pais (1997), and Sakaiya (1991), how these challenges are part of a context of change patterns that are unique for our time and markedly different from those that characterized the human condition a mere couple of decades ago. They require human beings to be able to function in entirely unpredictable situations. Lederman (1999) thus calls for schools to

> look across all disciplines, across the knowledge base of the sciences, across the wisdom of the humanities, the verities and explorations of the arts, for the ingredients that will enable our students to continually interact with a world in change, with the imminence of changes bringing essentially unforeseeable consequences. (p. 3)

By extension, the same rationale applies to any alternative to the school, such as distance education systems put in place to overcome the shortcomings of the school. However, it would be a mistake to look at the school, and its alternatives, in isolation. Schooling is not the same as learning. Schooling plays a role, and it can play a much more useful and effective role if it were profoundly reconceptualized, but that role is limited and relative to the role played by other factors that condition the learning environment at large. To appreciate the relative importance of the schooling tradition—including how that tradition is reflected in the practice of distance education—as well as to critically do away with those elements of the tradition that violate the attainment of agreed purposes, we must first develop a more comprehensive picture of what learning is.

LEARNING: THE COMPREHENSIVE PICTURE

One of the greatest impediments to the development of a learning society is the difficulty of overcoming the preconceptions about learning with which we grow up (J. Visser & Y. L. Visser, 2000). The need to broaden our views of learning has been amply discussed in a series of transdisciplinary debates, promoted and conducted under the auspices of UNESCO and the Learning Development Institute since 1999 (J. Visser et al., 1999; Meaning of Learning Project, 2000).

Further insight can be derived through disciplined inquiry into learning as perceived by those who learn. Such inquiry typically focuses on the entire human being or on the activity of an entire collaborative entity in a cultural-historical perspective. It thus involves units of analysis whose order of magnitude by far transcends the habitual research perspective which tends to focus on learning tasks that are narrowly defined in scope and time and that may involve only very specific learning behaviors assumed to be undertaken by isolated individuals. (A similar point is made by Cole, 1991, regarding the need to redefine the unit of analysis in the study of socially shared cognitions.) Research such as referred to above was reported by Y. L. Visser and J. Visser (2000); by J. Visser, Y. L. Visser, Amirault, Genge, and Miller (2002); and by M. Visser and J. Visser (2003, October) in their analysis of so-called learning stories. That research focused on the perceptions about learning from the perspective of individuals. John-Steiner (2000) went beyond the individual level, making the collaborative team or partnership the unit of analysis, in her study of creative collaboration. We learn from all the above studies that meaningful learning requires a focus on

- the development of felt ownership of knowledge;
- the emotional integration of any particular learning experience in an individual's perceived lifespan development;
- the generative nature of learning;
- the real-life context as the natural habitat for learning;
- the interaction with the learning of others as a basis for one's own learning;
- the power of learning to turn negative self-perceptions into positive ones;
- persistence as a strategy to manage life's challenges;
- "the balance between individuality and social connectedness" (Feldman, 2000).

The latter issue is particularly relevant in connection with the global concerns discussed in this chapter. It calls us to look beyond the content of education and ask questions about how we learn. Meaningful learning was found to be particularly facilitated when initially negative conditions could be transformed into positive challenges; when role models were present or emotionally significant support was available in the environment of the learner; or when there were opportunities for independent exploration of one's learning and metacognition.

CHALLENGES AHEAD

The prevailing focus in the rhetoric of distance education has for a long time been on such issues as cost-effectiveness, economies of scale, and parity of esteem, all of them defined with reference to the traditional school context. This has left the thinking about distance education in the fold of the dominant classroom model. Despite the advent of powerful new technologies and the increasing realization that the problems of today are essentially different from yesterday's problems, there is a disturbing lack of imagination in how discourse and practice remain locked up in the conceptions of the past. The abundant use of such terms as "online classroom" and "virtual school" is but one expression of how powerful a place the ideas of school and classroom continue to occupy in our language, and thus our thought processes. Even when new terms are introduced, such as *e-learning*, the reality behind them is often as sadly representative of the unaltered past— cast for the occasion in new molds—as the choice of the term itself is testimony to the absence of creative thinking.

Simonson (1999) calls for strategies that provide "different but equivalent learning experiences" (p. 29) to learners in face-to-face classes and in online classrooms. This so-called equivalency theory, while recognizing the differences in instructional contexts between the two modalities concerned, may do little to promote a fundamental rethinking of what goes on inside the learning space, whether virtual or real; the implicit assumption being that the face-to-face classroom is the norm and that equivalency rather than improvement should be sought.

Contrasting with the above is the sense of critical appreciation of the state of distance education in the world, emanated from a group of 23 experts from around the globe, convened by UNESCO, at a meeting in Karlsruhe, Germany. One of the recommendations made by that group states:

> Now that distance education has reached its desired level of recognition and esteem *vis-à-vis* traditional educational alternatives, time has come for it to take a critical look at itself, asking questions about how existing experience fits in with the requirements of and opportunities inherent in present day society and how it reflects the current state of knowledge about how people learn. It is recommended that such a critical attitude drive any future development in the field of distance education in UNESCO and its Member States. (UNESCO, 2001, p. 4)

The group framed its recommendation with particular reference to "the evolving notions of a learning society and of lifespan human development" (p. 4). It furthermore recommended that distance education be seen as "just one modality—or set of modalities—among many others that together shape the learning environment, which is multi-modal and aware of multiple dimensions of human intelligence, at the cognitive, meta-cognitive and affective level" (p. 4). In connection with the above recommendation, the group devoted particular attention to the opportunities inherent in the currently available technologies. Market forces, rather than considerations about how and why people learn, determine that such technologies will be used. In the absence of clear thinking, their use will likely result in the replication of past practices by new means. At best, this means that nothing changes; at worst, it means that with accelerated speed, and more forcefully than ever, bad practices will be consolidated and reinforced. The group thus recommended the inclusion of experts in communication and information technology in collaborative multidisciplinary partnerships involved in the reconceptualization of learning. Without doing so, it argued,

> there is the great risk that the use of improved technology will only reinforce and consolidate practices that, though unfortunately often part and parcel of established educational practice, have long been recognized to be counter to the development of humanity's critical and creative capacity and of the human ability to confront the complex problems of today's world. (p. 6)

The latter observation resonates with Salomon's (2000) criticism of "technocentrism," which "totally ignores some crucial social and human factors" (p. 4). He observes that, without taking these factors into account, "virtual distance learning . . . is in danger of yielding virtual results" (p. 4). Salomon thus urges an emphasis on two things: *tutelage* and *community of learners*. The former aspect has received attention in L. Visser's (1998) work on affective communication (see also L. Visser, Plomp, Amirault, & Kuiper, 2002) and in Gunawardena's (1995) work on social presence. The latter aspect has been emphasized by the group of people who gathered initially around the ideas promoted by UNESCO's Learning Without Frontiers (2000) program and who later converged around the vision of the Learning Development Institute (2001). It inspires particularly the dialogue originated by the Learning Development Institute (2005) concerning the roles and expectations of learners in a changing learning landscape.

COMPLEX COGNITION FOR A COMPLEX WORLD

We must develop a vision of learning that is ubiquitous, which is unrelated to conditions such as age, time, space, and circumstance of learning individuals; which manifests itself not only in the behavior of individuals but at diverse levels of complex organization; and that, in whatever context it takes place, does so as part of a pattern of interrelated learning events occurring in what can best be called a "learning landscape." Cognition is, and has always been, an ecological phenomenon. Being an ecological phenomenon, it is also evolutionary. The two notions are interrelated, as Levin (1999) points out: "Ecological interactions take place within an evolutionary context and in turn shape the ongoing evolutionary process" (p. 46).

Invoking terms such as *ecology* and *evolution* is not an exercise in inventing sophisticated metaphors. Webster's Third New International Dictionary (Gove, 1993) defines ecology as a "branch of science concerned with the *interrelationship* of organisms and their environments, esp. as manifested by natural cycles and rhythms, *community development* and structure, interaction between different kinds of organisms, geographic distribution and population alterations." (My emphasis)

The origin of the word is, according to the Encyclopaedia Britannica (1999), the Greek "*oikos*," which means "household, home, or place to live." These descriptions apply as much to the world of learning entities as they apply to the world of living organisms. This should come as no surprise. The capability to make sense of regularity among randomness—which, according to Gell-Mann (1994), is the essence of learning—is key to any life-form's chances of survival in an environment populated with other forms of life.

My use of the term *learning landscape* may be taken to be metaphorical. Like the real landscape, the learning landscape is the result of, on the one hand, the natural—that is, ecological—interplay of different learning entities seeking to establish themselves in the midst of others and, on the other hand, of the consciously planned action on the part of some actors to reshape and adjust what nature tends to produce. I use the term landscape deliberately because of its connotations, some of which are more poetic than operational. This, then, brings into play, in addition to the usual parameters of effectiveness and efficiency of the learning environment, also its aesthetic and ethical qualities. The planners and leaders whose actions impact the learning landscape may well want to consider this extended meaning of the metaphor and look for beauty and harmony in the learning landscape as a major indicator for the quality of the ecology of cognition. It is probably no exaggeration to say that, so far, the work of governmental educational planning agencies, as well as related entrepreneurial and institutional efforts, to create the infrastructural conditions for the facilitation of learning leaves considerable room for improvement in terms of the need to be environmentally aware of what else happens in the learning landscape. This observation obviously includes much of the distance education effort as well.

The term "learning landscape" reflects the idea of "complex cognition," a concept proposed by the author at a Santa Fe Institute seminar (J. Visser, 2000). Cognition is a complex phenomenon in the sense that it evolves according to the laws that govern the behavior of complex adaptive systems. The conditions that underlie such behavior are well known (see, e.g., Gell-Mann, 1995; Holland, 1995). The stock market, the weather, and biological systems are examples of it.

The notion of distributed cognitions approximates the idea of "complex cognition." However, as Salomon (1993) points out, the meaning attributed to the term *distributed cognitions* varies considerably, depending on the theoretical perspective adopted by different researchers. On one end of the spectrum there is the view that "cognition *in general* should be . . . conceived as principally distributed," the "proper unit of psychological analysis . . . [being] the joint . . . socially mediated action in a cultural context" (p. xv). This view contrasts with the common perception that cognitions reside inside individuals' heads. On the other end of the spectrum one finds the conception that "'solo' and distributed cognitions are still distinguished from each other and are taken to be in an interdependent dynamic interaction" (p. xvi). This juxtaposition of views is resolved in the concept of complex cognition, which makes the distinction irrelevant, integrating the diverse points of view in a single notion. Cognition is individually owned and socially shared at the same time.

DISTANCE EDUCATION IN THE PERSPECTIVE OF GLOBAL ISSUES AND CONCERNS

The global issues and concerns referred to in this chapter—the profound questions about how we live together on our tiny planet and share its resources, sustaining life as we came to know it and became conscious of our place in it; playing our role in how, in time, perhaps, a next phase in its evolution may emerge—find no response in our designed learning systems. Yet, most people share these concerns and feel they can no longer be dismissed or simply be seen as an afterthought of our more specific attempts at developing human capacity. The history of how the educational establishment, including the distance education variety of it, has failed to address such most-crucial challenges as the ones inherent in Article 26 of the Universal Declaration of Human Rights is proof of the fruitlessness of attempts to use our traditional learning systems in an isolated fashion while dealing with global issues and concerns. Such attempts must be undertaken, as urged in the earlier-quoted UNESCO report, in a wider framework, namely that of the learning society and of lifespan human development, taking full account of the convoluted ways in which humans learn (UNESCO, 2001).

The important question then is: How can distance education contribute to improving the ecological coherence of the learning environment so that it will allow meaningful learning to evolve in response to the crucial global issues and concerns that mark the beginning of the third millennium? The question branches off in a variety of directions, some of which will be highlighted below. To bring some order in the observations and conclusions that follow, I shall deal with them, respectively, in four levels: (a) society at large, (b) collaboration among institutions and organizations within society, (c) the organization of specific institutions, and (d) the learning process.

Implications at the Societal Level

At the level of society at large, the responsibility for the creation of the conditions of learning is a distributed one. This view contrasts with the common idea that such a responsibility resides solely or mostly with ministries or departments of education. Obviously, the latter idea comes from the misconception that education and learning are one and the same thing. It is important to make a distinction between the two and to look at the instructional landscape as a sub-landscape of the learning landscape.

Instruction is—or should be—a designed way to facilitate learning for specifically defined purposes. The preoccupation with instruction results in a wide variety of instructional opportunities. Within the conception, advocated in this chapter, that society at large is responsible for the totality of learning that goes on within it, the various instructional opportunities should be aware of each other and interconnected with each other. They form, as an organically interlinked whole of designed opportunities to learn, the instructional landscape.

The instructional landscape does not stand on its own. Many other sub-landscapes join together to make up the learning landscape, in a way similar to how Appadurai (1990) describes the dynamics of global diversity in terms of different "scapes." Other sub-landscapes included in the learning landscape are, for instance, the media landscape (see Allen, Otto, & Hoffman, 2004) and the socio-cultural organization landscape, of which the family is part. A truly ecologically functioning learning landscape will be characterized by the smooth integration among all the various sub-landscapes—together with their subordinated sub-landscapes—that compose the learning landscape.

Because of its potential flexibility and openness, the distance education modality can play an important role in bringing about ecological integration within the learning landscape. Doing so would be a more laudable goal—and a truly more exciting challenge—than the current emphasis on replication, for ever-expanding markets, of outdated learning structures by new means.

Implications at the Level of Interinstitutional Collaboration

While in some parts of the world there may seem to be no limit to the resources that can be brought to bear on addressing the problems of human learning, whosoever takes the trouble to look at the world at large will soon discover that there is an important challenge in creating sustainable solutions that benefit large numbers of people. Sustainability in this context means that the cost of what we do at a particular time will not be charged to a future we are unable or unwilling to visualize or take responsibility for. It should also be noted that solutions that benefit many people do not necessarily have to rely on mass-produced and mass-delivered options.

There is enormous potential for promoting and facilitating learning in the networking of those who have a passion to learn (e.g., Rossman, 1993, 2002). This applies to both individuals and institutions. Anything that detracts from the likelihood that interinstitutional collaboration would occur, such as the artificial opposition between learning at a distance and in the face-to-face mode, is thus counter to exploring this potential.

The tendencies of some institutional environments towards expansion (e.g., Daniel, 2000), sometimes through the merger with smaller entities, may seem to contribute to creating larger networks. However, there is the risk that the strong presence of large conglomerates reduces the diversity of the learning landscape, thus taking away one of the most powerful resources in the learning habitat. To the extent that the learning landscape functions in ecologically sound ways—in other words, to the extent that diverse sub-landscapes are the active ingredients of the learning landscape—such homogenizing forces may be counteracted by heterogeneous dialogues resulting from interaction with different ideological and cultural traditions (Appadurai, 1990).

There may, as yet, not be enough evidence to draw definite conclusions about how the various tendencies towards globalization will affect diversity. It would be prudent, though, to keep an open eye towards what may be happening and to assess such possible impact on an ongoing basis. It is equally prudent to encourage ways of networking that deliberately thrive on diversity (i.e., multi-nodal collaboration among institutions that have a distinct identity) as opposed to building networks that are run out of a central node (e.g., Semenov, 2005).

Against the backdrop of the above cautionary remarks, I posit that increased networking around the globe is an important condition for the formation of dynamic learning communities that are sufficiently global in outlook to become a basis for learning to live together (Delors et al., 1996) with the global concerns of our time. For this to be possible, collaborating institutions must once again become what they used to be: universities, places of inquiry not limited by the boundaries of bureaucracy and traditional divisions among disciplines. UNESCO's UNITWIN/UNESCO Chairs (n.d.) program is an interesting example in the above regard.

Implications at the Institutional/Organizational Level

The closing observation in the previous paragraph is also the first recommendation under the present heading. The model of monolithic, bureaucratized, and compartmentalized institutions dominates the institutional heritage of the 19th and 20th centuries. Such institutions now find themselves needing to become players in a networked environment, often having great difficulty responding adequately to the challenge.

In using the term *universities* above, I do not intend to restrict my considerations to higher-education institutions. The connection between higher education and higher learning (i.e., learning at a higher level of metacognitive awareness and capability) is rather weak, whence the meaning of the adjective "higher" in higher education seems to have little relevance as a qualifying concept for the kind of learning that is promoted by higher-education institutions.

To play an effective role in shaping the increasingly networked learning landscape of the 21st century, institutions whose mission is to promote and facilitate learning must enhance their ability to interact constructively with their changing environment. In terms of the redefinition of learning called for in this chapter (see also J. Visser, 2001), this means that such institutions must conceive of themselves as learning organizations. The literature in this area is vast and so well known that there is hardly a need to mention such names as Senge (1990); Argyris (1993); Senge, Kleiner, Roberts, Ross, and Smith (1994); Marquardt (1996); or Hesselbein, Goldsmith, and Beckhard, (1997).

The change of attitude implied in becoming a learning organization should go hand-in-hand with the development of systemic awareness and abilities in the institution, both in terms of its internal processes and with regard to its role vis-à-vis other institutions and the learning landscape at large. It must equally focus on the profoundly human (as contrasted with bureaucratic) mission inherent in fostering learning, a particularly acute challenge for institutions whose traditions are rooted in the philosophy of the industrial era (Peters, 1994). Clearly, this is a change that affects everyone in the institution: students, faculty, administrative staff, and management.

Implications at the Learning Process Level

The most important implications are at the level of the learning process. Very little impact on our ability to deal with global issues and concerns is likely to result from our continued preoccupation with knowledge as a thing, as opposed to knowledge as a process. To reorient the learning process away from its habitual focus on acquiring isolated pieces of knowledge, the overriding vision in learning must be on problems (e.g., Jonassen, 1994; Hmelo, 1998; Bransford, Brown, & Cocking, 2000 [particularly Ch. 2]), transdisciplinarity (Nicolescu, 1999, 2002), and consilience (Wilson, 1998).

Reintroducing this overriding concern in our conscious efforts to promote the development of human learning does not mean a radical doing-away with everything that has to do with disciplines, content-based curricula, or even rote learning of particular facts. There is abundant evidence to support the idea that such things have their relative usefulness. However, that usefulness gets reduced when it is the only focus in learning and when it cannot be embedded in a larger frame of relevance.

The overall focus on problems, transdisciplinarity, and consilience is a vital condition, also, for learning to become, once again, dialogue. It is equally a prerequisite for the development of critical thinking, creativity, and the socialization and contextualization of cognition. Moreover, placing students, and those with whom they learn, eye-to-eye with the real world of whole problems and interconnected knowledge and associated emotions regarding those problems, will be most beneficial to bring back yet another important aspect of our humanity in the learning process: the fact that we function with our entire bodies, not just the neocortex.

The challenge to the distance education community in considering the above implications lies in the need to move past the customary rhetoric of cost-effectiveness and economies of scale. Such notions are based on the idea that the existing principles of instruction are adequate and merely require the redesign of the processes of their application to benefit larger audiences in affordable ways. I have tried to argue that the problems with the development of learning in the context of today's challenges are much more complex and fundamental. They require the field to be reinvented. The difficulty in meeting that challenge is psychological rather than substantial. The problems are known and the tools are there.

Note: An expanded version of this chapter is available at http://www.learndev.org/dl/DEhdbk2ndEd.pdf

REFERENCES

Allen, B. S., Otto, R. G., & Hoffman, B. (1996). Media as lived environments: The ecological psychology of educational technology. In D. H. Jonassen (Ed.), *Handbook of research for educational communications and technology* (2nd ed., pp. 215–241). Mahwah, NJ: Lawrence Erlbaum Associates.

Amin, S. (2006). The Millennium Development Goals: A Critique from the South. *Monthly Review, 57*(10). Retrieved January 29, 2007, from http://monthlyreview.org/0306amin.htm

Appadurai, A. (1990). Disjuncture and difference in the global cultural economy. *Public Culture, 2*(2), 1–24.

Argyris, C. (1993). *On organizational learning.* Cambridge, MA: Blackwell.

Bransford, J. D., Brown, A. L., & Cocking, R. R. (Eds.) (2000). *How people learn: Brain, mind, experience, and school* [Report of the Committee on Developments in the Science of Learning, Commission on Behavioral and Social Sciences and Education, National Research Council] Washington, DC: National Academy Press.

Clarke, A. C. (1992). *How the world was one: Beyond the global village.* London: Victor Gollancz Ltd.

Cole, M. (1991). Conclusion. In L. B. Resnick, J. M. Levine, & S. D. Teasley (Eds.), *Perspectives on socially shared cognition* (pp. 398–417). Washington, DC: American Psychological Association.

Creed, C., & Perraton, H. (2001). *Distance education in the E-9 countries: The development and future of distance education programmes in the nine high-population countries.* Paris: UNESCO.

Daniel, J. (2000, July). *The university of the future and the future of universities.* Paper presented at the Improving University Learning and Teaching 25th International Conference, Frankfurt, Germany.

Delors, J., Al Mufti, I., Amagi, I., Carneiro, R., Chung, F., Geremek, B., et al. (1996). *Learning: The treasure within* [Report to UNESCO of the International Commission on Education for the Twenty-first Century]. Paris: UNESCO.

Edström, L. O., Erdos, R., & Prosser, R. (Eds.) (1970). *Mass education: Studies in adult education and teaching by correspondence in some developing countries.* Stockholm, Sweden: The Dag Hammerskjöld Foundation.

Encyclopaedia Britannica (1999). *Encyclopaedia Britannica CD 99: Knowledge for the information age. Multimedia edition,* [CD-ROM]. Chicago: Encyclopedia britanica, Inc.

Erdos, R. F. (1967). *Teaching by correspondence* [a UNESCO Source Book]. London; Paris: Longmans, Green & Co Limited; UNESCO.

Faure, E., Herrera, F., Kaddoura, A-R., Lopes, H., Petrovsky, A. V., Rahnema, M., et al. (1972). *Learning to be: The world of education today and tomorrow* [Report to UNESCO of the International Commission on the Development of Education]. Paris: UNESCO.

Feldman, D. H. (2000). Foreword. In V. John-Steiner, *Creative collaboration* (pp. ix–xiii). New York: Oxford University Press.

Gagné, R. M. (1965/1985). *The conditions of learning* (1st/4th ed.). New York,: Holt, Rinehart and Winston.

Gagné, R. M., & Briggs, L. J. (1974). *Principles of instructional design*. New York: Holt, Rinehart and Winston.

Gell-Mann, M. (1994). *The quark and the jaguar: Adventures in the simple and the complex*. New York: W. H. Freeman and Company.

Gell-Mann, M. (1995). What is complexity? *Complexity, 1*(1), 16–19.

Gove, P. B. (Ed.) (1993). *Webster's third new international dictionary of the English language* (unabridged edition). Springfield, MA: Merriam-Webster, Inc.

Gunawardena, C. N. (1995). Social presence theory and implications for interaction and collaborative learning in computer conferences. *International Journal of Educational Telecommunications, 1*(2/3), 147–166.

Hesselbein, F., Goldsmith, M., & Beckhard, R. (Eds.) (1997). *The organization of the future*. San Francisco: Jossey-Bass.

Hmelo, C. E. (1998). Problem-based learning: Effects on the early acquisition of cognitive skill in medicine. *The Journal of the Learning Sciences, 7*(2), 173–208.

Holland, J. H. (1995). Can there be a unified theory of complex adaptive systems? In H. J. Morowitz & J. L. Singer (Eds.), *The mind, the brain, and complex adaptive systems* (pp. 45–50). Reading, MA: Addison-Wesley.

Jamison, D. T., & McAnany, E. G. (1978). *Radio for education and development*. Beverly Hills, CA: Sage.

Jamison, D. T., Klees, S. J., & Wells, S. J. (1978). *The costs of educational media: Guidelines for planning and evaluation*. Beverly Hills, CA: Sage.

John-Steiner, V. (2000). *Creative collaboration*. New York: Oxford University Press.

Jonassen, D. (1994). Instructional design models for well-structured and ill-structured problem solving learning outcomes. *Educational Technology Research & Development, 45*(1), 65–94.

Koestler, A. (1989). *The ghost in the machine*, London: The Penguin Group. (Original work published 1967)

Learning Development Institute. (2001). Web site of the Learning Development Institute. Retrieved January 29, 2007, from http://www.learndev.org

Learning Development Institute. (2005). *Learners in a changing learning landscape: New roles and expectations*—A dialogue motivated by an ibstpi research project. Retrieved January 29, 2007, from http://www.learndev.org/ibstpi-AECT2005.html

Learning Without Frontiers. (2000). Web site of UNESCO's Learning Without Frontiers program. Retrieved January 29, 2007, from http://www.unesco.org/education/lwf/

Lederman, L. M. (1999, April). On the threshold of the 21st century: Comments on science education. In J. Visser (Chair), *Overcoming the underdevelopment of learning*. Symposium conducted at the Annual Meeting of the American Educational Research Association, Montreal, Quebec, Canada.

Levin, S. A. (1999). *Fragile dominion: Complexity and the commons*. Reading, MA: Perseus Books.

Marquardt, M. J. (1996). *Building the learning organization*. New York: McGraw Hill.

Meaning of Learning Project (2000, October). In J. Visser (Chair) *In search of the meaning of learning*. Symposium conducted at the International Conference of the Association for Educational Communications and Technology, Denver, CO. Retrieved January 29, 2007, from http://www.learndev.org/MoL.html

Nicolescu, B. (1999, April). The transdisciplinary evolution of learning. In J. Visser (Chair), *Overcoming the underdevelopment of learning. Symposium conducted* at the Annual Meeting of the American Educational Research Association, Montreal, Quebec, Canada.

Nicolescu, B. (2002). *Manifesto of transdisciplinarity*. New York: SUNY Press.

Pais, A. (1997). *A tale of two continents: A physicist's life in a turbulent world*. Princeton, NJ: Princeton University Press.

Pérez de Cuéllar, J., Arizpe, L., Fall, Y. K., Furgler, K., Furtado, C., Goulandris, N., et al. (1996). *Our creative diversity* [Report of the World Commission on Culture and Development]. Paris: UNESCO.

Perraton, H. (Ed.) (1976). *Food from learning: The International Extension College 1971–1976*. Cambridge, UK: International Extension College.

Peters, O. (1994). Distance education and industrial production: A comparative interpretation in outline (1967). In D. Keegan (Ed.), *The industrialization of teaching and learning* (pp. 107–127). London: Routledge.

Rossman, P. (1993). The emerging worldwide electronic university: Information age global education. Westport, CT: Praeger.

Rossman, P. (2002). *Transforming human society: The future of higher (lifelong) education: A vision of job training and education for everyone on the planet during this century, planning for all worldwide, a holistic view.* Retrieved January 29, 2007, from http://ecolecon.missouri.edu/globalresearch/index.html

Sakaiya, T. (1991). *The knowledge-value revolution, or, a history of the future* (translated by G. Fields and W. Marsh). Tokyo: Kodansha International. (Original work published 1985)

Salomon, G. (Ed.) (1993). *Distributed cognitions: Psychological and educational considerations.* Cambridge, UK: Cambridge University Press.

Salomon, G. (2000, June). *It's not just the tool, but the educational rationale that counts.* Invited keynote address at the 2000 Ed-Media Meeting, Montreal, Quebec, Canada.

Schramm, W. (1977). *Big media, little media: Tools and technologies for instruction.* Beverly Hills, CA: Sage.

Semenov, A. (2005). *Information and communication technologies in schools—A handbook for teachers, or How ICT can create new, open learning environments.* Paris: UNESCO.

Senge, P. M. (1990). *The fifth discipline: The art and practice of the learning organization.* New York: Doubleday.

Senge, P. M., Kleiner, A., Roberts, C., Ross, R. B., & Smith, B. J. (1994). *The fifth discipline fieldbook: Strategies and tools for building a learning organization.* New York: Doubleday.

Simonson, M. (2000). Making decisions: The use of electronic technology in online classrooms. *Principles of Effective Teaching in the Online Classroom: New Directions for Teaching and Learning, 84,* 29–34.

Sharma, Y. (2003). Literacy: a global problem-Written out of the script. *The New Courrier,* (April 2003). Retrieved January 29, 2007, from http://portal.unesco.org/en/ev.php@URL_ID=10513&URL_DO=DO_TOPIC&URL_SECTION=201.html

UNESCO (2000). *World education report 2000—The right to education: Towards education for all throughout life.* Paris: Author. Retrieved January 29, 2007, from http://www.unesco.org/education/information/wer/PDFeng/wholewer.PDF

UNESCO (2001, February). *Report on the UNESCO programme—Learntec 2001.* Report of the international expert meeting held in conjunction with Learntec 2001 in Karlsruhe, Germany.

UNESCO (2006). *Children out of school: Measuring exclusion from primary education.* Montreal, Quebec, Canada: Author.

UNESCO (1967a). *New educational media in action: Case studies for planners—I, II, & III.* Paris: Author.

UNESCO (1967b). *The new media: Memo to educational planners.* Paris: Author.

United Nations (1999). *Declaration and programme of action on a culture of peace,* General Assembly Resolution (A/53/243). New York: Author.

United Nations (2005). *UN Millennium Development Goals.* Retrieved January 29, 2007, from http://www.un.org/millenniumgoals/index.html

UNITWIN/UNESCO Chairs (n.d.) Web site of UNESCO's UNITWIN/UNESCO Chairs program. Retrieved January 29, 2007, from http://www.unesco.org/education/educprog/unitwin/index.html

Visser, J. (2000, November). *Learning in the perspective of complexity.* Paper presented at the Santa Fe Institute, Santa Fe, NM.

Visser, J. (2001). Integrity, completeness and comprehensiveness of the learning environment: Meeting the basic learning needs of all throughout life. In D. N. Aspin, J. D. Chapman, M. J. Hatton, & Y. Sawano (Eds.), *International Handbook of Lifelong Learning* (pp. 447–472). Dordrecht, The Netherlands: Kluwer Academic Publishers.

Visser, J., Berenfeld, B., Burnett, R., Diarra, C. M., Driscoll, M. P., Lederman, et al. (1999, April). *Overcoming the underdevelopment of learning.* Symposium conducted at the Annual Meeting of the American Educational Research Association, Montreal, Quebec, Canada.

Visser, J., & Visser, Y. L. (2000, October). On the difficulty of changing our perceptions about such things as learning. In J. Visser (Chair), *In Search of the Meaning of Learning. Symposium conducted* at the International Conference of the Association for Educational Communications and Technology, Denver, CO.

Visser, J., Visser, Y. L., Amirault, R. J., Genge, C. D., & Miller, V. (2002, April 1–5). *Second order learning stories*. Paper presented by at the annual meeting of the American Educational Research Association, New Orleans, LA.

Visser, L. (1998). *The development of motivational communication in distance education support*. Unpublished doctoral dissertation, University of Twente, Enschede, The Netherlands.

Visser, L., Plomp, T., Amirault, R., & Kuiper, W. (2002). Motivating Students at a Distance: The Case of an International Audience. *Educational Technology Research & Development, 50*(2), 94–110.

Visser, M., & Visser, J. (2003, October). *"We closed our books and put them away." Learning stories from Mozambique—A critical reflection on communicating about the reality and future of learning*. Paper presented at the International Conference of the Association for Educational Communications and Technology, Anaheim, CA.

Visser, Y. L., & Visser, J. (2000, October). *The learning stories project*. Paper presented at the International Conference of the Association for Educational Communications and Technology, Denver, CO.

Wislon, E. O. (1998). *Consilience: The unity of knowledge*. New York: Alfred A. Knopf.

Young, M., Perraton, H., Jenkins, J., & Dodds, T. (1980). *Distance teaching for the third world: The lion and the clockwork mouse*. London: Routledge/Kegan Paul Ltd.

49

Globalization and Emerging Technologies

Terry Evans
Deakin University, Australia

Daryl Nation
Monash University, Australia

The computer and communications media bring to the doorstep of distance education a range of matters which were either nonexistent before or were at least of minor significance. In essence, these matters can be considered under the rubric of globalization.

Evans (1997) considered the interrelationships between globalization and distance education, and he argued for a broad understanding of the former term, thus

> Globalisation implies that most people, if not all, are connected more or less contemporaneously with distant events, sometimes whether they like it or not. This "time-space compression" (Giddens, 1994, p. 7) is not just limited to communications and transport, but also to economic activity. The social and cultural implications . . . are intimately connected. (p. 18)

Many would argue that the human experience is altering fundamentally within a globalizing world—that is, a world where social, economic, cultural, and political activity is becoming more integrated and less demarcated by distances, national borders, and cultures. It is doing so not just because of the speed and interactivity of new communications media, but also because of the fusion of cultural conditions. For some, in this latter cultural sense, globalization is substantially Americanization, in that the dominant influence via the Internet is from the United States; however, this is an oversimplification in that prior to the Internet, other media also often reflected a significant American flavor (film, for example), and also another predominantly English language nation, the United Kingdom, has been globally influential through other media (i.e., popular music, television, and newspapers). Certainly, it seems that the domination of English as the global language has been further strengthened via the Internet and the Web (Crystal, 1997, 2001). As we shall illustrate, these matters are important for theory, practice and research in distance education.

Toward these ends, Edwards (1994), using Robertson's (1992) work, considered the impact of globalization on forms of distance education. He argued that it is not so much the fact of global connections that is important, "but (rather) in the contemporary world there is an intensification of the processes and the awareness of the globe as a single environment" (p. 10).

The tensions between the globalizing forces of contemporary life and the ways in which people live and learn (Giddens, 1991a, 1991b) can have major implications for open and distance education theory and practice, and for (distance) learners' self-identities (Evans 1989, 1995a, 1995b). Perhaps the best example of this is found in the interrelationships between the developed and the developing world where the possibilities and consequences of the new forms of distance education seem most alluring and yet most threatening. It is first worth noting that the term "developed nation" is misleading. "It conveys," as Evans (2003) suggested, "a sense that the 'developing' is over and that the countries in question have reached a stage of being developed: there is no further room to improve" (p. 31). Contrarily, a fundamental characteristic of a "developed country" is that it is speeding simultaneously along various lines of development; it is actually a *compulsively developing* one, one which values change and progress as central in its national culture (original emphasis). It is as if the so-called "developed nations" actually have a "compulsive development culture."

Likewise, compared to developed nations, developing nations are not usually developing at the same pace and do not possess a "compulsive development culture." Indeed, it could be argued that without some miraculous or equally profound progress, a developing nation is unlikely even to keep pace with the speed of development in the developed world. It has often been considered that appropriate forms of distance education may be able to assist developing nations to leapfrog some developmental stages by taking developed world educational programs and inserting them "in-country." In this way, the learners benefit from a standard of program that their own nation's educational infrastructure cannot provide. There are examples where this has been of general benefit (Perraton, 1993, 2000); however, as Evans (1997) noted, there is a series of "access versus invasion" dilemmas to be broached, especially when distance education is facilitated by the new educational technologies. For example, Papua New Guinea (PNG) is a developing nation that has had a longstanding involvement with distance education at both the school and higher education levels. It has used distance education in an attempt to deal with not only the serious needs for education in the country, but also to cope with the poor communications, isolation, and remoteness of many of the communities involved. As Guy (1991, 1997) commented, the access to developed world distance education courses is not without its invasive consequences, especially in a nation which is founded on over 800 language and cultural groups; however, the current PNG government is not recoiling from distance education, but rather sees the new educational technologies as enabling access to education to be provided in even the remotest PNG communities where no electricity, telephone, roads, or airstrips exist. The answer is seen to rest on solar electricity, computers, and satellite communications to enable people to access a world of (distance) education.

The rhetoric of globalization abounds in educational contexts today. The rhetoricians address the two main platforms of educational endeavor: the pedagogical and the curricular. At the pedagogical level, educators are encouraged to see their practices as being mediated, usually through electronic communications, along global lines. It is said that communications media, both directly and indirectly, are able take their teaching to learners around the globe, or conversely, they may use global resources via these media, to foster or enhance their own teaching. At the curricular level, it is said that no longer can the teacher just teach about the local, but rather global matters must be covered in order that the learners become knowledgeable global citizens. The rhetoric of globalization has its parallels (if not origins) in the transnational corporations, governments, governmental agencies (especially trans-governmental agencies such as UNESCO and the World Bank), and nongovernmental organizations. Much of the rhetoric is underpinned by the arguments and values of economic rationalism, whereby the worth of individuals, products, and services is determined by their economic value in the (increasingly global) marketplace; however, the consequences for the languages, cultures, and communities involved are difficult to predict other than that they are likely to be profound, and at least in some respects, deleterious.

Developed nations face their own dilemmas concerning the globalizing forces of distance education. There is a reflexiveness embedded in the globalizing forces of (distance) education. As the PNG example illustrates, distance education is not only affected by globalization, but it also operates as a globalizing entity in itself, and in so doing, adds its own particular influences. As we have argued previously (Evans & Nation, 1996, pp. 163–165), this is a version of what might be called the "global-local" tension within globalization, which operates through to the level of the individual person. As Giddens (1994) made clear, the "intensified reflexivity" of globalization creates the conditions for "a world of clever people" where "individuals more or less have to engage with the wider world if they are to survive in it. Information produced by specialists (including scientific knowledge) can no longer be wholly confined to specific groups, but becomes routinely interpreted and acted on by lay individuals in the course of everyday actions" (p. 7). "Clever people" need to be able to read, understand, analyze, and act locally on the basis of their learning:

> Not only does this say something about the need for high levels of education for the population, but it implies that the curricula involved need to reflect both global and local needs. We can also infer that, due to the reflexive, and therefore dynamic, nature of globalization, people need to engage in lifelong education in order to participate fully in social life. (Evans & Nation, 1996, p. 164)

In many respects, one might expect that the advent of the new educational technologies has enabled distance education to enter a new phase and become an even more powerful area of theory, practice and research; however, just as globalization operates reflexively between the local and the global, and just as the "access" to distance education can be an "invasion" for developing nation, so the new educational technologies present new possibilities for distance education. But also, as we argue below, they sow the seeds of the demise of distance education as a field of research, theory and practice.

WHITHER DISTANCE EDUCATION?

In some respects, distance education is a relatively recent area of educational research, theory, and practice. As was previously noted, its name was formalized in the 1970s, although the history of its practices goes back beyond the turn of the 20th century. It has operated under various terms, with probably "correspondence education" being its most enduring predecessor. It can be seen that distance education (using this term to cover all its preceding forms) both relies upon, and is demanded by, the modern industrial world. It was this world that provided the means of printing and reproduction, and the means of communication and transport to enable distance education to operate. Likewise, it was the ever-expanding developed areas of the world, together with the demands for people with appropriate education and training to operate the newly pioneered areas, that initiated the need for education and training to occur "at a distance." The "traditional" forms of face-to-face education were found wanting in many respects, although they did offer some direct and indirect forms of assistance, whether it was through boarding education or through providing the people to develop or support the new distance education.

In this sense, it can be seen that the modernization that led to what some call the first generation of educational technologies used in distance education (Bates, 1991; Garrison, 1985; Nipper, 1989) created the opportunities and conditions for its existence. The second generation of audiovisual media supplemented these and enhanced distance education considerably. Arguably, the rise of the large open universities world wide in the late 20th century can be traced to the development of the U.K. Open University (UKOU), which itself was inextricably linked to the use of (BBC) radio and television. The impetus the UKOU gave to distance education during the 1970s and 1980s was largely connected to its systems for the development and use of print and audiovisual media, although there were other very significant factors, too—not the least of which was the need for greater access to educational opportunities for all people. Things were somewhat different in the United States which, with exceptions, seemed to remain somewhat immune to these forms of distance education. American distance education typically pursued interactive audio and video links for remote class tutoring, rather than the print-based tutoring and assessment, supported by other media, which is commonplace in international distance education.

Since the emergence of the computer-based communications technologies, distance educators have seen their capacity to create their wares enhanced. In particular, the database, graphics, word-processing, communications, and multi-media capacities have provided large, sometimes untapped resources for distance educators; however, the scorpion of computer-based communications technology has a sting in its tail that may prove more than just painful for distance education. Despite the size and influence of some of the world's mega universities (Daniel, 1996), distance education has remained a relatively marginal endeavor in educational policy and practice. The "traditional" universities have increasingly become aware of the importance of computer-based communications technology to their existences, too, not just for educational purposes directly (although this is probably where the sting could be terminal for distance education), but also for their marketing, business, and administration needs.

Some years ago, Smith and Kelly (1987) encouraged a debate as to whether distance education might shift from the "margins to the mainstream" of education. Certainly, there were some clear reasons for thinking that this was a possibility—for example, in that distance education appealed to an important and expanding number of "mature-age" learners needing to undertake continuing education. However, a decade later, Evans, Nation, Renner, and Tregenza (1997) issued a rather different prognosis for distance education. Partly on the basis of their research into reforms in "traditional" universities, they addressed the Open and Distance Learning Association of Australia's 1997 conference:

> We do not wish to romanticise *distance education*, indeed, we remain critical of various aspects. However, the current circumstances lead us to wonder whether it is time for ODLAA members and other fellow travellers, to assert themselves on national and institutional policy agendas so that the research theory and practice which has been nurtured over previous years is not lost, and maybe then re-invented, by people who are ignorant of its importance and potential for taking (tertiary) education into the next millennium. (p. 152)

The problem identified is twofold. Conventional universities continue to embrace the new educational technologies, especially the two Web-based learning management platforms *Blackboard* and *WebCT*, which merged in business terms in 2005, threatening the emergence of a monopolistic monolith dominating the educational infrastructure. In effect, these universities teach their students "at a distance," in part, at least, without the benefit of the expertise and understanding that decades of the research, theory and practice in distance education could provide.

Additionally, we can see that the sorts of changes that new technologies have brought to society, work, and finance more generally have impacted on the nature of education in ways that effect distance education. As we previously argued, distance education itself is a product of modernity. Its forms of administration, production, and distribution are characteristic of modern (Fordist) societies, much in the way Peters (1983) described (somewhat controversially) nearly two decades ago; however, the new technologies and the way that they have been deployed by business, government, and other institutions have yielded significant, and sometimes fundamental, changes to the way work and society operates. Some refer to this new condition as "post-modernity" or "late-modernity." Within this context, various forms of education have been spawned that draw, to a greater or lesser extent, from education. These are forms such as "open learning," "flexible learning," "fleximode," "open campus," or "virtual campus." Edwards (1994, 1997) saw open learning and flexible learning as consequences of post-modernity. Likewise, Campion (1992) and Campion and Renner (1991) explained these new configurations in post-Fordist terms. These authors are critical of these shifts in terms of their impact on the quality of education and learning; indeed, Campion (1996) is particularly so. Others, such as Jakupec (1996, 1997), Nicoll (1997), and Kirkpatrick (1997), are similarly critical, especially in terms of seeing these new forms of distance education being influenced by, or having arisen from, the dominance of "economic rationalist" neoconservative politics, which commenced in the 1980s and has gathered pace into the 21st century.

These critiques of the various late-modern offshoots of distance education are often founded on the assumption that the types of learning which are fostered by these approaches are likely to be of the repetitive, "banking" kind eschewed by Freire and others in the 1970s (see Freire, 1972). The expectation of the critics is that learning will be reduced to "serving the system" and not be of a kind which "empowers" learners. These concerns are supported by a good deal of evidence that suggests that new forms of distance education (and many other forms of education and training) are coming under the influence of what we might call "neo-instructional industrialism"—that is, the old industrial approaches to distance education re-jigged into online forms (Bishop, 2002; Conrad, 2003; Simpson, 2005; Willems, 2005). This should be seen as a trend to be resisted and avoided. Indeed, if distance education is to survive these threats, it will need to be on the basis that it is rejuvenated in a way that uses the new educational technologies to foster dialogue and critique. In order to do so, it will need to address the challenge of the constructivists who are becoming influential in the design of new forms of distance education, and who have dominated theory and practice in the efforts of conventional universities seriously attempting to embrace online teaching and learning. We take up this matter in more detail following.

THE IMPACT OF CONSTRUCTIVISM

Since the early 1990s, constructivism has ridden a populist wave to become a fashionable theoretical position on which to build educational practices. For many it seemed to represent a significant, even radical, departure from previous approaches. Certainly, this is understandable for those who were trying to break away from largely behaviorist-influenced or behaviorist-derived approaches to educational technology, such as "programmed learning," which had gained favor in the 1970s and 1980s. The increasing "technologization" of teaching, learning, and assessment during this period made some educational psychologists with humanist, rather than behaviorist, leanings increasingly nervous.

Constructivism's origins, as is often the case with "modern" theories, have long and deep roots into epistemological histories. Candy (1991) took the view that its origins can be recognized as early as the 5th century B.C. in Greece. In terms of current approaches, however, there were significant contributors to the field in the second half of the 20th century. In psychology, Kelly (1955) propounded a form of personal construct theory in the mid-1950s. In sociology, Berger and Luckmann (1967) popularized the notion of the social construction of reality in the mid–1960s. In educational psychology, Piaget (1971) had a profound influence on teacher education and early schooling which can be seen to reflect and articulate constructivist ideas. In Australia, Connell's (1971) work on the child's construction of politics provided another valuable thread to the notion of construction. Arguably, in philosophy, the hermeneutic propositions of Husserl (1965) are again congruent with the meaning-making elements of constructivism.

The resurgence in interest in what might be called "constructualist" thought is largely attributed to Glasersfeld (1995), who added a new "radical" edge to the notion of constructivism. Then, as we have argued, it was the next decade when constructivism took off as a movement. It has been highly popular in science education for children, and to a lesser extent, in educational and instructional design for adults, including distance education. Jegede (1992) is a scholar of both science education and distance education, and so it is not surprising that he was amongst the vanguard of those in distance education who advocated that constructivism be taken seriously for the research and practice of teaching and learning in distance education; however, perhaps the most notable statement in terms of the impact of constructivism on distance education came from Hawkridge (1999). He was the foundation director of the Institute of Educational Technology at the UKOU (arguably one the most important developments in distance education of the 20th century). He is also an eminent scholar in the field of educational technology.

Hawkridge (1999) identified three challenges which remained to be met:

> First, educational technologists should understand and apply constructivism rather than behaviourism in their development of teaching and learning systems. Second, they should develop systems for teaching and learning that match the opportunities offered by the hardware and software of modern computers and telecommunications, including the Web. Third, they should answer the moral and ethical challenges from those who criticise educational technologists for not caring enough about teachers and students, for not endorsing an emancipatory view of education. (pp. 299–300)

This summary grows from earlier analyses by Hawkridge (1976, 1979, 1981, 1983, 1991) in which he reflects critically on the mission of educational technologists, addresses the views of critics, and continues to suggest changes in approaches related to changing conditions in education and society and progress in educational theory and practice. We have addressed these analyses in considerable detail previously (Evans & Nation, 1993a, 1993b, 1996, 2000); however, it is important to note here that some of the challenges to educational technology were also similar to challenges made to aspects of contructivism's earlier forms. For example, Berger and Luckmann's (1967) work in sociology generally lost favour under the weight of Marxist and neo-Marxian critiques of interactionist sociology. The absence of notions of social structure (class), power, and authority in the individualist theories of social constructionism, symbolic interactionism, and so forth rendered them unpopular by the mid- to late-1970s. Of course, the structuralist theories were themselves rendered unpopular by the various theoretical positions of postmodernism, post-structuralism, and feminism. Hence, we would argue, that constructivist principles are likely to be only partially successful in achieving Hawkridge's mission. Indeed, they are especially likely to be so if the proponents and exponents of constructivism in distance education and educational technology do not recognize both the useful related work which has been done in and/or through distance education since the early 1970s—which was not labeled constructivism, but which represents a relevant and strong base on which to build—and also that constructivism is limited by its weakness in terms of both the recognition of, and articulation with, social theories.

This is not to deny that the transformation in thinking demonstrated by reconstructed behaviorists is important for the future of distance education (and education, more broadly); however, the fact is that most of those espousing "constructivism" remain unwilling or unable to recognize the need for substantial analyses of the economic, political, and social contexts within which teaching and learning occur and, even more so, that they seem unable to grasp the rich potential of investigations from a diverse range of related disciplines. In our view, failing to make these connections will only remake distance education into a softer, individualistic form of instructional industrialism.

Having said this, considerable progress has been made to bridge the paradigmatic chasm between those who can be regarded as "instructional industrialists" and proponents of "critically reflexive education." It is especially noteworthy that Jonassen, an heir to the Gagnéian cognitivist tradition, is an instructive case. A recent publication, written with two colleagues, and addressed to aspiring school teachers, begins:

> Constructivism is a relatively new idea in education. It is an even newer idea to educational technology. It is so new to some educational circles that some people perceive it as a fad. We think not. Constructivism is an old idea to sociology and art. And as a way of understanding the learning phenomenon it is ageless. People have always constructed personal and socially acceptable meaning for events and objects in the world. . . . People naturally construct meaning. Formal educational enterprises that rely on the efficient transmission of prepackaged chunks of information are not natural. They are pandemic. The modern age values understanding less than it does the efficient transmission of culturally accepted beliefs. It doesn't have to be that way. Modernism can support meaning making as well. This book looks at how modern technologies, such as computers and video, can be used to engage learners in personal and socially constructed meaning making . . . *Learning With Technology* is about how educators can use technologies to support constructive learning. In the past, technology has largely been used in education to learn *from*. Technology programs were developed with the belief that they could convey information (and hopefully understanding) more effectively than teachers. But constructivists believe that you cannot convey understanding. That can only be constructed by learners. So this book argues that technologies are more effectively used as tools to construct knowledge *with*. The point of the book is that technology is a tool to think and learn *with*. (Jonassen, Peck, & Wilson, 1999, p. iii)

We have argued elsewhere that the notion of technologies as tools is somewhat impoverished, and that technologies are more usefully seen as the sciences, arts, and crafts of using tools (Evans & Nation, 1993b; 1996). A computer or chalk can both be educational technologies. Notwithstanding this, Jonassen et al. (1999) are espousing what distance educators such as Morgan (1997) have identified as the "new educational technology." Despite the importance of Jonassen et al.'s recognition of the social elements in educational technologies, the allegation of the novelty of constructivist ideas in educational theory and practice illustrates the point of weakness we mentioned above in relation to Hawkridge's summation of 30 years of educational technology. Accepting that Jonassen et al. acknowledge that sociology has an enduring record for espousing the importance of the "social construction of knowledge," it would be even more useful if they could point to substantial contributions in this regard, such as those made by Basil Bernstein, Geoffrey Esland, and Michael Young in the late-1960s and early-1970s and given general currency through OU courses in Education (Bernstein, 1971; Esland, 1971;

Young, 1971). These contributions have continued to develop and retain their vitality today (e.g., Young, 1998). It is worth discussing one of these contributions in more detail, because it illustrates the weakness in terms of both educational technology and science education.

In 1971, Esland identified the potential for educational psychology to create and facilitate the theory and research that could act as a basis for understanding teachers and learners as constructors of meaning. He did so in the course of a study of the emergence of curriculum reforms such as "Nuffield science," which were influenced very heavily by the work of Jerome Bruner and Jean Piaget. From this "epistemological perspective," children and adolescents are "little scientists" who can be led to discover what scientists have come "to know." Esland's study demonstrated that these reforms to teaching and learning in schools often founded on the rocks of "psychometric" approaches in the tradition of behaviorism and Gagné. He noted the tendency for psychometricians to incorporate Bruner and Piaget's ideas into their models and, in the process, to lose or misunderstand their emphasis on the meaning-making capacities of learners. Bruner's (1960) early work, with its conformity to the scientism of '60s and '70s academic psychology, also contributed to this misunderstanding. His mature work demonstrates much more clearly that an understanding of meaning making is the central aspect of educational psychology, and that anthropology, art, literature, music, sociology, and other social sciences all have important contributions to make to any complete analysis (Bruner, 1986; 1990).

For some years we have asserted that the social theorist Anthony Giddens offers a most effective basis for a thoroughly connected understanding of meaning making in economic, political and social contexts (Evans & Nation, 1996, pp. 163–165; 2000, pp. 164–168). For example, Giddens has continued in the tradition of interdisciplinarity that Bruner valued in the Harvard Department of Social Relations. He has produced some powerful eclectic theoretical works that allow others to analyze, articulate, and explain their own research, reflections, and theorizing in terms which recognize the power of human agency within the changing social, economic and political conditions. Giddens's understanding of the "reflexivity of modernity" offers a substantial theoretical basis for "the learning society" that is rapidly becoming "the challenge we face" as individuals making our way in the world personally, domestically, economically, politically, and socially, and as members of organizations (such as "educational enterprises") attempting to reform the world (Giddens, 1991a, pp. 36–45). With Kasperson (2000, pp. vi–vii), we agree that many can be bewildered by Giddens' overwhelming style—at least in his "technical works."

There are encouraging signs that some influential thinkers in distance education are beginning a constructive engagement with the challenges put forward by those who espouse the critically reflective approach. The work of Garrison and Anderson (2003) and Laurillard (2002) are excellent examples. Both have attempted to go beyond narrow neo-constructivism. Garrison and Anderson have drawn heavily on the recent revival of interest in John Dewey's pragmatic educational psychology, which regards teaching and learning as a "transactional experience." Laurillard has attempted to meld constructivism and phenomenography as a means of creating effective forms of "educational conversations" using a variety of media. Both works are frequently cited, but all too frequently, many of their disciples seem to confuse "mouse clicking interactivity" and "instant feedback" from a databank of answers to FAQs as meaningful educational transactions; however, it is also obvious that those who espouse the more radical forms of "critical reflexivity" still have some convincing to do.

CONTINUING A CRITICAL DEBATE

The emergence and success of the UKOU in the 1970s signaled that distance education could hold a preeminent place in higher education both nationally and internationally. As latecomers to the field, the British educational authorities were able to draw upon the experience of those in Europe and the "New World" who had pioneered the establishment of a variety of programs of "correspondence education," based in various organizational contexts, in colleges and universities in the late 19th and early 20th centuries. Unlike most of these pioneering programs, the Open University was a "single purpose" institution devoted exclusively to educating part time students whose circumstances or desires meant that they could not attend campus-based programs.

In many respects, the fledgling New World democracies recognized that education had to be taken to their citizens at the pioneering frontiers of their lands. They saw it as necessary and practical to "take the classroom" to the adults and children, from various religious and cultural backgrounds, who were building the new nations. The initiative for many of these developments was essentially local and/or national, but like most educational endeavors, there was always an international element in evidence. These were expressed though the emergence of organizations such as the ICDE and its predecessors. They played an important part in the development of the "open university movement" in the 1980s. The fact that universities were the focus of many of the developments was also influential, but never so exclusively, in the birth of research and scholarship aimed at understanding and improving policy and practice in the field.

In an age of "hyper (un)reality," in which incantations about the necessity and inevitability of "global," "mega," and/or "virtual universities" are part of many cultural, economic, political, and social discourses, it is essential for practitioners, policy makers, researchers, and theorists to maintain educational technologies as a central interest. We have ceased to be surprised that educators and their clients need to be reminded that "technologies" emerged in the Stone Age, and that the "new" communications and information technologies are simply the latest manifestations of a phenomenon that is always integral to education. The preeminent task for practitioners and scholars is to pursue the job of understanding and improving their use on the most substantial scale possible.

From our first involvement in "distance education," we have valued the confluence of knowledge from practice, research, and theory. Our approach, centering critical reflections on the practice of ourselves and our colleagues, has been founded on a rich tradition of scholarship developed by pioneers such as Charles Wedemeyer.

It is heartening to realize that this *Handbook* has given considerable emphasis to contributors who have been willing to value the richness of these traditions in research and theory.

REFERENCES

Bates, T. (1991). Third generation distance education. *Research in Distance Education, 3*(2), 10–15.

Berger, J., & Luckmann, T. S. (1967). *The social construction of reality.* Harmondsworth, UK: Penguin.

Bernstein, B. (1971). On the classification and framing of educational knowledge. In M. F. D. Young (Ed.), *Knowledge and control: New directions for the sociology of education* (pp. 47–69). London: Collier-Macmillan.

Bishop, A. (2002). Come into my parlour said the spider to the fly: Critical reflections on Web-based education from a student's perspective. *Distance Education, 23*(2), 231–236.

Bruner, J. S. (1960). The Process of Education, Cambridge, Mass, USA: Harvard University Press.

Bruner, J. (1986). *Actual minds, possible worlds.* Cambridge, MA: Harvard University Press.

Bruner, J. (1990). *Acts of meaning.* Cambridge, MA: Harvard University Press.

Campion, M. (1992). Revealing links: Post-Fordism, postmodernism and distance education. In T. D. Evans & P. A. Juler (Eds.), *Research in distance education, 2* (pp. 45–51). Geelong, VIC, Australia: Deakin University Press.

Campion, M. (1996). Open learning, closing minds. In T. D. Evans & D. E. Nation (Eds.), *Opening education: Policies and practices from open and distance education* (pp. 147–161). London: Routledge.

Campion, M., & Renner, W. (1991).The supposed demise of Fordism: Implications for distance education and higher education *Distance Education, 13*(1), 7–28.

Candy, P. C. (1991). *Self-direction for lifelong learning: A comprehensive guide to theory and practice.* San Francisco: Jossey-Bass.

Connell, R. W. (1971). *The child's construction of politics.* Melbourne, VIC, Australia: Melbourne University Press.

Conrad, D. (2003). From the spider's perspective: Revisiting Bishop's reflections on Web-based learning. *Distance Education, 24*(1), 123–126.

Crystal, D. (1997). *English as a global language.* Cambridge, UK: Cambridge University Press.

Crystal, D. (2001). *Language and the Internet.* Cambridge, UK: Cambridge University Press.

Daniel, J. (1996). *The Mega-universities and the knowledge media.* London: Kogan Page.

Edwards, R. (1994). From a distance? Globalisation, space-time compression and distance education. *Open Learning, 9*(3), 9–17.

Edwards, R. (1997). *Changing Places? Flexibility, lifelong learning and a learning society.* London: Routledge.

Esland, G. M. (1971). Teaching and learning as the organization of knowledge. In M. F. D. Young (Ed.), *Knowledge and control: New directions for the sociology of education* (pp. 70–115). London: Collier-Macmillan.

Evans, T. D. (1989). Taking place: The social construction of place, time and space and the (re) making of distances in distance education. *Distance Education, 10*(2), 170–183.

Evans, T. D. (1995a). Globalisation, post-Fordism and open and distance education. *Distance Education 16*(3), 256–269.

Evans, T. D. (1995b). Matters of modernity, late modernity and self-identity in distance education. *European Journal of Psychology of Education 10*(2), 169–180.

Evans, T. D. (1997). (En)Countering globalisation: issues for open and distance educators. In L. Rowan, L. Bartlett & T. D. Evans (Eds.), *Shifting Borders: Globalisation, localisation and open and distance education* (pp. 11–22). Geelong, VIC, Australia: Deakin University Press.

Evans, T. D. (2003). Policy and planning in the developed countries: Coping with compulsive development cultures. In S. Panda (Ed.), *Planning and management of open and flexible learning* (pp. 13–19). London: Kogan Page.

Evans, T. D., & Nation, D. E. (1993a). Distance education, educational technology and open learning: Converging futures and closer integration with conventional education. *Distance education futures: The proceedings of the Australian & South Pacific External Studies Association biennial forum*, Adelaide: University of South Australia.

Evans, T. D., & Nation, D. E. (1993b). Educational technologies: Reforming open and distance education. In T. D. Evans & D. E. Nation (Eds.), *Reforming open and distance education* (pp. 196–214). London: Kogan Page.

Evans, T. D., & Nation, D. E. (1996). Educational futures: Globalisation, educational technology and lifelong learning. In T. D. Evans & D. E. Nation (Eds.), *Opening education: Policies and practices from open and distance education* (pp. 162–176). London: Routledge.

Evans, T. D., & Nation, D. E. (2000). Understanding changes to university teaching. In T. D. Evans & D. E. Nation (Eds.), *Changing university teaching: Reflections on creating educational technologies* (pp. 160–175). London: Kogan Page.

Evans, T. D., Nation, D. E., Renner, W., & Tregenza, K. (1997). The end of the line or a new future for open and distance education? Issues for practitioners, researchers and theorists from a study of educational reform in post-secondary education. *Open and Distance Learning Association of Australia*, Launceston, TAS, Australia: University of Tasmania.

Freire, P. (1972). *Pedagogy of the oppressed*, Harmondsworth, UK: Penguin.

Garrison, D. R. (1985). Three generations of technological innovation in distance education. *Distance Education, 6*(2), 235–41.

Garrison, D. R., & Anderson, T. (2003). *E-Learning in the 21st Century.* London: RoutledgeFalmer.

Giddens, A. (1991a). *The Consequences of modernity.* Cambridge, UK: Polity Press.

Giddens, A. (1991b). *Modernity and self-identity: Self and society in the late modern age.* Cambridge, UK: Polity Press.

Giddens, A. (1994). *Beyond left and right: The future of radical politics.* Cambridge, UK: Polity Press.

Glasersfeld, E. V. (Ed.). (1995). *Radical constructivism: A way of knowing and learning.* London: Falmer.

Guy, R. (1991). Distance education and the developing world. In T. D. Evans & B. King (Eds.), *Beyond the text: Contemporary writing on distance education* (pp. 152–175). Geelong, VIC, Australia: Deakin University Press.

Guy, R. (1997). Contesting borders: Knowledge, power and pedagogy in distance education in Papua New Guinea. In L. Rowan, L. Bartlett, & T. D. Evans (Eds.), *Shifting borders: Globalisation, localisation and open and distance education* (pp. 53–64). Geelong, VIC, Australia: Deakin University Press.

Hawkridge, D. (1976). Next year Jerusalem! The rise of educational technology. *British Journal of Educational Technology, 12*(1), 7–30.

Hawkridge, D. (1979). Persuading the Dons. *British Journal of Educational Technology, 3*(10), 164–174.

Hawkridge, D. (1981). The telesis of educational technology. *British Journal of Educational Technology, 12*(1), 4–18.

Hawkridge, D. (1983). *New information technology in education.* Beckenham, UK: Croom Helm.

Hawkridge, D. (1991). Challenging educational technology. *Educational Training and Technology International, 28*(2), 1–22.

Hawkridge, D. (1999). Thirty years on, *BJET!* and educational technology. *British Journal of Educational Technology, 30*(4), 293–304.

Husserl, E. (1965). *Phenomenology and the crisis in philosophy.* New York: Harper Torch Books.

Jakupec, V. (1996). Reforming distance education through economic rationalism: a critical analysis of reforms to Australia higher education. In T. D. Evans & D. E. Nation (Eds.), *Opening education: Policies and practices from open and distance education* (pp. 77–89). London: Routledge.

Jakupec, V. (1997). Guest editorial. *Studies in Continuing Education, 19*(2), 95–99.

Jegede, O. (1992). Constructivist epistemology and its implications for contemporary research in distance learning. In T. D. Evans & P. A. Juler (Eds.), *Research in distance education 2* (pp. 21–29). Geelong, VIC, Australia: Deakin University Press.

Jonassen, D. H., Peck, K. L., & Wilson, B. G. (1999). *Learning with technology: A constructivist perspective.* Upper Saddle River, NJ: Merrill-Prentice Hall.

Kasperson, L. (2000). *Anthony Giddens: An introduction to a social theorist.* Oxford, UK: Blackwell.

Kelly, G. A. (1955). *The psychology of personal constructs.* New York: Norton.

Kirkpatrick, D. (1997). Becoming flexible: Contested territories. *Studies in Continuing Education 19*(2), 160–73.

Laurillard, D. (2002). *Rethinking university teaching: A conversational framework for the effective use of learning technologies* (2nd ed.). London: RoutledgeFalmer.

Morgan, A. R. (1997). Still seeking the silent revolution? Research, theory and practice in open and distance education. In T. D. Evans, V. Jakupec, & D. Thompson (Eds.), *Research in distance education 4* (pp. 7–17). Geelong, VIC, Australia: Deakin University Press

Nicoll, K. (1997). 'Flexible learning'—unsettling practices. *Studies in Continuing Education, 19*(2), 100–111.

Nipper, S. (1989). Third generation distance learning and computer conferencing. In R. Mason & A. Kaye (Eds.), *Mindweave* (pp. 63–73). Oxford, UK: Pergamon Press.

Perraton, H. (Ed.) (1993). *Distance education for teacher training.* London, Routledge.

Perraton, H. (2000). *Open and distance learning in the developing world.* London: Routledge.

Peters, O. (1983). Distance teaching and industrial production: a comparative interpretation in outline. In D. Sewart, D. Keegan, & B. Holmberg (Eds.), *Distance education: International perspectives* (pp. 95–113). London: Croom Helm.

Piaget, J. (1971). *Structuralism.* London: Routledge and Kegan Paul.

Robertson, R. (1992). *Globalisation: Social theory and global culture.* London: Sage.

Simpson, O. (2005). Web-based learning: Are we becoming obsessed? *Distance Education, 26*(1), 153–157.

Smith, P., & Kelly, M. (Eds.) (1987). *Distance education and the mainstream.* London: Croom Helm.

Willems, J. (2005). Flexible learning: implications of 'when-ever', 'where-ever' and 'what-ever'. *Distance Education, 26*(3), 429–435.

Young, M. F. D. (1971). An approach to the study of curricula as socially organised knowledge. In M. F. D. Young (Ed.), *Knowledge and control: New directions in the sociology of knowledge* (pp. 19–46). London: Collier-Macmillan.

Young, M. F. D. (1998). *The curriculum of the future.* London: Falmer Press.

Author Index

Page numbers not in parentheses refer to the reference lists at the end of each chapter. The numbers in parentheses refer to citations in the text.

K

Kabel, S., 336 (*334*)
Kaddoura, A-R., 645 (*635, 636*)
Kafai, Y. B., 351 (*346*)
Kahan, S., 147 (*143, 145*), 541 (*537*)
Kalmon, S., 168 (*157, 164*)
Kalyuga, S., 134 (*128*)
Kambutu, J. N., 388 (*381, 382, 386*)
Kaml, C. A., 388 (*381*)
Kanter, R., 579 (*571*)
Kanuka, H., 86, 88 (*79, 83, 84*), 103 (*99*), 320 (*312*)
Kapitzke, C., 167 (*160, 162*)
Kaplan, L., 448 (*337, 444*)
Kaplan, R., 579 (*574*), 605 (*595*)
Kapur, K., 307 (*304*)
Karunanayaka, S., 257 (*251, 252, 254*)
Kaser, J. S., 179 (*169*)
Kasperson, L., 659 (*656*)
Kastor, G., 178 (*174*)
Katz, R. N., 86 (*83*)
Kaufman, D. F., 134 (*131*)
Kaufman, H., 513 (*503, 504*)
Kaufman, R., 374, 375 (*363, 364, 365, 366, 367, 368, 369, 371, 372, 373*), 435 (*424*)
Kaye, A. R., 87 (*78*)
Kaye, T., 86 (*78*)
Kearley, J., 214 (*208, 210*)
Kearsley, G., 12 (*5, 6, 9*), 54 (*45, 46, 47*), 68 (*59, 64*), 75 (*69, 72*), 307 (*304*), 374 (*372*), 402 (*395*), 435 (*425*), 489 (*475, 487*), 514 (*505*)
Keefe, J. W., 351 (*339*)
Keegan D., 11, 12, 13 (*4, 5, 9*), 68 (*57, 63*), 75 (*72*), 87 (*84*), 103 (*96, 97*), 231 (*226*), 514 (*505, 506*), 619 (*612*)
Keen, M. A., 388 (*378, 379, 380, 381, 382, 385*)
Keeton, C. L., 388 (*380, 382, 386*)
Keeva, S., 541 (*539*)
Keisch, D., 282 (*278*)
Kelley, K., 214 (*208, 210, 211*)
Kells, H. R., 417 (*403*)
Kelly, G. A., 659 (*654*)
Kelly, M., 256 (*247*), 659 (*652*)
Kelsey, Y., 178 (*174*)
Kelson, A. C., 256 (*248, 254*)
Kember, D., 120 (*116*), 191 (*184*), 256 (*248*)
Kemp, W. C., 191 (*182, 189*)
Kendrick, A. A., 527 (*520*)
Kennedy, D., 307 (*298*)
Kennedy, H., 202 (*195*)
Kennepohl, D., 307 (*302*)
Kent, M. V., 146 (*137*)
Keough, E., 54 (*47*)
Kerr, E. B., 156 (*150*)
Ketelhut, D., 351 (*339, 344, 346*)
Khan, B., 41 (*32*), 591 (*584*)

Kiesler, S., 605 (*594*)
Kilbane, C., 309 (*301*)
Killion, J., 488 (*484*)
Kim, A. J., 147 (*142*)
Kim, H., 134 (*127, 132*), 283 (*273, 275, 282*)
Kim, J., 134 (*123*)
Kim, K.-J., 605 (*600, 601*)
Kim, M., 134 (*123*), 283 (*272, 273, 275, 282*)
Kim-Rupnow, W. S., 202 (*195, 196, 197, 199*)
Kinash, S., 202 (*195*)
King, J., 320 (*313*), 361, 362 (*355, 356, 361*)
Kiple, J., 213 (*208, 212*)
Kirby, E., 489 (*482*)
Kirk, J. J., 388 (*378, 379*)
Kirkley, S. E., 245 (*233*)
Kirkpatrick, A., 203 (*195*)
Kirkpatrick, D., 87 (*83*), 256 (*249*), 659 (*653*)
Kirkwood, A., 256 (*253*)
Kirschner, P. A., 256 (*254*), 320 (*313*)
Kitsantas, A., 283 (*272*)
Kleemann, G., 41 (*32*)
Klees, S. J., 646 (*635*)
Kleiman, G., 167 (*162*), 489 (*484*)
Klein, J. D., 41 (*33*), 284 (*273*)
Kline, J. P., 191 (*190*)
Klopfer, E., 351 (*346*)
Knight, J., 591 (*584, 585, 586, 588*)
Knowles, M., 120 (*109, 110, 111*), 634 (*623*)
Koble, M., 13 (*10*), 41 (*31, 33, 34*)
Koestler, A., 646 (*638*)
Koh, M. H., 136 (*125*)
Koku, E., 307, 309 (*303*)
Kolloff, M., 245 (*238*)
Kolodner, J. L., 256 (*252*)
Komura, T., 167 (*163*)
Koper, R., 307 (*301*), 336 (*333*)
Koronios, A., 257 (*251*)
Koschmann, T., 245 (*240*), 256 (*248, 254*)
Kowslowski, D., 179 (*177*)
Köymen, U., 120 (*118*), 156 (*152*)
Kozma, R., 134 (*123*), 168 (*159, 162*), 256 (*250*), 307 (*300*)
Krajcik, J., 284 (*274*)
Kramarae, C., 179 (*170, 171, 175, 177*)
Kreijns, K., 256 (*254*), 320 (*313*)
Krippendorff, K., 41 (*33*)
Kruepke, K. A., 156 (*149, 151*)
Kuehn, S. A., 156 (*149*)
Kuhn, D., 87 (*81, 82*)
Kuhn, T. S., 54 (*51*)
Kuiper, E., 180 (*173*)
Kulhavy, R. W., 256 (*249*)
Kulik, C.-L. C., 255, 257 (*249*)
Kulik, J. A., 255, 257 (*249*)
Kulkarni, S. R., 469 (*452*)
Kuplowska, O., 489 (*481*)

Subject Index